LITERARY CRITICISM AND THEORY

THE GREEKS TO THE PRESENT

Edited
and with
Introductions by
ROBERT CON DAVIS
LAURIE FINKE

New York & London

Literary Criticism and Theory: The Greeks to the Present

Longman Inc., 95 Church Street, White Plains, N.Y. 10601

Associated companies:
Longman Group Ltd., London
Longman Cheshire Pty., Melbourne
Longman Paul Pty., Auckland
Copp Clark Pitman, Toronto
Pitman Publishing Inc., New York

Longman English and Humanities Series
Series Editor: Lee A. Jacobus

Executive editor: Gordon T. R. Anderson
Production editor: Camilla T. K. Palmer
Text design: Jill Francis Wood
Cover design: Susan J. Moore
Production supervisor: Kathleen Ryan

Library of Congress Cataloging-in-Publication Data

Critical texts : literary theory from the Greeks through the present / edited by Robert Con Davis and Laurie Finke.

p. cm.—(Longman English and humanities series)
Bibliography: p.
Includes index.
ISBN 0-8013-0183-1
1. Criticism. I. Davis, Robert Con, 1948– . II. Finke, Laurie. III. Series.
PN86.C75 1989
801′.95—dc19 88-9089
CIP

ISBN 0-8013-0183-1
94 93 92 91 90 89 9 8 7 6 5 4 3 2 1

Chronological Table of Contents

Topical Table of Contents

WOMEN AND CRITICISM

HISTORY, POLITICS, AND CRITICISM

SEMIOTICS, STRUCTURALISM, AND POSTSTRUCTURALISM

PSYCHOLOGY, THE SUBJECT, AND CRITICISM

GENRE CRITICISM

Drama

Poetry

The Novel

Aesthetics and Formalism

Preface

About a year and a half ago the editors of this volume began discussing the feasibility of producing an innovative and useful collection covering the history of criticism from ancient Greece through the present. We knew all the books then on the market, some quite good when they were new; but we also knew that these books were now seriously dated, either in their selections or approach to the material. On the other hand, many of the most recent books had weak representation, no pedagogical apparatus, and, quite often, rigid canonical expectations. And the "new" books tended not to engage contemporary discourse and its challenges to the critical canon. We had talked to our publisher about editing a new criticism anthology, but we felt strongly that we did not want to duplicate books already available and had no interest in creating a book for which there was no need.

We had begun our talk in December at the Modern Language Association Convention and continued debating the task until March before deciding that we *could* produce an innovative and useful introduction to Western literary criticism—a book for the reader seriously interested in literary criticism and cultural studies. We felt that as a medievalist interested in Enlightenment and modern criticism and a modernist interested in classical and contemporary criticism we were the right editors for such an expansive book and, further, that the timing (the cultural moment of 1988) allowed for the broad perspective on criticism up through the late 1980s—in several senses the end of a critical era—that would be important to our work.

We are hopeful that this volume accomplishes what we wanted: that is, (1) to introduce readers to a great variety of critical approaches, (2) to give them a sense of criticism's complex genealogy, and (3) to give them a basis from which to inquire further about past and future directions in criticism. The difficulty of producing a book that does these things, modest as they may sound, surprised us a good bit. We faced the sheer mass of Western critical texts—on poetry, drama, fiction, and theory generally—and the enormous proliferation of modern criticism, especially the explosion of critical discourse in the last twenty-five years. Beyond the bulk of material to be covered, however, we saw the real need to include texts just now moving to the cultural foreground (in whatever period) as newly important for critical discourse. These texts are by women and minorities and those concerned with politics and institutional questions—critics and writers such as Aristophanes, Christine de Pisan, Anne Finch, Aphra Behn, Eliza Haywood, George Eliot, William Morris, Kenneth Burke, Raymond Williams, Mary Ellman, Sandra M. Gilbert, Hélène Cixous, Barbara Christian, and Robert Stepto.

Our inclusion of texts by these and others reflects the shifting of a paradigm and our own belief in the need to frame critical discourse as far as possible to indicate—and on occasion implicitly to support—the agents for change that have been at work in Western culture. The standards for selection, including subsequent influence, importance to a period or movement, historical significance, clarity, objectivity, and so on, have changed, or are at present rapidly changing. Informed readers now want to investigate counter and oppositional traditions in culture and ask where women, poor people, and racial and ethnic minorities fit within or may engage the critical tradition. And they want to know how these counter and oppositional traditions relate to the dominant discourses and political preoccupations of Western culture.

The book we have edited, we think, succeeds in engaging these many concerns. In choosing these essays, we consulted many friends and expert advisers (their names come up later) and received valuable help. Even so, a trace of arbitrariness in the selections will always remain, as even our most careful choices will demonstrate when compared to the many other useful texts we might have chosen instead. We dealt with this real and persistent difficulty—there is no way to escape it—by repeatedly challenging ourselves and each other to find representative but also the most accessible texts, texts that will in many ways repay the investment of reading them. We also tried to remember, though, that criticism—as the late Paul de Man once said—by its very nature either exists in crisis or else ceases to exist at all. With this precept in mind, we were also careful not to shy away from difficult, rough-hewn, but uniquely important pieces. With every such piece we have tried to smooth the way for the beginning reader of criticism with background information and historical perspectives; but a few crisis/critical texts (Derrida's "Father of Logos," for example) will be difficult even when they are exhilarating, and we have tried not to avoid or somehow denature this difficulty. In those cases we have given what help we could and then have moved aside to respect the reader's need to read, confront, and work through a text.

We have tried, finally, not to reproduce the format of criticism collections narrowly parochial and traditional in their selections—and if possible, not their underlying value schemes either—but we have also been mindful not to "ghettoize" the very critical texts we wished to foreground in critical discourse. We have not created sections, or critical ghettoes, for women and others concerned with cultural politics and theory but have included such critics prominently all through this book. The introductory essay for the twentieth-century section, for example, does not isolate women's studies as an area of criticism but includes it and assumes the continuing impact and decisive shifts of feminism all through the discourse about modernism, poststructuralism, and cultural studies.

CRITICISM AND CRITICAL AUTHORITY

As an aid to the reader, we have written introductory essays and made lists for further reading before each of the book's six sections. More important are the "guide" essays in Part II that introduce four broad areas of critical discourse in the history of criticism: (1) women and criticism; (2) history, politics, and criticism; (3) semiotics and criticism; and (4) psychology and criticism. These original essays by prominent contemporary theorists—Kristina Straub, Robert Markley, Ronald Schleifer, and Herman Rapaport—will give readers unique access to important dimensions of the history of criticism. They also introduce authoritative, editorial voices that contribute to the telling of how criticism should be read and regarded.

These authoritative voices are a key feature of this book and a crucial aspect of our pedagogical strategy for teaching the subject of criticism. The essays bring editorial voices *other than our own* into this book and demonstrate the "dialogic," multifaceted nature of current critical studies and the lack of a single perspective capable of organizing all critical activity. Add to this the fact that many of the headnotes to the critical texts were written by scholars and advanced graduate students in diverse areas of study.

This book, in other words, has the equivalent of multiple editors (male and female) who give testimony on how to read and understand criticism and who are, further, critics in specialties ranging from early (classical through restoration) to modern (eighteenth-century through the present) literary studies. Also, these are working scholars in semiotics and cultural studies, gender studies, feminist theory, psychology, history, and politics. Literary criticism must be understood as a polyphony of discourses, as an intertextual and interdisciplinary activity. Critical discourse at its best advances itself by challenging its own dominant voices—especially the singular, isolated (bound within a single discipline) voicings of "truth."

THE CHRONOLOGICAL APPROACH TO CRITICISM

The historical approach, beginning with classical criticism and working forward, can be useful but it is not the only way of reading this book. At its best, this approach gradually builds a context, or several contexts, for thinking about and practicing criticism, and it allows for considerable variation. Readers might well go through the book's first two sections to get a brief introduction to a few standard preoccupations of criticism (representation, genre, character, style, motif, and so on) and then, upon beginning the Renaissance section, start selectively reading essays from other periods that contrast and connect with the Renaissance pieces as they engage such issues as poetics, history, politics, and so on. In other words, as a reader moves forward in the book and gains a basis for critical comparison, increasingly he or she will profit from reading simultaneously in more than one section at a time. In this manner, one must juggle the complexities of critical comparison only after building confidence through reading already done—that is, after making the connections that allow one to know what is going on.

THE TOPICAL APPROACH

We have included the Topical Table of Contents, in fact, so that just such extensive multiple connections across periods can be made easily while any one section is being read—either while going through the book chronologically or by following particular topics across periods. The introductory essays for each historical period, thus—in addition to creating a perspective, or several perspectives, on that period—also make specific connections among periods and diverse critical issues.

The guide essays, as we mentioned already, not only examine many critical texts with attention to historical development but then interpret the material of those texts according to the dictates of a certain focus or topic, such as psychological understanding or attitudes toward women. These essays cover a broad range of issues important to the study of criticism, and each essay demonstrates how major lines of critical inquiry can be pursued in some detail through the essays of this book and beyond. This demonstration and the information provided in each case will greatly enhance the topical approach to critical discourse and make this book more generally useful.

THIS BOOK IN THE CLASSROOM

This book is designed also to function as a primary text for a history of criticism course, a contemporary criticism course, a course in cultural studies, or a course with critical readings on a special topic such as *mimesis*, poetics, aesthetics, gender relations, and the history and politics of literature. This text covers many such topics and a broad spectrum of approaches to literary and cultural studies as well as forges a historical path—rather, several historical paths—through the history of criticism from Athens in the fifth century B.C. through the late 1980s in the United States and Europe. As such, this book will provide more than enough material for a semester's reading in a college course in criticism.

It will be helpful to couple this text with several brief literary texts (poems, short stories, or essays) for constant reference and the application of critical precepts as the course progresses. One such text, a sonnet by Shakespeare, for example, could serve as the constant reference and test case as the class explores different interpretive schemes and possibilities. Also useful, of course, will be the texts students themselves have read and wish to interpret in light of the critical strategies they are becoming aware of.

SUPPLEMENTING THIS BOOK WITH OTHER BOOKS

While this book is designed to be the primary text in a criticism course, it will on occasion be useful to add one or two books that expand on an approach represented in the book already or that supplement the readings from a particular period. One influential essay in our book, for example, is Northrop Frye's "The Function of Criticism at the Present Time"—an essay at first published separately and then revised to be the introductory chapter of Frye's *Anatomy of Criticism*—a landmark text in the modern conceptualizing of criticism as a cultural institution. Frye's *Anatomy* would be an excellent additional text because it expands what our book already shows about archetypal criticism and because it has been influential in modern literary theory for its formulation of the nature of critical discourse. Our text, furthermore, provides the context of twentieth-century criticism needed for a thorough reading of Frye's book. From the same year, 1957, there is also Frank Kermode's *Romantic Image*, an important discussion of the practice and epistemology of British romantic poetry. A number of books would be particularly good texts to add, including Virginia Woolf's *A Room of One's Own*, C. S. Lewis's *Allegory of Love*, Ian Watt's *The Rise of the Novel*, M. H. Abrams's *The Mirror and the Lamp*, Kate Millett's *Sexual Politics*, Alice Jardine's *Gynesis*, and Jonathan Culler's *Structuralist Poetics*, *On Deconstruction*, and *Framing the Sign*. In each case the additional book expands on a concern already articulated in this book and does so in a way that is provocative and yet quite accessible to students.

ACKNOWLEDGMENTS

A number of friends helped us as we formulated and reformulated this book over the last year. Our greatest debts, though, are clearly to Robert Markley and Ronald Schleifer, who generously gave advice and suggestions—and routinely challenged our conclusions—at every step of the way and whose ideas and words (and, on occasion, sentences) appear all through our introductory essays. Gordon T. R. Anderson, J. Fisher Solomon, and Lee Jacobus were also instrumental at a very early stage in helping us shape the basic concept of this book. These friends (Gordon Anderson is also our editor) have significantly raised the quality and usefulness of this book, and we sincerely thank them.

We also benefited from the good counsel of Herman Rapaport and Kristina Straub, who frequently looked beyond their guide essays to help us think about the book's scope and aims. We got invaluable advice, too, from Nancy Armstrong, John Callahan, James Comas, Sandra M. Gilbert, David Gross, Ellen Pollock, James C. Raymond, Thomas A. Sebeok, Elaine Showalter, and Isaiah Smithson.

While we wrote and are responsible for the introductory essays and other editorial material in this book, a few friends wrote headnotes for some of the essays, and we thank them. They are as follows: Aristotle (*On Interpretation*)—Thomas Argiro; Rousseau, George Eliot (with S. Rose), Corneille—Stephen Kane; Burke, Foucault—James Comas; Aristotle (*Poetics*), Arnold, Brooks, Todorov—Thomas Elliott; Frye—Justin Everett; Bakhtin—Elizabeth Hinds and Thomas Bowden; Pater—Abigail Keegan; Pope, Johnson—Robert Markley; Wordsworth—Valerie Moore; Auerbach, Ellman—Betty Neal; Freud, Christian, Stepto—Jeannie Rhodes; George Eliot (Stephen Kane), Morris—Suzanne Rose; Emerson—Karl Rystad; Miller—Ronald Schleifer; Woolf, Cixous—Maureen Schaffer; Williams—John Springer; Longinus, Coleridge, Derrida, Barthes—Susan Williams; Gilbert—Joyce Zonana.

Finally, we thank Lewis and Clark College and the University of Oklahoma for supporting this project in many ways, from moral support to clerical help and with much in between. At Lewis and Clark College we specifically wish to thank the College of Arts and Sciences for a Faculty Research Grant to support this project. At the University of Oklahoma we thank Dean Robert Hemenway, Dean Kenneth Hoving, and the English Department Chair Dr. George D. Economou for their support. Dr. Economou also translated some Greek phrases in Aristotle's *Poetics* and supplied notes, and we thank him. We would also like to thank Kent Kraft for translating various passages from Greek, Latin, French, German, and Italian. At Lewis and Clark, departmental secretary Carol Patrick was immensely helpful, as were Paula Stacy and Resa Masopust at Oklahoma. Our research assistants Christie Leiter, Jeannie Rhodes, and Stephen Kane were essential to the completion of this project, and we are profoundly grateful for their good work and cheerful patience.

ROBERT CON DAVIS
LAURIE FINKE

Acknowledgments and Source Notes

(The following are presented in the order in which they appear in the book. Those that are public domain have a "source note" which lists volume, date, and publisher, but it will NOT say "reprinted by permission of . . .")

"The Frogs" by Aristophanes from *Four Plays of Aristophanes*, translated by James H. Mantinband, pp. 232–311. Copyright © 1983 by University Press of America. Reprinted by permission.

Excerpts from "The Republic" by Plato from *The Republic of Plato*, translated by F. M. Cornford, pp. 68–92. Copyright 1941 © by Oxford University Press. Reprinted by permission of Oxford University Press.

"Poetics" by Aristotle. Chicago: Henry Regnery Co., 1949.

Excerpts from "On Interpretation" by Aristotle from *Aristotle's On Interpretation*, translated by Jean T. Oesterle, pp. 73, 77, 89, 95, 101–102, 109–110, 121, 125, and 130. Copyright © 1962 by Marquette University Press. Reprinted by permission of Marquette University Press.

"Art of Poetry" by Horace, translated by John B. Quinn, from *Horace: Odes, Episodes, and Art of Poetry*. St. Louis, Mo.: Blackwell Wielandy, 1936.

"On the Sublime" by Longinus from *Longinus on the Sublime*, translated by A. O. Prickard, pp. 1–29. Copyright © 1926 by Oxford University Press. Reprinted by permission of Oxford University Press.

Reprinted with permission of Macmillan Publishing Co. from Saint Augustine, *On Christian Doctrine*, translated by D. W. Robertson, pp. 34–38, 43–53, 78–84, and 86–89. Copyright © 1985 by Macmillan Publishing Co.

Excerpts from "The Didascalicon" by Hugh of St. Victor from *The Didascalicon of Hugh of St. Victor*, translated by Jerome Taylor, pp. 120–122 and 147–150. Copyright © 1960 by Columbia University Press. Reprinted by permission.

Excerpts from "The Summa Theologica" by St. Thomas Aquinas from *Basic Writings of Saint Thomas Aquinas*, Vol. 1, edited by Anton C. Pegis, published by Random House, pp. 14–17. Copyright © 1945 by Richard J. Pegis for the estate of Anton C. Pegis. Reprinted by permission.

"On Eloquence" and "Letter to Can Grande" by Dante Alighieri from *Literary Criticism of Dante Alighieri*, translated by Robert S. Haller, pp. 3–4, 31–40, 42–48, and 98–104. Reprinted by permission of University of Nebraska Press. Copyright © 1973 by the University of Nebraska Press.

Excerpts from "Genealogy of the Gentile Gods" by Giovanni Boccaccio reprinted with permission of Macmillan Publishing Company from *Boccaccio on Poetry*, translated by Charles E. Osgood. Copyright © 1956 by Macmillan Publishing Company; copyright renewed 1984.

Excerpts from "Debat Sur La Roman De La Rose" by Christine de Pisan from "Christine's Response to the Treatise on *The Romance of the Rose* by John Montreuil," translated by Nadia Margolis, in *Medieval Women's Visionary Literature*, edited by Elizabeth Petroff, published by Oxford University Press. Copyright © 1984 by Nadia Margolis. Reprinted by permission.

"Apology for Poetry" by Sir Phillip Sidney, edited by Geoffrey Shepherd. London: Thomas Nelson and Sons, 1965.

"The Arte of English Poesy" by George Puttenham, edited by Gladys Doidge Willcox and Alice Walker. Cambridge: Cambridge University Press, 1936.

"Preface to Volpone" by Ben Jonson from *Works*, vol. 5, edited by C. H. Hereford and Percy Simpson. Oxford: Oxford University Press, 1925.

Excerpts from "Of the Three Unities of Action, Time, and Place" by Pierre Corneille from *The Continental Model: Selected French Essays of the Seventeenth Century*, edited by Scott Elledge and Donald Schier, pp. 101–115. Copyright © 1970 by the University of Minnesota Press. Reprinted by permission.

"Essay of Dramatic Poetry" by John Dryden from *Essays of John Dryden*, edited by W. P. Ker. Oxford: Clarendon Press, 1900.

"Preface" to *The Lucky Chance* and "Epistle" to *The Dutch Lover* by Aphra Behn from *The Works of Aphra Behn*, edited by Montague Summers. London: William Heinemann, 1915.

Excerpts reprinted from "An Essay Concerning Human Understanding" by John Locke, edited by Peter H. Nidditch (1975), by permission of Oxford University Press. Copyright © 1975 by Oxford University Press.

"Introduction" and "Preface" to *The Poems* by Anne Finch, countess of Winchilsea, edited by Myra Reynolds. Chicago: University of Chicago Press, 1903.

"Essay on Criticism" by Alexander Pope from *Complete Poetical Works*, Cambridge Edition. Boston and New York: Houghton Mifflin Co., 1903.

The Spectator by Joseph Addison from *The Works of Joseph Addison*, edited by B. P. Hurd. Philadelphia: J. B. Lippincott and Co., 1864.

The Female Spectator by Eliza Haywood, Vol. 1. London: for T. Gardner, 1775.

Excerpts reprinted from *The New Science of Giambattista Vico: Unabridged Translation of the Third Edition (1744) with the Addition of "Practice of the New Science,"* translated by Thomas Goddard Bergin and Max Harold Fisch. Copyright © 1948 by Cornell University Press. Reprinted by permission of the publisher, Cornell University Press.

"A Philosophical Inquiry into the Origin of Our Ideas of the Sublime and Beautiful" by Edmund Burke, *The Harvard Classics*, vol. 24. New York: P. F. Collier and Son, 1909.

Excerpts from "Observations on the Feeling of the Beautiful and Sublime" by Immanuel Kant, translated by John T. Goldthwait, pp. 45–96. Copyright © 1960 by the Regents of the University of California. Reprinted by permission of the publisher, the University of California Press.

"Preface to Shakespeare" by Samuel Johnson from *Harvard Classics: Prefaces and Prologues to Famous Books*. New York: P. F. Collier and Sons, 1910.

Excerpts from "Emile, Or, On Education" by Jean Jacques Rousseau, translated by Allan Bloom, pp. 341–344 and 362–365. Copyright © 1979 by Basic Books, Inc. Reprinted by permission of Basic Books, Inc., Publishers.

Excerpts from "Biographia Literaria by Samuel Taylor Coleridge, edited by J. Shawcross. Oxford: Clarendon Press, 1907.

"Preface to the Lyrical Ballads" by William Wordsworth from *Wordsworths's Literary Criticism*, edited by Nowell C. Smith. London: Henry Frowde, Oxford University Press, 1905.

"A Defense of Poetry" by Percy Bysshe Shelley from *Shelley's Literary and Philosophical Criticism*, edited by J. Shawcross. Oxford: Oxford University Press, 1909.

"Silly Novels by Lady Novelists" by George Eliot from *The Essays of George Eliot*, edited by Thomas Pinney, published by Columbia University Press, pp. 300–324. Copyright © 1963 by Thomas Pinney. Reprinted by permission.

"The Function of Criticism at the Present Time" by Matthew Arnold from *Matthew Arnold*, edited by John Bryson. London: Rupert Hart-Davis, 1954.

"The American Scholar" by Ralph Waldo Emerson from *The Works of Ralph Waldo Emerson*, vol. 2. Philadelphia: Nottingham Soc., N.D.

"Art Under Plutocracy" by William Morris from *Political Writings of William Morris*, edited by A. L. Morton. London: Lawrence and Wishart, 1984.

"On Music and Words" by Friedrich Nietzsche from *The Complete Works of Friedrich Nietsche, Early Greek Philosophy and Other Essays*, translated by Maximilliam Mugge. London: Macmillan Publishing Co., Inc., 1924.

"Wordsworth" by Walter Pater from *Essays on Literature and Art*, edited by Jennifer Uglow. London: Dent, 1973.

Excerpt from "The Theme of the Three Caskets" from *The Standard Edition of the Complete Psychological Works of Sigmund Freud*, edited and translated by James Strachey; also from *Collected Papers*, Vol. 4, by Sigmund Freud, Authorized Translation under the supervision of Joan Riviere. Published by Basic Books, Inc. by arrangement with The Hogarth Press Ltd. and The Institute of Psycho-Analysis, London. Reprinted by permission of the publishers and Sigmund Freud Copyrights Ltd.

"Tradition and the Individual Talent" by T. S. Eliot from *Selected Essays* by T. S. Eliot. Copyright © 1950 by Harcourt Brace Jovanovich, Inc.; renewed 1978 by Esme Valerie Eliot. Reprinted by permission of Harcourt Brace Jovanovich and Faber and Faber Ltd.

"Discourse in Life and Discourse in Art" by V. N. Voloshinov from *Freudianish: A Marxist Critique*, translated by I. R. Titunik. Copyright © 1976 by Academic Press, Inc. Reprinted by permission of Academic Press, Inc.

Excerpt from *A Room of One's Own* by Virginia Woolf, pp. 99–118, copyright © 1929 by Harcourt Brace Jovanovich, Inc.; renewed 1957 by Leonard Woolf. Reprinted by permission of Harcourt Brace Jovanovich, the Hogarth Press, and the estate of Virginia Woolf.

"Literature as Equipment for Living" by Kenneth Burke from *The Philosophy of Literary Form*, copyright © 1973 the Regents of the University of California. Reprinted by permission of the University of California Press.

"Odysseus' Scar" by Erich Auerbach from *Mimesis: The Representation of Reality in Western Literature*, translated by Willard R. Trask. Copyright © 1953; © 1981 renewed by Princeton University Press. Reprinted by permission of Princeton University Press.

Excerpt from *The Well Wrought Urn* by Cleanth Brooks, pp. 67–79; copyright © 1947, 1975 by Cleanth Brooks. Reprinted by permission of Harcourt Brace Jovanovich and Dobson Books Ltd.

"The Function of Criticism at the Present Time" by Northrup Frye from *Our Sense of Identity: A Book of Canadian Essays*, edited by Malcolm Ross; published by Toronto University Press, 1954. Copyright © 1954 by Northrup Frye. Reprinted by permission of the author.

Excerpt from *The Fantastic* by Tzvetan Todorov, pp. 41–57, translated by Richard Howard. Copyright © 1973 by Case Western Reserve University Press; © 1970 Editions du Seuil. Reprinted by permission of Case Western Reserve University and Georges Borchardt, Inc.

Excerpt from *Thinking About Women* by Mary Ellman, pp. 27–54. Copyright © 1968 by Mary Ellman. Reprinted by permission of Harcourt Brace Jovanovich and Macmillan, London and Basingstoke.

"Images of Black Women in Afro-American Literature" by Barbara Christian from *Black Feminist Criticism*, pp. 2–30. Copyright © 1985 by Pergamon Press. Reprinted by permission of Pergamon Press.

"From Work to Text" by Roland Barthes, translated from the French by Josue V. Harari, from *Textual Strategies: Perspectives in Post-Structuralist Criticism,* edited by Josue V. Harari, pp. 73–81. Copyright © 1979 by Cornell University. Reprinted by permission of the publisher, Cornell University Press, and Methuen & Co., London.

"What Is an Author?" by Michel Foucault, translated from the French by Josue V. harari, from *Textual Strategies: Perspectives in Post-Structuralist Criticism,* edited by Josue V. Harari, pp. 141–160. Copyright © 1979 by Cornell University. Used by permission of the publisher, Cornell University, and Methuen & Co., London.

"The Laugh of the Medusa" by Hélène Cixous, translated by Cohen and Cohen, from *Signs,* vol. 1, no. 4, pp. 875–893. Copyright © 1976 by the University of Chicago Press. Reprinted by permission of The University of Chicago Press and the author.

"The Father of Logos" by Jacques Derrida, translated by Barbara Johnson, from *Disseminations,* pp. 75–84. Copyright © 1981 by The University of Chicago Press. Reprinted by permission of The University of Chicago Press, the Athlone Press, and the author.

"Interpreting the Varorium" by Stanley Fish from *Critical Inquiry,* vol. 2, no. 3, pp. 465–486. Copyright © 1980 by The University of Chicago Press. Reprinted by permission of the University of Chicago Press and the author.

Excerpts from *Keywords: A Vocabulary of Culture and Society* by Raymond Williams. Copyright © 1976 by Raymond Williams. Reprinted by permission of Oxford University Press, Inc., and William Collins Sons & Co., Ltd.

"Life's Empty Pack: Notes Toward a Literary Daughteronomy" by Sandra Gilbert from *Critical Inquiry,* vol. 11, no. 3, pp. 355–384. Copyright © 1985 by The University of Chicago Press. Reprinted by permission of The University of Chicago Press and the author.

"The Search for Grounds in Literary Study" by J. Hillis Miller from *Genre,* vol. 17, no. 1/2, pp. 19–36. Copyright © 1984 by the University of Oklahoma Press. Reprinted by permission of the University of Oklahoma Press.

"Distrust of the Reader in Afro-American Narratives" by Robert B. Stepto from *Reconstructing American Literary History,* edited by Sacvan Berkovitch. Copyright © 1986 by Harvard University Press. Reprinted by permission of Harvard University Press.

"The Race for Theory" by Barbara Christian from *Cultural Critique,* Spring 1987, pp. 51–63. Copyright © 1987 by *Cultural Critique.* Reprinted by permission.

PART 1

CRITICAL TEXTS

CHAPTER ONE

Classical Literary Criticism

The modern British philosopher Alfred North Whitehead once suggested that all of Western philosophy is an elaborate footnote to Plato's work. Such dramatic exaggerations, though in a sense absurd, nonetheless convey important insights about cultural influence and continuity, and about the importance of the classical world in the Western tradition. It would be especially dangerous, however, to make the same claim—even granting the exaggeration—about the relationship between classical criticism and the history of literary studies. Western criticism in its many forms mirrors the complex historical and cultural changes that constitute the Western tradition; and that tradition, or set of traditions, has been shaped and influenced too broadly by too many different cultures, east and west, to be taken only as an expression or elaboration of the classical world.

Having said that, however, the briefest survey of classical literary theory and commentary—from Plato and Aristotle through Horace (the great teacher of Greek literary ideals in Rome), from the broadest view of the political use and social value of poetry through Longinus' descriptions of effective style and rhetoric—points up an extraordinarily rich range of concerns for literary criticism. Virtually no fundamental issue of literary study, whether semiotic, psychological, or political, is absent from classical thought; and the literary criticism of ancient Greece and Rome is a valuable survey of what literary studies can be. It is also a central exploration of the very nature and purpose of literary studies: why we should read and write texts to begin with, how literature helps to constitute and serve society, and what value literary texts have for community and culture generally. Finally, classical literary criticism and theory also provide the formative questions that have shaped Western criticism.

Accordingly, the phenomenon of literary criticism—that is, the specific, self-conscious examination of the function and value of literature—can be said to begin in Athens in the fifth century B.C., a period notable for tremendous political and cultural change. There is the superb example of Aristophanes' play *The Frogs*, which is about the judging of Euripides and Aeschylus according to contemporary standards of morality and theater craft. More important for criticism, however, is the escalating trend in this century for ideas about personal and private value to consolidate under the concept of the state and the "good" that it advances. Once this cultural and social development is complete, a trend strongly associated with Plato and Aristotle, the ideal of the "good" and the reality of the polity, or actual political and cultural organization, merge into one. Eric Havelock notes in *The Liberal Temper in Greek Politics* that the tendency to consolidate the value structure of Greek society grew strong enough in the fifth century to suppress liberal alternatives to it—the ideological positions of the Sophists that promoted noncentralized authority and challenged the absolute coordination of the state and all cultural and personal life. "It was Aristotle's vigorous and successful purpose," as Havelock explains, "to kill [liberal] theory and replace it by one of statehood. For statehood and state are definable in terms of permanent patterns of power; while "society" for the [Greek] liberals was ultimately something different, something in which power-patterns existed pragmatically and temporarily." Plato, Aristotle, and others thus advanced the goal of living one's life according to official state moral precepts that were thought to be synonymous with goodness; and the success of their effort is evident in the great age of Greek philosophy.

This suppression, however, accompanied a growing conservative belief in an absolute standard of morality, a growing picture of the official value of life lived in service to an overriding and unassailable communal authority. By many accounts, once accomplished, this consolidation produced a renaissance in Greek culture, especially a highly energized body of philosophy that articulated standards for the good life and the instrumental function of the human community in reaching it.

Decisive for literary criticism during this transition was the massive turn of Greek culture from poetry (and art generally) toward philosophy, a turn away from the writing and reading of poetic narratives like Homer's *Iliad* and *Odyssey* and Hesiod's *Theogony* as fundamental modes—highly imaginative and often visionary—for ordering and evaluating the world. Henceforth, fifth-century Athens developed alternative ways of knowing and methods of inquiry that would discover "truth" in a different manner from the poetic narratives. The rigors of philosophy and influential texts such as Plato's *Republic* and Aristotle's *Poetics, Politics* and *On Interpretation*—texts that manifest abstract and highly rational speculation as instruments for discovering what is valuable, moral, and, ultimately, "good" in the world—are evidence of the success of this transformation. From this transformation, particularly in the *Poetics*, we get the concept of "genre," or species of literature, that is fundamental for conceptions of poetry, drama, epic, and so on.

Embodied in this change is the critical attitude conveyed in the credo over Plato's academy door: "Let no one enter here who is not a geometer"—that is, let no one enter who does not recognize high abstraction and linear (noncontradictory) reasoning as the hallmarks of the inquiry into truth in the new Greek world. The ideal of the geometer-philosopher is epitomized in Socrates and the Socratic method of skeptical inquiry and relentless interrogation of an argument's underlying assumptions. In this way, the ideal of the geometer-philosopher pushed the value of rationalism and rational method to a previously unknown height. Once abstraction and pure generality became designated instruments for finding truth, literary criticism as a reflection on the abstract nature, order, and function of literature became possible—much as philosophy, in the specifically Greek sense of that term, also became possible for Greek and Western culture in the fifth century.

Also apparent in this beginning of literary criticism in ancient Greek culture is the assumption of a specific use for criticism, a stress on its instrumental nature as it serves a transcendent moral good. This is made clear in Plato's argument in *The Republic* that society must regulate what children read, the "first business" of education being "to supervise the making of fables and legends" so as to succeed in "moulding [children's] souls with these stories." This Platonic conception of criticism with a pedagogic function derives from the need for moral regulation by those who are legitimately the guardians—or geometers—of culture.

The community needs defending in the first place because literature itself (what the Greeks call "poetry") has such great power. Poetry, in fact, is too powerful, Plato worries, in that it shapes experience and represents or depicts reality in unconventional and unpredictable ways, therein compelling potentially wayward beliefs and allegiances with tremendous force. In short, since humans act on the beliefs and emotions evoked by poetry, there is a need to guide poetry with external constraints to prevent the misuse of this powerful force. Otherwise, through the experiences of poetry people will think and act in a variety of chance and potentially harmful ways. Such moral distraction, in turn, will disrupt the communal fabric by eroding the consensus view—what the Greeks saw as a correct "imitation"—of reality. Social disorder, chaos, and destruction will likely follow.

Criticism, then, has the moral end of leading people toward the "good" that society endeavors to attain ever greater knowledge of. Prior to the fifth century B.C., this good was thought to reside in dramatic, explanatory stories—like those of the *Iliad*, the *Odyssey*, and the *Theogony*—about the exploits of the gods when the world was created and civilization was being fashioned. These stories—especially those by Homer—tell about Zeus as the champion of the civilized community and the enfranchiser of civil order, law, and justice. In this role Zeus does not so much provide a model of behavior as an origin for the Cosmos and draws the boundaries of conduct that humans may obey and, in so doing, honor the divine parent, "the father of men." The moral good of humans consists, therefore, in their willing adherence to the world's political and social scheme as they successfully occupy their allotted position in it. In so doing, they affirm—through the success of their own lives—the conservative and unchangeable truth of the god-given order.

Plato further imagines that literary criticism should provide guidance for what citizens should read and think, especially when they are at a young and impressionable age. Criticism, in effect, should be a propaedeutic guide for what to read and how to understand poetry; and, in so being, it should channel personal and social inclinations toward communal goals. That is, since poetry cannot predetermine its own effect, criticism has a profoundly didactic and regulative social mission, a corrective service to perform for literature in light of literature's essentially amoral and dangerously powerful nature. In other words, poetry could not be allowed to win what Plato in *The Republic* called "the ancient feud between poetry and philosophy."

After the fifth century, the concept of moral goodness was conveyed more through an abstract principle of balance, a complex ideal of rational economy encompassing the chaotic variety of the mutable world as well as the unchanging ideals—the "truths," "forms," and divine patterns—that govern the Cosmos. From this point forward the Greeks sought after truth through the deployment of abstract Socratic reasoning, the deductive inquiry that, in being relentlessly skeptical, uncovers ignorance and error. Thus, as the critic and philosopher discover error in the mutable world, they affirm the abstract principles of reasoning that reflect truth, which themselves should not be—and technically cannot be—subject to change. The notion of truth as conveyed through rational balance was also shown in the symmetry achieved by classical rhetoric; that is, in parallel phrases and clauses that—in their symmetrical perfection—seemed to embody rationality's very form and essence. This form, by extension, conveys a dimension of truth and "the *force* in eloquence," as Longinus says later in the first century A.D., that "could not be known without that light which we receive from [well-formed and responsible] art."

What emerges from the renaissance of fifth-century Athens, however, is not something totally new. It is a highly abstract and philosophical version of the *scala naturae*, the underlying scheme of the Greek worldview. The overt conception of a world "scale" gets formal description in Plato's *Symposium* as "a scale or ladder of being" constituting, as Arthur O. Lovejoy says, a "graded series of creatures down which the divine life in its overflow had descended." This overflow "might be conceived to constitute also the stages of man's ascent to the divine life." The scale extends to and connects everything from the gods to chaos, from the most- to the least-perfect substance in the world. In between are the subdivine and then human orders. Each order, in turn, reflects a scale of organization that ranges from most- to least-perfect in composition. At the top of the human scale are the representatives of the gods and the "good," and at the bottom are those with no power. The king stands in for the divine father and shares the gods' responsibility to uphold civilization and hold back chaos. Ultimately a king has the same oppositional relationship to chaos as do the gods. This principle of gradation—implicit in the classical world as the *scala naturae* and made explicit in the late Middle Ages and early Renaissance as the Great Chain of Being, wherein a hierarchical scheme organizes the entire Cosmos—is key to understanding Greek morality and ethics.

In this way, the Greek Cosmos, as it hierarchically elaborates the concept of the good, is an order, or a kind of text, that humans try to decipher correctly. When people decipher it properly, they are acting morally. When they succeed in finding and acting in accordance with their place in the Cosmos, they are advancing themselves and the community's fortunes toward the "good." It is in this context that classical literary criticism must be viewed—as a cultural instrument for enhancing the community's grasp of its position in the Cosmos. A correct understanding of the Cosmos and its hierarchical construction constitutes *imitation*, an accurate rendering of the relationships, or ratios, of truth as manifested in the Cosmos. All human endeavors, and certainly the arts (at least to Aristotle's mind), should strive to imitate what is true and "just" in the world. Literary criticism that fulfills this function—that is, for Aristotle but not for Plato—is itself good; that which does not blocks the path to the life lived morally.

It is somewhat predictable, finally, that the abstract concept of the "good" developed in the fifth century would engender considerable skepticism about all human endeavors, especially literature and art, that have the potential to do other than serve a rationalized version of "good." Any given narrative poem and or work of art, in short, *may* serve the "good," or it may not. Aristophanes takes a pragmatic view of this dilemma in *The Frogs*, when he weighs how close Euripides and Aeschylus come to achieving valuable moral ends. Unfortunately, or so Plato and other Greeks thought, the visionary and polymorphous nature of poetry does not compel this service. Poetry, as Plato imagined it, draws from the power of the soul, but, alas, it too easily goes astray. Literary criticism, it follows, as practiced by Plato, Aristotle, Aristophanes, Horace, and Longinus, exists for precisely the purpose of correcting (at whatever degree of severity) the constitutional inadequacy of poetry.

Accordingly, whether the consideration is a genre distinction—the very concept of which the Greeks initiated—or the elements of poetry (according to Aristotle, *ethos*—character, *dianoia*—thought, *lexis*—expression, *melopoiia*—music, *opsis*—spectacle, and *mythos*—plot), literary criticism necessarily aims to guide poetry and interpretive understandings of it into a relationship with the Cosmos that is at once moral and inherently good.

FURTHER READING

D'Alton, J. F. *Roman Literary Theory and Criticism*. New York: Russell and Russell, 1962.

Dodds, E. R. *The Greeks and the Irrational*. Berkeley: University of California Press, 1950.

Ehnmark, Erland. *The Idea of God in Homer: Inaugural Dissertation*. Uppsala: Almquist and Wiksells Boktryckeri, AB, 1935.

Greene, William Chase. *Moira: Fate, Good, and Evil in Greek Thought*. Cambridge, Mass.: Harvard University Press, 1944.

Hack, Roy Kenneth. *God in Greek Philosophy to the Time of Socrates*. Princeton, N.J.: Princeton University Press for the University of Cincinnati, 1931.

Havelock, Eric A. *The Greek Concept of Justice: From Its Shadow in Homer to Its Substance in Plato*. Cambridge, Mass.: Harvard University Press, 1978.

———. *The Liberal Temper in Greek Politics*. New Haven, Conn.: Yale University Press, 1957.

Lefkowitz, Mary R. *Heroines and Hysterics*. New York: St. Martin's Press, 1981.

Lloyd-Jones, Hugh. *The Justice of Zeus*. Berkeley: University of California Press, 1983.

Lovejoy, Arthur O. *The Great Chain of Being: A Study of the History of an Idea*. New York: Harper & Row, 1960 (orig. 1936).

Rose, H. J. *A Handbook of Greek Mythology*. London: Methuen, 1928.

Russell, D. A., and M. Winterbottom, eds. *Ancient Literary Criticism: The Principal Texts in New Translations*. Oxford, Eng.: Clarendon Press, 1973.

Sikes, E.E. *The Greek View of Poetry*. New York: Barnes and Noble, 1931.

Vernant, Jean-Pierre. *Myth and Society in Ancient Greece*. Trans. Janet Lloyd. Sussex, Eng.: Harvester Press; Atlantic Highlands, N.J.: Humanities Press, 1980.

———. *The Origins of Greek Thought*. Ithaca, N.Y.: Cornell University Press, 1982.

Aristophanes 445–380 B.C.

Aristophanes was one of the greatest comic playwrights in Athens, and his eleven plays are the only surviving examples we have of New Comedy. Supposedly typical of New Comedy, his plays were broadly satirical and mixed political, social, and literary commentary; they did not shy away from either personal attacks on public figures or rich topical allusion. While his plays are immersed in references to his period, Aristophanes is known for the great inventiveness and brightness of his work—especially his wry and irreverent characters. His well-known plays are *The Acharnians* (425 B.C.), *The Knights* (424 B.C.), *The Clouds* (423 B.C.), *The Birds* (414 B.C.), *Lysistrata* (411 B.C.), and *The Frogs* (405 B.C.).

The Frogs presents the traditional Greek and Roman comic situation of a dialogue between an ironic and a posturing figure—in this case, a clever slave, Xanthias, and the god Dionysus, a self-important and puffed-up figure of authority. Much of the activity in this play centers on the exchange between the two and the ironic insights that come from the slave's wit. The plot revolves around Dionysus' decision to revitalize Athenian drama by traveling to Hades and bringing back Euripides. However, upon comparing Euripides with the playwright Aeschylus, Dionysus judges Euripides' work to be affected and false in style and theme; he therefore brings back Aeschylus from

Hades instead. This play is a good example of non-Platonic literary criticism from the fifth century B.C. that is not fundamentally skeptical of literature itself.

The Frogs

Cast of Characters

The God Dionysus
Xanthias, his slave
Heracles
A corpse
Charon, ferryman over the River Styx
Chorus of Frogs
Chorus of Initiates
Aeacus
Landlady
Plathane, her servant
Maidservant
Pluto
Aeschylus
Euripides

Dionysus, *disguised as Heracles (with lion's skin and club) and his servant* Xanthias, *carrying the baggage on a donkey*

Xanthias: Shall I tell one of those surefire old jokes now, boss,
that never fail to leave the audience in stitches?

Dionysus: Yes, anything you like, except "I'm getting crushed!"
Avoid that one, I'm getting sick and tired of it.

Xan.: No other jokes at all?

Dion.: Don't say "My aching back!"

Xan.: What about a really funny one?

Dion.: For God's sake.
Willingly, by all means, only please don't—

Xan.: Don't what?

Dion.: Don't shift your pole and say "I want to take a crap!"

Xan.: I can't say that I'm carrying such a heavy load
and if no one relieves me, I have got to shit?

Dion.: No, no, please don't, until I'm ready to throw up.

Xan.: What use is it for me to carry this big burden
if I can't tell a good old joke like Phyrnichus,[1]
Ameipsias and Lysis have in all their plays,
where people carrying burdens get all the jokes?

Dion.: Well, don't! I tell you, every time I see these plays
and hear these tired bits of comic business,
I always leave the theater a full year older!

Xan.: Oh, thrice unhappy neck of mine which now is getting
crushed, but cannot say so, because that would be a joke.

Dion.: What insolence, what arrogance the fellow shows,
when I, great Dionysus, son of Wine-Carafe[2]

must walk myself, and toil, and let this bumpkin ride,
so he won't become tired, or carry anything!

XAN.: What, I'm not carrying anything?

DION.: No, things are carrying you!

XAN.: I'm carrying this.

DION.: How?

XAN. With greatest difficulty!

DION.: Not so, the donkey carries everything that you are carrying.

XAN.: The donkey doesn't carry bags that *I* am carrying!

DION.: But how can you be carrying when you yourself are carried?

XAN.: Don't know. I only know I've got an "aching back"!

DION.: Well, if it does no good when the donkey carries you
why don't you change places and carry him awhile?

XAN.: Oh why, oh why, couldn't I have fought at Arginusae,[3]
then you'd never get away with acting like this!

DION.: Dismount, you villain! All this weary walking now
has brought me to the door that I've been looking for.
Porter, porter, hey, where's the porter?

HERACLES [*entering from his house*]:
Who is banging on my door like a drunken Centaur?[4]
My goodness, what is this, and who have we here?

DION.: Boy!

XAN.: What is it?

DION.: Didn't you see?

XAN.: See what boss?

DION.: How scared he was?

XAN.: Yes, he's scared you're out of your mind!

HER.: Ha, ha, oh, by Demeter, I cannot help laughing,
even though I bite my lips I cannot help it!

DION.: Come here, my good sir, for I have need of you.

HER.: I'm sorry but I still cannot refrain from laughing!
A lion's skin over a robe of yellow silk,
an actor's buskin and the club of Heracles![5]
Where have you been?

DION.: I've been at sea with Cleisthenes.[6]

HER.: At war?

DION.: We sank some vessels of the enemy.
At least a dozen or thirteen of them we sank.

HER.: You two?

DION.: Indeed.

XAN.: "And then I woke up from a sound sleep."

DION.: And on the ship's deck I was sitting there and reading
Euripides' *Andromeda*, when all at once
a sudden yearning struck me to the very heart.

HER.: How large was it?

DION.: Quite small, only the size of Molon.[7]

HER.: For a woman?

DION.: No, not that.

HER.: A boy, then?

DION.: No, not at all.

HER.: For a man?

DION.: Oh, go on!

HER.: Was it for Cleisthenes?[8]

DION.: Don't make fun of me, brother, I'm really in great trouble;

this yearning is consuming me, wearing me away.

HER.: Tell me, little brother.

DION.: No, no, I can't describe it.

Well, I'll try to explain by telling you in riddles:

Have you ever had a great longing for split-pea soup?

HER.: Split-pea soup? Oh, yes I have, thousands of times!

DION.: Well, do you understand? Or shall I explain again?

HER.: Not about the soup, I understand that fine.[9]

DION.: Well, that's the kind of longing that consumes me now,

for Euripides!

HER.: Euripides, but he's dead!

DION.: And no one can persuade me not to go to Hades

and bring him back.

HER.: You mean, to the place of the Dead?

DION.: And lower still, if there's a place that's lower still.

HER.: What for?

DION.: I want a really clever, genuine poet,

"For most of them are dead, only the bad still live!"[10]

HER.: But what about poor Iophon?[11]

DION.: He is the only one

remaining that's any good—if indeed he is good!

For even about him, I'm not exactly certain.

HER.: But why don't you restore old Sophocles to life

before Euripides, if you must bring someone back?

DION.: Not until I've seen what Iophon can do

all by himself, without his father there to help him.

Besides, Euripides is a tricky, crafty knave,

he'll easily escape from there, while Sophocles,

content on Earth, will be content in Hades, too.

HER.: And Agathon?[12]

DION.: Agathon? He's gone far away,

a good man and a good poet, missed by all his friends.

HER.: Where has he gone?

DION.: To join the banquets of the blessed.[13]

HER.: And Xenocles?[14] What about him?

DION.: Oh, the devil take Xenocles!

HER.: Pythangelus?

XAN.: And no one has a word for me

with all the skin rubbed off my "poor aching back"!

HER.: But don't you have a bunch of pleasant little lads

all writing tragedies, by tens of thousands now,

all much more wordy than Euripides himself?

DION.: Just gleanings, rotten grapes, and chattering gossips all,

all birds a-twittering, mutilators of their art!

They get one chorus, that's the last we see of them,

after once pissing on the Tragic Muse, that's all!

You'll never find a true creative genius there,

uttering a true word—not one of them with balls!

HER.: With balls?

DION.: I mean the kind of man who'd take a risk
or have the hardihood to coin some new expressions:
"Ether, Zeus' chamber," or "The lengthy foot of Time,"[15]
"Twas not my mind that took an oath, it was my tongue
committed perjury all on its own account."

HER.: That pleases you?

DION.: Pleases me? I'm downright crazy about it!

HER.: But it's all knavish tricks, as you must know yourself.

DION.: "Don't house in my mind, you have your own house!"[16]

HER.: Really, it's witless stuff, pretentious and all bad!

DION.: Teach me to eat!

XAN.: And no one has a word for me!

DION.: The reason I came dressed in all this paraphernalia,
disguised as you—so I could find out who were your hosts,
the ones you stayed with when you kidnapped Cerberus,[17]
in case I need them—tell me, who were your hosts,
where are the harbors and where are the bakery shops,
the brothels, inns, detours, the fountains and the roads,
the towns and dwellings, and hostesses, and where are
the fewest bedbugs?

XAN.: And no one has a word for me!

HER.: Brave man, you really dare to make that fearsome journey?

DION.: Never mind all that, just tell me what's the best way—
the quickest road to take a fellow down to Hades,
and, please, I don't want anything too hot or cold!

HER.: Well, which of them had I better tell you the first?
There's one in which you use the rope and stool and jump
—and hang yourself!

DION.: Oh, no, thanks, that's too throttling!

HER.: Well, there is another well-worn road, with mortar and with pestle . . .

DION.: Oh, hemlock, you mean!

HER.: Exactly so.

DION.: Oh, no, oh, no, that's much too cold and wintry for me!
Why, right away, your shins are frozen to the bone!

HER.: Well, then, how would you like a steep and swift descent?

DION.: That's just for me; you know, I'm not a famous walker.

HER.: So then, go to the Cerameicus . . .

DION.: Yes, and then what?

HER.: You climb up to the tower's very top . . .

DION.: What then?

HER.: You watch them starting the torch races there,
and when the crowds are all a-shouting "Let them go!"
then go, yourself!

DION.: Go where?

HER.: Why, right over the top!

DION.: Who, me? I'd lose two bags of brains! Thanks very much,
I'd never try that way!

HER.: Then which way will you try?

DION.: The way you went yourself.

HER.: That way is quite a journey!

The first thing that you'll see is an enormous lake[18]—
unfathomable . . .

DION.: How am I to cross over it?

HER.: An aged man will row you in a tiny boat,[19]
after collecting two obols as the fare from you.[20]

DION.: Oh, my! What power those two obols have all over
the world! How did they get there?

HER.: Theseus brought them.[21]
And then you'll see the serpents and the mighty monsters,
millions of them.

DION.: Stop trying to frighten me,
I'm going anyway!

HER.: Then mud and slime and filth
and ever-flowing dung, and lying there in it,
whoever wronged a stranger or a guest on earth,
or made love to a boy and didn't pay him for it,
whoever beat his mother up or hit his father
on the jaw, whoever swore an oath falsely,
or plagiarized a speech of Morsimus.[22]

DION.: And there belongs, I'll wager, with those criminals,
whoever dances Pyrrhic dances of Cinesias.[23]

HER.: But then you'll hear the sacred sound of sweetest flutes,
and lovely sunlight you will see, like we have here,
and myrtle groves, and happy throngs who are applauding
triumphantly, great crowds of men and women, too.[24]

DION.: And who will they be?

HER.: They'll be the Initiates.

XAN.: I'm the Donkey that's to be Initiated!
But, I won't stand it, no, not for another minute!

HER.: They will tell you everything you want to know:
they live right there, beside the road you're going to travel,
right beside the gates of Pluto's dwellingplace.
So fare you well brother.

[Exit HERACLES*]*

DION.: And the best of health
to you as well. Now, boy, let's pick up the baggage.

XAN.: Before I've put it down?

DION.: Yes, and be quick about it!

XAN.: Why don't you hire a body, like the one they are
carrying out right now—to be your porter, sir?

DION.: And if I cannot find one?

XAN.: Then I'll do it.

[Enter A FUNERAL*]*

DION.: All right.
Why, here's a funeral, they're carrying out the corpse.
Hey there, you, deceased one, I'm speaking to you sir, now!
Would you be willing to carry our baggage down to Hades?

CORPSE: What are they?

DION.: These you see here.

CORPSE: Two drachmas for the lot?

DION.: Oh, no, that's much too much!

CORPSE: Then on with the procession!

DION.: Stop a minute, see if we can't make a bargain.

CORPSE: Two drachmas, cash, or don't waste my time talking!
DION.: How about nine obols?
CORPSE: I'd rather live again!
[*Exit* FUNERAL]
XAN.: What an arrogant rascal—the devil take him, then!
I'll take the stuff myself!
DION.: That's a noble fellow!
Let's find the ferry.
[*Enter* CHARON]
CHARON: Avast there! Bring her alongside!
XAN.: What's that, for goodness sake?
DION.: That's a lake, by Zeus!
The one he spoke about, and there's the ferryboat!
XAN.: Yes, by Poseidon, and that must be old Charon himself!
DION.: Charon! Ahoy there, Charon, Charon, ahoy!
CHARON: Who's for Rest from Troubles, Pain, and other Sorrows,
Who's for Lethe's Plain, and who's for Donkey-Shearing?
Cereberus, Going to the Dogs, and Taenarus?
DION.: I am.
CHA.: Hurry aboard.
DION.: Where are you really bound for?
Going to the Dogs?
CHA.: Yes, and all on your account.
Just step on board.
DION.: This way, Boy!
CHA.: But, I don't take slaves!
Unless they fought at sea to get their freedom first.[25]
XAN.: I couldn't go, I had some trouble with my eyes.
CHA.: Then you must go on foot, and circle round the lake.
XAN.: Where must I go?
CHA.: Beside the Withering Stone
near to the Resting Place.
DION.: You understand?
XAN.: I do.
Oh, woe is me, what evil omen crossed my path!
[*Exit* XANTHIAS]
CHA.: Sit to your oar. Any more passengers for Charon?
Hurry. Hey, there, what are you doing?
DION.: What am I doing?
I'm sitting on my oar, just as you told me to!
CHA.: No, No! Get up again and sit down *there,* Fatso!
DION.: Like this?
CHA.: And stretch your arms out in front of you.
DION.: Like this?
CHA.: Stop fooling. Plant your feet right there
and pull for all your're worth.
DION.: How am I to pull?
I am not a rower or a Salaminian![26]
How am I to row?
Cha.: Easily, for you will hear at once
a lovely song as soon as you begin.
DION.: What from?
CHA.: From marvelous Cycnoranae!
DION.: Then give me the word!
CHA.: Ahoy there! Heave ho!
CHORUS OF FROGS:
Brekekekex coäx coäx
Brekekekex coäx coäx!
We are sons of lake and spring!

listen to our voices ring,
here we are and here we sing,
coäx coäx
coäx coäx
We are praising Dionysus,
he, the god who good wine prizes,
here we are with no disguises
as the wine in the jug arises.
Brekekekex coäx coäx
Brekekekex coäx coäx!
DION.: I begin to have an aching back,
you're putting me upon the rack!
FROGS: Brekekekex coäx coäx!
DION.: A lot you care for our aching backs!
FROGS: Brekekekex coäx coäx!
DION.: Something in your song there lacks,
You say nothing but Coäx!
FROGS: Brekekekex coäx coäx!
That's right, Mister Busy Man!
We are loved by Goatfoot Pan,
And the Muses with their Lyre,
And Apollo the Muses' sire,
for the reedy panpipes' sake,
growing right here in our lake,
and the lyre, grown in the mire,
Brekekekex coäx coäx
Brekekekex coäx coäx!
DION.: Look, blisters on my hands they wax,
and my ass, no sweat it lacks.
FROGS: Brekekex coäx coäx!
DION.: Enough of you and your loud quacks!
Stop, you creatures, with your cracks!
FROGS: Brekekex coäx coäx!
On we must go, yes, on and on,
singing louder, one by one,
as in bygone sunny days
we have sung our songs of praise,
singing in the calm and storm,
and in the slime so nice and warm,
raising our shrill voices double,
accompanied by bursting bubble!
Brekekekex coäx coäx.
DION.: Go on, with your dreadful quacks,
I don't care if you break your backs!
Brekekekex coäx coäx
FROGS: Then we'll sing our tuneful song
all the day and all night long!
FROGS and DION: Brekekekex coäx coäx!
Brekekekex coäx coäx!
DION.: Well, you never will outdo me!
FROGS: What do you think you can do to me?
We can croak all night, all day.
DION.: I can also shout this way!
And my wind and lungs I'll tax,
Brekekekex coäx coäx!
At last I'll end your endless coäx.
And then I will make you relax
and stop with your eternal quacks,
Brekekekex coäx coäx!
CHA.: Easy there, easy there, pull on your oar!
Pay your fare and get off.
DION.: Here you are, two obols.
Where are you, Xanthias? Xanthias, where are you?
XAN. [*entering*]: Here I am.
DION.: Come here then.
XAN.: Glad to see you, boss!
DION.: What do we have here?
XAN.: Only darkness and filth and mud!
DION.: But did you see the father-beaters that he spoke of
and all the perjurers that he said we would see?
XAN.: Yes, didn't you?
DION.: Poseidon, yes, there they are! [*Points at the audience*]
What do we do now?
XAN.: We have to move along, this is the place that Heracles said was all full
of horrible beasts and monsters.
DION.: Devil

take the man!
He's just putting it on to frighten us away.
He's jealous because he knows what a brave god I am
—for after all, who is as proud as Heracles?
I wish for nothing more than to meet some awful creature,
some dangerous adventure, to make the trip worthwhile!
XAN.: Yes, by Zeus, what's that? I think I hear a noise!
DION.: What is it?
XAN.: There behind us.
DION.: To the rear march!
XAN.: Now it's in front of us.
DION.: Then forward march, my man!
XAN.: There it is now, a most ferocious monster, there!
DION.: What kind of monster?
XAN.: Oh, terrible, it keeps on changing shape.
First it's a bull, then it's a mule, then it becomes
a gorgeous woman.
DION.: Where is she? I want to see her!
XAN.: She's not a woman any more, she's now a bitch.
DION.: Must be Empusa![27]
XAN.: Oh, its face is all aflame with fire.
DION.: Does it have one leg of bronze?
XAN.: Yes, by Poseidon, and the other one of bullshit.
DION.: Oh, where can I run?
XAN.: Oh, where can I run?
DION.: Oh, my Priest,[28] protect me! And, we'll have dinner together!
XAN.: Oh, Heracles, we're done for!
DION.: Oh, don't call me that!
Call me by any other name, but not by that one.
XAN.: Well, Dionysus, then!
DION.: Oh, no, that's even worse!
XAN.: Go away, monster! Come this way now, boss.
DION.: What is it?
XAN.: Take courage, all is calm now
and we can say as once Hegelochus did say,
"After the storm, how *weasily* the sun comes out!"[29]
Empusa's gone!
DION.: Swear it.
XAN.: By Zeus she's gone.
DION.: Swear again.
XAN.: Again, by Zeus.
DION.: Again.
XAN.: Again, by Zeus!
O goodness me, how pale I was when I saw it,
but he was scared shitless—and on me, at that!
DION.: Whence came all these calamities that have befallen me,
which of the gods shall I blame for my ill-fortune now?
Air, Zeus's chamber, or the Lengthy Foot of time?[30]
Hey, there!
[*Flute music heard offstage*]
XAN.: What is it?
DION.: Don't you hear it?
XAN.: Hear what?
DION.: The sound of flutes?
XAN.: Yes, and the smell of torches, too.
Wafting towards us in a most mysterious way.
DION.: Then let's crouch down and listen to the music now.

[CHORUS OF INITIATES *enters, with torches*]
CHORUS: Iacchus, O Iacchus!
Iacchus, O Iacchus!
XAN.: I know, Master, it's those blessed Mystics
he told us of, they are playing and rejoicing here
singing their Iacchus, according to Diagoras.[31]
DION.: Yes, I think so. The best thing for us to do
is to keep quiet and find out what's going on.
CHORUS: Iacchus, dwelling in your lovely temples,
Iacchus, O Iacchus!
Dancing among the verdant trees
in your Sacred Mysteries,
binding on your forehead now
wreaths of lovely myrtle bough,
dancing with the charming Graces
in these pure and holy places,
as the mystic choirs advance
figuring in the joyous dance.
XAN.: Oh, great Queen, great Demeter's holy child
what a lovely whiff of pork[32] my nostrils have beguiled!
DION.: If you keep quiet and do not gripe
perhaps they'll give you a piece of tripe!
CHORUS: Rise from your sleep, you fervent bands,
with your torches in your hands!
Iacchus, O Iacchus!
Iacchus, O Iacchus!
Lucifer, the Morning Star
shines o'er mead and field afar,
away with sorrow and with grief,
dance with gladness and relief,
raise the gleaming firebrands,
hold them in your lovely hands,
dancing in your joyous bands,
lead the Chorus, fair indeed,
to the verdant flowery mead!
May all wicked thoughts be kept far away from Mystic Choir
all the Uninitiated, all the hearts impure and dire,[33]
all who ne'er took part in orgies, learned the Muses' holy dances,
ne'er took part in Bacchic rites the beef-eating Cratinus advances,[34]
who engage in ribaldries, delighting in untimely jest,
who do not make peace with neighbors, and from factions never rest,
fanning flames of hatred, all desirous of petty gain,
taking bribes and graft, while Athens is tossed by wind and rain;
whoever sells out forts to foemen, like Thorcyon, that rat,[35]
sending contraband from Aegina to Epidaurus, just like that,
trading in sails and tar and such, for specific commission rate,
or who persuades someone to give supplies to enemies that we all hate!—
or he who craps on Hecate's shrines—and he a chorusmaster, too!
Or any public figure, lampooned by us in comedies, who
would try to confiscate the poet's pay—I give them warning all, today,
I warn them once, I warn them twice, I warn them thrice, unholy throng!
Hands off our Mystic Chorus! Up, friends and give us all your song!
Songs for day and night as well, fitting for this festival!
Come one, come all,
To the verdant bowers,
bearing fresh flowers,
come, come forth!
Leap, dance, play and rejoice,
you're feasted, now sing with happy voice!
Raise her on high
praise her to the sky

the savior-goddess praise,
who says she will
save our city still,
no matter what Thorcyon says!
Change the measure, change the hymn,
change the solemn beat.
Let us sing to the goddess Demeter, harvest
queen, giver of wheat:
Lady Queen of holy rites,
preserve your faithful choral throng,
dancing with the sacred lights
revelling with holy song,
and in earnest and in just
may we celebrate your name,
joking, mocking, all the rest,
may we win, and be free from blame!
Let us call the beautiful God, with loud
triumphant ode,
travelling with sacred chorus all along the
Sacred Road.
Iacchus, Iacchus, honor our song.
Come, be with the holy throng.
Come, beside the Holy Maid
unweary and unafraid.
Come and join us as we dance
Be with us, our joy enhance!
With torn garments, just for fun,
and for laughter—you are the one,
dancing with feet unshod
revelling, you, the joyous God!
Holy Iacchus, do this
come and join our dance and chorus,
be with us as we sing and dance
our festivities enhance!
A pretty girl was in the crowd
as they danced and sang aloud
in the throng with all the rest,
we could see her snow-white breast!
Holy Iacchus, as we dance,
be with us, our joy enhance!

DION.: I'd like to dance with you!

XAN.: Yes,
master, me too!

CHORUS: Let us all join in the row,
mocking Archidemus now,
who comes up from underneath
before he's lost his baby teeth!
And he holds important posts
here among grim Hades' ghosts!
While Cleisthenes tears out his hair,
bewailing his dead lover there,
mourning for the dead Sebinus
with laments worthy of Linus,
while Callias, that worthy he-man
has become a doughty seaman,
with a sewn-up lion's hide,
hiding female parts inside!

DION.: Can you tell me, be so kind,
where can I King Pluto find?
We are strangers on your shore,
we have not been here before.

CHORUS: You need not go any farther,
than you have gone. Nay, good sire,
rather,
you are standing right before
Pluto's subterranean door.

DION.: Pick the trunks up, now, my
boy!

XAN.: Oh, I hope it brings you joy!
Zeus' Corinthians are in there.

CHORUS: Let us dance the sacred dances
through the flowery glades,
as the holy throng advances
all you matrons and you maids,
revelling throughout the night,
in the torches' flickering light,
through the meads and roses wending,
in the choral strophes blending
with the holy Fates to lead
as we trip it through the mead!
For the sun is shining bright
and we dance in its pure light.
We have beheld the Mysteries
in such sacred rites as these;
pure our hearts with nothing loath
toward the friend and stranger both.

DION.: How am I supposed to knock on
Pluto's door?
I don't know how they knock in this
accursed land!

XAN.: Stop dawdling. Go ahead and try the door. Remember,
you're supposed to act like Heracles as well.

DION.: Hey, there!

AEACUS [*at door*]: Who's calling?

DION.: The Hero Heracles!

AEAC.: Oh, shameless and abandoned, foulest rascal, you!
You rotten, rottener, and rottenest of all men!
You, the one who seized our Cerberus and choked him
and fled away and vanished, taking our watchdog
whom I was watching! But, I've got you now, you villain!
So close the blackest rocks of Stygian caverns now,
the peaks of Acheron, dripping with fresh blood
will lock you in, Cocytus' whirling hounds of Hell,
Enchidan's hundred heads, will tear your insides out,
piece by piece, the Tartesian Lamprey make a Lung-prey
of your own lungs, Tithrasian Gorgons then shall come
and make a meal out of your kidneys, mashing them
into a bloody, gory, sloppy slaughter-house—
just you wait here, I'll run and fetch my monsters for you!

[*Exit* AEACUS]

XAN.: Hey, what are you doing?

DION.: I've shat myself, invoke the god.[36]

XAN.: Get up, they'll laugh at you, quickly Master, get up
before they see you!

DION.: I can't; I'm in a swoon!
Give me a cold wet sponge to put next to my heart.

XAN.: Here it is.

DION.: Where? Where?

XAN.: By all the Golden Gods!
Is *that* where your heart is?

DION.: Yes, I was so afraid
it fell and fell until it reached my deepest entrails.

XAN.: You are the biggest coward of gods or men!

DION.: Who, me?
A coward wouldn't do a thing like that!

XAN.: What else?

DION.: A coward would have lain right there in all the stench,
but me, I stood right up and wiped myself with it.

XAN.: Heroic, by Poseidon!

DION.: You can say that again!
Weren't you the least bit scared by all his awful threats
and ravings?

XAN.: Me? I never cared the slightest bit!

DION.: Well, then, if that's the kind of hero you would be,
why not be me, just take the club of Heracles,
and lion's skin, since you're so free of fear and terror.
I'll be the porter then and carry all the luggage.

XAN.: Agreed. Hand them over. No probem, none at all.

[*They change costumes*]

And now just watch the new Xanthoheracles
and see if I'm a lily-livered coward, too!

DION.: No, by Zeus, you're a Melitean whipping-boy.
I'll be the one to carry all the luggage now.

[*Enter a* MAIDSERVANT *of Persephone*]

MAID: O, dearest Heracles, come in, my love, come in!
My mistress, when she heard that you were coming down,
baked several loaves of bread, the kind that you love best,
made two or three big pots of nice fresh split-pea soup,
and roasted a whole ox, with honey-cakes and buns!
So come . . .

XAN.: Oh, no thanks.

MAID: But, you must, you can't escape!
She's braising birds for you, and making fruit preserves
and candied spices, and the fruits that you like best,
and mixing bowls of sweetest wine. So come along,
come in with me.

XAN.: appreciate it . . .

MAID.: Not another word!
I will not let you go. Besides, we have a flute girl,
and two or three young dancing girls that we have picked
just for you . . .

XAN.: What's that you said? Dancing girls?

MAID: Yes, fresh young virgins, newly depilated, too.
So come, my dear, the first course is already served,
the tables are all there and waiting for the feast!

XAN.: Well then, go in and tell those dancing girls you spoke of
that Heracles Himself is ready to make his appearance.

[*Exit* MAID]

Here, boy, pick up the bags and follow me inside.

DION.: Oh, stop it, you're not serious, and just because
I dressed you up as Heracles for a little joke?
Come now, stop fooling around, Xanthias, my dear fellow,
pick up the baggage now and bring it right inside.

XAN.: What's that? You're going to take away the gift that you
have given me yourself?

DION.: Going to nothing, I am.
Give me the lion's skin.

[*Takes it*]

XAN.: Help, bear witness, gods,
that I have been attacked!

DION.: You calling on the gods!
What a vain and silly idea to try to be
Alcmena's son—and you a mortal and a slave

XAN.: So be it then. But, maybe if the gods are willing,
the time will come when you'll again have need of me!

CHORUS: There's a man who's really smart,
of cleverness he's made an art;
he sailed over the stormy seas,
careful always to keep his ease,
never like a painted boat,
in one position fixed, afloat.
But always veering with the wind
regardless of how much he's sinned,
always shifting with the breeze
like good old Theramenes.[37]

DION.: Funny enough to make your hair curl,
to see him with a dancing girl,
on the cushions, what a fool!
While I'm playing with my tool,
then perhaps he'd turn on me,
(such a lazy one is he!)
an uppercut from underneath
knocking out my two front teeth!

[*Enter* LANDLADY, *and her maid*, PLATHANE]

LANDLADY: Plathane, Plathane, here comes that wicked man!
the one who came to our inn, as you may well remember,
and ate up sixteen loaves . . .

PLATHANE: Why so it is, you're right!
The very same one!

XAN.: Someone's going to get it now.

LAND.: And twenty dishes of boiled meat, he ate, as well,
at half an obol each.

XAN.: Oh, someone's really in for it!

LAND.: And all that garlic!

DION.: You are talking nonsense, woman.
You don't know what you're talking about!

LAND.: You really thought
I wouldn't know you with those high shoes on your feet?
I haven't even mentioned all that fish you ate,
and all the new fresh cheeses that you gobbled up.
You even ate the wicker baskets they were in!
And when I mentioned how much money it would cost,
he glared and bellowed at me like an angry bull!

XAN.: Yes, yes, indeed, that's just the way he always is.

LAND.: And then he drew his sword and looked just like a madman!

PLAT.: Yes, so he did.

LAND.: And we were all just scared to death!
We climbed into the loft, the maid and I, but he
just rushed out and took the matting and escaped!

XAN.: That's him all right, but something surely must be done.

LAND.: Quick, run and call my patron Cleon to my aid.[38]

PLAT.: And fetch out old Hyperbolus, if you can find him,
and then we'll beat him.

LAND.: Oh, my, what a filthy snout!
I'd like to take a good big rock and smash to pieces
those awful teeth with which you chomped up all my goodies!

PLAT.: And I would like to throw you in the Deadman's Hole!

LAND.: I'd like to get a good sharp sickle and cut out
that gullet that has eaten all my sausages!
But I shall go to Cleon; he will bring a summons
and wring the payments out of you, you good-for-nothing!

DION.: May I perish straightway if I don't love Xanthias!

XAN.: Yes, yes, I know! Well, you can just stop talking now!
I won't be Heracles!

DION.: Oh, please don't say such things,
my dear little Xanthias!

XAN.: But how can I, a slave
and mortal, too, be Alcmena's intrepid son!

DION.: I know, you're angry at me, and I deserve it well,
and if you beat me up, I will not say a word!
But if I take the costume from you one more time,
destruction seize myself, my wife, and all my children,
and even Archidemus, bleary-eyed old bat!

XAN.: That oath I like; I'll take it on such terms as these.

CHORUS: Now again you'll be quite glad
wearing clothes that first you had,
with the club and lion's skin,
again to play the hero in!
Glare and roar like Heracles,
wearing trappings such as these,
and when you're in a bad fix,
no more pusillanimous tricks;
if you do, O worst of men,
then you'll be a slave again!

XAN.: Thank you for that noble thought,
I for myself some time have bought.
If something good should happen to me,
he'll want to change again, you'll see!
And while I'm wearing clothes like these,
I'll be as brave as Heracles!
Another danger, from inside,
now the door is opening wide.

[*Enter* AEACUS *and* SLAVES]

AEACUS: Seize that dognapper! Put the shackles on him now
and lead him off to justice!

DION.: Someone's going to get it!

XAN.: Stop that, do not go another step!

AEAC.: What, you'll fight?
Come, Ditylas, Sceblyas, and Pardocas, this way!
Give this fellow a taste of fisticuffs, you men!

DION.: How terrible to fight a man this way
and steal things besides!

AEAC.: Unnatural, that's what!

DION.: Monstrous, terrible!

XAN.: Now, by Zeus, I swear to you
if I was ever here before or stole a thing,
even the value of one tiny little hair,
may I perish straightway—and here's a splendid offer:
take this slave of mine and put him to the torture,
and if you find me guilty, hang me straightaway![39]

AEAC.: Torture, but how?

XAN.: Any way at all that you please:
Bind him, scourge him, flog him with bristles if you like,
fill his nostrils up with sharpest vinegar,
pile bricks upon his chest, yes, anything you please,
only don't beat him up with leeks and scallions.[40]

AEAC.: That's fair enough, and if I happen to make him lame,
I'll give you compensation for the harm I've done.

XAN.: Not necessary. Take him out and beat him senseless.

AEAC.: I'll do it here and now before your very eyes.
Put down your luggage, you, and just be sure to tell
the whole, entire truth.

DION.: One moment, I warn you all:
I'm an immortal, and no one may touch my person
without taking the consequences.[41]

AEAC.: What's that you say?

DION.: I'm Dionysus, son of Zeus, immortal god!
And he's my slave.

AEAC.: Did you hear that?

XAN.: Oh, yes, I did,
that's all the better reason to beat him, *a fortiori*.
If he's a god, he will not feel a single thing!

DION.: But you claim you're a god yourself, as well as I,
so why should you not be beaten up, the same as I am?

XAN.: Fair enough. So let this be the acid test:
whichever one of us you first hear crying out,
or wincing, then you know that he is no true god.
AEAC.: Indeed, you're acting like a real gentleman,
you certainly believe in justice. Strip them, slaves!
XAN.: How will you test us?
AEAC.: I can do it easily.
I'll simply give you equal blow for equal blow.
XAN.: That's fine. [*He is hit*] Now see if I so much as wince.
AEAC.: I just hit you.
XAN.: No, you didn't!
AEAC.: It certainly seems not!
Now I'll hit the other. [*Hits* DIONYSUS]
DION.: Tell me when you hit me.
AEAC.: But I've hit you already!
DION.: Didn't make me sneeze!
AEAC.: Well, I don't know. I'll try the other one again.
XAN.: Be quick about it. [*Gets hit*] Oh, goodness!
AEAC.: Why oh goodness? Did it hurt you?
XAN.: Heavens, no! I was only thinking of
the Diomeian Feast of Heracles, that's all!
AEAC.: Such holiness! Now the other's turn [*Hits* DIONYSUS]
DION.: Ow-ow-ow!
AEAC.: What's the ow-ow-ow!
DION.: I just saw the cavalry!
AEAC.: Then why the tears?
DION.: I got a whiff of onions.
AEAC.: It didn't hurt you?
DION.: Oh, no, not a bit!
AEAC.: Well, I'll try the other one. [*Hits* XANTHIAS] Take that!
XAN.: Ai-ai-ai!
AEAC.: What's the matter?
XAN.: I have a thorn in my foot.
AEAC.: What does that mean? Now the other one. [*Hits* DIONYSUS]
DION.: Oh, Lord . . . "Apollo, of Delos and of Python's Rock!"
XAN.: He flinched, you heard!
DION.: Not at all, I merely quoted
iambic verses from the poetry of Hipponax!
XAN.: You're being too soft. Give him a good hard blow for once.
AEAC.: A good idea, by Zeus. Turn your belly this way. [*Hits him*]
DION.: Oh Poseidon!
XAN.: There, he flinched!
DION.: "Oh, Poseidon, who reigns
over the rocky crags and blue Aegean waters!"
AEAC.: By Demeter, I still don't know which is which,
one of you's a real god, but I can't tell which.
So come inside, the boss and his wife Persephone
will soon find out, since they are gods, in fact, themselves!
DION.: What a good idea! I wish you'd thought of that
before you started giving us those mighty blows!
[*Exeunt* DIONYSUS, XANTHIAS, *and* AEACUS]
CHORUS: Muse, come with our Chorus now
to this most sacred place,
to see Athenians endow
all the arts with grace.

More pride than Cleophon[42]
to whose ambiguous mouth
the Thracian swallow now has gone
winging her way to the South,
crying with her mournful notes,
that he'll die, even with equal votes.
The sacred Chorus is supposed, with counsel wise and just
to come to the assistance of the city, as it must.
Now all Athenians must stand equal, that is only fair,
even if some, following Phrynichus[43] have lost their share.
But all of these will now confess and surely be forgiven
for their misdemeanors, once they gallantly have striven;
give them back the vote, it isn't right that slaves and chattels
just because they bravely fought in one or two sea battles,
straightway should be freemen, citizens of Plataea now,
(not that this is blameworthy, in this to you we bow).
This is something that was wisely done, yes and nobly, too,
but you must remember those who fought at sea for you;
they should all be pardoned, for that one and single sin,
don't forget they are your kinsmen, see the trouble they are in!
So forget your anger, you, the wisest and best of Greece,
and let us accept as kinsmen and Athenians, in peace,
all the ones who fight our battles for the real Athenian glory,
for if we act proud and haughty, future men will tell the story
how Athenians floundered in the billows and stormy waves.
They will reckon that we acted, not like freemen, but like knaves
and that wicked little monkey
with the manners of a donkey
—shifty little Cleigenes,
with his evil properties,
dealing with Cimolian clay,
mixed with lye from day to day,
with his thieving naughty song,
he won't be around for long!
He carries a club, wherever he goes
so as not, while drunk, to be robbed of his clothes!
One thing we have noticed, and it really seems to us as funny,
that the city acts the very same with men and money.
We have noble men, and coins of purest ancient gold,
unalloyed, untarnished, and their fame comes down from days of old,
all unequalled and most perfect, beautiful in every way,
works of art, each one of them, the fairest things we have today.
All of Greece has nothing that can equal them for their great beauty,
nor Barbarians either, but we do not use them—no, for duty,
all we use is worthless money, made of cheapest, basest metal!
Likewise with our fellow-townsmen, men of finest, worthiest fettle,
nobly born and bred, most honorable in their lasting fame,
trained in music and in science, many a chorus, many a game,
these we thrust aside, preferring men of newer, cheaper race,
mongrel sons of half-breed fathers, with a sallow, yellow face;
men that we, in earlier days, would scarcely deign to use at all,
even for the scapegoat-sacrifice—you see

how far we fall!
But, O foolish men, you still have time to change your stupid ways,
and to use the useful—it will be a thing worthy of praise!
Let us fight with courage and with wisdom, if we still must hang,
let the tree be made of good wood, spare us then dishonor's pang!

AEAC.: By Savior Zeus, but he's a real true gentleman,
that master of yours!

XAN.: A gentleman, of course he is!
He's all for wine and women—nothing else exists!

AEAC.: But not to have given you the beating of your life,
a slave disguising himself in the costume of his master?

XAN.: Just let him try it!

AEAC.: Spoken like a true slave indeed!
That's just the way that I would act if I were you.

XAN.: You like it?

AEAC.: Like it? I love it, when I have the chance
to curse my master when his back is turned, in secret!

XAN.: How about cursing after you have felt the lash
and hurry out-of-doors?

AEAC.: Yes, I like that as well.

XAN.: And prying, busy-bodying?

AEAC.: By Zeus, that's the best of all!

XAN.: Oh, Zeus, the God of Kinship! What about listening
to master's secrets?

AEAC.: Oh, I'm crazy about that!

XAN.: And telling it to everybody?

AEAC.: By all the gods,
when I do that, I'm super-crazy with the joy of it!

XAN.: Phoebus Apollo, give me your right hand, my friend!
Kiss me and let me kiss you. [*Noise within*] But tell me this,
By Zeus, the Lord of Rascals, what is all that noise,
all that hullabaloo, and fracas and melee inside the house?

AEAC.: That's Aeschylus and Euripides.

XAN.: What?

AEAC.: Yes, there's a mighty to-do going on inside,
the dead are having a big dissension, taking sides.

XAN.: How come?

AEAC.: Well, we have a custom here, you know,
with all the Liberal Arts and all the Humanities,
that the foremost, chiefest Master of each and every Art
gets free maintenance in the Prytaneum here [44]
and sits by Pluto's side.

XAN.: Aha, I understand.

AEAC.: Until another comes, who's his superior,
and then he must give way, and make a place for him.

XAN.: And how has this arrangement affected Aeschylus?

AEAC.: Well, Aeschylus held the Throne of Tragedy, you see
because he was the best . . .

XAN.: He *was*? But, who is now?

AEAC.: Well, when Euripides came down here, he gave
free shows to all the highwaymen,

cutthroats, and robbers,
thieves, burglars, parricides—the sort that we have here
in Hades, and when they heard his sophistries and logic,
and pleas and counterpleas, and clever twists and turns,
they all went mad for him and thought he was the greatest!
So he grew very proud and claimed the Tragic Throne
where Aeschylus had sat before.

XAN.: They didn't stone him off?

AEAC.: Oh, no, the people clamored for a trial then
to see which of the two was master of his art.

XAN.: Those jailbirds?

AEAC.: Yes, the clamor rose to heaven itself!

XAN.: What? Nobody took the part of good old Aeschylus?

AEAC.: Well, goodness is scarce, you know, the same as you are here! [*Points to the audience*]

XAN.: And what will Pluto do to settle the whole matter?

AEAC.: He's going to hold a trial with their tragedies
to see which one is better.

XAN.: But Sophocles, did he
not want to claim the Tragic Throne for his own self?

AEAC.: Oh, no, not he! When he came here, he gave a kiss
to Aeschylus, and clasped his hand most graciously,
and Aeschylus gave half the throne to him, you see,
but now, according to Cleidemides, he's going
to watch and wait. If Aeschylus wins, he'll be content,
but, if, on the other hand, the victory should go
to Euripides, he'll fight, all for the sake of Art!

XAN.: So that's it, eh?

AEAC.: Yes, you'll see quite soon, you know,
all sorts of wonderful things are going to happen now,
they'll weigh the tragedies, line by line, upon the scales!

XAN.: Weigh tragedy like meat in butcher's scales? Oh, no!

AEAC.: And rulers, yardsticks, tape measures, protractors, too,
and miter boxes . . .

XAN.: One would think they're making bricks!

AEAC.: And compasses and wedges. Euripides, you see,
is going to test the tragedies, yes, word by word!

XAN.: I would think that Aeschylus didn't like this much!

AEAC.: He glowered with a gaze just like an angry bull!

XAN.: Who'll be the judge?

AEAC.: Yes, that made for some difficulty.
Decent critics were very difficult to find.
Aeschylus didn't like the Athenians, somehow.

XAN.: Too many thieves and robbers, I suppose he thought.

AEAC.: And all the others he said were simply trash, unable
to judge on poetry. Finally they picked your master,
for he has great experience in the tragic art.
But we had better go in now, for when the masters
have business to do, it's bad business for the slaves!

[*Exeunt*]

CHORUS: The Lord of the Thunder will be angry indeed
when the boar who is also the bore
is whetting his tusks for the imminent fight
with twisting and sophistry galore!
Plume-helmeted words shall wave in the breeze
and fragments and splinters shall fall,
when the Architect of Thoughts and the Wielder of Words
to the battle their forces shall call.
Manes and crests shall arise with the scowls
from a horrible beetling brow,
and epithets wielded aloft like swords,
and planks heaved up in the row.
Here is the tongueworker, versifier, poet,
and sophist of slippery tongue,
making mincemeat of language, and well does he know it,
of the labor of wind and of lung!

[*Change of scene. Hall of Pluto.* PLUTO, *enthroned,* AESCHYLUS, EURIPIDES, DIONYSUS *in the foreground*]

EURIPIDES: Don't try to tell me for I'll not give way to him,
I say that I am more the master of the Tragic Art!

DION.: Well, Aeschylus, why don't you speak? Refute him now.

EUR.: He wants to open with a long and pregnant silence,
the kind of tricks he uses in all his tragedies!

DION.: Come, my dear fellow, please don't talk so big!

EUR.: I know the man, I've made a thorough study of him,
savage barbarian, and stubborn as a mule,
his mouth without a bridle, fetter, curb, control,
an un-out-talkable and pomp-bundle-worded man.[45]

AESCHYLUS: You think so, child of the Goddess of the Greengrocer.[46]
You dare speak thus of me, you chattering gossipmonger,
you beggar-ragmaker, with all your pathetic props!
Oh, you shall eat your words!

DION.: Stop, give over Aeschylus,
don't work yourself into a tizzy just for that!

AES.: I'll not be still until I've exposed this cripple-maker
and shown him up in all his arrogance, once for all!

DION.: Bring out a black-fleeced lamb, boys, right away,
for we've a hurricane about to burst upon us.[47]

AES.: You and your Cretan Monodies that you've introduced,[48]
and the immoral love affairs you've brought onstage!

DION.: Just a minute, please, oh, noble Aeschylus,
and you, Euripides, poor wretch, if you've got sense,
get out of this hailstorm, as quickly as you can,
before some headstrong words will take you by surprise
and knock the insides out of your poor—*Telephus!*[49]
You, Aeschylus, control your passions, and be examined
coolly, with cool head; two poets should not jabber
like lowly fishwives yelling their fool heads off!
But you are roaring like a burning oak tree now!

EUR.: I'm ready, here I am, I'm completely prepared
to bite or to be bitten, whatever he should desire.
I have my words and lyrics and my

nerves and sinews,
I have my *Aeolus* and also my *Peleus*.
Here is my *Meleager* and even my *Telephus!*

DION.: And how about you, Aeschylus, do you consent?

AES.: I really should object, and ask for a change of venue,
for here it's no fair fight.

DION.: Why do you say that?

ARES.: Because my writings haven't all died when I died,
but his expired when he did, so he has them handy!
However, if that's the way you want it, so be it!

DION.: Go, someone, bring me frankincense and fire, forthwith,
so I may pray for guidance in this battle of wits,
this contest for the mastery in Poetic Art,
and in the meantime you may sing a hymn to the Muses.

CHORUS: Oh, Muses, daughters of Zeus and Memory
look down from your lofty heights and see the battle of these dramatists
meeting today in the lists.
They'll wrestle with their words and lines,
and pay their penalties and fines,
they'll take the various plays apart;
look out, now they're going to start;
now is the contest and all know it
to see which is the greater poet;

DION.: Will not the two of you put up your prayers now?

AES.: Demeter, Nourisher of my spirit, come to me,
and make me worthy of your rites and mysteries.

DION.: [*To* EURIPIDES] And how about some incense for you?

EUR.: Oh, thank you, no.
The gods I pray to are not coined in that mint.

DION.: What, you have a new currency of your own?

EUR.: Indeed, I have.

DION.: Well, then you pray to those private gods of your own.

EUR.: Ether, my foot! Larynx and Glottal, Stop, and Wit,
and Keen Scent of Reason, may you grant to me
power to win the victory in this dramatic contest!

CHORUS: We are yearning to be learning
of the citadels of song,
weapons rattle for the battle
tempers now for war are strong.
Each of them is nimble-minded,
neither to the truth is blinded,
one will use his words, well-chosen
and will try his foe to cozen,
while the other will uproot trees,
using words as big as these,
each of them will shatter, batter
his foe into gory bits of matter!

DION.: Now then, begin your arguments, and you must both begin
with logic and no metaphors, no sophistries, to win!

EUR.: You're on! Later I shall deal with my own artistic merit;
first of all I want to dig out like a well-trained ferret
to show you what a quack he is, how Aeschylus, all the while,
tricked the silly public, used to Phrynichus's style,
He'd put a solitary veiled figure on the stage,
Achilles, or Niobe,[50] who never would begin to engage
a soul in conversation, but stood like paintings in their grief.

DION.: Why, so they did!

EUR.: Then came the

Chorus, for lyric relief,
and while they sang four choral odes the actors never spoke a word!
DION.: But how I loved that Silence, it was just what I preferred!
Much better than the chatter that you get today . . .
EUR.: You didn't see why he did it?
DION.: True, I didn't, so now please tell me!
EUR.: He simply wished to keep the audience in nerve-wracking suspense
to see if Niobe would ever speak at all, after her reticence!
DION.: The sly old fox, he tricked us!
[*To* AESCHYLUS] What are you about?
Why do you rage and rant like that?
EUR.: Because he's been found out!
Then, after all that nonsense, and halfway through the play
we'd hear a dozen wild-bull words that the chief actor would say,
fierce crested ones with shaggy brows, and you could see he'd try
in ways no one had ever heard.
AES.: Oh, alas!
DION.: Please be quiet!
EUR.: But not a single one was clear.
DION.: [*To* AESCHYLUS] Please stop grinding your teeth!
EUR.: Scamanders and Moated Ditches, Griffin-Eagles underneath!
And Flashing Bronze and Hippocrene expressions, unclear to me.
DION.: I went for many sleepless nights, I couldn't seem to see
or understand why any character like noble Hector
had anything to do with a Rufous Hippalector.[51]
AES.: You idiot, it was a sign on the ship's prow, and none—
DION.: I thought it was Eryxis,[52] Philoxenus' son!
EUR.: But why, into a tragedy, would anyone bring a rooster?
AES.: You fool, what did your character do when anyone seduced her?
EUR.: At least I had no Hippalectors or Tragelaphs in *my* plays,[53]
like you see on Persian tapestries with their smarmy ways!
When I got the Drama from you, it was bloated and swollen up,
weighted down with heavy words, as when you've had too much to sup.
I took it in hand and put in on a two-week crash diet,
broth and wordlets and book-juice, you really ought to try it.[54]
I gave it lots of monodies, seasoned by Cephisophon.[55]
I never used capricious diction, or fostered any confusion.
My first character came on and explained every allusion,
and all the origins.
AES.: They were better than your own, I hope!
EUR.: Then from the very beginning, all my people had to work;
the mistress talked and talked and the slave-girl went berserk!
Master, maiden, old ladies, all of them talked forever.
AES.: And for that you don't deserve to die?
EUR.: No, by Apollo, never!
This is only what we learn from studying democracy!
DION.: You'd better lay off that subject—you and your hypocrisy!
EUR.: Next, I taught the city to speak.
AES.: Yes, you did, and the best
thing you could have done would be to suffer cardiac arrest!

EUR.: I gave them rules and canons, and I taught them how to love,
think, question, understand, plot and push and shove,
and to question everything that came from "up above"!

AES.: You did!

EUR.: I put on stage scenes from life of every day,
where I would be detected if I slipped in any way;
I never bullied and blustered or frightened anyone
with Magic Swans and Ethiops with terrifying costumes on.
Look at our pupils, and just see how different they are.
His is uncouth Meganaetus, Phormisus, the silliest by far,
the greatest trumpet-spear-and-beard, and splitter within the pine—[56]
but smart Cleitophon and clever Theramenes—these are mine!

DION.: Oh, Theramenes,[57] a clever man, he comes out smelling like a rose!
His friends may suffer, but Theramenes never seems to have any foes!
He simply changes his name from Kite to Knight—what do you suppose!

EUR.: I taught them such bright ways as these,
with all my clever sophistries,
to figure out the Why and How,
as most men are doing now.
They manage their own households too,
now that they know who is who!
They are getting really hot
with why is why and what is what!

DION.: Yes, indeed, for now a man
comes home shouting loud as he can,
"Where's the pitcher, Where's the pot?
Who ate the fish when it was hot?
Who ate the olives and the leek?
And the garlic which did reek?"
Before they got so very smart
they'd no understanding, and no art,
but mammacouths and blockheads all
like Melitides in his stall.[58]

CHORUS: Look around you, O great Achilles!
It's enough to give a man the Willies!
Do not let your angry spirit
whirl you right away—don't hear it!
Do not be blown off your course
by your feelings of remorse,
shorten canvas, reef your sails,
trim them for oncoming gales!
When the softer breezes blow
then the time will come, you know,
to gird yourself, so get you hence,
come out and fight in your defense!
Oh Aeschylus, who first did build us lofty towering verse,
and tragedies strong did write, now your lofty art rehearse.

AES.: It really makes me mad to think that I must fight with him,
but lest I seem to fall beneath this peasant's lowly whim,
tell me, why is a poet famous, since you are so witty?

EUR.: If he can give some good advice that's needed by the city
to make the people better.

AES.: But if you do the reverse,
finding men who are good and true and making them be worse,
then what do you deserve?

DION.: Don't ask, he deserves death!

AES.: Just think of what he got from me—men of heroic breath,
born and bred like noblemen, and loyal to the State,
instead of loiterers and loafers, such as we've seen of late,
men who lived with spears and helmets, brightly waving crests,
armor strong and mighty, and stout hearts in their breasts.

EUR.: Heavens, he's filling an armorer's shop, and neither more nor less,
If they were so very brave, how was that your business?
DION.: Answer him, Aeschylus, do not such anger and spleen display.
AES.: "A tragedy full of Ares."
DION.: Which?
AES.: *Seven Against Thebes* is the play.
Anyone who saw that play was mad for bloodshed and for war.
DION.: But that was very bad of you, the Thebans were mightier and more
and fought more bravely, and all your fault, my friend, take that!
AES.: You could have done the same yourselves, if you'd the brains of a gnat!
The next thing I did was teach you glory, instead of other diversions;
glory, military prowess, you learned that from *The Persians!*
DION.: Oh, yes, I enjoyed Darius' ghost, I really loved it, oh boy!
When the chorus waved their arms and all yelled "iau-oi!"[59]
AES.: That's what poetry is for! Just notice, from the very start,
how useful the works of the poets have been to all men in their art!
First Orpheus showed us mysteries; we learned about the vulture
and medicine from Musaeus; then Hesiod taught us agriculture:
when to reap and when to sow, and Homer won all his glory
by singing of honor and battle-glee, telling them in his story—
marching, fighting, and so on.
DION.: But not to Pantacles;
he never was able to profit from poems such as these,
He put his helmet on his head, then tried to fasten a plume.
AES.: But, he taught other brave men like Lamachus[60] how to meet doom!
Many brave heroes live on in my plays, to read them wouldn't hurt you:
Patroclus and Teucer and such as these, men of illustrious virtue!
Read them and you'll jump when the trumpet calls to war.
But I never wrote about Phaedras and Stheneboeas, or any other such whore![61]
No love-interest in any of my dramas that are so mighty.
EUR.: No, indeed! Your style was not the sort to attract Queen Aphrodite.
AES.: Better so, but she found too much of that with you and all your friends
and threw you on the ground yourself.[62]
DION.: So. That is how he ends!
You showed us cuckolds, then the same thing happened, alas, to you!
EUR.: But tell me, what harm to anyone my poor Stheneboea could do!
AES.: Many a noble wife, out of shame and chagrin, took poison
all on account of Bellerophon, the hero they took such joys in!
EUR.: But did I invent the story of Phaedra? It's true and well you know it!
AES.: Not so, for tales of sin and vice are not fit tales for the poet.
Poets are, for the world at large, the wise preceptors and preachers,
from whom men must learn as little boys must learn at school from their teachers!
We must only tell of good things . . .
EUR.: In words like Mt. Lycabettus?
And blocks of marble from Parnes? Where, Oh, where will that get us?
Why can't we speak as people do?
AES.: But, don't you see, you fool

for subjects great and mighty, great words
must be the tool!
Heroes should speak in heroic language,
not like your feeble whims,
since heroic are the garments that cover
their mighty limbs!
This was the way *I* did it, but you spoiled
it.
EUR.: I? How?
AES.: By bringing on kings in tatters and
rags, that's what they look like now.
With all your pathetic props . . .
EUR.: Whatever
was wrong with that?
AES.: The wealthy men have followed your
scheme, and they say, nice and pat,
"I can't pay for a trireme, I'm much too
poor, you know!"
DION.: While under the rags they'll be
wearing a woolen vest, where it doesn't
show!
And when they get exempted they're off
to the fishmonger's shop.
AES.: In speeches and sophistries you've
trained them all, and they'll never stop.
This is what's emptied the wrestling
ground and made their hips so narrow;
they'll all answer back and chatter like any
twittering sparrow!
It's nothing like the days of old when men
would bend to the oar,
eating their hardtack, calling "Stroke"—
just that and nothing more!
DION.: And fart on the face of the rowers
below and shit on the very next one.
Now they dispute and argue all day from
sun til rising sun.
Instead of being ready to row
they just go where the tides will flow!
AES.: He's the root of every evil thing,
that we have seen taking wing,
bawds and whores and pimps so fine!
Women in labor in the shrine,
brother-sister incest free,
arguing "to be is not to be!"
So the city's full today
of monkeys chattering away,
winning drawn-out legal cases,
never running torchlight races!
DION.: You're right! For at the Panathenea
I saw a running man, and he a
puffy, flabby gentleman
running as hard as ever he can.
Then the Potters turned on him
slapping, hitting, turning grim,
til he gave a puff and cough,
blew out his torch and then ran off!
CHORUS: Awful battle, awful war,
but what are they fighting for?
One is fighting up a storm,
the other rallies to keep warm.
Forward, march! Don't just sit there!
Now your wit's keen edge you'll bare!
Now's the time, like graceful birds
to let fly with your winged words!
Battle with your sophistries,
so that you'll the people please.
Don't be afraid the audience
will not take your meanings hence,
they are very knowing folks,
They'll catch on to all your jokes,
they have all read various books,
each one knows just where he looks.
They are witty, they are sharp,
you don't need on things to harp.
So just speak what's on your mind
and they will the meanings find!
EUR.: Well, then, let's start out with the
prologues now,
for after all, that's how the play begins on
stage!
I shall try to show the judges that
Aeschylus
has expositions that are always quite
obscure.
DION.: Which one to start with?
EUR.: All of them
but first we'll try

the famous first lines from the *Oresteia*, please.[63]

DION.: Then silence, everyone. Speak, noble Aeschylus.

AES.: [*Quotes opening lines of the* Choephori]:
"Hermes, Guide of the Dead, seeing a father's rites,
be thou my savior and ally, I call to thee
as I am coming and returning to this land . . ."

DION.: Anything wrong so far?

EUR.: Only a dozen errors!

DION.: How come? A dozen faults in only three lines?

EUR.: Because each line contains twenty mistakes or more!

DION.: Be silent, Aeschylus, please, because if you are not
you're going to run up debts of more than three iambics.

AES.: Silent for *him?*

DION.: Yes, if you'll be guided by my advice.

EUR.: Here, right away, the faults have mounted heavenwards.

AES.: You see how silly you were?

DION.: Go ahead, I don't care.

AES.: Where was the mistake?

EUR.: Begin the lines again.

AES.: "Hermes, Guide of the Dead, seeing a father's rites . . ."

EUR.: Orestes says all this standing beside the tomb
of his dead father?

AES.: That's what I say he does.

EUR.: Then does he mean that Hermes, when the father died
by craft and stealth and murdered by a woman's hand,
that Hermes, god of craft, was witness to the deed?

AES.: No, no, not he. Erounian Hermes, Guide of the Dead,
that was the god he called on, and then he adds
that Hermes got the job by inheriting it from his father.

EUR.: That makes it even worse! For if this Hermes
derives the job of caring for the dead from his father . . .

DION.: That means that they're a pair of ghouls and grave-robbers.

AES.: Dionysus, something's wrong with the wine you're drinking.

DION.: Give him another and you [*to* EURIPIDES] look out for the mistakes.

AES.: "Be thou my savior and ally, I call to thee
as I am coming and returning to this land."

EUR.: The clever Aeschylus is saying the same thing twice!

DION.: How twice?

EUR.: Just listen and I'll explain my meaning clearly.
"I come," he says, "I am returning" to this land;
to come is to return; they're both exactly the same!

DION.: Yes, indeed, by Zeus, as if you asked the neighbor
"Give me a kneading-trough, or else a trough to knead in!"

AES.: They're not the same, you godforsaken chatterbox!
They're not the same at all, I said just what I meant!

DION.: Explain to me just what you mean when you say that.

AES.: A man who's not an exile "comes" into a land,

with no particular connotation good or bad;
an exile both "returns" and "comes." Do you understand?

DION.: Good, by Apollo. [*To* EURIPIDES] Euripides, what do you say?

EUR.: I don't admit Orestes can be said to "return,"
he comes in secret, no one has recalled him home.

DION.: Good, by Hermes! [*Aside*] What in the world's he talking about?

EUR.: Give us another line, please.

DION.: Oh yes, Aeschylus,
another line, and you [*To* EURIPIDES], mark down the mistakes.

AES.: "Here upon this tomb, I call you, beloved father,
to hear and listen."

EUR.: There he goes again, redundant!
To "hear" and "listen" mean exactly the same thing!

DION.: But he was speaking to the dead, you foolish man
who cannot hear us even though we call them thrice.[64]

AES.: Well, what about *your* prologues?

EUR.: Any ones you like,
and if you find a single useless repetition
or redundancy, you can spit in my face!

DION.: Oh, good, let us begin, I can hardly wait to hear
your flawless, nonredundant, perfect prologues now!

EUR.: "King Oedipus was first a happy man . . ."[65]

AES.: A lie, by Zeus! He was nothing of the sort!
Before his birth Apollo had foretold that he
was foreordained to be his father's murderer.
So how could he be called a happy man at first?

EUR.: "Then he became the most unhappy of all mortals."

AES.: No, by the gods! He never was anything else!
As soon as he was born his feet were pinned together,
and he himself was exposed in an earthen pot
in winter's depth, lest he should prove his father's killer.
And then with swollen feet[66] he limped to Polybus,
and while still young he married a woman old enough
to be his mother—then he put out both his eyes!
So how can you say Oedipus was a happy man?

DION.: Happy, if he had been a colleague of Erasinides![67]

EUR.: Nonsense! My prologues haven't anything wrong with them!

AES.: Now, by Zeus, I'll take your prologues, not line by line,
but, with the aid of all the blessed gods in heaven,
I'll spoil them all, and with just one small flask of oil![68]

EUR.: You'll spoil my prologues with a flask of oil?

AES.: Just one!
Your prologues are so constructed that each and every one
has room for "flask" or "bottle" or "bag"
in your iambics. Wait, I'll show you how.

EUR.: You will?

AES.: Yes, I certainly will.

DION.: Well, then, let us begin.

EUR.: "Aegyptus, as the ancient legends tell the tale,

was sailing with his fifty sons upon the sea,
but when he touched at Argos . . ."

AES.: he lost his flask of oil!

EUR.: There's the flask of oil! However did he do it?

DION.: Give him another prologue, let him try again.

EUR.: "Dionysus, with fawnskins and thyrsuses,
along the summits of Mount Parnassos' heights,
while dancing with the nymphs . . ."

AES.: he lost his flask of oil!

DION.: Alas, I'm smitten![69] And with that lousy flask of oil!

EUR.: Nothing, nothing at all! I've got another one,
he'll never squeeze that oil-flask into this one—watch!
"No man is happy in all respects and everything;
one is of noble birth, but lives in poverty,
another one, baseborn, has . . ."

AES.: lost his flask of oil!

DION.: Euripides!

EUR.: Yes?

DION.: You'd better give up now, my friend,
a hurricane is coming from that flask of oil!

EUR.: No, by Demeter! I don't give one little damn!
Watch me knock it out of his hands this time, you'll see!

DION.: Well, then, proceed, but look out for those hidden oil-flasks!

EUR.: "Once as Cadmus, the son of old Agenor,
was leaving Sidon . . ."

AES.: he lost his flask of oil!

DION.: For goodness sake, why don't you buy that oil-flask from him,
before it breaks your prologues all to pieces?

EUR.: ME buy from HIM?

DION.: Yes, if you take my advice!

EUR.: Nonsense, I have lots of prologues I haven't used
where he cannot insert that rotten flask of oil:
"Once Pelops, son of Tantalus, as he was driving
his mares to Pisa . . ."

AES.: he lost his flask of oil!

DION.: You see, he's stuck that oil-flask right in there again!
Why don't you quit while you're ahead, Euripides?
All it will cost you is one paltry little obol!

EUR.: No, by Zeus, not yet! I still have lots of prologues:
"Oeneus, while harvesting . . ."

AES.: Lost his flask of oil!

EUR.: You might at least have let me finish one whole line!
"Oeneus, while harvesting his abundant crops of grain, offered a sacrifice . . ."

AES.: Lost his flask of oil!

DION.: What, while sacrificing? Who's the thief who stole it?

EUR.: Never mind. Let us try another prologue:
"Zeus, as the tale is told with truthfulness . . ."

DION.: No use, he'll just cut in with that accursed oil-flask!

These oil-flasks are regular excrescences
growing on your prologues like styes upon the eye!
Let's get on to the lyrics now, for Heaven's sake!

EUR.: Oh sure! I can easily demonstrate how bad they are,
for all the melodies and the lyrics are the same!

CHORUS: Now we shall see mighty things
coming at us from the wings
for what is he going to do?
Will he blame the poet who
always won the greatest praise
more than any in our days?
Now indeed I really wonder
how he will let loose his thunder
at the King without a peer,
he's the one for whom I fear!

EUR.: Only too soon you will see
Aeschylus's monotony!
I'll strip his meters down to one hexameter!

DION.: And I'll take pebbles and I'll keep an accurate count.

[Flute music]

EUR.: "Archilles, Lord of Phthia, hear the mankilling battle,
why comest thou not with smiting spear to the rescue?[70]
Hermes, we are worshipping here by the lonely lake,
why comest thou not with smiting spear to the rescue?"

DION.: That's two times now that you've been smitten, Aeschylus!

EUR.: "Hearken to me, Atreides, the nobles of all the Achaeans,
why comest thou not with smiting spear to the rescue?"

DION.: That makes three smittens,
Aeschylus, that you've been dealt.

EUR.: "Hearken, the Beekeepers will open now fair Artemis' portals.
Why comest thou not with smiting spear to the rescue?
And I shall sing of the pathway of Fate for all mortal men,
why comest thou not with smiting spear to the rescue?"

DION.: By Zeus, that's a lot of smiting spears, truly!
I'm making tracks for the bathroom now, because my poor kidneys
have taken far too much of all this smiting now!

EUR.: Just wait until you've heard another bunch of songs
that Aeschylus has written, accompanied by the lyre.

DION.: Well, then, go on, but please, no more of those awful smitings!

EUR.: "How the twin-throned Achaean powers, the youth of Hellas,
phlatto-thratto-phlatto-thrat![71]
Sending the Sphinx, the ill-boding one, the Bloodhound of Fate,
phlatto-thratto-phlatto-thrat!
With hand and spear the high-flying birds in the upper air
phlatto-thratto-phlatto-thrat!
Providing their prey for the swift-winged dogs of the ether,
phlatto-thratto-phlatto-thrat!
And leaning his mighty weight upon thee Greater Ajax,
phlatto-thratto-phlatto-thrat!

DION.: What's all this phlattothrat? Does it come from Marathon
where you have plucked all these twisted strands of verse from?

AES.: From the Fairest to the Fairest I brought them hither,
because I didn't want to pluck the flowers from
the self-same meadows where that Ohrynichus plucks his!

He gets his songs from all the latest brothel music,
Meletan drinking songs and Carian flute-pipings,
dirges and dances, let me show you what he does:
Bring me a lyre, but no, what need of lyres for that?
The girl who plays the castanets will do as well.
Come forth, Euripidean Muse, present yourself,
you're the sort of Muse that's fit for suchlike verses!

DION.: Don't tell me that she's a Lesbian Muse, oh no!

AES.: Halcyons by the shining waves,[72]
alternating shrieks and raves,
while the water moisture brings
to your feathers and your wi-i-i-ings!
Spiders weaving warp and woof
upon the timbers on the ro-o-o-of;
weaving all your silken bands
with your fingers and your hands.
Minstrel weaving on your loom
in the sunny little room;
dolphins, they who leap and skip
in the path of each swift ship;
oracles and all the seers,
races of the strong man's peers,
and the grapes that cares beguiled,
come, embrace me, oh, my child!
Do you see this foot?

DION.: Yes.

AES.: And this?

DION.: Of course.

AES.: This is the sort of stuff you write,
you, who against *my* songs would fight!
You with all your old perversions
from Cyrene's whores' diversions!
But that really isn't all—
listen to his monodies' gall![73]
Oh, thou mysterious night!
What means this fearsome sight?
From the world of ghosts and dreams,
where Death's pale fire flickers and gleams
where Death tells his age-old tales
with his enormous fingernails!
Come maidens, light the lamps, dip your pitchers in the stream,
give me water to wash away the horror of this awful dream!
Oh, thou god of the Sea,
what has befallen me?
Oh, to what have they reduced her?
Glyce has stolen away my rooster!
Mania and Nymphs, help me now,
wretched me, how I've suffered, how!
As I spun my wo-o-o-ol
and my hands were ful-u-u-u-ll!
I wanted to go to the Agora
tomorrow morning, though it is far,
but he began to fly away,
leaving me cares, all day! All day!
Tears, tears, from my eyes I shed,
wishing, alas, that I was dead!
Come, you sons of Ida and Crete,
taking your bows, in the forest meet
make a circle around the house,
quiet, quiet as a mouse!
Come Artemis, come Dictinna,
bring your dogs to seek their dinner,
hunting through the house with me,
careful, oh, so carefully!
And come Hecate, with your light,
Zeus' daughter, in your might,
help me find nocturnal Psyche,
the rooster stolen by old Glyce.

DION.: Enough of the monodies.

AES.: I agree, enough for me as well.
Now let us proceed to the Weighing in the Scales,
the Final Test of Meritorious Poetry,
to see which one of us has the weightiest words![74]

DION.: Then both of you come here, and I will weigh the verse,
as if it was a pound of cheese that we were weighing.
[*A huge pair of scales is brought out*]
CHORUS: Oh what labor, oh, what work!
something that we cannot shirk!
Who except these daring two
would think of such a thing to do?
What brilliance, what intelligence!
I'd never believe it would make sense!
It's so incredible that I
thought the whole thing was a lie!
DION.: Now each of you must stand beside the scale.
AESCHYLUS and EURIPIDES: Like this?
DION.: And hold it firmly while you speak your line, and don't
let go the scale until you hear me call "Cuckoo"!
AES. and EUR.: Ready!
DION.: Now speak the lines into the scale.
EUR.: "Would that the good ship Argo never had winged away."[75]
AES.: "River Spercheius, and the haunts of grazing cattle."
DION.: Cuckoo! Let go. Oh, Aeschylus' side sinks down
much further.
EUR.: Why should that be so, please tell me?
DION.: He threw in the river to wet his wool, just like
some crooked wool seller, to make it weigh much more,
while your line had wings in it, to fly away!
EUR.: Well, let's try another, and we'll see who wins.
DION.: Ready on the scales?
AES. and EUR.: Ready.
DION.: Recite your lines.
EUR.: "Persuasion has no temple, save for eloquent words."
AES.: "Of all the gods, 'tis Death alone that loves no gifts."
DION.: Let go, let go. Aeschylus wins again, because
he put in Death, the heaviest of all the ills!
EUR.: But I put in "Persuasion," a most charming word!
DION.: Perhaps; but it has neither weight nor sense, you see!
Come, think of some heavy-laden line of yours, my friend!
Something big and strong, to make your side go down.
EUR.: Let's see, where do I have such a line?
DION.: I'll tell you where,
"Archilles threw two singles and a four," that's where!
Come recite your lines, this is your last chance!
EUR.: "His right hand held an iron mace as weighty weapon."
AES.: "Chariot piled on chariot, and corpse on corpse!"
DION.: There! Aeschylus wins again!
EUR.: He does? How is that?
DION.: He threw two chariots and two corpses in the scales;
a hundred Egyptians couldn't carry all that load!
AES.: Come now, no more of this line-by-line weighting,
let him himself, his wife and children, and Cephisophon
get into the scale with the collected books as well;
two lines of mine will outweigh the entire lot!
DION.: Oh, how can I decide? I like both of these men;

I don't want to be an enemy of either one,
for one's so clever, and I so love the other one!
PLUTO: But then your entire trip will have been in vain.
DION.: And if I decide?
PLUTO: Well, you can take away with you
whichever one you choose, so it won't be a total loss!
DION.: Very well. Now listen to me, everyone,
I came here for a poet.
EUR.: What do you mean by that?
DION.: To save our city and to keep the choral games,
so whichsoever of you two shall best advise
the city, he's the one to come to earth with me.
Now, firstly, Alcibiades,[76] let each of you say
which should be done about him, the city is in trouble.
EUR.: And what is the city's opinion about the man?
DION.: Her opinion?
She loves and hates him, and she wants him back again.
But tell me, what is your advice about the fellow?
EUR.: I have a citizen slow to aid his native land,
and swift to do her harm, who can find many ways
to help himself, but none at all to help the city.
DION.: Good for you, by Poseidon!
What do you say, Aeschylus?
AES.: It's better not to rear a lion within the State,[77]
but once you've got him, best to give in to his ways.
DION.: By Savior Zeus, I still cannot make up my mind!
The one is so damned clever, the other so very clear!
But tell me once again, what is your plan for safety
for Athens in her present troubles? Let each one speak.
EUR.: Cleocritus should take the wings of Cinesias,
and waft with them over the flat waves of the sea . . .
DION.: Very funny, I admit, but what's the good of that?
EUR.: Then if there's a naval engagement they can pour
vinegar in the eyes of the foemen's troops!
I know and I can tell you.
DION.: Tell me, Euripides
EUR.: Put Trust in place of Mistrust, that's all you have to do.
Mistrust in place of Trust.
DION.: How? I don't get that.
Please be a little more explicit and not so smart.
EUR.: If we mistrust the citizens whom now we trust,
and use the ones we are not using at this time,
this is how we can save our beloved Athens.
We're getting nowhere fast the way that we are going.
Let's try the opposite, then we shall find salvation.
DION.: Good, by Palamedes! Oh, you wisest of all men,
is this your own plan or that of Cephisophon?
EUR.: This one's my own, the vinegar was

his idea!
DION.: And you, Aeschylus?
AES.: Tell me, whom does the city use?
Good and faithful men?
DION.: Are you out of your mind?
She hates them!
AES.: And does she love the bad, ones?
DION.: No, but she uses them because she has to.
AES.: How can such a city ever find salvation?
She doesn't want to use her silks or woolens, either!
DION.: You have to find a way, by Zeus, if you return.
AES.: There I shall speak; here I've nothing else to say.
DION.: No, no, you must speak out while you are here below.
AES.: When they shall count the enemy's land as their own land
and theirs the foemen's, when they realize their ships
are their only treasures, and their treasures worthless.
DION.: But that all goes for jurymen's fees—they drink it up.[78]
PLUTO: Your judgment, please.
DION.: I'm ready, this is how I'll judge.
I'll simply pick the one of them I love the most!
EUR.: Remember all the gods by whom you swore those oaths
that you would bring me back again—and choose your friend!
DION.: "My tongue has sworn an oath"[79]
but I'll pick Aeschylus!
EUR.: What have you done to me, you wretch?
DION.: I've given the prize
to Aeschylus; why not?
EUR.: How can you ever dare
to look me in the eye, you godforsaken traitor!
DION.: "What's shameful if the audience don't think it so?"
EUR.: Have you no heart at all? And will you leave me dead?
DION.: "Who knows if life be death and death itself be life,
and breath is soup and sleep a wooly fleece of sheep?"
PLUTO: Come inside, Dionysus.
DION.: Why should I come in?
PLUTO: The two of you shall dine with me before you go.
DION.: A good idea, I've no objection, none whatever.
CHORUS: Blessed are the ones who find
they have an intelligent mind.
He, the poet of great worth
ascends again to upper Earth.
Uttering the decrees of Fate,
he'll be a blessing to the State.
A solace to her bitter tears,
bringing Athenians rousing cheers.
Not sitting with Socrates,
talking with such men as these,
stripping Drama's lofty art,
despoiling her in every part,
quibbling sophistic phrases
as he the audience amazes.
Only the most arrant fool
would want to learn at such a school!
Let us not hear such a one,
for he wouldn't be much fun!
PLUTO: Farewell, Aeschylus, go your way,
save the Athenian State today,
with your words and counsels wise,
fools and villains you'll chastise.
This is for old Cleophon,
it's just the thing for such a one.

Myrmex and Archenomus,
this for them, without a fuss!
May they all come straight down here
to my house of deadly cheer;
if to loiter there they dare,
I shall come and get them there,
branded like the slaves they'll go,
be they fast or be they slow,
and that vilest one will haunt us
Leucolophus son of Adeimantus![80]

Aes.: I will do so, and I bestow
to Sophocles my throne below.
For his is the next to me
until again these realms I see.
As for that wretch Euripides
with his twisted sophistries,
don't let him sit on my chair,
unwilling or willing, he mustn't dare!

Pluto: And now with your mystic choir
and the holy torches' fire
let Aeschylus' mellifluous songs
escort the sacred festival throngs!

Chorus: The triumphant poet is rising again
to earth.
Grant him all the success that's merited
by his worth.
May he find for Athens plans to guide
her well,
freeing us from the agony and fear in
which we dwell
and let Cleophon[81] go off and fight his
war
far away with his cohorts; that's all that
he's good for!

End of the play.

Notes

1. The first two are comic playwrights; the third is unknown.

2. Aristophanes' favorite device of *para-prosdokion*, or surprise; we should expect "Dionysus, son of Zeus."

3. Slaves who fought in this naval battle were set free.

4. Known for their rowdy behavior, especially when drunk.

5. The club and lion's skin were the traditional attributes of Heracles; the buskin was the raised shoe of the tragic actor.

6. A notorious homosexual, constantly ridiculed by Aristophanes.

7. Either a very tall or very short actor.

8. See note 6 above.

9. Heracles as a notorious glutton.

10. A line from Euripides' lost play *Oeneus*.

11. The son of Sophocles; the implication being that Sophocles was at least partly responsible for the plays of his son. Sophocles and Euripides both died in 405 B.C.

12. A well-known tragedian. *Agathon* means "good."

13. He was living as the court of Archelaus in Macedon.

14. A tragic poet of little worth.

15. These are all parodies of the lines of Euripides. The last is the famous line from *Hippolytus* (612). In line 1471 of this play, the same line is again parodied. Aristophanes refused to forget that unfortunate line, or to let anyone else forget it.

16. Another parody of Euripides.

17. The theft of Cerberus, the watchdog of Hades, was one of the Labors of Heracles.

18. The Acherusian Lake, entrance to the Underworld.

19. Charon, ferryman of the dead over the River Styx.

20. Charon's fare was one obol; the admission to the Festival at which the play was performed was two obols.

21. Because Theseus is the only other person known to Heracles to have visited Hades.

22. A worthless tragedian, frequently ridiculed by Aristophanes.

23. A dithyrambic poet, also worthless. He also appears in *The Birds* (l. 1373).

24. However much Aristophanes may make fun of the gods themselves, he always takes the Mysteries seriously.

25. Cf. note 3, line 33, above.

26. Since Salamis is an island, its inhabitants would naturally be accustomed to rowing.

27. Empusa: A monster that changed her shape.

28. The Priest of Dionysus sat in the front row of the theater.

29. This tragic actor mispronounced a line from the *Orestes* of Euripides, saying, "I see a weasel" instead of "I see a calm."

30. Cf. note 15, line 100, above.

31. A lyric poet. Iacchus is another name for Dionysus.

32. Pigs were sacrificed at the initiation rites.

33. This chorus bears a striking resemblance to the songs "I've Got a Little List," and "My Object All Sublime" from Gilbert and Sullivan's *Mikado*. Both are long lists of undesirable persons marked down for extinction or punishment.

34. A successful comic poet, whose play won a victory over Aristophanes' *The Clouds* in 423 B.C.

35. This person is otherwise unknown.

36. The formula for libations.

37. A shifting and unreliable politician nicknamed *Cothurunus*, meaning a sandal that could be worn on either foot.

38. Cleon and Hyperbolus were demagogues, and at the time of this play, they were both dead.

39. Slaves were sometimes tortured to gain confessions implicating their masters.

40. A ceremonial type of scourging.

41. It is difficult not to see this as a satire on a scene in Euripides' *Bacchae*, in which Dionysus gives a very similar warning to Pentheus.

42. A demagogue.

43. One of the 400 Tyrants.

44. A town hall in Athens where distinguished people were entertained. Socrates, in the *Apology*, suggests that his punishment should be maintenance in the Prytaneum.

45. Euripides is using Aeschylean compound words.

46. For some reason, it was supposed to be either funny or disgraceful that Euripides' mother was a grocer.

47. The traditional sacrifice in time of storms.

48. A type of melody introduced by Euripides, here called immoral by the old-fashioned Aeschylus.

49. *Telephus*, an unsuccessful play of Euripides, is substituted for the expected word *kephalon*.

50. In two of the lost plays; but Prometheus and Cassandra, in the *Prometheus Bound* and the *Agamemnon*, respectively, are good examples of this Long Silence of Aeschylus.

51. Occurs in a lost play of Aeschylus, *The Myrmidons*.

52. The identity of this person is unknown.

53. Aeschylus was famous for his long compound words. These comic ones mean "horse-rooster" and "goat-deer," respectively.

54. Euripides, we are told, had an unusually large library.

55. A slave of Euripides, thought to have helped him with some of his plays.

56. Like the robber Sinis, who tied people to two pine trees and split them in two.

57. Theramenes (cf. note 35 above), like the famous Vicar of Bray, kept changing his affiliation, so that he was always in the favor of the ruling party, no matter who they were. Euripides is very proud to have such a famous relativist as his pupil; Aeschylus scorns such shifting allegiances.

58. Melitides, an Athenian proverbial for his stupidity. A "mammacouth" is a blockhead.

59. Actually, no such thing occurs in *The Persians*.

60. A general in the Sicilian expedition of 415 B.C.

61. Stheneboea, in the lost play named for her, tried to seduce Bellerophon. Phaedra, from the *Hippolytus*, probably the lost *Veiled Hippolytus*, since the term "whore" is scarcely applicable to the extant version. The point about the immorality in Euripides' plays is also mentioned in *The Clouds* and elsewhere.

62. Referring to Euripides' supposedly unhappy marriage.

63. Actually, the following lines are not the first lines of the *Oresteia* trilogy, but those of the *Choephori*, the second play. It is interesting to note that in the manuscript this passage is missing and has been restored by means of this passage in *The Frogs*.

64. This threefold call to the dead is attested by Homer (*Odyssey* 9. 65), Vergil (*Aeneid* 6. 506), and in the poem by Catullus at his brother's grave, where the word *frater* appears three times in the poem at equal intervals (Catullus 101).

65. From the lost *Antigone* of Euripides.

66. *Oedipus* means "swollen feet" in Greek.

67. If he was blind, he would not have had to fight at Arginusae and been condemned, as Erasinides was, to death by the ungrateful Athenians for his failure to bury the dead.

68. In each of the prologues quoted, six syllables containing a verb will complete both the syntax and the meter, nonsensical though the meaning may be. This is true of about half of the plays of Euripides that we possess. It is also true of about half the extant plays of both Aeschylus and Sophocles; so that the criticism, if it be one, is really of the prologue in general, rather than against Euripides. Two other points: perhaps Aristophanes is saying that Euripides' style is so commonplace and pedestrian that the oil-flask would not be out of place. But, apart from this, there must have been some joke, some sexual double entendre, concerning the oil-flask itself, because it keeps cropping up in the comedies, in places where its only purpose could have been to get a laugh.

69. This is the offstage cry of Agamemnon (Aeschylus, *Choephori* 1343) and of Clytemnestra (Sophocles, *Electra* 1415) as they are being slain.

70. About this and the following repetition, Aristophanes seems to be making two points. One is the metrical monotony of the lyrics of Aeschylus, the other his tendency to repeat the same line, making less sense with each repetition. Nothing in the extant plays justifies this criticism, certainly not the *"ailinon ailinon eipe, to de'eu nikato"* in the *Agamemnon*. Euripides also has repeated refrains.

71. Supposed to imitate the strumming of the lyre.

72. Making fun of Euripidean meters and *melismas*, which "prostituted" the older rhythms and corrupted their simplicity.

73. There follows a brilliant parody of the

wild, emotional lyrics of Euripides, much in the latter's style, although the meaning, of course, is pure nonsense.

74. Aeschylus is eager for this test, because he knows perfectly well that, with his ponderous vocabulary and long compound words, he will be the winner.

75. First line of *Medea*. Other lines are from lost plays.

76. Alcibiades was then in exile, living in the Chersonese.

77. See Aeschylus, *Agamemnon* 717, suggested, if not exactly quoted, here.

78. Making fun of the litigation and bibulousness of the Athenians.

79. Another parody of the *Hippolytus* line. Cf. note on line 101. There follow several more Euripidean parodies, one from the *Aeolus,* one from the *Polyeides,* one from the *Phrixus*. All these plays are lost.

80. A naval commander who betrayed the fleet to the Spartans.

81. Twice he tried to persuade Athens to reject an advantageous offer of peace.

Plato

427–348 B.C.

Perhaps the most towering figure of Greek and Western philosophy, and also still one of the most controversial, Plato is responsible for a number of positions that have shaped our beliefs about culture and critical thought—including the question of how there comes to be a world at all. Like Aristotle, his student, he tried to envision a single person's life within the community as having claims on a transcendent "good." The central insight that Plato advances in this regard is the concept of the "ideas," or ideal forms, that cast their shadow from "beyond" to make up the mutable and contingent world as we know it. The world exists by virtue of these ideal forms. This notion of an ideal realm of ideas—a realm somehow separate from the world of actuality—informs much of what Plato formulated on a great variety of subjects. His ideas are generally put forth in dialogue form, with the figure of Socrates, his teacher, often voicing Plato's own view. Among Plato's works are *Crito, Euthyphro, Gorgias, The Republic, Symposium,* and the *Timaeus.*

In Book II, Chapter 9, of *The Republic* Plato gives his rationale for the part literature and art will play in the ideal state as he conceives it. His thinking on this subject reflects a unified approach to art, education, and the civic good, and also a skepticism about what art accomplishes if it is not employed to attain certain preconceived social ends. Plato thus imagines literature for children to be exclusively teaching communal values and instructing children about adult life. For adults, Plato imagines that art and literature have the potential to teach the finer distinctions of character and disposition that will enable one to interact more decisively (and morally) with others. In this way, literature, like virtually every conceivable aspect of culture, is in service to the "good" as the Greeks conceived it.

THE REPUBLIC

from *BOOK II, CHAPTER 9*

The words "fiction," "fictitious," are used to represent the Greek *pseudos,* which has a much wider sense than our "lie": it covers any statement describing events which never in fact occurred, and so applies to all works of imagination, all fictitious narratives ("stories") in myth or allegory, fable or parable, poetry or romance. As Plato does not confuse fiction with falsehood or identify truth with literal statements of fact, *pseudos* should be rendered by "fiction" or "falsehood" according to the context, and sometimes by "lie." It can also mean "error" when it corresponds to the passive verb *epseusthai* = "to be deceived" or "mistaken."

This chapter has been shortened by condensation and by omitting a number of passages from the poets which Plato rejects as impious or immoral.

What is this education to be, then? Perhaps we shall hardly invent a system better than the one which long experience has worked out, with its two branches for the cultivation of the mind and of the body. And I suppose we shall begin with the mind, before we start physical training.

Naturally.

Under that head will come stories:[1] and of these there are two kinds: some are true, others fictitious. Both must come in, but we shall begin our education with the fictitious kind.

I don't understand, he said.

Don't you understand, I replied, that we begin by telling children stories, which, taken as a whole, are fiction, though they contain some truth? Such story-telling begins at an earlier age than physical training; that is why I said we should start with the mind.

You are right.

And the beginning, as you know, is always the most important part, especially in dealing with anything young and tender. That is the time when the character is being moulded and easily takes any impress one may wish to stamp on it.

Quite true.

Then shall we simply allow our children to listen to any stories that anyone happens to make up, and so receive into their minds ideas often the very opposite of those we shall think they ought to have when they are grown up?

No, certainly not.

It seems, then, our first business will be to supervise the making of fables and legends, rejecting all which are unsatisfactory; and we shall induce nurses and mothers to tell their children only those which we have approved, and to think more of moulding their souls with these stories than they now do of rubbing their limbs to make them strong and shapely. Most of the stories now in use must be discarded.

What kind do you mean?

If we take the great ones, we shall see in them the pattern of all the rest, which are bound to be of the same stamp and to have the same effect.

No doubt; but which do you mean by the great ones?

The stories in Hesiod and Homer and the poets in general, who have at all times composed fictitious tales and told them to mankind.

Which kind are you thinking of, and what fault do you find in them?

The worse of all faults, especially if the story is ugly and immoral as well as false—misrepresenting the nature of gods and heroes, like an artist whose picture is utterly unlike the object he sets out to draw.

That is certainly a serious fault; but give me an example.

A signal instance of false invention about the highest matters is that foul story, which Hesiod repeats, of the deeds of Uranus and the vengeance of Cronos;[2] and then there is the tale of Cronos's doings and of his son's treatment of him. Even if such tales were true, I should not have supposed they should be lightly told to thoughtless young people. If they cannot be altogether suppressed, they should only be revealed in a mystery, to which access should be as far as possible restricted by requiring the sacrifice, not of a pig, but of some victim such as very few could afford.[3]

It is true: those stories are objectionable.

Yes, and not to be repeated in our commonwealth, Adeimantus. We shall not tell a child that, if he commits the foulest crimes or goes to any length in punishing his father's misdeeds, he will be doing nothing out of the way, but only what the first and greatest of the gods have done before him.

I agree; such stories are not fit to be repeated.

Nor yet any tales of warfare and intrigues and battles of gods against gods, which are equally untrue. If our future Guardians are to think it a disgrace to quarrel lightly with one another, we shall not let them embroider robes with the Battle of the Giants[4] or tell them of all the other feuds of gods and heroes with their kith and kin. If by any means we can make them believe that no one has ever had a quarrel with a fellow citizen and it is a sin to have one, that is the sort of thing our old men and women should tell children from the first; and as they grow older, we must make the poets write for them in the same strain. Stories like those of Hera being bound by her son, or of Hephaestus flung from heaven by his father for taking his mother's part when she was beaten, and all those battles of the gods in Homer, must not be admitted into our state, whether they be allegorical or not. A child cannot distinguish the allegorical sense from the literal, and the ideas he takes in at that age are likely to become indelibly fixed; hence the great importance of seeing that the first stories he hears shall be designed to produce the best possible effect on his character.

Yes, that is reasonable. But if we were asked which of these stories in particular are of the right quality, what should we answer?

I replied: You and I, Adeimantus, are not, for the moment, poets, but founders of a commonwealth. As such, it is not our business to invent stories ourselves, but only to be clear as to the main outlines to be followed by the poets in making their stories and the limits beyond which they must not be allowed to go.

True; but what are these outlines for any account they may give of the gods?

Of this sort, said I. A poet, whether he is writing epic, lyric, or drama, surely ought always to represent the divine nature as it really is. And the truth is that that nature is good and must be described as such.

Unquestionably.

Well, nothing that is good can be harmful;

and if it cannot do harm, it can do no evil; and so it cannot be responsible for any evil.

I agree.

Again, goodness is beneficent, and hence the cause of well-being.

Yes.

Goodness, then, is not responsible for everything, but only for what is as it should be. It is not responsible for evil.[5]

Quite true.

It follows, then, that the divine, being good, is not, as most people say, responsible for everything that happens to mankind, but only for a small part; for the good things in human life are far fewer than the evil, and, whereas the good must be ascribed to heaven only, we must look elsewhere for the cause of evils.

I think that is perfectly true.

So we shall condemn as a foolish error Homer's description of Zeus as the "dispenser of both good and ill."[6] We shall disapprove when Pandarus' violation of oaths and treaties is said to be the work of Zeus and Athena, or when Themis and Zeus are said to have caused strife among the gods. Nor must we allow our young people to be told by Aeschylus that "Heaven implants guilt in man, when his will is to destroy a house utterly." If a poet writes of the sorrows of Niobe or the calamities of the house of Pelops or of the Trojan war, either he must not speak of them as the work of a god, or, if he does so, he must devise some such explanation as we are now requiring: he must say that what the god did was just and good, and the sufferers were the better for being chastised. One who pays a just penalty must not be called miserable, and his misery then laid at heaven's door. The poet will only be allowed to say that the wicked were miserable because they needed chastisement, and the punishment of heaven did them good. If our commonwealth is to be well-ordered, we must fight to the last against any member of it being suffered to speak of the divine, which is good, being responsible for evil. Neither young nor old must listen to such tales, in prose or verse. Such doctrine would be impious, self-contradictory, and disastrous to our commonwealth.

I agree, he said, and I would vote for a law to that effect.

Well then, that shall be one of our laws about religion. The first principle to which all must conform in speech or writing is that heaven is not responsible for everything, but only for what is good.

I am quite satisfied.

Now what of this for a second principle? Do you think of a god as a sort of magician who might, for his own purposes, appear in various shapes, now actually passing into a number of different forms, now deluding us into believing he has done so; or is his nature simple and of all things the least likely to depart from its proper form?

I cannot say offhand.

Well, if a thing passes out of its proper form, must not the change come either from within or from some outside cause?

Yes.

Is it not true, then, that things in the most perfect condition are the least affected by changes from outside? Take the effect on the body of food and drink or of exertion, or the effect of sunshine and wind on a plant: the healthiest and strongest suffer the least change. Again, the bravest and wisest spirit is least disturbed by external influence. Even manufactured things—furniture, houses, clothes—suffer least from wear and tear when they are well made and in good condition. So this immunity to change from outside is characteristic of anything which, thanks to art or nature or both, is in a satisfactory state.

That seems true.

But surely the state of the divine nature must be perfect in every way, and would therefore be the last thing to suffer transformations from any outside cause.

Yes.

Well then, would a god change or alter himself?

If he changes at all, it can only be in that way.

Would it be a change for the better or for the worse?

It could only be for the worse; for we cannot admit any imperfection in divine goodness or beauty.

True; and that being so, do you think, Adeimantus, that anyone, god or man, would deliberately make himself worse in any respect?

That is impossible.

Then a god cannot desire to change himself. Being as perfect as he can be, every god, it seems, remains simply and for ever in his own form.

That is the necessary conclusion.

If so, my friend, the poets must not tell us that "the gods go to and fro among the cities of men, disguised as strangers of all sorts from far countries"; nor must they tell any of those false tales of Proteus and Thetis transforming themselves, or bring Hera on the stage in the guise of a priestess collecting alms for "the life-giving children of Inachus, the river of Argos."[7] Mothers, again, are not to follow these suggestions and scare young children with mischievous stories of spirits that go about by night in all sorts of outlandish shapes. They would only be blaspheming the gods and at the same time making cowards of their children.

No, that must not be allowed.

But are we to think that the gods, though they do not really change, trick us by some magic into believing that they appear in many different forms?

Perhaps.

What? said I; would a god tell a falsehood or act one by deluding us with an apparition?

I cannot say.

Do you not know that the true falsehood—if that is a possible expression—is a thing that all gods and men abominate?

What do you mean?

This, I replied: no one, if he could help it, would tolerate the presence of untruth in the most vital part of his nature concerning the most vital matters. There is nothing he would fear so much as to harbour falsehood in that quarter.

Still I do not understand.

Because you think I mean something out of the ordinary. All I mean is the presence of falsehood in the soul concerning reality. To be deceived about the truth of things and so to be in ignorance and error and to harbour untruth in the soul is a thing no one would consent to. Falsehood in that quarter is abhorred above everything.

It is indeed.

Well then, as I was saying, this ignorance in the soul which entertains untruth is what really deserves to be called the true falsehood; for the spoken falsehood is only the embodiment or image of a previous condition of the soul, not pure unadulterated falsity. Is it not so?

It is.

This real falsehood, then, is hateful to gods and men equally. But is the spoken falsehood always a hateful thing? Is it not sometimes helpful—in war, for instance, or as a sort of medicine to avert some fit of folly or madness that might make a friend attempt some mischief? And in those legends we were discussing just now, we can turn fiction to account; not knowing the facts about the distant past, we can make our fiction as good an embodiment of truth as possible.

Yes, that is so.

Well, in which of these ways would falsehood be useful to a god? We cannot think of him as embodying truth in fiction for lack of information about the past.

No, that would be absurd.

So there is no room in his case for poetical inventions. Would he need to tell untruths because he has enemies to fear?

Of course not.

Or friends who are mad or foolish?

No; a fool or a madman could hardly enjoy the friendship of the gods.

Gods, then, have no motive for lying. There can be no falsehood of any sort in the divine nature.

None.

We conclude, then, that a god is a being of entire simplicity and truthfulness in word and in deed. In himself he does not change, nor does he delude others, either in dreams or in waking moments, by apparitions or oracles or signs.

I agree, after all you have said.

You will assent, then, to this as a second principle to guide all that is to be said or written about the gods: that they do not transform themselves by any magic or mislead us by illusions or lies. For all our admiration of Homer, we shall not approve his story of the dream Zeus sent to Agamemnon;[8] nor yet those lines of Aeschylus where Thetis tells how Apollo sang at her wedding:

> Boding good fortune for my child, long life
> From sickness free, in all things blest by heaven,
> His song, so crowned with triumph, cheered my heart.
> I thought those lips divine, with prophecy
> Instinct, could never lie. But he, this guest,
> Whose voice so rang with promise at the feast,
> Even he, has slain my son.

If a poet writes of the gods in this way, we shall be angry and refuse him the means to produce his play. Nor shall we allow such poetry to be used in educating the young, if we mean our Guardians to be godfearing and to reproduce the divine nature in themselves so far as man may.

I entirely agree with your principles, he said, and I would have them observed as laws.

So far, then, as religion is concerned, we have settled what sorts of stories about the gods may, or may not, be told to children who are to hold heaven and their parents in reverence and to value good relations with one another.

Yes, he said; and I believe we have settled right.

We also want them to be brave. So the stories they hear should be such as to make them unafraid of death. A man with that fear in his heart cannot be brave, can he?

Surely not.

And can a man be free from that fear and prefer death in battle to defeat and slavery, if he believes in a world below which is full of terrors?

No.

Here again, then, our supervision will be needed. The poets must be told to speak well of that other world. The gloomy descriptions they now give must be forbidden, not only as untrue, but as injurious to our future warriors. We shall strike out all lines like these:

> I would rather be on earth as the hired servant of another, in the house of a landless man with little to live on, than be king over all the dead;[9]

or these:

> Alack, there is, then, even in the house of Death a spirit or a shade; but the wits dwell in it no more.[10]

We shall ask Homer and the poets in general not to mind if we cross out all passages of this sort. If most people enjoy them as good poetry, that is all the more reason for keeping them from children or grown men who are to be free, fearing slavery more than death.

I entirely agree.

We must also get rid of all that terrifying language, the very sound of which is enough to make one shiver: "loathsome Styx," "the River of Wailing," "infernal spirits," "anatomies," and so on. For other purposes such language may be well enough; but we are afraid that fever consequent upon such shivering fits may melt down the fine-tempered spirit of our Guardians. So we will have none of it; and we shall encourage writing in the opposite strain.

Clearly.

Another thing we must banish is the wailing and lamentations of the famous heroes. For this reason: if two friends are both men of high character, neither of them will think that death has any terrors for his comrade; and so he will not mourn for his friend's sake, as if something terrible had befallen him.

No.

We also believe that such a man, above all, possesses within himself all that is necessary for a good life and is least dependent on others, so that he has less to fear from the loss of a son or brother or of his wealth or any other possession. When such misfortune comes, he will bear it patiently without lamenting.

True.

We shall do well, then, to strike out descriptions of the heroes bewailing the dead, and make over such lamentations to women (and not to women of good standing either) and to men of low character, so that the Guardians we are training for our country may disdain to imitate them.

Quite right.

Once more, then, we shall ask Homer and the other poets not to represent Achilles, the son of a goddess, as "tossing from side to side, now on his face, now on his back," and then as rising up and wandering distractedly on the seashore, or pouring ashes on his head with both hands, with all those tears and wailings the poet describes; nor to tell how Priam, who was near akin to the gods, "rolled in the dung as he made entreaty, calling on each man by name."[11] Still more earnestly shall we ask them not to represent gods as lamenting, or at any rate not to dare to misrepresent the highest god by making him say: "Woe is me that Sarpedon, whom I love above all men, is fated to die at the hands of Patroclus." For if our young men take such unworthy descriptions seriously instead of laughing at them, they will hardly feel themselves, who are but men, above behaving in that way or repress any temptation to do so. They would not be ashamed of giving way with complaints and outcries on every trifling occasion; and that would be contrary to the principle we have deduced and shall adhere to, until someone can show us a better.

It would.

Again, our Guardians ought not to be overmuch given to laughter. Violent laughter tends to provoke an equally violent reaction. We must not allow poets to describe men of worth being overcome by it; still less should Homer speak of the gods giving way to "unquenchable laughter" at the sight of Hephaestus "bustling from room to room." That will be against your principles.

Yes, if you choose to call them mine.

Again, a high value must be set upon truthfulness. If we were right in saying that gods have no use for falsehood and it is useful to mankind only in the way of a medicine, obviously a medicine should be handled by no one but a physician.

Obviously.

If anyone, then, is to practise deception, either on the country's enemies or on its citizens, it must be the Rulers of the commonwealth, acting for its benefit; no one else may meddle with this privilege. For a private person to mislead such Rulers we shall declare to be a worse offence than for a patient to mislead his doctor or an athlete his trainer about his bodily condition, or for a seaman to misinform his captain about the state of the ship or of the crew. So, if anyone else in our commonwealth "of all that practise crafts, physician, seer, or carpenter," is caught not telling the truth, the Rulers will punish him for introducing a practice as fatal and subversive in a state as it would be in a ship.

It would certainly be as fatal, if action were suited to the word.

Next, our young men will need self-control; and for the mass of mankind that chiefly means obeying their governors, and themselves governing their appetite for the pleasures of eating and drinking and sex. Here again we shall disapprove of much that we find in Homer.[12]

I agree.

Whereas we shall allow the poets to represent any examples of self-control and fortitude on the part of famous men, and admit such lines as these: "Odysseus smote his breast, chiding his heart: Endure, my heart; thou has borne worse things than these."

Yes, certainly.

Nor again must these men of ours be lovers of money, or ready to take bribes. They must not hear that "gods and great princes may be won by gifts."

No, that sort of thing cannot be approved.

If it were not for my regard for Homer, I should not hesitate to call it downright impiety to make Achilles say to Apollo: "Thou has wronged me, thou deadliest of gods; I would surely requite thee, if I had but the power." And all those stories of Achilles dragging Hector round the tomb of Patroclus and slaughtering captives on the funeral pyre we shall condemn as false, and not let our Guardians believe that Achilles, who was the son of a goddess and of the wise Peleus, third in descent from Zeus, and the pupil of the sage Chiron, was so disordered that his heart was a prey to two contrary maladies, mean covetousness and arrogant contempt of gods and men.

You are right.

We have now distinguished the kinds of stories that may and may not be told about gods and demigods, heroes, and the world below. There remains the literature concerned with human life.

Clearly.

We cannot lay down rules for that at our present stage.

Why not?

Because, I suspect, we shall find both poets and prose-writers guilty of the most serious misstatements about human life, making out that wrongdoers are often happy and just men miserable; that injustice pays, if not detected; and that my being just is to another man's advantage, but a loss to myself. We shall have to prohibit such poems and tales and tell them to compose others in the contrary sense. Don't you think so?

I am sure of it.

Well, as soon as you admit that I am right there, may I not claim that we shall have reached agreement on the subject of all this inquiry?

That is a fair assumption.

Then we must postpone any decision as to how the truth is to be told about human life, until we have discovered the real nature of justice and proved that it is intrinsically profitable to its possesser, no matter what reputation he may have in the eyes of the world.

That is certainly true.

§ 2. THE INFLUENCE OF DRAMATIC RECITATION

Plato now passes from the content of literature used in school to its form. The Greek schoolboy was not allowed to repeat Homer or Aeschylus in a perfunctory gabble, but was expected to throw himself into the story and deliver the speeches with the tones and gesture of an actor. (The professional reciter, Ion, describes how, when he was reciting Homer, his eyes watered and his hair stood on end, *Ion* 535 c.) The word for this dramatic representation is *mimesis*. This has also the wider sense of "imitation," and towards the end of this section it is used of the realistic copying of natural sounds and noises in music. But at first Plato is chiefly concerned with the actor's assumption of a character. The actor does not "imitate" Othello, whom he has never seen; he represents or embodies or reproduces the character created by Shakespeare. In some degree the spectator also identifies himself with a character he admires. Plato held that, in childhood particularly, such imaginative identification may leave its permanent mark on the characters of actor and audience. He will return to this subject in Chapters XXXVI and XXXVII. This section has been considerably abbreviated.

So much for the content of literature. If we consider next the question of form, we shall then have covered the whole field.

I don't understand what you mean by form, said Adeimantus.

I must explain, then, said I. Let me put it in this way. Any story in prose or verse is always a setting forth of events, past, present, or future, isn't it?

Yes.

And that can be done either in pure narrative or by means of representation or in both ways.

I am still rather in the dark.

I seem to be a poor hand at explaining; I had better give a particular illustration.[13] You remember the beginning of the *Iliad*, which describes how Chryses begged Agamemnon to release his daughter, and Agamemnon was angry, and Chryses called on his god to avenge the refusal on the Greeks. So far the poet speaks in his own person, but later on he speaks in the character of Chryses and tries to make us feel that the words come, not from Homer, but from an aged priest. Throughout the *Iliad* and *Odyssey*, the events are set forth in these two different forms. All the time, both in the speeches and in the narrative parts in between, he is telling his story; but where he is delivering a speech in character, he tries to make his manner resemble that of the person he has introduced as speaker. Any poet who does that by means of voice and gesture, is telling his story by way of dramatic representation; whereas, if he makes no such attempt to suppress his own personality, the events are set forth in simple narrative.

Now I understand.

Observe, then, that, if you omit the intervening narrative and leave only the dialogue, you get the opposite form.

Yes, I see; that occurs in tragedy, for instance.

Exactly, said I. Now I think you see the distinction I failed to make clear. All storytelling, in prose or poetry, is in one of three forms. It may be wholly dramatic: tragedy, as you say, or comedy. Or the poet may narrate the events in his own person; perhaps the best example of that is the dithyramb.[14] Or again both methods may be used, as in epic and several other kinds of poetry.

Yes, he said, I see now what you meant.

Remember, too, I began by saying that, having done with the content, we had still to consider the form. I meant that we should have to decide whether to allow our poets to tell their story in dramatic form, wholly, or in part (and, if so, in what parts), or not at all.

You mean, I suspect, the question whether we shall admit tragedy and comedy into our commonwealth.

Perhaps, I replied, or the question may be wider still. I do not know yet; but we must go wherever the wind of the argument carries us.[15]

That is good advice.

Here then, Adeimantus, is a question for you to consider: Do we want our Guardians to be capable of playing many parts? Perhaps the answer follows from our earlier principle that a man can only do one thing well; if he tries his hand at several, he will fail to make his mark in any of them. Does not that principle apply to acting? The same man cannot act many parts so well as he can act one.

No, he cannot.

Then he will hardly be able to pursue some worthy occupation and at the same time represent a variety of different characters. Even in the case of two forms of representation so closely allied as tragedy and comedy, the same poet cannot write both with equal success. Again, the recitation of epic poetry and acting on the stage are distinct professions; and even on the stage different actors perform in tragedy and comedy.

That is so.

And human talent, Adeimantus, seems to be split up into subdivisions even minuter than these; so that no man can successfully represent many different characters in the field of art or pursue a corresponding variety of occupations in real life.

Quite true.

If, then, we are to hold fast to our original principle that our Guardians shall be set free from all manual crafts to be the artificers of their country's freedom, with the perfect mastery which comes of working only at what conduces to that end, they ought not to play any other part in dramatic representation any more than in real life; but if they act, they should, from childhood upward, impersonate only the appropriate types of character, men who are brave, religious, self-controlled, generous. They are not to do anything mean or dishonourable; no more should they be practised in representing such behaviour, for fear of becoming infected with the reality. You must have noticed how the reproduction of another person's gestures or tones of voice or states of mind, if persisted in from youth up, grows into a habit which becomes second nature.

Yes, I have.

So these charges of ours, who are to grow up into men of worth, will not be allowed to enact the part of a woman, old or young, railing against her husband, or boasting of a happiness which she imagines can rival the gods', or overwhelmed with grief and misfortune; much less a woman in love, or sick, or in labour; nor yet slaves of either sex, going about their menial work; nor men of a low type, behaving with cowardice and all the qualities contrary to those we mentioned, deriding one another and exchanging coarse abuse, whether drunk or sober, and otherwise using language and behaviour that are an offence against themselves as well as their neighbours; nor must they copy the words and actions of madmen. Knowledge they must have of baseness and insanity both in men and women, but not reproduce such behaviour in life or in art.

Quite true.

Again, are they to impersonate men working at some trade, such as a smith's, or rowing a galley or giving the time to the oarsmen?

How should they, when they are not even to take any notice of such occupations?

And may they take part in performances which imitate horses neighing and bulls bellowing or the noise of rivers and sea and thunder?[16]

We have already forbidden them to represent the ravings of insanity.

If I understand you, then, there are two contrasted forms of expression in which any series of events may be set forth: one which will always be used by a man of fine character and breeding, the other by one whose nature and upbringing are of a very different sort.[17]

Yes, there are those two forms.

One of them involves little change and variety; when the words have been fitted to a suitable musical mode and rhythm, the recitation can keep almost to the same mode and rhythm throughout, the modulations required being slight. The other, on the contrary, involves every sort of variation and demands the use of all the modes and rhythms there are.

Quite true.

Now all writers and composers fall into one or other of these styles, or a mixture of both. What shall we do? Are we to admit into our commonwealth one or other of the extreme styles, or the mixed one, or all three?

If my judgement is to prevail, the simple one which serves to represent a fine character.

On the other hand, Adeimantus, the mixed style has its attractions; and children and their attendants, not to mention the great mass of the public, find the opposite of the one you chose the most attractive of all.

No doubt they do.

But perhaps you think it will not suit our commonwealth, where no man is to be two or more persons or a jack of all trades; this being the reason why ours is the only state in which we shall find a shoemaker who cannot also take command of a ship, a farmer who does not leave his farm to serve on juries, a soldier who is not a tradesman into the bargain.

Quite true.

Suppose, then, that an individual clever enough to assume any character and give imitations of anything and everything should visit our country and offer to perform his compositions, we shall bow down before a being with such miraculous powers of giving pleasure; but we shall tell him that we are not allowed to have any such person in our commonwealth; we shall crown him with fillets of wool, anoint his head with myrrh, and conduct him to the borders of some other country. For our own benefit, we shall employ the poets and story-tellers of the more austere and less attractive type, who will reproduce only the manner of a person of high character and, in the substance of their discourse, conform to those rules we laid down when we began the education of our warriors.

Yes, we shall do that, if it lies in our power.

So now, my dear Adeimantus, we have discussed both the content and the form of literature, and we have finished with that part of education.

Yes, I think so.

§ 3. MUSICAL ACCOMPANIMENT AND METRE

Plato approves of the old practice of writing lyric poetry only to be sung to music, and music only as an accompaniment to song. Hence he speaks of words, musical mode (*harmonia*), and rhythm (metre in poetry and time in music) as inseparable parts of "song." There was no harmony in the modern sense; and the melody followed the words very closely. At first there was normally one note to each syllable, and every syllable was conventionally treated as either "long" or "short," the long being equal to two shorts. By Plato's time the growing practice of using the poem as a libretto and distorting the words to suit the music had already excited protest.

In the older lyric poetry, of Aeschylus and Pindar for example, certain rhythms and certain modes were associated with particular moods of feeling and types of character, and, as the poetry passed from one mood or type to another, both metre and mode were suitably modulated. Accordingly, the limitations already imposed on the content of poetry entail corresponding limitations on the choice of metre and on the musical accompaniment.

This section has been abbreviated by the omission of technicalities of Greek music and metre, which are still imperfectly understood.

There remains the question of style in song and poetry set to music. It must be easy now for anyone to discover the rules we must make as to their character, if we are to be consistent.

Glaucon laughed. I am afraid "anyone" does not include me, Socrates. At the moment I cannot quite see what the rules should be, though I have my suspicions.

You can see this much at any rate, that song consists of three elements: words, musical mode, and rhythm.

Yes.

And so far as the words go, it will make no difference whether they are set to music or not; in either case they must conform to the rules we have already made for the content and form of literature.

True.

And the musical mode and the rhythm should fit the words?

Of course.

And we said that we did not want dirges and laments. Which are the modes that express sorrow? Tell me; you are musical.

Modes like the Mixed Lydian and Hyperlydian.

Then we may discard those; men, and even women of good standing, will have no use for them.

Certainly.

Again, drunkenness, effeminacy, and inactivity are most unsuitable in Guardians. Which are the modes expressing softness and the ones used at drinking-parties?

There are the Ionian and certain Lydian modes which are called "slack."

You will not use them in the training of your warriors?

Certainly not. You seem to have the Dorian and the Phrygian left.

I am not an expert in the modes, I said; but leave me one which will fittingly represent the tones and accents of a brave man in warlike action or in any hard and dangerous task, who, in the hour of defeat or when facing wounds and death, will meet every blow of fortune with steadfast endurance. We shall need another to express peaceful action under no stress of hard necessity; as when a man is using persuasion or entreaty, praying to the gods or instructing and admonishing his neighbour, or again submitting himself to the instruction and persuasion of others; a man who is not overbearing when any such action has proved successful, but behaves always with wise restraint and is content with the outcome. These two modes you must leave: the two which will best express the accents of courage in the face of stern necessity and misfortune, and of temperance in prosperity won by peaceful pursuits.

The modes you want, he replied, are just the two I mentioned.

Our songs and airs, then, will not need instruments of large compass capable of modulation into all the modes, and we shall not maintain craftsmen to make them, in particular the flute, which has the largest compass of all. That leaves the lyre and the cithara for use in the town; and in the country the herdsmen may have some sort of pipe.

That seems to be the conclusion.

At any rate, it is no innovation to prefer Apollo to Marsyas in the choice of instruments.

Surely not.

It strikes me, said I, that, without noticing it, we have been purging our commonwealth of that luxurious excess we said it suffered from.

A wise proceeding, he replied.

Let us go through with it, then. Next after the modes will come the principle governing rhythm, which will be, not to aim at a great variety of metres, but to discover the rhythms appropriate to a life of courage and self-control; and we shall then adapt metre and melody to the words expressing a life of that sort, not the words to the metre and melody. What these rhythms are, it is for you to explain, as you explained the modes.

Really, he replied, I cannot do that. I have observed that there are three fundamental types of rhythm to which all metres may be reduced, just as there are four intervals at the base of all the modes;[18] but what kind of life each rhythm is suited to express, I cannot say.

Well, said I, we shall consult Damon[19] on this question, which metres are expressive of meanness, insolence, frenzy, and other such evils, and which rhythms we must retain to express their opposites. It would take a long time to settle all that.

It would indeed.

§ 4. THE AIM OF EDUCATION IN POETRY AND MUSIC

Plato here passes from the simplification of poetry and music as used in early education to consider the whole field of art and craftsmanship and its influence on character. In his *Protagoras,* (326 A), a conversation imagined as taking place in the previous century, Plato had made Protagoras speak of children's training in music as introducing rhythm and harmony into their souls and having a socializing influence; "for the whole life of man stands in need of rhythm and harmony." This is not represented as a novel doctrine, but as if it were already a commonplace. The fragments of Damon suggest that it may have been formulated by him.

The ultimate end of all education is insight into the harmonious order (*cosmos*) of the whole world. This earliest stage ends here in the perception of those "images" of moral or spiritual excellences which, when combined with bodily beauty in a living person, are the proper object of love (*eros*). They are apparitions, in the sensible world, of the Forms ("Ideas"), their archetypes in the world of unseen reality, beyond the threshold which the future philosopher will cross at the next stage of his advance.

One thing, however, is easily settled, namely that grace and seemliness of form and movement go with good rhythm; ungracefulness and unseemliness with bad.

Naturally.

And again, good or bad rhythm and also tunefulness or discord in music go with the quality of the poetry; for they will be modelled after its form, if, as we have said, metre and music must be adapted to the sense of the words.

Well, they must be so adapted.

And the content of the poetry and the manner in which it is expressed depend, in their turn, on moral character.

Of course.

Thus, then, excellence of form and content in discourse[20] and of musical expression and rhythm, and grace of form and movement, all depend on goodness of nature, by which I mean, not the foolish simplicity sometimes called by courtesy "good nature," but a nature in which goodness of character has been well and truly established.

Yes, certainly.

So, if our young men are to do their proper work in life, they must follow after these qualities wherever they may be found. And they are to be found in every sort of workmanship, such as painting, weaving, embroidery, architecture, the making of furniture; and also in the human frame and in all the works of nature: in all these grace and seemliness may be present or absent. And the absence of grace, rhythm, harmony is nearly allied to baseness of thought and expression and baseness of character; whereas their presence goes with that moral excellence and self-mastery of which they are the embodiment.

That is perfectly true.

Then we must not only compel our poets, on pain of expulsion, to make their poetry the express image of noble character; we must also supervise craftsmen of every kind and forbid them to leave the stamp of baseness, licence, meanness, unseemliness, on painting and sculpture, or building, or any other work of their hands; and anyone who cannot obey shall not practise his art in our commonwealth. We would not have our Guardians grow up among representations of moral deformity, as in some foul pasture where, day after day, feeding on every poisonous weed they would, little by little, gather insensibly a mass of corruption in their very souls. Rather we must seek those craftsmen whose instinct guides them to whatsoever is lovely and gracious; so that our young men, dwelling in a wholesome climate, may drink in good from every quarter, whence, like a breeze bearing health from happy regions, some influence from noble works constantly falls upon eye and ear from childhood upward, and imperceptibly draws them into sympathy and harmony with the beauty of reason, whose impress they take.

There could be no better upbringing than that.

Hence, Glaucon, I continued, the decisive importance of education in poetry and music: rhythm and harmony sink deep into the recesses of the soul and take the strongest hold there, bringing that grace of body and mind which is only to be found in one who is brought up in the right way. Moreover, a proper training in this kind makes a man quick to perceive any defect or ugliness in art or in nature. Such deformity will rightly disgust him. Approving all that is lovely, he will welcome it home with joy into his soul and, nourished thereby, grow into a man of a noble spirit. All that is ugly and disgraceful he will rightly condemn and abhor while he is still too young to understand the reason; and when reason comes, he will greet her as a friend with whom his education has made him long familiar.

I agree, he said; that is the purpose of education in literature and music.

Now in learning to read, I went on, we

were proficient when we could recognize the few letters there are wherever they occur in all the multitude of different words, never thinking them beneath our notice in the most insignificant word, but bent upon distinguishing them everywhere, because we should not be scholars until we had got thus far.

True.

Also we must know the letters themselves before we can recognize images of them, reflected (say) in water or in a mirror. The same skill and practice are needed in either case.

Yes.

Then, is it not true, in the same way, that we and these Guardians we are to bring up will never be fully cultivated until we can recognize the essential Forms of temperance, courage, liberality, high-mindedness, and all other kindred qualities, and also their opposites, wherever they occur.[21] We must be able to discern the presence of these Forms themselves and also of their images in anything that contains them, realizing that, to recognize either, the same skill and practice are required, and that the most insignificant instance is not beneath our notice.

That must surely be so.

And for him who has eyes to see it, there can be no fairer sight than the harmonious union of a noble character in the soul with an outward form answering thereto and bearing the same stamp of beauty.

There cannot.

And the fairest is also the most lovable.

Of course.

So the man who has been educated in poetry and music will be in love with such a person, but never with one who lacks this harmony.

Not if the defect should lie in the soul; if it were only some bodily blemish, he would accept that with patience and goodwill.

I understand, said I; you are or have been in love with a person like that, and I agree. But tell me: is excessive pleasure compatible with temperance?

How can it be, when it unsettles the mind no less than pain?

Or with virtue in general?

Certainly not.

It has more to do with insolence and profligacy?

Yes.

And is there any pleasure you can name that is greater and keener than sexual pleasure?

No; nor any that is more like frenzy.

Whereas love rightfully is such a passion as beauty combined with a noble and harmonious character may inspire in a temperate and cultivated mind. It must therefore be kept from all contact with licentiousness and frenzy; and where a passion of this rightful sort exists, the lover and his beloved must have nothing to do with the pleasure in question.

Certainly not, Socrates.

It appears, then, that in this commonwealth we are founding you will have a law to the effect that a lover may seek the company of his beloved and, with his consent, kiss and embrace him like a son, with honourable intent, but must never be suspected of any further familiarity, on pain of being thought ill-bred and without any delicacy of feeling.

I quite agree.

Then is not our account of education in poetry and music now complete? It has ended where it ought to end, in the love of beauty.

I agree. . . .

NOTES

1. In a wide sense, tales, legends, myths, narratives in poetry or prose.

2. Hesiod, *Theogony*, 154 ff. A primitive

myth of the forcing apart of Sky (Uranus) and Earth (Gaia) by their son Cronos, who mutilated his father. Zeus, again, took vengeance on his father Cronos for trying to destroy his children. These stories were sometimes cited to justify ill-treatment of parents.

3. The usual sacrifice at the Eleusinian Mysteries was a pig, which was cheap. In a mystery unedifying legends might be given an allegorical interpretation, a method which had been applied to Homer since the end of the sixth century.

4. Such a robe was woven by maidens for the statue of Athena at the Great Panathenaea.

5. The words of Lachesis in the concluding myth [of *The Republic*] illustrate Plato's meaning.

6. Some further instances from Homer are here omitted.

7. The allusions are to the *Odyssey* and to a lost play of Aeschylus.

8. *Iliad* 2.1 ff.

9. Spoken by the ghost of Achilles, *Odyssey* 9.489.

10. Spoken by Achilles when the ghost of Patroclus eludes his embrace, *Iliad* 23.103. Other lines from Homer describing the misery of the dead are omitted.

11. When Priam saw Achilles maltreating the body of Hector, *Iliad* 23.414.

12. In order to save space, illustrations from Homer of the self-indulgence of heroes and gods and of disrespect for rulers are omitted here and below.

13. The explanation, necessitated by the ambiguity of the Greek *mimesis*, is shortened in the translation.

14. The most important type of lyric poetry in Plato's time.

15. In Chap. XXXV poetry and painting will in fact be criticized as "representation" in a wider sense.

16. This probably refers to the realistic dithyrambic poetry of the fourth century, and more particularly to the musical accompaniment. Philoxenus' dithyramb *Cyclops* represented the bleating of Polyphemus' flock; the *Nautilus* of Timotheus depicted a storm at sea.

17. Plato's point being now sufficiently clear, the translation omits a passage in which he says that a man of well-regulated character will confine himself to impersonating men of a similar type and will consequently use pure narrative for the most part. A vulgar person, on the other hand, will impersonate any type and even give musical imitations of the cries of animals and inanimate noises. Plato began by speaking of recitation as a part of early education, but he now proposes to exclude poetry and music of the second kind from the state altogether.

18. The meaning is uncertain, but the three perfect consonances (octave, fourth, fifth) and the tone may be intended.

19. A famous musician, the friend of Pericles. An obscure account of certain metres is here omitted.

20. *Eulogia* is given an unusual sense in order to bring in the associations of *eulogos* as "reasonable," the poetry being the intellectual element.

21. For the Platonic doctrine of Forms see Chap. XIX.

Aristotle 384–322 B.C.

The son of a doctor, Aristotle had a lifelong interest in medical science. His years as a student at Plato's Academy were characterized by a questioning, highly analytical mind that earned him the nickname "the Brain." Plato, Aristotle's teacher, had already charged the poets in his *Republic* with two great weaknesses: "imitation" and "pity and fear." The *Poetics* is Aristotle's answer to Plato's accusations. His other chief works are the *Physics, Metaphysics, De Anima, Nichomachean Ethics, Politics,* and *Rhetoric.*

What we know as the *Poetics* is in fact the surviving lecture notes of what may have been a series of lectures given by Aristotle. They lack the coherence typical of Aristotle's other works, and there is evidence that originally there were two books of the *Poetics*, one of which we have now lost; but even at that, the *Poetics* has had an important critical influence on literary theory.

When Aristotle turned to poetry and the nature of great literature, his analytical abilities allowed him to offer insights that have offered each generation of critics either the answers to their questions or the point from which they could move in an attempt to discover other answers. Key issues—including the nature of tragedy and its essential elements, the relationship between plot and character, the significance of pity and fear, and the nature and role of imitation—have made Aristotle's *Poetics* the starting point for countless theories and the foundation, ultimately, from which much Western literary criticism develops.

POETICS

1

I propose to treat of poetry in itself and of its several species, noting the essential quality of each; to inquire into the structure of the plot as requisite to a good poem; into the number and nature of the parts of which each species consists; and similarly into whatever else falls within the same inquiry. Following, then, the order of nature, let us begin with the principles which come first.

Epic poetry and Tragedy, Comedy also and dithyrambic poetry, and the greater part of the music of the flute and of the lyre, are all in their general conception modes of imitation. They differ, however, from one another in three respects—the means, the objects, the manner of imitation being in each case distinct.

For as there are persons who, by conscious art or mere habit, imitate and represent various objects through the medium of color and form, or again by the voice; so in the arts above mentioned taken as a whole, the imitation is produced by rhythm, language, and "harmony," either singly or combined.

Thus in the music of the flute and the lyre "harmony" and rhythm alone are employed; also in other arts, such as that of the pipe, which are essentially similar to these. In dancing, rhythm alone is used without "harmony"; for even dancing imitates character, emotion, and action, by rhythmical movement.

The art which imitates by means of language alone, and that either in prose or verse—which verse, again, may either combine different metres or consist of but one kind—has hitherto been without a name. For there is no common term we could apply to the mimes of Sophron and Xenarchus and to the Socratic dialogues; or, again, to poetic imitations in iambic, elegiac, or any similar metre. People do, indeed, commonly connect the idea of poetry or "making" with that of verse, and speak of elegiac poets, or of epic (that is, hexameter) poets; implying that it is not imitation that makes them poets, but the metre that entitles them to the common name. Even if a treatise on medicine or natural philosophy be brought out in verse, the name of poet is by custom given to the author; and yet Homer and Empedocles have nothing in common except the metre: the former, therefore, is properly styled poet, the latter, physicist rather than poet.

So too if a writer should, in his poetic imitation, combine every variety of metre, like Chaeremon—whose *Centaur* is a rhapsody in which all metres are mingled—we must, according to usage, call him simply poet. So much then for these distinctions.

There are, again, certain kinds of poetry which employ all the means above mentioned—namely, rhythm, melody and metre. Such are dithyrambic and nomic poetry, and also Tragedy and Comedy; but between them the difference is, that in the first two cases these means are all employed at the same time, in the latter, separately.

Such, then, are the differences of the arts with respect to means of imitation.

2

Since the objects of imitation are persons acting, and these persons must be either of a higher or a lower type (for moral character mainly answers to these divisions, goodness and badness being the distinguishing marks of moral differences), it follows that we must represent men either as better than in real life, or worse, or as they are. It is the same in painting. Polygnotus depicted men as nobler than they are, Pauson as less noble, Dionysius drew them true to life.

Now it is evident that each of the modes of imitation above mentioned will exhibit these differences, and become a distinct kind in imitating objects that are thus distinct. Such diversities may be found even in dancing, flute-playing, and lyre-playing. So again in prose compositions, and in verse unaccompanied by music. Homer, for example, makes men better than they are; Cleophon as they are; Hegemon the Thasian, the inventor of parodies, and Nicochares, the author of the *Deliad*, worse than they are. The same thing holds good of dithyrambs and nomes; here too one may portray lower types, as Timotheus and Philoxenus represented their Cyclopes. The same distinction marks off Tragedy from Comedy; for Comedy aims at representing men as worse, Tragedy as better than in actual life.

3

There is still a third difference—the manner in which each of these objects may be imitated. For the means being the same, and the objects the same, the poet may imitate by narration—in which case he can either take another personality as Homer does, or speak in his own person, unchanged—or he may imitate by making all his actors live and move before us.

These, then, as we said at the beginning, are the three differences which distinguish artistic imitation—the means, the objects, and the manner. So that from one point of view, Sophocles is an imitator of the same kind as Homer—for both imitate higher types of character; from another point of view, of the same kind as Aristophanes—for both imitate persons acting and doing. Hence, some say, the name of "drama" is given to such poems, as representing action. For the same reason the Dorians claim the invention both of Tragedy and Comedy. The claim to Comedy is put forward by the Megarians—not only by those of Greece proper, who allege that it originated under their democracy, but also by the Megarians of Sicily; the poet Epicharmus, who lived not long before Chionides and Magnes, being from their country. Tragedy too is claimed by certain Dorians of the Peloponnese. In each case they appeal to the evidence of language. Villages, they say, are by them called *κῶμαι*, by the Athenians *δῆμοι*: and they assume that the name Comedians is derived not from *κωμάζειν* "to revel," but from the performers wandering about the villages (*κῶμαι*), when still excluded from the city. They add also that the Dorian word for "doing" is *δρᾶν*, and the Athenian, *πράττειν*.

This may suffice as to the number and nature of the various modes of imitation.

4

Poetry in general seems to have sprung from two causes, each of them lying deep in our nature. First, the instinct of imitation is implanted in man from childhood, one difference between him and other animals being that he is the most imitative of creatures; and through imitation he acquires his earliest learning. And, indeed, every one feels a natural pleasure in things imitated. There is evidence of this in the effect produced by works of art. Objects which in themselves we view with pain, we delight to contemplate when reproduced with absolute fidelity: such as the forms of the most ignoble beasts and of dead bodies. The cause of this again is, that to learn is a lively pleasure, not only to philosophers but to men in general; whose capacity, however, of learning is more limited. Thus the reason why men enjoy seeing a likeness is, that in contemplating it they are engaged in learning—they reason and infer what each object is: "this," they say, "is the man." For if you happen not to have seen the original, the pleasure will be due not to the imitation at such, but to the execution, the colouring, or some such other cause.

Imitation, then, is one instinct of our nature. Next, there is the instinct for harmony and rhythm, metre being manifestly a species of rhythm. Persons, therefore, with this natural gift little by little improved upon their early efforts, till their rude improvisations gave birth to Poetry.

Poetry now branched off in two directions, according to the individual character of the writers. The more elevated poets imitated noble actions, and the actions of good men. The more trivial sort imitated the actions of meaner persons, at first composing satires, as the former did hymns to the gods and the praises of famous men. A poem of the satirical kind cannot indeed be put down to any author earlier than Homer; though many such writers probably there were. But from Homer onward, instances can be cited—his *Margites,* for example, and other similar compositions. The iambic metre was here introduced, as best fitted to the subject: hence the measure is still called the iambic or lampooning measure, being that in which the lampoons were written.

Thus the older poets were distinguished as writers either of heroic or of iambic verse. As, in the serious style, Homer is preeminent among poets, standing alone not only in the excellence, but also in the dramatic form of his imitations, so he too first sketched out the main lines of Comedy, by dramatising the ludicrous instead of writing personal satire. His *Margites* bears the same relations to Comedy that the *Iliad* and *Odyssey* do to Tragedy. But when Tragedy and Comedy had once appeared, writers applied themselves to one or other species of poetry, following their native bent. They composed comedies in place of lampoons, and Tragedies in place of Epic poems, the newer forms of poetry being higher and more highly esteemed than the old.

Whether Tragedy has as yet perfected its proper types or not; and whether it is to be judged in itself, or in relation also to the stage—this raises another question. Be that as it may, Tragedy—as also Comedy—was at first mere improvisation. The one originated with the leaders of the dithyrambic, the other with those of the phallic songs, which are still in use in many of our cities. Tragedy advanced by slow degrees; each new element that showed itself was in turn developed. Having passed through many changes, it found its natural form, and there it stopped.

Aeschylus first introduced a second actor; he diminished the importance of the Chorus, and assigned the leading part to the dialogue. Sophocles raised the number of actors to three, and added scene-painting. It was not till late that the short plot was discarded for one of greater compass, and the grotesque diction of the earlier satyric form, for the stately manner of Tragedy. The iambic measure then replaced the trochaic tetrameter, which was originally employed when the poetry was of the satyric order, and had greater affinities with dancing. Once dialogue had come in, Nature herself discovered the appropriate measure. For the iambic is, of all measures, the most colloquial: we see it in the fact that conversational speech runs into iambic form more frequently than into any other kind of verse; rarely into hexameters, and only when we drop the colloquial intonation. The number of "episodes" or acts was also increased, and the other embellishments added, of which tradition tells. These we need not here discuss; to enter into them in detail would, probably, be tedious.

5

Comedy is, as we have said, an imitation of characters of a lower type—not, however, in the full sense of the word bad; for the Ludicrous is merely a subdivision of the ugly. It may be defined as a defect or ugliness which is not painful or destructive. Thus, for example, the comic mask is ugly and distorted, but does not cause pain.

The successive changes through which Tragedy passed, and the authors of these changes are not unknown. It is otherwise with Comedy, which at first was not seriously treated. It was late before the Archon appointed a comic chorus; the performers were till then voluntary. From the time, however, when Comedy began to assume certain fixed forms, comic poets, distinctively so called, are recorded. Who introduced masks, or prologues, or increased the number of actors—these and other similar details remain unknown. As for the plot, it came originally from Sicily; but of Athenian writers Crates was the first who, abandoning the "iambic" or lampooning form, generalised his themes and plots.

Epic poetry agrees with Tragedy in so far as it is an imitation in verse of characters of a higher type. They differ, in that Epic poetry admits but one kind of metre, and is narrative in form. They differ, again, in length: for Tragedy endeavours, as far as possible, to confine itself to a single revolution of the sun, or but slightly to exceed this limit; whereas the Epic action has no limits of time. This, then, is a second point of difference; though at first the same freedom was admitted in Tragedy as in Epic poetry.

Of their constituent parts some are common to both, some peculiar to Tragedy. Whoever, therefore, knows what is good or bad Tragedy, knows also about Epic poetry: for all the parts of an Epic poem are found in Tragedy, but what belongs to Tragedy is not all found in the Epic poem.

6

Of the poetry which imitates in hexameter verse, and of Comedy, we will speak hereafter. Let us now discuss Tragedy, resuming its formal definition, as resulting from what has been already said.

Tragedy, then, is an imitation of an action that is serious, complete, and of a certain magnitude; in language embellished with each kind of artistic ornament, the several kinds being found in separate parts of the play; in the form of action, not of narrative; through pity and fear effecting the proper purgation of these emotions. By "language embellished," I mean language into which rhythm, "harmony," and song enter. By "the several kinds in separate parts," I mean, that some parts are rendered through the medium of verse alone, others again with the aid of song.

Now as tragic imitation implies persons acting, it necessarily follows, in the first place, that Scenic equipment will be a part of Tragedy. Next, Song and Diction, for these are the means of imitation. By "Diction" I mean the mere metrical arrangement of the words: as for "Song," it is a term whose full sense is well understood.

Again, Tragedy is the imitation of an action; and an action implies personal agents, who necessarily possess certain qualities both of character and thought. It is these that determine the qualities of actions themselves; these—thought and character—are the two natural causes from which actions spring: on these causes, again, all success or failure depends. Hence, the Plot is the imitation of the action—for by plot I here mean the arrangement of the incidents. By Character I mean that in virtue of which we ascribe certain qualities to the agents. By Thought, that whereby a statement is proved, or a general truth expressed. Every Tragedy, therefore, must have six parts, which parts determine its quality—namely, Plot, Character, Diction, Thought, Scenery, Song. Two of the parts constitute the means of imitation, one the manner, and three the objects of imitation. And these complete the list. These elements have been employed, we may say, by almost all poets; in fact, every play contains Scenic accessories as well as Character, Plot, Diction, Song, and Thought.

But most important of all is the structure of the incidents. For Tragedy is an imitation, not of men, but of an action and of life—of happiness and misery; and happiness and misery consist in action, the end of human life being a mode of action, not a quality. Now the characters of men determine their qualities, but it is by their actions that they are happy or the reverse. Dramatic action, therefore, is not with a view to the representation of character: character comes in as subsidiary to the action. Hence the incidents and the plot are the end of a tragedy; and the end is the chief thing of all. Again, without action there cannot be a tragedy; there may be without character. The tragedies of most of our modern poets fail in the rendering of character; and of poets in general this is often true. It is the same in painting; and here lies the difference between Zeuxis and Polygnotus. Polygnotus delineates character well: the style of Zeuxis is devoid of ethical quality. Again, if you string together a set of speeches expressive of character, and well finished in point of diction and thought, you will not produce the essential tragic effect nearly so well as with a play, which, however deficient in these respects, yet has a plot and artistically constructed incidents. Besides which, the most powerful elements of emotional interest in Tragedy—Reversals of Fortune, and Recognition scenes—are parts of the plot. A further proof is, that novices in the art are able to elaborate their diction and ethical portraiture, before they can frame the incidents. It is the same with almost all early poets.

The Plot, then, is the first principle, and, as it were, the soul of the tragedy: Character holds the second place. A similar fact is seen in painting. The most beautiful colours, laid on confusedly, will not give as much pleasure as the chalk outline of a portrait. Thus Tragedy is the imitation of an action, and of the agents, mainly with a view to the action.

Third in order is the Thought—that is, the faculty of saying what is possible and pertinent in given circumstances. In the case of the dramatic dialogue, this is the function of the political or the rhetorical art: for the older poets make their characters speak the language of the rhetoricians. Character is that which reveals moral purpose: it shows what kind of things, in cases of doubt, a man chooses or avoids. A dialogue, therefore, which in no way indicates what the speaker chooses or avoids, is not expressive of character. Thought, on the other hand, is that whereby we prove that something is or is not, or state a general maxim.

Fourth comes the Diction; by which I mean, as has been already said, the expression of our meaning in words; and its essence is the same both in verse and prose.

Of the remaining elements Song holds the chief place among the embellishments.

The Scenery has, indeed, an emotional attraction of its own, but, of all the parts, it is the least artistic, and connected least with poetic theory. For the power of Tragedy, we may be sure, is felt even apart from representation and actors. Besides, the production of scenic effects depends more on the art of the stage manager than on that of the poet.

7

These principles being established, let us now discuss the proper structure of the Plot, since this is the first, and also the most important part of Tragedy.

Now, according to our definition, Tragedy is an imitation of an action, that is complete, and whole, and of a certain magnitude; for there may be a whole that is wanting in magnitude. A whole is that which has beginning, middle, and end. A beginning is that which does not itself follow anything but causal necessity, but after which something naturally is or comes to be. An end, on the contrary, is that which itself naturally follows some other thing, either by necessity, or in the regular course of events, but has nothing following it. A middle is that which follows something as some other thing follows it. A well constructed plot, therefore, must neither begin nor end at haphazard, but conform to the type here described.

Again, if an object be beautiful—either a living organism or a whole composed of parts—it must not only have its parts in orderly arrangement, it must also be of a certain magnitude. Hence no exceedingly small animal can be beautiful; for the view of it is confused, the object being seen in an almost imperceptible moment of time. Nor, again, can an animal of vast size be beautiful; for as the eye cannot take it all in at once, the unity and sense of the whole is lost for the spectator. So it would be with a creature a thousand miles long. As, therefore, in animate bodies and living organisms, a certain magnitude is necessary, and that such as may be easily embraced in one view; so in the plot, a certain length is necessary, and that length one that may be easily embraced by the memory. The limit of length in relation to dramatic competition and sensuous presentment, is no part of artistic theory. For suppose a hundred tragedies had to be played against one another, the performance would be regulated by the hour-glass—a method, indeed, that is familiar enough otherwise. But the limit as fixed by the nature of the drama itself is this:—the greater the length, the more beautiful will the piece be in respect of such magnitude, provided that the whole be perspicuous. And as a general rule, the proper magnitude is comprised within such limits, that the sequence of events, according to the law of probability or necessity, will admit of a change from bad fortune to good, or from good fortune to bad.

8

Unity of plot does not, as some persons think, consist in the unity of the hero. For infinitely various are the incidents in one man's life, which cannot be reduced to unity; and so, too, there are many actions of one man out of which we cannot make one action. Hence the error, as it appears, of all poets who have composed a Heracleid, a Theseid, or other poems of the kind. They imagine that as Heracles was one man, the story of Heracles ought also to be a unity. But Homer, as in all else he is of surpassing merit, here too—whether from art or natural genius—seems to have happily discerned the truth. In composing the *Odyssey* he did not bring in all the adventures of Odysseus—such as his wound on Parnassus, or his feigned madness at the mustering of the host—incidents between which there was no necessary or probable connexion: but he made the *Odyssey*, and likewise the *Iliad*, to centre round an action, that in our sense of the word is one. As therefore, in the other imitative arts, the imitation is one, when the object imitated is one, so the plot, being an imitation of an action, must imitate one action and that a whole, the structural union of the parts being such that, if any one of them is displaced or removed, the whole will be disjointed and disturbed. For that which may be present or absent without being perceived, is not an organic part of the whole.

9

It is, moreover, evident from what has been said, that it is not the function of the poet to relate what has happened, but what may happen—what is possible according to the law of probability or necessity. The poet and the historian differ not by writing in verse or in prose. The work of Herodotus might be put into verse, and it would still be a species of history, with metre no less than without it. The true difference is that one relates what has happened, the other what may happen. Poetry, therefore, is a more philosophical and a higher thing than history: for poetry tends to express the universal, history the particular. The universal tells us how a person of given character will on occasion speak or act, according to the law of probability or necessity; and it is this universality at which Poetry aims in giving expressive names to the characters. The particular is—for example—what Alcibiades did or suffered. In Comedy that is now apparent: for here the poet first constructs the plot on the lines of probability, and then assumes any names he pleases—unlike the lampooners who write about a particular individual. But tragedians still keep to real names, the reason being that what is possible is credible: what has not happened we do not at once feel sure to be possible: but what has happened is manifestly possible; otherwise it would not have happened. Still there are some tragedies in which one or two names only are well known, the rest being fictitious. In others, none are well known—as in Agathon's *Flower*, where incidents and names alike are fictitious, and yet it pleases. We must not, therefore, at all costs keep to the received legends, which are the usual subjects of Tragedy. Indeed, it would be absurd to attempt it; for even familiar subjects are familiar only to a few, and yet give pleasure to all. It clearly follows that the poet or "maker" should be the maker of plots rather than of verses; since he is a poet because he imitates, and what he imitates are actions. And if he chances to take an historical subject, he is none the less a poet; for there is no reason why some real events should not have that internal probability or possibility which entitles the author to the name of poet.

Of all plots and actions the episodic are the worst. I call a plot episodic in which the episodes or acts succeed one another without probable or necessary sequence. Bad poets compose such pieces by their own fault, good poets, to please the players; for, as they write for competing rivals, they draw out the plot beyond its capacity, and are often forced to break the natural continuity.

But again, Tragedy is an imitation not only of a complete action, but of events terrible and pitiful. Such an effect is best produced when the events come on us by surprise; and the effect is heightened when, at the same time, they follow from one another. The tragic wonder will then be greater than if they happened of themselves or by accident; for even accidents are most striking when they have an air of design. We may instance the statue of Mitys at Argos, which fell upon his murderer while he was looking at it, and killed him. Such events seem not to be due to mere chance. Plots, therefore, constructed on these principles are necessarily the best.

10

Plots are either simple or complicated; for such too, in their very nature, are the actions of which the plots are an imitation. An action which is one and continuous in the sense above defined, I call Simple, when the turning point is reached without Reversal of Fortune or Recognition: Complicated, when it is reached with Reversal of Fortune, or Recognition or both. These last should arise from the internal structure of the plot, so that what follows should be the necessary or probable result of the preceding action.

It makes all the difference whether one event is the consequence of another, or merely subsequent to it.

11

A reversal of fortune is, as we have said, a change, by which a train of action produces the opposite of the effect intended; and that, according to our rule of probability or necessity. Thus in the *Oedipus*, the messenger, hoping to cheer Oedipus, and to free him from his alarms about his mother, reveals his origin, and so produces the opposite effect. Again in the *Lynceus*, Lynceus is being led out to die, and Danaus goes with him, meaning to slay him; but the outcome of the action is, that Danaus is killed and Lynceus saved.

A Recognition, as the name indicates, is a change from ignorance to knowledge, producing love or hate between the persons destined by the poet for good or bad fortune. The best form of recognition is coincident with a reversal of fortune, as in the *Oedipus*. There are indeed other forms. Even inanimate things of the most trivial kind may sometimes be objects of recognition. Again, the discovery may be made whether a person has or has not done something. But the form which is most intimately connected with the plot and action is, as we have said, the recognition of persons. This, combined with a reversal of fortune, will produce either pity or fear; and actions producing these effects are those which, as we have assumed, Tragedy represents. Moreover, fortune or misfortune will depend upon such incidents. Recognition, then, being between persons, it may happen that one person only is recognised by the other—when the latter is already known—or the recognition may need to be on both sides. Thus Iphigenia is revealed to Orestes by the sending of the letter; but another means is required to make Orestes known to Iphigenia.

Two parts, then, of the Plot—Reversal of Fortune and Recognition—turn upon surprises. A third part is the Tragic Incident. The two former have been discussed. The Tragic Incident is a destructive or painful action, such as death on the stage, bodily torments, wounds and the like.

12

[The parts of tragedy, which must be treated as elements of the whole, have been already mentioned. We now come to the quantitative parts—the separate parts into which Tragedy is divided—namely, Prologos, Episode, Exodos, Choral element; this last being divided into Parodos and Stasimon. These two are sung by the whole Chorus. The songs of the actors on the stage, and the Commoi, are sung by individuals.

The Prologos is that entire part of a tragedy which precedes the Parodos of the Chorus. The Episode is that entire part of a tragedy which is between whole choral songs. The Exodos is that entire part of a tragedy which has no choral song after it. Of the Choral part the Parodos is the first undivided utterance of the Chrous: the Stasimon is a choral ode without anapaests or trochees: the Commos is a joint lamentation of chorus and actors. The parts of Tragedy which must be treated as elements of the whole have been already mentioned. The quantitative parts—the separate parts into which it is divided—are here enumerated.]

13

As the sequel to what has already been said, we must proceed to consider what the poet should aim at, and what he should avoid, in constructing his plots; and by what means Tragedy must best fulfill its function.

A perfect tragedy should, as we have seen, be arranged on the complicated not the simple plan. It should, moreover, imitate actions which excite pity and fear, this being the distinctive mark of tragic imitation. It follows plainly, in the first place, that the change of fortune presented must not be the spectacle of a perfectly good man brought from prosperity to adversity: for this moves neither pity nor fear; it simply shocks us. Nor, again, that of a bad man passing from adversity to prosperity: for nothing can be more alien to the spirit of Tragedy; it possesses no single tragic quality; it neither satisfies the moral sense, nor calls forth pity or fear. Nor, again, should the downfall of the utter villain be exhibited. A plot of this kind would, doubtless, satisfy the moral sense, but it would inspire neither pity nor fear; for pity is aroused by unmerited misfortune, fear by the misfortune of a man like ourselves. Such an event, therefore, will be neither pitiful nor terrible. There remains, then, the character between these two extremes—that of a man who is not eminently good and just, yet whose misfortune is brought about not by vice or depravity, but by some error or frailty. He must be one who is highly renowned and prosperous—a personage like Oedipus, Thyestes, or other illustrious men of such families.

A well constructed plot should, therefore, be single, rather than double as some maintain. The change of fortune should be not from bad to good, but, reversely, from good to bad. It should come about as the result not of vice, but of some great error or frailty, in a character either such as we have described, or better rather than worse. The practice of the stage bears out our view. At first the poets recounted any legends that came in their way. Now, tragedies are founded on the story of a few houses—on the fortunes of Alcmaeon, Oedipus, Orestes, Meleager, Thyestes, Telephus, and those others who have done or suffered something terrible. A tragedy, then, to be perfect according to the rules of art should be of this construction. Hence they are in error who censure Euripides just because he follows this principle in his plays, many of which end unhappily. It is, as we have said, the right ending. The best proof is that on the stage and in dramatic competition, such plays, if they are well represented, are most tragic in their effect; and Euripides, faulty as he is in the general management of his subject, yet is felt to be the most tragic of poets.

In the second rank comes the kind of tragedy which some place first. Like the *Odyssey*, it has a double thread of plot, and also an opposite catastrophe for the good and for the bad. It is generally thought to be the best owing to the weakness of the spectators; for the poet is guided in what he writes by the wishes of his audience. The pleasure, however, thence derived is not the true tragic pleasure. It is proper rather to Comedy, where those who, in the piece, are the deadliest enemies—like Orestes and Aegisthus—go forth reconciled at last, and no one slays or is slain.

14

Fear and pity may be aroused by the spectacle or scenic presentment; but they may also result from the inner structure of the piece, which is the better way, and indicates a superior poet. For the plot ought to be so constructed that, even without the aid of the eye, any one who is told the incidents will thrill with horror and pity at the turn of events. This is precisely the impression we should receive from listening to the story of the *Oedipus*. But to produce this effect by the mere spectacle is a less artistic method, and dependent on extraneous aids. Those who employ spectacular means to create a sense not of the terrible but of the monstrous, are strangers to the purpose of Tragedy; for we must not demand of Tragedy every kind of pleasure, but only that which is proper to it. And since the pleasure which the poet should afford is that which comes from pity and fear through imitation, it is evident that this quality must be stamped upon the incidents.

Let us then determine what are the circumstances which impress us as terrible or pitiful.

Actions capable of this effect must happen between persons who are either friends or enemies or indifferent to one another. If an enemy kills an enemy, there is nothing to excite pity either in the act or the intention—except so far as the suffering in itself is pitiful. So again with indifferent persons. But when the tragic incident occurs between those who are near or dear to one another—if, for example, a brother kills, or intends to kill, a brother, a son his father, a mother her son, a son his mother, or any other deed of the kind is done—here we have the situations which should be sought for by the poet. He may not indeed destroy the framework of the received legends—the fact, for instance, that Clytemnestra was slain by Orestes and Eriphyle by Alcmaeon—but he ought to show invention of his own, and skilfully adapt the traditional material. What is meant by skilfully, let us explain more clearly.

The action may be done willingly and with full knowledge on the part of the agents, in the manner of the older poets. It is thus, in fact, that Euripides makes Medea slay her children. Or, again, the deed of horror may be done, but done in ignorance, and the tie of kinship or friendship be discovered afterwards. The *Oedipus* of Sophocles is an example. Here, indeed, the incident is outside the drama proper; but cases occur where it falls within the action of the play: we may cite the *Alcmaeon* of Astydamas, or Telegonus in the *Wounded Odysseus*. Again, there is a third case, where some one is just about to do some irreparable deed through ignorance, and makes the discovery before it is done. These are the only possible ways. For the deed must either be done or not done—and that wittingly or unwittingly. But of all these ways, to be about to act knowing the consequences, and then not to act, is the worst. It is shocking without being tragic, for no disaster follows. It is, therefore, never, or very rarely, found in poetry. One instance, however, is in the *Antigone*, where Haemon intends to kill Creon. The next and better way is that the deed should be perpetrated. Still better, that it should be perpetrated in ignorance, and the discovery made afterwards. There is then nothing to shock us, while the discovery produces a startling effect. But the absolutely best way is the last mentioned. Thus in the *Cresphontes*, Merope is in the act of putting her son to death, but, recognising who he is, spares his life. So in the *Iphigenia*, the sister recognises the brother just in time. Again in the *Helle*, the son recognises the mother when on the point of giving her up. This, then, is why a few families only, as has been already observed, furnish the subjects of tragedy. It was not art, but happy chance, that led poets by tentative discovery to impress the tragic quality upon their plots. They are compelled, therefore, to have recourse to those houses in which tragic disasters have occurred.

Enough has now been said concerning the structure of the incidents, and the proper constitution of the plot.

15

In respect of character there are four things to be aimed at. First, and most important, it must be good. Now any speech or action that manifests a certain moral purpose will be expressive of character: the character will be good if the purpose is good. This rule applies to persons of every class. Even a woman may be good, and also a slave; though the woman may be said to be an inferior being, and the slave is absolutely bad. The second thing to aim at is propriety. There is a type of manly valour; but for a woman to be valiant in this sense, or terrible, would be inappropriate. Thirdly, character must be true to life: for this is a distinct thing from goodness and propriety, as here described. The fourth point is consistency: for even though the original character, who suggested the type, be inconsistent, still he must be consistently inconsistent. As an example of character needlessly bad, we have Menelaus in the *Orestes*: of character incongruous and inappropriate, the lament of Odysseus in the *Scylla*, and the speech of Melanippe: of inconsistency, the *Iphigenia at Aulis*—for the suppliant Iphigenia in no way resembles her later self.

As in the structure of the plot, so too in the portraiture of character, the poet should always aim either at the necessary or the probable. Thus a person of a given character should speak or act in a given way, by the rule either of necessity or of probability; just as this event should follow that by necessary or probable sequence. It is therefore evident that the unravelling of the plot, no less than the complication, must be brought about by the plot itself, and not by Machinery—as in the *Medea*, or in the Return of the Greeks in the *Iliad*. Machinery should be employed only for events external to the drama—either such as are previous to it and outside the sphere of human knowledge, or subsequent to it and which need to be foretold and announced; for to the gods we ascribe the power of seeing all things. Within the action there must be nothing irrational. If the irrational cannot be excluded, it should be outside the scope of the tragedy. Such is the irrational element in the *Oedipus* of Sophocles.

Again, since Tragedy is an imitation of persons who are above the common level, the example of good portrait-painters should be followed. They, while reproducing the distinctive form of the original, make a likeness which is true to life and yet more beautiful. So too the poet, in representing men quick or slow to anger, or with other defects of character, should preserve the type and yet ennoble it. In this way Achilles is portrayed by Agathon and Homer.

These are rules the poet should observe. Nor should he neglect those appeals to the senses, which, though not among the essentials, are the concomitants of poetry; for here too there is much room for error. But of this we have said enough in our published treatises.

16

What recognition is has been already explained. We will now enumerate its kinds.

First, the least artistic form, which, from poverty of wit, is commonly employed—recognition by signs. Of these some are congenital—such as "the spear which the earth-born race bear on their bodies," or the stars introduced by Carcinus in his *Thyestes*. Others are acquired after birth; and of these some are bodily marks, as scars; some external tokens, as necklaces, or the little ark in the *Tyro* by which the discovery is effected. Even these admit of more or less skilful treatment. Thus in the recognition of Odysseus by his scar, the discovery is made in one way by the nurse, in another by the herdsmen. This use of tokens for purposes of proof—and, indeed, any formal proof with or without tokens—is an inartistic mode of recognition. A better kind is that which results from the turn of fortune; as in the Bath scene in the *Odyssey*.

Next come the recognitions invented at will by the poet, and on that account wanting in art. For example, Orestes in the *Iphigenia* reveals the fact that he is Orestes. She, indeed, makes herself known by the letter; but he, by speaking himself, and saying what the poet, not what the plot requires. This, therefore, is nearly allied to the fault above mentioned:—for Orestes might as well have brought tokens with him. Another similar instance is the 'voice of the shuttle' in the *Tereus* of Sophocles.

The third form of recognition is when the sight of some object calls up a train of memory: as in the *Cyprians* of Dicaeogenes, where the hero breaks into tears on seeing a picture; or again in the *Lay* of Alcinous, where Odysseus, hearing the minstrel play the lyre, recalls the past and weeps; and hence the recognition.

The fourth kind is by process of reasoning. Thus in the *Choephori*:—"Some one resembling me has come; no one resembles me but Orestes: therefore Orestes has come." Again, there is the discovery made by Iphigenia in the play of Polyeidus the Sophist. It was natural for Orestes to reason thus with himself:—"As my sister was sacrificed, so too it is my lot to be sacrificed." So, again, in the *Tydeus* of Theodectes:—"I came to find my son, and I must perish myself." So too in the *Phineidae*: the women, on seeing the plate, inferred their fate:—"Here we are fated to die, for here we were exposed." Again, there is a recognition combined with a false inference on the part of one of the characters, as in the *Odysseus, the False Messenger*. A man said he would know the bow,—which, however, he had not seen. This remark led Odysseus to imagine that the other would recognise him through the bow, and so suggested a false inference.

But, of all recognitions, the best is that which arises from the incidents themselves, where the startling effect is produced by probable means. Such is that in the *Oedipus* of Sophocles, and in the *Iphigenia*; for it was natural that Iphigenia should wish to send a letter by Orestes. These recognitions stand on their own merits, and do not need the aid of tokens invented for the purpose, or necklaces. Next come the recognitions by process of reasoning.

17

In constructing the plot and working it out with the help of language, the poet should place the scene, as far as possible, before his eyes. In this way, seeing everything with the utmost vividness, as if he were a spectator of the action, he will discover what is in keeping with it, and be most unlikely to overlook inconsistencies. The need of such a rule is shown by the fault found in Carcinus. Amphiaraus was on his way from the temple. This fact escaped the observation of one who did not see the situation. On the stage, however, the piece failed, the audience being offended at the oversight.

Again, the poet should work out his play, to the best of his power, with appropriate gestures; for those who feel emotion are most impressive by force of sympathy. One who is agitated storms, one who is angry rages, with the most lifelike reality. Hence poetry implies either a happy gift of nature or a strain of madness. In the one case a man can take the mould of any character; in the other, he is lifted out of his proper self.

The poet, whether he accepts the traditional subjects, or invents new ones, should, in shaping them himself, first sketch the general outline of the play, and then fill in the episodes and amplify in detail. The general plan of the Iphigenia, for instance, may be thus seen. A young girl is sacrificed; she disappears mysteriously from the eyes of those who sacrificed her; she is transported to another country, where the custom is to offer up all strangers to the goddess. To this ministry she is appointed. Some time later her brother chances to arrive. The fact that the oracle for some reason ordered him to go there, is outside the general plan of the play. The purpose, again, of his coming is outside the action proper. However, he comes, he is seized, and, when on the point of being sacrificed, reveals who he is. The mode of recognition may be either that of Euripides or of Polyeidus, in whose play he exclaims very naturally:—"So it was not my sister only, but I too, who was doomed to be sacrificed"; and by that remark he is saved.

After this, the names being once assumed, it remains to fill in the episodes. We must see that they are relevant to the action. In the case of Orestes, for example, there is the madness which led to his capture, and his deliverance by means of the purificatory rite. In a drama, the episodes are short, but it is these that give extension to the Epic poem. Thus the story of the *Odyssey* can be stated briefly. A certain man is absent from home for many years; he is jealously watched by Poseidon, and left desolate. Meanwhile his home is in a wretched plight—suitors are wasting his substance and plotting against his son. At length, tempest-tost, he arrives and reveals who he is; he attacks his enemies, destroys them and is preserved himself. This is the essence of the plot; the rest is episode.

18

Every tragedy falls into two parts—Complication and Unravelling or *Dénouement*. Incidents extraneous to the action are frequently combined with a portion of the action proper to form the Complication; the rest is the Unravelling. By the Complication I mean all that comes between the beginning of the action and the part which marks the turning point from bad fortune to good or good fortune to bad. The Unravelling is that which comes between the beginning of the change and the end. Thus, in the *Lynceus* of Theodectes, the Complication consists of the incidents presupposed in the drama, the seizure of the child, and then the arrest of the parents. The Unravelling extends from the accusation of murder to the end.

There are four kinds of Tragedy—first, the Complicated, depending entirely on reversal of fortune and recognition; next, the Simple; next, the Pathetic (where the motive is passion)—such as the tragedies on Ajax and Ixion; next, the Ethical (where the motives are ethical)—such as the *Phthiotides* and the *Peleus*.

We here exclude the supernatural kind, such as the *Phorcides*, the *Prometheus*, and tragedies whose scene is in the lower world. The poet should endeavour, if possible, to combine all poetic merits; or failing that, the greatest number and those the most important; the more so, in face of the cavilling criticism of the day. For whereas there have hitherto been good poets, each in his own branch, the critics now expect one man to surpass all others in their several lines of excellence.

In speaking of a tragedy as the same or different, the best test to take is the plot. Identity exists where the Complication and Unravelling are the same. Many poets tie the knot well, but unravel it ill. Both arts, however, should always be mastered.

Again, we should remember what has been often said, and not make a Tragedy into an Epic structure. By an Epic structure I mean one with a multiplicity of plots: as if, for instance, you were to make a tragedy out of the entire story of the *Iliad*. In the Epic poem, owing to its length, each part assumes its proper magnitude. In the drama the result is far from the expectation. The proof is that the poets who have dramatised the whole story of the Fall of Troy, instead of selecting portions, like Euripides; or who—unlike Aeschylus—have taken the whole tale of Niobe, either fail utterly or figure badly on the stage. Even Agathon has been known to fail from this one defect. In his reversals of fortune, however, he shows a marvellous skill in the effort to hit the popular taste—to produce a tragic effect that satisfies the moral sense. This effect is produced when the clever rogue, like Sisyphus, is cheated, or the brave villain defeated. Such an event is probable in Agathon's sense of the word: "it is probable," he says, "that many things should happen contrary to probability."

The Chorus too should be regarded as one of the actors; it should be an integral part of the whole, and share in the action, in the manner not of Euripides but of Sophocles. As for the later poets, their choral songs pertain as little to the subject of the piece as to that of any other tragedy. They are, therefore, sung as mere interludes—a practice first begun by Agathon. Yet what difference is there between introducing such choral interludes, and transferring a speech, or even a whole act, from one play to another?

19

It remains to speak of the Diction and the Thought, the other parts of Tragedy having been already discussed. Concerning the Thought, we may assume what is said in the Rhetoric; to which inquiry the subject more strictly belongs. Under Thought is included every effect which has to be produced by speech; in particular—proof and refutation; the exitation of the feelings, such as pity, fear, anger, and the like; the heightening or extenuating of facts. Further, it is evident that the dramatic incidents must be treated from the same points of view as the dramatic speeches, when the object is to evoke the sense of pity, fear, grandeur, or probability. The only difference is, that the incidents should speak for themselves without verbal exposition; while the effects aimed at in a speech should be produced by the speaker, and as a result of the speech. For what were the need of a speaker, if the proper impression were at once conveyed, quite apart from what he says?

Next, as regards Diction. One branch of the inquiry treats of the Figures of Speech. But this province of knowledge belongs to the art of Declamation, and to the masters of that science. It includes, for instance—what is a command, a prayer, a narrative, a threat, a question, an answer, and so forth. To know or not to know these things involves no serious censure upon the poet's art. For who can admit the fault imputed to Homer by Protagoras—that in the words, "Sing, goddess, of the wrath," he gives a command under the idea that he utters a prayer? For to call on some one to do or not to do is, he says, a command. We may, therefore, pass this over as an inquiry that belongs to another art, not to poetry.

20

Language in general includes the following parts:—the Letter, the Syllable, the Connecting words, the Noun, the Verb, the Inflexion, the Sentence or Phrase.

A Letter is an indivisible sound, yet not every such sound, but only one from which an intelligible sound can be formed. For even brutes utter indivisible sounds, none of which I call a letter. Letters are of three kinds—vowels, semi-vowels, and mutes. A vowel is that which without contact of tongue or lip has an audible sound. A semi-vowel, that which with such contact has an audible sound, as S and R. A mute, that which with such contact has by itself no sound, but joined to a vowel becomes audible, as G and D. These are distinguished according to the form assumed by the mouth, and the place where they are produced; according as they are aspirated or smooth, long or short; as they are acute, grave, or of an intermediate tone; which inquiry belongs in detail to the metrical treatises.

A Syllable is a non-significant sound, composed of a mute and a vowel or of a mute, a semi-vowel, and a vowel: for GA without R is a syllable, as it also is with R—GRA. But the investigation of these differences belongs also to metrical science.

A Connecting word is a non-significant sound, which neither causes nor hinders the union of many sounds into one significant sound; it may be placed at either end or in the middle of a sentence. Or, a non-significant sound, which out of several sounds, each of them significant, is capable of forming one significant sound—as ἀμφί, περί,[1] and the like. Or, a non-significant sound, which marks the beginning, end, or division of a sentence; such, however, that it cannot correctly stand by itself at the beginning of a sentence—as μέν, ἤτοι, δέ.[2]

A Noun is a composite significant sound, not marking time, of which no part is in itself significant; for in double or compound words we do not employ the separate parts as if each were in itself significant. Thus in *theodorus*, "god-given," the δῶρον or "gift" is not in itself significant.

A Verb is a composite significant sound, marking time, in which, as in the noun, no part is in itself significant. For "man," or "white" does not express the idea of "when"; but "he walks," or "he has walked" does connote time, present or past.

Inflexion belongs both to the noun and verb, and expresses either the relation "of," "to," or the like; or that of number, whether one or many, as "man" or "men"; or the mode of address—a question, it may be, or a command. "Did he go?" and "go" are verbal inflexions of this kind.

A Sentence or Phrase is a composite sound, some of whose parts are in themselves significant; for every such combination of words is not composed of verbs and nouns—the definition of man, for example—but it may dispense with the verb. Still it will always have some significant part, as the word "Cleon" in "Cleon walks." A sentence or phrase may form a unity in two ways—either as signifying one thing, or as consisting of several parts linked together. Thus the *Iliad* is one by the linking together of parts, the definition of man by the unity of the thing signified.

21

Words are of two kinds, simple and double. By simple I mean those composed of non-significant elements, such as γῆ. By double or compound, those composed either of a significant and non-significant element (though within the whole word this distinction disappears), or of elements that are both significant. A word may likewise be triple, quadruple, or multiple in form, as are most magniloquent compounds, such as *Hermocaico-xanthus*.[3]

Every word is common or proper, strange, metaphorical, ornamental, newly-coined, extended, contracted, or altered.

By a common or proper word I mean one which is in general use among a people; by a strange word, one which is in use in another country. Plainly, therefore, the same word may be at once strange and common, but not in relation to the same people. The word *σίγυνον*, "lance," is to the Cyprians a common word but to us a strange one.

Metaphor is the application of an alien name by transference either from genus to species, or from species to genus, or from species to species, or by analogy, that is, proportion. Thus from genus to species, as: "There stands my ship"; for to be at anchor is a species of standing. From species to genus, as: "Verily ten thousand noble deeds hath Odysseus wrought"; for ten thousand is a species of large number, and is here used for a large number generally. From species to species, as: "Drew away the life with the blade of bronze," and "Cleft the water with the vessel of unyielding bronze." Here *ἀρύσαι*, "to draw away," is used for *ταμεῖν*, "to cleave," and *ταμεῖν* again for *ἀρύσαι*—each being a species of taking away. Analogy or proportion is when the second term is to the first as the fourth to the third. We may then use the fourth for the second, or the second for the fourth. Sometimes too we qualify the metaphor by adding the term to which the proper word is relative. Thus the cup is to Dionysus as the shield to Ares. The cup may, therefore, be called "the shield of Dionysus," and the shield "the cup of Ares." Or, again, as old age is to life, so is evening to day. Evening may therefore be called "the old age of the day," and old age, "the evening of life" or, in the phrase of Empedocles, "life's setting sun." In some cases one of the terms of the proportion has no specific name; still, the metaphor may be used. For instance, to scatter seed is called sowing: but the action of the sun in scattering his rays is nameless. Still this action bears to the sun the same relation that sowing does to him who scatters the grain. Hence the expression of the poet, "sowing the god-created light." There is another way in which this kind of metaphor may be employed. We may apply an alien term, and then deny of that term one of its proper attributes; as if we were to call the shield, not "the cup of Ares," but "the wine-less cup."

A newly-coined word is one which has never yet been in use, but is invented by the poet himself. Some such words there appear to be: as *ἐρνύγες*, "sprouters," for *κέρατα*, "horns," and *ἀρητήρ*, "supplicator," for *ἱερεύς*, "priest."

A word is extended when its own vowel is exchanged for a longer one, or when a syllable is inserted. A word is contracted when some part of it is removed. Instances of extension are—*πόληος* for *πόλεως*, Πηλῆος for Πηλέος, and Πηληιάδεω for Πηλείδου:[4] of contraction—*κρῖ*, *δῶ*, and *ὄψ*, as in *μία γίνεται ἀμφοτέρων ὄψ*.[5]

An altered word is one in which part of the ordinary form is left unchanged, and part is re-cast; as in *δεξιτερὸν κατὰ μαζόν*, *δεξιτερόν* is for *δεξιόν*.[6]

[Nouns in themselves are either masculine, feminine, or neuter. Masculine are such as end in *ν*, *ρ*, *ς*, or in some letter compounded with *ς*—these being two, *η* and *ξ*. Feminine, such as end in vowels that are always long, as *ψ* and *ω*, and—of vowels that admit of lengthening—those in *α*. Thus the number of letters in which nouns masculine and feminine end is the same; for *ψ* and *ξ* are equivalent to endings in *ς*. No noun ends in a mute or a vowel short by nature. Three only end in *ι*—*μέλι*, *κόμμι*, *πέπερι*:[7] five end in *υ*. Neuter nouns end in these two latter vowels; also in *ν* and *ς*.]

22

The perfection of style is to be clear without being mean. The style which uses only common or proper words is in the highest degree clear; at the same time it is mean:—witness the poetry of Cleophon and of Sthenelus. That diction, on the other hand, is lofty and raised above the commonplace which employs unusual words. By unusual, I mean words rare or strange, metaphorical, extended—anything, in short, that differs from the normal idiom. Yet a style wholly composed of such words is either a riddle or a jargon; a riddle, if it consists of metaphors; a jargon, if it consists of rare or strange words. For the essence of a riddle is to express true facts under impossible combinations. Now this cannot be done by any arrangement of ordinary words, but by the use of metaphor it can. Such is the riddle:—"A man I saw who on another man had glued the bronze by aid of fire," and others of the same kind. A diction that is made up of rare or strange terms is a jargon. A certain infusion, therefore, of these elements is necessary to style; for the rare or strange word, the metaphorical, the ornamental, and the other kinds above mentioned, will raise it above the commonplace and mean, while the use of proper words will make it perspicuous. But nothing contributes more to produce a clearness of diction that is remote from commonness than the extension, contraction, and alteration of words. For by deviating in exceptional cases from the normal idiom, the language will gain distinction; while, at the same time, the partial conformity with usage will give perspicuity. The critics, therefore, are in error who censure these licenses of speech, and hold the author up to ridicule. Thus Eucleides, the elder, declared that it would be an easy matter to be a poet if you might lengthen syllables at will. His travesty consisted in the mere form of the verse, for example:

> Ἐπιχάρην ε ἶδον Μαραθῶνάδε βαδίζοντα,[8]

or,

> οὐκ ἄν γ' ἐράμενος τὸν ἐκείνου ἐλλέβορον.

To employ such lengthening at all obtrusively is grotesque. Here, as in all modes of poetic diction, there must be moderation. Even metaphors, rare or strange words, or any similar forms of speech, would produce the like effect if used without propriety, and with the express purpose of being ludicrous. How great a difference is made by the appropriate use of lengthening, may be seen in Epic poetry by the insertion of ordinary forms in the verse. So, again, if we take a rare or strange word, a metaphor, or any similar mode of expression, and replace it by the common or proper word, the truth of our observation will be manifest. For example, Aeschylus and Euripides each composed the same iambic line. But the alteration of a single word by Euripides, who employed the rarer term instead of the ordinary one, makes one verse appear beautiful and the other trivial. Aeschylus in his *Philoctetes* says:

> The cancer, which feeds upon the flesh of his foot.

Euripides substitutes θοινᾶται "feasts on" for ἐσθίει "feeds on." Again, in the line,

> But now being of slight consequence, and a weakling, and in disgrace,

the difference will be felt if we substitute the common words,

> And now being little, and feeble, and shamed.

Or, if for the line,

> Having placed a simple chair and a small table,

we read,

> Having placed an ugly chair and a tiny table.

Or, for "Shores roar," "Shores scream."

Again, Ariphrades ridiculed the tragedians for using phrases which no one would employ in ordinary speech: for example, δωμάτων ἄπο instead of ἀπὸ δωμάτων, σέθεν, ἐγὼ δέ νιν, Ἀχιλλέως πέρι instead of περὶ

Αχιλλέως, and the like.[9] It is precisely because such phrases are not part of the common idiom that they give distinction to the style. This, however, he failed to see.

It is a great matter to observe propriety in these several modes of expression—compound words, rare or strange words, and so forth. But the greatest thing by far is to have a genius for metaphor. This alone cannot be had from another; it is the mark of a gifted nature—for to make good metaphors implies an eye for resemblances.

Of the various kinds of words, the compound are best adapted to dithyrambs, rare words to heroic poetry, metaphors to iambic. In heroic poetry, indeed, all these varieties are serviceable. But in iambic verse, which reproduces, as far as may be, familiar speech, the most appropriate words are those which belong to conversational idiom. These are—the common or proper, the metaphorical, the ornamental.

Concerning Tragedy and imitation by means of action, this may siffice.

23

As to that poetic imitation which is narrative in form and employs a single metre, the plot manifestly ought to be constructed on dramatic principles. It should have for its subject a single action, whole and complete, with a beginning, a middle, and an end. It will thus resemble a living organism and produce its proper pleasure. Herein it differs from the ordinary histories, which of necessity present not a single action, but a single period, and all that happened within that period to one person or to many, little connected together as the events may be. For as the sea-fight at Salamis and the battle with the Carthaginians in Sicily took place at the same time, but did not tend to one result, so in the sequence of events, one thing sometimes follows another, and yet the two may not work up to any common end. Such is the practice, we may say, of most poets. Here again, then, as has been already observed, the transcendent excellence of Homer is manifest. He never attempts to make the whole war of Troy the subject of his poem, though that war had a beginning and an end. It would have been too vast a theme, and not easily embraced in a single view. If again, he had kept it within moderate limits, it must have been complicated by the variety of the incidents. As it is, he selects a single portion, and admits many episodes from the general story of the war—such as the Catalogue of the ships and others—thus diversifying the poem. All other poets take a single hero, a single period, or an action single indeed, but with a multiplicity of parts. Thus did the author of the *Cypria* and of the *Little Iliad*. For this reason the *Iliad* and the *Odyssey* each furnish the subject of one tragedy, or, at most, of two; while the *Cypria* furnishes many, and the *Little Iliad* eight—the *Award of the Arms*, the *Philoctetes*, the *Neoptolemus*, *Eurypylus*, the *Mendicant Odysseus*, the *Laconian Women*, the *Fall of Ilium*, the *Departure of the Fleet*.

24

Again, epic poetry must have the same species as Tragedy: it must be simple, complicated, "ethical," or "pathetic." The parts also, with the exception of song and scenery, are the same; for it requires reversals of fortune, recognitions, and tragic incidents. Moreover, the thoughts and the diction must be artistic. In all these respects Homer is our earliest and sufficient model. Indeed each of his poems has a twofold character. The *Iliad* is at once simple and "pathetic," and the *Odyssey* complicated (for recognition scenes run through it), and at the same time "ethical." Moreover, in diction and thought he is unequalled.

Epic poetry differs from Tragedy in the scale on which it is constructed, and in its metre. As regards scale or length, we have already laid down an adequate limit. We must be able to embrace in a single view the beginning and the end; which might be done if the scale of the whole were reduced as compared with that of the ancient Epic, and the poem made equal in length to the tragedies, taken collectively, which are exhibited at one sitting.

Epic poetry has, however, a great—a special—capacity for enlarging its dimensions, and we can see the reason. In Tragedy we cannot imitate several actions carried on at one and the same time. We must confine ourselves to the action on the stage and the part taken by the players. But in Epic poetry, owing to the narrative form, many events simultaneously transacted can be represented; and these, if relevant to the subject, add mass and dignity to the poem. This particular merit conduces to grandeur of effect; it also serves to divert the mind of the hearer and to relieve the story with varying episodes. For sameness of incident soon produces satiety, and makes tragedies fail on the stage.

As for the metre, the heroic has proved its fitness by the test of experience. If a narrative poem in any other metre were now composed, it would be found incongruous. For the heroic of all measures is the stateliest and the most imposing; and hence it most readily admits rare words and metaphors; as indeed the narrative mode of imitation is in this respect singular. On the other hand, the iambic and the trochaic tetrameter are stirring measures, the latter being suited to dancing, the former to action. Still more absurd would it be to mix together different metres, as was done by Chaeremon. Hence no one has ever composed a poem on a great scale in any other than heroic verse. Nature herself, as we have said, teaches the choice of the proper measure.

Homer, admirable in all respects, has the special merit of being the only poet who appreciates the part he should take himself. The poet in his own person should speak as little as possible; it is not this that makes him an imitator. Other poets appear themselves upon the scene throughout, and imitate but little and rarely. Homer, after a few prefatory words, at once brings in a man, or woman, or other personage; none of them wanting in characteristic qualities, but each with a character of his own.

The element of the wonderful is admitted in Tragedy. The irrational, on which the wonderful depends for its chief effects, has wider scope in Epic poetry, because there the person acting is not seen. Thus, the pursuit of Hector would be ludicrous if placed upon the stage—the Greeks standing still and not joining in the pursuit, and Achilles beckoning to them to keep back. But in the Epic poem the absurdity is unnoticed. Now the wonderful is pleasing: as may be inferred from the fact that, in telling a story, every one adds something startling of his own, knowing that his hearers like it. It is Homer who has taught other poets the true art of fiction. The secret of it lies in a fallacy. For, assuming that if one thing is or becomes, a second is or becomes, men imagine that, if the second is, the first likewise is or becomes. But this is a false inference. Hence, where the first thing is untrue, it is quite unnecessary, provided the second be true, to add that the first is or has become. For the mind, knowing the second to be true, falsely infers the truth of the first. There is an example of this in the book of the *Odyssey* containing the Bath Scene.

Accordingly, the poet should prefer probable impossibilities to improbable possibilities. The tragic plot must not consist of incidents which the reason rejects. These incidents should, if possible, be excluded; or, at least, they should be outside the action of the play. Such, in the *Oedipus,* is the ignorance of the hero as to the manner of Laius' death. The irrational parts should not be within the drama—as in the *Electra,* the messenger's account of the Pythian games; or, in the *Mysians,* the man who comes from Tegea to Mysia without speaking. The plea that otherwise the plot would have been ruined, is ridiculous. Such a plot should not in the first instance be constructed. But once it has been framed and an air of likelihood imparted to it, the absurdity itself should be tolerated. Take the irrational incidents connected with the landing on Ithaca in the *Odyssey.* How intolerable they might have been would be apparent if an inferior poet were to treat the subject. As it is, the absurdity is veiled by the poetic charm with which the poet invests it.

The diction should be elaborated in the pauses of the action, where there is no expression of character or thought. On the other hand, character and thought are merely obscured by a diction that is over brilliant.

25

With respect to critical difficulties and their solutions, the number and nature of the sources from which they may be drawn may be thus exhibited.

The poet being an imitator, like a painter or any other artist, must of necessity imitate one of three objects—things as they were or are, things as they are said or thought to be, or things as they ought to be. The vehicle of expression is language—either common words or rare words or metaphors. There are also many modifications of language, which we concede to the poets. Add to this, that the standard of correctness is not the same in poetry and politics, any more than in poetry and any other art. Within the art of poetry itself there are two kinds of faults—those which touch its essence, and those which are accidental. If a poet has proposed to himself to imitate something, but has imitated it incorrectly through want of capacity, the error is inherent in the poetry. But if the failure is due to the thing he has proposed to do—if he has represented a horse as throwing out both his right legs at once, or introduced technical inaccuracies in medicine, it may be, or in any other art—the error is not essential to the poetry. By such considerations as these we should answer the objections raised by the critics.

First we will suppose the poet has represented things impossible according to the laws of his own art. It is an error; but the error may be justified, if the end of the art be thereby attained (the end being that already mentioned)—if, that is, the effect of this or any other part of the poem is thus rendered more striking. A case in point is the pursuit of Hector. If, however, the end might have been as well, or better, attained without violating the special rules of the poetic art, the error is not justified: for every kind of error should, if possible, be avoided.

Again, does the error touch the essentials of the poetic art, or some accident of it? For example—not to know that a hind has no horns is a less serious matter than to paint it inartistically.

Further, if it be objected that the description is not true to fact, the poet may perhaps reply—"But the objects are as they ought to be": just as Sophocles said that he drew men as they ought to be drawn; Euripides, as they are. In this way the objection may be met. If, however, the representation be of neither kind, the poet may answer—"This is what is commonly said." This applies to tales about the gods. It may well be that these stories are not higher than fact nor yet true to fact: they are, very possibly, what Xenophanes says of them. But anyhow, "this is what is said." Again, a description may be no better than the fact: "still, it was the fact"; as in the passage about the arms: "Upright upon their butt-ends stood the spears." This was the custom then, as it now is among the Illyrians.

Again, in examining whether what has been said or done by some one is right or wrong, we must not look merely to the particular speech or action, and ask whether it is in itself good or bad. We must also consider by whom it is said, to whom, when, in whose interest, or for what end; whether, for instance, it be for the sake of attaining some greater good, or averting some greater evil.

Other difficulties may be resolved by due regard to the diction. We may note a rare word, as in *οὐρῆας μὲν πρῶτον*, where the poet perhaps employs *οὐρῆας* not in the sense of mules, but of sentinels. So again, of Dolon: "ill-favoured indeed he was to look upon." It is not meant that his body was ill-shaped, but that his face was ugly; for the Cretans use the word *εὐειδές*, "well-favoured," to denote a fair face. Again *ζωρότερον δὲ κέραιε*, mix the drink livelier," does not mean "mix it stronger" as for hard drinkers, but "mix it quicker."

Sometimes an expression is metaphorical, as "Now all gods and men were sleeping through the night"—while at the same time the poet says: "Often indeed as he turned his gaze to the Trojan plain, he marvelled at the sound of flutes and pipes." "All" is here used metaphorically for "many," all being a species of many. So in the verse—"alone she hath no part . . ," *οἴη*, "alone," is metaphorical; for the best known may be called the only one.

Again, objections may be removed by a change of accent, as Hippias of Thasos did in the lines—*δίδομεν* (*διδόμεν*) *δέ οἱ*, and *τὸ μὲν οὐ* (*οὑ*) *καταπύθεται ὄμβρῳ.*[10]

Or again, by punctuation, as in Empedocles—"Of a sudden things became mortal that before had learnt to be immortal, and things unmixed before mixed."

Or again, by ambiguity of construction—as in *παρῴχηκεν δὲ πλέω νύξ*, where the word *πλέω* is ambiguous.

Or by the usage of language. Thus some mixed drinks are called *οἶνος*, "wine." Hence Ganymede is said "to pour the wine to Zeus," though the gods do not drink wine. So too workers in iron ore are called *χαλκέας*, or workers in bronze. This, however, may also be taken as a metaphor.

Again, when a word seems to involve some inconsistency of meaning, we should consider how many senses it may bear in the particular passage. For example: "there was stayed the spear of bronze"—we should ask in how many ways we may take "being checked there." The true mode of interpretation is the precise opposite of what Glaucus mentions. Critics, he says, jump at certain groundless conclusions; they pass adverse judgment and then proceed to reason on it; and, assuming that the poet has said whatever they happen to think, find fault if a thing is inconsistent with their own fancy. The question about Icarius has been treated in this fashion. The critics imagine he was a Lacedaemonian. They think it strange, therefore, that Telemachus should not have met him when he went to Lacedaemon. But the Cephallenian story may perhaps be the true one. They allege that Odysseus took a wife from among themselves, and that her father was Icadius not Icarius. It is merely a mistake, then, that gives plausibility to the objection.

In general, the impossible must be brought under the law of poetic truth, or of the higher reality, or of received opinion. With respect to poetic truth, a probable impossibility is to be preferred to a thing improbable and yet possible. If, again, we are told it is impossible that there should be men such as Zeuxis painted: "Yes," we say, "but the impossible is the higher thing; for the pattern before the mind must surpass the reality." To justify the irrational, we appeal to what is commonly said to be. In addition to which, we urge that the irrational sometimes does not violate reason; just as "it is probable that a thing may happen contrary to probability."

Inconsistencies should be examined by the same rules as in dialectical refutation—whether the same thing is meant, in the same relation, and in the same sense; whether the poet contradicts either what he says himself, or what is tacitly assumed by a person of intelligence.

The element of the irrational, and, similarly, depravity of character, are justly censured when there is no inner necessity for introducing them. Such is the irrational element in the *Aegeus* of Euripides, and the badness of Menelaus in the *Orestes*.

Thus, there are five sources from which critical objections are drawn. Things are censured either as impossible, or irrational, or morally hurtful, or inconsistent, or inaccurate in respect of some special art. The answers should be sought under the twelve heads above mentioned.

26

The question may be raised whether the Epic or Tragic mode of imitation is the higher. If the more refined art is the higher, and the more refined in every case is that which appeals to the better sort of audience, the art which imitates indiscriminately is manifestly most unrefined. The audience is supposed to be incapable of apprehension, unless something of their own is thrown in by the performers, who therefore execute divers movements. Bad flute-players pirouette, if they have to express the motion of the discus, or drag the coryphaeus about when they play the accompaniment of *Scylla*. Tragedy, it is said, has this same defect. We may compare the opinion that the older actors entertained of their successors. Mynniscus used to call Callippides "ape" on account of the extravagance of his action, and the same view was held of Pindarus. Tragic art, then, as a whole, stands to Epic in the same relation as these different generations of actors do to one another. Epic poetry, we are told, is addressed to a cultivated audience, who do not need gesture; Tragedy, to an inferior public. Being then unrefined, it is evidently on a lower level.

Now, in the first place, this censure attaches not to the poetic but to the histrionic art; for gesticulation may be equally overdone in epic recitation, as by Sosistratus, or in lyrical competition, as by Mnasitheus the Opuntian. Next, all action is not to be condemned—any more than all dancing—but only that of bad performers. Such was the fault found in Callippides, as also in others of our own day, who are censured for representing ill-bred women. Again, Tragedy like Epic poetry produces its effect even without action; its quality can be found out by reading. If, then, in all other respects it is superior, this fault, we say, is not inherent in it.

And superior it is, because it has all the epic elements—it may even use the epic metre—with the music and scenic effects as important accessories; and these afford the most vivid combination of pleasures. Further, it has vividness of impression in reading as well as in representation. Moreover, the art attains its end within narrower limits; for the concentrated effect is more pleasurable than one which is spread over a long time and so diluted. What, for example, would be the effect of the *Oedipus* of Sophocles, if it were cast into a form as long as the *Iliad*? Once more, the Epic imitation has less unity; as is shown by this—that any Epic poem will furnish subjects for several tragedies. Now if the story be worked into a unity, it will, if concisely told, appear truncated; or, if it conform to the proper Epic scale, it will seem weak and watery. What I mean by a story composed of several actions may be illustrated from the *Iliad* and *Odyssey*, which have many parts, each with a certain magnitude of its own. Yet these poems are as perfect as possible in structure; each is, in the truest sense, an imitation of a single action.

If, then, Tragedy is superior to Epic poetry in all these respects, and, moreover, fulfils its specific function better as an art—for each art ought to produce, not any chance pleasure, but the pleasure proper to it, as already stated—it plainly follows that Tragedy is the higher art, as attaining its end more perfectly.

Thus much may suffice concerning Tragic and Epic poetry in general; their several species and parts, with the number of each and their differences; the causes that make a poem good or bad; the objections of the critic and the answers to these objections.

Notes

1. *ἀμφί*: preposition meaning "on both sides," "around"; *περί*: preposition meaning "all around," "about."

2. *μεύ, ἤτοι, δέ*: conjunctive particles.

3. *Hermo-caico-xanthus:* a compounding of the names of three rivers, Hermus, Caïcus, and Xanthus.

4. *πόληος* and *πηλιάδεω* are epic genitives of the word "many" and the patronym "son of Peleus" (Achilles), respectively.

5. *κρῖ* for *κριθή*, "barley"; *δῶ* for *δῶμα*, "house"; and *ὄψ* for *ὄψις*, "eye" or "face." The latter appears in a phrase quoted from Empedocles.

6. *δεξιόν* means "the right"; the quoted phrase is from Homer, *Iliad* V.393, which says Hera has been wounded "in the right breast."

7. *μέλι, κόμμι, πεπερι* mean "honey," "gum," and "pepper," respectively.

8. Eucleides' lines, "I saw Ephicares walking to Marathon," and a phrase that refers without clear meaning to a lover and the herb hellebore, are prodic hexameters that do not scan properly. Eucleides may have been a drama critic.

9. The phrases for which Ariphrades (unknown) ridiculed the tragedians reverse the customary order of preposition before noun, "before the house" and "about Achilles." *σέθεν* and *νιν* are epic, therefore old, forms of pronouns.

10. The solutions of Hippias and Thasos concern *Iliad* II.15 and XXIII.328. Like the expressions mentioned in the two preceding paragraphs, all of which are from the *Iliad*, these passages represent ambiguities and the possibility of metaphorical expression. Scholars seem to agree that Aristotle's suggestions are not always convincing. The two examples that follow the quotation from Empedocles are also from the *Iliad*, X.252–53 and XXI.592.

Aristotle 384–322 B.C.

In recent years, as literary scholars have endeavored to sort out the complex difficulties of ascertaining both the explicit and implicit meanings of literary texts, the name of Aristotle has continually reappeared as both an authority and a point of contention. Rhetoricians, philosophers, and literary scholars as diverse as Coleridge and Nietzsche, Kenneth Burke and Matthew Arnold have all used Aristotle as a ground for interpretive models. The more contemporary scholars who have paid tribute to and/or taken issue with Aristotle's ideas would be far too numerous to list here, and it suffices to say that Aristotle's thoughts on how the human mind sorts out contrarieties and oppositions in both texts and "reality" still remain hugely important and compelling issues for rhetoricians, semioticians, and literary critics.

These selections, excerpted from *On Interpretation*, are poignant examples of the thoroughness with which Aristotle sought to work out the necessary qualifications of how something may be defined as true or false, or having or not having certain qualities. Aristotle reasons that "if every affirmation or negation is true or false, then everything does or does not belong to a thing necessarily." By emphasizing this test, he polarizes meaning in an oppositional system. In our own era, which emphasizes the inevitability of "indeterminacy," Aristotle is the voice of certainty. He says, for example, that ". . . since speech is true as it corresponds to things, it is clear that when things are such that they are indeterminate to either of two, and opposites are possible, the corresponding contradiction must be similar. This is the case in those things that do not always exist or always not exist. Of these it is necessary that one part of the contradiction be true or false, not, however, this or that part, but either of the two indeterminately. One may be more likely to be true, but it is not yet actually true or false."

This important systematizing of "opposition" in interpretation points up the relevance of Aristotle not only to basic problems of interpretation but to more complex issues underlying structuralist and poststructuralist thought.

Aristotle's crucial contribution to literary theory, so aptly illustrated by these selections, is his revealing exposition on the "differences" at work in the "naturalness" of meaning. These passages show how cultural assumptions about "is" vs. "is not" resurface in the interpretive act and shape the way we understand texts in the context of the world.

from On Interpretation

Lesson IX: The Opposition of Affirmation and Negation Absolutely

17a 26 Since it is possible to enunciate that what belongs to a subject does not belong to it and what does not, does, and that what does belong to it, does, and what does not, does not, and to enunciate these in regard to those times outside of the present as well as of the present, it would be possible to deny whatever someone affirms and to affirm what he denies. It is evident, therefore, that there is a negation opposed to every affirmation and an affirmation opposed to every negation.

17a 33 We will call this opposed affirmation and negation "contradiction."

17a 34 I mean by "opposed" the enunciation of the same thing of the same subject—not equivocally however, nor in any of the other ways that we have distinguished in reference to the specious difficulties of the sophists.

Lesson X: The Division of the Proposition on the Part of the Subject and the Opposition of Affirmation and Negation in Universal and in Indefinite Propositions

17a 38 Since some of the things we are concerned with are universal and others singular—by "universal" I mean that which is of such a nature as to be predicated of many, and by "singular" that which is not; for example "man" is universal, "Callias" singular—

17b 1 we have to enunciate either of a universal or of a singular that something belongs or does not belong to it.

17b 3 If, then, it is universally enunciated of a universal that something belongs or does not belong to it, the enunciations will be contraries. By "universally enunciated of a universal" I mean such enunciations as "Every man is white," "No man is white."

17b 7 On the other hand, when the enunciations are of a universal but not universally enunciated, they are not contraries, although it is possible for the things signified to be contraries.

17b 8 I mean by "enunciated of a universal but not universally" such enunciations as "Man is white," "Man is not white." For, while "man" is a universal, it is not used as universal in the enunciation, for "every" does not signify the universal but signifies that it is taken universally.

17b 12 But as regards the predicate the universal universally predicated is not true; for no affirmation will be true in which a universal predicate is predicated universally, for example, "Every man is every animal."

Lesson XI: The Opposition of Universal and Particular Enunciations and the Relation of an Opposed Affirmation and Negation to Truth and Falsity

17b 16 Affirmation is opposed to negation in the way I call contradictory when the one signifying universally is opposed to the same one not signifying universally, as in "Every man is white" and "Not every man is white"; "No man is white" and "Some man is white."

17b 20 They are opposed contrarily when the universal affirmation is opposed to the universal negation; as in "Every man is just" and "No man is just."

17b 22 Hence in the case of the latter it is impossible that both be at once true, but it is possible for the contradictories of these contraries to be at once true with respect to the same subject, as in "Not every man is white" and "Some man is white."

17b 26 Whenever there are contradictions with respect to universals signifying universally, one must be true, the other false; this is also the case when there are contradictions with respect to singulars, as in "Socrates is white" and "Socrates is not white."

17b 29 But when the contradictions are of universals not signifying universally, one is not always true and the other false; for it is at once true to say that man is white and man is not white, and man is beautiful and man is not beautiful.

17b 33 For if he is ugly, he is not beautiful; and if he is becoming something, he is not yet it.

17b 34 At first sight this might seem paradoxical, because "Man is not white" seems to signify the same thing as "No man is white"; but it neither signifies this, nor are they at once true necessarily.

Lesson XII: There is Only One Negation Opposed to One Affirmation

17b 37 It is evident that there is one negation of one affirmation;

17b 39 for the negation must deny the same thing that the affirmation affirms, and of the same subject, either something singular, or something universal, and either universally or not universally.

18a 2 For example, the negation of "Socrates is white" is "Socrates is not white." (If something else is said of the subject or the same thing of a different subject, it will not be opposed to it but different from it.) The negation opposed to "Every man is white" is "Not every man is white"; to "Some man is white," "No man is white"; to "Man is white," "Man is not white."

18a 7 We have said that there is no negation opposed contradictorily to one affirmation, and what these are; and that the others are contraries, and what these are; and that in every contradiction one is not always true and the other false, and what the reason is for this, and when it is the case that one is true and the other false.

18a 12 Affirmation or negation is one when one thing is signified of one thing, whether the subject is universal and is taken universally or not; as in "Every man is white" and "Not every man is white"; "Man is white" and "Man is not white"; "No man is white" and "Some man is white"; provided the "white" signifies one thing.

18a 18 But if one name is imposed for two things, from which there is not one thing, the affirmation is not one. For example, if someone were to impose the name "cloak" on horse and man, the enunciation "Cloak is white" would not be one affirmation, nor would "Cloak is not white" be one negation.

18a 21 For this is no different from saying "Horse and man is white," and this no different from saying, "Horse is white" and "Man is white." If, then, these signify many things and are many, it is evident that the first enunciation ["Cloak is white"] signifies many things—or nothing, for there is not such a thing as a horse-man.

18a 26 Consequently, in such enunciations it is not necessary that one contradictory be true and the other false.

Lesson XIII: Truth and Falsity in Opposed Singular Propositions about the Future in Contingent Matter

18a 28 In enunciations about that which is or has taken place, the affirmation or the negation must be true or false. And in enunciations of universals as universal, one is always true and the other false, and also in enunciations of singulars, as has been said; but in enunciations of universals not taken universally, it is not necessary that one be true and the other false. We have already spoken of these.

However, in enunciations about future singular things the case is not the same.

18a 34 For if every affirmation or negation is true or false, then everything belongs or does not belong to a thing necessarily;

18a 35 for if one person says a thing will be such, and another says it will not be this very thing, clearly one of them must be speaking the truth if every affirmation is true or false. For it will not both belong and not belong to the thing simultaneously in such cases.

18a 39 For if it is true to say that a thing is white or not white, it must necessarily be white or not white. And if it is white or not white, it was true to affirm or deny it. And if it does not belong to it, it is false to say that it does, and if it is false to say that it does, then it does not belong to it. Consequently, it is necessary that either the affirmation or negation be true. If this is so, then nothing either is, or takes place fortuitously or indeterminately in relation to two alternatives, or will be or will not be; but everything takes place of necessity and is not indeterminate to either of two alternatives (for the supposition is that either the one who affirms it or the one who denies it is speaking the truth). Whereas if everything does not take place of necessity, it could take place or not take place as well, for what is indeterminate to either of two alternatives happens or will happen no more in this way than not.

18b 9 Furthermore, on such a supposition, if something is now white, it was true to say formerly that it will be white; therefore it was always true to say of anything that has taken place that it will be. But if it was always true to say that it is or will be, it is not possible for this not to be, nor that it will not be; and when a thing cannot not take place, it is impossible that it not take place, and when it is impossible that it not take place, it is necessary that it take place; all things that will be, then, must necessarily take place. Therefore, nothing will be indeterminate to either of two alternatives, nor fortuitous; for if it were fortuitous it would not take place of necessity.

18b 17 But still it is not possible to say that neither is true; that is, to say that a thing neither will take place nor will not take place.

18b 18 In the first place, though the affirmation be false, the negation will not be true, and though the negation be false, the affirmation will not be true.

18b 20 Secondly, if it is true to say that a thing is white and large, both necessarily belong to it; and if they will belong to it the next day, they will necessarily belong to it the next day. But if a thing neither will be nor will not be tomorrow, it would not be indeterminate to either of two alternatives. For example, in the case of a naval battle, it would be necessary that the naval battle neither take place nor not take place tomorrow.

Lesson XIV: Contingency in Things and the Roots of Contingency in Relation to Singular Propositions about the Future in Contingent Matter

18b 26 These absurd consequences and others like them result if of every affirmation and negation, whether in regard to universals taken universally or in regard to singulars, one of the opposites must be true and the other false: that nothing is indeterminate to either of two in things that come about but all are and take place of necessity; consequently, there will be no need to deliberate nor to take pains about something, as though if we were to do this, such a thing would follow and if we were not to do this, it would not follow.

18b 33 For nothing prevents one person from saying that this will be so in ten thousand years and another person saying it will not; and on the aforesaid supposition, whichever of these was truly said at that time will take place of necessity.

18b 36 Moreover, it makes no difference whether people have actually made the contradictory statements or not; for it is evident that things either will take place or will not even if one person has not affirmed and the other denied it. For it is not because of the affirming or denying that it will be or will not be, whether in ten thousand years or any other space of time.

Therefore, if throughout all time it was the case that one thing or the other was truly said, it would be necessary that this take place; and of every one of the things that takes place it was always the case that it would necessarily take place. For what anyone truly says will be, cannot not take place; and of that which takes place, it was always true to say that it would be.

19a 6 But these things appear to be impossible; for we see that both our deliberation about doing something and our action are principles of future events;

19a 9 and that universally in the things not always in act there is a potentiality to be and not to be. In these there is the possibility either of being or not being, and so they may either take place or not take place.

19a 12 We can point to many clear instances of this. For example, this cloak could be cut in half, and yet might not be but wear out first; likewise it is possible that it not be cut in half, for it could not wear out first if it were not possible that it not be cut.

19a 16 So it is, too, in other things that are said to take place according to this kind of potentiality.

19a 18 It is evident, then, that not all things are or take place of necessity, but some are indeterminate to either of two, in which case the affirmation is no more true than the negation; others take place more in one way than another, as in that which takes place for the most part, and yet it is possible for the other one to take place and the more frequent one not.

Lesson XV: It is Concluded that Propositions Are True as They Correspond to the Way in Which Things Are in Reality

19a 23 Now that which is, when it is, necessarily is, and that which is not, when it is not, necessarily is not. But it is not necessary for everything that is, to be, nor is it necessary for that which is not, not to be. For these are not the same: that everything be necessarily when it is and to be simply from necessity. And the case is similar with respect to that which is not.

19a 27 And this is also the case with respect to contradiction. It is necessary that everything be or not be; and that it will be or will not be; however, taking them separately, it is not possible to say one of the two is necessary. For example, it is necessary that there will or will not be a naval battle tomorrow; however, it is not necessary that a naval battle take place tomorrow, nor is it necessary that it not take place. Yet it is necessary that it either take place or not take place.

19a 32 And so, since speech is true as it corresponds to things, it is clear that when things are such that they are indeterminate to either of two, and opposites are possible, the corresponding contradiction must be similar. This is the case in those things that do not always exist or always not exist. Of these it is necessary that one part of the contradiction be true or false, not however this or that part, but either of the two indeterminately. One may be more likely to be true, but it is not yet actually true or false.

19a 39 Therefore it is clear that it is not necessary that of every affirmation and negation of opposites, one is true and one false. For the case is not the same in regard to those things that are and those that are not but could be or not be. It is as we have just stated.

Book II—Lesson I: The Distinction and Order of Simple Enunciations in Which the Finite or the Infinite Name Is Posited only on the Part of the Subject

19b 5 Since an affirmation signifies something about something, and the subject is either the name or that which has no name, and one thing must be signified about one thing in an affirmation

19b 7 (we have already stated what a name is and that which has no name: I do not call "non-man" a name but an infinite name—for an infinite name also signifies one thing in a certain way—nor "non-matures" a verb, but an infinite verb),

19b 10 every affirmation will be made up of a name and a verb or an infinite name and a verb.

19b 12 There can be no affirmation or negation without a verb; for according to what has been established, "is," "will be," or "was," or "becomes," or any others such as these are verbs since they signify with time.

19b 14 Therefore the primary affirmation and negation is "Man is," "Man is not"; then, "Non-man is," "Non-man is not"; and then "Every man is," "Not every man is"; "Every non-man is," "Not every non-man is"; and there are similar affirmations and negations with regard to times outside of the present.

Lesson II: The Number and Relationship of Simple Enunciations in Which the Verb "Is" Is Predicated as a Third Element and the Subject Is the Finite Name not Universally Taken

19b 19 But when "is" is predicated as a third element in the enunciation, there are two oppositions.

19b 20 I mean by this that in an enunciation such as "Man is just," the "is" is a third name or verb contained in the affirmation.

19b 22 In this case, therefore, there will be four enunciations, two of which will correspond in their sequence, in respect of affirmation and negation, with the privations but two will not.

19b 24 I mean that the "is" will be added either to "just" or to "nonjust"; and so also in the case of the negative. Thus there will be four.

19b 27 The following diagram will make this clear.

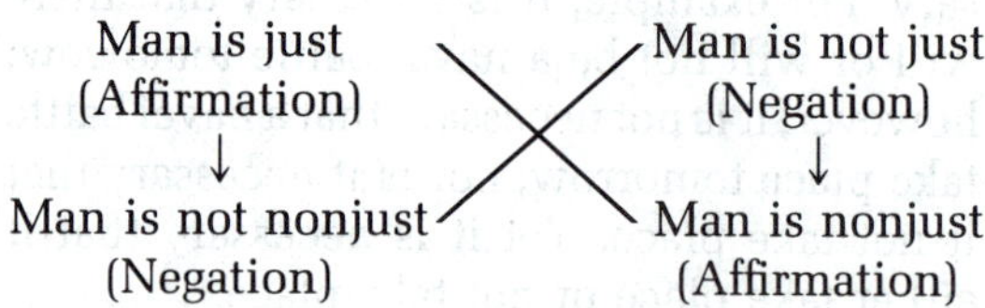

Here the "is" and the "is not" are added to "just" and "nonjust." This, then, is the way these are arranged, as we have said in the *Analytics*.

Lesson IV: Some Doubts About What Has Been Said Are Presented and Solved

20a 16 Since the negation contrary to "Every animal is just," is the one signifying "No animal is just," it is evident that these will never be at once true, or in reference to the same thing, but the opposites of these will sometimes be true, i.e., "Not every animal is just" and "Some animal is just."

20a 20 Now the enunciation "No man is just" follows upon the enunciation "Every man is nonjust"; and "Not every man is nonjust," which is its opposite, follows upon "Some man is just," for its opposite [i.e. the opposite of "every man"] must be "some man."

20a 23 And it is also clear with respect to the singular that if a question is asked and a negative answer is the true one, there is also a true affirmation. Take the example, "Is Socrates wise?" and the answer, "No"; then, "Socrates is nonwise." But in the case of universals, the affirmative inference is not true, but the negation is true. For example, in the question, "Is every man wise?" and the true answer, "No," the inference "Then every man is nonwise" is clearly false, but "Not every man is wise" is true. The latter is the opposite, the former the contrary.

20a 31 The antitheses in infinite names and verbs, as in "non-man" and "nonjust," might seem to be negations without a name or a verb; they are not, however. For the negation must always be either true or false; but the person who says "non-man" says nothing more than one who says "man," and he is even further from saying something true or false if something is not added.

20a 37 Moreover, "Every non-man is just" does not signify the same thing as any of the other enunciations, nor does the opposite of this. "Not every non-man is just."

20a 39 But "Every non-man is nonjust" signifies the same thing as "No non-man is just."

20b 1 When the names and verbs are transposed, the enunciations signify the same thing; for example, "Man is white" and "White is man."

20b 3 For if this is not the case there will be more than one negation of the same enunciation; but it has been shown that there is only one negation of one affirmation, for the negation of "Man is white" is "Man is not white," and if "White is man" is not the same as "Man is white," the negation of it ["White is man"] will be "White is not non-man" and "White is not man." The former, however, is the negation of "White is non-man"; the latter of "Man is white." Therefore, there will be two [negations] of one [affirmation]. It is clear, therefore, that when the name and the verb are transposed the signification of the affirmation and negation is the same.

Horace

65 B.C.–A.D. 8

Horace was one of the greatest of the Roman poets and satirists. His father was a freed slave who became a tax collecter and then went to great lengths to educate his son. Horace thus studied in Rome and Athens. While in Athens he became disastrously involved in Greek politics and was forced to return to Rome, where he began his career as a poet. He soon gained the patronage of Maecenas and henceforth wrote his poetry uninterrupted until his death. Prolific and inventive, he was perhaps the greatest representative of Greek sensibility and literary convention in Italy. His major works include the *Satires* (35 B.C.), the *Epodes* (30 B.C.), the second *Satires* (29 B.C.), the *Odes* (24 B.C.), and the *Epistles* (20 B.C.). A fourth book of *Odes*, another book of *Epistles*, and the *Ars Poetica* appeared in 13 B.C.

Horace's poetry in general gives a vivid sense of the life of Augustan Rome during a time of great cultivation and accomplishment. He had what Petronius called "painstaking felicity" of expression and was a master poetic technician. For the English tradition of poetry, in fact, Horace came to represent decorum and restrained eloquence, especially in England during the sixteenth and seventeenth centuries. Particularly influential in the *Art of Poetry* is Horace's emphasis on the specifics of poetry as a craft. "Might a praiseworthy poem be made," you inquire,/ "By one's genius or training? Without a rich vein/ Art will fail, as will talents untrained, I maintain;/ For each seeks the support of the other perforce." Horace thus values nature—or what will much later be called "genius"—but stresses the nurture of rigorous poetic preparation, a benefit that his own often subtle but not ostentatious poetry attests to.

THE ART OF POETRY

If a painter should choose to unite to the head
Of a woman the neck of a horse, and thence spread
Divers scales on the members conjoined, to degrade
From above a hideous fish, a fair maid,
Could you stifle a laugh when invited to look?
And, believe me, dear Pisos, as such is a book
Whose materials, friends, as fantastic as dreams
Of the sick, are arranged so no unity seems
From beginning to end. "But the canons declare
To both painters and poets the right aught to dare!"
We concede it and pardon such faults as we find
Save in matings where opposite traits are combined
As of serpents with birds, and of tigers with sheep!
Or when treating a theme of magnificent sweep
Should one daub on his purples with gaudy design
In depicting "Diana's Own Grove and her Shrine,"
Or "Fountains that favor the Grain and the Vine,"
Or "The Arch of the Rainbow," or "Scenes on the Rhine,"
It were neither the place nor the time! Why display
"A Lone Cypress," (his masterpiece, sooth!), if one pay
For "My Rescue from Shipwreck at Sea?" Or why turn
A decanter from what you began as an urn?
Let the plot be a simple and unified one!

But the most of us poets, my worthies, should shun
Certain faults in applying the rule: I am terse,
Then my language is vague; seeking smoothness of verse,—
It is weak; if I soar,—it is meaningless sound;
If too fearful of tempests,—it creeps on the ground!
Or one seeks, just to differ, a novel design,—
With the dolphins in forests, and boars on the brine!
The avoidance of faults comes from practice and rule.
The worst artisan nigh the Aemilian School,
Will delineate deftly soft hair and trim nails
On his bronze but his work as a whole simply fails
Through his lack of proportion. Were I to compose
As he does I would rather endure a hooked nose
And be praised for jet eyes and my glossy black hair.
Before writing, long ponder your themes and prepare
As befitting your talents such topics to use
As your shoulders can bear; and if ably you choose
The arrangement will please and your meaning be clear.

A bard's genius and charm will, I hold, thus appear,—
That he sing in due sequence, at once, what is fit;
But the most, for the moment, withhold or omit
To be culled, to embellish his forthcoming lay.

And eke choice and refined in his verbal array,
One will write with distinction, if aptly a phrase
Of commonplace words a new meaning conveys.
If one must the arcana of science unfold
In expressions unheard by Cethegus, of old,
Then a license is given, if sparingly used;
For new words although recent will e'er be excused
If derived from the Greek and the changes be scant.
Shall our race to Caecilius and Plautus e'en grant
Aught denied unto Varius and Virgil? Wherefore
Am I envied if aptly I add a few more,
Since the language of Cato and Ennius improved
Latin lore by new terms? It will aye be approved
To impress a coined word with a current design!
As the leaves become changed at each yearly decline
And the earliest, first, so with age words decay,
Though like children from birth they develop each day!
We are destined to Death, we and ours; e'en the deep
Land embedded that keeps from the fleet the winds' sweep,—
(A king's plan!); or waste marsh land long fit for light keels
That now feeds local towns and the plough's burden feels;
Or the stream whose rough channel once coursed through the field

Has been changed to a better. Things mortal shall yield!
But the vigor of language is less likely to last;
Many words are reborn that had once been outcast;
Some will fade though now favored, if usage so rules
As the tyrant of speech that controls them as tools.

The adventures and battles of chieftains and kings
Can be written in measures as Homer well sings.
The first dirge was in distichs unequally long
That was later a scheme for a votary's song.
The grammarians argue to this very day
Who was first to compose in a sorrowful lay.
In iambics, Archilochus choler expressed;
Then the slippers and buskins considered them best,
When adapted to dialogue even to sway
The loud din of the mob with the zest of the play.
But the Muse has ordained with a lyre must be sung
All the gods and their children, the loves of the young,
The victorious boxers, and steeds, and good wines.
If I fail to preserve proper style and good lines
In my work, why do I, then, a poet's name earn?
Why prefer through false shame not to know than to learn?
As the comic refuses a tragical strain
So the Feast of Thyestes contemns measures plain
And a treatment approaching a humorous vein.
Let each theme its appropriate balance retain;
Yet, at times, even Comedy haughtily speaks,

And a Chremes when angered harangues with puffed cheeks;
And so, often do Peleus and Telephus grieve
In a prosy discourse when poor exiles they leave
Their majestic, sonorous, grandiloquent art
Not unmindful of moving the spectator's heart;
For with beautiful verses must charm be combined
To impel to their bidding the auditor's mind,
As from mirth to bring laughter, from sorrow bring tears
To his face. You must grieve till it truly appears
Ere I weep, that in me your afflictions sink deep,
Be you Peleus or Telephus; yet, I shall sleep
Or just laugh if the reading is poor. It is fit
That the facial expressions be suited to it;
As for anger, with scowls, and for sorrows, be sad;
For the serious, grave, for the sportive, be glad;
Then our nature reacts from within to reveal
The resentment, or joy, or the anguish we feel
As the mind is aroused by the mimicker's art.
If the tones of his voice are not changed for each part
Then the Romans will laugh be they footmen or knights.
He should note if a god, or a hero recites,
Or a venerable sage, or a light-hearted boy,
Or a matron of note, or a maid-servant coy,
Or a traveling man, or a grower of leek
Or a Colchian or Syrian, a Cretan or Greek;
Let traditions be kept; and if types you may rear
Be distinctive; as, say, of Achilles' career,—
As fleetfooted, relentless, quick-tempered, and brave,
Unrestrained by all laws save his sword itself gave;
As Medea, vindictive; and Ino, the Sad;
False, Ixion; vexed, Io; Orestes, gone mad!

Should you dramatize something untried and present
A new character, let it persist to its bent
From beginning to end, as consistent throughout.
Common topics are hard to compose; so no doubt
You do well to extract from the Iliad your own
Than first venture a theme both unsung and unknown;
And though public, you set up a personal right
By avoiding its cycles well beaten and trite,
Or translator's too verbal rendition of lines,
Or a plagiarist's, that to abridgment inclines,
But his shame or its form does its metre withhold.
And suppose you begin as a Cyclist of old:
"I shall sing Priam's fate and his noble campaign";—
Will this braggart produce aught to merit such strain?
A big mountain in labor to a mouse it gave birth!
Much more neatly he opens with manifest worth:—
"Sing, O Muse, of the hero when Troy had been burned,
That had viewed many lands ere he homeward returned";—
For he aims not for smoke, but from smoke to give light
That its wonders will forcibly dazzle the sight,—

As the Cyclopes, Scylla, Antiphates dread,—
(Not,—"How Diomed left Meleager" when dead,
Nor,—"The War Against Troy" with an egg for its source);
But he hastens the end, as he sweeps on his course
To the climax, with his hearers assuming as known
Many things, whilst he leaves the dull topics alone,
Or embellishes them as with truth so to blend
That the verity holds to the middle and end.

And now hear what the public and I do ordain
If you want e'en one man in his seat to remain
Till the actor announces "Applaud!" from the stage;
Let the habits of persons conform to their age,
And their characters change with their years and their bents;
Thus, the boy that now voices replies and indents
With firm footstep the ground loves with comrades to play;
Waxes angry, soon cools, and so varies each day.
Beardless youth is delighted when free from his guard,
With horses and hounds and the Campus' green sward;
He is prone unto vice, to advisers is cold,
Unconcerned for the useful and lavish of gold;
Full of passion and vain, and most fickle of mood.
But then age and man's spirit assume a new brood
Of desires, as for friendship and wealth and fame's boon,
With due care for his acts, lest amends be made soon.
Disadvantages hamper the old. If one choose
Aught to seek, like the miser he's fearful to use
What he finds; or is timid or faint in affairs;
Never ready, expectant, impressive, and cares
For the future; is peevish and plaintive, with praise
For the past but with censure for youths of our days.
Many blessings accompany years that advance
That departing years lose. Let there never perchance
Be assigned the old parts to a youth, nor a man's
To a boy, but adjust them through suitable plans.
Then in dramas some things are enacted, some told.
The impressions through hearing, less vividly hold
A spectator's attention than those of the sight,
To which he was a witness. Nor would it be right
To present on the stage much that should not be shown
That will soon through narration be properly known:—
Thus, Medea's destroying her children in view
Of the public, or Atreus' preparing his stew;
Or make Cadmus, a snake, or fair Procne a bird,—
Contradicting my sense, I detest as absurd!

Let your drama consist of five acts,—five alone
If you wish it success and oft to be shown.
Let no deity meddle unless he may seek
Worthy knots to undo; nor a fourth person speak.
Let the Chorus consider important its role

As an actor's; to sing as a part of the whole—
Between acts—what explains and connects with the plot
Let it favor the good and incline to their lot;
Reconcile the resentful; be kind to the meek;
Let it praise moderation, true justice, and eke,
The observance of laws, and a permanent peace;
Let it safeguard its trust, pray to God,(— and not cease),—
That the poor be made happy and tyrants be downed.

Ancient flutes that now rival the horn were not bound
With brass trimmings as now; but were slender, for use
Of the chorus, and plain with few notes to produce,—
Nor yet ample in volume to fill a large hall;
Then the people were easily counted, and small
Their assembly, but reverent, frugal, and chaste.
But they later, when victors, converted the waste
Into farms, and enlarged the town wall, and appeased
Their good Genius on Feast Days, with wine, as they pleased;
More licentious became both their music and plays.
How else might idle rustics untrained to their ways
With the townsfolk commingle—the rude with refined?
So the flutist, abandon and gesture, combined
With his art as he danced in long robes on the stage.
Simple harps did new musical notes disengage
And the chorus gave quickly a pompous harangue
With the advice on the useful and future, and sang
Its opinions in Delphic oracular strain.

Who first wrote tragic verse a rank goat to obtain
Soon presented his Satyrs as naked and bold
And essayed e'en to jest as the actions unfold,
And through novelties make some spectators benign
That were drunk from the ritual orgies and wine.
Though befitting that Satyrs appear always gay
And divert from the tragic with jesting and play,
Yet whoever the god or the hero displayed
In his purple and gold that was lately arrayed
Must not sink to coarse speech of the dives underground,
Or avoiding it, raise to the clouds hollow sound.
As a matron, when ordered to dance at a Fete
Among roystering Satyrs, must act quite sedate,
So must tragedy frivolous babbling disdain.
Should I write a Satyric, I'd choose not the plain
And indigenous words, my dear Pisos, alone;
Nor essay to depart from a tragical tone,
Whether Davus is speaking, or Pythias bold
That inveigled from Simo a talent of gold,
Or Silenus, the guard, that on Bacchus attends.

From known themes, I develop my play, so that, friends,
These expecting to equal it, toil and erase
But in vain; from one gets from his plot as much grace

As the force, its unfolding and sequences share.
In my judgment the Fauns of the woods must beware
Not to sport as town-bred and forensically trained,
Nor to simper in juvenile lilts unrestrained,
Nor to prattle in language too vulgar and trite
And offend every Senator, rich man, and Knight;—
Nay, though all the parched-pea-and-nut buyers in town
With their favor approve and award it a crown!
When two syllables join, the first, short,—the next long,
An iambus is formed, a quick measure for song;
And the verse is a trimeter, counting six beats,
When each foot from the first an iambus repeats.
Not long since as more serious plays were composed,
The iambics, adopting the spondees, disposed
Them with friendship, as partners in many a place
Save the second and fourth; in which metrical grace
The famed measures of Accius and Ennius are scant.
To deliver slow verse on the stage is to rant;
As it shows undue haste and an indolent part
Or complete disregard for the rules of the art.
Since the faults of a poem few judges detect,
And our poets though worthless are given respect
Shall I wander and write as I please? And suppose
I may think all perceive the defects? As to those,
On my guard, I am cautious each blemish to shun
But no praise I deserve. Let Greek models be done
For your practice, by hand both by day and by night.
"Did the wit and the measures of Plautus, delight
Our ancestors?" Ay, truly, with tolerance,—too!—
Not to say, they admired in their folly! As you
And I know a coarse joke from keen wit, if we hear,
And can tell proper cadence by fingers and ear.

The inventor of tragedy, Thespis, they say,
Did in wagons his scenery and actors convey,
Who performed with their faces discolored with lees.
Later Aeschylus masked and costumed them to please,
And constructed a small wooden stage where he taught
Them in buskins to speak with due force as they ought.
Then Old Comedy followed with no little praise,
But through licence adopted degenerate ways
That impelled a suppression by law; to its shame
Did the Chorus then quit when forbade to defame.
But our poets left nothing untried and e'en dared
(Quite successfully, too) to depart as they fared
From Greek paths to exhibit our manners at home,
By examples of Nobles and Commons of Rome.
No more famous for valor or glories of war,

Than for poets, would Latium be, save they mar
Their productions through lack of a file or delay.
O ye, Blood of Pompilius, condemn any play
That erasures and time have not pruned from defect,
And revised so that none can a blemish detect.

"Because genius is more advantageous than art,
And in Helicon, poets with sense have no part,"
As Democritus taught, many haunt hidden vales
And cease bathing, or trimming their beards and their nails;
They secure the name *Poet,* and eke the prized wreaths,
If their polls though uncured by three Anticyr heaths
Be ne'er bent to the barber Licinus. I smile
At my folly each Spring to get rid of my bile,—
I'd be foremost, but not for the toll to be paid!

Hence I serve like a whetstone that sharpens the blade
Without being a cutter itself; thus the art
And its rules, though no playwright myself, I'll impart:
How materials spring; how arranged and combined;
What is pleasing; what strength or what weakness we find.
Now good sense is the poet's first rule and his guide.
When Socratical texts to a theme are applied
And the subjects reviewed, proper words will then blend;
One has learned what is due to his country or friend;
How should parents, or brothers, or hosts be esteemed;
What the duty of judges or senators deemed;
How a general acts; and thus quickly he knows
How he should every character fitly dispose.

I'll direct the intelligent poet to view
Human conduct and life, that his words will ring true.
Oft a play without ornament, smoothness, and art,
But replete with conceits and appeals to the heart
Gives the people more pleasure or profit for life
Than do meaningless verses with melody rife.
The Greek genius is due for its well-rounded strain
To the Muse, since the Greeks sought for glory not gain!
Roman boys through long processes learn how to tell
The proportional parts of a shilling, as,—"Well—
Young Albinus, five pence are diminished by one,
What remains?—You once knew it!"—"A third."— Quite well done!
You will guard your estate!—One is added, what then?"
"A half!", Lo, once this canker of wealth seizes men
Do we hope for a poem one ought to preserve
With the unguent of cedar and in cypress conserve?

As the poets design to instruct or delight
Or present situations, both pleasing and bright,

Let your precepts be brief that the words quickly told,
The keen minds will receive and in memory hold,—
Since superfluous verbiage soon is forgot;
Let your fancies to please be with realism fraught.
Do not think any story you tell is deemed true.
Nor from Lamia's belly withdraw unto view
A live child she had eaten! No Senators deem
It instructive; and Knights do not have an esteem
For obscenity. Make it a point to unite
Sweet and useful for readers' advice and delight.
Such a book will bring money and cross o'er the main
And for ages its author's repute will sustain.

Yet mistakes will occur we may wish were unknown;
As no string aye performs with precision of tone,
But oft renders a sharp when a flat is essayed,
Whilst a bow sometimes misses the target displayed.
But when beauties are rife in a poem, and few
Are its faults, I condone these, dear Pisos, as due
To a trifling neglect or man's nature. "*What next?*"
Should a copyist err, although warned, in his text,
He deserves a reproof; and a laugh alone greets
A musician that mars the same note in all beats;
So a shirker that brags in the Choerilan style,
With a verse or two fine, I admire with a smile
Of contempt! The good Homer at times slumbers light,
But, you know, in long work, that is proper and right.

As with pictures, some poems the closer you stand
Are more pleasing, but some more remote should be scanned;
One appears best in shadows, and one in clear light
Unafraid of a critic's discerning insight;
And some please us once, some, an indefinite time.
Though, dear youth, as the elder, you plan the sublime
Through your father's advice, and your talent and skill,
Yet remember this truth: Mediocrity still
Is esteemed in some things; as, a lawyer may plead
And fall short of our famous Messala, or read
With less power than Casselius Aulus, yet he
Has his value. No men, or e'en gods, through decree
Nor can book-posts make excellent, average bards;
As at banquets, symphonic cacophonous chords,
And rank perfumes, and poppy with honey from Sard
Are offensive, since these from the feast could be barred;
So a poem for mental enjoyment designed
Should it veer from its heights, to the depths is inclined.
One unskilled with the foils, from the Campus refrains,
And from tennis, or quoits, or the hoop, lest the trains
Of spectators foregathered may scoff unrestrained;
Yet he dares to write verses!—why not,—though untrained?—
He is well-born and free and is rated at twice

The estate of a Knight and untainted by vice!
Save Minerva so wills you can say and do naught;
Then decide and resolve, if you e'er should write aught,
To recite it to Maecio's critical ears,
To your father's, and mine, and retain it nine years.
From your parchment encased you can always erase
Words unpublished, that issued you could not efface.

The Defender of Deities, Orpheus, the Blest,
The tree dwellers from carnage and vile food repressed,
And 'twas said e'en wild tigers and lions he stilled;
And that eke when Amphion his city did build
He moved stones where he chose at the sound of his shell.
This was Wisdom of yore: To discriminate well
What is public from private; from sacred, profane;
To keep men from loose ties, and true wedlock sustain;
To wall towns; and engrave on wood tablets their laws.
Divine honors arose for these poets because
Of their poems. Great Homer, succeeding was next,
With Tyrtaeus whose verses excited and vexed
Men to warfare. In verse, were the oracles made,
And life's conduct prescribed, a king's favor essayed
With Thessalian music, and at Festivale, eke,
And at close of long toil; be not bashful to seek
Both the singer Apollo and Muse with her lyre.

"Might a praiseworthy poem be made," you inquire,
"By one's genius or training?" Without a rich vein
Art will fail, as will talents untrained, I maintain;
For each seeks the support of the other perforce.
The aspirant that reaches the goal on the course,
As a boy, suffered changes of cold and heat,
Shunning Venus and wine; so the bards that compete
For Pythons, learnt a dread teacher's sharp tone.
Now one says: "I compose the best poems e'er known;
Let the itch get the last; to be left would be base;
And for me to confess to no learning,—Disgrace!"

As a crier that draws to his bargains a crowd,
So the bard rich in fields, and with money endowed
And large loans, attracts flatters thither for gain;
And besides if he can with fine feasts entertain
And give bail for a client (though poor), and so change
One involved from a grievous lawsuit, it were strange
If he then could distinguish his friends,—false from true.

If you give to some one or expect so to do,
Do not read your new verses to him; in his glee;
He will shout: "They are pretty! Correct! Good to me!"
He will pale and his tears will gush forth in a stream;

He will jump, and by stamping express his esteem!
As hired mourners in outbursts at funerals rave
With more noise, than do those with true sorrow behave,
So pretenders react with more praise than a friend!
We are told that some rulers with goblets commend
As they rack one with wine whom they strive to disclose
Whether worthy of friendship. If plays you compose,
Do not let foxy minds ever lead you astray!

If one read to Quintilius, "Correct this, I pray,
And eke this," he would say: and if thus you replied,
You had tried many times but in vain, "Then decide
To erase and to forge the ill verses anew";
Should you rather defend your mistakes than renew,
He would waste no more time or his scrupulous pains,
But would leave you and yours to your own matchless strains.

As a prudent good man will condemn faulty lines,
Censure roughness, delete the redundant by signs
(With his calamus turned), cull ambitious display,
And compel one to clear any vagueness away;
He will challenge the doubtful, and show what to mend,
And be like Aristarchus; nor say: "Why offend
With such trifles a friend?" For these trifles will lead
To a rank, ill-received, and ridiculous screed.
As when those with the itch or the jaundice appear,
Or a maudlin or lunatic, wise men through fear
Will make haste to avoid them, so bards when not sane
They will leave to a boyish and roystering train.
Such a one while he belches his verses may stray
And fall down, as a sportsman intent on his prey,
In a pit or a ditch; though he cried, "Help me, friends!"
For some time, there is none that in pity attends.

If one cares to bring aid and to offer a rope,
I would say: "Do you know whether he without hope
Chose to cast himself down there to die? We are told
Whilst he sought to be god and immortal, that cold
Did Empedocles leap into Aetna aflame!
Yes, a poet may perish if such is his aim;
To prevent one from dying that seeks it, is ill!
He has done this before, and if drawn out he will
Be no wiser, nor put his death-glory aside.
As to verses, I cannot explain why he tried,
Unless he had profaned his sires' ashes or changed
The bidental enclosure. And bear-like he ranged
As with power to break all the bolts of his den,
And reciting his verses he routed all men.
Whom he catches he holds and with reading he kills,
As a leech grips the skin, till its bloodsac it fills."

Longinus *ca.* A.D. 1

At the 1948 Johns Hopkins University Lectures in Criticism, the poet and critic Allen Tate (1899–1979) claimed that Longinus was the first literary critic. In his lecture on Longinus, he defended his claim by saying that—unlike Aristotle—Longinus focused his critical work on the broad range of literature and the issue of the relation of language itself to its subject matter. He went further, citing as an example the analysis of Sappho's "Ode to Anactoria" that appears in Chapter X of *On the Sublime*, an analysis that explores the effects of the ode in terms of its structure. Given the nineteenth-century assessment of Longinus, which interpreted his theory in light of the romantic adaptation of the Kantian sublime found in *The Critique of Judgment*, Tate's view seems novel. It sounds a caution for us to question those interpreters of Longinus who rely on a Kantian notion of the sublime when assessing Longinian theory and its contemporary significance. Such assessments may not come to terms with the complexity of his theory.

But Longinus himself is not an easy subject for evaluation. He was long thought to be Cassius Longinus, a Roman-Greek minister to Zenobia, queen of Palmyra, but this person certainly did not write the *Peri hypsous* (*On the Sublime*.) Also troublesome yet is the work's English title, which was originally, in the first English translation (John Hall, 1652), *Of the Height of Eloquence* and sometimes *On Elevation in Poetry*. The trouble is that "sublime" is not a cognate for *hypsous*, which means "on high" in the sense of height, as in "top." Thus the work's current title (*On the Sublime*) obscures the Longinian focus on the elevation of language as "a kind of supreme excellence of discourse." In doing so, the title leaves the theoretical work more vulnerable to the Kantian gloss on the meaning of the sublime.

However, despite the historical confusions and most of the differences among its interpreters, there is some general agreement about the *Peri hypsous*. We know that Longinus was concerned with the conditions of the sublime in a literary work and what effect those conditions have on the work's audience. We know also that Longinus intended to refute a certain Caecilius, who seems to have claimed that great writers are born, not made—a claim consistent with Platonic and Aristotelian views. Longinus thought instead that a writer's style is created by natural talent as well as acquired through a kind of practice or experience, not through any schooling in prescriptive rules. And we know to attribute to Longinus a deliberate theoretical break between rhetoric and literature insofar as rhetoric meant merely the art of persuasion.

This rupture in some ways foretold the position of contemporary rhetorical studies as it rejects the narrow restriction of rhetoric to fields of argumentation and forms of persuasive discourse. Today a reassessment of Longinus might usefully contribute to the expanding discussion of what rhetoric is, particularly in regard to the broader recognition of its vital role in literary criticism and philosophy.

from On the Sublime

I

The treatise written by Caecilius "concerning Sublimity" appeared to us, as you will remember, dear Postumius Teretianus, when we looked into it together, to fall below the level of the general subject, failing especially in grasp of vital points; and to give his readers but little of that assistance which should be the first aim of every writer. In any technical treatise two points are essential; the first, that the writer should show what the thing proposed for inquiry is; the second, but in effect the more important, that he should tell us by what specific methods that thing may be made our own. Now Caecilius endeavours to show us by a vast number of instances what the sublime is, as though we did not know; the process by which we may raise our natural powers to a required advance in scale he unaccountably passed over as unnecessary. So far as he is concerned, perhaps we ought to praise the man for his ingenuity and pains, not to blame him for the omissions. Since, however, you lay your commands upon me, that I should take up the subject in my turn, and without fail put something on paper about Sublimity as a favour to yourself, give me your company; let us see whether there is anything in the views which I have formed really serviceable to men in public life. You, comrade, will help me by passing judgement, with perfect frankness, upon all particulars; you can and you ought. It was well answered by one who wished to show wherein we resemble gods: "in doing good," said he, "and in speaking truth."

Writing to you, my dear friend, with your perfect knowledge of all liberal study, I am almost relieved at the outset from the necessity of showing at any length that Sublimity is always an eminence and excellence in language; and that from this, and this alone, the greatest poets and writers of prose have attained the first place and have clothed their fame with immortality. For it is not to persuasion but to ecstasy that passages of extraordinary genius carry the hearer: now the marvellous, with its power to amaze, is always and necessarily stronger than that which seeks to persuade and to please: to be persuaded rests usually with ourselves, genius brings force sovereign and irresistible to bear upon every hearer, and takes its stand high above him. Again, skill in invention and power of orderly arrangement are not seen from one passage nor from two, but emerge with effort out of the whole context; Sublimity, we know, brought out at the happy moment, parts all the matter this way and that, and like a lightning flash, reveals, at a stroke and in its entirety, the power of the orator. These and suchlike considerations I think, my dear Terentianus, that your own experience might supply.

II

We, however, must at once raise this further question; is there any art of sublimity or of its opposite? For some go so far as to think all who would bring such terms under technical rules to be entirely mistaken. "Genius," says one, "is inbred, not taught; there is one art for the things of genius, to be born with them." All natural effects are spoilt, they think, by technical rules, and become miserable skeletons. I assert that the reverse will prove true on examination, if we consider that Nature, a law to herself as she mostly is in all that is passionate and lofty, yet is no creature of random impulse delighting in mere absence of method; that she is indeed herself the first and originating principle which underlies all things, yet rules of degree, of fitting occasion, of unerring practice, and of application can be determined by method and are its contribution; in a sense all greatness is exposed to a danger of its own, if left to itself without science to control, "unsteadied, unballasted," abandoned to mere velocity and uninstructed venture; greatness needs the spur often, it also needs the bit. What Demosthenes shows to be true of the common life of men—that of all good things the greatest is good fortune, but a second, not inferior to the first, is good counsel, and that where the latter is wanting the former is at once cancelled—we may properly apply to literature; here Nature fills the place of good fortune, Art of good counsel. Also, and this is most important, it is only from Art that we can learn the very fact that certain effects in literature rest on Nature and on her alone. If, as I said, the critic who finds fault with earnest students, would take all these things into his account, he would in my opinion no longer deem inquiry upon the subjects before us to be unnecessary or unfruitful.

[*Here the equivalent of about six pages of this translation has been lost.*]

III

Stay they the furnace! quench the far-flung blaze!
For if I spy one crouching habitant,
I'll twist a lock, one lock of storm-borne flame,
And fire the roof, and char the halls to ash:
Not yet, not now my noble strain is raised[1]

All this is tragic no longer, but burlesque of tragic; "locks," "to vomit up to heaven," "Boreas turned flute player," and the rest. It is turbid in expression, and confused in imagery, not forcible; and if you examine each detail in clear light, you see a gradual sinking from the terrible to the contemptible. Now when in tragedy, which by its nature is pompous and admits bombast, tasteless rant is found to be unpardonable, I should be slow to allow that it could be in place in true history. Thus we laugh at Gorgias[2] of Leontini for writing "Xerxes the Zeus of the Persians" and "vultures, those living tombs," and at some passages in Callisthenes[3] as being stilted, not sublime, and even more at some in Cleitarchus;[4] he is a mere fantastic, he "puffs," to apply the words of Sophocles, "on puny pipes, *but* with no mellowing gag."[5] So with Amphicrates, Hegesias, and Matris;[6] they often appear to themselves to be possessed, really they are no inspired revellers but children at play. We may take it that turgidity is of all faults perhaps the most difficult to avoid. It is a fact of Nature that all men who aim at grandeur, in avoiding the reproach of being weak and dry, are, we know not how, borne off into turgidity, caught by the adage:—"To lapse from greatness were a generous fault."[7] As in bodies, so in writings, all swellings which are hollow and unreal are bad, and very possibly work round to the opposite condition, for "nothing," they say, "so dry as a man with dropsy."

While tumidity thus tends to overshoot the sublime, puerility is the direct opposite of all that is great; it is in every sense low and small spirited, and essentially a most ignoble fault. What then is puerility? Clearly it is a pedantic conceit, which overdoes itself and becomes frigid at the last. Authors glide into this when they make for what is unusual, artificial, above all, agreeable, and so run on the reefs of nonsense and affectation. By the side of these is a third kind of vice, found in passages of strong feeling, and called by Theodorus[8] "Parenthyrsus." This is passion out of place and unmeaning, where there is no call for passion, or unrestrained where restraint is needed. Men are carried aside, as if under strong drink, into expressions of feeling which have nothing to do with the subject, but are personal to themselves and academic: then they play clumsy antics before an audience which has never been moved; it cannot be otherwise, when the speakers are in an ecstasy, and the hearers are not. But we reserve room to speak of the passions elsewhere.

IV

Of the second fault which we mentioned, frigidity, Timaeus[9] is full; an able author in other respects, and not always wanting in greatness of style; learned, acute, but extremely critical of the faults of others, while insensible to his own; often sinking into mere childishness from an incessant desire to start new notions. I will set down one or two instances only from this author, since Caecilius has been before me with most of them. Praising Alexander the Great, he writes: "who annexed all Asia in fewer years than Isocrates[10] took to write his *Panegyricus* in support of war against the Persians." Truly a wonderful comparison between the Macedonian and the Sophist: yes, Timaeus, clearly the Lacedaemonians were far out-matched by Isocrates in valour, for they took Messene in thirty years, he composed his *Panegyricus* in ten! Then how he turns upon the Athenians captured in Sicily: "Because they committed impiety against Hermes, and defaced his images, they suffered punishment for it, largely on account of one man, a descendant, on the father's side, of the injured god, Hermocrates, son of Hermon." This makes me wonder, dear Terentianus, that he does not also write of the tyrant Dionysius: "He had shown impiety towards Zeus[11] and Heracles; therefore he was deprived of his kingdom by Dion and Heraclides." What need to speak of Timaeus, when those heroes Xenophon and Plato, although they were of Socrates' own school, sometimes forgot themselves in such paltry attempts to please. Thus Xenophon writes in the *Constitution of the Lacedaemonians*: "I mean to say that you can no more hear their voices than if they were made of stone, no more draw their eyes aside than if they were made of brass; you might think them more modest than the maiden-pupils in their eyes." It was worthy of Amphicrates,[12] not of Xenophon, to call the pupils in our eyes "modest maidens": but what a notion, to believe that the eyes of a whole row were modest, whereas they say that immodesty in particular persons is expressed by nothing so much as by the eyes. Addressing a forward person, "Wine laden dog-eyed!" says Homer.[13] Timaeus, however, as if clutching at stolen goods, has not left to Xenophon even this point of frigidity. He says, speaking of Agathocles, that he even carried off his cousin, who had been given in marriage to another man, from the solemnity of Unveiling; "Now who would have done this, who had maidens, not harlots, in his eyes?" Nay, Plato, the divine, as at other times he is, wishing to mention tablets, says: "they will write and store in the temples memorials of cypress wood," and again "concerning walls, O Megillus, I would take the Spartan view, to allow our walls to sleep on the ground where they lie, and not be raised again."[14] And Herodotus is hardly clear of this fault, when he calls beautiful women "pains to the eyes";[15] though he has some excuse, for the speakers in Herodotus are barbarians and in drink: still, not even through the mouths of such characters is it well, out of sheer pettiness, to cut a clumsy figure before all time.

V

All these undignified faults spring up in literature from a single cause, the craving for intellectual novelties, on which, above all else, our own generation goes wild. It would almost be true to say that the sources of all the good in us are also the sources of all the bad. Thus beauties of expression, and all which is sublime, I will add, all which is agreeable, contribute to success in our writing; and yet every one of these becomes a principle and a foundation, as of success, so of its opposite. Much the same is to be said of changes of construction, hyperboles, plurals for singulars; we will show in the sequel the danger which seems to attend each. Therefore it is necessary at once to raise the question directly, and to show how it is possible for us to escape the vices thus intimately mingled with the sublime.

VI

It is possible, my friend, to do this, if we could first of all arrive at a clear and discriminating knowledge of what true sublimity is. Yet this is hard to grasp: judgement of style is the last and ripest fruit of much experience. Still, if I am to speak in the language of precept, it is perhaps not impossible, from some such remarks as follow, to attain to a right decision upon the matter.

VII

We must, dear friend, know this truth. As in our ordinary life nothing is great which it is a mark of greatness to despise; as fortunes, offices, honours, kingdoms, and such like, things which are praised so pompously from without, could never appear, at least to a sensible man, to be surpassingly good, since actual contempt for them is a good of no mean kind (certainly men admire, more than those who have them, those who might have them, but in greatness of soul let them pass); even so it is with all that is elevated in poetry and prose writings; we have to ask whether it may be that they have that image of greatness to which so much careless praise is attached, but on a close scrutiny would be found vain and hollow, things which it is nobler to despise than to admire. For it is a fact of Nature that the soul is raised by true sublimity, it gains a proud step upwards, it is filled with joy and exultation, as though itself had produced what it hears. Whenever therefore anything is heard frequently by a man of sense and literary experience, which does not dispose his mind to high thoughts, nor leave in it material for fresh reflection, beyond what is actually said; while it sinks, if you look carefully at the whole context, and dwindles away, this can never be true sublimity, being preserved so long only as it is heard. That is really great which gives much food for fresh reflection; which it is hard, nay impossible, to resist; of which the memory is strong and indelible. You may take it that those are beautiful and genuine effects of sublimity which please always, and please all. For when men of different habits, lives, ambitions, ages, all take one and the same view about the same writings, the verdict and pronouncement of such dissimilar individuals give a powerful assurance, beyond all gainsaying, in favour of that which they admire.

VIII

Now there are five different sources, so to call them, of lofty style, which are the most productive; power of expression being presupposed as a foundation common to all five types, and inseparable from any. First and most potent is the faculty of grasping great conceptions, as I have defined it in my work on Xenophon. Second comes passion, strong and impetuous. These two constituents of sublimity are in most cases native-born, those which now follow come through art: the proper handling of figures, which again seem to fall under two heads, figures of thought, and figures of diction; then noble phraseology, with its subdivisions, choice of words, and use of tropes and of elaboration; and fifthly, that cause of greatness which includes in itself all that preceded it, dignified and spirited composition. Let us now look together at what is included under each of these heads, premising that Caecilius has passed over some of the five, for instance, passion. If he did so under the idea that sublimity and feeling are one and the same thing, coexistent and of common origin, he is entirely wrong. For some passions may be found which are distinct from sublimity and are humble, as those of pity, grief, fear; and again, in many cases, there is sublimity without passion; take, besides countless other instances, the poet's own venturesome lines on the Aloadae:

> Upon Olympus Ossa, leafy Pelion
> On Ossa would they pile, a stair to heaven;[16]

and the yet grander words which follow:

> Now had they worked their will.

In the Orators, again, speeches of panegyric, pomp, display, exhibit on every hand majesty and the sublime, but commonly lack passion: hence Orators of much passion succeed least in panegyric, and again the panegyrists are not strong in passion. Or if, on the other hand, Caecilius did not think that passion ever contributes to sublimity, and, therefore, held it undeserving of mention, he is quite in error. I should feel confidence in maintaining that nothing reaches great eloquence so surely as genuine passion in the right place; it breathes the vehemence of frenzy and divine possession, and makes the very words inspired.

IX

After all, however, the first element, great natural genius, covers far more ground than the others: therefore, as to this also, even if it be a gift rather than a thing acquired, yet so far as is possible we must nurture our souls to all that is great, and make them, as it were, teem with noble endowment. How? you will ask. I have myself written in another place to this effect:—Sublimity is the note which rings from a great mind. Thus it is that, without any utterance, a notion, unclothed and unsupported, often moves our wonder, because the very thought is great: the silence of Ajax in the book of the Lower World is great, and more sublime than any words.[17] First, then, it is quite necessary to presuppose the principle from which this springs: the true Orator must have no low ungenerous spirit, for it is not possible that they who think small thoughts, fit for slaves, and practise them in all their daily life, should put out anything to deserve wonder and immortality. Great words issue, and it cannot be otherwise, from those whose thoughts are weighty. So it is on the lips of men of the highest spirit that words of rare greatness are found. . . .

[*Here about eighteen pages have been lost.*]

But how does Homer make great all that belongs to gods?

> Far as the region of blank air in sight
> Of one who sitting on some beacon height
> Views the long wine-dark barrens of the deep,
> Such space the horses of the realm of light
> Urged by the gods, as on they strain and sweep,
> While their hoofs thunder aloft, bound over at one leap.[18]

He measures their leap by the interval of the boundaries of the world. Who might not justly exclaim, when he marked this extravagance in greatness, that, if the horses of the gods make two leaps, leap after leap, they will no longer find room within the world. Passing great too are the appearances in the Battle of the Gods:—

> Heaven sent its clarion forth: Olympus too:[19]
> . . . .
> Trembled too Hades in his gloomy reign,
> And leapt up with a scream, lest o'er his head
> Poseidon cleave the solid earth in twain,
> And open the pale kingdom of the dead
> Horrible, foul with blight, which e'en Immortals dread.[20]

You see, comrade, how, when earth is torn up from its foundations, and Tartarus itself laid bare, and the Universe suffers overthrow and dissolution, all things at once, heaven and hell, things mortal and immortal, mingle in the war and the peril of that fight. Yet all this is terrible indeed, though, unless taken as allegory, thoroughly impious and out of proportion. For when Homer presents to us woundings of the gods, their factions, revenges, tears, bonds, sufferings, all massed together, it seems to me that, as he has done his uttermost to make the men of the Trojan war gods, so he has made the gods men. Only for us, when we are miserable, a harbour from our ills is reserved in death; the gods, as he draws them, are everlasting, not in their nature, but in their unhappiness. Far better than the "Battle of the Gods" are the passages which show us divinity as something undefiled and truly great, with no admixture; for instance, to take a passage which has been worked out by many before us, the lines on Poseidon:

> Tall mountains and wild woods, from height to height,
> The city and the vessels by the main . . .
> Rocked to the immortal feet that, hurrying, bare
> Poseidon in his wrath . . .
> . . . the light wheels along the sea-plain rolled;
> From cave and lair the creatures of the deep
> Flocked to sport round him, and the crystal heap
> Of waters in wild joy disparting know
> Their lord, and as the fleet pair onward sweep . . .[21]

Thus too the lawgiver of the Jews, no common man,[22] when he had duly conceived the power of the Deity, showed it forth as duly. At the very beginning of his Laws, "God said," he writes—What? "Let there be light, and there was light, let there be earth, and there was earth." Perhaps I shall not seem wearisome, comrade, if I quote to you one other passage from the poet, this time on a human theme, that you may learn how he accustoms his readers to enter with him into majesties which are more than human. Gloom and impenetrable night suddenly cover the battle of the Greeks before him: then Ajax, in his helplessness, says:—

> Zeus, sire, do thou the veil of darkness rend,
> And make clear daylight, that our eyes may see:
> Then in the light e'en slay us—.[23]

Here is the very truth of the passion of Ajax: he does not pray to live—such a petition were too humble for the hero—but when in impracticable darkness he could dispose his valour to no good purpose, chafing that he stands idle for the battle, he prays for light at the speediest, sure of finding therein at the worst a burial worthy of his valour, even if Zeus be arrayed against him. Truly the spirit of Homer goes along with every struggle, in full and carrying gale; he feels the very thing himself, he rages;—

> Not fire in densest mountain glade,
> Nor spear-armed Ares e'er raged dreadfuller:
> Foam started from his lips, . . .[24]

Yet he shows throughout the *Odyssey* (for there are many reasons why we must look closely into passages from that poem also), that, when a great genius begins to decline, the love of story-telling is a mark of its old age. It is clear from many other indications that this work was the second; but more particularly from the fact that he introduces throughout the *Odyssey* remnants of the sufferings before Ilium, as so many additional episodes of the Trojan war; aye, and renders to its heroes fresh lamentations and words of pity, as though awarded in some far distant time. Yes, the *Odyssey* is nothing but an epilogue of the *Iliad*:—

> There the brave Aias and Achilleus lie;
> Patroclus there, whose wisdom matched the gods on high;
> There too Antilochus my son . . .[25]

From the same cause, I think, writing the *Iliad* in the heyday of his spirit, he made the whole structure dramatic and combative; that of the *Odyssey* is in the main narrative, which is the special mark of age. So it is that in the *Odyssey* one might liken Homer to a setting sun; the intensity is gone, but there remains the greatness. Here the tone of those great lays of Ilium is no longer maintained—the passages on one level of sublimity with no sinking anywhere, the same stream of passion poured upon passion, the readiness of turn, the closeness to life, the throng of images all drawn from the truth: as when Ocean retires into himself, and is left lonely around his proper bounds, only the ebbings of his greatness are left to our view, and a wandering among the shallows of the fabulous and the incredible. While I say this, I have not forgotten the storms in the *Odyssey*, nor the story of the Cyclops,[26] nor certain other passages; I am describing an old age, but the old age of Homer. Still in all these, as they follow one another, fable prevails over action. I entered upon this digression, as I said, in order to show how very easily great genius, when the prime is passed, is turned aside to trifling: there are the stories of the wine-skin, of the companions turned by Circe to swine[27] (whom Zoilus[28] called "porkers in tears"), of Zeus fed by doves like a young bird,[29] of Ulysses ten days without food on the wreck,[30] there are the incredible details of the slaying of the Suitors.[31] What can we call these but in very truth "dreams of Zeus? A second reason why the incidents of the *Odyssey* also should be discussed is this; that you may recognize how the decline of passion in great writers and poets passes away into character-drawing: the sketches of the life in the household of Ulysses much resemble a comedy of character.

X

I will now ask you to consider with me whether we may possibly arrive at anything further, which has power to make our writings sublime. Since with all things are associated certain elements, constituents which are essentially inherent in the substance of each, one factor of sublimity must necessarily be the power of choosing the most vital of the included elements, and of making these, by mutual superposition, form as it were a single body. On one side the hearer is attracted by the choice of ideas, on another by the accumulation of those which have been chosen. Thus Sappho, in all cases, takes the emotions incident to the frenzy of love from the attendant symptoms and from actual truth. But wherein does she show her great excellence? In her power of first selecting and then closely combining those which are conspicuous and intense:—

Blest as the immortal gods is he
The youth whose eyes may look on thee,
Whose ears thy tongue's sweet melody
 May still devour.

Thou smilest too!—sweet smile, whose charm
Has struck my soul with wild alarm,
And, when I see thee, bids disarm
 Each vital power.

Speechless I gaze: the flame within
Runs swift o'er all my quivering skin;
My eyeballs swim; with dizzy din
 My brain reels round;
And cold drops fall; and tremblings frail
Seize every limb; and grassy pale
I grow; and then—together fail
 Both sight and sound.[32]

Do you not marvel how she seeks to gather soul and body into one, hearing and tongue, eyes and complexion; all dispersed and strangers before: now, by a series of contradictions, she is cold at once and burns, is irrational, is sensible (for she is either in terror or at the point of death),[33] so that it may not appear to be a single passion which is upon her, but an assemblage of passions? All the symptoms are found severally in lovers; to the choice of those which are conspicuous, and to their concentration into one, is due the pre-eminent merit here. So it is, I think, with the Poet and his storms; he picks out the grimmest of the attendant circumstances. The author of the *Arimaspeia* thinks these lines terrible:—

Here too is mighty marvel for our thought:
Mid seas men dwell, on water, far from land:
Wretches they are, for sorry toil is theirs;
Eyes on the stars, heart on the deep they fix.
Oft to the gods, I ween, their hands are raised,
Their inward parts in evil case upheaved.[34]

Any one, I think, will see that there is more embroidery than terror in it all. Now for Homer; take one instance out of many:—

As when a wave swoln by the wild wind's
 blore[35]
Down from the clouds upon a ship doth light,
And the whole hulk with scattering foam is
 white,
And through the sails all tattered and forlorn
Roars the fell blast: the seamen with affright
Shake, out from death a hand-breadth they
 are borne.[36]

Aratus has attempted to transfer this very notion:—

Tiny the plank which thrusts grim death
 away.[37]

Only the result is petty and smooth, not terrible. Moreover, he makes the danger limited, by the words "the plank thrusts death away": and so it does! Again our Poet does not limit the terror to one occurrence; he gives us the picture of men meeting destruction continually, wellnigh in every wave. Yet again, by forcing together prepositions naturally inconsistent, and compelling them to combine (I refer to the words "out from death"), he has so strained the verse as to match the trouble which fell upon them; has so pressed it together as to give the very presentment of that trouble; has stamped, I had almost said, upon the language the form and features of the peril: "out from death a hand-breadth they are borne." Just so Archilochus[38] in describing the shipwreck, and Demosthenes, when the news of Elateia comes: "For it was evening," he says.[39] They chose the expressions of real eminence, looking only to merit (if one may use the word), took them out clean, and placed them one upon another, introducing between them nothing trivial, or undignified, or low. For such things mar the whole effect, much as, in building, massive blocks, intended to cohere and hold together in one, are spoilt by stop-gaps and rubble.

XI

Closely connected with the excellencies which I have named is that called Amplification; in which, when the facts and issues admit of several fresh beginnings and fresh halting-places, in periodic arrangement, great phrases come rolling upon others which have gone before, in a continuously ascending order. Whether this be done by way of enlarging upon commonplace topics, or of exaggeration, or of intensifying facts or reasoning, or of handling deeds done or suffering endured (for there are numberless varieties of amplification), the orator must in any case know that none of these can possibly stand by itself without sublimity as a perfect structure. The only exceptions are where pity or depreciation are required; in all other processes of amplification, take away the sublime, and you will take soul out of body; they are effective no longer, and become nerveless and hollow unless braced by passages of sublimity. But, for clearness' sake, I must shortly lay down wherein the difference lies between my present precepts, and what I said above (there I spoke of a sketch embracing the principal ideas and arranging them into one); and the broad difference between Amplification and Sublimity.

XII

I am not satisfied with the definition given by the technical writers. Amplification is, they say, language which invests the subject with greatness. Of course this definition may serve in common for sublimity, and passion, and tropes, since they, too, invest the language with greatness of a particular kind. To me it seems that they differ from one another in this, that Sublimity lies in intensity, Amplification also in multitude; consequently sublimity often exists in a single idea, amplification necessarily implies quantity and abundance. Amplification is—to define it in outline—an accumulation of all the parts and topics inherent in a subject, strengthening the fabric of the argument by insistence; and differs in this from rhetorical proof that the latter seeks to demonstrate the point required. . . .

[*Here about six pages have been lost.*]

In richest abundance, like a very sea, Plato often pours into an open expanse of grandeur. Hence it is, I think, that, if we look to style, the Orator, appealing more strongly to passions, has a large element of fire and of spirit aglow; Plato, calm in his stately and dignified magnificence, I will not say, is cold, but is not so intense. It is on these and no other points, as it seems to me, dear Terentianus (that is, if we as Greeks are allowed to form an opinion), that Cicero and Demosthenes differ in their grand passages. Demosthenes' strength is in sheer height of sublimity, that of Cicero in its diffusion. Our countryman, because he burns and ravages all in his violence, swift, strong, terrible, may be compared to a lightning flash or a thunderbolt, Cicero, like a spreading conflagration, ranges and rolls over the whole field; the fire which burns is within him, plentiful and constant, distributed at his will now in one part, now in another, and fed with fuel in relays. These are points on which you can best judge: certainly the moment for the sublimity and tension of Demosthenes is where accumulated invective and strong passion are in play, and generally where the hearer is to be hard struck: the moment for diffusion is where he is to be flooded with detail, as it is always appropriate in enlargement upon commonplaces, in perorations and digressions, and in all passages written for the style and for display, in scientific and physical exposition, and in several other branches of literature. . . .

Notes

1. From the lost *Oreithyia* of Aeschylus (p. 281, Nauck).

2. A Sicilian teacher of rhetoric (about 480–370 B.C.), a speaker in the dialogue of Plato which bears his name.

3. Philosopher, historian, and rhetorician, a pupil of Aristotle (died about 328 B.C.).

4. Cleitarchus, historian of Alexander the Great.

5. Sophocles had written "he puffs no longer on puny pipes, but with fierce bellows and no mouthpiece (to modify sound)." The lines, in their original form, are quoted by Cicero of Pompey (ad *Att.* ii. 16, 2).

6. Amphicrates: an Athenian rhetorician and sophist, who died at the court of Tigranes, about 70 B.C. Hegesias: a rhetorician, native of Magnesia, probably of the third century B.C., who wrote on Alexander the Great. Matris of Thebes: author of an encomium on Hercules; mentioned by Diodorus Siculus, and therefore not later than the Augustan period.

7. A proverb, doubtless familiar in a metrical form.

8. Of Gadara, or Rhodes: a rhetorician, and instructor of the Emperor Tiberius (*Suetonius*, Tib. 57).

9. A Sicilian historian (about 352–256 B.C.), severely criticized by Polybius.

10. A great, but somewhat tedious, Athenian orator (436–338 B.C.), The *Panegyricus* was originally composed for the Olympic festival of 380.

11. Zeus gives in the genitive Dios, &c.

12. Athenian soldier and historian (about 444–354 B.C.).

13. *Iliad* i. 225.

14. Plato, *Laws*, vi. p. 778D.

15. Herodotus, v. 18.

16. *Odyssey* xi, 315 and 317.

17. *Odyssey* xi. 543.

18. *Iliad* v. 770.

19. *Iliad* xxi. 388, perhaps mixed up with v. 750.

20. *Iliad* xx. 61–5.

21. These lines are taken from *Iliad* xiii, 18–29, with omissions, and with the exception of the second, which is read in xx. 60.

22. Moses, in Genesis 1:3.

23. *Iliad* xvii, 645.

24. *Iliad* xv. 605.

25. *Odyssey* iii. 109.

26. Odyssey Book ix.

27. *Odyssey* x. 17 &c.; 229, &c.

28. A grammarian of uncertain date, probably of the fourth century B.C. He was a bitter and malignant critic, and earned the name of "Scourge of Homer."

29. *Odyssey* xii. 62.

30. *Odyssey* xii, end.

31. *Odyssey* xxii.

32. This ode of Sappho, the great woman-poet of Lesbos (about 600 B.C.), written in the metre which bears her name, has only been preserved to us in this treatise. It has been partly translated by Catullus into Latin, in the same metre. The version in the text is by J. Herman Merivale (1833).

33. The text of the original appears to be faulty here.

34. Aristeas, an early poet of Proconnesus, wrote an epic on the Arimaspi (a one-eyed people of the far North, mentioned by Herodotus, who says, iv. 26, that their name was formed by the Greeks from two Scythian words, "Arima," one, and "spous," an eye).

35. blore, i.e., blast.

36. *Iliad* xv. 624.

37. Aratus, living about 270 B.C., the author of two Greek astronomical poems, one of which was translated by Cicero. The words quoted by St. Paul, Acts xvii, 28, occur in Aratus, and also in another poet.

38. Archilochus of Paros (about 800 B.C.), the reputed inventor of the iambic metre. Two extant fragments describe shipwreck.

39. The passage which follows (*De Cor.* 169) is perhaps the most famous in Demosthenes, and should be read in its context.

CHAPTER TWO

The Middle Ages

The term *Middle Ages* (and its Latinate adjective *medieval*, which also means "middle ages") has been used only since the seventeenth century to designate the centuries roughly between the fall of Rome and the discovery of the New World. During these centuries, modern Europe assumed its present shape. It was transformed from a predominantly Latinate and religious culture to a vernacular and secular culture, as the centers of cultural activity gradually shifted from the monasteries to the cities and courts of European princes. The term *Middle Ages*, however, fosters the impression that this was a transitional and "dark age" during which little, if anything, happened, a period sandwiched in between the glories of ancient Greece and Rome and the enlightened Renaissance, when classical values resurfaced. But such beliefs obscure the importance of this period to the development of modern European literature and culture. The accomplishments of the greatest medieval poets—Dante, Boccaccio, Chaucer—attest to the vitality of the period's poetry. But the contributions of medieval thought to problems of language and poetics, its "literary criticism," are less well understood. One might argue that by tackling the question of how texts mean, the magisterial syntheses of Christian philosophy and doctrine by early medieval fathers of the Church such as Augustine, John Cassian, and Origen and by twelfth-century philosophers such as Aquinas, Hugh of St. Victor, and Bernard of Clairvaux, although they are rarely read except by the specialist, helped to shape the modern practice of literary criticism. In this respect, their accomplishments rivalled those of the period's great poets.

The dominance of Latin as the language of learning during the Middle Ages creates an impression of homogeneity during this period that is belied by the cultural diversity that contributed to the transformations taking place. One of the great tasks of medieval literary criticism was to articulate a poetics of the vernacular, to make languages like French, Italian, and English respectable vehicles for poetry. This was partly accomplished through the poetry produced by vernacular poets like Chrétien de Troyes (in French), Dante (in Italian), and Chaucer (in English). But it also required the vigorous advocacy of critics like Dante and Boccaccio. So entrenched was the prejudice against the vernacular languages that as late as 1589 a Renaissance writer like George Puttenham felt compelled to defend English as an appropriate language for poetry.

The richness and diversity of medieval criticism, however, has not always been appreciated. In the history of criticism, the period of over a thousand years between Longinus and Sidney has frequently been bypassed altogether because it is seen as having produced no great literary criticism. Literary critics often see the Middle Ages as devoid of speculation on literary problems, many anthologies of criticism even failing to include the Middle Ages in their surveys. What few treatises and apologies exist, critics argue, are not consistent with the texts produced by the great medieval poets. Poetic practice and critical practice did not coincide. The piety that dominated the period is assumed to be incompatible with what one commentator has called "the true aims and content of poetry" (Haller, 1973). But such arguments presume that what the twentieth century approves of as "the aims and true content of poetry" was the same for the twelfth or fourteenth centuries. It requires poetry be seen as a universal and unchanging essence rather than as a set of conventions imbued with the historical and cultural beliefs of the times producing them.

In the last decade, the rehabilitation of allegory in the wake of poststructuralist notions of language has prompted a rethinking of medieval literary theory, suggesting that the Middle Ages, in fact, has much to say about the meaning of meaning: about how texts mean, how meaning relates to the author's intention, how meaning is controlled and disseminated, and how we understand texts that are culturally or linguistically alien to us. Medieval writers, it turns out, wrote sophisticated discussions about *hermeneutics,* the art or science of interpretation, that address these very problems. But since hermeneutics was originally confined to the interpretation of sacred scriptures and only later was expanded to include other cultural texts, including literary texts, many such treatises deal only with religious texts, primarily the Bible, and are, therefore, often dismissed as marginal, outside the concerns of literary criticism. In the interpretation of sacred scriptures, however, the outlines of a medieval literary theory begin to emerge, along with the views medieval writers held about the ways in which texts represent the world—in particular, how medieval writers read the Book of God's Word (the Bible) as a divinely authorized reflection of the Book of God's Works (nature).

Hugh of St. Victor in his treatise on reading, *Didascalicon,* describes the basis of all medieval literary theory as precisely the reflection, or imitation, of God's Works in his Words.

> . . . this whole visible world is a book written by the finger of God, that is, created by divine power; and individual creatures are as figures therein, not

> devised by human will but instituted by divine authority to show forth the wisdom of the invisible things of God. But just as some illiterate man looks at the figures but does not recognize the letters: just so the foolish natural man, who does not perceive the things of God, sees outwardly in these visible creatures the appearances but does not inwardly understand the reason. But he who is spiritual and can judge of all things, while he considers outwardly the beauty of the work inwardly conceives how marvelous is the wisdom of the Creator (*Didascalicon*).

Hugh's analogy between nature and a book written by the finger of God encapsulates the medieval theory of reading. Because he is an "author" who is fully in control of his intentions, God has woven meaning into the text (literally the fabric) of the world. The "spiritual man," unlike the "foolish natural man," learns to read correctly those meanings. There is only one true and correct meaning in any text, including the text of nature, but that meaning is always hidden and must be uncovered by those who know the "key." Thus, the act of reading leads not to the discovery of a pale imitation of nature, but to a discovery of the ways in which reading a text and reading the world are parallel activities. The text is not a representation of the world; rather the world is ordered and functions like a text.

In spite of the popularity of this analogy, however, medieval writers, particularly religious writers, viewed poetry with an alarm and distrust inherited from the Neoplatonic ideals of early Christianity. Just as Plato excludes the poets from his Republic because they are liars who present as true an "imitation and shadowy image" of reality, so Augustine, in his *Confessions*, denounces "poetic fables" and their false representation of the world:

> Again, if I should ask which of these would be forgotten with greater inconvenience to our life, to read and write or those poetic fables, who does not discern the answer of every man who has not completely lost his mind? Therefore, as a boy I sinned when I preferred those inane tales to more useful studies, or rather when I hated the one and loved the other (*Confessions* I. xiii).

Whether they attacked or defended poetry and "fables," most classical and medieval writers shared basic assumptions about the truth of language's representation of the world and the uselessness of false representations.

An example of the medieval abhorence of "false" representation occurs in the fifteenth-century French poet Christine de Pisan's defense of women against the depredations of *The Romance of the Rose*. Begun in the late thirteenth century by Guillaume de Lorris and completed around 1305 by Jean de Meun, *The Romance of the Rose* is an elaborate courtly allegory that depicts a young man falling in love with a rose (woman), then planning and carrying out his seduction with the help and advice of several allegorical guides. Christine attacks the poem as "utter idleness," a useless work and a waste of time not only because it is morally promiscuous but because it is linguistically promiscuous as well. Jean de Meun in particular "spoke superfluously," in "derision of holy predication." Christine's words echo every linguistic conservative's fear of the excesses of language—poetic language in particular—cut loose from proper signification. Sexual excess and linguistic excess—that is, sexual and social intercourse that is not tied to meaningful (re)production—become one and the same thing for many medieval writers. Because Jean de Meun's language does not behave properly, Christine argues, his representation of women in the poem, his misogyny, is a false representation. If Christine's concern with "speaking right" strikes many modern readers as an insufficient reason to condemn a poem as highly valued as *The Romance of the Rose*, Christine's critique of Jean de Meun's representation of women is, nonetheless, thoroughly grounded in medieval theories of representation and signification.

This distrust of and antipathy toward poetry and other "false" representation derives from medieval theories about language, which held that language proceeds directly from God and is a divinely ordained reflection of the Logos (i.e., the Word as God—"In the beginning was the Word and the Word was with God and the Word was God"). In its original form, language was a transparent sign of truth because language accurately portrayed the world. Even after Babel, when God confused languages, a language retained vestigial and imperfect resemblances to the world. Signs (words) were conventional, but they did "imitate"—represent—nature. Before the seventeenth century, the function of language in the West was not seen as a binary and arbitrary connection between words and things, but a ternary one linking words, the content a word indicated, and the preordained similitudes (resemblances) that linked words to what they designated. In Augustinian linguistics, for instance, the relationship between word and thing is guaranteed by the Incarnation, a perfect melding of divine meaning and material representation. In glossing the biblical text "and the Word was made Flesh," for example, Augustine defines a characteristic Christian perception of the correspondence between language and thought.

> It is as when we speak. In order that what we are thinking may reach the mind of the listener through the fleshly ears, that which we have in mind is expressed in words and is called speech. But our thought is not transformed into sounds: it remains entire in itself and assumes the form of words by means of which it may reach the ears without any deterioration in itself. In the same way the Word of God was made flesh without change that He might dwell among us (*On Christian Doctrine*).

Language, for Augustine, does not exist in and of itself; it exists only to convey a meaning that preexists it. If language always transparently signifies a fixed Truth, then it must be both serious and single-minded and it cannot exist independent of the Truth it must, by definition, convey. This assumption lies behind Augustine's denunciation of "poetic fables" and his belief that language can never be reflexive or playful as poetry is but must be transparent, must efface itself in pointing to similitudes that in turn suggest an eternal and unchanging Truth.

But, try as they might to assert the "truth" of language and the uselessness of poetic fictions, medieval writers simply could not ignore the fact that the master text of Christianity, the Bible, uses both poetry and fables frequently. Thus Petrarch, in a letter to his brother Gherardo, a Carthusian monk, defends his own poetry, predictably, by explicitly demonstrating that it is harmonious with piety and religion.

> I judge, from what I know of your religious fervor, that you will feel a sort of repugnance toward the poem which I enclose in this letter, deeming it quite out of harmony with all your professions, and in direct opposition to your whole mode of thinking and living . . . you will object and say, ". . . the fact remains that the sweetness of your poetry is inconsistent with the severity of my life." Ah but you are mistaken my brother. Why even the Old Testament fathers made use of poetry, both heroic and other kinds.

Most medieval writers after Augustine accepted his theory of language and at least acted as if words could represent the world truthfully, but they were constantly confronting a serious contradiction: the basis of language's ability to represent was God, but God himself was unrepresentable. Augustine recognizes, but passes over this contradiction.

> Have we spoken or announced anything worthy of God? Rather I feel that I have done nothing but wish to speak: if I have spoken I have not said what I wished to say. Whence do I know this except because God is ineffable? (*On Christian Doctrine*).

Clearly, if God is unrepresentable then the fiction of language's perfect representation of Truth is called into question. The two great "books" of medieval culture, the Bible and the book of nature show God only indirectly, "through a glass darkly," or negatively, as Aquinas suggests, by showing us what he cannot be.

Poetry, it follows, could not so easily be denounced as lies since it is one way of indirectly representing God. Macrobius, for example, asserts that while "Philosophy does not discountenance all stories nor does it accept all," fictions may yet justify themselves as a means to a greater end.

> Fables—the very word acknowledges their falsity—serve two purposes: either merely to gratify the ear or to encourage the reader to good works. . . . This whole category of fables that promise only to gratify the ear a philosophic treatise avoids and relegates to children's nurseries (*Commentary on the Dream of Scipio* I. ii).

On the other hand, the fable promising good works, proper to a philosophic treatise, is not an end in itself, but a form of instruction. The distinction is pertinent because poetry that merely "gratifies the ear"—that is, language that is self-reflexive, that does not represent the truth—is dismissed as "useless," a trifle for children. Only if there is some kernel of meaning, some truth to be found within it, can poetry be described as useful and hence to be tolerated. The meaning, and not the language, should attract the reader; the beauty of language is a superfluous, and even dangerous, indulgence because it is promiscuous. Poetry can only be countenanced as a "pious fraud" by which to "entice the wanton minds of men" to discover "delicate Minerva secretly lurking beneath the mask of pleasure" (Richard du Bury, *Philobiblon*).

Within such a context poetry must be defended, as Boccaccio does, as a language that "proceeds from the bosom of God." The heroic songs and psalms of the Old Testament, as well as Christ's parables in the New Testament, function as metaphoric mediations, creating similitudes between this world and the next ("The kingdom of heaven is like . . ."). Such similitudes are necessary, in Augustine's words, so that "by means of corporal and temporal things we may comprehend the eternal and spiritual" (*On Christian Doctrine*). But the one-to-one correspondence between word and thing suggested by Augustinian linguistics cannot, by itself, account for the presence of similitudes, nor can it tell a reader how to find meaning in the obscurities and difficulties of the biblical text, Augustine's primary task in *On Christian Doctrine*. Such a task requires an explanation of metaphoric language, or what Augustine calls "figurative signs." If the discovery of a word's truth is the discovery of similitude rather than correspondence, then the word remains secondary even when the referent is not immediately related to the Divine Logos. When it seems otherwise, it is because a "figurative sign" or a metaphor has insinuated itself into the relationship between the word and the Logos. Thus, the Latin word *bos* ("ox") might refer to a large draft animal with horns. But it might also refer metaphorically to one of the evangelists. The interpretive task is multileveled, so that at least one other level of signification is inserted into the process: the words yield up a sense that, by virtue of its difference from the words, points to a third, "true" meaning. This is the medieval concept of allegory. Accordingly, allegory (or allegoresis as the process is sometimes called), a trope, or figure of speech, in classical oratory, functioned in the Middle Ages primarily as a critical tool to explain and control the dissemination of meanings in sacred scriptures and only later became a literary genre in itself. In the *Institutio oratoria*, Quintillian defines allegory as meaning "one thing in the words, another in the sense." This definition, the basis of all rhetorical definitions of allegory in the Middle Ages and Renaissance, hierarchically orders meaning and significance, promising that the text will yield up stable meanings if the initiated reader applies the proper "code" to translate the message. Allegorical texts, in this way, produce stable meanings and mirror unequivocal truths. Allegory inserts another level of meaning into the signifying process, but it never seriously questions the existence of a kernel, a truth, at the origin of that process.

While the concern of medieval hermeneutics with fixing the meaning of the Bible might strike the modern reader as simply an abstract philosophic argument or, at times, a set of trivial debates over whether in the Song of Songs the Bride's navel stood for the seven acts of mercy, the seventh day of rest, or the seven gifts of the Holy Spirit, it was very much a part of the

Church's strategy for consolidating and maintaining its position of authority in medieval Europe. In the fourth century, Augustine's powerful synthesis of doctrine and hermeneutics provided an intellectual foundation for a relatively new Church anxious to consolidate its spiritual and temporal authority against a host of heresies threatening to splinter Christianity into competing sects. By the twelfth century, the Church faced a new set of political and social threats to its hegemony: changes in the economy, a growing reliance on money, urbanization, the movement of centers of learning from the monasteries to the cities, and the reintroduction of classical learning, particularly Aristotelianism, which presented a threat to the Neoplatonism of early Christianity. One intellectual response to these changes was Scholasticism: a method of discovering the truth of "texts" by means of a dialectic based on Aristotelian logic.

The twelfth-century habit of schematizing created distinctions among the kinds of meaning other than literal that could be found beneath the letter of biblical texts; this process came to be known as biblical exegesis. The most widespread "system" was the system of fourfold allegory, which created four levels of interpretation for biblical texts. Although this system was first articulated in the fourth century by John Cassian, by the twelfth century it had become standardized. Scriptural texts were to be read on the historical or literal level first; then on the allegorical or spiritual, the tropological or moral, and the anagogical levels. In the New Testament story of Christ's raising of Lazarus from the dead, for example, the medieval exegete would recognize, first, that on the historical or literal level of the story is the record of an event that actually took place. Christ raised Lazarus from the dead at the request of Lazarus' sister. On the allegorical or spiritual level, the story prefigures Christ's death, descent into hell, and resurrection. On the tropological or moral level, it represents the sacrament of Penance, whereby the individual soul is raised from the death of sin. Lazarus signifies a man in mortal sin who repents, confesses, and receives absolution. Finally, on the anagogical level, the raising of Lazarus prefigures the resurrection of the body after the last judgment. In this way a whole complex of ideas about sin, repentance, death, rewards, and punishments is held together as one vast system of meaning. But the system of exegesis never achieved the level of finality suggested by this example. It remained fluid in spite of all attempts to fix individual meanings. Most medieval writers insisted that the four levels were not necessarily present in each and every passage of the Bible and not every writer conceived of the four levels in exactly the same way. Hugh of St. Victor, for instance, uses only three levels in his exegesis of biblical texts. All medieval writers insisted upon the presence of "deeper" significances in every passage, but they did not always agree on what that meaning was. At least theoretically, the meanings of every passage in the Bible could be systematized and hierarchalized, and at least theoretically, the plurality of meanings could be contained within a single interpretation. The practice often proved otherwise. Particularly after the twelfth century, new and often creative glosses of Biblical texts proliferated.

Although the twelfth century saw the rise of vernacular literature throughout Europe, it is only in the fourteenth century that serious consideration was given to literature written in languages other than Latin. The cultural implications of the movement from Latin to vernacular literature were enormous, since all sorts of texts, including the Bible, became available to a much wider public. By the fourteenth century, the system of allegorical interpretation came increasingly to be applied to other nonbiblical texts, the most notable example being Dante's appropriation of the system to explain and justify his method in *The Divine Comedy*. But Boccaccio, in his own defense of poetry, refers to the system as well when he remarks that in poetry "sense is revealed from under the veil of fiction."

What was once religious orthodoxy became critical practice. Vernacular poets like Dante and Boccaccio turned to contemporary religious exegesis for both a vocabulary and a justification for their poetics primarily because there was virtually nothing else available to them. All vernacular writers of the period at least give lip service to the belief that poetry functions as a veil or cover of some sort that simultaneously withholds and reveals moral truths. Even Chaucer's erstwhile rhetorician and literary theorist in *The Canterbury Tales*, the Nun's Priest, writes,

> . . . al that written is
> To oure doctrine it is ywrit, ywiss,
> Taketh the fruit, and let the chaf be stille (VII. 4631–4633).

To assume, however, that the medieval vernacular poet merely imitated uncritically received doctrines and practices of religious authorities is to greatly underestimate the accomplishments of both medieval poetry and criticism, reducing them to religious propaganda. The debate over the value of an exegetical method such as that outlined in Dante's "Letter to Can Grande" occupied medieval scholars for nearly two decades in the 1960s and 1970s (see Bethurum), but recent critics have put the debate into perspective by arguing that poets, far from merely imitating or "copying" material received from the religious tradition, used their poetry to interpret and to shape received authorities. That is, they conceived of allegoresis not as a uniform, standardizing code to be mechanically applied to literary works, but as a rich and heterogeneous source of inspiration that occasionally even acted as an insurrectionary force within medieval culture.

FURTHER READING

Chenu, M. D. *Nature, Man, and Society in the Twelfth Century: Essays in New Theological Perspectives in the Latin West.* Jerome Taylor and Lester K. Little, eds. and trans. Chicago: University of Chicago Press, 1968.

Colish, Marcia. *The Mirror of Language: A Study in the Medieval Theory of Language.* Lincoln: University of Nebraska Press, 1968.

Curtius, Ernst Robert. *European Literature and the Latin Middle Ages*. Willard R. Trask, trans. Princeton, N.J.: Princeton University Press, 1953.

Finke, Laurie A., and Martin B. Shichtman, eds. *Medieval Texts and Contemporary Readers*. Ithaca, N.Y.: Cornell University Press, 1987.

Gellrich, Jesse. *The Idea of the Book in the Middle Ages: Language Theory, Mythology, and Fiction*. Ithaca, N.Y.: Cornell University Press, 1985.

Haller, Robert S., trans. and ed. *Literary Criticism of Dante Alighieri*. Lincoln: University of Nebraska Press, 1973.

Kelly, Joan. "Early Feminist Theory and the Querelle des Femmes," in *Women, History, and Theory*. Chicago: University of Chicago Press, 1985.

Kermode, Frank. *The Genesis of Secrecy: On the Interpretation of Narrative*. Cambridge, Mass.: Harvard University Press, 1979.

Miller, Robert P. "Medieval Literary Theory." In R. P. Miller, ed., *Chaucer: Sources and Background*. New York: Oxford University Press, 1977, pp. 38–89.

Osgood, Charles, trans. *Boccaccio on Poetry*. New York: Liberal Arts Press, 1956.

Quilligan, Maureen. *The Language of Allegory: Defining the Genre*. Ithaca, N.Y.: Cornell University Press, 1980.

Robertson, D. W. *A Preface to Chaucer: Studies in Medieval Perspective*. Princeton, N.J.: Princeton University Press, 1962.

Smalley, Beryl. *The Study of the Bible in the Middle Ages*. Notre Dame, Ind.: University of Notre Dame Press, 1964.

Todorov, Tzvetan. *Theories of the Symbol*. Catherine Porter, trans. Ithaca, N.Y.: Cornell University Press, 1982.

Vance, Eugene. *From Topic to Tale: Logic and Narrativity in the Middle Ages*. Minneapolis: University of Minnesota Press, 1987.

Ward, Charles F. *The Epistles on the Romance of the Rose and Other Documents in the Debate*. Chicago: University of Chicago Press, 1911.

Augustine of Hippo A.D. 354–430

In *On Christian Doctrine* Augustine deals with problems that may strike us as surprisingly literary: the nature of signification, the problem of how readers make meaning of texts, and of how interpretations are validated. Augustine of Hippo wrote *On Christian Doctrine* at a time when Christianity, in its earliest stages, needed a means of authorizing interpretations of its central text, the Bible, to avert the danger of division into a series of sects without a unifying system. Augustine forged, out of a hodgepodge of sometimes unconnected, and even contradictory, stories, a body of doctrine.

Augustine, bishop of Hippo and doctor of the Church, was born in a North African Roman province in A.D. 354. He was not baptized, although his mother, Saint Monica, was devoutly Christian. What we know of his life comes primarily from his own *Confessions,* which were written around 400. He studied in the rhetoric schools of Carthage, where he was attracted to Manichaeism, a Gnostic sect notable for its extreme metaphysical and moral dualism, and its belief that evil is as powerful as good. The two greatest intellectual influences upon Augustine before his conversion to Christianity were Manichaeism and Greek philosophy, especially the works of the Neoplatonists. From 376 to 383 Augustine taught in Carthage and then went to Rome, where he set up as a teacher of rhetoric. In 384 he was appointed municipal professor of rhetoric by the city of Milan, where he came under the influence of the bishop of Milan, Ambrose. In 387 Augustine was baptized by Ambrose. He resigned his rhetoric position and returned to North Africa, where in 391 he was ordained a priest and in 395 became bishop of Hippo.

Augustine was an extremely prolific writer (his bibliography numbers about 1,000 works). Many of those works became standard authorities in the Middle Ages, cited by virtually every later medieval author. Besides his *Confessions* and his magisterial philosophy of history, *City of God* (413–26), he wrote several commentaries on the Bible (most notably on Genesis and the Psalms) and polemics against prominent heresies of the time, including the Manichaeans. He died on August 28, 430.

On Christian Doctrine was begun around 396, at about the time Augustine was made bishop of Hippo, and was completed in 427, just three years before his death. In it Augustine undertakes to explain "certain precepts" for treating the Scriptures to those students of the Bible "able and willing to learn" (Prologue). It is, then, an exercise in practical literary criticism, a treatise on how to interpret the Bible correctly. Although Augustine's principle critical touchstone, "Scripture teaches us nothing but charity, nor condemns anything except cupidity" (88), may strike us as more theological than literary, the effort of formulating this ethic involved him in some quite modern literary problems. Augustine never forgot his training in rhetoric, although it became increasingly problematic for him after his conversion. In *On Christian Doctrine,* he is not so much concerned with *what* the Bible means as with *how* it means. The obscurities and ambiguities of the biblical text had to be accounted for and interpretations stabilized to meet the threat of division posed by various heretical sects. Augustine begins with a theory of signification that distinguishes between signs (which point to something other than themselves) and things (which do not). He further distinguishes between natural signs (which signify without intending to, as smoke, for instance, signifies fire) and conventional (man-made) signs. Words (conventional signs), properly interpreted, are reliable guides to faith because their reference is assured by the Logos, by God. But proper interpretation of biblical obscurities requires more than simply a knowledge of signs. It also involves the reader in problems of translation, rhetorical and grammatical obscurities, and the interpretation of figurative signs (words that can point to more than one referent). Augustine finally admits that no system of interpretation can ever totally fix the meaning of the text. He demonstrates the efficacy of his hermeneutics through powerful readings of many difficult passages, but in the end recognizes that meaning is a process that the reader, guided by the principle of charity, must construct.

from ON CHRISTIAN DOCTRINE

from *BOOK TWO*

I

1. Just as I began, when I was writing about things by warning that no one should consider them except as they are, without reference to what they signify beyond themselves, now when I am discussing signs I wish it understood that no one should consider them for what they are but rather for their value as signs which signify something else. A sign is a thing which causes us to think of something beyond the impression the thing itself makes upon the senses. Thus if we see a track, we think of the animal that made the track; if we see smoke, we know that there is a fire which causes it; if we hear the voice of a living being, we attend to the emotion it expresses; and when a trumpet sounds, a soldier should know whether it is necessary to advance or to retreat, or whether the battle demands some other response.

2. Among signs, some are natural and others are conventional. Those are natural which, without any desire or intention of signifying, make us aware of something beyond themselves, like smoke which signifies fire. It does this without any will to signify, for even when smoke appears alone, observation and memory of experience with things bring a recognition of an underlying fire. The track of a passing animal belongs to this class, and the face of one who is wrathful or sad signifies his emotion even when he does not wish to show that he is wrathful or sad, just as other emotions are signified by the expression even when we do not deliberately set out to show them. But it is not proposed here to discuss signs of this type. Since the class formed a division of my subject, I could not disregard it completely, and this notice of it will suffice.

II

3. Conventional signs are those which living creatures show to one another for the purpose of conveying, in so far as they are able, the motion of their spirits or something which they have sensed or understood. Nor is there any other reason for signifying, or for giving signs, except for bringing forth and transferring to another mind the action of the mind in the person who makes the sign. We propose to consider and to discuss this class of signs in so far as men are concerned with it, for even signs given by God and contained in the Holy Scriptures are of this type also, since they were presented to us by the men who wrote them. Animals also have signs which they use among themselves, by means of which they indicate their appetites. For a cock who finds food makes a sign with his voice to the hen so that she runs to him.

And the dove calls his mate with a cry or is called by her in turn, and there are many similar examples which may be adduced. Whether these signs, or the expression or cry of a man in pain, express the motion of the spirit without intention of signifying or are truly shown as signs is not in question here and does not pertain to our discussion, and we remove this division of the subject from this work as superfluous.

III

4. Among the signs by means of which men express their meanings to one another, some pertain to the sense of sight, more to the sense of hearing, and very few to the other senses. For when we nod, we give a sign only to the sight of the person whom we wish by that sign to make a participant in our will. Some signify many things through the motions of their hands, and actors give signs to those who understand with the motions of all their members as if narrating things to their eyes. And banners and military standards visibly indicate the will of the captains. And all of these things are like so many visible words. More signs, as I have said, pertain to the ears, and most of these consist of words. But the trumpet, the flute, and the harp make sounds which are not only pleasing but also significant, although as compared with the number of verbal signs the number of signs of this kind are few. Few words have come to be predominant among men for signifying whatever the mind conceives if they wish to communicate it to anyone. However, Our Lord gave a sign with the odor of the ointment with which His feet were anointed;[1] and the taste of the sacrament of His body and blood signified what He wished;[2] and when the woman was healed by touching the hem of His garment,[3] something was signified. Nevertheless, a multitude of innumerable signs by means of which men express their thoughts is made up of words. And I could express the meaning of all signs of the type here touched upon in words, but I would not be able at all to make the meanings of words clear by these signs.

IV

5. But because vibrations in the air soon pass away and remain no longer than they sound, signs of words have been constructed by means of letters. Thus words are shown to the eyes, not in themselves but through certain signs which stand for them. These signs could not be common to all peoples because of the sin of human dissension which arises when one people seizes the leadership for itself. A sign of this pride is that tower erected in the heavens where impious men deserved that not only their minds but also their voices should be dissonant.[4]

V

6. Thus it happened that even the Sacred Scripture, by which so many maladies of the human will are cured, was set forth in one language, but so that it could be spread conveniently through all the world it was scattered far and wide in the various languages of translators that it might be known for the salvation of peoples who desired to find in it nothing more than the thoughts and desires of those who wrote it and through these the will of God, according to which we believe those writers spoke.

VI

7. But many and varied obscurities and ambiguities deceive those who read casually, understanding one thing instead of another; indeed, in certain places they do not find

anything to interpret erroneously, so obscurely are certain sayings covered with a most dense mist. I do not doubt that this situation was provided by God to conquer pride by work and to combat disdain in our minds, to which those things which are easily discovered seem frequently to become worthless. For example, it may be said that there are holy and perfect men with whose lives and customs as an exemplar the Church of Christ is able to destroy all sorts of superstitions in those who come to it and to incorporate them into itself, men of good faith, true servants of God, who, putting aside the burden of the world, come to the holy laver of baptism and, ascending thence, conceive through the Holy Spirit and produce the fruit of a twofold love of God and their neighbor. But why is it, I ask, that if anyone says this he delights his hearers less than if he had said the same thing in expounding that place in the Canticle of Canticles where it is said of the Church, as she is being praised as a beautiful woman, "Thy teeth are as flocks of sheep, that are shorn, which come up from the washing, all with twins, and there is none barren among them"?[5] Does one learn anything else besides that which he learns when he hears the same thought expressed in plain words without this similitude? Nevertheless, in a strange way, I contemplate the saints more pleasantly when I envisage them as the teeth of the Church cutting off men from their errors and transferring them to her body after their hardness has been softened as if by being bitten and chewed. I recognize them most pleasantly as shorn sheep having put aside the burdens of the world like so much fleece, and as ascending from the washing, which is baptism, all to create twins, which are the two precepts of love, and I see no one of them sterile of this holy fruit.

8. But why it seems sweeter to me than if no such similitude were offered in the divine books, since the thing perceived is the same, is difficult to say and is a problem for another discussion. For the present, however, no one doubts that things are perceived more readily through similitudes and that what is sought with difficulty is discovered with more pleasure. Those who do not find what they seek directly stated labor in hunger; those who do not seek because they have what they wish at once frequently become indolent in disdain. In either of these situations indifference is an evil. Thus the Holy Spirit has magnificently and wholesomely modulated the Holy Scriptures so that the more open places may deter a disdainful attitude. Hardly anything may be found in these obscure places which is not found plainly said elsewhere. . . .

X

15. There are two reasons why things written are not understood: they are obscured either by unknown or by ambiguous signs. For signs are either literal or figurative. They are called literal when they are used to designate those things on account of which they were instituted; thus we say *bos* [ox] when we mean an animal of a herd because all men using the Latin language call it by that name just as we do. Figurative signs occur when that thing which we designate by a literal sign is used to signify something else; thus we say "ox" and by that syllable understand the animal which is ordinarily designated by that word, but again by that animal we understand an evangelist, as is signified in the Scripture, according to the interpretation of the Apostle, when it says, "Thou shalt not muzzle the ox that treadeth out the corn."[6]

XI

16. Against unknown literal signs the sovereign remedy is a knowledge of languages. And Latin-speaking men, whom we have

here undertaken to instruct, need two others for a knowledge of the Divine Scriptures, Hebrew and Greek, so that they may turn back to earlier exemplars if the infinite variety of Latin translations gives rise to any doubts. Again, in these books we frequently find untranslated Hebrew words, like *amen, alleluia, racha, hosanna,* and so on, of which some, although they could be translated, have been preserved from antiquity on account of their holier authority, like *amen* and *alleluia;* others, like the other two mentioned above, are said not to be translatable into another language. For there are some words in some languages which cannot be translated into other languages. And this is especially true of interjections which signify the motion of the spirit rather than any part of a rational concept. And these two belong to this class: *racha* is said to be an expression of indignation and *hosanna* an expression of delight. But a knowledge of these two languages is not necessary for these few things, which are easy to know and to discover, but, as we have said, it is necessary on account of the variety of translations. We can enumerate those who have translated the Scriptures from Hebrew into Greek, but those who have translated them into Latin are innumerable. In the early times of the faith when anyone found a Greek codex, and he thought that he had some facility in both languages, he attempted to translate it.

XII

17. This situation would rather help than impede understanding if readers would only avoid negligence. For an inspection of various translations frequently makes obscure passages clear. For example, one translator renders a passage in the prophet Isaias: "Despise not the family of thy seed"; but another says: "Despise not thy own flesh."[7] Either confirms the other, for one may be explained by means of the other. Thus the "flesh" may be taken literally, so that one may find himself admonished that no one should despise his own body, and the "family of seed" may be taken figuratively so that it is understood to mean "Christians" born spiritually from the seed of the Word which produced us. But a collation of the translations makes it probable that the meaning is a literal precept that we should not despise those of our own blood, since when we compare "family of the seed" with "flesh," blood relations come especially to mind. Whence, I think, comes the statement of the Apostle, who said, "If, by any means, I may provoke to emulation them who are my flesh, and may save some of them,"[8] that is, so that, emulating those who had believed, they also might believe. He calls the Jews his "flesh" because of blood relationship. Again, a text of the prophet Isaias reads: "If you will not believe, you shall not understand," and in another translation: "If you will not believe, you shall not continue."[9] Which of these is to be followed is uncertain unless the text is read in the original language. But both of them nevertheless contain something of great value for the discerning reader. It is difficult for translators to become so disparate that they do not show a similarity in one area of meaning. Thus, although understanding lies in the sight of the Eternal, faith nourishes as children are nourished with milk in the cradles of temporal things. Now "we walk by faith and not by sight."[10] Unless we walk by faith, we shall not be able to come to that sight which does not fail but continues through a cleansed understanding uniting us with Truth. On account of this principle one said, "If you will not believe, you shall not continue," and the other said, "If you will not believe, you shall not understand."

18. Many translators are deceived by ambi-

guity in the original language which they do not understand, so that they transfer the meaning to something completely alien to the writer's intention. Thus some codices have "their feet are sharp to shed blood," for the word *oxús* in Greek means both "sharp" and "swift." But he sees the meaning who translates "their feet swift to shed blood";[11] the other, drawn in another direction by an ambiguous sign, erred. And such translations are not obscure; they are false, and when this is the situation the codices are to be emended rather than interpreted. The same situation arises when some, because *móschos* in Greek means "calf," do not know that *moscheúmata* means "transplantings," and have translated it "calves." This error appears in so many texts that one hardly finds anything else written, although the sense is very clear and is supported by the succeeding words. For the expression "bastard slips shall not take deep root"[12] makes better sense than to speak of "calves," which walk on the earth and do not take root in it. The rest of the context, moreover, supports this translation.

XIII

19. Since the meaning which many interpreters, according to their ability and judgment, seek to convey is not apparent unless we consult the language being translated, and since many translators err from the sense of the original authors unless they are very learned, we must either seek a knowledge of those languages from which Scripture is translated into Latin or we must consult the translations of those who translate word for word, not because they suffice but because by means of them we may test the truth or falsity of those who have sought to translate meanings as well as words. For often not only single words but whole locutions are translated because they cannot be expressed in Latin if one wishes to adhere to the ancient and customary idiom of the Latin language. These unidiomatic expressions do not impede the understanding, but they offend those who take more delight in things when the signs for them are governed by a certain correctness. For what is called solecism is nothing else than an arrangement of words which does not conform to the law followed by those who have spoken before us with some authority. Whether one says "among men" by saying *inter homines* or by saying *inter hominibus* does not affect the person considering things rather than signs. In the same way, what else is a barbarism except a word pronounced with letters or sounds different from those which those who spoke Latin before us were accustomed to use? Whether *ignoscere* [to forgive] is spoken with a long or short third syllable makes little difference to a man asking God to forgive his sins, in whatever way he can pronounce the word. What then is integrity of expression except the preservation of the customs of others, confirmed by the authority of ancient speakers?

20. The more men are offended by these things, the weaker they are. And they are weaker in that they wish to seem learned, not in the knowledge of things, by which we are truly instructed, but in the knowledge of signs, in which it is very difficult not to be proud. For even the knowledge of things frequently raises the neck unless it is disciplined by the yoke of the Lord. It does not impede the understanding of the reader to find written: "What is the land in which these dwell upon it, whether it is good or evil, and what are the cities in which these dwell in them?"[13] I consider this to be the idiom of an alien tongue rather than the expression of a more profound meaning. There is also the expression that we cannot now take away from the chant of the people: "but upon him shall my sanctification flourish."[14] Nothing

is detracted from the meaning, although the more learned hearer may wish to correct it so that the *florebit* is spoken instead of *floriet*, and nothing impedes the correction but the custom of the chanters. These things may easily be disregarded if one does not wish to pay attention to that which does not detract from a sound understanding. Then there is the expression of the Apostle: "the foolishness of God is wiser than men; and the weakness of God is stronger than men."[15] If anyone wished to keep the Greek idiom and say "The foolishness of God is wiser of men, and the weakness of God is stronger of men," the labor of the vigilant reader would lead him to the true meaning, but a somewhat slower reader might either not understand it or misunderstand it. For not only is such a phrase incorrect in the Latin language, it also obscures the truth in ambiguity. Thus the foolishness of men or the weakness of men might seem wiser or stronger than God's. And even *sapientius est nominibus* [wiser than men] does not lack ambiguity, although it contains no solecism. Without the illumination of the idea being conveyed it is not clear whether *hominibus* is ablative or dative. It would be better to say *sapientius est quam homines* and *fortius est quam homines*, which express the ideas "wiser than men" and "stronger than men" without any possible ambiguity.

XIV

21. We shall speak later of ambiguous signs; now we are discussing unknown signs, of which there are two forms, in so far as they apply to words. For either an unknown word or an unknown expression may impede the reader. If these come from foreign languages we must consult one who speaks those languages, or learn them ourselves if we have leisure and ability, or make a comparison of various translations. If we do not know certain words or expressions in our own language, we become familiar with them by reading and hearing them. Nothing is better commended to the memory than those types of words and expressions which we do not know, so that when one more learned appears who may be questioned, or when a passage appears in reading where the preceding or following context makes their meaning clear, we may easily with the aid of the memory refer to them and learn them. Such is the force of habit even in learning that those who are nourished and educated in the Holy Scriptures wonder more at other expressions and think them poorer Latin than those used in the Scriptures, even though these do not appear in the writings of the Latin authors. In this matter of learning a comparison and weighing of various translations is also useful. But falsity should be rejected. For those who desire to know the Sacred Scriptures should exercise their ingenuity principally that texts not emended should give way to those emended, at least among those which come from one source of translation.

XV

22. Among these translations the *Itala* is to be preferred, for it adheres to the words and is at the same time perspicacious regarding meaning.[16] And in emending Latin translations, Greek translations are to be consulted, of which the Septuagint carries most authority in so far as the Old Testament is concerned. In all the more learned churches it is now said that this translation was so inspired by the Holy Spirit that many men spoke as if with the mouth of one. It is said and attested by many of not unworthy faith that, although the translators were separated in various cells while they worked, nothing was to be found in any version that was not found in the same words and with the same

order of words in all of the others. Who would compare any other authority with this, or, much less, prefer another? But even if they conferred and arrived at a single opinion on the basis of common judgment and consent, it is not right or proper for any man, no matter how learned, to seek to emend the consensus of so many older and more learned men. Therefore, even though something is found in Hebrew versions different from what they have set down, I think we should cede to the divine dispensation by which they worked to the end that the books which the Jewish nation refused to transmit to other peoples, either out of envy or for religious reasons, might be revealed so early, by the authority and power of King Ptolemy, to the nations which in the future were to believe in Our Lord. It may be that the Holy Spirit judged that they should translate in a manner befitting the people whom they addressed and that they should speak as if with one voice. Yet, as I have said before, a comparison with those translators who adhered most closely to the words of the original is not without use in explaining their meaning. Latin translations of the Old Testament, as I set out to say, are to be emended on the authority of the Greeks, and especially on the authority of those who, although there were seventy, are said to have spoken as if with one voice. Moreover, if the books of the New Testament are confusing in the variety of their Latin translations, they should certainly give place to the Greek versions, especially to those which are found among more learned and diligent Churches.

XVI

23. Among figurative signs, if any impede the reader, he should study them partly with reference to a knowledge of languages and partly with reference to a knowledge of things. Thus the pool of Siloe, where the Lord commanded the man whose eyes he had anointed with clay made of spittle to wash, has some value as a similitude and undoubtedly suggests some mystery [e.g., baptism], but the name Siloe in an unknown language, if it had not been interpreted for us by the Evangelist,[17] would have concealed a very important perception. In the same way many Hebrew names which are not explained by the authors of those books undoubtedly have considerable importance in clarifying the enigmas of the Scriptures, if someone were able to interpret them. Some men, expert in that language, have rendered no small benefit to posterity by having explained all of those words taken from the Scriptures without reference to place and have translated Adam, Eve, Abraham, Moses, and names of places like Jerusalem, Sion, Jericho, Sinai, Lebanon, Jordan, or whatever other names in that language are unknown to us; and since these things have been made known, many figurative expressions in the Scriptures have become clear.

24. An ignorance of things makes figurative expressions obscure when we are ignorant of the natures of animals, or stones, or plants, or other things which are often used in the Scriptures for purposes of constructing similitudes. Thus the well-known fact that a serpent exposes its whole body in order to protect its head from those attacking it illustrates the sense of the Lord's admonition that we be wise like serpents.[18] That is, for the sake of our head, which is Christ, we should offer our bodies to persecutors lest the Christian faith be in a manner killed in us, and in an effort to save our bodies we deny God. It is also said that the serpent, having forced its way through narrow openings, sheds its skin and renews its vigor. How well this conforms to our imitation of the wisdom of the serpent when we shed the "old man," as the Apostle says, and put on the "new";[19] and we shed

it in narrow places, for the Lord directs us, "Enter ye in at the narrow gate."[20] Just as a knowledge of the nature of serpents illuminates the many similitudes which Scripture frequently makes with that animal, an ignorance of many other animals which are also used for comparisons is a great impediment to understanding. The same thing is true of stones, or of herbs or of other things that take root. For a knowledge of the carbuncle which shines in the darkness also illuminates may obscure places in books where it is used for similitudes, and an ignorance of beryl or of diamonds frequently closes the doors of understanding. In the same way it is not easy to grasp that the twig of olive which the dove brought when it returned to the ark[21] signifies perpetual peace unless we know that the soft surface of oil is not readily corrupted by an alien liquid and that the olive tree is perennially in leaf. Moreover, there are many who because of an ignorance of hyssop—being unaware of its power either to purify the lungs or, as it is said, to penetrate its roots to the rocks in spite of the fact that it is a small and humble plant—are not able at all to understand why it is said, "Thou shalt sprinkle me with hyssop, and I shall be cleansed."[22]

25. An ignorance of numbers also causes many things expressed figuratively and mystically in the Scriptures to be misunderstood. Certainly, a gifted and frank person cannot avoid wondering about the significance of the fact that Moses, Elias, and the Lord Himself all fasted for forty days.[23] The knot, as it were, of this figurative action cannot be untied without a knowledge and consideration of this number. For it contains four tens, to indicate the knowledge of all things involved in times. The day and the year both run their courses in a quaternion: the day in hours of morning, noon, evening, and night; the year in the months of spring, summer, autumn, and winter. But while we live in these times we should abstain and fast from temporal delight because of the eternity in which we wish to live, for in the very courses of time the doctrine in accordance with which we condemn temporal things and desire the eternal is suggested. Again, the number ten signifies a knowledge of the Creator and the creature; for the trinity is the Creator and the septenary indicates the creature by reason of his life and body. For with reference to life there are three, whence we should love God with all our hearts, with all our souls, and with all our minds; and with reference to the body there are very obviously four elements of which it is made. Thus when the number ten is suggested to us with reference to time, or, that is, when it is multiplied by four, we are admonished to live chastely and continently without temporal delight, or, that is, to fast for forty days. This is the Law, represented in the person of Moses; the Prophets, whose person is acted by Elias; and the Lord Himself all admonish. He, as if bearing the testimony of the Law and the Prophets, appeared between these two on the Mount to His three watching and amazed disciples.[24] Then it may be asked how the number fifty, which is very sacred in our religion because of the feast of Pentecost, proceeds from forty; or how, when it is tripled because of the three times—before the Law, during the Law, and under Grace—or because of the name of the Father, the Son, and the Holy Spirit, and the number of the most high Trinity is added, it refers to the mystery of the most pure Church and arrives at the number of the hundred and fifty-three fish which the net caught "on the right side" after the Resurrection of the Lord.[25] In the same way many other numbers and patterns of numbers are placed by way of similitudes in the sacred books as secrets which are often closed to readers because of ignorance of numbers.

26. An ignorance of some things concern-

ing music also halts and impedes the reader. A certain writer has well explained some figures of things on the basis of the difference between the psaltery and the harp. It may be inquired not unreasonably among the learned whether the psalterium of ten strings follows any musical law which demands strings of that number, or, if no such law exists, whether that number should be considered more sacred either on account of the Ten Commandments (if a question is raised about that number, we can apply it to the Creator and the creature), or whether it is used because of the explanation of the number ten we have used above. And the number mentioned in the Gospel in connection with the building of the temple, forty-six years,[26] somehow has a musical sound, and, when it is applied to the structure of Our Lord's body, it causes some heretics to confess the Son of God to be clothed not falsely but with a true and human body.[27] And we find both number and music given an honorable position in many places in the Sacred Scriptures. . . .

from *BOOK THREE*

I

1. A man fearing God diligently seeks His will in the Holy Scriptures. And lest he should love controversy, he is made gentle in piety. He is prepared with a knowledge of languages lest he be impeded by unknown words and locutions. He is also prepared with an acquaintance with certain necessary things lest he be unaware of their force and nature when they are used for purposes of similitudes. He is assisted by the accuracy of texts which expert diligence in emendation has procured. Thus instructed, he may turn his attention to the investigation and solution of the ambiguities of the Scriptures. That he may not be deceived by ambiguous signs we shall offer some instruction. It may be, however, that he will deride those ways which we wish to point out as puerile either because of the greatness of his acumen or the brilliance of his illumination. Nevertheless, as I set out to say, he who has a mind to be instructed by us, in so far as he may be instructed by us, will know that the ambiguity of Scripture arises either from words used literally or figuratively, both of which types we have discussed in the second book.

II

2. When words used literally cause ambiguity in Scripture, we must first determine whether we have mispunctuated or misconstrued [with reference to Latin, "mispronounced"][28] them. When investigation reveals an uncertainty as to how a locution should be pointed or construed, the rule of faith should be consulted as it is found in the more open places of the Scriptures and in the authority of the Church. We explained this sufficiently when we spoke of things in the first book. But if both meanings, or all of them, in the event that there are several, remain ambiguous after the faith has been consulted, then it is necessary to examine the context of the preceding and following parts surrounding the ambiguous place, so that we may determine which of the meanings among those which suggest themselves it would allow to be consistent.

3. Now, consider some examples. This heretical punctuation does not allow that the Word is God: "In the beginning was the Word,

and the Word was with God, and God was," so that the sense of what follows is different: "This Word was in the beginning with God." But this is to be refuted according to the rule of faith which teaches us the equality of the Trinity, so that we say: "And the Word was God. The same was in the beginning with God."[29]

4. Neither aspect of the ambiguity is contrary to the faith, so that the context must be used as a guide where the Apostle says: "What I shall do I know not. But I am straitened between two: having a desire to be dissolved and to be with Christ, (for this is) a thing by far the better. But to abide still in the flesh, is needful for you."[30] It is uncertain whether this should be punctuated so as to read "having a desire for two things," or so as to read "straitened between two," so that the passage continues, "having a desire to be dissolved and to be with Christ." But since there follows "for this is a thing by far the better," he clearly says that he has a desire for the better thing, as if he were urged by two things, for one of which he has a desire and for the other of which there is a necessity. That is, he has a desire to be with Christ, but a necessity to remain in the flesh. This ambiguity is decided by one word showing a logical connection, "for" [and, in English, the expression "this is"]. The translators who have omitted this particle have been inclined toward the opinion that he was not only urged by two things but that he also desired two things. Therefore the passage should be punctuated as follows: "What I shall do I know not. But I am straitened between two." This is followed by the phrase "having a desire to be dissolved and to be with Christ." And as if answering the question why he should have more of a desire for this, he says, "for this is a thing by far the better." Why is he urged by two things? Because there is a necessity that he remain, whence he adds, "But to abide still in the flesh, is needful for you" [i.e., "on your account"].

5. But when neither the principles of the faith nor the context is sufficient to explain an ambiguity, there is nothing to prevent our punctuating the passage in any of the various possible ways. For example, the following passage occurs in Corinthians: "Having therefore these promises, dearly beloved, let us cleanse ourselves from all defilement of the flesh and of the spirit, perfecting sanctification in the fear of God. Understand us. We have corrupted no man."[31] There is a question as to whether we should interpret the text to mean "let us cleanse ourselves from all defilement of the flesh and of the spirit," according to the lesson of "that she may be holy both in body and spirit,"[32] or, on the other hand, whether we should say "let us cleanse ourselves of all defilement of the flesh," and continue "and perfecting sanctification of the spirit in the fear of God; understand us." Distinctions in interpretation of this kind may be made at the will of the reader.

III

6. The principles that I have described for the treatment of ambiguous pointing serve also for ambiguous constructions. For these also, unless the reader is weakened by too much carelessness, are to be corrected according to the rule of faith, or according to the context established by the preceding and following passages; or, if neither of these is sufficient for correction and some doubt still remains, whatever blameless interpretation the reader wishes may be used. If faith did not remove the possibility on the grounds that we do not believe that God will accuse His elect nor that Christ will condemn them, we might read as a question, "Who shall ac-

cuse against the elect of God," and add as an answer, "God that justifieth."[33] And we might ask again, "Who is he that shall condemn?" and answer, "Christ Jesus that died."[34] But since it is utter madness to believe this, the passages should be interpreted so that the first element is a question, the second a rhetorical question. The ancients distinguished a question from a rhetorical question by saying that there are many possible answers to a question, but that a rhetorical question may be answered only negatively or affirmatively. The verses should be pronounced so that after the question, "Who shall accuse against the elect of God?," that which follows is inflected as a question, "God that justifieth?," with an implied negative reply. And in the same way we ask, "Who is he that shall condemn?," and add as a rhetorical question implying once more a negative reply, "Christ Jesus that died, yea that is risen also again; who is at the right hand of God, who also maketh intercession for us?" But in that place where the Apostle says, "What then shall we say? That the Gentiles, who followed not after justice, have attained to justice,"[35] the context does not make sense unless the first part, "What then shall we say?," is expressed as a question and the last part, "That the Gentiles, who followed not after justice, have attained to justice," is added as a reply. However, in inflecting the question of Nathanael, "Can anything of good come from Nazareth?,"[36] I do not see how we can determine whether the whole should be stated affirmatively with interrogatory inflection only in the phrase "from Nazareth" or whether the interrogatory inflection should be applied to the whole expression. Faith impedes neither of these interpretations.

7. There is sometimes an ambiguity in the doubtful sound of syllables, and this matter also pertains to pronunciation. For example, in the passage "My bone [Latin, *os*] is not hidden from thee, which thou hast made in secret,"[37] it is not clear to the reader whether *os* should be pronounced with a short or with a long vowel. If he makes it short, the plural form is *ossa* [bones], if he makes it long, the plural form is *ora* [mouths]. But such things may be decided by looking at the passage in an earlier language. The Greek text in this instance reads not *stóma* [mouth], but *ostéon* [bone]. As in this example, the vulgar form of speech is sometimes clearer than the more correct literary form. Indeed, I should prefer to say "My bone [*ossum meum*] is not hidden from thee," rather than to express it in a less clear but more correct Latin. But sometimes the significance of a doubtful syllable is made clear by the use of a word in the same context having a related meaning, as in this passage: "Of which I foretell [i.e., warn] you as I have foretold to you, that they who do such things shall not obtain the kingdom of God."[38] If he had simply said "of which I foretell" [Latin, *praedico*], without adding "as I have foretold" [Latin, *sicut praedixi*], it would not have been clear without reference to earlier texts whether the middle syllable of *praedico* should be long [meaning "I foretell"] or short [meaning "I announce"]. But it is evident since he said "I have foretold" [*praedixi*] and not "I have announced" [*praedicavi*] that it should be pronounced long.

IV

8. Not only ambiguities of this type but also those which do not depend on punctuation or pronunciation should be treated in the same way. Consider the passage from Thessalonians: "Therefore we were comforted, brethren, in you."[39] It is doubtful whether "brethren" [Latin, *fratres*] should be read as a vocative [as in the translation above] or

as an accusative [so as to read "on this account we have comforted the brethren among you"]. But in Greek the two cases do not have the same form, and when the Greek text is examined, the word is found to be vocative. But if the translator had been willing to say, *Propterea, consolationem habuimus, fratres, in vobis* [instead of *consolati sumus*], the translation would have been less literal but also less doubtful as to meaning. Or, if he had added *nostri* [i.e., "our brethren"], almost no one would have doubted that *fratres* should be construed as a vocative. But an addition of this kind would be more dangerous. It has been done in that passage from Corinthians where the Apostle says, "I die daily . . . by your glory, brethren, which I have in Christ Jesus."[40] A certain translator says, "I die daily, I protest, by your glory," because a mood of adjuration is evident in the Greek text without any ambiguous sound. Only rarely and with difficulty may we find ambiguities in the literal meanings of the scriptural vocabulary which may not be solved either by examining the context which reveals the author's intention, or by comparing translations, or by consulting a text in an earlier language.

V

9. But the ambiguities of figurative words, which are now to be treated, require no little care and industry. For at the outset you must be very careful lest you take figurative expressions literally. What the Apostle says pertains to this problem: "For the letter killeth, but the spirit quickeneth."[41] That is, when that which is said figuratively is taken as though it were literal, it is understood carnally. Nor can anything more appropriately be called the death of the soul[42] than that condition in which the thing which distinguishes us from beasts, which is the understanding, is subjected to the flesh in the pursuit of the letter. He who follows the letter takes figurative expressions as though they were literal and does not refer the things signified to anything else. For example, if he hears of the Sabbath, he thinks only of one day out of the seven that are repeated in a continuous cycle; and if he hears of Sacrifice, his thoughts do not go beyond the customary victims of the flocks and fruits of the earth. There is a miserable servitude of the spirit in this habit of taking signs for things, so that one is not able to raise the eye of the mind above things that are corporal and created to drink in eternal light. . . .

IX

13. He is a slave to a sign who uses or worships a significant thing without knowing what it signifies. But he who uses or venerates a useful sign divinely instituted whose signifying force he understands does not venerate what he sees and what passes away but rather that to which all such things are to be referred. Such a man is spiritual and free, even during that time of servitude in which it is not yet opportune to reveal to carnal minds those signs under whose yoke they are to be tamed. The Patriarchs and the Prophets were spiritual men of this kind, as were also all those among the people of Israel through whom the Holy Spirit ministered to us the help and solace of the Scriptures. In these times, since there has been revealed to us a clear sign of our liberty in the Resurrection of the Lord, we are not heavily burdened with the use of certain signs whose meaning we understand; rather we have a few in place of many, which the teaching of the Lord and the Apostles has transmitted to us, and these are very easy to perform, very sublime in

implication, and most upright in observance. Such are the sacrament of Baptism and the celebration of the Body and Blood of the Lord. When anyone instructed perceives one of these, he knows what it refers to so that he venerates it not in carnal servitude but in spiritual freedom. But just as it is a servile infirmity to follow the letter and to take signs for the things that they signify, in the same way it is an evil of wandering error to interpret signs in a useless way. However, he who does not know what a sign means, but does know that it is a sign, is not in servitude. Thus it is better to be burdened by unknown but useful signs than to interpret signs in a useless way so that one is led from the yoke of servitude only to thrust his neck into the snares of error.

X

14. To this warning that we must beware not to take figurative or transferred expressions as though they were literal, a further warning must be added lest we wish to take literal expressions as though they were figurative. Therefore a method of determining whether a locution is literal or figurative must be established. And generally this method consists in this: that whatever appears in the divine Word that does not literally pertain to virtuous behavior or to the truth of faith you must take to be figurative. Virtuous behavior pertains to the love of God and of one's neighbor; the truth of faith pertains to a knowledge of God and of one's neighbor. For the hope of everyone lies in his own conscience in so far as he knows himself to be becoming more proficient in the love of God and of his neighbor. Concerning these things we have spoken in the first book.

15. But since humanity is inclined to estimate sins, not on the basis of the importance of the passion involved in them, but rather on the basis of their own customs, so that they consider a man to be culpable in accordance with the way men are reprimanded and condemned ordinarily in their own place and time, and, at the same time, consider them to be virtuous and praiseworthy in so far as the customs of those among whom they live would so incline them, it so happens that if Scripture commends something despised by the customs of the listeners, or condemns what those customs do not condemn, they take the Scriptural locution as figurative if they accept it as an authority. But Scripture teaches nothing but charity, nor condemns anything except cupidity, and in this way shapes the minds of men. Again, if the minds of men are subject to some erroneous opinion, they think that whatever Scripture says contrary to that opinion is figurative. But it asserts nothing except the catholic faith as it pertains to things past, future, and present. It is a history of past things, an announcement of future things, and an explanation of present things; but all these things are of value in nourishing and supporting charity and in conquering and extirpating cupidity.

16. I call "charity" the motion of the soul toward the enjoyment of God for His own sake, and the enjoyment of one's self and of one's neighbor for the sake of God; but "cupidity" is a motion of the soul toward the enjoyment of one's self, one's neighbor, or any corporal thing for the sake of something other than God. That which uncontrolled cupidity does to corrupt the soul and its body is called a "vice"; what it does in such a way that someone else is harmed is called a "crime."[43] And these are the two classes of all sins, but vices occur first. When vices have emptied the soul and led it to a kind of extreme hunger, it leaps into crimes by means of which impediments to the vices may be removed or the vices themselves sus-

tained. On the other hand, what charity does to the charitable person is called "utility"; what it does to benefit one's neighbor is called "beneficence." And here utility occurs first, for no one may benefit another with that which he does not have himself. The more the reign of cupidity is destroyed, the more charity is increased. . . .

Notes

1. John 12. 3–8. For the "odor of the ointment, see 3. 12. 18.
2. Matt. 26. 28; Luke 22. 19–20.
3. Matt. 9. 20–22.
4. Cf. Gen. 11. 1–9.
5. Cant. [Song of Sol.] 4. 2.
6. Deut. 25. 4. For the apostolic interpretation, see 1 Cor. 9. 9; 1 Tim. 5. 18.
7. Isa. 58. 7 (Ancient and Vulgate versions).
8. Rom. 11. 14.
9. Isa. 7. 9 (Ancient and Vulgate versions).
10. 2 Cor. 5. 7.
11. Rom. 3. 15 (from Prov. 1. 16).
12. Wisd. 4. 3.
13. Cf. Num. 13. 20.
14. Ps. 131. 18 [132. 18], with *floriet* instead of *efflorebit* as in the Vulgate.
15. 1 Cor. 1. 25.
16. For a discussion of St. Augustine's preferences among Scriptural texts, see Maurice Pontet, *L'exégèse de Saint Augustin prédicateur* (Paris, 1946), pp. 220 ff.
17. John. 9. 7.
18. Matt. 10. 16.
19. Eph. 4. 22–25; Col. 3. 9–10.
20. Matt. 7. 13.
21. Gen. 8. 11.
22. Ps. 50. 9 [51. 7].
23. Exod. 24. 18; 3 Kings [1 Kings] 19. 8; Matt. 4. 2.
24. Matt. 17. 3.
25. John 21. 6–11.
26. John 2. 20.
27. Cf. 2. 28. 42. The number 46 was taken as a sign of Christ's human body, since A D A M may be thought of as 1 plus 4 plus 1 plus 40.
28. On "pronunciation" here translated in other terms, see H. I. Marrou, *Saint Augustin et la fin de la culture antique* (Paris, 1938), p. 21.
29. John 1. 1–2.
30. Phil. 1. 22–24.
31. 2 Cor. 7. 1–2.
32. 1 Cor. 7. 34.
33. Rom. 8. 33.
34. Rom. 8. 34.
35. Rom. 9. 30.
36. John 1. 46.
37. Ps. 138. 15 [139. 15].
38. Gal. 5. 21.
39. 1 Thess. 3. 7.
40. 1 Cor. 15. 31.
41. 2 Cor. 3. 6.
42. Cf. Rom. 8. 6.
43. *Flagitium* is here translated as "vice," and *facinus* is translated as "crime."

Hugh of St. Victor *ca.* 1099–1140

Hugh of St. Victor is regarded as one of the leading theologians of Europe's twelfth-century renaissance. His *Didascalicon,* a treatise on reading in the tradition of *On Christian Doctrine,* refashioned Augustinian hermeneutics for the scholastic mind of the twelfth century. As with so many medieval writers, very little is known about Hugh of St. Victor beyond what he wrote. He was probably born towards the end of the eleventh century and educated in the area of Saxony. At age 18 he was sent to Paris, where he took his monastic vows at the newly founded Augustinian abbey of St. Victor and eventually became master of its school. Besides the *Didascalicon,* he wrote commentaries on the Bible and a number of mystical works, the most famous of which is the treatise *De sacramentis Christianae fidei* ("*The Sacraments of the Christian Faith*"). He died on February 20 in either 1140 or 1141.

A book about reading, *Didascalicon* is a compendium of the medieval arts. Originally a practical guide for students who came to the school at the Abbey of St. Victor, it was widely copied throughout Europe in the succeeding centuries. It surveyed what students should read and the order, manner, and purpose that should govern their reading both in the arts and in Sacred Scripture. Because of the work's concern with integrating various areas of learning with the study of Sacred Scriptures and with the scientific pursuit of a whole complex of arts, it is characteristic of the twelfth-century renaissance, a time when the centers of education moved from rural monasteries to the cathedral schools of the emerging cities.

The passages selected deal with the proper manner of reading Sacred Scriptures. Like Augustine before him, Hugh argues that the Bible is polysemous, allowing for several different meanings. In explicating the Scriptures, Hugh would have the reader consider in order the letter, the sense, and the sentence of a text. The letter refers to such matters as grammar, style, and rhetoric. The sense refers to the most obvious meaning conveyed by the letter. The sentence is the "hidden," or deeper, level of meanings contained in the literal level. But what Augustine's system opened up to new interpretations, Hugh's pushed toward definition and closure. Where for Augustine meaning could disseminate from a sign in several, even unpredictable, directions (so long as one adhered to the principle of charity), for Hugh meanings are organized hierarchically and vertically on three levels: the historical or literal, the allegorical (which refers to the spiritual meaning that underlies the literal meaning), and the tropological (which refers to moral conduct). While this system of biblical interpretation was first articulated by John Cassian in the fourth century, it reached the height of its popularity in the twelfth century in treatises like this one. Hugh is careful to insist that all three meanings cannot be dogmatically sought in every passage of Scripture, although there are several passages in which all three meanings can be found. This system of allegorical interpretation was later adapted by vernacular writers like Dante and applied to other texts besides the Bible, supplying the basis for later medieval theories of allegory.

from DIDASCALICON

FROM BOOK FIVE

Chapter One: Concerning Properties of Sacred Scripture and the Manner of Reading It

It should not be burdensome to the eager student that we set forth the number and order and names of the Sacred Books in such a variety and number of ways, for it often happens that these least matters, when unknown, obscure one's knowledge of great and useful things. Therefore, let the student prepare himself once and for all by fixing these matters in the forefront of his mind, in certain little formulae, so to say, so that thereafter he will be able to run the course before him with free step and will not have to search out new elementary facts as he comes to individual books. With these matters set in order, we shall treat successively all the other things which will seem of value for the task before us.

Chapter Two: Concerning the Threefold Understanding

First of all, it ought to be known that Sacred Scripture has three ways of conveying meaning—namely, history, allegory, and tropology. To be sure, all things in the divine utterance must not be wrenched to an interpretation such that each of them is held to contain history, allegory, and tropology all at once. Even if a triple meaning can appropriately be assigned in many passages, nevertheless it is either difficult or impossible to see it everywhere. "On the zither and musical instruments of this type not all the parts which are handled ring out with musical sounds; only the strings do this. All the other things on the whole body of the zither are made as a frame to which may be attached, and across which may be stretched, those parts which the artist plays to produce sweetness of song." Similarly, in the divine utterances are placed certain things which are intended to be understood spiritually only, certain things that emphasize the importance of moral conduct, and certain things said according to the simple sense of history. And yet, there are some things which can suitably be expounded not only historically but allegorically and tropologically as well. Thus is it that, in a wonderful manner, all of Sacred Scripture is so suitably adjusted and arranged in all its parts through the Wisdom of God that whatever is contained in it either resounds with the sweetness of spiritual understanding in the manner of strings; or, containing utterances of mysteries set here and there in the course of a historical narrative or in the substance of a literal context, and, as it were, connecting these up into one object, it binds them together all at once as the wood does which curves under the taut strings; and, receiving their sound into itself, it reflects it more sweetly to our ears—a sound which the string alone has not yielded, but which the wood too has formed by the shape of its body. Thus also is honey more pleasing because enclosed in the comb, and whatever is sought with greater effort is also found with greater desire. It is necessary, therefore, so to handle the Sacred Scripture that we do not try to find history everywhere, nor allegory everywhere, nor tropology everywhere but rather that we assign individual things fittingly in their own places, as reason demands. Often, however, in one and the same literal context, all may be found together, as when a truth of history both hints at some mystical meaning by way of allegory, and equally shows by way of tropology how we ought to behave.

Chapter Three: That Things, Too, Have a Meaning in Sacred Scripture

It ought also to be known that in the divine utterance not only words but even things have a meaning—a way of communicating not usually found to such an extent in other writings. The philosopher knows only the significance of words, but the significance of things is far more excellent than that of words, because the latter was established by usage, but Nature dictated the former. The latter is the voice of men, the former the voice of God speaking to men. The latter, once uttered, perishes; the former, once created, subsists. The unsubstantial word is the sign of man's perceptions; the thing is a resemblance of the divine Idea. What, therefore, the sound of the mouth, which all in the same moment begins to subsist and fades away, is to the idea in the mind, that the whole extent of time is to eternity. The idea in the mind is the internal word, which is shown forth by the sound of the voice, that is, by the external word. And the divine Wisdom, which the Father has uttered out of his heart, invisible in Itself, is recognized through creatures and in them. From this is most surely gathered how profound is the understanding to be sought in the Sacred Writings, in which we come through the word to a concept, through the concept to a thing, through the thing to its idea, and through its idea arrive at Truth. Because certain less well instructed persons do not take account of this, they suppose that there is nothing subtle in these matters on which to exercise their mental abilities, and they turn their attention to the writings of philosophers precisely because, not knowing the power of Truth, they do not understand that in Scripture there is anything beyond the bare surface of the letter.

That the sacred utterances employ the meaning of things, moreover, we shall demonstrate by a particular short and clear example. The Scripture says: "Watch, because your adversary the Devil goeth about as a roaring lion." Here, if we should say that the lion stands for the Devil, we should mean by "lion" not the word but the thing. For if the two words "devil" and "lion" mean one and the same thing, the likeness of that same thing to itself is not adequate. It remains, therefore, that the word "lion" signifies the animal, but that the animal in turn designates the Devil. And all other things are to be taken after this fashion, as when we say that worm, calf, stone, serpent, and other things of this sort signify Christ. . . .

From Book Six

Chapter Eight: Concerning the Order of Exposition

Exposition includes three things: the letter, the sense, and the deeper meaning (*sententia*). The letter is found in every discourse, for the very sounds are letters; but sense and a deeper meaning are not found together in every discourse. Some discourses contain only the letter and sense, some only the letter and a deeper meaning, some all these three together. But every discourse ought to contain at least two. That discourse in which something is so clearly signified by the mere telling that nothing else is left to be supplied for its understanding contains only letter and sense. But that discourse in which the hearer can conceive nothing from the mere telling unless an exposition is added thereto contains only the letter and a deeper meaning in which, on the one hand, something is plainly signified and, on the other, something else is left which must be supplied for its understanding and which is made clear by exposition.

Chapter Nine: Concerning the Letter

Sometimes the letter is perfect, when, in order to signify what is said, nothing more than what has been set down needs to be added or taken away—as, "All wisdom is from the Lord God"; sometimes it is compressed, when something is left which must be supplied—as, "The Ancient to the lady Elect"; sometimes it is in excess, when, either in order to inculcate an idea or because of a long parenthetical remark, the same thought is repeated or another and unnecessary one is added, as Paul, at the end of his Epistle to the Romans, says: "Now to him . . ." and then, after many parenthetical remarks, concludes, "to whom is honor and glory." The other part of this passage seems to be in excess. I say "in excess," that is, not necessary for making the particular statement. Sometimes the literal text is such that unless it is stated in another form it seems to mean nothing or not to fit, as in the following: "The Lord, in heaven the throne of him," that is, "the throne of the Lord in heaven"; "the sons of men, the teeth of those are weapons and arrows," that is, "the teeth of the sons of men"; and "man, like grass the days of him," that is, "man's days": in these examples the nominative case of the noun and the genitive case of the pronoun are put for a single genitive of the noun; and there are many other things which are similar. To the letter belong construction and continuity.

Chapter Ten: Concerning the Sense

Some sense is fitting, other unfitting. Of unfitting sense, some is incredible, some impossible, some absurd, some false. You find many things of this kind in the Scriptures, like the following: "They have devoured Jacob." And the following: "Under whom they stoop that bear up the world." And the following: "My soul hath chosen hanging." And there are many others.

There are certain places in Divine Scripture in which, although there is a clear meaning to the words, there nevertheless seems to be no sense, either because of an unaccustomed manner of expression or because of some circumstance which impedes the understanding of the reader, as is the case, for example, in that passage in which Isaias says: "In that day seven women shall take hold of one man, saying: We will eat our own bread, and wear our own apparel: only let us be called by thy name. Take away our reproach." The words are plain and open. You understand well enough, "Seven women shall take hold of one man." You understand, "We will eat our own bread." You understand, "We will wear our own apparel." You understand, "Only let us be called by thy name." You understand, "Take away our reproach." But possibly you cannot understand what the sense of the whole thing together is. You do not know what the Prophet wanted to say, whether he promised good or threatened evil. For this reason it comes about that you think the passage, whose literal sense you do not see, has to be understood spiritually only. Therefore, you say that the seven women are the seven gifts of the Holy Spirit, and that these take hold of one man, that is, Christ, in whom it pleased all fulness of grace to dwell because he alone received these gifts without measure; and that he alone takes away their reproach so that they may find someone with whom to rest, because no one else alive asked for the gifts of the Holy Spirit.

See now, you have given a spiritual interpretation, and what the passage may mean to say literally you do not understand. But the Prophet could also mean something literal by these words. For, since he had spoken above about the slaughter of the transgressing people, he now adds that so great would be the destruction of that same people and to such an extent were their men to be wiped out that seven women will hardly find one husband, for only one woman usually has one man; and, while now women are usually sought after by men, then, in contrary fashion, women will seek after men; and, so that one man may not hesitate to marry seven women at the same time, since he might not have the wherewithal to feed and clothe them, they say to him: "We will eat our own bread, and wear our own apparel." It will not be necessary for you to be concerned about our well-being, "only let us be called by thy name," so that you may be called our husband and *be* our husband so that we may not be heralded as rejected women, and die sterile, without children—which at that time was a great disgrace. And that is why they say, "Take away our reproach."

You find many things of this sort in the Scriptures, and especially in the Old Testament—things said according to the idiom of that language and which, although they are clear in that tongue, seem to mean nothing in our own.

Chapter Eleven: Concerning the Deeper Meaning

The divine deeper meaning can never be absurd, never false. Although in the sense, as has been said, many things are found to disagree, the deeper meaning admits no contradiction, is always harmonious, always true. Sometimes there is a single deeper meaning for a single expression; sometimes there are several deeper meanings for a single expression; sometimes there is a single deeper meaning for several expressions; sometimes there are several deeper meanings for several expressions. "When, therefore, we read the Divine Books, in such a great multitude of true concepts elicited from a few words and fortified by the sound rule of the Catholic faith, let us prefer above all what it seems certain that the man we are reading thought. But if this is not evident, let us certainly prefer what the circumstances of the writing do not disallow and what is consonant with sound faith. But if even the circumstances of the writing cannot be explored and examined, let us at least prefer only what sound faith prescribes. For it is one thing not to see what the writer himself thought, another to stray from the rule of piety. If both these things are avoided, the harvest of the reader is a perfect one. But if both cannot be avoided, then, even though the will of the writer may be doubtful, it is not useless to have elicited a deeper meaning consonant with sound faith." "So too, if, regarding matters which are obscure and farthest removed from our comprehension, we read some of the Divine Writings and find them susceptible, in sound faith, to many different meanings, let us not plunge ourselves into headlong assertion of any one of these meanings, so that if the truth is perhaps more carefully opened up and destroys that meaning, we are overthrown; for so we should be battling not for the thought of the Divine Scriptures but for our own thought, and this in such a way that we wished the thought of the Scriptures to be identical with our own, whereas we ought rather to wish our thought identical with that of the Scriptures.". . .

Thomas Aquinas 1224–1274

The *Summa theologica* of Thomas Aquinas marks the culmination of the Scholastic philosophy of the Middle Ages, a compelling synthesis of faith and reason, of Platonism and Aristotelianism, of Hellenic and Christian thought. His expositions of Aristotle's philosophic works were instrumental in the efforts of Christian scholarship to assimilate the newly discovered works of Aristotle in the thirteenth century. Born in either 1224 or 1225 in Italy, Thomas Aquinas (known as the Angelic Doctor) entered the Dominican Order at age 22. By his early thirties he had a reputation as a brilliant scholar and teacher at the University of Paris. From 1248 to 1252, he studied with the philosopher Albertus Magnus at Cologne, and between 1269 and 1272 he taught once again at the University of Paris as professor of theology. These were his most productive years. He continued working on expositions of Aristotle and on the Bible and wrote shorter treatises on theological and philosophical subjects. A large portion of the *Summa theologica* dates from this period. By 1272 Thomas had returned to Italy to become master of theology at the University of Naples. He died in 1274 on his way to Lyons and was canonized in 1323.

Aquinas was a prolific writer but by far and away his most profound and enduring work is the *Summa theologica*, an encyclopedic compendium of all knowledge pertinent to the Christian religion conveyed "in a manner that is adaptable to the teaching of beginners" (Prologue). The method of the *Summa theologica* is the model of scholastic thinking. Every problem is presented as an open question, and opposing views are considered before Aquinas offers his own resolution. In the section below, Articles 9 and 10 of Question 1 "On Sacred Doctrine: What Kind It Is and What It Covers," Aquinas deals with the interpretation of Sacred Scripture, and in particular with its obscurities and ambiguities. Aquinas has inherited the Platonic distrust of poetry characteristic of medieval religious writers, but must nonetheless deal with the fact that Sacred Scripture uses poetic language frequently. While poetry uses metaphors "For the sake of lively description," Scripture uses them of necessity. If poetry, "the least of all sciences," promotes deception, Scripture reveals spiritual truths through corporeal metaphors. Like Augustine, he endorses the possibility that the Bible contains multiple meanings. Like Hugh, he organizes these different meanings vertically and hierarchically in a fourfold scheme: literal, spiritual, moral, and anagogical.

from SUMMA THEOLOGICA

QUESTION 1

NINTH ARTICLE

Whether Holy Scripture Should Use Metaphors?

We proceed thus to the Ninth Article:—

Objection 1. It seems that Holy Scripture should not use metaphors. For that which is proper to the lowest science seems not to befit this science, which holds the highest place of all. But to proceed by the aid of various similitudes and figures is proper to poetic, the least of all the sciences. Therefore it is not fitting that this science should make use of such similitudes.

Obj. 2. Further, this doctrine seems to be intended to make truth clear. Hence a reward is held out to those who manifest it: *They that explain me shall have life everlasting* (*Ecclus.* xxiv. 31). But by such similitudes truth is obscured. Therefore to put forward divine truths under the likeness of corporeal things does not befit this doctrine.

Obj. 3. Further, the higher creatures are, the nearer they approach to the divine likeness. If therefore any creature be taken to represent God, this representation ought chiefly to be taken from the higher creatures, and not from the lower; yet this is often found in the Scriptures.

On the contrary, It is written (*Osee* xii. 10): *I have multiplied visions, and I have used similitudes by the ministry of the prophets.* But to put forward anything by means of similitudes is to use metaphors. Therefore sacred doctrine may use metaphors.

I answer that, It is befitting Holy Scripture to put forward divine and spiritual truths by means of comparisons with material things. For God provides for everything according to the capacity of its nature. Now it is natural to man to attain to intellectual truths through sensible things, because all our knowledge originates from sense. Hence in Holy Scripture spiritual truths are fittingly taught under the likeness of material things. This is what Dionysius says: *We cannot be enlightened by the divine rays except they be hidden within the covering of many sacred veils.* It is also befitting Holy Scripture, which is proposed to all without distinction of persons—*To the wise and to the unwise I am a debtor* (*Rom.* i. 14)—that spiritual truths be expounded by means of figures taken from corporeal things, in order that thereby even the simple who are unable by themselves to grasp intellectual things may be able to understand it.

Reply Obj. 1. Poetry makes use of metaphors to produce a representation, for it is natural to man to be pleased with representations. But sacred doctrine makes use of metaphors as both necessary and useful.

Reply Obj. 2. The ray of divine revelation is not extinguished by the sensible imagery wherewith it is veiled, as Dionysius says; and its truth so far remains that it does not allow the minds of those to whom the revelation has been made, to rest in the likenesses, but raises them to the knowledge of intelligible truths; and through those to whom the revelation has been made others also may receive instruction in these matters. Hence those things that are taught metaphorically in one part of Scripture, in other parts are taught more openly. The very hiding of truth in figures is useful for the exercise of thoughtful minds, and as a defense against the ridicule of the unbelievers, according to the words, *Give not that which is holy to dogs* (*Matt.* vii. 6).

Reply Obj. 3. As Dionysius says, it is more fitting that divine truths should be expounded under the figure of less noble than of nobler bodies; and this for three reasons. First, because thereby men's minds are the better freed from error. For then it is clear that these things are not literal descriptions of divine truths, which might have been open to doubt had they been expressed under the figure of nobler bodies, especially in the case of those who could think of nothing nobler than bodies. Second, because this is more befitting the knowledge of God that we have in this life. For what He is not is clearer to us than what He is. Therefore similitudes drawn from things farthest away from God form within us a truer estimate that God is above whatsoever we may say or think of Him. Third, because thereby divine truths are the better hidden from the unworthy.

Tenth Article

Whether in Holy Scripture a Word May Have Several Senses?

We proceed thus to the Tenth Article:—

Objection 1. It seems that in Holy Scripture a word cannot have several senses, historical or literal, allegorical, tropological or moral, and anagogical. For many different senses in one text produce confusion and deception and destroy all force of argument. Hence no argument, but only fallacies, can be deduced from a multiplicity of propositions. But Holy Scripture ought to be able to state the truth without any fallacy. Therefore in it there cannot be several senses to a word.

Obj. 2. Further, Augustine says that *the Old Testament has a fourfold division: according to history, etiology, analogy, and allegory*. Now these four seem altogether different from the four divisions mentioned in the first objection. Therefore it does not seem fitting to explain the same word of Holy Scripture according to the four different senses mentioned above.

Obj. 3. Further, besides these senses, there is the parabolical, which is not one of these four.

On the contrary, Gregory says: *Holy Scripture by the manner of its speech transcends every science, because in one and the same sentence, while it describes a fact, it reveals a mystery*.

I answer that, The author of Holy Scripture is God, in Whose power it is to signify His meaning, not by words only (as man also can do), but also by things themselves. So, whereas in every other science things are signified by words, this science has the property that the things signified by the words have themselves also a signification. Therefore that first signification whereby words signify things belongs to the first sense, the historical or literal. That signification whereby things signified by words have themselves also a signification is called the spiritual sense, which is based on the literal, and presupposes it. Now this spiritual sense has a threefold division. For as the Apostle says (*Heb.* x. 1) the Old Law is a figure of the New Law, and Dionysius says *the New Law itself is a figure of future glory*. Again, in the New Law, whatever our Head has done is a type of what we ought to do. Therefore, so far as the things of the Old Law signify the things of the New Law, there is the allegorical sense; so far as the things done in Christ, or so far as the things which signify Christ, are signs of what we ought to do, there is the moral sense. But so far as they signify what relates to eternal glory, there is the anagogical sense. Since the literal sense is that which the author intends, and since the author of Holy Scripture is God, Who by one act comprehends all things by His intellect, it is not unfitting, as Augustine says, if, even according to the literal sense, one word in Holy Scripture should have several senses.

Reply Obj. 1. The multiplicity of these senses does not produce equivocation or any other kind of multiplicity, seeing that these senses are not multiplied because one word signifies several things, but because the things signified by the words can be themselves signs of other things. Thus in Holy Scripture no confusion results, for all the senses are founded on one—the literal—from which alone can any argument be drawn, and not from those intended allegorically, as Augustine says. Nevertheless, nothing of Holy Scripture perishes because of this, since nothing necessary to faith is contained under the spiritual sense which is not elsewhere put forward clearly by the Scripture in its literal sense.

Reply Obj. 2. These three—history, etiology, analogy—are grouped under the literal sense. For it is called history, as Augustine expounds, whenever anything is simply related; it is called etiology when its cause is assigned, as when Our Lord gave the reason why Moses allowed the putting away of wives—namely, because of the hardness of men's hearts (*Matt.*, xix, 8); it is called analogy whenever the truth of one text of Scripture is shown not to contradict the truth of another. Of these four, allegory alone stands for the three spiritual senses. Thus Hugh of St. Victor includes the anagogical under the allegorical sense, laying down three senses only—the historical, the allegorical and the tropological.

Reply Obj. 3. The parabolical sense is contained in the literal, for by words things are signified properly and figuratively. Nor is the figure itself, but that which is figured, the literal sense. When Scripture speaks of God's arm, the literal sense is not that God has such a member, but only what is signified by this member, namely, operative power. Hence it is plain that nothing false can ever underlie the literal sense of Holy Scripture. . . .

Dante Alighieri 1265–1321

It is not surprising that the author of the most revered work of medieval poetry, *The Divine Comedy*, should have written extensively and incisively on poetic theory. What is perhaps more surprising is the current belief that what he wrote about poetics bears little or no relationship to his practice. Born in Florence in 1265, Dante Alighieri was a pupil of the Florentine encyclopedist and statesman Brunetto Latini, who in the *Commedia* is confined to the seventh circle of Hell for his sins against nature (sodomy). Dante's involvement in Florentine politics led to his banishment in 1302; he spent the rest of his life in exile. About 1316 he joined the court of Can Grande della Scala, the imperial vicar of Verona. He dedicated the third part of his *Commedia*, the *Paradiso*, to his patron. Sometime after 1318, he moved to Ravenna, where he died in

1321. Dante's most important poetic works include *La vita nuova* ("*New Life*," 1293), a cycle of poems that celebrate his youthful love for Beatrice, who later appears as his guide in *Paradiso;* and *Commedia* (1307–21), which subsequent generations referred to as *The Divine Comedy* and which relates the journey of Dante the pilgrim from Hell, through Purgatory, to a vision of the Divine in Heaven. The *Convivio* (1304–1307), and *De vulgari eloquentia* (1304–1309) represent Dante's most important critical writing.

In his criticism, Dante confronts two problems: how to make vernacular poetry artistic and how to give it meaning. *On Eloquence in the Vernacular* examines the creative possibilities of the various vernacular languages and dialects as poetic languages. Until the end of the thirteenth century, Latin had been the reigning language of culture in the West. Beginning in the twelfth century with the troubadour poets of southern France, poets began to experiment with the vernacular languages of Europe as vehicles for poetry. Dante's *La vita nuova* is one such experiment in Italian. But Dante's choice to write his *Commedia* in Italian was controversial, Italian not being considered a language weighty enough to bear a subject of such importance. This treatise is a defense—ironically, written in Latin—of the artistry of vernacular poetry. It argues that all forms of discourse, from the humblest domestic conversations to the most exalted poetry could be derived from principles suited to common speech. In the dedicatory epistle to Can Grande della Scala, he examines the relationship between general critical principles and detailed interpretation of specific parts of a text. In justifying his poetic practice in *Paradiso,* and in the *Commedia* as a whole to his patron, Can Grande, Dante extends the four levels of allegorical interpretation articulated in earlier religious works to vernacular texts. The commentary shows, however, that specific interpretations were not expected to follow the theory of levels in any dogmatic or wooden way. The fact that the poem would be interpreted literally and on three allegorical levels (allegorical, tropological, and anagogical) does not imply that every section and symbol has to have all four meanings. This fourfold system of allegorical interpretation was not, for Dante, simply a way of showing off his artistic or interpretive cleverness; nor was it merely an after-the-fact justification of his work. Rather, it constituted a way of thinking about the world, a vision that saw the world as a Book, full of symbolic meaning to be interpreted according to God's plan.

from On Eloquence in the Vernacular

from *BOOK 1*

Chapter 1

Since I find that no one, before me, has treated systematically the doctrines of eloquence in the vernacular, and since I see that such eloquence is unquestionably needed by almost everyone, for not only men, but even women and children (to the extent that nature allows) strive for it, I shall try, with the inspiration from heaven of the Word, to enhance the speech of vernacular speakers, wishing in some manner to enlighten the discernment of those who, like the blind, roam the streets thinking for the most part that what is really behind is in front; and not only drawing upon the waters of my own natural talent to fill this large vessel, but mixing in the best of what I can extract or compile from others, in order to offer for drinking a most sweet honey-water.

But because it is required of any field of study not that it prove, but that it delineate its subject so that what it is concerned with may be known, I say (quickly coming to the point) that what I call "vernacular speech" is that which babies become accustomed to from those around them when they first begin to articulate speech; or, as it could be put more succinctly, I would claim as vernacular speech that which we learn without any rules in imitating our nurse.

We can also acquire another speech which is dependent on this one called by the Romans "grammar." The Greeks and other peoples, but not all peoples, have this sort of secondary speech; and furthermore, very few people attain fluency in this speech because we do not adapt ourselves to its rules and teachings without concentrated attention over a long period of time.

Of these two [kinds of speech], then, the vernacular is the nobler; both because it is enjoyed by the whole world (though it has been divided into [languages with] differing words and paradigms), and because it is natural to us while the other is more an artificial product.

And my purpose is to treat systematically this more noble kind of speech. . . .

from *BOOK 2*

Chapter 1

Calling once again upon the quickness of my natural talent, and taking my pen up again for beneficial works, I first declare that the illustrious Latin vernacular is suitable for use in both prose and verse. But because the prose writers mostly pick up this vernacular from those who have knit it in verse, and because what is knit in verse seems to have remained the model for prose writers, and not the reverse (which facts would seem to confer a certain superiority on verse), let us purify[1] the form [of this vernacular] which is put into meter, ordering our discussion as we promised at the end of the first book.

Let us inquire first whether all verse writers in the vernacular ought to use this vernacular. It would seem so on the surface, because it is required of all verse writers that they embellish their verses to the extent that they are able. And since nothing more embellishes than the illustrious vernacular, it would seem that every verse writer ought to make use of it. Furthermore, if something which is the best of its kind is mixed with something inferior to it, the superior thing does not simply not detract from the inferior, it actually improves it. Therefore any verse writer, even though he might write very crudely, who mixes this vernacular with his crudity would seem to do not just a good thing, but even the required thing: those with little ability can use much more assistance than those with much. And thus it appears that all writers of verse should be allowed to make use of it.

But this conclusion is absolutely false: even the most excellent poets should not use[2] it all the time, as can be gathered from my discussion below. Such a vernacular demands men of its own level, just like our other customs and fashions: magnificence demands men of great power; the purple, noble men; and, by the same token, this vernacular seeks out those with the greatest natural talent and learning, as will be made clear later. For what is appropriate to us is so because of the qualities of either our genus, or species, or individual natures, such as the capacities for feeling, or laughing, or making war. But this vernacular is not appropriate to us because of our genus, since it is not appropriate to animals; nor because of our species, since it is not appropriate to all men, as there can be no doubt no one would claim that it is appropriate to mountaineers with their rustic pursuits—so it must be appropriate to individual natures. Now things are appropriate to an individual as they suit his particular level of dignity, as is true of trading, fighting, and ruling. Thus, if things are appropriate to a level of dignity, which is to say, to those who are worthy (and some men may be worthy, others worthier, and still others worthiest), then clearly good things are appropriate to the worthy, better to the worthier, and the best to the worthiest. And since a dialect is no less a necessary instrument for [the expression of] our thoughts than a horse is to a soldier, and since the best horse is appropriate to the best soldier, the best dialect is appropriate to the best thoughts. But the best thoughts can exist only where there is learning and natural talent. Therefore the best dialect is appropriate only to those who have the greatest learning and talent. So the best dialect is not appropriate to every writer of verse (as so many of them write verse without having either learning or talent), and therefore neither is the best vernacular. It follows that if it does not fit everybody's capacities, it should not be made use of by everybody, on the grounds that no one should act with impropriety.

And as for the statement that everyone ought to embellish his verses to the extent of his ability, I affirm its truth. But we do not say that a decked-out cow or a garlanded pig have been embellished: we rather laugh at them, considering them vulgarized; for embellishment is the addition of something appropriate. Concerning the statement that a superior thing mixed with an inferior brings it assistance, I say that it is true whenever the distinction between the two is broken down, as when we melt gold and silver together. But if the two remain distinct, the inferior will be made more contemptible, as when beautiful women are mixed with ugly ones. And therefore since the verse-writer's meanings always remain distinct from the words with which they are mixed, they will appear not better, but worse, when accompanied with the best vernacular, for the same reason that an ugly woman looks worse when she is dressed in gold or silk.

Chapter 2

Now that I have established that not all verse writers, but only the most excellent, should make use of the illustrious vernacular, my next step is to establish whether all subjects should or should not be treated in it, and, if not, to separate out those which are worthy of it.

For this task it must first be discovered what we mean by the word "worthy." And we call something worthy which has dignity, just as we call something noble which has nobility. And just as we know what someone is by his clothing, insofar as the clothing identifies him, by knowing what the clothing means, so we know what is worthy by knowing what dignity is. And dignity, then, is the effect or the end of desert: we say that someone has achieved dignity for a good when he has deserved well, and for an evil when he has deserved evil. Someone who has fought well as a knight has the dignity appropriate to victory, someone who has ruled well, the dignity appropriate to sovereignty, and, as well, a liar has the dignity appropriate to disgrace, and a murderer, the dignity appropriate to that which causes death. But since there are degrees among those who deserve well, and among their opposites as well, some deserving well, some better, and some the best, some evil, some worse, and some the worst; and since these degrees are distinguished by the end of the deserts, which, as I said, we call dignity, it follows that there will be degrees of greater or lesser among dignities, some being great, some greater, and some the greatest; and consequently it is evident that some things will be worthy, some worthier, and some the worthiest. And since these degrees of dignity are not applied to the same, but to different objects, so that we would say that something was more worthy when it was worthy of a greater object, most worthy when of the greatest object (since nothing can be more worthy of the same object), it is clear that, in the nature of things, the best things are worthy of the best. And so since that vernacular which I call illustrious is the best of all of them, it follows that only the best subjects should be treated in it, which we would then call "the worthiest" among possible subjects.

I will now therefore search out what these worthiest subjects might be. To see clearly which they are, it should be noted that man travels a threefold road according as he has been granted three souls, the vegetable, the animal, and the rational. For he seeks what is useful insofar as his nature is vegetative, and in this respect shares his nature with plants; he seeks what is delightful insofar as his nature is animate, and in this respect shares his nature with the beasts; and seeks what is honest, insofar as his nature is rational, and in this respect he is alone or is perhaps of the same nature with the angels. It is evident that in all of our actions, we act for these three ends. And because in all three of the cases, certain ends are greater, others the greatest, it is clear that those ends which are the greatest in their kind should be written about with the best available means, and consequently in the best vernacular.

But it should be explained what these greatest ends are. First, if we consider carefully the intention of all things which seek usefulness, we would find among those things sought for their usefulness that the best end is nothing other than self-preservation.[3] Secondly, we would say in considering those things sought for the sake of delight, that that thing is most delightful which gives delight as the most precious object of the appetite: and this is the enjoyment of love.[4] Third, in considering those things which are sought for their honesty, no one may doubt that the best end is virtue. For this reason, these three (that is, self-preservation, the enjoyment of love, and virtue), are certainly those "splendidly great things" which should be written about using the best available means; or rather, the things which to the greatest extent tend toward them, which are prowess in arms, the flames of love, and the direction of the will.

I have found, if I can trust my memory, that the illustrious men have written poetry in the vernacular on these subjects alone: Bertran de Born, on arms; Arnault Daniel, on love; Girautz de Borneilh, on rectitude; Cino di Pistoia, on love; his friend, on rectitude. Bertran, for example, has written the poem,

> *No posc mudar c'un cantar no exparja*[5]

Arnault, the poem,

> *L'aura amara fa·l bruol brancuz*
> *clarzir*[6]

Girautz, the poem,

> *Per solaz reveillar*
> *che s'es trop endormitz.*[7]

Cino, the poem,

> *Digno sono eo de morte.*[8]

His friend, the poem,

> *Doglia mi reca ne lo core ardire.*[9]

I myself have found no Latin poets, up to this time, who have written on the subject of arms. But having looked over these poems, it should be clear which subjects are to be written about in poems in the greatest vernacular.

Chapter 3

Now I shall endeavor to establsh in what sort of metrical form those subjects which are worthy of so great a vernacular should be confined.

Therefore, wishing to indicate the metrical form in which they are worthy to be bound, I would first have it borne in mind that those who have written poetry in the vernacular have published their poems in many different metrical forms, some of them in *canzoni*, some in ballades, some in sonnets, and others in irregular and illegitimate metrical forms, as I will demonstrate later. But from among these metrical forms I would single out the *canzone* as the most excellent form; and for this reason, if the most excellent things are as I proved earlier, worthy of the most excellent, then the subjects which are worthy of the most excellent vernacular are also worthy of the most excellent metrical form, and consequently should be written about in *canzoni*.

And that the metrical form of the *canzone* is such as I say it is can be established, upon investigation, in several ways. In the first place, although everything we write in verse is a song,[10] only *canzoni* happen to have this word in their name, which would never have continued to be the case had it not been planned so from the earliest times. Moreover, whatever brings about by itself that for which it was made is clearly more noble than what requires help from outside itself. But *canzoni* in themselves accomplish all that they are supposed to do, which ballades do not. The latter have need of dancers to keep time, who thus bring out their form. Therefore, *canzoni* should be considered nobler than ballades, and consequently their metrical form should be considered the noblest of all, since no one may doubt that the ballade surpasses the sonnet in nobility.

Furthermore, something is clearly nobler when it confers greater honor on its maker. But *canzoni* confer greater honor on their makers than ballades; therefore they are nobler, and consequently their metrical form is the noblest of all. Furthermore, whatever is noblest will be preserved with the greatest care. But among all the forms which are sung, *canzoni* are preserved with the greatest care, as would be clear upon the sampling of books. Therefore *canzoni* are the noblest, and consequently their metrical form is noblest. To this can be added that, among the products of art, the noblest is the one which includes the whole art. Therefore, since all forms which are sung are products of art, and since the whole art is included in the *canzone* alone, *canzoni* are the noblest, and thus their metrical form is noblest of all. And that the whole art of singing in poetic style can be found in the *canzone* is clear in this, that whatever element of art is included in other forms is included in the *canzone*, but not the reverse of this. And the evidence of these things which I say is clearly available to sight, for everything coming from the very heights of those most illustrious minds writing poetry which issues at the lips can be found in the *canzone* alone. Therefore, as to the question before us, it is evident that the subjects which are worthy of the highest vernacular ought to be written about in the *canzone*.

Chapter 4

Having labored to set apart those poets and those subjects worthy of the courtly vernacular, as well as that metrical form which I think worthy of such honor that it alone is appropriate to the highest vernacular, I should now, before moving on to other questions, explain in detail the metrical form of the *canzone*, which many poets appear to employ more by intuition[11] than through art; and so for that form which has up to this time been adopted by intuition, let us open up the workshop of its art, putting aside any discussion of the form of the ballade or sonnet, which I intend to take up in the fourth book of this work (where I will treat the middle vernacular).

Looking back over what I have already said, I note that I have often called those who write verse in the vernacular, "poets." I have presumed to do so, without reservation, and for good reason; for they are undoubtedly poets, if we consider the true definition of poetry, which is nothing other than "a fiction expressed in verse according to [the arts of] rhetoric and music." These poets, however, differ from the great poets, those who follow the rules, in that the great ones have written poems in a language and with an art which follows rules, while these [vernacular poets] as I said, do so intuitively. For this reason it happens that the more closely we imitate those great poets, the more correctly we write poetry. And therefore, where we intend to write works in a learned manner, we should follow their learned poetic.

So I would state first of all that everyone should make the weight of his material equal to [the strength of] his shoulders, as it may happen otherwise that he will fall in the mud because of the excessive weight on his shoulders. This is what Horace, our master, advises when he states, at the beginning of the *Art of Poetry*, "Choose your material. . . ."[12]

Next I should distinguish, among those subjects suitable for writing, which of them should be sung in the tragic, which in the comic, and which in the elegiac style. Tragedy is an example of something in the higher style, comedy of something in the lower style, and elegy is to be understood as having the style of the miserable. If these subjects seem to be suitable for the tragic style, then the illustrious vernacular will also be employed, and consequently, they must be bound in the *canzone*. If, on the other hand, they seem to be suitable for the comic style, then sometimes the middle, sometimes the low vernacular is to be employed, which distinction I am saving for treatment in the fourth book. But if they are suitable for the elegiac style then we should employ only the low vernacular.

But let us leave aside for the present the other styles and discuss the tragic style in its proper place. It is clear that we are using the true tragic style when the gravity of the meaning is in accord with the splendor of the lines, with the elevation of the constructions, and with the excellence of the words. It is for this reason (remembering that I have already proved the highest things worthy of the highest) that the style which I call tragic is clearly the highest style. It is for this reason, too, that the subjects which I pick out as suitable for poetry in the highest style, these being self-preservation, the enjoyment of love, and virtue (along with whatever activities not trivialized by some accidental quality which we undertake in pursuit of these ends), must be sung about in this style alone.

But let anyone reading this be cautious and discern what I have said; when he intends to sing about these three subjects in their essence, or about those activities which are connected directly and essentially with these subjects, having drunk from the Helicon and having tightened the strings to perfect pitch, *only then* let him begin confidently to move the plectrum. But the skill in using this caution and discernment, this is the difficulty, this the labor, which he can never achieve without the exercise of his talents and the assiduous study of the art and the acquiring of facility in learning. And those who can achieve this are the ones whom the poet calls in the sixth book of the *Aeneid*[13] the "favorites of God," the ones "raised up to heaven by the ardor of their virtue," and the "sons of the gods" (though he speaks figuratively). And thus those fools are refuted who, immune equally from art or learning, trusting in their native talent alone, burst into song, using the highest subjects and the highest style. Since they are geese by nature or out of laziness, they should cease from such presumption, and not try to imitate the star-seeking eagles. . . .

Chapter 6

I have now located the illustrious vernacular, the noblest of all vernaculars; I have picked out those subjects which are worthy of being sung in this vernacular, of which three are the noblest as I demonstrated above; I have selected for them the form of the *canzone* as the highest form of all; and, in order to make my teaching the more complete, I have just provided for it a style and a poetic line. I shall now deal with the construction [of the *canzone*].

It should be noted first that what I call a "construction" is a joining together of words according to rules, such as, for example, "*Aristotiles phylosophatus est tempore Alexandri.*"[14] For there are five words here, joined together according to rules, and they make a single construction. The lowest-level consideration in the case of constructions is whether or not the parts are in [grammatical] agreement. And because, if you will recall the original principles of my digression, we are hunting only for the highest things, constructions not in agreement have no place in our hunt because they deserve to be placed low on a scale of goodness. Shame on them, then, shame on those men ignorant [of agreement] who in the future dare to burst forth with *canzoni!* I would hold them in contempt as I would the blind, trying to distinguish colors. And, as is quite clear, it is constructions in agreement which we are seeking.

But before we can obtain what we are searching for, we are presented with a problem of no little difficulty, which is to distinguish the construction most filled with elegance. For there several grades among constructions, as for example, the flavorless, used by the unlearned, as in "*Petrus amat multum dominan Bertam.*"[15] There is also that which has flavor alone, used by the austere scholar or teacher, as in "*Piget me cunctis pietate maiorem, quicunque in exilio tabescentes patriam tantum sompniando revisunt.*"[16] And there is that which is both flavorful and charming, which is used by those who have a superficial knowledge of rhetoric, as in "*Laudabilis discretio marchionis Estensis, et sua magnificentia preparata, cunctis illum facit esse dilectum.*"[17] And then there is that construction which is both flavorful and charming, and, in addition, elevated, which is used by illustrious writers, as in "*Eiecta maxima parte florum de sinu tuo, Florentia, nequicquam Trinacriam Totila secundus adivit.*"[18] This I would call the highest grade among constructions, and, since we have been hunting, as I have said, for the best, this is that construction which we seek.

It will be found that this construction alone has been woven into the illustrious *canzoni*, as in this one of Girautz de Borneilh:

Si per mon Sobretots non fos;[19]

or in this one, by Folquetz of Marseilles:

Tan m'abellis l'amoros pensamen;[20]

or this, by Arnault Daniel:

Sols sui che sai lo sobraffan chem sorz;[21]

or this, by Aimeric de Belenoi:

Nuls hom non pot complir addrechamen;[22]

or this, by Aimeric de Pegulhan:

Si com l'arbres che per sobrecarcar;[23]

or this, by the King of Navarre [Thibaut of Champagne]:

Ire d'amor qui en mon cor repaire;[24]

or this one, by the Judge [Guido delle Colonne] of Messina:

Anchor che l'aigua per lo foco lassi;[25]

or this one by Guido Guinizelli;

Tegno de folle' impresa a lo ver dire;[26]

or this, by Guido Cavalcanti:

Poi che de doglia cor conven ch'io porti;[27]

or this one, by Cino di Pistoia:

Avegna che io aggia più per tempo;[28]

or this, by his friend:

Amor che ne la mente mi ragiona.[29]

You should not be surprised, reader, at the number of authors I have recalled for you; for only through such examples could I indicate to you what I call the highest construction. And, to familiarize oneself with this construction, it would perhaps be most useful to look at the poets who follow the rules [of art], meaning Virgil, Ovid in the *Metamorphoses*, Statius, and Lucan, as well as those others who have used prose of the highest style, such as Titus Livius, Pliny, Frontinus, Paulus Orosius,[30] and many others, whom loving eagerness invites me to frequent. But at any rate, let the followers of ignorance cease from their praise of Guittone d'Arezzo and certain others who have never lost the habit of using the words and constructions of the common people.

Chapter 7

The next question which presents itself to my orderly treatise demands that I explain now which are the grandiose words, those worthy of forming the basis for the highest style.

I will begin by declaring that to be able to discern different kinds of words is not the least accomplishment of reason, since, as I see it, it is possible to find many different varieties among them. Some words impress one as childish, some as womanish, others as manly; among these last, some seem rustic, others urban; and of those we call urban, some seem smooth-haired or even oily, others shaggy or even bristly. It is the smooth-haired and shaggy among these which we call grandiose, which we call those oily or bristly whose sounds are excessive in some direction. By the same token, among great actions, we say that some are the works of magnanimity, others of vanity, this second term being applied where, although the action might look superficially as if it had risen higher, it had really, according to right reason, not risen higher, but fallen down the other side as soon as it had crossed the line which marks off virtue.

Think carefully, then, reader, how much is required of you in the straining which separates out the outstanding words. For if you have in mind the illustrious vernacular, that which should be used, as I said earlier, for the tragic style by poets of the vernacular (and these it is my object to fashion), you will take care that only the noblest words remain in your sieve. You can by no means number among those either the childish, like *mamma* and *babbo, mate* and *pate,*[31] because of their simplicity; or the womanish, like *dolciada* or *placevole,*[32] because of their softness; or the rustic, like *greggia* or *cetra,*[33] because of their harshness; or the oily and bristly, like *femina* or *corpo.*[34] You will see, then, that only the smooth-haired and shaggy among the urban words are left to you, these being the noblest and members of the illustrious vernacular. And I call those words smooth-haired which are three-syllables or very near to the measure of three syllables, have no aspiration, no acute accent or circumflex, no double consonants with x or z, no doubling of two liquids or placing of one liquid after a mute—which are, as it were, polished, and are emitted by a speaker with a certain sweetness, examples of which are *amore, donna, disio, vertute, donare, letitia, salute, securtate,* and *defesa.*[35]

On the other hand, I would call all other words, besides the smooth-haired, which would seem to be either necessary or ornamental to the illustrious vernacular, "shaggy." And I call those words necessary which cannot be avoided, including certain monosyllables such as *si, no, me, te, se, a, e, i', ò* and *u',*[36] as well as interjections, and a great many others. Then I would call those words ornamental which, when mixed with the smooth-haired, produce an attractive harmony in combination, though they themselves have some harshness because of aspiration, or accent, or double consonants or liquids or length, such words being *terra, honore, speranza, gravitate, alleviato, impossibilità, impossibilitate, benaventuratissimo, inanimatissimamente, disaventuratissimamente, sovramagnificentissimamente,*[37] this last having eleven syllables. It would be possible to find words or names with more syllables than this, but because such words would exceed the capacity of all of our poetic lines, they would not seem to be appropriate to our present discussion. An example would be *honorificabilitudinitate,*[38] which ends at the twelfth syllable in the [Italian] vernacular, but at the thirteenth in two of its case endings in [Latin] grammar.

But I leave for later my instructions concerning the manner in which the smooth-haired and shaggy words of this sort should be harmonized in poetic lines. What I have already said about the sublimity of words should suffice for someone of natural discernment. . . .

from *THE LETTER TO CAN GRANDE*

Therefore, if one should wish to present an introduction to a part of a work, it is necessary to present some conception of the whole work of which it is a part. For this reason, I, who wish to present something in the form of an introduction to the above mentioned part of the whole *Comedy*, have decided to preface it with some discussion of the whole work, in order to make the approach to the part easier and more complete. There are six questions, then, which should be asked at the beginning about any doctrinal work: what is its subject, its form, its agent, its end, the title of the book, and its branch of philospathy. In three cases the answers to these questions will be different for the part of the work I propose to give you than for the whole, that is, in the cases of its subject, form, and title, while in the other three, as will be clear upon inspection, they will be the same. Thus these first three should be specifically asked in a discussion of the whole work, after which the way will be clear for an introduction to the part. Let us, then, ask the last three questions not only about the whole but also about the offered part itself.

For the clarification of what I am going to say, then, it should be understood that there is not just a single sense in this work: it might rather be called *polysemous*, that is, having several senses. For the first sense is that which is contained in the letter, while there is another which is contained in what is signified by the letter. The first is called literal, while the second is called allegorical, or moral or anagogical. And in order to make this manner of treatment clear, it can be applied to the following verses: "When Israel went out of Egypt, the house of Jacob from a barbarous people, Judea was made his sanctuary, Israel his dominion."[39] Now if we look at the letter alone, what is signified to us is the departure of the sons of Israel from Egypt during the time of Moses; if at the allegory, what is signified to us is our redemption through Christ; if at the moral sense, what is signified to us is the conversion of the soul from the sorrow and misery of sin to the state of grace; if at the anagogical, what is signified to us is the departure of the sanctified soul from bondage to the corruption of this world into the freedom of eternal glory. And although these mystical senses are called by various names, they may all be called allegorical, since they are all different from the literal or historical. For allegory is derived from the Greek *alleon*, which means in Latin *alienus* ("belonging to another") or *diversus* ("different").

This being established, it is clear that the subject about which these two senses play must also be twofold. And thus it should first be noted what the subject of the work is when taken according to the letter, and then what its subject is when understood allegorically. The subject of the whole work, then, taken literally, is the state of souls after death, understood in a simple sense; for the movement of the whole work turns upon this and about this. If on the other hand the work is taken allegorically, the subject is man, in the exercise of his free will, earning or becoming liable to the rewards or punishments of justice.

And the form is twofold: the form of the treatise and the form of the treatment. The form of the treatise is threefold, according to its three kinds of divisions. The first division is that which divides the whole work into three canticles. The second is that which divides each canticle into cantos. The third, that which divides the cantos into rhymed units. The form or manner of treatment is poetic, fictive, descriptive, digressive, and transumptive, and it as well consists in definition, division, proof, refutation, and the giving of examples.

The title of the work is, "Here begins the Comedy of Dante Alighieri, a Florentine by birth but not in character." To understand the title, it must be known that comedy is derived from *comos*, "a village," and from *oda*, "a song," so that a comedy is, so to speak, "a rustic song." Comedy, then, is a certain genre of poetic narrative differing from all others. For it differs from tragedy in its matter, in that tragedy is tranquil and conducive to wonder at the beginning, but foul and conducive to horror at the end, or catastrophe, for which reason it is derived from *tragos*, meaning "goat," and *oda*, making it, as it were, a "goat song," that is, foul as a goat is foul. This is evident in Seneca's tragedies. Comedy, on the other hand, introduces a situation of adversity, but ends its matter in prosperity, as is evident in Terence's comedies. And for this reason some writers have the custom of saying in their salutations, by way of greeting, "a tragic beginning and a comic ending to you." And, as well, they differ in their manner of speaking. Tragedy uses an elevated and sublime style, while comedy uses an unstudied and low style, which is what Horace implies in the *Art of Poetry* where he allows comic writers occasionally to speak like the tragic, and also the reverse of this:

> Yet sometimes even comedy elevates its voice,
> and angry Chremes rages in swelling tones;
> and in tragedy Telephus and Peleus often lament
> in prosaic speeches. . . .[40]

So from this it should be clear why the present work is called the *Comedy*. For, if we consider the matter, it is, at the beginning, that is, in Hell, foul and conducive to horror, but at the end, in Paradise, prosperous, conducive to pleasure, and welcome. And if we consider the manner of speaking, it is unstudied and low, since its speech is the vernacular, in which even women communicate. There are, besides these, other genres of poetic narrative, such as pastoral verse, elegy, satire, and the hymn of thanksgiving, as could also be gathered from Horace in his *Art of Poetry*. But there is no purpose to discussing these at this time.

Now it can be explained in what manner the part I have offered you may be assigned a subject. For if the subject of the whole work, on the literal level, is the state of souls after death, in an absolute, not in a restricted sense, then the subject of this part is the same state, but restricted to the state of blessed souls after death. And if the subject of the whole work, considered allegorically, is man, through exercise of free will, earning or becoming liable to the rewards or punishments of justice, then it is evident that the subject in this part is restricted to man's becoming eligible, to the extent he has earned them, for the rewards of justice.

And in the same manner the form of this part follows from the form ascribed to the whole. For if the form of the whole treatise is threefold, then the form in this part is twofold, that is, the division into cantos and into rhymed units. This part could not have the first division as its form, since this part itself is [a product] of the first division.

The title of the book also follows; for while the title of the whole book is, as was said earlier, "Here begins the Comedy, *etc.*," the title of this part is, "Here begins the third canticle of Dante's *Comedy, etc.*, which is called *Paradise*."

Having settled these three questions, where the answer was different for the part than for the whole, it remains to deal with the other three, where the answers will not be different for either the part or the whole. The agent, then, in the whole and in the part, is he who has been mentioned above; and he is clearly so throughout.

The end of the whole and of the part could be multiple, that is, both immediate and ultimate. But, without going into details, it can be briefly stated that the end of the whole as of the part is to remove those living in this life from the state of misery and to lead them to the state of happiness.

The branch of philosophy which determines the procedure of the work as a whole and in this part is moral philosophy, or ethics, inasmuch as the whole and this part have been conceived for the sake of practical results, not for the sake of speculation. So even if some parts or passages are treated in the manner of speculative philosophy, this is not for the sake of theory, but for a practical purpose, following that principle which the Philosopher advances in the second book of the *Metaphysics*, that "practical men sometimes speculate about things in their particular and temporal relations."[41]

Having presented these basic principles, I will now offer a sample exposition of the literal level; and I should say ahead of time that the exposition of the literal level consists in nothing else than the making explicit of the form of the work. Thus this part, or the third canticle which is called *Paradise*, is divided into two parts, that is, into a prologue and an executive part. The second part begins where it says "Through diverse outlets rises on mortals. . . ."[42]

[The glory of him who moves all things
Penetrates through the universe, and shines
More in one part, and less in another.
In that heaven which receives more of his light
I was, and I saw things which to relate
He who descends below neither knows how nor is able;
Because, approaching near to its desire,
Our intellect goes so deeply
That the memory cannot follow so far.
In truth, as much as I could make a treasure of
In my mind of [what I saw] in the holy kingdom
Will be now the matter of my song.
O good Apollo, for this final labor
Make me through your power to be made a vessel
As you require before you will give the beloved laurel!
Up to this point one summit of Parnassus
Has been enough for me, but now with both
I am required to enter the remaining arena.
Enter my breast, and breathe through me
As when you drew Marsyas[43]
From the sheath of his members!
O divine virtue, if you will grant me this,
So that a shadow of the blessed kingdom,
Sealed in my head, I may express,
You shall see me come to the tree of your pleasure,
And then crown myself with those leaves
Which my matter and you make me worthy of.
So rarely, father, it is gathered
For the triumph of a Caesar or a Poet
(Because of the sin and shame of human desires)

That the Peneian leaf[44] must bear [a child/ fruit] within
Of joy to the joyous Delphic god,
Whenever it makes anyone thirst for itself.
From a small spark a great flame follows:
Perhaps behind me with a better voice
Prayer will be made so that Cyrrha[45] may respond.
Through diverse outlets rises on mortals
The light of the world. . . .]

Concerning the first of these parts, it should be noted that, although in a general way it could be called an exordium, it should, in this particular case, be termed a prologue. This is what the Philosopher would seem to imply in the third book of the *Rhetoric*, where he says, "The proem is the exordium of an oration, corresponding to the prologue of a poem or to the prelude in flute-playing."[46] It should be further noted that this introductory section, which can be called in general the exordium, becomes a different thing in the hands of a poet than it is in the hands of an orator. For orators usually give some sample of what they are about to say, in order to make the minds of their listeners receptive. Poets, on the other hand, not only do this, but also follow it with some sort of invocation. And this is right for them since they require so much more of their invocation and must therefore ask the superior powers for a thing, resembling a divine gift, beyond the ordinary capacity of man. And so the prologue under consideration is divided into two parts, the first outlining what is about to be said, the second invoking Apollo. And the second part begins with the line, "O good Apollo, for this final labor. . . ."

Concerning the first of these parts, it should be noted that three things are required of a good exordium, as Cicero says in the *New Rhetoric;* it must render the listener well-disposed, attentive, and willing to learn, particularly when the matter is of a type which excites amazement, as Cicero himself says.[47] And since the matter dealt with in the treatise under consideration is of the type which excites amazement, it is the purpose of the first part of the exordium, or prologue, to bring about these three conditions of the listener with relation to the source of the amazement. For the author says that he is about to relate what he saw in the first heaven and was able to retain in his mind. This statement fulfills all three of the requirements; for the usefulness of the relation makes the listener well-disposed; its capacity to excite amazement makes him attentive; and its being possible makes him willing to learn. The author implies usefulness when he says he is about to recount that which is to the greatest extent attractive to human desire, namely, the joys of Paradise; he touches on the source of amazement when he promises to tell of things as remote as they are sublime, namely, the conditions of the kingdom of heaven; and he shows that it is within the realm of possibility when he says he will tell what he could retain in his mind; for if he could do so, others could as well. All three of these things are touched on in the passage where he says that he has been in the first heaven, and that he intends to tell, concerning the kingdom of heaven, whatever, like a treasure, he was able to retain in his mind. Having thus noted the goodness and completeness of the first part of the prologue, let us proceed to a literal exposition.

Notes

1. This verb (*carminare*), translated "purify," literally refers to that process by which wool is cleansed and separated into strands. The weaving or knitting of a fabric is one of the two principal metaphors for the making of poetry in this treatise, the other being the tying together of a bundle of sticks.

2. The verb *induere* translated here as "use" means, literally, "to put on clothes"; it thus makes more compelling the comparison between the suitability of a man and his clothing and the suitability of a thought to the language in which it is expressed.

3. The word *salus* has the primary meaning of "health" or "well-being," but it is used by Dante here in one of its secondary senses to mean "self-preservation" or "safety."

4. Dante's word is *venus,* derived of course from the name of the goddess of love, and meaning here, as in classical writings, the enjoyment of the act of love.

5. "I cannot choose but send forth a song"; a poem in honor of King Richard the Lion-Hearted, celebrating his victory over the French king Philippe II, who aided Richard's brother, John. The date of the victory was 1194.

6. "The bitter air makes the leafy trees / grow thin"; a poem on the sufferings and anxieties of love.

7. "To waken solace, which is too often asleep"; a poem on the decay of ancient gallantry and manners.

8. "I am worthy of death"; an elaborate conceit, in which the poet claims to deserve death for having "stolen" Love from his lady's eyes.

9. "Sorrow causes me to burn in my heart"; a poem in condemnation of love and in praise of virtue.

10. The term *canzone* is clearly derived from the Italian word for "to sing" (*cantare*). The term itself may mean, quite simply, "a song," as well as, more particularly, a certain poetic form.

11. The word *casus* means "chance" or "accident," which, for the poet lacking an art to guide him, is the same as "intuition."

12. Lines 38–39.

13. Virgil, *Aeneid* 6.126–30.

14. "Aristotle philosophized in the time of Alexander." The rules to which Dante refers are those which determine the agreement of words in case, number, and gender.

15. "Peter likes Mistress Bertha very much."

16. "I, greater in pity than others, am sorry for those, who, wasting away in exile, see their native land only while dreaming." The sentence is flavorful because of its artificial grammatical order; it has an appositive (*cunctis pietate maiorem*), and two participial phrases in apparent, but not grammatical, parallelism.

17. "Laudable is the discernment of the Marquis of Este, and his generosity well calculated, who makes himself loved by all." The "flavor" comes from the artificial order, with the main clause at the end, and from the observance of the *cursus* in the members. The "charm" comes from the irony of the statement, which makes it figurative. This statement, like the others of the last four, makes specific reference to events related to Dante's exile and to the political condition of Italy: the "Marquis of Este" to whom he refers is the same "Azzo" he mentions at 1.12.5.

18. "The greatest part of the flower having been thrown out from your breast, Florence, in vain a second Totila will go to Sicily." The "flavor" lies in the artificiality of the grammar: the participial clause at the beginning, and the complexity of the ordering in the main clause. The "charm" lies in the figures: the personification of, and apostrophe to, Florence; the pun of *florum* and *Florentia;*

the alliteration of *Totila* and *Trinacriam* (Trinacria itself being a figure for Sicily); the allusion to Totila, presumed to have destroyed Florence during earlier barbarian invasions, and here made equivalent to Charles of Valois. It is "elevated" because of its moral gravity, and because all of these figures are carefully calculated to support that gravity.

19. "If it were not for my All-excelling one."

20. "The cares of love so greatly delight me."

21. "I am the only one who knows the superfrustration of love which issues. . . ."

22. "No man can satisfactorily fulfill. . . ."

23. "Just like the tree which, from being overloaded. . . ."

24. "The disdain of love, who dwells in my heart." This poem is really by Gace Brulé.

25. "Although some water might have lost, because of fire. . . ."

26. "I hold him of foolish daring, to tell the truth."

27. "Since it has happened that I bear a heart of sorrow."

28. "Although it has been a very long time. . . ."

29. "Love, who in my mind discourses with me."

30. Titus Livius (Livy) (59 B.C.–A.D. 17) was the writer of an enormous history of Rome, admired for its scope and accuracy as well as for its style. "Pliny" probably refers to both Pliny the elder (A.D. 23/4–79) and his nephew Pliny the Younger (61–114). The preface to Pliny the Elder's *Natural History* was highly regarded as a stylistic model, as were the *Letters* of Pliny the Younger. Frontinus (A.D. 30–104) was the author of a treatise called *The Strategems*, which deals with the uses and qualities of military officers. Paulus Orosius (fl. A.D. 414–18) wrote a *History* of Rome which was an apology for Christianity, rebutting the charge that the new religion caused the fall of Rome.

31. "Mama" and "papa," "mommy" and "daddy" would be the English equivalents.

32. "Sweetness" and "pleasant." Dante objects to a liquid preceded by a mute as in *placevole*, and also, apparently, to a liquid followed by a palatal, as in *dulciada;* to the colloquial endings of these words, in contrast to the more regular *dolcezza* and *piacente* (only the latter of which would be a "noble" word); and to the irregular derivation of *placevole* from the Latin: the usual derivation would change *pl-* to *pi-*.

33. "Herd" and "lute." Both are, as well, examples of liquids preceded by mutes (*greggia* and *cetra*), and of a doubling and syncopation which produce what Dante would call harshness.

34. "Woman" and "body." *Femina*, with the accent on the first syllable, and with long vowels in every syllable, seems to Dante too soft in pronunciation, while *corpo* not only has a grouping of liquid and a mute, but also the repetition of an open vowel. These two words also have overtones absolutely incompatible with "elevation" since *femina*, as against *donna*, implies feminine bestiality, and *corpo*, as against *persona*, implies a body without an animating soul.

35. The words mean, respectively, "love," "lady," "desire," "virtue," "to give," "joy," "well-being," "security," and "defended." It is no accident that these are, in meaning, some of the key words of the high style: Dante clearly thought that there was an intimate connection between sound and meaning, so that the words his theory eliminated on the grounds that their sounds were too oily or bristly would also be eliminated on the grounds that their meanings were too coarse and vulgar. At the same time he eliminates certain forms of these words themselves with his phonological rules. *Vertute* and *securtate* had variant forms, *vertù* and *securtà*, which are apparently examples of what Dante means by the "acute accent"; and *donare*, because of the long *a*, could also appear as *donar*, which is apparently what he meant by a circumflex.

36. Meaning, respectively, "so," "not," "me," "you" (sing.), "if," "to" (or "has"), "and" (or "is"), "the," "or," and "where."

37. Meaning, respectively, "land," "honor," "hope," "gravity," "eased," "impossibility," "impossibly," "most fortunately," "in a most unlively manner," "in a most unfortunate manner," "in a most overmagnificent manner." They are rejected on the grounds, respectively, of a doubling of two liquids (*terra*); aspiration (*honore*); the letter z in a double consonant cluster (*speranza*); a liquid after a mute (*gravitate*); a double liquid (*alleviato*); an accent, and perhaps too many syllables (*impossibilita*); and, the others, too many syllables.

38. "In the manner of something having the capacity to bestow honor." The two cases in Latin are the ablative and dative plurals: *honorificabilitudinatibus*.

39. Psalm 113:1–2 (114:1–2 in the King James version).

40. Horace *Art of Poetry* 93–96.

41. Aristotle *Metaphysics* 2.1.

42. *Paradise* 1.37. The entire passage (line 1–38) which is the subject of Dante's exposition is printed immediately below, for the convenience of the reader.

43. The satyr Marsyas challenged Apollo to a musical contest. Defeated, he was punished for his presumption by being flayed. See Ovid, *Metamorphoses* 6.382–400.

44. Daphne, daughter of the river god Peneus, who was transformed into the laurel.

45. Seaport of Delphi, here standing for Apollo's residence.

46. Aristotle *Rhetoric* 3.14.

47. The *New Rhetoric* is the *Rhetorica ad Herrenium*, long attributed to Cicero: see Book 1, chapter 41. Cf. the *De inventione* 1.15.20 and 22.

Giovanni Boccaccio 1313–1375

Boccaccio is perhaps best known for the bawdy and comic tales of the *Decameron* and so it is easy to forget that he is also the scholar-humanist who wrote the *Genealogy of the Gentile Gods*, an encyclopedic compendium of pagan mythology. An extremely prolific writer, he is, along with Dante and Petrarch, one of the great triumvirate of Italian scholar-poets.

What little is known of Boccaccio's works is largely dependent upon so-called autobiographical passages in his fiction, most of which now appear fictitious as well. He was the son of a Florentine businessman. In about 1328 he was sent to Naples to study business and law, but these pursuits interested him less than the pursuit of poetry. The most significant works of his early career are the long romances: *Filocolo* (*ca.* 1336), *Filostrato* (*ca.* 1338), and *Teseide* (1340–41). About 1353 he published the *Decameron.* Although this work is now the basis for his reputation, throughout the Renaissance his successors were primarily interested in his romances and his scholarly works, which became handbooks for poets who followed him.

De genealogia deorum gentilium ("*Genealogy of the Gentile Gods*") was written and revised between 1350 and 1374. It is an encyclopedic compendium of materials available on pagan mythology. The first thirteen books of the *Genealogy* describe the pagan myths, often providing allegorical interpretations of them. In Book XV Boccaccio justifies his own method and style. Book XIV, from which this selection is taken, is his defense of poetry. In it, Boccaccio compiles, as had never been done before, ideas about poetry that had prevailed for a thousand years and more. Thus articulated, these ideas would unite with Aristotle's *Poetics* (not recovered until the fifteenth century) to form the substance of literary theory for the Renaissance.

Boccaccio's acerbic wit and sharp eye for satire is evident even in his most "scholarly" of works. His invective against the "noisy sophists" who condemn poetry is characteristic of the writer of the *Decameron;* he calls them "giant hulks" and "fine cattle" who "bellow"; he lambastes their "ineptitudes" and "boorish vociferations against the truth." Boccaccio takes on the three primary charges leveled against poetry: that is useless, untruthful, and obscure. He defines poetry as "a fervid and exquisite invention, with fervid expression in speech or writing, of that which the mind has invented"; poetry "streams forth from the bosom of God." Like Dante and other poets before him, he sees the purpose of poetry as the revelation of truths under a "veil" of fiction. The power of fiction lies in its ability to delight and instruct. The argument is given force by linking it with the argument for scriptural allegory, which also disguises truth under a veil of fiction. Boccaccio frequently cites Augustine to make the point that in reading poetry one strips away the layers of fiction to reveal the sense hidden within the invention.

Boccaccio's answer to the charge that poets are liars raises the hidden problem of representation more cogently than any other medieval writer. He is not satisfied merely to restate the usual defense that poetry, while untruthful on the surface, contains "hidden" moral meanings that redeem its lies, nor simply to reiterate Aquinas's dictim that truths acquired through labor are more valuable because they are comprehended with more difficulty than plain truths. Boccaccio's definition of lies as false representations—"a close counterfeit of the truth which serves to destroy the true and substitute the false"—answers the old Platonic charge that poets present false representations by arguing that they do not attempt literal representation at all, that poetry in fact makes no attempt to imitate literal truths; therefore it cannot be called a lie. Boccaccio is one of the first literary critics to call into question Platonic commonplaces about art "imitating" life, thus setting the stage for Renaissance debates over poetry's imitation of nature.

from Genealogy of the Gentile Gods: Book XIV

VI. Poetry Is a Useful Art

I am about to enter the arena, a manikin against these giant hulks—who have armed themselves with authority to say that poetry is either no art at all or a useless one. In the circumstances, for me first to discuss the definition and function of poetry would be hunting a mare's nest. But since the fight must be fought I wish these past masters of all the arts would declare upon what particular point they desire the contest to bear. Yet I know full well that with a sneer and a brazen front they will unblushingly utter the same ineptitudes as before. Come, O merciful God, give ear to their foolish objections and guide their steps into a better way.

They say, then, in condemnation of poetry, that it is naught. If such is the case, I should like to know why, through generation after generation, so many great men have sought the name of poet. Whence come so many volumes of poems? If poetry is naught, whence came this word poetry? Whatever answer they make, they are going out of their way, I think, since they can give no rational answer that is not directly against their present vain contention. It is absolutely certain, as I shall show later, that poetry, like other studies, is derived from God, Author of all wisdom; like the rest it got its name from its effect. From this name "poetry" at length comes the glorious name of "poet"; and from "poet," "poem." In that case poetry apparently is not wholly naught, as they said.

If then it prove a science, what more will those noisy sophists have to say? They will either retract a little, or rather, I think, flit lightly over the gap thus opening in their argument to the second point of their objection, and say that if poetry *is* a mere art, it is a useless one. How rank! How silly! Better to have kept quiet than hurl themselves with their frivolous words into deeper error. Why, do not the fools see that the very meaning of this word "art" or "faculty" always implies a certain plenitude? But of this elsewhere. Just now I wish that these accomplished gentlemen would show how poetry can reasonably be called futile when it has, by God's grace, given birth to so many famous books, so many memorable poems, clearly conceived, and dealing with strange marvels. They will keep quiet at this, I think, if their vain itch for display will let them.

Keep quiet, did I say? Why they would rather die than confess the truth in silence, not to say with the tip of their tongues. They will dart off on another tack, and by their own arbitrary interpretation, will say, with slight addition, that poetry must be regarded a futile and empty thing, nay, damnable, detestable, because the poems which come of it sing the adulteries of the gods they celebrate, and beguile the reader into unspeakable practices. Though this interpretation is easy to refute—since nothing can be empty that is filled with adulteries—in any case it may be borne with a calm mind; nay their contention based upon it may be granted in all reason, since I readily acknowledge that there are poems of the kind they describe, and if the bad kind were to corrupt the good, then the victory would be theirs. But, I protest; if Praxiteles or Phidias, both experts in their art, should choose for a statue the immodest subject of Priapus on his way to Iole by night, instead of Diana glorified in her chastity; or if Apelles, or our own Giotto—whom Apelles in his time did not excel—

should represent Venus in the embrace of Mars instead of the enthroned Jove dispensing laws unto the gods, shall we therefore condemn these arts? Downright stupidity, I should call it!

The fault for such corruption lies in the licentious mind of the artist. Thus for a long time there have been "poets," if such deserve the name, who, either to get money or popularity, study contemporary fashions, pander to a licentious taste, and at the cost of all self-respect, the loss of all honor, abandon themselves to these literary fooleries. Their works certainly should be condemned, hated, and spurned, as I shall show later. Yet if a few writers of fiction erred thus, poetry does not therefore deserve universal condemnation, since it offers us so many inducements to virtue, in the monitions and teaching of poets whose care it has been to set forth with lofty intelligence, and utmost candor, in exquisite style and diction, men's thoughts on things of heaven.

But enough! Not only is poetry more than naught, but it is a science worthy of veneration; and, as often appears in the foregoing as well as in succeeding pages, it is an art or skill, not empty, but full of the sap of natural vigor for those who would through fiction subdue the senses with the mind. So, not to be tedious, it would seem that at the first onset of this conflict these leaders have turned tail, and, with slight effort on my part, have abandoned the arena. But it is my present duty to define Poetry, that they may see for themselves how stupid they are in their opinion that poetry is an empty art.

VII. The Definition of Poetry, Its Origin, and Function

This poetry, which ignores triflers cast aside, is a sort of fervid and exquisite invention, with fervid expression, in speech or writing, of that which the mind has invented. It proceeds from the bosom of God, and few, I find, are the souls in whom this gift is born; indeed so wonderful a gift it is that true poets have always been the rarest of men. This fervor of poesy is sublime in its effects: it impels the soul to a longing for utterance; it brings forth strange and unheard-of creations of the mind; it arranges these meditations in a fixed order, adorns the whole composition with unusual interweaving of words and thoughts; and thus it veils truth in a fair and fitting garment of fiction. Further, if in any case the invention so requires, it can arm kings, marshal them for war, launch whole fleets from their docks, nay, counterfeit sky, land, sea, adorn young maidens with flowery garlands, portray human character in its various phases, awake the idle, stimulate the dull, restrain the rash, subdue the criminal, and distinguish excellent men with their proper meed of praise: these, and many other such, are the effects of poetry. Yet if any man who has received the gift of poetic fervor shall imperfectly fulfil its function here described, he is not, in my opinion, a laudable poet. For, however deeply the poetic impulse stirs the mind to which it is granted, it very rarely accomplishes anything commendable if the instruments by which its concepts are to be wrought out are wanting—I mean, for example, the precepts of grammar and rhetoric, an abundant knowledge of which is opportune. I grant that many a man already writes his mother tongue admirably, and indeed has performed each of the various duties of poetry as such; yet over and above this, it is necessary to know at least the principles of the other Liberal Arts, both moral and natural, to possess a strong and abundant vocabulary, to behold the monuments and relics of the Ancients, to have in one's memory the histories of the nations, and to be familiar with the geography of various lands, of seas, rivers and mountains.

Furthermore, places of retirement, the lovely handiwork of Nature herself, are favorable to poetry, as well as peace of mind and desire for wordly glory; the ardent period of life also has very often been of great advantage. If these conditions fail, the power of creative genius frequently grows dull and sluggish.

Now since nothing proceeds from this poetic fervor, which sharpens and illumines the powers of the mind, except what is wrought out by art, poetry is generally called an art. Indeed the word poetry has not the origin that many carelessly suppose, namely *poio, pois,* which is but Latin *fingo, fingis;* rather it is derived from a very ancient Greek word *poetes,* which means in Latin exquisite discourse (*exquisita locutio*). For the first men who, thus inspired, began to employ an exquisite style of speech, such, for example, as song in an age hitherto unpolished, to render this unheard-of discourse sonorous to their hearers, let it fall in measured periods; and lest by its brevity it fail to please, or, on the other hand, become prolix and tedious, they applied to it the standard of fixed rules, and restrained it within a definite number of feet and syllables. Now the product of this studied method of speech they no longer called by the more general term poesy, but poem. Thus as I said above, the name of the art, as well as its artificial product, is derived from its effect.

Now though I allege that this science of poetry has ever streamed forth from the bosom of God upon souls while even yet in their tenderest years, these enlightened cavillers will perhaps say that they cannot trust my words. To any fair-minded man the fact is valid enough from its constant recurrence. But for these dullards I must cite witnesses to it. If, then, they will read what Cicero, a philosopher rather than a poet, says in his oration delivered before the senate in behalf of Aulus Licinius Archias, perhaps they will come more easily to believe me. He says: "And yet we have it on the highest and most learned authority, that while other arts are matters of science and formula and technique, poetry depends solely upon an inborn faculty, is evoked by a purely mental activity, and is infused with a strange supernal inspiration."

But not to protract this argument, it is now sufficiently clear to reverent men, that poetry is a practical art, springing from God's bosom and deriving its name from its effect, and that it has to do with many high and noble matters that constantly occupy even those who deny its existence. If my opponents ask when and in what circumstances, the answer is plain: the poets would declare with their own lips under whose help and guidance they compose their inventions when, for example, they raise flights of symbolic steps to heaven, or make thick-branching trees spring aloft to the very stars, or go winding about mountains to their summits. Haply, to disparage this art of poetry now unrecognized by them, these men will say that it is rhetoric which the poets employ. Indeed, I will not deny it in part, for rhetoric has also its own inventions. Yet, in truth, among the disguises of fiction rhetoric has no part, for whatever is composed as under a veil, and thus exquisitely wrought, is poetry and poetry alone. . . .

IX. It Is Rather Useful than Damnable to Compose Stories

These fine cattle bellow still further to the effect that poets are tale-mongers, or, to use the lower and more hateful term which they sometimes employ in their resentment—liars. No doubt the ignorant will regard such an imputation as particularly objectionable. But I scorn it. The foul language of some men cannot infect the glorious name of the illustrious. Yet I grieve to see these revilers in a purple rage let themselves loose upon the innocent. If I conceded that poets deal in stories, in that they are composers of fiction, I think I hereby incur no further disgrace than a philosopher would in drawing up a syllogism. For if I show the nature of a fable or story, its various kinds, and which kinds these "liars" employ, I do not think the composers of fiction will appear guilty of so monstrous a crime as these gentlemen maintain. First of all, the word "fable" (*fabula*) has an honorable origin in the verb *for, faris*, hence "conversation" (*confabulatio*), which means only "talking together" (*collocutio*). This is clearly shown by Luke in his Gospel, where he is speaking of the two disciples who went to the village of Emmaus after the Passion. He says,

"And they talked together of all these things which had happened.

"And it came to pass, that, while they communed together, and reasoned, Jesus himself drew near, and went with them."

Hence, if it is a sin to compose stories, it is a sin to converse, which only the veriest fool would admit. For nature has not granted us the power of speech unless for purposes of conversation, and the exchange of ideas.

But, they may object, nature meant this gift for a useful purpose, not for idle nonsense; and fiction is just that—idle nonsense. True enough, if the poet had intended to compose a mere tale. But I have time and time again proved that the meaning of fiction is far from superficial. Wherefore, some writers have framed this definition of fiction (*fabula*): Fiction is a form of discourse, which, under guise of invention, illustrates or proves an idea; and, as its superficial aspect is removed, the meaning of the author is clear. If, then, sense is revealed from under the veil of fiction, the composition of fiction is not idle nonsense. Of fiction I distinguish four kinds: The first superficially lacks all appearance of truth; for example, when brutes or inanimate things converse. Aesop, an ancient Greek, grave and venerable, was past master in this form; and though it is a common and popular form both in city and country, yet Aristotle, chief of the Peripatetics, and a man of divine intellect, did not scorn to use it in his books. The second kind at times superficially mingles fiction with truth, as when we tell of the daughters of Minyas at their spinning, who, when they spurned the orgies of Bacchus, were turned to bats; or the mates of the sailor Acestes, who for contriving the rape of the boy Bacchus, were turned to fish. This form has been employed from the beginning by the most ancient poets, whose object it has been to clothe in fiction divine and human matters alike; they who have followed the sublimer inventions of the poets have improved upon them; while some of the comic writers have perverted them, caring more for the approval of a licentious public than for honesty. The third kind is more like history than fiction, and famous poets have employed it in a variety of ways. For however much the heroic poets seem to be writing history—as Vergil in his description of Aeneas tossed by the storm, or Homer in his account of Ulysses bound to the mast to escape the lure of the Sirens' song—yet their hidden meaning is far other than appears on the surface. The better of the comic poets, Terence and Plautus, for example, have also employed this form, but they intend naught other than the literal meaning of their lines. Yet by their art they portray varieties of human nature and conversation, incidentally teaching the reader and putting him on his guard. If the events they describe have not actually taken place, yet since they are common, they could have occurred, or might at some time. My opponents need not be so squeamish—Christ, who is God, used this sort of fiction again and again in his parables!

The fourth kind contains no truth at all, either superficial or hidden, since it consists only of old wives' tales.

Now, if my eminent opponents condemn the first kind of fiction, then they must include the account in Holy Writ describing the conference of the trees of the forest on choosing a king. If the second, then nearly the whole sacred body of the Old Testament will be rejected. God forbid, since the writings of the Old Testament and the writings of the poets seem as it were to keep step with each other, and that too in respect to the method of their composition. For where history is lacking, neither one concerns itself with the superficial possibility, but what the poet calls fable or fiction our theologians have named figure. The truth of this may be seen by fairer judges than my opponents, if they will but weigh in a true scale the outward literary semblance of the visions of Isaiah, Ezekiel, Daniel, and other sacred writers on the one hand, with the outward literary semblance of the fiction of poets on the other. If they find any real discrepancy in their methods, either of implication or exposition, I will accept their condemnation. If they condemn the third form of fiction, it is the same as condemning the form which our Savior Jesus Christ, the Son of God, often used when He was in the flesh, though Holy Writ does not call it "poetry," but "parable"; some call it "exemplum," because it is used as such.

I count as naught their condemnation of the fourth form of fiction, since it proceeds from no consistent principle, nor is fortified by the reinforcement of any of the arts, nor carried logically to a conclusion. Fiction of this kind has nothing in common with the works of the poets, though I imagine these objectors think poetry differs from it in no respect.

I now ask whether they are going to call the Holy Spirit, or Christ, the very God, liars, who both in the same Godhead have uttered fictions. I hardly think so, if they were wise. I might show them, your Majesty, if there were time, that difference of names constitutes no objection where methods agree. But they may see for themselves. Fiction, which they scorn because of its mere name, has been the means, as we often read, of quelling minds aroused to a mad rage, and subduing them to their pristine gentleness. Thus, when the Roman plebs seceded from the senate, they were called back from the sacred mount to the city by Menenius Agrippa, a man of great influence, all by means of a story. By fiction, too, the strength and spirit of great men worn out in the strain of serious crises, have been restored. This appears, not by ancient instance alone, but constantly. One knows of princes who have been deeply engaged in important matters, but after the noble and happy disposal of their affairs of state, obey, as it were, the warning of nature, and revive their spent forces by calling about them such men as will renew their weary minds with diverting stories and conversation. Fiction has, in some cases, sufficed to lift the opressive weight of adversity and furnish consolation, as appears in Lucius Apuleius; he tells how the highborn maiden Charis, while bewailing her unhappy condition as captive among thieves, was in some degree restored through hearing from an old woman the charming story of Psyche. Through fiction, it is well known, the mind that is slipping into inactivity is recalled to a state of better and more vigorous fruition. Not to mention minor instances, such as my own, I once heard Giacopo Sanseverino, Count of Tricarico and Chiarmonti, say that he had heard his father tell of Robert, son of King Charles,—himself in after time the famous King of Jerusalem and Sicily—how as a boy he was so dull that it took the utmost skill and patience of his master to teach him the mere elements of letters. When all his friends were nearly in despair of his doing anything, his master, by the most subtle skill, as were, lured his mind with the fables of Aesop into so grand a passion for study and knowledge, that in a brief time he not only learned the Liberal Arts familiar to Italy, but entered with wonderful keenness of mind into the very inner mysteries of sacred philosophy. In short, he made of himself a king whose superior in learning men have not seen since Solomon.

Such then is the power of fiction that it pleases the unlearned by its external appearance, and exercises the minds of the learned with its hidden truth; and thus both are edified and delighted with one and the same perusal. Then let not these disparagers raise their heads to vent their spleen in scornful words, and spew their ignorance upon poets! If they have any sense at all, let them look to their own speciousness before they try to dim the splendor of others with the cloud of their maledictions. Let them see, I pray, how pernicious are their jeers, fit to rouse the laughter only of girls. When they have made themselves clean, let them purify the tales of others, mindful of Christ's commandment to the accusers of the woman taken in adultery, that he who was without sin should cast the first stone. . . .

XII. The Obscurity of Poetry Is Not Just Cause for Condemning It

These cavillers further object that poetry is often obscure, and that poets are to blame for it, since their end is to make an incomprehensible statement appear to be wrought with exquisite artistry; regardless of the old rule of the orators, that a speech must be simple and clear. Perverse notion! Who but a deceiver himself would have sunk low enough not merely to hate what he could not understand, but incriminate it, if he could? I admit that poets are at times obscure. At the same time will these accusers please answer me? Take those philosophers among whom they shamelessly intrude; do they always find their close reasoning as simple and clear as they say an oration should be? If they say yes, they lie; for the works of Plato and Aristotle, to go no further, abound in difficulties so tangled and involved that from their day to the present, though searched and pondered by many a man of keen insight, they have yielded no clear nor consistent meaning. But why do I talk of philosophers? There is the utterance of Holy Writ, of which they especially like to be thought expounders; though proceeding from the Holy Ghost, is it not full to overflowing with obscurities and ambiguities? It is indeed, and for all their denial, the truth will openly assert itself. Many are the witnesses, of whom let them be pleased to consult Augustine, a man of great sanctity and learning, and of such intellectual power that, without a teacher, as he says himself, he learned many arts, besides all that the philosophers teach of the ten categories. Yet he did not blush to admit that he could not understand the beginning of Isaiah. It seems that obscurities are not confined to poetry. Why then do they not criticise philosophers as well as poets? Why do they not say that the Holy Spirit wove obscure sayings into his works, just to give them an appearance of clever artistry? As if He were not the sublime Artificer of the Universe! I have no doubt they are bold enough to say such things, if they were not aware that philosophers already had their defenders, and did not remember the punishment prepared for them that blaspheme against the Holy Ghost. So they pounce upon the poets because they seem defenseless, with the added reason that, where no punishment is imminent, no guilt is involved. They should have realized that when things perfectly clear seem obscure, it is the beholder's fault. To a half-blind man, even when the sun is shining its brightest, the sky looks cloudy. Some things are naturally so profound that not without difficulty can the most exceptional keenness in intellect sound their depths; like the sun's globe, by which, before they can clearly discern it, strong eyes are sometimes repelled. On the other hand, some things, though naturally clear perhaps, are so veiled by the artist's skill that scarcely anyone could by mental effort derive sense from them; as the immense body of the sun when hidden in clouds cannot be exactly located by the eye of the most learned astronomer. That some of the prophetic poems are in this class, I do not deny.

Yet not by this token is it fair to condemn them; for surely it is not one of the poet's various functions to rip up and lay bare the meaning which lies hidden in his inventions. Rather where matters truly solemn and memorable are too much exposed, it is his office by every effort to protect as well as he can and remove them from the gaze of the irreverent, that they cheapen not by too common familiarity. So when he discharges this duty and does it ingeniously, the poet earns commendation, not anathema.

Wherefore I again grant that poets are at times obscure, but invariably explicable if approached by a sane mind; for these cavillers view them with owl eyes, not human. Surely no one can believe that poets invidiously veil the truth with fiction, either to deprive the reader of the hidden sense, or to appear the more clever; but rather to make truths which would otherwise cheapen by exposure the object of strong intellectual effort and various interpretations, that in ultimate discovery they shall be more precious. In a far higher degree is this the method of the Holy Spirit; nay, every right-minded man should be assured of it beyond any doubt. Besides it is established by Augustine in the *City of God*, Book Eleven, when he says:

> The obscurity of the divine word has certainly this advantage, that it causes many opinions about the truth to be started and discussed, each reader seeing some fresh meaning in it.

Elsewhere he says of Psalm 126:

> For perhaps the words are rather obscurely expressed for this reason, that they may call forth many understandings, and that men may go away the richer, because they have found that closed which might be opened in many ways, than if they could open and discover it by one interpretation.

To make further use of Augustine's testimony (which so far is adverse to these recalcitrants), to show them how I apply to the obscurities of poetry his advice on the right attitude toward the obscurities of Holy Writ, I will quote his comment on Psalm 146:

> There is nothing in it contradictory: somewhat there is which is obscure, not in order that it may be denied thee, but that it may exercise him that shall afterward receive it.

But enough of the testimony of holy men on this point, I will not bore my opponents by again urging them to regard the obscurities of poetry as Augustine regards the obscurities of Holy Writ. Rather I wish that they would wrinkle their brows a bit, and consider fairly and squarely, how, if this is true of sacred literature addressed to all nations, in far greater measure is it true of poetry, which is addressed to the few.

If by chance in condemning the difficulty of the text, they really mean its figures of diction and oratorical colors and the beauty which they fail to recognize in alien words, if on this account they pronounce poetry obscure—my only advice is for them to go back to the grammar schools, bow to the ferule, study, and learn what license ancient authority granted the poets in such matters, and give particular attention to such alien terms as are permissible beyond common and homely use. But why dwell so long upon the subject? I could have urged them in a sentence to put off the old mind, and put on the new and noble; then will that which now seems to them obscure look familiar and open. Let them not trust to concealing their gross confusion of mind in the precepts of the old orators; for I am sure the poets were ever mindful of such. But let them observe that oratory is quite different, in arrangement of words, from fiction, and that fiction has been consigned to the discretion of the inventor as being the legitimate work of another art than oratory. "In poetic narrative above all, the poets maintain majesty of style and corresponding dignity." As saith Francis Petrarch in the Third Book of his *Invectives*, contrary to my opponents' supposition, "Such majesty and dignity are not intended to hinder those who wish to understand, but rather propose a delightful task, and are designed to enhance the reader's pleasure and support his memory. What we acquire with difficulty and keep with care is always the dearer to us"; so continues Petrarch. In fine, if their minds are dull, let them not blame the poets but their own sloth. Let them not keep up a silly howl against those whose lives and actions contrast most favorably with their own. Nay, at the very outset they have taken fright at mere appearances, and bid fair to spend themselves for nothing. Then let them retire in good time, sooner than exhaust their torpid minds with the onset and suffer a violent repulse.

But I repeat my advice to those who would appreciate poetry, and unwind its difficult involutions. You must read, you must persevere, you must sit up nights, you must inquire, and exert the utmost power of your mind. If one way does not lead to the desired meaning, take another; if obstacles arise, then still another; until, if your strength holds out, you will find that clear which at first looked dark. For we are forbidden by divine command to give that which is holy to dogs, or to cast pearls before swine.

XIII. Poets Are Not Liars

These enemies of poetry further utter the taunt that poets are liars. This position they try to maintain by the hackneyed objection that poets write lies in their narratives, to wit, that a human being was turned into a stone—a statement in every aspect contrary to the truth. They urge besides that poets lie in asserting that there are many gods, though it is established in all certainty that there is but One—the True and Omnipotent. They add that the greatest Latin poet, Vergil, told the more or less untrue story of Dido, and allege other like instances. I fancy they think their point is already won, and so indeed it would be, were there no one to repel their boorish vociferations with the truth. Yet further discussion seems hardly necessary for I supposed that I had already answered this objection above, where at sufficient length I defined a story, its kinds, what sorts the poets employ, and wherefore.

But if the matter is to be resumed, I insist that, whatever those fellows think, poets are not liars. I had supposed that a lie was a certain very close counterfeit of the truth which served to destroy the true and substitute the false. Augustine mentions eight kinds of lies, of which some are, to be sure, graver than others, yet none, if we employ them consciously, free from sin and the mark of infamy that denotes a liar. If the enemies of poetry will consider fairly the meaning of this definition, they will become aware that their charge of falsehood is without force, since poetic fiction has nothing in common with any variety of falsehood, for it is not a poet's purpose to deceive anybody with his inventions; furthermore poetic fiction differs from a lie in that in most instances it bears not only no close resemblance to the literal truth, but no resemblance at all; on the contrary, it is quite out of harmony and agreement with the literal truth.

Yet there is one kind of fiction very like the truth, which as I said, is more like history than fiction, and which by most ancient agreement of all peoples has been free from taint of falsehood. This is so in virtue of their consent from of old that anyone who could might use it as an illustration in which the literal truth is not required, nor its opposite forbidden. And if one considers the function of the poet already described, clearly poets are not constrained by this bond to employ literal truth on the surface of their inventions; besides, if the privilege of ranging through every sort of fiction be denied them, their office will altogether resolve itself into naught.

Again: if all my preceding argument should deserve reprobation—and I hardly think it possible—yet this fact remains irrefutable, that no one can in the proper discharge of his duty incur by that act the taint of infamy. If the judge, for example, lawfully visits capital punishment upon malefactors, it is not called homicide. Neither is a soldier who wastes the enemy's fields called a robber. Though a lawyer gives his client advice not wholly just, yet if he breaks not the bounds of the law he does not deserve to be called a falsifier. So also a poet, however he may sacrifice the literal truth in invention, does not incur the ignominy of a liar, since he discharges his very proper function not to deceive, but only by way of invention.

Yet if they will insist that whatever is not literally true is, however uttered, a lie, I accept it for purposes of argument; if not, I will spend no more energy in demolishing this objection of theirs. Rather I will ask them to tell me what name should be applied to those parts of the Revelation of John the Evangelist—expressed with amazing majesty of inner sense, though often at first glance quite contrary to the truth—in which he has veiled the great mysteries of God. And what will they call John himself? What too will they call the other writers who have employed the same style to the same end? I certainly should not dare answer for them "lies" and "liars," even if I might. Yet I know well they will say what I myself in part am about to say—should anyone ask me—that John and the other prophets were men of absolute truthfulness, a point already conceded. My opponents will add that their writings are not fiction but rather figures, to use the correct term, and their authors are figurative writers. O silly subterfuge! As if I were likely to believe that two things to all appearances exactly alike should gain the power of different effects by mere change or difference of name.

But not to dispute the point, I grant they are figures. Then, let me ask, does the truth which they express lie on their surface? If they wish me to think it does, what else is it but a lie thus to veil the eyes of my understanding, as they also veil the truth beneath? Well then, if these sacred writers must be called liars, though not held such, since indeed they are none, no more are poets to be considered liars who lean with their whole weight upon mere invention.

Yet without question poets do say in their works that there are many gods, when there is but One. But they should not therefore be charged with falsehood, since they neither believe nor assert it as a fact, but only as a myth or fiction, according to their wont. Who is witless enough to suppose that a man deeply versed in philosophy hasn't any more sense than to accept polytheism? As sensible men we must easily admit that the learned have been most devoted investigators of the truth, and have gone as far as the human mind can explore; thus they know beyond any shadow of doubt that there is but one God. As for poets, their own works clearly show that they have attained to such knowledge. Read Vergil and you will find the prayer:

> If any vows, Almighty Jove, can bend Thy will—

an epithet which you will never see applied to another god. The multitude of other gods they looked upon not as gods, but as members or functions of the Divinity; such was Plato's opinion, and we call him a theologian. But to these functions they gave a name in conformity with Deity because of their veneration for the particular function in each instance.

But I do not expect these disturbers to hold their peace here. They will cry out the louder that poets have written many lies about this one true God—whom, as I have just said, they recognize —and on that count deserve to be called liars. Of course I do not doubt that pagan poets had an imperfect sense of the true God, and so sometimes wrote of him what was not altogether true—a lie, as their accusers call it. But for all that I think they should hardly be called liars. There are two kinds of liars: first, those who knowingly and wilfully lie, whether to injure another person or not, or even to help him. These should not be called merely liars, but, more appropriately, "wilful deceivers." The second class are those who have told a falsehood without knowing it. Among these last a further distinction is in order. For in some cases ignorance is neither to be excused nor endured. For example, the law forbids any man privately to hold a citizen prisoner. John Doe has detained Richard Roe, his debtor, and pleads exemption from fine through ignorance of the law; but since such ignorance of the law seems stupid and negligent, it can constitute no defense. Likewise a Christian who is of age should find no protection in ignorance of the articles of faith. On the other hand there are those whose ignorance is excusable, such as boys ignorant of philosophy or a mountaineer ignorant of navigation, or a man congenitally blind who does not know his letters. Such are the pagan poets who, with all their knowledge of the Liberal Arts, poetry, and philosophy, could not know the truth of Christianity; for that light of the eternal truth which lighteth every man that cometh into the world had not yet shone forth upon the nations. Not yet had these servants gone throughout all the earth bidding every man to the supper of the Lamb. To the Israelites alone had this gift been granted of knowing the true God aright, and truly worshipping Him. But they never invited anyone to share the great feast with them, nor admitted any of the Gentiles at their doors. And if pagan poets wrote not the whole truth concerning the true God, though they thought they did, such ignorance is an acceptable excuse and they ought not to be called liars.

But my opponents will say, that whatever ignorance occasioned the lie, he who told it, is none the less a liar. True; but I repeat, they who sinned in pardonable ignorance are not to be damned by the same token as the offenders whose ignorance was crass and negligent; for the law, both in its equity and its austerity, holds them excused, wherefore, they incur not the brand of a lie.

If these disparagers still insist in spite of everything that poets are liars, I accuse the philosophers, Aristotle, Plato, and Socrates of sharing their guilt. Now, I expect, these expert critics will again lift their voices to heaven and cry to the sound of harp and cithera that this objection of theirs has suffered no harm. Fools! Though one small shield be shattered, the whole front does not waver. Let them not exult, but remember how often they have now been belabored and beaten back.

Their objection to Vergil—that no wise man would ever consent to tell the story of Dido—is utterly false. With his profound knowledge of such lore, he was well aware that Dido had really been a woman of exceptionally high character, who would rather die by her own hand than subdue the vow of chastity fixed deep in her heart to a second marriage. But that he might attain the proper effect of his work under the artifice of a poetic disguise, he composed a story in many respects like that of this historic Dido, according to the privilege of poets established by ancient custom. Possibly someone more worthy of a reply than my opponents—perhaps even thou, O Prince—may ask to what purpose this was necessary for Vergil. By way of fitting answer let me then say that his motive was fourfold.

First, that in the same style which he had adopted for the *Aeneid* he might follow the practice of earlier poets, particularly Homer, whom he imitated in this work. For poets are not like historians, who begin their account at some convenient beginning and describe events in the unbroken order of their occurrence to the end. Such, we observe, was Lucan's method, wherefore many think of him rather as a metrical historian than a poet. But poets, by a far nobler device, begin their proposed narrative in the midst of the events, or sometimes even near the end; and thus they find excuse for telling preceding events which seem to have been omitted. Thus Homer, in the *Odyssey*, begins, as it were, near the end of Ulysses's wanderings and shows him wrecked upon the Phaeacian shore, then has him tell King Alcinous everything that had happened to him hitherto since he left Troy. Vergil chose the same method in describing Aeneas as a fugitive from the shore of Troy after the city was razed. He found no place so appropriate on which to land him before he reached Italy as the coast of Africa; for at any nearer point he had been sailing continuously among his enemies the Greeks. But since the shore of Africa was at that time still the home of rude and barbarous rustics, he desired to bring his hero to somebody worthy of regard who might receive him and urge him to tell of his own fate and that of the Trojans. Such a one above all he found in Dido, who, to be sure, is supposed to have dwelt there not then, but many generations later; yet Dido he presents as already living, and makes her the hostess of Aeneas; and we read how at her command he told the story of his own troubles and those of his friends.

Vergil's second purpose, concealed within the poetic veil, was to show with what passions human frailty is infested, and the strength with which a steady man subdues them. Having illustrated some of these, he wished particularly to demonstrate the reasons why we are carried away into wanton behavior by the passion of concupiscence; so he introduces Dido, a woman of distinguished family, young, fair, rich, exemplary, famous for her purity, ruler of her city and people, of conspicuous wisdom and eloquence, and, lastly, a widow, and thus from former experience in love, the more easily disposed to that passion. Now all these qualifications are likely to excite the mind of a high-born man, particularly an exile and castaway thrown destitute upon an unknown shore. So he represents in Dido the attracting power of the passion of love, prepared for every opportunity, and in Aeneas one who is readily disposed in that way and at length overcome. But after showing the enticements of lust, he points the way of return to virtue by bringing in Mercury, messenger of the gods, to rebuke Aeneas, and call him back from such indulgence to deeds of glory. By Mercury, Vergil means either remorse, or the reproof of some outspoken friend, either of which rouses us from slumber in the mire of turpitude, and calls us back into the fair and even path to glory. Then we burst the bonds of unholy delight, and, armed with new fortitude, we unfalteringly spurn all seductive flattery, and tears, prayers, and such, and abandon them as naught.

Vergil's third purpose, is to extol, through his praise of Aeneas, the *gens Julia* in honor of Octavius; this he does by showing him resolutely and scornfully setting his heel upon the wanton and impure promptings of the flesh and the delights of women.

It is Vergil's fourth purpose to exalt the glory of the name of Rome. This he accomplishes through Dido's execrations at her death; for they imply the wars between Carthage and Rome, and prefigure the triumphs which the Romans gained thereby—a sufficient glorification of the city's name.

Thus it appears that Vergil is not a liar, whatever the unthinking suppose; nor are the others liars who compose in the same manner. . . .

XIX. It Is Untrue that Plato Would Abolish All Poets from His Republic

A mere trifle it seems to these barkers—the exposure of their vain attempt to drive the poets out of the homes and hands of men. For see! they rally and rush to the attack, and flourishing like a weapon the authority of Plato they belch out with hideous roar, that Plato ordered the poets banished from the cities. Then, as if Plato were weak and needed help, they add as their own reason, that poets may vitiate the commonwealth with their immorality. Though I have already answered this objection at sufficient length, I shall not now shrink from a fuller reply. For I admit that the authority of this philosopher is of the highest order; and deserves all respect if rightly understood; but these men pervert or altogether misprise his meaning, as I shall prove.

I have said that the poets prefer to dwell in solitude, wherefore their disparagers called them backwoodsmen and boors. But if poets chose the hurly-burly of towns, what would these backbiters say of them? They would call them tyrants! It seems that they have changed their minds, and now call the poets dwellers in cities; if so, they are wrong. It is an established fact that Homer, after wandering the world over, settled at last in extreme poverty on the shore of Arcadia, amid crags and mountain-forests; and there, overtaken by blindness, but with "mind irradiate," conceived those great and marvellous works; works anointed not with the sweetness of Hybla, but of Castaly—the *Iliad* and the *Odyssey*. And Vergil, who was no less a genius than Homer, forsook Rome, then mistress of the world, and deserted Octavius, ruler of all the earth, whose friendship was the poet's peculiar and happy privilege, all to seek out an abode not far from the famous principality of Naples in central Campania, a spot even in that day abounding in beauty and comfort; and there, according to the account of John Barillus, a man of much intelligence, he chose a spot still and removed, near a lonely shore, between the cape of Posilipo and the old Greek colony Pozzuolo, whither none would come except to visit him. There he composed both his *Georgics* and the divine *Aeneid*. And when at Vergil's death, Octavius wished to commemorate his choice of this lonely spot, he caused his bones to be brought from Brundisium, and buried close by his favorite retreat near the road still called the Puteolan Way; thus his bones lie near the abode of his choice.

But I will not confine myself to ancient examples, for, however happy and authentic, my opponents will none of them. Francis Petrarch, a man of heaven-sent genius, and the greatest poet of our time, scorned the western Babylon, and ignored the favor of the Pope, for which nearly every Christian longs and contends his utmost—not to say the favor of bonneted cardinals and other princes—and departed to a secluded valley, in an exceptionally lonely part of France, where the Sorga, the greatest of springs, takes its rise. There, in meditation and composition, he spent nearly the whole flower of his youth, content with one servant. The proofs of his deed still remain and will so remain for a long time—a little house and garden, and, as long as God pleases, a number of living witnesses. These examples suffice to show what a waste of effort it is to try to drive poets out of the city whence they have departed of their own choice.

I wish my opponents would say whether they think that Plato, in his *Republic*, passed the stricture they mention upon Homer, so that Homer would have been an exile from his ideal city. Whatever they say, I cannot think so, having read so much in praise of Homer. The most sacred laws of the Caesars call him father of all virtues; and time and again their proposers, to win reverence for them, and support them with holy testimonial have mingled with them lines from Homer. Thus at the close of the proem of the Justinian Code occurs such a quotation, as likewise under the titles, On Justice and Law On Contract of Sale, On Legacies and Trusts, and so forth: the curious may see it for themselves in the Pandects of Pisa. It was Homer whom many of the leading cities of Greece would have dignified as their citizen, though he had died in poverty; nay, they contended with one another for this honor. This is clearly shown in Cicero's speech for Archias where he says: "Homer is claimed as their fellow-citizen by the men of Colophon, while the Chians demand, and the Salaminians aspire to the same honor; Smyrna also insists that he is here, and has gone so far as to dedicate a shrine to him. Many others are there who likewise strive and contend for the same honor." Nor is Cicero the only witness; I remember reading it in an old Greek verse familiar to the learned which says: "Seven cities dispute for the honor of Homer's birth—Samos, Smyrna, Chios, Colophon, Pylos, Argos and Athens." Nay Plato himself calls Homer to witness in the very book of the *Republic* in which he condemns poets, and elsewhere. If then the laws call him the father of virtues, and glory of the law, and if he is claimed as citizen of so many states, and if Plato, our very monitor, cites him to prove a point, isn't it utter folly to think so wise a man as he would have ordered such a poet to be excluded from his commonwealth?

Are we to believe that by the same token Ennius must be banished? He was a man who lived content in honest poverty, and yet was greatly endeared to the Scipios by his goodness; and they, besides their distinction of noble birth and exploits in war, were at home in philosophy, and singularly pure in character. They so loved the poet that at his death they desired that he be buried in the tomb of their family, and his ashes mingled with those of their fathers and their own. Then I for one will never agree with these idiots; nay, rather am I convinced that Plato would have wished his state brim-full of such as these. What of Solon, who in his old age, after he had made the laws of Athens, devoted himself to poetry? Must he be also expelled who restored a broken and ruined city to civil and moral health? There again is Vergil, who withal was so pure that he blushed in mind as well as in countenance when he overheard an indecent remark among his coevals or others, and thus won the nickname "Parthenias," that is, "virgin," or more correctly "virginity." It is often said that his works contain as many admonitions to virtue as they do words. To save his divine poem from being burned according to his own dying command, Octavius interrupted the cares of his vast empire to compose some prohibitory verses, which are still extant. The poet's name enjoys such honor at his native Mantua that when Augustus moved his ashes, and the Mantuans were not suffered to have the keeping of them as they wished, they began to honor the little farm where he had lived, and named it after him as if it had been alive; and the old men of the place still point it out to the younger generation as something sacred and venerable. They even take care to call strangers' attention to it, as if to augment their own glory. Such things do not happen unprecedented by conspicuous virtue. Shall we suppose then, that Plato would have men of such virtue expelled from the state? Blockheads! I could say as much of Horace, and Persius of Volterra, and Juvenal of Aquinum, all to prove that it never entered Plato's mind to expel such men. But it is my purpose to cite contemporary instances, immediately visible, so that they can not repudiate them by any possible tergiversation. Can one imagine that Plato would have been mad enough to banish Francis Petrarch? From his youth Petrarch has lived celibate, and such has been his horror at impure and illicit love, that his friends know him for a perfect model of saintly and honorable living. A lie is his mortal enemy, and he abhors all the vices. Truth finds in him her sanctuary, and virtue her adornment and delight. He is a pattern of Catholic piety—dutiful, gentle, devout, and so modest that he is called a second Parthenias. He is, besides, the present glory of the art of poetry, an eloquent and sweet-tongued speaker, a man to whom the whole heart of Philosophy is open and familiar, of penetration more than human, endowed with tenacious memory, and enjoying knowledge commensurate with the mind of man. His prose, and his more extensive works in verse, are so splendid, so redolent with sweetness, so loaded down with the bright bloom of his eloquence, so honey-sweet with rounded cadence, so pungent with the sap of his wonderful wisdom, that they seem like the creations of a divine not a human genius. What more could one say? For surely he exceeds human limits and far outstrips the powers of man. Such praise I utter not of an ancient who died centuries ago, rather of one who, please God, is alive and well; of one whom you, my snarling monsters, if you trust not my words, may see with your own eyes, and seeing, believe. I have no fear that he will share the common fate of great men, whose presence, as Claudian says, impairs their fame. Nay, rather, I insist that his actual presence far surpasses his reputation. So dignified is his bearing, so flowing and delightful his discourse, so gentle his manners, so tranquil his old age, that one may say of him what Seneca writes of Socrates, that his hearers were even more edified by his character than by his words. I pause in my eulogy of this great man to ask these objectors whether such are the poets Plato would banish from his state. If men of this kind are shut out, what sort would even Plato admit in their stead? Will they be panderers, body-snatchers, parasites, roisterers, fishmongers, or jailbirds and the like?

Long life and happiness to Plato's state, if she rids herself of poets to receive such as the safeguards of life and morals. But let us never suppose the learned man meant what these "interpreters" say he did; for I can only believe that great poets and their kind are to be rightly regarded not as merely citizens of his state and all others, but as the princes and rulers thereof.

But they will spleen and say: "If not these, then what poets would Plato expel?" There is only one answer to such nonsense. Find out for yourselves, you incompetents! To be sure, allowance must be made for ignorance of all sorts. Every art, like every liquor, hath its lees; the lees may be but so much foul draff; yet an art, like a liquor, without lees is cheapened. What, for example, is truer than Philosophy, mistress of all sciences and arts? Yet she hath had as her dregs, so to speak, the Cynics and Epicureans—not to mention any more—who having got themselves tangled up in unspeakable errors, proceeded in various ways to defame her more like enemies than supporters. But shall we say that for the sake of these we must abandon also Socrates, Xenocrates, Anaxagoras, Panetius, and others adorned with the fair title of Philosopher? Such is the way of the knave and the fool! What is holier than the Christian religion? Yet she hath her Donatists, her Macedons, her Fotini, and far worse dregs of heresy than they; and we do not therefore regard Basil, and St. John Chrysostom, and Ambrose, and Pope Leo, and many another holy and reverend man as profane. Thus also poetry, like the other arts, contains likewise its dregs. There have been certain so-called comic poets, who, to be sure, included a few upright men such as Terence and Plautus, but who for the most part defiled the bright glory of poetry with their filthy creations. Even Ovid at times makes one of these. Whether from innate foulness of mind, or greed for money, or desire of popularity, they wrote dirty stories and presented them on the stage, and thus prompted lascivious men to crime, unsettled those who were established in virtue, and weakened the moral order of the whole state. What was worst of all, though the pagan religion was already in other respects reprehensible, yet they seduced various peoples into the practice of such licentious rites that its own disciples had to blush for it. It is such poets, I repeat, that paganism no less than Christianity abhors, and such it is that Plato would banish. Indeed I think they ought to be not expelled, but exterminated. But for the sake of these, must Hesiod also go, and Euripides, and Statius, and Claudian, and the like? I think not. I beseech these cavillers, then, to make a distinction, to avoid their hateful and unworthy prejudice, to single out for their attacks the really undeserving, and leave honorable men in peace. . . .

Christine de Pisan 1365–1429

Christine de Pisan was the first European woman to earn a living by writing; her works are full of outspoken condemnations of the misogynistic representations of women that were prevalent in her day, attacking even so popular a work as *The Romance of the Rose*. She was born in Venice in 1365. Shortly after, her father, Tommaso di Benvenute da Pizzano, became court astrologer to Charles V of France. Christine was able to profit from her family's ties to the court to get a good education. At age 15 she married Estienne de Castel, a court notary, who died in 1389. Widowed at 25, with three children to support, Christine turned to writing to earn a living. The work for which she is best known is the *City of Ladies* (1405), a long, elaborate, and sometimes mind-numbingly boring allegory that, like Chaucer's *Legend of Good Women*, praises the accomplishments of women while countering the misogyny that was prevalent in clerical writing. Her other writings include *La vision de Christine*, an autobiography of sorts (1405), *The Book of Three Virtues*, and *Le Livre de la Mutacion de Fortune*, another stab at autobiography.

In 1399 she wrote *The Epistle of the God of Love*, in which she deplored the popularity of *The Romance of the Rose*, one of the central works of medieval French literature, and the representation of women it promoted. Around 1402, Christine became involved in a debate, with several Parisian humanists, over the merits of Jean de Meun's continuation of the poem. It is now thought that the provost of Lille, Jean de Montrevil, initiated the affair by writing an enthusiastic commentary on the *Romance*, which he had read during the spring of 1401, and by sending a copy to Christine. She then replied, in the letter included here, with an attack on several aspects of the poem, especially the slander heaped on women not only by Jean de Meun but by the whole tradition of misogynistic literature. Christine's criticisms of the poem were seconded by at least one very important Parisian, Jean Gerson, the chancellor of the University of Paris. Her principle opponents were Jean de Montrevil and two brothers, Gontier and Pierre Col, the former a royal secretary and the latter a member of the chapter of Notre Dame.

In her letter to John of Montrevil, Christine attacks *The Romance of the Rose*, perhaps somewhat priggishly, for being immoral in general and for slandering women. If her complaint that Reason "names the secret parts of the body" sounds to modern ears more like Phyllis Schlafly than Kate Millet, a useful context in which to understand Christine's critique might be current feminist controversies over the censorship of pornography. There is some scholarly debate over whether or not to see Christine as a feminist or protofeminist (see bibliography). While she does attack the misogyny of clerical writing in several of her works, her vision of women's proper role is ultimately more conservative than would make most feminists comfortable. What is most interesting about Christine's attack on *The Romance of the Rose* and its representation of women is that its critique is grounded in a fear of the excesses of poetic language cut loose from proper signification. Jean de Meun "spoke superfluously," and "in derision of holy predication." Because de Meun does not have the proper respect for signification, he misrepresents his subject—women. His ultimately misogynistic portrayals of women are untrue precisely because he has not understood the proper use of language. At bottom, Christine's theory of representation, of the representation of women, is thoroughly Platonic and it is this, more than anything, that accounts for her conservative view of woman's role.

Response to the Treatise on *The Romance of the Rose* by John of Montrevil

To that most adept and knowledgeable person, Master John Johannes, secretary to our lord, the King.

Most reverend, honorable sir, to you my lord Provost of Lille, dearest sire and master, wise in all customs and morals, lover of science, learned in holy matters and expert in rhetoric, from me, Christine de Pizan, a woman ignorant of subtle understanding and agile sentiment—for which things your wisdom has never held the paltriness of my reasoning in contempt, I thus wish to beg your indulgence despite my feminine debility. And since it has pleased you to send me, for which I thank you, a small treatise composed in fine rhetoric and convincing arguments (this done in your own words in reproving, or so it seems to me, several of those finding fault with the compilation of *The Romance of the Rose* in several places and vigorously defending and approving this work and its authors, especially Meun), I, having read and considered our aforementioned prose and understood its meaning inasmuch as the feebleness of my paltry intellect would enable me—to the extent that, without a response having been requested of me, I, moved rather by my contrary opinion of your words and in accord with the especially astute and discerning cleric to whom your epistle is addressed—mean to say, divulge and manifestly uphold that, your good grace notwithstanding, you have committed a great error without reason in giving such perfect praise to the aforesaid work, which could better be called utter idleness than a useful work, in my judgment. And how often you reprove those who would contradict your opinion, saying that "it is a great thing thus to understand that which another says to be true; he has better constructed and held up his assumptions by dint of long and diligent study," etc., may I not be judged presumptuous in daring to repudiate and reprove so serious and subtle an author; but let it be noted that the firm and forceful conviction that moves me against several particularities which are or are said to be understood—and, moreover, a thing that is said out of inner conviction and not by order of the law can be argued without prejudice. And however much I do not possess great knowledge nor am I schooled in the use of subtle styles of language (from which I might know how to arrange words pleasingly and in polished style and order to make my ideas shine forth), I will not allow to be said in any way whatsoever a vulgar opinion of my understanding, merely because I do not know how to express it in ornate, well-ordered words.

So why have I said above that this work

"could better be called idleness . . ."? Without fail it seems to me that anything without worth, although it has been treated, done and accomplished by great labor and trouble, can be called idle or worse than idle inasmuch as worse evil comes of it. And since already for a long time for the great common renown of the said romance I have desired to see it, after knowledge and recognition had caused me to understand somewhat these subtle matters, I read and considered it at length and in great detail to the best of my understanding. It is true that for the material that was not to my liking in several areas I hopped over it like a bird over a snare: I thus did not dwell on it much. Nevertheless there remained in my memory several matters treated in it that my judgment greatly condemned and still cannot approve in spite of the contrary praise of other people. It is very true that my paltry understanding considers that which is expressed with levity and delight, in several sections, to be rather solemn discourse in what it really means—and in very attractive terms and graceful leonine verses: nor could it be said more subtly nor in more measured terms than that means by which he intends to treat his subject. But in dealing with the disputed position, without fail, in my opinion, he treats this dishonestly in several parts—and equally in the character which he calls Reason, who names the secret parts of the body explicity. And to the extent to which you defend and convey his position, and allege that in all things God has created there is no ugliness and consequently their names must not be evaded, I say and confess that God did indeed create all things pure and clean in themselves, and at that time it was not unseemly to name them: but by the pollution of sin did man become impure, from which the original sin still inhabits us (so testify the Holy Scriptures). Thus by way of comparison I can allege: God made Lucifer the most beautiful of all the angels and gave him a solemn and beautiful name, he who was then by his sin dragged down to hideousness; in his case the name as beautiful as it was originally now strikes terror in the ears of all who hear it because of the reputation of its bearer.

Moreover you propose that Jesus Christ, "In speaking of female sinners, called them *meretrix*," etc. And that in his calling them by this name I can deduce via your argument that this term *meretrix* is not at all unsuitable for naming the vileness of the thing itself—for in Latin it can be said in still more vile terms. And that shame must be pushed aside in speaking publicly of those things of which nature herself is ashamed, I reply that, given the esteem in which both you and the author are held, you are commiting a great error against the noble virtue of shame, which by its very nature refrains from libertinage and dishonesty in sayings and deeds; and that it is a great vice beyond the realm of honest practice and good morals as found in many places throughout the Holy Scriptures. And that the name should not be repudiated "any more than if it were the holy relics themselves being named," I confess to you that it is not the name which makes a thing dishonest. For this reason, to my fragile mind, it should be spoken of with sobriety—and not without necessity—for a particular reason, as in the treatment of illness or other such necessity. And just as our ancestors hid them, so would we in deed and in word.

And I still cannot remain silent about that which disturbs me: that the lofty personage of Reason, whom he himself calls the daughter of God, must be the one to enunciate in such words and in the form of a proverb that which I have noted in this chapter, wherein she says to the Lover that "in the battle of love . . . it is better to deceive than be deceived." I daresay here that John of Meun's Reason abjures her Father in so saying, for she has given herself too much to another doctrine. For if one were better than the other, it would follow that both were worthy: which cannot be. I thus hold to the contrary that, to tell the truth, it is less bad to be deceived than to deceive.

Now let us go further in considering the material or the manner of speaking, which has caused many to reproach on good advice. Great Good Lord! What horribleness! What dishonesty! And such contradictory teachings does he record in the chapter on the Duenna! But for Heaven's sake! What else can one find here but sophistic exhortations full of ugliness and utterly vile reminiscence? Look here! Among you who have beautiful daughters and wish to initiate them to a life of virtue, take them under your wing, and procure for them and advise them to read *The Romance of the Rose* in order to teach them to discern good from evil—what am I saying? But evil from good! And what use or advantage can it be for the listener to hear such vileness? Then in the chapter on Jealousy, good Lord! What great benefit can be noted, what need to record the dishonest and ugly words which are all too frequently on the lips of those unfortunates smitten with this malady? What good example or initiation can this possibly provide? And the ugliness noted down there about women, some say that in justifying this by saying that it is spoken by the Jealous Husband, and truly it is as if God were speaking through Jeremiah. But unfailingly, whatever deceitful additions he may have added, they cannot—thank God!—in any way make conditions for women more bitter or unfavorable. So much for that! And when I think of the ruses, false appearances, and hidden deceptions in marriage or in other situations that one may gather from this treatise, I adjudge these most certainly to be good and worthwhile narratives to hear!

But the character whom he names Genius the priest says marvelous things: no doubt the works of Nature would all have failed long ago if he had not commended them! But for Heaven's sake! Who is this man who has the nerve to assure me that this great progression full of vituperation that he calls a sermon could possibly be worthwhile, as though in derision of holy predication, which he says Genius is doing, wherein you find so much dishonesty, sophistic names and words provoking Nature's secrets—those which should be kept in silence and not named, since one does not see at all discontinued the activities that maintain the common order which cannot fail: for, if it were otherwise, it would be well and good for the perpetuation of the human race, to find and speak those provocative and exciting words to urge mankind to continue such activity.

The author goes on to say, as far as I can remember, to what end I cannot cease to marvel: for to the aforementioned sermon he joins, as a kind of figure, Paradise and the pleasures found within it. He says rightly that here is where the virtuous shall go, and then concludes so that all may understand—without sparing man or woman—how to accomplish and put to practice the works of Nature; not in that it goes against the law, as one would expect him to say—but very plainly!—that in so doing they will be saved. And in this he seems to wish to maintain that there is no sin in *Luxuria*, that it is thus a virtue—which is an error and contrary to the laws of God. Oh! What sowing and what doctrine! What can one expect to reap from all this! I believe that many people have retreated from the world and entered religion or have become hermits for this holy reading, or have withdrawn from a life of wrongdoing to be saved from such advice, which never comes, I daresay at the risk of offending someone, except through abandonment of one's character to corruption and vice—which may cause great suffering and sin.

And still, for the sake of God! Let us look a little beyond: in what manner valuable or constructive can he be justified in so excessively, impetuously, and most dishonestly accusing, blaming and slandering women as committing many serious vices and whose habits are full of every kind of perversion; and by so many attacks as conveyed by as many characters as one could ever hope to absorb. For if you wished to tell me that the Jealous Husband acts out of passion, I would not understand him to be in the service of Genius, who so often recommends and counsels one to sleep with women without forgetting that activity which he so frequently praises; and this same character says to all others many vituperations against women, and says in fact: "Flee! Oh flee the venomous serpent!" and then says to continue as before with that activity. There is here a great and evil contradiction in commanding us to flee that which he wishes us to follow and to follow that which he wishes us to flee. Rather, if women are that perverse, one should not order us to approach them at all; for whoever fears trouble should take pains to evade it.

And because of this he strongly forbids telling secrets to women—about whom he is so desirous to know, as he records, such that I do not believe that devils can find as much hodgepodge, rubbish, and wasted words to equal that so carefully arranged therein—yet I beg of those who make such opinions a reality and who uphold them to tell me when they have once seen men accused, dead, hanged, or attacked in the street because of accusations made by their wives: I think they will find them to have suffered for other reasons. Notwithstanding that it is good and praiseworthy advice that everyone should keep his secrets close for safety's sake, for there are vicious people everywhere; and that in many cases, as I have heard tell, someone has been accused and then hanged because of having been betrayed by a friend in whom he had placed his confidence, but I think that before justice there have been few such rumors, or complaints of horrible evils, or great betrayals and diabolical behavior as he maliciously and secretly knows women to have committed—what kind of secret is it that is true of no one! And as I have said earlier on this subject in a poem of mine called *The Epistle to the God of Love:* where are the countries or kingdoms which exile people for their evil deeds? But without speaking in common agreement, let us say of those great crimes one can accuse even the worst those who deceive the most: what can these women do if you don't give them a chance to deceive you? If they ask you for the silver from your purse, which they do not take nor steal from you, don't give it to them if you do not wish to! And if you say that you were besotted at the time, don't let yourself get drunk! What are these women going to do, track you down in your home and take it from you by force? It would be good to know just how women deceive you.

And moreover, he spoke so superfluously and offensively about married women who deceived their husbands—a situation he could not know firsthand and so spoke of it in so many generalizations: to what good end can this lead, what good can come of it? I know not what to think other than that it prevents happiness and harmony, and renders husbands who hear so much rubbish and twaddle, if they decide to believe it, suspicious and unloving with their wives. Heavens! What an exhortation! How worthwhile it is! Actually, since he blamed all women in general, I am forced to believe that he has never made the acquaintance nor known the company of an honorable and virtuous woman, but rather has frequented only dissolute and disreputable ones—as self-indulgent men are wont to do—and thus claims that all women are of the lowly kind, since he has never known the other. If only he had criticised the dishonest ones and had advised the avoidance of this sort alone, his teachings would be good and just. But no! He accuses all women of this without exception. But if the author takes it upon himself so much beyond the limits of reason to accuse them or judge them untruthfully, no blame should be imputed to them but rather to him who tells a lie so far beyond the boundaries of truth that it is totally unbelieveable, as the contrary manifestly appears. For if he and all his accomplices in this matter had sworn to it, none would suffer, for there have already been, there are and will be many of the most valiant women, more honest, better raised and even more learned, whose greatest worth is revered throughout the world where that author has never been—even in wordly affairs and most refined customs—and several who were the cause of reconciliation of their husbands, and conducted their affairs for them and kept their inner passions and secrets within, even though their husbands were crude and unloving. Of this one finds proof enough in the Bible and in other ancient histories, such as Sarah, Rebecca, Esther, Judith, and many others; even in our time have we seen in France many valiant women, great ladies and others of our ladies of France: the holy devoted Queen Joan, Queen Blanche, the Duchess of Orléans, daughter of the King of France, the Duchess of Anjou who is now named the Queen of Sicily—all of whom had such beauty, chastity, honesty, and wisdom—and still others; and the least known valiant noblewomen, such as my lady of Ferte, the wife of my lord Peter of Craon—who performed many laudable deeds, and several others, all of whom would make too long an account to relate here.

And do not believe, dear sir, that no one else could have an opinion on this matter, or that I say or put in order these said defenses for the purpose of gaining favorable treatment as a woman: for in truth my motive is nothing more than to uphold pure truth, since I know a certain body of accepted knowledge to be contrary to the aforementioned points denied by me; and in that I am indeed a woman, I can better bear witness on this aspect than he who has no experience of it, and who thus speaks only out of supposition and haphazard guessing.

By all means, for the love of Heaven!—let this be considered the end of this said treatise. For as the proverb says, "At the end all things are finished." So let it be seen and noted to whom it may be useful the most horrible and shameful conclusion—and I do mean shameful!—but so dishonest that I dare say that no one loving virtue and honesty would hear it without being confounded by shame and outraged at thus hearing discerned and disjointed and put into dishonest fictions that which reason and shame should restrain good people from even thinking; moreover, I daresay that even the Goliards would be shocked to read or hear it in public, in proper places, or before people of virtuous reputation. What is the point of a work one dares not read or speak of in proper form at the table of queens, princesses and worthy noblewomen—without their having to cover their faces as they blush with shame! And if you wish to excuse this by saying that it was in the style of a lovely novella that it pleased him to represent the goal of love by these figures, I'll reply to you that there's nothing new in what he's telling us! Don't we already know how men inhabit women by nature? If he were to relate to us how bears or lions or birds or other strange beasts came to be, that would serve to make us laugh in a fable, but he still tells us nothing new. No doubt such occurrences have been related more pleasantly, much more sweetly, and in more courtly terms, more likely to please charming honest lovers and all other virtuous people.

Thus, according to my limited abilities and feeble judgment, without being more prolix in language, although more can be said and better, I cannot attribute any good use to the said treatise; for so much do I seem to notice in it that many pains were taken to no advantage. Although my judgment confesses Master John to be a very great cleric, subtle and eloquent, capable of producing a work of great merit and lofty sentiment if he were to apply himself to it—in this case it's a pity—I suppose that the great carnality with which his work is filled caused him to abandon at will that which would have led him to a profitable end, as all operations come to be known by their inclinations. This notwithstanding, I would never reprove *The Romance of the Rose* as a whole, for there are certainly some good things well stated in it. And this moreover is the work's greatest danger: for evil is rendered more believable by putting it together with good to make it more respectable; in this way many subtle authors have on several occasions planted the seeds by error by mixing and coating it with bits of truth and virtue. Just as his priest Genius says: "Flee! flee woman, the evil serpent lurking under the grass!" I can say: "Flee! flee the covert malice beneath the shadow of goodness and virtue!"

For this reason I say to you, in conclusion, most dear sir, and to all of your allies and accomplices who praise it so much and who wish to magnify its worth to such an extent that you would devalue all other volumes and would dare lower your esteem of them before it, that it is not worthy of a judgment being imputed to it, with all due respect to your good grace; and that you do a great injustice to all valuable books: for a work without usefulness to the common or private good—no matter how delightful or at what labor and cost—is not worthy of praise. And just as in olden times when the triumphant Romans would give neither praise nor honors to anything that was not useful to the public, let ut look at their example before attempting to crown this romance. For I find, it seems to me, these aforementioned things and others considered, better that it be shrouded in fire than crowned with laurel, even though you call it a "mirror of good living, a model for political self-government and for living religiously and wisely;" on the contrary, with all respect, I say that it is an exhortation to vice seeking to comfort a dissolute life, a doctrine full of deception, a path to damnation, public defamation, a cause of suspicion and heresy, shame in several people, and perhaps a source of error.

And I well know that on this point in excusing it you will answer me that in it good deeds are extolled and that evil is presented only so as to be avoided. Likewise I can explain to you by means of a better reason that human nature, which in itself is inclined toward evil, has no need for us to call attention to the lame foot in order to learn to walk more correctly; and as for speaking of all the good that can be noted in said book, certainly too many virtuous things, better said, more respectable and more useful—even in political and moral life—are found in many other volumes done by philosophers and doctors of our faith, such as Aristotle, Seneca, Saint Paul, Saint Augustine, and others—this you know—which more validly and completely attest and teach virtue and how to flee vices than Master John of Meun would know to do: but not so willingly are these authors seen or retained by mortals of the flesh, as when it greatly pleases the drunkard taken ill for whom the physician prescribes that he drink plenty of fluids, and so willingly for the pleasure of drinking does he allow himself to believe it will no longer do him any harm. And so I become certain that you—to whom God has prescribed it!—and all others returned to the light and purity of a clear conscience by the grace of God, without the blemish or pollution of sin nor even its intention, if you clean by the sting of contrition (an act causing to be seen clearly the secret of conscience and condemning free will as the arbiter of truth), you will make another judgment of *The Romance of the Rose* and might even wish, perhaps, that you had never seen it.

So it should thus suffice. And may folly, arrogance, or presumption not be imputed to me for daring, I a woman, to take up and refute such a subtle author and whittle down the praise of him, when he, only one man, dared to undertake the defamation and blasphemy, without exception, of an entire sex.

CHAPTER THREE

Renaissance to Restoration

The period of one hundred years between the defeat of the Spanish Armada (1589) and the Glorious Revolution (1688) saw the emergence of a characteristically English literature as well as a specifically English literary criticism. The criticism of this period—a period framed by Sidney and Shakespeare at one end and Milton and Dryden at the other—developed from the Renaissance doctrines of humanism and neoclassicism that were first advanced in Italy and later in France. During the late sixteenth and the seventeenth century, England became recognized as an important center of European culture. Many of the great poet-critics of this period were British; and while English criticism was often representative, and even imitative, of Continental critical trends, it diverged at important points from Continental practice. Increasingly during the century, English critics came to set themselves apart from Continental theorists, concerning themselves with describing the distinctive practice of English poets rather than with formulating rules for all poets to follow. By Dryden's time, the differences between Continental theory and English practice were marked.

The seventeenth century was a period of social and political turmoil in England. After the ascension of James I in 1603, relations between the throne and an increasingly vocal Puritan majority in the House of Commons grew strained. The reign of James's son, Charles I (1625–42), was characterized by economic and political conflict culminating in the English Civil War (1642–45) that pitted the king against Parliament. After the execution of Charles I in 1649, Oliver Cromwell became virtual dictator of England (1653–58), followed by a period of unrest and the subsequent restoration of Charles II in 1660. In 1688, Charles' younger brother, the Catholic monarch, James II, was forced from the throne by the country's Protestant majority and William and Mary took his place. This history of political upheaval was reflected in fundamental changes in the practice of literature and in the ways literature itself was conceptualized as an art before and after the Civil War. Early in the seventeenth century the practice of poetry and criticism was seen as the proper avocation of gentlemen and courtiers; by the end of the century, the idea of the critic as commentator upon, and arbiter of, social "taste" had been born. The poetry that Sidney envisioned buttressed and legitimated aristocratic values and virtues; Dryden's "dramatic poetry" was but one aspect of a cultural program that would define and negotiate a new relationship between an entrenched aristocracy and an emerging professional middle class.

The concept of what it meant to be a poet also underwent important changes during this period. The technology of the printing press gradually led to a new cultural role for the poet. No longer an aristocratic courtier whose works circulated privately in manuscript for the amusement and edification of others who shared his sociopolitical values, the poet became a professional writer who exposed his work publicly. As early as the 1590s, London literary circles, particularly the theater, were dominated by writers from middle-class backgrounds—Shakespeare, Robert Greene, Christopher Marlowe, Ben Jonson—who used their writing to enhance their financial and social positions. Throughout the seventeenth century, the printing press acted as a leveler, opening up the profession of writing to a new class of writers. After 1641, when press censorship broke down during the Civil War, large numbers of writers who had previously been denied access to printing published their works. In 1640, twenty-two books were published in London; two years later in 1642, after the end of censorship, 1,966 books came out. After the Restoration, the offspring of the middle class and the gentry used writing to gain entry to court circles and political preferment, among them John Dryden, William Wycherley, George Etherege, Aphra Behn, and William Congreve. The professionalization of the writer, in one respect, helps to define the ways in which Renaissance notions of literature underwent a significant historical transformation.

In this context, it is worth examining briefly what is usually meant by the terms *Renaissance* and *Restoration* and the ways in which these terms promote particular views of the periods they designate. Both terms promote the myth of a return to a pristine origin, a nostalgia for an idealized past. The term *Renaissance* celebrates the "rebirth" of the knowledge of the ancients; it promotes the fiction of a break with the ignorance of the medieval past. In *The Advancement of Learning* (1604), Francis Bacon opposes the knowledge of the classics against "the Bishop of Rome and the degenerate traditions of the [Catholic] Church." He describes the need "to awake all Antiquity and . . . to make a party against the present time," with the result that "the ancient Authors . . . which had long time slept in Libraries, began generally to be read."

The classical texts read and cited by English literary critics were filtered primarily through the Platonic neoclassicism of Italian humanism. The most important classical works for Renaissance literary critics were Horace's *Ars poetica* and Aristotle's *Poetics*, the latter becoming generally available in translation only in the latter half of the sixteenth century. The revival of Aristotle's *Poetics* and the emergence of the neoclassical "rules" for writing poetry occurred in Italy before they spread to England late in the sixteenth century. The stricter Italian Aristotelians regarded the *Poetics* as a prescriptive document and attempted to formulate rules for the various genres of poetry; Julius Caesar Scaliger's *Poetice libri septem* (*"Seven Books of Poetics"*) (1561) became the authoritative text of early neoclassicism in both England and France.

The word *restoration* also calls up a nostalgia for the glories of the ancient past, most notably of Augustus Caesar. The period after 1660 is built on the myth of "restoring" the monarchy to the glories of the "past age" (Dryden's term) after the sociopolitical turmoil of the Civil War. While the Restoration is usually treated by literary critics as a kind of anteroom to the eighteenth century, it is itself a significant era in the development of English criticism. In part because the English court was in exile in France during the period of Cromwell's Interregnum government (1645–1660), English literary criticism after the Restoration initially turned to France, rather than Italy, for its interpretation of the classics. France set the fashions in literary criticism, particularly in the theater, where the plays and theoretical writings of dramatists like Racine and Corneille sparked a heated debate over the supposedly Aristotelian conception of the unities of time, place, and action that did not subside until well into the eighteenth century.

Much of the literary criticism of the sixteenth century, like George Puttenham's *Arte of English Poesie,* is concerned with the technical aspects of poetics and rhetoric: versification, the argument over quantitative versus qualititative meter, figures, and tropes. But the fundamental aesthetic problems of late sixteenth- and seventeenth-century literary criticism center on the object or material cause of poetry's representation: is it real or fictive? Sidney's definition of poetry in the *Apology* sets an agenda for the discussion of this question that brings together many of the learned commonplaces of Renaissance criticism. He writes:

> Poesy therefore is an art of imitation, for so Aristotle termeth it in his word *mimesis,* that is to say, a representing, counterfeiting, or figuring forth—to speak metaphorically, a speaking picture—with this end, to teach and delight.

Sidney's definition is less notable for its originality (it is drawn almost word for word from Scaliger's *Poetice,* which in turn was indebted to Aristotle's *Poetics* and Horace's *Ars poetica*) than for the insight it gives into the critical controversies of the century. This definition touches on three issues that dominate literary criticism until virtually the end of the eighteenth century: the nature of imitation, the problem of defining nature, and the injunction that poetry serve moral ends (the Horatian dictum of *utile et dulce*). In order to understand the relevance of Renaissance and Restoration theory to literary practice, it is necessary to understand the contexts that framed these arguments, the grounds on which the meanings of these terms—imitation, nature, and moral utility—were contested.

Much literary criticism during this period was a response to Puritan attacks on poetry, and on the theater in particular. These responses attempted to use the authority of classical texts to defend literature from the charge that it was obscene and blasphemous. Sidney's *Apology* is no exception; it is thought to be a response to an attack on poetry by Stephen Gosson (1579), which was dedicated "To the right noble Gentleman, Master Philip Sidney, Esquire." Because texts like Sidney's were designed as "apologies," the defenders of poetry were implicitly forced to accept the terms of the Puritan critics of art in order to refute their arguments. Although all seventeenth-century critics dutifully recite the Horatian dictum that poetry must *both* instruct and delight, the emphasis in the criticism is almost exclusively on the moral efficacy of poetry. Ben Jonson, for instance, writes in his Dedication to *Volpone* of the "impossibility of any man's being the good poet without being first a good man." Both Sidney and Jonson had to structure their arguments to make literature seem primarily a form of moral instruction.

Similarly, the principle of imitation, although not definitions of it, reigns unchallenged over literary theory from the Renaissance virtually to the end of the eighteenth century. No aesthetic writing of this period, either on the Continent or in England, fails to mention this principle. But not all critics meant the same thing by imitation, nor did they necessarily agree on the object of that representation. At the center of the controversy over imitation was a debate over the nature of nature. Critics argued about what constituted nature and about the status of representations of that "reality." At stake was the constitution of knowledge itself. The medieval view of imitation stressed the need to follow *auctoritas*, to make representations embody the principles of received authorities. This view of imitation found its way into Renaissance criticism as an injunction to imitate the classical poets, Homer and Virgil in particular. What Roger Ascham, Elizabeth I's tutor, meant in *The Scholemaster* by imitation was "to follow for learning of tongues and sciences the best authors." For critics of the sixteenth and seventeenth centuries, poetry was less an expression of what the twentieth-century critic might call "personality" than an "objective imitation" either of nature itself or, even better, of nature mediated through the agency of a classical model. This view of imitation is never entirely abandoned in the seventeenth century; it finds its way after 1660 into Dryden's criticism. But it does give way in the later seventeenth century to a debate over poetry's imitation of nature, a debate that takes up the question of Aristotelian *mimesis*. The tension between two views of the imitation of nature—what we might term tradition versus experience—dominates the criticism of the seventeenth and eighteenth centuries.

Neoplatonic *mimesis* held that the nature the poet imitated was the ideal, not the real. In the Renaissance the ideal of Nature was God's cosmological plan. Sidney perhaps best represents this viewpoint when he argues that "right poets" "imitate to teach and delight, and to imitate borrow nothing of what is, hath been, or shall be; but range, only reined with learned discretion, into the divine consideration of what may be or should be" (*An Apology for Poetry*). This view of *mimesis* is based on a belief in providential design; because the universe is the product of divine wisdom, the purpose of the poet is ultimately to affirm the rule of justice and order. Therefore, the ideal that Sidney invokes—what may or should be—is more "real" than what is. But the Neoplatonic idealism inherent in Sidney's conception of nature was not a purely aesthetic formulation. It was part of an ideology that effectively masked the operation of power within the Tudor court. Economically and politically, the Renaissance was marked by the loss of feudal prerogatives and the consolidation of state power within a small privileged elite surrounding the monarch, who became a ritual symbol of that power. The ascent from the world of the senses to the world of ideas effectively focused attention away from the real operations of power in the court to the world of universal ideals, preventing the courtier from confronting the fact of his own servitude.

Ideology, however, seldom operates without contradiction. Sidney's conceptions of mimesis raises thorny questions about the nature of this ideal reality. At times it seems as if what ought to be—the ideal—has the status of the real, at least the reality of the Platonic "form." It exists, although it is hidden by the appearances of the workaday historical world. This is the basis of Sidney's claim that poetry is a truer imitation of nature than history, which is constrained by what happened: the wicked are often rewarded and the good punished. Poetry knows no such constraints and so provides a grasp of the universal design and order that history cannot. But other statements in the *Apology* call into question the reality of the poetic ideal by suggesting that this ideal is the product of the poet's own imagination. The poet creates a world that is better than the one in which he actually lives. If the poet ranges "only within the zodiac of his own wit," if he "nothing affirms and therefore never lieth," then he is not imitating some preexistent eternal ideal, a reality hidden beneath appearances, but one that he creates and whose status is purely fictive. The moral utility of such a poetry, however, is greatly reduced if the "nature" imitated is not real.

This is precisely how Francis Bacon describes the relationship between poetry and "revealed providence":

> The use of this Fained History [i.e., poetry] hath been to give some shadow of satisfaction to the mind of Man in those points wherein the Nature of things doth deny it, the world being in proportion inferior to the soul; by reason whereof there is agreeable to the spirit of Man a more ample Greatness, a more exact Goodness, and a more absolute variety than can be found in the Nature of things . . . because *true History* propoundeth the successes and issues of actions not so agreeable to the merits of Virtue and Vice, therefore *Poesie* faines them more just in Retribution and more according to Revealed Providence (*Advancement of Learning*).

For Bacon, the ideal represented, or imitated, by poetry is entirely fictive; it is merely "Feined History." If poetry can represent divine retribution and providence in a way history cannot, as Sidney suggests, it does so only by creating "shadows," which Bacon juxtaposes to "the Nature of things" described by history.

Bacon thus retains the opposition between history and poetry, but claims that poetry is inferior to "the nature of things"; its moral persuasiveness is undercut by its fictitiousness. Bacon's critique of poetry leads to a questioning of idealist representations of "nature" in the seventeenth century. The crucial issue for critics becomes defining what "the nature of things" is. If it is not the ideal cosmological conception of Nature Sidney advocates, it is also not the strict empiricism usually (although inaccurately) attributed to Bacon by some historians. During and after the Civil War, debates about "the nature of things" become crucial political issues, intertwined with debates about the power of the monarchy. These debates cut across what we in the twentieth century consider disciplinary boundaries, occupying, by the end of the century, not only literary theorists such as Dryden, but philosophers such as John Locke and scientists such as Robert Boyle and Isaac Newton.

Writing after the English Civil War, Dryden tackles the same question as his predecessors: what exactly is the "nature of things?" What is the "nature" that the poet imitates? *An Essay of Dramatic Poesy* demonstrates the range of meanings the word *nature* could hold for a critic in the late seventeenth century. If the four interlocutors in Dryden's dialogue all agree that a play is "a lively imitation of nature," each understands something radically different by that phrase. The discussion of the three unities, which figures prominently in the *Essay*, hinges on the meaning of nature. Although this debate may strike the modern reader as sometimes downright silly, it was nonetheless a hotly and seriously contested issue in the late seventeenth century, particularly in tragedy, as Corneille's defensiveness about his own dramatic practice suggests. The French neoclassicists insisted upon strict adherence to the unities of time, place, and action, even though these "rules" were based on a misreading of Aristotle's *Poetics*. These rules, which required that the action of a play should be confined to twenty-four hours at most, that the scene should be set in a single place, and that the action represented be a single action and not a series of actions, were justified as being a truer representation of nature, as more like the way things really occur in life. Of course the great English playwrights of the early seventeenth century—particularly Shakespeare—did not fare so well when judged by this strict standard of verisimilitude. If audiences ought not to be asked to believe that a stage that is in one scene Egypt should in the next be Rome, that is exactly what Shakespeare does in *Anthony and Cleopatra*. If it is not plausible to believe that in the space of a three-hour play thirty or forty years can have passed, that is precisely what Shakespeare asks his audience to believe in his history plays. Words like *plausibility* and *believability* suggest a faithful representation of the world, what the French neoclassicists called *vraisemblance*. Behind the debate over the three unities lies a more fundamental debate about the nature of nature and the proper representation of it.

Dryden's use of the dialogue form in the *Essay* enables him to explore the tensions that existed by the end of the seventeenth century between "scientific" knowledge and received philosophical and religious ideals. Each of his interlocutors admits that the "more useful experiments in philosophy [read science], more noble secrets in optics, medicine, anatomy, [and] astronomy," have revealed "a new nature." But none of them, including Dryden's own persona, Neander, sees this "new knowledge" as a necessarily "better" imitation of nature. All four feel the need to reassert the truth of a providential design that orders and controls nature. Crites, for instance, dismisses advances in scientific knowledge as irrelevant for art, arguing that the ancients have been "faithful and wise observers of nature, which is so torn and ill-represented in our [i.e., modern] plays." Eugenius asserts that the modern poets, because they have "the life" before them, can "arrive still nearer to perfection" than the ancient poets whose imitation of nature was "narrow," "as if they imitated only an eye or an hand, and did not dare to venture on the lines of a face or the proportion of a body." But Eugenius does not argue that the poet should be a mere copyist. While he accuses the ancients of "swerving from the rules of their own art by misrepresenting nature" (it is Eugenius who points out that the French, and not the Greeks, formulated the three unities), he also accuses them of ignoring the moral demands of poetic justice by showing "a prosperous wickedness and an unhappy piety." The moralistic invocation of poetic justice—punishing vice and rewarding virtue—is the hallmark of idealist views of nature, ingrained in the seventeenth-century consciousness because it was the key ingredient in defenses of the theater against attacks on its immorality, which even after the Restoration were still frequent. Although Lisideius, in defending the stricter French neoclassicism, comes close to a "realist" conception of nature, he too eventually recognizes the demands of poetic justice. Shakespeare's habit of cramming thirty or forty years into one play is a distortion of historical verisimilitude. It is "not to imitate or paint Nature, but rather to draw her in miniature, to take her in little; to look upon her through the wrong end of a perspective, and receive her images not only much less, but infinitely more imperfect than the life." But he does not go so far as to demand strict adherence to some empirical standard of verisimilitude; indeed, he seems somewhat uncomfortable with the opportunities to observe nature afforded by such technologies as microscopes and telescopes. Idealism creeps into his argument in the form of the "pleasing fallacy" of poetic justice. The playwright "dispenses with the severity of history, to reward the virtue which has been rendered to us there unfortunate."

Neander's comments on nature reveal the extent to which the debate over the imitation of nature was cultural and political as well as aesthetic. In this section of the *Essay*, Dryden reveals the tension between his nationalistic fervor for the English stage and his attraction to the aristocratic ideals of the court in which he sought patronage. He criticizes French drama for its inability to imitate the humours and passions of the individual, for displaying "the beauties of a statue, but not of a man" and praises Ben Jonson for his "knowledge and observation of particular persons," his ability to capture in his "humours" the peculiar and extravagant affectation and turn it to comic purpose. But Jonsonian *mimesis* is low *mimesis*—the imitation of the crude and vulgar. Beaumont and Fletcher more nearly imitated the polite and witty "conversation of gentlemen." The imitation of nature, for Dryden, grows out of social circumstances. The courtly society with whom Dryden curried favor required a more idealized version of nature than Jonsonian comedy provided. This is why Neander argues that heroic verse in tragedy is more "natural" than blank verse. It is "Nature wrought up to a higher pitch." Ultimately, for "a play to be like Nature, is to be set above it." The courtly idealism that marks Dryden's defense of rhyme in tragedy is, at first glance, reminiscent of Sidney's idealism, but it is, in fact, quite different, just as the court for which Dryden wrote was different from Elizabeth's, considerably reduced in power and influence.

At the end of the century, the appearance of a new group of writers traditionally excluded from both literature and literary criticism began to expose the aristocratic and elitist ideologies underpinning of the debate over poetry's moral utility and imitation of nature. The last decades of the seventeenth century witnessed a renewed inquiry into the intellectual abilities and education of women as well as the emergence of the first group of professional women writers, many of them playwrights, conscious of themselves as an intellectual group and of their precarious positions in the theatrical world of late seventeenth- and early eighteenth-century London. Aphra Behn was one of the most outspoken of this group. Her "defense" of her own writing, articulated in the "Epistle to the Reader" that prefaces *The Dutch Lover*, exposes contemporary criticism's absolute reliance on the imitation of received authorities, particularly the "master texts" of classical antiquity, which were available only to the educated and ruling elite. As a woman, Behn did not have training in Latin and Greek and, therefore, no access to an education in the classics. As a successful playwright, however, she had more than a little self-interest in the newly emerging avocation of criticism and the proliferation of critics "whose Business it is to find Fault." Her defense of *The Dutch Lover* undermines every commonplace of seventeenth-century criticism by setting her practical experience as a playwright against the "rules" of neoclassical orthodoxy. The moral utility of poetry is the first precept attacked:

> I am myself well able to affirm that one of all our English Poets, and least the Dramatique (so I think you call them) can be justly charg'd with too great reformation of men's minds or manners, and for that I may appeal to general experiment, if those who are the most assiduous Disciples of the Stage, do not make the fondest and the lewdest Crew about this Town.

Behn has a similar contempt for those "who do discourse as formally about the rules of it [drama], as if 'twere the grand affair of human life." The "musty rules of Unity" are certainly intelligible, even to an unlearned woman, but they are, on the whole, more inconvenient than necessary, a hindrance to the most important "rule of Plays," "making them pleasant." Behn reveals more than any critic of the seventeenth century about the difficulties faced by a practicing dramatist in the Restoration theater, particularly one who must operate outside of "proper" society. Her essays are peopled by theater managers and licensors who threaten to suppress her plays, audiences who shout them down, directors who rewrite her lines, and actors who mangle them.

As historians of literary criticism continue to look at more nontraditional kinds of documents by women—prefaces, letters, dedications, journals, diaries—women's roles in shaping the literary tastes of seventeenth- and eighteenth-century England may emerge more clearly. In particular, the conventional notions of what was important to consumers of literature during this period may be radically altered and we may begin to see the role the woman writer played in the shift in the eighteenth century from a criticism focused on the moral utility of poetry to one investigating the sources of aesthetic pleasure.

FURTHER READING

Boyd, John D. *The Function of Mimesis and Its Decline*. Cambridge, Mass.: Harvard University Press, 1968.

Chapman, G. W., ed. *Literary Criticism in England, 1660–1800*. Englewood Cliffs, N.J.: Prentice Hall, 1966.

Cotton, Nancy. *Women Playwrights in England, c. 1363–1750*. East Brunswick, N.J.: Associated University Presses, 1980.

Daiches, David. *Critical Approaches to Literature*. London: Longman, 1956.

Dollimore, Jonathan. *Radical Tragedy: Religion, Ideology, and Power in the Dramas of Shakespeare and His Contemporaries*. Chicago: University of Chicago Press, 1984.

Greville, Fulke. *Poems and Dramas*. Geoffrey Bullough, ed. 2 vols. Edinburgh and London: Oliver and Boyd, 1939.

Hardison, O. B., Jr. *English Literary Criticism: The Renaissance*. Englewood Cliffs, N.J.: Prentice Hall, 1963.

Kahn, Victoria. *Rhetoric, Prudence, and Skepticism in the Renaissance*. Ithaca, N.Y.: Cornell University Press, 1985.

Kelly, Joan. "Did Women Have a Renaissance?" In Kelly, *Women, History, and Theory*. Chicago: University of Chicago Press, 1984.

Morgan, Fidelis. *The Female Wits*. London: Virago Press, 1981.

Smith, Gregory. *Elizabethan Critical Essays*. London: Oxford University Press, 1904.

Springarn, J. E. *Critical Essays of the Seventeenth Century*. London: Oxford University Press, 1907.

Todorov, Tzvetan. *Theories of the Symbolic.* Catherine Porter, trans. Ithaca, N.Y.: Cornell University Press, 1982.

Wimsatt, William K., Jr., and Cleanth Brooks. *Literary Criticism: A Short History.* New York: Vintage Books, 1957.

Zimbardo, Rose. "Dramatic Imitation of Nature in the Restoration's Seventeenth-Century Predecessors." In Robert Markley and Laurie Finke, eds., *From Renaissance to Restoration: Metamorphoses of the Drama.* Cleveland: Bellflower Press, 1984, pp. 57–86.

Sir Philip Sidney 1554–1586

Sir Philip Sidney is usually recognized as the first of the English poet-critics; his *An Apology for Poetry* represents the first complete synthesis of Renaissance ideas about poetry. Sidney was the embodiment of the aristocratic ideals of the Renaissance. He was a man of war, man of affairs, soldier, courtier, poet, and amateur scholar. Born on November 29, 1554, he was the son of Sir Henry Sidney, three times lord deputy of Ireland, and of Lady Mary, the eldest daughter of John Dudley, duke of Northumberland, and sister to Robert Dudley, earl of Leicester, who would become one of the most spectacular and powerful of Elizabeth I's advisors. Sidney entered Shrewsbury school in 1564, at age 10. In 1568 he matriculated at Christ Church, Oxford (where his contemporaries included such Elizabethan notables as Fulke Greville, Richard Carew, Walter Raleigh, Richard Hooker, John Lyly), but he never took a degree, leaving in 1572. He completed his education by traveling abroad. Returning to England in 1575, Sidney led the life of a prominent courtier under the guidance of his uncle, the earl of Leicester. He was the center of a learned literary group investigating the resources of English as a literary language. In 1580 when Sidney was dismissed from court, he retreated to the estates of his sister, Mary Herbert, the countess of Pembroke, where he wrote his long prose pastoral romance, the *Arcadia.* In 1581 Sidney returned to London, where he eventually became a member of Parliament and married Frances Walsingham, daughter of Sir Francis Walsingham, Elizabeth's secretary of state. In 1583 he was knighted by the queen. Sidney's dedication to Protestantism led him to the Low Countries, where he fought against Spain in several battles. On September 22, 1586, he was wounded in the thigh in battle and died shortly before his thirty-second birthday.

In keeping with his sense of the decorum expected of a courtier, Sidney's major works were never published in his lifetime; instead they circulated privately in manuscript. Besides the *Arcadia* (which was first published in 1590), he also wrote the first of the great English sonnet cycles, *Astrophel and Stella,* which was published in 1591.

An Apology for Poetry, published in 1596, is the classical formulation of Renaissance literary theory primarily because of its grace and clarity, its scope, and its typicality. Unlike Puttenham and others before him, Sidney is not concerned with formulating the technical rules of poetry or rhetoric; rather, he treats the subject of poetry generally. At the same time, Sidney's debts are clear; he is a synthesizer, not a trailblazer. His classicism, particularly his understanding of Aristotle's and Horace's poetics, is filtered through the Italian humanists of the previous century. Indeed, one frequently hears echoes of Boccaccio's defense of poetry in the *Genealogy of the Gentile Gods*. Although the *Apology* takes the form of a classical oration, including its division into seven parts, it is perhaps most easily understood as treating three major topics. The first part defends the dignity of poetry, culminating in Sidney's definition of poetry, drawn from Aristotle, as the "art of imitation," a representing or counterfeiting whose purpose is to "teach and delight." The second part demonstrates the superiority of poetry to philosophy and history because it combines the moral precepts of the one with the examples of the other, all the while cloaking the lesson with the pleasurable devices of art to make it more palatable. The final part deals with the specific objections raised against poetry, and in particular the charge that the poet is a liar. Sidney follows Boccaccio on this point: "The poet he nothing affirms and therefore never lieth." The poet's imitations, his representations are not lies, as Plato would have it, because he makes no truth claims for them.

AN APOLOGY FOR POETRY

When the right virtuous Edward Wotton[1] and I were at the Emperor's court together, we gave ourselves to learn horsemanship of John Pietro Pugliano, one that with great commendation had the place of an esquire in his stable. And he, according to the fertileness of the Italian wit, did not only afford us the demonstration of his practice, but sought to enrich our minds with the contemplations therein which he thought most precious. But with none I remember mine ears were at any time more loaden, than when (either angered with slow payment, or moved with our learner-like admiration) he exercised his speech in the praise of his faculty. He said soldiers were the noblest estate of mankind, and horsemen the noblest of soldiers. He said they were the masters of war and ornaments of peace, speedy goers and strong abiders, triumphers both in camps and courts. Nay, to so unbelieved a point he proceeded, as that no earthly thing bred such wonder to a prince as to be a good horseman. Skill of government was but a *pedanteria*[2] in comparison. Then would he add certain praises, by telling what a peerless beast a horse was, the only serviceable courtier without flattery, the beast of most beauty, faithfulness, courage, and such more, that if I had not been a piece of a logician before I came to him, I think he would have persuaded me to have wished myself a horse. But thus much at least with his no few words he drave into me, that self-love is better than any gilding to make that seem gorgeous wherein ourselves are parties.

Wherein, if Pugliano's strong affection and weak arguments will not satisfy you, I will give you a nearer example of myself, who (I know not by what mischance) in these my not old years and idlest times having slipped into the title of a poet, am provoked to say something unto you in the defence of that my unelected vocation, which if I handle with more good will than good reasons, bear with me, since the scholar is to be pardoned that followeth the steps of his master. And yet I must say that, as I have just cause to make a pitiful defence of poor Poetry, which from almost the highest estimation of learning is fallen to be the laughing-stock of children, so have I need to bring some more available proofs, since the former is by no man barred of his deserved credit, the silly latter hath had even the names of philosophers used to the defacing of it, with great danger of civil war among the Muses.

And first, truly, to all them that, professing learning, inveigh against Poetry, may justly be objected that they go very near to ungratefulness, to seek to deface that which, in the noblest nations and languages that are known, hath been the first light-giver to ignorance, and first nurse, whose milk by little and little enabled them to feed afterwards of tougher knowledges. And will they now play the hedgehog that, being received into the den, drave out his host? Or rather the vipers, that with their birth kill their parents? Let learned Greece in any of her manifold sciences be able to show me one book before Musaeus, Homer, and Hesiod, all three nothing else but poets. Nay, let any history be brought that can say any writers were there before them, if they were not men of the same skill, as Orpheus, Linus, and some other are named, who, having been the first of that country that made pens deliverers of their knowledge to their posterity, may justly challenge to be called their fathers in learning: for not only in time they had this priority (although in itself antiquity be venerable) but went before them, as causes to draw with their charming sweetness the wild untamed wits to an admiration of knowledge. So, as Amphion was said to move stones with his poetry to build Thebes, and Orpheus to be listened to by beasts—indeed stony and beastly people—so among the Romans were Livius Andronicus, and Ennius. So in the Italian language the first that made it aspire to be a treasure-house of science were the poets Dante, Boccaccio, and Petrarch. So in our English were Gower and Chaucer, after whom, encouraged and delighted with their excellent fore-going, others have followed, to beautify our mother tongue, as well in the same kind as in other arts.

This did so notably show itself, that the philosophers of Greece durst not a long time appear to the world but under the masks of poets. So Thales, Empedocles, and Parmenides sang their natural philosophy in verses; so did Pythagoras and Phocylides their moral counsels; so did Tyrtaeus in war matters, and Solon in matters of policy: or rather they, being poets, did exercise their delightful vein in those points of highest knowledge, which before them lay hid to the world. For that wise Solon was directly a poet it is manifest, having written in verse the notable fable of the Atlantic Island, which was continued by Plato.

And truly even Plato whosoever well considereth shall find that in the body of his work, though the inside and strength were Philosophy, the skin as it were and beauty depended most of Poetry: for all standeth upon dialogues wherein he feigneth many honest burgesses of Athens to speak of such matters, that, if they had been set on the rack, they would never have confessed them; besides his poetical describing the circumstances of their meetings, as the well ordering of a banquet, the delicacy of a walk, with interlacing mere tales, as Gyges' Ring, and others, which who knoweth not to be flowers of poetry did never walk into Apollo's garden.

And even historiographers (although their lips sound of things done, and verity be written in their foreheads) have been glad to borrow both fashion and perchance weight of poets. So Herodotus entitled his History by the name of the nine Muses; and both he and all the rest that followed him either stole or usurped of Poetry their passionate describing of passions, the many particularities of battles, which no man could affirm, or, if that be denied me, long orations put in the mouths of great kings and captains, which it is certain they never pronounced.

So that truly neither philosopher nor historiographer could at the first have entered into the gates of popular judgments, if they had not taken a great passport of Poetry, which in all nations at this day, where learning flourisheth not, is plain to be seen; in all which they have some feeling of Poetry.

In Turkey, besides their law-giving divines, they have no other writers but poets. In our neighbour country Ireland, where truly learning goeth very bare, yet are their poets held in a devout reverence. Even among the most barbarous and simple Indians where no writing is, yet have they their poets who make and sing songs, which they call *areytos*, both of their ancestors' deeds and praises of their gods—a sufficient probability that, if ever learning come among them, it must be by having their hard dull wits softened and sharpened with the sweet delights of Poetry; for until they find a pleasure in the exercises of the mind, great promises of much knowledge will little persuade them that know not the fruits of knowledge. In Wales, the true remnant of the ancient Britons, as there are good authorities to show the long time they had poets, which they called *bards*, so through all the conquests of Romans, Saxons, Danes, and Normans, some of whom did seek to ruin all memory of learning from among them, yet do their poets even to this day last; so as it is not more notable in soon beginning than in long continuing.

But since the authors of most of our sciences were the Romans, and before them the Greeks, let us a little stand upon their authorities, but even so far as to see what names they have given unto this now scorned skill.

Among the Romans a poet was called *vates*, which is as much as a diviner, foreseer, or prophet, as by his conjoined words *vaticinium* and *vaticinari* is manifest: so heavenly a title did that excellent people bestow upon this heart-ravishing knowledge. And so far were they carried into the admiration thereof, that they thought in the chanceable hitting upon any such verses great foretokens of their following fortunes were placed. Whereupon grew the word of *Sortes Virgilianae*, when by sudden opening Virgil's book they lighted upon any verse of his making as it is reported by many: whereof the Histories of the Emperors' Lives are full, as of Albinus, the governor of our island, who in his childhood met with this verse,

> *Arma amens capio nec sat rationis in armis;*[3]

and in his age performed it: which, although it were a very vain and godless superstition, as also it was to think that spirits were commanded by such verses—whereupon this word charms, derived of *carmina*, cometh—so yet serveth it to show the great reverence those wits were held in. And altogether not without ground, since both the oracles of Delphos and Sibylla's prophecies were wholly delivered in verses. For that same exquisite observing of number and measure in words, and that high flying liberty of conceit proper to the poet, did seem to have some divine force in it.

And may not I presume a little further, to show the reasonableness of this word *vates*, and say that the holy David's Psalms are a divine poem? If I do, I shall not do it without the testimony of great learned men, both ancient and modern. But even the name psalms will speak for me, which being interpreted, is nothing but songs; then, that it is fully written in metre, as all learned hebricians agree, although the rules be not yet fully found; lastly and principally, his handling his prophecy, which is merely poetical. For what else is the awaking his musical instruments, the often and free changing of persons, his notable *prosopopeias*,[4] when he maketh you, as it were, see God coming in His majesty, his telling of the beasts' joyfulness, and hills leaping, but a heavenly poesy, wherein almost he showeth himself a passionate lover of that unspeakable and everlasting beauty to be seen by the eyes of the mind, only cleared by faith? But truly now having named him, I fear me I seem to profane that holy name, applying it to Poetry, which is among us thrown down to so ridiculous an estimation. But they that with quiet judgments will look a little deeper into it, shall find the end and working of it such as, being rightly applied, deserveth not to be scourged out of the Church of God.

But now let us see how the Greeks named it, and how they deemed of it. The Greeks called him "a poet," which name hath, as the most excellent, gone through other languages. It cometh of this word *poiein*, which is "to make": wherein I know not whether by luck or wisdom, we Englishmen have met with the Greeks in calling him "a maker": which name, how high and incomparable a title it is, I had rather were known by marking the scope of other sciences than by my partial allegation.

There is no art delivered to mankind that hath not the works of Nature for his principal object, without which they could not consist, and on which they so depend, as they become actors and players, as it were, of what Nature will have set forth. So doth the astronomer look upon the stars, and, by that he seeth, setteth down what order Nature hath taken therein. So do the geometrician and arithmetician in their diverse sorts of quantities. So doth the musician in times tell you which by nature agree, which not. The natural philosopher thereon hath his name, and the moral philosopher standeth upon the natural virtues, vices, and passions of man; and "follow Nature" (saith he) "therein, and thou shalt not err." The lawyer saith what men have determined; the historian what men have done. The grammarian speaketh only of the rules of speech; and the rhetorician and logician, considering what in Nature will soonest prove and persuade, thereon give artificial rules, which still are compassed within the circle of a question according to the proposed matter. The physician weigheth the nature of a man's body, and the nature of things helpful or hurtful unto it. And the metaphysic, though it be in the second and abstract notions, and therefore be counted supernatural, yet doth he indeed build upon the depth of Nature.

Only the poet, disdaining to be tied to any such subjection, lifted up with the vigour of his own invention, doth grow in effect into another nature, in making things either better than Nature bringeth forth, or, quite anew, forms such as never were in Nature, as the Heroes, Demigods, Cyclops, Chimeras, Furies, and such like: so as he goeth hand in hand with Nature, not enclosed within the narrow warrant of her gifts, but freely ranging only within the zodiac of his own wit.

Nature never set forth the earth in so rich tapestry as divers poets have done; neither with pleasant rivers, fruitful trees, sweet-smelling flowers, nor whatsoever else may make the too much loved earth more lovely. Her world is brazen, the poets only deliver a golden.

But let those things alone, and go to man—for whom as the other things are, so it seemeth in him her uttermost cunning is employed—and know whether she have brought forth so true a lover as Theagenes, so constant a friend as Pylades, so valiant a man as Orlando, so right a prince as Xenophon's Cyrus, so excellent a man every way as Virgil's Aeneas. Neither let this be jestingly conceived, because the works of the one be essential, the other in imitation or fiction; for any understanding knoweth the skill of the artificer standeth in that *Idea* or fore-conceit of the work, and not in the work itself. And that the poet hath that *Idea* is manifest, by delivering them forth in such excellency as he hath imagined them. Which delivering forth also is not wholly imaginative, as we are wont to say by them that build castles in the air; but so far substantially it worketh, not only to make a Cyrus, which had been but a particular excellency as Nature might have done, but to bestow a Cyrus upon the world to make many Cyruses, if they will learn aright why and how that maker made him.

Neither let it be deemed too saucy a comparison to balance the highest point of man's wit with the efficacy of Nature; but rather give right honour to the heavenly Maker of that maker, who having made man to His own likeness, set him beyond and over all the works of that second nature: which in nothing he showeth so much as in Poetry, when with the force of a divine breath he bringeth things forth far surpassing her doings, with no small argument to the incredulous of that first accursed fall of Adam: since our erected wit maketh us know what perfection is, and yet our infected will keepeth us from reaching unto it. But these arguments will by few be understood, and by fewer granted. Thus much (I hope) will be given me, that the Greeks with some probability of reason gave him the name above all names of learning.

Now let us go to a more ordinary opening of him, that the truth may be more palpable: and so I hope, though we get not so unmatched a praise as the etymology of his names will grant, yet his very description, which no man will deny, shall not justly be barred from a principal commendation.

Poesy therefore is an art of imitation, for so Aristotle termeth it in his word *mimesis*, that is to say, a representing, counterfeiting, or figuring forth—to speak metaphorically, a speaking picture—with this end, to teach and delight.

Of this have been three several kinds. The chief, both in antiquity and excellency, were they that did imitate the inconceivable excellencies of God. Such were David in his Psalms; Solomon in his Song of Songs, in his Ecclesiastes, and Proverbs; Moses and Deborah in their Hymns; and the writer of Job: which, beside other, the learned Emanuel Tremellius and Franciscus Junius do entitle the poetical part of the Scripture. Against these none will speak that hath the Holy Ghost in due holy reverence. In this kind, though in a full wrong divinity, were Orpheus, Amphion, Homer in his Hymns, and many other, both Greeks and Romans. And this poesy must be used by whosoever will follow St. James's counsel in singing psalms when they are merry, and I know is used with the fruit of comfort by some, when, in sorrowful pangs of their death-bringing sins, they find the consolation of the never-leaving goodness.

The second kind is of them that deal with matters philosophical: either moral, as Tyrtaeus, Phocylides, and Cato; or natural, as Lucretius and Virgil's Georgics; or astronomical, as Manilius and Pontanus; or historical, as Lucan: which who mislike, the fault is in their judgements quite out of taste, and not in the sweet food of sweetly uttered knowledge.

But because this second sort is wrapped within the fold of the proposed subject, and takes not the course of his own invention, whether they properly be poets or no let grammarians dispute, and go to the third, indeed right poets, of whom chiefly this question ariseth. Betwixt whom and these second is such a kind of difference as betwixt the meaner sort of painters, who counterfeit only such faces as are set before them, and the more excellent, who having no law but wit, bestow that in colours upon you which is fittest for the eye to see: as the constant though lamenting look of Lucretia, when she punished in herself another's fault; wherein he painteth not Lucretia whom he never saw, but painteth the outward beauty of such a virtue. For these third be they which most properly do imitate to teach and delight, and to imitate borrow nothing of what is, hath been, or shall be; but range, only reined with learned discretion, into the divine consideration of what may be and should be. These be they that, as the first and most noble sort may justly be termed *vates*, so these are waited on in the excellentest languages and best understandings, with the foredescribed name of poets; for these indeed do merely make to imitate, and imitate both to delight and teach: and delight to move men to take that goodness in hand, which without delight they would fly as from a stranger, and teach, to make them know that goodness whereunto they are moved: which being the noblest scope to which ever any learning was directed, yet want there not idle tongues to bark at them.

These be subdivided into sundry more special denominations. The most notable be the Heroic, Lyric, Tragic, Comic, Satiric, Iambic, Elegiac, Pastoral, and certain others, some of these being termed according to the matter they deal with, some by the sorts of verses they liked best to write in; for indeed the greatest part of poets have apparelled their poetical inventions in that numbrous kind of writing which is called verse—indeed but apparelled, verse being but an ornament and no cause to Poetry, since there have been many most excellent poets that never versified, and now swarm many versifiers that need never answer to the name of poets. For Xenophon, who did imitate so excellently as to give us *effigiem justi imperii*, "the portraiture of a just empire," under the name of Cyrus (as Cicero saith of him), made therein an absolute heroical poem. So did Heliodorus in his sugared invention of that picture of love in Theagenes and Chariclea; and yet both these writ in prose: which I speak to show that it is not rhyming and versing that maketh a poet—no more than a long gown maketh an advocate, who though he pleaded in armour should be an advocate and no soldier. But it is that feigning notable images of virtues, vices, or what else, with that delightful teaching, which must be the right describing note to know a poet by, although indeed the senate of poets hath chosen verse as their fittest raiment, meaning, as in matter they passed all in all, so in manner to go beyond them: not speaking (table talk fashion or like men in a dream) words as they chanceably fall from the mouth, but peizing each syllable of each word by just proportion according to the dignity of the subject.

Now therefore it shall not be amiss first to weigh this latter sort of Poetry by his works, and then by his parts, and if in neither of these anatomies he be condemnable, I hope we shall obtain a more favourable sentence. This purifying of wit, this enriching of memory, enabling of judgment, and enlarging of conceit, which commonly we call learning, under what name soever it come forth, or to what immediate end soever it be directed, the final end is to lead and draw us to as high a perfection as our degenerate souls, made worse by their clayey lodgings, can be capable of. This, according to the inclination of the man, bred many formed impressions. For some that thought this felicity principally to be gotten by knowledge, and no knowledge to be so high and heavenly as acquaintance with the stars, gave themselves to Astronomy; others, persuading themselves to be demigods if they knew the causes of things, became natural and supernatural philosophers; some an admirable delight drew to Music; and some the certainty of demonstration to the Mathematics. But all, one and other, having this scope—to know, and by knowledge to lift up the mind from the dungeon of the body to the enjoying his own divine essence. But when by the balance of experience it was found that the astronomer looking to the stars might fall into a ditch, that the inquiring philosopher might be blind in himself, and the mathematician might draw forth a straight line with a crooked heart, then lo, did proof, the overruler of opinions, make manifest that all these are but serving sciences, which, as they have each a private end in themselves, so yet are they all directed to the highest end of the mistress-knowledge, by the Greeks called *architectonike*, which stands (as I think) in the knowledge of a man's self, in the ethic and politic consideration, with the end of well-doing and not of well-knowing only: even as the saddler's next end is to make a good saddle, but his farther end to serve a nobler faculty, which is horsemanship; so the horseman's to soldiery, and the soldier not only to have the skill, but to perform the practice of a soldier. So that, the ending end of all earthly learning being virtuous action, those skills, that most serve to bring forth that, have a most just title to be princes over all the rest.

Wherein if we can, show we the poet's nobleness, by setting him before his other competitors, among whom as principal challengers step forth the moral philosophers, whom, me thinketh, I see coming towards me with a sullen gravity, as though they could not abide vice by daylight, rudely clothed for to witness outwardly their contempt of outward things, with books in their hands against glory, whereto they set their names, sophistically speaking against subtlety, and angry with any man in whom they see the foul fault of anger. These men casting largesse as they go of definitions, divisions, and distinctions, with a scornful interrogative do soberly ask whether it be possible to find any path so ready to lead a man to virtue as that which teacheth what virtue is—and teacheth it not only by delivering forth his very being, his causes, and effects, but also by making known his enemy, vice, which must be destroyed, and his cumbersome servant, passion, which must be mastered, by showing the generalities that containeth it, and the specialities that are derived from it; lastly, by plain setting down, how it extendeth itself out of the limits of a man's own little world to the government of families, and maintaining of public societies.

The historian scarcely giveth leisure to the

moralist to say so much, but that he, loaden with old mouse-eaten records, authorising himself (for the most part) upon other histories, whose greatest authorities are built upon the notable foundation of hearsay; having much ado to accord differing writers and to pick truth out of partiality; better acquainted with a thousand years ago than with the present age, and yet better knowing how this world goeth than how his own wit runneth; curious for antiquities and inquisitive of novelties; a wonder to young folks and a tyrant in table talk, denieth, in a great chafe, that any man for teaching of virtue, and virtuous actions is comparable to him. "I am *testis temporum, lux veritatis, vita memoriae, magistra vitae, nuncia vetustatis.*[5] The philosopher," saith he, "teacheth a disputative virtue, but I do an active. His virtue is excellent in the dangerless Academy of Plato, but mine showeth forth her honourable face in the battles of Marathon, Pharsalia, Poitiers, and Agincourt. He teacheth virtue by certain abstract considerations, but I only bid you follow the footing of them that have gone before you. Old-aged experience goeth beyond the fine-witted philosopher, but I give the experience of many ages. Lastly, if he make the song-book, I put the learner's hand to the lute; and if he be the guide, I am the light."

Then would he allege you innumerable examples, conferring story by story, how much the wisest senators and princes have been directed by the credit of history, as Brutus, Alphonsus of Aragon, and who not, if need be? At length the long line of their disputation maketh a point in this, that the one giveth the precept, and the other the example.

Now whom shall we find (since the question standeth for the highest form in the school of learning) to be moderator? Truly, as me seemeth, the poet; and if not a moderator, even the man that ought to carry the title from them both, and much more from all other serving sciences. Therefore compare we the poet with the historian and with the moral philosopher; and if he go beyond them both, no other human skill can match him. For as for the divine, with all reverence it is ever to be excepted, not only for having his scope as far beyond any of these as eternity exceedeth a moment, but even for passing each of these in themselves. And for the lawyer, though *jus* be the daughter of justice, and justice the chief of virtues, yet because he seeketh to make men good rather *formidine poenae* than *virtutis amore;*[6] or, to say righter, doth not endeavour to make men good, but that their evil hurt not others; having no care, so he be a good citizen, how bad a man he be: therefore as our wickedness maketh him necessary, and necessity maketh him honourable, so is he not in the deepest truth to stand in rank with these who all endeavour to take naughtiness away and plant goodness even in the secretest cabinet of our souls. And these four are all that any way deal in that consideration of men's manners, which being the supreme knowledge, they that best breed it deserve the best commendation.

The philosopher therefore and the historian are they which would win the goal, the one by precept, the other by example. But both, not having both, do both halt. For the philosopher, setting down with thorny argument the bare rule, is so hard of utterance and so misty to be conceived, that one that hath no other guide but him shall wade in him till he be old before he shall find sufficient cause to be honest. For his knowledge standeth so upon the abstract and general, that happy is that man who may understand him, and more happy that can apply what he doth understand. On the other side, the historian, wanting the precept, is so tied, not to what should be but to what is, to the particular truth of things and not to the general reason of things, that his example draweth no necessary consequence, and therefore a less fruitful doctrine.

Now doth the peerless poet perform both: for whatsoever the philosopher saith should be done, he giveth a perfect picture of it in some one by whom he presupposeth it was done, so as he coupleth the general notion with the particular example. A perfect picture I say, for he yieldeth to the powers of the mind an image of that whereof the philosopher bestoweth but a wordish description, which doth neither strike, pierce, nor possess the sight of the soul so much as that other doth.

For as in outward things, to a man that had never seen an elephant or a rhinoceros, who should tell him most exquisitely all their shapes, colour, bigness, and particular marks; or of a gorgeous palace, the architecture, with declaring the full beauties might well make the hearer able to repeat, as it were by rote, all he had heard, yet should never satisfy his inward conceits with being witness to itself of a true lively knowledge; but the same man, as soon as he might see those beasts well painted, or the house well in model, should straightways grow, without need of any description, to a judicial comprehending of them: so no doubt the philosopher with his learned definition—be it of virtue, vices, matters of public policy or private government—replenisheth the memory with many infallible grounds of wisdom, which, notwithstanding, lie dark before the imaginative and judging power, if they be not illuminated or figured forth by the speaking picture of poesy.

Tully taketh much pains, and many times not without poetical helps, to make us know the force love of our country hath in us. Let us but hear old Anchises speaking in the midst of Troy's flames, or see Ulysses in the fulness of all Calypso's delights bewail his absence from barren and beggarly Ithaca. Anger, the Stoics say, was a short madness: let but Sophocles bring you Ajax on a stage, killing and whipping sheep and oxen, thinking them the army of Greeks, with their chieftains Agamemnon and Menelaus, and tell me if you have not a more familiar insight into anger than finding in the schoolmen his genus and difference. See whether wisdom and temperance in Ulysses and Diomedes, valour in Achilles, friendship in Nisus and Euryalus, even to an ignorant man carry not an apparent shining; and, contrarily, the remorse of conscience in Oedipus, the soon repenting pride of Agamemnon, the self-devouring cruelty in his father Atreus, the violence of ambition in the two Theban brothers, the sour-sweetness of revenge in Medea; and, to fall lower, the Terentian Gnatho and our Chaucer's Pandar so expressed that we now use their names to signify their trades; and finally, all virtues, vices, and passions so in their own natural seats laid to the view, that we seem not to hear of them, but clearly to see through them.

But even in the most excellent determination of goodness, what philosopher's counsel can so readily direct a prince, as the feigned Cyrus in Xenophon; or a virtuous man in all fortunes, as Aeneas in Virgil; or a whole commonwealth, as the way of Sir Thomas More's *Utopia?* I say the way, because where Sir Thomas More erred, it was the fault of the man and not of the poet, for that way of patterning a commonwealth was most absolute, though he perchance hath not so absolutely performed it. For the question is, whether the feigned image of poesy or the regular instruction of philosophy hath the more force in teaching: wherein if the philosophers have more rightly showed themselves philosophers than the poets have attained to the high top of their profession, as in truth,

Mediocribus esse poetis,
Non dii, non homines, non concessere columnae;[7]

it is, I say again, not the fault of the art, but that by few men that art can be accomplished.

Certainly, even our Saviour Christ could as well have given the moral commonplaces of uncharitableness and humbleness as the divine narration of Dives and Lazarus; or of disobedience and mercy, as that heavenly discourse of the lost child and the gracious father; but that His throughsearching wisdom knew the estate of Dives burning in hell, and of Lazarus being in Abraham's bosom, would more constantly (as it were) inhabit both the memory and judgment. Truly, for myself, me seems I see before my eyes the lost child's disdainful prodigality, turned to envy a swine's dinner: which by the learned divines are thought not historical acts, but instructing parables.

For conclusion, I say the philosopher teacheth, but he teacheth obscurely, so as the learned only can understand him; that is to say, he teacheth them that are already taught. But the poet is the food for the tenderest stomachs, the poet is indeed the right popular philosopher, whereof Aesop's tales give good proof; whose pretty allegories, stealing under the formal tales of beasts, make many, more beastly than beasts, begin to hear the sound of virtue from these dumb speakers.

But now may it be alleged that if this imagining of matters be so fit for the imagination, then must the historian needs surpass, who bringeth you images of true matters, such as indeed were done, and not such as fantastically or falsely may be suggested to have been done. Truly, Aristotle himself, in his discourse of poesy, plainly determineth this question, saying that Poetry is *philosophoteron* and *spoudaioteron*, that is to say, it is more philosophical and more studiously serious than history. His reason is, because poesy dealeth with *katholou*, that is to say, with the universal consideration, and the history with *kathekaston*,[8] the particular: "now," saith he, "the universal weighs what is fit to be said or done, either in likelihood or necessity (which the poesy considereth in his imposed names), and the particular only marks whether Alcibiades did, or suffered, this or that." Thus far Aristotle: which reason of his (as all his) is most full of reason.

For indeed, if the question were whether it were better to have a particular act truly or falsely set down, there is no doubt which is to be chosen, no more than whether you had rather have Vespasian's picture right as he was, or, at the painter's pleasure, nothing resembling. But if the question be for your own use and learning, whether it be better to have it set down as it should be, or as it was, then certainly is more doctrinable the feigned Cyrus of Xenophon than the true Cyrus in Justin, and the feigned Aeneas in Virgil than the right Aeneas in Dares Phrygius: as to a lady that desired to fashion her countenance to the best grace, a painter should more benefit her to portray a most sweet face, writing Canidia upon it, than to paint Canidia as she was, who, Horace sweareth, was foul and ill favoured.

If the poet do his part aright, he will show you in Tantalus, Atreus, and such like, nothing that is not to be shunned; in Cyrus, Aeneas, Ulysses, each thing to be followed; where the historian, bound to tell things as things were, cannot be liberal (without he will be poetical) of a perfect pattern, but, as in Alexander or Scipio himself, show doings, some to be liked, some to be misliked. And then how will you discern what to follow but by your own discretion, which you had without reading Quintus Curtius? And whereas a man may say, though in universal consideration of doctrine the poet prevaileth, yet that the history, in his saying such a thing was done, doth warrant a man more in that he shall follow—the answer is manifest: that if he stand upon that *was*—as if he should argue, because it rained yesterday, therefore it should rain to-day—then indeed it hath some advantage to a gross conceit; but if he know an example only informs a conjectured likelihood, and so go by reason, the poet doth so far exceed him as he is to frame his example to that which is most reasonable, be it in warlike, politic, or private matters; where the historian in his bare *was* hath many times that which we call fortune to overrule the best wisdom. Many times he must tell events whereof he can yield no cause; or, if he do, it must be poetical.

For that a feigned example hath as much force to teach as a true example (for as for to move, it is clear, since the feigned may be tuned to the highest key of passion), let us take one example wherein a poet and a historian do concur. Herodotus and Justin do both testify that Zopyrus, King Darius' faithful servant, seeing his master long resisted by the rebellious Babylonians, feigned himself in extreme disgrace of his king: for verifying of which, he caused his own nose and ears to be cut off, and so flying to the Babylonians, was received, and for his known valour so far credited, that he did find means to deliver them over to Darius. Much like matter doth Livy record of Tarquinius and his son. Xenophon excellently feigneth such another stratagem performed by Abradatas in Cyrus' behalf. Now would I fain know, if occasion be presented unto you to serve your prince by such an honest dissimulation, why you do not as well learn it of Xenophon's fiction as of the other's verity? And truly so much the better, as you shall save your nose by the bargain; for Abradatas did not counterfeit so far. So then the best of the historian is subject to the poet; for whatsoever action, or faction, whatsoever counsel, policy, or war stratagem the historian is bound to recite, that may the poet (if he list) with his imitation make his own, beautifying it both for further teaching, and more delighting, as it pleaseth him: having all, from Dante's heaven to his hell, under the authority of his pen. Which if I be asked what poets have done so, as I might well name some, yet say I and say again, I speak of the art, and not of the artificer.

Now, to that which commonly is attributed to the praise of histories, in respect of the notable learning is gotten by marking the success, as though therein a man should see virtue exalted and vice punished—truly that commendation is peculiar to Poetry, and far off from history. For indeed Poetry ever setteth virtue so out in her best colours, making Fortune her well-waiting handmaid, that one must needs be enamoured of her. Well may you see Ulysses in a storm, and in other hard plights; but they are but exercises of patience and magnanimity, to make them shine the more in the near-following prosperity. And of the contrary part, if evil men come to the stage, they ever go out (as the tragedy writer answered to one that misliked the show of such persons) so manacled as they little animate folks to follow them. But the historian, being captived to the truth of a foolish world, is many times a terror from well-doing, and an encouragement to unbridled wickedness.

For see we not valiant Miltiades rot in his fetters? the just Phocion and the accomplished Socrates put to death like traitors? the cruel Severus live prosperously? the excellent Severus miserably murdered? Sylla and Marius dying in their beds? Pompey and Cicero slain then when they would have thought exile a happiness? See we not virtuous Cato driven to kill himself, and rebel Caesar so advanced that his name yet, after 1600 years, lasteth in the highest honour?

And mark but even Caesar's own words of the forenamed Sylla (who in that only did honestly, to put down his dishonest tyranny), *literas nescivit,*[9] as if want of learning caused him to do well. He meant it not by Poetry, which, not content with earthly plagues, deviseth new punishments in hell for tyrants, nor yet by Philosophy, which teacheth *occidendos esse;*[10] but no doubt by skill in History, for that indeed can afford your Cypselus, Periander, Phalaris, Dionysius, and I know not how many more of the same kennel, that speed well enough in their abominable injustice or usurpation. I conclude therefore, that he excelleth History, not only in furnishing the mind with knowledge, but in setting it forward to that which deserveth to be called and accounted good: which setting forward, and moving to well-doing, indeed setteth the laurel crown upon the poet as victorious, not only of the historian, but over the philosopher, howsoever in teaching it may be questionable.

For suppose it be granted (that which I suppose with great reason may be denied) that the philosopher, in respect of his methodical proceeding, doth teach more perfectly than the poet, yet do I think that no man is so much *philophilosophos*[11] as to compare the philosopher in moving with the poet.

And that moving is of a higher degree than teaching, it may be this appear, that it is well nigh the cause and the effect of teaching. For who will be taught, if he be not moved with desire to be taught? and what so much good doth that teaching bring forth (I speak still of moral doctrine) as that it moveth one to do that which it doth teach? For, as Aristotle saith, it is not *gnosis* but *praxis*[12] must be the fruit. And how *praxis* cannot be, without being moved to practise, it is no hard matter to consider.

The philosopher showeth you the way, he informeth you of the particularities, as well of the tediousness of the way, as of the pleasant lodging you shall have when your journey is ended, as of the many by-turnings that may divert you from your way. But this is to no man but to him that will read him, and read him with attentive studious painfulness; which constant desire whosoever hath in him, hath already passed half the hardness of the way, and therefore is beholding to the philosopher but for the other half. Nay truly, learned men have learnedly thought that where once reason hath so much overmastered passion as that the mind hath a free desire to do well, the inward light each mind hath in itself is as good as a philosopher's book; seeing in Nature we know it is well to do well, and what is well and what is evil, although not in the words of art which philosophers bestow upon us; for out of natural conceit the philosophers drew it. But to be moved to do that which we know, or to be moved with desire to know, *hoc opus, hic labor est.*[13]

Now therein of all sciences (I speak still of human, and according to the human conceits) is our poet the monarch. For he doth not only show the way, but giveth so sweet a prospect into the way, as will entice any man to enter into it. Nay, he doth, as if your journey should lie through a fair vineyard, at the first give you a cluster of grapes, that full of that taste, you may long to pass further. He beginneth not with obscure definitions, which must blur the margent with interpretations, and load the memory with doubtfulness; but he cometh to you with words set in delightful proportion, either accompanied with, or prepared for, the well enchanting skill of music; and with a tale forsooth he cometh unto you, with a tale which holdeth children from play, and old men from the chimney corner. And, pretending no more, doth intend the winning of the mind from wickedness to virtue: even as the child is often brought to take most wholesome things by hiding them in such other as have a pleasant taste: which, if one should begin to tell them the nature of aloes or rhubarb they should receive, would sooner take their physic at their ears than at their mouth. So is it in men (most of which are childish in the best things, till they be cradled in their graves): glad they will be to hear the tales of Hercules, Achilles, Cyrus, and Aeneas; and, hearing them, must needs hear the right description of wisdom, valour, and justice; which, if they had been barely, that is to say philosophically, set out, they would swear they be brought to school again.

That imitation whereof Poetry is, hath the most conveniency to Nature of all other, insomuch that, as Aristotle saith, those things which in themselves are horrible, as cruel battles, unnatural monsters, are made in poetical imitation delightful. Truly, I have known men, that even with reading *Amadis de Gaule* (which God knoweth wanteth much of a perfect poesy) have found their hearts moved to the exercise of courtesy, liberality, and especially courage. Who readeth Aeneas carrying old Anchises on his back, that wisheth not it were his fortune to perform so excellent an act? Whom do not the words of Turnus move, the tale of Turnus having planted his image in the imagination?

> *Fugientem haec terra videbit?*
> *Usque adeone mori miserum est?*[14]

Where the philosophers, as they scorn to delight, so must they be content little to move—saving wrangling whether virtue be the chief or the only good, whether the contemplative or the active life do excel—which Plato and Boethius well knew, and therefore made mistress Philosophy very often borrow the masking raiment of Poesy. For even those hard-hearted evil men who think virtue a school name, and know no other good but *indulgere genio*,[15] and therefore despise the austere admonitions of the philosopher, and feel not the inward reason they stand upon, yet will be content to be delighted—which is all the good-fellow poet seemeth to promise—and so steal to see the form of goodness (which seen they cannot but love) ere themselves be aware, as if they took a medicine of cherries.

Infinite proofs of the strange effects of this poetical invention might be alleged; only two shall serve, which are so often remembered as I think all men know them. The one of Menenius Agrippa, who, when the whole people of Rome had resolutely divided themselves from the senate, with apparent show of utter ruin, though he were (for that time) an excellent orator, came not among them upon trust of figurative speeches or cunning insinuations, and much less with farfetched maxims of Philosophy, which (especially if they were Platonic) they must have learned geometry before they could well have conceived; but forsooth he behaves himself like a homely and familiar poet. He telleth them a tale, that there was a time when all the parts of the body made a mutinous conspiracy against the belly, which they thought devoured the fruits of each other's labour: they concluded they would let so unprofitable a spender starve. In the end, to be short (for the tale is notorious, and as notorious that it was a tale), with punishing the belly they plagued themselves. This applied by him wrought such effect in the people, as I never read that ever words brought forth but then so sudden and so good an alteration; for upon reasonable conditions a perfect reconcilement ensued. The other is of Nathan the prophet, who, when the holy David had so far forsaken God as to confirm adultery with murder, when he was to do the tenderest office of a friend, in laying his own shame before his eyes, sent by God to call again so chosen a servant, how doth he it but by telling of a man whose beloved lamb was ungratefully taken from his bosom?—the application most divinely true, but the discourse itself feigned; which made David (I speak of the second and instrumental cause) as in a glass to see his own filthiness, as that heavenly psalm of mercy well testifieth.

By these, therefore, examples and reasons, I think it may be manifest that the poet, with that same hand of delight, doth draw the mind more effectually than any other art doth. And so a conclusion not unfitly ensueth: that, as virtue is the most excellent resting place for all worldly learning to make his end of, so Poetry, being the most familiar to teach it, and most princely to move towards it, in the most excellent work is the most excellent workman.

But I am content not only to decipher him by his works (although works in commendation or dispraise must ever hold an high authority), but more narrowly will examine his parts; so that, as in a man, though all together may carry a presence full of majesty and beauty, perchance in some one defectious piece we may find a blemish. Now in his parts, kinds, or species (as you list to term them), it is to be noted that some poesies have coupled together two or three kinds, as tragical and comical, whereupon is risen the tragi-comical. Some, in the like manner, have mingled prose and verse, as Sannazzaro and Boethius. Some have mingled matters heroical and pastoral. But that cometh all to one in this question, for, if severed they be good, the conjunction cannot be hurtful. Therefore, perchance forgetting some and leaving some as needless to be remembered, it shall not be amiss in a word to cite the special kinds, to see what faults may be found in the right use of them.

Is it then the Pastoral poem which is misliked? For perchance where the hedge is lowest they will soonest leap over. Is the poor pipe disdained, which sometime out of Meliboeus' mouth can show the misery of people under hard lords or ravening soldiers? And again, by Tityrus, what blessedness is derived to them that lie lowest from the goodness of them that sit highest; sometimes, under the pretty tales of wolves and sheep, can include the whole considerations of wrongdoing and patience; sometimes show that contention for trifles can get but a trifling victory: where perchance a man may see that even Alexander and Darius, when they strave who should be cock of this world's dunghill, the benefit they got was that the afterlivers may say,

Haec memini et victum frustra contendere Thirsin:
Ex illo Corydon, Corydon est tempore nobis.[16]

Or is it the lamenting Elegiac? which in a kind heart would move rather pity than blame, who bewails with the great philosopher Heraclitus the weakness of mankind and the wretchedness of the world; who surely is to be praised, either for compassionate accompanying just causes of lamentation, or for rightly painting out how weak be the passions of woefulness. Is it the bitter but wholesome Iambic? which rubs the galled mind, in making shame the trumpet of villainy with bold and open crying out against naughtiness. Or the Satiric? who

Omme vafer vitium ridenti tangit amico;[17]

who sportingly never leaveth until he make a man laugh at folly, and at length ashamed to laugh at himself, which he cannot avoid, without avoiding the folly; who, while

circum praecordia ludit,[18]

giveth us to feel how many headaches a passionate life bringeth us to; how, when all is done,

Est Ulubris, animus si nos non deficit aequus.[19]

No, perchance it is the Comic, whom naughty play-makers and stage-keepers have justly made odious. To the argument of abuse I will answer after. Only thus much now is to be said, that the Comedy is an imitation of the common errors of our life, which he representeth in the most ridiculous and scornful sort that may be, so as it is impossible that any beholder can be content to be such a one.

Now, as in geometry the oblique must be known as well as the right, and in arithmetic the odd as well as the even, so in the actions of our life who seeth not the filthiness of evil wanteth a great foil to perceive the beauty of virtue. This doth the Comedy handle so in our private and domestical matters, as with hearing it we get as it were an experience, what is to be looked for of a niggardly Demea, of a crafty Davus, of a flattering Gnatho, of a vainglorious Thraso; and not only to know what effects are to be expected, but to know who be such, by the signifying badge given them by the comedian. And little reason hath any man to say that men learn evil by seeing it so set out; since, as I said before, there is no man living but, by the force truth hath in Nature, no sooner seeth these men play their parts, but wisheth them *in pistrinum;*[20] although perchance the sack of his own faults lie so behind his back that he seeth not himself dance the same measure; whereto yet nothing can more open his eyes than to find his own actions contemptibly set forth.

So that the right use of Comedy will (I think) by nobody be blamed, and much less of the high and excellent Tragedy, that openeth the greatest wounds, and showeth forth the ulcers that are covered with tissue; that maketh kings fear to be tyrants, and tyrants manifest their tyrannical humours; that, with stirring the affects of admiration and commiseration, teacheth the uncertainty of this world, and upon how weak foundations gilden roofs are builded; that maketh us know,

Qui sceptra saevus duro imperio regit,
Timet timentes, metus in auctorem redit.[21]

But how much it can move, Plutarch yieldeth a notable testimony of the abominable tyrant Alexander Pheraeus, from whose eyes a tragedy, well made and represented, drew abundance of tears, who without all pity had murdered infinite numbers, and some of his own blood; so as he that was not ashamed to make matters for tragedies, yet could not resist the sweet violence of a tragedy. And if it wrought no further good in him, it was that he, in despite of himself, withdrew himself from hearkening to that which might mollify his hardened heart. But it is not the Tragedy they do mislike; for it were too absurd to cast out so excellent a representation of whatsoever is most worthy to be learned.

Is it the Lyric that most displeaseth? who with his tuned lyre and well-accorded voice, giveth praise, the reward of virtue, to virtuous acts; who gives moral precepts, and natural problems; who sometimes raiseth up his voice to the height of the heavens, in singing the lauds of the immortal God. Certainly, I must confess my own barbarousness, I never heard the old song of Percy and Douglas that I found not my heart moved more than with a trumpet; and yet is it sung but by some blind crowder, with no rougher voice than rude style; which, being so evil apparelled in the dust and cobwebs of that uncivil age, what would it work, trimmed in the gorgeous eloquence of Pindar? In Hungary I have seen it the manner at all feasts, and other such meetings, to have songs of their ancestors' valour, which that right soldierlike nation think the chiefest kindlers of brave courage. The incomparable Lacedemonians did not only carry that kind of music ever with them to the field, but even at home, as such songs were made, so were they all content to be the singers of them; when the lusty men were to tell what they did, the old men what they had done, and the young men what they would do. And where a man may say that Pindar many times praiseth highly victories of small moment, matters rather of sport than virtue; as it may be answered, it was the fault of the poet, and not of the poetry, so indeed the chief fault was in the time and custom of the Greeks, who set those toys at so high a price that Philip of Macedon reckoned a horserace won at Olympus among his three fearful felicities. But as the unimitable Pindar often did, so is that kind most capable and most fit to awake the thoughts from the sleep of idleness, to embrace honourable enterprises.

There rests the Heroical, whose very name (I think) should daunt all backbiters; for by what conceit can a tongue be directed to speak evil of that which draweth with it no less champions than Achilles, Cyrus, Aeneas, Turnus, Tydeus, and Rinaldo? who doth not only teach and move to a truth, but teacheth and moveth to the most high and excellent truth; who maketh magnanimity and justice shine throughout all misty fearfulness and foggy desires; who, if the saying of Plato and Tully be true, that who could see virtue would be wonderfully ravished with the love of her beauty—this man sets her out to make her more lovely in her holiday apparel, to the eye of any that will deign not to disdain until they understand. But if anything be already said in the defence of sweet Poetry, all concurreth to the maintaining the Heroical, which is not only a kind, but the best and most accomplished kind of Poetry. For as the image of each action stirreth and instructeth the mind, so the lofty image of such worthies most inflameth the mind with desire to be worthy, and informs with counsel how to be worthy. Only let Aeneas be worn in the tablet of your memory, how he governeth himself in the ruin of his country; in the preserving his old father, and carrying away his religious ceremonies; in obeying the god's commandment to leave Dido, though not only all passionate kindness, but even the human consideration of virtuous gratefulness, would have craved other of him; how in storms, how in sports, how in war, how in peace, how a fugitive, how victorious, how besieged, how besieging, how to strangers, how to allies, how to enemies, how to his own; lastly, how in his inward self, and how in his outward government; and I think, in a mind not prejudiced with a prejudicating humour, he will be found in excellency fruitful, yea, even as Horace saith,

melius Chrysippo et Crantore.[22]

But truly I imagine it falleth out with these poet-whippers, as with some good women, who often are sick, but in faith they cannot tell where. So the name of Poetry is odious to them, but neither his cause nor effects, neither the sum that contains him, nor the particularities descending from him, give any fast handle to their carping dispraise.

Since then Poetry is of all human learning the most ancient and of most fatherly antiquity, as from whence other learnings have taken their beginnings; since it is so universal that no learned nation doth despise it, nor no barbarous nation is without it; since both Roman and Greek gave divine names unto it, the one of "prophesying," the other of "making," and that indeed that name of "making" is fit for him, considering that whereas other arts retain themselves within their subject, and receive, as it were, their being from it, the poet only bringeth his own stuff, and doth not learn a conceit out of a matter, but maketh matter for a conceit; since neither his description nor his end containeth any evil, the thing described cannot be evil; since his effects be so good as to teach goodness and to delight the learners; since therein (namely in moral doctrine, the chief of all knowledges) he doth not only far pass the historian, but, for instructing, is well nigh comparable to the philosopher, and, for moving, leaves him behind him; since the Holy Scripture (wherein there is no uncleanness) hath whole parts in it poetical, and that even our Saviour Christ vouchsafed to use the flowers of it; since all his kinds are not only in their united forms but in their severed dissections fully commendable; I think (and think I think rightly) the laurel crown appointed for triumphing captains doth worthily (of all other learnings) honour the poet's triumph.

But because we have ears as well as tongues, and that the lightest reasons that may be will seem to weigh greatly, if nothing be put in the counterbalance, let us hear, and, as well as we can, ponder, what objections may be made against this art, which may be worthy either of yielding or answering.

First, truly I note not only in these *mysomousoi*, poet-haters, but in all that kind of people who seek a praise by dispraising others, that they do prodigally spend a great many wandering words in quips and scoffs, carping and taunting at each thing which, by stirring the spleen, may stay the brain from a through-beholding the worthiness of the subject. Those kind of objections, as they are full of very idle easiness, since there is nothing of so sacred a majesty but that an itching tongue may rub itself upon it, so deserve they no other answer, but, instead of laughing at the jest, to laugh at the jester. We know a playing wit can praise the discretion of an ass, the comfortableness of being in debt, and the jolly commodity of being sick of the plague. So of the contrary side, if we will turn Ovid's verse,

Ut lateat virtus proximitate mali,

that "good lie hid in nearness of the evil," Agrippa will be as merry in showing the vanity of science as Erasmus was in commending of folly. Neither shall any man or matter escape some touch of these smiling railers. But for Erasmus and Agrippa, they had another foundation, than the superficial part would promise. Marry, these other pleasant faultfinders, who will correct the verb before they understand the noun, and confute others' knowledge before they confirm their own, I would have them only remember that scoffing cometh not of wisdom; so as the best title in true English they get with their merriments is to be called good fools, for so have our grave forefathers ever termed that humorous kind of jesters.

But that which giveth greatest scope to their scorning humours is rhyming and versing. It is already said (and, as I think, truly said) it is not rhyming and versing that maketh poesy. One may be a poet without versing, and a versifier without poetry. But yet presuppose it were inseparable (as indeed it seemeth Scaliger judgeth) truly it were an inseparable commendation. For if *oratio* next to *ratio*, speech next to reason, be the greatest gift bestowed upon mortality, that cannot be praiseless which doth most polish that blessing of speech; which considers each word, not only (as a man may say) by his forcible quality, but by his best measured quantity, carrying even in themselves a harmony—without, perchance, number, measure, order, proportion be in our time grown odious. But lay aside the just praise it hath, by being the only fit speech for Music (Music, I say, the most divine striker of the senses), thus much is undoubtedly true, that if reading be foolish without remembering, memory being the only treasurer of knowledge, those words which are fittest for memory are likewise most convenient for knowledge.

Now, that verse far exceedeth prose in the knitting up of the memory, the reason is manifest: the words (besides their delight, which hath a great affinity to memory) being so set as one word cannot be lost but the whole work fails; which accuseth itself, calleth the remembrance back to itself, and so most strongly confirmeth it. Besides, one word so, as it were, begetting another, as, be it in rhyme or measured verse, by the former a man shall have a near guess to the follower. Lastly, even they that have taught the art of memory have showed nothing so apt for it as a certain room divided into many places well and thoroughly known. Now, that hath the verse in effect perfectly, every word having his natural seat, which seat must needs make the words remembered. But what needeth more in a thing so known to all men? Who is it that ever was a scholar that doth not carry away some verses of Virgil, Horace, or Cato, which in his youth he learned, and even to his old age serve him for hourly lessons? But the fitness it hath for memory is notably proved by all delivery of arts: wherein for the most part, from Grammar to Logic, Mathematic, Physic, and the rest, the rules chiefly necessary to be borne away are compiled in verses. So that verse being in itself sweet and orderly, and being best for memory, the only handle of knowledge, it must be in jest that any man can speak against it.

Now then go we to the most important imputations laid to the poor poets. For aught I can yet learn, they are these. First, that there being many other more fruitful knowledges, a man might better spend his time in them than in this. Secondly, that it is the mother of lies. Thirdly, that it is the nurse of abuse, infecting us with many pestilent desires, with a siren's sweetness drawing the mind to the serpent's tale of sinful fancy—and herein, especially, comedies give the largest field to ear (as Chaucer saith); how both in other nations and in ours, before poets did soften us, we were full of courage, given to martial exercises, the pillars of manlike liberty, and not lulled asleep in shady idleness with poets' pastimes. And lastly, and chiefly, they cry out with an open mouth as if they outshot Robin Hood, that Plato banished them out of his commonwealth. Truly, this is much, if there be much truth in it.

First, to the first, that a man might better spend his time is a reason indeed; but it doth (as they say) but *petere principium:*[23] for if it be, as I affirm, that no learning is so good as that which teacheth and moveth to virtue, and that none can both teach and move thereto so much as Poetry, then is the conclusion manifest that ink and paper cannot be to a more profitable purpose employed. And certainly, though a man should grant their first assumption, it should follow (methinks) very unwillingly, that good is not good because better is better. But I still and utterly deny that there is sprung out of earth a more fruitful knowledge.

To the second therefore, that they should be the principal liars, I answer paradoxically, but truly, I think truly, that of all writers under the sun the poet is the least liar, and, though he would, as a poet can scarcely be a liar. The astronomer, with his cousin the geometrician, can hardly escape, when they take upon them to measure the height of the stars. How often, think you, do the physicians lie, when they aver things good for sicknesses, which afterwards send Charon a great number of souls drowned in a potion before they come to his ferry? And no less of the rest, which take upon them to affirm. Now for the poet, he nothing affirms, and therefore never lieth. For, as I take it, to lie is to affirm that to be true which is false; so as the other artists, and especially the historian, affirming many things, can, in the cloudy knowledge of mankind, hardly escape from many lies. But the poet (as I said before) never affirmeth. The poet never maketh any circles about your imagination, to conjure you to believe for true what he writes. He citeth not authorities of other histories, but even for his entry calleth the sweet Muses to inspire into him a good invention; in truth, not labouring to tell you what is or is not, but what should or should not be. And therefore, though he recount things not true, yet because he telleth them not for true, he lieth not—without we will say that Nathan lied in his speech before-alleged to David; which as a wicked man durst scarce say, so think I none so simple would say that Aesop lied in the tales of his beasts; for who thinks that Aesop writ it for actually true were well worthy to have his name chronicled among the beasts he writeth of. What child is there that, coming to a play, and seeing *Thebes* written in great letters upon an old door, doth believe that it is Thebes? If then a man can arrive, at that child's age, to know that the poets' persons and doings are but pictures what should be, and not stories what have been, they will never give the lie to things not affirmatively but allegorically and figuratively written. And therefore, as in History looking for truth, they go away full fraught with falsehood, so in Poesy looking but for fiction, they shall use the narration but as an imaginative ground-plot of a profitable invention.

But hereto is replied, that the poets give names to men they write of, which argueth a conceit of an actual truth, and so, not being true, proves a falsehood. And doth the lawyer lie then, when under the names of "John a Stile" and "John a Noakes" he puts his case? But that is easily answered. Their naming of men is but to make their picture the more lively, and not to build any history: painting men, they cannot leave men nameless. We see we cannot play at chess but that we must give names to our chessmen; and yet, methinks, he were a very partial champion of truth that would say we lied for giving a piece of wood the reverend title of a bishop. The poet nameth Cyrus or Aeneas no other way than to show what men of their fames, fortunes, and estates should do.

Their third is, how much it abuseth men's wit, training it to wanton sinfulness and lustful love: for indeed that is the principal, if not the only, abuse I can hear alleged. They say the Comedies rather teach than reprehend amorous conceits. They say the Lyric is larded with passionate sonnets, the Elegiac weeps the want of his mistress, and that even to the Heroical Cupid hath ambitiously climbed. Alas, Love, I would thou couldst as well defend thyself as thou canst offend others. I would those on whom thou dost attend could either put thee away, or yield good reason why they keep thee. But grant love of beauty to be a beastly fault (although it be very hard, since only man, and no beast, hath that gift to discern beauty); grant that lovely name of Love to deserve all hateful reproaches (although even some of my masters the philosophers spent a good deal of their lamp-oil in setting forth the excellency of it); grant, I say, whatsoever they will have granted, that not only love, but lust, but vanity, but (if they list) scurrility, possesseth many leaves of the poets' books; yet think I, when this is granted, they will find their sentence may with good manners put the last words foremost, and not say that Poetry abuseth man's wit, but that man's wit abuseth Poetry.

For I will not deny but that man's wit may make Poesy, which should be *eikastike*, which some learned have defined, "figuring forth good things," to be *phantastike*, which doth contrariwise infect the fancy with unworthy objects; as the painter, that should give to the eye either some excellent perspective, or some fine picture, fit for building or fortification, or containing in it some notable example, as Abraham sacrificing his son Isaac, Judith killing Holofernes, David fighting with Goliath, may leave those, and please an ill-pleased eye with wanton shows of better hidden matters. But what, shall the abuse of a thing make the right use odious? Nay truly, though I yield that Poesy may not only be abused, but that being abused, by the reason of his sweet charming force, it can do more hurt than any other army of words, yet shall it be so far from concluding that the abuse should give reproach to the abused, that contrariwise it is a good reason, that whatsoever, being abused, doth most harm, being rightly used (and upon the right use each thing conceiveth his title), doth most good.

Do we not see the skill of Physic (the best rampire to our often-assaulted bodies), being abused, teach poison, the most violent destroyer? Doth not knowledge of Law, whose end is to even and right all things, being abused, grow the crooked fosterer of horrible injuries? Doth not (to go to the highest) God's word abused breed heresy, and His name abused become blasphemy? Truly a needle cannot do much hurt, and as truly (with leave of ladies be it spoken) it cannot do much good. With a sword thou mayest kill thy father, and with a sword thou mayest defend thy prince and country. So that, as in their calling poets the fathers of lies they say nothing, so in this their argument of abuse they prove the commendation.

They allege herewith, that before poets began to be in price our nation hath set their hearts' delight upon action, and not upon imagination, rather doing things worthy to be written, than writing things fit to be done. What that beforetime was, I think scarcely Sphinx can tell, since no memory is so ancient that hath the precedence of Poetry. And certain it is that, in our plainest homeliness, yet never was the Albion nation without poetry. Marry, this argument, though it be levelled against poetry, yet is it indeed a chain-shot against all learning, or bookishness, as they commonly term it. Of such mind were certain Goths, of whom it is written that, having in the spoil of a famous city taken a fair library, one hangman (belike fit to execute the fruits of their wits who had murdered a great number of bodies), would have set fire on it. "No," said another very gravely, "take heed what you do, for while they are busy about these toys, we shall with more leisure conquer their countries."

This indeed is the ordinary doctrine of ignorance, and many words sometimes I have heard spent in it; but because this reason is generally against all learning, as well as Poetry, or rather, all learning but Poetry; because it were too large a digression to handle, or at least too superfluous (since it is manifest that all government of action is to be gotten by knowledge, and knowledge best by gathering many knowledges, which is reading), I only, with Horace, to him that is of that opinion,

jubeo stultum esse libenter;[24]

for as for Poetry itself, it is the freest from this objection.

For Poetry is the companion of the camps. I dare undertake, Orlando Furioso, or honest King Arthur, will never displease a soldier: but the quiddity of *ens* and *prima materia* will hardly agree with a corslet. And therefore, as I said in the beginning, even Turks and Tartars are delighted with poets. Homer, a Greek, flourished before Greece flourished. And if to a slight conjecture a conjecture may be opposed, truly it may seem, that as by him their learned men took almost their first light of knowledge, so their active men received their first motions of courage. Only Alexander's example may serve, who by Plutarch is accounted of such virtue, that Fortune was not his guide but his footstool; whose acts speak for him, though Plutarch did not,—indeed the phoenix of warlike princes. This Alexander left his schoolmaster, living Aristotle, behind him, but took dead Homer with him. He put the philosopher Callisthenes to death for his seeming philosophical, indeed mutinous, stubbornness, but the chief thing he ever was heard to wish for was that Homer had been alive. He well found he received more bravery of mind by the pattern of Achilles than by hearing the definition of fortitude. And therefore, if Cato misliked Fulvius for carrying Ennius with him to the field, it may be answered that, if Cato misliked it, the noble Fulvius liked it, or else he had not done it: for it was not the excellent Cato Uticensis (whose authority I would much more have reverenced), but it was the former, in truth a bitter punisher of faults, but else a man that had never well sacrificed to the graces. He misliked and cried out upon all Greek learning, and yet, being four score years old, began to learn it, belike fearing that Pluto understood not Latin. Indeed, the Roman laws allowed no person to be carried to the wars but he that was in the soldiers' roll, and therefore, though Cato misliked his unmustered person, he misliked not his work. And if he had, Scipio Nasica, judged by common consent the best Roman, loved him. Both the other Scipio brothers, who had by their virtues no less surnames than of Asia and Afric, so loved him that they caused his body to be buried in their sepulchre. So as Cato's authority being but against his person, and that answered with so far greater than himself, is herein of no validity.

But now indeed my burden is great; now Plato's name is laid upon me, whom, I must confess, of all philosophers I have ever esteemed most worthy of reverence, and with great reason: since of all philosophers he is the most poetical. Yet if he will defile the fountain out of which his flowing streams have proceeded, let us boldly examine with what reasons he did it. First, truly a man might maliciously object that Plato, being a philosopher, was a natural enemy of poets. For indeed, after the philosophers had picked out of the sweet mysteries of Poetry the right discerning true points of knowledge, they forthwith, putting it in method, and making a school-art of that which the poets did only teach by a divine delightfulness, beginning to spurn at their guides, like ungrateful prentices, were not content to set up shops for themselves, but sought by all means to discredit their masters; which by the force of delight being barred them, the less they could overthrow them, the more they hated them. For indeed, they found for Homer seven cities strave who should have him for their citizen; where many cities banished philosophers as not fit members to live among them. For only repeating certain of Euripides' verses, many Athenians had their lives saved of the Syracusans, when the Athenians themselves thought many philosophers unworthy to live. Certain poets, as Simonides and Pindar, had so prevailed with Hiero the First, that of a tyrant they made him a just king; where Plato could do so little with Dionysius, that he himself of a philosopher was made a slave. But who should do thus, I confess, should requite the objections made against poets with like cavillation against philosophers; as likewise one should do that should bid one read *Phaedrus* or *Symposium* in Plato, or the discourse of love in Plutarch, and see whether any poet do authorize abominable filthiness, as they do. Again, a man might ask out of what commonwealth Plato did banish them. In sooth, thence where he himself alloweth community of women. So as belike this banishment grew not for effeminate wantonness, since little should poetical sonnets be hurtful when a man might have what woman he listed. But I honour philosophical instructions, and bless the wits which bred them: so as they be not abused, which is likewise stretched to Poetry.

St. Paul himself (who yet, for the credit of poets, allegeth twice two poets, and one of them by the name of a prophet), setteth a watchword upon Philosophy,—indeed upon the abuse. So doth Plato upon the abuse, not upon Poetry. Plato found fault that the poets of his time filled the world with wrong opinions of the gods, making light tales of that unspotted essence, and therefore would not have the youth depraved with such opinions. Herein may much be said; let this suffice: the poets did not induce such opinions, but did imitate those opinions already induced. For all the Greek stories can well testify that the very religion of that time stood upon many and many-fashioned gods, not taught so by the poets, but followed according to their nature of imitation. Who list may read in Plutarch the discourses of Isis and Osiris, of the cause why oracles ceased, of the divine providence, and see whether the theology of that nation stood not upon such dreams which the poets indeed superstitiously observed and truly (since they had not the light of Christ) did much better in it than the philosophers, who, shaking off superstition, brought in atheism. Plato therefore (whose authority I had much rather justly construe than unjustly resist) meant not in general of poets, in those words of which Julius Scaliger saith, *Qua authoritate barbari quidam atque hispidi abuti velint ad poetas e republica exigendos;*[25] but only meant to drive out those wrong opinions of the Deity (whereof now, without further law, Christianity hath taken away all the hurtful belief), perchance (as he thought) nourished by the then esteemed poets. And a man need go no further than to Plato himself to know his meaning: who, in his dialogue called *Ion*, giveth high and rightly divine commendation to Poetry. So as Plato, banishing the abuse, not the thing—not banishing it, but giving due honour unto it—shall be our patron and not our adversary. For indeed I had much rather (since truly I may do it) show their mistaking of Plato (under whose lion's skin they would make an ass-like braying against Poesy) than go about to overthrow his authority; whom, the wiser a man is, the more just cause he shall find to have in admiration; especially since he attributeth unto Poesy more than myself do, namely, to be a very inspiring of a divine force, far above man's wit, as in the afore-named dialogue is apparent.

Of the other side, who would show the honours have been by the best sort of judgments granted them, a whole sea of examples would present themselves: Alexanders, Caesars, Scipios, all favourers of poets; Laelius, called the Roman Socrates, himself a poet, so as part of *Heautontimorumenos* in Terence was supposed to be made by him; and even the Greek Socrates, whom Apollo confirmed to be the only wise man, is said to have spent part of his old time in putting Aesop's fables into verses. And therefore, full evil should it become his scholar Plato to put such words in his master's mouth against poets. But what need more? Aristotle writes the Art of Poesy: and why, if it should not be written? Plutarch teacheth the use to be gathered of them, and how, if they should not be read? And who reads Plutarch's either history or philosophy, shall find he trimmeth both their garments with guards of Poesy. But I list not to defend Poesy with the help of her underling Historiography. Let it suffice that it is a fit soil for praise to dwell upon; and what dispraise may set upon it, is either easily overcome, or transformed into just commendation.

So that, since the excellencies of it may be so easily and so justly confirmed, and the low-creeping objections so soon trodden down: it not being an art of lies, but of true doctrine; not of effeminateness, but of notable stirring of courage; not of abusing man's wit, but of strengthening man's wit; not banished, but honoured by Plato; let us rather plant more laurels for to engarland our poets' heads (which honour of being laureate, as besides them only triumphant captains wear, is a sufficient authority to show the price they ought to be had in) than suffer the ill-favouring breath of such wrong-speakers once to blow upon the clear springs of Poesy.

But since I have run so long a career in this matter, methinks, before I give my pen a full stop, it shall be but a little more lost time to inquire why England (the mother of excellent minds) should be grown so hard a stepmother to poets, who certainly in wit ought to pass all other, since all only proceedeth from their wit, being indeed makers of themselves, not takers of others. How can I but exclaim,

> *Musa, mihi causas memora, quo numine laeso?*[26]

Sweet Poesy, that hath anciently had kings, emperors, senators, great captains, such as, besides a thousand others, David, Adrian, Sophocles, Germanicus, not only to favour poets, but to be poets; and of our nearer times can present for her patrons a Robert, king of Sicily, the great King Francis of France, King James of Scotland; such cardinals as Bembus and Bibbiena: such famous preachers and teachers as Beza and Melanchthon; so learned philosophers as Fracastorius and Scaliger; so great orators as Pontanus and Muretus; so piercing wits as George Buchanan; so grave counsellors as, besides many, but before all, that Hospital of France, than whom (I think) that realm never brought forth a more accomplished judgment, more firmly builded upon virtue—I say these, with numbers of others, not only to read others' poesies, but to poetise for others' reading—that Poesy, thus embraced in all other places, should only find in our time a hard welcome in England, I think the very earth lamenteth it, and therefore decketh our soil with fewer laurels than it was accustomed. For heretofore poets have in England also flourished, and, which is to be noted, even in those times when the trumpet of Mars did sound loudest. And now that an overfaint quietness should seem to strew the house for poets, they are almost in as good reputation as the mountebanks at Venice. Truly even that, as of the one side it giveth great praise to Poesy, which like Venus (but to better purpose) hath rather be troubled in the net with Mars than enjoy the homely quiet of Vulcan; so serves it for a piece of a reason why they are less grateful to idle England, which now can scarce endure the pain of a pen. Upon this necessarily followeth, that base men with servile wits undertake it, who think it enough if they can be rewarded of the printer. And so as Epaminondas is said, with the honour of his virtue to have made an office, by his exercising it, which before was contemptible, to become highly respected, so these, no more but setting their names to it, by their own disgracefulness disgrace the most graceful Poesy. For now, as if all the Muses were got with child to bring forth bastard poets, without any commission they do post over the banks of Helicon, till they make the readers more weary than post-horses; while, in the meantime, they,

> *Queis meliore luto finxit praecordia Titan,*[27]

are better content to suppress the outflowing of their wit, than, by publishing them, to be accounted knights of the same order.

But I that, before ever I durst aspire unto the dignity, am admitted into the company of the paper-blurrers, do find the very true cause of our wanting estimation is want of desert, taking upon us to be poets in despite of Pallas. Now wherein we want desert were a thankworthy labour to express; but if I knew, I should have mended myself. But I, as I never desired the title, so have I neglected the means to come by it. Only, overmastered by some thoughts, I yielded an inky tribute unto them. Marry, they that delight in Poesy itself should seek to know what they do, and how they do; and especially look themselves in an unflattering glass of reason, if they be inclinable unto it. For Poesy must not be drawn by the ears; it must be gently led, or rather it must lead; which was partly the cause that made the ancient-learned affirm it was a divine gift, and no human skill: since all other knowledges lie ready for any that hath strength of wit; a poet no industry can make, if his own genius be not carried unto it; and therefore is it an old proverb, *orator fit, poeta nascitur.*[28] Yet confess I always that as the fertilest ground must be manured, so must the highest-flying wit have a Daedalus to guide him. That Daedalus, they say, both in this and in other, hath three wings to bear itself up into the air of due commendation: that is, Art, Imitation, and Exercise. But these, neither artificial rules nor imitative patterns, we much cumber ourselves withal. Exercise indeed we do, but that very fore-backwardly: for where we should exercise to know, we exercise as having known; and so is our brain delivered of much matter which never was begotten by knowledge. For there being two principal parts—matter to be expressed by words and words to express the matter—in neither we use Art or Imitation rightly. Our matter is *quodlibet* indeed, though wrongly performing Ovid's verse,

> *Quicquid conabor dicere, versus erit:*[29]

never marshalling it into an assured rank, that almost the readers cannot tell where to find themselves.

Chaucer, undoubtedly, did excellently in his *Troilus and Criseyde;* of whom, truly, I know not whether to marvel more, either that he in that misty time could see so clearly, or that we in this clear age walk so stumblingly after him. Yet had he great wants, fit to be forgiven in so reverent antiquity. I account the *Mirror of Magistrates* meetly furnished of beautiful parts, and in the Earl of Surrey's lyrics many things tasting of a noble birth, and worthy of a noble mind. The *Shepherd's Calendar* hath much poetry in his eclogues, indeed worthy the reading, if I be not deceived. That same framing of his style to an old rustic language I dare not allow, since neither Theocritus in Greek, Virgil in Latin, nor Sannazzaro in Italian did affect it. Besides these, do I not remember to have seen but few (to speak boldly) printed, that have poetical sinews in them: for proof whereof, let but most of the verses be put in prose, and then ask the meaning, and it will be found that one verse did but beget another, without ordering at the first what should be at the last; which becomes a confused mass of words, with a tingling sound of rhyme, barely accompanied with reason.

Our Tragedies and Comedies (not without cause cried out against), observing rules neither of honest civility nor of skilful Poetry, excepting *Gorboduc* (again, I say, of those that I have seen), which notwithstanding, as it is full of stately speeches and well-sounding phrases, climbing to the height of Seneca's style, and as full of notable morality, which it doth most delightfully teach, and so obtain the very end of Poesy, yet in truth it is very defectious in the circumstances, which grieveth me, because it might not remain as an exact model of all tragedies. For it is faulty both in place and time, the two necessary companions of all corporal actions. For where the stage should always represent but one place, and the uttermost time presupposed in it should be, both by Aristotle's precept and common reason, but one day, there is both many days, and many places, inartificially imagined.

But if it be so in *Gorboduc*, how much more in all the rest? where you shall have Asia of the one side, and Afric of the other, and so many other under-kingdoms, that the player, when he cometh in, must ever begin with telling where he is, or else the tale will not be conceived. Now ye shall have three ladies walk to gather flowers and then we must believe the stage to be a garden. By and by we hear news of shipwreck in the same place, and then we are to blame if we accept it not for a rock. Upon the back of that comes out a hideous monster with fire and smoke, and then the miserable beholders are bound to take it for a cave. While in the meantime two armies fly in, represented with four swords and bucklers, and then what hard heart will not receive it for a pitched field?

Now of time they are much more liberal, for ordinary it is that two young princes fall in love. After many traverses, she is got with child, delivered of a fair boy, he is lost, groweth a man, falls in love, and is ready to get another child, and all this in two hours' space: which, how absurd it is in sense, even sense may imagine, and Art hath taught, and all ancient examples justified, and at this day, the ordinary players in Italy will not err in. Yet will some bring in an example of *Eunuchus* in Terence, that containeth matter of two days, yet far short of twenty years. True it is, and so was it to be played in two days, and so fitted to the time it set forth. And though Plautus hath in one place done amiss, let us hit with him, and not miss with him. But they will say, How then shall we set forth a story, which containeth both many places and many times? And do they not know that a tragedy is tied to the laws of Poesy, and not of History; not bound to follow the story, but, having liberty, either to feign a quite new matter, or to frame the history to the most tragical conveniency? Again, many things may be told which cannot be showed, if they know the difference betwixt reporting and representing. As, for example, I may speak (though I am here) of Peru, and in speech digress from that to the description of Calicut; but in action I cannot represent it without Pacolet's horse. And so was the manner the ancients took, by some *nuncius* to recount things done in former time or other place.

Lastly, if they will represent an history, they must not (as Horace saith) begin *ab ovo*, but they must come to the principal point of that one action which they will represent. By example this will be best expressed. I have a story of young Polydorus, delivered for safety's sake, with great riches, by his father Priam to Polymnestor, king of Thrace, in the Trojan war time. He, after some years, hearing the overthrow of Priam, for to make the treasure his own, murdereth the child. The body of the child is taken up by Hecuba. She, the same day, findeth a sleight to be revenged most cruelly of the tyrant. Where now would one of our tragedy writers begin, but with the delivery of the child? Then should he sail over into Thrace, and so spend I know not how many years, and travel numbers of places. But where doth Euripides? Even with the finding of the body, leaving the rest to be told by the spirit of Polydorus. This need no further to be enlarged; the dullest wit may conceive it.

But besides these gross absurdities, how

all their plays be neither right tragedies, nor right comedies, mingling kings and clowns, not because the matter so carrieth it, but thrust in clowns by head and shoulders, to play a part in majestical matters, with neither decency nor discretion, so as neither the admiration and commiseration, nor the right sportfulness, is by their mongrel tragi-comedy obtained. I know Apuleius did somewhat so, but that is a thing recounted with space of time, not represented in one moment; and I know the ancients have one or two examples of tragi-comedies, as Plautus hath *Amphitrio*. But, if we mark them well, we shall find, that they never, or very daintily, match hornpipes and funerals. So falleth it out that, having indeed no right comedy, in that comical part of our tragedy, we have nothing but scurrility, unworthy of any chaste ears, or some extreme show of doltishness, indeed fit to lift up a loud laughter, and nothing else: where the whole tract of a comedy should be full of delight, as the tragedy should be still maintained in a well-raised admiration.

But our comedians think there is no delight without laughter; which is very wrong, for though laughter may come with delight, yet cometh it not of delight, as though delight should be the cause of laughter; but well may one thing breed both together. Nay, rather in themselves they have, as it were, a kind of contrariety: for delight we scarcely do but in things that have a conveniency to ourselves or to the general nature; laughter almost ever cometh of things most disproportioned to ourselves and nature. Delight hath a joy in it, either permanent or present. Laughter hath only a scornful tickling. For example, we are ravished with delight to see a fair woman, and yet are far from being moved to laughter. We laugh at deformed creatures, wherein certainly we cannot delight. We delight in good chances, we laugh at mischances; we delight to hear the happiness of our friends, or country, at which he were worthy to be laughed at that would laugh. We shall, contrarily, laugh sometimes to find a matter quite mistaken and go down the hill against the bias, in the mouth of some such men, as for the respect of them one shall be heartily sorry, yet he cannot choose but laugh; and so is rather pained than delighted with laughter. Yet deny I not but that they may go well together: for as in Alexander's picture well set out we delight without laughter, and in twenty mad antics we laugh without delight; so in Hercules, painted with his great beard and furious countenance, in woman's attire, spinning at Omphale's commandment, it breedeth both delight and laughter. For the representing of so strange a power in love procureth delight: and the scornfulness of the action stirreth laughter.

But I speak to this purpose, that all the end of the comical part be not upon such scornful matters as stirreth laughter only, but, mixed with it, that delightful teaching which is the end of Poesy. And the great fault even in that point of laughter, and forbidden plainly by Aristotle, is that they stir laughter in sinful things, which are rather execrable than ridiculous; or in miserable, which are rather to be pitied than scorned. For what is it to make folks gape at a wretched beggar, or a beggarly clown; or, against law of hospitality, to jest at strangers, because they speak not English so well as we do? What do we learn? since it is certain

> *Nil habet infelix paupertas durius in se,*
> *Quam quod ridiculos homines facit.*[30]

But rather a busy loving courtier; a heartless threatening Thraso; a self-wise-seeming schoolmaster; an awry-transformed traveller: these if we saw walk in stage names, which we play naturally, therein were delightful laughter, and teaching delightfulness: as in the other, the tragedies of Buchanan do justly bring forth a divine admiration. But I have lavished out too many words of this play matter. I do it because, as they are excelling parts of Poesy, so is there none so much used in England, and none can be more pitifully abused; which, like an unmannerly daughter showing a bad education, causeth her mother Poesy's honesty to be called in question.

Other sorts of Poetry almost have we none, but that lyrical kind of songs and sonnets: which, Lord, if He gave us so good minds, how well it might be employed, and with how heavenly fruit, both private and public, in singing the praises of the immortal beauty, the immortal goodness of that God who giveth us hands to write and wits to conceive; of which we might well want words, but never matter; of which we could turn our eyes to nothing, but we should ever have new-budding occasions. But truly many of such writings as come under the banner of unresistible love, if I were a mistress, would never persuade me they were in love; so coldly they apply fiery speeches, as men that had rather read lovers' writings (and so caught up certain swelling phrases which hang together like a man which once told me the wind was at north-west and by south, because he would be sure to name winds enough), than that in truth they feel those passions, which easily (as I think) may be betrayed by that same forcibleness or *energia* (as the Greeks call it) of the writer. But let this be a sufficient though short note, that we miss the right use of the material point of Poesy.

Now, for the outside of it, which is words, or (as I may term it) diction, it is even well worse. So is that honey-flowing matron eloquence apparelled, or rather disguised, in a courtesan-like painted affectation: one time with so far-fetched words, they may seem monsters, but must seem strangers, to any poor Englishman; another time with coursing of a letter, as if they were bound to follow the method of a dictionary; another time with figures and flowers extremely winter-starved. But I would this fault were only peculiar to versifiers, and had not as large possession among prose-printers, and (which is to be marvelled) among many scholars, and (which is to be pitied) among some preachers. Truly I could wish, if at least I might be so bold to wish in a thing beyond the reach of my capacity, the diligent imitators of Tully and Demosthenes (most worthy to be imitated) did not so much keep Nizolian paper-books of their figures and phrases, as by attentive translation (as it were) devour them whole, and make them wholly theirs. For now they cast sugar and spice upon every dish that is served to the table, like those Indians, not content to wear earrings at the fit and natural place of the ears, but they will thrust jewels through their nose and lips, because they will be sure to be fine.

Tully, when he was to drive out Catiline, as it were with a thunderbolt of eloquence, often used that figure of repetition, *Vivit. Vivit? Imo vero etiam in senatum venit*, &c.[31] Indeed, inflamed with a well-grounded rage, he would have his words (as it were) double out of his mouth, and so do that artificially which we see men do in choler naturally. And we, having noted the grace of those words, hale them in sometime to a familiar epistle, when it were too too much collar to be choleric. How well store of *similiter cadences* doth sound with the gravity of the pulpit, I would but invoke Demosthenes' soul to tell, who with a rare daintiness useth them. Truly they have made me think of the sophister that with too much sublety would prove two eggs three, and though he might be counted a sophister, had none for his labour. So these men bringing in such a kind of eloquence, well may they obtain an opinion of a seeming fineness, but persuade few—which should be the end of their fineness.

Now for similitudes in certain printed discourses, I think all herbarists, all stories of beasts, fowls, and fishes are rifled up, that they come in multitudes to wait upon any of our conceits; which certainly is as absurd a surfeit to the ears as is possible: for the force of a similitude not being to prove anything to a contrary disputer, but only to explain to a willing hearer; when that is done, the rest is a most tedious prattling, rather over-swaying the memory from the purpose whereto they were applied, than any whit informing the judgment, already either satisfied, or by similitudes not to be satisfied. For my part, I do not doubt, when Antonius and Crassus, the great forefathers of Cicero in eloquence, the one (as Cicero testifieth of them) pretended not to know art, the other not to set by it, because with a plain sensibleness they might win credit of popular ears; which credit is the nearest step to persuasion; which persuasion is the chief mark of Oratory—I do not doubt (I say) but that they used these tracks very sparingly; which, who doth generally use, any man may see doth dance to his own music, and so be noted by the audience more careful to speak curiously than to speak truly.

Undoubtedly (at least to my opinion undoubtedly) I have found in divers smally learned courtiers a more sound style than in some professors of learning; of which I can guess no other cause, but that the courtier, following that which by practice he findeth fittest to nature, therein (though he know it not) doth according to art, though not by art: where the other, using art to show art, and not to hide art (as in these cases he should do), flieth from nature, and indeed abuseth art.

But what? methinks I deserve to be pounded for straying from Poetry to Oratory: but both have such an affinity in this wordish consideration, that I think this digression will make my meaning receive the fuller understanding—which is not to take upon me to teach poets how they should do, but only, finding myself sick among the rest, to show some one or two spots of the common infection grown among the most part of writers; that, acknowledging ourselves somewhat awry, we may bend to the right use both of matter and manner: whereto our language giveth us great occasion, being indeed capable of any excellent exercising of it. I know some will say it is a mingled language. And why not so much the better, taking the best of both the other? Another will say it wanteth grammar. Nay truly, it hath that praise, that it wanteth not grammar: for grammar it might have, but it needs it not; being so easy of itself, and so void of those cumbersome differences of cases, genders, moods, and tenses, which I think was a piece of the Tower of Babylon's curse, that a man should be put to school to learn his mother-tongue. But for the uttering sweetly and properly the conceits of the mind, which is the end of speech, that hath it equally with any other tongue in the world; and is particularly happy in compositions of two or three words together, near the Greek, far beyond the Latin: which is one of the greatest beauties can be in a language.

Now of versifying there are two sorts, the one ancient, the other modern: the ancient marked the quantity of each syllable, and according to that framed his verse; the modern observing only number (with some regard of the accent), the chief life of it standeth in that like sounding of the words, which we call rhyme. Whether of these be the most excellent, would bear many speeches: the ancient (no doubt) more fit for music, both words and time observing quantity, and more fit lively to express divers passions, by the low or lofty sound of the well-weighed syllable. The latter likewise, with his rhyme, striketh a certain music to the ear; and, in fine, since it doth delight, though by another way, it obtains the same purpose: there being in either sweetness, and wanting in neither majesty. Truly the English, before any other vulgar language I know, is fit for both sorts: for, for the ancient, the Italian is so full of vowels that it must ever be cumbered with elisions; the Dutch so, of the other side, with consonants, that they cannot yield the sweet sliding fit for a verse; the French in his whole language hath not one word that hath his accent in the last syllable saving two, called *antepenultima;* and little more hath the Spanish, and therefore very gracelessly may they use dactyls. The English is subject to none of these defects.

Now for the rhyme, though we do not observe quantity, yet we observe the accent very precisely, which other languages either cannot do, or will not do so absolutely. That *caesura*, or breathing place in the midst of the verse, neither Italian nor Spanish have, the French and we never almost fail of. Lastly, even the very rhyme itself the Italian cannot put in the last syllable, by the French named the masculine rhyme, but still in the next to the last, which the French call the female, or the next before that, which the Italians term *sdrucciola*. The example of the former is *buono: suono*, of the *sdrucciola*, *femina: semina*. The French, of the other side, hath both the male, as *bon: son*, and the female, as *plaise: taise*, but the *sdrucciola* he hath not: where the English hath all three, as *due: true*, *father: rather*, *motion: potion;* with much more which might be said, but that I find already the triflingness of this discourse is much too much enlarged.

So that since the ever-praiseworthy Poesy is full of virtue-breeding delightfulness, and void of no gift that ought to be in the noble name of learning; since the blames laid against it are either false or feeble; since the cause why it is not esteemed in England is the fault of poet-apes, not poets; since, lastly, our tongue is most fit to honour Poesy, and to be honoured by Poesy; I conjure you all that have had the evil luck to read this ink-wasting toy of mine, even in the name of the Nine Muses, no more to scorn the sacred mysteries of Poesy, no more to laugh at the name of poets, as though they were next inheritors to fools, no more to jest at the reverent title of a rhymer; but to believe, with Aristotle, that they were the ancient treasurers of the Grecians' divinity; to believe, with Bembus, that they were first bringers-in of all civility; to believe, with Scaliger, that no philosopher's precepts can sooner make you an honest man than the reading of Virgil; to believe, with Clauserus, the translator of Cornutus, that it pleased the heavenly Deity, by Hesiod and Homer, under the veil of fables, to give us all knowledge, Logic, Rhetoric, Philosophy natural and moral, and *quid non?;* to believe, with me, that there are many mysteries contained in Poetry, which of purpose were written darkly, lest by profane wits it should be abused; to believe, with Landino, that they are so beloved of the gods that whatsoever they write proceeds of a divine fury; lastly, to believe themselves, when they tell you they will make you immortal by their verses.

Thus doing, your name shall flourish in the printers' shops; thus doing, you shall be of kin to many a poetical preface; thus doing, you shall be most fair, most rich, most wise, most all; you shall dwell upon superlatives. Thus doing, though you be *libertino patre natus*, you shall suddenly grow *Herculea proles*,

Si quid mea carmina possunt.[32]

Thus doing, your soul shall be placed with Dante's Beatrix, or Virgil's Anchises. But if (fie of such a but) you be born so near the dull-making cataract of Nilus that you cannot hear the planet-like music of Poetry, if you have so earth-creeping a mind that it cannot lift itself up to look to the sky of Poetry, or rather, by a certain rustical disdain, will become such a mome as to be a Momus of Poetry; then, though I will not wish unto you the ass's ears of Midas, nor to be driven by a poet's verses (as Bubonax was) to hang himself, nor to be rhymed to death, as is said to be done in Ireland; yet thus much curse I must send you, in the behalf of all poets, that while you live, you live in love, and never get favour for lacking skill of a sonnet, and, when you die, your memory die from the earth for want of an epitaph.

NOTES

1. Edward Wotton (1548–1626), the first Baron Wotton of Marley, was a courtier and diplomat, half-brother of the Stuart diplomat and poet, Sir Henry Wotton (1568–1639). A friend of Sidney's, he was a beneficiary of Sidney's will and a pallbearer at his funeral.

2. Pedantry, or schoolbook knowledge.

3. "I seize upon arms, while frenzied; nor is there enough reason for arms" (*Aeneid* II. 314).

4. Personifications.

5. "The witness of the ages, the light of truth, the life of memory, the governess of life, the herald of antiquity" (Cicero, *De oratore* II. 9. 36).

6. "By fear of punishment rather than love of virtue" (Horace, *Epistles* I. 16. 52–53).

7. "Mediocre poets are not endured by gods, men, or booksellers" (Horace, *Art of Poetry* 372–73).

8. *Philosophoteron*, "philosophic"; *spoudaioteron*, "of grave import"; *katholou*, "of universals"; *kathekaston*, "of singular or particulars."

9. "He did not know literature."

10. "They are to be killed."

11. A lover of the philosophers.

12. Not abstract knowledge, but action.

13. "This is the work, this is the labor" (*Aeneid* VI. 129).

14. "Shall this land see [Turnus] fleeing away? Is it so wretched a thing to die as that?" (*Aeneid* VII. 645–46).

15. "To indulge one's nature."

16. "I recall those things, and that the conquered Thyrsis strove in vain: From that time, Corydon for us is Corydon" (Virgil, *Eclogue* VII. 69–70).

17. "The rogue touches every vice while causing his friend to laugh" (Persius, *Satires* I. 116–17).

18. "He plays around the heart-strings" (ibid.).

19. "Happiness is found in Ulabrae [an extinct or dead city] if we have a sane mind" (Horace, *Epistles* I. xi. 30).

20. A Roman mill to which slaves were often condemned as punishment.

21. "The savage ruler who wields the sceptre with a hard hand fears his frightened subjects, and fear thus returns to the author of it" (Seneca, *Oedipus* 705–6).

22. "Better than do Chrysippus and Crantor" (Horace, *Epistles* I. 2. 4).

23. "To beg the question."

24. "I ask him to be as much of a fool as he wishes" (Horace, *Satires* I. 1. 63).

25. "The rude and barbarous would abuse such an authority in order to drive the poets out of the state" (*Poetice* 1. 2).

26. "O Muse, tell me in what way was her divinity being injured" (*Aeneid* I. 8).

27. "Whose hearts Titan has fashioned of finer clay" (Juvenal, *Satires* XIV. 35).

28. "An orator is made, a poet born."

29. "Whatever I tried to say was verse" (Ovid, *Tristia* IV. x, 26).

30. "Unhappy poverty has nothing worse than that it makes men ridiculous" (Juvenal, *Satires* III. 152–53).

31. "He lives. Lives?—He even comes into the senate."

32. "Thus doing, though you be the son of a former slave, you shall suddenly grow Herculean offspring, if my poems are able to do anything." The Latin phrases are from Horace, Ovid, and Virgil, respectively.

George Puttenham *ca.* 1529–1590

Puttenham's *The Arte of English Poesie* is one of the most ambitious and comprehensive undertakings in Elizabethan criticism. It demonstrates how the origins of English criticism are bound up with the awakening of linguistic consciousness. It is the most fully documented guide to Tudor approaches to poetry. Unlike Sidney's *Apology*, it is unconcerned with the abstract theory and Platonic ideals that occupied most Renaissance theory.

The Arte of English Poesie appeared anonymously in 1589, but is generally attributed to "Puttenham." Both George Puttenham (*ca.* 1529–1590) and his older brother Richard (1520–1601) have been independently credited with writing *The Arte*. Although it is impossible to claim either with any authority, the evidence seems stronger for George. Little, if anything, is known about George Puttenham's early life. He matriculated at the age of 17 at Christ Church, Cambridge, in 1546 and left without taking a degree. However, his tenure at Cambridge is one piece of evidence cited in favor of his authorship. The liberal and progressive spirit and the linguistic bias of *The Arte* suggests a Cambridge influence, particularly that of the classicist Roger Ascham. Little else is known about Puttenham except that he traveled abroad and was admitted to the Middle Temple in 1556 at a time when the Inns of Court were centers of literary activity. He died in 1590.

Although it was published in 1589, *The Arte of English Poesie* is difficult to date with any certainty. It was probably begun as early as the mid-1560s, but later parts, particularly Book III, can be assigned to the 1580s. After a short preliminary book justifying the existence of poetry as the expression of social and individual needs, Puttenham addresses himself in Book II to an examination of English poetry, its stanzaic forms and prosody. The third book of *The Arte*, "Of Ornament," is concerned with language, particularly its study and organization as the medium of poetry. Like Dante, Puttenham is thinking about the creative possibilities of the vernacular language. Chapter 4, "Of Language," suggests that Englishmen were still coming to terms with the use of "vulgar English" as a literary language, despite the effects of the printing press, which was standardizing the language at the same time it was widely disseminating books in English. But Puttenham's thinking about language extends beyond simply the difficulties of forging a literary language out of the language of gentlemen. His discussion of style is one of the first extended critical treatments of this slippery concept. Although he draws upon the taxonomy of classical rhetoric into high, middle, and low styles, Puttenham shows how style is more than simply the merger of a particular subject with a set of figures. Rather, it is, for him, the felicitous conjunction of the "image of the man" (the *mentis character*), the subject matter, and the language. Style is the "mettle of [the poet's] mind" and the "warp and woof of his conceit."

from The Arte of English Poesie[1]

Chapter 4: Of Language

Speech is not natural to man except for his ability to speak, and that he is by nature apt to utter all his conceits with sounds and voices diversified in many manner of ways, by means of the many and fit instruments he has by nature to that purpose, as a broad and voluble tongue, thin and movable lips, teeth even and not jagged, thick ranged, a round vaulted palate, and a long throat, besides an excellent capacity of wit that makes him more disciplinable and imitative than any other creature. Then, as to the form and action of his speech, it comes to him by art and teaching, and by use or exercise. But after a speech is fully fashioned to the common understanding, and accepted by consent of a whole country and nation, it is called a language, and receives no allowed alteration but by extraordinary occasions by little and little, as it were, insensibly bringing in of many corruptions that creep along with the time—of all which matters, we have more largely spoken in our books of the origins and pedigree of the English tongue. Then when I say language, I mean the speech wherein the poet or maker writes, be it Greek or Latin, or as our case is, the vulgar English. And when it is peculiar to a country it is called the mother speech of that people—the Greeks term it *idioma;* so is ours at this day the Norman English. Before the conquest of the Normans it was the Anglo-Saxon, and before that the British, which as some will, is at this day the Welsh, or as others affirm, the Cornish; I for my part think neither of both, as they be now spoken and pronounced.

This part in our maker or poet must be heedily[2] looked unto, that it be natural, pure, and the most usual of all his country, and for the same purpose rather that which is spoken in the king's court or in the good towns and cities within the land, than in the marshes and frontiers, or in port towns, where strangers haunt for traffic's sake, or yet in universities, where scholars use much peevish affectation of words out of the primitive languages, or finally, in any uplandish village or corner of a realm, where is no resort but of poor rustical or uncivil people. Neither shall he follow the speech of a craftsman or carter, or other of the inferior sort, though he be inhabitant[3] or bred in the best town and city in this realm, for such persons do abuse good speech by strange accents or ill-shaped sounds, and false orthography. But he shall follow generally the better brought-up sort, such as the Greeks call [*charientes*], men civil and graciously behaved and bred.

Our maker therefore these days shall not follow *Piers Plowman* nor *Gower* nor *Lydgate* nor yet *Chaucer*, for their language is now out of use with us; neither shall he take the terms of Northernmen such as they use in daily talk, whether they be noblemen or gentlemen, or of their best clerks, all is a matter; nor, in effect, any speech used beyond the river of Trent—though no man can deny but that theirs is the purer English Saxon at this day, yet it is not so courtly nor so current as our Southern English is, no more is the far westernmost speech. You shall therefore take the usual speech of the court, and that of London and the shires lying about London within sixty miles, and not much above. I say not this but that in every shire of England there be gentlemen and others that speak, but especially write, as good Southern as we of Middlesex or Surrey do; but not the common people of every shire, to whom the gentlemen and also their learned clerks do for the most part condescend. But herein we are already ruled by the English dictionaries and other books written by learned men, and therefore it needs no other direction in that behalf.

Albeit peradventure some small admonition be not impertinent, for we find in our English writers many words and speeches amendable, and you shall see in some many inkhorn terms,[4] so ill-affected, brought in by men of learning as preachers and schoolmasters, and many strange terms of other languages by secretaries and merchants and travelers, and many dark words and not usual nor well-sounding, though they be daily spoken in court. Wherefore great heed must be taken by our maker in this point, that his choice be good. And peradventure the writer hereof be in that behalf no less faulty than any other, using many strange and unaccustomed words and borrowings from other languages, and in that respect himself no meet magistrate to reform the same errors in any other person. But since he is not unwilling to acknowledge his own fault, and can the better tell how to amend it, he may seem a more excusable corrector of other men's. He intends, therefore, for an indifferent way and universal benefit, to tax himself first and before any others. . . .

[Here Puttenham gives an account of the borrowings he has used in his own treatise, justifying what he has above condemned "for our speech wants words to such sense so well to be used," which ends in the following.]

But peradventure (and I could bring a reason for it) many other like words borrowed out of the Latin and French were not so well to be allowed by us, as these words: *audacious,* for bold; *fecundity,* for eloquence; *egregious,* for great or notable; *implete,* for replenished; *attemptat,* for attempt; *compatible,* for agreeable in nature; and many more. But herein the noble poet Horace has said enough to satisfy us all in these few verses:

Multa renascentur quæ iam cecidere cadent [quibus]
quæ nunc sunt in honore vocabula si volet usus
Quem penes arbitrium est & vis & norma loquendi.

Which I have thus Englished, but nothing with so good grace, nor so briefly as the Poet wrote:

> Many a word fallen shall again arise
> And such as now been held in highest prize
> Will fall as fast, when use and custom will
> Only umpires of speech, for force and skill.

Chapter 5: Of Style

Style is a constant and continual phrase or tenor of speaking and writing, extending to the whole tale or process of the poem or history, and not properly to any piece or member of a tale; but is of words, speeches, and sentences together, a certain contrived form and quality, many times natural to the writer, many times his peculiar by election and art, and such as either he keeps by skill or holds on by ignorance, and will not or peradventure cannot easily alter into any other. So we say that Cicero's style and Sallust's were not one, nor Caesar's and Livy's, nor Homer's and Hesiod's, nor Herodotus' and Thucydides', nor Euripides' and Aristophanes', nor Erasmus' and Budeus' styles. And because this continual course and manner of writing or speech shows the matter and disposition of the writer's mind more than one or few words or sentences can show, therefore there be [those] that have called style the image of man [*mentis character*], for man is but his mind, and as his mind is tempered and qualified, so are his speeches and language at large, and his inward conceits be the mettle of his mind, and his manner of utterance the very warp and woof of his conceits, more plain, or busy and intricate, or otherwise affected after the rate.

Most men say that not any one point in all *Physiognomy* is so certain, as to judge a man's manners by his eye—but more assuredly, in my opinion, by his daily manner of speech and ordinary writing. For if the man be grave, his speech and style is grave; if light-headed, his style and language also light. If the mind be haughty and hoate,[5] the speech and style is also vehement and stirring; if it be cold and temperate, the style is also very modest; if it be humble, or base and meek, so is also the language and style. And yet peradventure not altogether so, but that every man's style is for the most part according to the matter and subject of the writer, or so ought to be, and conformable thereunto.

Then again may it be said as well that men do choose their subjects according to the mettle of their minds, and therefore a high-minded man chooses high and lofty matter to write of; the base courage,[6] matter base and low; the mean and modest mind, mean and moderate matters after the rate. Howsoever it be, we find that under these three principal complexions (if I may with leave so term them)—high, mean, and base style—there be contained many other humors or qualities of style, as the plain and obscure, the rough and smooth, the facile and hard, the plentiful and barren, the rude and eloquent, the strong and feeble, the vehement and cold styles, all which in their evil are to be reformed, and the good to be kept and used. But generally, to have the style decent and comely it behooves the maker or poet to follow the nature of his subject. That is, if his matter be high and lofty that the style be so too; if mean, the style also to be mean; if base, the style humble and base accordingly. And they that do otherwise use it—applying to mean matter, high and lofty style, and to high matters, style either mean or base, and to base matters, the mean or high style—do utterly disgrace their poetry and show themselves nothing skillful in their art, nor having regard to the decency which is the chief praise of any writer. Therefore, to rid all lovers of learning from that error, I will as near as I can set down which matters be high and lofty, which be but mean, and which be low and base, to the intent the styles may be fashioned to the matters, and keep their *decorum* and good proportion in every respect.

I am not ignorant that many good clerks be contrary to my opinion, and say that the lofty style may be decently used in a mean and base subject and countrariwise, which I do in part acknowledge, but with a reasonable qualification. For Homer has so used it in his trifling work of *Batrachomyomachia*—that is, in his treatise of the war betwixt the frogs and the mice; Virgil also, in his *Bucolics* and in his *Georgics*, whereof the one is counted mean, the other base—that is, the husbandman's discourses and the shepherd's. But hereunto serves a reason in my simple conceit. For first, to that trifling poem of Homer. Though the frog and the mouse be but little and ridiculous beasts, yet to treat of war is a high subject, and a thing in every respect terrible and dangerous to them that it alights on, and therefore of learned duty asks martial grandiloquence if it be set forth in his kind and nature of war, even betwixt the basest creatures that can be imagined. So also is the ant or pismire, and they be but little creeping things, not perfect beasts but *insects*, or worms. Yet in describing their nature and instinct and their manner of life approaching to the form of a commonwealth, and their properties not unlike to the virtues of most excellent governors and captains, it asketh a more majesty of speech than would the description of any other beast's life or nature—and perchance of many matters pertaining unto the baser sort of men—because it resembleth the history of a civil regiment, and of them all the chief and most principal, which is monarchy.

So also in his *Bucolics* (which are but pastoral speeches and the basest of any other poem in their own proper nature) Virgil used a somewhat swelling style when he came to insinuate the birth of Marcellus, heir apparent to the emperor Augustus, as child to his sister, aspiring by hope and greatness of the House to the succession of the Empire, and establishment thereof in that family. Whereupon Virgil could do no less than to use such manner of style, whatsoever condition the poem were of, and this was decent, and no fault or blemish, to confound the tenors of the styles for that cause. But now when I remember me again that this *Eclogues* (for I have read it somewhere) was conceived by Octavian the Emperor to be written to the honor of Pollio—a citizen of Rome and of no great nobility—the same was misliked again as an implicative,[7] nothing decent nor proportionable to Pollio, his fortunes, and calling; in which respect I might say likewise the style was not to be such as if it had been for the Emperor's own honor, and those of the blood imperial, than which subject there could not be among the Roman writers a higher nor graver to treat upon.

So can I not be removed from my opinon, but still methinks that in all decency the style ought to conform with the nature of the subject, otherwise if a writer will seem to observe no *decorum* at all, nor pass[8] how he fashion his tale to his matter, who doubteth but he may in the lightest cause speak like a pope, and in the gravest matters prate like a parrot, and find words and phrases enough to serve both turns, and neither of them commendably. For neither is all that may be written of kings and princes such as ought to keep a high style, nor all that may be written upon a shepherd to keep the low, but according to the matter reported, if that be of high or base nature. For every petty pleasure and vain delight of a king are not to be accounted high matter for the height of his estate, but mean and perchance very base and vile. Nor so a poet or historiographer could decently with a high style report the vanities of Nero, the ribaldries of Caligula, the idleness of Domitian and the riots of Heliogabalus. But well [could he report] the magnanimity and honorable ambition of Caesar, the prosperities of Augustus, the gravity of Tiberius, the bounty of Trajan, the wisdom of Aurelius, and generally all that which concerned the highest honors of emperors, their birth, alliances, government, exploits in war and peace, and other public affairs. For they be matter stately and high, and require a style to be lifted up and advanced by choice of words, phrases, sentences, and figures high, lofty, eloquent, and magnificent in proportion. So be the mean matters to be carried with all words and speeches of smoothness and pleasant moderation, and finally the base things to be held within their tether by a low, mild, and simple manner of utterance, creeping rather than climbing, and marching rather than mounting upwards with the wings of the stately subjects and style.

Chapter 6: Of the High, Low, and Mean Subject

The matters, therefore, that concern the gods and divine things, are highest of all other to be couched in writing; next to them the noble *gestes* and great fortunes of princes, and the notable accidents of time, as the greatest affairs of war and peace. These be all high subjects, and therefore are delivered over to the poets hymnical and historical who be occupied either in divine lauds or in heroical reports.

The mean matters be those that concern mean men, their life and business—as lawyers, gentlemen, and merchants, good householders and honest citizens—and which sound neither to matters of state nor of war, nor leagues nor great alliances, but smatch[9] all the common conversation, as of the civiler and better sort of men.

The base and low matters be the doings of the common artificer, servingman, yeoman, groom, husbandman, day-laborer, sailor, shepherd, swineherd, and such-like of homely callings, degrees, and up-bringings.

So that in every of the said three degrees, not the self-same virtues be equally to be praised nor the same vices equally to be dispraised, nor their loves, marriages, quarrels, contracts, and other behaviors be like high nor do require to be set forth with the like style, but every one in his degree and decency. Which made that all hymns and histories and tragedies were written in the high style, all comedies and interludes and other common poetries of love and such-like in the mean style, all eclogues and pastoral poems in the low and base style; otherwise they had been utterly disproportioned. Likewise, for the same cause, some phrases and figures be only peculiar to the high style, some to the base or mean, some common to all three, as shall be declared more at large hereafter when we come to speak of figures and phrases. Also, some words and speeches and sentences do become the high style that do not become the other two, and contrariwise, as shall be said when we talk of words and sentences.

Finally, some kind of measure and concord do not beseem the high style, that well become the mean and low, as we have said speaking of concord and measure. But generally the high style is disgraced and made foolish and ridiculous by all words affected, counterfeit, and puffed up, as it were a wind-ball carrying more countenance than matter, and cannot be better resembled than to these midsummer pageants in London, where, to make the people wonder, are set forth great and ugly giants marching as if they were alive and armed at all points; but within they are stuffed full of brown paper and tow, which the shrewd boys, underpeering, do guilefully discover and turn to a great derision. Also, all dark and unaccustomed words, or rustical and homely, and sentences that hold too much of the merry and light or infamous and unshamefaced, are to be accounted of the same sort, for such speeches become not princes nor great estates, nor them that write of their doings to utter or report and intermingle with the grave and weighty matters.

NOTES

1. Text modernized by Stephen Kane.
2. With attention (OED).
3. A resident (OED).
4. A learned or pedantic word or expression.
5. A nonce spelling, almost certainly from *haut*, meaning "lofty or proud" (OED).
6. The heart and, by extension, disposition (OED).
7. That which implies, a statement implying something more than it expressly states (OED).
8. Concern oneself with, trouble, care (OED).
9. Smack of (OED).

Ben Jonson 1572–1637

Ben Jonson is the first English man of letters to exhibit a nearly complete and consistent neoclassicism. A celebrity in the literary world of the early seventeenth century, he was a man of letters, a poet, a writer of court masques, a grammarian, a dramatist, and a literary theorist. In his later years, he influenced a number of younger poets and dramatists, the "sons of Ben." Born in 1572, he was the posthumous son of a minister. He was educated at Westminster, where the headmaster was the scholar and antiquarian William Camden. But instead of moving on to Oxford or Cambridge, he was apprenticed to his stepfather as a bricklayer. Later he served as a soldier in the Low Countries, where he killed a soldier in hand-to-hand combat. Upon his return to England, he married and was for a time an actor. He fought a duel with a fellow actor and escaped the gallows only by pleading "benefit of clergy." In 1597 he began writing plays for Philip Henslowe, the owner of the Rose Theater.

Jonson became the greatest writer and contriver of the lavish Renaissance court entertainments known as masques, producing thirty-three of them for James I, in collaboration with the famous architect and stage designer Inigo Jones. He also invented the grotesque comic interlude known as the antimasque. But it is as a dramatist that Jonson is primarily remembered. His greatest works are his comedies: *Volpone* (1606); *Epicoene, or The Silent Woman* (1609); *The Alchemist* (1610); and *Bartholomew Fair* (1614). His two Roman tragedies, *Sejanus* (1603) and *Catiline* (1611), were less successful. By 1616, when he published a folio edition of his *Workes*, Jonson had reached the height of his fame. During the same year he was granted a pension and made poet laureate by James I. Both Oxford and Cambridge gave him honorary degrees. But under Charles I he found less favor and, as a result of a falling out with Inigo Jones, was replaced as court masque writer. He died on August 6, 1637, and was buried at Westminster Abbey.

Jonson's Epistle to *Volpone*—significantly—is dedicated to the "two sisters" of learning, the universities of Oxford and Cambridge. It is, in an important sense, a deliberate effort to claim for Jonson's play—and for drama in general—a moral and aesthetic seriousness. In the early seventeenth century, drama, particularly comedy, was generally considered a socially suspect form of art: popular, vulgar, and lacking the moral and artistic significance of epic and tragedy. By emphasizing the moral utility of *Volpone*, Jonson effectively challenges traditional prejudices against comedy and elevates it to the level of morally serious art.

DEDICATION TO *VOLPONE*[1]

To the most noble and most equal Sisters, the two famous universities, for their love and acceptance shown to his poem in the presentation, Ben Jonson, the grateful acknowledger, dedicates both it and himself.

Never, most equal Sisters, had any man a wit so presently excellent as that it could raise itself, but there must come both matter, occasion, commenders, and favorers to it. If this be true (and that, the fortune of all writers doth daily prove it), it behooves the careful to provide well toward these accidents, and, having acquired them, to preserve that part of reputation most tenderly wherein the benefit of a friend is also defended. Hence is it that I now render myself grateful and am studious to justify the bounty of your act, to which, though your mere authority were satisfying, yet, it being an age wherein poetry and the professors of it hear so ill on all sides, there will a reason be looked for in the subject.

It is certain, nor can it with any forehead be opposed, that the too-much license of poetasters in this time hath much deformed their mistress, that every day their manifold and manifest ignorance doth stick unnatural reproaches upon her. But for their petulance, it were an act of the greatest injustice either to let the learned suffer or [to let] so divine a skill—which indeed should not be attempted with unclean hands—to fall under the least contempt. For if men will impartially and not asquint look toward the offices and function of a poet, they will easily conclude to themselves the impossibility of any man's being the good poet without first being a good man. He that is said to be able to inform young men to all good disciplines, inflame grown men to all great virtues, keep old men in their best and supreme state or, as they decline to childhood, recover them to their first strength; [he] that comes forth the interpreter and arbiter of nature, a teacher of things divine no less than human, a master in manners; and [he that] can alone (or with a few) effect the business of mankind—this, I take him, is no subject for pride and ignorance to exercise their railing rhetoric upon.

But it will here be hastily answered that the writers of these days are other things; that not only their manners but their natures are inverted, and nothing remaining with them of the dignity of Poet but the abused name, which every scribe usurps; that now, especially in dramatic, or, as they term it, stage poetry, nothing but ribaldry, profanation, blasphemy, all license of offense to God and man is practiced. I dare not deny a great part of this (and am sorry I dare not) because in some men's abortive features (and would they had never boasted the light) it is overtrue. But that all are embarked in this bold adventure for hell is a most uncharitable thought and, uttered, a more malicious slander.

For my particular, I can, and from a most clear conscience, affirm that I have ever trembled to think toward the least profaneness, have loathed the use of such foul and unwashed bawdry as is now made the food of the scene. And howsoever, I cannot escape from some the imputation of sharpness, but that they will say I have taken a pride or lust to be bitter, and not my youngest infant[2] but hath come into the world with all his teeth. I would ask of these supercilious *politiques*, what nation, society, or general order or state I have provoked? What public person? Whether I have not, in all these, preserved their dignity, as my own person, safe? My works are read, allowed—I speak of those that are entirely mine. Look into them. What broad reproofs have I used? Where have I been particular? Where personal?—except to a mimic, cheater, bawd, or buffoon, creatures (for their insolences) worthy to be taxed? Yet to which of these so pointingly, as he might not either ingenuously have confessed or wisely dissembled his disease?

But it is not rumor can make men guilty, much less entitle me to other men's crimes. I know that nothing can be so innocently written or carried but may be made obnoxious to construction. Marry, while I bear mine innocence about me, I fear it not. Application[3] is now grown a trade with many, and there are [those] that profess to have a key for the deciphering of everything. But let wise and noble persons take heed how they be too credulous, or give leave to these invading interpreters to be overfamiliar with their fames—[these interpreters] who cunningly, and often, utter their own virulent malice under other men's simplest meanings.

As for those that will, by faults which charity hath raked up or common honesty concealed, make themselves a name with the multitude, or, to draw their rude and beastly claps, care not whose living faces they entrench with their petulant styles: may they do it without a rival. For me, I choose rather to live graved in obscurity than share with them in so preposterous a fame. Nor can I blame the wishes of those severe and wiser patriots who, providing the hurts these licentious spirits may do in a state, desire rather to see fools and devils and those antique relics of barbarism retrieved, with all other ridiculous and exploded follies, than [to] behold the wounds of private men, of princes and nations. For, as Horace makes Trebatius speak, among these

> *Sibi quisq; timet, quanquam est intactus, & odit.*[4]

And men may justly impute such rages, if continued, to the writer, as his sports.

The increase of which lust in liberty, together with the present trade of the stage in all their misc'line[5] interludes, what learned or liberal soul doth not already abhor? Where nothing but the filth of the time is uttered, and that with such impropriety of phrase, such plenty of solecisms, such dearth of sense, so bold prolepses, so wracked metaphors, with brothelry able to violate the ear of a pagan and blasphemy to turn the blood of a Christian to water. I cannot but be serious in a cause of this nature, wherein my fame, and the reputations of diverse honest and learned, are the question; when a name[6] so full of authority, antiquity, and all great mark is—through their insolence—become the lowest scorn of the age; and [when] those men [are] subject to the petulancy of every vernaculous orator, that were wont to be the care of kings and happiest monarchs.

This it is that hath not only rapped me to present indignation but made me studious heretofore, and by all my actions to stand off from them: which may most appear in this, my latest work (which you, most learned Arbitresses, have seen, judged, and to my crown, approved), wherein I have labored, for their instruction and amendment, to reduce[7] not only the ancient forms, but manners of the scene, the easiness, the propriety, the innocence, and last, the doctrine—which is the principal end of poetry, to inform men in the best reason of living. And though my catastrophe may, in the strict rigor of comic law, meet with censure, as turning back to my promise, I desire the learned and charitable critic to have so much faith in me to think it was done of industry. For with what ease I could have varied it nearer his scale (but that I fear to boast my own faculty) I could here insert. But my special aim being to put the snaffle[8] in their mouths that cry out, "We never punish vice in our interludes," etc., I took the more liberty—though not without some lines of example drawn even in the ancients themselves, the goings out of whose comedies are not always joyful, but oft-times the bawds, the servants, the rivals, yea, and the masters, are mulcted[9]—and [took this liberty] fitly, it being the office of a comic poet to imitate justice, and instruct to life as well as purity of language, or stir up gentle affections. To which, I shall take the occasion elsewhere to speak.

For the present, most reverenced Sisters, as I have cared to be thankful for your affections past, and here made the understanding acquainted with some ground of your favors, let me not despair their continuance to the maturing of some worthier fruits. Wherein, if my muses be true to me, I shall raise the despised head of poetry again, and, stripping her out of those rotten and base rags wherewith the times have adulterated her form, restore her to her primitive habit, feature, and majesty, and render her worthy to be embraced and kissed of all the great and master-spirits of our world. As for the vile and slothful, who never effected an act worthy of celebration, or are so inward with their own vicious natures as they worthily fear her and think it a high point of policy to keep her in contempt with their declamatory and windy invectives: she shall out of just rage incite her servants (who are *genus irritabile*) to spout ink in their faces that shall eat farder than their marrow, into their fames; and not Cinnamus the barber,

with his art, shall be able to take out the brands,
but they shall live, and be read, 'til the wretches die,
as things worst deserving of themselves in
chief, and then of all mankind.

Notes

1. Text modernized by Stephen Kane.
2. i.e., *Sejanus.*
3. The identification of characters in a play with actual persons.
4. From Horace, *Satires* II. i, 23; in *Poetaster*, Jonson provides a loose translation:

   In satires, each man (though untouched) complains

   As he were hurt; and hates such biting strains (III. v).
5. A mixture or medley (OED).
6. The name or profession of a poet.
7. To reproduce.
8. A simple bridle or bit (OED), here used figuratively.
9. Punished, usually by a fine (OED).

Pierre Corneille 1606–1684

Along with Racine and Molière, Pierre Corneille was one of the masters of the French classical theater; preceding them, he was a pioneer. Born into a well-to-do Norman family of lawyers and clerics, Corneille became a licentiate in law, and from 1628 to 1650 was king's counselor in a Rouen office. A series of successful comedies and tragicomedies began to appear in 1629. But his best-known works, his "classical tetralogy," all appeared within a few years of each other: *Le Cid* (1637), *Horace* (1640), *Cinna* (1641), and *Polyeucte* (1643). These were tragedies of interior emotion more than action, marked by closely articulated conflicts between duty and feeling, tradition and personal honor. Happily married and father of seven, Corneille moved to Paris in 1647. He continued to produce plays until his late sixties, but declined in popular favor after the classical period.

Here, writing for a 1660 edition of his collected works, Corneille discusses the so-called three unities, or classical unities, to which the best plays were believed to adhere. This prevailing critical paradigm derived from a misreading of Aristotle's *Poetics.* "Unity of action" outlawed nonessential plot developments, unexplained entrances and exits, and improbable resolutions; "unity of time" circumscribed the time span a play could cover; "unity of place" limited a play's setting to one location. All of these were considered necessary because drama "is an imitation, or rather a portrait of human actions" that will "gain in excellence as [it resembles] the original more closely." Interestingly, Corneille's own *Le Cid* was suppressed in part because it violated these unities. In this essay he strategically, even legalistically, interprets the doctrine to defend his plays. Yet, unlike later writers such as Dryden and Johnson, he never calls the fundamental paradigm into question.

Of the Three Unities of Action, Time, and Place

The two preceding discourses and the critical examination of the plays which my first two volumes contain have furnished me so many opportunities to explain my thoughts on these matters that there would be little left for me to say if I absolutely forbade myself to repeat.

I hold then, as I have already said, that in comedy, unity of action consists in the unity of plot or the obstacle to the plans of the principal actors, and in tragedy in the unity of peril, whether the hero falls victim to it or escapes. It is not that I claim that several perils cannot be allowed in the latter or several plots or obstacles in the former, provided that one passes necessarily from one to the other; for then escape from the first peril does not make the action complete since the escape leads to another danger; and the resolution of one plot does not put the actors at rest since they are confounded afresh in another. My memory does not furnish me any ancient examples of this multiplicity of perils linked each to each without the destruction of the unity of action; but I have noted independent double action as a defect in *Horace* and in *Théodore*, for it is not necessary that the first kill his sister upon gaining his victory nor that the other give herself up to martyrdom after having escaped prostitution; and if the death of Polyxène and that of Astyanax in Seneca's *Trojan Women* do not produce the same irregularity I am very much mistaken.

In the second place, the term unity of action does not mean that tragedy should show only one action on the stage. The one which the poet chooses for his subject must have a beginning, a middle, and an end; and not only are these three parts separate actions which find their conclusion in the principal one, but, moreover, each of them may contain several others with the same subordination. There must be only one complete action, which leaves the mind of the spectator serene; but that action can become complete only through several others which are less perfect and which, by serving as preparation, keep the spectator in a pleasant suspense. This is what must be contrived at the end of each act in order to give continuity to the action. It is not necessary that we know exactly what the actors are doing in the intervals which separate the acts, nor even that they contribute to the action when they do not appear on the stage; but it is necessary that each act leave us in the expectation of something which is to take place in the following one.

If you asked me what Cléopâtre is doing in *Rodogune* between the time when she leaves her two sons in the second act until she rejoins Antiochus in the fourth, I should be unable to tell you, and I do not feel obliged to account for her; but the end of this second act prepares us to see an amicable effort by the two brothers to rule and to hide Rodogune from the venomous hatred of their mother. The effect of this is seen in the third act, whose ending prepares us again to see another effort by Antiochus to win back these two enemies one after the other and for what Séleucus does in the fourth, which compels that unnatural mother [Cléopâtre] to resolve upon what she tries to accomplish in the fifth, whose outcome we await with suspense.

In *Le Menteur* the actors presumably make

use of the whole interval between the third and fourth acts to sleep; their rest, however, does not impede the continuity of the action between those two acts because the third does not contain a complete event. Dorante ends it with his plan to seek ways to win back the trust of Lucrèce, and at the very beginning of the next he appears so as to be able to talk to one of her servants and to her, should she show herself.

When I say that it is not necessary to account for what the actors do when they are not on stage, I do not mean that it is not sometimes very useful to give such an accounting, but only that one is not forced to do it, and that one ought to take the trouble to do so only when what happens behind the scenes is necessary for the understanding of what is to take place before the spectators. Thus I say nothing of what Cléopâtre did between the second and the fourth acts, because during all that time she can have done nothing important as regards the principal action which I am preparing for; but I point out in the very first lines of the fifth act that she has used the interval between these latter two for the killing of Séleucus, because that death is part of the action. This is what leads me to state that the poet is not required to show all the particular actions which bring about the principal one; he must choose to show those which are the most advantageous, whether by the beauty of the spectacle or by the brilliance or violence of the passions they produce, or by some other attraction which is connected with them, and to hide the others behind the scenes while informing the spectator of them by a narration or by some other artistic device; above all, he must remember that they must all be so closely connected that the last are produced by the preceding and that all have their source in the protasis which ought to conclude the first act. This rule, which I have established in my first *Discourse,* although it is new and contrary to the usage of the ancients, is founded on two passages of Aristotle. Here is the first of them: "There is a great difference," he says, "between events which succeed each other and those which occur because of others." The Moors come into the *Cid* after the death of the Count and not because of the death of the Count; and the fisherman comes into *Don Sanche* after Charles is suspected of being the Prince of Aragon and not because he is suspected of it; thus both are to be criticized. The second passage is even more specific and says precisely "that everything that happens in tragedy must arise necessarily or probably from what has gone before."

The linking of the scenes which unites all the individual actions of each act and of which I have spoken in criticizing *La Suivante* is a great beauty in a poem and one which serves to shape continuity of action through continuity of presentation; but, in the end, it is only a beauty and not a rule. The ancients did not always abide by it although most of their acts have but two or three scenes. This made things much simpler for them than for us, who often put as many as nine or ten scenes into each act. I shall cite only two examples of the scorn with which they treated this principle: one is from Sophocles, in *Ajax*, whose monologue before he kills himself has no connection with the preceding scene; the other is from the third act of Terence's *The Eunuch,* where Antipho's soliloquy has no connection with Chremes and Pythias who leave the stage when he enters. The scholars of our century, who have taken the ancients for models in the tragedies they have left us, have even more neglected that linking than did the ancients, and one need only glance at the plays of Buchanan, Grotius, and Heinsius, of which I spoke in the discussion of *Polyeucte,* to agree on that point. We have so far accustomed our audiences to this careful linking of scenes that they cannot now witness a detached scene without considering it a defect; the eye and even the ear are outraged by it even before the mind has been able to reflect upon it. The fourth act of *Cinna* falls below the others through this flaw; and what formerly was not a rule has become one now through the assiduousness of our practice.

I have spoken of three sorts of linkings in the discussion of *La Suivante:* I have shown myself averse to those of sound, indulgent to those of sight, favorable to those of presence and speech; but in these latter I have confused two things which ought to be separated. Links of presence and speech both have, no doubt, all the excellence imaginable; but there are links of speech without presence and of presence without speech which do not reach the same level of excellence. An actor who speaks to another from a hiding-place wthout showing himself forms a link of speech without presence which is always effective; but that rarely happens. A man who remains on stage merely to hear what will be said by those whom he sees making their entrance forms a link of presence without speech; this is often clumsy and falls into mere pretense, being contrived more to accede to this new convention which is becoming a precept than for any need dictated by the plot of the play. Thus, in the third act of *Pompée*, Achorée, after having informed Charmion of the reception Caesar gave to the king when he presented to him the head of that hero, remains on the stage where he sees the two of them come together merely to hear what they will say and report it to Cléopâtre. Ammon does the same thing in the fourth act of *Andromède* for the benefit of Phinée, who retires when he sees the king and all his court arriving. Characters who become mute connect rather badly scenes in which they play little part and in which they count for nothing. It is another matter when they hide in order to find out some important secret from those who are speaking and who think they are not overheard, for then the interest which they have in what is being said, added to a reasonable curiosity to find out what they cannot learn in any other way, gives them an important part in the action despite their silence; but in these two examples Ammon and Achorée lend so cold a presence to the scenes they overhear that, to be perfectly frank, whatever feigned reason I give them to serve as pretext for their action, they remain there only to connect the scenes with those that precede, so easily can both plays dispense with what they do.

Although the action of the dramatic poem must have its unity, one must consider both its parts: the complication and the resolution. "The complication is composed," according to Aristotle, "in part of what has happened off stage before the beginning of the action which is there described, and in part from what happens on stage; the rest belongs to the resolution. The change of fortune forms the separation of these two parts. Everything which precedes it is in the first part, and this change, with what follows it, concerns the other." The complication depends entirely upon the choice and industrious imagination of the poet and no rule can be given for it, except that in it he ought to order all things according to probability or necessity, a point which I have discussed in the second *Discourse;* to this I add one piece of advice, which is that he involve himself as little as possible with things which have happened before the action he is presenting. Such narrations are annoying, usually because they are not expected, and they disturb the mind of the spectator, who is obliged to burden his memory with what has happened ten or twelve years before in order to understand what he is about to see; but narrations which describe things which happen and take place behind the scenes once the action has started always produce a better effect because they are awaited with some curiosity and are a part of the action which is being shown. One of the reasons why so many illustrious critics favor *Cinna* above anything else I have done is that it contains no narration of the past, the one Cinna makes in describing his plot to Emilie being rather an ornament which tickles the mind of the spectators than a necessary marshaling of the details they must know and impress upon their memories for the understanding of what is to come. Emilie informs them adequately in the first two scenes that he is conspiring against Augustus in her favor, and if Cinna merely told her that the plotters are ready for the following day he would advance the action just as much as by the hundred lines he uses to tell both what he said to them and the way in which they received his words. There are plots which begin at the very birth of the hero like that of *Héraclius*, but these great efforts of the imagination demand an extraordinary attention of the spectator and often keep him from taking a real pleasure in the first performances, so much do they weary him.

In the resolution I find two things to avoid: the mere change of intention and the machine. Not much skill is required to finish a poem when he who has served as the obstacle to the plans of the principal actors for four acts desists in the fifth without being constrained to do so by any remarkable event; I have spoken of this in the first *Discourse* and I shall add nothing to that here. The machine requires no more skill when it is used only to bring down a god who straightens everything out when the actors are unable to do so. It is thus that Apollo functions in the *Orestes*: this prince and his friend Pylades, accused by Tyndarus and Menelaus of the death of Clytemnestra and condemned after prosecution by them, seize Helen and Hermione; they kill, or think they kill the first, and threaten to do so the same with the other if the sentence pronounced against them is not revoked. To smooth out these difficulties Euripides seeks nothing subtler than to bring Apollo down from heaven, and he, by absolute authority, orders that Orestes marry Hermione and Pylades Electra; and lest the death of Helen prove an obstacle to this, it being improbable that Hermione would marry Orestes since he had just killed her mother, Apollo informs them that she is not dead, that he has protected her from their blows and carried her off to heaven at the moment when they thought they were killing her. This use of the machine is entirely irrelevant, being founded in no way on the rest of the play, and makes a faulty resolution. But I find a little too harsh the opinion of Aristotle, who puts on the same level the chariot Medea uses to flee from Corinth after the vengeance she has taken on Creon. It seems to me there is a sufficient basis for this in the fact that she has been made a magician and that actions of hers as far surpassing natural forces as that one have been mentioned in the play. After what she did for Jason at Colchis and after she had made his father Aeson young again following his return, and after she had attached invisible fire to the gift she gave to Creusa, the flying chariot is not improbable and the poem has no need of other preparation for that extraordinary effect. Seneca gives it preparation by this line which Medea speaks to her nurse:

> *Tuum quoque ipsa corpus hinc mecum aveham;*

and by this one which she speaks to Aegeus:

> I shall follow you tomorrow by a new road.

Thus the condemnation of Euripides, who took no precautions, may be just and yet not fall on Seneca or on me; and I have no need to contradict Aristotle in order to justify myself on this point.

From the action I turn to the acts, each of which ought to contain a portion of it, but not so equal a portion that more is not reserved for the last than for the others and less given to the first than to the others. Indeed, in the first act one may do no more than depict the moral nature of the characters and mark off how far they have got in the story which is to be presented. Aristotle does not prescribe the number of the acts; Horace limits it to five; and although he prohibits having fewer, the Spaniards are obstinate enough to stop at three and the Italians often do the same thing. The Greeks used to separate the acts by the chanting of the chorus, and since I think it reasonable to believe that in some of their poems they made it chant more than four times, I should not want to say they never exceeded five. This way of distinguishing the acts was less handy than ours, for either they paid attention to what the chorus was chanting or they did not; if they did, the mind of the spectators was too tense and had no time in which to rest; if they did not, attention was too much dissipated by the length of the chant, and when a new act began, an effort of memory was needed to recall to the imagination what had been witnessed and at what point the action had been interrupted. Our orchestra presents neither of these two inconveniences; the mind of the spectator relaxes while the music is playing and even reflects on what he has seen, to praise it or to find fault with it depending on whether he has been pleased or displeased; and the short time the orchestra is allowed to play leaves his impressions so fresh that when the actors return he does not need to make an effort to recall and resume his attention.

The number of scenes in each act has never been prescribed by rule, but since the whole act must have a certain number of lines which make its length proportionate to that of the others, one may include in it more or fewer scenes depending on whether they are long or short to fill up the time which the whole act is to consume. One ought, if possible, to account for the entrance and exit of each actor; I consider this rule indispensable, especially for the exit, and think there is nothing so clumsy as an actor who leaves the stage merely because he has no more lines to speak.

I should not be so rigorous for the entrances. The audience expects the actor, and although the setting represents the room or the study of whoever is speaking, yet he cannot make his appearance there unless he comes out from behind the tapestry, and it is not always easy to give a reason for what he has just done in town before returning home, since sometimes it is even probable that he has not gone out at all. I have never seen anybody take offense at seeing Emilie begin *Cinna* without saying why she has come to her room; she is presumed to be there before the play begins, and it is only stage necessity which makes her appear from behind the scenes to come there. Thus I should willingly dispense from the rigors of the rule the first scene of each act but not the others, because once an actor is on the stage anyone who enters must have a reason to speak to him or, at least, must profit from the opportunity to do so when it offers. Above all, when an actor enters twice in one act, in comedy or in tragedy, he must either lead one to expect that he will soon return when he leaves the first time, like Horace in the second act and Julie in the third act of *Horace*, or explain on returning why he has come back so soon.

Aristotle wishes the well-made tragedy to be beautiful and capable of pleasing without the aid of actors and quite aside from performance. So that the reader may more easily experience that pleasure, his mind, like that of the spectator, must not be hindered, because the effort he is obliged to make to conceive and to imagine the play for himself lessens the satisfaction which he will get from it. Therefore, I should be of the opinion that the poet ought to take great care to indicate in the margin the less important actions which do not merit being included in the lines, and which might even mar the dignity of the verse if the author lowered himself to express them. The actor easily fills this need on the stage, but in a book one would often be reduced to guessing and sometimes one might even guess wrong, unless one were informed in this way of these little things. I admit that this is not the practice of the ancients; but you must also allow me that because they did not do it they have left us many obscurities in their poems which only masters of dramatic art can explain; even so, I am not sure they succeed as often as they think they do. If we forced ourselves to follow the method of the ancients completely, we should make no distinction between acts and scenes because the Greeks did not. This failure on their part is often the reason that I do not know how many acts there are in their plays, nor whether at the end of an act the player withdraws so as to allow the chorus to chant, or whether he remains on stage without any action while the chorus is chanting, because neither they nor their interpreters have deigned to give us a word of indication in the margin.

We have another special reason for not neglecting that helpful little device as they did: this is that printing puts our plays in the hands of actors who tour the provinces and whom we we can thus inform of what they ought to do, for they would do some very odd things if we did not help them by these notes. They would find themselves in great difficulty at the fifth act of plays that end happily, where we bring together all the actors on the stage (a thing which the ancients did not do); they would often say to one what is meant for another, especially when the same actor must speak to three or four people one after the other. When there is a whispered command to make, like Cléopâtre's to Laonice which sends her to seek poison an aside would be necessary to express this in verse if we were to do without the marginal indications, and that seems to me much more intolerable than the notes, which give us the real and only way, following the opinion of Aristotle, of making the tragedy as beautiful in the reading as in performance, by making it easy for the reader to imagine what the stage presents to the view of the spectators.

The rule of the unity of time is founded on this statement of Aristotle "that the tragedy ought to enclose the duration of its action in one journey of the sun or try not to go much beyond it." These words gave rise to a famous dispute as to whether they ought to be understood as meaning a natural day of twenty-four hours or an artificial day of twelve; each of the two opinions has important partisans, and, for myself, I find that there are subjects so difficult to limit to such a short time that not only should I grant the twenty-four full hours but I should make use of the license which the philosopher gives to exceed them a little and should push the total without scruple as far as thirty. There is a legal maxim which says that we should broaden the mercies and narrow the rigors of the law, *odia restringenda, favores ampliandi;* and I find that an author is hampered enough by this constraint which forced some of the ancients to the very edge of the impossible. Euripides, in *The Suppliants*, makes Theseus leave Athens with an army, fight a battle beneath the walls of Thebes, which was ten or twelve leagues away, and return victorious in the following act; and between his departure and the arrival of the messenger who comes to tell the story of his victory, the chorus has only thirty-six lines to speak. That makes good use of such a short time. Aeschylus makes Agamemnon come back from Troy with even greater speed. He had agreed with Clytemnestra, his wife, that as soon as the city was taken he would inform her by signal fires built on the intervening mountains, of which the second would be lighted as soon as the first was seen, the third at the sight of the second, and so on; by this means she was to learn the great news the same night. However, scarcely had she learned it from the signal fires when Agamemnon arrives, whose ship, although battered by a storm, if memory serves, must have traveled as fast as the eye could see the lights. *The Cid* and *Pompée*, where the action is a little precipitate, are far from taking so much license; and if they force ordinary probability in some way, at least they do not go as far as such impossibilities.

Many argue against this rule, which they call tyrannical, and they would be right if it were founded only on the authority of Aristotle; but what should make it acceptable is the fact that common sense supports it. The dramatic poem is an imitation, or rather a portrait of human actions, and it is beyond doubt that portraits gain in excellence in proportion as they resemble the original more closely. A performance lasts two hours and would resemble reality perfectly if the action it presented required no more for its actual occurrence. Let us then not settle on twelve or twenty-four hours, but let us compress the action of the poem into the shortest possible period, so that the performance may more closely resemble reality and thus be more nearly perfect. Let us give, if that is possible, to the one no more than the two hours which the other fills. I do not think that *Rodogune* requires much more, and perhaps two hours would be enough for *Cinna*. If we cannot confine the action within the two hours, let us take four, six, or ten, but let us not go much beyond twenty-four for fear of falling into lawlessness and of so far reducing the scale of the portrait that it no longer has its proportionate dimensions and is nothing but imperfection.

Most of all, I should like to leave the matter of duration to the imagination of the spectators and never make definite the time the action requires unless the subject needs this precision, but especially not when probability is a little forced, as in the *Cid*, because precision serves only to make the crowded action obvious to the spectator. Even when no violence is done to a poem by the necessity of obeying this rule, why must one state at the beginning that the sun is rising, that it is noon at the third act, and that the sun is setting at the end of the last act? This is only an obtrusive affectation; it is enough to establish the possibility of the thing in the time one gives to it and that one be able to determine the time easily if one wishes to pay attention to it, but without being compelled to concern oneself with the matter. Even in those actions which take no longer than the performance it would be clumsy to point out that a half hour has elasped between the beginning of one act and the beginning of the next.

I repeat what I have said elsewhere, that when we take a longer time, as, for instance, ten hours, I should prefer that the eight extra be used up in the time between the acts and that each act should have as its share only as much time as performance requires especially when all scenes are closely linked together. I think, however, that the fifth act, by special privileges, has the right to accelerate time so that the part of the action which it presents may use up more time than is necessary for performance. The reason for this is that the spectator is by then impatient to see the end, and when the outcome depends on actors who are off stage, all the dialogue given to those who are on stage awaiting news of the others drags and action seems to halt. There is no doubt that from the point where Phocas exits in the fifth act of *Héraclius* until Amyntas enters to relate the manner of his death, more time is needed for what happens off stage than for the speaking of the lines in which Héraclius, Martian, and Pulchérie complain of their misfortune. Prusias and Flaminius, in the fifth act of *Nicomède*, do not have the time they would need to meet at sea, take counsel with each other, and return to the defense of the queen; and the Cid has not enough time to fight a duel with Don Sanche during the conversations of the Infanta with Léonor and of Chimène with Elvire. I was aware of this and yet have had no scruples about this acceleration of which, perhaps, one might find several examples among the ancients, but the laziness of which I have spoken will force me to rest content with this one, which is from the *Andria* of Terence. Simo slips his son Pamphilus into the house of Glycerium in order to get the old man, Crito, to come out and to clear up with him the question of the birth of his mistress, who happens to be the daughter of Chremes. Pamphilus enters the house, speaks to Crito, asks him for the favor and returns with him; and during this exit, this request, and this re-entry, Simo and Chremes, who remain on stage, speak only one line each, which could not possibly give Pamphilus more than time enough to ask where Crito is, certainly not enough to talk with him and to explain to him the reasons for which he should reveal what he knows about the birth of the unknown girl.

When the conclusion of the action depends on actors who have not left the stage and about whom no one is awaiting news, as in *Cinna* and *Rodogune*, the fifth act has no need of this privilege because then all the action takes place in plain sight, as does not happen when part of it occurs off stage after the beginning of the act. The other acts do not merit the same freedom. If there is not time enough to bring back an actor who has made his exit, or to indicate what he has done since that exit, the accounting can be postponed to the following act; and the music, which separates the two acts, may use up as much time as is necessary; but in the fifth act no postponement is possible: attention is exhausted and the end must come quickly.

I cannot forget that although we must reduce the whole tragic action to one day, we can nevertheless make known by a narration or in some other more artful way what the hero of the tragedy has been doing for several years, because there are plays in which the crux of the plot lies in an obscurity of birth which must be brought to light, as in *Oedipus*. I shall not say again that the less one burdens oneself with past actions, the more favorable the spectator will be, because of the lesser degree of trouble he is given when everything takes place in the present and no demands are made on his memory except for what he has seen; but I cannot forget that the choice of a day both illustrious and long-awaited is a great ornament to a poem. The opportunity for this does not always present itself, and in all that I have written until now you will find only four of that kind: the day in *Horace* when two nations are to decide the question of supremacy of empire by a battle; and the ones in *Rodogune*, *Andromède*, and *Don Sanche*. In *Rodogune* it is a day chosen by two sovereigns for the signature of a treaty of peace between the hostile crowns, for a complete reconciliation of the two rival governments through a marriage, and for the elucidation of a more than twenty-year-old secret concerning the right of succession of one of the twin princes on which the fate of the kingdom depends, as does the outcome of both their loves. The days in *Andromède* and *Don Sanche* are not of lesser importance, but, as I have just said, such opportunities do not often present themselves, and in the rest of my works I have been able to choose days remarkable only for what chance makes happen on them and not by the use to which public arrangements destined them long ago.

As for the unity of place, I find no rule concerning it in either Aristotle or Horace. This is what leads many people to believe that this rule was established only as a consequence of the unit of one day, and leads them to imagine that one can stretch the unit of place to cover the points to which a man may go and return in twenty-four hours. This opinion is a little too free, and if one made an actor travel post-haste, the two sides of the theater might represent Paris and Rouen. I could wish, so that the spectator is not at all disturbed, that what is performed before him in two hours might actually be able to take place in two hours, and that what he is shown in a stage setting which does not change might be limited to a room or a hall depending on a choice made beforehand; but often that is so awkward, if not impossible, that one must necessarily find some way to enlarge the place as also the time of the action. I have shown exact unity of place in *Horace*, *Polyeucte*, and *Pompée*, but for that it was necessary to present either only one woman, as in *Polyeucte;* or to arrange that the two who are presented are such close friends and have such closely related interests that they can be always together, as in *Horace;* or that they may react as in *Pompée* where the stress of natural curiosity drives Cléopâtre from her apartments in the second act and Cornélie in the fifth; and both enter the great hall of the king's palace in anticipation of the news they are expecting. The same thing is not true of *Rodogune:* Cléopâtre and she have interests which are too divergent to permit them to express their most secret thoughts in the same place. I might say of that play what I have said of *Cinna*, where, in general, everything happens in Rome and, in particular, half of the action takes place in the quarters of Auguste and half of it in Emilie's apartments. Following that arrangement, the first act of this tragedy would be laid in Rodogune's antechamber, the second, in Cléopâtre's apartments, the third, in Rodogune's; but if the fourth act can begin in Rodogune's apartments it cannot finish there, and what Cléopâtre says to her two sons one after the other would be badly out of place there. The fifth act needs a throne room where a great crowd can be gathered. The same problem is found in *Héraclius*. The first act could very well take place in Phocas's quarters, the second, in Léontine's apartments; but if the third begins in Pulchérie's rooms, it cannot end there, and it is outside the bounds of probability that Phocas should discuss the death of her brother in Pulchérie's apartments.

The ancients, who made their kings speak in a public square, easily kept a rigorous unity of place in their tragedies. Sophocles, however, did not observe it in his *Ajax*, when the hero leaves the stage to find a lonely place in which to kill himself and does so in full view of the people; this easily leads to the conclusion that the place where he kills himself is not the one he has been seen to leave, since he left it only to choose another.

We do not take the same liberty of drawing kings and princesses from their apartments, and since often the difference and the opposition on the part of those who are lodged in the same palace do not allow them to take others into their confidence or to disclose their secrets in the same room, we must seek some other compromise about unity of place if we want to keep it intact in our poems; otherwise we should have to decide against many plays which we see succeeding brilliantly.

I hold, then, that we ought to seek exact unity as much as possible, but as this unity does not suit every kind of subject, I should be very willing to concede that a whole city has unity of place. Not that I should want the stage to represent the whole city, that would be somewhat too large, but only two or three particular places enclosed within its walls. Thus the scene of *Cinna* does not leave Rome, passing from the apartments of Auguste to the house of Emilie. *Le Menteur* takes place in the Tuileries and in the Place Royale at Paris, and *La Suite* shows us the prison and Mélisse's house at Lyons. *The Cid* increases even more the number of particular places without leaving Seville; and since the close linking of scenes is not observed in that play, the stage in the first act is supposed to represent Chimène's house, the Infante's apartments in the king's palace, and the public square; the second adds to these the king's chamber. No doubt there is some excess in this freedom. In order to rectify in some way this multiplication of places when it is inevitable, I should wish two things done: first, that the scene should never change in a given act but only between the acts, as is done in the first three acts of *Cinna;* the other, that these two places should not need different stage settings and that neither of the two should ever be named, but only the general place which includes them both, as Paris, Rome, Lyons, Constantinople, and so forth. This would help to deceive the spectator, who, seeing nothing that would indicate the difference in the places, would not notice the change, unless it was maliciously and critically pointed out, a thing which few are capable of doing, most spectators being warmly intent upon the action which they see on the stage. The pleasure they take in it is the reason why they do not seek out its imperfections lest they lose their taste for it; and they admit such an imperfection only when forced, when it is too obvious, as in *Le Menteur* and *La Suite,* where the different settings force them to recognize the multiplicity of places in spite of themselves.

But since people of opposing interests cannot with verisimilitude unfold their secrets in the same place, and since they are sometimes introduced into the same act through the linking of scenes which the unity of place necessarily produces, one must find some means to make it compatible with the contradiction which rigorous probability finds in it, and consider how to preserve the fourth act of *Rodogune* and the third of *Héraclius,* in both of which I have already pointed out the contradiction which lies in having enemies speak in the same place. Jurists allow legal fictions, and I should like, following their example, to introduce theatrical fictions by which one could establish a theatrical place which would not be Cléopâtre's chamber nor Rodogune's, in the play of that name, nor that of Phocas, of Léontine or of Pulchérie in *Héraclius,* but a room contiguous to all these other apartments, to which I should attribute these two privileges: first, that each of those who speaks in it is presumed to enjoy the same secrecy there as if he were in his own room; and second, that whereas in the usual arrangement it is sometimes proper for those who are on stage to go off, in order to speak privately with others in their rooms, these latter might meet the former on stage without shocking convention, so as to preserve both the unity of place and the linking of scenes. Thus Rodogune, in the first act, encounters Laonice, whom she must send for so as to speak with her; and, in the fourth act, Cléopâtre encounters Antiochus on the very spot where he has just moved Rodogune to pity, even though in utter verisimilitude the prince ought to seek out his mother in her own room since she hates the princess too much to come to speak to him in Rodogune's, which, following the first scene, would be the locus of the whole act, if one did not introduce that compromise which I have mentioned into the rigorous unity of place.

Many of my plays will be at fault in the unity of place if this compromise is not accepted, for I shall abide by it always in the future when I am not able to satisfy the ultimate rigor of the rule. I have been able to reduce only three plays, *Horace, Polyeucte,* and *Pompée,* to the requirements of the rule. If I am too indulgent with myself as far as the others are concerned, I shall be even more so for those which may succeed on the stage through some appearance of regularity. It is easy for critics to be severe; but if they were to give ten or a dozen plays to the public, they might perhaps slacken the rules more than I do, as soon as they have recognized through experience what constraint their precision brings about and how many beautiful things it banishes from our stage. However that may be, these are my opinions, or if you prefer, my heresies concerning the principal points of the dramatic art, and I do not know how better to make the ancient rules agree with modern pleasures. I do not doubt that one might easily find better ways of doing that, and I shall be ready to accept them when they have been put into practice as successfully as, by common consent, mine have been.

John Dryden 1631–1700

As a poet, critic, and playwright, John Dryden dominates the second half of the seventeenth century, contributing to the refinement and extension of English neoclassicism. In *The Life of Dryden*, Samuel Johnson attributes to him "the improvement, perhaps the completion of our meter, the refinement of our language, and much of the correctness of our sentiments." Born in Northamptonshire of a Puritan family in 1631, Dryden attended Westminster and graduated from Trinity College, Cambridge, in 1654. He settled in London, where he quickly made his reputation as a playwright. In 1660 he was appointed to the Royal Society, but was dropped six years later for nonpayment of dues. In 1668, he was appointed poet laureate. After the accession of James II in 1685, Dryden converted to Catholicism, but lost his position as laureate when the Catholic James was deposed in 1688. At the end of his life, he had to turn once again to earning his living by writing. He died on May 1, 1700, and was buried in Westminster Abbey.

Dryden was the most prolific writer of the Restoration. He wrote in almost every genre available to the Restoration writer, including heroic tragedy, comedy, satire, encomium, essay, and translation. His best works include *All for Love,* a heroic revision of Shakespeare's *Antony and Cleopatra; Marriage-à-la-Mode,* among his comedies; and the great satire *Absolom and Achitophel.* Dryden took a very active part in the London literary scene. Indeed in satire he is considered second only to Pope. He satirized his chief poetic rival, Thomas Shadwell, in *Mac Flecknoe* (1682), and was himself the butt of Lord Buckingham's satire of the heroic tragedy in *The Rehearsal* (1671–72). In 1679, he was beaten up by thugs in Rose Alley, Covent Garden, probably because he was suspected of writing a satiric attack on Lord Rochester and two of the king's mistresses.

An Essay of Dramatic Poesy, published in 1668, is a dramatization of a debate among four men who are floating on a barge in the Thames during a naval battle between the English and the Dutch. The debate form enables Dryden to present different critical perspectives on almost all of the major topics of seventeenth-century criticism, including the imitation of nature and the three unities, as well as the relative merits of ancient and modern drama, the French and English stage, and rhymed and blank verse tragedy. Crites—who was probably meant to be Sir Robert Howard, Dryden's brother-in-law and sometime collaborator—defends the extreme classical view that contemporary drama can do no better than to imitate the rules laid down by the ancients. Eugenius—probably Dryden's friend and patron Charles Sackville, Lord Buckhurst—upholds the modern drama as superior to the ancient poets. Lisideius—an anagram for Sir Charles Sedley—argues for the superiority of French drama over the English because it has more perfectly realized the classical rules, particularly the three unities. With the entrance of Neander (the new man, Dryden himself) into the debate, the *Essay* turns to its major argument. Neander defends the diversity and effectiveness of the English stage, whose roots he traces to Shakespeare rather than to Aristotle or Corneille. Freed from the strict classicism of the French drama, which offered only "the beauties of a statue," the English drama is "animated with the soul of Poesy." He illustrates his point through an analysis of Ben Jonson's *Silent Woman*—the first example of a sustained "close reading" in English criticism—as an example of how neoclassical ideals could be combined with English common sense to create a richer, more lively "imitation of nature."

An Essay of Dramatic Poesy

It was that memorable day, in the first summer of the late war, when our navy engaged the Dutch; a day wherein the two most mighty and best appointed fleets which any age had ever seen, disputed the command of the greater half of the globe, the commerce of nations, and the riches of the universe. While these vast floating bodies, on either side, moved against each other in parallel lines, and our countrymen, under the happy conduct of his Royal Highness, went breaking, by little and little, into the line of the enemies; the noise of the cannon from both navies reached our ears about the City, so that all men being alarmed with it and in a dreadful suspense of the event which we knew was then deciding, every one went following the sound as his fancy led him; and leaving the town almost empty, some took towards the park, some cross the river, others down it; all seeking the noise in the depth of silence.

Among the rest, it was the fortune of Eugenius, Crites, Lisideius, and Neander, to be in company together; three of them persons whom their wit and quality have made known to all the town; and whom I have chose to hide under these borrowed names, that they may not suffer by so ill a relation as I am going to make of their discourse.

Taking then a barge which a servant of Lisideius had provided for them, they made haste to shoot the bridge, and left behind them that great fall of waters which hindered them from hearing what they desired: after which, having disengaged themselves from many vessels which rode at anchor in the Thames, and almost blocked up the passage towards Greenwich, they ordered the watermen to let fall their oars more gently; and then, every one favouring his own curiosity with a strict silence, it was not long ere they perceived the air break about them like the noise of distant thunder, or of swallows in a chimney: those little undulations of sound, though almost vanishing before they reached them, yet still seeming to retain somewhat of their first horror, which they had betwixt the fleets. After they had attentively listened till such time as the sound by little and little went from them, Eugenius, lifting up his head, and taking notice of it, was the first who congratulated to the rest that happy omen of our Nation's victory: adding, we had but this to desire in confirmation of it, that we might hear no more of that noise, which was now leaving the English coast. When the rest had concurred in the same opinion, Crites, a person of a sharp judgment, and somewhat too delicate a taste in wit, which the world have mistaken in him for ill-nature, said, smiling to us, that if the concernment of this battle had not been so exceeding great, he could scarce have wished the victory at the price he knew he must pay for it, in being subject to the reading and hearing of so many ill verses as he was sure would be made upon it. Adding, that no argument could scape some of those eternal rhymers, who watch a battle with more diligence than the ravens and birds of prey; and the worst of them surest to be first in upon the quarry: while the better able either out of modesty writ not at all, or set that due value upon their poems, as to let them be often called for and long expected! "There are some of those impertinent people you speak of," answered Lisideius, "who to my knowledge are already so provided, either way, that they can produce not only a Panegyric upon the victory, but, if need be, a Funeral Elegy on the Duke; and after they have crowned his valour with many laurels, at last deplore the odds under which he fell concluding that his courage deserved a better destiny." All the company smiled at the conceit of Lisideius; but Crites, more eager than before, began to make particular exceptions against some writers, and said, the public magistrate ought to send betimes to forbid them; and that it concerned the peace and quiet of all honest people, that ill poets should be as well silenced as seditious preachers. "In my opinion," replied Eugenius, "you pursue your point too far; for as to my own particular, I am so great a lover of poesy, that I could wish them all rewarded, who attempt but to do well; at least, I would not have them worse used than Sylla the Dictator did one of their breathren heretofore:—*Quem in concione vidimus* (says Tully) *cum ei libellum malus poeta de populo subjecisset, quod epigramma in eum fecisset tantummodo alternis versibus longiusculis, statim ex iis rebus quas tunc vendebat jubere ei præmium tribui, sub ea conditione ne quid postea scriberet.*"[1] "I could wish with all my heart," replied Crites, "that many whom we know were as bountifully thanked upon the same condition,—that they would never trouble us again. For amongst others, I have a mortal apprehension of two poets, whom this victory, with the help of both her wings, will never be able to escape." " 'Tis easy to guess whom you intend," said Lisideius; "and without naming them, I ask you, if one of them does not perpetually pay us with clenches upon words, and a certain clownish kind of raillery? if now and then he does not offer at a catachresis or Clevelandism, wresting and torturing a word into another meaning: in fine, if he be not one of those whom the French would call *un mauvais buffon;* one that is so much a well-willer to the satire, that he spares no man; and though he cannot strike a blow to hurt any, yet ought to be punished for the malice of the action, as our witches are justly hanged, because they think themselves so; and suffer deservedly for believing they did mischief, because they meant it." "You have described him," said Crites, "so exactly, that I am afriad to come after you with my other extremity of poetry. He is one of those who, having had some advantage of education and converse, knows better than the other what a poet should be, but puts it into practice more unluckily than any man; his style and matter are everywhere alike: he is the most calm, peaceable writer you ever read: he never disquiets your passions with the least concernment, but still leaves you in as even a temper as he found you; he is a very Leveller in poetry: he creeps along with ten little words in every line, and helps out his numbers with *For to*, and *Unto*, and all the pretty expletives he can find, till he drags them to the end of another line; while the sense is left tired half way behind it: he doubly starves all his verses, first for want of thought, and then of expression; his poetry neither has wit in it, nor seems to have it; like him in Martial:

> *Pauper videri* Cinna *vult, et est pauper.*[2]

"He affects plainness, to cover his want of imagination: when he writes the serious way, the highest flight of his fancy is some miserable antithesis, or seeming contradiction; and in the comic he is still reaching at some thin conceit, the ghost of a jest, and that too flies before him, never to be caught; these swallows which we see before us on the Thames are the just resemblance of his wit: you may observe how near the water they stoop, how many proffers they make to dip, and yet how seldom they touch it; and when they do, 'tis but the surface: they skim over it but to catch a gnat, and then mount into the air and leave it."

"Well, gentlemen," said Eugenius, "you may speak your pleasure of these authors; but though I and some few more about the town may give you a peaceable hearing, yet assure yourselves, there are multitudes who would think you malicious and them injured: especially him whom you first described; he is the very Withers of the city: they have bought more editions of his works than would serve to lay under all their pies at the Lord Mayor's Christmas. When his famous poem first came out in the year 1660, I have seen them reading it in the midst of 'Change time; nay so vehement they were at it, that they lost their bargain by the candles' ends; but what will you say, if he has been received amongst the great ones? I can assure you he is, this day, the envy of a great Person who is lord in the art of quibbling; and who does not take it well, that any man should intrude so far into his province." "All I would wish," replied Crites, "is that they who love his writings, may still admire him, and his fellow poet: *Qui Bavium non odit, &c.*,[3] is curse sufficient." "And farther," added Lisideius, "I believe there is no man who writes well, but would think himself very hardly dealt with, if their admirers should praise anything of his: *Nam quos contemnimus, corum quoque laudes contemnimus.*"[4] "There are so few who write well in this age," says Crites, "that methinks any praises should be welcome; they neither rise to the dignity of the last age, nor to any of the Ancients: and we may cry out of the writers of this time, with more reason than Petronius of his, *Pace vestrâ liceat dixisse, primi omnium eloquentiam perdidistis:*[5] you have debauched the true old poetry so far, that Nature, which is the soul of it, is not in any of your writings."

"If your quarrel," said Eugenius, "to those who now so write, be grounded only on your reverence to antiquity, there is no man more ready to adore those great Greeks and Romans than I am: but on the other side, I cannot think so contemptibly of the age I live in, or so dishonourably of my own country, as not to judge we equal the Ancients in most kinds of posey, and in some surpass them; neither know I any reason why I may not be as zealous for the reputation of our age, as we find the Ancients themselves in reference to those who lived before them. For you hear your Horace saying,

> *Indignor quidquam reprehendi, non quia crasse*
> *Compositum, illepidève putetur, sed quia nuper.*

And after:

> *Si meliora dies, ut vina, poemata reddit,*
> *Scire velim, pretium chartis quotus arroget annus?*[6]

"But I see I am engaging in a wide dispute, where the arguments are not like to reach close on either side; for Poesy is of so large an extent, and so many both of the Ancients and Moderns have done well in all kinds of it, that in citing one against the other, we shall take up more time this evening than each man's occasions will allow him: therefore I would ask Crites to what part of Poesy he would confine his arguments, and whether he would defend the general cause of the Ancients against the Moderns, or oppose any age of the Moderns against this of ours?"

Crites, a little while considering upon this demand, told Eugenius he approved his propositions, and if he pleased, he would limit their dispute to Dramatic Poesy; in which he thought it not difficult to prove, either that the Ancients were superior to the Moderns, or the last age to this of ours.

Eugenius was somewhat surprised, when he heard Crites make choice of that subject. "For ought I see," said he, "I have undertaken a harder province than I imagined; for though I never judged the plays of the Greek or Roman poets comparable to ours, yet, on the other side, those we now see acted come short of many which were written in the last age: but my comfort is, if we are o'ercome, it will be only by our own countrymen: and if we yield to them in this one part of poesy, we more surpass them in all the other: for in the epic or lyric way, it will be hard for them to show us one such amongst them, as we have many now living, or who lately were so: they can produce nothing so courtly writ, or which expresses so much the conversation of a gentleman, as Sir John Suckling; nothing so even, sweet, and flowing, as Mr. Waller; nothing so majestic, so correct, as Sir John Denham; nothing so elevated, so copious, and full of spirit, as Mr. Cowley; as for the Italian, French, and Spanish plays, I can make it evident, that those who now write surpass them; and that the Drama is wholly ours."

All of them were thus far of Eugenius his opinion, that the sweetness of English verse was never understood or practised by our fathers; even Crites himself did not much oppose it: and every one was willing to acknowledge how much our poesy is improved by the happiness of some writers yet living; who first taught us to mould our thoughts into easy and significant words; to retrench the superfluities of expression, and to make our rime so properly a part of the verse, that it should never mislead the sense, but itself be led and governed by it.

Eugenius was going to continue this discourse, when Lisideius told him it was necessary, before they proceeded further, to take a standing measure of their controversy; for how was it possible to be decided who writ the best plays, before we know what a play should be? But, this once agreed on by both parties,each might have recourse to it, either to prove his own advantages, or to discover the failings of his adversary.

He had no sooner said this, but all desired the favour of him to give the definition of a play; and they were the more importuante, because neither Aristotle, nor Horace, nor any other, who writ of that subject, had ever done it.

Lisideius, after some modest denials, at last confessed he had a rude notion of it; indeed, rather a description than a definition; but which served to guide him in his private thoughts, when he was to make a judgment of what others writ: that he conceived a play ought to be, *A just and lively image of human nature, representing its passions and humours, and the changes of fortune to which it is subject, for the delight and instruction of mankind.*

This definition, though Crites raised a logical objection against it; that it was only *a genere et fine,* and so not altogether perfect; was yet well received by the rest: and after they had given order to the watermen to turn their barge, and row softly, that they might take the cool of the evening in their return, Crites, being desired by the company to begin, spoke on behalf of the Ancients, in this manner:

"If confidence presage a victory, Eugenius, in his own opinion, has already triumphed over the Ancients: nothing seems more easy to him, than to overcome those whom it is our greatest praise to have imitated well; for we do not only build upon their foundation, but by their models. Dramatic Poesy had time enough, reckoning from Thespis (who first invented it) to Aristophanes, to be born, to grow up, and to flourish in maturity. It has been observed of arts and sciences, that in one and the same century they have arrived to a great perfection; and no wonder, since every age has a kind of universal genius, which inclines those that live in it to some particular studies: the work then being pushed on by many hands, must of necessity go forward.

"Is it not evident, in these last hundred years (when the study of philosophy has been the business of all the Virtuosi in Christendom), that almost a new Nature has been revealed to us?—that more errors of the school have been detected, more useful experiments in philosophy have been made, more noble secrets in optics, medicine, anatomy, astronomy, discovered, than in all those credulous and doting ages from Aristotle to us?—so true is it, that nothing spreads more fast than science, when rightly and generally cultivated.

"Add to this, the more than common emulation that was in those times of writing well; which though it be found in all ages and all persons that pretend to the same reputation, yet Poesy, being then in more esteem than now it is, had greater honours decreed to the professors of it, and consequently the rivalship was more high between them; they had judges ordained to decide their merit, and prizes to reward it; and historians have been diligent to record of Eschylus, Euripides, Sophocles, Lycophron, and the rest of them, both who they were that vanquished in these wars of the threatre, and how often they were crowned: while the Asian kings and Grecian commonwealths scarce afforded them a nobler subject than the unmanly luxuries of a debauched court, or giddy intrigues of a factious city. *Alit æmulatio ingenia,* (says Paterculus,) *et nunc invidia, nunc admiratio incitationem accendit:* Emulation is the spur of wit; and sometimes envy, sometimes admiratin, quickens our endeavours.

"But now, since the rewards of honour are taken away, that virtuous emulation is turned into direct malice; yet so slothful, that it contents itself to condemn and cry down others, without attempting to do better: 'tis a reputation too unprofitable, to take the necessary pains for it; yet, wishing they had it is incitement enough to hinder others from it. And this, in short, Eugenius, is the reason why you have now so few good poets, and so many severe judges. Certainly, to imitate the Ancients well, much labour and long study is required; which pains, I have already shown, our poets would want encouragement to take, if yet they had ability to go through with it. Those Ancients have been faithful imitators and wise observers of that Nature which is so torn and ill represented in our plays; they have handed down to us a perfect resemblance of her; which we, like ill copiers, neglecting to look on, have rendered monstrous, and disfigured. But, that you may know how much you are indebted to those your masters, and be ashamed to have so ill requited them, I must remember you, that all the rules by which we practise the Drama at this day, (either such as relate to the justness and symmetry of the plot, or the episodical ornaments, such as descriptions, narrations, and other beauties, which are not essential to the play,) were delivered to us from the observations which Aristotle made, of those poets, which either lived before him, or were his contemporaries: we have added nothing of our own, except we have the confidence to say our wit is better; of which none boast in this our age, but such as understand not theirs. Of that book which Aristotle has left us, *περὶ τῆς Ποιητικῆς*,[7] Horace his *Art of Poetry* is an excellent comment, and, I believe, restores to us that Second Book of his concerning *Comedy,* which is wanting in him.

"Out of these two have been extracted the famous Rules, which the French call *Des*

Trois Unitez, or, the Three Unities, which ought to be observed in every regular play; namely, of Time, Place, and Action.

"The Unity of Time they comprehend in twenty-four hours, the compass of a natural day, or as near as it can be contrived; and the reason of it is obvious to every one,—that the time of the feigned action, or fable of the play, should be proportioned as near as can be to the duration of that time in which it is represented: since therefore, all plays are acted on the theatre in a space of time much within the compass of twenty-four hours, that play is to be thought the nearest imitation of nature, whose plot or action is confined within that time; and, by the same rule which concludes this general proportion of time, it follows, that all the parts of it are to be equally subdivided; as namely, that one act take not up the supposed time of half a day, which is out of proportion to the rest; since the other four are then to be straitened within the compass of the remaining half: for it is unnatural that one act, which being spoke or written is not longer than the rest, should be supposed longer by the audience; 'tis therefore the poet's duty, to take care that no act should be imagined to exceed the time in which it is represented on the stage; and that the intervals and inequalities of time be supposed to fall out between the acts.

"This rule of time, how well it has been observed by the Ancients, most of their plays will witness; you see them in their tragedies, (wherein to follow this rule, is certainly most difficult,) from the very beginning of their plays, falling close into that part of the story which they intend for the action or principal object of it, leaving the former part to be delivered by narration: so that they set the audience, as it were, at the post where the race is to be concluded; and, saving them the tedious expectation of seeing the poet set out and ride the beginning of the course, you behold him not till he is in sight of the goal, and just upon you.

"For the second Unity, which is that of Place, the Ancients meant by it, that the scene ought to be continued through the play, in the same place where it was laid in the beginning: for the stage on which it is represented being but one and the same place, it is unnatural to conceive it many; and those far distant from one another. I will not deny but, by the variation of painted scenes, the fancy, which in these cases will contribute to its own deceit, may sometimes imagine it several places, with some appearance of probability; yet it still carries the greater likelihood of truth, if those places be supposed so near each other, as in the same town or city; which may all be comprehended under the larger denomination of one place; for a greater distance will bear no proportion to the shortness of time which is allotted in the acting, to pass from one of them to another; for the observation of this, next to the Ancients, the French are to be most commended. They tie themselves so strictly to the Unity of Place, that you never see in any of their plays, a scene changed in the middle of an act: if the act begins in a garden, a street, or chamber, 'tis ended in the same place; and that you may know it to be the same, the stage is so supplied with persons, that it is never empty all the time: he that enters the second, has business with him who was on before; and before the second quits the stage, a third appears who has business with him. This Corneille calls *la liaison des scenes*, the continuity or joining of the scenes; and 'tis a good mark of a well-contrived play, when all the persons are known to each other, and every one of them has some affairs with all the rest.

"As for the third Unity, which is that of Action, the Ancients meant no other by it than what the logicians do by their *finis*, the end or scope of any action; that which is the first in intention, and last in execution: now the poet is to aim at one great and complete action, to the carrying on of which all things in his play, even the very obstacles, are to be subservient; and the reason of this is as evident as any of the former.

"For two actions, equally laboured and driven on by the writer, would destroy the unity of the poem; it would be no longer one play, but two: not but that there may be many actions in a play, as Ben Johnson has observed in his *Discoveries;* but they must be all subservient to the great one, which our language happily expresses in the name of *under-plots:* such as in Terence's *Eunuch* is the difference and reconcilement of Thais and Phædria, which is not the chief business of the play, but promotes the marriage of Chærea and Chremes's sister, principally intended by the poet. There ought to be but one action, says Corneille, that is, one complete action which leaves the mind of the audience in a full repose; but this cannot be brought to pass but by many other imperfect actions, which conduce to it, and hold the audience in a delightful suspence of what will be.

"If by these rules (to omit many other drawn from the precepts and practice of the Ancients) we should judge our modern plays, 'tis probable that few of them would endure the trial: that which should be the business of a day, takes up in some of them an age; instead of one action, they are the epitomes of a man's life; and for one spot of ground (which the stage should represent) we are sometimes in more countries than the map can show us.

"But if we will allow the Ancients to have contrived well, we must acknowledge them to have writ better; questionless we are deprived of a great stock of wit in the loss of Menander among the Greek poets, and of Cæcilius, Afranius, and Varius, among the Romans; we may guess at Menander's excellency by the plays of Terence, who translated some of his; and yet wanted so much of him, that he was called by C. Caesar the half-Menander; and may judge of Varius, by the testimonies of Horace, Martial, and Velleius Paterculus. 'Tis probable that these, could they be recovered, would decide the controversy; but so long as Aristophanes in the old Comedy, and Plautus in the new are extant, while the tragedies of Euripides, Sophocles, and Seneca, are to be had, I can never see one of those plays which are now written, but it increases my admiration of the Ancients. And yet I must acknowledge farther, that to admire them as we ought, we should understand them better than we do. Doubtless many things appear flat to us, whose wit depended on some custom or story, which never came to our knowledge; or perhaps on some criticism in their language, which being so long dead, and only remaining in their books, 'tis not possible they should make us know it perfectly. To read Macrobius, explaining the propriety and elegancy of many words in Virgil, which I had before passed over without consideration, as common things, is enough to assure me that I ought to think the same of Terence; and that in the purity of his style (which Tully so much valued that he ever carried his works about him) there is yet left in him great room for admiration, if I knew but where to place it. In the mean time I must desire you to take notice, that the greatest man of the last age (Ben Johnson) was willing to give place to them in all things: he was not only a professed imitator of Horace, but a learned plagiary of all the others; you track him every where in their snow: if Horace, Lucan, Petronius Arbiter, Seneca, and Juvenal, had their own from him, there are few serious thoughts which are new in him: you will pardon me, therefore, if I presume he loved their fashion, when he wore their clothes. But since I have otherwise a great veneration for him, and you, Eugenius, prefer him above all other poets, I will use no farther argument of you than his example: I will produce Father Ben to you, dressed in all the ornaments and colours of the Ancients; you will need no other guide to our party, if you follow him; and whether you consider the bad plays of our age, or regard the good ones of the last, both the best and worst of the modern poets will equally instruct you to esteem the Ancients."

Crites had no sooner left speaking, but Eugenius, who had waited with some impatience for it, thus began:

"I have observed in your speech, that the former part of it is convincing as to what the Moderns have profited by the rules of the Ancients; but in the latter you are careful to conceal how much they have excelled them; we own all the helps we have from them, and want neither veneration nor gratitude while we acknowledge that to overcome them we must make use of the advantages we have received from them: but to these assistances we have joined our own industry; for, had we sat down with a dull imitation of them, we might then have lost somewhat of the old perfection, but never acquired any that was new. We draw not therefore after their lines, but those of Nature; and having the life before us, besides the experience of all they knew, it is no wonder if we hit some airs and features which they have missed. I deny not what you urge of arts and sciences, that they have flourished in some ages more than others; but your instance in philosophy makes for me: for if natural causes be more known now than in the time of Aristotle, because more studied, it follows that poesy and other arts may, with the same pains, arrive still nearer to perfection; and, that granted, it will rest for you to prove that they wrought more perfect images of human life than we; which seeing in your discourse you have avoided to make good, it shall now be my task to show you some part of their defects, and some few excellencies of the Moderns. And I think there is none among us can imagine I do it enviously, or with purpose to detract from them; for what interest of fame or profit can the living lose by the reputation of the dead? On the other side, it is a great truth which Velleius Paterculus affirms: *Audita visis libentius laudamus; et præsentia invidia, præterita admiratione prosequimur; et his nos obrui, illis instrui credimus:*[8] that praise or censure is certainly the most sincere, which unbribed posterity shall give us.

"Be pleased then in the first place to take notice, that the Greek poesy, which Crites has affirmed to have arrived to perfection in the reign of the Old Comedy, was so far from it, that the distinction of it into acts was not known to them; or if it were, it is yet so darkly delivered to us that we cannot make it out.

"All we know of it is, from the singing of their Chorus; and that too is so uncertain, that in some of their plays we have reason to conjecture they sung more than five times. Aristotle indeed divides the integral parts of a play into four. First, the *Protasis*, or entrance, which gives light only to the characters of the persons, and proceeds very little into any part of the action. Secondly, the *Epitasis*, or working up of the plot; where the play grows warmer, the design or action of it is drawing on, and you see something promising that it will come to pass. Thirdly, the *Catastasis*, or counterturn, which destroys that expectation, imbroils the action in new difficulties, and leaves you far distant from that hope in which it found you; as you may have observed in a violent stream resisted by a narrow passage,—it runs round to an eddy, and carries back the waters with more swiftness than it brought them on. Lastly, the *Catastrophe,* which the Grecians called λύσις, the French *le denouement,* and we the discovery or unravelling of the plot: there you see all things settling again upon their first foundations; and, the obstacles which hindered the design or action of the play once removed, it ends with that resemblance of truth and nature, that the audience are satisfied with the conduct of it. Thus this great man delivered to us the image of a play; and I must confess it is so lively, that from thence much light has been derived to the forming it more prefectly into acts and scenes: but what poet first limited to five the number of the acts, I know not; only we see it so firmly established in the time of Horace, that he gives it for a rule in comedy; *Neu brevior quinto, neu sit productior actu.*[9] So that you see the Grecians cannot be said to have consummated this art; writing rather by entrances, than by acts, and having rather a general indigested notion of a play, than knowing how and where to bestow the particular graces of it.

"But since the Spaniards at this day allow but three acts, which they call *Jornadas,* to a play, and the Italians in many of theirs follow them, when I condemn the Ancients, I declare it is not altogether because they have not five acts to every play, but because they have not confined themselves to one certain number: it is building an house without a model; and when they succeeded in such undertakings, they ought to have sacrificed to Fortune, not to the Muses.

"Next, for the plot, which Aristotle called *τὸ μυθος,*[10] and often *τῶν πραγμάτων σύνθεσις,*[11] and from him the Romans *Fabula,* it has already been judiciously observed by a late writer, that in their tragedies it was only some tale derived from Thebes or Troy, or at least something that happened in those two ages; which was worn so threadbare by the pens of all the epic poets, and even by tradition itself of the talkative Greeklings, (as Ben Johnson calls them,) that before it came upon the stage, it was already known to all the audience: and the people, so soon as ever they heard the name of Œdipus, knew as well as the poet, that he had killed his father by a mistake, and committed incest with his mother, before the play; that they were now to hear of a great plague, an oracle, and the ghost of Laius: so that they sat with a yawning kind of expectation, till he was to come with his eyes pulled out, and speak a hundred or two of verses in a tragic tone, in complaint of his misfortunes. But one (Œdipus, Hercules, or Medea, had been tolerable: poor people, they scaped not so good cheap; they had still the *chapon bouillé*[12] set before them till their appetities were cloyed with the same dish, and, the novelty being gone, the pleasure vanished; so that one main end of Dramatic Poesy in its definition, which was to cause delight, was of consequence destroyed.

"In their comedies, the Romans generally borrowed their plots from the Greek poets; and theirs was commonly a little girl stolen or wandered from her parents, brought back unknown to the same city, there got with child by some lewd young fellow, who, by the help of his servant, cheats his father; and when her time comes, to cry *Juno Lucina, fer opem,*[13] one or other sees a little box or cabinet which was carried away with her, and so discovers her to her friends, if some god do not prevent it, by coming down in a machine, and take the thanks of it to himself.

"By the plot you may guess much of the characters of the persons. An old father, who would willingly, before he dies, see his son well married; his debauched son, kind in his nature to his wench, but miserably in want of money; a servant or slave, who has so much wit to strike in with him, and help to dupe his father; a braggadochio captain, a parasite, and a lady of pleasure.

"As for the poor honest maid, whom all the story is built upon, and who ought to be one of the principal actors in the play, she is commonly a mute in it: she has the breeding of the old Elizabeth way, for maids to be seen and not to be heard; and it is enough you know she is willing to be married, when the fifth act requires it.

"These are plots built after the Italian mode of houses; you see through them all at once: the characters are indeed the imitations of Nature, but so narrow, as if they had imitated only an eye or an hand, and did not dare to venture on the lines of a face, or the proportion of a body.

"But in how strait a compass soever they have bounded their plots and characters, we will pass it by, if they have regularly pursued them, and perfectly observed those three Unities of Time, Place, and Action; the knowledge of which you say is derived to us from them. But in the first place give me leave to tell you, that the Unity of Place, however it might be practised by them, was never any of their rules: we neither find it in Aristotle, Horace, or any who have written of it, till in our age the French poets first made it a precept of the stage. The Unity of Time, even Terence himself (who was the best and most regular of them) has neglected: his *Heautontimorumenos*, or *Self-Punisher*, takes up visibly two days; therefore, says Scaliger, the two first acts concluding the first day were acted overnight; the three last on the ensuing day; and Euripides, in tying himself to one day, has committed an absurdity never to be forgiven him; for in one of his tragedies he has made Theseus go from Athens to Thebes, which was about forty English miles, under the walls of it give battle, and appear victorious in the next act; and yet, from the time of his departure to the return of the Nuntius, who gives the relation of his victory, Æthra and the Chorus have but thirty-six verses; that is not for every mile a verse.

"The like error is as evident in Terence his *Eunuch*, when Laches, the old man, enters in a mistake the house of Thais; where, betwixt his exit and the entrance of Pythias, who comes to give an ample relation of the garboyles he has raised within, Parmeno, who was left upon the stage, has not above five lines to speak. *C'est bien employer un temps si court,*[14] says the French poet, who furnished me with one of the observations: and almost all their tragedies will afford us examples of the like nature.

" 'Tis true, they have kept the continuity, or, as you called it, *liaison des scenes*, somewhat better: two do not perpetually come in together, talk, and go out together; and other two succeed them, and do the same throughout the act, which the English call by the name of single scenes; but the reason is, because they have seldom above two or three scenes, properly so called, in every act; for it is to be accounted a new scene, not every time the stage is empty; but every person who enters, though to others, makes it so; because he introduces a new business. Now the plots of their plays being narrow, and the persons few, one of their acts was written in a less compass than one of our well-wrought scenes; and yet they are often deficient even in this. To go no further than Terence; you find in the *Eunuch* Antipho entering single in the midst of the third act, after Cremes and Pythias were gone off; in the same play you have likewise Dorias beginning the fourth act alone; and after she had made a relation of what was done at the Soldier's entertainment (which by the way was very inartificial, because she was presumed to speak directly to the audience, and to acquaint them with what was necessary to be known, but yet should have been so contrived by the poet as to have been told by persons of the drama to one another, and so by them to have come to the knowledge of the people), she quits the stage, and Phædria enters next, alone likewise: he also gives you an account of himself, and of his returning from the country, in monologue; to which unnatural way of narration Terence is subject in all his plays. In his *Adelphi*, or Brothers, Syrus and Demea enter after the scene was broken by the departure of Sostrata, Geta, and Canthara; and indeed you can scarce look into any of his comedies, where you will not presently discover the same interruption.

"But as they have failed both in laying of their plots, and managing of them, swerving from the rules of their own art by misrepresenting Nature to us, in which they have ill satisfied one intention of a play, which was delight; so in the instructive part they have erred worse: instead of punishing vice and rewarding virtue, they have often shown a prosperous wickedness, and an unhappy piety: they have set before us a bloody image of revenge in Medea, and given her dragons to convey her safe from punishment; a Priam and Astyanax murdered, and Cassandra ravished, and the lust and murder ending in the victory of him who acted them: in short, there is no indecorum in any of our modern plays, which if I would excuse, I could not shadow with some authority from the Ancients.

"And one farther note of them let me leave you: tragedies and comedies were not writ then as they are now, promiscuously, by the same person; but he who found his genius bending to the one, never attempted the other way. This is so plain, that I need not instance to you, that Artistophanes, Plautus, Terence, never any of them writ a tragedy; Æschylus, Euripides, Sophocles, and Seneca, never meddled with comedy: the sock and buskin were not worn by the same poet. Having then so much care to excel in one kind, very little is to be pardoned them, if they miscarried in it; and this would lead me to the consideration of their wit, had not Crites given me sufficient warning not to be too bold in my judgment of it; because, the languages being dead, and many of the customs and little accidents on which it depended lost to us, we are not competent judges of it. But though I grant that here and there we may miss the application of a proverb or a custom, yet a thing well said will be wit in all languages; and though it may lose something in the translation, yet to him who reads it in the original, 'tis still the same: he has an idea of its excellency, though it cannot pass from his mind into any other expression or words than those in which he finds it. When Phædria, in the *Eunuch*, had a command from his mistress to be absent two days, and, encouraging himself to go through with it, said, *Tandem ego non illa caream, si sit opus, vel totum triduum?*[15]—Parmeno, to mock the softness of his master, lifting up his hands and eyes, cries out, as it were in admiration, *Hui! universum triduum!*[16] the elegancy of which *universum*, though it cannot be rendered in our language, yet leaves an impression on our souls: but this happens seldom in him; in Plautus oftener, who is infinitely too bold in his metaphors and coining words, out of which many times his wit is nothing; which questionless was one reason why Horace falls upon him so severely in those verses:—

> *Sed proavi nostri Plautinos et numeros et*
> *Laudavere sales, nimium patienter utrumque,*
> *Ne dicam stolide.*[17]

For Horace himself was cautious to obtrude a new word on his readers, and makes custom and common use the best measure of receiving it into our writings.

Multa renascentur quae iam cecidere, cadenique
Quae nunc sunt in honore vocabula, si volet usus,
Quem penes arbitrium est, et jus, et norma loquendi.[18]

"The not observing this rule is that which the world has blamed in our satyrist, Cleveland: to express a thing hard and unnaturally, is his new way of elocution. 'Tis true, no poet but may sometimes use a catachresis: Virgil does it—

Mistaque ridenti colocasia fundet acantho—

in his eclogue of *Pollio;* and in his 7th *Æneid.*

. . . mirantur et undae,
Miratur nemus insuctum fulgentia longe
Scuta virum fluvio pictasque innare carinas.[19]

And Ovid once so modestly, that he asks leave to do it:

. . . quem, si verbo audacia detur,
Haud metuam summi dixisse Palatia caeli:

calling the court of Jupiter by the name of Augustus his palace; though in another place he is more bold, where he says,—*et longas visent Capitolia pompas.*[20] But to do this always, and never be able to write a line without it, though it may be admired by some few pedants, will not pass upon those who know that wit is best conveyed to us in the most easy language; and is most to be admired when a great thought comes dressed in words so commonly received, that it is understood by the meanest apprehensions, as the best meat is the most easily digested: but we cannot read a verse of Cleveland's without making a face at it, as if every word were a pill to swallow: he gives us many times a hard nut to break our teeth, without a kernel for our pains. So that there is this difference betwixt his *Satires* and doctor Donne's; that the one gives us deep thoughts in common language, though rough cadence; the other gives us common thoughts in abstruse words: 'tis true, in some places his wit is independent of his words, as in that of the *Rebel Scot:*

Had *Cain* been *Scot,* God would have chang'd his doom;
Not forc'd him wander, but confin'd him home.

"*Si sic omnia dixisset!*[21] This is wit in all languages: 'tis like Mercury, never to be lost or killed:—and so that other—

For beauty, like white powder, makes no noise,
And yet the silent hypocrite destroys.

You see, the last line is highly metaphorical, but it is so soft and gentle, that it does not shock us as we read it.

"But, to return from whence I have digressed, to the consideration of the Ancients' writing, and their wit; of which by this time you will grant us in some measure to be fit judges. Though I see many excellent thoughts in Seneca, yet he of them who had a genius most proper for the stage, was Ovid; he had a way of writing so fit to stir up a pleasing admiration and concernment, which are the objects of a tragedy, and to show the various movements of a soul combating betwixt two different passions, that, had he lived in our age, or in his own could have writ with our advantages, no man but must have yielded to him; and therefore I am confident the *Medea* is none of his: for, though I esteem it for the gravity and sententiousness of it, which he himself concludes to be suitable to a tragedy,—*Omne genus scripti gravitate tragaedia vincit,*[22]—yet it moves not my soul enough to judge that he, who in the epic way wrote things so near the drama as the story of Myrrha, of Caunus and Biblis, and the rest, should stir up no more concernment where he most endeavoured it. The masterpiece of Seneca I hold to be that scene in the *Troades*, where Ulysses is seeking for Astyanax to kill him; there you see the tenderness of a mother so represented in Andromache, that it raises compassion to a high degree in the reader, and bears the nearest resemblance of any thing in their tragedies to the excellent scenes of passion in Shakespeare, or in Fletcher: for love-scenes, you will find few among them; their tragic poets dealt not with that soft passion, but with lust, cruelty, revenge, ambition, and those bloody actions they produced; which were more capable of raising horror than compassion in an audience: leaving love untouched, whose gentleness would have tempered them, which is the most frequent of all the passions, and which being the private concernment of every person, is soothed by viewing its own image in a public entertainment.

"Among their comedies, we find a scene or two of tenderness, and that where you would least expect it, in Plautus; but to speak generally, their lovers say little, when they see each other, but *anima mea, vita mea:* *ζωη καὶ ψυχη*,[23] as the women in Juvenal's time used to cry out in the fury of their kindness: then indeed to speak sense were an offence. Any sudden gust of passion (as an extasy of love in an unexpected meeting) cannot better be expressed than in a word and a sigh, breaking one another. Nature is dumb on such occasions; and to make her speak, would be to represent her unlike herself. But there are a thousand other concernments of lovers, as jealousies, complaints, contrivances, and the like, where not to open their minds at large to each other, were to be wanting to their own love, and to the expectation of the audience; who watch the movements of their minds, as much as the changes of their fortunes. For the imaging of the first is properly the work of a poet; the latter he borrows of the historian."

Eugenius was proceeding in that part of his discourse, when Crites interrupted him. "I see," said he, "Eugenius and I are never like to have this question decided betwixt us; for he maintains the Moderns have acquired a new perfection in writing; I can only grant they have altered the mode of it. Homer described his heroes men of great appetites, lovers of beef broiled upon the coals, and good fellows; contrary to the practice of the French Romances, whose heroes neither eat, nor drink, nor sleep, for love. Virgil makes Æneas a bold avower of his own virtues:

> *Sum pius Æneas, fama super aethera notus;*[24]

which in the civility of our poets is the character of a fanfaron or Hector: for with us the knight takes occasion to walk out, or sleep, to avoid the vanity of telling his own story, which the trusty squire is ever to perform for him. So in their love-scenes, of which Eugenius spoke last, the Ancients were more hearty, we more talkative: they writ love as it was then the mode to make it; and I will grant thus much to Eugenius, that perhaps one of their poets, had he lived in our age, *si foret hoc nostrum fato delapsus in ævum*[25] (as Horace says of Lucilius), he had altered many things: not that they were not as natural before, but that he might accommodate himself to the age he lived in. Yet in the mean time, we are not to conclude any thing rashly against those great men, but preserve to them the dignity of masters, and give that honour to their memories, *quos Libitina sacravit*,[26] part of which we expect may be paid to us in future times."

This moderation of Crites, as it was pleasing to all the company, so it put an end to that dispute; which Eugenius, who seemed to have the better of the argument, would urge no farther: but Lisideius, after he had acknowledged himself of Eugenius his opinion concerning the Ancients, yet told him, he had forborne, till his discourse were ended, to ask him why he preferred the English plays above those of other nations? and whether we ought not to submit our stage to the exactness of our next neighbours?

"Though," said Eugenius, "I am at all times ready to defend the honour of my country against the French, and to maintain, we are as well able to vanquish them with our pens, as our ancestors have been with their swords; yet, if you please," added he, looking upon Neander, "I will commit this cause to my friend's management; his opinion of our plays is the same with mine: and besides, there is no reason, that Crites and I, who have now left the stage, should re-enter so suddenly upon it; which is against the laws of comedy."

"If the question had been stated," replied Lisideius, "who had writ best, the French or English, forty years ago, I should have been of your opinion, and adjudged the honour to our nation; but since that time" (said he, turning towards Neander) "we have been so long together bad Englishmen, that we had not leisure to be good poets. Beaumont, Fletcher, and Johnson (who were only capable of bringing us to that degree of perfection which we have) were just then leaving the world; as if (in an age of so much horror) wit, and those milder studies of humanity, had no farther business among us. But the Muses, who ever follow peace, went to plant in another country: it was then that the great Cardinal of Richelieu began to take them into his protection; and that, by his encouragement, Corneille, and some other Frenchmen, reformed their theatre, which before was as much below ours, as it now surpasses it and the rest of Europe. But because Crites in his discourse for the Ancients has prevented me, by touching upon many rules of the stage which the Moderns have borrowed from them, I shall only, in short, demand of you, whether you are not convinced that of all nations the French have best observed them? In the Unity of Time you find them so scrupulous, that it yet remains a dispute among their poets, whether the artificial day of twelve hours, more or less, be not meant by Aristotle, rather than the natural one of twenty-four; and consequently, whether all plays ought not to be reduced into that compass. This I can testify, that in all their dramas writ within these last twenty years and upwards, I have not observed any that have extended the time to thirty hours: in the Unity of Place they are full as scrupulous; for many of their critics limit it to that very spot of ground where the play is supposed to begin; none of them exceed the compass of the same town or city. The Unity of Action in all plays is yet more conspicuous; for they do not burden them with underplots, as the English do: which is the reason why many scenes of our tragi-comedies carry on a design that is nothing of kin to the main plot; and that we see two distinct webs in a play, like those in ill-wrought stuffs; and two actions, that is, two plays, carried on together, to the confounding of the audience; who, before they are warm in their concernments for one part, are diverted to another; and by that means espouse the interest of neither. From hence likewise it arises, that the one half of our actors are not known to the other. They keep their distances, as if they were Mountagues and Capulets, and seldom begin an acquaintance till the last scene of the fifth act, when they are all to meet upon the stage. There is no theatre in the world has any thing so absurd as the English tragi-comedy; 'tis a drama of our own invention, and the fashion of it is enough to proclaim it so; here a course of mirth, there another of sadness and passion, a third of honour, and fourth a duel: thus, in two hours and a half, we run through all the fits of Bedlam. The French affords you as much variety on the same day, but they do it not so unseasonably, or *mal à propos,* as we: our poets present you the play and the farce together; and our stages still retain somewhat of the orginal civility of the *Red Bull:*

> *Atque ursum et pugiles media inter carmina poscunt.*[27]

The end of tragedies or serious plays, says Aristotle, is to beget admiration, compassion, or concernment; but are not mirth and compassion things incompatible? and is it not evident that the poet must of necessity destroy the former by intermingling of the latter? that is, he must ruin the sole end and object of his tragedy, to introduce somewhat that is forced in, and is not of the body of it. Would you not think that physician mad, who, having prescribed a purge, should immediately order you to take restringents upon it?

"But to leave our plays, and return to theirs. I have noted one great advantage they have had in the plotting of their tragedies; that is, they are always grounded upon some known history: according to that of Horace, *Ex noto fictum carmen sequar,*[28] and in that they have so imitiated the Ancients, that they have surpassed them. For the Ancients, as was observed before, took for the foundation of their plays some poetical fiction, such as under that consideration could move but little concernment in the audience, because they already knew the event of it. But the French goes farther:

> *Atque ita mentitur, sic veris falsa remiscet,*
> *Primo ne medium, medio ne discrepet imum.*[29]

He so interweaves truth with probable fiction, that he puts a pleasing fallacy upon us; mends the intrigues of fate, and dispenses with the severity of history, to reward that virtue which has been rendered to us there unfortunate. Sometimes the story has left the success so doubtful, that the writer is free, by the privilege of a poet, to take that which of two or more relations will best suit with his design: as for example, the death of Cyrus, whom Justin and some others report to have perished in the Scythian war, but Xenophon affirms to have died in his bed of extreme old age. Nay more, when the event is past dispute, even then we are willing to be deceived, and the poet, if he contrives it with appearance of truth, has all the audience of his party; at least during the time his play is acting: so naturally we are kind to virtue, when our own interest is not in question, that we take it up as the general concernment of mankind. On the other side, if you consider the historical plays of Shakespeare, they are rather so many chronicles of kings, or the business many times of thirty or forty years, cramped into a representation of two hours and an half; which is not to imitate or paint Nature, but rather to draw her in miniature, to take her in little; to look upon her through the wrong end of a perspective, and receive her images not only much less, but infinitely more imperfect than the life: this, instead of making a play delightful, renders it ridiculous:—

> *Quodcunque ostendis mihi sic, incredulus odi.*[30]

For the spirit of man cannot be satisfied but with truth, or at least verisimility: and a poem is to contain, if not *τᾲ ἐτυμα,* yet *ἐτύμοισιν ὁμοῖα,*[31] as one of the Greek poets has expressed it.

"Another thing in which the French differ from us and from the Spaniards, is, that they do not embarrass, or cumber themselves with too much plot; they only represent so much of a story as will constitute one whole and great action sufficient for a play; we, who undertake more, do but multiply adventures; which, not being produced from one another, as effects from causes, but barely following, constitute many actions in the drama, and consequently make it many plays.

"But by pursuing close one argument, which is not cloyed with many turns, the French have gained more liberty for verse, in which they write; they have leisure to dwell on a subject which deserves it; and to represent the passions (which we have acknowledged to be the poet's work), without being hurried from one thing to another, as we are in the plays of Calderon, which we have seen lately upon our theatres, under the name of Spanish plots. I have taken notice but of one tragedy of ours, whose plot has that uniformity and unity of design in it, which I have commended in the French; and that is *Rollo,* or rather, under the name of Rollo, the story of Bassianus and Geta in Herodian: there indeed the plot is neither large nor intricate, but just enough to fill the minds of the audience, not to cloy them. Besides, you see it founded upon the truth of history, only the time of the action is not reduceable to the strictness of the rules; and you see in some places a little farce mingled, which is below the dignity of the other parts; and in this all our poets are extremely peccant: even Ben Johnson himself, in *Sejanus* and *Catiline,* has given us this oleo of a play, this unnatural mixture of comedy and tragedy; which to me sounds just as ridiculously as the history of David with the merry humours of Golias. In *Sejanus* you may take notice of the scene betwixt Livia and the physician, which is a pleasant satire upon the artifical helps of beauty: in *Catiline* you may see the parliament of women; the little envies of them to one another; and all that passes betwixt Curio and Fulvia: scenes admirable in their kind, but of an ill mingle with the rest.

"But I return again to the French writers, who, as I have said, do not burden themselves too much with plot, which has been reproached to them by an *ingenious person* of our nation as a fauit; for, he says, they commonly make but one person considerable in a play; they dwell on him, and his concernments, while the rest of the persons are only subservient to set him off. If he intends this by it, that there is one person in the play who is of greater dignity than the rest, he must tax, not only theirs, but those of the Ancients, and which he would be loth to do, the best of ours; for it is impossible but that one person must be more conspicuous in it than any other, and consequently the greatest share in the action must devolve on him. We see it so in the management of all affairs: even in the most equal aristocracy, the balance cannot be so justly poised, but some one will be superior to the rest, either in parts, fortune, interest, or the consideration of some glorious exploit; which will reduce the greatest part of business into his hands.

"But, if he would have us to imagine, that in exalting one character the rest of them are neglected, and that all of them have not some share or other in the action of the play, I desire him to produce any of Corneille's tragedies, wherein every person, like so many servants in a well-governed family, has not some employment, and who is not necessary to the carrying on of the plot, or at least to your understanding it.

"There are indeed some protatick persons in the Ancients, whom they make use of in their plays, either to hear or give the relation: but the French avoid this with great address, making their narrations only to, or by such, who are some way interested in the main design. And now I am speaking of relations, I cannot take a fitter opportunity to add this in favour of the French, that they often use them with better judgment and more *à propos* than the English do. Not that I commend narrations in general,—but there are two sorts of them. One, of those things which are antecedent to the play, and are related to make the conduct of it more clear to us. But 'tis a fault to choose such subjects for the stage as will force us on that rock, because we see they are seldom listened to by the audience, and that is many times the ruin of the play; for, being once let pass without attention, the audience can never recover themselves to understand the plot: and indeed it is somewhat unreasonable that they should be put to so much trouble, as that, to comprehend what passes in their sight, they must have recourse to what was done, perhaps, ten or twenty years ago.

"But there is another sort of relations, that is, of things happening in the action of the play, and supposed to be done behind the scenes; and this is many times both convenient and beautiful; for by it the French avoid the tumult which we are subject to in England, by representing duels, battles, and the like; which renders our stage too like the theatres where they fight prizes. For what is more ridiculous than to represent an army with a drum and five men behind it; all which the hero of the other side is to drive in before him; or to see a duel fought, and one slain with two or three thrusts of the foils, which we know are so blunted, that we might give a man an hour to kill another in good earnest with them.

"I have observed that in all our tragedies, the audience cannot forbear laughing when the actors are to die; it is the most comic part of the whole play. All *passions* may be lively represented on the stage, if to the well-writing of them the actor supplies a good commanded voice, and limbs that move easily, and without stiffness; but there are many *actions* which can never be imitated to a just height: dying especially is a thing which none but a Roman gladiator could naturally perform on the stage, when he did not imitate or represent, but naturally do it; and therefore it is better to omit the representation of it.

"The words of a good writer, which describe it lively, will make a deeper impression of belief in us than all the actor can persuade us to, when he seems to fall dead before us; as a poet in the description of a beautiful garden, or a meadow, will please our imagination more than the place itself can please our sight. When we see death represented, we are convinced it is but fiction; but when we hear it related, our eyes, the strongest witnesses, are wanting, which might have undeceived us; and we are all willing to favour the sleight, when the poet does not too grossly impose on us. They therefore who imagine these relations would make no concernment in the audience, are deceived, by confounding them with the other, which are of things antecedent to the play: those are made often in cold blood, as I may say, to the audience; but these are warmed with our concernments, which were before awakened in the play. What the philosophers say of motion, that, when it is once begun, it continues of itself, and will do so to eternity, without some stop put to it, is clearly true on this occasion: the soul, being already moved with the characters and fortunes of those imaginary persons, continues going of its own accord; and we are no more weary to hear what becomes of them when they are not on the stage, than we are to listen to the news of an absent mistress. But it is objected, that if one part of the play may be related, then why not all? I answer, some parts of the action are more fit to be represented, some to be related. Corneille says judiciously, that the poet is not obliged to expose to view all particular actions which conduce to the principal: he ought to select such of them to be seen, which will appear with the greatest beauty, either by the magnificence of the show, or the vehemence of passions which they produce, or some other charm which they have in them; and let the rest arrive to the audience by narration. 'Tis a great mistake in us to believe the French present no part of the action on the stage; every alteration or crossing of a design, every new-sprung passion, and turn of it, is a part of the action, and much the noblest, except we conceive nothing to be action till they come to blows; as if the painting of the hero's mind were not more properly the poet's work than the strength of his body. Nor does this anything contradict the opinion of Horace, where he tells us,

Segnius irritant animos demissa per aurem,
Quam quæ sunt oculis subjecta fidelibus.[32]

For he says immediately after,

. . . Non tamen intus
Digna geri promes in scenam; multaque tolles
Ex oculis, quae mox narret facundia præsens.[33]

Among which many he recounts some:

Ne pueros coram populo Medea trucidet,
Aut in avem Progne mutetur, Cadmus in anguem; &c.[34]

That is, those actions which by reason of their cruelty will cause aversion in us, or by reason of their imposibility, unbelief, ought either wholly to be avoided by a poet, or only delivered by narration. To which we may have leave to add such as to avoid tumult (as was before hinted), or to reduce the plot into a more reasonable compass of time, or for defect of beauty in them, are rather to be related than presented to the eye. Examples of all these kinds are frequent, not only among all the Ancients, but in the best received of our English poets. We find Ben Johnson using them in his *Magnetick Lady*, where one comes out from dinner, and relates the quarrels and disorders of it, to save the undecent appearance of them on the stage, and to abbreviate the story; and this in express imitation of Terence, who had done the same before him in his *Eunuch*, where Pythias makes the like relation of what had happened within at the Soldier's entertainment. The relations likewise of Sejanus's death, and the prodigies before it, are remarkable; the one of which was hid from sight, to avoid the horror and tumult of the representation; the other, to shun the introducing of things impossible to be believed. In that excellent play, *The King and no King*, Fletcher goes yet farther; for the whole unravelling of the plot is done by narration in the fifth act, after the manner of the Ancients; and it moves great concernment in the audience, though it be only a relation of what was done many years before the play. I could multiply other instances, but these are sufficient to prove that there is no error in choosing a subject which requires this sort of narrations; in the ill managing of them, there may.

"But I find I have been too long in this discourse, since the French have many other excellencies not common to us; as that you never see any of their plays end with a conversion, or simple change of will, which is the ordinary way which our poets use to end theirs. It shows little art in the conclusion of a dramatic poem, when they who have hindered the felicity during the four acts, desist from it in the fifth, without some powerful cause to take them off; and though I deny not but such reasons may be found, yet it is a path that is cautiously to be trod, and the poet is to be sure he convinces the audience that the motive is strong enough. As for example, the conversion of the Usurer in *The Scornful Lady*, seems to me a little forced; for, being an Usurer, which implies a lover of money to the highest degree of covetousness (and such the poet has represented him), the account he gives for the sudden change is, that he has been duped by the wild young fellow; which in reason might render him more wary another time, and make him punish himself with harder fare and coarser clothes, to get it up again: but that he should look on it as a judgment, and so repent, we may expect to hear of in a sermon, but I should never endure it in a play.

"I pass by this; neither will I insist on the care they take, that no person after his first entrance shall ever appear, but the business which brings him upon the stage shall be evident; which, if observed, must needs render all the events in the play more natural; for there you see the probability of every accident, in the cause that produced it; and that which appears chance in the play, will seem so reasonable to you, that you will there find it almost necessary: so that in the exits of the actors you have a clear account of their purpose and design in the next entrance (though, if the scene be well wrought, the event will commonly deceive you), for there is nothing so absurd, says Corneille, as for an actor to leave the stage, only because he has no more to say.

"I should now speak of the beauty of their rhyme, and the just reason I have to prefer that way of writing in tragedies before ours in blank-verse; but because it is partly received by us, and therefore not altogether peculiar to them, I will say no more of it in relation to their plays. For our own, I doubt not but it will exceedingly beautify them; and I can see but one reason why it should not generally obtain, that is because our poets write so ill in it. This indeed may prove a more prevailing argument than all others which are used to destroy it, and therefore I am only troubled when great and judicious poets, and those who are acknowledged such, have writ or spoke against it: as for others, they are to be answered by that one sentence of an ancient author:—*Sed ut primo ad consequendos eos quos priores ducimus, accendimur, ita ubi aut præteriri, aut æquari eos posse desperavimus, studium cum spe senescit: quod, scilicet, assequi non potest, sequi desinit; . . . præteritoque eo in quo eminere non possumus, aliquid in quo nitamur, conquirimus.*"[35]

Lisideius concluded in this manner; and Neander, after a little pause, thus answered him:

"I shall grant Lisideius, without much dispute, a great part of what he has urged against us; for I acknowledge that the French contrive their plots more regularly, and observe the laws of comedy, and decorum of the stage (to speak generally), with more exactness than the English. Farther, I deny not but he has taxed us justly in some irregularities of ours, which he has mentioned; yet, after all, I am of opinion that neither our faults nor their virtues are considerable enough to place them above us.

"For the lively imitation of Nature being in the definition of a play, those which best fulfil that law ought to be esteemed superior to the others. 'Tis true, those beauties of the French poesy are such as will raise perfection higher where it is, but are not sufficient to give it where it is not: they are indeed the beauties of a statue, but not of a man, because not animated with the soul of Poesy, which is imitation of humour and passions: and this Lisideius himself, or any other however biassed to their party, cannot but acknowledge, if he will either compare the humours of our comedies, or the characters of our serious plays, with theirs. He that will look upon theirs which have been written till these last ten years, or thereabouts, will find it an hard matter to pick out two or three passable humours amongst them. Corneille himself, their arch-poet, what has he produced except *The Liar*, and you know how it was cried up in France; but when it came upon the English stage, though well translated, and that part of Dorant acted to so much advantage by Mr. Hart as I am confident it never received in its own country, the most favourable to it would not put it in competition with many of Fletcher's or Ben Johnson's. In the rest of Corneille's comedies you have little humour; he tells you himself, his way is, first to show two lovers in good intelligence with each other; in the working up of the play to embroil them by some mistake, and in the latter end to clear it, and reconcile them.

"But of late years Molière, the younger Corneille, Quinault, and some others, have been imitating afar off the quick turns and graces of the English stage. They have mixed their serious plays with mirth, like our tragicomedies, since the death of Cardinal Richelieu; which Lisideius and many others not observing, have commended that in them for a virtue which they themselves no longer practice. Most of their new plays are, like some of ours, derived from the Spanish novels. There is scarce one of them without a veil, and a trusty Diego, who drolls much after the rate of the *Adventures*. But their humours, if I may grace them with that name, are so thin-sown, that never above one of them comes up in any play. I dare take upon me to find more variety of them in some one play of Ben Johnson's, than in all theirs together; as he who has seen *The Alchymist, The Silent Woman*, or *Bartholomew Fair*, cannot but acknowledge with me.

"I grant the French have performed what was possible on the ground-work of the Spanish plays; what was pleasant before, they have made regular: but there is not above one good play to be writ on all those plots; they are too much alike to please often; which we need not the experience of our own stage to justify. As for their new way of mingling mirth with serious plot, I do not, with Lisideius, condemn the thing, though I cannot approve their manner of doing it. He tells us, we cannot so speedily recollect ourselves after a scene of great passion and concernment, as to pass to another of mirth and humour, and to enjoy it with any relish: but why should he imagine the soul of man more heavy than his senses? Does not the eye pass from an unpleasant object to a pleasant in a much shorter time than is required to this? and does not the unpleasantness of the first commend the beauty of the latter? The old rule of logic might have convinced him, that contraries, when placed near, set off each other. A continued gravity keeps the spirit too much bent; we must refresh it sometimes, as we bait in a journey, that we may go on with greater ease. A sense of mirth, mixed with tragedy, has the same effect upon us which our music has betwixt the acts; and that we find a relief to us from the best plots and language of the stage, if the discourses have been long. I must therefore have stronger arguments, ere I am convinced that compassion and mirth in the same subject destroy each other; and in the mean time cannot but conclude, to the honour of our nation, that we have invented, increased, and perfected a more pleasant way of writing for the stage, than was ever known to the ancients or moderns of any nation, which is tragi-comedy.

"And this leads me to wonder why Lisideius and many others should cry up the barrenness of the French plots, above the variety and copiousness of the English. Their plots are single; they carry on one design, which is pushed forward by all the actors, every scene in the play contributing and moving towards it. Our plays, besides the main design, have underplots or by-concernments, of less considerable persons and intrigues, which are carried on with the motion of the main plot: just as they say the orb of the fixed stars, and those of the planets, though they have motions of their own, are whirled about by the motion of the *Primum Mobile,* in which they are contained. That similitude expresses much of the English stage; for if contrary motions may be found in nature to agree; if a planet can go east and west at the same time, one way by virtue of his own motion, the other by the force of the First Mover, it will not be difficult to imagine how the under-plot, which is only different, not contrary to the great design, may naturally be conducted along with it.

"Eugenius has already shown us, from the confession of the French poets, that the Unity of Action is sufficiently preserved, if all the imperfect actions of the play are conducing to the main design; but when those petty intrigues of a play are so ill ordered, that they have no coherence with the other, I must grant that Lisideius has reason to tax that want of due connexion; for co-ordination in a play is as dangerous and unnatural as in a state. In the mean time he must acknowledge, our variety, if well ordered, will afford a greater pleasure to the audience.

"As for his other argument, that by pursuing one single theme they gain an advantage to express and work up the passions, I wish any example he could bring from them would make it good; for I confess their verses are to me the coldest I have ever read. Neither, indeed, is it possible for them, in the way they take, so to express passion, as that the effects of it should appear in the concernment of an audience, their speeches being so many declamations, which tire us with the length; so that instead of persuading us to grieve for their imaginary heroes, we are concerned for our own trouble, as we are in the tedious visits of bad company; we are in pain till they are gone. When the French stage came to be reformed by Cardinal Richelieu, those long harangues were introduced, to comply with the gravity of a churchman. Look upon the *Cinna* and the *Pompey;* they are not so properly to be called plays, as long discourses of reason of state; and *Polieucte* in matters of religion is as solemn as the long stops upon our organs. Since that time it is grown into a custom, and their actors speak by the hour-glass, as our parsons do; nay, they account it the grace of their parts, and think themselves disparaged by the poet, if they may not twice or thrice in a play entertain the audience with a speech of an hundred or two hundred lines. I deny not but this may suit well enough with the French; for as we, who are a more sullen people come to be diverted at our plays, so they, who are of an airy and gay temper, come thither to make themselves more serious: and this I conceive to be one reason why comedy is more pleasing to us, and tragedies to them. But to speak generally: it cannot be denied that short speeches and replies are more apt to move the passions and beget concernment in us, than the other; for it is unnatural for any one in a gust of passion to speak long together, or for another in the same condition to suffer him, without interruption. Grief and passion are like floods raised in little brooks by a sudden rain; they are quickly up; if the concernment be poured unexpectedly in upon us, it overflows us: but a long sober shower gives them leisure to run out as they came in, without troubling the ordinary current. As for Comedy, repartee is one of its chiefest graces; the greatest pleasure of the audience is a chace of wit, kept up on both sides, and swiftly managed. And this our forefathers, if not we, have had in Fletcher's plays, to a much higher degree of perfection than the French poets can arrive at.

"There is another part of Lisideius his discourse, in which he has rather excused our neighbours, than commended them; that is, for aiming only to make one person considerable in their plays. 'Tis very true what he has urged, that one character in all plays, even without the poet's care, will have advantage of all the others; and that the design of the whole drama will chiefly depend on it. But this hinders not that there may be more shining characters in the play; many persons of a second magnitude, nay, some so very near, so almost equal to the first, that greatness may be opposed to greatness, and all the persons be made considerable, not only by their quality, but their action. 'Tis evident that the more the persons are, the greater will be the variety of the plot. If then the parts are managed so regularly, that the beauty of the whole be kept entire, and that the variety become not a perplexed and confused mass of accidents, you will find it infinitely pleasing to be led in a labyrinth of design, where you see some of your way before you, yet discern not the end till you arrive at it. And that all this is practicable, I can produce for examples many of our English plays: as *The Maid's Tragedy, The Alchymist, The Silent Woman:* I was going to have named *The Fox,* but that the unity of design seems not exactly observed in it; for there appear two actions in the play; the first naturally ending with the fourth act; the second forced from it in the fifth: which yet is the less to be condemned in him, because the disguise of Volpone, though it suited not with his character as a crafty or covetous person, agreed well enough with that of a voluptuary; and by it the poet gained the end he aimed at, the punishment of vice, and the reward of virtue, which that disguise produced. So that to judge equally of it, it was an excellent fifth act, but not so naturally proceeding from the former.

"But to leave this, and pass to the latter part of Lisideius his discourse, which concerns relations: I must acknowledge with him, that the French have reason when they hide that part of the action which would occasion too much tumult on the stage, and choose rather to have it made known by narration to the audience. Farther, I think it very convenient, for the reasons he has given, that all incredible actions were removed; but, whether custom has so insinuated itself into our countrymen, or nature has so formed them to fierceness, I know not; but they will scarcely suffer combats and other objects of horror to be taken from them. And indeed, the indecency of tumults is all which can be objected against fighting: for why may not our imagination as well suffer itself to be deluded with the probability of it, as with any other thing in the play? For my part, I can with as great ease persuade myself that the blows which are struck, are given in good earnest, as I can, that they who strike them are kings or princes, or those persons which they represent. For objects of incredibility, I would be satisfied from Lisideius, whether we have any so removed from all appearance of truth, as are those of Corneille's *Andromede;* a play which has been frequented the most of any he has writ. If the Perseus, or the son of an heathen god, the Pegasus, and the Monster, were not capable to choke a strong belief, let him blame any representation of ours hereafter. Those indeed were objects of delight; yet the reason is the same as to the probability: for he makes it not a Ballette or masque, but a play, which is to resemble truth. But for death, that it ought not to be represented, I have, besides the arguments alleged by Lisideius, the authority of Ben Johnson, who has forborn it in his tragedies; for both the death of Sejanus and Catiline are related: though in the latter I cannot but observe one irregularity of that great poet; he has removed the scene in the same act from Rome to Catiline's army, and from thence again to Rome; and besides, has allowed a very inconsiderable time, after Catiline's speech, for the striking of the battle, and the return of Petreius, who is to relate the event of it to the senate: which I should not animadvert on him, who was otherwise to a painful observer of *τὸ πρέπον*, or the *decorum* of the stage, if he had not used extreme severity in his judgment on the incomparable Shakespeare for the same fault.—To conclude on this subject of relations; if we are to be blamed for showing too much of the action, the French are as faulty for discovering too little of it: a mean betwixt both should be observed by every judicious writer, so as the audience may neither be left unsatisfied by not seeing what is beautiful, or shocked by beholding what is either incredible or undecent.

"I hope I have already proved in this discourse, that though we are not altogether so punctual as the French, in observing the laws of Comedy, yet our errors are so few, and little, and those things wherein we excel them so considerable, that we ought of right to be preferred before them. But what will Lisideius say, if they themselves acknowledge they are too strictly tied up by those laws, for breaking which he has blamed the English? I will allege Corneille's words, as I find them in the end of his Discourse of the Three Unities:—*Il est facile aux speculatifs d'estre severes, &c.* ' 'Tis easy for speculative persons to judge severely; but if they would produce to public view ten or twelve pieces of this nature, they would perhaps give more latitude to the rules than I have done, when, by experience, they had known how much we are bound up and constrained by them, and how many beauties of the stage they banished from it.' To illustrate a little what he has said: by their servile observations of the Unities of Time and Place, and integrity of scenes, they have brought on themselves that dearth of plot, and narrowness of imagination, which may be observed in all their plays. How many beautiful accidents might naturally happen in two or three days, which cannot arrive with any probability in the compass of twenty-four hours? There is time to be allowed also for maturity of design, which, amongst great and prudent persons, such as are often represented in Tragedy, cannot, with any likelihood of truth, be brought to pass at so short a warning. Farther; by tying themselves strictly to the Unity of Place, and unbroken scenes, they are forced many times to omit some beauties which cannot be shown where the act began; but might, if the scene were interrupted, and the stage cleared for the persons to enter in another place; and therefore the French poets are often forced upon absurdities; for if the act begins in a chamber, all the persons in the play must have some business or other to come thither, or else they are not to be shown that act; and sometimes their characters are very unfitting to appear there. As, suppose it were the king's bed-chamber; yet the meanest man in the tragedy must come and dispatch his business there, rather than in the lobby or courtyard (which is fitter for him), for fear the stage should be cleared, and the scenes broken. Many times they fall by it in a greater inconvenience; for they keep their scenes unbroken, and yet change the place; as in one of their newest plays, where the act begins in the street. There a gentleman is to meet his friend; he sees him with his man, coming out from his father's house; they talk together, and the first goes out: the second, who is a lover, has made an appointment with his mistress; she appears at the window, and then we are to imagine the scene lies under it. This gentleman is called away, and leaves his servant with his mistress; presently her father is heard from within; the young lady is afraid the servingman should be discovered, and thrusts him in through a door, which is supposed to be her closet. After this, the father enters to the daughter, and now the scene is in a house; for he is seeking from one room to another for this poor Philipin, or French Diego, who is heard from within, drolling and breaking many a miserable conceit upon his sad condition. In this ridiculous manner the play goes on, the stage being never empty all the while: so that the street, the window, the houses, and the closet, are made to walk about, and the persons to stand still. Now what, I beseech you, is more easy than to write a regular French play, or more difficult than write an irregular English one, like those of Fletcher, or of Shakespeare?

"If they content themselves, as Corneille did, with some flat design, which, like an ill riddle, is found out ere it be half proposed, such plots we can make every way regular, as easily as they; but whene'er they endeavour to rise to any quick turns and counterturns of plot, as some of them have attempted, since Corneille's plays have been less in vogue, you see they write as irregularly as we, though they cover it more speciously. Hence the reason is perspicuous, why no French plays, when translated, have, or ever can succeed on the English stage. For, if you consider the plots, our own are fuller of variety; if the writing, ours are more quick and fuller of spirit; and therefore 'tis a strange mistake in those who decry the way of writing plays in verse, as if the English therein imitated the French. We have borrowed nothing from them; our plots are weaved in English looms: we endeavour therein to follow the variety and greatness of characters which are derived to us from Shakespeare and Fletcher; the copiousness and well-knitting of the intrigues we have from Johnson; and for the verse itself we have English precedents of elder date than any of Corneille's plays. Not to name our old comedies before Shakespeare, which were all writ in verse of six feet, or Alexandrines, such as the French now use, I can show in Shakespeare, many scenes of rhyme together, and the like in Ben Johnson's tragedies: in *Catiline* and *Sejanus* sometimes thirty or forty lines, I mean besides the Chorus, or the monologues; which, by the way, showed Ben no enemy to this way of writing, especially if you look upon his *Sad Shepherd*, which goes sometimes on rhyme, sometimes on blank verse, like an horse who eases himself on trot and amble. You find him likewise commending Fletcher's pastoral of *The Faithful Shepherdess*, which is for the most part rhyme, though not refined to that purity to which it hath since been brought. And these examples are enough to clear us from a servile imitation of the French.

"But to return from whence I have digressed: I dare boldly affirm these two things of the English drama;—First, that we have many plays of ours as regular as any of theirs, and which, besides, have more variety of plot and characters; and secondly, that in most of the irregular plays of Shakespeare or Fletcher (for Ben Johnson's are for the most part regular) there is a more masculine fancy and greater spirit in the writing, than there is in any of the French. I could produce, even in Shakespeare's and Fletcher's works, some plays which are almost exactly formed: as *The Merry Wives of Windsor*, and *The Scornful Lady;* but because (generally speaking) Shakespeare, who writ first, did not perfectly observe the laws of Comedy, and Fletcher, who came nearer to perfection, yet through carelessness made many faults; I will take the pattern of a perfect play from Ben Johnson, who was a careful and learned observer of the dramatic laws, and from all his comedies I shall select *The Silent Woman;* of which I will make a short examen, according to those rules which the French observe."

As Neander was beginning to examine *The Silent Woman*, Eugenius, looking earnestly upon him; "I beseech you, Neander," said he, "gratify the company, and me in particular, so far, as before you speak of the play, to give us a character of the author; and tell us frankly your opinion, whether you do not think all writers, both French and English, ought to give place to him."

"I fear," replied Neander, "that in obeying your commands I shall draw a little envy on myself. Besides, in performing them, it will be first necessary to speak somewhat of Shakespeare and Fletcher, his rivals in poesy; and one of them, in my opinion, at least his equal, perhaps his superior.

"To begin, then, with Shakespeare. He was the man who of all modern, and perhaps ancient poets, had the largest and most comprehensive soul. All the images of Nature were still present to him, and he drew them, not laboriously, but luckily; when he describes any thing, you more than see it, you feel it too. Those who accuse him to have wanted learning, give him the greater commendation: he was naturally learn'd; he needed not the spectacles of books to read Nature; he looked inwards, and found her there. I cannot say he is every where alike; were he so, I should do him injury to compare him with the greatest of mankind. He is many times flat, insipid; his comic wit degenerating into clenches, his serious swelling into bombast. But he is always great, when some great occasion is presented to him; no man can say he ever had a fit subject for his wit, and did not then raise himself as high above the rest of poets,

> *Quantum lenta solent inter viburna cupressi.*[36]

The consideration of this made Mr. Hales of Eaton say, that there was no subject of which any poet ever writ, but he would produce it much better treated of in Shakespeare; and however others are now generally preferred before him, yet the age wherein he lived, which had contemporaries with him Fletcher and Johnson, never equalled them to him in their esteem: and in the last King's court, when Ben's reputation was at highest, Sir John Suckling, and with him the greater part of the courtiers, set our Shakespeare far above him.

"Beaumont and Fletcher, of whom I am next to speak, had, with the advantage of Shakespeare's wit, which was their precedent, great natural gifts, improved by study: Beaumont especially being so accurate a judge of plays, that Ben Johnson, while he lived, submitted all his writings to his censure, and, 'tis thought, used his judgment in correcting, if not contriving, all his plots. What value he had for him, appears by the verses he writ to him; and therefore I need to speak no farther of it. The first play that brought Fletcher and him in esteem was their *Philaster*: for before that, they had written two or three very unsuccessfully, as the like is reported of Ben Johnson, before he writ *Every Man in his Humour*. Their plots were generally more regular than Shakespeare's, especially those which were made before Beaumont's death; and they understood and imitated the conversation of gentlemen much better; whose wild debaucheries, and quickness of wit in repartees, no poet can ever paint as they have done. Humour, which Ben Johnson derived from particular persons, they made it not their business to describe: they represented all the passions very lively, but above all, love. I am apt to believe the English language in them arrived to its highest perfection: what words have since been taken in, are rather superfluous than ornamental. Their plays are now the most pleasant and frequent entertainments of the stage;

two of theirs being acted through the year for one of Shakespeare's or Johnson's: the reason is, because there is a certain gaiety in their comedies, and pathos in their more serious plays, which suits generally with all men's humours. Shakespeare's language is likewise a little obsolete, and Ben Johnson's wit comes short of theirs.

"As for Johnson, to whose character I am now arrived, if we look upon him while he was himself (for his last plays were but his dotages), I think him the most learned and judicious writer which any theatre ever had. He was a most severe judge of himself, as well as others. One cannot say he wanted wit, but rather that he was frugal of it. In his works you find little to retrench or alter. Wit, and langugage, and humour also in some measure, we had before him; but something of art was wanting to the Drama, till he came. He managed his strength to more advantage than any who preceded him. You seldom find him making love in any of his scenes, or endeavouring to move the passions; his genius was too sullen and saturnine to do it gracefully, especially when he knew he came after those who had performed both to such an height. Humour was his proper sphere; and in that he delighted most to represent mechanic people. He was deeply conversant in the Ancients, both Greek and Latin, and he borrowed boldly from them: there is scarce a poet or historian among the Roman authors of those times whom he has not translated in *Sejanus* and *Catiline*. But he has done his robberies so openly, that one may see he fears not to be taxed by any law. He invades authors like a monarch; and what would be theft in other poets, is only victory in him. With the spoils of these writers he so represents old Rome to us, in its rites, ceremonies, and customs, that if one of their poets had written either of his tragedies, we had seen less of it than in him. If there was any fault in his language, 'twas that he weaved it too closely and laboriously, in his serious plays: perhaps too, he did a little too much Romanize our tongue, leaving the words which he translated almost as much Latin as he found them: wherein, though he learnedly followed the idiom of their language, he did not enough comply with the idiom of ours. If I would compare him with Shakespeare, I must acknowledge him the more correct poet, but Shakespeare the greater wit. Shakespeare was the Homer, or father of our dramatic poets; Johnson was the Virgil, the pattern of elaborate writing; I admire him, but I love Shakespeare. To conclude of him; as he has given us the most correct plays, so in the precepts which he has laid down in his *Discoveries*, we have as many and profitable rules for perfecting the stage, as any wherewith the French can furnish us.

"Having thus spoken of the author, I proceed to the examination of his comedy, *The Silent Woman*.

Examen of the Silent Woman

"To begin first with the length of the action; it is so far from exceeding the compass of a natural day, that it takes not up an artificial one. 'Tis all included in the limits of three hours and an half, which is no more than is required for the presentment on the stage. A beauty perhaps not much observed; if it had, we should not have looked on the Spanish translation of *Five Hours* with so much wonder. The scene of it is laid in London; the latitude of place is almost as little as you can imagine; for it lies all within the compass of two houses, and after the first act, in one. The continuity of scenes is observed more than in any of our plays, except his own *Fox* and *Alchymist*. They are not broken above twice or thrice at most in the whole comedy; and in the two best of Corneille's plays, the *Cid* and *Cinna*, they are interrupted once apiece. The action of the play is entirely one; the end or aim of which is the settling Morose's estate on Dauphine. The intrigue of it is the greatest and most noble of any pure unmixed comedy in any language; you see it in many persons of various characters and humours, and all delightful; as first, Morose, or an old man, to whom all noise but his own talking is offensive. Some who would be thought critics, say this humour of his is forced; but to remove that objection, we may consider him first to be naturally of a delicate hearing, as many are, to whom all sharp sounds are unpleasant; and secondly, we may attribute much of it to the peevishness of his age, or the wayward authority of an old man in his own house, where he may make himself obeyed; and this the poet seems to allude to in his name Morose. Besides this, I am assured from divers persons, that Ben Johnson was actually acquainted with such a man, one altogether as ridiculous as he is here represented. Others say, it is not enough to find one man of such an humour; it must be common to more, and the more common the more natural. To prove this, they instance in the best of comical characters, Falstaff: there are many men resembling him; old, fat, merry, cowardly, drunken, amorous, vain, and lying. But to convince these people, I need but tell them, that humour is the ridiculous extravagance of conversation, wherein one man differs from all others. If then it be common, or communicated to many, how differs it from other men's? or what indeed causes it to be ridiculous so much as the singularity of it? As for Falstaff, he is not properly one humour, but a miscellany of humours or images, drawn from so many several men: that wherein he is singular is his wit, or those things he says *præter expectatum*, unexpected by the audience; his quick evasions, when you imagine him surprised, which, as they are extremely diverting of themselves, so receive a great addition from his person; for the very sight of such an unwieldy old debauched fellow is a comedy alone. And here, having a place so proper for it, I cannot but enlarge somewhat upon this subject of humour into which I am fallen. The ancients has little of it in their comedies; for the *τὸ γελοῖον*[37] of the Old Comedy, of which Aristophanes was chief, was not so much to imitate a man, as to make the people laugh at some odd conceit, which had commonly somewhat of unnatural or obscene in it. Thus, when you see Socrates brought upon the stage, you are not to imagine him made ridiculous by the imitation of his actions, but rather by making him perform something very unlike himself; something so childish and absurd, as by comparing it with the gravity of the true Socrates, makes a ridiculous object for the spectators. In their New Comedy which succeeded, the poets sought indeed to express the *ἦθος*,[38] as in their tragedies the *πάθος*[39] of mankind. But this *ἦθος* contained only the general characters of men and manners; as old men, lovers, servingmen, courtezans, parasites, and such other persons as we see in their comedies; all which they made alike: that is, one old man or father, one lover, one courtezan, so like another, as if the first of them had begot the rest of every sort: *Ex homine hunc natum dicas*.[40] The same custom they observed likewise in their tragedies. As for the French, though they have the word *humeur* among them, yet they have small use of it in their comedies or farces; they being but ill imitations of the *ridiculum*, or that which stirred up laughter in the Old Comedy. But among the English 'tis otherwise: where by humour is meant some extravagant habit, passion, or affection, particular (as I said before) to some one person, by the oddness of which, he is immediately distinguished from the rest of the men; which being lively and naturally represented, most frequently begets that malicious pleasure in the audience which is testified by laughter; as all things which are deviations from common customs are ever the aptest to produce it: though by the way this laughter is only accidental, as the person represented is fantastic or bizarre; but pleasure is essential to it, as the imitation of what is natural. The description of these humours, drawn from the knowledge and observation of particular persons, was the peculiar genius and talent of Ben Johnson; to whose play I now return.

"Besides Morose, there are at least nine or ten different characters and humours in *The Silent Woman;* all which persons have several concernments of their own, yet are all used by the poet, to the conducting of the main design to perfection. I shall not waste time in commending the writing of this play; but I will give you my opinion, that there is more wit and acuteness of fancy in it than in any of Ben Johnson's. Besides, that he has here described the conversation of gentlemen in the persons of True-Wit, and his friends, with more gaiety, air, and freedom, than in the rest of his comedies. For the contrivance of the plot, 'tis extreme elaborate, and yet withal easy; for the λύσιζ, or untying of it, 'tis so admirable, that when it is done, no one of the audience would think the poet could have missed it; and yet it was concealed so much before the last scene, that any other way would sooner have entered into your thoughts. But I dare not take upon me to commend the fabric of it, because it is altogether so full of art, that I must unravel every scene in it to commend it as I ought. And this excellent contrivance is still the more to be admired, because 'tis comedy, where the persons are only of common rank, and their business private, not elevated by passions or high concernments, as in serious plays. Here every one is a proper judge of all he sees, nothing is represented but that with which he daily converses: so that by consequences all faults lie open to discovery, and few are pardonable. 'Tis this which Horace has judiciously observed:

> *Creditur, ex medio quia res arcessit, habere*
> *Sudoris minimum; sed habet Comedia tanto*
> *Plus oneris, quanto veniæ minus.*[41]

But our poet who was not ignorant of these difficulties, had prevailed himself of all advantages; as he who designs a large leap takes his rise from the highest ground. One of these advantages is that which Corneille has laid down as the greatest which can arrive to any poem, and which he himself could never compass above thrice in all his plays; viz. the making choice of some signal and long-expected day, whereon the action of the play is to depend. This day was that designed by Dauphine for the settling of his uncle's estate upon him; which to compass, he contrives to marry him. That the marriage had been plotted by him long beforehand, is made evident by what he tells True-Wit in the second act, that in one moment he had destroyed what he had been raising many months.

"There is another artifice of the poet, which I cannot here omit, because by the frequent practice of it in his comedies he has left it to us almost as a rule; that is, when he has any character or humour wherein he would show a *coup de Maistre,* or his highest skill, he recommends it to your observation by a pleasant description of it before the person first appears. Thus, in *Bartholomew Fair* he gives you the pictures of Numps and Cokes, and in this those of Daw, Lafoole, Morose, and the Collegiate Ladies; all which you hear described before you see them. So that before they come upon the stage, you have a longing expectation of them, which prepares you to receive them favourably; and when they are there, even from their first appearance you are so far acquainted with them, that nothing of their humour is lost to you.

"I will observe yet one thing further of this admirable plot; the business of it rises in every act. The second is greater than the first; the third than the second; and so forward to the fifth. There too you see, till the very last scene, new difficulties arising to obstruct the action of the play; and when the audience is brought into despair that the business can naturally be effected, then, and not before, the discovery is made. But that the poet might entertain you with more variety all this while, he reserves some new characters to show you, which he opens not till the second and third act. In the second Morose, Daw, the Barber, and Otter; in the third the Collegiate Ladies: all which he moves afterwards in bywalks, or under-plots, as diversions to the main design, lest it should grow tedious, though they are still naturally joined with it, and somewhere or other subservient to it. Thus, like a skilful chess-player, by little and little he draws out his men, and makes his pawns of use to his greater persons.

"If this comedy and some others of his were translated into French prose (which would now be no wonder to them, since Molière has lately given them plays out of verse, which have not displeased them), I believe the controversy would soon be decided betwixt the two nations, even making them the judges. But we need not call our heroes to our aid; be it spoken to the honour of the English, our nation can never want in any age such who are able to dispute the empire of wit with any people in the universe. And though the fury of a civil war, and power for twenty years together abandoned to a barbarous race of men, enemies of all good learning, had buried the Muses under the ruins of monarchy; yet, with the restoration of our happiness, we see revived Poesy lifting up its head, and already shaking off the rubbish which lay so heavy on it. We have seen since his Majesty's return, many dramatic poems which yield not to those of any foreign nation, and which deserve all laurels but the English. I will set aside flattery and envy: it cannot be denied but we have had some little blemish either in the plot or writing of all those plays which have been made within these seven years (and perhaps there is no nation in the world so quick to discern them, or so difficult to pardon them, as ours): yet if we can persuade ourselves to use the candour of that poet, who, though the most severe of critics, has left us this caution by which to moderate our censures—

> . . . *ubi plura nitent in carmine, non ego paucis*
> *Offendar maculis;*—[42]

if, in consideration of their many and great beauties, we can wink at some slight and little imperfections, if we, I say, can be thus equal to ourselves, I ask no favour from the French. And if I do not venture upon any particular judgment of our late plays, 'tis out of the consideration which an ancient writer gives me: *vivo rum, ut magna admiratio, ita censura difficilis:*[43] betwixt the extremities of admiration and malice, 'tis hard to judge uprightly of the living. Only I think it may be permitted me to say, that as it is no lessening to us to yield to some plays, and those not many, of our own nation in the last age, so can it be no addition to pronounce of our present poets, that they have far surpassed all the Ancients, and the modern writers of other countries."

This, my Lord, was the substance of what was then spoke on that occasion; and Lisideius, I think, was going to reply, when he was prevented thus by Crites: "I am confident," said he, "that the most material things that can be said have been already urged on either side; if they have not, I must beg of Lisideius that he will defer his answer till another time: for I confess I have a joint quarrel to you both, because you have concluded, without any reason given for it, that rhyme is proper for the stage. I will not dispute how ancient it hath been among us to write this way; perhaps our ancestors knew no better till Shakespeare's time. I will grant it was not altogether left by him, and that Fletcher and Ben Johnson used it frequently in their Pastorals, and sometimes in other plays. Farther, I will not argue whether we received it originally from our own countrymen, or from the French; for that is an inquiry of as little benefit, as theirs who, in the midst of the great Plague, were not so solicitous to provide against it, as to know whether we had it from malignity of our own air, or by transportation from Holland. I have therefore only to affirm, that it is not allowable in serious plays; for comedies, I find you already concluding with me. To prove this, I might satisfy myself to tell you, how much in vain it is for you to strive against the stream of the people's inclination; the greatest part of which are prepossessed so much with those excellent plays of Shakespeare, Fletcher, and Ben Johnson, which have been written out of rhyme, that except you could bring them such as were written better in it, and those too by persons of equal reputation with them, it will be impossible for you to gain your cause with them, who will still be judges. This it is to which, in fine, all your reasons must submit. The unanimous consent of an audience is so powerful, that even Julius Cæsar (as Macrobius reports of him), when he was perpetual dictator, was not able to balance it on the other side. But when Laberius, a Roman Knight, at his request contended in the Mime with another poet, he was forced to cry out, *Etiam favente me victus es, Laberi.*[44] But I will not on this occasion take the advantage of the greater number, but only urge such reasons against rhyme, as I find in the writings of those who have argued for the other way. First then, I am of opinion, that rhyme is unnatural in a play, because dialogue there is presented as the effect of sudden thought: for a play is the imitation of Nature; and since no man without premeditation speaks in rhyme, neither ought he to do it on the stage. This hinders not but the fancy may be there elevated to an higher pitch of thought than it is in ordinary discourse; for there is a probability that men of excellent and quick parts may speak noble things *ex tempore*: but those thoughts are never fettered with the numbers or sound of verse without study, and therefore it cannot be but unnatural to present the most free way of speaking in that which is the most constrained. For this reason, says Aristotle, 'tis best to write tragedy in that kind of verse which is the least such, or which is nearest prose: and this amongst the Ancients was the iambic, and with us is blank verse, or the measure of verse kept exactly without rhyme. These numbers therefore are fittest for a play; the others for a paper of verses, or a poem; blank verse being as much below them, as rhyme is improper for the Drama. And if it be objected that neither are blank verses made *ex tempore*, yet, as nearest nature, they are still to be preferred.—But there are two particular exceptions, which many besides myself have had to verse; by which it will appear yet more plainly how improper it is in plays. And the first of them is grounded on that very reason for which some have commended rhyme; they say, the quickness of repartees in argumentative scenes receives an ornament from verse. Now what is more unreasonable than to imagine that a man should not only light upon the wit, but the rhyme too, upon the sudden?

This nicking of him who spoke before both in sound and measure, is so great an happiness, that you must at least suppose the persons of your play to be born poets: *Arcades omnes, et cantare pares, et respondere parati*: they must have arrived to the degree of *quicquid conabar dicere*;[45]—to make verses almost whether they will or no. If they are any thing below this, it will look rather like the design of two, than the answer of one: it will appear that your actors hold intelligence together; that they perform their tricks like fortune-tellers, by confederacy. The hand of art will be too visible in it, against that maxim of all professions, *Ars est celare artem*,[46] that it is the greatest perfection of art to keep itself undiscovered. Nor will it serve you to object, that however you manage it, 'tis still known to be a play; and, consequently, the dialogue of two persons understood to be the labour of one poet. For a play is still an imitation of Nature; we know we are to be deceived, and we desire to be so; but no man ever was deceived but with a probability of truth; for who will suffer a gross lie to be fastened on him? Thus we sufficiently understand, that the scenes which represent cities and countries to us are not really such, but only painted on boards and canvas; but shall that excuse the ill painture or designment of them? Nay, rather ought they not to be laboured with so much the more diligence and exactness, to help the imagination? since the mind of man does naturally tend to, and seek after truth; and therefore the nearer any thing comes to the imitation of it, the more it pleases.

"Thus, you see, your rhyme is uncapable of expressing the greatest thoughts naturally, and the lowest it cannot with any grace: for what is more unbefitting the majesty of verse, than to call a servant, or bid a door be shut in rhyme? And yet this miserable necessity you are forced upon. But verse, you say, circumscribes a quick and luxuriant fancy, which would extend itself too far on every subject, did not the labour which is required to well-turned and polished rhyme, set bounds to it. Yet this argument, if granted, would only prove that we may write better in verse, but not more naturally. Neither is it able to evince that; for he who wants judgment to confine his fancy in blank verse, may want it as much in rhyme: and he who has it will avoid errors in both kinds. Latin verse was as great a confinement to the imagination of those poets, as rhyme to ours; and yet you find Ovid saying too much on every subject. *Nescivit* (says Seneca) *quoa bene cessit relinquere*:[47] of which he gives you one famous instance in his description of the deluge:

> *Omnia pontus erat, deerant quoque litora ponto.*
>
> Now all was sea, nor had that sea a shore.

Thus Ovid's fancy was not limited by verse, and Virgil needed not verse to have bounded his.

"In our own language we see Ben Johnson confining himself to what ought to be said, even in the liberty of blank verse; and yet Corneille, the most judicious of the French poets, is still varying the same sense an hundred ways, and dwelling eternally on the same subject, though confined by rhyme. Some other exceptions I have to verse; but being these I have named are for the most part already public, I conceive it reasonable they should first be answered."

"It concerns me less than any," said Neander (seeing he had ended), "to reply to this discourse; because when I should have proved that verse may be natural in plays, yet I should always be ready to confess, that those which I have written in this kind come short of that perfection which is required. Yet since you are pleased I should undertake this province, I will do it, though with all imaginable respect and deference, both to that person from whom you have borrowed your strongest arguments, and to whose judgment, when I have said all, I finally submit. But before I proceed to answer your objections, I must first remember you, that I exclude all Comedy from my defence; and next that I deny not but blank verse may be also used; and content myself only to assert, that in serious plays where the subject and characters are great, and the plot unmixed with mirth, which might allay or divert these concernments which are produced, rhyme is there as natural and more effectual than blank verse.

"And now having laid down this as a foundation,—to begin with Crites, I must crave leave to tell him, that some of his arguments against rhyme reach no farther than, from the faults or defects of ill rhyme, to conclude against the use of it in general. May not I conclude against blank verse by the same reason? If the words of some poets who write in it, are either ill chosen, or ill placed, which makes not only rhyme, but all kind of verse in any language unnatural, shall I, for their vicious affectation, condemn those excellent lines of Fletcher, which are written in that kind? Is there any thing in rhyme more constrained than this line in blank verse, *I heaven invoke, and strong resistance make?* where you see both the clauses are placed unnaturally, that is, contrary to the common way of speaking, and that without the excuse of a rhyme to cause it: yet you would think me very ridiculous, if I should accuse the stubbornness of blank verse for this, and not rather the stiffness of the poet. Therefore, Crites, you must either prove that words, though well chosen, and duly placed, yet render not rhyme natural in itself; or that, however natural and easy the rhyme may be, yet it is not proper for a play. If you insist on the former part, I would ask you, what other conditions are required to make rhyme natural in itself, besides an election of apt words, and a right disposing of them? For the due choice of your words expresses your sense naturally, and the due placing them adapts the rhyme to it. If you object that one verse may be made for the sake of another, though both the words and rhyme be apt, I answer, it cannot possibly so fall out; for either there is a dependance of sense betwixt the first line and the second, or there is none: if there be that connection, then in the natural position of the words the latter line must of necessity flow from the former; if there be no dependance, yet still the due ordering of words makes the last line as natural in itself as the other: so that the necessity of a rhyme never forces any but bad or lazy writers to say what they would not otherwise. 'Tis true, there is both care and art required to write in verse. A good poet never concludes upon the first line, till he has sought out such a rhyme as may fit the sense, already prepared to heighten the second: many times the close of the sense falls into the middle of the next verse, or farther off, and he may often prevail himself of the advantages in English which Virgil had in Latin; he may break off in the hemistich, and begin another line. Indeed, the not observing these two last things, makes plays which are writ in verse so tedious: for though, most commonly, the sense is to be confined to the couplet, yet nothing that does *perpetuo tenore fluere*, run in the same channel, can please always. 'Tis like the murmuring of a stream, which not varying in the fall, causes at first attention, at last drowsiness. Variety of cadences is the best rule; the greatest help to the actors, and refreshment to the audience.

"If then verse may be made natural in itself, how becomes it improper to a play? You say the stage is the representation of Nature, and no man in ordinary conversation speaks in rhyme. But you foresaw when you said this, that it might be answered—neither does any man speak in blank verse, or in measure without rhyme. Therefore you concluded, that which is nearest Nature is still to be preferred. But you took no notice that rhyme might be made as natural as blank verse, by the well placing of the words, &c. All the difference between them, when they are both correct, is, the sound in one, which the other wants; and if so, the sweetness of it, and all the advantage resulting from it, which are handled in the Preface to *The Rival Ladies*, will yet stand good. As for that place of Aristotle, where he says, plays should be writ in that kind of verse which is nearest prose, it makes little for you; blank verse being properly but measured prose. Now measure alone, in any modern language, does not constitute verse; those of the Ancients in Greek and Latin consisted in quantity of words, and a determinate number of feet. But when, by the inundation of the Goths and Vandals into Italy, new languages were brought in and barbarously mingled with the Latin, of which the Italian, Spanish, French, and ours (made out of them and the Teutonic) are dialects, a new way of poesy was practised; new, I say, in those countries, for in all probability it was that of the conquerors in their own nations. This new way consisted in measure or number of feet, and rhyme; the sweetness of rhyme, and observation of accent, supplying the place of quantity in words, which could neither exactly be observed by those Barbarians, who knew not the rules of it, neither was it suitable to their tongues, as it had been to the Greek and Latin. No man is tied in modern poesy to observe any farther rule in the feet of his verse, but that they be dissyllables; whether spondee, trochee, or iambic, it matters not; only he is obliged to rhyme. Neither do the Spanish, French, Italian, or Germans, acknowledge at all, or very rarely, any such kind of poesy as blank verse amongst them. Therefore, at most 'tis but a poetic prose, a *sermo pedestris;* and as such, most fit for comedies, where I acknowledge rhyme to be improper. Farther; as to that quotation of Aristotle, our couplet verses may be rendered as near prose as blank verse itself, by using those advantages I lately named, as breaks in a hemistich, or running the sense into another line, thereby making art and order appear as loose and free as nature: or not tying ourselves to couplets strictly, we may use the benefit of the Pindaric way practised in *The Siege of Rhodes:* where the numbers vary, and the rhyme is disposed carelessly, and far from often chiming. Neither is that other advantage of the Ancients to be despised, of changing the kind of verse when they please, with the change of the scene, or some new entrance; for they confine not themselves always to iambics, but extend their liberty to all lyric numbers, and sometimes even to hexameter. But I need not go so far to prove that rhyme, as it succeeds to all other offices of Greek and Latin verse, so especially to this of plays, since the custom of all nations at this day confirms it, all the French, Italian, and Spanish tragedies are generally writ in it; and sure the universal consent of the most civilized parts of the world ought in this, as it doth in other customs, to include the rest.

"But perhaps you may tell me, I have proposed such a way to make rhyme natural, and consequently proper to plays, as is unpracticable; and that I shall scarce find six or eight lines together in any play, where the words are so placed and chosen as is required to make it natural. I answer, no poet need constrain himself at all times to it. It is enough he makes it his general rule; for I deny not but sometimes there may be a greatness in placing the words otherwise; and sometimes they may sound better, sometimes also the variety itself is excuse enough. But if, for the most part, the words be placed as they are in the negligence of prose, it is sufficient to denominate the way practicable; for we esteem that to be such, which in the trial oftener succeeds than misses. And thus far you may find the practice made good in many plays: where you do not, remember still, that if you cannot find six natural rhymes together, it will be as hard for you to produce as many lines in blank verse, even among the greatest of our poets, against which I cannot make some reasonable exception.

"And this, Sir, calls to my remembrance the beginning of your discourse, where you told us we should never find the audience favourable to this kind of writing, till we could produce as good plays in rhyme, as Ben Johnson, Fletcher, and Shakespeare, had writ out of it. But it is to raise envy to the living, to compare them with the dead. They are honoured, and almost adored by us, as they deserve; neither do I know any so presumptuous of themselves as to contend with them. Yet give me leave to say thus much, without injury to their ashes; that not only we shall never equal them, but they could never equal themselves, were they to rise and write again. We acknowledge them our fathers in wit; but they have ruined their estates themselves, before they came to their children's hands. There is scarce an humour, a character, or any kind of plot, which they have not blown upon. All comes sullied or wasted to us: and were they to entertain this age, they could not make so plenteous treatments out of such decayed fortunes. This therefore will be a good argument to us, either not to write at all, or to attempt some other way. There is no bays to be expected in their walks: *tentanda via est, qua me quoque possum tollere humo.*[48]

"This way of writing in verse they have only left free to us; our age is arrived to a perfection in it, which they never knew; and which (if we may guess by what of theirs we have seen in verse, as *The Faithful Shepherdess,* and *Sad Shepherd*) 'tis probable they never could have reached. For the genius of every age is different; and though ours excel in this, I deny not but that to imitate Nature in that perfection which they did in prose, is a greater commendation than to write in verse exactly. As for what you have added, that the people are not generally inclined to like this way; if it were true, it would be no wonder, that betwixt the shaking off an old habit, and the introducing of a new, there should be difficulty. Do we not see them stick to Hopkins' and Sternhold's psalms, and forsake those of David, I mean Sandys his translation of them? If by the people you understand the multitude, the *οἱ πολλοί,*[49] 'tis no matter what they think; they are sometimes in the right, sometimes in the wrong: their judgment is a mere lottery. *Est ubi plebs recte putat, est ubi peccat.*[50] Horace says it of the vulgar, judging poesy. But if you mean the mixed audience of the populace and the noblesse, I dare confidently affirm that a great part of the latter sort are already favourable to verse; and that no serious plays written since the King's return have been more kindly received by them, than *The Siege of Rhodes,* the *Mustapha, The Indian Queen,* and *Indian Emperor.*

"But I come now to the inference of your first argument. You said the dialogue of plays is presented as the effect of sudden thought, but no man speaks suddenly, or ex *tempore,* in rhyme; and you inferred from thence, that rhyme, which you acknowledge to be proper to epic poesy, cannot equally be proper to dramatic, unless we could suppose all men born so much more than poets, that verses should be made in them, not by them.

"It has been formerly urged by you, and

confessed by me, that since no man spoke any kind of verse *ex tempore*, that which was nearest Nature was to be preferred. I answer you, therefore, by distinguishing betwixt what is nearest to the nature of Comedy, which is the imitation of common persons and ordinary speaking, and what is nearest the nature of a serious play: this last is indeed the representation of Nature, but 'tis Nature wrought up to an higher pitch. The plot, the characters, the wit, the passions, the descriptions, are all exalted above the level of common converse, as high as the imagination of the poet can carry them, with proportion to verisimility. Tragedy, we know, is wont to image to us the minds and fortunes of noble persons, and to portray these exactly; heroic rhyme is nearest Nature, as being the noblest kind of modern verse.

Indignatur enim privatis et prope socco
Dignis carminibus narrari cœna Thyestæ.

says Horace: and in another place,

Effutire leves indigna tragædia versus.[51]

Blank verse is acknowledged to be too low for a poem, nay more, for a paper of verses; but if too low for an ordinary sonnet, how much more for Tragedy, which is by Aristotle, in the dispute betwixt the epic poesy and the dramatic, for many reasons he there alleges, ranked above it?

"But setting this defence aside, your argument is almost as strong against the use of rhyme in poems as in plays: for the epic way is every where interlaced with dialogue, or discoursive scenes; and therefore you must either grant rhyme to be improper there, which is contrary to your assertion, or admit it into plays by the same title which you have given it to poems. For though Tragedy be justly preferred above the other, yet there is a great affinity between them, as may easily be discovered in that definition of a play which Lisideius gave us. The *genus* of them is the same, a just and lively image of human nature, in its actions, passions, and traverses of fortune: so is the end, namely, for the delight and benefit of mankind. The characters and persons are still the same, viz. the greatest of both sorts; only the manner of acquainting us with those actions, passions, and fortunes, is different. Tragedy performs it *viva voce*, or by action, in dialogue; wherein it excels the Epic Poem, which does it chiefly by narration, and therefore is not so lively an image of human nature. However, the agreement betwixt them is such, that if rhyme be proper for one, it must be for the other. Verse, 'tis true, is not the effect of sudden thought; but this hinders not that sudden thought may be represented in verse, since those thoughts are such as must be higher than Nature can raise them without premeditation, especially to a continuance of them, even out of verse; and consequently you cannot imagine them to have been sudden either in the poet or in the actors. A play, as I have said, to be like Nature, is to be set above it; as statues which are placed on high are made greater than the life, that they may descend to the sight in their just proportion.

"Perhaps I have insisted too long on this objection; but the clearing of it will make my stay shorter on the rest. You tell us, Crites, that rhyme appears most unnatural in repartees, or short replies: when he who answers, it being presumed he knew not what the other would say, yet makes up that part of the verse which was left incomplete, and supplies both the sound and measure of it. This, you say, looks rather like the confederacy of two, than the answer of one.

"This, I confess, is an objection which is in every one's mouth, who loves not rhyme: but suppose, I beseech you, the repartee were made only in blank verse, might not part of the same argument be turned against you?

for the measure is as often supplied there, as it is in rhyme; the latter half of the hemistich as commonly made up, or a second line subjoined as a reply to the former; which any one leaf in Johnson's plays will sufficiently clear to you. You will often find in the Greek tragedians, and in Seneca, that when a scene grows up into the warmth of repartees, which is the close fighting of it, the latter part of the trimeter is supplied by him who answers; and yet it was never observed as a fault in them by any of the ancient or modern critics. The case is the same in our verse, as it was in theirs; rhyme to us being in lieu of quantity to them. But if no latitude is to be allowed a poet, you take from him not only his licence of *quidlibet audendi*,[52] but you tie him up in a straiter compass than you would a philosopher. This is indeed *Musas colere severiores*.[53] You would have him follow Nature, but he must follow her on foot: you have dismounted him from his Pegasus. But you tell us, this supplying the last half of a verse, or adjoining a whole second to the former, looks more like the design of two, than the answer of one. Supposing we acknowledge it: how comes this confederacy to be more displeasing to you, than in a dance which is well contrived? You see there the united design of many persons to make up one figure: after they have separated themselves in many petty divisions, they rejoin one by one into a gross: the confederacy is plain amongst them, for chance could never produce any thing so beautiful; and yet there is nothing in it, that shocks your sight. I acknowledge the hand of art appears in repartee, as of necessity it must in all kinds of verse. But there is also the quick and poynant brevity of it (which is an high imitation of Nature in those sudden gusts of passion) to mingle with it; and this, joined with the cadency and sweetness of the rhyme, leaves nothing in the soul of the hearer to desire. 'Tis an art which appears; but it appears only like the shadowings of painture, which being to cause the rounding of it, cannot be absent; but while that is considered, they are lost: so while we attend to the other beauties of the matter, the care and labour of the rhyme is carried from us, or at least drowned in its own sweetness, as bees are sometimes buried in their honey. When a poet has found the repartee, the last perfection he can add to it, is to put it into verse. However good the thought may be, however apt the words in which 'tis couched, yet he finds himself at a little unrest, while rhyme is wanting: he cannot leave it till that comes naturally, and then is at ease, and sits down contented.

"From replies, which are the most elevated thoughts of verse, you pass to the most mean ones, those which are common with the lowest of household conversation. In these, you say, the majesty of verse suffers. You instance in the calling of a servant, or commanding a door to be shut, in rhyme. This, Crites, is a good observation of yours, but no argument: for it proves no more but that such thoughts should be waved, as often as may be, by the address of the poet. But suppose they are necessary in the places where he uses them, yet there is no need to put them into rhyme. He may place them in the beginning of a verse, and break it off, as unfit, when so debased, for any other use; or granting the worst,—that they require more room than the hemistich will allow, yet still there is a choice to be made of the best words, and least vulgar (provided they be apt) to express such thoughts. Many have blamed rhyme in general, for this fault, when the poet with a little care might have redressed it. But they do it with no more justice, than if English Poesy should be made ridiculous for the sake of the Water Poet's rhymes. Our language is noble, full, and significant; and I know not why he who is master of it may not clothe ordinary things in it as decently as the Latin, if he use the same diligence in his choice of words. *Delectus verborum origo est eloquentiae.*[54] It was the saying of Julius Cæsar, one so curious in his, that none of them can be changed but for a worse. One would think, *unlock the door,* was a thing as vulgar as could be spoken; and yet Seneca could make it sound high and lofty in his Latin:

> *Reserate clusos regii postest laris.*
> Set wide the palace gates.

"But I turn from this exception, both because it happens not above twice or thrice in any play that those vulgar thoughts are used; and then too, were there no other apology to be made, yet the necessity of them, which is alike in all kind of writing, may excuse them. Besides that the great eagerness and precipitation with which they are spoken makes us rather mind the substance than the dress; that for which they are spoken, rather than what is spoke. For they are always the effect of some hasty concernment, and something of consequence depends on them.

"Thus, Crites, I have endeavoured to answer your objections; it remains only that I should vindicate an argument for verse, which you have gone about to overthrow. It had formerly been said, that the easiness of blank verse renders the poet too luxuriant, but that the labour of rhyme bounds and circumscribes an overfruitful fancy; the sense there being commonly confined to the couplet, and the words so ordered that the rhyme naturally follows them, not they the rhyme. To this you answered, that it was no argument to the question in hand; for the dispute was not which way a man may write best, but which is most proper for the subject on which he writes.

"First, give me leave, Sir, to remember you, that the argument against which you raised this objection, was only secondary: it was built on this hypothesis, that to write in verse was proper for serious plays. Which supposition being granted (as it was briefly made out in that discourse, by showing how verse might be made natural), it asserted, that this way of writing was an help to the poet's judgment, by putting bounds to a wild overflowing fancy. I think, therefore, it will not be hard for me to make good what it was to prove. But you add, that were this let pass, yet he who wants judgment in the liberty of his fancy, may as well show the defect of it when he is confined to verse; for he who has judgment will avoid errors, and he who has it not, will commit them in all kinds of writing.

"This argument, as you have taken it from a most acute person, so I confess it carries much weight in it: but by using the word judgment here indefinitely, you seem to have put a fallacy upon us. I grant, he who has judgment, that is, so profound, so strong, so infallible a judgment, that he needs no helps to keep it always poised and upright, will commit no faults either in rhyme or out of it. And on the other extreme, he who has a judgment so weak and crazed that no helps can correct or amend it, shall write scurvily out of rhyme, and worse in it. But the first of these judgments is no where to be found, and the latter is not fit to write at all. To speak therefore of judgment as it is in the best poets; they who have the greatest proportion of it, want other helps than from it, within. As for example, you would be loth to say, that he who was endued with a sound judgment had no need of History, Geography, or Moral Philosophy, to write correctly. Judgment is indeed the master-workman in a play; but he requires many subordinate hands, many tools to his assistance. And verse I affirm to be one of these; 'tis a rule and line by which he keeps his building compact and even, which otherwise lawless imagination would raise either irregularly or loosely. At least, if the poet commits errors with this help, he would make greater and more without it: 'tis, in short, a slow and painful, but the surest kind of working. Ovid, whom you accuse for luxuriancy in verse, had perhaps been farther guilty of it, had he writ in prose. And for your instance of Ben Johnson, who, you say, writ exactly without the help of rhyme; you are to remember, 'tis only an aid to a luxuriant fancy, which his was not: as he did not want imagination, so none ever said he had much to spare. Neither was verse then refined so much to be an help to that age, as it is to ours. Thus then the second thoughts being usually the best, as receiving the maturest digestion from judgment, and the last and most mature product of those thoughts being artful and laboured verse, it may well be inferred, that verse is a great help to a luxuriant fancy; and this is what that argument which you opposed was to evince."

Neander was pursuing this discourse so eagerly, that Eugenius had called to him twice or thrice, ere he took notice that the barge stood still, and that they were at the foot of Somerset Stairs, where they had appointed it to land. The company were all sorry to separate so soon, though a great part of the evening was already spent; and stood a-while looking back on the water, which the moon-beams played upon, and made it appear like floating quick-silver: at last they went up through a crowd of French people, who were merrily dancing in the open air, and nothing concerned for the noise of guns which had alarmed the town that afternoon. Walking thence together to the Piazze, they parted there; Eugenius and Lisideius to some pleasant appointment they had made, and Crites and Neander to their several lodgings.

Notes

1. "When in the assembly we saw . . . that a bad poet from the crowd offered him a complimentary poem in rough elegaics, he immediately ordered that a reward from the goods he was now selling should be given to him on condition that he should never afterwards write."

2. "Cinna pretends to be poor—and, in fact, he is poor."

3. "Who does not hate Bavius?"

4. "For we despise the praise of people whom we despise."

5. "With your permission, let me say that you were the first of all to lose your eloquence."

6. "I resent anything's being condemned merely because it is new and not because it is considered to be crudely or coarsely written" and "If time improves poems, as it does wines, I should like to know how many years give value to literature" (Horace, *Epistles* II., i., 76 and 34).

7. *Peri tes Poietikes: "The Poetics."*

8. "What is heard we praise more willingly than what is seen, and we follow the present with envy, the past with admiration; and we believe ourselves harmed by the former but edified by the latter."

9. "Let it be neither shorter than five acts, nor longer."

10. *To mythos*: compare English "myth."

11. *Ton pragmaton synthesis*: "the putting together of the action."

12. Literally, "boiled capon."

13. "Juno, goddess of childbirth, bring help."

14. "So short a time is well used."

15. "Shall I not do without her for even three days if necessary?"

16. "Alas, all of three days!"

17. "But our ancestors praised the meter and wit of Plautus, admiring each of them tolerantly if not stupidly" (*Art of Poetry*, 270–72).

18. "Many words now disused will revive, and many now esteemed will wither, if custom demands; for custom determines the right usage in language" (ibid.).

19. "The bean shall flower, joined with the laughing acanthus" (*Eclogues* IV. 20); and "Woods and the waters wonder at the shining shields and painted ships on the waves" (*Aeneid* VII, 91).

20. "If I may be allowed a bold metaphor, I should not fear to call it the imperial palace"; and "the capitol will see long processions" (Ovid, *Metamorphoses* I. 175, 561).

21. "If only he had said everything thus."

22. "Tragedy exceeds every other kind of writing in gravity."

23. "My soul, my life": *Zoe kai psyche*.

24. "I am pious Aeneas, whose fame is known above the heavens" (*Aeneid* I. 378–79).

25. "If he had been dropped into our age by fate."

26. "Which Libitina has consecrated."

27. "In the middle of plays they ask for a bear and boxers."

28. "From a well-known story, I should bring a poem" (*Art of Poetry*).

29. "He so lies, and mixes the false with the true, that you cannot tell apart the beginning, middle, or end" (ibid.).

30. "Whatever you show me in this way I find unbelievable and disgusting" (ibid.).

31. *Ta etuma; etumoisin omoia:* "True things, things like the truth."

32. "What we hear through our ears stirs us less strongly than what we see through our eyes" (*Art of Poetry*).

33. "You should not bring on stage what should be done off it: many things should be kept out of sight, and instead told with a vivid eloquence" (ibid.).

34. "Medea should not cut up her children in front of the audience, Procne should not be changed into a bird there, nor Cadmus into a snake, etc." (ibid.).

35. "Just as we are inspired to follow those we consider most worthy, so—when we despair of excelling or equalling them—our enthusiasm and hope diminish. For what it cannot attain, it ceases to follow; . . . after we have abandoned what we are unable to excel in, we look for something else for which to strive" (Velleius Paterculus, I. 17).

36. "As cypresses raise themselves above scraggly shrubs."

37. *To geloion:* "the laughable."

38. *Ethos:* "character."

39. *Pathos:* "emotion."

40. "You would say that one was born from another."

41. "Comedy is thought to demand the least work; for it draws its subjects from ordinary life. But the less indulgence it has, the more work it requires" (*Epistles* II. 1).

42. "When many beauties shine out in a poem, I shall not be offended at small faults" (Horace, *Art of Poetry* 351).

43. "Just as admiration for the living is great, it is difficult to criticize them."

44. "You are defeated even with me on your side, Laberius."

45. "All Arcadians, prepared to sing on equal terms and reply"; "Of singing whatever they attempted" (Virgil, *Eclogues* VII. 4).

46. "It is an art to conceal art."

47. "He did not know how to end when he should have" (*Controversies* IX. 5).

48. "I must explore new ways to raise my name aloft" (Virgil, *Georgics* III. 8–9).

49. *Hoi polloi*: "the masses."

50. "Sometimes the people think rightly, sometimes not" (*Epistles* II. i, 63).

51. "The banquet of Thyestes should not be told in the familiar verses appropriate to comedy"; and "It is not proper for tragedy to babble forth light verse" (*Art of Poetry* 90–91, 231).

52. "Of taking any liberty he wishes."

53. "To cultivate the more serious Muses."

54. "The origin of eloquence is the proper choice of words."

Aphra Behn *ca.* 1640–1688

Aphra Behn was the first Englishwoman to write professionally—that is, to earn her living by writing. As such she was the model for the commercial woman writer outside of the circle of propriety. She was born around 1640 in Kent, near Canterbury. Her maiden name may have been either Amies, Johnson, or Cooper. During her youth, she went with her family to Surinam (Dutch Guiana) where her father or a relative of her father was supposed to serve as lieutenant governor of the colony. The lieutenant governor died en route but the family arrived in 1663; Behn stayed on until the spring of 1664. After her return to England she married Mr. Behn. Nothing is known of her husband or what became of him, although there is speculation that he died of the plague in 1665. In 1666 Behn was persuaded by Thomas Killigrew, licensee of the King's Theater, to act as a spy in the Dutch wars. The English government failed to pay even Behn's living expenses while she was in Holland, and she had to borrow money to survive. When she returned to London in 1667, she was imprisoned for failure to pay her debts. Nothing is known of how she regained her freedom, but in 1670 she began her career as a writer.

After John Dryden ("our most unimitable laureate"), Aphra Behn was the most prolific writer of the Restoration. During her career she produced at least eighteen plays, as well as many poems and prose works. Her best and most successful plays were *The Rover* and *The Lucky Chance*. She wrote the first antislave novel, *Orinooko*, based on her experiences in Surinam. This novel was later made into a play by Thomas Southern. On April 16, 1688, five days after the coronation of William and Mary, Aphra Behn died. She was buried in Westminster Abbey.

In pleading for "my Masculine Part the Poet in me," Aphra Behn eloquently and forthrightly defends the right of women to compete as writers on equal terms with men. In the epistles and prefaces to her plays, Behn attacks the overt sexual biases of the criticism of her day that condemned a play simply because of the sex of its author, but she also calls into question the elitism implicit in English neoclassicism from Sidney to Dryden. She is the first English critic to reject outright the Horatian platitude that literature must both instruct and delight. The "Epistle to the Reader" that prefaces *The Dutch Lover* argues that poetry, and drama in particular, rarely if ever improves anyone's morality, nor indeed were plays written with such an end in mind. Their purpose is to entertain and this is the true measure of their success. Behn's "apology" for her poetry does not draw upon the authority of classical tradition—Aristotle, Plato, Horace. Indeed, she states that, as a woman, she would not have had access to the classical education required to make such an argument. Unencumbered by the weight of the classical defense of poetry, she is able to expose, with brutal honesty, the realities of competing in the theatrical world of Restoration London. Those realities included theater managers, licensors, actors, hostile audiences, and censorious and loud critics. Behn's outspokenness and her refusal to conform to the dictates of modesty and propriety demanded of women in her day led later generations of critics to dismiss her as licentious and immoral, "a harlot who danced through uncleanness and dared others to follow."

Preface to *The Lucky Chance*

The little Obligation I have to some of the witty Sparks and Poets of the Town, has put me on a Vindication of this Comedy from those Censures that Malice, and ill Nature have thrown upon it, tho in vain: The Poets I heartily excuse, since there is a sort of Self-Interest in their Malice, which I shou'd rather call a witty Way they have in this Age, of Railing at every thing they find with pain successful, and never to shew good Nature and speak well of any thing; but when they are sure 'tis damn'd, then they afford it that worse Scandal, their Pity. And nothing makes them so thorough-stitcht an Enemy as a full Third Day, that's Crime enough to load it with all manner of Infamy; and when they can no other way prevail with the Town, they charge it with the old never failing Scandal—That 'tis not fit for the Ladys: As if (if it were as they falsly give it out) the Ladys were oblig'd to hear Indecencys only from their Pens and Plays and some of them have ventur'd to treat 'em as Coursely as 'twas possible, without the least Reproach from them; and in some of their most Celebrated Plays have entertained 'em with things, that if I should here strip from their Wit and Occasion that conducts 'em in and makes them proper, their fair Cheeks would perhaps wear a natural Colour at the reading them: yet are never taken Notice of, because a Man writ them, and they may hear that from them they blush at from a Woman—But I make a Challenge to any Person of common Sense and Reason—that is not wilfully bent on ill Nature, and will in spight of Sense wrest a double *Entendre* from every thing, lying upon the Catch for a Jest or a Quibble, like a Rook for a Cully; but any unprejudic'd Person that knows not the Author, to read any of my Comedys and compare 'em with others of his Age, and if they find one Word that can offend the chastest Ear, I will submit to all their peevish Cavills; but Right or Wrong they must be Criminal because a Woman's; condemning them without having the Christian Charity, to examine whether it be guilty or not, with reading, comparing, or thinking; the Ladies taking up any Scandal on Trust from some conceited Sparks, who will in spight of Nature be Wits and *Beaus;* then scatter it for Authentick all over the Town and Court, poysoning of others Judgments with their false Notions, condemning it to worse than Death, Loss of Fame. And to fortifie their Detraction, charge me with all the Plays that have ever been offensive; though I wish with all their Faults I had been the Author of some of those they have honour'd me with.

For the farther Justification of this Play; it being a Comedy of Intrigue Dr. *Davenant* out of Respect to the Commands he had from Court, to take great Care that no Indecency should be in Plays, sent for it and nicely look't it over, putting out anything he but imagin'd the Criticks would play with. After that, Sir *Roger L'Estrange* read it and licens'd it, and found no such Faults as 'tis charg'd with: Then Mr. *Killigrew,* who more severe than any, from the strict Order he had, perus'd it with great Circumspection; and lastly the Master Players, who you will I hope in some Measure esteem Judges of Decency and their own Interest, having been so many Years Prentice to the Trade of Judging.

I say, after all these Supervisors the Ladys may be convinc'd, they left nothing that could offend, and the Men of their unjust Reflections on so many Judges of Wit and Decencys. When it happens that I challenge any one, to point me out the least Expression of what some have made their Discourse, they cry, *That Mr.* Leigh *opens his Night Gown, when he comes into the Bride-chamber;* if he do, which is a Jest of his own making, and which I never saw, I hope he has his Cloaths on underneath? And if so, where is the Indecency? I have seen in that admirable Play of *Oedipus,* the Gown open'd wide, and the Man shown in his Drawers and Waist coat, and never thought it an Offence before. Another crys, *Why we know not what they mean, when the Man takes a Woman off the Stage, and another is thereby cuckolded;* is that any more than you see in the most Celebrated of your Plays? as the *City Politicks,* the *Lady Mayoress,* and the *Old Lawyers Wife,* who goes with a Man she never saw before, and comes out again the joyfull'st Woman alive, for having made her Husband a Cuckold with such Dexterity, and yet I see nothing unnatural nor obscene: 'tis proper for the Characters. So in that lucky Play of the *London Cuckolds,* not to recite Particulars. And in that good Comedy of *Sir Courtly Nice,* the *Taylor to the young Lady*—in the fam'd Sir *Fopling Dorimont* and *Bellinda,* see the very Words—in *Valentinian,* see the Scene between the *Court Bawds.* And *Valentianian* all loose and ruffld a Moment after the Rape, and all this you see without Scandal, and a thousand others The *Moor of Venice* in many places. The *Maids Tragedy*—see the Scene of undressing the Bride, and between the *King* and *Amintor,* and after between the *King* and *Evadne*—All these I Name as some of the best Plays I know; If I should repeat the Words exprest in these Scenes I mention, I might justly be charg'd with course ill Manners, and very little Modesty, and yet they so naturally fall into the places they are designed for, and so are proper for the Business, that there is not the least Fault to be found with them; though I say those things in any of mine wou'd damn the whole Peice, and alarm the Town. Had I a Day or two's time, as I have scarce so many Hours to write this in (the Play, being all printed off and the Press waiting,) I would sum up all your Beloved Plays, and all the Things in them that are past with such Silence by; because written by Men: such Masculine Strokes in me, must not be allow'd. I must conclude those Women (if there be any such) greater Critics in that sort of Conversation than my self, who find any of that sort in mine, or any thing that can justly be reproach't. But 'tis in vain by dint of Reason or Comparison to convince the obstinate Criticks, whose Business is to find Fault, if not by a loose and gross Imagination to create them, for they must either find the Jest, or make it; and those of this sort fall to my share, they find Faults of another kind for the Men Writers. And this one thing I will venture to say, though against my Nature, because it has a Vanity in it: That had the Plays I have writ come forth under any Mans Name, and never known to have been mine; I appeal to all unbyast Judges of Sense, if they had not said that Person had made as many good Comedies, as any one Man that has writ in our Age; but a Devil on't the Woman damns the Poet.

Ladies, for its further Justification to you, be pleas'd to know, that the first Copy of this Play was ready by several Ladys of very great Quality, and unquestioned Fame, and received their most favourable Opinion, not one charging it with the Crime, that some have been pleas'd to find in the Acting. Other Ladys who saw it more than once, whose Quality and Vertue can sufficiently justifie any thing they design to favour, were pleas'd to say, they found an Entertainment in it very far from scandalous; and for the Generality of the Town, I found by my Receipts it was not thought so Criminal. However, that shall not be an Incouragement to me to trouble the Criticks with new Occasion of affronting me, for endeavouring at least to divert; and at this rate, both the few Poets that are left, and the Players who toil in vain will be weary of their Trade.

I cannot omit to tell you, that a Wit of the Town, a Friend of mine at *Wills* Coffee House, the first Night of the Play, cry'd it down as much as in him lay, who before had read it and assured me he never saw a prettier Comedy. So complaisant one pestilent Wit will be to another, and in the full Cry make his Noise too; but since 'tis to the witty Few I speak, I hope the better Judges will take no Offence, to whom I am oblig'd for better Judgments; and those I hope will be so kind to me, knowing my Conversation not at all addicted to the Indecencys alledged, that I would much less practice it in a Play, that must stand the Test of the censoring World. And I must want common Sense, and all the Degrees of good Manners, renouncing my Fame, all Modesty and Interest for a silly Sawcy fruitless Jest, to make Fools laugh, and Women blush, and wise Men asham'd; My self all the while, if I had been guilty of this Crime charg'd to me, remaining the only stupid, insensible. Is this likely, is this reasonable to be believ'd by any body, but the wilfully blind? All I ask, is the Priviledge for my Masculine Part the Poet in me, (if any such you will allow me) to tread in those successful Paths my Predecessors have so long thriv'd in, to take those Measures that both the Ancient and Modern Writers have set me, and by which they have pleas'd the World so well: If I must not, because of my Sex, have this Freedom, but that you will usurp all to your selves; I lay down my Quill, and you shall hear no more of me, no not so much as to make Comparisons, because I will be kinder to my Brothers of the Pen, than they have been to a defenceless Woman; for I am not content to write for a Third day only. I value Fame as much as if I had been born a *Hero;* and if you rob me of that, I can retire from the ungrateful World, and scorn its fickle Favours.

An Epistle to the Reader (from *The Dutch Lover*)

Good, Sweet, Honey, Sugar-Candied Reader,

Which I think is more than anyone has called you yet, I must have a word or two with you before you do advance into the Treatise; but 'tis not to beg your pardon for diverting you from your affairs, by such an idle Pamphlet as this is, for I presume you have not much to do and therefore are to be obliged to me for keeping you from worse employment, and if you have a better you may get you gone about your business: but if you will misspend your Time, pray lay the fault upon yourself; for I have dealt pretty fairly in the matter, told you in the Title Page what you are to expect within. Indeed, had I hung a sign of the Immortality of the Soul, of the Mystery of Godliness, or of Ecclesiastical Policie, and then had treated you with Indiscerpibility and Essential Spissitude (words, which though I am no competent Judge of, for want of Languages, yet I fancy strongly ought to mean just nothing) with a company of Apocryphal midnight Tales cull'd out of the choicest Insignificant Authors; If I had only proved in Folio that Apollonius was a naughty knave, or had presented you with two or three of the worst principles transcrib'd out of the peremptory and ill-natur'd (though prettily ingenious) Doctor of Malmsbury undigested and ill-manag'd by a silly, saucy, ignorant, impertinent, ill educated Chaplain I were then indeed sufficiently in fault; but having inscrib'd Comedy on the beginning of my Book, you may guess pretty near what penny-worths you are like to have, and ware your money and your time accordingly. I would not yet be understood to lessen the dignity of Playes, for surely they deserve a place among the middle if not the better sort of Books; for I have heard the most of that which bears the name of Learning, and which has abused such quantities of Ink and Paper, and continually employs so many ignorant, unhappy souls for ten, twelve, twenty years in the University (who yet poor wretches think they are doing something all the while) as Logick etc. and several other things (that shall be nameless lest I misspell them) are much more absolutely nothing than the errantest Play that e'er was writ. Take notice, Reader, I do not assert this purely upon my own knowledge, but I think I have known it very fully prov'd, both sides being fairly heard, and even some ingenious opposers of it most abominably baffl'd in the Argument: Some of which I have got so perfectly by rote, that if this were a proper place for it, I am apt to think myself could almost make it clear; and as I would not undervalue Poetry, so neither am I altogether of their judgement who believe no wisdom in the world beyond it. I have often heard indeed (and read) how much the World was anciently oblig'd to it for most of that which they call'd Science, which my want of letters makes me less assured of than others happily may be: but I have heard some wise men say that no considerable part of useful knowledge was this way communicated, and on the other way, that it hath serv'd to propogate so many idle superstitions, as all the benefits it hath or can be guilty of, can never make sufficient amends for; which unaided by the unlucky charms of Poetry, could never have possest a thinking Creature such as man. However true this is, I am myself well able to affirm that none of all our English Poets, and least the Dramatique (so I think you call them) can be justly charg'd with too great reformation of men's minds or manners, and for that I may appeal to general experiment, if those who are the most assiduous Disciples of the Stage, do not make the fondest and the lewdest Crew about this Town; for if you should unhappily converse them through the year, you will not find one Dram of sense amongst a Club of them, unless you will allow for such a little Link-Boy's Ribaldry thick larded with unseasonable oaths & impudent defiance of God, and all things serious; and that at such a senseless damn'd unthinking rate, as, if 'twere well distributed, would spoil near half the Apothecaries trade, and save the sober people of the Town the charge of Vomits; And it was smartly said (how prudently I cannot tell) by a late learned Doctor, who, though himself no great asserter of a Deity, (as you'll believe by that which follows) yet was observed to be continually persuading of this sort of men (if I for once may call them so) of the necessity and truth of our Religion; and being ask'd how he came to bestir himself so much this way, made answer that it was because their ignorance and indiscreet debauch made them a scandal to the profession of Atheism. And for their wisdom and design I never knew it reach beyond the invention of some notable expedient, for the speedier ridding them of their Estate, (a devilish clog to Wit and Parts), than other grouling Mortals know, or battering half-a-dozen fair new Windows in a Morning after their debauch, whilst the dull unjantee Rascal they belong to is fast asleep. But I'll proceed no farther in their character, because that miracle of Wit (in spite of Academick frippery) the mighty Echard hath already done it to my satisfaction; and whoever undertakes a Supplement to anything he hath discourst, had better for their reputation be doing nothing.

Besides this Theam is worn too thread-bare by the whiffling would-be Wits of the Town, and of both the stone-blind-eyes of the Kingdom. And therefore to return to that which I before was speaking of, I will have leave to say that in my judgement the increasing number of our latter Plays have not done much more towards the amending of men's Morals, or their Wit, than hath the frequent Preaching, which this last age hath been pester'd with, (indeed without all Controversie they have done less harm) nor can I once imagine what temptation anyone can have to expect it from them; for sure I am no Play was ever writ with that design. If you consider Tragedy, you'll find their best of Characters unlikely patterns for a wise man to pursue: For he that is the Knight of the Play, no sublunary feats must serve his Dulcinea; for if he can't bestrid the Moon, he'll ne'er make good his business to the end, and if he chance to be offended, he must without considering right or wrong confound all things he meets, and put you half-a-score likely tall fellows into each pocket; and truly if he come not something near this Pitch I think the Tragedy's not worth a farthing; for Playes were certainly intended for the exercising of men's passions not their understandings, and he is infinitely far from wise that will bestow one moment's meditation on such things: And as for Comedie, the finest folks you meet with there are still unfitter for your imitation, for though within a leaf or two of the Prologue, you are told that they are people of Wit, good Humour, good Manners, and all that: yet if the Authors did not kindly add their proper names, you'd never know them by their Characters; for whatsoe'er's the matter, it hath happen'd so spightfully in several Playes, which have been prettie well received of late, that even those persons that were meant to be the ingenious Censors of the Play, have either prov'd the most debauch'd, or most unwittie people in the Company: nor is this error very lamentable, since as I take it Comedie was never meant, either for a converting or a conforming Ordinance: In short, I think a Play the best divertisement that wise man have: but I do also think them nothing so who do discourse as formallie about the rules of it, as if 'twere the grand affair of humane life. This being my opinion of Plays, I studied only to make this as entertaining as I could, which whether I have been successful in, my gentle Reader, you may for your shilling judge. To tell you my thoughts of it, were to little purpose, for were they very ill, you may be sure I would not have expos'd it; nor did I so till I had first consulted most of those who have a reputation for judgment of this kind; who were at least so civil (if not kind) to it as did encourage me to venture it upon the Stage, and in the Press: Nor did I take their single word for it, but us'd their reasons as a confirmation of my own.

Indeed that day 'twas Acted first, there comes me into the Pit, a long, lither, phlegmatick, white, ill-favour'd, wretched Fop, an Officer in Masquerade newly transported with a Scarf & Feather out of France, a sorry Animal that has nought else to shield it from the uttermost contempt of all mankind, but that respect which we afford to Rats and Toads, which though we do not well allow to live, yet when considered as a part of God's Creation, we make honourable mention of them. A thing, Reader—but no more of such a Smelt: This thing, I tell ye, opening that which serves it for a mouth, out issued such a noise as this to those that sate about it, that they were to expect a woful Play, God damn him, for it was a woman's. Now how this came about I am not sure, but I suppose he brought it piping hot from some who had with him the reputation of a villanous Wit: for Creatures of his size of sense talk without all imagination, such scraps as they pick up from other folks. I would not for a world be taken arguing with such a propertie as this; but if I thought there were a man of any tolerable parts, who could upon mature deliberation distinguish well his right hand from his left, and justly state the difference between the number of sixteen and two, yet had this prejudice upon him; I would take a little pains to make him know how much he errs. For waving the examination why women having equal education with men, were not as capable of knowledge, of whatsoever sort as well as they: I'll only say as I have touch'd before, that Plays have no great room for that which is men's great advantage over women, that is Learning; We all well know that the immortal Shakespeare's Plays (who was not guilty of much more of this than often falls to women's share) have better pleas'd the World than Johnson's works, though by the way 'tis said that Benjamin was no such Rabbi neither, for I am inform'd that his Learning was but Grammar high; (sufficient indeed to rob poor Salust of his best orations) and it hath been observ'd that they are apt to admire him most confoundedly, who have just such a scantling of it as he had; and I have seen a man the most severe of Johnson's Sect, sit with his Hat remov'd less than a hair's breadth from one sullen posture for almost three hours at *The Alchymist;* who at that excellent Play of *Harry the Fourth* (which yet I hope is far enough from Farce) hath very hardly kept his Doublet whole; but affectation hath always had a greater share both in the action and discourse of men than truth and judgement have; and for our Modern ones, except our most unimitable Laureat, I dare to say I know of none that write at such a formidable rate, but that a woman may well hope to reach their greatest heights. Then for their musty rules of Unity, and God knows what besides, if they meant anything, they are enough intelligible and as practible by a woman; but really methinks they that disturb their heads with any other rule of Playes besides the making them pleasant, and avoiding of scurrility, might much better be employed in studying how to improve men's too imperfect knowledge of that ancient English Game which hight long Laurence: And if comedy should be the picture of ridiculous mankind I wonder anyone should think it such a sturdy task, whilst we are furnish'd with such precious Originals as him I lately told you of; if at least that Character do not dwindle into Farce, and so become too mean an entertainment for those persons who are us'd to think. Reader, I have a complaint or two to make to you and I have done; Know then that this Play was hugely injur'd in the Acting, for 'twas done so imperfectly as never any was before, which did more harm to this then it could have done to any of another sort; the Plot being busie (though I think not intricate) and so requiring a continual attention, which being interrupted by the intolerable negligence of some that acted in it, must needs much spoil the beauty on't. My Dutch Lover spoke but little of what I intended for him, but supplied it with a great deal of idle stuff, which I was wholly unacquainted with until I had heard it first from him; so that Jack-pudding ever us'd to do: which though I knew before, I gave him yet the Part, because I knew him so acceptable to most o'th' lighter Periwigs about the Town, and he indeed did vex me so, I could almost be angry: Yet, but Reader, you remember, I suppose, a fusty piece of Latine that has past from hand to hand this thousand years they say (and how much longer I can't tell) in favour of the dead. I intended him a habit much more notably ridiculous, which if ever it be important was so here, for many of the Scenes in the three last Acts depended upon the mistakes of the Colonel for Haunce, which the ill-favour'd likeness of their Habits is suppos'd to cause. Lastly my Epilogue was promis'd me by a Person who had surely made it good, if any, but he failing of his word, deput'd one, who has made it as you see, and to make out your penyworth you have it here. The Prologue is by misfortune lost. Now, Reader, I have eas'd my mind of all I had to say, and so sans farther complyment, Adieu.

John Locke 1632–1704

John Locke's *Essay Concerning Human Understanding* has long been recognized as one of the great works of seventeenth-century English literature—an epoch-making work in the history of philosophy and a founding text of British empiricism. It exerted a considerable influence on aesthetic theory in the eighteenth century, particularly on those theorists, like Addison and Burke, who sought a psychological explanation for aesthetic pleasure.

Locke was born on August 29, 1632, the son of John Locke, Sr., an attorney and small landowner. He was educated at Westminster School, where he received a thorough grounding in Latin and Greek. In 1652 he attended Christ Church, Oxford, receiving a B.A. in 1656. Afterward he became a senior student, lecturing in Greek and rhetoric, a position he retained until 1684, when he was removed by Charles II after his patron, the earl of Shaftesbury, fell. In 1665 he went abroad as the secretary to Charles's ambassador to the elector of Brandenberg, and on his return he studied medicine. In 1667 he became a personal physician and tutor in the household of his patron, Lord Ashley, earl of Shaftesbury, an enemy to Charles II and James II and the Achitophel of Dryden's satire *Absalom and Achitophel.* Locke became a fellow of the Royal Society in 1668 but, because of his political affiliations with the earl of Shaftesbury, spent most of the 1670s and 1680s in political exile, first in France and then in Holland. After the Whig victory in the Glorious Revolution, he returned to England and prospered. All of his major works, including the *Letter for Toleration, Two Treatises of Civil Government,* and his most famous work, *An Essay Concerning Human Understanding,* were published after 1688. In 1696 he became the commissioner for trade. Soon after, he retired from London to his retreat in Essex, where he died in 1704.

An Essay Concerning Human Understanding is an essay in the sense that Montaigne uses the term—that is, an attempt or "trial," examining the human mind through the discriminating analysis of one mind in particular. "I pretend not to teach," wrote Locke, "but to enquire." The *Essay* promotes "natural knowledge," arguing that nothing, not even language, must be interposed between the mind and nature. In the "Epistle to his Readers," Locke writes, " 'tis Ambition enough to be employed as an Under-Labourer in clearing the Ground a little, and removing some of the Rubbish that lies in the way of knowledge." That "rubbish" to be cleared away, for Locke, is the largely mistaken trust in language and words, as well as the imperfections and abuses of language. Locke felt compelled to devote an entire book (III) to "the nature, use, and signification of language." In it he argues that as all knowledge comes only from sense impressions and from reflections on those impressions, language can only express, or "stand for," ideas in the mind. Although in his account of language, nonfunctional uses of language—poetry and rhetoric, for instance—are equated with the abuses and imperfections of language, Locke's articulation of a philosophy of mind and cognition lays the philosophic foundation for eighteenth-century speculations by writers such as Addison and Burke on such critical and aesthetic concepts as taste, wit, and judgment.

from Book III of *An Essay Concerning Human Understanding*

Chapter I: Of Words or Language in General

§1. God having designed Man for a sociable Creature, made him not only with an inclination, and under a necessity to have fellowship with those of his own kind; but furnished him also with Language, which was to be the great Instrument, and common Tye of Society. *Man* therefore had by Nature his Organs so fashioned, as to be *fit to frame articulate Sounds*, which we call Words. But this was not enough to produce Language; for Parrots, and several other Birds, will be taught to make articulate Sounds distinct enough, which yet, by no means, are capable of Language.

§2. Besides articulate Sounds therefore, it was farther necessary, that he should be *able to use these Sounds, as Signs of internal Conceptions;* and to make them stand as marks for the *Ideas* within his own Mind, whereby they might be made known to others, and the Thoughts of Men's Minds be conveyed from one to another.

§3. But neither was this sufficient to make Words so useful as they ought to be. It is not enough for the perfection of Language, that Sounds can be made signs of *Ideas*, unless those *signs* can be so made use of, as *to comprehend several particular Things:* For the multiplication of Words would have perplexed their Use, had every particular thing need of a distinct name to be signified by. To remedy this inconvenience, Language had yet a farther improvement in the use of general Terms, whereby one word was made to mark a multitude of particular existences: Which advantageous use of Sounds was obtain'd only by the difference of the *Ideas* they were made signs of. Those names becoming general, which are made to stand for general *Ideas*, and those remaining particular, where the *Ideas* they are used for are particular.

§4. Besides these Names which stand for *Ideas*, there be other words which Men make use of, not to signify any *Idea*, but the want or absence of some *Ideas* simple or complex, or all *Ideas* together; such as are *Nihil* in Latin, and in English, *Ignorance* and *Barrenness*. All which negative or privative Words, cannot be said properly to belong to, or signify no *Ideas:* for then they would be perfectly insignificant Sounds; but they relate to positive *Ideas*, and signify their absence.

§5. It may also lead us a little towards the Original of all our Notions and Knowledge, if we remark, how great a dependance our *Words* have on common sensible *Ideas;* and how those, which are made use of to stand for Actions and Notions quite removed from sense, *have their rise from thence, and from obvious sensible* Ideas *are transferred to more abstruse significations*, and made to stand for *Ideas* that come not under the cognizance of our senses; *v.g.* to *Imagine, Apprehend, Comprehend, Adhere, Conceive, In-*

still, Disgust, Disturbance, Tranquillity, etc. are all Words taken from the Operations of sensible Things, and applied to certain Modes of Thinking. *Spirit,* in its primary signification, is Breath; *Angel,* a Messenger: And I doubt not, but if we could trace them to their sources, we should find, in all Languages, the names, which stand for Things that fall not under our Senses, to have had their first rise from sensible *Ideas.* By which we may give some kind of guess, what kind of Notions they were, and whence derived, which filled their Minds, who were the first Beginners of Languages; and now Nature, even in the naming of Things, unawares suggested to Men the Originals and Principles of all their Knowledge: whilst, to give Names, that might make known to others any Operations they felt in themselves, or any other *Ideas,* that came not under their Senses, they were fain to borrow Words from ordinary known *Ideas* of Sensation, by that means to make others the more easily to conceive those Operations they experimented in themselves, which made no outward sensible appearances; and then when they had got known and agreed Names, to signify those internal Operations of their own Minds, they were sufficiently furnished to make known by Words, all their other *Ideas;* since they could consist of nothing, but either of outward sensible Perceptions, or of the inward Operations of their Minds about them; we having, as has been proved, no *Ideas* at all, but what originally come either from sensible Objects without, or what we feel within our selves, from the inward Workings of our own Spirits, which we are conscious to our selves of within.

§6. But to understand better the use and force of Language, as subservient to Instruction and Knowledge, it will be convenient to consider,

First, To what it is that Names, in the use of Language, are immediately applied.

Secondly, Since all (except proper) Names are general, and so stand not particularly for this or that single Thing; but for sorts and ranks of Things, it will be necessary to consider, in the next place, what the Sorts and Kinds, or, if you rather like the Latin Names, *what the Species and Genera of Things* are; wherein they consist; and how they come to be made. These being (as they ought) well looked into, we shall the better come to find the right use of Words; the natural Advantages and Defects of Language; and the remedies that ought to be used, to avoid the inconveniencies of obscurity or uncertainty in the signification of Words, without which, it is impossible to discourse with any clearness, or order, concerning Knowledge: Which being conversant about Propositions, and those most commonly universal ones, has greater connexion with Words, than perhaps is suspected.

These Considerations therefore, shall be the matter of the following Chapters.

Chapter II: Of the Signification of Words

§1. Man, though he have great variety of Thoughts, and such, from which others, as well as himself, might receive Profit and Delight; yet they are all within his own Breast, invisible, and hidden from others, nor can of themselves be made appear. The Comfort, and Advantage of Society, not being to be had without Communication of Thoughts, it was necessary, that Man should find out some external sensible Signs, whereby those invisible *Ideas*, which his thoughts are made up of, might be made known to others. For this purpose, nothing was so fit, either for Plenty or Quickness, as those articulate Sounds, which with so much Ease and Variety, he found himself able to make. Thus we may conceive how *Words*, which were by Nature so well adapted to that purpose, come to be made use of by Men, as *the Signs* of their *Ideas;* not by any natural connexion, that there is between particular articulate Sounds and certain *Ideas*, for then there would be but one Language amongst all Men; but by a voluntary Imposition, whereby such a Word is made arbitrarily the Mark of such an *Idea*. The use then of Words, is to be sensible Marks of *Ideas;* and the *Ideas* they stand for, are their proper and immediate Signification.

§2. The use Men have of these Marks, being either to record their own Thoughts for the Assistance of their own Memory; or as it were, to bring out their *Ideas*, and lay them before the view of others: *Words in their primary or immediate Signification, stand for nothing, but the* Ideas *in the Mind of him that uses them,* how imperfectly soever, or carelesly those *Ideas* are collected from the Things, which they are supposed to represent. When a Man speaks to another, it is, that he may be understood; and the end of Speech is, that those Sounds, as Marks, may make known his *Ideas* to the Hearer. That then which Words are the Marks of, are the *Ideas* of the Speaker: Nor can any one apply them, as Marks, immediately to any thing else, but the *Ideas*, that he himself hath: For this would be to make them Signs of his own Conceptions, and yet apply them to other *Ideas;* which would be to make them Signs, and not Signs of his *Ideas* at the same time; and so in effect, to have no Signification at all. Words being voluntary Signs, they cannot be voluntary Signs imposed by him on Things he knows not. That would be to make them Signs of nothing, Sounds without Signification. A Man cannot make his Words the Signs either of Qualities in Things, or of Conceptions in the Mind of another, whereof he has none in his own. Till he has some *Ideas* of his own, he cannot suppose them to correspond with the Conceptions of another Man; nor can he use any Signs for them: For thus they would be the Signs of he knows not what, which is in Truth to be the Signs of nothing. But when he represents to himself other Men's *Ideas*, by some of his own, if he consent to give them the same Names, that other Men do, 'tis still to his own *Ideas;* to *Ideas* that he has, and not to *Ideas* that he has not.

§3. This is so necessary in the use of Language, that in this respect, the Knowing, and the Ignorant; the Learned, and Unlearned, use the *Words* they speak (with any meaning) all alike. They, *in every Man's Mouth, stand for the* Ideas *he has*, and which he would express by them. A Child having taken notice of nothing in the Metal he hears called Gold, but the bright shining yellow colour, he applies the Word Gold only to his own *Idea* of that Colour, and nothing else; and therefore calls the same Colour in a Peacocks Tail, Gold. Another that hath better observed, adds to shining yellow, great Weight: And then the Sound Gold, when he uses it, stands for a complex *Idea* of a shining Yellow and very weighty Substance. Another adds to those Qualities, Fusibility: and then the Word Gold to him signifies a Body, bright, yellow, fusible, and very heavy. Another adds Malleability. Each of these uses equally the Word Gold, when they have Occasion to express the *Idea*, which they have apply'd it to: But it is evident, that each can apply it only to his own *Idea;* nor can he make it stand, as a Sign of such a complex *Idea*, as he has not.

§4. But though Words, as they are used by Men, can properly and immediately signify nothing but the *Ideas*, that are in the Mind of the Speaker; yet they in their Thoughts give them a secret reference to two other things.

First, they suppose their Words to be Marks of the Ideas *in the Minds also of other Men, with whom they communicate:* For else they should talk in vain, and could not be understood, if the Sounds they applied to one *Idea*, were such, as by the Hearer, were applied to another, which is to speak two Languages. But in this, Men stand not usually to examine, whether the *Idea* they, and those they discourse with have in their Minds, be the same: But think it enough, that they use the Word, as they imagine, in the common Acceptation of that Language; in which case they suppose, that the *Idea*, they make it a Sign of, is precisely the same, to which the Understanding Men of that Country apply that Name.

§5. *Secondly*, Because *Men* would not be thought to talk *barely* of their own Imaginations, but of Things as really they are; therefore they *often suppose their Words to stand also for the reality of Things*. But this relating more particularly to Substances, and their Names as perhaps the former does to simple *Ideas* and Modes, we shall speak of these two different ways of applying Words more at large, when we come to treat of the Names of mixed Modes, and Substances, in particular: Though give me leave here to say, that it is a perverting the use of Words, and brings unavoidable Obscurity and Confusion into their Signification, whenever we make them stand for any thing, but those *Ideas* we have in our own Minds.

§6. Concerning Words also it is farther to be considered. *First*, That they being immediately the Signs of Mens *Ideas;* and, by that means, the Instruments whereby Men communicate their Conceptions, and express to one another those Thoughts and Imaginations, they have within their own Breasts, *there comes by constant use, to be such a Connexion between certain Sounds, and the* Ideas *they stand for*, that the Names heard, almost as readily excite certain *Ideas*, as if the Objects themselves, which are apt to produce them, did actually affect the Senses. Which is manifestly so in all obvious sensible Qualities; and in all Substances, that frequently, and familiarly occur to us.

§7. *Secondly*, That though the proper and immediate Signification of Words, are *Ideas* in the Mind of the Speaker; yet because by familiar use from our Cradles, we come to learn certain articulate Sounds very perfectly, and have them readily on our Tongues, and always at hand in our Memories; but yet are not always careful to examine, or settle their Significations perfectly, it *often* happens that *Men*, even when they would apply themselves to an attentive Consideration, do *set their Thoughts more on Words than Things*. Nay, because Words are many of them learn'd, before the *Ideas* are known for which they stand: Therefore some, not only Children, but Men, speak several Words, no otherwise than parrots do, only because they have learn'd them, and have been accustomed to those Sounds. But so far as Words are of Use and Signification, so far is there a constant connexion between the Sound and the *Idea;* and a Designation, that the one stand for the other: without which Application of them, they are nothing but so much insignificant Noise.

§8. *Words* by long and familiar use, as has been said, come to excite in Men certain *Ideas*, so constantly and readily, that they are apt to suppose a natural connexion between them. But that they *signify* only Men's peculiar *Ideas*, and that *by a perfectly arbi-*

trary Imposition, is evident, in that they often fail to excite in others (even that use the same Language) the same *Ideas*, we take them to be the Signs of: And every Man has so inviolable a Liberty, to make Words stand for what *Ideas* he pleases, that no one hath the Power to make others have the same *Ideas* in their Minds, that he has, when they use the same Words, that he does. And therefore the great *Augustus* himself, in the Possession of that Power which ruled the World, acknowledged, he could not make a new Latin Word: which was as much as to say, that he could not arbitrarily appoint, what *Idea* any Sound should be a Sign of, in the Mouths and common Language of his Subjects. 'Tis true, common use, by a tacit Consent, appropriates certain Sounds to certain *Ideas* in all Languages, which so far limits the signification of that Sound, that unless a Man applies it to the same *Idea*, he does not speak properly: And let me add, that unless a Man's Words excite the same *Ideas* in the Hearer, which he makes them stand for in speaking, he does not speak intelligibly. But whatever be the consequence of any Man's using of Words differently, either from their general Meaning, or the particular Sense of the Person to whom he addresses them, this is certain, their signification, in his use of them, is limited to his *Ideas*, and they can be Signs of nothing else. . . .

Chapter X: Of the Abuse of Words

§1. Besides the Imperfection that is naturally in Language, and the obscurity and confusion that is so hard to be avoided in the Use of Words, there are several *wilful Faults and Neglects*, which Men are guilty of, in this way of Communication, whereby they render these signs less clear and distinct in their signification, than naturally they need to be.

§2. *First*, In this kind, the first and most palpable abuse is, the using of Words, without clear and distinct *Ideas;* or, which is worse, signs without any thing signified. Of these there are two sorts:

I. One may observe, in all Languages, certain Words, that if they be examined, will be found, in their first Original, and their appropriated Use, not to stand for any clear and distinct *Ideas*. These, for the most part, the several *Sects* of Philosophy and Religion have introduced. For their Authors, or Promoters, either affecting something singular, and out of the way of common apprehensions, or to support some strange Opinions, or cover some Weakness of their Hypothesis, seldom fail to *coin* new Words, and such as, when they come to be examined, may justly be called *insignificant Terms*. For having either had no determinate Collection of *Ideas* annexed to them, when they were first invented; or at least such as, if well examined, will be found inconsistent, 'tis no wonder if afterwards, in the vulgar use of the same party, they remain empty Sounds, with little or no signification, amongst those who think it enough to have them often in their Mouths, as the distinguishing Characters of their Church, or School, without much troubling their Heads to examine, what are the precise *Ideas* they stand for. I shall not need here to heap up Instances, every one's reading and conversation will sufficiently furnish him: Or if he wants to be better stored, the great

Mint-Masters of these kind of Terms, I mean the Schoolmen and Metaphysicians, (under which, I think, the disputing natural and moral Philosophers of these latter Ages, may be comprehended,) have wherewithal abundantly to content him.

§3. II. Others there be, who extend this abuse yet farther, who take so little care to lay by Words, which in their primary notation have scarce any clear and distinct *Ideas* which they are annexed to, that by an unpardonable negligence, they familiarly *use Words,* which the Propriety of Language has affixed to very important *Ideas, without any distinct meaning* at all. *Wisdom, Glory, Grace,* etc. are Words frequent enough in every Man's Mouth; but if a great many of those who use them, should be asked, what they mean by them? they would be at a stand, and not know what to answer: A plain proof, that though they have learned those Sounds, and have them ready at their Tongues end, yet there are no determined *Ideas* laid up in their Minds, which are to be expressed to others by them.

§4. *Men,* having been *accustomed* from their Cradles *to learn Words,* which are easily got and retained, *before they knew,* or had framed *the complex Ideas,* to which they were annexed, or which were to be found in the things *they* were thought to *stand* for, they *usually continue to do so* all their Lives, and without taking the pains necessary to settle in their Minds determined *Ideas,* they use their Words for such unsteady and confused Notions as they have, contenting themselves with the same Words other People use; as if their very sound necessarily carried with it constantly the same meaning. This, though men make a shift with, in the ordinary Occurrences of Life, where they find it necessary to be understood, and therefore they make signs till they are so; Yet this insignificancy in their Words, when they come to Reason concerning either their Tenents or Interest, manifestly fills their Discourse with abundance of empty unintelligible noise and jargon, especially in moral Matters, where the Words, for the most part, standing for arbitrary and numerous Collections of *Ideas,* not regularly and permanently united in Nature, their bare Sounds are often only thought on, or at least very obscure and uncertain Notions annexed to them. Men take the Words they find in use amongst their Neighbours; and that they may not seem ignorant what they stand for, use them confidently, without much troubling their heads about a certain fixed meaning; whereby, besides the ease of it, they obtain this advantage, That as in such Discourses they seldom are in the right, so they are as seldom to be convinced, that they are in the wrong; it being all one to go about to draw those Men out of their Mistakes, who have no setled Notions, as to dispossess a Vagrant of his Habitation, who has no setled abode. This I guess to be so; and every one may observe in himself and others, whether it be, or no.

§5. *Secondly,* Another great abuse of Words is, *Inconstancy* in the use of them. It is hard to find a Discourse written of any Subject, especially of Controversie, wherein one shall not observe, if he read with attention, the same Words (and those commonly the most material in the Discourse, and upon which the Argument turns) used sometimes for one Collection of simple *Ideas,* and sometimes for another, which is a perfect abuse of Language, Words being intended for signs of my *Ideas,* to make them known to others, not by any natural signification, but by a voluntary imposition, 'tis plain cheat and abuse, when I make them stand sometimes for one thing, and sometimes for another; the wilful doing whereof, can be imputed to nothing but great Folly, or greater dishonesty. And a Man, in his Accompts with another, may, with as much fairness, make the Characters of Numbers stand sometimes for one, and sometimes for another Collection of Unites: *v.g.* this Character 3, stand sometimes for three, sometimes for four, and sometimes for eight; as in his Discourse, or Reasoning, make the same Words stand for different Collections of simple *Ideas*. If Men should do so in their Reckonings, I wonder who would have to do with them? One who would speak thus, in the Affairs and Business of the World, and call 8 sometimes seven, and sometimes nine, as best served his Advantage, would presently have clapp'd upon him one of the two Names Men constantly are disgusted with. And yet in Arguings, and learned contests, the same sort of proceeding passes commonly for Wit and Learning: but to me it appears a greater dishonesty, than the misplacing of Counters, in the casting up a Debt; and the cheat the greater, by how much Truth is of greater concernment and value, than money.

§6. *Thirdly*, Another abuse of Language is, an *affected Obscurity*, by either applying old Words, to new and unusual Significations; or introducing new and ambiguous Terms, without defining either; or else putting them so together, as may confound their ordinary meaning. Though the Peripatetick Philosophy has been most eminent in this way, yet other Sects have not been wholly clear of it. There is scarce any of them that are not cumbred with some Difficulties, (such is the imperfection of Humane Knowledge,) which they have been fain to cover with Obscurity of Terms, and to confound the Signification of Words, which, like a Mist before Peoples Eyes, might hinder their weak parts from being discovered. That *Body* and *Extension*, in common use, stand for two distinct *Ideas*, is plain to any one that will but reflect a little. For were their Signification precisely the same, it would be as proper, and as intelligible to say, the *Body of an Extension*, as *the Extension of a Body;* and yet there are those who find it necessary to confound their signification. To this abuse, and the mischiefs of confounding the Signification of Words, Logick, and the liberal Sciences, as they have been handled in the Schools, have given Reputation; and the admired Art of Disputing, hath added much to the natural imperfection of Languages, whilst it has been made use of, and fitted, to perplex the signification of Words, more than to discover the Knowledge and Truth of Things: And he that will look into that sort of learned Writings, will find the Words there much more obscure, uncertain, and undetermined in their Meaning, than they are in ordinary Conversation.

§7. This is unavoidably to be so, where Men's Parts and Learning, are estimated by their Skill in *Disputing*. And if Reputation and Reward shall attend these Conquests, which depend mostly on the fineness and niceties of Words, 'tis no Wonder if the Wit of Man so employ'd, should perplex, involve, and subtilize the signification of Sounds, so as never to want something to say, in opposing or defending any Question; the Victory being adjudged not to him who had Truth on his side, but the last word in the Dispute.

§8. This, though a very useless Skill, and that which I think the direct opposite to the ways of Knowledge, hath yet passed hitherto under the laudable and esteemed Names of *Subtlety* and *Acuteness;* and has had the applause of the Schools, and encouragement of one part of the learned Men of the World. And no wonder, since the Philosophers of old, (the disputing and wrangling Philosophers I mean, such as *Lucian* wittily, and with reason taxes,) and the Schoolmen since, aiming at Glory and Esteem, for their great and universal Knowledge, easier a great deal to be pretended to, than really acquired, found this a good Expedient to cover their

Ignorance, with a curious and unexplicable Web of perplexed Words, and procure to themselves the admiration of others, by unintelligible Terms, the apter to produce wonder, because they could not be understood: whilst it appears in all History, that these profound Doctors were no wiser, nor more useful than their Neighbours; and brought but small advantage to humane Life, or the Societies, wherein they lived: Unless the coining of new Words, where they produced no new Things to apply them to, or the perplexing or obscuring the signification of old ones, and so bringing all things into question and dispute, were a thing profitable to the Life of Man, or worthy Commendation and Reward.

§9. For, notwithstanding these learned Disputants, these all-knowing Doctors, it was to the unscholastick Statesman, that the Governments of the World owed their Peace, Defence, and Liberties; and from the illiterate and contemned Mechanick, (a Name of Disgrace) that they received the improvements of useful Arts. Nevertheless, this artificial Ignorance, and *learned Gibberish,* prevailed mightily in these last Ages, by the Interest and Artifice of those, who found no easier way to that pitch of Authority and Dominion they have attained, than by amusing the Men of Business, and Ignorant, with hard Words, or imploying the Ingenious and Idle in intricate Disputes, about unintelligible Terms, and holding them perpetually entangled in that endless Labyrinth. Besides, there is no such way to gain admittance, or give defence to strange and absurd Doctrines, as to guard them round about with Legions of obscure, doubtful, and undefined Words. Which yet make these Retreats, more like the Dens of Robbers, or Holes of Foxes, than the Fortresses of fair Warriours: which if it be hard to get them out of, it is not for the strength that is in them, but the Briars and Thorns, and the Obscurity of the Thickets they are beset with. For Untruth being unacceptable to the Mind of Man, there is no other defence left for Absurdity, but Oscurity.

§10. Thus learned Ignorance, and this Art of keeping, even inquisitive Men, from true Knowledge, hath been propagated in the World, and hath much perplexed, whilst it pretended to inform the Understanding. For we see, that other well-meaning and wise Men, whose Education and Parts had not acquired that *acuteness,* could intelligibly express themselves to one another; and in its plain use, make a benefit of Language. But though unlearned Men well enough understood the Words *White* and *Black, etc.* and had constant Notions of the *Ideas* signified by those Words; yet there were Philosophers found, who had learning and *subtlety* enough to prove, that *Snow* was *black; i.e.* to prove, that *White* was *Black.* Whereby they had the Advantage to destroy the Instruments and Means of Discourse, Conversation, Instruction, and Society; whilst with great Art and *Subtlety* they did no more but perplex and confound the signification of Words, and thereby render Language less useful, than the real Defects of it had made it, a Gift, which the illiterate had not attained to.

§11. These learned Men did equally instruct Men's Understandings, and profit their Lives, as he who should alter the signification of known Characters, and, by a subtle Device of Learning, far surpassing the Capacity of the Illiterate, Dull, and Vulgar, should, in his Writing, shew, that he could put *A.* for *B.* and *D.* for *E, etc.* to the no small admiration and benefit of his Reader. It being as sensless to put *Black,* which is a Word agreed on to stand for one sensible *Idea,* to put it, I say, for another, or the contrary *Idea, i.e.* to call *Snow Black,* as to put this mark *A.* which is a Character agreed on to stand for one modification of Sound, made by a certain motion of the Organs of Speech, for *B.* which is agreed on to stand for another Modification of Sound, made by another certain motion of the Organs of Speech.

§12. Nor hath this mischief stopped in logical Niceties, or curious empty Speculations; it hath invaded the great Concernments of Humane Life and Society; obscured and perplexed the material Truths of Law and Divinity; brought Confusion, Disorder, and Uncertainty into the Affairs of Mankind; and if not destroyed, yet in great measure rendred useless, those two great Rules, Religion and Justice. What have the greatest part of the Comments and Disputes, upon the Laws of GOD and Man served for, but to make the meaning more doubtful, and perplex the sense? What have been the effect of those multiplied curious Distinctions, and acute Niceties, but Obscurity and Uncertainty, leaving the Words more unintelligible, and the Reader more at a loss? How else comes it to pass, that Princes, speaking or writing to their Servants, in their ordinary Commands, are easily understood; speaking to their People, in their Laws, are not so? And, as I remarked before, doth it not often happen, that a Man of an ordinary Capacity, very well understands a Text, or a Law, that he reads, till he consults an Expositor, or goes to Council; who by that time he hath done explaining them, makes the Words signifie either nothing at all, or what he pleases.

§13. Whether any by Interests of these Professions have occasioned this, I will not here examine; but I leave it to be considered, whether it would not be well for Mankind, whose concernment it is to know Things as they are, and to do what they ought; and not to spend their Lives in talking about them, or tossing Words to and fro; Whether it would not be well, I say, that the use of Words were made plain and direct; and that Language, which was given us for the improvement of Knowledge, and bond of Society, should not be employ'd to darken Truth, and unsettle Peoples Rights; to raise Mists, and render unintelligible both Morality and Religion? Or that at least, if this will happen, it should not be thought Learning or Knowledge to do so?

§14. *Fourthly,* Another great *abuse of Words is, the taking them for Things.* This, though it, in some degree, concerns all names in general; yet more particularly affects those of Substances. To this Abuse, those Men are most subject, who confine their Thoughts to any one System, and give themselves up into a firm belief of the Perfection of any received Hypothesis: whereby they come to be persuaded, that the Terms of that Sect, are so suited to the Nature of Things, that they perfectly correspond with their real Existence. Who is there, that has been bred up in the Peripatetick Philosophy, who does not think the Ten Names, under which are ranked the Ten Predicaments, to be exactly conformable to the Nature of Things? Who is there, of that School, that is not persuaded, that *substantial Forms, vegetative Souls, abhorrence of a Vacuum, intentional Species,* etc. are something real? These Words Men have learned from their very entrance upon Knowledge, and have found their Masters and Systems lay great Stress upon them: and therefore they cannot quit the Opinion, that they are conformable to Nature, and are the Representations of something that really exists. The *Platonists* have their *Soul of the World,* and the *Epicureans* their *endeavour towards Motion* in their Atoms, when at rest. There is scarce any Sect in Philosophy has not a distinct set of Terms, that others understand not. But yet this Gibberish, which in the weakness of Humane Understanding, serves so well to palliate Men's Ignorance, and cover their Errours, comes by familiar use amongst those of the same Tribe, to seem the most important part of Language, and of all other the Terms the most significant: And should *Aërial* and *Ætherial Vehicles* come once, by the prevalency of that Doctrine, to be generally received any where, no doubt those Terms would make impressions on Men's Minds, so as to establish them in the persuasion of the reality of such Things, as much as *peripatetick Forms*, and *intentional Species* have heretofore done.

§15. How much *names taken for Things*, are apt to *mislead the Understanding*, the attentive reading of philosophical Writers would abundantly discover; and that, perhaps, in Words little suspected of any such misuse. I shall instance in one only, and that a very familiar one. How many intricate Disputes have there been about *Matter*, as if there were some such thing really in Nature, distinct from *Body;* as 'tis evident, the Word *Matter* stands for an *Idea* dinstinct from the *Idea* of Body? For if the *Ideas* these two Terms stood for, were precisely the same, they might indifferently in all places be put one for another. But we see, that tho' it be proper to say, There is *one Matter of all Bodies*, one cannot say, There is *one Body of all Matters:* We familiarly say, one *Body* is bigger than another, but it sounds harsh (and I think is never used) to say, one *Matter* is bigger than another. Whence comes this then? *Viz.* from hence, that though *Matter* and *Body*, be not really distinct, but where-ever there is the one, there is the other; yet *Matter* and *Body*, stand for two different Conceptions, whereof the one is incomplete, and but a part of the other. For *Body* stands for a solid extended figured Substance, whereof *Matter* is but a partial and more confused Conception, it seeming to me to be used for the Substance and Solidity of Body, without taking in its Extension and Figure: And therefore it is that speaking of *Matter*, we speak of it always as one, because in truth, it expresly contains nothing but the *Idea* of a solid Substance, which is every where the same, every where uniform. This being our *Idea* of *Matter*, we no more conceive, or speak of different *Matters* in the World, than we do of different Solidities; though we both conceive, and speak of different Bodies, because Extension and Figure are capable of variation. But since Solidity cannot exist without Extension, and Figure, the taking *Matter* to be the name of something really existing under that Precision, has no doubt produced those obscure and unintelligible Discourses and Disputes, which have filled the Heads and Books of Philosophers concerning *Materia prima;* which Imperfection or Abuse, how far it may concern a great many other general Terms, I leave to be considered. This, I think, I may at least say, that we should have a great many fewer Disputes in the World, if Words were taken for what they are, the Signs of our *Ideas* only, and not for Things themselves. For when we argue about *Matter*, or any the like Term, we truly argue only about the *Idea* we express by that Sound, whether that precise *Idea* agree to any thing really existing in Nature, or no. And if Men would tell, what Ideas they make their Words stand for, there could not be half that Obscurity or Wrangling, in the search or support of Truth, that there is.

§16. But whatever inconvenience follows from this mistake of Words, this I am sure, that by constant and familiar use, they charm Men into Notions far remote from the Truth of Things. 'Twould be a hard Matter, to persuade any one, that the Words which his Father or Schoolmaster, the Parson of the Parish, or such a Reverend Doctor used, signified nothing that really existed in Nature: Which, perhaps, is *none of the least Causes, that Men are so hardly drawn to quit their Mistakes*, even in Opinions purely Philosophical, and where they have no other Interest but Truth. For the Words, they have a long time been used to, remaining firm in their Minds, 'tis no wonder, that the wrong Notions annexed to them, should not be removed.

§17. *Fifthly,* Another *Abuse of Words, is the setting them in the place of Things, which they do or can by no means signify.* We may observe, that in the general names of Substances, whereof the nominal Essences are only known to us, when we put them into Propositions, and affirm or deny any thing about them, we do most commonly tacitly suppose, or intend, they should stand for the real Essence of a certain sort of Substances. For when a Man says *Gold is Malleable,* he means and would insinuate something more than this, that *what I call Gold is malleable,* (though truly it amounts to no more) but would have this understood, *viz.* that *Gold;* i.e. *what has the real Essence of Gold is malleable,* which amounts to thus much, that *Malleableness depends on, and is inseparable from the real Essence of Gold.* But a Man, not knowing wherein that real Essence consists, the connexion in his Mind of Malleableness, is not truly with an Essence he knows not, but only with the Sound Gold he puts for it. Thus when we say, that *Animal rationale* is, and *Animal implume bipes latis unguibus,* is not a good definition of a Man; 'tis plain, we suppose the Name *Man* in this case to stand for the real Essence of a Species, and would signifie, that a *rational Animal* better described that real Essence, than *a two-leg'd Animal with broad Nails, and without Feathers.* For else, why might not *Plato* as properly make the Word *ἄνθρωπος* or *Man* stand for his complex *Idea,* made up of the *Ideas* of a Body, distinguished from others by a certain shape and other outward appearances, as *Aristotle,* make the complex *Idea,* to which he gave the Name *ἄνθρωπος* or *Man,* of Body, and the Faculty of reasoning join'd together; unless the Name *ἄνθρωπος* or *Man,* were supposed to stand for something else, than what it signifies; and to be put in the place of some other thing, than the *Idea* a Man professes he would express by it?

§18. 'Tis true, the names of Substances would be much more useful, and Propositions made in them much more certain, were the real Essences of Substances the *Ideas* in our Minds, which those words signified. And 'tis for want of those real Essences, that our Words convey so little Knowledge or Certainty in our Discourses about them: And therefore the Mind, to remove that Imperfection as much as it can, makes them, by a secret Supposition, to stand for a Thing, having that real Essence, as if thereby it made some nearer approaches to it. For though the Word *Man* or *Gold,* signify nothing truly but a complex *Idea* of Properties, united together in one sort of Substances: Yet there is scarce any Body in the use of these Words, but often supposes each of those names to stand for a thing having the real Essence, on which those Properties depend. Which is so far from diminishing the Imperfection of our Words, that by a plain Abuse, it adds to it, when we would make them stand for something, which not being in our complex *Idea,* the name we use, can no ways be the sign of.

§19. This shews us the Reason, Why in *mixed Modes* any of the *Ideas* that make the Composition of the complex one, being left out, or changed; it is allowed to be another thing, *i.e.* to be of another Species, as is plain in *Chance-medly, Man-slaughter, Murther, Parricide,* etc. The Reason whereof is, because the complex *Idea* signified by that name, is the real, as well as nominal Essence; and there is no secret reference of that name to any other Essence, but that. But in *Substances* is it not so. For though in that called *Gold,* one puts into his complex *Idea,* what another leaves out; and *Vice Versâ:* yet Men do not usually think, that therefore the Species is changed: Because they secretly in their Minds referr that name, and suppose it annexed to a real immutable Essence of a thing existing, on which those Properties depend. He that adds to his complex *Idea* of *Gold*, that of Fixedness or Solubility in *Aqua Regia*, which he put not in it before, is not thought to have changed the Species; but only to have a more perfect *Idea*, by adding another simple *Idea*, which is always in fact, joined with those other, of which his former complex *Idea* consisted. But this reference of the name to a thing, whereof we have not the *Idea*, is so far from helping at all, that it only serves the more to involve us in Difficulties. For by this tacit reference to the real Essence of that Species of Bodies, the Word *Gold* (which by standing for a more or less perfect Collection of simple *Ideas*, serves to design that sort of Body well enough in civil Discourse) comes to have no signification at all, being put for somewhat, whereof we have no *Idea* at all, and so can signify nothing at all, when the Body it self is away. For however it may be thought all one; yet, if well considered, it will be found a quite different thing, to argue about *Gold* in name, and about a parcel of the Body it self, *v.g.* a piece of *Leaf-Gold* laid before us; though in Discourse we are fain to substitute the name for the thing.

§20. That which, I think, very much disposes Men to substitute their names for the real Essences of *Species*, is the supposition before mentioned, that Nature works regularly in the Production of Things, and sets the Boundaries to each of those *Species*, by giving exactly the same real internal Constitution to each individual, which we rank under one general name. Whereas any one who observes their different Qualities can hardly doubt, that many of the Individuals, called by the same name, are, in their internal Constitution, as different one from another, as several of those which are ranked under different specifick Names. *This supposition*, however *that the same precise internal Constitution goes always with the same specifick name, makes Men forward to take* those *names for the Representatives* of those real *Essences*, though indeed they signify nothing but the complex *Ideas* they have in their Minds when they use them. So that, if I may so say, signifying one thing, and being supposed for, or put in the place of another, they cannot but, in such a kind of use, cause a great deal of Uncertainty in Men's Discourses; especially in those, who have throughly imbibed the Doctrine of *substantial Forms*, Whereby they firmly imagine the several Species of Things to be determined and distinguished.

§21. But however preposterous and absurd it be, to make our names stand for *Ideas* we have not, or (which is all one) Essences that we know not, it being in effect to make our Words the signs of nothing; yet 'tis evident to any one, whoever so little reflects on the use Men make of their Words, that there is nothing more familiar. When a Man asks, whether this or that thing he sees, let it be a Drill, or a monstrous *Fœtus*, be a *Man*, or no; 'tis evident, the Question is not, Whether that particular thing agree to his complex *Idea*, expressed by the name *Man*: But whether it has in it the real Essence of a Species of Things, which he supposes his name *Man* to stand for. In which way of using the names of Substances, there are these false suppositions contained.

First, That there are certain precise Essences, according to which Nature makes all particular Things, and by which they are distinguished into *Species*. That every Thing has a real Constitution, whereby it is what it is, and on which its sensible Qualities depend, is past doubt: But I think it has been proved, that this makes not the distinction of *Species*, as we rank them; nor the boundaries of their names.

Secondly, This tacitly also insinuates, as if we had *Ideas* of these proposed Essences. For to what purpose else is it, to enquire whether this or that thing have the real Essence of the Species *Man*, if we did not suppose that there were such a specifick Essence known? Which yet is utterly false: And therefore such Application of names, as would make them stand for *Ideas* which we have not, must needs cause great Disorder in Discourses and Reasonings about them, and be a great inconvenience in our Communication by Words.

§22. *Sixthly*, There remains yet another more general, though, perhaps, less observed *Abuse of Words;* and that is, that Men having by a long and familiar use annexed to them certain *Ideas*, they are apt *to imagine so near and necessary a connexion between the names and the signification* they use them in, that they forwardly suppose one cannot but understand what their meaning is; and therefore one ought to acquiesce in the Words delivered, as if it were past doubt, that in the use of those common received sounds, the Speaker and Hearer had necessarily the same precise *Ideas*. Whence presuming, that when they have in Discourse used any Term, they have thereby, as it were, set before others the very thing they talk of. And so likewise taking the Words of others, as naturally standing for just what they themselves have been accustomed to apply them to, they never trouble themselves to explain their own, or understand clearly others meaning. From whence commonly proceeds Noise, and Wrangling, without Improvement or Information; whilst Men take Words to be the constant regular marks of agreed Notions, which in truth are no more but the voluntary and unsteady signs of their own *Ideas*. And yet Men think it strange, if in Discourse, or (where it is often absolutely necessary) in Dispute, one sometimes asks the meaning of their Terms: Though the Arguings one may every day observe in Conversation, make it evident, that there are few names of complex *Ideas*, which any two Men use for the same just precise Collection. 'Tis hard to name a Word, which will not be a clear instance of this. *Life* is a Term, none more familiar. Any one almost would take it for an Affront, to be asked what he meant by it. And yet if it comes in Question, whether a Plant, that lies ready formed in the Seed, have Life; whether the Embrio in an Egg before Incubation, or a Man in a Swound without Sense or Motion, be alive, or no, it is easy to perceive, that a clear distinct settled *Idea* does not always accompany the Use of so known a Word, as that of *Life* is. Some gross and confused Conceptions Men indeed ordinarily have, to which they apply the common Words of their Language, and such a loose use of their words serves them well enough in their ordinary Discourses and Affairs. But this is not sufficient for philosophical Enquiries. Knowledge and Reasoning require precise determinate *Ideas*. And though Men will not be so importunately dull, as not to understand what others say, without demanding an explication of their Terms; nor so troublesomely critical, as to correct others in the use of the Words they receive from them: yet where Truth and Knowledge are concerned in the Case, I know not what Fault it can be to desire the explication of Words, whose Sense seems dubious; or why a Man should be ashamed to own his Ignorance, in what Sense another Man uses his Words, since he has no other way of certainly knowing it, but by being informed. This Abuse of taking Words upon Trust, has no where spread so far, nor with so ill Effects, as amongst Men of Letters. The multiplication and obstinacy of Disputes, which has so laid waste the intellectual

World, is owing to nothing more, than to this ill use of Words. For though it be generally believed, that there is great diversity of Opinions in the Volumes and Variety of Controvesies, the World is distracted with; yet the most I can find, that the contending learned Men of different Parties do, in their Arguings one with another, is, that they speak different languages. For I am apt to imagine, that when any of them quitting Terms, think upon Things, and know what they think, they think all the same: Though perhaps, what they would have, be different.

§23. To conlude this Consideration of the Imperfection, and Abuse of Language; the *ends of Language in our Discourse with others*, being chiefly these three: *First, To make known* one Man's Thoughts or *Ideas* to another. *Secondly*, To do it *with* as much ease and *quickness*, as is possible; and!*bm Thirdly*, Thereby *to convey* the *Knowledge* of Things. Language is either abused, or deficient, when it fails in any of these Three.

First, Words fail in the first of these Ends, and lay not open one Man's *Ideas* to anothers view. *First*, When Men have names in their Mouths without any determined *Ideas* in their Minds, whereof they are the signs: or *Secondly*, When they apply the common received names of any Language to *Ideas*, to which the common use of that Language does not apply them: or *Thirdly*, When they apply them very unsteadily, making them stand now for one, and by and by for another *Idea*.

§24. *Secondly*, Men fail of conveying their Thoughts, with all the quickness and ease that may be, when they have complex *Ideas*, without having distinct names for them. This is sometimes the Fault of the Language it self, which has not in it a Sound yet apply'd to such a Signification: and sometimes the Fault of the Man, who has not yet learn'd the name for that *Idea* he would shew another.

§25. *Thirdly*, There is no Knowledge of Things conveyed by Men's Words, when their *Ideas* agree not to the Reality of Things. Though it be a Defect, that has its Original in our *Ideas*, which are not so conformable to the Nature of Things, as Attention, Study, and Application might make them: Yet it fails not to extend it self to our Words too, when we use them as Signs of real Beings, which yet never had any Reality or Existence.

§26. *First*, He that hath Words of any Language, without distinct *Ideas* in his Mind, to which he applies them, does, so far as he uses them in Discourse, only make a noise without any Sense or Signification; and how learned soever he may seem by the use of hard Words, or learned Terms, is not much more advanced thereby in Knowledge, than he would be in Learning, who had nothing in his Study but the bare Titles of Books, without possessing the Contents of them. For all such Words, however put into Discourse, according to the right Construction of Grammatical Rules, or the Harmony of well turned Periods, do yet amount to nothing but bare Sounds, and nothing else.

§27. *Secondly*, he that has complex *Ideas*, without particular names for them, would be in no better a Case than a Bookseller, who had in his Ware-house Volumes, that lay there unbound, and without Titles; which he could therefore make known to others, only by shewing the loose Sheets, and communicate them only by Tale. This Man is hindred in his Discourse, for want of Words to communicate his complex *Ideas*, which he is therefore forced to make known by an enumeration of the simple ones that compose them; and so is fain often to use twenty Words, to express what another Man signifies in one.

§28. *Thirdly*, He that puts not constantly the same Sign for the same *Idea*, but uses the same Words sometimes in one, and sometimes in another Signification, ought to pass in the Schools and Conversation, for as fair a Man, as he does in the Market and Exchange, who sells several Things under the same Name.

§29. *Fourthly*, He that applies the Words of any Language to *Ideas*, different from those, to which the common use of that Country applies them, however, his own Understanding may be fill'd with Truth and Light, will not by such Words be able to convey much of it to others, without defining his Terms. For however, the Sounds are such as are familiarly known, and easily enter the Ears of those who are accustomed to them; yet standing for other *Ideas* than those they usually are annexed to, and are wont to excite in the Mind of the Hearers, they cannot make known the Thoughts of him who thus uses them.

§30. *Fifthly*, he that hath imagined to himself Substances such as never have been, and fill'd his Head with *Ideas* which have not any correspondence with the real Nature of Things, to which yet he gives settled and defined names, may fill his Discourse, and, perhaps, another Man's Head, with the fantastical Imaginations of his own Brain; but will be very far from advancing thereby one jot in real and true Knowledge.

§31. He that hath Names without *Ideas*, wants meaning in his Words, and speaks only empty Sounds. He that hath complex *Ideas* without names for them, wants Liberty and Dispatch in his Expressions, and is necessitated to use Periphrases. He that uses his Words loosly and unsteadily, will either be not minded, or not understood. He that applies his Names to *Ideas*, different from their common use, wants Propriety in his Language, and speaks Gibberish. And he that hath *Ideas* of Substances, disagreeing with the real Existence of Things, so far wants the Materials of true Knowledge in his Understanding, and hath, instead thereof, *Chimæras*.

§32. In our Notions concerning Substances, we are liable to all the former Inconveniences: *v.g.* 1. He that uses the word *Tarantula*, without having any Imagination or *Idea* of what it stands for, pronounces a good Word; but so long means nothing at all by it. 2. He that, in a new-discovered Country, shall see several sorts of Animals and Vegetables, unknown to him before, may have as true *Ideas* of them, as of a Horse, or a Stag; but can speak of them only by a description, till he shall either take the names the Natives call them by, or give them Names himself. 3. He that uses the word *Body* sometimes for pure Extension, and sometimes for Extension and Solidity together, will talk very fallaciously. 4. He that gives the name *Horse*, to that *Idea* which common usage calls *Mule*, talks improperly, and will not be understood. 5. He that thinks the Name *Centaur* stands for some real Being, imposes on himself, and mistakes Words for Things.

§33. In Modes and Relations generally, we are liable only to the four first of these Inconveniencies, (*viz.*) 1. I may have in my Memory the Names of Modes, as *Gratitude*, or *Charity*, and yet not have any precise *Ideas* annexed in my Thoughts to those Names. 2. I may have *Ideas*, and not know the Names that belong to them; *v.g.* I may have the *Idea* of a Man's drinking, till his Colour and Humour be altered, till his Tongue trips, and his Eyes look red, and his Feet fail him; and yet not know, that it is to be called *Drunkenness*. 3. I may have the *Ideas* of Vertues, or Vices, and Names also, but apply them amiss: *v.g.* When I apply the Name *Frugality* to that *Idea* which others call and signify by this sound, *Covetousness*. 4. I may use any of those names with inconstancy. 5. But in Modes and Relations, I cannot have *Ideas* disagreeing to the Existence of Things: for Modes being complex *Ideas*, made by the Mind at pleasure; and Relation being but my way of considering, or comparing two Things together, and so also an *Idea* of my own making, these *Ideas* can scarce be found to disagree with any Thing existing; since they are not in the Mind, as the Copies of Things regularly made by nature, nor as Properties inseparably flowing from the internal Constitution or Essence of any Substance; but, as it were, Patterns lodg'd in my Memory, with names annexed to them, to denominate Actions and Relations by, as they come to exist. But the mistake is commonly in my giving a wrong name to my Conceptions; and so using Words in a different sense from other People, I am not understood, but am thought to have wrong *Ideas* of them, when I give wrong Names to them. Only if I put in my *Ideas* of mixed Modes or Relations, any inconsistent *Ideas* together, I fill my Head also with *Chimæras;* since such *Ideas*, if well examined, cannot so much as exist in the Mind, much less any real Being, be ever denominated from them.

§34. Since Wit and Fancy finds easier entertainment in the World, than dry Truth and real Knowledge, *figurative Speeches*, and allusion in Language, will hardly be admitted, as *an* imperfection or *abuse* of it. I confess, in Discourses, where we seek rather Pleasure and Delight, than Information and Improvement, such Ornaments as are borrowed from them, can scarce pass for Faults. But yet, if we would speak of Things as they are, we must allow, that all the Art of Rhetorick, besides Order and Clearness, all the artificial and figurative application of Words Eloquence hath invented, are for nothing else but to insinuate wrong *Ideas*, move the Passions, and thereby mislead the Judgment; and so indeed are perfect cheat: And therefore however laudable or allowable Oratory may render them in Harangues and popular Addresses, they are certainly, in all Discourses that pretend to inform or instruct, wholly to be avoided; and where Truth and Knowledge are concerned, cannot but be thought a great fault, either of the Language or Person that makes use of them. What, and how various they are, will be superfluous here to take notice; the Books of Rhetorick which abound in the world, will instruct those, who want to be informed: Only I cannot but observe, how little the preservation and improvement of Truth and Knowledge, is the Care and Concern of Mankind; since the Arts of Fallacy are endow'd and preferred. 'Tis evident how much Men love to deceive, and be deceived, since Rhetorick, that powerful instrument of Error and Deceit, has its established Professors, is publickly taught, and has always been had in great Reputation: And, I doubt not, but it will be thought great boldness, if not brutality in me, to have said thus much against it. *Eloquence*, like the fair Sex, has too prevailing Beauties in it, to suffer it self ever to be spoken against. And 'tis in vain to find fault with those Arts of Deceiving, wherein Men find pleasure to be Deceived. . . .

Anne Finch, Countess of Winchilsea 1661–1720

Anne Finch has the dubious distinction of having been satirized for her "scribbling" by such "wits" as Jonathan Swift, Alexander Pope, and John Gay. She also counted such men among her friends. Born in 1661, she was the daughter of a country aristocrat, Sir William Kingsmill of Sidmonton near Southampton. Her father died when she was five months old and her mother when she was three years. In 1683 she became a maid of honor to Mary of Modena, wife of the duke of York (later James II). In 1684 she married Heneage Finch, a gentleman of the bedchamber to the duke of York and second son of the second earl of Winchilsea. Both of the Finches were loyal adherents of James II and lost everything when their patron, James II, was deposed in the Revolution of 1688. In 1690 Finch's nephew had become the earl of Winchilsea and the Finches retired to the family seat of Eastwell in Kent. Anne spent much of her retirement writing. She became something of a literary celebrity, based upon the manuscript circulation of her poetry. Her husband succeeded to the title as fourth earl on the death of his nephew in 1712. Anne Finch died childless in 1720.

Finch began writing poetry about 1685. She wrote in most of the popular forms of her day, including love songs, sacred songs, Pindarics, satires, epistles, fables, and translations. She wrote two plays, *The Triumphs of Love and Marriage* and *Aristomenes,* although neither was intended for the stage. She even wrote one critical essay. Her most considerable work, a poem entitled *The Spleen,* written in 1701, chronicles the depression from which she frequently suffered. In 1713 she published a volume of her collected poetry, anonymously at first and then under her own name.

The "Introduction" and "Preface" to this volume illustrate one possible reaction to the belief that it was both unfeminine and improper for a woman to write poetry. Finch's pose of superfeminine modesty is realized in her abhorence of vulgar public display. Like the courtier of the Elizabethan period, the "proper" woman writer of this period ought not to contaminate herself with the "public view" that would naturally result from publication. Her poems were written to be circulated among friends. Finch's model for the female poet is Katherine Philips (Orinda), a playwright, poet, and contemporary of Aphra Behn's, who first articulated this pose. The woman writer who would remain within the circle of propriety must avoid competition with men. Her muse must fly "with contracted wing," limiting itself to the most inoffensive subject matter. Romantic love is a fit subject for a woman poet, but not sexual love. Above all else, she must not give any cause for scandal. Finch's response to what has been called the woman poet's "anxiety of authorship," the belief that women cannot be poets, is to fashion a lineage for herself, a string of successful female poets that stretches back to the Bible. Finch's critical writing asserts a woman's right to create poetry, at the same time it attempts to neutralize the threat such an assertion might pose to the male monopoly on creativity.

Introduction and Preface to *The Poems*

The Introduction

Did I, my lines intend for publick view,
How many censures, wou'd their faults persue,
Some wou'd, because such words they do affect,
Cry they're insipid, empty, uncorrect.
And many, have attain'd, dull and untaught
The name of Witt, only by finding fault.
True judges, might condemn their want of witt,
And all might say, they're by a Woman writt.
Alas! a woman that attempts the pen,
Such an intruder on the rights of men,
Such a presumptuous Creature, is esteem'd,
The fault, can by no vertue be redeem'd.
They tell us, we mistake our sex and way;
Good breeding, fassion, dancing, dressing, play
Are the accomplishments we shou'd desire;
To write, or read, or think, or to enquire
Wou'd cloud our beauty, and exaust our time,
And interrupt the Conquests of our prime;
Whilst the dull mannage, of a servile house
Is held by some, our outmost art, and use.
  Sure 'twas not ever thus, nor are we told
Fables, of Women that excell'd of old;
To whom, by the diffusive hand of Heaven
Some share of witt, and poetry was given.
On that glad day, on which the Ark return'd,
The holy pledge, for which the land had mourn'd,
The joyfull Tribes, attend itt on the way,
The Levites do the sacred Charge convey,
Whilst various Instruments, before itt play;
Here, holy Virgins in the Concert joyn,
The louder notes, to soften, and refine,
And with alternate verse, compleat the Hymn Devine.
Loe! the yong Poet, after Gods own heart,
By Him inspired, and taught the Muses Art,
Return'd from Conquest, a bright Chorus meets,
That sing his slayn ten thousand in the streets.
In such loud numbers they his acts declare,
Proclaim the wonders, of his early war,
That Saul upon the vast applause does frown,
And feels, itts mighty thunder shake the Crown.
What, can the threat'n'd Judgment now prolong?
Half of the Kingdom is already gone;
The fairest half, whose influence guides the rest,
Have David's Empire, o're their hearts confess't.
  A Woman here, leads fainting Israel on,
She fights, she wins, she tryumphs with a song,
Devout, Majestick, for the subject fitt,
And far above her arms, exalts her witt,
Then, to the peacefull, shady Palm withdraws,
And rules the rescu'd Nation, with her Laws.
How are we fal'n, fal'n by mistaken rules?
And Education's, more then Nature's fools,

Debarr'd from all improve-ments of the mind,
And to be dull, expected and dessigned;
And if some one, wou'd Soar above the rest,
With warmer fancy, and ambition press't,
So strong, th' opposing faction still appears,
The hopes to thrive, can ne're outweigh the fears,
Be caution'd then my Muse, and still retir'd;
Nor be dispis'd, aiming to be admir'd;
Conscious of wants, still with contracted wing,
To some few freinds, and to thy sorrows sing;
For groves of Lawrell, thou wert never meant;
Be dark enough thy shades, and be thou there content.

The Preface

Beaumont in the beginni[n]g of a Coppy of Verses to his freind Fletcher (upon the ill successe of his Faithfull Shepheardesse) tells him,

> I know too well! that no more, then the man
> That travells throo' the burning Deserts, can
> When he is beaten with the raging Sun,
> Half smother'd in the dust, have power to run
> From a cool River, which himself doth find,
> E're he be slack'd; no more can he, whose mind
> Joys in the Muses, hold from that delight,
> When Nature, and his full thoughts, bid him write.

And this indeed, I not only find true by my own experience, but have also too many witt-nesses of itt against me, under my own hand in the following Poems; which tho' never meritting more then to be once read, and then carlessly scatter'd or consum'd; are grown by the partiality of some of my freinds, to the formidable appearance of a Volume; tho' but in Manuscript, and have been solicited to a more daring manefestation, which I shall ever resist, both from the knowledge of their incapassity, of bearing a publick tryal; and also, upon recalling to my memory, some of the first lines I ever writt, which were part of an invocation of Apollo, whose wise and limitted answer to me, I did there suppose to be

> I grant thee no pretence to Bays,
> Nor in bold print do thou appear;
> Nor shalt thou reatch Orinda's prayse,
> Tho' all thy aim, be fixt on her.

And tho' I have still avoided the confident producing anything of mine in thatt manner, yett have I come too neer itt, and been like those imperfect penitents, who are ever re-lenting, and yett ever returning to the same offences. For I have writt, and expos'd my uncorrect Rimes, and immediatly repented; and yett have writt again, and again suffer'd them to be seen; tho' att the expence of more uneasy reflections, till at last (like them) wea-ried with uncertainty, and irresolution, I rather chuse to be harden'd in an errour, then to be still att the trouble of endeavering to over come itt: and now, neither deny myself the pleasure of writing, or any longer make a mistery of that to my freinds and acquain-tance, which does so little deserve itt; tho' itt is still a great satisfaction to me, that I was not so far abandon'd by my prudence, as out of a mistaken vanity, to lett any at-tempts of mine in Poetry, shew themselves whilst I liv'd in such a publick place as the Court, where every one wou'd have made their remarks upon a Versifying maid of Hon-our; and far the greater number with preju-dice, if not contempt. And indeed, the appre-hension of this, had so much wean'd me from the practice and inclination to itt; that had nott an utter change in my Condition, and Circumstances, remov'd me into the solitude, & security of the Country, and the generous kindnesse of one that possest the most de-lightfull seat in itt; envited him, from whom I was inseperable, to partake of the pleasures of itt, I think I might have stopp'd ere it was too late, and suffer'd those few compositions I had then by me, to have sunk into that oblivion, which I ought to wish might be the lott of all that have succeeded them. But when I came to Eastwell, and cou'd fix my eyes only upon objects naturally inspiring soft and Poeticall immaginations, and found the Owner of itt, so indulgent to that Art, so knowing in all the rules of itt, and att his pleasure, so capable of putting them in practice; and also most obligingly favorable to some lines of mine, that had fall'n under his Lordship's perusal, I cou'd no longer keep within the limitts I had prescrib'd myself, nor be wisely reserv'd, in spite of inclination, and such powerfull temptations to the contrary. Again I engage my self in the service of the Muses, as eagerly as if

From their new Worlds, I know not where,
Their golden Indies in the air—

they cou'd have supply'd the material losses, which I had lately sustain'd in this. And now, whenever I contemplate all the several beautys of this Park, allow'd to be (if not of the Universal yett) of our British World infinitely the finest,

A pleasing wonder throo' my fancy moves,
Smooth as her lawnes, and lofty as her Groves.
Boundlesse my Genius seems, when my free sight,
Finds only distant skys to stop her flight.
Like mighty Denhams, then, methinks my hand,
Might bid the Landskip, in strong numbers stand,
Fix all itts charms, with a Poetick skill,
And raise itts Fame, above his Cooper's hill.

This, I confesse, is whatt in itts self itt deserves, but the unhappy difference is, that he by being a real Poet, cou'd make that place (as he sais) a Parnassus to him; whilst I, that behold a real Parnassus here, in that lovely Hill, which in this Park bears that name, find in my self, so little of the Poet, that I am still restrain'd from attempting a description of itt in verse, tho' the agreeablenesse of the subject, has often prompted me most strongly to itt.

But now, having pleaded an irresistable impulse, as my excuse for writing, which was the cheif design of this Preface, I must also expresse my hopes of excaping all suspition of vanity, or affectation of applause from itt; since I have in my introduction, deliver'd my sincere opinion that when a Woman meddles with things of this nature,

so strong, th' opposing faction still appears,
The hopes to thrive, can ne're outweigh the fears.

And, I am besides sensible, that Poetry has been of late so explain'd, the laws of itt being putt into familiar languages, that even those of my sex, (if they will be so presumptuous as to write) are very accountable for their transgressions against them. For what rule of Aristotle, or Horace is there, that has not been given us by Rapin, Despreaux, D'acier, my Lord Roscomon, etc.? What has Mr. Dryden omitted, that may lay open the very misteries of this Art? and can there any where be found a more delightsome, or more usefull piece of Poetry, then that,

correct Essay,
Which so repairs, our old Horatian way.

If then, after the persual of these, we fail, we cannott plead any want, but that of capacity, or care, in both of which I own myself so very defective, y[t] whenever any things of mine, escape a censure, I allways attribute itt, to the good nature or civility of the Reader; and not to any meritt in the Poems, which I am satisfy'd are so very imperfect, and uncorrect, that I shall not attempt their justifycation.

For the subjects, I hope they are att least innofensive; tho' sometimes of Love; for keeping within those limmitts which I have observ'd, I know not why itt shou'd be more faulty, to treat of that passion, then of any other violent excursion, or transport of the mind. Tho' I must confesse, the great reservednesse of Mrs. Philips in this particular, and the prayses I have heard given her upon that account, together with my desire not to give scandal to the most severe, has often discourag'd me from making use of itt, and given me some regrett for what I had writt of that kind, and wholy prevented me from putting the Aminta of Tasso into English verse, from the verbal translation that I procured out of the Italian, after I had finish'd the first act extreamly to my satisfaction; and was convinc'd, that in the original, itt must be as soft and full of beautys, as ever anything of that nature was; but there being nothing mixt with itt, of a serious morality, or usefullnesse, I sacrafis'd the pleasure I took in itt, to the more sollid reasonings of my own mind; and hope by so doing to have made an attonement, to my gravest readers, for the two short pieces of that Pastoral, taken from the French, the songs, and other few lighter things, which yett remain in the following sheetts.

As to Lampoons, and all sorts of abusive verses, I ever so much detested, both the underhand dealing and uncharitablenesse which accompanys them, that I never suffer'd my small talent, to be that way employ'd; tho' the facility of doing itt, is too well known to many, who can but make two words rime; and there wants not some provocation often, either from one's own resentments, or those of others, to put such upon itt, as are any way capable of that mean sort of revenge. The only coppy of mine that tends towards this, is the letter to Ephelia, in answer to an invitation to the Town; but, as that appears to have been long written, by the mention made of my Lord Roscommon, under the name of Piso, given to him first, in a Panegerick, of Mr. Wallers, before his Art of Poetry; so I do declare, that att the time of composing itt, there was no particular person meant by any of the disadvantageous Caracters; and the whole intention of itt, was in general to expose the Censorious humour, foppishnesse and coquetterie that then prevail'd. And I am so far from thinking there is any ill in this, that I wish itt oftener done, by such hands as might sufficiently ridicule, and wean us from those mistakes in our manners, and conversation.

Plays, were translated by our most vertuous Orinda; and mine, tho' originals, I hope are not lesse reserv'd. The Queen of Cyrpus, I once thought to have call'd the Triumphs of Love and Innocence; and doubted not but the latter part of the Title, wou'd have been as aptly apply'd as the former. Aristomenes is wholy Tragicall, and, if itt answer my intention, moral and inciting to Vertue. What they are as to the performance, I leave to the judgment of those who shall read them; and if any one can find more faults then I think to be in y^{m}; I am much mistaken. I will only add, that when they were compos'd, itt was far from my intention ever to own them, the first was for my own private satisfaction, only an Essay wheither I cou'd go throo' with such a peice of Poetry. The other, I was led to, by the strong impressions, which some wonderfull circumstances in the life of Aristomenes, made upon my fancy; and cheifly the sweetnesse of his temper, observable in itt, wrought upon me; for which reason tho' itt may be I did not so Poetically, I chose rather to represent him Good, then Great; and pitch'd upon such parts of the relation, and introduc'd such additional cirumstances of my own, as might most illustrate that, and shew him to be (as declared by the Oracle) the best of Men. I know not what effect they will have upon others, but I must acknowledge, that the giving some interruption to those melancholy thoughts, which posesst me, not only for my own, but much more for the misfortunes of those to whom I owe all immaginable duty, and gratitude, was so great a benefitt; that I have reason to be satisfy'd with the undertaking, be the performance never so inconsiderable. And indeed, an absolute solitude (which often was my lott) under such dejection of mind, cou'd not have been supported, had I indulg'd myself (as was too natural to me) only in the contemplation of present and real afflictions, which I hope will plead my excuse, for turning them for releif, upon such as were immaginary, & relating to Persons no more in being. I had my end in the writing, and if they please not those who will take the pains to peruse them, itt will be a just accusation to my weaknesse, for letting them escape out of their concealment; but if attended with a better successe, the satisfaction any freind of mine, may take in them, will make me think my time past, not so unprofitably bestowed, as otherwise I might; and which I shall now endeavour to redeem, by applying myself to better employments, and when I do write to chuse, my subjects generally out of Devinity, or from moral and serious occasions; which made me place them last, as capable of addition; For when we have run throo' all the amusements of life, itt will be found, that there is but one thing necessary; and they only Wise, who chuse the better part. But since there must be also, some relaxation, some entertaining of the spiritts,

> Whilst Life by Fate is lent to me,
> Whilst here below, I stay,
> Religion, my sole businesse be,
> And Poetry, my play.

The Appology

'Tis true I write and tell me by what Rule
I am alone forbid to play the fool
To follow through the Groves a wand'ring Muse
And fain'd Idea's for my pleasures chuse
Why shou'd it in my Pen be held a fault
Whilst Mira paints her face, to paint a thought
Whilst Lamia to the manly Bumper flys
And borrow'd Spiritts sparkle in her Eyes
Why shou'd itt be in me a thing so vain
to heat with Poetry my colder Brain
But I write ill and there-fore shou'd forbear
Does Flavia cease now at her fortieth year
In ev'ry Place to lett that face be seen
Which all the Town rejected at fifteen
Each Woman has her weaknesse; mind [*sic*] indeed
Is still to write tho' hoplesse to succeed
Nor to the Men is this so easy found
Ev'n in most Works with which the Witts abound
(So weak are all since our first breach with Heav'n)
There's lesse to be Applauded then forgiven.

CHAPTER FOUR
The Eighteenth Century

The modern concept of literary criticism emerged early in the eighteenth century out of the bourgeois public sphere, a group of social institutions—primarily clubs, journals, coffeehouses, and periodicals—in which private individuals (mostly men) came together for the free and equal exchange of rational discourse. These exchanges created the illusion of a consensus, a polite and informed public opinion, that exerted considerable social and political force. The public sphere included a set of discourses about virtually every aspect of social and cultural life: manners and morals, politics and economics, literature and philosophy; these subjects were envisioned not as separate disciplines, but as a unified body of received opinion, "a totalizing project of moral education" (Stallybrass and White, 1985). In the coffeehouses, clubs, and periodicals of the early eighteenth century, men of property came together as equals, as "men of reason." The claims made for the equalizing power of reason served to mediate, at least superficially, the conflicts between a landed and privileged aristocracy and a wealthy, but often politically impotent, middle class. Reason did not distinguish between aristocrat and commoner; power and position could no longer confer cultural authority. Instead the public sphere brought individuals together in a community bound by its belief in the universal and timeless appeals of reason, taste, and morality.

In the eighteenth century, notions like "the reading public," the author, critical judgment, and taste were beginning to emerge as contested issues; and it is perhaps at this point of emergence that the stakes literary criticism has in these terms can best be appreciated. The public sphere contributed to the increasing professionalization of literary criticism, particularly in Britain. Periodicals, such as Steele's *Tatler*, Addison and Steele's *Spectator*, and Johnson's *Rambler*, played an important role in providing, if only for relatively brief runs, vehicles intended to shape and direct public taste. Criticism, which as late as Dryden's *Essay* had been one of the prerogatives of upper-class existence, by the middle of the eighteenth century became a means for middle-class authors and readers to exert their claim to sharing cultural authority with the aristocracy and land-holding gentry. In effect, by the time of Pope's *Essay on Criticism* (1711), critics could make the claim—as Pope does—that their work was as necessary to cultural literacy as the work of poets and dramatists. In different ways, Vico, Pope, Addison, Johnson, Rousseau, Burke, and other eighteenth-century critics assert that criticism serves important sociocultural functions in regulating not simply the "rules" of neoclassical decorum but the flow of information within society.

The importance of the public sphere for the development of modern criticism has not always been apparent in traditional histories of literary criticism because these histories have tended to focus only on the *literary* production of the period's central figures: Pope, Addison, and Johnson. Furthermore, the questions that they ask about these figures' oeuvres are often more appropriate to twentieth-century ideas about literature. Rarely do they consider the ends that literature and literary criticism served in the eighteenth century. But a brief glimpse at the literary production of someone like Eliza Haywood, who, as a woman, was an "outsider" in the eighteenth-century world of educated and propertied men and who remains an outsider in the canon of literary criticism, suggests the need to rethink traditional arguments about the development of modern literary criticism, in particular its elevation of reason as the disinterested standard for criticism.

In 1744, Haywood began *The Female Spectator*, a periodical designed to imitate Addison and Steele's *Spectator*. In 1745 the journal was reissued in four volumes. Its moral agenda is most clearly revealed in the dedication to the first volume, which promises "to rectify some small errors which, small as they may seem at first, may, if indulged, grow into greater." Even a cursory reading of *The Female Spectator* reveals the breadth of writing in the public sphere. Haywood writes on matters as apparently trivial as snuff, coffee, and tea, as apparently feminine as courtship and women's education, and as apparently monumental as aesthetics and philosophy, without distinguishing separate categories among these things. Her literary criticism is not a discourse sealed off from other cultural discourses, but a part of a whole series of codes designed to consolidate the power and influence of the middle class, and to define its unique virtues. For instance, in Book VI, the "theme" of which is good nature and manners, she exposes the viciousness of much contemporary criticism by relating the "story" of a young playwright who anonymously submits his new play *Mariamne* to the judgment of a "certain noble person," an "arbiter of wit." The critic responds "wittily,"

> Poet, whoe'er thou art, G-d d--n thee;
> Go hang thyself and burn thy Mariamne

Of course, the poet heeds his advice (see Kristina Straub's essay in this volume). Haywood's comments on this "piece of ill-nature" suggest that the "disinterestedness" so cherished by "men of reason" was often a mask for their self-interest. Only the interested are disinterested.

The basic argument that one encounters again and again in eighteenth-century criticism is that the expansion of the reading public to include groups that traditionally had been ignored or discounted—notably women and the middle classes—created the need for "arbiters of taste" (to use Addison's term) to instruct these new classes of readers about what constitutes work of literary and cultural value. As Pope suggests in his *Essay on Criticism,* the critic has two important socioliterary functions: to preserve and defend the standard of "nature" as derived from the ancients (particularly Homer), and to maintain the authoritative "judgment" of those men of learning (specifically Pope and his friends) who uphold a neoclassical political ideal of a stable, hierarchically ordered civilization. In this respect, the kind of criticism that Pope envisions does not consist either of laying down rules or of describing passively the virtues of past writers; instead, it is an active force that selectively preserves canonical works and demonstrates the universal application of the "nature" that they represent. It is no coincidence that Pope spent a number of years translating Homer's *Iliad* and *Odyssey* and editing an edition of Shakespeare's plays. Both endeavors made him a good deal of money and both also offered him the opportunity to re-envision major parts of his literary heritage, to make current these works of his past and to offer them as part of a broad vision of what civilization should be.

Like other eighteenth-century critics, then, Pope is concerned not simply with appreciating individual elements of works or attacking what he considers particular defects but with offering a set of universal principles—grounded in his conception of "nature"—that transcend specific historical limitations. In his "Preface to Shakespeare," Johnson holds that all truths are "general," that nothing restricted to specific circumstances of time and place—customs, manners, political intrigues—can last as a work of art. For Johnson, Shakespeare is a great genius precisely to the extent that he escapes particular observations, the "barbarities" of his own culture, and the suffocating influence of the neoclassical unities to write directly to his audiences and readers across the centuries. Shakespeare transcends the sorts of historical limitations that, Johnson maintains, hamper the efforts of other dramatists. Because he is a living part of an ongoing cultural tradition, he transcends the sorts of territorial disputes that Johnson sees as inimical to true, or great, or timeless art.

In cultural terms, then, critics like Addison, Johnson, Pope, and, in a different way, Haywood are concerned with demonstrating to their readers the kinds of values they are expected to hold as consumers of literature. What is tricky about this process of education—and what accounts for much of the productive tension within eighteenth-century criticism—is that these middle-class writers are faced with the prospect of adapting aristocratic literary traditions to their own purposes. In brief, eighteenth-century critics frequently see themselves as the guardians of the *moral* values of their culture. Although the middle class, particularly in England during the eighteenth century, grew increasingly powerful economically, its political influence was often less than we might expect; consequently, its claims to power sharing with the aristocracy rested on a variety of interlocking claims about the benefits of its industriousness; its hard-working devotion to the enrichment of the country as a whole; its prudence, moderation, common sense, temperance, stability, and virtue—in short, about its moral superiority to the profligate aristocracy. This argument, which we see demonstrated, for example, in Daniel Defoe's novel *Robinson Crusoe* (1719), underlies much of the criticism that emerges in the first half of the eighteenth century. These values, however, paradoxically are invoked in support of the kind of conservative vision that marks Pope's *Essay*. The literary tradition symbolized by Homer and Shakespeare is, in effect, translated into the kinds of terms that make it largely consistent with the middle-class "taste" that Addison defends and celebrates.

At the same time, however, eighteenth-century criticism was anything but a bloodless affair. Addison, Pope, Haywood, Johnson, Burke, and others worked within an intensely political climate; their assertions of the universal values of literature are themselves political statements, arguments about the ways in which "nature" should be constituted. In the guise of an omniscient observer, Addison's *Spectator* offers a polemic for Whiggish, middle-class values of common sense and moral rectitude; Haywood's *Female Spectator*, with its fiction of a collective authorship, provides a very different view of the literary culture of the time. A number of the "letters" addressed to *The Female Spectator* deal with the problems of those individuals who feel shut out by the social and literary establishment of the time. Throughout his career, Pope's basic satiric persona is that of the beseiged literary moralist fighting off the onslaught of illiterate or unskilled barbarians, an image carried to brilliant mock-heroic lengths in his satiric masterpiece *The Dunciad*. Almost without exception, eighteenth-century critics see their function as that of an isolated moralist out to refine or reform the tastes of the times. Their very isolation becomes a political statement of the importance they attach to their defense of cultural values. The authoritative tone that we find in Addison, Pope, and Johnson represents an attempt to turn their particular political positions into "timeless" assessments of what literature, "taste," and criticism should be.

Frequently, this drama of the critic's role as defender of the cultural faith is worked out in criticism in efforts to define the relationship of individual genius to its historical context (Johnson on Shakespeare, for example) and the relationship of literature as a cultural product to "timeless" values (Vico). In contrast to the kind of criticism produced during the sixteenth and seventeenth centuries (particularly in Continental Europe), eighteenth-century criticism frequently does away with or shunts aside metaphysical justifications for its assessments of literary value. Even among those critics like Addison, Pope, and Johnson who are devoutly religious, the moral function of literature is defined largely in cultural and political terms. Universal principles are not inbred in humankind but must be reasserted in every generation, as Pope suggests in his spirited defense of the ancients. The classics—particularly Homer—become the touchstone for eighteenth-century criticism, rather than Christian semiotics, because the former offer a vision of an ordered civilization, a regulated society. Indeed, many eighteenth-century critics seems to feel that the world can (or ideally should) be ordered in the same way as a poem. Writing early in the eighteenth century, the third earl of Shaftesbury, an aristocrat, Whig, and contemporary of Addison's, offered the strongest possible justification for this view: "to *philosophize,* in a just Signification, is but To carry *Good-Breeding* a step higher. For the Accomplishment of Breeding is, To learn whatever is *decent* in Company, or *beautiful* in Arts: and the Sum of Philosophy is, To learn what is *just* in Society, and *beautiful* in Nature, and the Order of the World" (*Characteristicks of Men, Manners, Opinions, and Times*). Polished language, "good breeding," "manners," social grace, aesthetic perfection, natural harmony, and universal order form a natural progression in Shaftesbury's mind.

These connections among aesthetic beauty, natural order, and sociopolitical stability are evident in a number of critical works of the period, notably Pope's *Essay,* but also in attempts by Addison, Burke, and, later, Kant to describe the various effects of aesthetic pleasure, the human experience of beauty. In the eighteenth century beauty *meant* balance, symmetry, and order, both natural and sociopolitical. The aesthetic experience depended heavily on the proper exercise of wit, judgment, and taste. Only through an analysis of the universal bases of these faculties could the human capacity to enjoy beauty could be understood. It was important that these faculties be conceptualized as universal, that, in Burke's words, "the standard of reason and taste is the same in all human creatures." The critic's job was to articulate these faculties' "fixed principles" and "invariable and certain laws." It was also important, at least for the British critics, that these faculties be firmly rooted in the human experience of the world. Locke's *Essay Concerning Human Understanding* provides the philosophical underpinnings for this argument. If all human knowledge derives from the senses, as Locke argues, or from interiorizations of sensory experience, then our knowledge of beauty can only be described with reference to what Locke calls "sensible ideas." Both Addison and Burke cite the same passage from Locke's *Essay* to distinguish between wit and judgment and both premise their theories of aesthetic pleasure upon the belief that wit and taste have their origins in sensory experience; in Addison's words, it is impossible for "any thought to be beautiful which is not just, and has not its foundations in the nature of things." This logical empiricism dominates discussions of what Addison calls the "pleasures of the imagination" until Kant, whose aesthetic treatise, *Observations on the Feeling of the Beautiful and Sublime* (1763), shifts the terms of the debate over aesthetic value from the realm of sensory experience to that of "feeling" and, in so doing, anticipates romantic discussions of beauty and the imagination.

The Enlightenment's compelling vision of human perfectability through reason, and its concomitant view of history as linear and progressive, would seem to have been promoted in one way or another by virtually all eighteenth-century theorists and philosophers, even though, as we have tried to suggest, this view of human nature buttressed a conservative social order while, at the same time, suppressing the claims of marginal groups like women and the lower and unpropertied classes. One has to go to Italy, a virtual backwater of culture in the eighteenth century, to find any challenge to the hegemony of Cartesian logic (based on the philosophy of René Descartes) and British empiricism (based on Locke). *The New Science* of the cultural historian Giambattista Vico (who emerged from a lower-class background to gain a professorial chair at the University of Naples) attempts to counter the claims of rationalism by arguing for the priority of the irrational, by valuing poetic and mythological ways of knowing over those of philosophy and the law, as well as positing a circular view of history.

The significance of eighteenth-century criticism, however, transcends whatever limitations it may have as the product of a particular moment in cultural history. First, criticism is effectively institutionalized; no longer the plaything of gentlemen or of broad-based defenses of poetry, it becomes an arena of debate about what values a literate civilization should promote. Second, it becomes, in effect, a genre of literature in itself. Criticism becomes an accepted form in which to write and to put forth a view of human existence. Third, criticism concerns itself with describing relationships between works produced at particular moments in history and the "general" or universal values that appeal to a variety of readers long after the works were written. This concern leads astute critics like Johnson to focus on the political and cultural dimensions of individual authors and works. This politicizing of criticism in the eighteenth century leads, fourth, to questions about the relationship of aesthetic order to social and cultural order: Can (or should) society be regulated the way a poem is structured? Does criticism imply, as Pope and Shaftesbury would have it, an authoritarian connection between art and life? And finally, the criticism of the eighteenth century, like that of the Renaissance and seventeenth century, raises important questions about the construction of "nature." Are there, in effect, multiple natures that are constructed by authors and critics or is nature immutable, the subject of endless speculation only because no writer, as Dryden maintains, can show all of its aspects? These questions, raised so forcefully in eighteenth-century criticism, are still part of the critical enterprise today.

FURTHER READING

Anderson, Howard, and John S. Shea. *Studies in Criticism and Aesthetics, 1660–1800: Essays in Honor of Samuel Holt Monk.* Minneapolis: University of Minnesota Press, 1967.

Boyd, John D. *The Function of Mimesis and Its Decline.* Cambridge, Mass.: Harvard University Press, 1968.

Chapman, G. W., ed. *Literary Criticism in England, 1660–1800.* Englewood Cliffs, N.J.: Prentice-Hall, 1966.

Eagleton, Terry. *The Function of Criticism: From the Spectator to Post-Structuralism.* London: Verso, 1984.

Folkenflik, Robert. *Samuel Johnson, Biographer.* Ithaca, N.Y.: Cornell University Press, 1987.

Ginsberg, Robert, ed. *The Philosopher as Writer: The Eighteenth Century.* London: Associated University Presses, 1987.

Hagstrom, Jean. *Johnson's Literary Criticism.* Chicago: University of Chicago Press, 1967.

Hohendahl, P. U. *The Institution of Criticism.* Ithaca, N.Y.: Cornell University Press, 1982.

Hume, Robert. *Dryden's Criticism.* Ithaca, N.Y.: Cornell University Press, 1970.

Stallybrass, Peter, and Allon White. *The Politics and Poetics of Transgression.* Ithaca, N.Y.: Cornell University Press, 1985.

Todorov, Tzvetan. *Theories of the Symbolic.* Catherine Porter, trans. Ithaca, N.Y.: Cornell University Press, 1982.

Weinsheimer, Joel. *Imitation.* London: Routledge and Kegan Paul, 1983.

Wimsatt, William K., Jr., and Cleanth Brooks. *Literary Criticism: A Short History.* New York: Vintage, 1957.

Alexander Pope 1688–1744

Alexander Pope is perhaps the most influential of the early eighteenth-century poets, a master of the satiric couplet and a witty and often passionate defender of conservative social, political, and aesthetic values. The son of a Roman Catholic merchant, Pope was a child prodigy who attracted the attention of a number of older poets and men of letters, including William Walsh and William Wycherley. His early poems, "Pastorals" (1709), *The Rape of the Lock* (1712, revised 1714), and "Eloisa to Abelard" (1717), established him as a major poet. In 1713 Pope began work on his translations of Homer, published as *The Iliad* (6 vols., 1715–20) and *The Odyssey* (5 vols., 1725–26). These works helped secure Pope's financial independence. He edited Shakespeare's *Works* (1725) and later published the *Moral Essays* (1731–35), *An Essay on Man* (1733–34), and several versions of his satiric masterpiece, *The Dunciad* (1728, 1729, 1742, 1743), an attack on his numerous literary adversaries.

Pope's *Essay on Criticism* (1711) is both a compendium of neoclassical critical views and a defense of the social function of criticism as a bulwark of order, stability, and political quietism. For Pope, criticism regulates the artistic depiction of "nature," "the source, and end, and test of Art." Nature, though, is idealized in the poem with "the ancients," particularly Homer; it comes, in effect, loaded with ideological presuppositions. The images that dominate the poem are ones of restraint, control, and even repression. In Pope's mind, the function of literature is to reassert rather than challenge "universally" acknowledged truths; "true wit," he tells us, "gives us back the image of our mind." The sociopolitical implications of Pope's arguments are evident in his yoking of art, morality, and classical authority: "Learning and Rome alike in empire grew." The "fundamental laws" of wit in the *Essay* place familiar observations about language as the "dress" of thought and "the sound [of poetry] . . . as an Echo to the sense" within a complex defense of cultural and political authority. The significance of the poem lies in its depiction of criticism as a means of preserving traditional cultural values in a time of socioeconomic change. By asserting the importance of criticism, Pope elevates the critic to the status of guardian of civilized values—an argument that, in various forms, persists through the nineteenth and twentieth centuries.

An Essay on Criticism

Part I

'T is hard to say if greater want of skill
Appear in writing or in judging ill;
But of the two less dangerous is th' offence
To tire our patience than mislead our sense:
Some few in that, but numbers err in this;
Ten censure wrong for one who writes amiss;
A fool might once himself alone expose;
Now one in verse makes many more in prose.
'T is with our judgments as our watches, none
Go just alike, yet each believes his own.
In Poets as true Genius is but rare,
True Taste as seldom is the Critic's share;
Both must alike from Heav'n derive their light,
These born to judge, as well as those to write.
Let such teach others who themselves excel,
And censure freely who have written well;
Authors are partial to their wit, 't is true,
But are not Critics to their judgment too?
Yet if we look more closely, we shall find
Most have the seeds of judgment in their mind:
Nature affords at least a glimm'ring light;
The lines, tho' touch'd but faintly, are drawn right:
But as the slightest sketch, if justly traced,
Is by ill col'ring but the more disgraced,
So by false learning is good sense defaced:
Some are bewilder'd in the maze of schools,
And some made coxcombs Nature meant but fools:
In search of wit these lose their common sense,

And then turn Critics in their own defence:
Each burns alike, who can or cannot write,
Or with a rival's or an eunuch's spite.
All fools have still an itching to deride,
And fain would be upon the laughing side.
If Mævius scribble in Apollo's spite,
There are who judge still worse than he can write.
  Some have at first for Wits, then Poets pass'd;
Turn'd Critics next, and prov'd plain Fools at last.
Some neither can for Wits nor Critics pass,
As heavy mules are neither horse nor ass.
Those half-learn'd witlings, numerous in our isle,
As half-form'd insects on the banks of Nile;
Unfinish'd things, one knows not what to call,
Their generation 's so equivocal;
To tell them would a hundred tongues require,
Or one vain Wit's, that might a hundred tire.
  But you who seek to give and merit fame,
And justly bear a Critic's noble name,
Be sure yourself and your own reach to know,
How far your Genius, Taste, and Learning go,
Launch not beyond your depth, but be discreet,
And mark that point where Sense and Dulness meet.
  Nature to all things fix'd the limits fit,
And wisely curb'd proud man's pretending wit.
As on the land while here the ocean gains,
In other parts it leaves wide sandy plains;
Thus in the soul while Memory prevails,
The solid power of Understanding fails;
Where beams of warm Imagination play,
The Memory's soft figures melt away.
One Science only will one genius fit;
So vast is Art, so narrow human wit:
Not only bounded to peculiar arts,
But oft in those confin'd to single parts.
Like Kings we lose the conquests gain'd before,
By vain ambition still to make them more:
Each might his sev'ral province well command,
Would all but stoop to what they understand.
  First follow Nature, and your judgment frame
By her just standard, which is still the same;
Unerring Nature, still divinely bright,
One clear, unchanged, and universal light,
Life, force, and beauty must to all impart,
At once the source, and end, and test of Art.
Art from that fund each just supply provides,
Works without show, and without pomp presides.
In some fair body thus th' informing soul
With spirits feeds, with vigour fills the whole;
Each motion guides, and every nerve sustains,
Itself unseen, but in th' effects remains.
Some, to whom Heav'n in wit has been profuse,
Want as much more to turn it to its use;
For Wit and Judgment often are at strife,
Tho' meant each other's aid, like man and wife.
'T is more to guide than spur the Muse's steed,
Restrain his fury than provoke his speed:
The winged courser, like a gen'rous horse,
Shows most true mettle when you check his course.
  Those rules of old, discover'd, not devised,
Are Nature still, but Nature methodized;
Nature, like Liberty, is but restrain'd
By the same laws which first herself ordain'd.
  Hear how learn'd Greece her useful rules indites
When to repress and when indulge our flights:
High on Parnassus' top her sons she show'd,

And pointed out those arduous paths they trod;
Held from afar, aloft, th' immortal prize,
And urged the rest by equal steps to rise.
Just precepts thus from great examples giv'n,
She drew from them what they derived from Heav'n.
The gen'rous Critic fann'd the poet's fire,
And taught the world with reason to admire.
Then Criticism the Muse's handmaid prov'd,
To dress her charms, and make her more belov'd:
But following Wits from that intention stray'd:
Who could not win the mistress woo'd the maid;
Against the Poets their own arms they turn'd,
Sure to hate most the men from whom they learn'd.
So modern 'pothecaries, taught the art
By doctors' bills to play the doctor's part,
Bold in the practice of mistaken rules,
Prescribe, apply, and call their masters fools.
Some on the leaves of ancient authors prey;
Nor time nor moths e'er spoil'd so much as they;
Some drily plain, without invention's aid,
Write dull receipts how poems may be made;
These leave the sense their learning to display,
And those explain the meaning quite away.
You then whose judgment the right course would steer,
Know well each ancient's proper character;
His fable, subject, scope in every page;
Religion, country, genius of his age:
Without all these at once before your eyes,
Cavil you may, but never criticise.
Be Homer's works your study and delight,
Read them by day, and meditate by night;
Thence form your judgment, thence your maxims bring,
And trace the Muses upward to their spring.
Still with itself compared, his text peruse;
And let your comment be the Mantuan Muse.
When first young Maro in his boundless mind
A work t' outlast immortal Rome design'd,
Perhaps he seem'd above the critic's law,
And but from Nature's fountains scorn'd to draw;
But when t' examine ev'ry part he came,
Nature and Homer were, he found, the same.
Convinced, amazed, he checks the bold design,
And rules as strict his labour'd work confine
As if the Stagyrite o'erlook'd each line.
Learn hence for ancient rules a just esteem;
To copy Nature is to copy them.
Some beauties yet no precepts can declare,
For there 's a happiness as well as care.
Music resembles poetry; in each
Are nameless graces which no methods teach,
And which a master-hand alone can reach.
If, where the rules not far enough extend,
(Since rules were made but to promote their end)
Some lucky license answer to the full
Th' intent proposed, that license is a rule.
Thus Pegasus, a nearer way to take,
May boldly deviate from the common track.
Great Wits sometimes may gloriously offend,
And rise to faults true Critics dare not mend;
From vulgar bounds with brave disorder part,
And snatch a grace beyond the reach of Art,
Which, without passing thro' the judgment, gains
The heart, and all its end at once attains.
In prospects thus some objects please our eyes,
Which out of Nature's common order rise,
The shapeless rock, or hanging precipice.
But tho' the ancients thus their rules invade,
(As Kings dispense with laws themselves have made)

Moderns, beware! or if you must offend
Against the precept, ne'er transgress its end;
Let it be seldom, and compell'd by need;
And have at least their precedent to plead;
The Critic else proceeds without remorse,
Seizes your fame, and puts his laws in force.
  I know there are to whose presumptuous thoughts
Those freer beauties, ev'n in them, seem faults.
Some figures monstrous and misshaped appear,
Consider'd singly, or beheld too near,
Which, but proportion'd to their light or place,
Due distance reconciles to form and grace.
A prudent chief not always must display
His powers in equal ranks and fair array,
But with th' occasion and the place comply,
Conceal his force, nay, seem sometimes to fly.
Those oft are stratagems which errors seem,
Nor is it Homer nods, but we that dream.
  Still green with bays each ancient altar stands
Above the reach of sacrilegious hands,
Secure from flames, from Envy's fiercer rage,
Destructive war, and all-involving Age.
See from each clime the learn'd their incense bring!
Hear in all tongues consenting pæans ring!
In praise so just let ev'ry voice be join'd,
And fill the gen'ral chorus of mankind.
Hail, Bards triumphant! born in happier days,
Immortal heirs of universal praise!
Whose honours with increase of ages grow,
As streams roll down, enlarging as they flow;
Nations unborn your mighty names shall sound,
And worlds applaud that must not yet be found!
O may some spark of your celestial fire
The last, the meanest of your sons inspire,
(That on weak wings, from far, pursues your flights,
Glows while he reads, but trembles as he writes)
To teach vain Wits a science little known,
T' admire superior sense, and doubt their own.

Part II

Of all the causes which conspire to blind
Man's erring judgment, and misguide the mind,
What the weak head with strongest bias rules,
Is Pride, the never failing vice of fools.
Whatever Nature has in worth denied
She gives in large recruits of needful Pride:
For as in bodies, thus in souls, we find
What wants in blood and spirits swell'd with wind:
Pride, where Wit fails, steps in to our defence,
And fills up all the mighty void of Sense:
If once right Reason drives that cloud away,
Truth breaks upon us with resistless day.
Trust not yourself; but your defects to know,
Make use of ev'ry friend—and ev'ry foe.
  A little learning is a dangerous thing;
Drink deep, or taste not the Pierian spring:
There shallow draughts intoxicate the brain,
And drinking largely sobers us again.
Fired at first sight with what the Muse imparts,
In fearless youth we tempt the heights of arts,
While from the bounded level of our mind
Short views we take, nor see the lengths behind:
But more advanc'd, behold with strange surprise
New distant scenes of endless science rise!
So pleas'd at first the tow'ring Alps we try,

Mount o'er the vales, and seem to tread the sky;
Th' eternal snows appear already past,
And the first clouds and mountains seem the last:
But those attain'd, we tremble to survey
The growing labours of the lengthen'd way;
Th' increasing prospect tires our wand'ring eyes,
Hills peep o'er hills, and Alps on Alps arise!

A perfect judge will read each work of wit
With the same spirit that its author writ;
Survey the whole, nor seek slight faults to find
Where Nature moves, and Rapture warms the mind:
Nor lose, for that malignant dull delight,
The gen'rous pleasure to be charm'd with wit.
But in such lays as neither ebb nor flow,
Correctly cold, and regularly low,
That shunning faults one quiet tenor keep,
We cannot blame indeed—but we may sleep.
In Wit, as Nature, what affects our hearts
Is not th' exactness of peculiar parts;
'T is not a lip or eye we beauty call,
But the joint force and full result of all.
Thus when we view some well proportion'd dome,
(The world's just wonder, and ev'n thine, O Rome!)
No single parts unequally surprise,
All comes united to th' admiring eyes;
No monstrous height, or breadth, or length, appear;
The whole at once is bold and regular.

Whoever thinks a faultless piece to see,
Thinks what ne'er was, nor is, nor e'er shall be.
In every work regard the writer's end,
Since none can compass more than they intend;
And if the means be just, the conduct true,
Applause, in spite of trivial faults, is due.
As men of breeding, sometimes men of wit,
T' avoid great errors must the less commit;
Neglect the rules each verbal critic lays,
For not to know some trifles is a praise.
Most critics, fond of some subservient art,
Still make the whole depend upon a part:
They talk of Principles, but Notions prize,
And all to one lov'd folly sacrifice.

Once on a time La Mancha's Knight, they say,
A certain bard encount'ring on the way,
Discours'd in terms as just, with looks as sage,
As e'er could Dennis, of the Grecian Stage:
Concluding all were desperate sots and fools
Who durst depart from Aristotle's rules.
Our author, happy in a judge so nice,
Produced his play, and begg'd the knight's advice;
Made him observe the Subject and the Plot,
The Manners, Passions, Unities; what not?
All which exact to rule were brought about,
Were but a combat in the lists left out.
"What! leave the combat out?" exclaims the knight.
"Yes, or we must renounce the Stagyrite."
"Not so, by Heaven! (he answers in a rage)
Knights, squires, and steeds must enter on the stage."
"So vast a throng the stage can ne'er contain."
"Then build a new, or act it in a plain."

Thus critics of less judgment than caprice,
Curious, not knowing, not exact, but nice,
Form short ideas, and offend in Arts
(As most in Manners), by a love to parts.

Some to Conceit alone their taste confine,
And glitt'ring thoughts struck out at every line;
Pleas'd with a work where nothing's just or fit,
One glaring chaos and wild heap of wit.

Poets, like painters, thus unskill'd to trace
The naked nature and the living grace,
With gold and jewels cover every part,
And hide with ornaments their want of Art.
True Wit is Nature to advantage dress'd,
What oft was thought, but ne'er so well express'd;
Something whose truth convinced at sight we find,
That gives us back the image of our mind.
As shades more sweetly recommend the light,
So modest plainness sets off sprightly wit:
For works may have more wit than does them good,
As bodies perish thro' excess of blood.

Others for language all their care express,
And value books, as women men, for dress:
Their praise is still—the Style is excellent;
The Sense they humbly take upon content.
Words are like leaves; and where they most abound,
Much fruit of sense beneath is rarely found.
False eloquence, like the prismatic glass,
Its gaudy colours spreads on every place;
The face of Nature we no more survey,
All glares alike, without distinction gay;
But true expression, like th' unchanging sun,
Clears and improves whate'er it shines upon;
It gilds all objects, but it alters none.
Expression is the dress of thought, and still
Appears more decent as more suitable.
A vile Conceit in pompous words express'd
Is like a clown in regal purple dress'd:
For diff'rent styles with diff'rent subjects sort,
As sev'ral garbs with country, town, and court.
Some by old words to fame have made pretence,
Ancients in phrase, mere moderns in their sense;
Such labour'd nothings, in so strange a style,
Amaze th' unlearn'd, and make the learned smile;
Unlucky as Fungoso in the play,
These sparks with awkward vanity display
What the fine gentleman wore yesterday;
And but so mimic ancient wits at best,
As apes our grandsires in their doublets drest.
In words as fashions the same rule will hold,
Alike fantastic if too new or old:
Be not the first by whom the new are tried,
Nor yet the last to lay the old aside.

But most by Numbers judge a poet's song,
And smooth or rough with them is right or wrong.
In the bright Muse tho' thousand charms conspire,
Her voice is all these tuneful fools admire;
Who haunt Parnassus but to please their ear,
Not mend their minds; as some to church repair,
Not for the doctrine, but the music there.
These equal syllables alone require,
Tho' oft the ear the open vowels tire,
While expletives their feeble aid do join,
And ten low words oft creep in one dull line:
While they ring round the same unvaried chimes,
With sure returns of still expected rhymes,
Where'er you find "the cooling western breeze,"
In the next line, it "whispers thro' the trees;"
If crystal streams "with pleasing murmurs creep,"
The reader's threaten'd (not in vain) with "sleep;"
Then, at the last and only couplet, fraught
With some unmeaning thing they call a thought,
A needless Alexandrine ends the song,
That, like a wounded snake, drags its slow length along.
Leave such to tune their own dull rhymes, and know

What's roundly smooth, or languishingly slow;
And praise the easy vigour of a line
Where Denham's strength and Waller's sweetness join.
True ease in writing comes from Art, not Chance,
As those move easiest who have learn'd to dance.
'T is not enough no harshness gives offence;
The sound must seem an echo to the sense.
Soft is the strain when zephyr gently blows,
And the smooth stream in smoother numbers flows;
But when loud surges lash the sounding shore,
The hoarse rough verse should like the torrent roar.
When Ajax strives some rock's vast weight to throw,
The line, too, labours, and the words move slow:
Not so when swift Camilla scours the plain,
Flies o'er th' unbending corn, and skims along the main.
Hear how Timotheus' varied lays surprise,
And bid alternate passions fall and rise!
While at each change the son of Libyan Jove
Now burns with glory, and then melts with love;
Now his fierce eyes with sparkling fury glow,
Now sighs steal out, and tears begin to flow:
Persians and Greeks like turns of nature found,
And the world's Victor stood subdued by sound!
The power of music all our hearts allow,
And what Timotheus was is Dryden now.
  Avoid extremes, and shun the fault of such
Who still are pleas'd too little or too much
At ev'ry trifle scorn to take offence;
That always shows great pride or little sense:
Those heads, as stomachs, are not sure the best
Which nauseate all, and nothing can digest.
Yet let not each gay turn thy rapture move;
For fools admire, but men of sense approve:
As things seem large which we thro' mist descry,
Dulness is ever apt to magnify.
  Some foreign writers, some our own despise;
The ancients only, or the moderns prize.
Thus Wit, like Faith, by each man is applied
To one small sect, and all are damn'd beside.
Meanly they seek the blessing to confine,
And force that sun but on a part to shine,
Which not alone the southern wit sublimes,
But ripens spirits in cold northern climes;
Which from the first has shone on ages past,
Enlights the present, and shall warm the last;
Tho' each may feel increases and decays,
And see now clearer and now darker days.
Regard not then if wit be old or new,
But blame the False and value still the True.
  Some ne'er advance a judgment of their own,
But catch the spreading notion of the town;
They reason and conclude by precedent,
And own stale nonsense which they ne'er invent.
Some judge of authors' names, not works, and then
Nor praise nor blame the writings, but the men.
Of all this servile herd, the worst is he
That in proud dulness joins with quality;
A constant critic at the great man's board,
To fetch and carry nonsense for my lord.
What woful stuff this madrigal would be
In some starv'd hackney sonneteer or me!
But let a lord once own the happy lines,
How the Wit brightens! how the Style refines!
Before his sacred name flies every fault,

And each exalted stanza teems with thought!
The vulgar thus thro' imitation err,
As oft the learn'd by being singular;
So much they scorn the crowd, that if the throng
By chance go right, they purposely go wrong.
So schismatics the plain believers quit,
And are but damn'd for having too much wit.
Some praise at morning what they blame at night,
But always think the last opinion right.
A Muse by these is like a mistress used,
This hour she 's idolized, the next abused;
While their weak heads, like towns unfortified,
'Twixt sense and nonsense daily change their side.
Ask them the cause; they 're wiser still they say;
And still to-morrow 's wiser than to-day.
We think our fathers fools, so wise we grow;
Our wiser sons no doubt will think us so.
Once school-divines this zealous isle o'erspread;
Who knew most sentences was deepest read.
Faith, Gospel, all seem'd made to be disputed,
And none had sense enough to be confuted.
Scotists and Thomists now in peace remain
Amidst their kindred cobwebs in Ducklane.
If Faith itself has diff'rent dresses worn,
What wonder modes in Wit should take their turn?
Oft, leaving what is natural and fit,
The current Folly proves the ready Wit;
And authors think their reputation safe,
Which lives as long as fools are pleas'd to laugh.
Some, valuing those of their own side or mind,
Still make themselves the measure of mankind:
Fondly we think we honour merit then,
When we but praise ourselves in other men.
Parties in wit attend on those of state,
And public faction doubles private hate.
Pride, Malice, Folly, against Dryden rose,
In various shapes of parsons, critics, beaux:
But sense survived when merry jests were past;
For rising merit will buoy up at last.
Might he return and bless once more our eyes,
New Blackmores and new Milbournes must arise.
Nay, should great Homer lift his awful head,
Zoilus again would start up from the dead.
Envy will Merit as its shade pursue,
But like a shadow proves the substance true;
For envied Wit, like Sol eclips'd, makes known
Th' opposing body's grossness, not its own.
When first that sun too powerful beams displays,
It draws up vapours which obscure its rays;
But ev'n those clouds at last adorn its way,
Reflect new glories, and augment the day.
Be thou the first true merit to befriend;
His praise is lost who stays till all commend.
Short is the date, alas! of modern rhymes,
And 't is but just to let them live betimes.
No longer now that Golden Age appears,
When patriarch wits survived a thousand years:
Now length of fame (our second life) is lost,
And bare threescore is all ev'n that can boast:
Our sons their fathers' failing language see,
And such as Chaucer is shall Dryden be.
So when the faithful pencil has design'd
Some bright idea of the master's mind,
Where a new world leaps out at his command,
And ready Nature waits upon his hand;
When the ripe colours soften and unite,
And sweetly melt into just shade and light;

When mellowing years their full perfection give,
And each bold figure just begins to live,
The treach'rous colours the fair art betray,
And all the bright creation fades away!
  Unhappy Wit, like most mistaken things,
Atones not for that envy which it brings:
In youth alone its empty praise we boast,
But soon the short-lived vanity is lost;
Like some fair flower the early Spring supplies,
That gaily blooms, but ev'n in blooming dies.
What is this Wit, which must our cares employ?
The owner's wife that other men enjoy;
Then most our trouble still when most admired,
And still the more we give, the more required;
Whose fame with pains we guard, but lose with ease,
Sure some to vex, but never all to please,
'T is what the vicious fear, the virtuous shun;
By fools 't is hated, and by knaves undone!
  If Wit so much from Ignorance undergo,
Ah, let not Learning too commence its foe!
Of old those met rewards who could excel,
And such were prais'd who but endeavour'd well;
Tho' triumphs were to gen'rals only due,
Crowns were reserv'd to grace the soldiers too.
Now they who reach Parnassus' lofty crown
Employ their pains to spurn some others down;
And while self-love each jealous writer rules,
Contending wits become the sport of fools;
But still the worst with most regret commend,
For each ill author is as bad a friend.
To what base ends, and by what abject ways,
Are mortals urged thro' sacred lust of praise!
Ah, ne'er so dire a thirst of glory boast,
Nor in the critic let the man be lost!
Good nature and good sense must ever join;
To err is human, to forgive divine.
  But if in noble minds some dregs remain,
Not yet purged off, of spleen and sour disdain,
Discharge that rage on more provoking crimes,
Nor fear a dearth in these flagitious times.
No pardon vile obscenity should find,
Tho' Wit and Art conspire to move your mind;
But dulness with obscenity must prove
As shameful sure as impotence in love.
In the fat age of pleasure, wealth, and ease
Sprung the rank weed, and thrived with large increase:
When love was all an easy monarch's care,
Seldom at council, never in a war;
Jilts ruled the state, and statesmen farces writ;
Nay wits had pensions, and young lords had wit;
The Fair sat panting at a courtier's play,
And not a mask went unimprov'd away;
The modest fan was lifted up no more,
And virgins smil'd at what they blush'd before.
The following license of a foreign reign
Did all the dregs of bold Socinus drain;
Then unbelieving priests reform'd the nation,
And taught more pleasant methods of salvation;
Where Heav'n's free subjects might their rights dispute,
Lest God himself should seem too absolute;
Pulpits their sacred satire learn'd to spare,
And vice admired to find a flatt'rer there!
Encouraged thus, Wit's Titans braved the skies,
And the press groan'd with licens'd blasphemies.
These monsters, Critics! with your darts engage,

Here point your thunder, and exhaust your rage!
Yet shun their fault, who, scandalously nice,
Will needs mistake an author into vice:
All seems infected that th' infected spy,
As all looks yellow to the jaundic'd eye.

Part III

Learn then what morals Critics ought to show,
For 't is but half a judge's task to know.
'T is not enough Taste, Judgment, Learning join;
In all you speak let Truth and Candour shine;
That not alone what to your Sense is due
All may allow, but seek your friendship too.
  Be silent always when you doubt your Sense,
And speak, tho' sure, with seeming diffidence.
Some positive persisting fops we know,
Who if once wrong will needs be always so;
But you with pleasure own your errors past,
And make each day a critique on the last.
  'T is not enough your counsel still be true;
Blunt truths more mischief than nice falsehoods do.
Men must be taught as if you taught them not,
And things unknown proposed as things forgot.
Without good breeding truth is disapprov'd;
That only makes superior Sense belov'd.
  Be niggards of advice on no pretence,
For the worst avarice is that of Sense.
With mean complacence ne'er betray your trust,
Nor be so civil as to prove unjust.
Fear not the anger of the wise to raise;
Those best can bear reproof who merit praise.
  'T were well might critics still this freedom take,
But Appius reddens at each word you speak,
And stares tremendous, with a threat'ning eye,
Like some fierce tyrant in old tapestry.
Fear most to tax an honourable fool,
Whose right it is, uncensured to be dull:
Such without Wit, are poets when they please,
As without Learning they can take degrees.
Leave dangerous truths to unsuccessful satires,
And flattery to fulsome dedicators;
Whom, when they praise, the world believes no more
Than when they promise to give scribbling o'er.
'T is best sometimes your censure to restrain,
And charitably let the dull be vain;
Your silence there is better than your spite,
For who can rail so long as they can write?
Still humming on their drowsy course they keep,
And lash'd so long, like tops, are lash'd asleep.
False steps but help them to renew the race,
As, after stumbling, jades will mend their pace.
What crowds of these, impenitently bold,
In sounds and jingling syllables grown old,
Still run on poets, in a raging vein,
Ev'n to the dregs and squeezings of the brain,
Strain out the last dull droppings of their sense,
And rhyme with all the rage of impotence!
  Such shameless bards we have; and yet 't is true
There are as mad abandon'd critics too.
The bookful blockhead ignorantly read,
With loads of learned lumber in his head,
With his own tongue still edifies his ears,
And always list'ning to himself appears.

All books he reads, and all he reads assails,
From Dryden's Fables down to Durfey's Tales.
With him most authors steal their works, or buy;
Garth did not write his own Dispensary.
Name a new play, and he's the poet's friend;
Nay, show'd his faults—but when would poets mend?
No place so sacred from such fops is barr'd,
Nor is Paul's church more safe than Paul's churchyard:
Nay, fly to altars; there they'll talk you dead;
For fools rush in where angels fear to tread.
Distrustful sense with modest caution speaks,
It still looks home, and short excursions makes;
But rattling nonsense in full volleys breaks
And never shock'd, and never turn'd aside,
Bursts out, resistless, with a thund'ring tide.

But where's the man who counsel can bestow,
Still pleas'd to teach, and yet not proud to know?
Unbiass'd or by favour or by spite;
Not dully prepossess'd nor blindly right;
Tho' learn'd, well bred, and tho' well bred sincere;
Modestly bold, and humanly severe;
Who to a friend his faults can freely show,
And gladly praise the merit of a foe;
Bless'd with a taste exact, yet unconfin'd,
A knowledge both of books and humankind;
Gen'rous converse; a soul exempt from pride;
And love to praise, with reason on his side?
Such once were critics; such the happy few
Athens and Rome in better ages knew.
The mighty Stagyrite first left the shore,
Spread all his sails, and durst the deeps explore;
He steer'd securely, and discover'd far,
Led by the light of the Mæonian star.
Poets, a race long unconfin'd and free,
Still fond and proud of savage liberty,
Receiv'd his laws, and stood convinc'd 't was fit
Who conquer'd Nature should preside o'er Wit.

Horace still charms with graceful negligence,
And without method talks us into sense;
Will, like a friend, familiarly convey
The truest notions in the easiest way.
He who, supreme in judgment as in wit,
Might boldly censure as he boldly writ,
Yet judg'd with coolness, though he sung with fire;
His precepts teach but what his works inspire.
Our critics take a contrary extreme,
They judge with fury, but they write with phlegm;
Nor suffers Horace more in wrong translations
By Wits, than Critics in as wrong quotations.
See Dionysius Homer's thoughts refine,
And call new beauties forth from ev'ry line!
Fancy and art in gay Petronius please,
The Scholar's learning with the courtier's ease.

In grave Quintilian's copious work we find
The justest rules and clearest method join'd.
Thus useful arms in magazines we place,
All ranged in order, and disposed with grace;
But less to please the eye than arm the hand,
Still fit for use, and ready at command.

Thee, bold Longinus! all the Nine inspire,
And bless their critic with a poet's fire:
An ardent judge, who, zealous in his trust,
With warmth gives sentence, yet is always just;
Whose own example strengthens all his laws,

And is himself that great sublime he draws.
Thus long succeeding critics justly reign'd,
License repress'd, and useful laws ordain'd:
Learning and Rome alike in empire grew,
And arts still follow'd where her eagles flew;
From the same foes at last both felt their doom,
And the same age saw learning fall and Rome.
With tyranny then superstition join'd,
As that the body, this enslaved the mind;
Much was believ'd, but little understood,
And to be dull was construed to be good;
A second deluge learning thus o'errun,
And the monks finish'd what the Goths begun.
At length Erasmus, that great injur'd name,
(The glory of the priesthood and the shame!)
Stemm'd the wild torrent of a barb'rous age,
And drove those holy Vandals off the stage.
But see! each Muse in Leo's golden days
Starts from her trance, and trims her wither'd bays.
Rome's ancient genius, o'er its ruins spread,
Shakes off the dust, and rears his rev'rend head.
Then sculpture and her sister arts revive;
Stones leap'd to form, and rocks began to live;
With sweeter notes each rising temple rung;
A Raphael painted and a Vida sung:
Immortal Vida! on whose honour'd brow
The poet's bays and critic's ivy grow:
Cremona now shall ever boast thy name,
As next in place to Mantua, next in fame!
But soon by impious arms from Latium chased,
Their ancient bounds the banish'd Muses pass'd;
Thence arts o'er all the northern world advance,
But critic learning flourish'd most in France;
The rules a nation born to serve obeys,
And Boileau still in right of Horace sways.
But we, brave Britons, foreign laws despised,
And kept unconquer'd and uncivilized;
Fierce for the liberties of wit, and bold,
We still defied the Romans, as of old.
Yet some there were, among the sounder few
Of those who less presumed and better knew,
Who durst assert the juster ancient cause,
And here restor'd Wit's fundamental laws.
Such was the Muse whose rules and practice tell
"Nature's chief masterpiece is writing well."
Such was Roscommon, not more learn'd than good,
With manners gen'rous as his noble blood;
To him the wit of Greece and Rome was known,
And every author's merit but his own.
Such late was Walsh—the Muse's judge and friend,
Who justly knew to blame or to commend;
To failings mild but zealous for desert,
The clearest head, and the sincerest heart.
This humble praise, lamented Shade! receive;
This praise at least a grateful Muse may give:
The Muse whose early voice you taught to sing,
Prescribed her heights, and pruned her tender wing,
(Her guide now lost), no more attempts to rise,
But in low numbers short excursions tries;
Content if hence th' unlearn'd their wants may view,
The learn'd reflect on what before they knew;
Careless of censure, nor too fond of fame;
Still pleas'd to praise, yet not afraid to blame;
Averse alike to flatter or offend;
Not free from faults, nor yet too vain to mend.

Joseph Addison 1672–1719

Joseph Addison is best known as a critic and essayist whose wide-ranging contributions to *The Spectator* include essays on conduct, morals, political doctrine, philosophy, science, and literature. The diversity of his reading—which included Descartes, Locke, and Newton, as well as the fashionable French criticism—made him a powerful synthesizer and disseminator of Augustan culture. The son of the dean of Lichfield, Addison was born in 1672 and educated at Charterhouse and Magdalene College, Oxford, where he was a fellow. He lived primarily in France until 1703. Upon his return, he became connected with the Whig party, was appointed undersecretary of state in 1706, and was a member of Parliament from 1708 until his death in 1719.

Addison is the first English critic who was never really a poet. Although he wrote some verses, it was the kind of poetry that educated men were supposed to be able to write. His most renowned work, the blank-verse tragedy *Cato*, owes its popularity in the eighteenth century more to politics than to its merits as drama. Addison earned his literary reputation primarily as a critic and essayist in the newly emerging genre of the periodical. He became a regular contributor to Richard Steele's *Tatler*. In 1711, he and Steele jointly began publishing *The Spectator*, a daily periodical to which Addison contributed over 300 numbers.

Addison's essays on literary and aesthetic topics illustrate the critical tastes of informed English society at the beginning of the eighteenth century. In "True and False Wit," Addison engages a subject that had been of great interest to critics since Dryden—the nature of wit. Like his predecessors, Addison sees wit as a synthesis of ideas (not words), as a uniting of opposites, a *discordia concors*, "to delight and surprise the reader" and opposes it to judgment, which he sees as analysis. The basis of all wit, for Addison, is truth. His definition of wit is rooted in the contemplation of ideas, which reveal truth, as opposed to words, which can be false. "Pleasures of the Imagination" is an early attempt at a psychological theory of aesthetic pleasure that anticipates critical discussions of the sublime and beautiful that occupy late eighteenth-century and romantic criticism. Addison limits his subject to the pleasures of the imagination that derive from sight and that arise from "greatness" or sublimity, from "the new or uncommon," or from beauty. He distinguishes primary pleasures of the imagination—those in which the viewer sees and comprehends objects directly—and secondary pleasures, in which an absent object is recalled through the agency of art. The secondary pleasures of the imagination, though secondary and merely representations, are often more pleasing than direct viewing. The poet, in particular, is conceived of as "mending and perfecting Nature," of making the ugly agreeable, as Milton does in *Paradise Lost* by rendering the tortures of Hell pleasing to the imagination.

Addison's analysis of the psychological aspects of literary judgment, although somewhat primitive, seems in conception surprisingly modern, particularly in its attempt to probe the bases of artistic representation.

from The Spectator

No. 62 Friday, May 11

TRUE AND FALSE WIT

Scribendi recte sapere est et principium et fons.
HORACE

Sound judgment is the ground of writing well.
ROSCOMMON

Mr. Locke has an admirable reflection upon the difference of wit and judgment, whereby he endeavours to shew the reason why they are not always the talents of the same person. His words are as follows: "And hence, perhaps, may be given some reason of that common observation, that men who have a great deal of wit, and prompt memories, have not always the clearest judgment, or deepest reason. For wit lying most in the assemblage of ideas, and putting those together with quickness and variety, wherein can be found any resemblance and congruity, thereby to make up pleasant pictures and agreeable visions in the fancy; judgment on the contrary, lies quite on the other side, in separating carefully one from another, ideas wherein can be found the least difference, thereby to avoid being mis-led by similitude, and by affinity, to take one thing for another. This is a way of proceeding quite contrary to metaphor and allusion; wherein, for the most part, lies that entertainment and pleasantry of wit which strikes so lively on the fancy, and is therefore so acceptable to all people." (*Essay*, Bk 2, ch 11)

This is, I think, the best and most philosophical account that I have ever met with of wit, which generally, though not always consists in such a resemblance and congruity of ideas as this author mentions. I shall only add to it, by way of explanation that every resemblance of ideas is not that which we call wit, unless it be such an one that gives delight and surprise to the reader; these two properties seem essential to wit, more particularly the last of them. In order, therefore, that the resemblance in the ideas be wit, it is necessary that the ideas should not lie too near one another in the nature of things; for where the likeness is obvious, it gives no surprise. To compare one man's singing to that of another, or to represent the whiteness of any object by that of milk and snow, or its variety of its colours by those of the rainbow, cannot be called wit, unless, besides this obvious resemblance, there be some further congruity discovered in the two ideas, that is capable of giving the reader some surprise. Thus, when a poet tells us, the bosom of his mistress is as white as snow, there is no wit in the comparison; but when he adds, with a sigh, that it is as cold too, it then grows into wit. Every reader's memory may supply him with innumerable instances of the same nature. For this reason, the similitudes in heroic poets, who endeavour rather to fill the mind with great conceptions, than to divert it with such as are new and surprising, have seldom any thing in them that can be called wit. Mr. Locke's account of wit, with this short explanation, comprehends most of the species of wit; as metaphors, similitudes, allegories, ænigmas, mottos, parables, fables, dreams, visions, dramatic writings, burlesque, and all the methods of allusion: as there are many other pieces of wit (how remote soever they may appear at first sight from the foregoing description) which upon examination will be found to agree with it.

As true wit generally consists in this resemblance and congruity of ideas, false wit chiefly consists in the resemblance and congruity sometimes of single letters, as in anagrams, chronograms, lipograms, and acrostics: sometimes of syllables, as in echoes and doggerel rhymes: sometimes of words, as in puns and quibbles; and sometimes of whole sentences or poems, cast into the figures of eggs, axes, or altars: nay, some carry the notion of wit so far, as to ascribe it even to external mimicry; and to look upon a man as an ingenious person, that can resemble the tone, posture, or face of another.

As true wit consists in the resemblance of ideas, and false wit in the resemblance of words, according to the foregoing instances; there is another kind of wit, which consists partly in the resemblance of ideas, and partly in the resemblance of words; which, for distinction sake, I shall call mixt wit. This kind of wit is that which abounds in Cowley, more than in any author that ever wrote. Mr. Waller has likewise a great deal of it. Mr. Dryden is very sparing in it. Milton had a genius much above it. Spenser is in the same class with Milton. The Italians, even in their epic poetry, are full of it. Monsieur Boileau, who formed himself upon the ancient poets, has every where rejected it with scorn. If we look after mixt wit among the Greek writers, we shall find it no where but in the epigrammatists. There are, indeed, some strokes of it in the little poem ascribed to Musæus, which by that as well as many other marks, betrays itself to be a modern composition. If we look into the Latin writers, we find none of this mixt wit in Virgil, Lucretius, or Catullus; very little in Horace; but a great deal of it in Ovid; and scarce any thing else in Martial.

Out of the innumerable branches of mixt wit, I shall chuse one instance which may be met with in all the writers of this class. The passion of love in its nature has been thought to resemble fire; for which reason the words fire and flame are made use of to signify love. The witty poets, therefore, have taken an advantage from the doubtful meaning of the word fire, to make an infinite number of witticisms. Cowley observing the cold regard of his mistress's eyes, and at the same time their power of producing love in him, considers them as burning-glasses made of ice; and finding himself able to live in the greatest extremities of love, concludes the torrid zone to be habitable. When his mistress has read his letter written in juice of lemon by holding it to the fire, he desires her to read it over a second time by love's flames. When she weeps, he wishes it were inward heat that distilled those drops from the limbec. When she is absent, he is beyond eighty; that is, thirty degrees nearer the pole than when she is with him. His ambitious love is a fire that naturally mounts upwards; his happy love is the beams of heaven, and his unhappy love flames of hell. When it does not let him sleep, it is a flame that sends up no smoke; when it is opposed by counsel and advice, it is a fire that rages the more by the wind's blowing upon it. Upon the dying of a tree in which he had cut his loves, he observes that his written flames had burnt up and withered the tree. When he resolves to give over his passion, he tells us that one burnt like him for ever dreads the fire. His heart is an Ætna, that instead of Vulcan's shop, incloses Cupid's forge in it. His endeavouring to drown his love in wine, is throwing oil upon the fire. He would insinuate to his mistress, that the fire of love, like that of the sun (which produces so many living creatures) should not only warm but beget. Love in another place cooks pleasure at his fire. Sometimes the poet's heart is frozen in every breast, and sometimes scorched in every eye. Sometimes he is drowned in tears, and burnt in love, like a ship set on fire in the middle of the sea.

The reader may observe in every one of these instances, that the poet mixes the qualities of fire with those of love; and in the same sentence speaking of it both as a passion, and as real fire, surprises the reader with those seeming resemblances or contradictions that make up all the wit in this kind of writing. Mixt wit, therefore, is a composition of pun and true wit, and is more or less perfect as the resemblance lies in the ideas, or in the words: its foundations are laid partly in falsehood, and partly in truth: reason puts in her claim for one half of it, and extravagance for the other. The only province, therefore, for this kind of wit, is epigram, or those little occasional poems, that in their own nature are nothing else but a tissue of epigrams. I cannot conclude this head of mixt wit, without owning that the admirable poet out of whom I have taken the examples of it, had as much true wit as any author that ever writ; and, indeed, all other talents of an extraordinary genius.

It may be expected, since I am upon this subject, that I should take notice of Mr. Dryden's definition of wit; which, with all the deference that is due to the judgment of so great a man, is not so properly a definition of wit, as of good writing in general. Wit, as he defines it, is "a propriety of words and thoughts adapted to the subject." If this be a true definition of wit, I am apt to think that Euclid was the greatest wit that ever set pen to paper: it is certain there never was a greater propriety of words and thoughts adapted to the subject, than what that author has made use of in his *Elements*. I shall only appeal to my reader if this definition agrees with any notion he has of wit. If it be a true one, I am sure Mr. Dryden was not only a better poet, but a greater wit, than Mr. Cowley; and Virgil a much more facetious man than either Ovid or Martial.

Bouhours, whom I look upon to be the most penetrating of all the French critics, has taken pains to shew, that it is impossible for any thought to be beautiful which is not just, and has not its foundation in the nature of things: that the basis of all wit is truth; and that no thought can be valuable, of which good sense is not the ground-work. Boileau has endeavoured to inculcate the same notion in several parts of his writings, both in prose and verse. This is that natural way of writing, that beautiful simplicity, which we so much admire in the compositions of the ancients; and which nobody deviates from, but those who want strength of genius to make a thought shine in its own natural beauties. Poets who want this strength of genius to give that majestic simplicity to nature, which we so much admire in the works of the ancients, are forced to hunt after foreign ornaments, and not to let any piece of wit of what kind soever escape them. I look upon these writers as Goths in poetry, who, like those in architecture, not being able to come up to the beautiful simplicity of the old Greeks and Romans, have endeavoured to supply its place with all the extravagancies of an irregular fancy.

Mr. Dryden makes a very handsome observation of Ovid's writing a letter from Dido to Æneas, in the following words: "Ovid (says he, speaking of Virgil's fiction of Dido and Æneas) takes it up after him, even in the same age, and makes an ancient heroine of Virgil's new-created Dido; dictates a letter for her just before her death to the ungrateful fugitive; and, very unluckily for himself, is for measuring a sword with a man so much superior in force to him on the same subject: I think I may be judge of this, because I have translated both. The famous author of the *Art of Love* has nothing of his own; he borrows all from a greater master in his own profession, and, which is worse, improves nothing which he finds: nature fails him, and being forced to his old shift, he has recourse to witticism. This passes, indeed, with his soft admirers, and gives him the preference to Virgil in their esteem."

Were not I supported by so great an authority as that of Mr. Dryden, I should not venture to observe, that the taste of most of our English poets, as well as readers, is extremely Gothic. He quotes Monsieur Segrais for a threefold distinction of the readers of poetry; in the first of which he comprehends the rabble of readers, whom he does not treat as such with regard to their quality, but to their numbers, and the coarseness of their taste. His words are as follow: "Segrais has distinguished the readers of poetry, according to their capacity of judgment, into three classes. (He might have said the same of writers, too, if he had pleased.) In the lowest form he places those whom he calls *Les Petits Esprits;* such things as are our upper-gallery audience in a play-house, who like nothing but the husk and rind of wit, prefer a quibble, a conceit, an epigram, before solid sense, and elegant expression: these are mob readers. If Virgil and Martial stood for parliament men, we know already who would carry it. But though they make the greatest appearance in the field, and cry the loudest, the best on't is, they are but a sort of French Huguenots, or Dutch boors, brought over in herds, but not naturalized; who have not lands of two pounds per annum in Parnassus, and therefore are not privileged to poll. Their authors are of the same level, fit to represent them on a mountebank's stage, or to be masters of the ceremonies in a bear-garden; yet these are they who have the most admirers. But it often happens, to their mortification, that as their readers improve their stock of sense (as they may by reading better books, and by conversation with men of judgment), they soon forsake them."

I must not dismiss this subject without observing, that as Mr. Locke, in the passage above-mentioned, has discovered the most fruitful source of wit, so there is another of a quite contrary nature to it, which does likewise branch itself out into several kinds. For not only the resemblance, but the opposition of ideas does very often produce wit; as I could shew in several little points, turns, and antitheses, that I may possibly enlarge upon in some future speculation.

No. 412 Monday, June 23

PLEASURES OF THE IMAGINATION

Divisum sic breve fiet opus.
Martial Epigrams iv. 83

The work, divided aptly, shorter grows.

I shall first consider those pleasures of the imagination, which arise from the actual view and survey of outward objects: and these, I think, all proceed from the sight of what is great, uncommon, or beautiful. There may, indeed, be something so terrible or offensive, that the horror or loathsomeness of an object may over-bear the pleasure which results from its greatness, novelty, or beauty; but still there will be such a mixture of delight in the very disgust it gives us, as any of these three qualifications are most conspicuous and prevailing.

By greatness, I do not only mean the bulk of any single object, but the largeness of a whole view, considered as one entire piece. Such are the prospects of an open champaign country, a vast uncultivated desert, of huge heaps of mountains, high rocks and precipices, or a wide expanse of waters, where we are not struck with the novelty or beauty of the sight, but with that rude kind of magnificence which appears in many of these stupendous works of nature. Our imagination loves to be filled with an object, or to grasp at any thing that is too big for its capacity. We are flung into a pleasing astonishment at such unbounded views, and feel a delightful stillness and amazement in the soul at the apprehension of them. The mind of man naturally hates every thing that looks like a restraint upon it, and is apt to fancy itself under a sort of confinement, when the sight is pent up in a narrow compass, and shortened on every side by the neighbourhood of walls or mountains. On the contrary, a spacious horizon is an image of liberty, where the eye has room to range abroad, to expatiate at large on the immensity of its views, and to lose itself amidst the variety of objects that offer themselves to its observation. Such wide and undetermined prospects are as pleasing to the fancy, as the speculations of eternity or infinitude are to the understanding. But if there be a beauty or uncommonness joined with this grandeur, as in a troubled ocean, a heaven adorned with stars and meteors, or a spacious landscape cut out into rivers, woods, rocks, and meadows, the pleasure still grows upon us, as it rises from more than a single principle.

Every thing that is new or uncommon raises a pleasure in the imagination, because it fills the soul with an agreeable surprise, gratifies its curiosity, and gives it an idea of which it was not before possest. We are indeed so often conversant with one set of objects, and tired out with so many repeated shows of the same things, that whatever is new or uncommon contributes a little to vary human life, and to divert our minds, for a while, with the strangeness of its appearance: it serves us for a kind of refreshment, and takes off from that satiety we are apt to complain of in our usual and ordinary entertainments. It is this that bestows charms on a monster, and makes even the imperfections of nature please us. It is this that recommends variety, where the mind is every instant called off to something new, and the attention not suffered to dwell too long, and waste itself on any particular object. It is this, likewise, that improves what is great or beautiful, and makes it afford the mind a double entertainment. Groves, fields, and meadows are at any season of the year pleasant to look upon, but never so much as in the opening of spring, when they are all new and fresh, with their first gloss upon them, and not yet too much accustomed and familiar to the eye. For this reason there is nothing that more enlivens a prospect than rivers, jetteaus, or falls of water, where the scene is perpetually shifting, and entertaining the sight every moment with something that is new. We are quickly tired of looking upon hills and vallies, where every thing continues fixed and settled in the same place and posture, but find our thoughts a little agitated and relieved at the sight of such objects as are ever in motion, and sliding away from beneath the eye of the beholder.

But there is nothing that makes its way more directly to the soul than beauty, which immediately diffuses a secret satisfaction and complacency through the imagination, and gives a finishing to any thing that is great or uncommon. The very first discovery of it strikes the mind with an inward joy, and spreads a chearfulness and delight through all its faculties. There is not perhaps any real beauty or deformity more in one piece of matter than another, because we might have been so made, that whatsoever now appears loathsome to us, might have shewn itself agreeable; but we find by experience, that there are several modifications of matter, which the mind, without any previous consideration, pronounces at first sight beautiful or deformed. Thus we see, that every different species of sensible creatures has its different notions of beauty, and that each of them is most affected with the beauties of its own kind. This is no where more remarkable than in birds of the same shape and proportion, where we often see the male determined in his courtship by the single grain or tincture of a feather, and never discovering any charms but in the colour of its species. . . .

There is a second kind of beauty that we find in the several products of art and nature, which does not work in the imagination with that warmth and violence as the beauty that appears in our proper species, but is apt, however, to raise in us a secret delight, and a kind of fondness for the places or objects in which we discover it. This consists either in the gaiety or variety of colours, in the symmetry and proportion of parts, in the arrangement and disposition of bodies, or in a just mixture and concurrence of all together. Among these kinds of beauty the eye takes most delight in colours. We no where meet with a more glorious or pleasing show in nature, than what appears in the heavens at the rising and setting of the sun, which is wholly made up of those different stains of light than shew themselves in clouds of a different situation. For this reason we find the poets, who are always addressing themselves to the imagination, borrowing more of their epithets from colours than from any other topic.

As the fancy delights in every thing that is great, strange, or beautiful, and is still more pleased the more it finds of these perfections in the same object, so is it capable of receiving new satisfaction by the assistance of another sense. Thus any continued sound, as the music of birds, or a fall of water, awakens every moment the mind of the beholder, and makes him more attentive to the several beauties of the place that lie before him. Thus if there arises a fragrancy of smells or perfumes, they heighten the pleasure of the imagination, and make even the colours and verdure of the landscape appear more agreeable; for the ideas of both senses recommend each other, and are pleasanter together than when they enter the mind separately; as the different colours of a picture, when they are well disposed, set off one another, and receive an additional beauty from the advantage of their situation.

No. 416 Friday, June 27

PLEASURES OF THE IMAGINATION

Quantenus hoc simile est oculis, quod mente videmus.

Lucretius iv. 754

Objects still appear the same
To mind and eye, to colour, and in frame.

Creech

I at first divided the pleasures of the imagination, into such as arise from objects that are actually before our eyes, or that once entered in at our eyes, and are afterwards called up into the mind either barely by its own operations, or on occasion of something without us, as statues or descriptions. We have already considered the first division, and shall therefore enter on the other, which, for distinction sake, I have called the secondary pleasures of the imagination. When I say the ideas we receive from statues, descriptions, or such like occasions, are the same that were once actually in our view, it must not be understood that we had once seen the very place, action, or person, which are carved or described. It is sufficient, that we have seen places, persons, or actions, in general, which bear a resemblance, or at least some remote analogy with what we find represented. Since it is in the power of the imagination, when it is once stocked with particular ideas, to enlarge, compound, and vary them at her own pleasure.

Among the different kinds of representation, statuary is the most natural, and shews us something likest the object that is represented. To make use of a common instance, let one who is born blind take an image in his hands, and trace out with his fingers the different furrows and impressions of the chissel, and he will easily conceive how the shape of a man, or beast, may be represented by it; but should he draw his hand over a picture, where all is smooth and uniform, he would never be able to imagine how the several prominences and depressions of a human body could be shewn on a plain piece of canvass, that has in it no unevenness or irregularity. Description runs yet further from the things it represents than painting; for a picture bears a real resemblance to its original, which letters and syllables are wholly void of. Colours speak all languages, but words are understood only by such a people or nation. For this reason, though men's necessities quickly put them on finding out speech, writing is probably of a later invention than painting; particularly we are told, that in America when the Spaniards first arrived there, expresses were sent to the emperor of Mexico in paint, and the news of his country delineated by the strokes of a pencil, which was a more natural way than that of writing, though at the same time much more imperfect, because it is impossible to draw the little connections of speech, or to give the picture of a conjunction or an adverb. It would be yet more strange, to represent visible objects by sounds that have no ideas annexed to them, and to make something like description in music. Yet it is certain, there may be confused imperfect notions of this nature raised in the imagination by an aritifical composition of notes; and we find that great masters in the art are able, sometimes, to set their hearers in the heat and hurry of a battle, to overcast their minds with melancholy scenes and apprehensions of deaths and funerals, or to lull them into pleasing dreams of groves and elysiums.

In all these instances, this secondary pleasure of the imagination proceeds from that action of the mind, which compares the ideas arising from the original objects, with the ideas we receive from the statue, picture, description, or sound that represents them. It is impossible for us to give the necessary reason, why this operation of the mind is attended with so much pleasure, as I have before observed on the same occasion: but we find a great variety of entertainments derived from this single principle: for it is this that not only gives us a relish of statuary, painting, and description, but makes us delight in all the actions and arts of mimicry. It is this that makes the several kinds of wit pleasant, which consists, and I have formerly shewn, in the affinity of ideas: and we may add, it is this also that raises the little satisfaction we sometimes find in the different sorts of false wit; whether it consists in the affinity of letters, as in anagram, acrostic; or of syllables, as in doggerel rhymes, echos; or of words, as in puns, quibbles; or of a whole sentence or poem, to wings and altars. The final cause, probably, of annexing pleasure to this operation of the mind, was to quicken and encourage us in our searches after truth, since the distinguishing one thing from another, and the right discerning betwixt our ideas, depends wholly upon our comparing them together, and observing the congruity or disagreement that appears among the several works of nature.

But I shall here confine myself to those pleasures of the imagination, which proceed from ideas raised by words, because most of the observations that agree with descriptions, are equally applicable to painting and statuary.

Words, when well chosen, have so great a force in them, that a description often gives us more lively ideas than the sight of things themselves. The reader finds a scene drawn in stronger colours, and painted more to the life in his imagination, by the help of words, than by an actual survey of the scene which they describe. In this case, the poet seems to get the better of nature; he takes, indeed, the landscape after her, but gives it more vigorous touches, heightens its beauty, and so enlivens the whole piece, that the images which flow from the objects themselves appear weak and faint, in comparison of those that come from the expressions. The reason, probably, may be, because in the survey of any object we have only so much of it painted on the imagination, as comes in at the eye; but in its description, the poet gives us as free a view of it as he pleases, and discovers to us several parts, that either we did not attend to, or that lay out of our sight when we first beheld it. As we look on any object, our idea of it is, perhaps, made up of two or three simple ideas; but when the poet represents it, he may either give us a more complex idea of it, or only raise in us such ideas as are most apt to affect the imagination.

It may be here worth our while to examine how it comes to pass that several readers, who are all acquainted with the same language, and know the meaning of the words they read, should nevertheless have a different relish of the same descriptions. We find one transported with a passage which another runs over with coldness and indifference, or finding the representation extremely natural, where another can perceive nothing of likeness and conformity. This different taste must proceed, either from the perfection of imagination in one more than another, or from the different ideas that several readers affix to the same words. For, to have a true relish, and form a right judgment of a description, a man should be born with a good imagination, and must have well weighed the force and energy that lies in the several words of a langauge, so as to be able to distinguish which are most significant and expressive of their proper ideas, and what additional strength and beauty they are capable of receiving from conjunction with others. The fancy must be warm, to retain the print of those images it hath received from outward objects; and the judgment discerning, to know what expressions are most proper to clothe and adorn them to the best advantage. A man who is deficient in either of these respects, though he may receive the general notion of a description, can never see distinctly all its particular beauties: as a person, with a weak sight, may have the confused prospect of a place that lies before him, without entering into its several parts, or discerning the variety of its colours in their full glory and perfection.

No. 418 Monday, June 30

PLEASURES OF THE IMAGINATION

ferat et rubus asper amomum.

Virgil, Eclogues iii. 89

The rugged thorn shall bear the fragrant rose.

The pleasures of these secondary views of the imagination, are of a wider and more universal nature than those it has when joined with sight; for not only what is great, strange, or beautiful, but any thing that is disagreeable, when looked upon, pleases us, in an apt description. Here, therefore, we must inquire after a new principle of pleasure, which is nothing else but the action of the mind, which compares the ideas that arise from words, with the ideas that arise from the objects themselves; and why this operation of the mind is attended with so much pleasure, we have before considered. For this reason, therefore, the description of a dunghill is pleasing to the imagination, if the image be presented to our minds by suitable expressions; though, perhaps this may be more properly called the pleasure of the understanding than of the fancy, because we are not so much delighted with the image that is contained in the description, as with the aptness of the description to excite the image.

But if the description of what is little, common, or deformed, be acceptable to the imagination, the description of what is great, surprising, or beautiful, is much more so; because here we are not only delighted with comparing the representation with the original, but are highly pleased with the original itself. Most readers, I believe, are more charmed with Milton's description of Paradise, than of Hell: they are both, perhaps, equally perfect in their kind, but in the one the brimstone and sulphur are not so refreshing to the imagination, as the beds of flowers and the wilderness of sweets in the other.

There is yet another circumstance which recommends a description more than all the rest, and that is, if it represents to us such objects as are apt to raise a secret ferment in the mind of the reader, and to work, with violence, upon his passions. For, in this case, we are at once warmed and enlightened, so that the pleasure becomes more universal, and is several ways qualified to entertain us. Thus, in painting, it is pleasant to look on the picture of any face, where the resemblance is hit, but the pleasure increases, if it be the picture of a face that is beautiful, and is still greater, if the beauty be softened with an air of melancholy or sorrow. The two leading passions which the more serious parts of poetry endeavour to stir up in us, are terror and pity. And here, by the way, one would wonder how it comes to pass, that such passions as are very unpleasant at all other times, are very agreeable when excited by proper descriptions. It is not strange, that we should take delight in such passages as are apt to produce hope, joy, admiration, love, or the like emotion in us, because they never rise in the mind without an inward pleasure which attends them. But how comes it to pass, that we should take delight in being terrified or dejected by a description, when we find so much uneasiness in the fear or grief which we receive from any other occasion?

If we consider, therefore, the nature of this pleasure, we shall find that it does not arise so properly from the description of what is terrible, as from the reflection we make on ourselves at the time of reading it. When we look on such hideous objects, we are not a little pleased to think we are in no danger of them. We consider them at the same time, as dreadful and harmless; so that the more frightful appearance they make, the greater is the pleasure we receive from the sense of our own safety. In short, we look upon the terrors of a description, with the same curiosity and satisfaction that we survey a dead monster.

Informe cadaver
Protrahitur: nequeunt expleri corda tuendo
Terribiles oculos, vultum, villosaque setis
Pectora semiferi, atque extinctos faucibus ignes.

VIRGIL, Æneid viii. v. 264

They drag him from his den
The wond'ring neighbourhood, with glad surprise,
Beheld his shagged breast, his giant size,
His mouth that flames no more, and his extinguished eyes.

DRYDEN

It is for the same reason that we are delighted with the reflecting upon dangers that are past, or in looking on a precipice at a distance, which would fill us with a different kind of horror; if we saw it hanging over our heads.

In the like manner, when we read of torments, wounds, deaths, and like dismal accidents, our pleasure does not flow so properly from the grief which such melancholy descriptions give us, as from the secret comparison which we make between ourselves and the person who suffers. Such representations teach us to set a just value upon our own condition, and make us prize our good fortune which exempts us from the like calamities. This is, however, such a kind of pleasure as we are not capable of receiving, when we see a person actually lying under the tortures that we meet with in a description; because in this case, the object presses too close upon our senses, and bears so hard upon us, that it does not give us time or leisure to reflect on ourselves. Our thoughts are so intent upon the miseries of the sufferer, that we cannot turn them upon our own happiness. Whereas, on the contrary, we consider the misfortunes we read in history or poetry, either as past, or as fictitious, so that the reflection upon ourselves rises in us insensibly, and overbears the sorrow we conceive for the sufferings of the afflicted.

But because the mind of man requires something more perfect in matter, than what it finds there, and can never meet with any sight in nature which sufficiently answers its highest ideas of pleasantness; or, in other words, because the imagination can fancy to itself things more great, strange, or beautiful, than the eye ever saw, and is still sensible of some defect in what it has seen; on this account it is the part of a poet to humour the imagination in its own notions, by mending and perfecting nature where he describes a reality, and by adding greater beauties than are put together in nature, where he describes a fiction.

He is not obliged to attend her in the slow advances which she makes from one season to another, or to observe her conduct, in the successive production of plants and flowers. He may draw into his description all the beauties of the spring and autumn, and make the whole year contribute something to render it more agreeable. His rose-trees, woodbines, and jessamines, may flower together, and his beds be covered at the same time with lilies, violets, and amaranths. His soil is not restrained to any particular set of plants, but is proper either for oaks or myrtles, and adapts itself to the products of every climate. Oranges may grow wild in it; myrrh may be met with in every hedge, and if he thinks it proper to have a grove of spices, he can quickly command sun enough to raise it. If all this will not furnish out an agreeable scene, he can make several new species of flowers, with richer scents and higher colours, than any that grow in the gardens of nature. His concerts of birds may be as full and harmonious, and his woods as thick and gloomy as he pleases. He is at no more expence in a long vista, than a short one, and can as easily throw his cascades from a precipice of half a mile high, as from one of twenty yards. He has his choice of the winds, and can turn the course of his rivers in all the variety of meanders, that are most delightful to the reader's imagination. In a word, he has the modelling of nature in his own hands, and may give her what charms he pleases, provided he does not reform her too much, and run into absurdities, by endeavouring to excel.

Eliza Haywood 1693–1756

Eliza Haywood, immortalized in Pope's *Dunciad,* is best known as the editor of *The Female Spectator,* in which her essays on manners, morals, education, philosophy, and literature "in imitation of my learned brother," Joseph Addison, attempted to reform and refine the public tastes of mid-century London society. Born around 1693, Haywood was the daughter of a London tradesman named Fowler. She married an unknown man named Haywood and after he abandoned them she wrote to support herself and her two children. She first appeared in the public eye in 1715 as an actress in Dublin. Soon after, she came to London. Between 1720 and 1733 she wrote some plays, both comedies and tragedies, that were acted at Lincoln's Inn Fields and Drury Lane with moderate success. She collaborated on the libretto of an opera, an adaptation of Fielding's *Tragedy of Tragedies,* called *Opera of Operas, or Tom Thumb,* which was acted at the Haymarket and Drury Lane theaters. She also wrote several notorious novels revealing thinly disguised scandals. These earned her some of the bitterest and coarsest satires in Pope's *Dunciad.* Haywood was an extremely proficient writer; in all, she produced some eighty titles in several genres before she died in 1756.

Between April 1744 and March 1746 in association with some friends, she issued, in twenty-four monthly installments, *The Female Spectator,* a collection of moral tales and reflections modeled on Addison's *Spectator*. These essays, many of them written in the form of fictitious letters from readers and correspondents, range in subject from philosophy, education, and literature to fashion, tea, and courtship and were intended primarily to refine the manners and morals of her readers. In the following selection, under the guise of a fictive letter from Distrario, Haywood examines the causes of the degeneration of the English stage as a result of the Stage Licensing Act: "The name of a dramatic poet [is] at present so contemptible that no person of real abilities will choose to be distinguished by it." Like Aphra Behn, she exposes the politics that denied many playwrights access to the theater. The Licensing Act of 1737 limited the number of theaters in London to two and required that all plays be examined by the Lord Chamberlain's office before they could be produced. Haywood's burlesque portrait of a would-be playwright shows the power of the licensers, the managers who held virtual monopolies, and the principal actors to determine what kinds of plays would be written and who would profit by them. This censorship effectively choked off the "genius in the growth of our own times." Few new plays were produced; instead older, "safer" plays were revived. The result, as Haywood points out, was a resurgence in the popularity of Shakespeare's plays, which were frequently revived, although usually rewritten to fit the taste and temper of the times. Haywood's solution, an office that would require the performance of good plays, rather than the censoring of dangerous ones, although facetious, exposes the problems of aesthetic judgment and the difficulties involved in legislating taste.

from The Female Spectator

BOOK VIII

To *The Female Spectator*

Madam,

The justice you have done in recommending dramatic performances, before any other of the present more encouraged diversions of the town, renders your monthly essays a proper vehicle to convey the groans of the stage to the ears of the public; nor can those gentlemen who unhappily have devoted themselves to the Muses, find any means of making their complaint with so much probability of success, as through your nervous and pathetic strains.

Be not startled, I beseech you, at the sight of this long epistle, nor imagine it is my intention to trouble you with any animadversion on the late or present contest between the patentees and players; the town is already sufficiently pestered with cases and replies, and I am afraid these idle quarrels among themselves will rather contribute to bring acting in general into contempt, than be of any service to the persons concerned in them.

No, madam, my aim is to obviate the more real misfortunes of the theatres, and show how the drama is wounded through the sides of those by whom alone it can exist with any honour or reputation.

There are two reasons commonly assigned why the nobility and better sort of people have of late years very much withdrawn that encouragement they used to vouch safe to the stage. The first is, that the part in which Wilks, Booth, Cibber senior, Oldfield, Porter, and some other appeared in with great propriety, are but ill supplied by their successors; but I cannot look on this as any real objection, because it would be both cruel and unjust; actors cannot always retain the same faculties any more than other people, much less can they be immortal: besides, there are at this time several whose merit ought not to be absorbed in the regard we pay to the memory of those who went before them. And if even they are less excellent, I do not perceive but the audiences are satisfied with their endeavours to please us, by imitating them as far as lies in their power. The second, were it founded on truth, would be of weight indeed; and that is, that there are now no gentlemen of any abilities that will write for the stage, and that the town is obliged to be content with seeing the same things over and over again for several reasons together, without any one new subject of entertainment being exhibited. The latter part of this objection is founded on too known a fact not to give some credit to the former, especially when propagated by those whose interest one would imagine it was to inculcate a contrary opinion; but this it is to take upon me to confute, by displaying those latent motives which have occasioned a report so injurious to the present age, that I wonder nobody has yet taken the pains to examine into it.

First, let us ask the question whether there are, or are not, any surviving geniuses truly qualified to write for the stage?—I believe nobody will answer in the negative, because nothing could be more easy than to prove the contrary. This being granted, let us ask farther, whence it comes to pass that every one should now despise an avocation, which was once attended with considerable profit, and so much reputation, that some of our greatest men have valued themselves more on their talents this way, than on their coronets? Strange it seems that the name of a dramatic poet should at present be so contemptible, than no person of real abilities will choose to be distinguished by it!

Yet it is easily accounted for, if the tedious delays, the shocking rebuffs, the numberless difficulties an author is almost sure to meet with, in his attempt to introduce any new thing on the stage, were laid open and considered as they ought.

A person of condition would make but an odd figure, if, after having taken pains to oblige the town, and do honour to the stage, he should be made to dance attendance at the levee of an imperious patentee for days, weeks, nay months together, and receive no other answers than that he had not had time to look over his play; that he had mislaid it;—or perhaps affects to forget he ever saw it:—at last, the actors must be consulted, and it often happens that those among them who are least capable of judging, are called into the cabinet council. If any one of these happens to dislike the character he imagines will be allotted for him, then the whole piece is condemned; and the conclusion of the season, or it is possible at that of two or three succeeding ones, the author has it returned, and is told, it is not theatrical enough; a term invented by this august assembly, to conceal their inability of pointing out the real faults, and the meaning which can neither be defined by themselves or anybody else.

But you will say, Why should they behave in this manner?—Is it not the interest of both manager and actors to receive a good play, which will be certain of putting money in the pocket of the one, and securing the payment of the salaries of the other?

To which I answer, that it is doubtless their true interest; but avarice and idolence render many people blind to what is so:—the manager flatters himself, that if the town cannot have new plays, they will come to old ones, and he should thereby save the profits of the third night: and the actors (those I mean of them who are at what they call the top of the business, for the others have no influence) having their salaries fixed, think they have no occasion to take the trouble of studying new parts, since they know they must be paid equally the same without it.

These, madam, are the false ill-judged maxims by which both patentee and company are swayed to reject the most excellent pieces submitted to their censure, and are the motives which deter, as far as it relates to them, an author from offering any thing to the stage.

Yet while I condemn the little inclination those gentlemen for the most part testify to oblige the town, or give encouragement to the poets, I must do them the justice to say, that it has not been always owing to them that so many improving and delightful entertainments have been deprived of seeing the light. There is another more terrific cloud from a superior quarter hangs over the author's hopes, and threatens the destruction of his most sanguine expectations.

I believe neither yourself, nor any of your readers will be at a loss to understand I mean the license-office, at the head of which a great person is placed, who cannot be supposed to have leisure to inspect everyone, nor indeed any of the pieces brought before him; and there is much more than a bare possibility, that his deputies may, either through weakness or partiality, err in their judgment and give an unfair report, nay, some go so far as to imagine they are under a secret compact with the managers of both houses to reject indiscriminately every thing that comes, except recommended by the higher powers; but this I am far from being able to lay to their charge, nor do indeed think either the one or the other capable of entering into any such combination.

But to what, unless one of the foregoing reasons, can we impute forbidding the tragedies of *Edward and Eleonora, Gustavus Vasa,* and some other excellent performances, founded on the most interesting parts of history, supported by various turns and surprising incidents, and illustrated with all the strength and beauty of language; especially the former, which, for every thing that can render a piece improving and entertaining, finds itself not excelled (I had almost said equalled) by any thing either of the ancient or modern writers!—Yet was this admirable play, when just ready to make its appearance, forbid to be acted, the longing expectations of the pubic were disappointed, and we had been totally deprived of so elegant an entertainment, did not, thank Heaven, the liberty of the press still continue in some measure with us.

Though stripped of all the ornaments of dress and action, it gives in the reading a lasting and undeniable proof that it is neither want of abilities, or an idolence in exerting those abilities, but permission to exhibit them in a proper manner, that the stage at present affords so little matter of attraction.

But I will now come to the point, which chiefly induced me to trouble the *Female Spectator* with this letter; and having enumerated the many hardships authors in general go through in attempting to get their plays acted, I will proceed as briefly as the circumstance will admit, to lay before you those which myself in particular have laboured under.

I must inform you, madam, that I have written several things, which have not only been well received by the public, but have also been favoured with the approbation of some of our best judges; and that it was no less owing to their encouragement than my own ambition, that I resolved to try the force of my genius in the dramatic way, which, according to one of the greatest of our English poets,

> is a bold pretence
> To learning, breeding, wit and eloquence.

I ventured at it, notwithstanding; and, undeterred by example, launched into that sea, on whose rocks and quicksands so many much more skillful pilots than myself have been wrecked before my eyes.

To confess the truth, I was greatly emboldened by the favour and friendship of a person of condition, a courtier, and who I imagined had interest enough both with the licenser and players to introduce whatever he should recommend. But to return:—

As my genius inclined me chiefly to the sublime, my first attempt was tragedy. —The part of the history I made choice of, was the famous combat between Edward, surnamed Ironside, King of England, and the great Canute of Denmark. —There appeared to me so true a magnanimity and paternal affection for his people in that heroic prince, when to save the effusion of their blood, he set all his own, as well as kingdom at stake, and fought hand to hand with one who had no equal but himself in strength and courage, while both armies stood admiring spectators only of his wondrous valour, that I thought a more proper subject could not have employed my pen. —I am not apt to be vain of my performances, but the friend abovementioned assured me I had done my part as a poet; and withal said, he was sorry I had not pitched upon some other story;—that this would never do;—that it would be looked upon as too romantic;—that customs were entirely changed since the days of Ironside;—that kings were now too sacred to hazard their persons in that manner;—and concluded with advising me not to expose it, as it would never pass the office, and might render me obnoxious.

This was a very great mortification to me; however, I submitted to his judgment, and changed the scene to the last part of that glorious monarch's life, where himself and kingdom were betrayed and given up to ruin by the treachery and avarice of his first minister and favourite, Edric duke of Mercia: but alas! my patron disapproved of this more than the former, and told me, a first minister, especially an ill one, ought never to be represented on the stage; because seditious people might take upon them to draw parallels, thereby lessening the reverence due to those in power.

I then took the liberty of intreating he would recommend some part of history for me to write upon; but he told me as to that, he had not leisure to think of such things; all he could do was to advise me either to find out or invent some agreeable fable, where no king or prime minister or any sort had any business to be introduced; and above all things not to lay the scene in any of the independent commonwealths, 'because,' said he, 'it may naturally draw you into some expressions that may favour of republicanism.'

Some months I passed in considering what he had said, and searching history in order to find out, if possible, some event, the representation of which might be liable to none of these objections; but the thing was in itself an utter impossibility, and all my endeavors served only to convince me it was so.

My ambition of acquiring the name of a dramatic author not being quelled by the disappointments I received, still flattered me with better success in the comic vein.—A whim which I thought would be entertaining enough, came into my head, and I threw it immediately into scenes, which I afterwards divided into five acts, and gave the piece the title of *The Blunderers*, from two odd fellows I had introduced, who made whatever was bad still worse.

But, good Madam Spectator, how shall I describe the passion my friend was in at seeing this title! 'If I did not know,' said he, 'that you were an honest man, I should take you for the most arrant rascal in the world: What is it you mean by calling your comedy *The Blunderers*? Are you insensible that the Jacobites, and enemies to the government, aspersed the late ministry with the name of Blunderers, and are they not beginning to load the present with the same odious appellation?—I am surprised a poet can have so thick a head.'

Though what he accused me of, had never before come into my thoughts, I was now sensible I had committed an error, and having confessed as much, told him, that the title need be no objection to the play itself, which might with the same propriety be called *The Bubbles*, there being several characters in it which it might well deserve that name.

This, instead of appealing, as I expected it would have done, his rage, more inflamed it.—'How,' cried he, 'then I perceive you are aiming at popularity: you cannot be so ignorant as not to know, by *The Bubbles* will be understood the common people:—and I have no more to say to you or your productions.'

He left me in speaking these words, nor could I prevail on him to renew our former familiarity for a long time; and I was so much disquieted at the thoughts of having so foolishly forfeited the interest I before had with him, that I had no capacity for writing anything. At length, however, he was reconciled; I recovered his esteem, and with it my inclination for the drama, but told him, that the mistakes I had been guilty of had determined me not to go upon my own bottom till I had more experience, but would build on the plan of some old author, whose fable could no way be brought into comparison with the present transactions.

This he seeming to approve of, I mentioned a comedy wrote nearly a century and a half ago, by one Drawbridge Court Belchier, a gentleman it seems much applauded for his poetic works in the age he lived: the title of it is, *Hans Beerpot; or, The Invisible Comedy of See Me, and See Me Not;* which I had no sooner repeated, than he cried out, 'You must not think of it; it will be taken for a reflection on the Dutch, who, you know, though they have of late played a little the Will o' the Wisp with us, are, notwithstanding, our good friends and allies, and must not be affronted.'

I knocked under, in token of yielding myself in the wrong; and having read over a great many old comedies, in order to find one for my purpose, I asked what he thought of a play of Middleton's called, *A Mad World, my Masters,* at which he shook his head and answered, 'That may affect some princes of Germany; I would not have you meddle with it.'

I then told him, 'that *The Knight of the Burning Pestle,* wrote by Beaumont and Fletcher, could not give offense to any party.' 'You are deceived,' said he; 'who knows but it may, with some ignorant people, bring the noblest orders of knighthood into contempt?'

'Well, then,' resumed I, '*The Isle of Gulls,* wrote by Mr. Day in the reign of our Elizabeth of immortal memory, may surely be modernized, without incurring the censure of any party.'

'Fye, fye,' replied he peevishly, 'you are as ill a judge of other men's productions as of your own—such a play would be looked upon as a most scandalous libel.'

Quite impatient to hit on something out of the reach of evil, I proposed the revival of *Breneralt; or, The Discontented Colonel*, a play of Sir John Suckling's; but that, it seems, bordered too near on some late military disgusts.—*The Glass of Government*, by Gascoigne, might also be construed into an arrogant attempt to point out defects which ought to be concealed. *The Supposes*, by the same author, might affront a certain great man, who is thought to build all his schemes on supposition. By *The Hog Has Lost His Pearl*, though wrote by Taylor, in the year 1611, I should infallibly be understood to insinuate a present loss of British liberty.—Mr. Broom's play of *The Court Beggar* would be a glaring insult on some of the chief nobility round Whitehall, and some other places; and *The Court Secret*, by Shirley, was a thing too delicate to be pried into. *The Doubtful Heir*, by the same gentleman, and *The Fall of Tarquin*, by Hunt, were equally rejected by this state-critic, though without explaining his reasons for doing so on these two last.

Judge, madam, how much I was vexed and confounded at hearing innuendos, which one could not have imagined should ever enter into the heart of man; but as I was resolved to try this pretended friend to the utmost, I told him that since it was so impossible a thing either to write a new tragedy or comedy, or to revive what had been rewritten so many ages past without giving offence, I would content myself with modernizing an interlude of more than two hundred years old, composed by John Heywood, and entitled, *The Four P's*. On that he paused a little, but at last replied gravely that he could by no means encourage me in any such attempt; for, said he, 'by the four P's may be implied Prince, Power, Parliament, and Pension; or, perhaps, People, Poverty, Prison, and Petition:—no, Sir,' continued he, 'avoid all such seditious allegories, I beseech you, or we must no longer be acquainted.'

This put me beyond all patience, and I could not forbear answering with some warmth, that I found he endeavoured to pick meanings where they were never intended. 'If the four P's,' said I, 'contain any allegory, why must it needs be a seditious one? Why may they not as well be understood to mean Penitence, Pardon, Peace, and Plenty? Or if that should seem a little strained in the present age, may it not with greater propriety be turned on the coquet part of the fair sex, and stand for Proud, Pretty, Prating, and Playful?'

This argument, though certainly reasonable, had no manner of weight with him, any more than some other I made use of for the same purpose; and only served to convince myself that there was no possibility of writing anything but what might be liable to censure from those who made it their business to find matter for it.

Thus, madam, I have pointed out the obstacles which lie in the way of a dramatic author, and you will easily conceive the little probability there is that a person of fortune will descend to that servile dependence and solicitation now required for the admission of his play; and a poet whose support is his muse, is deterred from risking, on so precarious a hope, that time, which he is sure to be largely paid for, if employed in the service of some persons, not altogether convenient to name.

Without some better regulation therefore on the part of the theatres, and some abatement of the present severity of that of the licenser, the town must despair of seeing any new thing exhibited, the drama be entirely neglected, and the stage in a short time become a desert.

Nothing can be more worthy the pen of a 'Female Spectator' than to set this affair in a proper light; that good-nature you have so amiably described, requires it of you in behalf of distressed authors;—justice demands you should stand up in defense of an institution calculated for public service;—and reason will, I doubt not, engage you to exert yourself on so laudable an occasion.

I am, MADAM,
Very much your admirer, and
Most obedient humble servent,
DISTRARIO.

We were pretty much divided in our opinions on the first perusal of this letter; but at last agreed, that though the complaints contained in it might be, and it is highly probable are, perfectly just, yet Distrario may perhaps have taken the latitude allowed to poets, and represented things somewhat higher than the life. We know not how to think that either of the patentees, who are both of them gentlemen of families, and doubtless have had an education conformable to their birth, should be able to bring themselves to treat, even the least meritorious of those who endeavor to serve them, and oblige the town, with that haughtiness and contempt he seems to accuse them of. Good manners is a debt we owe to ourselves, as well as to others, and whoever neglects to pay it, forfeits all the pretensions he might otherwise have both to the love and respect of the world. A civil refusal takes off the asperity of the disappointment, and is given with the same ease as a more rough and poignant one: sure, therefore, those who are at the head of an eternal scene of politeness, cannot so far vary from what they have continually before their eyes. But as this is a punctilio, which regards only the persons of the poets, who are very well able to return in kind any flights they may imagine put upon them, and is of much less consequence to the public than those their productions meet with, it were to be wished that some of the great world would vouchsafe to interest themselves in this affair, and not leave it at the option of those who live by the good-humour of the town, to deprive it of any entertainment it has a right to expect from them.

As therefore is an office to forbid the exhibitions of such new plays as by it are judged to have anything in them offensive or indecent, it would not, methinks, be unbecoming the wisdom of the legislature to erect one for the commanding and enforcing such to be acted, as on perusal are found proper to entertain a polite and virtuous audience.

Such an office, under the direction of gentlemen qualified to judge of dramatic performances, would take away all occasion of complaint from the poets, and be a motive to induce many gentlemen to write for the stage, who, if it be as Distrario says, are now deterred from it.

Besides, to prevent the shock an author feels in having his piece rejected, as well as all jealousies of partiality in the affair, every one might send his play, without ever being known from what hand it came, till it had been approved, and was ordered to be acted.

It is certain, that according to the opinion we have of the man, we are greatly prejudiced in favour or dislike of his work; yet this is in truth a piece of injustice, which we ought not to indulge ourselves in.—It is possible to excel in one kind of writing, yet be very bad in another:—few there are, if any, whose talents are universal. Mr. Pope, whose poetical works will always be read with an equal share of pleasure and admiration, had, notwithstanding, no genius for dramatic writing; and Mr. Rymer, that awful critic on the productions of his contemporaries, that great pretender to a reformation of the stage, by attempting to give a proof of what plays ought to be, has only shown how little he was qualified to write one. This, I believe, will be allowed by every one who has read his *Edgar*, a piece which, after all his long labour, can but at best be called correctly dull, since the two chief beauties of tragedy, pity and surprize, are entirely wanting in it: yet doubtless the town were in high expectations of something wonderful, from a pen which had been so severe on the performance of others.

I therefore cannot help smiling within myself, when on the first talk of a new play being in rehearsal, the name of the author is presently inquired into, and a strict scrutiny made into the merit of his former works; and if he has written anything, though never so foreign to the stage, which has the good fortune to succeed, people cry out, "Oh, if it is his, it must be good!" and following this conclusion, run the first night to give an applause to that which perhaps after they had seen, and well considered, they are ashamed of having countenanced.

Nor am I less concerned, and even shocked, when I hear with what contempt the performance of a young author, who is in a manner but clambering up the hill of fame, is treated by some who speak of it;—how they throw aside his tickets, and cry, "What obscure fellow is this? What stuff does he invite us to?" and either not go to his play at all, or go with a prepossession, which will not suffer them to give it a fair hearing.

This is a piece of cruelty in some who would be thought good judges, yet are entirely governed by prejudice; and I have known has been practiced long before those new hardships Distrario complains of were ever known.

Such an office, therefore, as I have mentioned, where plays should be candidly examined, without any regard to the merits of their authors in other respects, or even knowing who they were, would remedy all these inconveniences to the poets, and also be a means of obliging the town with three or four at least new pieces every season at each theatre.

As to the power of forbidding plays to be acted, now lodged in the licenser, it must be granted, that in an age so dissolute as this, there ought to be some restraint on the latitude poets might otherwise take, and some whom I could name have taken, in expectation of crowded audiences of the looser part of both sexes; but then, methinks, this restriction should have its bounds. Whatever is offensive to the Majesty of heaven, or of its vicegerents on earth, would, indeed, be very unfit subjects to be exhibited on a stage; but to reject a valuable play for the sake of such strained innuendoes does as the friend of Distrario suggested, seems to overthrow that decent liberty, which in all ages, and in all free nations, has ever been allowed.

The stage by its institution is the school of virtue, and the scourge of vice; and when either of these noble purposes is defeated, it is no wonder that persons of true sense and honour choose to absent themselves, and oblige their families to do so too.

The tragedies of *Edward and Eleonora*, *Gustavus Vasa*, *Arminius*, and some other forbidden by this office from being acted, have dared the test of examination by appearing in print; and I never yet found any one person who could penetrate into the motives which denied us the pleasure of seeing them represented.

If the true *amor patriae* be a virtue these times are not ashamed of, how must every breast glow with a noble ardour at the illustrious example of Gustavus Vasa, and his brave *Dalecarlians*? If the desire of attaining glory and renown for worthy actions be a principle which ought to be inculcated in the young, and cherished in the old, Arminius affords lessons for the laudable ambition:—and if courage in distress, resignation to Heaven, faith, love, piety, and zeal, and every virtue that can illustrate the character of a Christian hero, be deserving our regard, where can we find a greater influence, than in our gallant Edward?

The ladies, above all, have reason to regret the ill treatment of this excellent performance, since none was ever wrote could do greater honour to the sex.—The amiable Eleonora is a character, which I believe no other history can parallel, and her behavior a shining proof that greatness of mind, fortitude, constancy, and all those perfections which constitute a true magnanimity, are not confined to the male gender.

It was however thought proper to suppress these plays, and many others, as far as the power of the licenser extended, and it is not our province to examine into his reasons for so doing; but may allow, with Distrario, that when such as these were not permitted, it is very difficult for an author to find or invent any story which may not be liable to some objection, and suffer the same fate.

If the eye could be satisfied with seeing, or the ear with hearing always the same things over and over repeated, it must be owned there are many old plays, which the best of our modern poets would not perhaps be able to excel; but Nature delights in variety; and though it would be unjust and ungrateful to strip the laurels from the brows of Shakespeare, Johnson, Beaumont and Fletcher, Dryden, Otway, Lee, Congreve, and several other deservedly admired authors, to adorn those who shall succeed them, yet we love to see a genius the growth of our own times, and might find sufficient trophies for the merits of such, without any injury to their predecessors.

Those most impatient for new plays desire not, however, that those which for so many years have continued to divert and please, should now be sunk and buried in oblivion.—The poets I have mentioned will always preserve the same charms, and would do so yet more were they less frequently exhibited.—Some of Shakespeare's comedies, and all his tragedies, have beauties in them almost inimitable; but then it must be confessed, that he sometimes gave a loose to the luxuriancy of his fancy; so that his plays may be compared to fine gardens full of the most beautiful flowers, but choaked up with weeds through the too great richness of the soil: those therefore which have had those weeds plucked up by the skillful hands of his successors, are much the most elegant entertainments.

For which reason I was a little surprized, when I heard that Mr. Cibber, junior, had revived the tragedy of *Romeo and Juliet*, as it was first acted; *Caius Marius* being the same play, only modernized, and cleared of some part of its rubbish, by Otway, appearing to so much more advantage, that it is not to be doubted, but that the admirable author, had he lived to see the alteration, would have been highly thankful and satisfied with it.

It were indeed to be wished, that the same kind corrector had been somewhat more severe, and lopped off not only some superfluous scenes, but whole characters, which rather serve to diminish than add to the piece, particularly those of the Nurse and Sulpitius, neither of them being in the least conducive to the conduct of the fable, and all they say favouring more of comedy than tragedy.—It is, methinks, inconsistent with the character of a Roman senator and patrician, to suffer himself to be entertained for half an hour together with such idle chat as would scarce pass among old women in a nursery: nor does the wild or loose discourse of Sulpitius at all agree with the austerity of the times he is supposed to live in, or any way improve the morals of an audience. The description also of the apothecary, though truly poetical, and his meagre appearance, always occasion a loud laugh, and but ill dispose us to take the solemnity of the ensuing scene.

Mr. Otway was doubtless fearful of going too far, or he had removed everything which prevents this piece from being perfect. It must be owned he has improved and heightened every beauty that could receive addition, and been extremely tender in preserving all those intire which are above the reach of amendment. Nor is his judgment in this particular less to be admired than his candour. Some poets, perhaps, to show their own abilities, would have put a long soliloquy into the mouth of young Marius, when he finds Lavinia at her window, at a time of night when it was but just possible for him to distinguish it was she; whereas this judicious emendator leaves his author here as he found him; and indeed what could so emphatically express the feeling of a lover on such an occasion, as is couched in this short acclamation!

> Oh 'tis my love!
> See how she hangs upon the cheek of night,
> Like a rich jewel in an Ethiop's ear.

Nor is the tenderness and innocence of Lavinia less conveyed to us, when in the fulness of her heart, and unsuspecting she was overheard by any body, she cries out,

> O Marius! Marius! wherefore art thou Marius!
> Renounce thy family, deny thy name,
> And in exchange take all Lavinia.

I mention these two places merely because they strike my own fancy in a peculiar manner; for the whole piece abounds with other equally strong, natural, and pathetic, and is, in my opinion, and that of many others, the very best and most agreeable of all the tragedies of that excellent author.

Johnson's comedies, though they have less of fire and fancy than most of those of the foregoing author, yet are infinitely more correct, therefore stand in need of little other alteration than what the omission of some scenes which render them too long for performance, must necessarily occasion, and which is the fault of most of those who wrote in former ages.

Beaumont and Fletcher have left us many excellent plays; those of them which are modernized afford us very agreeable matter of entertainment; and there are many others, which would be no less pleasing, if revived with a very few alterations.

So also of Shirley, Broom, Massinger, and other ancient poets, under the care of a skilful hand, might come in for their share of applause. But I must still agree with Distrario, that in complaisance to the part, the stage ought not to be shut from the present; that living geniuses should at least be admitted to a probation; and that our immediate descendants should not have it in their power to accuse us of a partiality our ancestors were not guilty of.

But I am very much afraid the apprehensions Distrario labours under on this head are too justly founded, and that the person whom he consulted on the choice of his fable, spoke no more than the sentiments of those in a superior class; and if this should happen to be the case, it will be in vain for us to hope for any new performance in the dramatic way that will be worth our seeing.

It seems, however, extremely strange that it should be a crime to represent on the stage, those transactions which are in history, and every body has the privilege of reading and commenting on in any other kind of writing.

But it may be thought impertinent by some, and too arrogant by others, in me to pretend to argue on a matter equally impossible to account for, as to remedy; I shall therefore forbear any farther discourse upon it, and proceed to the next letter on the table.

Giambattista Vico 1668–1744

Giambattista Vico was an Italian philosopher of cultural history whose *New Science* was a reaction against the rationalistic theories of history and language current in the eighteenth century. Although his work received little attention during his life, its focus on the languages of poetry, myth, and ritual anticipated romantic criticism, modern anthropology, and contemporary archetypal criticism.

Vico was born on June 23, 1668, in Naples. His father was a bookseller, and the family home was a mud-floored, ground-level room that served as bookshop, living room, and kitchen. Vico attended various schools, including a Jesuit college, for short periods of time, but was largely self-taught. In his early studies, he was most influenced by Plato, the Roman historian Tacitus, and the Italian statesman and political philosopher Machiavelli. Vico frequented the fashionable salons in Naples, where he met many of the most influential scholars of his day. Gradually this circle became attracted to the ideas of Descartes, Spinoza, and Locke, which were penetrating Naples by the end of the seventeenth century. In 1699 Vico obtained a chair of rhetoric at the University of Naples. The outlines of the work he was to call *Scienza nuova* ("*The New Science*") first appeared in 1720–21 in a legal treatise. The outline, written in Latin, appeared in a chapter entitled "Nova Scientia Tentatur" ("The New Science Attempted"). The work finally appeared in 1725 under the title *Scienza nuova* but was unsuccessful. Vico spent the rest of his life revising and restructuring his work. The definitive edition did not appear until after his death in 1744.

The New Science speculates on the origins "of divine and human institutions." It counters the prevailing eighteenth-century rationalism of Descartes, Spinoza, and Locke, by seeing the origins of history and abstract philosophy in the poetic rather than vice versa. Unlike Locke, for whom figurative language was a sometimes dangerous deviation from the proper use of language, Vico sees the language of poetry, ritual, and myth as prior to the transparent language of philosophy and history. Poetry, far from being an imitation of historical "reality," preceded history and was, in fact, the first history. Vico divides the history of the "gentile nations" (by which he means pagans) into three ages: the age of the gods, the age of heroes, and the age of men. Each is distinguished by its own language: the first by the language of myth, symbol, and ritual; the second by poetry; and the last by the utilitarian language of philosophy and history. As his "search for the true Homer" suggests, the ancient poets, and Homer in particular, are central to Vico's scheme because they function as a bridge between the heroic age of myth, symbol, and ritual and the present "demotic" age of law, history, and philosophy.

from THE NEW SCIENCE

31. This New Science or metaphysic, studying the common nature of nations in the light of divine providence, discovers the origins of divine and human institutions among the gentile nations, and thereby establishes a system of the natural law of the gentes, which proceeds with the greatest equality and constancy through the three ages which the Egyptians handed down to us as the three periods through which the world has passed up to their time. These are: (1) The age of the gods, in which the gentiles believed they lived under divine governments, and everything was commanded them by auspices and oracles, which are the oldest institutions in profane history. (2) The age of the heroes, in which they reigned everywhere in aristocratic commonwealths, on account of a certain superiority of nature which they held themselves to have over the plebs. (3) The age of men, in which all men recognized themselves as equal in human nature, and therefore there were established first the popular commonwealths and then the monarchies, both of which are forms of human government.

32. In harmony with these three kinds of nature and government, three kinds of language were spoken which compose the vocabulary of this Science: (1) That of the time of the families when gentile men were newly received into humanity. This, we shall find, was a mute language of signs and physical objects having natural relations to the ideas they wished to express. (2) That spoken by means of heroic emblems, or similitudes, comparisons, images, metaphors, and natural descriptions, which make up the great body of the heroic language which was spoken at the time the heroes reigned. (3) Human language using words agreed upon by the people, a language of which they are absolute lords, and which is proper to the popular commonwealths and monarchical states; a language whereby the people may fix the meaning of the laws by which the nobles as well as the plebs are bound. Hence, among all nations, once the laws had been put into the vulgar tongue, the science of laws passed from the control of the nobles. Hitherto, among all nations, the nobles, being also priests, had kept the laws in a secret language as a sacred thing. That is the natural reason for the secrecy of the laws among the Roman patricians until popular liberty arose.

Now these are the same three languages that the Egyptians claimed had been spoken before in their world, corresponding exactly both in number and in sequence to the three ages that had run the course before them. (1) The hieroglyphic or sacred or secret language, by means of mute acts. This is suited to the uses of religion, for which observance is more important than discussion. (2) The symbolic, by means of similitudes, such as we have just seen the heroic language to have been. (3) The epistolary or vulgar, which served the common uses of life. These three types of language are found among the Chaldeans, Scythians, Egyptians, Germans, and all the other ancient gentile nations; although hieroglyphic writing survived longest among the Egyptians, because for a longer time than the others they were closed to all foreign nations (as for the same reason it still survives among the Chinese, and hence we have a proof of the vanity of their imagined remote antiquity.

33. We here bring to light the beginnings

not only of languages but also of letters, which philology has hitherto despaired of finding. We shall give a specimen of the extravagant and monstrous opinions that have been held up to now. We shall observe that the unhappy cause of this effect is that philologists have believed that among the nations languages first came into being and then letters; whereas (to give here a brief indication of what will be fully proved in this volume) letters and languages were born twins and proceeded apace through all their three stages. These beginnings are precisely exhibited in the causes of the Latin language, as set forth in the first edition of the *New Science* (which is the second of the three passages on whose account we do not regret that book). By the reasoning out of these causes many discoveries have been made in ancient Roman history, government, and law, as you will observe a thousand times, O reader, in this volume. From this example, scholars of oriental languages, of Greek, and, among the modern languages, particularly of German, which is a mother language, will be enabled to make discoveries of antiquities far beyond their expectations and ours.

34. We find that the principle of these origins both of languages and of letters lies in the fact that the first gentile peoples, by a demonstrated necessity of nature, were poets who spoke in poetic characters. This discovery, which is the master key of this Science, has cost us the persistent research of almost all our literary life, because with our civilized natures we [moderns] cannot at all imagine and can understand only by great toil the poetic nature of these first men. The [poetic] characters of which we speak were certain imaginative genera (images for the most part of animate substances, of gods or heroes, formed by their imagination) to which they reduced all the species or all the particulars appertaining to each genus; exactly as the fables of human times, such as those of late comedy, are intelligible genera reasoned out by moral philosophy, from which the comic poets form imaginative genera (for the best ideas of the various human types are nothing but that) which are the persons of the comedies. These divine or heroic characters were true fables or myths, and their allegories are found to contain meanings not analogical but univocal, not philosophical but historical, of the peoples of Greece of those times.

Since these genera (for that is what the fables in essence are) were formed by most vigorous imaginations, as in men of the feeblest reasoning powers, we discover in them true poetic sentences, which must be sentiments clothed in the greatest passions and therefore full of sublimity and arousing wonder. Now the sources of all poetic locution are two: poverty of language and need to explain and be understood. Heroic speech followed immediately on the mute language of acts and objects that had natural relations to the ideas they were meant to signify, which was used in the divine times. Lastly, in the necessary natural course of human institutions, language among the Assyrians, Syrians, Phoenicians, Egyptians, Greeks, and Latins began with heroic verses, passed thence to iambics, and finally settled into prose. This gives certainty to the history of the ancient poets and explains why in the German language, particularly in Silesia, a province of peasants, there are many natural versifiers, and in the Spanish, French and Italian languages the first authors wrote in verse. . . .

SECTION I

SEARCH FOR THE TRUE HOMER

[Chapter I] The Esoteric Wisdom Attributed to Homer

781. Let us concede to Homer what certainly must be granted, that he had to conform to the quite vulgar feelings and hence the vulgar customs of the barbarous Greece of his day, for such vulgar feelings and vulgar customs provide the poets with their proper materials. Let us therefore concede to him what he narrates: that the gods are esteemed according to their strength, as by his supreme strength Jove attempts to show, in the fable of the great chain, that he is the king of men and gods. On the basis of this vulgar opinion he makes it credible that Diomed can wound Venus and Mars with the help of Minerva, who, in the contest of the gods, despoils Venus and strikes Mars with a rock (and Minerva forsooth was the goddess of philosophy in vulgar belief, and uses weapons so worthy of the wisdom of Jove!). Let us allow him to tell of the inhuman custom (so contrary to what the writers on the natural law of the gentes claim to have been eternally practiced among the nations) which then prevailed among the barbarous peoples of Greece (who are held to have spread humanity through the world): to wit, that of poisoning arrows (for Ulysses goes to Ephyra to seek poisonous herbs for this purpose, and further, that of denying burial to enemies slain in battle, leaving their unburied bodies instead as a prey to dogs and vultures (on which account the unhappy Priam found so costly the ransom of his son's body, though the naked corpse of Hector had already been dragged by Achilles's chariot three times around the walls of Troy).

782. Nevertheless, if the purpose of poetry is to tame the ferocity of the vulgar whose teachers the poets are, it was not the part of a wise man, versed in such fierce feelings and customs, to arouse admiration of them in the vulgar in order that they should take pleasure in them and be confirmed in them by that pleasure. Nor was it the part of a wise man to arouse pleasure in the villainous vulgar at the villainies of the gods, to say nothing of the heroes. As, for example, we read of Mars in the midst of the contest calling Minerva a dog-fly, and of Minerva punching Diana (i.e., Venus), and of Agememnon and Achilles, the latter the greatest of the Greek heroes and the former the head of the Greek league, and both of them kings, calling each other dogs, as servants in popular comedies would scarcely do nowadays.

783. But what name under heaven more appropriate than sheer stupidity can be given to the wisdom of his captain, Agamemnon? For he has to be compelled by Achilles to do his duty in restoring Chryseis to Chryses, her father, priest of Apollo, the god who, on account of this rape, was decimating the Greek army with a cruel pestilence. And then, holding himself offended, Agamemnon thought to regain his honor by an act of justice of a piece with his wisdom, by wrongfully stealing Briseis from Achilles, who bore in his person the fate of Troy, so that, on his withdrawing in anger with his men and ships, Hector might make short work of the Greeks still surviving the pestilence. Here is the Homer hitherto considered the architect of Greek polity or civility, starting with such an episode the thread with which he weaves the whole *Iliad*, the principal actors of which are such a captain [as Agamemnon] and such a hero as we have shown Achilles

to be when we spoke of the Heroism of the First Peoples. Here is the Homer unrivaled in creating poetic characters, the greatest of which are so discordant with this civil human nature of ours, yet perfectly decorous in relation to the punctilious heroic nature.

784. What are we then to say of his representing his heroes as delighting so much in wine, and, whenever they are troubled in spirit, finding all their comfort, yes, and above all others the wise Ulysses, in getting drunk? Fine precepts for consolation, most worthy of a philosopher!

785. [J. C.] Scaliger [*Poetices* 5.3] is indignant at finding almost all his comparisons to be taken from beasts and other savage things. But even if we admit that they were necessary to Homer in order to make himself better understood by the wild and savage vulgar, nevertheless to attain such success in them—for his comparisons are incomparable—is certainly not characteristic of a mind chastened and civilized by any sort of philosophy. Nor could the truculent and savage style in which he describes so many, such varied, and such bloody battles, so many and such extravagantly cruel kinds of butchery as make up all the sublimity of the *Iliad* in particular, have originated in a mind touched and humanized by any philosophy.

786. The constancy, moreover, which is developed and fixed by the study of the wisdom of the philosophers, could not have depicted gods and heroes of such instability. For some, though deeply moved and distressed, are quieted and calmed by the slightest contrary suggestion; others, though boiling with violent wrath, if they chance to recall some sad event, break into bitter tears. (Just so, in the returned barbarism of Italy, at the end of which came Dante, the Tuscan Homer, who also sang only of history, we read of Cola di Rienzo, whose biography we said above exhibited vividly the customs of the Greek heroes as described by Homer, that when he spoke of the unhappy Roman state oppressed by the great of that time, both he and his hearers broke down in uncontrollable tears.[1]) Others, conversely, when deep in grief, if some pleasant diversion offers itself, like the banquet of Alcinous in the case of the wise Ulysses, completely forget their troubles and give themselves over to hilarity. Others, quiet and calm, at some innocent remark which is not to their humor, react with such violence and fly into such a blind rage as to threaten the speaker with a frightful death. So it is with Achilles when he receives Priam in his tent on the afore-mentioned occasion when the latter, protected by Mercury, has come through the Greek camp by night and all alone in order to ransom the body of Hector. Achilles receives him at dinner and, because of a little phrase that does not please him and which has fallen inadvertently from the mouth of the unhappy father grieving for such a valorous son, flies into a rage. Forgetting the sacred laws of hospitality, unmindful of the simple faith in which Priam has come all alone to him because he trusts completely in him alone, unmoved by the many great misfortunes of such a king or by pity for such a father or by the veneration due to so old a man, heedless of the common lot which avails more than anything else to arouse compassion, he allows his bestial wrath to reach such a point as to thunder at him that he will cut off his head. The same Achilles, even while impiously determined not to forgive a private injury at the hands of Agamemnon (which, grave though it was, could not justly be avenged by the ruin of their fatherland and of their entire nation), is pleased—he who carries with him the fate of Troy—to see all the Greeks fall to ruin and suffer miserable defeat at Hector's hands; nor is he moved by love of country or by his nation's glory to bring them any aid. He does it, finally, only to satisfy a purely private grief, the slaying of his friend Patroclus by

Hector. And not even in death is he placated for the loss of his Briseis until the unhappy beautiful royal maiden Polyxena, of the ruined house of the once rich and puissant Priam, but now become a miserable slave, has been sacrificed before his tomb, and his ashes, thirsting for vengeance, have drunk up the last drop of her blood [Euripides, *Hecuba* 37, 220f]. To say nothing of what is really past understanding: that a philosopher's gravity and propriety of thought could have been possessed by a man who amused himself by inventing so many fables worthy of old women entertaining children, as those with which Homer stuffed his other poem, the *Odyssey*.

787. Such crude, course, wild, savage, volatile, unreasonable or unreasonably obstinate, frivolous, and foolish customs as we set forth in Book Two in the Corollaries on the Heroic Nature, can pertain only to men who are like children in the weakness of their minds, like women in the vigor of their imaginations, and like violent youths in the turbulence of their passions; whence we must deny to Homer any kind of esoteric wisdom. These are the considerations which first gave rise to the doubts that put us under the necessity of seeking out the true Homer. . . .

[Chapter IV] Homer's Matchless Faculty for Heroic Poetry

806. The complete absence of philosophy which we have shown in Homer, and our discoveries concerning his fatherland and his age, arouse in us a strong suspicion that he may perhaps have been quite simply a man of the people. This suspicion is confirmed by Horace's observation in his *Art of Poetry* concerning the desperate difficulty of creating fresh characters or persons of tragedy after Homer, on account of which he advises poets to take their characters from Homer's poems. Now this grave difficulty must be taken in conjunction with the fact that the personages of the New Comedy are all of artificial creation; indeed, there was an Athenian law requiring the New Comedy to appear on the stage with characters entirely fictitious, and the Greeks managed this so successfully that the Latins, for all their pride, despaired of competing, as Quintilian acknowledged in saying: *Cum graecis de comoedia non contendimus*, "We do not rival the Greeks in comedy."

807. To Horace's difficulty we must add two others of wider scope. For one thing, how is it that Homer, who came first, was such an inimitable heroic poet, while tragedy, which was born later, began with the crudeness familiar to everybody and which we shall later describe more in detail? And for another, how is it that Homer, who preceded philosophy and the poetic and critical arts, was yet the most sublime of all the sublime poets, and that after the invention of philosophies and of the arts of poetry and criticism there was no poet who could come within a long distance of competing with him? However, putting aside our two difficulties, that of Horace combined with what we have said of the New Comedy should have spurred scholars like Patrizzi, Scaliger, and Castelvetro and other valiant masters of the poetic art to investigate the reason for the difference.

808. The reason cannot be found elsewhere than in the origin of poetry, as discovered above in the Poetic Wisdom, and consequently in the discovery of the poetic characters in which alone consists the essence of poetry itself. For the New Comedy portrays our present human customs, on which the Socratic philosophy had meditated, and hence, from the latter's general maxims concerning human morals, the Greek poets, profundly steeped in that doctrine (as was Menander for example, in comparison with whom Terence was called even by the

Latins "half a Menander"), could create certain luminous examples of ideal human types, by the light and splendor of which they might awaken the vulgar, who are as quick to learn from convincing examples as they are incapable of understanding from reasoned maxims. The Old Comedy took arguments or subjects from real life and made plays of them just as they were, as the wicked Aristophanes once did with the good Socrates, thus bringing on his ruin. But tragedy puts on the scene heroic hatred, scorn, wrath, and revenge, which spring from sublime natures which naturally are the source of sentiments, modes of speech, and actions in general that are wild, crude, and terrible. Such arguments are clothed with an air of marvel, and all these matters are in closest conformity among themselves and uniform in their subjects. Such works the Greeks could produce only in the time of their heroism, at the end of which Homer must have come. This is shown by the following metaphysical criticism. The fables, which at their birth had come forth direct and proper, reached Homer distorted and perverted. As may be seen throughout the Poetic Wisdom above set forth, they were all at first true histories, which were gradually altered and corrupted, and in their corrupt form finally came down to Homer. Hence he must be assigned to the third age of the heroic poets. The first age invented the fables to serve as true narratives, the primary and proper meaning of the word *mythos*, as defined by the Greeks themselves, being "true narration." The second altered and corrupted them. The third and last, that of Homer, received them thus corrupted.

809. But, to return to our purpose, for the reason assigned by us to this effect, Aristotle in his *Poetics* says that only Homer knew how to invent poetic falsehoods. For his poetic characters, which are incomparable for the sublime appropriateness which Horace admires in them, were imaginative universals, as defined above in the Poetic Metaphysics, to which the peoples of Greece attached all the various particulars belonging to each genus. To Achilles, for example, who is the subject of the *Iliad*, they attached all the properties of heroic valor, and all the feelings and customs arising from these natural properties, such as those of quick temper, punctiliousness, wrathfulness, implacability, violence, the arrogation of all right to might, as they are summed up by Horace in his description of this character. To Ulysses, the subject of the *Odyssey*, they attached all the feelings and customs of heroic wisdom; that is, those of wariness, patience, dissimulation, duplicity, deceit, always preserving propriety of speech and indifference of action, so that others may of themselves fall into error and may be the causes of their own deception. And to these two characters, according to kind, they attached those actions of particular men which were conspicuous enough to arouse and move the still dull and stupid Greeks to note them and refer them to their kinds. These two characters, since they had been created by an entire nation, could only be conceived as naturally uniform (in which uniformity, agreeable to the common sense of an entire nation, alone consists the decorum or beauty and charm of a fable); and, since they were created by powerful imaginations, they could not be created as anything but sublime. Hence derive two eternal properties of poetry: one that poetic sublimity is inseparable from popularity, and the other that peoples who have first created heroic characters for themselves will afterward apprehend human customs only in terms of characters made famous by luminous examples.

Note

1. *La vita di Cola Rienzo*, ed. Zefirino Re, Firenze, 1854, p. 31.

Edmund Burke 1729–1797

Although he never achieved the same prominence in aesthetic theory that he did as a statesman, orator, and political philosopher, Edmund Burke exerted considerable influence on later psychological theories of artistic value and beauty—particularly those of the German philosophers Kant and Lessing.

Born in Dublin, the second son of an Irish Protestant lawyer and his Catholic wife, Burke was educated at the Quaker school in Balitore. He entered Trinity College, Dublin, in 1744, earned a B.A. in 1748, and in 1750 was admitted to the Middle Temple in London, where he was sent to study law. He never actually practiced; instead, he turned to writing and in 1756 he published *A Vindication of Natural Society* and *A Philosophical Enquiry*. In 1764, he became secretary to the marquis of Rockingham (then prime minister) and was subsequently elected to the House of Commons. He spent most of his parliamentary career, until 1794, in opposition as a member of a group known as the "Rockingham Whigs." In 1770 he published his first major political work, *Thoughts on the Present Discontents*, in which he criticized the growing power of George III and the court. He is best known for his speeches in support of Irish Catholics, American colonists, and the native inhabitants of British India and for his opposition to the American policies of Lord North, the slave trade, and the doctrines of the French Revolution. This last issue obsessed him during the final years of his life. One of his last major works, *Reflections on the Revolution in France* (1790), a passionate defense of conservative ideals, develops at some length his abhorence of the ideals of the French Revolution. He ended his political career in virtual isolation but vigorously supporting the war against France; he died on July 9, 1797.

A Philosophical Enquiry into the Origins of Our Ideas of the Sublime and Beautiful (1756), although an early work, illustrates the shift of interest, characteristic of late eighteenth-century criticism, from the moral utility of poetry to the psychological effects of the work of art. The attempt in the introduction, "On Taste," follows Locke in tracing the abstraction back to its origins in "sensible ideas," that is, in the sense of taste. Burke defines taste as "that faculty or faculties of the mind, which are affected with, or which form a judgment of, the works of imagination and the elegant arts." If the sense of taste can be shown to be invariable in all humans, if what is sweet and sour can be discriminated by all, then the "taste" that judges aesthetic pleasure ought to be constant as well. An artistic judgment that differs from the "invariable and certain laws" of taste, then, does not reveal a difference in taste, but an ignorant or vitiated taste. If knowledge is improved, judgment is altered and taste is corrected. This examination of the faculty that regulates aesthetic pleasure lays the groundwork for Burke's analysis of the sublime and the beautiful, a comparison that depends on a network of unstated but powerful gender distinctions that are, once again, traced back to their origin in "nature" and the senses. The sublime is masculine and the beautiful feminine. Burke's analysis contributes to the attempt in eighteenth-century criticism to fix canons of judgment, to "discover" supposedly universal and timeless values of beauty that transcend historical situations or individual cases.

from A Philosophical Inquiry into the Origin of Our Ideas of the Sublime and Beautiful

Introductory Discourse

On Taste

On a superficial view, we may seem to differ very widely from each other in our reasonings, and no less in our pleasures: but notwithstanding this difference, which I think to be rather apparent than real, it is probable that the standard both of reason and taste is the same in all human creatures. For if there were not some principles of judgment as well as of sentiment common to all mankind, no hold could possibly be taken either on their reason or their passions, sufficient to maintain the ordinary correspondence of life. It appears indeed to be generally acknowledged, that with regard to truth and falsehood there is something fixed. We find people in their disputes continually appealing to certain tests and standards, which are allowed on all sides, and are supposed to be established in our common nature. But there is not the same obvious concurrence in any uniform or settled principles which relate to taste. It is even commonly supposed that this delicate and aërial faculty, which seems too volatile to endure even the chains of a definition, cannot be properly tried by any test, nor regulated by any standard. There is so continual a call for the exercise of the reasoning faculty, and it is so much strengthened by perpetual contention, that certain maxims of right reason seem to be tacitly settled amongst the most ignorant. The learned have improved on this rude science, and reduced those maxims into a system. If taste has not been so happily cultivated, it was not that the subject was barren, but that the labourers were few or negligent; for, to say the truth, there are not the same interesting motives to impel us to fix the one, which urge us to ascertain the other. And, after all, if men differ in their opinion concerning such matters, their difference is not attended with the same important consequences; else I make no doubt but that the logic of taste, if I may be allowed the expression, might very possibly be as well digested, and we might come to discuss matters of this nature with as much certainty, as those which seem more immediately within the province of mere reason. And indeed, it is very necessary, at the entrance into such an inquiry as our present, to make this point as clear as possible; for if taste has no fixed principles, if the imagination is not affected according to some invariable and certain laws, our labour is likely to be employed to very little purpose; as it must be judged a useless, if not an absurd undertaking, to lay down rules for caprice, and to set up for a legislator of whims and fancies.

The term taste, like all other figurative terms, is not extremely accurate; the thing which we understand by it is far from a simple and determinate idea in the minds of most men, and it is therefore liable to uncertainty and confusion. I have no great opinion of a definition, the celebrated remedy for the cure of this disorder. For, when we define, we seem in danger of circumscribing nature within the bounds of our own notions, which we often take up by hazard, or embrace on trust, or form out of a limited and partial consideration of the object before us; instead of extending our ideas to take in all that nature comprehends, according to her manner of combining. We are limited in our inquiry by the strict laws to which we have submitted at our setting out.

A definition may be very exact, and yet go but a very little way towards informing us of the nature of the thing defined; but let the virtue of a definition be what it will, in the order of things, it seems rather to follow than to precede our inquiry, of which it ought to be considered as the result. It must be acknowledged, that the methods of disquisition and teaching may be sometimes different, and on very good reason undoubtedly; but, for my part, I am convinced that the method of teaching which approaches most nearly to the method of investigation is incomparably the best; since, not content with serving up a few barren and lifeless truths, it leads to the stock on which they grew; it tends to set the reader himself in the track of invention, and to direct him into those paths in which the author has made his own discoveries, if he should be so happy as to have made any that are valuable.

But to cut off all pretence for cavilling, I mean by the word Taste no more than that faculty or those faculties of the mind, which are affected with, or which form a judgment of, the works of imagination and the elegant arts. This is, I think, the most general idea of that word, and what is the least connected with any particular theory. And my point in this inquiry is, to find whether there are any principles, on which the imagination is affected, so common to all, so grounded and certain, as to supply the means of reasoning satisfactorily about them. And such principles of taste I fancy there are; however paradoxical it may seem to those, who on a superficial view imagine, that there is so great a diversity of tastes, both in kind and degree, that nothing can be more indeterminate.

All the natural powers in man, which I know, that are conversant about external objects, are the senses; the imagination; and the judgment. And first with regard to the senses. We do and we must suppose, that as the conformation of their organs are nearly or altogether the same in all men, so the manner of perceiving external objects is in all men the same, or with little difference. We are satisfied that what appears to be light to one eye, appears light to another; that what seems sweet to one palate, is sweet to another; that what is dark and bitter to this man, is likewise dark and bitter to that; and we conclude in the same manner of great and little, hard and soft, hot and cold, rough and smooth, and indeed of all the natural qualities and affections of bodies. If we suffer ourselves to imagine, that their senses present to different men different images of things, this sceptical proceeding will make every sort of reasoning on every subject vain and frivolous, even that sceptical reasoning itself which had persuaded us to entertain a doubt concerning the agreement of our perceptions. But as there will be little doubt that bodies present similar images to the whole species, it must necessarily be allowed, that the pleasures and the pains which every object excites in one man, it must raise in all mankind, whilst it operates naturally, simply, and by its proper powers only; for if we deny this, we must imagine that the same cause, operating in the same manner, and on subjects of the same kind, will produce different effects; which would be highly absurd. Let us first consider this point in the sense of taste, and the rather, as the faculty in question has taken its name from that sense. All men are agreed to call vinegar sour, honey sweet, and aloes bitter; and as they are all agreed in finding these qualities in those objects, they do not in the least differ concerning their effects with regard to pleasure and pain. They all concur in calling sweetness pleasant, and sourness and bitterness unpleasant. Here there is no diversity in their sentiments; and that there is not, appears fully from the consent of all men in the metaphors which are taken from the sense of taste. A sour temper, bitter expressions, bitter curses, a bitter fate, are terms well and strongly understood by all. And we are altogether as well understood when we say, a sweet disposition, a sweet person, a sweet condition, and the like. It is confessed, that custom and some other causes have made many deviations from the natural pleasures or pains which belong to these several tastes: but then the power of distinguishing between the natural and the acquired relish remains to the very last. A man frequently comes to prefer the taste of tobacco to that of sugar, and the flavour of vinegar to that of milk; but this makes no confusion in tastes, whilst he is sensible that the tobacco and vinegar are not sweet, and whilst he knows that habit alone has reconciled his palate to these alien pleasures. Even with such a person we may speak, and with sufficient precision, concerning tastes. But should any man be found who declares, that to him tobacco has a taste like sugar, and that he cannot distinguish between milk and vinegar; or that tobacco and vinegar are sweet, milk bitter, and sugar sour; we immediately conclude that the organs of this man are out of order, and that his palate is utterly vitiated. We are as far from conferring with such a person upon tastes, as from reasoning concerning the relations of quantity with one who should deny that all the parts together were equal to the whole. We do not call a man of this kind wrong in his notions, but absolutely mad. Exceptions of this sort, in either way, do not at all impeach our general rule, nor make us conclude that men have various principles concerning the relations of quantity or the taste of things. So that when it is said, taste cannot be disputed, it can only mean, that no one can strictly answer what pleasure or pain some particular man may find from the taste of some particular thing. This indeed cannot be disputed; but we may dispute, and with sufficient clearness too, concerning the things which are naturally pleasing or disagreeable to the sense. But when we talk of any peculiar or acquired relish, then we must know the habits, the prejudices, or the distempers of this particular man, and we must draw our conclusion from those.

This agreement of mankind is not confined to the taste solely. The principle of pleasure derived from sight is the same in all. Light is more pleasing than darkness. Summer, when the earth is clad in green, when the heavens are serene and bright, is more agreeable than winter, when everything makes a different appearance. I never remember that anything beautiful, whether a man, a beast, a bird, or a plant, was ever shown, though it were to a hundred people, that they did not all immediately agree that it was beautiful, though some might have thought that it fell short of their expectation, or that other things were still finer. I believe no man thinks a goose to be more beautiful than a swan, or imagines that what they call a Friezland hen excels a peacock. It must be observed, too, that the pleasures of the sight are not near so complicated, and confused, and altered by unnatural habits and associations, as the pleasures of the taste are; because the pleasures of the sight more commonly acquiesce in themselves; and are not so often altered by considerations which are independent of the sight itself. But things do not spontaneously present themselves to the palate as they do to the sight; they are generally applied to it, either as food or as medicine; and, from the qualities which they possess for nutritive or medicinal purposes, they often form the palate by degrees, and by force of these associations. Thus opium is pleasing to Turks, on account of the agreeable delirium it produces. Tobacco is the delight of Dutchmen, as it diffuses a torpor and pleasing stupefaction. Fermented spirits please our common people, because they banish care, and all consideration of future or present evils. All of these would lie absolutely neglected if their properties had originally gone no further than the taste; but all these together, with tea and coffee, and some other things, have passed from the apothecary's shop to our tables, and were taken for health long before they were thought of for pleasure. The effect of the drug has made us use it frequently; and frequent use, combined with the agreeable effect, has made the taste itself at last agreeable. But this does not in the least perplex our reasoning; because we distinguish to the last the acquired from the natural relish. In describing the taste of an unknown fruit, you would scarcely say that it had a sweet and pleasant flavour like tobacco, opium, or garlic, although you spoke to those who were in the constant use of these drugs, and had great pleasure in them. There is in all men a sufficient remembrance of the original natural causes of pleasure, to enable them to bring all things offered to their senses to that standard, and to regulate their feelings and opinions by it. Suppose one who had so vitiated his palate as to take more pleasure in the taste of opium than in that of butter or honey, to be presented with a bolus of squills; there is hardly any doubt but that he would prefer the butter or honey to this nauseous morsel, or to any bitter drug to which he had not been accustomed; which proves that his palate was naturally like that of other men in all things, that it is still like the palate of other men in many things, and only vitiated in some particular points. For in judging of any new thing, even of a taste similar to that which he has been formed by habit to like, he finds his palate affected in a natural manner, and on the common principles. Thus the pleasure of all the senses, of the sight, and even of the taste, that most ambiguous of the senses, is the same in all, high and low, learned and unlearned.

Besides the ideas, with their annexed pains and pleasures, which are presented by the sense; the mind of man possesses a sort of creative power of its own; either in representing at pleasure the images of things in the order and manner in which they were received by the senses, or in combining those images in a new manner, and according to a different order. This power is called imagination; and to this belongs whatever is called wit, fancy, invention, and the like. But it must be observed, that this power of the imagination is incapable of producing anything absolutely new; it can only vary the disposition of those ideas which it has received from the senses. Now the imagination is the most extensive province of pleasure and pain, as it is the region of our fears and our hopes, and of all our passions that are connected with them; and whatever is calculated to affect the imagination with these commanding ideas, by force of any original natural impression, must have the same power pretty equally over all men. For since the imagination is only the representation of the senses, it can only be pleased or displeased with the images, from the same principle on which the sense is pleased or displeased with the realities; and consequently there must be just as close an agreement in the imaginations as in the senses of men. A little attention will convince us that this must of necessity be the case.

But in the imagination, besides the pain or pleasure arising from the properties of the natural object, a pleasure is perceived from the resemblance which the imitation has to the original: the imagination, I conceive, can have no pleasure but what results from one or other of these causes. And these causes operate pretty uniformly upon all men, because they operate by principles in nature, and which are not derived from any particular habits or advantages. Mr. Locke very justly and finely observes of wit, that it is chiefly conversant in tracing resemblances: he remarks, at the same time, that the business of judgment is rather in finding differences. It may perhaps appear, on this supposition, that there is no material distinction between the wit and the judgment, as they both seem to result from different operations of the same faculty of *comparing*. But in reality, whether they are or are not dependent on the same power of the mind, they differ so very materially in many respects, that a perfect union of wit and judgment is one of the rarest things in the world. When two distinct objects are unlike to each other, it is only what we expect; things are in their common way; and therefore they make no impression on the imagination: but when two distinct objects have a resemblance, we are struck, we attend to them, and we are pleased. The mind of man has naturally a far greater alacrity and satisfaction in tracing resemblances than in searching for differences: because by making resemblances we produce *new images;* we unite, we create, we enlarge our stock; but in making distinctions we offer no food at all to the imagination; the task itself is more severe and irksome, and what pleasure we derive from it is something of a negative and indirect nature. A piece of news is told me in the morning; this, merely as a piece of news, as a fact added to my stock, gives me some pleasure. In the evening I find there was nothing in it. What do I gain by this, but the dissatisfaction to find that I have been imposed upon? Hence it is that men are much more naturally inclined to belief than to incredulity. And it is upon this principle, that the most ignorant and barbarous nations have frequently excelled in similitudes, comparisons, metaphors, and allegories, who have been weak and backward in distinguishing and sorting their ideas. And it is for a reason of this kind, that Homer and the Oriental writers, though very fond of similitudes, and though they often strike out such as are truly admirable, seldom take care to have them exact; that is, they are taken with the general resemblance, they paint it strongly, and they take no notice of the difference which may be found between the things compared.

Now, as the pleasure of resemblance is that which principally flatters the imagination, all men are nearly equal in this point, as far as their knowledge of the things represented or compared extends. The principle of this knowledge is very much accidental, as it depends upon experience and observation, and not on the strength or weakness of any natural faculty; and it is from this difference in knowledge, that what we commonly, though with no great exactness, call a difference in taste proceeds. A man to whom sculpture is new, sees a barber's block, or some ordinary piece of statuary, he is immediately struck and pleased, because he sees something like a human figure; and, entirely taken up with this likeness, he does not at all attend to its defects. No person, I believe, at the first time of seeing a piece of imitation ever did. Some time after, we suppose that this novice lights upon a more artificial work of the same nature; he now begins to look with contempt on what he admired at first; not that he admired it even then for its unlikeness to a man, but for that general, though inaccurate, resemblance which it bore to the human figure. What he admired at different times in these so different figures, is strictly the same; and though his knowledge is improved, his taste is not altered. Hitherto his mistake was from a want of knowledge in art, and this arose from his inexperience; but he may be still deficient from a want of knowledge in nature. For it is possible that the man in question may stop here, and that the masterpiece of a great hand may please him no more than the middling performance of a vulgar artist: and this not for want of better or higher relish, but because all men do not observe with sufficient accuracy on the human figure to enable them to judge properly of an imitation of it. And that the critical taste does not depend upon a superior principle in men, but upon superior knowledge, may appear from several instances. The story of the ancient painter and the shoemaker is very well known. The shoemaker set the painter right with regard to some mistakes he had made in the shoe of one of his figures, and which the painter, who had not made such accurate observations on shoes, and was content with a general resemblance, had never observed. But this was no impeachment to the taste of the painter; it only showed some want of knowledge in the art of making shoes. Let us imagine, that an anatomist had come into the painter's working-room. His piece is in general well done, the figure in question in a good attitude, and the parts well adjusted to their various movements; yet the anatomist, critical in his art, may observe the swell of some muscle not quite just in the peculiar action of the figure. Here the anatomist observes what the painter had not observed; and he passes by what the shoemaker had remarked. But a want of the last critical knowledge in anatomy no more reflected on the natural good taste of the painter or of any common observer of his piece, than the want of an exact knowledge in the formation of a shoe. A fine piece of a decollated head of St. John the Baptist was shown to a Turkish emperor; he praised many things, but he observed one defect; he observed that the skin did not shrink from the wounded part of the neck. The sultan on this occasion, though his observation was very just, discovered no more natural taste than the painter who executed this piece, or than a thousand European connoisseurs, who probably never would have made the same observation. His Turkish Majesty had indeed been well acquainted with that terrible spectacle, which the others could only have represented in their imagination. On the subject of their dislike there is a difference between all these people, arising from the different kinds and degrees of their knowledge; but there is something in common to the painter, the shoemaker, the anatomist, and the Turkish emperor, the pleasure arising from a natural object, so far as each perceives it justly imitated; the satisfaction in seeing an agreeable figure; the sympathy proceeding from a striking and affecting incident. So far as taste is natural, it is nearly common to all.

In poetry, and other pieces of imagination, the same parity may be observed. It is true, that one man is charmed with Don Bellianis, and reads Virgil coldly: whilst another is transported with the Eneid, and leaves Don Bellianis to children. These two men seem to have a taste very different from each other; but in fact they differ very little. In both these pieces, which inspire such opposite sentiments, a tale exciting admiration is told; both are full of action, both are passionate; in both are voyages, battles, triumphs, and continual changes of fortune. The admirer of Don Bellianis perhaps does not understand the refined language of the Eneid, who, if it was degraded into the style of the Pilgrim's Progress, might feel it in all its energy, on the same principle which made him an admirer of Don Bellianis.

In his favourite author he is not shocked with the continual breaches of probability, the confusion of times, the offences against manners, the trampling upon geography; for he knows nothing of geography and chronology, and he has never examined the grounds of probability. He perhaps reads of a shipwreck on the coast of Bohemia; wholly taken up with so interesting an event, and only solicitous for the fate of his hero, he is not in the least troubled at this extravagant blunder. For why should he be shocked at a shipwreck on the coast of Bohemia, who does not know but that Bohemia may be an island in the Atlantic ocean? and after all, what reflection is this on the natural good taste of the person here supposed?

So far then as taste belongs to the imagination, its principle is the same in all men; there is no difference in the manner of their being affected, nor in the causes of the affection; but in the *degree* there is a difference, which arises from two causes principally; either from a greater degree of natural sensibility, or from a closer and longer attention to the object. To illustrate this by the procedure of the senses, in which the same difference is found, let us suppose a very smooth marble table to be set before two men; they both perceive it to be smooth, and they are both pleased with it because of this quality. So far they agree. But suppose another, and after that another table, the latter still smoother than the former, to be set before them. It is now very probable that these men, who are so agreed upon what is smooth, and in the pleasure from thence, will disagree when they come to settle which table has the advantage in point of polish. Here is indeed the great difference between tastes, when men come to compare the excess or diminution of things which are judged by degree and not by measure. Nor is it easy, when such a difference arises, to settle the point, if the excess or diminution be not glaring. If we differ in opinion about two quantities, we can have recourse to a common measure, which may decide the question with the utmost exactness; and this, I take it, is what gives mathematical knowledge a greater certainty than any other. But in things whose excess is not judged by greater or smaller, as smoothness and roughness, hardness and softness, darkness and light, the shades of colours, all these are very easily distinguished when the difference is any way considerable, but not when it is minute, for want of some common measures, which perhaps may never come to be discovered. In these nice cases, supposing the acuteness of the sense equal, the greater attention and habit in such things will have the advantage. In the question about the tables, the marble-polisher will unquestionably determine the most accurately. But notwithstanding this want of a common measure for settling many disputes relative to the senses, and their representative the imagination, we find that the principles are the same in all, and that there is no disagreement until we come to examine into the pre-eminence or difference of things, which brings us within the province of the judgment.

So long as we are conversant with the sensible qualities of things, hardly any more than the imagination seems concerned; little more also than the imagination seems concerned when the passions are represented, because by the force of natural sympathy they are felt in all men without any recourse to reasoning, and their justness recognized in every breast. Love, grief, fear, anger, joy, all these passions have, in their turns, affected every mind; and they do not affect it in an arbitrary or casual manner, but upon certain, natural, and uniform principles. But as many of the works of imagination are not confined to the representation of sensible objects, nor to efforts upon the passions, but extend themselves to the manners, the characters, the actions, and designs of men, their relations, their virtues, and vices, they come within the province of the judgment, which is improved by attention, and by the habit of reasoning. All these make a very considerable part of what are considered as the objects of taste; and Horace sends us to the schools of philosophy and the world for our instruction in them. Whatever certainty is to be acquired in morality and the science of life; just the same degree of certainty have we in what relates to them in the works of imitation. Indeed it is for the most part in our skill in manners, and in the observances of time and place, and of decency in general, which is only to be learned in those schools to which Horace recommends us, that what is called taste, by way of distinction, consists; and which is in reality no other than a more refined judgment. On the whole it appears to me, that what is called taste, in its most general acceptance, is not a simple idea, but is partly made up of a perception of the primary pleasures of sense, of the secondary pleasures of the imagination, and of the conclusions of the reasoning faculty, concerning the various relations of these, and concerning the human passions, manners, and actions. All this is requisite to form taste, and the ground-work of all these is the same in the human mind; for as the senses are the great originals of all our ideas, and consequently of all our pleasures, if they are not uncertain and arbitrary, the whole ground-work of taste is common to all, and therefore there is a sufficient foundation for a conclusive reasoning on these matters.

Whilst we consider taste merely according to its nature and species, we shall find its principles entirely uniform; but the degree in which these principles prevail in the several individuals of mankind, is altogether as different as the principles themselves are similar. For sensibility and judgment, which are the qualities that compose what we commonly call a *taste*, vary exceedingly in various people. From a defect in the former of these qualities arises a want of taste; a weakness in the latter constitutes a wrong or a bad one. There are some men formed with feelings so blunt, with tempers so cold and phlegmatic, that they can hardly be said to be awake during the whole course of their lives. Upon such persons the most striking objects make but a faint and obscure impression. There are others so continually in the agitation of gross and merely sensual pleasures, or so occupied in the low drudgery of avarice, or so heated in the chase of honours and distinction, that their minds, which had been used continually to the storms of these violent and tempestuous passions, can hardly be put in motion by the delicate and refined play of the imagination. These men, though from a different cause, become as stupid and insensible as the former; but whenever either of these happen to be struck with any natural elegance or greatness, or with these qualities in any work of art, they are moved upon the same principle.

The cause of a wrong taste is a defect of judgment. And this may arise from a natural weakness of understanding, (in whatever the strength of that faculty may consist,) or, which is much more commonly the case, it may arise from a want of proper and well-directed exercise, which alone can make it strong and ready. Besides that ignorance, inattention, prejudice, rashness, levity, obstinacy, in short, all those passions, and all those vices, which pervert the judgment in other matters, prejudice it no less in this its more refined and elegant province. These causes produce different opinions upon everything which is an object of the understanding, without inducing us to suppose that there are no settled principles of reason. And indeed, on the whole, one may observe that there is rather less difference upon matters of taste among mankind, than upon most of those which depend upon the naked reason; and that men are far better agreed on the excellency of a description in Virgil, than on the truth or falsehood of a theory of Aristotle.

A rectitude of judgment in the arts, which may be called a good taste, does in a great measure depend upon sensibility; because, if the mind has no bent to the pleasures of the imagination, it will never apply itself sufficiently to works of that species to acquire a competent knowledge in them. But, though a degree of sensibility is requisite to form a good judgment, yet a good judgment does not necessarily arise from a quick sensibility of pleasure; it frequently happens that a very poor judge, merely by force of a greater complexional sensibility, is more affected by a very poor piece, than the best judge by the most perfect; for as everything new, extraordinary, grand, or passionate, is well calculated to affect such a person, and that the faults do not affect him, his pleasure is more pure and unmixed; and as it is merely a pleasure of the imagination, it is much higher than any which is derived from a rectitude of the judgment; the judgment is for the greater part employed in throwing stumbling-blocks in the way of the imagination, in dissipating the scenes of its enchantment, and in tying us down to the disagreeable yoke of our reason: for almost the only pleasure that men have in judging better than others, consists in a sort of conscious pride and superiority, which arises from thinking rightly; but then, this is an indirect pleasure, a pleasure which does not immediately result from the object which is under contemplation. In the morning of our days, when the senses are unworn and tender, when the whole man is awake in every part, and the gloss of novelty fresh upon all the objects that surround us, how lively at that time are our sensations, but how false and inaccurate the judgments we form of things? I despair of ever receiving the same degree of pleasure from the most excellent performance of genius, which I felt at that age from pieces which my present judgment regards as trifling and contemptible. Every trivial cause of pleasure is apt to affect the man of too sanguine a complexion: his appetite is too keen to suffer his taste to be delicate; and he is in all respects what Ovid says of himself in love,

> *Molle meum levibus cor est violabile telis,*
> *Et semper causa est, cur ego semper amem.*[1]

One of this character can never be a refined judge; never what the comic poet calls *elegans formarum spectator*. The excellence and force of a composition must always be imperfectly estimated from its effect on the minds of any, except we know the temper and character of those minds. The most powerful effects of poetry and music have been displayed, and perhaps are still displayed, where these arts are but in a very low and imperfect state. The rude hearer is affected by the principles which operate in these arts even in their rudest condition; and he is not skilful enough to perceive the defects. But as the arts advance towards their perfection, the science of criticism advances with equal pace, and the pleasure of judges is frequently interrupted by the faults which are discovered in the most finished compositions.

Before I leave this subject I cannot help taking notice of an opinion which many persons entertain, as if the taste were a separate faculty of the mind, and distinct from the judgment and imagination; a species of instinct, by which we are struck naturally, and at the first glance, without any previous reasoning, with the excellencies, or the defects, of a composition. So far as the imagination and the passions are concerned, I believe it true, that the reason is little consulted; but where disposition, where decorum, where congruity are concerned, in short, wherever the best taste differs from the worst, I am convinced that the understanding operates, and nothing else; and its operation is in reality far from being always sudden, or, when it is sudden, it is often far from being right. Men of the best taste, by consideration, come frequently to change these early and precipitate judgments, which the mind, from its aversion to neutrality and doubt, loves to form on the spot. It is known that the taste (whatever it is) is improved exactly as we improve our judgment, by extending our knowledge, by a steady attention to our object, and by frequent exercise. They who have not taken these methods, if their taste decides quickly, it is always uncertainly; and their quickness is owing to their presumption and rashness, and not to any sudden irradiation, that in a moment dispels all darkness from their minds. But they who have cultivated that species of knowledge which makes the object of taste, by degrees, and habitually, attain not only a soundness, but a readiness of judgment, as men do by the same methods on all other occasions. At first they are obliged to spell, but at last they read with ease and with celerity; but this celerity of its operation is no proof that the taste is a distinct faculty. Nobody, I believe, has attended the course of a discussion, which turned upon matters within the sphere of mere naked reason, but must have observed the extreme readiness with which the whole process of the argument is carried on, the grounds discovered, the objections raised and answered, and the conclusions drawn from premises, with a quickness altogether as great as the taste can be supposed to work with; and yet where nothing but plain reason either is or can be suspected to operate. To multiply principles for every different appearance, is useless, and unphilosophical too in a high degree.

This matter might be pursued much further; but it is not the extent of the subject which must prescribe our bounds, for what subject does not branch out to infinity? It is the nature of our particular scheme, and the single point of view in which we consider it, which ought to put a stop to our researches.

Sect. VII.—Of the Sublime

Whatever is fitted in any sort to excite the ideas of pain and danger, that is to say, whatever is in any sort terrible, or is conversant about terrible objects, or operates in a manner analogous to terror, is a source of the *sublime;* that is, it is productive of the strongest emotion which the mind is capable of feeling. I say the strongest emotion, because I am satisfied the ideas of pain are much more powerful than those which enter on the part of pleasure. Without all doubt, the torments which we may be made to suffer are much greater in their effect on the body and mind, than any pleasures which the most learned voluptuary could suggest, or than the liveliest imagination, and the most sound and exquisitely sensible body, could enjoy. Nay, I am in great doubt whether any man could be found, who would earn a life of the most perfect satisfaction, at the price of ending it in the torments, which justice inflicted in a few hours on the late unfortunate regicide in France. But as pain is stronger in its operation than pleasure, so death is in general a much more affecting idea than pain; because there are very few pains, however exquisite, which are not preferred to death: nay, what generally makes pain itself, if I may say so, more painful, is, that it is considered as an emissary of this king of terrors. When danger or pain press too nearly, they are incapable of giving any delight, and are simply terrible; but at certain distances, and with certain modifications, they may be, and they are, delightful, as we every day experience. The cause of this I shall endeavour to investigate hereafter. . . .

Sect. X.—Of Beauty

The passion which belongs to generation, merely as such, is lust only. This is evident in brutes, whose passions are more unmixed, and which pursue their purposes more directly than ours. The only distinction they observe with regard to their mates, is that of sex. It is true, that they stick severally to their own species in preference to all others. But this preference, I imagine, does not arise from any sense of beauty which they find in their species, as Mr. Addison supposes, but from a law of some other kind, to which they are subject; and this we may fairly conclude, from their apparent want of choice amongst those objects to which the barriers of their species have confined them. But man, who is a creature adapted to a greater variety and intricacy of relation, connects with the general passion the idea of some *social* qualities, which direct and heighten the appetite which he has in common with all other animals; and as he is not designed like them to live at large, it is fit that he should have something to create a preference, and fix his choice; and this in general should be some sensible quality; as no other can so quickly, so powerfully, or so surely produce its effect. The object therefore of this mixed passion, which we call love, is the *beauty* of the *sex*. Men are carried to the sex in general, as it is the sex, and by the common law of nature; but they are attached to particulars by personal *beauty*. I call beauty a social quality; for where women and men, and not only they, but when other animals give us a sense of joy and pleasure in beholding them, (and there are many that do so,) they inspire us with sentiments of tenderness and affection towards their persons; we like to have them near us, and we enter willingly into a kind of relation with them, unless we should have strong reasons to the contrary. But to what end, in many cases, this was designed, I am unable to discover; for I see no greater reason for a connexion between man and several animals who are attired in so engaging a manner, than between him and some others who entirely want this attraction, or possess it in a far weaker degree. But it is probable, that Providence did not make even this distinction, but with a view to some great end; though we cannot perceive distinctly what it is, as his wisdom is not our wisdom, nor our ways his ways. . . .

Sect. XXVII.—The Sublime and Beautiful Compared

On closing this general view of beauty, it naturally occurs, that we should compare it with the sublime; and in this comparison there appears a remarkable contrast. For sublime objects are vast in their dimensions, beautiful ones comparatively small: beauty should be smooth and polished; the great, rugged and negligent; beauty should shun the right line, yet deviate from it insensibly; the great in many cases loves the right line, and when it deviates it often makes a strong deviation: beauty should not be obscure; the great ought to be dark and gloomy: beauty should be light and delicate; the great ought to be solid, and even massive. They are indeed ideas of a very different nature, one being founded on pain, the other on pleasure; and however they may vary afterwards from the direct nature of their causes, yet these causes keep up an eternal distinction between them, a distinction never to be forgotten by any whose business it is to affect the passions. In the infinite variety of natural combinations, we must expect to find the qualities of things the most remote imaginable from each other united in the same object. We must expect also to find combinations of the same kind in the works of art. But when we consider the power of an object upon our passions, we must know that when anything is intended to affect the mind by the force of some predominant property, the affection produced is like to be the more uniform and perfect, if all the other properties or qualities of the object be of the same nature, and tending to the same design, as the principal.

> If black and white blend, soften, and unite
> A thousand ways, are there no black and white?

If the qualities of the sublime and beautiful are sometimes found united, does this prove that they are the same; does it prove that they are any way allied; does it prove even that they are not opposite and contradictory? Black and white may soften, may blend; but they are not therefore the same. Nor, when they are so softened and blended with each other, or with different colours, is the power of black as black, or of white as white, so strong as when each stands uniform and distinguished.

Note

1. "My soft heart is easily wounded,
   And the reason is that I always love."

Immanual Kant 1724–1804

Immanuel Kant was perhaps the most important philosopher of the second half of the eighteenth century in Germany. His attempt to forge comprehensive systems of knowledge, aesthetics, and ethics were enormously influential for nineteenth-century philosophy, particularly in continental Europe. His aesthetic philosophy was central to the development of German romanticism.

Born on April 22, 1724, at Königsberg in East Prussia, Kant was the fourth of eleven children. His parents were Lutherans and his early education was the Pietist school directed by his pastor. In 1740 at the age of sixteen, he entered the University of Königsberg to study theology, but after the death of his father and his failure to secure a post at the university, he left to become a private tutor. He finally completed his degree in 1755 and became a lecturer at the University of Königsberg, where he would remain for the rest of his life. In 1770, Kant was finally appointed to the chair of logic and metaphysics, a position he held until a few years before his death in 1804.

Kant is best known for his critical philosophy, which includes his three greatest works: *The Critique of Pure Reason* (1781), *The Critique of Practical Reason* (1788), and *The Critique of Judgment* (1790). These works mark the culmination of a prolific forty-year period, during which he published works in several disciplines, including philosophy, the natural sciences, anthropology, and education. *Observations on the Feeling of the Beautiful and Sublime* (1764), Kant's only aesthetic work besides *The Critique of Judgment*, is representative of his precritical aesthetic thinking. Its style is simple, yet polished, in sharp contrast to the abstract rational idealism of the *Critiques*. The treatise consists of four sections, of which three are included below. In the first section, Kant introduces the concepts of the sublime and beautiful; in the second section, he describes how these characteristics are exhibited. In the third he examines how the sublime and beautiful appear in the two sexes, and in the fourth, he examines how they appear in the different nations. Kant's treatise is the culmination of the eighteenth-century attempts to comprehend the nature of the human experience of beauty, both in art and in nature. He differs from his English counterparts in attributing the sublime and beautiful to *feeling* rather than *sense*, as Burke and Addison, drawing upon Locke, had done. The feeling of beauty or sublimity is not a uniform response to all beauties or sublimities, a simple signal of their presence, but a complex of feeling that pervades the whole mind. It is not uniform, but diverse; not localized, but pervasive.

from OBSERVATIONS ON THE FEELING OF THE BEAUTIFUL AND SUBLIME

OF THE DISTINCT OBJECTS OF THE FEELING OF THE BEAUTIFUL AND SUBLIME

SECTION ONE

The various feelings of enjoyment or of displeasure rest not so much upon the nature of the external things that arouse them as upon each person's own disposition to be moved by these to pleasure or pain. This accounts for the joy of some people over things that cause aversion in others, or the amorous passion so often a puzzle to everybody, or the lively antipathy one person feels toward something that to another is quite indifferent. The field of observation of these peculiarities of human nature extends very wide, and still conceals a rich source for discoveries that are just as pleasurable as they are instructive. For the present I shall cast my gaze upon only a few places that seem particularly exceptional in this area, and even upon these more with the eye of an observer than of a philosopher.

Because a person finds himself happy only so far as he gratifies an inclination, the feeling that makes him capable of enjoying great pleasures, without needing exceptional talents to do so, is certainly no trifle. Stout persons, whose favorite authors are their cooks and whose works of fine taste are in their cellars, will thrive on vulgar obscenities and on a coarse jest with just as lively a delight as that upon which persons of noble sensitivity pride themselves. An indolent man who loves having books read aloud to him because it is so pleasant to fall asleep that way, the merchant to whom all pleasures are trifling except those a clever man enjoys when he calculates his profits, one who loves the opposite sex only so far as he counts it among things to enjoy, the lover of the hunt, whether he hunt flies like Domitian or ferocious beasts like A. . . . ,—all these have a feeling that makes them capable of enjoying pleasures after their own fashion, without presuming to envy others or even being able so much as to conceive of other pleasures. But to that kind of feeling, which can take place without any thought whatever, I shall here pay no attention. There is still another feeling of a more delicate sort, so described either because one can enjoy it longer without satiation and exhaustion; or because it presupposes a sensitivity of the soul, so to speak, which makes the soul fitted for virtuous impulses; or because it indicates talents and intellectual excellences. It is this feeling of which I wish to consider one aspect. I shall moreover exclude from it that inclination that is fixed upon high intellectual insights, and the thrill that was possible to a Kepler, who, as Bayle reports, would not have sold one of his discoveries for a princedom. The latter sensation is quite toodelicate to belong in the present sketch, which will concern only the sensuous feeling of which also more ordinary souls are capable.

Finer feeling, which we now wish to consider, is chiefly of two kinds: the feeling of the *sublime* and that of the *beautiful*. The stirring of each is pleasant, but in different ways. The sight of a mountain whose snow-covered peak rises above the clouds, the description of a raging storm, or Milton's portrayal of the infernal kingdom, arouse enjoyment but with horror; on the other hand, the sight of flower-strewn meadows, valleys with winding brooks and covered with grazing flocks, the description of Elysium, or Homer's portrayal of the girdle of Venus, also occasion a pleasant sensation but one that is joyous and smiling. In order that the former impression could occur to us in due strength, we must have a *feeling of the sublime*, and, in order to enjoy the latter well, a *feeling of the beautiful*. Tall oaks and lonely shadows in a sacred grove are sublime; flower beds, low hedges and trees trimmed in figures are beautiful. Night is sublime, day is beautiful. Temperaments that possess a feeling for the sublime are drawn gradually, by the quiet stillness of a summer evening as the shimmering light of the stars breaks through the brown shadows of night and the lonely moon rises into view, into high feelings of friendship, of disdain for the world, of eternity. The shining day stimulates busy fervor and a feeling of gaiety. The sublime *moves*, the beautiful *charms*. The mien of a man who is undergoing the full feeling of the sublime is earnest, sometimes rigid and astonished. On the other hand the lively sensation of the beautiful proclaims itself through shining cheerfulness in the eyes, through smiling features, and often through audible mirth. The sublime is in turn of different kinds. Its feeling is sometimes accompanied with a certain dread, or melancholy; in some cases merely with quiet wonder; and in still others with a beauty completely pervading a sublime plan. The first I shall call the *terrifying sublime*, the second the *noble*, and the third the *splendid*. Deep loneliness is sublime, but in a way that stirs terror.[1] Hence great far-reaching solitudes, like the colossal Komul Desert in Tartary, have always given us occasion for peopling them with fearsome spirits, goblins, and ghouls.

The sublime must always be great; the beautiful can also be small. The sublime must be simple; the beautiful can be adorned and ornamented. A great height is just as sublime as a great depth, except that the latter is accompanied with the sensation of shuddering, the former with one of wonder. Hence the latter feeling can be the terrifying sublime, and the former the noble. The sight of an Egyptian pyramid, as Hasselquist reports, moves one far more than one can imagine from all the descriptions; but its design is simple and noble. St. Peter's in Rome is splendid; because on its frame, which is large and simple, beauty is so distributed, for example, gold, mosaic work, and so on, that the feeling of the sublime still strikes through with the greatest effect; hence the object is called splendid. An arsenal must be noble and simple, a residence castle splendid, and a pleasure palace beautiful and ornamented.

A long duration is sublime. If it is of time past, then it is noble. If it is projected into an incalculable future, then it has something of the fearsome in it. A building of the remotest antiquity is venerable. Haller's description of the coming eternity stimulates a mild horror, and of the past, transfixed wonder.

OF THE ATTRIBUTES OF THE BEAUTIFUL AND SUBLIME IN MAN IN GENERAL

Section Two

Understanding is sublime, wit is beautiful. Courage is sublime and great, artfulness is little but beautiful. Caution, said Cromwell, is a burgomaster's virtue. Veracity and honesty are simple and noble; jest and pleasant flattery are delicate and beautiful. Graciousness is the beauty of virtue. Unselfish zeal to serve is noble; refinement (*politesse*) and courtesy are beautiful. Sublime attributes stimulate esteem, but beautiful ones, love. People in whom especially the feeling for the beautiful rises seek their sincere, steadfast, and earnest friends only in need, but choose jesting, agreeable, and courteous companions for company. There is many a person whom one esteems much too highly to be able to love him. He inspires admiration, but is too far above us for us to dare approach him with the familiarity of love.

Those in whom both feelings join will find that the emotion of the sublime is stronger than that of the beautiful, but that unless the latter alternates with or accompanies, it, it tires and cannot be so long enjoyed.[2] The lively feelings to which the conversation in a select company occasionally rises must dissolve intermittently in cheerful jest, and laughing delights should make a beautiful contrast with the moved, earnest expression, allowing both kinds of feelings to alternate freely. Friendship has mainly the character of the sublime, but love between the sexes, that of the beautiful. Yet tenderness and deep esteem give the latter a certain dignity and sublimity; on the other hand, gay jest and familiarity heighten the hue of the beautiful in this emotion. *Tragedy* is distinguished from *comedy*, according to my view, chiefly in that in the first the feeling for the sublime is stirred, and in the second, that for the beautiful. In the first are portrayed magnanimous sacrifices for another's welfare, bold resolution in peril, and proven loyalty. There love is sad, fond, and full of respect; the misfortune of others stirs feelings of sympathy in the breast of the spectator and causes his generous heart to beat for the distress of others. He is gently moved, and feels the dignity of his own nature. On the other hand, comedy sets forth delicate intrigues, prodigious entanglements, and wits who know how to extricate themselves, fools who let themselves be shown up, jests and amusing characters. Here love is not sorrowful; it is pleasurable and familiar. Yet just as in other cases, the noble in this also can be united to a certain degree with the beautiful.

Even depravities and moral failings often bear, for all that, some features of the sublime or beautiful, at least so far as they appear to our sensory feeling without being tested by reason. The anger of someone fearsome is sublime, like Achilles' wrath in the *Iliad*. In general, a hero of Homer's is the terrifying sublime; one of Vergil's, on the other hand, is noble. Open bold revenge, following a great offense, bears something of the great about it; and as unlawful as it may be, nevertheless its telling moves one with both horror and gratification. When Shah Nadir was set upon at night in his tent by some conspirators, as Hanway reports, after he had already received some wounds and was defending himself in despair, he cried out, "Mercy! I will pardon you all!" One among them answered, as he raised his saber on high, "You have shown no mercy, and you deserve none." Resolute audacity in a rogue is of the greatest danger, but it moves in the telling, and even if he is dragged to a disgraceful death he nevertheless ennobles it to some extent by going to it defiantly and with disdain. On the other side, a scheme contrived deceitfully, even when it is bent on some piece of knavery, has something about it which is delicate, and is laughed at. The amorous inclination (*coquetterie*) in a delicate sense, that is, an endeavor to fascinate and charm, in an otherwise decorous person is perhaps reprehensible but still beautiful, and usually is set above the respectable, earnest bearing.

The figure of persons who please by their outward appearance falls sometimes into one, sometimes into the other sort of feeling. A large stature gains regard and esteem, a small one rather familiarity. In fact, dark coloring and black eyes are more closely related to the sublime, blue eyes and blonde coloring to the beautiful. A somewhat greater age conforms more with the qualities of the sublime, but youth with those of the beautiful. It is the same way with the distinction determined by stations; and in all the points suggested, even the costumes must accord with this distinction of feeling. Great, portly persons must observe simplicity, or at most, splendor, in their apparel; the little can be adorned and embellished. For age, darker colors and uniformity in apparel are seemly; youth radiates through lighter colored and vividly contrasting garments. Among the classes with similar power and rank, the cleric must exhibit the greatest simplicity, the statesman the most splendor. The paramour may adorn himself as he pleases.

There is also something in external circumstances which, at least according to the folly of men, concerns these sensations. High birth and title generally find people bowed in respect. Wealth without merit is honored even by the disinterested, presumably because with its idea we associate projects of great actions which can be carried out by its means. This respect falls occasionally to many a rich scoundrel, who will never perform such actions and has no concept of the noble feeling that alone can make riches valuable. What increases the evil of poverty is contempt, which cannot be completely overcome even by merits, at least not before common eyes, unless rank and title deceive this coarse feeling and to some extent impose upon its advantage.

In human nature, praiseworthy qualities never are found without concurrent variations that must run through endless shadings to the utmost imperfection. The quality of the *terrifying sublime*, if it is quite unnatural, is adventurous.[3] Unnatural things, so far as the sublime is supposed in them, although little or none at all may actually be found, are *grotesque*. Whoever loves and believes the fantastic is a *visionary;* the inclination toward whims makes the *crank*. On the other side, if the noble is completely lacking the feeling of the beautiful degenerates, and one calls it *trifling*. A male person of this quality, if he is young, is named a *fop;* if he is of middle age, he is a *dandy*. Since the sublime is most necessary to the elderly, an *old dandy* is the most contemptible creature in nature, just as a young crank is the most offensive and intolerable. Jests and liveliness pertain to the feeling of the beautiful. Nevertheless, much understanding can fittingly shine through, and to that extent they can be more or less related to the sublime. He in whose sprightliness this admixture is not detectable *chatters*. He who perpetually chatters is *silly*. One easily notices that even clever persons occasionally chatter, and that not a little intellect is needed to call the understanding away from its post for a short time without anything going wrong thereby. He whose words or deeds neither entertain nor move one is *boring*. The bore, if he is nevertheless zealous to do both, is *insipid*. The insipid one, if he is conceited, is a fool.[4]

I shall make this curious sketch of human frailties somewhat more understandable by examples; for he to whom Hogarth's engraving stylus is wanting must compensate by description for what the drawing lacks in expression. Bold acceptance of danger for our own, our country's or our friends' rights is sublime. The crusades and ancient knighthood were adventurous; duels, a wretched remnant of the latter arising from a perverted concept of chivalry, are grotesque. Melancholy separation from the bustle of the world due to a legitimate weariness is noble. Solitary devotion by the ancient hermits was adventurous. Monasteries and such tombs, to confine the living saints, are grotesque. Subduing one's passions through principles is sublime. Castigation, vows, and other such monks' virtues are grotesque. Holy bones, holy wood, and all similar rubbish, the holy stool of the High Lama of Tibet not excluded, are grotesque. Of the works of wit and fine feeling, the epic poems of Vergil and Klopstock fall into the noble, of Homer and Milton into the adventurous. The *Metamorphoses* of Ovid are grotesque; the fairy tales of French foolishness are the most miserable grotesqueries ever hatched. Anacreontic poems are generally very close to the trifling.

Works of understanding and ingenuity, so far as their objects also contain something for feeling, likewise take some part in the differences now being considered. Mathematical representation of the infinite magnitude of the universe, the meditations of metaphysics upon eternity, Providence, and the immortality of our souls contain a certain sublimity and dignity. On the other hand, philosophy is distorted by many empty subtleties, and the superficial appearance of profundity cannot prevent our regarding the four syllogistic figures as scholastic trifling.

Among moral attributes true virtue alone is sublime. There are nevertheless good moral qualities that are amiable and beautiful, and, so far as they harmonize with virtue, will also be regarded as noble, although they cannot properly be included within the virtuous disposition. The judgment concerning this is subtle and complex. Of course one cannot call that state of mind virtuous which is a source of such actions as might be grounded in virtue itself but whose actual cause accords with virtue only accidentally, and which may often, by its very nature, conflict with the general rules of virtue. A certain tenderheartedness, which is easily stirred into a warm feeling of *sympathy*, is beautiful and amiable; for it shows a charitable interest in the lot of other men, to which principles of virtue likewise lead. But this good-natured passion is nevertheless weak and always blind. For suppose that this feeling stirs you to help a needy person with your expenditure. But you are indebted to another, and doing this makes it impossible for you to fulfill the stern duty of justice. Thus the action obviously cannot spring from a virtuous design; for such could not possibly induce you to sacrifice a higher obligation to this blind fascination. On the other hand, when universal affection toward the human species has become a principle within you to which you always subordinate your actions, then love toward the needy one still remains; but now, from a higher standpoint, it has been placed in its true relation to your total duty. Universal affection is a ground of your interest in his plight, but also of the justice by whose rule you must now forbear this action. Now as soon as this feeling has arisen to its proper universality, it has become sublime, but also colder. For it is not possible that our heart should swell from fondness for every man's interest and should swim in sadness at every stranger's need; else the virtuous man, incessantly dissolving like Heraclitus in compassionate tears, nevertheless with all this goodheartedness would become nothing but a tenderhearted idler.[5]

The second sort of the charitable feeling which is beautiful and amiable, indeed, but not yet the foundation of a true virtue, is *complaisance*, an inclination to be agreeable to others by friendliness, by consent to their demands, and by conformity of our conduct with their intentions. This ground of a delightful sociability is beautiful, and the pliancy of such a heart good-natured. But it is not at all a virtue, for where higher principles do not set bounds for it and weaken it, all the depravities can spring from it. For—not to mention that this complaisance toward those with whom we are concerned is very often an injustice toward others who are outside this little circle—if one takes this incitement alone, such a man can have all the depravities, not out of immediate inclination but because he likes to live so as to please others. Out of kindhearted fellowship he will be a liar, an idler, a drunkard, or the like, for he does not act by the rules that are directed to good conduct in general, but rather by an inclination that in itself is beautiful but becomes trifling when it is without support and without principles.

Accordingly, true virtue can be grafted only upon principles such that the more general they are, the more sublime and noble it becomes. These principles are not speculative rules, but the consciousness of a feeling that lives in every human breast and extends itself much further than over the particular grounds of compassion and complaisance. I believe that I sum it all up when I say that it is the *feeling of the beauty and the dignity of human nature*. The first is a ground of universal affection, the second of universal esteem; and if this feeling had the greatest perfection in some one human heart, this man would of course love and prize even himself, but only so far as he is one of all those over whom his broadened and noble feeling is spread. Only when one subordinates his own inclination to one so expanded can our charitable impulses be used proportionately and bring about the noble bearing that is the beauty of virtue.

In view of the weakness of human nature and of the little force which the universal moral feeling would exercise over most hearts, Providence has placed in us as supplements to virtue assisting drives, which, as they move some of us even without principles, can also give to others who are ruled by these latter a greater thrust and a stronger impulse toward beautiful actions. Sympathy and complaisance are grounds of beautiful deeds, which would perhaps be altogether suppressed by the preponderance of a coarser selfishness; but these are not immediate grounds of virtue, as we have seen, although because they are ennobled by the relationship with it, even they gain its name. I can therefore call them *adoptive virtues*, but that which rests upon principles, *genuine virtue*. The former are beautiful and charming; the latter alone is sublime and venerable. One calls a disposition in which the first feelings rule a *kind heart*, and the man of that sort *goodhearted;* on the other hand, one rightly denotes the man who is virtuous on principle a *noble heart*, and calls him alone a *righteous* person. These adoptive virtues have, nevertheless, a great similarity to the true virtues, since they contain the feeling of an immediate pleasure in charitable and benevolent actions. The goodhearted man will go about peaceably and courteously, out of immediate complaisance without further design, and will feel sincere condolence in the misery of another.

But since even this moral sympathy is not yet enough to stimulate inert human nature to actions for the common good, Providence has placed within us still another feeling that is fine and can set us in motion or can effect a balance with coarser selfishness and common sensuality. This is the *sense of honor*, and its consequence, *shame*. The opinion others might have of our worth and their judgment of our actions is a motivation of great weight which coaxes many a sacrifice out of us. What a large part of mankind would neither have done out of an immediately arising impulse of goodheartedness, nor out of principles, happens often enough simply on account of external appearance, out of a delusion very useful although in itself very shallow—as if the judgment of others determined the worth of ourselves and our actions. What happens out of this impulse is not in the least virtuous, on account of which everyone who wants to be considered so deliberately conceals the motivation of ambition. This inclination is not even so closely related to genuine virtue as goodheartedness, because it cannot be moved immediately by the beauty of actions, but rather through their appearance of propriety when laid before strange eyes. Since nevertheless the sense of honor is a fine feeling, I can accordingly call the semblance of virtue which is motivated by it the *gloss of virtue*.

If we compare the dispositions of men, so far as one of these three kinds of feeling governs in them and determines the moral character, we shall find that each one of them stands in a closer relation with some one of the temperaments as ordinarily classified, and further that a greater deficiency of the moral feeling would be the share of the phlegmatic. Not as if the essential attribute in the character of these different temperaments depends upon the traits under consideration—for we are not concerned in this discussion with the coarser feeling, of selfishness for example, or common sensuality, and so forth, and it is of such inclinations that account is taken in the customary classification—but rather because the aforesaid finer moral feelings are apt to join more easily with one or the other of these temperaments and for the most part actually are so united.

A profound feeling for the beauty and dignity of human nature and a firmness and determination of the mind to refer all one's actions to this as to a universal ground is earnest, and does not at all join with a changeable gaiety nor with the inconstancy of a frivolous person. It even approaches melancholy, a gentle and noble feeling so far as it is grounded upon the awe that a hard-pressed soul feels when, full of some great purpose, he sees the danger he will have to overcome, and has before his eyes the difficult but great victory of self-conquest. Thus genuine virtue based on principles has something about it which seems to harmonize most with the *melancholy* frame of mind in the moderated understanding.

Goodheartedness, a beauty and a sensitive ability of the heart to be moved with sympathy or benevolence in individual cases according to the appearance presented, is very much subject to the variation of circumstances; and as the motive of the mind does not rest upon a universal principle, it easily takes on changed forms according to whether the objects offer one or the other aspect. And as this inclination amounts to a feeling for the beautiful, it appears to unite most naturally with the temperament we call *sanguine*, which is changeable and given over to amusements. It is in this temperament that we shall have to seek the well-liked qualities we have called adoptive virtues.

The sense of honor has usually been taken

as a mark of the *choleric* complexion, and the description of this character will give occasion to seek out the moral consequences of that fine feeling, which for the most part are aimed only at the gloss.

Never is a man without all traces of finer sensation; but a greater deficiency of it, a comparative apathy, occurs in the character of the *phlegmatic,* whom one deprives moreover of even the gross motives, such as lust for wealth, which nevertheless we can leave to him anyhow, together with other related inclinations, because they do not belong in this outline.

Let us now consider more closely the feelings of the sublime and beautiful, particularly so far as they are moral, under the accepted classification of the temperaments.

He whose feeling places him among the melancholy is not so named because, robbed of the joys of life, he aggrieves himself into dark dejection, but because when his feelings are aroused beyond a certain degree, or for various causes adopt a false direction, they are more easily terminated in that than in some other condition. He has above all a *feeling for the sublime.* Even beauty, for which he also has a perception, must not only delight him but move him, since it also stirs admiration in him. The enjoyment of pleasures is more earnest with him, but is none the smaller on that account. All emotions of the sublime have more fascination for him than the deceiving charms of the beautiful. His well-being will rather be satisfaction than pleasure. He is resolute. On that account he orders his sensations under principles. They are so much the less subject to inconstancy and change, the more universal this principle is to which they are subordinated, and the broader the high feeling is under which the lower are included. All particular grounds of inclination are subject to many exceptions and variations, so far as they are not derived from such a superior ground. The merry and friendly Alceste says: "I love and treasure my wife, for she is beautiful, affectionate, and clever." But how will it be when she becomes deformed by illness, and surly with age, and after the first fascination disappears seems no cleverer to you than anyone else? If the ground is no longer there, what can become of the inclination? On the other hand, let us take the kindly and steady Adraste, who thinks to himself, "I will treat this person lovingly and with respect, for she is my wife." This sentiment is noble and generous. Henceforth uncertain charms may alter; she will, however, still be his wife. The noble ground remains and is not so much subject to the inconstancy of external things. Of such a nature are principles in comparison to impulses, which simply well up upon isolated occasions; and thus the man of principles is in counteraction with him who is seized opportunely by a goodhearted and loving motive. But what if the secret tongue of his heart speaks in this manner: "I must come to the aid of that man, for he suffers; not that he were perhaps my friend or companion, nor that I hold him amenable to repaying the good deed with gratitude later on. There is now no time to reason and delay with questions; he is a man, and whatever befalls men, that also concerns me." Then his conduct sustains itself on the highest ground of benevolence in human nature, and is extremely sublime, because of its unchangeability as well as of the universality of its application.

I shall proceed with my observations. The man of melancholy frame of mind cares little for what others judge, what they consider good or true; he relies in this matter simply on his own insight. Because his grounds of motivation take on the nature of principles, he is not easily brought to other ideas; occasionally his steadfastness degenerates into self-will. He looks upon the change of fashions with indifference and their glitter with disdain. Friendship is sublime, and therefore belongs to his feeling. He can perhaps lose an inconstant friend; but the latter loses him not so soon. Even the remembrance of extinguished friendship is still estimable to him. Affability is beautiful, thoughtful silence sublime. He is a good guardian of his own and others' secrets. Truthfulness is sublime, and he hates lies or dissimulation. He has a high feeling of the dignity of human nature. He values himself and regards a human being as a creature who merits respect. He suffers no depraved submissiveness, and breathes freedom in a noble breast. All chains, from the gilded ones worn at court to the heavy irons of galley slaves, are abominable to him. He is a strict judge of himself and others, and not seldom is weary of himself as of the world.

In the deterioration of this character, earnestness inclines toward dejection, devotion toward fanaticism, love of freedom to enthusiasm. Insult and injustice kindle vengefulness in him. He is then much to be feared. He defies peril, and disdains death. By the perversity of his feeling and the lack of an enlightened reason he takes up the adventurous—inspirations, visions, attacks. If the understanding is still weaker, he hits upon the grotesque—meaningful dreams, presentiments, and miraculous portents. He is in danger of becoming a visionary or a crank.

He of the sanguine frame of mind has a predominating feeling for the beautiful. Hence his joys are laughing and lively. If he is not gay, then he is discontented, and he little knows peaceful silence. Multiplicity is beautiful, and he loves change. He seeks joy in himself and about himself, amuses others, and is a good companion. He has much moral sympathy. Others' joyfulness makes him pleased, and their sorrow, downhearted. His moral feeling is beautiful, but without principles, and always depends immediately upon the impression of the moment which objects make upon him. He is a friend of all men, or what is to say the same thing, really never a friend although he is goodhearted and benevolent. He does not dissemble. Today he will entertain you with his friendliness and good sorts, and tomorrow when you are ill or in adversity he will feel true and unfeigned compassion, but will slip gently away until the circumstances have changed. He must never be a judge. The laws generally seem too strict to him, and he lets himself be corrupted by tears. He is a poor clergyman, never downright good and never downright bad. He often yields to excess and is wicked, more from complaisance than from inclination. He is generous and charitable but a poor accountant of what he owes, because he has much sensation for kindness but little for justice. No one has such a good opinion of his own heart as he. Even if you do not esteem him, you will still have to love him. In the greater deterioration of his character he falls into the trifling; he is dawdling and childish. If age does not perhaps diminish his vivacity or bestow more understanding upon him, he is in danger of becoming an old dandy.

He whom one supposes to be of the choleric disposition has a predominant feeling for that sort of the sublime which one may call the splendid. It is actually only the gloss of sublimity and a strong conspicuous color which conceals the inner content of a thing or person who perhaps is only evil and common, and deludes and moves by appearance. Just as a building that imitates stone carving by means of a whitewashing makes as noble an impression as if it were really made of stone, and just as pasted-on cornices and pilasters give the idea of solidity although they have little hold and support nothing—in the same way do alloyed virtues glitter, a tinsel of wisdom and painted merit.

The choleric one considers his worth and the worth of his possessions and actions to lie in the propriety or the appearance with which he strikes the eye. With respect to the inner nature and the reasons for action which the object itself contains, he is cold, neither warmed by true benevolence nor moved by respect.[6] His conduct is artful. He must know how to take up all sorts of standpoints, in order to appraise his own bearing from the different positions of onlookers, because he seldom asks what he is, but only what he appears. On that account he must know well the effect upon the general taste and the various impressions which his behavior will have on those around him. As he has to be cold-blooded in this sly awareness and must not let himself be blinded by love, compassion, and sympathy, he will avoid many follies and vexations into which a sanguine person falls, who is fascinated by his immediate sensation. On that account he generally appears more understanding than he really is. His benevolence is politeness, his respect ceremony, his love concocted flattery. He is always full of himself when he takes up the position of a lover or a friend, and is never either the one nor the other. He seeks to dazzle by fashions, but because everything about him is artificial and contrived, he is stiff and awkward in them. He behaves far more according to principles than the sanguine, who is simply moved by haphazard impressions; but these are not principles of virtue but of reputation, and he has no feeling for the beauty or the worth of actions, but for the judgment that the world might pass on them. Because his behavior, so far as one does not look at the source from which it springs, is moreover almost as generally useful as virtue itself, before ordinary eyes he gains the same high esteem as the virtuous; but before subtler eyes he conceals himself carefully, because he well knows that the disclosure of his secret motive of seeking repute would destroy respect for him. He is therefore very much given to dissembling, hypocritical in religion, a flatterer in society, and he capriciously changes his political affiliation according to changing circumstances. He is glad to be a slave of the great, in order thereby to be a tyrant over the petty. *Naïveté,* this noble or beautiful simplicity that bears upon itself the seal of nature and not of art, is quite foreign to him. Hence if his taste degenerates his appearance becomes *flagrant,* that is to say, swaggering in an obnoxious way. He belongs as much because of his style as of his ornamentation among the galimatias (the exaggerated), a sort of the grotesque, which is the same with respect to the splendid as the adventurous or irresponsible is with respect to the earnest sublime. In insults he falls back upon duels or lawsuits, and in civic relations upon ancestry, precedence, and title. As long as he is only vain, that is, seeks reputation and strives to catch the eye, so long can he still be tolerated; but if he becomes inflated despite an utter lack of real excellences and talents, then he is what he would least rather be considered—namely, a fool.

Since in the phlegmatic mixture no ingredients of the sublime or beautiful usually enter in any noticeable degree, this disposition does not belong in the context of our deliberations.

Of whichever sort these finer feelings might be which we have treated thus far, whether sublime or beautiful, they have the common fate that in the judgment of him who has no definite feeling in that respect, they always appear senseless and absurd. A man of a quiet and self-interested diligence has, so to speak, none of the organs with which to experience the noble bent in a poem or in a heroic virtue. He would rather read a Robinson than a Grandison, and holds Cato for an obstinate fool. In the same way, to persons of a somewhat earnest disposition, that seems trifling which to others is charming, and the beguiling naïveté of a pastoral love affair to them is insipid and childish. Furthermore, even if the mind is not completely without a univocal finer feeling, the degrees of its sensitivity are still very different, and we will see that the one finds something noble and decorous which seems to the other great but adventurous. Opportunities that offer themselves to spy out something of the feeling of another in nonmoral affairs can also give us occasion to elucidate, with fair probability, his sensation with respect to the higher mental qualities and even those of the heart. Whoever is bored with beautiful music gives a strong presumption that the beauties of literature and the delicate fascinations of love will have little power over him.

There is a certain spirit of minutiae (*esprit des bagatelles*) which exhibits a kind of fine feeling but aims at quite the opposite of the sublime. A taste for something because it is very *artful* and laborious—verses that can be read both forward and backward, riddles, clocks in finger rings, flea chains, and so on. A taste for everything that is overparticular and in painful fashion *orderly*, although without use—for example, books that stand neatly arrayed in long rows in bookcases, and an empty head that looks at them and takes delight, rooms that like optical cabinets are prim and washed extremly clean, together with an inhospitable and morose host who inhabits them. A taste for all that is *rare*, little though its inherent worth otherwise might be—Epictetus' lamp, a glove of King Charles the Twelfth; in a way, coin collecting is classed with these. Such persons stand under great suspicion that in knowledge they will be grubs and cranks, but in morals they will be without feeling for all that is beautiful or noble in a free way.

We do an injustice to another who does not perceive the worth or the beauty of what moves or delights us, if we rejoin that *he does not understand* it. Here it does not matter so much what the *understanding* comprehends, but what the feeling senses. Nevertheless the capacities of the soul have so great a connection that for the most part one can elucidate the talents of insight from the manifestation of feeling. For it would be in vain to have bestowed these talents upon him who has many intellectual excellences, if he had not at the same time a strong feeling for the true noble or beautiful, which must be the motive to employ these gifts well and regularly.[7]

Now it is customary to call *useful* only what can provide a sufficiency for our coarser sensation, which can supply us a surplus in eating and drinking, display in clothing and in furniture, and lavishness in entertainment, although I do not see why everything that my most lively feeling craves should not just as well be counted among the useful things. But everything, nevertheless, being taken on the usual terms, he whom *self-interest* governs is a man with whom one must never reason concerning the finer taste. In this respect a hen is frankly better than a parrot, a kitchen pot is more useful than a porcelain vessel, all the witty heads in the world have not the value of a peasant, and the effort to discover the distance of the fixed stars can be set aside until it has been decided how to drive the plow to best advantage. But what folly it is to let oneself into such a dispute, where it is impossible to reach a common agreement of the feelings, because feeling is by no means uniform! Nevertheless a man of the most coarse and common sensation will be able to perceive that the charms and pleasures of life which appear to be the most superfluous attract our greatest care, and that we would have few motives remaining for such abundant toils if we wanted to exclude those. Similarly, virtually no one is so gross as not to sense that a moral action, at least when done to another person, moves all the more the further it is from self-interest, and the more those nobler impulsions stand out in it.

If I examine alternately the noble and the weak side of men, I reprimand myself that I am unable to take that standpoint from which these contrasts present the great portrait of the whole of human nature in a stirring form. For I willingly concede that so far as it belongs to the design of nature on the whole, these grotesque postures cannot give anything but a noble expression, although one is indeed much too shortsighted to see them in this relation. Nevertheless, in order to cast a weak glance upon this, I believe I can set down what follows. Among men there are but few who behave according to *principles*—which is extremely good, as it can so easily happen that one errs in these principles, and then the resulting disadvantage extends all the further, the more universal the principle and the more resolute the person who has set it before himself. Those who act out of *goodhearted impulses* are far more numerous, which is most excellent, although this by itself cannot be reckoned as a particular merit of the person. Although these virtuous instincts are sometimes lacking, on the average they perform the great purpose of nature just as well as those other instincts that so regularly control the animal world. But most men are among those who have their best-loved selves fixed before their eyes as the only point of reference for their exertions, and who seek to turn everything around *self-interest* as around the great axis. Nothing can be more advantageous than this, for these are the most diligent, orderly, and prudent; they give support and solidity to the whole, while without intending to do so they serve the common good, provide the necessary requirements, and supply the foundation over which finer souls can spread beauty and harmony. Finally the *love of honor* has been disseminated to *all* men's hearts, although in unlike measure, which must give to the whole a beauty that is charming unto admiration. For although ambition is a foolish fancy so far as it becomes a rule to which one subordinates the other inclinations, nevertheless as an attendant impulse it is most admirable. For since each one pursues actions on the great stage according to his dominating inclinations, he is moved at the same time by a secret impulse to take a standpoint outside himself in thought, in order to judge the outward propriety of his behavior as it seems in the eyes of the onlooker. Thus the different groups unite into a picture of splendid expression, where amidst great multiplicity unity shines forth, and the whole of moral nature exhibits beauty and dignity.

OF THE DISTINCTION OF THE BEAUTIFUL AND SUBLIME IN THE INTERRELATIONS OF THE TWO SEXES

Section Three

He who first conceived of woman under the name of the *fair sex* probably wanted to say something flattering, but he has hit upon it better than even he himself might have believed. For without taking into consideration that her figure in general is finer, her features more delicate and gentler, and her mien more engaging and more expressive of friendliness, pleasantry, and kindness than in the male sex, and not forgetting what one must reckon as a secret magic with which she makes our passion inclined to judgments favorable to her—even so, certain specific traits lie especially in the personality of this sex which distinguish it clearly from ours and chiefly result in making her known by the mark of the beautiful. On the other side, we could make a claim on the title of the *noble sex*, if it were not required of a noble disposition to decline honorific titles and rather to bestow than to receive them. It is not to be understood by this that woman lacks noble qualities, or that the male sex must do without beauty completely. On the contrary, one expects that a person of either sex brings both together, in such a way that all the other merits of a woman should unite solely to enhance the character of the beautiful, which is the proper reference point; and on the other hand, among the masculine qualities the sublime clearly stands out as the criterion of his kind. All judgments of the two sexes must refer to these criteria, those that praise as well as those that blame; all education and instruction must have these before its eyes, and all efforts to advance the moral perfection of the one or the other—unless one wants to disguise the charming distinction that nature has chosen to make between the two sorts of human being. For here it is not enough to keep in mind that we are dealing with human beings; we must also remember that they are not all alike.

Women have a strong inborn feeling for all that is beautiful, elegant, and decorated. Even in childhood they like to be dressed up, and take pleasure when they are adorned. They are cleanly and very delicate in respect to all that provokes disgust. They love pleasantry and can be entertained by trivialities if only these are merry and laughing. Very early they have a modest manner about themselves, know how to give themselves a fine demeanor and be self-possessed—and this at an age when our well-bred male youth is still unruly, clumsy, and confused. They have many sympathetic sensations, goodheartedness, and compassion, prefer the beautiful to the useful, and gladly turn abundance of circumstance into parsimony, in order to support expenditure on adornment and glitter. They have very delicate feelings in regard to the least offense, and are exceedingly precise to notice the most trifling lack of attention and respect toward them. In short, they contain the chief cause in human nature for the contrast of the beautiful qualities with the noble, and they refine even the masculine sex.

I hope the reader will spare me the reckoning of the manly qualities, so far as they are parallel to the feminine, and be content only to consider both in comparison with each other. The fair sex has just as much understanding as the male, but it is a *beautiful understanding*, whereas ours should be a *deep understanding*, an expression that signifies identity with the sublime.

To the beauty of all actions belongs above all the mark that they display facility, and appear to be accomplished without painful toil. On the other hand, strivings and surmounted difficulties arouse admiration and belong to the sublime. Deep meditation and a long-sustained reflection are noble but difficult, and do not well befit a person in whom unconstrained charms should show nothing else than a beautiful nature. Laborious learning or painful pondering, even if a woman should greatly succeed in it, destroy the merits that are proper to her sex, and because of their rarity they can make of her an object of cold admiration; but at the same time they will weaken the charms with which she exercises her great power over the other sex. A woman who has a head full of Greek, like

Mme. Dacier, or carries on fundamental controversies about mechanics, like the Marquise de Châtelet, might as well even have a beard; for perhaps that would express more obviously the mien of profundity for which she strives. The beautiful understanding selects for its objects everything closely related to the finer feeling, and relinquishes to the diligent, fundamental, and deep understanding abstract speculations or branches of knowledge useful but dry. A woman therefore will learn no geometry; of the principle of sufficient reason or the monads she will know only so much as is needed to perceive the salt in a satire which the insipid grubs of our sex have censured. The fair can leave Descartes his vortices to whirl forever without troubling themselves about them, even though the suave Fontenelle wished to afford them company among the planets; and the attraction of their charms loses none of its strength even if they know nothing of what Algarotti has taken the trouble to sketch out for their benefit about the gravitational attraction of matter according to Newton. In history they will not fill their heads with battles, nor in geography with fortresses, for it becomes them just as little to reek of gunpowder as it does the males to reek of musk.

It appears to be a malicious stratagem of men that they have wanted to influence the fair sex to this perverted taste. For, well aware of their weakness before her natural charms and of the fact that a single sly glance sets them more in confusion than the most difficult problem of science, so soon as woman enters upon this taste they see themselves in a decided superiority and are at an advantage that otherwise they hardly would have, being able to succor their vanity in its weakness by a generous indulgence toward her. The content of woman's great science, rather, is humankind, and among humanity, men. Her philosophy is not to reason, but to sense. In the opportunity that one wants to give to women to cultivate their beautiful nature, one must always keep this relation before his eyes. One will seek to broaden their total moral feeling and not their memory, and that of course not by universal rules but by some judgment upon the conduct that they see about them. The examples one borrows from other times in order to examine the influence the fair sex has had in culture, the various relations to the masculine in which it has stood in other ages or in foreign lands, the character of both so far as it can be illustrated by these, and the changing taste in amusements—these comprise her whole history and geography. For the ladies, it is well to make it a pleasant diversion to see a map setting forth the entire globe or the principal parts of the world. This is brought about by showing it only with the intention of portraying the different characters of peoples that dwell there, and the differences of their taste and moral feeling, especially in respect to the effect these have upon the relations of the sexes—together with a few easy illustrations taken from the differences of their climates, or their freedom or slavery. It is of little consequence whether or not the women know the particular subdivisions of these lands, their industry, power, and sovereigns. Similarly, they will need to know nothing more of the cosmos than is necessary to make the appearance of the heavens on a beautiful evening a stimulating sight to them, if they can conceive to some extent that yet more worlds, and in them yet more beautiful creatures, are to be found. Feeling for expressive painting and for music, not so far as it manifests artistry but sensitivity—all this refines or elevates the taste of this sex, and always has some connection with moral impulses. Never a cold and speculative instruction but always feelings, and those indeed which remain as close as possible to the situation of her sex. Such instruction is very rare because it demands talents, experience, and a heart full of feeling; and a woman can do very well without any other, as in fact without this she usually develops very well by her own efforts.

The virtue of a woman is a *beautiful virtue.*[8] That of the male sex should be a *noble virtue.* Women will avoid the wicked not because it is unright, but because it is ugly; and virtuous actions mean to them such as are morally beautiful. Nothing of duty, nothing of compulsion, nothing of obligation! Woman is intolerant of all commands and all morose constraint. They do something only because it pleases them, and the art consists in making only that please them which is good. I hardly believe that the fair sex is capable of principles, and I hope by that not to offend, for these are also extremely rare in the male. But in place of it Providence has put in their breast kind and benevolent sensations, a fine feeling for propriety, and a complaisant soul. One should not at all demand sacrifices and generous self-restraint. A man must never tell his wife if he risks a part of his fortune on behalf of a friend. Why should he fetter her merry talkativeness by burdening her mind with a weighty secret whose keeping lies solely upon him? Even many of her weaknesses are, so to speak, *beautiful faults.* Offense or misfortune moves her tender soul to sadness. A man must never weep other than magnanimous tears. Those he sheds in pain or over circumstances of fortune make him contemptible. *Vanity,* for which one reproaches the fair sex so frequently, so far as it is a fault in that sex, yet is only a beautiful fault. For—not to mention that the men who so gladly flatter a woman would be left in a strait if she were not inclined to take it well—by that they actually enliven their charms. This inclination is an impulsion to exhibit pleasantness and good demeanor, to let her merry wit play, to radiate through the changing devices of dress, and to heighten her beauty. Now in this there is not at all any offensiveness toward others, but rather so much courtesy, if it is done with good taste, that to scold against it with peevish rebukes is very ill-bred. A woman who is too inconstant and deceitful is called a coquette; which expression yet has not so harsh a meaning as what, with a changed syllable, is applied to man, so that if we understand each other, it can sometimes indicate a familiar flattery. If vanity is a fault that in a woman much merits excuse, a *haughty bearing* is not only as reproachable in her as in people in general, but completely disfigures the character of her sex. For this quality is exceedingly stupid and ugly, and is set completely in opposition to her captivating, modest charms. Then such a person is in a slippery position. She will suffer herself to be judged sharply and without any pity; for whoever presumes an esteem invites all around him to rebuke. Each disclosure of even the least fault gives everyone a true joy, and the word *coquette* here loses its mitigated meaning. One must always distinguish between vanity and conceit. The first seeks approbation and to some extent honors those on whose account it gives itself the trouble. The second believes itself already in full possession of approbation, and because it never strives to gain any, it wins none.

If a few ingredients of vanity do not deform a woman in the eyes of the male sex, still, the more apparent they are, the more they serve to divide the fair sex among themselves. Then they judge one another very severely, because the one seems to obscure the charms of the other, and in fact, those who make strong presumptions of conquest actually are seldom friends of one another in a true sense.

Nothing is so much set against the beautiful as disgust, just as nothing sinks deeper beneath the sublime than the ridiculous. On this account no insult can be more painful to a man than being called a *fool*, and to a woman, than being called *disgusting*. The English *Spectator* maintains that no more insulting reproach could be made to a man than if he is considered a liar, and to a woman none more bitter than is she is held unchaste. I will leave this for what it is worth so far as it is judged according to strictness in morals. But here the question is not what of itself deserves the greatest rebuke, but what is actually felt as the harshest of all. And to that point I ask every reader whether, when he sets himself to thinking upon this matter, he must not assent to my opinion. The maid Ninon Lenclos made not the least claims upon the honor of chastity, and yet she would have been implacably offended if one of her lovers should have gone so far in his pronouncements; and one knows the gruesome fate of Monaldeschi, on account of an insulting expression of that sort, at the hands of a princess who had wanted to be thought no Lucretia. It is intolerable that one should never once be capable of doing something wicked if one actually wanted to, because then even the omission of it remains only a very ambiguous virtue.

In order to remove ourselves as far as possible from these disgusting things, *neatness*, which of course well becomes any person, in the fair sex belongs among the virtues of first rank and can hardly be pushed too high among them, although in a man it sometimes rises to excess and then becomes trifling.

Sensitivity to *shame* is a secrecy of nature addressed to setting bounds to a very intractable inclination, and since it has the voice of nature on its side, seems always to agree with good moral qualities even if it yields to excess. Hence it is most needed, as a supplement to principles, for there is no instance in which inclination is so ready to turn Sophist, subtly to devise complaisant principles, as in this. But at the same time it serves to draw a curtain of mystery before even the most appropriate and necessary purposes of nature, so that a too familiar acquaintance with them might not occasion disgust, or indifference at least, in respect to the final purpose of an impulse onto which the finest and liveliest inclinations of human nature are grafted. This quality is especially peculiar to the fair sex and very becoming to it. There is also a coarse and contemptible rudeness in putting delicate modesty to embarrassment or annoyance by the sort of vulgar jests called obscenities. However, although one may go as far around the secret as one ever will, the sexual inclination still ultimately underlies all her remaining charms, and a woman, ever as a woman, is the pleasant object of a well-mannered conversation; and this might perhaps explain why otherwise polite men occasionally take the liberty to let certain fine allusions show through, by a little mischief in their jests, which make us call them *loose* or *waggish*. Because they neither affront by searching glances nor intend to injure anyone's esteem, they believe it justified to call the person who receives it with an indignant or brittle mien a *prude*. I mention this practice only because it is generally considered as a somewhat bold trait in polite conversation, and also because in point of fact much wit has been squandered upon it; however, judgment according to moral strictness does not belong here, because what I have to observe and explain in the sensing of the beautiful is only the appearances.

The noble qualities of this sex, which still, as we have already noted, must never disguise the feeling of the beautiful, proclaim themselves by nothing more clearly and surely than by *modesty*, a sort of noble simplicity and innocence in great excellences. Out of it shines a quiet benevolence and respect toward others, linked at the same time with a certain *noble trust* in oneself, and a reasonable self-esteem that is always to be found in a sublime disposition. Since this fine mixture at once captivates by charms and moves by respect, it puts all the remaining shining qualities in security against the mischief of censure and mockery. Persons of this temperament also have a heart for friendship, which in a woman can never be valued highly enough, because it is so rare and moreover must be so exceedingly charming.

As it is our purpose to judge concerning feelings, it cannot be unpleasant to bring under concepts, if possible, the difference of the impression that the form and features of the fair sex make on the masculine. This complete fascination is really overlaid upon the sex instinct. Nature pursues its great purpose, and all refinements that join together, though they may appear to stand as far from that as they will, are only trimmings and borrow their charm ultimately from that very source. A healthy and *coarse taste*, which always stays very close to this impulse, is little tempted by the charms of demeanor, of facial features, of eyes, and so on, in a woman, and because it really pertains only to sex, it oftentimes sees the delicacy of others as empty flirting.

If this taste is not fine, nevertheless it is not on that account to be disdained. For the largest part of mankind complies by means of it with the great order of nature, in a very simple and sure way.[9] Through it the greatest number of marriages are brought about, and indeed by the most diligent part of the human race; and because the man does not have his head full of fascinating expressions, languishing eyes, noble demeanor, and so forth, and understands nothing of all this, he becomes that much the more attentive to householders' virtues, thrift and such, and to the dowry. As for what relates to the somewhat finer taste, on whose account it might be necessary to make a distinction among the exterior charms of women, this if fixed either upon what in the form and the expression of the face is moral, or upon what is nonmoral. In respect to the last-named sort of pleasantness, a lady is called *pretty*. A well-proportioned figure, regular features, colors of eyes and face which contrast prettily, beauties pure and simple which are also pleasing in a bouquet and gain a cool approbation. The face itself says nothing, although it is pretty, and speaks not to the heart. What is moral in the expression of the features, the eyes, and mien pertains to the feeling either of the sublime or of the beautiful. A woman in whom the agreeableness beseeming her sex particularly makes manifest the moral expression of the sublime is called *beautiful* in the proper sense; so far as the moral composition makes itself discernible in the mien or facial features, she whose features show qualities of beauty is *agreeable*, and if she is that to a high degree, *charming*. The first, under a mien of composure and a noble demeanor, lets the glimmer of a beautiful understanding play forth through discreet glances, and as in her face she portrays a tender feeling and a benevolent heart, she seizes possession of the affection as well as the esteem of a masculine heart. The second exhibits merriment and wit in laughing eyes, something of fine mischief, the playfulness of jest and sly coyness. She charms, while the first moves; and the feeling of love of which she is capable and which she stimulates in others is fickle but beautiful, whereas the feeling of the first is tender, combined with respect, and constant. I do not want to engage in too detailed an analysis of this sort, for in doing so the author always appears to depict his own inclination. I shall still mention, however, that the liking many women have for a healthy but pale color can be explained here. For this generally accompanies a disposition of more inward feeling and delicate sensation, which belongs to the quality of the sublime; whereas the rosy and blooming complexion proclaims less of the first, but more of the joyful and merry disposition—but it is more suitable to vanity to move and to arrest, than to charm and to attract. On the other hand there can be very pretty persons completely without moral feeling and without any expression that indicates feeling; but they will neither move nor charm, unless it might be the coarse taste of which we have made mention, which sometimes grows somewhat more refined and then also selects after its fashion. It is too bad that this sort of beautiful creatures easily fall into the fault of *conceit*, through the consciousness of the beautiful figure their mirror shows them, and from a lack of finer sensations, for then they make all indifferent to them except the flatterer, who has ulterior motives and contrives intrigues.

Perhaps by following these concepts one can understand something of the different effect the figure of the same woman has upon the tastes of men. I do not concern myself with what in this impression relates too closely to the sex impulse and may be of a piece with the particular sensual illusion with which the feeling of everyone clothes itself, because it lies outside the compass of finer taste. Perhaps what M. Buffon supposes may be true: that the figure that makes the first impression, at the time when this impulse is still new and is beginning to develop, remains the pattern all feminine figures in the future must more or less follow so as to be able to stir the fanciful ardor, whereby a rather coarse inclination is compelled to choose among the different objects of a sex. Regarding the somewhat finer taste, I affirm that the sort of beauty we have called the *pretty figure* is judged by all men very much alike, and that opinions about it are not so different as one generally maintains. The Circassian and Georgian maidens have always been considered extremely pretty by all Europeans who travel through their lands. The Turks, the Arabs, the Persians are apparently of one mind in this taste, because they are very eager to beautify their races through such fine blood, and one also notes that the Persian race has actually succeeded in this. The merchants of Hindustan likewise do not fail to draw great profit from a wicked commerce in such beautiful creatures, for they supply them to the self-indulgent rich men of their land. And it appears that, as greatly as the caprice of taste in these different quarters of the world may diverge, still, whatever is once known in any of these as especially pretty will also be considered the same in all the others. But whenever what is moral in the features mingles in the judgment upon the fine figure, the taste of different men is always very different, both because their moral feeling itself is dissimilar, and also on account of the different meaning that the expression of the face may have in every fancy. One finds that those formations that at first glance do not have any particular effect, because they are not pretty in any decided way, generally appear far more to captivate and to grow constantly more beautiful as soon as they begin to please upon nearer acquaintance. On the other hand, the pretty appearance that proclaims itself at once is later received with greater indifference. This probably is because moral charms, when they are evident, are all the more arresting because they are set in operation only on the occasion of moral sensations, and let themselves be discovered in this way, each disclosure of a new charm causing one to suspect still more of these; whereas all the agreeable features that do not at all conceal themselves, after exercising their entire effect at the beginning, can subsequently do nothing more than to cool off the enamored curiosity and bring it gradually to indifference.

Along with these observations, the following comment naturally presents itself. The quite simple and coarse feeling in the sexual inclination leads directly to the great purpose of nature, and as it fulfills her claims it is fitted to make the person himself happy without digression; but because of its great universality it degenerates easily into excess and dissoluteness. On the other hand, a very refined taste serves to take away the wildness of an impetuous inclination, and although it limits this to few objects, to make it modest and decorous, such an inclination usually misses the great goal of nature. As it demands or expects more than nature usually offers, it seldom takes care to make the person of such delicate feeling happy. The first disposition becomes uncouth, because it is attracted to all the members of a sex; the second becomes oversubtle, because actually it is attracted to none. It is occupied only with an object that the enamored inclination creates in thought, and ornaments with all the noble and beautiful qualities that nature seldom unites in one human being and still more seldom brings to him who can value them and perhaps would be worthy of such a possession. Thence arises the postponement and finally the full abandonment of the marital bond; or what is perhaps just as bad, a peevish regret after making a choice that does not fulfill the great expectations one had made oneself—for not seldom the Aesopian cock finds a pearl when a common barleycorn would have been better suited to him.

From this we can perceive in general that as charming as the impressions of the delicate feeling may be, one still might have cause to be on guard in its refinement, lest by excessive sensibility we subtly fabricate only much discontent and a source of evil. To noble souls I might well propose to refine as much as they can the feeling with respect to qualities that become them, or with respect to actions that they themselves perform, but to maintain this taste in its simplicity respecting what they enjoy or expect from others—if only I saw how this were possible to achieve. But if it were approached, they would make others happy and also be happy themselves. It is never to be lost sight of that in whatever way it might be, one must make no very high claims upon the raptures of life and the perfection of men; for he who always expects only something ordinary has the advantage that the result seldom refutes his hope, but sometimes he is surprised by quite unexpected perfections.

Finally age, the great destroyer of beauty, threatens all these charms; and if it proceeds according to the natural order of things, gradually the sublime and noble qualities must take the place of the beautiful, in order to make a person always worthy of a greater respect as she ceases to be attractive. In my opinion, the whole perfection of the fair sex in the bloom of years should consist in the beautiful simplicity that has been brought to its height by a refined feeling toward all that is charming and noble. Gradually, as the claims upon charms diminish, the reading of books and the broadening of insight could refill unnoticed the vacant place of the Graces with the Muses, and the husband should be the first instructor. Nevertheless, when the epoch of growing old, so terrible to every woman, actually approaches, she still belongs to the fair sex, and that sex disfigures itself if in a kind of despair of holding this character longer, it gives way to a surly and irritable mood.

An aged person who attends a gathering with a modest and friendly manner, is sociable in a merry and sensible way, favors with a pleasant demeanor the pleasures of youth in which she herself no longer participates, and, as she looks after everything, manifests contentment and benevolence toward the joys that are going on around her, is yet a finer person that a man of like age and perhaps even more attractive than a girl, although in another sense. Indeed the platonic love might well be somewhat too mystical, which an ancient philosopher asserted when he said of the object of his inclination, "The Graces reside in her wrinkles, and my soul seems to hover upon my lips when I kiss her withered mouth"; but such claims must then be relinquished. An old man who acts infatuated is a fool, and the like presumptions of the other sex at that age are disgusting. It never is due to nature when we do not appear with a good demeanor, but rather to the fact that we turn her upside down.

In order to keep close to my text, I want to undertake a few reflections on the influence one sex can have upon the other, to beautify or ennoble its feeling. Woman has a superior feeling for the beautiful, so far as it pertains to herself; but for the noble, so far as it is encountered in the male sex. Man on the other hand has a decided feeling for the noble, which belongs to his qualities, but for the beautiful, so far as it is to be found in woman. From this it must follow that the purposes of nature are directed still more to ennoble man, by the sexual inclination, and likewise still more to beautify woman. A woman is embarrassed little that she does not possess certain high insights, that she is timid, and not fit for serious employments, and so forth; she is beautiful and captivates, and that is enough. On the other hand, she demands all these qualities in a man, and the sublimity of her soul shows itself only in that she knows to treasure these noble qualities so far as they are found in him. How else indeed would it be possible that so many grotesque male faces, whatever merits they may possess, could gain such well-bred and fine wives! Man on the other hand is much more delicate in respect to the beautiful charms of woman. By their fine figure, merry naïveté, and charming friendliness he is sufficiently repaid for the lack of book learning and for other deficiencies that he must supply by his own talents. Vanity and fashion can give these natural drives a false direction and make out of many a male a *sweet gentleman*, but out of a woman either a prude or an Amazon; but still nature always seeks to reassert her own order. One can thereby judge what powerful influences the sexual inclination could have especially upon the male sex, to ennoble it, if instead of many dry instructions the moral feeling of woman were seasonably developed to sense properly what belongs to the dignity and the sublime qualities of the other sex, and were thus prepared to look upon the trifling fops with disdain and to yield to no other qualities than the merits. It is also certain that the power of her charms on the whole would gain through that; for it is apparent that their fascination for the most part works only upon nobler souls; the others are not fine enough to sense them. Just as the poet Simonides said, when someone advised him to let the Thessalians hear his beautiful songs: "These fellows are too stupid to be beguiled by such a man as I am." It has been regarded moreover as an effect of association with the fair sex that men's customs have become gentler, their conduct more polite and refined, and their bearing more elegant; but the advantage of this is only incidental.[10] The principal object is that the man should become more perfect as a man, and the woman as a wife; that is, that the motives of the sexual inclination work according to the hint of nature, still more to ennoble the one and to beautify the qualities of the other.

If all comes to the extreme, the man, confident in his merits, will be able to say: "Even if you do not love me, I will constrain you to esteem me," and the woman, secure in the might of her charms, will answer: "Even if you do not inwardly admire me, I will still constrain you to love me." In default of such principles one sees men take on femininity in order to please, and woman occasionally (although much more seldom) affect a masculine demeanor in order to stimulate esteem; but whatever one does contrary to nature's will, one always does very poorly.

In matrimonial life the united pair should, as it were, constitute a single moral person, which is animated and governed by the understanding of the man and the taste of the wife. For not only can one credit more insight founded on experience to the former, and more freedom and accuracy in sensation to the latter; but also, the more sublime a disposition is, the more inclined it is to place the greatest purpose of its exertions in the contentment of a beloved object, and likewise the more beautiful it is, the more it seeks to requite these exertions by complaisance. In such a relation, then, a dispute over precedence is trifling and, where it occurs, is the surest sign of a coarse or dissimilarly matched taste. If it comes to such a state that the question is of the right of the superior to command, then the case is already utterly corrupted; for where the whole union is in reality erected solely upon inclination, it is already half destroyed as soon as the "duty" begins to make itself heard. The presumption of the woman in this harsh tone is extremely ugly, and of the man is base and contemptible in the highest degree. However, the wise order of things so brings it about that all these niceties and delicacies of feeling have their whole strength only in the beginning, but subsequently gradually become duller through association and domestic concerns, and then degenerate into familiar love. Finally, the great skill consists in still preserving sufficient remainders of those feelings so that indifference and satiety do not put an end to the whole value of the enjoyment on whose account it has solely and alone been worth the trouble to enter such a union. . . .

Notes

[The following notes are by Immanuel Kant and were included in the original edition of this essay—Ed.]

1. I should like to give just one example of the noble awe that the description of complete loneliness can inspire, and I draw for that purpose upon some passages from "Carazan's Dream" in the *Bremen Magazine*, volume IV, page 539. In proportion as his riches increased, this wealthy miser had closed off his heart from compassion and love toward all others. Meantime, as the love of man grew cold in him, the diligence of his prayer and his religious observances increased. "One evening, as by my lamp I drew up my accounts and calculated my profits, sleep overpowered me. In this state I saw the Angel of Death come over me like a whirlwind. He struck me before I could plead to be spared his terrible stroke. I was petrified, as I perceived that my destiny throughout eternity was cast, and that to all the good I had done nothing could be added, and from all the evil I had committed, not a thing could be taken away. I was led before the throne of him who dwells in the third heaven. The glory that flamed before me spoke to me thus: 'Carazan, your service of God is rejected. You have closed your heart to the love of man, and have clutched your treasures with an iron grip. You have lived only for yourself, and therefore you shall also live the future in eternity alone and removed from all communion with the whole of Creation.' At this instant I was swept away by an unseen power, and driven through the shining edifice of Creation. I soon left countless worlds behind me. As I neared the outermost end of nature, I saw the shadows of the boundless void sink down into the abyss before me. A fearful kingdom of eternal silence, loneliness, and darkness! Unutterable horror overtook me at this sight. I gradually lost sight of the last star, and finally the last glimmering ray of light was extinguished in outer darkness! The mortal terrors of despair increased with every moment, just as every moment increased my distance from the last inhabited world. I reflected with unbearable anguish that if ten thousand times a thousand years more should have carried me along beyond the bounds of all the universe I would still always be looking ahead into the infinite abyss of darkness, without help or hope of any return—. In this bewilderment I thrust out my hands with such force toward the objects of reality that I awoke. And now I have been taught to esteem mankind; for in that terrifying solitude I would have preferred even the least of those whom in the pride of my fortune I had turned from my door to all the treasures of Golconda—"

2. The sensations of the sublime exert the powers of the soul more strongly, and therefore tire sooner. One will be able to read a pastoral poem longer at a time than Milton's *Paradise Lost,* and La Bruyère longer than Young. It seems to me to be especially a fault of the latter, as a moral poet, that he too uniformly maintains a sublime tone; for the strength of the impression can be renewed only through interspersing gentler passages. In the beautiful, nothing tires more than laborious craftsmanship which betrays itself there. The effort to charm is experienced as painful and toilsome.

3. So far as sublimity or beauty exceeds the known average, one tends to call it *fictitious.*

4. One soon observes that this praiseworthy company divides into two compartments, that of the cranks and that of the dandies. A learned crank is discreetly called a *pedant.* If he assumes an obstinate appearance of wisdom, like the *dunce* of ancient and recent times, then the cap with bells becomes him well. The class of dandies is more often encountered in high society. Perhaps it is still better than the first. At their expense one has much to gain and much with which to amuse oneself. For all that, in this caricature each makes a wry mouth at the other, and knocks with his empty head on the head of his brother.

[*Dunce*: " 'Duns' or 'Dunsman' was a name early applied by their opponents to the followers of Duns Scotus, the Scotists, and hence was equivalent to one devoted to sophistical distinctions and subtleties. When, in the 16th century, the Scotists obstinately opposed the 'new learning,' the term 'duns' or 'dunce' became in the mouths of the humanists and reformers, a term of abuse, a synonym for one incapable of scholarship, a dull blockhead."—*Encyclopaedia Britannica,* 11th ed. (New York, 1910).]

5. Upon a closer consideration one finds that as amiable as the compassionate quality might be, it still does not have the dignity of a virtue. A suffering child, an unfortunate though upright lady will fill our heart with this sadness, while at the same time we hear with indifference the news of a terrible battle in which, obviously, a considerable number of the human species must suffer undeservedly under horrible evil. Many a prince who has averted his face from sadness for a single unfortunate person has at the same time, and often from a vain motive, given the command to make war. Here there is no proportion in the result; how then can anyone say that the universal love of man is the cause?

6. He even considers himself happy only to the extent that he supposes he is considered so by others.

7. One will also see that a true fineness of feeling is counted as a merit in a man. If someone can down a good dinner of meat or sweets, and then sleep incomparably well, we will indeed count it as a sign of a good digestion, but not as a merit. On the other hand, whoever can devote a part of his mealtime to listening to a piece of music or can absorb himself in a pleasant diversion with a painting, or who likes to read some witty piece even if it be only a poetical trifle, has in almost everyone's eyes the position of a more refined man, of whom one has a more favorable and laudatory opinion.

8. Above, in a strict judgment this was called adoptive virtue; here, where on account of the character of the sex it deserves a favorable justification, it is generally called a beautiful virtue.

9. As all things in the world have their bad side, regarding this taste it is only to be regretted that easier than another it degenerates into dissoluteness. For as any other can extinguish the fire one person has lighted, there are not enough obstacles that can confine an intractable inclination.

10. This advantage itself is really much reduced by the observation that one will have made, that men who are too early and too frequently introduced into company where woman sets the tone generally become somewhat trifling, and in male society they are boring or even contemptible because they have lost the taste for conversation, which must be merry, to be sure, but still of actual content—witty, to be sure, but also useful through its earnest discourse.

Samuel Johnson 1709–1784

To a great extent, Samuel Johnson, as critic, poet, editor, lexicographer, and journalist, dominated the middle third of the eighteenth century. The son of a Lichfield bookseller, Johnson survived childhood illnesses (which left him with impaired vision) and years of poverty and obscurity to emerge as an important London literary figure with his *Life of Richard Savage* (1744); *The Vanity of Human Wishes* (1749); *London* (1738), a collection of satiric poems in imitation of Juvenal; and his monumental *Dictionary of the English Language* (1755, revised 1773). Between 1750 and 1752 he wrote almost single-handedly the twice-weekly periodical, *The Rambler*, and later contributed numerous pieces for *The Adventurer* (1753) and *The Universal Chronicle*; his contributions to the latter were reprinted as *The Idler* (1761).

Other important works include *A Journey to the Western Islands of Scotland* (1775) and *The Lives of the English Poets* (1779–81). After his death, his friend James Boswell (1740–1795) published *The Life of Johnson*, a biography that helped to solidify Johnson's image as a brilliant thinker and an engaging, occasionally irascible, personality.

Johnson's "Preface to Shakespeare" is the most significant of the critical and editorial introductions to Shakespeare (and there were many) written in the eighteenth century. It demonstrates both Johnson's commitment to the Horatian idea that literature should instruct and entertain its audience and to his originality as a reader of Shakespeare's plays. Johnson stresses that Shakespeare, virtually alone of modern dramatists, writes plays that offer timeless portrayals of human nature rather than self-interested portraits of particular individuals, customs, or political factions. "From his works," says Johnson, "may be collected a system of civil and economical prudence"; they are filled "with practical axioms and domestic wisdom." Johnson's emphasis on Shakespeare's plays as a "mirror of life" is essential to his attack on previous critics—Thomas Rhymer, John Dennis, Corneille, and Voltaire—who impose on Shakespeare rigid notions of dramatic decorum. Like Dryden, Johnson remains alert to the particular theatrical effects of Shakespeare's art and to their sociocultural implications for subsequent generations of readers. His "Preface," then, illustrates the ways in which Johnson's neoclassicism transcends rigid notions of what literature should be and offers a brilliant response to the cultural significance of Shakespeare's plays.

Preface to Shakespeare

That praises are without reason lavished on the dead, and that the honours due only to excellence are paid to antiquity, is a complaint likely to be always continued by those, who, being able to add nothing to truth, hope for eminence from the heresies of paradox; or those, who, being forced by disappointment upon consolatory expedients, are willing to hope from posterity what the present age refuses, and flatter themselves that the regard which is yet denied by envy, will be at last bestowed by time.

Antiquity, like every other quality that attracts the notice of mankind, has undoubtedly votaries that reverence it, not from reason, but from prejudice. Some seem to admire indiscriminately whatever has been long preserved, without considering that time has sometimes co-operated with chance; all perhaps are more willing to honour past than present excellence; and the mind contemplates genius through the shades of age, as the eye surveys the sun through artificial opacity. The great contention of criticism is to find the faults of the moderns, and the beauties of the ancients. While an author is yet living we estimate his powers by his worst performance, and when he is dead, we rate them by his best.

To works, however, of which the excellence is not absolute and definite, but gradual and comparative; to works not raised upon principles demonstrative and scientifick, but appealing wholly to observation and experience, no other test can be applied than length of duration and continuance of esteem. What mankind have long possessed they have often examined and compared; and if they persist to value the possession, it is because frequent comparisons have confirmed opinion in its favour. As among the works of nature no man can properly call a river deep, or a mountain high without the knowledge of many mountains, and many rivers; so in the productions of genius, nothing can be stiled excellent till it has been compared with other works of the same kind. Demonstration immediately displays its power, and has nothing to hope or fear from the flux of years; but works tentative and experimental must be estimated by their proportion to the general and collective ability of man, as it is discovered in a long succession of endeavours. Of the first building that was raised, it might be with certainty determined that it was round or square; but whether it was spacious or lofty must have been referred to time. The Pythagorean scale of numbers was at once discovered to be perfect; but the poems of *Homer* we yet know not to transcend the common limits of human intelligence, but by remarking, that nation after nation, and century after century, has been able to do little more than transpose his incidents, new-name his characters, and paraphrase his sentiments.

The reverence due to writings that have long subsisted arises therefore not from any credulous confidence in the superior wisdom of past ages, or gloomy persuasion of the degeneracy of mankind, but is the consequence of acknowledged and indubitable positions, that what has been longest known has been most considered, and what is most considered is best understood.

The Poet, of whose works I have undertaken the revision, may now begin to assume the dignity of an ancient, and claim the privilege of established fame and prescriptive veneration. He has long outlived his century, the term commonly fixed as the test of literary merit. Whatever advantages he might once derive from personal allusions, local customs, or temporary opinions, have for many years been lost; and every topick of merriment, or motive of sorrow, which the modes of artificial life afforded him, now only obscure the scenes which they once illuminated. The effects of favour and competition are at an end; the tradition of his friendships and his enemies has perished; his works support no opinion with arguments, nor supply any faction with invectives; they can neither indulge vanity nor gratify malignity; but are read without any other reason than the desire of pleasure, and are therefore praised only as pleasure is obtained; yet, thus unassisted by interest or passion, they have past through variations of taste and changes of manners, and, as they devolved from one generation to another, have received new honours at every transmission.

But because human judgment, though it be gradually gaining upon certainty, never becomes infallible; and approbation, though long continued, may yet be only the approbation of prejudice or fashion; it is proper to inquire, by what peculiarities of excellence *Shakespeare* has gained and kept the favour of his countrymen.

Nothing can please many, and please long, but just representations of general nature. Particular manner, can be known to few, and therefore few only can judge how nearly they are copied. The irregular combinations of fanciful invention may delight a-while, by that novelty of which the common satiety of life sends us all in quest; but the pleasures of sudden wonder are soon exhausted, and the mind can only repose on the stability of truth.

Shakespeare is above all writers, at least above all modern writers, the poet of nature; the poet that holds up to his readers a faithful mirrour of manners and of life. His characters are not modified by the customs of particular places, unpractised by the rest of the world; by the peculiarities of studies or professions, which can operate but upon small numbers; or by the accidents of transient fashions or temporary opinions: they are the genuine progeny of common humanity, such as the world will always supply, and observation will always find. His persons act and speak by the influence of those general passions and principles by which all minds are agitated, and the whole system of life is continued in motion. In the writings of other poets a character is too often an individual; in those of *Shakespeare* it is commonly a species.

It is from this wide extension of design that so much instruction is derived. It is this which fills the plays of *Shakespeare* with practical axioms and domestic wisdom. It was said of *Euripides,* that every verse was a precept; and it may be said of *Shakespeare,* that from his works may be collected a system of civil and oeconomical prudence. Yet his real power is not shewn in the splendour of particular passages, but by the progress of his fable, and the tenour of his dialogue; and he that tries to recommend him by select quotations, will succeed like the pedant in *Hierocles,* who, when he offered his house to sale, carried a brick in his pocket as a specimen.

It will not easily be imagined how much *Shakespeare* excells in accommodating his sentiments to real life, but by comparing him with other authors. It was observed of the ancient schools of declamation, that the more diligently they were frequented, the more was the student disqualified for the world, because he found nothing there which he should ever meet in any other place. The same remark may be applied to every stage but that of *Shakespeare.* The theatre, when it is under any other direction, is peopled by such characters as were never seen, conversing in a language which was never heard, upon topicks which will never rise in the commerce of mankind. But the dialogue of this author is often so evidently determined by the incident which produces it, and is pursued with so much ease and simplicity, that it seems scarcely to claim the merit of fiction, but to have been gleaned by diligent selection out of common conversation, and common occurrences.

Upon every other stage the universal agent is love, by whose power all good and evil is distributed, and every action quickened or retarded. To bring a lover, a lady and a rival into the fable; to entangle them in contradictory obligations, perplex them with oppositions of interest, and harrass them with violence of desires inconsistent with each other; to make them meet in rapture and part in agony; to fill their mouths with hyperbolical joy and outrageous sorrow; to distress them as nothing human ever was distressed; to deliver them as nothing human ever was delivered; is the business of a modern dramatist. For this probability is violated, life is misrepresented, and language is depraved. But love is only one of many passions; and as it has no great influence upon the sum of life, it has little operation in the dramas of a poet, who caught his ideas from the living world, and exhibited only what he saw before him. He knew, that any other passion, as it was regular or exorbitant, was a cause of happiness or calamity.

Characters thus ample and general were not easily discriminated and preserved, yet perhaps no poet ever kept his personages more distinct from each other. I will not say with *Pope,* that every speech may be assigned to the proper speaker, because many speeches there are which have nothing characteristical; but perhaps, though some may be equally adapted to every person, it will be difficult to find any that can be properly transferred from the present possessor to another claimant. The choice is right, when there is reason for choice.

Other dramatists can only gain attention by hyperbolical or aggravated characters, by fabulous and unexampled excellence or depravity, as the writers of barbarous romances invigorated the reader by a giant and a dwarf; and he that should form his expectations of human affairs from the play, or from the tale, would be equally deceived. *Shakespeare* has no heroes; his scenes are occupied only by men, who act and speak as the reader thinks that he should himself have spoken or acted on the same occasion: Even where the agency is supernatural the dialogue is level with life. Other writers disguise the most natural passions and most frequent incidents; so that he who contemplates them in the book will not know them in the world: *Shakespeare* approximates the remote, and familiarizes the wonderful; the event which he represents will not happen, but if it were possible, its effects would probably be such as he has assigned; and it may be said, that he has not only shewn human nature as it acts in real exigencies, but as it would be found in trials, to which it cannot be exposed.

This therefore is the praise of *Shakespeare*, that his drama is the mirrour of life; that he who has mazed his imagination, in following the phantoms which other writers raise up before him, may here be cured of his delirious extasies, by reading human sentiments in human language, by scenes from which a hermit may estimate the transactions of the world, and a confessor predict the progress of the passions.

His adherence to general nature has exposed him to the censure of criticks, who form their judgments upon narrow principles. *Dennis* and *Rhymer* think his *Romans* not sufficiently *Roman;* and *Voltaire* censures his kings as not completely royal. *Dennis* is offended, that *Menenius*, a senator of *Rome*, should play the buffoon; and *Voltaire* perhaps thinks decency violated when the *Danish* Usurper is represented as a drunkard. But *Shakespeare* always makes nature predominate over accident; and if he preserves the essential character, is not very careful of distinctions superinduced and adventitious. His story requires Romans or kings, but he thinks only on men. He knew that *Rome*, like every other city, had men of all dispositions; and wanting a buffoon, he went into the senate-house for that which the senate-house would certainly have afforded him. He was inclined to shew an usurper and a murderer not only odious but despicable, he therefore added drunkenness to his other qualities, knowing that kings love wine like other men, and that wine exerts its natural power upon kings. These are the petty cavils of petty minds; a poet overlooks the casual distinction of country and condition, as a painter, satisfied with the figure, neglects the drapery.

The censure which he has incurred by mixing comick and tragick scenes, as it extends to all his works, deserves more consideration. Let the fact be first stated, and then examined.

Shakespeare's plays are not in the rigorous and critical sense either tragedies or comedies, but compositions of a distinct kind; exhibiting the real state of sublunary nature, which partakes of good and evil, joy and sorrow, mingled with endless variety of proportion and innumerable modes of combination; and expressing the course of the world, in which the loss of one is the gain of another; in which, at the same time, the reveller is hasting to his wine, and the mourner burying his friend; in which the malignity of one is sometimes defeated by the frolick of another; and many mischiefs and many benefits are done and hindered without design.

Out of this chaos of mingled purposes and casualties the ancient poets, according to the laws which custom had prescribed, selected some the crimes of men, and some their absurdities; some the momentous vicissitudes of life, and some the lighter occurrences; some the terrours of distress, and some the gayeties of prosperity. Thus rose the two modes of imitation, known by the names of *tragedy* and *comedy*, compositions intended to promote different ends by contrary means, and considered as so little allied, that I do not recollect among the *Greeks* or *Romans* a single writer who attempted both.

Shakespeare has united the powers of exciting laughter and sorrow not only in one mind, but in one composition. Almost all his plays are divided between serious and ludicrous characters, and, in the successive evolutions of the design, sometimes produce seriousness and sorrow, and sometimes levity and laughter.

That this is a practice contrary to the rules of criticism will be readily allowed; but there is always an appeal open from criticism to nature. The end of writing is to instruct; the end of poetry is to instruct by pleasing. That the mingled drama may convey all the instruction of tragedy or comedy cannot be denied, because it includes both in its alterations of exhibition and approaches nearer than either to the appearance of life, by shewing how great machinations and slender designs may promote or obviate one another, and the high and the low co-operate in the general system by unavoidable concatenation.

It is objected, that by this change of scenes the passions are interrupted in their progression, and that the principal event, being not advanced by a due gradation of preparatory incidents, wants at last the power to move, which constitutes the perfection of dramatick poetry. This reasoning is so specious, that it is received as true even by those who in daily experience feel it to be false. The interchanges of mingled scenes seldom fail to produce the intended vicissitudes of passion. Fiction cannot move so much, but that the attention may be easily transferred; and though it must be allowed that pleasing melancholy be sometimes interrupted by unwelcome levity, yet let it be considered likewise, that melancholy is often not pleasing, and that the disturbance of one man may be the relief of another; that different auditors have different habitudes; and that, upon the whole, all pleasure consists in variety.

The players, who in their edition divided our authour's works into comedies, histories, and tragedies, seem not to have distinguished the three kinds by any very exact or definite ideas.

And action which ended happily to the principal persons, however serious or distressful through its intermediate incidents, in their opinion, constituted a comedy. This idea of a comedy continued long amongst us; and plays were written, which, by changing the catastrophe, were tragedies to-day, and comedies to-morrow.

Tragedy was not in those times a poem of more general dignity or elevation than comedy; it required only a calamitous conclusion, with which the common criticism of that age was satisfied, whatever lighter pleasure it afforded in its progress.

History was a series of actions, with no other than chronological succession, independent on each other, and without any tendency to introduce or regulate the conclusion. It is not always very nicely distinguished from tragedy. There is not much nearer approach to unity of action in the tragedy of *Antony and Cleopatra*, than in the history of *Richard the Second*. But a history might be continued through many plays; as it had no plan, it had no limits.

Through all these denominations of the drama, *Shakespeare's* mode of composition is the same; an interchange of seriousness and merriment, by which the mind is softened at one time, and exhilarated at another. But whatever be his purpose, whether to gladden or depress, or to conduct the story, without vehemence or emotion, through tracts of easy and familiar dialogue, he never fails to attain his purpose; as he commands us, we laugh or mourn, or sit silent with quiet expectation, in tranquillity without indifference.

When *Shakespeare's* plan is understood, most of the criticisms of *Rhymer* and *Voltaire* vanish away. The play of *Hamlet* is opened, without impropriety, by two sentinels; *Iago* bellows at *Brabantio's* window, without injury to the scheme of the play, though in terms which a modern audience would not easily endure; the character of *Polonius* is seasonable and useful; and the Grave-diggers themselves may be heard with applause.

Shakespeare engaged in dramatick poetry with the world open before him; the rules of the ancients were yet known to few; but publick judgment was unformed; he had no example of such fame as might force him upon imitation, nor criticks of such authority as might restrain his extravagance: He therefore indulged his natural disposition, and his disposition, as *Rhymer* has remarked, led him to comedy. In tragedy he often writes, with great appearance of toil and study, what is written at last with little felicity; but in his comick scenes, he seems to produce without labour what no labour can improve. In tragedy he is always struggling after some occasion to be comick; but in comedy he seems to repose, or to luxuriate, as in a mode of thinking congenial to his nature. In his tragick scenes there is always something wanting, but his comedy often surpasses expectation or desire. His comedy pleases by the thoughts and the language, and his tragedy for the greater part by incident and action. His tragedy seems to be skill, his comedy to be instinct.

The force of his comick scenes has suffered little diminution from the changes made by a century and a half, in manners or in words. As his personages act upon principles arising from genuine passion, very little modified by particular forms, their pleasures and vexations are communicable to all times and to all places; they are natural, and therefore durable; the adventitious peculiarities of personal habits, are only superficial dies, bright and pleasing for a little while, yet soon fading to a dim tinct, without any remains of former lustre; but the discriminations of true passion are the colours of nature; they pervade the whole mass, and can only perish with the body that exhibits them. The accidental compositions of heterogeneous modes are dissolved by the chance which combined them; but the uniform simplicity of primitive qualities neither admits increase, nor suffers decay. The sand heap by one flood is scattered by another, but the rock always continues in its place. The stream of time, which is continually washing the dissoluble fabricks of other poets, passes without injury by the adamant of *Shakespeare*.

If there be, what I believe there is, in every nation, a stile which never becomes obsolete, a certain mode of phraseology so consonant and congenial to the analogy and principles of its respective language as to remain settled and unaltered; this style is probably to be sought in the common intercourse of life, among those who speak only to be understood, without ambition of elegance. The polite are always catching modish innovations, and the learned depart from established forms of speech, in hope of finding or making better; those who wish for distinction forsake the vulgar, when the vulgar is right; but there is a conversation above grossness and below refinement, where propriety resides, and where this poet seems to have gathered his comick dialogue. He is therefore more agreeable to the ears of the present age than any other authour equally remote, and among his other excellencies deserves to be studied as one of the original masters of our language.

These observations are to be considered not as unexceptionally constant, but as containing general and predominant truth. *Shakespeare's* familiar dialogue is affirmed to be smooth and clear, yet not wholly without ruggedness or difficulty; as a country may be eminently fruitful, though it has spots unfit for cultivation: His characters are praised as natural, though their sentiments are sometimes forced, and their actions improbable; as the earth upon the whole is spherical, though its surface is varied with protuberances and cavities.

Shakespeare with his excellencies has likewise faults, and faults sufficient to obscure and overwhelm any other merit. I shall shew them in the proportion in which they appear to me, without envious malignity or superstitious veneration. No question can be more innocently discussed than a dead poet's pretensions to renown; and little regard is due to that bigotry which sets candour higher than truth.

His first defect is that to which may be imputed most of the evil in books or in men. He sacrifices virtue to convenience, and is so much more careful to please than to instruct, that he seems to write without any moral purpose. From his writings indeed a system of social duty may be selected, for he that thinks reasonably must think morally; but his precepts and axioms drop casually from him; he makes no just distribution of good or evil, nor is always careful to shew in the virtuous a disapprobation of the wicked; he carries his persons indifferently through right and wrong, and at the close dismisses them without further care, and leaves their examples to operate by chance. This fault the barbarity of his age cannot extenuate; for it is always a writer's duty to make the world better, and justice is a virtue independent on time or place.

The plots are often so loosely formed, that a very slight consideration may improve them, and so carelessly pursued, that he seems not always fully to comprehend his own design. He omits opportunities of instructing or delighting which the train of his story seems to force upon him, and apparently rejects those exhibitions which would be more affecting, for the sake of those which are more easy.

It may be observed, that in many of his plays the latter part is evidently neglected. When he found himself near the end of his work, and, in view of his reward, he shortened the labour to snatch the profit. He therefore remits his efforts where he should most vigorously exert them, and his catastrophe is improbably produced or imperfectly represented.

He had no regard to distinction of time or place, but gives to one age or nation, without scruple, the customs, institutions, and opinions of another, at the expence not only of likelihood, but of possibility. These faults *Pope* has endeavoured, with more zeal than judgment, to transfer to his imagined interpolators. We need not wonder to find *Hector* quoting *Aristotle*, when we see the loves of *Theseus* and *Hippolyta* combined with the *Gothick* mythology of fairies. *Shakespeare*, indeed, was not the only violator of chronology, for in the same age *Sidney*, who wanted not the advantages of learning, has, in his *Arcadia*, confounded the pastoral with the feudal times, the days of innocence, quiet and security, with those of turbulence, violence, and adventure.

In his comick scenes he is seldom very successful, when he engages his characters in reciprocations of smartness and contests of sarcasm; their jests are commonly gross, and their pleasantry licentious; neither his gentlemen nor his ladies have much delicacy, nor are sufficiently distinguished from his clowns by any appearance of refined manners. Whether he represented the real conversation of his time is not easy to determine; the reign of *Elizabeth* is commonly supposed to have been a time of stateliness, formality and reserve; yet perhaps the relaxations of that severity were not very elegant. There must, however, have been always some modes of gayety preferable to others, and a writer ought to chuse the best.

In tragedy his performance seems constantly to be worse, as his labour is more. The effusions of passion which exigence forces out are for the most part striking and energetick; but whenever he solicits his invention, or strains his faculties, the offspring of his throes is tumour, meanness, tediousness, and obscurity.

In narration he affects a disproportionate pomp of diction, and a wearisome train of circumlocution, and tells the incident imperfectly in many words, which might have been more plainly delivered in few. Narration in dramatick poetry is naturally tedious, as it is unanimated and inactive, and obstructs the progress of the action; it should therefore always be rapid, and enlivened by frequent interruption. *Shakespeare* found it an encumberance, and instead of lightening it by brevity, endeavoured to recommend it by dignity and splendour.

His declamations or set speeches are commonly cold and weak, for his power was the power of nature; when he endeavoured, like other tragick writers, to catch opportunities of amplification, and instead of inquiring what the occasion demanded, to show how much his stores of knowledge could supply, he seldom escapes without the pity or resentment of his reader.

It is incident to him to be now and then entangled with an unwieldy sentiment, which he cannot well express, and will not reject; he struggles with it a while, and if it continues stubborn, comprises it in words such as occur, and leaves it to be disentangled and evolved by those who have more leisure to bestow upon it.

Not that always where the language is intricate the thought is subtle, or the image always great where the line is bulky; the equality of words to things is very often neglected, and trivial sentiments and vulgar ideas disappoint the attention, to which they are recommended by sonorous epithets and swelling figures.

But the admirers of this great poet have never less reason to indulge their hopes of supreme excellence, than when he seems fully resolved to sink them in dejection, and mollify them with tender emotions by the fall of greatness, the danger of innocence, or the crosses of love. He is not long soft and pathetick without some idle conceit, or contemptible equivocation. He no sooner begins to move, than he counteracts himself; and terrour and pity, as they are rising in the mind, are checked and blasted by sudden frigidity.

A quibble is to *Shakespeare*, what luminous vapours are to the traveller; he follows it at all adventures; it is sure to lead him out of his way, and sure to engulf him in the mire. It has some malignant power over his mind, and its fascinations are irresistible. Whatever be the dignity or profundity of his disquisition, whether he be enlarging knowledge or exalting affection, whether he be amusing attention with incidents, or enchaining it in suspense, let but a quibble spring up before him, and he leaves his work unfinished. A quibble is the golden apple for which he will always turn aside from his career, or stoop from his elevation. A quibble, poor and barren as it is, gave him such delight, that he was content to purchase it, by the sacrifice of reason, propriety and truth. A quibble was to him the fatal *Cleopatra* for which he lost the world, and was content to lose it.

It will be thought strange, that, in enumerating the defects of this writer, I have not yet mentioned his neglect of the unities; his violation of those laws which have been instituted and established by the joint authority of poets and criticks.

For his other deviations from the art of writing I resign him to critical justice, without making any other demand in his favour, than that which must be indulged to all human excellence: that his virtues be rated with his failings: But, from the censure which this irregularity may bring upon him, I shall, with due reverence to that learning which I must oppose, adventure to try how I can defend him.

His histories, being neither tragedies nor comedies are not subject to any of their laws; nothing more is necessary to all the praise which they expect, than that the changes of action be so prepared as to be understood, that the incidents be various and affecting, and the characters consistent, natural, and distinct. No other unity is intended, and therefore none is to be sought.

In his other works he has well enough preserved the unity of action. He has not, indeed, an intrigue regularly perplexed and regularly unravelled: he does not endeavour to hide his design only to discover it, for this is seldom the order of real events, and *Shakespeare* is the poet of nature: But his plan has commonly what *Aristotle* requires, a beginning, a middle, and an end; one event is concatenated with another, and the conclusion follows by easy consequence. There are perhaps some incidents that might be spared, as in other poets there is much talk that only fills up time upon the stage; but the general system makes gradual advances, and the end of the play is the end of expectation.

To the unities of time and place he has shewn no regard; and perhaps a nearer view of the principles on which they stand will diminish their value, and withdraw from them the veneration which, from the time of *Corneille*, they have very generally received, by discovering that they have given more trouble to the poet, than pleasure to the auditor.

The necessity of observing the unities of time and place arises from the supposed necessity of making the drama credible. The criticks hold it impossible, that an action of months or years can be possibly believed to pass in three hours; or that the spectator can suppose himself to sit in the theatre, while ambassadors go and return between distant kings while armies are levied and towns besieged, while an exile wanders and returns, or till he whom they saw courting his mistress, shall lament the untimely fall of his son. The mind revolts from evident falsehood, and fiction loses its force when it departs from the resemblance of reality.

From the narrow limitation of time necessarily arises the contraction of place. The spectator, who knows that he saw the first act at *Alexandria*, cannot suppose that he sees the next at *Rome*, at a distance to which not the dragons of *Medea* could, in so short a time, have transported him; he knows with certainty that he has not changed his place, and he knows that place cannot change itself; that what was a house cannot become a plain; that what was *Thebes* can never be *Persepolis*.

Such is the triumphant language with which a critick exults over the misery of an irregular poet, and exults commonly without resistance of reply. It is time therefore to tell him by the authority of *Shakespeare*, that he assumes, as an unquestionable principle, a position, which, while his breath is forming it into words, his understanding pronounces to be false. It is false, that any representation is mistake for reality; that any dramatick fable in its materiality was ever credible, or, for a single moment, was ever credited.

The objection arising from the impossibility of passing the first hour at *Alexandria*, and the next at *Rome*, supposes, that when the play opens, the spectator really imagines himself at *Alexandria*, and believes that his walk to the theatre has been a voyage to *Egypt*, and that he lives in the days of *Antony* and *Cleopatra*. Surely he that imagines this may imagine more. He that can take the stage at one time for the palace of the *Ptolemies*, may take it in half an hour for the promontory of *Actium*. Delusion, if delusion be admitted, has no certain limitation; if the spectator can be once persuaded, that his old acquaintance are *Alexander* and *Cæsar*, that a room illuminated with candles is the plain of *Pharsalia*, or the bank of *Granicus*, he is in a state of elevation above the reach of reason, or of truth, and from the heights of empyrean poetry, may despise the circumscriptions of terrestrial nature. There is no reason why a mind thus wandering in extacy should count the clock, or why an hour should not be a century in that calenture of the brains that can make the stage a field.

The truth is, that the spectators are always in their senses, and know, from the first act to the last, that the stage is only a stage, and that the players are only players. They came to hear a certain number of lines recited with just gesture and elegant modulation. The lines relate to some action, and an action must be in some place; but the different actions that complete a story may be in places very remote from each other; and where is the absurdity of allowing that space to represent first *Athens*, and then *Sicily*, which was always known to be neither *Sicily* nor *Athens*, but a modern theatre?

By supposition, as place is introduced, times may be extended; the time required by the fable elapses for the most part between the acts; for, of so much of the action as is represented, the real and poetical duration is the same. If, in the first act, preparations for war against *Mithridates* are represented to be made in *Rome*, the event of the war may, without absurdity, be represented, in the catastrophe, as happening in *Pontus;* we know that there is neither war, nor preparation for war; we know that we are neither in *Rome* nor *Pontus;* that neither *Mithridates* nor *Lucullus* are before us. The drama exhibits successive imitations of successive actions; and why may not the second imitation represent an action that happened years after the first, if it be so connected with it, that nothing but time can be supposed to intervene? Time is, of all modes of existence, most obsequious to the imagination; a lapse of years is as easily conceived as a passage of hours. In contemplation we easily contract the time of real actions, and therefore willingly permit it to be contracted when we only see their imitation.

It will be asked, how the drama moves, if it is not credited. It is credited with all the credit due to a drama. It is credited, whenever it moves, as a just picture of a real original; as representing to the auditor what he would himself feel, if he were to do or suffer what is there feigned to be suffered or to be done. The reflection that strikes the heart is not, that the evils before us are real evils, but that they are evils to which we ourselves may be exposed. If there be any fallacy, it is not that we fancy the players, but that we fancy ourselves unhappy for a moment; but we rather lament the possibility than suppose the presence of misery, as a mother weeps over her babe, when she remembers that death may take it from her. The delight of tragedy proceeds from our consciousness of fiction; if we thought murders and treasons real, they would please no more.

Imitations produce pain or pleasure, not because they are mistaken for realities, but because they bring realities to mind. When the imagination is recreated by a painted landscape, the trees are not supposed capable to give us shade, or the fountains coolness; but we consider, how we should be pleased with such fountains playing beside us, and such woods waving over us. We are agitated in reading the history of *Henry* the Fifth, yet no man takes his book for the field of *Agencourt*. A dramatick exhibition is a book recited with concomitants that encrease or diminish its effect. Familiar comedy is often more powerful in the theatre, than on the page; imperial tragedy is always less. The humour of *Petruchio* may be heightened by grimace; but what voice or what gesture can hope to add dignity or force to the soliloquy of *Cato*.

A play read, affects the mind like a play acted. It is therefore evident, that the action is not supposed to be real; and it follows, that between the acts a longer or shorter time may be allowed to pass, and that no more account of space or duration is to be taken by the auditor of a drama, than by the reader of a narrative, before whom may pass in an hour the life of a hero, or the revolutions of an empire.

Whether *Shakespeare* knew the unities, and rejected them by design, or deviated from them by happy ignorance, it is, I think, impossible to decide, and useless to enquire. We may reasonably suppose, that, when he rose to notice, he did not want the counsels and admonitions of scholars and criticks, and that he at last deliberately persisted in a practice, which he might have begun by chance. As nothing is essential to the fable, but unity of action, and as the unities of time and place arise evidently from false assumptions, and, by circumscribing the extent of the drama, lessen its variety, I cannot think it much to be lamented, that they were not known by him, or not observed: Nor, if such another poet could arise, should I very vehemently reproach him, that his first act passed at *Venice*, and his next in *Cyprus*. Such violations of rules merely positive, become the comprehensive genius of *Shakespeare*, and such censures are suitable to the minute and slender criticism of *Voltaire:*

> *Non usque adeo permiscuit imis*
> *Longus summa dies, ut non, si voce Metelli*
> *Serventur leges, malint a Cæsare tolli.*[1]

Yet when I speak thus slightly of dramatick rules, I cannot but recollect how much wit and learning may be produced against me: before such authorities I am afraid to stand, not that I think the present question one of those that are to be decided by mere authority, but because it is to be suspected, that these precepts have not been so easily received but for better reasons than I have yet been able to find. The result of my enquiries, in which it would be ludicrous to boast of impartiality, is, that the unities of time and place are not essential to a just drama, that though they may sometimes conduce to pleasure, they are always to be sacrificed to the nobler beauties of variety and instruction; and that a play, written with nice observation of critical rules, is to be contemplated as an elaborate curiosity, as the product of superfluous and ostentatious art, by which is shewn, rather what is possible, than what is necessary.

He that, without diminution of any other excellence, shall preserve all the unities unbroken, deserves the like applause with the architect, who shall display all the orders of architecture in a citadel, without any deduction from its strength; but the principal beauty of a citadel is to exclude the enemy; and the greatest graces of a play, are to copy nature and instruct life.

Perhaps what I have here not dogmatically but deliberatively written, may recal the principles of the drama to a new examination. I am almost frighted at my own temerity; and when I estimate the fame and the strength of those that maintain the contrary opinion, am ready to sink down in reverential silence; as *Æneas* withdrew from the defence of *Troy*, when he saw *Neptune* shaking the wall, and *Juno* heading the besiegers.

Those whom my arguments cannot persuade to give their approbation to the judgment of *Shakespeare*, will easily, if they consider the condition of his life, make some allowance for his ignorance.

Every man's performances, to be rightly estimated, must be compared with the state of the age in which he lived, and with his own particular opportunities; and though to the reader a book be not worse or better for the circumstances of the authour, yet as there is always a silent reference of human works to human abilities, and as the enquiry, how far man may extend his designs, or how high he may rate his native force, is of far greater dignity than in what rank we shall place any particular performance, curiosity is always busy to discover the instruments, as well as to survey the workmanship, to know how much is to be ascribed to original powers, and how much to casual and adventitious help. The palaces of *Peru* or *Mexico* were certainly mean and incommodious habitations, if compared to the houses of *European* monarchs; yet who could forbear to view them with astonishment, who remembered that they were built without the use of iron?

The *English* nation, in the time of *Shakespeare*, was yet struggling to emerge from barbarity. The philology of *Italy* had been transplanted hither in the reign of *Henry* the Eighth; and the learned languages had been successfully cultivated by *Lilly*, *Linacer*, and *More*; by *Pole*, *Cheke*, and *Gardiner*; and afterwards by *Smith*, *Clerk*, *Haddon*, and *Ascham*. Greek was now taught to boys in the principal schools; and those who united elegance with learning, read, with great diligence, the *Italian* and *Spanish* poets. But literature was yet confined to professed scholars, or to men and women of high rank. The publick was gross and dark; and to be able to read and write, was an accomplishment still valued for its rarity.

Nations, like individuals, have their infancy. A people newly awakened to literary curiosity, being yet unacquainted with the true state of things, knows not how to judge of that which is proposed as its resemblance. Whatever is remote from common appearances is always welcome to vulgar, as to childish credulity; and of a country unenlightened by learning, the whole people is the vulgar. The study of those who then aspired to plebeian learning was laid out upon adventures, giants, dragons, and enchantments. *The Death of Arthur* was the favourite volume.

The mind, which has feasted on the luxurious wonders of fiction, has no taste of the insipidity of truth. A play which imitated only the common occurrences of the world, would, upon the admirers of *Palmerin* and *Guy of Warwick*, have made little impression; he that wrote for such an audience was under the necessity of looking round for strange events and fabulous transactions, and that incredibility, by which maturer knowledge is offended, was the chief recommendation of writings, to unskilful curiosity.

Our authour's plots are generally borrowed from novels, and it is reasonable to suppose, that he chose the most popular, such as were read by many, and related by more; for his audience could not have followed him through the intricacies of the drama, had they not held the thread of the story in their hands.

The stories, which we now find only in remoter authours, were in his time accessible and familiar. The fable of *As you like it*, which is supposed to be copied from *Chaucer's* Gamelyn, was a little pamphlet of those times; and old Mr. *Cibber* remembered the tale of *Hamlet* in plain *English* prose, which the criticks have now to seek in *Saxo Grammaticus*.

His *English* histories he took from *English* chronicles and *English* ballads; and as the ancient writers were made known to his countrymen by versions, they supplied him with new subjects; he dilated some of *Plutarch's* lives into plays, when they had been translated by *North*.

His plots, whether historical or fabulous, are always crouded with incidents, by which the attention of a rude people was more easily caught than by sentiment or argumentation; and such is the power of the marvellous even over those who despise it, that every man finds his mind more strongly seized by the tragedies of *Shakespeare* than of any other writer; others please us by particular speeches, but he always makes us anxious for the event, and has perhaps excelled all but *Homer* in securing the first purpose of a writer, by exciting restless and unquenchable curiosity and compelling him that reads his work to read it through. The shows and bustle with which his plays abound have the same original. As knowledge advances, pleasure passes from the eye to the ear, but returns, as it declines, from the ear to the eye. Those to whom our authour's labours were exhibited had more skill in pomps or processions than in poetical language, and perhaps wanted some visible and discriminated events, as comments on the dialogue. He knew how he should most please; and whether his practice is more agreeable to nature, or whether his example has prejudiced the nation, we still find that on our stage something must be done as well as said, and inactive declamation is very coldly heard, however musical or elegant, passionate or sublime.

Voltaire expresses his wonder, that our authour's extravagances are endured by a nation, which has seen the tragedy of *Cato*. Let him be answered, that *Addison* speaks the language of poets, and *Shakespeare*, of men. We find in *Cato* innumerable beauties which enamour us of its authour, but we see nothing that acquaints us with human sentiments or human actions; we place it with the fairest and the noblest progeny which judgment propagates by conjunction with learning, but *Othello* is the vigorous and vivacious offspring of observation impregnated by genius. *Cato* affords a splendid exhibition of artificial and fictitious manners, and delivers just and noble sentiments, in diction easy, elevated and harmonious, but its hopes and fears communicate no vibration to the heart; the composition refers us only to the writer; we pronounce the name of *Cato*, but we think on *Addison*.

The work of a correct and regular writer is a garden accurately formed and diligently planted, varied with shades, and scented with flowers; the composition of *Shakespeare* is a forest, in which oaks extend their branches, and pines tower in the air, interspersed sometimes with weeds and brambles, and sometimes giving shelter to myrtles and to roses; filling the eye with awful pomp, and gratifying the mind with endless diversity. Other poets display cabinets of precious rarities, minutely finished, wrought into shape, and polished into brightness. *Shakespeare* opens a mine which contains gold and diamonds in unexhaustible plenty, though clouded by incrustations, debased by impurities, and mingled with a mass of meaner minerals.

It has been much disputed, whether *Shakespeare* owed his excellence to his own native force, or whether he had the common helps of scholastick education, the precepts of critical science, and the examples of ancient authours.

There has always prevailed a tradition, that *Shakespeare* wanted learning, that he had no regular education, nor much skill in the dead languages. *Johnson*, his friend, affirms, that *he had small Latin, and no Greek;* who, besides that he had no imaginable temptation to falsehood, wrote at a time when the character and acquisitions of *Shakespeare* were known to multitudes. His evidence ought therefore to decide the controversy, unless some testimony of equal force could be opposed.

Some have imagined, that they have discovered deep learning in many imitations of old writers; but the examples which I have known urged, were drawn from books translated in his time; or were such easy coincidences of thought, as will happen to all who consider the same subjects; or such remarks on life or axioms of morality as float in conversation, and are transmitted through the world in proverbial sentences.

I have found it remarked, that, in this important sentence, *Go before, I'll follow,* we read a translation of, *I prae, sequar.* I have been told, that when *Caliban*, after a pleasing dream, says, *I cry'd to sleep again,* the authour imitates *Anacreon*, who had, like every other man, the same wish on the same occasion.

There are a few passages which may pass for imitations, but so few, that the exception only confirms the rule; he obtained them from accidental quotations, or by oral communication, and as he used what he had, would have used more if he had obtained it.

The *Comedy of Errors* is confessedly taken from the *Menæchmi* of *Plautus;* from the only play of *Plautus* which was then in *English*. What can be more probable, than that he who copied that, would have copied more; but that those which were not translated were inaccessible?

Whether he knew the modern languages is uncertain. That his plays have some *French* scenes proves but little; he might easily procure them to be written, and probably, even though he had known the language in the common degree, he could not have written it without assistance. In the story of *Romeo* and *Juliet* he is observed to have followed the *English* translation, where it deviates from the *Italian;* but this on the other part proves nothing against his knowledge of the original. He was to copy, not what he knew himself, but what was known to his audience.

It is most likely that he had learned *Latin* sufficiently to make him acquainted with construction, but that he never advanced to an easy perusal of the *Roman* authours. Concerning his skill in modern languages, I can find no sufficient ground of determination; but as no limitations of *French* or *Italian* authours have been discovered, though the *Italian* poetry was then high in esteem, I am inclined to believe, that he read little more than *English*, and chose for his fables only such tales as he found translated.

That much knowledge is scattered over his works is very justly observed by *Pope*, but it is often such knowledge as books did not supply. He that will understand *Shakespeare*, must not be content to study him in the closet, he must look for his meaning sometimes among the sports of the field, and sometimes among the manufactures of the shop.

There is however proof enough that he was

a very diligent reader, nor was our language then so indigent of books, but that he might very liberally indulge his curiosity without excursion into foreign literature. Many of the *Roman* authours were translated, and some of the *Greek;* the reformation had filled the kingdom with theological learning; most of the topicks of human disquisition had found *English* writers; and poetry had been cultivated, not only with diligence, but success. This was a stock of knowledge sufficient for a mind so capable of appropriating and improving it.

But the greater part of his excellence was the product of his own genius. He found the *English* stage in a state of the utmost rudeness; no essays either in tragedy or comedy had appeared, from which it could be discovered to what degree of delight either one or other might be carried. Neither character nor dialogue were yet understood. *Shakespeare* may be truly said to have introduced them both amongst us, and in some of his happier scenes to have carried them both to the utmost height.

By what gradations of improvement he proceeded, is not easily known; for the chronology of his works is yet unsettled. *Rowe* is of opinion, that *perhaps we are not to look for his beginning, like those of other writers, in his least perfect works; art had so little, and nature so large a share in what he did, that for ought I know,* says he, *the performances of his youth, as they were the most vigorous, were the best.* But the power of nature is only the power of using to any certain purpose the materials which diligence procures, or opportunity supplies. Nature gives no man knowledge, and when images are collected by study and experience, can only assist in combining or applying them. *Shakespeare,* however favoured by nature, could impart only what he had learned; and as he must increase his ideals, like other mortals, by gradual acquisition, he, like them, grew wiser as he grew older, could display life better, as he knew it more, and instruct with more efficacy, as he was himself more amply instructed.

There is a vigilance of observation and accuracy of distinction which books and precepts cannot confer; from this almost all original and native excellence proceeds. *Shakespeare* must have looked upon mankind with perspicacity, in the highest degree curious and attentive. Other writers borrow their characters from preceding writers, and diversify them only by the accidental appendages of present manners; the dress is a little varied, but the body is the same. Our authour had both matter and form to provide; for except the characters of *Chaucer,* to whom I think he is not much indebted, there were no writers in *English,* and perhaps not many in other modern languages, which shewed life in its native colours.

The contest about the original benevolence or malignity of man had not yet commenced. Speculation had not yet attempted to analyse the mind, to trace the passions to their sources, to unfold the seminal principles of vice and virtue, or sound the depths of the heart for the motives of action. All those enquiries, which from that time that human nature became the fashionable study, have been made sometimes with nice discernment, but often with idle subtilty, were yet unattempted. The tales, with which the infancy of learning was satisfied, exhibited only the superficial appearances of action, related the events but omitted the causes, and were formed for such as delighted in wonders rather than in truth. Mankind was not then to be studied in the closet; he that would know the world, was under the necessity of gleaning his own remarks, by mingling as he could in its business and amusements.

Boyle congratulated himself upon his high

birth, because it favoured his curiosity, by facilitating his access. *Shakespeare* had no such advantage; he came to *London* a needy adventurer, and lived for a time by very mean employments. Many works of genius and learning have been performed in states of life, that appear very little favourable to thought or to enquiry; so many, that he who considers them is inclined to think that he sees enterprise and perseverance predominating over all external agency, and bidding help and hindrance vanish before them. The genius of *Shakespeare* was not to be depressed by the weight of poverty, nor limited by the narrow conversation to which men in want are inevitably condemned; the incumbrances of his fortune were shaken from his mind, *as dewdrops from a lion's mane.*

Though he had so many difficulties to encounter, and so little assistance to surmount them, he has been able to obtain an exact knowledge of many modes of life, and many casts of native dispositions; to vary them with great multiplicity; to mark them by nice distinctions; and to shew them in full view by proper combinations. In this part of his performances he had none to imitate, but has himself been imitated by all succeeding writers; and it may be doubted, whether from all his successors more maxims of theoretical knowledge, or more rules of practical prudence, can be collected, than he alone has given to his country.

Nor was his attention confined to the actions of men; he was an exact surveyor of the inanimate world; his descriptions have always some peculiarities, gathered by contemplating things as they really exist. It may be observed, that the oldest poets of many nations preserve their reputation, and that the following generations of wit, after a short celebrity, sink into oblivion. The first, whoever they be, must take their sentiments and descriptions immediately from knowledge; the resemblance is therefore just, their descriptions are verified by every eye, and their sentiments acknowledged by every breast. Those whom their fame invites to the same studies, copy partly them, and partly nature, till the books of one age gain such authority, as to stand in the place of nature to another, and imitation, always deviating a little, becomes at last capricious and casual. *Shakespeare,* whether life or nature be his subject, shews plainly, that he has seen with his own eyes; he gives the image which he receives, not weakened or distorted by the intervention of any other mind; the ignorant feel his representations to be just, and the learned see that they are compleat.

Perhaps it would not be easy to find any authour, except *Homer,* who invented so much as *Shakespeare,* who so much advanced the studies which he cultivated, or effused so much novelty upon his age or country. The form, the characters, the language, and the shows of the *English* drama are his. *He seems,* says *Dennis, to have been the very original of our* English *tragical harmony, that is, the harmony of blank verse, diversified often by dissyllable and trissyllable terminations. For the diversity distinguishes it from heroick harmony, and by bringing it nearer to common use makes it more proper to gain attention, and more fit for action and dialogue. Such verse we make when we are writing prose; we make such verse in common conversation.*

I know not whether this praise is rigorously just. The dissyllable termination, which the critic rightly appropriates to the drama, is to be found, though, I think, not in *Gorboduc* which is confessedly before our author; yet in *Hieronnymo,* of which the date is not certain, but which there is reason to believe at least as old as his earliest plays. This however is certain, that he is the first who taught either tragedy or comedy to please, there being no theatrical piece of any older writer, of which the name is known, except to antiquaries and collectors of books, which are sought because they are scarce, and would not have been scarce, had they been much esteemed.

To him we must ascribe the praise, unless *Spenser* may divide it with him, of having first discovered to how much smoothness and harmony the *English* language could be softened. He has speeches, perhaps sometimes scenes, which have all the delicacy of *Rowe*, without his effeminacy. He endeavours indeed commonly to strike by the force and vigour of his dialogue, but he never executes his purpose better, than when he tries to sooth by softness.

Yet it must be at last confessed, that as we owe every thing to him, he owes something to us; that, if much of his praise is paid by perception and judgement, much is likewise given by custom and veneration. We fix our eyes upon his graces, and turn them from his deformities, and endure in him what we should in another loath or despise. If we endured without praising, respect for the father of our drama might excuse us; but I have seen, in the book of some modern critick, a collection of anomalies, which shew that he has corrupted language by every mode of depravation, but which his admirer has accumulated as a monument of honour.

He has scenes of undoubted and perpetual excellence, but perhaps not one play, which, if it were now exhibited as the work of a contemporary writer, would be heard to the conclusion. I am indeed far from thinking, that his works were wrought to his own ideas of perfection; when they were such as would satisfy the audience, they satisfied the writer. It is seldom that authours, though more studious of fame than *Shakespeare*, rise much above the standard of their own age; to add a little of what is best will always be sufficient for present praise, and those who find themselves exalted into fame, are willing to credit their encomiasts, and to spare the labour of contending with themselves.

It does not appear, that *Shakespeare* thought his works worthy of posterity, that he levied any ideal tribute upon future times, or had any further prospect, than of present popularity and present profit. When his plays had been acted, his hope was at an end; he solicited no addition of honour from the reader. He therefore made no scruple to repeat the same jests in many dialogues, or to entangle different plots by the same knot of perplexity, which may be at least forgiven him, by those who recollect, that of *Congreve's* four comedies, two are concluded by a marriage in a mask, by a deception, which perhaps never happened, and which, whether likely or not, he did not invent.

So careless was this great poet of future fame, that, though he retired to ease and plenty, while he was yet little *declined into the vale of years*, before he could be disgusted with fatigue, or disabled by infirmity, he made no collection of his works, nor desired to rescue those that had been already published from the depravations that obscured them, or secure to the rest a better destiny, by giving them to the world in their genuine state.

Of the plays which bear the name of *Shakespeare* in the late editions, the greater part were not published till about seven years after his death, and the few which appeared in his life are apparently thrust into the world without the care of the authour, and therefore probably without his knowledge.

Of all the publishers, clandestine or professed, their negligence and unskilfulness has by the late revisers been sufficiently shown. The faults of all are indeed numerous and gross, and have not only corrupted many passages perhaps beyond recovery, but have brought others into suspicion, which are only obscured by obsolete phraseology, or by the writer's unskilfulness and affection. To alter is more easy than to explain, and temerity is a more common quality than diligence. Those who saw that they must employ conjecture to a certain degree, were willing to indulge it a little further. Had the author published his own works, we should have sat quietly down to disentangle his intricacies, and clear his obscurities; but now we tear what we cannot loose, and eject what we happen not to understand.

The faults are more than could have happened without the concurrence of many causes. The stile of *Shakespeare* was in itself ungrammatical, perplexed and obscure; his works were transcribed for the players by those who may be supposed to have seldom understood them; they were transmitted by copiers equally unskilful, who still multiplied errours; they were perhaps sometimes mutilated by the actors, for the sake of shortening the speeches; and were at last printed without correction of the press.

In this state they remained, not as Dr. *Warburton* supposes, because they were unregarded, but because the editor's art was not yet applied to modern languages, and our ancestors were accustomed to so much negligence of *English* printers, that they could very patiently endure it. At last an edition was undertaken by *Rowe;* not because a poet was to be published by a poet, for *Rowe* seems to have thought very little on correction or explanation, but that our authour's works might appear like those of his fraternity, with the appendages of a life and recommendatory preface. *Rowe* has been clamorously blamed for not performing what he did not undertake, and it is time that justice be done him, by confessing, that though he seems to have had no thought of corruption beyond the printer's errours, yet he has made many emendations, if they were not made before, which his successors have received without acknowledgement, and which, if they had produced them, would have filled pages and pages with censures of the stupidity by which the faults were committed, with displays of the absurdities which they involved, with ostentatious expositions of the new reading, and self congratulations on the happiness of discovering it.

Of *Rowe,* as of all the editors, I have preserved the preface, and have likewise retained the authour's life, though not written with much elegance or spirit; it relates however what is now to be known, and therefore deserves to pass through all succeeding publications.

The nation had been for many years content enough with Mr. *Rowe's* performance, when Mr. *Pope* made them acquainted with the true state of *Shakespeare's* text, shewed that it was extremely corrupt, and gave reason to hope that there were means of reforming it. He collated the old copies, which none had thought to examine before, and restored many lines to their integrity; but, by a very compendious criticism, he rejected whatever he disliked, and thought more of amputation than of cure.

I know not why he is commended by Dr. *Warburton* for distinguishing the genuine from the spurious plays. In this choice he exerted no judgment of his own; the plays which he received, were given by *Hemings* and *Condel,* the first editors; and those which he rejected, though, according to the licentiousness of the press in those times, they were printed during *Shakespeare's* life, with his name, had been omitted by his friends, and were never added to his works before the edition of 1664, from which they were copied by the later printers.

This was a work which *Pope* seems to have thought unworthy of his abilities, being not able to suppress his contempt of *the dull duty of an editor.* He understood but half his undertaking. The duty of a collator is indeed dull, yet, like other tedious tasks, is very necessary; but an emendatory critick would ill discharge his duty, without qualities very different from dullness. In perusing a corrupted piece, he must have before him all possibilities of meaning, with all possibilities of expression. Such must be his comprehension of thought, and such his copiousness of language. Out of many readings possible, he must be able to select that which best suits with the state, opinions, and modes of language prevailing in every age, and with his authour's particular cast of thought, and turn of expression. Such must be his knowledge, and such his taste. Conjectural criticism demands more than humanity possesses, and he that exercises it with most praise has very frequent need of indulgence. Let us now be told no more of the dull duty of an editor.

Confidence is the common consequence of success. They whose excellence of any kind has been loudly celebrated, are ready to conclude, that their powers are universal. *Pope's* edition fell below his own expectations, and he was so much offended, when he was found to have left any thing for others to do, that he past the latter part of his life in a state of hostility with verbal criticism.

I have retained all his notes, that no fragment of so great a writer may be lost; his preface, valuable alike for elegance of composition and justness of remark, and containing a general criticism on his authour, so extensive, that little can be added, and so exact, that little can be disputed, every editor has an interest to suppress, but that every reader would demand its insertion.

Pope was succeeded by *Theobald*, a man of narrow comprehension and small acquisitions, with no native and intrinsick splendour of genius, with little of the artificial light of learning, but zealous for minute accuracy, and not negligent in pursuing it. He collated the ancient copies, and rectified many errours. A man so anxiously scrupulous might have been expected to do more, but what little he did was commonly right.

In his report of copies and editions he is not to be trusted, without examination. He speaks sometimes indefinitely of copies, when he has only one. In his enumeration of editions, he mentions the two first folios as of high, and the third folio as of middle authority; but the truth is, that the first is equivalent to all others, and that the rest only deviate from it by the printer's negligence. Whoever has any of the folios has all, excepting those diversities which mere reiteration of editions will produce. I collated them all at the beginning, but afterwards used only the first.

Of his notes I have generally retained those which he retained himself in his second edition, except when they were confuted by subsequent annotators, or were too minute to merit preservation. I have sometimes adopted his restoration of a comma, without inserting the panegyrick in which he celebrated himself for his atchievement. The exuberant excrescense of his diction I have often lopped, his triumphant exultations over *Pope* and *Rowe* I have sometimes suppressed, and his contemptible ostentation I have frequently concealed; but I have in some places shewn him, as he would have shewn himself, for the reader's diversion, that the inflated emptiness of some notes may justify or excuse the contraction of the rest.

Theobald, thus weak and ignorant, thus mean and faithless, thus petulant and ostentatious, by the good luck of having *Pope* for his enemy, has escaped, and escaped alone, with reputation, from this undertaking. So willingly does the world support those who solicite favour, against those who command reverence; and so easily is he praised, whom no man can envy.

Our authour fell then into the hands of

Sir *Thomas Hanmer*, the *Oxford* editor, a man, in my opinion, eminently qualified by nature for such studies. He had, what is the first requisite to emendatory criticism, that intuition by which the poet's intention is immediately discovered, and that dexterity of intellect which despatches its work by the easiest means. He had undoubtedly read much; his acquaintance with customs, opinions, and traditions, seems to have been large; and he is often learned without shew. He seldom passes what he does not understand, without an attempt to find or to make a meaning, and sometimes hastily makes what a little more attention would have found. He is solicitous to reduce to grammar, what he could not be sure that his authour intended to be grammatical. *Shakespeare* regarded more the series of ideas, than of words; and his language, not being designed for the reader's desk, was all that he desired it to be, if it conveyed his meaning to the audience.

Hanmer's care of the metre has been too violently censured. He found the measures reformed in so many passages, by the silent labours of some editors, with the silent acquiescence of the rest, that he thought himself allowed to extend a little further the license, which had already been carried so far without reprehension; and of his corrections in general, it must be confessed, that they are often just, and made commonly with the least possible violation of the text.

But, by inserting his emendations, whether invented or borrowed, into the page, without any notice of varying copies, he has appropriated the labour of his predecessors, and made his own edition of little authority. His confidence indeed, both in himself and others, was too great; he supposes all to be right that was done by *Pope* and *Theobald;* he seems not to suspect a critick of fallibility, and it was but reasonable that he should claim what he so liberally granted.

As he never writes without careful enquiry and diligent consideration, I have received all his notes, and believe that every reader will wish for more.

Of the last editor it is more difficult to speak. Respect is due to high place, tenderness to living reputation, and veneration to genius and learning; but he cannot be justly offended at that liberty of which he has himself so frequently given an example, nor very solicitous what is thought of notes, which, I suppose, since the ardour of composition is remitted, he no longer numbers among his happy effusions.

The original and predominant errour of his commentary, is acquiescence in his first thoughts; that precipitation which is produced by consciousness of quick discernment; and that confidence which presumes to do, by surveying the surface, what labour only can perform, by penetrating the bottom. His notes exhibit sometimes perverse interpretations, and sometimes improbable conjectures; he at one time gives the authour more profundity of meaning, than the sentence admits, and at another discovers absurdities, where the sense is plain to every other reader. But his emendations are likewise often happy and just; and his interpretation of obscure passages learned and sagacious.

Of his notes, I have commonly rejected those, against which the general voice of the publick has exclaimed, or which their own incongruity immediately condemns, and which, I suppose, the authour himself would desire to be forgotten. Of the rest, to part I have given the highest approbation, by inserting the offered reading in the text; part I have left to the judgment of the reader, as doubtful, though specious; and part I have censured without reserve, but I am sure without bitterness of malice, and I hope, without wantonness of insult.

It is no pleasure to me, in revising my volumes, to observe how much paper is wasted in confutation. Whoever considers the revolutions of learning, and the various questions of greater or less importance, upon which wit and reason have exercised their powers, must lament the unsuccessfulness of enquiry, and the slow advances of truth, when he reflects, that great part of the labour of every writer is only the destruction of those that went before him. The first care of the builder of a new system, is to demolish the fabricks which are standing. The chief desire of him that comments an authour, is to shew how much other commentators have corrupted and obscured him. The opinions prevalent in one age, as truths above the reach of controversy, are confuted and rejected in another, and rise again to reception in remoter times. Thus the human mind is kept in motion without progress. Thus sometimes truth and errour, and sometimes contrarieties of errour, take each other's place by reciprocal invasion. The tide of seeming knowledge which is poured over one generation, retires and leaves another naked and barren; the sudden meteors of intelligence which for a while appear to shoot their beams into the regions of obscurity, on a sudden withdraw their lustre, and leave mortals again to grope their way.

These elevations and depressions of reknown, and the contradictions to which all improvers of knowledge must for ever be exposed, since they are not escaped by the highest and brightest of mankind, may surely be endured with patience by criticks and annotators, who can rank themselves but as the satellites of their authours. How canst thou beg for life, says *Achilles* to his captive, when thou knowest that thou art now to suffer only what must another day be suffered by *Achilles*?

Dr. *Warburton* had a name sufficient to confer celebrity on those who could exalt themselves into antagonists, and his notes have raised a clamour too loud to be distinct. His chief assailants are the authours of *the Canons of criticism* and of the *Review* of Shakespeare's *text;* of whom one ridicules his errours with airy petulance, suitable enough to the levity of the controversy; the other attacks them with gloomy malignity, as if he were dragging to justice an assassin or incendiary. The one stings like a fly, sucks a little blood, takes a gay flutter, and returns for more; the other bites like a viper, and would be glad to leave inflammations and gangrene behind him. When I think on one, with his confederates, I remember the danger of *Coriolanus,* who was afraid that *girls with spits, and boys with stones, should slay him in puny battle;* when the other crosses my imagination, I remember the prodigy in *Macbeth.*

> An eagle tow'ring in his pride of place,
> Was by a mousing owl hawk'd at and kill'd.

Let me however do them justice. One is a wit, and one a scholar. They have both shown acuteness sufficient in the discovery of faults, and have both advanced some probable interpretations of obscure passages; but when they aspire to conjecture and emendation, it appears how falsely we all estimate our own abilites, and the little which they have been able to perform might have taught them more candour to the endeavours of others.

Before Dr. *Warburton's* edition, *Critical observations on* Shakespeare had been published by Mr. *Upton,* a man skilled in languages, and acquainted with books, but who seems to have had no great vigour of genius or nicety of taste. Many of his explanations are curious and useful, but he likewise, though he professed to oppose the licentious confidence of editors, and adhere to the old copies, is unable to restrain the rage of emendation, though his ardour is ill seconded by his skill. Every cold empirick, when his heart is expanded by a successful experiment, swells into a theorist, and the laborious collator at some unlucky moment frolicks in conjecture.

Critical, historical and explanatory notes have been likewise published upon *Shakespeare* by Dr. *Grey*, whose diligent perusal of the old *English* writers has enabled him to make some useful observations. What he undertook he has well enough performed, but as he neither attempts judicial nor emendatory criticism, he employs rather his memory than his sagacity. It were to be wished that all would endeavour to imitate his modesty who have not been able to surpass his knowledge.

I can say with great sincerity of all my predecessors, what I hope will hereafter be said of me, that not one has left *Shakespeare* without improvement, nor is there one to whom I have not been indebted for assistance and information. Whatever I have taken from them it was my intention to refer to its original authour, and it is certain, that what I have not given to another, I believed when I wrote it to be my own. In some perhaps I have been anticipated; but if I am ever found to encroach upon the remarks of any other commentator, I am willing that the honour, be it more or less, should be transferred to the first claimant, for his right, and his alone, stands above dispute; the second can prove his pretensions only to himself, nor can himself always distinguish invention, with sufficient certainty, from recollection.

They have all been treated by me with candour, which they have not been careful of observing to one another. It is not easy to discover from what cause the acrimony of a scholiast can naturally proceed. The subjects to be discussed by him are of very small importance; they involve neither property nor liberty; nor favour the interest of sect or party. The various readings of copies, and different interpretations of a passage, seem to be questions that might exercise the wit, without engaging the passions. But, whether it be, that *small things make mean men proud*, and vanity catches small occasions; or that all contrariety of opinion, even in those that can defend it no longer, makes proud men angry; there is often found in commentaries a spontaneous strain of invective and contempt, more eager and venomous than is vented by the most furious controvertist in politicks against those whom he is hired to defame.

Perhaps the lightness of the matter may conduce to the vehemence of the agency; when the truth to be investigated is so near to inexistence, as to escape attention, its bulk is to be enlarged by rage and exclamation: That to which all would be indifferent in its original state, may attract notice when the fate of a name is appended to it. A commentator has indeed great temptations to supply by turbulence what he wants of dignity, to beat his little gold to a spacious surface, to work that to foam which no art or diligence can exalt to spirit.

The notes which I have borrowed or written are either illustrative, by which difficulties are explained; or judicial by which faults and beauties are remarked; or emendatory, by which depravations are corrected.

The explanations transcribed from others, if I do not subjoin any other interpretation, I suppose commonly to be right, at least I intend by acquiescence to confess, that I have nothing better to propose.

After the labours of all the editors, I found many passages which appeared to me likely to obstruct the greater number of readers, and thought it my duty to facilitate their passage. It is impossible for an expositor not to write too little for some, and too much for others. He can only judge what is necessary by his own experience; and how long soever he may deliberate, will at last explain many lines which the learned will think impossible to be mistaken, and omit many for which the ignorant will want his help. These are censures merely relative, and must be quietly endured. I have endeavoured to be neither superfluously copious, nor scrupulously reserved, and hope that I have made my authour's meaning accessible to many who before were frighted from perusing him, and contributed something to the publick, by diffusing innocent and rational pleasure.

The compleat explanation of an authour not systematick and consequential, but desultory and vagrant, abounding in casual allusions and light hints, is not to be expected from any single scholiast. All personal reflections, when names are suppressed, must be in a few years irrecoverably obliterated; and customs, too minute to attract the notice of law, such as modes of dress, formalities of conversation, rules of visits, disposition of furniture, and practices of ceremony, which naturally find places in familiar dialogue, are so fugitive and unsubstantial, that they are not easily retained or recovered. What can be known, will be collected by chance, from the recesses of obscure and obsolete papers, perused commonly with some other view. Of this knowledge every man has some, and none has much; but when an authour has engaged the publick attention, those who can add any thing to his illustration, communicate their discoveries, and time produces what had eluded diligence.

To time I have been obliged to resign many passages, which, though I did not understand them, will perhaps hereafter be explained, having, I hope, illustrated some, which others have neglected or mistaken, sometimes by short remarks, or marginal directions, such as every editor has added at his will, and often by comments more laborious than the matter will seem to deserve; but that which is most difficult is not always most important, and to an editor nothing is a trifle by which his authour is obscured.

The poetical beauties or defects I have not been very diligent to observe. Some plays have more, and some fewer judicial observations, not in proportion to their difference of merit, but because I gave this part of my design to chance and to caprice. The reader, I believe, is seldom pleased to find his opinion anticipated; it is natural to delight more in what we find or make, than in what we receive. Judgement, like other faculties, is improved by practice, and its advancement is hindered by submission to dictatorial decisions, as the memory grows torpid by the use of a table book. Some initiation is however necessary; of all skill, part is infused by precept, and part is obtained by habit; I have therefore shewn so much as may enable the candidate of criticism to discover the rest.

To the end of most plays, I have added short strictures, containing a general censure of faults, or praise of excellence; in which I know not how much I have concurred with the current opinion; but I have not, by any affectation of singularity, deviated from it. Nothing is minutely and particularly examined, and therefore it is to be supposed, that in the plays which are condemned there is much to be praised, and in these which are praised much to be condemned.

The part of criticism in which the whole succession of editors has laboured with the greatest diligence, which has occasioned the most arrogant ostentation, and excited the keenest acrimony, is the emendation of corrupted passages, to which the publick attention having been first drawn by the violence of contention between *Pope* and *Theobald*, has been continued by the persecution, which, with a kind of conspiracy, has been since raised against all the publishers of *Shakespeare*.

That many passages have passed in a state of depravation through all the editions is indubitably certain; of these the restoration is only to be attempted by collation of copies or sagacity of conjecture. The collator's province is safe and easy, the conjecturer's perilous and difficult. Yet as the greater part of the plays are extant only in one copy, the peril must not be avoided, nor the difficulty refused.

Of the readings which this emulation of amendment has hitherto produced, some from the labours of every publisher I have advanced into the text; those are to be considered as in my opinion sufficiently supported; some I have rejected without mention, as evidently erroneous; some I have left in the notes without censure or approbation, as resting in equipoise between objection and defence; and some, which seemed specious but not right, I have inserted with a subsequent animadversion.

Having classed the observations of others, I was at last to try what I could substitute for their mistakes, and how I could supply their omissions. I collated such copies as I could procure, and wished for more, but have not found the collectors of these rarities very communicative. Of the editions which chance or kindness put into my hands I have given an enumeration, that I may not be blamed for neglecting what I had not the power to do.

By examining the old copies, I soon found that the later publishers, with all their boasts of diligence, suffered many passages to stand unauthorised, and contented themselves with *Rowe's* regulation of the text, even where they knew it to be arbitrary, and with a little consideration might have found it to be wrong. Some of these alterations are only the ejection of a word for one that appeared to him more elegant or more intelligible. These corruptions I have often silently rectified; for the history of our language, and the true force of our words, can only be preserved, by keeping the text of authours free from adulteration. Others, and those very frequent, smoothed the cadence, or regulated the measure; on these I have not exercised the same rigour; if only a word was transposed, or a particle inserted or omitted, I have sometimes suffered the line to stand; for the inconstancy of the copies is such, as that some liberties may be easily permitted. But this practice I have not suffered to proceed far, having restored the primitive diction wherever it could for any reason be preferred.

The emendations, which comparison of copies supplied, I have inserted in the text; sometimes where the improvement was slight, without notice, and sometimes with an account of the reasons of the change.

Conjecture, though it be sometimes unavoidable, I have not wantonly nor licentiously indulged. It has been my settled principle, that the reading of the ancient books is probably true, and therefore is not to be disturbed for the sake of elegance, perspicuity, or mere improvement of the sense. For though much credit is not due to the fidelity, nor any to the judgement of the first publishers, yet they who had the copy before their eyes were more likely to read it right, than we who read it only by imagination. But it is evident that they have often made strange mistakes by ignorance or negligence, and that therefore something may be properly attempted by criticism, keeping the middle way between presumption and timidity.

Such criticism I have attempted to practice, and where any passage appeared inextricably perplexed, have endeavoured to discover how it may be recalled to sense, with least violence. But my first labour is, always to turn the old text on every side, and try if there be any interstice, through which light can find its way; nor would *Huetius* himself condemn me, as refusing the trouble of research, for the ambition of alteration. In this modest industry I have not been unsuccessful. I have rescued many lines from the violations of temerity, and secured many scenes from the inroads of correction. I have adopted the *Roman* sentiment, that it is more honourable to save a citizen, than to kill an enemy, and have been more careful to protect than to attack.

I have preserved the common distribution of the plays into acts, though I believe it to be in almost all the plays void of authority. Some of those which are divided in the later editions have no division in the first folio, and some that are divided in the folio have no division in the preceding copies. The settled mode of the theatre requires four intervals in the play, but few, if any, of our authour's compositions can be properly distributed in that manner. An act is so much of the drama as passes without intervention of time or change of place. A pause makes a new act. In every real, and therefore in every imitative action, the intervals may be more or fewer, the restriction of five acts being accidental and arbitrary. This *Shakespeare* knew, and this he practised; his plays were written, and at first printed in one unbroken continuity, and ought now to be exhibited with short pauses, interposed as often as the scene is changed, or any considerable time is required to pass. This method would at once quell a thousand absurdities.

In restoring the author's works to their integrity, I have considered the punctuation as wholly in my power; for what could be their care of colons and commas, who corrupted words and sentences. Whatever could be done by adjusting points is therefore silently performed, in some plays with much diligence, in others with less; it is hard to keep a busy eye steadily fixed upon evanescent atoms, or a discursive mind upon evanescent truth.

The same liberty has been taken with a few particles, or other words of slight effect. I have sometimes inserted or omitted them without notice. I have done that sometimes, which the other editors have done always, and which indeed the state of the text may sufficiently justify.

The greater part of readers, instead of blaming us for passing trifles, will wonder that on mere trifles so much labour is expended, with such importance of debate, and such solemnity of diction. To these I answer with confidence, that they are judging of an art which they do not understand; yet cannot much reproach them with their ignorance, nor promise that they would become in general, by learning criticism, more useful, happier or wiser.

As I practised conjecture more, I learned to trust it less; and after I had printed a few plays, resolved to insert none of my own readings in the text. Upon this caution I now congratulate myself, for every day encreases my doubt of my emendations.

Since I have confined my imagination to the margin, it must not be considered as very reprehensible, if I have suffered it to play some freaks in its own dominion. There is no danger in conjecture, if it be proposed as conjecture; and while the text remains uninjured, those changes may be safely offered, which are not considered even by him that offers them as necessary or safe.

If my readings are of little value, they have not been ostentatiously displayed or importunately obtruded. I could have written longer notes, for the art of writing notes is not of difficult attainment. The work is performed, first by railing at the stupidity, negligence, ignorance, and asinine tastelessness of the former editors, and shewing, from all that goes before and all that follows, the inelegance and absurdity of the old reading; then by proposing something which to superficial readers would seem specious, but which the editor rejects with indignation; then by producing the true reading, with a long paraphrase, and concluding with loud acclamations on the discovery, and a sober wish for the advancement and prosperity of genuine criticism.

All this may be done, and perhaps done sometimes without impropriety. But I have always suspected that the reading is right, which requires many words to prove it wrong; and the emendation wrong, that cannot without so much labour appear to be right. The justness of a happy restoration strikes at once, and the moral precept may be well applied to criticism, *quod dubitas ne feceris.*[2]

To dread the shore which he sees spread with wrecks, is natural to the sailor. I had before my eye, so many critical adventures ended in miscarriage, that caution was forced upon me. I encountered in every page Wit struggling with its own sophistry, and Learning confused by the multiplicity of its views. I was forced to censure those whom I admired, and could not but reflect, while I was dispossessing their emendations, how soon the same fate might happen to my own, and how many of the readings which I have corrected may be by some other editor defended and established.

> Criticks, I saw, that other's names efface.
> And fix their own, with labour, in the place;
> Their own, like others, soon their place resign'd,
> Or disappear'd, and left the first behind.
>
> Pope

That a conjectural critick should often be mistaken, cannot be wonderful, either to others or himself, if it be considered, that in his art there is no system, no principal and axiomatical truth that regulates subordinate positions. His chance of errour is renewed at every attempt; an oblique view of the passage, a slight misapprehension of a phrase, a casual inattention to the parts connected, is sufficient to make him not only fail, but fail ridiculously; and when he succeeds best, he produces perhaps but one reading of many probable, and he that suggests another will always be able to dispute his claims.

It is an unhappy state, in which danger is hid under pleasure. The allurements of emendation are scarcely resistible. Conjecture has all the joy and all the pride of invention, and he that has once started a happy change, is too much delighted to consider what objections may rise against it.

Yet conjectural criticism has been of great use in the learned world; nor is it my intention to depreciate a study, that has exercised so many mighty minds, from the revival of learning to our own age, from the Bishop of *Aleria* to English *Bentley*. The criticks on ancient authours have, in the exercise of their sagacity, many assistances, which the editor of *Shakespeare* is condemned to want. They are employed upon grammatical and settled languages, whose construction contributes so much to perspicuity, that *Homer* has fewer passages unintelligible than *Chaucer*. The words have not only a known regimen, but invariable quantities, which direct and confine the choice. There are commonly more manuscripts than one; and they do not often conspire in the same mistakes. Yet *Scaliger* could confess to *Salmasius* how little satisfaction his emendations gave him. *Illudunt nobis conjecturæ nostræ, quarum nos pudet, posteaquam in meliores codices incidimus.*[3] And *Lipsius* could complain, that criticks were making faults, by trying to remove them, *Ut olim vitiis, ita nunc remediis laboratur.*[4] And indeed, where mere conjecture is to be used, the emendations of *Scaliger* and *Lip-*

sius, notwithstanding their wonderful sagacity and erudition, are often vague and disputable, like mine or *Theobald's*.

Perhaps I may not be more censured for doing wrong, than for doing little; for raising in the publick expectations, which at last I have not answered. The expectation of ignorance is indefinite, and that of knowledge is often tyrranical. It is hard to satisfy those who know not what to demand, or those who demand by design what they think impossible to be done. I have indeed disappointed no opinion more than my own; yet I have endeavoured to perform my task with no slight solicitude. Not a single passage in the whole work has appeared to me corrupt, which I have not attempted to restore; or obscure, which I have not endeavoured to illustrate. In many I have failed like others; and from many, after all my efforts, I have retreated, and confessed the repulse. I have not passed over, with affected superiority, what is equally difficult to the reader and to myself, but where I could not instruct him, have owned my ignorance. I might easily have accumulated a mass of seeming learning upon easy scenes; but it ought not to be imputed to negligence, that, where nothing was necessary, nothing has been done, or that, where others have said enough, I have said no more.

Notes are often necessary, but they are necessary evils. Let him, that is yet unacquainted with the powers of *Shakespeare*, and who desires to feel the highest pleasure that the drama can give, read every play from the first scene to the last, with utter negligence of all his commentators. When his fancy is once on the wing, let it not stoop at correction or explanation. When his attention is strongly engaged, let it disdain alike to turn aside to the name of *Theobald* and of *Pope*. Let him read on through brightness and obscurity, through integrity and corruption; let him preserve his comprehension of the dialogue and his interest in the fable. And when the pleasures of novelty have ceased, let him attempt exactness, and read the commentators.

Particular passages are cleared by notes, but the general effect of the work is weakened. The mind is refrigerated by interruption; the thoughts are diverted from the principal subject; the reader is weary, he suspects not why; and at last throws away the book, which he has too diligently studied.

Parts are not to be examined till the whole has been surveyed; there is a kind of intellectual remoteness necessary for the comprehension of any great work in its full design and its true proportions; a close approach shews the smaller niceties, but the beauty of the whole is discerned no longer.

It is not very grateful to consider how little the succession of editors has added to this authour's power of pleasing. He was read, admired, studied, and imitated, while he was yet deformed with all the improprieties which ignorance and neglect could accumulate upon him; while the reading was yet not rectified, nor his allusions understood; yet then did *Dryden* pronounce "that *Shakespeare* was the man, who, of all modern and perhaps ancient poets, had the largest and most comprehensive soul." All the images of nature were still present to him, and he drew them not laboriously, but luckily; when he describes any thing, you more than see it, you feel it too. Those who accuse him to have wanted learning, give him the greater commendation; he was naturally learned; he needed not the spectacles of books to read nature; he looked inwards, and found her there. I cannot say he is every where alike; were he so, I should do him injury to compare him with the greatest of mankind. He is many times flat and insipid; his comick wit degenerating into clenches, his serious swelling into bombast. But he is always great, when some great occasion is presented to him: No man can say, he ever had a fit subject for his wit, and did not then raise himself as high above the rest of poets,

> *Quantum lenta solent inter viburna cupressi.*[5]

It is to be lamented, that such a writer should want a commentary; that his language should become obsolete, or his sentiments obscure. But it is vain to carry wishes beyond the condition of human things; that which must happen to all, has happened to *Shakespeare*, by accident and time; and more than has been suffered by any other writer since the use of types, has been suffered by him through his own negligence of fame, or perhaps by that superiority of mind, which despised its own performances, when it compared them with its powers, and judged those works unworthy to be preserved, which the criticks of following ages were to contend for the fame of restoring and explaining.

Among these candidates of inferiour fame, I am now to stand the judgment of the publick; and wish that I could confidently produce my commentary as equal to the encouragement which I have had the honour of receiving. Every work of this kind is by its nature deficient, and I should feel little solicitude about the sentence, were it to be pronounced only by the skilful and the learned.

Notes

1. "A long period of time does not bring such confusion that the laws made by Metellus should needs be abolished by Caesar."
2. "When in doubt, refrain."
3. "Our conjectures make fools of us, putting us to shame, when we later discover better manuscripts."
4. "As before we toiled over corruptions, now we struggle with corrections."
5. "As cypresses raise themselves above scraggly shrubs."

Jean-Jacques Rousseau 1712–1778

Jean-Jacques Rousseau, often dubbed the father of both French romanticism and the French Revolution, left a body of writing more complex and ambivalent than these tags would suggest. A watchmaker's son raised in strict Calvinist Geneva, Rousseau embarked at the age of 16 on a lifetime of rebellious wandering. Much of this life is documented in his extraordinarily candid *Confessions* (1770); much of its emotional content is undoubtedly reflected in his hugely successful epistolary novel, *La Nouvelle Héloïse* (1791).

Rousseau's first creative work actually came as a composer of ballet and light opera. For the *Encyclopédie*, the mid-century embodiment of Enlightenment aspirations, he wrote the article on muscial notation. But in his first essays, *Discourses on the Sciences and Arts* (1750) and *Discourse on the Origin and Foundation of Inequality Among Mankind* (1754), he broke ranks with his contemporaries. In the first essay he argued that "progress" in the arts and sciences actually corrupts society; in the second, he posited a theoretical "natural man" and showed how political institutions had evolved to crush natural equality. Another major work, *The Social Contract* (1762), constructed a political framework to satisfy both the impulse to freedom and the demands of society. Yet to many twentieth-century observers, Rousseau's solution—his famous "General Will"—strongly resembles old Geneva and seems a prescription more for totalitarianism than for democracy.

Contradictions arise as well in *Émile* (1762). Most of the book, including the first excerpt here, describes how he would raise and educate a young man so as to produce an approximate natural man—independent, uncorrupted, unaffected, sincerely rather than institutionally moral. Like many of the English romantics to follow, Rousseau warns against overly "polished" literature and art, preferring the "pure literature" of antiquity to the "sewers" of contemporary philosophy and science. Yet cultivating taste ("the art of knowing all about petty things") is also necessary and requires a different literary experience. The second excerpt describes a *woman's* ideal upbringing. Though Rousseau's *Discourse on Inequality* accorded radical, equal autonomy to both men and women in the state of nature, by the *Émile* passages he declares that woman's nature is coquettish, submissive, and dependent on opinion, and that her education should follow logically from this premise. Women writers like Mary Wollstonecraft (*A Vindication of the Rights of Woman*) would later quarrel with these passages, while continuing to admire the revolutionary impact of Rousseau's work.

from ÉMILE; OR, ON EDUCATION

FROM BOOK IV

. . . If, in order to cultivate my disciple's taste, I had to choose between taking him to countries where there has not yet been any cultivation of taste and to others where taste has already degenerated, I would proceed in reverse order. That is, I would begin his tour with the latter countries and end with the former. This reason for this choice is that taste is corrupted by an excessive delicacy which creates a sensitivity to things that the bulk of men do not perceive. This delicacy leads to a spirit of discussion, for the more subtle one is about things, the more they multiply. This subtlety makes feelings more delicate and less uniform. Then as many tastes are formed as there are individuals. In the disputes about preference, philosophy and enlightenment are extended, and it is in this way that one learns to think. Fine observations can hardly be made except by people who get around a lot, given that those observations strike us only after all the others and that people unaccustomed to large societies exhaust their attention on the gross features of things. At the present time there is perhaps not a civilized place on earth where the general taste is worse than in Paris. Nevertheless it is in this capital that good taste is cultivated, and there appear few books esteemed in Europe whose author has not been in Paris for the purpose of forming himself. Those who think that it suffices to read the books produced there are mistaken. One learns much more in conversation with authors than in their books, and the authors themselves are not those from whom one learns the most. It is the spirit of societies which develops a thoughtful mind and extends our vision as far as it can go. If you have a spark of genius, go and spend a year in Paris. Soon you will be all that you can be, or you will never be anything.

One can learn to think in places where bad taste reigns; but one must not think as do those who have this bad taste—and it is quite difficult for this not to happen when one stays among them too long. With their assistance one must perfect the instrument which judges, while avoiding using it as they do. I shall be careful not to polish Émile's judgment so much as to spoil it, and when his feelings are refined enough to sense and compare men's diverse tastes, I shall bring him back to simpler objects to establish his own taste.

I shall go further still to preserve in him a pure and healthy taste. Amidst the tumult of dissipation I shall know how to arrange useful discussions with him; and by always directing these discussions toward objects which please him, I shall take care to make them as enjoyable to him as they are instructive. This is the time for reading, for reading enjoyable books. This is the time to teach him how to analyze speech, to make him sensitive to all the beauties of eloquence and diction. It is trivial to learn languages for their own sake; their use is not as important as people believe. But the study of languages leads to that of grammar. Latin has to be learned in order to know French. Both must be studied and compared in order to understand the rules of the art of speaking.

There is, moreover, a certain simplicity of taste that speaks straight to the heart and is found only in the writings of the ancients. In eloquence, in poetry, in every kind of literature Émile will again find the ancients—as he found them in history—rich in facts and sparing in judgments. Our authors, by contrast, say little and make many pronouncements. Constantly to give us their judgment as the law is not the way to form our judgment. The difference between the two tastes makes itself felt in all monuments, even including tombs. Our tombstones are covered with praise; on those of the ancients one read facts:

> *Sta viator, Heroem calcas*[1]

Even if I had found this epitaph on an ancient monument, I would have immediately guessed that it was modern; for nothing is so ordinary among us as heroes, but among the ancients they were rare. Instead of saying that a man was a hero, they would have said what he had done to become one. To the epitaph of this hero compare that of the effeminate Sardanapalus:

> *I built Tarsus and Anchialus in a day and now I am dead.*[2]

Which says more in your opinion? Our bombastic lapidary style is good only for inflating dwarfs. The ancients showed men as they are naturally, and one saw that they were men. Xenophon, honoring the memory of some warriors who were treacherously killed during the retreat of the ten thousand, says, "They died irreproachable in war and in friendship."[3] That is all. But consider what must have filled the author's heart in writing this short and simple eulogy. Woe unto him who does not find that entrancing!

One read these words carved in marble at Thermopylae:

> *Passer-by, tell them at Sparta that we died here to obey her holy laws.*[4]

It is quite obvious that it was not the Academy of Inscriptions which wrote that.

I am mistaken if my pupil, who sets so little store by words, does not immediately turn his attention to these differences, and if they do not influence his choice of reading. Drawn by the masculine eloquence of Demosthenes, he will say, "This is an orator." But in reading Cicero, he will say, "This is a lawyer."

In general, Émile will get more of a taste for the books of the ancients than for ours, for the sole reason that the ancients, since they came first, are closest to nature and their genius is more their own. Whatever La Motte and the Abbé Terrasson may have said, there is no true progress of reason in the human species, because all that is gained on one side is lost on the other: all minds always start from the same point, and since the time used in finding out what others have thought is wasted for learning to think for ourselves, we have acquired more enlightenment and less vigor of mind. We exercise our minds, like our arms, by having them do everything with tools and nothing by themselves. Fontenelle said that this whole dispute about ancients and moderns comes down to knowing whether the trees in the past were bigger than those today. If agriculture had changed, it would not be impertinent to ask this question.

After having thus helped Émile ascend to the sources of pure literature, I also show him its sewers in the reservoirs of modern compilers, newspapers, translations, and dictionaries. He casts a glance at all this, then leaves it never to return. In order to amuse him, I have him listen to the chatter of the academies; I see to it that he notices that the individuals who compose the academies are always worth more alone than as part of the group. He will draw for himself the implication about the utility of all these fine establishments.

I take him to the theater to study not morals but taste, for it is here that taste reveals itself to those who know how to reflect. "Leave aside precepts and morality," I would say to him, "it is not here that they are to be learned." The theater is not made for the truth. It is made to delight, to entertain men. There is no school in which one learns so well the art of pleasing men and of interesting the human heart. The study of the theater leads to that of poetry. They have exactly the same aim. If he has a spark of taste for it, with what pleasure he will cultivate the languages of the poets—Greek, Latin, and Italian! These studies will be entertainments without constraint for him, and thus he will profit all the more from them. They will be delicious to him at an age and in circumstances when his interest is aroused by the great charm of all the sorts of beauty capable of touching the heart. Picture my Émile, on the one hand, and a young college scamp, on the other, reading the fourth book of the *Aeneid*, or Tibullus, or Plato's *Banquet*. What a difference! How much the heart of the one is stirred by what does not even affect the other. O good young man, stop, suspend your reading. I see that you are too moved. I certainly want the language of love to please you, but I do not want it to lead you astray. Be a sensitive man, but also a wise one. If you are only one of the two, you are nothing. Moreover, I care little whether he succeeds or not at the dead languages, at letters, at poetry. He will be worth no less if he knows none of all that, and it is not with all these trifles that his education is concerned.

My principle aim in teaching him to feel and to love the beautiful of all sorts is to fix his affections and tastes on it, to prevent his natural appetites from becoming corrupted, and to see to it that he does not one day seek in his riches the means for being happy—means that he ought to find nearer to him. I have said elsewhere that taste is only the art of knowing all about petty things, and that is very true. But since the agreeableness of life depends on a tissue of petty things, such concerns are far from being matters of indifference. It is through such concerns that we learn to fill life with the good things within our reach in all the truth they can have for us. I am talking here not about the moral goods which depend on the good disposition of the soul, but only about what is connected with sensuality and with real voluptuousness, apart from prejudices and opinion. . . .

From Book V

. . . In his *Republic,* Plato gives women the same exercises as men.[5] I can well believe it! Having removed private families from his regime and no longer knowing what to do with women, he found himself forced to make them men. That noble genius had planned everything, foreseen everything. He was forestalling an objection that perhaps no one would have thought of making to him, but he provided a poor solution to the one which is made to him. I am not speaking of that alleged community of women; the often repeated reproach on this point proves that those who make it against him have never read him. I am speaking of that civil promiscuity which throughout confounds the two sexes in the same employments and in the same labors and which cannot fail to engender the most intolerable abuses. I speak of that subversion of the sweetest sentiments of nature, sacrificed to an artificial sentiment which can only be maintained by them—as though there were no need for a natural base on which to form conventional ties; as though the love of one's nearest were not the principle of the love one owes the state; as though it were not by means of the small fatherland which is the family that the heart attaches itself to the large one; as though it were not the good son, the good husband, and the good father who make the good citizen!

Once it is demonstrated that man and woman are not and ought not to be constituted in the same way in either character or temperament, it follows that they ought not to have the same education. In following nature's directions, man and woman ought to act in concert, but they ought not to do the same things. The goal of their labors is common, but their labors themselves are different, and consequently so are the tastes directing them. After having tried to form the natural man, let us also see how the woman who suits this man ought to be formed so that our work will not be left imperfect.

Do you wish always to be well guided? Then always follow nature's indications. Everything that characterizes the fair sex ought to be respected as established by nature. You constantly say, "Women have this or that failing which we do not have." Your pride deceives you. They would be failings for you; they are their good qualities. Everything would go less well if they did not have these qualities. Prevent these alleged failings from degenerating, but take care not to destroy them.

For their part, women do not cease to proclaim that we raise them to be vain and coquettish, that we constantly entertain them with puerilities in order to remain more easily their masters. They blame on us the failings for which we reproach them. What folly! And since when is it that men get involved in the education of girls? Who prevents their mothers from raising them as they please? They have no colleges. What a great misfortune! Would God that there were none for boys; they would be more sensibly and decently raised! Are your daughters forced to waste their time in silliness? Are they made in spite of themselves to spend half their lives getting dressed up, following the example you set them? Are you prevented from instructing them and having them instructed as you please? Is it our fault that they please us when they are pretty, that their mincing ways seduce us, that the art which they learn from you attracts us and pleases us, that we like to see them tastefully dressed, that we let them sharpen at their leisure the weapons with which they subjugate us? So, decide to raise them like men. The men will gladly consent to it! The more women want to resemble them, the less women will govern them, and then men will truly be the masters.

All the faculties common to the two sexes are not equally distributed between them; but taken together, they balance out. Woman is worth more as woman and less as man. Wherever she makes use of her rights, she has the advantage. Wherever she wants to usurp ours, she remains beneath us. One can respond to this general truth only with exceptions, the constant mode of argument of the gallant partisans of the fair sex.

To cultivate man's qualities in women and to neglect those which are proper to them is obviously to work to their detriment. Crafty women see this too well to be duped by it. In trying to usurp our advantages, they do not abandon theirs. But it turns out that they are unable to manage both well—because the two are incompatible—and they remain beneath their own level without getting up to ours, thus losing half their value. Believe me, judicious mother, do not make a decent man of your daughter, as though you would give nature the lie. Make a decent woman of her, and be sure that as a result she will be worth more for herself and for us.

Does it follow that she ought to be raised in ignorance of everything and limited to the housekeeping functions alone? Will man turn his companion into his servant? Will he deprive himself of the greatest charm of society with her? In order to make her more subject, will he prevent her from feeling anything, from knowing anything? Will he make her into a veritable automaton? Surely not. It is not thus that nature has spoken in giving women such agreeable and nimble minds. On the contrary, nature wants them to think, to judge, to love, to know, to cultivate their minds as well as their looks. These are the weapons nature gives them to take the place of the strength they lack and to direct ours. They ought to learn many things but only those that are suitable for them to know.

Whether I consider the particular purpose of the fair sex, whether I observe its inclinations, whether I consider its duties, all join equally in indicating to me the form of education that suits it. Woman and man are made for one another, but their mutual dependence is not equal. Men depend on women because of their desires; women depend on men because of both their desires and their needs. We would survive more easily without them than they would without us. For them to have what is necessary to their station, they depend on us to give it to them, to want to give it to them, to esteem them worthy of it. They depend on our sentiments, on the value we set on their merit, on the importance we attach to their charms and their virtues. By the very law of nature women are at the mercy of men's judgments, as much for their own sake as for that of their children. It is not enough that they be estimable; they must be esteemed. It is not enough for them to be pretty; they must please. It is not enough for them to be temperate; they must be recognized as such. Their honor is not only in their conduct but in their reputation; and it is not possible that a woman who consents to be regarded as disreputable can ever be decent. When a man acts well, he depends only on himself and can brave public judgment; but when a woman acts well, she has accomplished only half of her task, and what is thought of her is no less important to her than what she actually is. From this it follows that the system of woman's education ought to be contrary in this respect to the system of our education. Opinion is the grave of virtue among men and its throne among women.

The good constitution of children initially depends on that of their mothers. The first education of men depends on the care of women. Men's morals, their passions, their tastes, their pleasures, their very happiness also depend on women. Thus the whole education of women ought to relate to men. To please men, to be useful to them, to make herself loved and honored by them, to raise them when young, to care for them when grown, to counsel them, to console them, to make their lives agreeable and sweet—these are the duties of women at all times, and they ought to be taught from childhood. So long as one does not return to this principle, one will deviate from the goal, and all the precepts taught to women will be of no use for their happiness or for ours.

But although every woman wants to please men and should want to, there is quite a difference between wanting to please the man of merit, the truly lovable man, and wanting to please those little flatterers who dishonor both their own sex and the one they imitate. Neither nature nor reason can bring a woman to love in men what resembles herself; nor is it by adopting their ways that she ought to seek to make herself loved.

When women leave the modest and composed tone of their sex and adopt the airs of these giddy fellows, far from following their own vocation, they renounce it and divest themselves of the rights they think they are usurping, "If we acted differently," they say, "we would not please men." They lie. One has to be foolish to love fools. The desire to attract these people reveals the taste of the woman who indulges it. If there were no frivolous men, she would be eager to produce some; and she is much more responsible for their frivolities than they are for hers. The woman who loves true men and who wants to please them employs means appropriate to her intention. To be a woman means to be coquettish, but her coquetry changes its form and its object according to her views. Let us regulate her views according to those of nature, and woman will have the education which suits her.

Notes

1. "Stop, passerby, you are trampling on a hero." This was the epitaph of François de Mercy, defeated at the battle of Nordlingen in 1645 by Condé (with whom Émile's name may have some connection). Cf. Voltaire, the *Age of Louis XIV*, III.

2. Strabo, *Geography* XIV. v, 9.

3. Xenophon, *Anabasis* II. vi, 30. "No one ever laughed at them as cowards in war or blamed them in friendship" is the exact text.

4. Herodotus, *Histories* VII. 228. "Passerby, tell the Lacedaemonians that here we lie obedient to their word" is the exact text.

5. Plato, *Republic* V. 451D-452B, 457A.

CHAPTER FIVE

Nineteenth-Century Literary Criticism

We can think of nineteenth-century criticism as having a strong double inauguration in the work of the German critic Friedrich Schlegel and the great British romantic poet William Wordsworth. In Schlegel is the broadest view of criticism for the nineteenth century, a global perspective fixing the place of contemporary literature in relation to the past, especially the classical past of Greek and Roman literature. Classical Greek poetry, Schlegel believed, had an unselfconscious vitality that he thought could inspire and revitalize contemporary literature, a vitality he christened "romantic." In his work as philologist, historian, and critic he sought to keep alive for German literature an appreciation of this "romantic" living dimension of poetry. Criticism's role in this endeavor was to be "reconstructive" of the past. The critic, as Schlegel wrote, has the power and also the responsibility to "reconstruct, perceive, and characterize the more subtle peculiarities of a whole [literary experience]" that would otherwise be lost. Such an important reconstructive process "is the actual business and inner essence of criticism," surely criticism's highest achievement and its truly significant contribution to cultural life. Criticism, for Schlegel, is a program for resurrecting the past as part of what Matthew Arnold later in the nineteenth century would call "a disinterested endeavor to learn and propagate the best that is known and thought in the world."

Schlegel named this era *romantic* to indicate the special passion, enthusiasm, and innocent vitality he saw as abundantly evident in the ancient Greek poets. He applied this term to contemporary German writers and others who evinced the same exuberance. While the British romantic poets, curiously, did not see themselves as "romantic," they too—along with much early nineteenth-century European literature—fit well into Schlegel's description of moderns who must find their own sense of the past, who must refind for themselves a source of "past" exuberance and passion in the present.

Schlegel's "romantic" strategy stipulated simply that while Greek literature and its special traits were gone, modern culture could make up for such losses by "reconstructing" the past so as to bring its forms, and by extension its vitality, back to the present. As a "critic," in other words, Schlegel endeavored to meet an ethical mandate to make Greek poetry "whole" for the present. The critic's success in doing this allows those arriving late in history to "historicize" the present (an important word for Schlegel) and, therein, successfully position themselves in the present through a living orientation to the past.

Schlegel's attitude toward the past constituted his answer to the battle of the ancients and moderns—the theme of past/present conflict that dates from Greek antiquity. The main question of this traditional debate concerns whether those who came before knew best about life and art and, therefore, deserve our imitation of them; or if we living now know best how to live and should, therefore, exclusively follow our own dictates, our own directions for invention. Schlegel answered by saying that the classical Greek poets did have superior knowledge of life and art but that those in the present can still "reconstruct" what is needed from the past and make it real in the present. In this belief, and in the passion he brought to it, Schlegel inaugurated the specifically nineteenth-century attempt to bring forward—to make immediate, "to learn"—"the best that is known and thought in the world."

In Wordsworth there is a related but quite different critical impulse to cope with the cultural belatedness characteristic of the nineteenth-century version of the modern predicament. In the "Preface" to the *Lyrical Ballads*, for example, Wordsworth evokes his own romantic version of the ancients-and-moderns battle, but he reimagines and depicts this conflict in far more personal and psychological terms. Wordsworth, too, imagines that there is lost vitality in an unrecoverable past, and the present is indeed severed from the past to the degree that one is "free" almost without restriction to act, but, as a consequence, one is also alienated from the past. Wordsworth, however, depicts this cultural dilemma in the personal terms of nineteenth-century psychology, thereby translating history into psychology. In other words, the unrecoverable past (the time of the ancients) is precisely the innocent vitality of one's own childhood. The alienated present (the era of the moderns) is none other than adulthood with its knowledge and broad perspectives but stripped of the immediate force of innocence and exuberance. The substance of the battle of the ancients and moderns, then, is here recast as an interior struggle to reconnect with the past, a scenario of romantic sensibility.

Also like Schlegel, Wordsworth imagined a "reconstructive" process whereby vitality is regained from the past, in this case personally refound through a wrenching admission and assessment of loss. This recovery process is especially evident in what Harold Bloom has called the "therapeutic lyrics"—e.g., "Ode: Intimations of Immortality," "Tintern Abbey," the "Lucy" poems, and *The Prelude*—poems that stage the scene of recognizing lost innocence and that of recovering innocence in a transformed state. Wordsworth thus imagines poetry to form a grand cycle of personal reconstruction, wherein the connection with the past is continually refound in a dynamic spiraling of new experience in one's critical and emotional growth.

In this way, Schlegel and Wordsworth construct a romantic poetics that describes the interior dynamic of poetry itself but also the external development of literature in a broad cultural and historical frame. This poetics, immensely influential all through the nineteenth century, foreshadows Matthew Arnold's agenda for retrieval of the cultural past for use as the "best" of the present. It is also the model that informs T. S. Eliot's modernist sense of the "presentness" of the past as that which is actively "won" from what is otherwise lost in history.

Wordsworth and Samuel Taylor Coleridge schematized this romantic poetics in what they call the interaction of primary and secondary imagination and fancy, a scheme prescribing the psychological *and* aesthetic dimension of poetry. They saw *primary imagination* as an experiential foundation, an unmediated apprehension of the world. In their view sensory contact and its immediate configuration constitute a powerful if fundamentally untranslatable grasp of experience, a romantic version of that which is "sacred" or transcendent. *Secondary imagination* they saw as once removed from the primary grasp of the world, growing directly out of the primary but constituting experience shaped into rudimentary and primordial forms, elemental patterns that resemble what in the twentieth century will be called "archetypes." The secondary imagination is the ground out of which rises the articulable and the promptings of "genius." *Fancy,* thereafter, they defined as conscious thought, the deliberate manipulation of memories in patterns of understanding and reasoning. Having neither the power nor authenticity of primary and secondary imagination, fancy is a rational and articulate engagement with the world—a civilized but simultaneously denatured version of primordial or "sacred" experience.

Wordsworth and Coleridge then situated poetry as emanating from secondary imagination; it is neither a pure product of intellection, not merely a memory or a calculation, nor is it a primordial, untranslatable grasp of things, a primitive knowing. Poetry rests, rather, between the two as the product of a unified sensibility—an amalgam of feeling and thinking in what Schlegel calls a "whole" experience. But in that poetry is closer to primary experience—that is, primary imagination—than to civilized life, it makes sense that poetry should be inspired by those innocents (children and others of "simple" mind—people not highly "civilized") who are close to a basic sense of things. Wordsworth, accordingly, in the "Preface" to the *Lyrical Ballads* suggests that poetry should be an experience of rusticity, of the "middle and lower classes of society," an engagement with their "humble and rustic life." Poetry should favor such subjects, and, further, it will achieve the goal of inspired simplicity by rejecting eighteenth-century poetic forms and by redirecting its attention away from poetic decorum (elevated diction) and toward common speech. The break with these artificial conventions will enable poetry to attend to its true object, the "spontaneous overflow of powerful feelings."

Romantic poetics thus advances an extensive interpretation and approach to nineteenth-century culture. It postulates broadly that the significant living forms of culture emanate not from social activity and discourse but from below levels of social activity. The romantic critic or poet, in effect, looks out over society and sees the illusions of mundane life, of—in Wordsworth's term—the world lost in commerce and in every way "too much with us." True efficacy in the world, paradoxically, belongs, then, to that person who can respond to the deeper, "primary" dimension of experience, to the "esemplastic power" (in Coleridge's term) that operates in people to allow nature to inform imagination. Those of poetic sensibility, who see the truth of the world in (as William Blake said) a "grain of sand," may themselves appear simple and rustic, but they are—as Shelley says in "A Defence of Poetry"—"the unacknowledged legislators of the World." The poets can actually change the world because they have access to the truly significant power, the esemplastic power, that lies beneath the mundane facades of commerce and public life.

On the American side, there is perhaps no clearer indication of the extreme to which romantic critical sensibility develops than Ralph Waldo Emerson's conception of "Man Thinking" in "The American Scholar." Like Schlegel, Wordsworth, and Coleridge, Emerson develops a broad cultural theory through a romantic poetics, in this case reflecting, as he believed, American national experience and character. Emerson imagines the comprehensive ideal of America, the country and culture in its entirety, as comprising a "whole man"—"One Man." The limbs of this "whole man"—like a huge Paul Bunyan figure—represent different parts of American society, each part "parcelled out to individuals, each of whom aims to do his stint of the joint work, whilst each other performs his." For example, the legs and feet, presumably, are the locomotive force of the country. The arms are "Man on the farm." The hands are manual labor, and so on around the body. But while all parts of the One Man work together and form a whole society, "you must," Emerson writes, "take the whole society to find the whole man." He shows that the various parts of society cannot be aware of the entire mass of America, or the significance the whole might have.

But while there is unawareness in the various parts of America, Emerson goes on, above the body in the head is Man Thinking. Unique among the "body" parts, both scholar and poet, Man Thinking can "see" the complete national body and its significance. As the country's "head"—more accurately in Emerson's metaphor, its "eyes"—the scholar/poet has the ability to gaze on and comprehend "everything," all of America. In this way, Emerson creates a cultural hierarchy and erects a poetic caste system. It is only the scholar/poet, finally, detached and situated above the neck of America, who can "see" culture. The other parts that form the body only act, "subdivided and peddled out," without recognition of what they are "doing." In other words, like Wordsworth and Coleridge before him, Emerson argues that when one looks out over the surface of society, one sees the mechanics of activity, not the significance. Only from the special place removed, which the unified "whole" romantic sensibility alone can inhabit and "see" from, does the value and force of American life become apparent.

As Emerson's example shows, romantic criticism houses its poetics anthropomorphically as a cultural "Man," an isolated Man Thinking. This cultural colossus, like Rousseau's Emile or a Blakean figure, is a natural child and at home in the world—at home except when artificially dislodged by culture and its "civilized" illusions. The active development of romantic criticism based on these assumptions—deeply connected, as Emerson shows, with numerous American ideals and commitments—begins and continues later in America than in England, up through the 1850s and the American Renaissance and most notably in Walt Whitman's work.

Difficult to classify in late nineteenth-century criticism, and extremely influential in the twentieth century, is the work of German philosopher Friedrich Nietzsche. Nietzsche's "On Words and Music," for example, explores a recurring theme of his work, the relationship of the Dionysian (irrational) and Apollonian (rational) poles of experience, terms that also echo fancy and imagination. But like French linguist and semiotician Ferdinand de Saussure, American philosopher Charles Sanders Peirce, and other late-century theorists, Nietzsche posits not another romantic poetics but a view of culture as radically nonrational—to the point that culture escapes humanistic and anthropomorphic models all together. "In the multiplicity of languages," Nietzsche writes, is basic evidence "that word and thing do not necessarily coincide with one another completely [so that] the word is a symbol," an arbitrary symbol (or "sign") in the sense of being an arbitrary representation in language. This impersonality and arbitrariness Nietzsche reveals to be a dehumanizing, yet inevitable force in modern culture; the linguistic aspect of language assumed by romantic criticism to be the most familiar and intimate aspect of experience is, in fact, foreign and nonhuman—deeply arbitrary and without natural human import.

In this essay, further, Nietzsche connects music, because of its supposed nonrepresentational status, with the Dionysian and irrational impulse. Words, on the other hand, which he imagines to have more stable meanings, are tame and Apollonian. "On Words and Music," in fact, comes in a romantic phase of Nietzsche's work in which he imagines a radically new art emerging as music and words; Dionysus and Apollo, the irrational and rational, merge together—"this *par nobile fratrum* [of words and music]," as Nietzsche says, "[will] embrace one another!" Like the British romantics, in other words, Nietzsche here suggests a horizon for poetics that encompasses the extremes of, and suggests continuity between, nature and culture. In later work he will make a more radical choice and posit that the Dionysian, destructive impulse—pure disruption—underlies all art, all experience. In this later thinking, the echoes of "imagination" and "fancy" disappear from Nietzche's discourse. Particularly in *Thus Spake Zarathustra*, Nietzsche attempts to think radically "beyond" the romantic paradigm that dominates nineteenth-century criticism. He attempts to reconceive romantic poetics and recast its very structure—much as Michel Foucault and Jacques Derrida attempt to recast (deconstruct) the romantic image of Man Thinking in the twentieth century.

Literary criticism in the later nineteenth century, especially in Europe, turns from romanticism, in some cases violently rejecting it, and toward aesthetic, historical, semiotic, and naturalistic (deterministic) approaches. There is a continuation of historical criticism, begun in the middle century with French critic Hippolyte Taine and the English W. J. Courthope. In the later century, Henry James, Matthew Arnold, Walter Pater, and Oscar Wilde give major accounts of aestheticism and formalism—technical and aesthetically oriented explanations for the operation of novelistic and poetic narratives. As the century closes, especially in the work of the French symbolist poets Charles Baudelaire and Stéphane Mallarmé, criticism is strongly shaped by the experiments of avant-garde literature that foretell a new and emerging paradigm, the twentieth-century's encompassing age of modernism.

FURTHER READING

Abrams, M. H. *The Mirror and the Lamp: Romantic Theory and the Critical Tradition.* New York: Oxford University Press, 1953.

_____. *Natural Supernaturalism: Tradition and Revolution in Romantic Literature.* New York: Norton, 1971.

Babbitt, Irving. *Criticism in America.* New York: Haskell House, 1969.

_____. *Rousseau and Romanticism.* New York: Houghton Mifflin, 1919.

Bloom, Harold. *The Visionary Company.* Garden City, N.Y.: Doubleday, 1971.

Buckley, Jerome. *The Victorian Temper.* Cambridge, Mass.: Harvard University Press, 1951.

Bush, Douglas. *Mythology and the Romantic Tradition in English Poetry.* Cambridge, Mass.: Harvard University Press, 1937.

Gallagher, Catherine, and Thomas Laqueur, eds. *The Making of the Modern Body: Sexuality and Society in the Nineteenth Century.* Berkeley: University of California Press, 1987.

Gilbert, Sandra, and Susan Gubar. *The Madwoman in the Attic: The Woman Writer and the Nineteenth-Century Literary Imagination.* New Haven, Conn.: Yale University Press, 1979.

Kermode, Frank. *Romantic Image.* London: Routledge & Kegan Paul, 1957.

Matthiessen, F. O. *The American Renaissance.* New York: Oxford University Press, 1941.

Miller, J. Hillis. *The Disappearance of God: Five Nineteenth-Century Writers.* Cambridge, Mass.: Harvard University Press, 1963.

_____. *The Form of Victorian Fiction.* Notre Dame, Ind.: University of Notre Dame Press, 1968.

Pritchard, John Paul. *Criticism in America.* Norman: University of Oklahoma Press, 1956.

Praz, Mario. *The Hero in Eclipse in Victorian Fiction.* New York: Oxford University Press, 1956.

______. *The Romantic Agony.* Trans. Angus Davidson. 2nd ed. London: Oxford University Press, 1951.

Stang, Richard. *The Theory of the Novel in England: 1850–1870.* New York: Columbia University Press, 1959.

Thompson, Gary Richard, ed. *The Gothic Imagination: Essays in Dark Romanticism.* Pullman: Washington State University Press, 1974.

Warren, Alba H., Jr. *English Poetic Theory: 1825–1865.* Princeton, N.J.: Princeton University Press, 1950.

Wellek, René. *A History of Modern Criticism: 1750–1950.* Vol. II, *The Romantic Age.* New Haven, Conn.: Yale University Press, 1955.

______. *A History of Modern Criticism: 1750–1950.* Vol. III, *The Age of Transition.* New Haven, Conn.: Yale University Press, 1965.

______. *A History of Modern Criticism: 1750–1950.* Vol. IV, *The Later Nineteenth Century.* New Haven, Conn.: Yale University Press, 1965.

Wiley, Basil. *Nineteenth Century Studies: Coleridge to Matthew Arnold.* New York: Columbia University Press, 1950.

Samuel Taylor Coleridge 1772–1834

In late 1800, Samuel Taylor Coleridge and William Wordsworth (1770–1850) settled near each other in England's Lake District. They had collaborated on the 1798 publication of the *Lyrical Ballads,* and they were to work together on a second edition. Their discussions of a proposed preface to the second edition were the germination of Coleridge's own aesthetic theory. Wordsworth meanwhile wrote the preface they discussed, claiming later, however, that the theory was substantially Coleridge's.

Coleridge seems at once both a contemporary and an early nineteenth-century aesthetician. In his *Biographia Literaria,* we find him to be the artist (not unlike Joyce) who is scrupulously conscious of his role and the theoretical import of his work; and we also find him to be the philosopher (not unlike Derrida) who deliberately chooses to render his theory in rhetoric uncommon to philosophy itself. Nevertheless, though he may seem for this to be more readily familiar, he is the significantly less familiar early romantic poet. Disciplined in the German Enlightenment philosophy of Kant (system, regulation, and constitutive order) and bold enough to appropriate Schelling, Coleridge is a late eighteenth-century literatus who is, however, the nineteenth-century forerunner of those more conventional romantic types, Byron and Shelley. It was Coleridge who argued that the artist's assumption of a lofty alienation—a peculiarly English gloss on Kant's notion of "disinterest"—is necessary to the godlike creative activity that is the artist's mark of genius. Thus, for his particular focus on the artist's role *As Artist*, we can perhaps think of Coleridge as a man of his times as well as the first truly modern aesthetician.

His *Biographia Literaria* did not appear until July 1817, two years after its completion, because the printer had overestimated its page count and requested additional material to fill out the second volume that had quite literally ended in the middle. Considering that the discussions between Coleridge and Wordsworth took place in 1800, the *Biographia Literaria* was a very long time in the making. Coleridge even took three years (1800 to 1803) to decide on its autobiographical framework.

It was also in 1803 that Coleridge drew his distinction between imagination and fancy, a distinction central to the project of the *Biographia Literaria*. Imagination is of two types: primary (standard) and secondary (genius), but both seek to fuse conscious forces (mind) with unconscious forces (nature) and are therefore organic. Fancy is a thing of talent only; it is merely imitative and mechanical, an aggregate of perceptions. Always through imagination, the perceiver tries to put personal perceptions together with his or her perceptions of nature in a way that reconciles the two. This is a creative, symbolic act, even though fancy itself is not creative and attempts no reconciliation. Coleridge, rejecting Newton's scientific empiricism, which he identified with understanding, linked imagination to reason, leaving fancy to understanding. Keeping to these distinctions, Coleridge praised Shakespeare's genius, countering the neoclassical criticism that found Shakespeare unschooled and therefore flawed.

from **Biographia Literaria**

from Chapter IV

. . . During the last year of my residence at Cambridge, I became acquainted with Mr. Wordsworth's first publication entitled "Descriptive Sketches"; and seldom, if ever, was the emergence of an original poetic genius above the literary horizon more evidently announced. In the form, style, and manner of the whole poem, and in the structure of the particular lines and periods, there is an harshness and acerbity connected and combined with words and images all a-glow, which might recall those products of the vegetable world, where gorgeous blossoms rise out of the hard and thorny rind and shell, within which the rich fruit was elaborating. The language was not only peculiar and strong, but at times knotty and contorted, as by its own impatient strength; while the novelty and struggling crowd of images, acting in conjunction with the difficulties of the style, demanded always a greater closeness of attention, than poetry, (at all events, than descriptive poetry) has a right to claim. It not seldom therefore justified the complaint of obscurity. In the following extract I have sometimes fancied, that I saw an emblem of the poem itself, and of the author's genius as it was then displayed.

> 'Tis storm; and hid in mist from hour to hour,
> All day the floods a deepening murmur pour;
> The sky is veiled, and every cheerful sight:
> Dark is the region as with coming night;
> And yet what frequent bursts of overpowering light!
> Triumphant on the bosom of the storm,
> Glances the fire-clad eagle's wheeling form;
> Eastward, in long perspective glittering, shine
> The wood-crowned cliffs that o'er the lake recline;
> Wide o'er the Alps a hundred streams unfold,
> At once to pillars turn'd that flame with gold;
> Behind his sail the peasant strives to shun
> The West, that burns like one dilated sun,
> Where in a mighty crucible expire
> The mountains, glowing hot, like coals of fire.

The poetic PSYCHE, in its process to full development, undergoes as many changes as its Greek name-sake, the butterfly.[1] And it is remarkable how soon genius clears and purifies itself from the faults and errors of its earliest products; faults which, in its earliest compositions, are the more obtrusive and confluent, because as heterogeneous elements, which had only a temporary use, they constitute the very *ferment*, by which themselves are carried off. Or we may compare them to some diseases, which must work on the humours, and be thrown out on the surface, in order to secure the patient from their future recurrence. I was in my twenty-fourth year, when I had the happiness of knowing Mr. Wordsworth personally, and while memory lasts, I shall hardly forget the sudden effect produced on my mind, by his recitation of a manuscript poem, which still remains unpublished, but of which the stanza, and tone of style, were the same as those of the "Female Vagrant," as originally printed in the first volume of the "Lyrical Ballads." There was here no mark of strained thought, or forced diction, no crowd or turbulence of imagery; and, as the poet hath himself well described in his lines "on re-visiting the Wye," manly reflection, and human associations had given both variety, and an additional interest to natural objects, which in the passion and appetite of the first love they had seemed to him neither to need or permit. The occasional obscurities, which had risen from an imperfect control over the resources of his native language, had almost wholly disappeared, together with that worse defect of arbitrary and illogical phrases, at once hackneyed, and fantastic, which hold so distinguished a place in the *technique* of ordinary poetry, and will, more or less, alloy the earlier poems of the truest genius, unless the attention has been specifically directed to their worthlessness and incongruity.[2] I did not perceive anything particular in the mere style of the poem alluded to during its recitation, except indeed such difference as was not separable from the thought and manner; and the Spenserian stanza, which always, more or less, recalls to the reader's mind Spenser's own style, would doubtless have authorized, in my then opinion, a more frequent descent to the phrases of ordinary life, than could without an ill effect have been hazarded in the heroic couplet. It was not however the freedom from false taste, whether as to common defects, or to those more properly his own, which made so unusual an impression on my feelings immediately, and subsequently on my judgement. It was the union of deep feeling with profound thought; the fine balance of truth in observing, with the imaginative faculty in modifying the objects observed; and above all the original gift of spreading the tone, the *atmosphere*, and with it the depth and height of the ideal world around forms, incidents, and situations, of which, for the common view, custom had bedimmed all the lustre, had dried up the sparkle and the dew drops. "To find no contradiction in the union of old and new; to contemplate the ANCIENT of days and all his works with feelings as fresh, as if all had then sprang forth at the first creative fiat; characterizes the mind that feels the riddle of the world, and may help to unravel it. To carry on the feelings of childhood into the powers of manhood; to combine the child's sense of wonder and novelty with the appearances, which every day for perhaps forty years had rendered familiar;

> With sun and moon and stars throughout the year,
> And man and woman;

this is the character and privilege of genius, and one of the marks which distinguish genius from talents. And therefore is it the prime merit of genius and its most unequivocal mode of manifestation, so to represent familiar objects as to awaken in the minds of others a kindred feeling concerning them and that freshness of sensation which is the constant accompaniment of mental, no less than of bodily, convalescence. Who has not a thousand times seen snow fall on water? Who has not watched it with a new feeling, from the time that he has read Burns' comparison of sensual pleasure

> To snow that falls upon a river
> A moment white—then gone for ever!

In poems, equally as in philosophic disquisitions, genius produces the strongest impressions of novelty, while it rescues the most admitted truths from the impotence caused by the very circumstance of their universal admission. Truths of all others the most awful and mysterious, yet being at the same time of universal interest, are too often considered as *so* true, that they lose all the life and efficiency of truth, and lie bed-ridden in the dormitory of the soul, side by side with the most despised and exploded errors."—THE FRIEND, p. 76, No. 5.[3]

This excellence, which in all Mr. Wordsworth's writings is more or less predominant, and which constitutes the character of his mind, I no sooner felt, than I sought to understand. Repeated meditations led me first to suspect, (and a more intimate analysis of the human faculties, their appropriate marks, functions, and effects matured my conjecture into full conviction,) that fancy and imagination were two distinct and widely different faculties, instead of being, according to the general belief, either two names with one meaning, or, at furthest, the lower and higher degree of one and the same power. It is not, I own, easy to conceive a more opposite translation of the Greek *Phantasia* than the Latin Imaginatio; but it is equally true that in all societies there exists an instinct of growth, a certain collective, unconscious good sense working progressively to desynonymize[4] those words originally of the same meaning, which the conflux of dialects had supplied to the more homogeneous languages, as the Greek and German: and which the same cause, joined with accidents of translation from original works of different countries, occasion in mixt languages like our own. The first and most important point to be proved is, that two conceptions perfectly distinct are confused under one and the same word, and (this done) to appropriate that word exclusively to one meaning, and the synonyme (should there be one) to the other. But if (as will be often the case in the arts and sciences) no synonyme exists, we must either invent or borrow a word. In the present instance the appropriation has already begun, and been legitimated in the derivative adjective: Milton had a highly *imaginative,* Cowley a very *fanciful* mind. If therefore I should succeed in establishing the actual existences of two faculties generally different, the nomenclature would be at once determined. To the faculty by which I had characterized Milton, we should confine the term *imagination;* while the other would be contradistinguished as *fancy.* Now were it once fully ascertained, that this division is no less grounded in nature, than that of delirium from mania, or Otway's

> Lutes, lobsters, seas of milk, and ships of amber,

from Shakespear's

> What! have his daughters brought him to this pass?

or from the preceding apostrophe to the elements; the theory of the fine arts, and of poetry in particular, could not, I thought, but derive some additional and important light. It would in its immediate effects furnish a torch of guidance to the philosophical critic; and ultimately to the poet himself. In energetic minds, truth soon changes by domestication into power; and from directing in the discrimination and appraisal of the product, becomes influencive in the production. To admire on principle, is the only way to imitate without loss of originality.

It has been already hinted, that metaphysics and psychology have long been my hobby-horse. But to have a hobby-horse, and to be vain of it, are so commonly found together, that they pass almost for the same. I trust therefore, that there will be more good humour than contempt, in the smile with which the reader chastises my self-complacency, if I confess myself uncertain, whether the satisfaction from the perception of a truth new to myself may not have been rendered more poignant by the conceit, that it would be equally so to the public. There was a time, certainly, in which I took some little credit to myself, in the belief that I had been the first of my countrymen, who had pointed out the diverse meaning of which the two terms were capable, and analyzed the faculties to which they should be appropriated. Mr. W. Taylor's recent volume of synonymes I have not yet seen;[5] but his specification of the terms in question has been clearly shown to be both insufficient and erroneous by Mr. Wordsworth in the Preface added to the late collection of his "Lyrical Ballads and other poems." The explanation which Mr. Wordsworth has himself given will be found to differ from mine, chiefly perhaps, as our objects are different. It could scarcely indeed happen otherwise, from the advantage I have enjoyed of frequent conversation with him on a subject to which a poem of his own first directed my attention, and my conclusions concerning which, he had made more lucid to myself by many happy instances drawn from the operation of natural objects on the mind. But it was Mr. Wordsworth's purpose to consider the influences of fancy and imagination as they are manifested in poetry, and from the different effects to conclude their diversity in kind; while it is my object to investigate the seminal principle, and then from the kind to deduce the degree. My friend has drawn a masterly sketch of the branches with their *poetic* fruitage. I wish to add the trunk, and even the roots as far as they lift themselves above ground, and are visible to the naked eye of our common consciousness.

Yet even in this attempt I am aware, that I shall be obliged to draw more largely on the reader's attention, than so immethodical a miscellany can authorize; when in such a work (the *Ecclesiastical Polity*) of such a mind as Hooker's, the judicious author, though no less admirable for the perspicuity than for the port and dignity of his language; and though he wrote for men of learning in a learned age; saw nevertheless occasion to anticipate and guard against "complaints of obscurity," as often as he was about to trace his subject "to the highest well-spring and fountain." Which, (continues he) "because men are not accustomed to, the pains we take are more needful a great deal, than acceptable; and the matters we handle, seem by reason of newness (till the mind grow better acquainted with them) dark and intricate." I would gladly therefore spare both myself and others this labor, if I knew how without it to present an intelligible statement of my poetic creed; not as my *opinions*, which weigh for nothing, but as deductions from established premises conveyed in such a form, as is calculated either to effect a fundamental conviction, or to receive a fundamental confutation. If I may dare once more adopt the words of Hooker, "they, unto whom we shall seem tedious, are in no wise injured by us, because it is in their own hands to spare that labor, which they are not willing to endure." Those at least, let me be permitted to add, who have taken so much pains to render me ridiculous for a perversion of taste, and have supported the charge by attributing strange notions to me on no other authority than their own conjectures, owe it to themselves as well as to me not to refuse their attention to my own statement of the theory, which I *do* acknowledge; or shrink from the trouble of examining the grounds on which I rest it, or the arguments which I offer in its justification.

ON THE LAW OF ASSOCIATION—ITS HISTORY TRACED FROM ARISTOTLE TO HARTLEY.

Chapter V

There have been men in all ages, who have been impelled as by an instinct to propose their own nature as a problem, and who devote their attempts to its solution. The first step was to construct a table of distinctions, which they seem to have formed on the principle of the absence or presence of the WILL. Our various sensations, perceptions, and movements were classed as active or passive, or as media partaking of both. A still finer distinction was soon established between the voluntary and the spontaneous. In our perceptions we seem to ourselves merely passive to an external power, whether as a mirror reflecting the landscape, or as a blank canvas on which some unknown hand paints it. For it is worthy of notice, that the latter, or the system of idealism may be traced to sources equally remote with the former, or materialism; and Berkeley can boast an ancestry at least as venerable as Gassendi or Hobbs. These conjectures, however, concerning the mode in which our perceptions originated, could not alter the natural difference of *things* and *thoughts*. In the former, the cause appeared wholly external, while in the latter, sometimes our will interfered as the producing or determining cause, and sometimes our nature seemed to act by a mechanism of its own, without any conscious effort of the will, or even against it. Our inward experiences were thus arranged in three separate classes, the passive sense, or what the school-men call the merely receptive quality of the mind; the voluntary; and the spontaneous, which holds the middle place between both. But it is not in human nature to meditate on any mode of action, without enquiring after the law that governs it; and in the explanation of the spontaneous movements of our being, the metaphysician took the lead of the anatomist and natural philosopher. In Egypt, Palestine, Greece, and India the analysis of the mind had reached its noon and manhood, while experimental research was still in its dawn and infancy. For many, very many centuries, it has been difficult to advance a new truth, or even a new error, in the philosophy of the intellect or morals. With regard, however, to the laws that direct the spontaneous movements of thought and the principle of their intellectual mechanism there exists, it has been asserted, an important exception most honorable to the moderns, and in the merit of which our own country claims the largest share. Sir James Mackintosh, (who amid the variety of his talents and attainments is not of less repute for the depth and accuracy of his philosophical enquiries than for the eloquence with which he is said to render their most difficult results perspicuous, and the driest attractive,) affirmed in the lectures, delivered by him in Lincoln's Inn Hall, that the law of association as established in the contemporaneity of the original impressions, formed the basis of all true psychology; and any ontological or metaphysical science, not contained in such (i.e. empirical) psychology, was but a web of abstractions and generalizations. Of this prolific truth, of this great fundamental law, he declared Hobbs to have been the original *discoverer*, while its full application to the whole intellectual system we owed to David Hartley, who stood in the same relation to Hobbs as Newton to Kepler; the law of association being that to the mind, which gravitation is to matter.

Of the former clause in this assertion, as it respects the comparative merits of the ancient metaphysicians, including their commentators, the school-men, and of the modern French and British philosophers from Hobbs to Hume, Hartley, and Condillac, this is not the place to speak. So wide indeed is the chasm between this gentleman's philosophical creed and mine, that so far from being able to join hands, we could scarcely make our voices intelligible to each other: and to *bridge* it over, would require more time, skill, and power than I believe myself to possess. But the latter clause involves for the greater part a mere question of fact and history, and the accuracy of the statement is to be tried by documents rather than reasoning.

First, then, I deny Hobbs's claim in toto: for he had been anticipated by Des Cartes, whose work "De Methodo," preceded Hobbs's "De Natura Humana," by more than a year. But what is of much more importance, Hobbs builds nothing on the principle which he had announced. He does not even announce it, as differing in any respect from the general laws of material motion and impact: nor was it, indeed, possible for him so to do, compatibly with his system, which was exclusively material and mechanical. Far otherwise is it with Des Cartes; greatly as he too in his after writings (and still more egregiously his followers De la Forge, and others) obscured the truth by their attempts to explain it on the theory of nervous fluids, and material configurations. But, in his interesting work, "De Methodo," Des Cartes relates the circumstance which first led him to meditate on this subject, and which since then has been often noticed and employed as an instance and illustration of the law. A child who with its eyes bandaged had lost several of his fingers by amputation, continued to complain for many days successively of pains, now in this joint and now in that, of the very fingers which had been cut off. Des Cartes was led by this incident to reflect on the uncertainty with which we attribute any particular place to any inward pain or uneasiness, and proceeded after long consideration to establish it as a general law; that contemporaneous impressions, whether images or sensations, recall each other mechanically. On this principle, as a ground work, he built up the whole system of human language, as one continued process of association. He showed in what sense not only general terms, but generic images (under the name of abstract ideas) actually existed, and in what consists their nature and power. As one word may become the general exponent of many, so by association a simple image may represent a whole class. But in truth Hobbs himself makes no claims to any discovery, and introduces this law of association, or (in his own language) discursus mentalis, as an admitted fact, in the *solution* alone of which, this by causes purely physiological, he arrogates any originality. His system is briefly this; whenever the senses are impinged on by external objects, whether by the rays of light reflected from them, or by effluxes of their finer particles, there results a correspondent motion of the innermost and subtlest organs. This motion constitutes a *representation*, and there remains an *impression* of the same, or a certain disposition to repeat the same motion. Whenever we feel several objects at the same time, the *impressions* that are left, (or in the language of Mr. Hume, the *ideas*,) are linked together. Whenever therefore any one of the movements, which constitute a complex impression, is renewed through the senses, the others succeed mechanically. It follows of necessity therefore that Hobbs as well as Hartley and all others who derive association from the connection and interdependence of the supposed matter, the movements of which constitute our thoughts, *must* have reduced all its forms to the one law of time. But even the merit of announcing this law with philosophic precision cannot be fairly conceded to him. For the objects of any two ideas[6] need not have co-existed in the same sensation in order to become mutually associable. The same result will follow when one only of the two ideas has been represented by the senses, and the other by the memory.

Long however before either Hobbs or Des Cartes the law of association had been defined, and its important functions set forth by Melanchthon, Ammerbach, and Ludovicus Vives; more especially by the last. Phantasia, it is to be noticed, is employed by Vives to express the mental power of comprehension, or the *active* function of the mind; and imaginatio for the receptivity (vis receptiva) of impressions, or for the *passive* perception. The power of combination he appropriates to the former: "*quæ singula et simpliciter acceperat imaginatio, ea conjungit et disjungit phantasia.*" [Those things that the imagination had received one by one and simply, the phantasy unites and separates.] And the law by which the thoughts are spontaneously presented follows thus; "*quæ simul sunt a phantasia comprehensa, si alterutrum occurrat, solet secum alterum repræsentare.*" [Regarding things that have been perceived at the same time by the phantasy, if one of the two should present itself, it is customary that the other be reproduced with it.] To time therefore he subordinates all the other exciting causes of association. The soul proceeds "*a causa ad effectum, ab hoc ad instrumen-*

tum, a parte ad totum;" [from cause to effect, from this to the means of execution, from a part to the whole] thence to the place, from place to person, and from this to whatever preceded or followed, all as being parts of a total impression, each of which may recall the other. The apparent springs "*Saltus vel transitus etiam longissimos*" [even the longest leaps and transitions], he explains by the same thought having been a component part of two or more total impressions. Thus "*ex Scipione venio in cogitationem potentiæ Turcicæ, propter victorias ejus in eâ parte Asiæ in qua regnabat Antiochus*" [From Scipio I arrive at the idea of the Turkish power, because of his victories in that part of Asia in which Antiochus ruled].

But from Vives I pass at once to the source of his doctrines, and (as far as we can judge from the remains yet extant of Greek philosophy) as to the first, so to the fullest and most perfect enunciation of the associative principle, viz. to the writings of Aristotle; and of these in particular to the books "De Anima," "De Memoria," and that which is entitled in the old translations "Parva Naturalia." In as much as later writers have either deviated from, or added to his doctrines, they appear to me to have introduced either error or groundless supposition.

In the first place it is to be observed, that Aristotle's positions on this subject are unmixed with fiction. The wise Stagyrite speaks of no successive particles propagating motion like billiard balls, (as Hobbs); nor of nervous or animal spirits, where inanimate and irrational solids are thawed down, and distilled, or filtrated by ascension, into living and intelligent fluids, that etch and re-etch engravings on the brain, (as the followers of Des Cartes, and the humoral pathologists in general); nor of an oscillating ether which was to effect the same service for the nerves of the brain considered as solid fibres, as the animal spirits perform for them under the notion of hollow tubes (as *Hartley* teaches)—nor finally, (with yet more recent dreamers) of chemical compositions by elective affinity, or of an electric light at once the immediate object and the ultimate organ of inward vision, which rises to the brain like an Aurora Borealis, and there disporting in various shapes (as the balance of plus and minus, or negative and positive, is destroyed or re-established) images out both past and present. Aristotle delivers a just *theory* without pretending to an *hypothesis;* or in other words a comprehensive survey of the different facts, and of their relations to each other without *supposition,* i.e. a fact *placed under* a number of facts, as their common support and explanation; though in the majority of instances these hypotheses or suppositions better deserve the name of ὑποποιήσεις ["hypo poleses"], or *suffictions.* He uses indeed the word κινήσεις, to express what we call representations or ideas, but he carefully distinguishes them from material motion, designating the latter always by annexing the words ἐν τόπῳ, ["in space"], or κατὰ τόπον ["regarding space"]. On the contrary, in his treatise "De Anima," he excludes place and motion from all the operations of thought, whether representations or volitions, as attributes utterly and absurdly heterogeneous.

The *general law* of association, or, more accurately, the *common condition* under which all exciting causes act, and in which they may be generalized, according to Aristotle is this. Ideas by having been together acquire a power of recalling each other; or every partial representation awakes the total representation of which it had been a part. In the practical determination of this common principle to particular recollections, he admits five agents or occasioning causes: 1st, connection in time, whether simultaneous, preceding, or successive; 2nd, vicinity or connection in space; 3rd, interdependence or necessary connection, as cause and effect; 4th, likeness; and 5th, contrast. As an additional solution of the occasional seeming chasms in the continuity of reproduction he proves, that movements or ideas possessing one or the other of these five characters had passed through the mind as intermediate links, sufficiently clear to recall other parts of the same total impressions with which they had co-existed, though not vivid enough to excite that degree of attention which is requisite for distinct recollection, or as we may aptly express it, *after-consciousness*. In association then consists the whole mechanism of the reproduction of impressions, in the Aristotelian Psychology. It is the universal law of the *passive* fancy and *mechanical* memory; that which supplies to all other faculties their objects, to all thought the elements of its materials.

In consulting the excellent commentary of St. Thomas Aquinas on the Parva Naturalia of Aristotle, I was struck at once with its close resemblance to Hume's Essay on association. The main thoughts were the same in both, the *order* of the thoughts was the same, and even the illustrations differed only by Hume's occasional substitution of more modern examples. I mentioned the circumstance to several of my literary acquaintances, who admitted the closeness of the resemblance, and that it seemed too great to be explained by mere coincidence; but they thought it improbable that Hume should have held the pages of the angelic Doctor worth turning over. But some time after Mr. Payne, of the King's mews, shewed Sir James Mackintosh some odd volumes of St. Thomas Aquinas, partly perhaps from having heard that Sir James (then Mr.) Mackintosh had in his lectures passed a high encomium on this canonized philosopher, but chiefly from the fact, that the volumes had belonged to Mr. Hume, and had here and there marginal marks and notes of reference in his own hand writing. Among these volumes was that which contains the *Parva Naturalia*, in the old Latin version, swathed and swaddled in the commentary afore mentioned!

It remains then for me, first to state wherein Hartley differs from Aristotle; then, to exhibit the grounds of my conviction, that he differed only to err; and next as the result, to shew, by what influences of the choice and judgement the associative power becomes either memory or fancy; and, in conclusion, to appropriate the remaining offices of the mind to the reason, and the imagination. With my best efforts to be as perspicuous as the nature of language will permit on such a subject, I earnestly solicit the good wishes and friendly patience of my readers, while I thus go "sounding on my dim and perilous way."

Notes

[The following notes are by Samuel Taylor Coleridge and were included in the original edition of this essay—Ed.]

1. The fact that in Greek Psyche is the common name for the soul, and the butterfly, is thus alluded to in the following stanzas from an unpublished poem of the author:

> The butterfly the ancient Grecians made
> The soul's fair emblem, and its only name—
> But of the soul, escaped the slavish trade
> Of mortal life! For in this earthly frame
> Our's is the reptile's lot, much toil, much
> blame,
> Manifold motions making little speed,
> And to deform and kill the things, whereon
> we feed.
>
> S. T. C.

2. Mr. Wordsworth, even in his two earliest, "the Evening Walk and the Descriptive Sketches," is more free from this latter defect than most of the young poets his contemporaries. It may however be exemplified, together with the harsh and obscure construction, in which he more often offended, in the following lines:—

'Mid stormy vapours ever driving by,
Where ospreys, cormorants, and herons cry;
Where hardly given the hopeless waste to
  cheer,
Denied the bread of life, the foodful ear,
Dwindles the pear on autumn's latest spray,
And *apple sickens* pale in summer's ray;
Ev'n here content has fixed her smiling reign
With independence, child of high disdain.

I hope, I need not say, that I have quoted these lines for no other purpose than to make my meaning fully understood. It is to be regretted that Mr. Wordsworth has not republished these two poems entire.

3. As "the Friend" was printed on stampt sheets, and sent only by the post to a very limited number of subscribers, the author has felt less objection to quote from it, though a work of his own. To the public at large indeed it is the same as a volume in manuscript.

4. This is effected either by giving to the one word a general, and to the other an exclusive use; as "to put on the back" and "to indorse"; or by an actual distinction of meanings, as "naturalist," and "physician"; or by difference of relation, as "I" and "Me" (each of which the rustics of our different provinces still use in all the cases singular of the first personal pronoun). Even the mere difference, or corruption, in the *pronunciation* of the same word, if it have become general, will produce a new word with a distinct signification; thus "property" and "propriety"; the latter of which, even to the time of Charles II, was the *written* word for all the senses of both. Thus too "mister" and "master," both hasty pronunciations of the same word "magister," "mistress," and "miss," "if" and "give," &c. &c. There is a sort of *minim immortal* among the animalcula infusoria which has not naturally either birth, or death, absolute beginning, or absolute end: for at a certain period a small point appears on its back, which deepens and lengthens till the creature divides into two, and the same process recommences in each of the halves now become integral. This may be a fanciful, but it is by no means a bad emblem of the formation of words, and may facilitate the conception, how immense a nomenclature may be organized from a few simple sounds by rational beings in a social state. For each new supplication, or excitement of the same sound, will call forth a different sensation, which cannot but affect the pronunciation. The after recollection of the sound, without the same vivid sensation, will modify it still further; till at length all trace of the original likeness is worn away.

5. I ought to have added, with the exception of a single sheet which I accidentally met with at the printer's. Even from this scanty specimen, I found it impossible to doubt the talent, or not to admire the ingenuity of the author. That his distinctions were for the greater part unsatisfactory to *my* mind, proves nothing against their accuracy; but it may possibly be serviceable to him, in case of a second edition, if I take this opportunity of suggesting the query; whether he may not have been occasionally misled, by having assumed, as to me he appeared to have done, the non-existence of *any* absolute synonymes in our language? Now I cannot but think, that there are many which remain for our posterity to distinguish and appropriate, and which I regard as so much reversionary wealth in our mother-tongue. When two distinct meanings are confounded under one or more words, (and such must be the case, as sure as our knowledge is progressive and of course imperfect) erroneous consequences will be drawn, and what is true in one sense of the word will be affirmed as true in toto. Men of research, startled by the consequences, seek in the things themselves (whether in or out of the mind) for a knowledge of the fact, and having discovered the difference, remove the equivocation either by the substitution of a new word, or by the appropriation of one of the two more words, that had before been used promiscuously. When this distinction has been so naturalized and of such general currency that the language itself does as it were *think* for us (like the sliding rule which is the mechanic's safe substitute for arithmetical knowledge) we then say, that it is evident to *common sense*. Common sense, therefore, differs in different ages. What was born and christened in the schools passes by degrees in to the world at large, and becomes the property of the market and the tea-table. At least I can discover no other meaning of the term, *common sense*, if it is to convey any specific difference from sense and judgement in genere, and where it is not used scholastically for the *universal reason*. Thus in the reign of Charles II the philosophic world was called to arms by the moral sophism of Hobbs, and the ablest writers exerted themselves in the detection of an error, which a school-boy would now be able to confute by the mere recollection, that *compulsion* and *obligation* conveyed two ideas perfectly disparate, and that what appertained to the one, had been falsely transferred to the other by a mere confusion of terms.

6. I here use the word "idea" in Mr. Hume's sense on account of its general currency amongst the English metaphysicians; though against my own judgement, for I believe that the vague use of this word has been the cause of much error and more confusion. The word, *ἰδέα*, in its original sense as used by Pindar, Aristophanes, and in the Gospel of St. Matthew, represented by visual abstraction of a distant object, when we see the whole without distinguishing its parts. Plato adopted it as a technical term, and as the antithesis to *εἴδωλα*, or sensuous images; the transient and perishable emblems, or mental words, of ideas. The ideas themselves he considered by mysterious powers, living, seminal, formative, and exempt from time. In this sense the word became the property of the Platonic school; and it seldom occurs in Aristotle, without some such phrase annexed to it, as according to Plato, or as Plato says. Our English writers to the end of Charles 2nd's reign, or somewhat later, employed it either in the original sense, or platonically, or in a sense nearly correspondent to our present use of the substantive, Ideal, always however opposing it, more or less, to image, whether of present of absent objects. The reader will not be displeased with the following interesting exemplification from Bishop Jeremy Taylor. "St. Lewis the King sent Ivo Bishop of Chartres on an embassy, and he told, that he met a grave and stately matron on the way with a censer of fire in one hand, and a vessel of water in the other; and observing her to have a melancholy, religious, and phantastic deportment and look, he asked her what those symbols meant, and what she meant to do with her fire and water; she answered, my purpose is with the fire to burn paradise, and with my water to quench the flames of hell, that men may serve God purely for the love of God. But we rarely meet with such spirits which love virtue so metaphysically as *to abstract her from all sensible compositions, and love the purity of the idea.*" Des Cartes having introduced into his philosophy the fanciful hypothesis of *material ideas*, or certain configurations of the brain, which were as so many moulds to the influxes of the external world; Mr. Locke adopted the term, but extended its signification to whatever is the immediate object of the mind's attention or consciousness. Mr. Hume, distinguishing those representations which are accompanied with a sense of a present object, from those reproduced by the mind itself, designated the former by *impressions*, and confined the word *idea* to the latter.

William Wordsworth 1770–1850

William Wordsworth and his friend Samuel Taylor Coleridge were the harbingers of English romanticism, a movement that arose in reaction to the rationality and skepticism of the eighteenth century and was inspired by the American and French revolutions. Romanticism valued the emotional experience of the individual imagination, the relationship of the individual to nature, and the individual's experience of the "sublime." *Lyrical Ballads* (1798), the landmark collection of poetry by Wordsworth and Coleridge, ushered in the romantic age in English literature. Wordsworth's other works include *Poems in Two Volumes* (1807), *The Excursion* (1814), *Miscellaneous Poems* (1815), *The Borderers* (1842), and *The Prelude* (1850), which was published after his death. Wordsworth attended St. John's College at Cambridge but did not complete a degree. He walked through the Alps in France and Italy in 1790 and 1791, and during these tours he encountered popular revolutionary movements that would strongly influence his work. The poetry of his early and middle years was the most successful, and he was appointed poet laureate in 1843, but his increasing respectability was severely criticized by the second generation of romantic writers, who had been influenced by his early work. Byron, Shelley, Keats, and others abhorred his abandonment of the revolutionary ideals of his youth and his growing conservatism.

Written as an introduction to the second edition of *Lyrical Ballads* (1801), the "Preface" was Wordsworth's explanation of the poetry included in the volume. Wordsworth considered this poetry unique and separate from previous eighteenth-century works. In his essay Wordsworth put forth a new vision of poetry. His intent in writing the essay was to avoid being "censured for not having performed" what he "never intended." He desired his readers to understand his poetry as a complete break with the past, a poetry mirroring the ideals of the revolutions in France and America. For his subject matter he chose "incidents and situations from common life" that were to be written in a "language really used by men." Placing great emphasis on emotionalism, he thought poetry should be a "spontaneous overflow of powerful feelings." His new definition of a poet was not an individual superior to others, but a "man speaking to men," who everywhere carried with him "relationship and love."

In the "Preface," finally, Wordsworth was inaugurating a new tradition that emphasized the passion, dreams, and communal spirit of the common individual. This essay hailed the creation of a new paradigm in English literature and introduced the romantic movement, a movement full of self-awareness and the revolutionary spirit of change.

PREFACE to *Lyrical Ballads*

The first volume of these Poems has already been submitted to general perusal. It was published, as an experiment, which, I hoped, might be of some use to ascertain, how far, by fitting to metrical arrangement a selection of the real language of men in a state of vivid sensation, that sort of pleasure and that quantity of pleasure may be imparted, which a Poet may rationally endeavour to impart.

I had formed no very inaccurate estimate of the probable effect of those Poems: I flattered myself that they who should be pleased with them would read them with more than common pleasure: and, on the other hand, I was well aware, that by those who should dislike them, they would be read with more than common dislike. The result has differed from my expectation in this only, that a greater number have been pleased than I ventured to hope I should please. . . .

. . . .

Several of my Friends are anxious for the success of these Poems, from a belief, that if the views with which they were composed were indeed realized, a class of Poetry would be produced, well adapted to interest mankind permanently, and not unimportant in the quality, and in the multiplicity of its moral relations: and on this account they have advised me to prefix a systematic defence of the theory upon which the Poems were written. But I was unwilling to undertake the task, knowing that on this occasion the Reader would look coldly upon my arguments, since I might be suspected of having been principally influenced by the selfish and foolish hope of *reasoning* him into an approbation of these particular Poems: and I was still more unwilling to undertake the task, because, adequately to display the opinions, and fully to enforce the arguments, would require a space wholly disproportionate to a preface. For, to treat the subject with the clearness and coherence of which it is susceptible, it would be necessary to give a full account of the present state of the public taste in this country, and to determine how far this taste is healthy or depraved; which, again, could not be determined, without pointing out in what manner language and the human mind act and re-act on each other, and without retracing the revolutions, not of literature alone, but likewise of society itself. I have therefore altogether declined to enter regularly upon this defence; yet I am sensible, that there would be something like impropriety in abruptly obtruding upon the Public, without a few words of introduction, Poems so materially different from those upon which general approbation is at present bestowed.

It is supposed, that by the act of writing in verse an Author makes a formal engagement that he will gratify certain known habits of association; that he not only thus apprises the Reader that certain classes of ideas and expressions will be found in his book, but that others will be carefully excluded. This exponent or symbol held forth by metrical language must in different eras of literature have excited very different expectations: for example, in the age of Catullus, Terence, and Lucretius, and that of Statius or Claudian; and in our own country, in the age of Shakespeare and Beaumont and Fletcher, and that of Donne and Cowley, or Dryden, or Pope. I will not take upon me to determine the exact import of the promise which, by the act of writing in verse, an Author in the present day makes to his reader: but it will undoubtedly appear to many persons that I have not fulfilled the terms of an engagement thus voluntarily contracted. They who have been accustomed to the gaudiness and inane phraseology of many modern writers, if they persist in reading this book to its conclusion, will, no doubt, frequently have to struggle with feelings of strangeness and awkwardness: they will look round for poetry, and will be induced to inquire by what species of courtesy these attempts can be permitted to assume that title. I hope therefore the reader will not censure me for attempting to state what I have proposed to myself to perform; and also (as far as the limits of a preface will permit) to explain some of the chief reasons which have determined me in the choice of my purpose: that at least he may be spared any unpleasant feeling of disappointment, and that I myself may be protected from one of the most dishonourable accusations which can be brought against an Author; namely, that of an indolence which prevents him from endeavouring to ascertain what is his duty, or, when his duty is ascertained, prevents him from performing it.

The principal object, then, proposed in these Poems was to choose incidents and situations from common life, and to relate or describe them, throughout, as far as was possible in a selection of language really used by men, and, at the same time, to throw over them a certain colouring of imagination, whereby ordinary things should be presented to the mind in an unusual aspect; and, further, and above all, to make these incidents and situations interesting by tracing in them, truly though not ostentatiously, the primary laws of our nature: chiefly, as far as regards the manner in which we associate ideas in a state of excitement. Humble and rustic life was generally chosen, because, in that condition, the essential passions of the heart find a better soil in which they can attain their maturity, are less under restraint, and speak a plainer and more emphatic language; because in that condition of life our elementary feelings coexist in a state of greater simplicity, and, consequently, may be more accurately contemplated, and more forcibly communicated; because the manners of rural life germinate from those elementary feelings, and, from the necessary character of rural occupations, are more easily comprehended, and are more durable; and, lastly, because in that condition the passions of men are incorporated with the beautiful and permanent forms of nature. The language, too, of these men has been adopted (purified indeed from what appear to be its real defects, from all lasting and rational causes of dislike or disgust) because such men hourly communicate with the best objects from which the best part of language is originally derived; and because, from their rank in society and the sameness and narrow circle of their intercourse, being less under the influence of social vanity, they convey their feelings and notions in simple and unelaborated expressions. Accordingly, such a language, arising out of repeated experience and regular feelings, is a more permanent, and a far more philosophical language, than that which is frequently substituted for it by Poets, who think that they are conferring honour upon themselves and their art, in proportion as they separate themselves from the sympathies of men, and indulge in arbitrary and capricious habits of expression, in order to furnish food for fickle tastes, and fickle appetites, of their own creation.[1]

I cannot, however, be insensible to the present outcry against the triviality and meanness, both of thought and language, which some of my contemporaries have occasionally introduced into their metrical compositions; and I acknowledge that this defect, where it exists, is more dishonourable to the Writer's own character than false refinement or arbitrary innovation, though I should contend at the same time, that it is far less pernicious in the sum of its consequences. From such verses the Poems in these volumes will be found distinguished at least by one mark of difference, that each of them has a worthy *purpose.* Not that I always began to write with a distinct purpose formally conceived; but habits of meditation have, I trust, so prompted and regulated my feelings, that my descriptions of such objects as strongly excite those feelings, will be found to carry along with them a *purpose.* If this opinion be erroneous, I can have little right to the name of a Poet. For all good poetry is the spontaneous overflow of powerful feelings: and though this be true, Poems to which any value can be attached were never produced on any variety of subjects but by a man who, being possessed of more than usual organic sensibility, had also thought long and deeply. For our continued influxes of feeling are modified and directed by our thoughts, which are indeed the representatives of all our past feelings; and, as by contemplating the relation of these general representatives to each other, we discover what is really important to men, so, by the repetition and continuance of this act, our feelings will be connected with important subjects, till at length, if we be originally possessed of much sensibility, such habits of mind will be produced, that, by obeying blindly and mechanically the impulses of those habits, we shall describe objects, and utter sentiments, of such a nature, and in such connexion with each other, that the understanding of the Reader must necessarily be in some degree enlightened, and his affections strengthened and purified.

It has been said that each of these poems has a purpose. Another circumstance must be mentioned which distinguishes these Poems from the popular Poetry of the day; it is this, that the feeling therein developed gives importance to the action and situation, and not the action and situation to the feeling.

A sense of false modesty shall not prevent me from asserting, that the Reader's attention is pointed to this mark of distinction, far less for the sake of these particular Poems than from the general importance of the subject. The subject is indeed important! For the human mind is capable of being excited without the application of gross and violent stimulants; and he must have a very faint perception of its beauty and dignity who does not know this, and who does not further know, that one being is elevated above another, in proportion as he possesses this capability. It has therefore appeared to me, that to endeavour to produce or enlarge this capability is one of the best services in which, at any period, a Writer can be engaged; but this service, excellent at all times, is especially so at the present day. For a multitude of causes, unknown to former times, are now acting with a combined force to blunt the discriminating powers of the mind, and, unfitting it for all voluntary exertion, to reduce it to a state of almost savage torpor. The most effective of these causes are the great national events which are daily taking place, and the increasing accumulation of men in cities, where the uniformity of their occupations produces a craving for extraordinary incident, which the rapid communication of intelligence hourly gratifies. To this tendency of life and manners the literature and theatrical exhibitions of the country have conformed themselves. The invaluable works of our elder writers, I had almost said the works of Shakespeare and Milton, are driven into neglect by frantic novels, sickly and stupid German Tragedies, and deluges of idle and extravagant stories in verse.—When I think upon this degrading thirst after outrageous stimulation, I am almost ashamed to have spoken of the feeble endeavour made in these volumes to counteract it; and, reflecting upon the magnitude of the general evil, I should be oppressed with no dishonourable melancholy, had I not a deep impression of certain inherent and indestructible qualities of the human mind, and likewise of certain powers in the great and permanent objects that act upon it, which are equally inherent and indestructible; and were there not added to this impression a belief, that the time is approaching when the evil will be systematically opposed, by men of greater powers, and with far more distinguished success.

Having dwelt thus long on the subjects and aim of these Poems, I shall request the Reader's permission to apprise him of a few circumstances relating to their *style,* in order, among other reasons, that he may not censure me for not having performed what I never attempted. The Reader will find that personifications of abstract ideas rarely occur in these volumes; and are utterly rejected, as an ordinary device to elevate the style, and raise it above prose. My purpose was to imitate, and, as far as possible, to adopt the very language of men; and assuredly such personifications do not make any natural or regular part of that language. They are, indeed, a figure of speech occasionally prompted by passion, and I have made use of them as such; but have endeavoured utterly to reject them as a mechanical device of style, or as a family language which Writers in metre seem to lay claim to by prescription. I have wished to keep the Reader in the company of flesh and blood, persuaded that by so doing I shall interest him. Others who pursue a different track will interest him likewise; I do not interfere with their claim, but wish to prefer a claim of my own. There will also be found in these volumes little of what is usually called poetic diction; as much pains has been taken to avoid it as is ordinarily taken to produce it; this has been done for the reason already alleged, to bring my language near to the language of men; and further, because the pleasure which I have proposed to myself to impart, is of a kind very different from that which is supposed by many persons to be the proper object of poetry. Without being culpably particular, I do not know how to give my Reader a more exact notion of the style in which it was my wish and intention to write, than by informing him that I have at all times endeavoured to look steadily at my subject; consequently, there is I hope in these Poems little falsehood of description, and my ideas are expressed in language fitted to their respective importance. Something must have been gained by this practice, as it is friendly to one property of all good poetry, namely, good sense: but it has necessarily cut me off from a large portion of phrases and figures of speech which from father to son have long been regarded as the common inheritance of Poets. I have also thought it expedient to restrict myself still further, having abstained from the use of many expressions, in themselves proper and beautiful, but which have been foolishly repeated by bad Poets, till such feelings of disgust are connected with them as it is scarcely possible by any art of association to overpower.

If in a poem there should be found a series of lines, or even a single line, in which the language, though naturally arranged, and according to the strict laws of metre, does not differ from that of prose, there is a numerous class of critics, who, when they stumble upon these prosaisms, as they call them, imagine that they have made a notable discovery, and exult over the Poet as over a man ignorant of his own profession. Now these men would establish a canon of criticism which the Reader will conclude he must utterly reject, if he wishes to be pleased with these volumes. And it would be a most easy task to prove to him, that not only the language of a large portion of every good poem, even of the most elevated character, must necessarily, except with reference to the metre, in no respect differ from that of good prose, but likewise that some of the most interesting parts of the best poems will be found to be strictly the language of prose when prose is well written. The truth of this assertion might be demonstrated by innumerable passages from almost all the poetical writings, even of Milton himself. To illustrate the subject in a general manner, I will here adduce a short composition of Gray, who was at the head of those who, by their reasonings, have attempted to widen the space of separation betwixt Prose and Metrical composition, and was more than any other man curiously elaborate in the structure of his own poetic diction.

> In vain to me the smiling mornings shine,
> And reddening Phœbus lifts his golden fire:
> The birds in vain their amorous descant join,
> Or cheerful fields resume their green attire.
> These ears, alas! for other notes repine;
> *A different object do these eyes require:*
> *My lonely anguish melts no heart but mine:*
> *And in my breast the imperfect joys expire:*
> Yet morning smiles the busy race to cheer,
> And new-born pleasure brings to happier men;
> The fields to all their wonted tribute bear;
> To warm their little loves the birds complain.
> *I fruitless mourn to him that cannot hear,*
> *And weep the more because I weep in vain.*

It will easily be perceived, that the only part of this Sonnet which is of any value is the lines printed in Italics; it is equally obvious, that, except in the rhyme, and in the use of the single word "fruitless" for fruitlessly, which is so far a defect, the language of these lines does in no respect differ from that of prose.

By the foregoing quotation it has been shown that the language of Prose may yet be well adapted to Poetry; and it was previously asserted, that a large portion of the language of every good poem can in no respect differ from that of good Prose. We will go further. It may be safely affirmed, that there neither is, nor can be, any *essential* difference between the language of prose and metrical composition. We are fond of tracing the resemblance between Poetry and Painting, and, accordingly, we call them Sisters: but where shall we find bonds of connexion sufficiently strict to typify the affinity betwixt metrical and prose composition? They both speak by and to the same organs; the bodies in which both of them are clothed may be said to be of the same substance, their affections are kindred, and almost identical, not necessarily differing even in degree; Poetry[2] sheds no tears "such as Angels weep," but natural and human tears; she can boast of no celestial ichor that distinguishes her vital juices from those of prose; the same human blood circulates through the veins of them both.

If it be affirmed that rhyme and metrical arrangement of themselves constitute a distinction which overturns what has just been said on the strict affinity of metrical language with that of prose, and paves the way for other artificial distinctions which the mind voluntarily admits, I answer that the language of such Poetry as is here recommended is, as far as is possible, a selection of the language really spoken by men; that this selection, wherever it is made with true taste and feeling, will of itself form a distinction far greater than would at first be imagined, and will entirely separate the composition from the vulgarity and meanness of ordinary life; and, if metre be superadded thereto, I believe that a dissimilitude will be produced altogether sufficient for the gratification of a rational mind. What other distinction would we have? Whence is it to come? And where is it to exist? Not, surely, where the Poet speaks through the mouths of his characters: it cannot be necessary here, either for elevation of style, or any of its supposed ornaments: for, if the Poet's subject be judiciously chosen, it will naturally, and upon fit occasion, lead him to passions the language of which, if selected truly and judiciously, must necessarily be dignified and variegated, and alive with metaphors and figures. I forbear to speak of an incongruity which would shock the intelligent Reader, should the Poet interweave any foreign splendour of his own with that which the passion naturally suggests: it is sufficient to say that such addition is unnecessary. And, surely, it is more probable that those passages, which with propriety abound with metaphors and figures, will have their due effect, if, upon other occasions where the passions are of a milder character, the style also be subdued and temperate.

But, as the pleasure which I hope to give by the Poems now presented to the Reader must depend entirely on just notions upon this subject, and, as it is in itself of high importance to our taste and moral feelings, I cannot content myself with these detached remarks. And if, in what I am about to say, it shall appear to some that my labour is unnecessary, and that I am like a man fighting a battle without enemies, such persons may be reminded, that, whatever be the language outwardly holden by men, a practical faith in the opinions which I am wishing to establish is almost unknown. If my conclusions are admitted, and carried as far as they must be carried if admitted at all, our judgements concerning the works of the greatest Poets both ancient and modern will be far different from what they are at present, both when we praise, and when we censure: and our moral feelings influencing and influenced by these judgements will, I believe, be corrected and purified.

Taking up the subject, then, upon general grounds, let me ask, what is meant by the word Poet? What is a Poet? To whom does he address himself? And what language is to be expected from him?—He is a man speaking to men: a man, it is true, endowed with more lively sensibility, more enthusiasm and tenderness, who has a greater knowledge of human nature, and a more comprehensive soul, than are supposed to be common among mankind; a man pleased with his own passions and volitions, and who rejoices more than other men in the spirit of life that is in him; delighting to contemplate similar volitions and passions as manifested in the goings-on of the Universe, and habitually impelled to create them where he does not find them. To these qualities he has added a disposition to be affected more than other men by absent things as if they were present; an ability of conjuring up in himself passions, which are indeed far from being the same as those produced by real events, yet (especially in those parts of the general sympathy which are pleasing and delightful) do more nearly resemble the passions produced by real events, than anything which, from the motions of their own minds merely, other men are accustomed to feel in themselves:—whence, and from practice, he has acquired a greater readiness and power in expressing what he thinks and feels, and especially those thoughts and feelings which, by his own choice, or from the structure of his own mind, arise in him without immediate external excitement.

But whatever portion of this faculty we may suppose even the greatest Poet to possess, there cannot be a doubt that the language which it will suggest to him, must often, in liveliness and truth, fall short of that which is uttered by men in real life, under the actual pressure of those passions, certain shadows of which the Poet thus produces, or feels to be produced, in himself.

However exalted a notion we would wish to cherish of the character of a Poet, it is obvious, that while he describes and imitates passions, his employment is in some degree mechanical, compared with the freedom and power of real and substantial action and suffering. So that it will be the wish of the Poet to bring his feelings near to those of the persons whose feelings he describes, nay, for short spaces of time, perhaps, to let himself slip into an entire delusion, and even confound and identify his own feelings with theirs; modifying only the language which is thus suggested to him by a consideration that he describes for a particular purpose, that of giving pleasure. Here, then, he will apply the principle of selection which has been already insisted upon. He will depend upon this for removing what would otherwise be painful or disgusting in the passion; he will feel that there is no necessity to trick out or to elevate nature: and, the more industriously he applies this principle, the deeper will be his faith that no words, which *his* fancy or imagination can suggest, will be to be compared with those which are the emanations of reality and truth.

But it may be said by those who do not object to the general spirit of these remarks, that, as it is impossible for the Poet to produce upon all occasions language as exquisitely fitted for the passion as that which the real passion itself suggests, it is proper that he should consider himself as in the situation of a translator, who does not scruple to substitute excellencies of another kind for those which are unattainable by him; and endeavours occasionally to surpass his original, in order to make some amends for the general inferiority to which he feels that he must submit. But this would be to encourage idleness and unmanly despair. Further, it is the language of men who speak of what they do not understand; who talk of Poetry as of a matter of amusement and idle pleasure; who will converse with us as gravely about a *taste* for Poetry, as they express it, as if it were a thing as indifferent as a taste for rope-dancing, or Frontiniac or Sherry. Aristotle, I have been told, has said, that Poetry is the most philosophic of all writing: it is so: its object is truth, not individual and local, but general, and operative; not standing upon external testimony, but carried alive into the heart by passion; truth which is its own testimony, which gives competence and confidence to the tribunal to which it appeals, and receives them from the same tribunal. Poetry is the image of man and nature. The obstacles which stand in the way of the fidelity of the Biographer and Historian, and of their consequent utility, are incalculably greater than those which are to be encountered by the Poet who comprehends the dignity of his art. The Poet writes under one restriction only, namely, the necessity of giving immediate pleasure to a human Being possessed of that information which may be expected from him, not as a lawyer, a physician, a mariner, an astronomer, or a natural philosopher, but as a Man. Except this one restriction, there is no object standing between the Poet and the image of things; between this, and the Biographer and Historian, there are a thousand.

Nor let this necessity of producing immediate pleasure be considered as a degradation of the Poet's art. It is far otherwise. It is an acknowledgement of the beauty of the universe, an acknowledgement the more sincere, because not formal, but indirect; it is a task light and easy to him who looks at the world in the spirit of love: further, it is a homage paid to the native and naked dignity of man, to the grand elementary principle of pleasure, by which he knows, and feels, and lives, and moves. We have no sympathy but what is propagated by pleasure: I would not be misunderstood; but wherever we sympathize with pain, it will be found that the sympathy is produced and carried on by subtle combinations with pleasure. We have no knowledge, that is, no general principles drawn from the contemplation of particular facts, but what has been built up by pleasure, and exists in us by pleasure alone. The Man of science, the Chemist and Mathematician, whatever difficulties and disgusts they may have had to struggle with, know and feel this. However painful may be the objects with which the Anatomist's knowledge is connected, he feels that his knowledge is pleasure; and where he has no pleasure he has no knowledge. What then does the Poet? He considers man and the objects that surround him as acting and re-acting upon each other, so as to produce an infinite complexity of pain and pleasure; he considers man in his own nature and in his ordinary life as contemplating this with a certain quantity of immediate knowledge, with certain convictions, intuitions, and deductions, which from habit acquire the quality of intuitions; he considers him as looking upon this complex scene of ideas and sensations, and finding everywhere objects that immediately excite in him sympathies which, from the necessities of his nature, are accompanied by an overbalance of enjoyment.

To this knowledge which all men carry about with them, and to these sympathies in which, without any other discipline than that of our daily life, we are fitted to take delight, the Poet principally directs his attention. He considers man and nature as essentially adapted to each other, and the mind of man as naturally the mirror of the fairest and most interesting properties of nature. And thus the Poet, prompted by this feeling of pleasure, which accompanies him through the whole course of his studies, converses with general nature, with affections akin to those, which, through labour and length of time, the Man of science has raised up in himself, by conversing with those particular parts of nature which are the objects of his studies. The knowledge both of the Poet and the Man of science is pleasure; but the knowledge of the one cleaves to us as a necessary part of our existence, our natural and unalienable inheritance; the other is a personal and individual acquisition, slow to come to us, and by no habitual and direct sympathy connecting us with our fellow-beings. The Man of science seeks truth as a remote and unknown benefactor; he cherishes and loves it in his solitude: the Poet, singing a song in which all human beings join with him, rejoices in the presence of truth as our visible and hourly companion. Poetry is the breath and finer spirit of all knowledge; it is the impassioned expression which is in the countenance of all Science. Emphatically may it be said of the Poet, as Shakespeare hath said of man, "that he looks before and after." He is the rock of defence for human nature; an upholder and preserver, carrying everywhere with him relationship and love. In spite of difference of soil and climate, of language and manners, of laws and customs: in spite of things silently gone out of mind, and things violently destroyed; the Poet binds together by passion and knowledge the vast empire of human society, as it is spread over the whole earth, and over all time. The objects of the Poet's thoughts are everywhere; though the eyes and senses of man are, it is true, his favourite guides, yet he will follow wheresoever he can find an atmosphere of sensation in which to move his wings. Poetry is the first and last of all knowledge—it is as immortal as the heart of man. If the labours of Men of science should ever create any material revolution, direct or indirect, in our condition, and in the impressions which we habitually receive, the Poet will sleep then no more than at present; he will be ready to follow the steps of the Man of science, not only in those general indirect effects, but he will be at his side, carrying sensation into the midst of the objects of the science itself. The remotest discoveries of the Chemist, the Botanist, or Mineralogist, will be as proper objects of the Poet's art as any upon which it can be employed, if the time should ever come when these things shall be familiar to us, and the relations under which they are contemplated by the followers of these respective sciences shall be manifestly and palpably material to us as enjoying and suffering beings. If the time should ever come when what is now called science, thus familiarized to men, shall be ready to put on, as it were, a form of flesh and blood, the Poet will lend his divine spirit to aid the transfiguration, and will welcome the Being thus produced, as a dear and genuine inmate of the household of man.—It is not, then, to be supposed that any one, who holds that sublime notion of Poetry which I have attempted to convey, will break in upon the sanctity and truth of his pictures by transitory and accidental ornaments, and endeavour to excite admiration of himself by arts, the necessity of which must manifestly depend upon the assured meanness of his subject.

What has been thus far said applies to Poetry in general; but especially to those parts of composition where the Poet speaks through the mouths of his characters; and upon this point it appears to authorize the conclusion that there are few persons of good sense, who would not allow that the dramatic parts of composition are defective, in proportion as they deviate from the real language of nature, and are coloured by a diction of the Poet's own, either peculiar to him as an individual Poet or belonging simply to Poets in general; to a body of men who, from the circumstance of their compositions being in metre, it is expected will employ a particular language.

It is not, then, in the dramatic parts of composition that we look for this distinction of language; but still it may be proper and necessary where the Poet speaks to us in his own person and character. To this I answer by referring the Reader to the description before given of a Poet. Among the qualities there enumerated as principally conducing to form a Poet, is implied nothing differing in kind from other men, but only in degree. The sum of what was said is, that the Poet is chiefly distinguished from other men by a greater promptness to think and feel without immediate external excitement, and a greater power in expressing such thoughts and feelings as are produced in him in that manner. But these passions and thoughts and feelings are the general passions and thoughts and feelings of men. And with what are they connected? Undoubtedly with our moral sentiments and animal sensations, and with the causes which excite these; with the operations of the elements, and the appearances of the visible universe; with storm and sunshine, with the revolutions of the seasons, with cold and heat, with loss of friends and kindred, with injuries and resentments, gratitude and hope, with fear and sorrow. These, and the like, are the sensations and objects which the Poet describes, as they are the sensations of other men, and the objects which interest them. The Poet thinks and feels in the spirit of human passions. How, then, can his language differ in any material degree from that of all other men who feel vividly and see clearly? It might be *proved* that it is impossible. But supposing that this were not the case, the Poet might then be allowed to use a peculiar language when expressing his feelings for his own gratification, or that of men like himself. But Poets do not write for Poets alone, but for men. Unless therefore we are advocates for that admiration which subsists upon ignorance, and that pleasure which arises from hearing what we do not understand, the Poet must descend from this supposed height; and, in order to excite rational sympathy, he must express himself as other men express themselves. To this it may be added, that while he is only selecting from the real language of men, or, which amounts to the same thing, composing accurately in the spirit of such selection, he is treading upon safe ground, and we know what we are to expect from him. Our feelings are the same with respect to metre; for, as it may be proper to remind the Reader, the distinction of metre is regular and uniform, and not, like that which is produced by what is usually called POETIC DICTION, arbitrary, and subject to infinite caprices upon which no calculation whatever can be made. In the one case, the Reader is utterly at the mercy of the Poet, respecting what imagery or diction he may choose to connect with the passion; whereas, in the other, the metre obeys certain laws, to which the Poet and Reader both willingly submit because they are certain, and because no interference is made by them with the passion, but such as the concurring testimony of ages has shown to heighten and improve the pleasure which co-exists with it.

It will now be proper to answer an obvious question, namely, Why, professing these opinions, have I written in verse? To this, in addition to such answer as is included in what has been already said, I reply, in the first place, Because, however I may have restricted myself, there is still left open to me what confessedly constitutes the most valuable object of all writing, whether in prose or verse; the great and universal passions of men, the most general and interesting of their occupations, and the entire world of nature before me—to supply endless combinations of forms and imagery. Now, supposing for a moment that whatever is interesting in these objects may be as vividly described in prose, why should I be condemned for attempting to superadd to such description the charm which, by the consent of all nations, is acknowledged to exist in metrical language? To this, by such as are yet unconvinced, it may be answered that a very small part of the pleasure given by Poetry depends upon the metre, and that it is injudicious to write in metre, unless it be accompanied with the other artificial distinctions of style with which metre is usually accompanied, and that, by such deviation, more will be lost from the shock which will thereby be given to the Reader's associations than will be counterbalanced by any pleasure which he can derive from the general power of numbers. In answer to those who still contend for the necessity of accompanying metre with certain appropriate colours of style in order to the accomplishment of its appropriate end, and who also, in my opinion, greatly underrate the power of metre in itself, it might, perhaps, as far as relates to these Volumes, have been almost sufficient to observe, that poems are extant, written upon more humble subjects, and in a still more naked and simple style, which have continued to give pleasure from generation to generation. Now, if nakedness and simplicity be a defect, the fact here mentioned affords a strong presumption that poems somewhat less naked and simple are capable of affording pleasure at the present day; and, what I wished *chiefly* to attempt, at present, was to justify myself for having written under the impression of this belief.

But various causes might be pointed out why, when the style is manly, and the subject of some importance, words metrically arranged will long continue to impart such a pleasure to mankind as he who proves the extent of that pleasure will be desirous to impart. The end of Poetry is to produce excitement in co-existence with an overbalance of pleasure; but, by the supposition, excitement is an unusual and irregular state of the mind; ideas and feelings do not, in that state, succeed each other in accustomed order. If the words, however, by which this excitement is produced be in themselves powerful, or the images and feelings have an undue proportion of pain connected with them, there is some danger that the excitement may be carried beyond its proper bounds. Now the copresence of something regular, something to which the mind has been accustomed in various moods and in a less excited state, cannot but have great efficacy in tempering and restraining the passion by an intertexture of ordinary feeling, and of feeling not strictly and necessarily connected with the passion. This is unquestionably true; and hence, though the opinion will at first appear paradoxical, from the tendency of metre to divest language, in a certain degree, of its reality, and thus to throw a sort of half-consciousness of unsubstantial existence over the whole composition, there can be little doubt but that more pathetic situations and sentiments, that is, those which have a greater proportion of pain connected with them, may be endured in metrical composition, especially in rhyme, than in prose. The metre of the old ballads is very artless; yet they contain many passages which would illustrate this opinion; and, I hope, if the following Poems be attentively perused, similar instances will be found in them. This opinion may be further illustrated by appealing to the Reader's own experience of the reluctance with which he comes to the re-perusal of the distressful parts of *Clarissa Harlowe*, or *The Gamester*; while Shakespeare's writings, in the most pathetic scenes, never act upon us, as pathetic, beyond the bounds of pleasure—an effect which, in a much greater degree than might at first be imagined, is to be ascribed to small, but continual and regular impulses of pleasurable surprise from the metrical arrangement.—On the other hand (what it must be allowed will much more frequently happen) if the Poet's words should be incommensurate with the passion, and inadequate to raise the Reader to a height of desirable excitement, then (unless the Poet's choice of his metre has been grossly injudicious), in the feelings of pleasure which the Reader has been accustomed to connect with metre in general, and in the feeling, whether cheerful or melancholy, which he has been accustomed to connect with that particular movement of metre, there will be found something which will greatly contribute to impart passion to the words, and to effect the complex end which the Poet proposes to himself.

If I had undertaken a SYSTEMATIC defence of the theory here maintained, it would have been my duty to develop the various causes upon which the pleasure received from metrical language depends. Among the chief of these causes is to be reckoned a principle which must be well known to those who have made any of the Arts the object of accurate reflection; namely, the pleasure which the mind derives from the perception of similitude in dissimilitude. This principle is the great spring of the activity of our minds, and their chief feeder. From this principle the direction of the sexual appetite, and all the passions connected with it, take their origin: it is the life of our ordinary conversation; and upon the accuracy with which similitude in dissimilitude, and dissimilitude in similitude are perceived, depend our taste and our moral feelings. It would not be a useless employment to apply this principle to the consideration of metre, and to show that metre is hence enabled to afford much pleasure, and to point out in what manner that pleasure is produced. But my limits will not permit me to enter upon this subject, and I must content myself with a general summary.

I have said that poetry is the spontaneous overflow of powerful feelings: it takes its origin from emotion recollected in tranquillity: the emotion is contemplated till, by a species of reaction, the tranquillity gradually disappears, and an emotion, kindred to that which was before the subject of contemplation, is gradually produced, and does itself actually exist in the mind. In this mood successful composition generally begins, and in a mood similar to this it is carried on; but the emotion, of whatever kind, and in whatever degree, from various causes, is qualified by various pleasures, so that in describing any passions whatsoever, which are voluntarily described, the mind will, upon the whole, be in a state of enjoyment. If Nature be thus cautious to preserve in a state of enjoyment a being so employed, the Poet ought to profit by the lesson held forth to him, and ought especially to take care, that, whatever passions he communicates to his Reader, those passions, if his Reader's mind be sound and vigorous, should always be accompanied with an overbalance of pleasure. Now the music of harmonious metrical language, the sense of difficulty overcome, and the blind association of pleasure which has been previously received from works of rhyme or metre of the same or similar construction, an indistinct perception perpetually renewed of language closely resembling that of real life, and yet, in the circumstance of metre, differing from it so widely—all these imperceptibly make up a complex feeling of delight, which is of the most important use in tempering the painful feeling always found intermingled with powerful descriptions of the deeper passions. This effect is always produced in pathetic and impassioned poetry; while, in lighter compositions, the ease and gracefulness with which the Poet manages his numbers are themselves confessedly a principal source of the gratification of the Reader. All that it is *necessary* to say, however, upon this subject, may be effected by affirming, what few persons will deny, that, of two descriptions, either of passions, manners, or characters, each of them equally well executed, the one in prose and the other in verse, the verse will be read a hundred times where the prose is read once.

Having thus explained a few of my reasons for writing in verse, and why I have chosen subjects from common life, and endeavoured to bring my language near to the real language of men, if I have been too minute in pleading my own cause, I have at the same time been treating a subject of general interest; and for this reason a few words shall be added with reference solely to these particular poems, and to some defects which will probably be found in them. I am sensible that my associations must have sometimes been particular instead of general, and that, consequently, giving to things a false importance, I may have sometimes written upon unworthy subjects; but I am less apprehensive on this account, than that my language may frequently have suffered from those arbitrary connexions of feelings and ideas with particular words and phrases, from which no man can altogether protect himself. Hence I have no doubt, that, in some instances, feelings, even of the ludicrous, may be given to my Readers by expressions which appeared to me tender and pathetic. Such faulty expressions, were I convinced they were faulty at present, and that they must necessarily continue to be so, I would willingly take all reasonable pains to correct. But it is dangerous to make these alterations on the simple authority of a few individuals, or even of certain classes of men; for where the understanding of an Author is not convinced, or his feelings altered, this cannot be done without great injury to himself: for his own feelings are his stay and support; and, if he set them aside in one instance, he may be induced to repeat this act till his mind shall lose all confidence in itself, and become utterly debilitated. To this it may be added, that the critic ought never to forget that he is himself exposed to the same errors as the Poet, and, perhaps, in a much greater degree: for there can be no presumption in saying of most readers, that it is not probable they will be so well acquainted with the various stages of meaning through which words have passed, or with the fickleness or stability of the relations of particular ideas to each other; and, above all, since they are so much less interested in the subject, they may decide lightly and carelessly.

Long as the Reader has been detained, I hope he will permit me to caution him against a mode of false criticism which has been applied to Poetry, in which the language closely resembles that of life and nature. Such verses have been triumphed over in parodies, of which Dr. Johnson's stanza is a fair specimen:—

> I put my hat upon my head
> And walked into the Strand,
> And there I met another man
> Whose hat was in his hand.

Immediately under these lines let us place one of the most justly admired stanzas of the "Babes in the Wood."

> These pretty Babes with hand in hand
> Went wandering up and down;
> But never more they saw the Man
> Approaching from the Town.

In both these stanzas the words, and the order of the words, in no respect differ from the most unimpassioned conversation. There are words in both, for example, "the Strand," and "the Town," connected with none but the most familiar ideas; yet the one stanza we admit as admirable, and the other as a fair example of the superlatively contemptible. Whence arises this difference? Not from the metre, not from the language, not from the order of the words; but the *matter* expressed in Dr. Johnson's stanza is contemptible. The proper method of treating trivial and simple verses, to which Dr. Johnson's stanza would be a fair parallelism, is not to say, this is a bad kind of poetry, or, this is not poetry; but, this wants sense; it is neither interesting in itself, nor can *lead* to anything interesting; the images neither originate in that sane state of feeling which arises out of thought, nor can excite thought or feeling in the Reader. This is the only sensible manner of dealing with such verses. Why trouble yourself about the species till you have previously decided upon the genus? Why take pains to prove that an ape is not a Newton, when it is self-evident that he is not a man?

One request I must make of my reader, which is, that in judging these poems he would decide by his own feelings genuinely, and not by reflection upon what will probably be the judgement of others. How common is it to hear a person say, I myself do not object to this style of composition, or this or that expression, but, to such and such classes of people it will appear mean or ludicrous! This mode of criticism, so destructive of all sound unadulterated judgement, is almost universal: let the Reader then abide, independently, by his own feelings, and, if he finds himself affected, let him not suffer such conjectures to interfere with his pleasure.

If an Author, by any single composition, has impressed us with respect for his talents, it is useful to consider this as affording a presumption, that on other occasions where we have been displeased, he, nevertheless, may not have written ill or absurdly; and further, to give him so much credit for this one composition as may induce us to review what has displeased us, with more care than we should otherwise have bestowed upon it. This is not only an act of justice, but, in our decisions upon poetry especially, may conduce, in a high degree, to the improvement of our own taste; for an *accurate* taste in poetry, and in all the other arts, as Sir Joshua Reynolds has observed, is an *acquired* talent, which can only be produced by thought and a long continued intercourse with the best models of composition. This is mentioned, not with so ridiculous a purpose as to prevent the most inexperienced Reader from judging for himself (I have already said that I wish him to judge for himself), but merely to temper the rashness of decision, and to suggest, that, if Poetry be a subject on which much time has not been bestowed, the judgement may be erroneous; and that, in many cases, it necessarily will be so.

Nothing would, I know, have so effectually contributed to further the end which I have in view, as to have shown of what kind the pleasure is, and how that pleasure is produced, which is confessedly produced by metrical composition essentially different from that which I have here endeavoured to recommend: for the Reader will say that he has been pleased by such composition; and what more can be done for him? The power of any art is limited; and he will suspect, that, if it be proposed to furnish him with new friends, that can be only upon condition of his abandoning his old friends. Besides, as I have said, the Reader is himself conscious of the pleasure which he has received from such composition, composition to which he has peculiarly attached the endearing name of Poetry; and all men feel an habitual gratitude, and something of an honourable bigotry, for the objects which have long continued to please them: we not only wish to be pleased, but to be pleased in that particular way in which we have been accustomed to be pleased. There is in these feelings enough to resist a host of arguments; and I should be the less able to combat them successfully, as I am willing to allow, that, in order entirely to enjoy the Poetry which I am recommending, it would be necessary to give up much of what is ordinarily enjoyed. But, would my limits have permitted me to point out how this pleasure is produced, many obstacles might have been removed, and the Reader assisted in perceiving that the powers of language are not so limited as he may suppose; and that it is possible for poetry to give other enjoyments, of a purer, more lasting, and more exquisite nature. This part of the subject has not been altogether neglected, but it has not been so much my present aim to prove, that the interest excited by some other kinds of poetry is less vivid, and less worthy of the nobler powers of the mind, as to offer reasons for presuming, that if my purpose were fulfilled, a species of poetry would be produced, which is genuine poetry; in its nature well adapted to interest mankind permanently, and likewise important in the multiplicity and quality of its moral relations.

From what has been said, and from a perusal of the Poems, the Reader will be able clearly to perceive the object which I had in view: he will determine how far it has been attained; and, what is a much more important question, whether it be worth attaining: and upon the decision of these two questions will rest my claim to the approbation of the Public.

Notes

[The following notes are by William Wordsworth and were included in the original edition of this essay—Ed.]

1. It is worth while here to observe that the affecting parts of Chaucer are almost always expressed in language pure and universally intelligible even to this day.

2. I here use the word "Poetry" (though against my own judgement) as opposed to the word Prose, and synonymous with metrical composition. But much confusion has been introduced into criticism by this contradistinction of Poetry and Prose, instead of the more philosophical one of Poetry and Matter of Fact, or Science. The only strict antithesis to Prose is Metre; nor is this, in truth, a *strict* antithesis, because lines and passages of metre so naturally occur in writing prose, that it would be scarcely possible to avoid them, even were it desirable.

Percy Bysshe Shelley 1792–1822

The primary world event for this nineteenth-century romantic poet and social activist was the French Revolution. Under its influence, Shelley hoped to stir a libidinal desire in humanity to create a better world. In 1811, Shelley's coauthorship, with Thomas Jefferson Hogg, of "The Necessity of Atheism" cost him his Oxford education, and he was expelled. He then married Harriet Westbrook and went to Ireland to work for the Catholic emancipation movement and there distributed his "Address to the Irish People." After Westbrook's death in 1818, Shelley, viewed by all of London as an immoral anarchist because of his revolutionary activities and his relationship with Mary Wollstonecraft Godwin, married Godwin and moved with her to Italy. Shelley remained in exile until he was killed in a shipwreck in the Gulf of Spezia. His complete works, which consist primarily of poetry, are collected in ten volumes by Roger Ingpen and W. E. Peck (1927).

In "A Defence of Poetry" (1821), his only completed piece of critical prose, Shelley refutes Thomas Love Peacock's argument that the range of poetry is diminished by the advances of reason. By tracing the development of poetry in Western literature, he shows that without the "intervention" of poetic "excitements," the human mind could never have "been awakened to the invention of the grosser sciences."

Poetry allows the mind to integrate all forms of knowledge, for we feel what we perceive and imagine what we know. Shelley, like Blake, believed that the poet's individual imaginative vision renews language and recreates the world. In the early twentieth century, anti-Shelleyans derided his work for its idealism, its messianic claims for poetry, and its vagueness. W. B. Yeats, however, believed "A Defence of Poetry" to be the most important essay on the development of English poetry. Currently critics continue to debate the questions of Shelley's "sceptical idealism."

from A Defence of Poetry

Poetry, in a general sense, may be defined to be "the expression of the imagination": and poetry is connate with the origin of man. Man is an instrument over which a series of external and internal impressions are driven, like the alternations of an ever-changing wind over an Æolian lyre, which move it by their motion to ever-changing melody. But there is a principle within the human being, and perhaps within all sentient beings, which acts otherwise than in a lyre, and produces not melody alone, but harmony, by an internal adjustment of the sounds and motions thus excited to the impressions which excite them. It is as if the lyre could accommodate its chords to the motions of that which strikes them, in a determined proportion of sound; even as the musician can accommodate his voice to the sound of the lyre. . . .

In the youth of the world, men dance and sing and imitate natural objects, observing in these actions, as in all others, a certain rhythm or order. And, although all men observe a similar, they observe not the same order, in the motions of the dance, in the melody of the song, in the combinations of language, in the series of their imitations of natural objects. For there is a certain order or rhythm belonging to each of these classes of mimetic representation, from which the hearer and the spectator receive an intenser and purer pleasure than from any other: the sense of an approximation to this order has been called taste by modern writers. Every man in the infancy of art, observes an order which approximates more or less closely to that from which this highest delight results: but the diversity is not sufficiently marked, as that its gradations should be sensible, except in those instances where the predominance of this faculty of approximation to the beautiful (for so we may be permitted to name the relation between this highest pleasure and its cause) is very great. Those in whom it exists to excess are poets, in the most universal sense of the word; and the pleasure resulting from the manner in which they express the influence of society or nature upon their own minds, communicates itself to others, and gathers a sort of reduplication from the community. Their language is vitally metaphorical; that is, it marks the before unapprehended relations of things and perpetuates their apprehension, until words, which represent them, become, through time, signs for portions or classes of thought, instead of pictures of integral thoughts; and then, if no new poets should arise to create afresh the associations which have been thus disorganized, language will be dead to all the nobler purposes of human intercourse. . . .

But poets, or those who imagine and express this indestructible order, are not only the authors of language and of music, of the dance, and architecture, and statuary, and painting; they are the institutors of laws and the founders of civil society, and the inventors of the arts of life, and the teachers, who draw into a certain propinquity with the beautiful and the true, that partial apprehension of the agencies of the invisible world which is called religion. Hence all original religions are allegorical or susceptible of allegory, and, like Janus, have a double face of false and true. Poets, according to the circumstances of the age and nation in which they appeared, were called, in the earlier epochs of the world, legislators or prophets: a poet essentially comprises and unites both these characters. For he not only beholds intensely the present as it is, and discovers those laws according to which present things ought to be ordered, but he beholds the future in the present, and his thoughts are the germs of the flower and the fruit of latest time. Not that I assert poets to be prophets in the gross sense of the word, or that they can foretell the form as surely as they foreknow the spirit of events: such is the pretence of superstition, which would make poetry an attribute of prophecy, rather than prophecy an attribute of poetry. A poet participates in the eternal, the infinite, and the one; as far as relates to his conceptions, time and place and number are not. . . . But poetry in a more restricted sense expresses those arrangements of language, and especially metrical language, which are created by that imperial faculty, whose throne is curtained within the invisible nature of man. And this springs from the nature itself of language, which is a more direct representation of the actions and passions of our internal being, and is susceptible of more various and delicate combinations, than colour, form, or motion, and is more plastic and obedient to the control of that faculty of which it is the creation. For language is arbitrarily produced by the imagination, and has relation to thoughts alone; but all other materials, instruments, and conditions of art, have relations among each other, which limit and interpose between conception and expression. The former is as a mirror which reflects, the latter as a cloud which enfeebles, the light of which both are mediums of communication. . . .

The distinction between poets and prose writers is a vulgar error. . . . All the authors of revolutions in opinion are not only necessarily poets as they are inventors, nor even as their words unveil the permanent analogy of things by images which participate in the life of truth; but as their periods are harmonious and rhythmical, and contain in themselves the elements of verse; being the echo of the eternal music. Nor are those supreme poets, who have employed traditional forms of rhythm on account of the form and action of their subjects, less capable of perceiving and teaching the truth of things, than those who have omitted that form. Shakespeare, Dante, and Milton (to confine ourselves to modern writers) are philosophers of the very loftiest power.

A poem is the very image of life expressed in its eternal truth. There is this difference between a story and a poem, that a story is a catalogue of detached facts, which have no other connexion than time, place, circumstance, cause, and effect; the other is the creation of actions according to the unchangeable forms of human nature, as existing in the mind of the Creator, which is itself the image of all other minds. The one is partial, and applies only to a definite period of time, and a certain combination of events which can never again recur; the other is universal, and contains within itself the germ of a relation to whatever motives or actions have place in the possible varieties of human nature. Time, which destroys the beauty and the use of the story of particular facts, stripped of the poetry which should invest them, augments that of poetry, and for ever develops new and wonderful applications of the eternal truth which it contains. Hence epitomes have been called the moths of just history; they eat out the poetry of it. A story of particular facts is as a mirror which obscures and distorts that which should be beautiful: poetry is a mirror which makes beautiful that which is distorted. . . .

Having determined what is poetry, and who are poets, let us proceed to estimate its effects upon society.

Poetry is ever accompanied with pleasure: all spirits upon which it falls open themselves to receive the wisdom which is mingled with its delight. In the infancy of the world, neither poets themselves nor their auditors are fully aware of the excellence of poetry: for it acts in a divine and unapprehended manner, beyond and above consciousness; and it is reserved for future generations to contemplate and measure the mighty cause and effect in all the strength and splendour of their union. Even in modern times, no living poet ever arrived at the fullness of his fame; the jury which sits in judgment upon a poet, belonging as he does to all time, must be composed of his peers: it must be empanelled by time from the selectest of the wise of many generations. A poet is a nightingale, who sits in darkness and sings to cheer its own solitude with sweet sounds; his auditors are as men entranced by the melody of an unseen musician, who feel that they are moved and softened, yet know not whence or why. The poems of Homer and his contemporaries were the delight of infant Greece; they were the elements of that social system which is the column upon which all succeeding civilization has reposed. Homer embodied the ideal perfection of his age in human character; nor can we doubt that those who read his verses were awakened to an ambition of becoming like to Achilles, Hector, and Ulysses: the truth and beauty of friendship, patriotism, and persevering devotion to an object, were unveiled to their depths in these immortal creations: the sentiments of the auditors must have been refined and enlarged by a sympathy with such great and lovely impersonations, until from admiring they imitated, and from imitation they identified themselves with the objects of their admiration. Nor let it be objected, that these characters are remote from moral perfection, and that they are by no means to be considered as edifying patterns for general imitation. Every epoch, under names more or less specious, has deified its peculiar errors; Revenge is the naked idol of the worship of a semibarbarous age; and Self-deceit is the veiled image of unknown evil, before which luxury and satiety lie prostrate. But a poet considers the vices of his contemporaries as the temporary dress in which his creations must be arrayed, and which cover without concealing the eternal proportions of their beauty. An epic or dramatic personage is understood to wear them around his soul, as he may the ancient armour or modern uniform around his body; whilst it is easy to conceive a dress more graceful than either. The beauty of the internal nature cannot be so far concealed by its accidental vesture, but that the spirit of its form shall communicate itself to the very disguise, and indicate the shape it hides from the manner in which it is worn. A majestic form and graceful motions will express themselves through the most barbarous and tasteless costume. Few poets of the highest class have chosen to exhibit the beauty of their conceptions in its naked truth and splendour; and it is doubtful whether the alloy of costume, habit, etc., be not necessary to temper this planetary music for mortal ears.

The whole objection, however, of the immortality of poetry rests upon a misconception of the manner in which poetry acts to produce the moral improvement of man. Ethical science arranges the elements which poetry has created, and propounds schemes and proposes examples of civil and domestic life: nor is it for want of admirable doctrines that men hate, and despise, and censure, and deceive, and subjugate one another. But poetry acts in another and diviner manner. It awakens and enlarges the mind itself by rendering it the receptacle of a thousand unapprehended combinations of thought. Poetry lifts the veil from the hidden beauty of the world, and makes familiar objects be as if they were not familiar; it reproduces all that it represents, and the impersonations clothed in its Elysian light stand thenceforward in the minds of those who have once contemplated them, as memorials of that gentle and exalted content which extends itself over all thoughts and actions with which it coexists. The great secret of morals is love; or a going out of our own nature, and an identification of ourselves with the beautiful which exists in thought, action, or person, not our own. A man, to be greatly good, must imagine intensely and comprehensively; he must put himself in the place of another and of many others; the pains and pleasures of his species must become his own. The great instrument of moral good is the imagination; and poetry administers to the effect by acting upon the cause. Poetry enlarges the circumference of the imagination by replenishing it with thoughts of ever new delight, which have the power of attracting and assimilating to their own nature all other thoughts, and which form new intervals and interstices whose void for ever craves fresh food. Poetry strengthens the faculty which is the organ of the moral nature of man, in the same manner as exercise strengthens a limb. A poet therefore would do ill to embody his own conceptions of right and wrong, which are usually those of his place and time, in his poetical creations, which participate in neither. . . .

The poetry of Dante may be considered as the bridge thrown over the stream of time, which unites the modern and ancient world. The distorted notions of invisible things which Dante and his rival Milton have idealised, are merely the mask and the mantle in which these great poets walk through eternity enveloped and disguised. It is a difficult question to determine how far they were conscious of the distinction which must have subsisted in their minds between their own creeds and that of the people. Dante at least appears to wish to mark the full extent of it by placing Riphæus, whom Virgil calls *justissimus unus*, in Paradise, and observing a most heretical caprice in his distribution of rewards and punishments. And Milton's poem contains within itself a philosophical refutation of that system of which, by a strange and natural antithesis, it has been a chief popular support. Nothing can exceed the energy and magnificence of the character of Satan as expressed in *Paradise Lost*. It is a mistake to suppose that he could ever have been intended for the popular personification of evil. Implacable hate, patient cunning, and a sleepless refinement of device to inflict the extremest anguish on an enemy, these things are evil; and, although venial in a slave, are not to be forgiven in a tyrant; although redeemed by much that ennobles his defeat in one subdued, are marked by all that dishonours his conquest in the victor. Milton's Devil as a moral being is as far superior to his God, as one who perseveres in some purpose which he has conceived to be excellent in spite of adversity and torture, is to one who in the cold security of undoubted triumph inflicts the most horrible revenge upon his enemy, not from any mistaken notion of inducing him to repent of a perseverance in enmity, but with the alleged design of exasperating him to deserve new torments. Milton has so far violated the popular creed (if this shall be judged to be a violation) as to have alleged no superiority of moral virtue to his god over his devil. And this bold neglect of a direct moral purpose is the most decisive proof of the supremacy of Milton's genius. He mingled as it were the elements of human nature as colours upon a single pallet, and arranged them in the composition of his great picture according to the laws of epic truth, that is, according to the laws of that principle by which a series of actions of the external universe and of intelligent and ethical beings is calculated to excite the sympathy of succeeding generations of mankind. . . . All high poetry is infinite; it is as the first acorn, which contained all oaks potentially. Veil after veil may be undrawn, and the inmost naked beauty of the meaning never exposed. A great poem is a fountain for ever overflowing with the waters of wisdom and delight; and after one person and one age has exhausted all its divine effluence which their peculiar relations enable them to share, another and yet another succeeds, and new relations are ever developed, the source of an unforeseen and an unconceived delight. . . .

But poets have been challenged to resign the civic crown to reasoners and mechanists, on another plea. It is admitted that the exercise of the imagination is most delightful, but it is alleged that that of reason is more useful. Let us examine, as the grounds of this distinction, what is here meant by utility. Pleasure or good, in a general sense, is that which the consciousness of a sensitive and intelligent being seeks, and in which, when found, it acquiesces. There are two kinds of pleasure, one durable, universal and permanent; the other transitory and particular. Utility may either express the means of producing the former or the latter. In the former sense, whatever strengthens and purifies the affections, enlarges the imagination, and adds spirit to sense, is useful. But a narrower meaning may be assigned to the word utility, confining it to express that which banishes the importunity of the wants of our animal nature, the surrounding men with security of life, the dispersing the grosser delusions of superstition, and the conciliating such a degree of mutual forbearance among men as may consist with the motives of personal advantage.

Undoubtedly the promoters of utility, in this limited sense, have their appointed office in society. They follow the footsteps of poets, and copy the sketches of their creations into the book of common life. They make space, and give time. Their exertions are of the highest value, so long as they confine their administration of the concerns of the inferior powers of our nature within the limits due to the superior ones. But while the sceptic destroys gross superstitions, let him spare to deface, as some of the French writers have defaced, the eternal truths charactered upon the imaginations of men. Whilst the mechanist abridges, and the political economist combines, labour, let them beware that their speculations, for want of correspondence with those first principles which belong to the imagination, do not tend, as they have in modern England, to exasperate at once the extremes of luxury and want. They have exemplified the saying, "To him that hath, more shall be given; and from him that hath not, the little that he hath shall be taken away." The rich have become richer, and the poor have become poorer; and the vessel of the state is driven between the Scylla and Charybdis of anarchy and despotism. Such are the effects which must ever flow from an unmitigated exercise of the calculating faculty.

It is difficult to define pleasure in its highest sense; the definition involving a number of apparent paradoxes. For, from an inexplicable defect of harmony in the constitution of human nature, the pain of the inferior is frequently connected with the pleasures of the superior portions of our being. Sorrow, terror, anguish, despair itself, are often the chosen expressions of an approximation to the highest good. Our sympathy in tragic fiction depends on this principle; tragedy delights by affording a shadow of that pleasure which exists in pain. This is the source also of the melancholy which is inseparable from the sweetest melody. The pleasure that is in sorrow is sweeter than the pleasure of pleasure itself. And hence the saying, "It is better to go to the house of mourning than to the house of mirth." Not that this highest species of pleasure is necessarily linked with pain. The delight of love and friendship, the ecstacy of the admiration of nature, the joy of the perception and still more of the creation of poetry, is often wholly unalloyed.

The production and assurance of pleasure in this highest sense is true utility. Those who produce and preserve this pleasure are poets or poetical philosophers. . . .

We have more moral, political, and historical wisdom, than we know how to reduce into practice; we have more scientific and economical knowledge than can be accommodated to the just distribution of the produce which it multiplies. The poetry, in these systems of thought, is concealed by the accumulation of facts and calculating processes. There is no want of knowledge respecting what is wisest and best in morals, government, and political economy, or at least what is wiser and better than what men now practise and endure. But we let "*I dare not* wait upon *I would*, like the poor cat in the adage." We want the creative faculty to imagine that which we know; we want the generous impulse to act that which we imagine; we want the poetry of life: our calculations have outrun conception; we have eaten more than we can digest. The cultivation of those sciences which have enlarged the limits of the empire of man over the external world, has, for want of the poetical faculty, proportionally circumscribed those of the internal world; and man, having enslaved the elements, remains himself a slave. To what but a cultivation of the mechanical arts in a degree disproportioned to the presence of the creative faculty, which is the basis of all knowledge, is to be attributed the abuse of all invention for abridging and combining labour, to the exasperation of the inequality of mankind? From what other cause has it arisen that the discoveries which should have lightened, have added a weight to the curse imposed on Adam? Poetry, and the principle of Self, of which money is the visible incarnation, are the God and Mammon of the world. . . .

Poetry is indeed something divine. It is at once the centre and circumference of knowledge; it is that which comprehends all science, and that to which all science must be referred. It is at the same time the root and blossom of all other systems of thought; it is that from which all spring, and that which adorns all; and that which, if blighted, denies the fruit and the seed, and withholds from the barren world the nourishment and the succession of the scions of the tree of life. It is the perfect and consummate surface and bloom of all things; it is as the odour and the colour of the rose to the texture of the elements which compose it, as the form and splendour of unfaded beauty to the secrets of anatomy and corruption. What were virtue, love, patriotism, friendship,—what were the scenery of this beautiful universe which we inhabit; what were our consolations on this side of the grave—and what were our aspirations beyond it, if poetry did not ascend to bring light and fire from those eternal regions where the owl-winged faculty of calculation dare not ever soar? Poetry is not like reasoning, a power to be exerted according to the determination of the will. A man cannot say, "I will compose poetry." The greatest poet even cannot say it; for the mind in creation is as a fading coal, which some invisible influence, like an inconstant wind, awakens to transitory brightness; this power arises from within, like the colour of a flower which fades and changes as it is developed, and the conscious portions of our nature are unprophetic either of its approach or its departure. Could this influence be durable in its original purity and force, it is impossible to predict the greatness of the results; but when composition begins, inspiration is already on the decline, and the most glorious poetry that has ever been communicated to the world is probably a feeble shadow of the original conceptions of the poet. I appeal to the greatest poets of the present day, whether it is not an error to assert that the finest passages of poetry are produced by labour and study. The toil and the delay recommended by critics, can be justly interpreted to mean no more than a careful observation of the inspired moments, and an artificial connection of the spaces between their suggestions, by the intertexture of conventional expressions; a necessity only imposed by the limitedness of the poetical faculty itself: for Milton conceived the Paradise Lost as a whole before he executed it in portions. We have his own authority also for the muse having "dictated" to him the "unpremeditated song." And let this be an answer to those who would allege the fifty-six various readings of the first line of the Orlando Furioso. Compositions so produced are to poetry what mosaic is to painting. The instinct and intuition of the poetical faculty is still more observable in the plastic and pictorial arts: a great statue or picture grows under the power of the artist as a child in the mother's womb; and the very mind which directs the hands in formation, is incapable of accounting to itself for the origin, the gradations, or the media of the process.

Poetry is the record of the best and happiest moments of the happiest and best minds. We are aware of evanescent visitations of thought and feeling, sometimes associated with place or person, sometimes regarding our own mind alone, and always arising unforeseen and departing unbidden, but elevating and delightful beyond all expression: so that even in the desire and the regret they leave, there cannot but be pleasure, participating as it does in the nature of its object. It is as it were the interpenetration of a diviner nature through our own; but its footsteps are like those of a wind over the sea, which the coming calm erases, and whose traces remain only, as on the wrinkled sand which paves it. These and corresponding conditions of being are experienced principally by those of the most delicate sensibility and the most enlarged imagination; and the state of mind produced by them is at war with every base desire. The enthusiasm of virtue, love, patriotism, and friendship, is essentially linked with such emotions; and whilst they last, self appears as what it is, an atom to a universe. Poets are not only subject to these experiences as spirits of the most refined organization, but they can colour all that they combine with the evanescent hues of this ethereal world; a word, a trait in the representation of a scene or a passion, will touch the enchanted chord, and reanimate, in those who have ever experienced those emotions, the sleeping, the cold, the buried image of the past. Poetry thus makes immortal all that is best and most beautiful in the world; it arrests the vanishing apparitions which haunt the interlunations of life, and veiling them, or in language or in form, sends them forth among mankind, bearing sweet news of kindred joy to those with whom their sisters abide—

abide, because there is no portal of expression from the caverns of the spirit which they inhabit into the universe of things. Poetry redeems from decay the visitations of the divinity in man.

Poetry turns all things to loveliness; it exalts the beauty of that which is most beautiful, and it adds beauty to that which is most deformed; it marries exultation and horror, grief and pleasure, eternity and change; it subdues to union, under its light yoke, all irreconcilable things. It transmutes all that it touches, and every form moving within the radiance of its presence is changed by wondrous sympathy to an incarnation of the spirit which it breathes: its secret alchemy turns to potable gold the poisonous waters which flow from death through life; it strips the veil of familiarity from the world, and lays bare the naked and sleeping beauty, which is the spirit of its forms.

All things exist as they are perceived; at least in relation to the percipient. "The mind is its own place, and of itself can make a heaven of hell, a hell of heaven." But poetry defeats the curse which binds us to be subjected to the accident of surrounding impressions. And whether it spreads its own figured curtain, or withdraws life's dark veil from before the scene of things, it equally creates for us a being within our being. It makes us the inhabitant of a world to which the familiar world is a chaos. It reproduces the common universe of which we are portions and percipients, and it purges from our inward sight the film of familiarity which obscures from us the wonder of our being. It compels us to feel that which we perceive, and to imagine that which we know. It creates anew the universe, after it has been annihilated in our minds by the recurrence of impressions blunted by reiteration. It justifies the bold and true word of Tasso: *Non merita nome di creatore, se non Iddio ed il Poeta* [Only God and the poet are worthy of the name "Creator"].

A poet, as he is the author to others of the highest wisdom, pleasure, virtue and glory, so he ought personally to be the happiest, the best, the wisest, and the most illustrious of men. As to his glory, let time be challenged to declare whether the fame of any other institutor of human life be comparable to that of a poet. That he is the wisest, the happiest, and the best, inasmuch as he is a poet, is equally incontrovertible: the greatest poets have been men of the most spotless virtue, of the most consummate prudence, and, if we would look into the interior of their lives, the most fortunate of men: and the exceptions, as they regard those who possessed the poetic faculty in a high yet inferior degree, will be found on consideration to confine rather than destroy the rule. Let us for a moment stoop to the arbitration of popular breath, and usurping and uniting in our own persons the incompatible characters of accuser, witness, judge and executioner, let us decide without trial, testimony, or form, that certain motives of those who are "there sitting where we dare not soar," are reprehensible. Let us assume that Homer was a drunkard, that Virgil was a flatterer, that Horace was a coward, that Tasso was a madman, that Lord Bacon was a peculator, that Raphael was a libertine, that Spenser was a poet laureate. It is inconsistent with this division of our subject to cite living poets, but posterity has done ample justice to the great names now referred to. Their errors have been weighed and found to have been dust in the balance; if their sins "were as scarlet, they are now white as snow": they have been washed in the blood of the mediator and redeemer, time. Observe in what a ludicrous chaos the imputations of real or fictitious crime have been confused in the contemporary calumnies against poetry and poets; consider how little is, as it appears—or appears, as it is; look to your own motives, and judge not, lest ye be judged.

Poetry, as has been said, differs in this respect from logic, that it is not subject to the control of the active powers of the mind, and that its birth and recurrence have no necessary connection with the consciousness or will. It is presumptuous to determine that these are the necessary conditions of all mental causation, when mental effects are experienced insusceptible of being referred to them. The frequent recurrence of the poetical power, it is obvious to suppose, may produce in the mind a habit of order and harmony correlative with its own nature and with its effects upon other minds. But in the intervals of inspiration, and they may be frequent without being durable, a poet becomes a man, and is abandoned to the sudden reflux of the influences under which others habitually live. But as he is more delicately organized than other men, and sensible to pain and pleasure, both his own and that of others, in a degree unknown to them, he will avoid the one and pursue the other with an ardour proportioned to this difference. And he renders himself obnoxious to calumny, when he neglects to observe the circumstances under which these objects of universal pursuit and flight have disguised themselves in one another's garments.

But there is nothing necessarily evil in this error, and thus cruelty, envy, revenge, avarice, and the passions purely evil, have never formed any portion of the popular imputations on the lives of poets. . . .

In spite of the low-thoughted envy which would undervalue contemporary merit, our own will be a memorable age in intellectual achievements, and we live among such philosophers and poets as surpass beyond comparison any who have appeared since the last national struggle for civil and religious liberty. The most unfailing herald, companion, and follower of the awakening of a great people to work a beneficial change in opinion or institution, is poetry. At such periods there is an accumulation of the power of communicating and receiving intense and impassioned conceptions respecting man and nature. The persons in whom this power resides, may often, as far as regards many portions of their nature, have little apparent correspondence with that spirit of good of which they are the ministers. But even whilst they deny and abjure, they are yet compelled to serve, the power which is seated on the throne of their own soul. It is impossible to read the compositions of the most celebrated writers of the present day without being startled with the electric life which burns within their words. They measure the circumference and sound the depths of human nature with a comprehensive and all-penetrating spirit, and they are themselves perhaps the most sincerely astonished at its manifestations; for it is less their spirit than the spirit of the age. Poets are the hierophants of an unapprehended inspiration; the mirrors of the gigantic shadows which futurity casts upon the present; the words which express what they understand not; the trumpets which sing to battle and feel not what they inspire; the influence which is moved not, but moves. Poets are the unacknowledged legislators of the world.

George Eliot 1819–1880

George Eliot was one of the greatest English Victorian novelists. Eliot—the name was a pseudonym for Mary Anne Evans—was born in Warwickshire and educated at a series of boarding schools and through private Latin and German lessons allowed by her father. In her early twenties she began to encounter both people and ideas that pulled her from the religious and political orthodoxy of her upbringing.

Eliot was in her late thirties before she began writing fiction. Her novels include *Adam Bede* (1859), *The Mill on the Floss* (1860), *Middlemarch* (1871–72)—widely considered to be her masterpiece—and *Daniel Deronda* (1876). Psychological character analysis, realistic observation of a wide range of people and customs, broadly informed sympathy, and concern with moral problems are all characteristic of these works. Eliot lived with the journalist George Henry Lewes for twenty-five years in Germany and England, and her death followed his by two years.

Before turning to fiction, Eliot had written essays on a range of philosophical, political, and literary topics. One of these, "Silly Novels" (1856), acerbically lays out what Eliot presumably wanted to avoid in her own fledgling fiction career—"the frothy, the prosy, the pious, and the pedantic." Realism is her literary standard. The truly great writers "have thought it quite a sufficient task to exhibit men and things as they are," and have allowed meaning to arise from this depiction. The best literature does not encyclopedically expound information, which is only "the raw material of culture," but instead encourages and evokes sympathy, culture's "subtlest essence." Eliot also laments the effect these "silly novels" might have on "serious" women authors and on the cause of women's education. This base of liberal, moral, social concern may perhaps be her most characteristic trait.

Silly Novels by Lady Novelists

Silly novels by Lady Novelists are a genus with many species, determined by the particular quality of silliness that predominates in them—the frothy, the prosy, the pious, or the pedantic. But it is a mixture of all these—a composite order of feminine fatuity, that produces the largest class of such novels, which we shall distinguish as the *mind-and-millinery* species. The heroine is usually an heiress, probably a peeress in her own right, with perhaps a vicious baronet, an amiable duke, and an irresistible younger son of a marquis as lovers in the foreground, a clergyman and a poet sighing for her in the middle distance, and a crowd of undefined adorers dimly indicated beyond. Her eyes and her wit are both dazzling; her nose and her morals are alike free from any tendency to irregularity; she has a superb *contralto* and a superb intellect; she is perfectly well-dressed and perfectly religious; she dances like a sylph, and reads the Bible in the original tongues. Or it may be that the heroine is not an heiress—that rank and wealth are the only things in which she is deficient; but she infallibly gets into high society, she has the triumph of refusing many matches and securing the best, and she wears some family jewels or other as a sort of crown of righteousness at the end. Rakish men either bite their lips in impotent confusion at her repartees, or are touched to penitence by her reproofs, which, on appropriate occasions, rise to a lofty strain of rhetoric; indeed, there is a general propensity in her to make speeches, and to rhapsodize at some length when she retires to her bedroom. In her recorded conversations she is amazingly eloquent, and in her unrecorded conversations, amazingly witty. She is understood to have a depth of insight that looks through and through the shallow theories of philosophers, and her superior instincts are a sort of dial by which men have only to set their clocks and watches, and all will go well. The men play a very subordinate part by her side. You are consoled now and then by a hint that they have affairs, which keeps you in mind that the working-day business of the world is somehow being carried on, but ostensibly the final cause of their existence is that they may accompany the heroine on her "starring" expedition through life. They see her at a ball, and are dazzled; at a flower-show, and they are fascinated; on a riding excursion, and they are witched by her noble horsemanship; at church, and they are awed by the sweet solemnity of her demeanour. She is the ideal woman in feelings, faculties, and flounces. For all this, she as often as not marries the wrong person to begin with, and she suffers terribly from the plots and intrigues of the vicious baronet; but even death has a soft place in his heart for such a paragon, and remedies all mistakes for her just at the right moment. The vicious baronet is sure to be killed in a duel, and the tedious husband dies in his bed requesting his wife, as a particular favour to him, to marry the man she loves best, and having already dispatched a note to the lover informing him of the comfortable arrangement. Before matters arrive at this desirable issue our feelings are tried by seeing the noble, lovely, and gifted heroine pass through many *mauvais moments*, but we have the satisfaction of knowing that her sorrows are wept into embroidered pocket-handkerchiefs, that her fainting form reclines on the very best upholstery, and that whatever vicissitudes she may undergo, from being dashed out of her carriage to having her head shaved in a fever, she comes out of them all with a complexion more blooming and locks more redundant than ever.

We may remark, by the way, that we have been relieved from a serious scruple by discovering that silly novels by lady novelists rarely introduce us into any other than very lofty and fashionable society. We had imagined that destitute women turned novelists, as they turned governesses, because they had no other "lady-like" means of getting their bread. On this supposition, vacillating syntax and improbable incident had a certain pathos for us, like the extremely supererogatory pincushions and ill-devised nightcaps that are offered for sale by a blind man. We felt the commodity to be a nuisance, but we were glad to think that the money went to relieve the necessitous, and we pictured to ourselves lonely women struggling for a maintenance, or wives and daughters devoting themselves to the production of "copy" out of pure heroism,—perhaps to pay their husband's debts, or to purchase luxuries for a sick father. Under these impressions we shrank from criticising a lady's novel: her English might be faulty, but, we said to ourselves, her motives are irreproachable; her imagination may be uninventive, but her patience is untiring. Empty writing was excused by an empty stomach, and twaddle was consecrated by tears. But no! This theory of ours, like many other pretty theories, has had to give way before observation. Women's silly novels, we are now convinced, are written under totally different circumstances. The fair writers have evidently never talked to a tradesman except from a carriage window; they have no notion of the working-classes except as "dependents"; they think five hundred a-year a miserable pittance; Belgravia and "baronial halls" are their primary truths; and they have no idea of feeling interest in any man who is not at least a great landed proprietor, if not a prime minister. It is clear that they write in elegant boudoirs, with violet-coloured ink and a ruby pen; that they must be entirely indifferent to publishers' accounts, and inexperienced in every form of poverty except poverty of brains. It is true that we are constantly struck with the want of verisimilitude in their representations of the high society in which they seem to live; but then they betray no closer acquaintance with any other form of life. If their peers and peeresses are improbable, their literary men, tradespeople, and cottagers are impossible; and their intellect seems to have the peculiar impartiality of reproducing both what they *have* seen and heard, and what they have *not* seen and heard, with equal unfaithfulness.

There are few women, we suppose, who have not seen something of children under five years of age, yet in "Compensation," a recent novel of the mind-and-millinery species, which calls itself a "story of real life," we have a child of four and a half years old talking in this Ossianic fashion—

> "Oh, I am so happy, dear gran'mamma;—I have seen,—I have seen such a delightful person: he is like everything beautiful,—like the smell of sweet flowers, and the view from Ben Lomond;—or no, *better than that*—he is like what I think of and see when I am very, very happy; and he is really like mamma, too, when she sings; and his forehead is like *that distant sea,*" she continued, pointing to the blue Mediterranean; "there seems no end—no end; or like the clusters of stars I like best to look at on a warm fine night. . . . Don't look so . . . your forehead is like Loch Lomond, when the wind is blowing and the sun is gone in; I like the sunshine best when the lake is smooth. . . . So now—I like it better than ever . . . it is more beautiful still from the dark cloud that has gone over it, *when the sun suddenly lights up all the colours of the forests and shining purple rocks, and it is all reflected in the waters below.*"

We are not surprised to learn that the mother of this infant phenomenon, who exhibits symptoms so alarmingly like those of adolescence repressed by gin, is herself a phœnix. We are assured, again and again, that she had a remarkably original mind, that she was a genius, and "conscious of her originality," and she was fortunate enough to have a lover who was also a genius, and a man of "most original mind."

This lover, we read, though "wonderfully similar" to her "in powers and capacity," was "infinitely superior to her in faith and development," and she saw in him the " 'Agape'—so rare to find—of which she had read and admired the meaning in her Greek Testament; having, *from her great facility in learning languages,* read the Scriptures in their original *tongues.*" Of course! Greek and

Hebrew are mere play to a heroine; Sanscrit is no more than *a b c* to her; and she can talk with perfect correctness in any language except English. She is a polking polyglott, a Creuzer in crinoline. Poor men! There are so few of you who know even Hebrew; you think it something to boast of if, like Bolingbroke, you only "understand that sort of learning, and what is writ about it"; and you are perhaps adoring women who can think slightingly of you in all the Semitic languages successively. But, then, as we are almost invariably told, that a heroine has a "beautifully small head," and as her intellect has probably been early invigorated by an attention to costume and deportment, we may conclude that she can pick up the Oriental tongues, to say nothing of their dialects, with the same aërial facility that the butterfly sips nectar. Besides, there can be no difficulty in conceiving the depth of the heroine's erudition, when that of the authoress is so evident.

In "Laura Gay," another novel of the same school, the heroine seems less at home in Greek and Hebrew, but she makes up for the deficiency by a quite playful familiarity with the Latin classics—with the "dear old Virgil," "the graceful Horace, the humane Cicero, and the pleasant Livy"; indeed, it is such a matter of course with her to quote Latin, that she does it at a pic-nic in a very mixed company of ladies and gentlemen, having, we are told, "no conception that the nobler sex were capable of jealousy on this subject. And if, indeed," continues the biographer of Laura Gay, "the wisest and noblest portion of that sex were in the majority, no such sentiment would exist; but while Miss Wyndhams and Mr. Redfords abound, great sacrifices must be made to their existence." Such sacrifices, we presume, as abstaining from Latin quotations, of extremely moderate interest and applicability, which the wise and noble minority of the other sex would be quite as willing to dispense with as the foolish and ignoble majority. It is as little the custom of well-bred men as of well-bred women to quote Latin in mixed parties; they can contain their familiarity with "the humane Cicero" without allowing it to boil over in ordinary conversation, and even references to "the pleasant Livy" are not absolutely irrepressible. But Ciceronian Latin is the mildest form of Miss Gay's conversational power. Being on the Palatine with a party of sightseers, she falls into the following vein of well-rounded remark: "Truth can only be pure objectively, for even in the creeds where it predominates, being subjective, and parcelled out into portions, each of these necessarily receives a hue of idiosyncrasy, that is, a taint of superstition more or less strong; while in such creeds as the Roman Catholic, ignorance, interest, the bias of ancient idolatries, and the force of authority, have gradually accumulated on the pure truth, and transformed it, at last, into a mass of superstition for the majority of its votaries; and how few are there, alas! whose zeal, courage, and intellectual energy are equal to the analysis of this accumulation, and to the discovery of the pearl of great price which lies hidden beneath this heap of rubbish." We have often met with women much more novel and profound in their observations than Laura Gay, but rarely with any so inopportunely long winded. A clerical lord, who is half in love with her, is alarmed by the daring remarks just quoted, and begins to suspect that she is inclined to free-thinking. But he is mistaken; when in a moment of sorrow he delicately begs leave to "recall to her memory, a *depôt* of strength and consolation under affliction, which, until we are hard pressed by the trials of life, we are too apt to forget," we learn that she really has "recurrence to that sacred depôt," together with the tea-pot. There is a certain flavour of orthodoxy mixed with the parade of fortunes and fine carriages in "Laura Gay," but it is an orthodoxy mitigated by study of "the humane Cicero," and by an "intellectual disposition to analyse."

"Compensation" is much more heavily dosed with doctrine, but then it has a treble amount of snobbish worldliness and absurd incident to tickle the palate of pious frivolity. Linda, the heroine, is still more speculative and spiritual than Laura Gay, but she has been "presented," and has more, and far grander, lovers; very wicked and fascinating women are introduced—even a French *lionne;* and no expense is spared to get up as exciting a story as you will find in the most immoral novels. In fact, it is a wonderful *pot pourri* of Almack's, Scotch second-sight, Mr. Rogers's breakfasts, Italian brigands, death-bed conversions, superior authoresses, Italian mistresses, and attempts at poisoning old ladies, the whole served up with a garnish of talk about "faith and development," and "most original minds." Even Miss Susan Barton, the superior authoress, whose pen moves in a "quick decided manner when she is composing," declines the finest opportunities of marriage; and though old enough to be Linda's mother (since we are told that she refused Linda's father), has her hand sought by a young earl, the heroine's rejected lover. Of course, genius and morality must be backed by eligible offers, or they would seem rather a dull affair; and piety, like other things, in order to be *comme il faut,* must be in "society," and have admittance to the best circles.

"Rank and Beauty" is a more frothy and less religious variety of the mind-and-millinery species. The heroine, we are told, "if she inherited her father's pride of birth and her mother's beauty of person, had in herself a tone of enthusiastic feeling that perhaps belongs to her age even in the lowly born, but which is refined into the high spirit of wild romance only in the far descended, who feel that it is their best inheritance." This enthusiastic young lady, by dint of reading the newspaper to her father, falls in love with the *prime minister,* who, through the medium of leading articles and "the *resumé* of the debates," shines upon her imagination as a bright particular star, which has no parallax for her, living in the country as simple Miss Wyndham. But she forthwith becomes Baroness Umfraville in her own right, astonishes the world with her beauty and accomplishments when she bursts upon it from her mansion in Spring Gardens, and, as you foresee, will presently come into contact with the unseen *objet aimé.* Perhaps the words "prime minister" suggest to you a wrinkled or obese sexagenarian; but pray dismiss the image. Lord Rupert Conway has been "called while still almost a youth to the first situation which a subject can hold in the *universe,*" and even leading articles and a *resumé* of the debates have not conjured up a dream that surpasses the fact.

> The door opened again, and Lord Rupert Conway entered. Evelyn gave one glance. It was enough; she was not disappointed. It seemed as if a picture on which she had long gazed was suddenly instinct with life, and had stepped from its frame before her. His tall figure, the distinguished simplicity of his air—it was a living Vandyke, a cavalier, one of his noble cavalier ancestors, or one to whom her fancy had always likened him, who long of yore had, with an Umfraville, fought the Paynim far beyond sea. Was this reality?

Very little like it, certainly.

By-and-by, it becomes evident that the ministerial heart is touched. Lady Umfraville is on a visit to the Queen at Windsor, and,

> The last evening of her stay, when they returned from riding, Mr. Wyndham took her and a large party to the top of the Keep, to see the view. She was leaning on the battle-

> ments, gazing from that "stately height" at the prospect beneath her, when Lord Rupert was by her side. "What an unrivalled view!" exclaimed she.
>
> "Yes, it would have been wrong to go without having been up here. You are pleased with your visit?"
>
> "Enchanted! A Queen to live and die under, to live and die for!"
>
> "Ha!" cried he, with sudden emotion, and with a *eureka* expression of countenance, as if he had *indeed found a heart in unison with his own.*

The "*eureka* expression of countenance," you see at once to be prophetic of marriage at the end of the third volume; but before that desirable consummation, there are very complicated misunderstandings, arising chiefly from the vindictive plotting of Sir Luttrell Wycherley, who is a genius, a poet, and in every way a most remarkable character indeed. He is not only a romantic poet, but a hardened rake and a cynical wit; yet his deep passion for Lady Umfraville has so impoverished his epigrammatic talent, that he cuts an extremely poor figure in conversation. When she rejects him, he rushes into the shrubbery, and rolls himself in the dirt; and on recovering, devotes himself to the most diabolical and laborious schemes of vengeance, in the course of which he disguises himself as a quack physician, and enters into general practice, foreseeing that Evelyn will fall ill, and that he shall be called in to attend her. At last, when all his schemes are frustrated, he takes leave of her in a long letter, written, as you will perceive from the following passage, entirely in the style of an eminent literary man:

> Oh, lady, nursed in pomp and pleasure, will you ever cast one thought upon the miserable being who addresses you? Will you ever, as your gilded galley is floating down the unruffled stream of prosperity, will you ever, while lulled by the sweetest music—thine own praises,—hear the far-off sigh from that world to which I am going?

On the whole, however, frothy as it is, we rather prefer "Rank and Beauty" to the other two novels we have mentioned. The dialogue is more natural and spirited; there is some frank ignorance, and no pedantry; and you are allowed to take the heroine's astounding intellect upon trust, without being called on to read her conversational refutations of sceptics and philosophers, or her rhetorical solutions of the mysteries of the universe.

Writers of the mind-and-millinery school are remarkably unanimous in their choice of diction. In their novels, there is usually a lady or gentleman who is more or less of a upas tree: the lover has a manly breast; minds are redolent of various things; hearts are hollow; events are utilized; friends are consigned to the tomb; infancy is an engaging period; the sun is a luminary that goes to his western couch, or gathers the rain-drops into his refulgent bosom; life is a melancholy boon; Albion and Scotia are conversational epithets. There is a striking resemblance, too, in the character of their moral comments, such, for instance, as that "It is a fact, no less true than melancholy, that all people, more or less, richer or poorer, are swayed by bad example"; that "Books, however trivial, contain some subjects from which useful information may be drawn"; that "Vice can too often borrow the language of virtue"; that "Merit and nobility of nature must exist, to be accepted, for clamour and pretension cannot impose upon those too well read in human nature to be easily deceived"; and that, "In order to forgive, we must have been injured." There is, doubtless, a class of readers to whom these remarks appear peculiarly pointed and pungent; for we often find them doubly and trebly scored with the pencil, and delicate hands giving in their determined adhesion to these hardy novelties by a distinct *très vrai,* emphasized by many notes of exclamation. The colloquial style of these novels is often marked by much ingenious inversion, and a careful avoidance of such cheap phraseology as can be heard every day. Angry young gentlemen exclaim—" 'Tis ever thus, methinks"; and in the half-hour before dinner a young lady informs her next neighbour that the first day she read Shakspeare she "stole away into the park, and beneath the shadow of the greenwood tree, devoured with rapture the inspired page of the great magician." But the most remarkable efforts of the mind-and-millinery writers lie in their philosophic reflections. The authoress of "Laura Gay," for example, having married her hero and heroine, improves the event by observing that "if those sceptics, whose eyes have so long gazed on matter that they can no longer see aught else in man, could once enter with heart and soul into such bliss as this, they would come to say that the soul of man and the polypus are not of common origin, or of the same texture." Lady novelists, it appears, can see something else besides matter; they are not limited to phenomena, but can relieve their eyesight by occasional glimpses of the *noumenon,* and are, therefore, naturally better able than any one else to confound sceptics, even of that remarkable, but to us unknown school, which maintains that the soul of man is of the same texture as the polypus.

The most pitiable of all silly novels by lady novelists are what we may call the *oracular* species—novels intended to expound the writer's religious, philosophical, or moral theories. There seems to be a notion abroad among women, rather akin to the superstition that the speech and actions of idiots are inspired, and that the human being most entirely exhausted of common sense is the fittest vehicle of revelation. To judge from their writings, there are certain ladies who think that an amazing ignorance, both of science and of life, is the best possible qualification for forming an opinion on the knottiest moral and speculative questions. Apparently, their recipe for solving all such difficulties is something like this: Take a woman's head, stuff it with a smattering of philosophy and literature chopped small, and with false notions of society baked hard, let it hang over a desk a few hours every day, and serve up hot in feeble English, when not required. You will rarely meet with a lady novelist of the oracular class who is diffident of her ability to decide on theological questions,—who has any suspicion that she is not capable of discriminating with the nicest accuracy between the good and evil in all church parties,—who does not see precisely how it is that men have gone wrong hitherto,—and pity philosophers in general that they have not had the opportunity of consulting her. Great writers, who have modestly contented themselves with putting their experience into fiction, and have thought it quite a sufficient task to exhibit men and things as they are, she sighs over as deplorably deficient in the application of their powers. "They have solved no great questions"—and she is ready to remedy their omission by setting before you a complete theory of life and manual of divinity, in a love story, where ladies and gentlemen of good family go through genteel vicissitudes, to the utter confusion of Deists, Puseyites, and ultra-Protestants, and to the perfect establishment of that particular view of Christianity which either condenses itself into a sentence of small caps, or explodes into a cluster of stars on the three hundred and thirtieth page. It is true, the ladies and gentlemen will probably seem to you remarkably little like any you have had the fortune or misfortune to meet with, for, as a general rule, the ability of a lady novelist to describe actual life and her fellow-men, is in inverse proportion to her confident eloquence about God and the other world, and the means by which she usually chooses to conduct you to true ideas of the invisible is a totally false picture of the visible.

As typical a novel of the oracular kind as we can hope to meet with, is "The Enigma: a Leaf from the Chronicles of the Wolchorley House." The "enigma" which this novel is to solve, is certainly one that demands powers no less gigantic than those of a lady novelist, being neither more nor less than the existence of evil. The problem is stated, and the answer dimly foreshadowed on the very first page. The spirited young lady, with raven hair, says, "All life is an inextricable confusion"; and the meek young lady, with auburn hair, looks at the picture of the Madonna which she is copying, and—"*There* seemed the solution of that mighty enigma." The style of this novel is quite as lofty as its purpose; indeed, some passages on which we have spent much patient study are quite beyond our reach, in spite of the illustrative aid of italics and small caps; and we must await further "development" in order to understand them. Of Ernest, the model young clergyman, who sets every one right on all occasions, we read, that "he held not of marriage in the marketable kind, after a social desecration"; that, on one eventful night, "sleep had not visited his divided heart, where tumultuated, in varied type and combination, the aggregate feelings of grief and joy"; and that, "for the *marketable* human article he had no toleration, be it of what sort, or set for what value it might, whether for worship or class, his upright soul abhorred it, whose ultimatum, the self-deceiver, was to him THE *great spiritual lie*, 'living in a vain show, deceiving and being deceived'; since he did not suppose the phylactery and enlarged border on the garment to be *merely* a social trick." (The italics and small caps are the author's, and we hope they assist the reader's comprehension.) Of Sir Lionel, the model old gentleman, we are told that "the simple ideal of the middle age, apart from its anarchy and decadence, in him most truly seemed to live again, when the ties which knit men together were of heroic cast. The first-born colours of pristine faith and truth engraven on the common soul of man, and blent into the wide arch of brotherhood, where the primæval law of *order* grew and multiplied, each perfect after his kind, and mutually inter-dependent." You see clearly, of course, how colours are first engraven on a soul, and then blent into a wide arch, on which arch of colours—apparently a rainbow—the law of order grew and multiplied, each—apparently the arch and the law—perfect after his kind? If, after this, you can possibly want any further aid towards knowing what Sir Lionel was, we can tell you, that in his soul "the scientific combinations of thought could educe no fuller harmonies of the good and the true, than lay in the primæval pulses which floated as an atmosphere around it!" and that, when he was sealing a letter, "Lo! the responsive throb in that good man's bosom echoed back in simple truth the honest witness of a heart that condemned him not, as his eye, bedewed with love, rested, too, something of ancestral pride, on the undimmed motto of the family—'LOIAUTÉ'."

The slightest matters have their vulgarity fumigated out of them by the same elevated style. Commonplace people would say that a copy of Shakspeare lay on a drawing-room table; but the authoress of "The Enigma," bent on edifying periphrasis, tells you that there lay on the table, "that fund of human thought and feeling, which teaches the heart through the little name, 'Shakspeare.' " A watchman sees a light burning in an upper window rather longer than usual, and thinks that people are foolish to sit up late when they have an opportunity of going to bed; but, lest this fact should seem too low and common, it is presented to us in the following striking and metaphysical manner: "He marvelled—as man *will* think for others in a necessarily separate personality, consequently (though disallowing it) in false mental premise,—how differently *he* should act, how gladly *he* should prize the rest so lightly held of within." A footman—an ordinary Jeames, with large calves and aspirated vowels—answers the door-bell, and the opportunity is seized to tell you that he was a "type of the large class of pampered menials, who follow the curse of Cain—'vagabonds' on the face of the earth, and whose estimate of the human class varies in the graduated scale of money and expenditure. . . . These, and such as these, O England, be the false lights of thy morbid civilization!" We have heard of various "false lights," from Dr. Cumming to Robert Owen, from Dr. Pusey to the Spirit-rappers, but we never before heard of the false light that emanates from plush and powder.

In the same way very ordinary events of civilized life are exalted into the most awful crises, and ladies in full skirts and *manches à la Chinoise*, conduct themselves not unlike the heroines of sanguinary melodramas. Mrs. Percy, a shallow woman of the world, wishes her son Horace to marry the auburn-haired Grace, she being an heiress; but he, after the manner of sons, falls in love with the raven-haired Kate, the heiress's portionless cousin; and, moreover, Grace herself shows every symptom of perfect indifference to Horace. In such cases, sons are often sulky or fiery, mothers are alternately manœuvring and waspish, and the portionless young lady often lies awake at night and cries a good deal. We are getting used to these things now, just as we are used to eclipses of the moon, which no longer set us howling and beating tin kettles. We never heard of a lady in a fashionable "front" behaving like Mrs. Percy under these circumstances. Happening one day to see Horace talking to Grace at a window, without in the least knowing what they are talking about, or having the least reason to believe that Grace, who is mistress of the house and a person of dignity, would accept her son if he were to offer himself, she suddenly rushes up to them and clasps them both, saying, "with a flushed countenance and in an excited manner"—"This is indeed happiness; for, may I not call you so, Grace?—my Grace—my Horace's Grace!—my dear children!" Her son tells her she is mistaken, and that he is engaged to Kate, whereupon we have the following scene and tableau:

> Gathering herself up to an unprecedented height,(!) her eyes lightning forth the fire of her anger:—
>
> "Wretched boy!" she said, hoarsely and scornfully, and clenching her hand, "Take then the doom of your own choice! Bow down your miserable head and let a mother's—"
>
> "Curse not!" spake a deep low voice from behind, and Mrs. Percy started, scared, as though she had seen a heavenly visitant appear, to break upon her in the midst of her sin.
>
> Meantime, Horace had fallen on his knees at her feet, and hid his face in his hands.
>
> Who, then, is she—who! Truly his "guardian spirit" hath stepped between him and the fearful words, which, however unmerited, must have hung as a pall over his future existence;—a spell which could not be unbound—which could not be unsaid.
>
> Of an earthly paleness, but calm with the still, iron-bound calmness of death—the only calm one there,—Katherine stood; and her words smote on the ear in tones whose appallingly slow and separate intonation rung on the heart like the chill, isolated tolling of some fatal knell.
>
> "He would have plighted me his faith, but

I did not accept it; you cannot, therefore—you *dare* not curse him. And here," she continued, raising her hand to heaven, whither her large dark eyes also rose with a chastened glow, which, for the first time, *suffering* had lighted in those passionate orbs,—"here I promise, come weal, come woe, that Horace Wolchorley and I do never interchange vows without his mother's sanction—without his mother's blessing!"

Here, and throughout the story, we see that confusion of purpose which is so characteristic of silly novels written by women. It is a story of quite modern drawing-room society—a society in which polkas are played and Puseyism discussed; yet we have characters, and incidents, and traits of manner introduced, which are mere shreds from the most heterogeneous romances. We have a blind Irish harper "relic of the picturesque bards of yore," startling us at a Sunday-school festival of tea and cake in an English village; we have a crazy gipsy, in a scarlet cloak, singing snatches of romantic song, and revealing a secret on her deathbed which, with the testimony of a dwarfish miserly merchant, who salutes strangers with a curse and a devilish laugh, goes to prove that Ernest, the model young clergyman, is Kate's brother; and we have an ultra-virtuous Irish Barney, discovering that a document is forged, by comparing the date of the paper with the date of the alleged signature, although the same document has passed through a court of law, and occasioned a fatal decision. The "Hall" in which Sir Lionel lives is the venerable country-seat of an old family, and this, we suppose, sets the imagination of the authoress flying to donjons and battlements, where "lo! the warder blows his horn"; for, as the inhabitants are in their bedrooms on a night certainly within the recollection of Pleaceman X., and a breeze springs up, which we are at first told was faint, and then that it made the old cedars bow their branches to the greensward, she falls into this mediæval vein of description (the italics are ours): "The banner *unfurled it* at the sound, and shook its guardian wing above, while the startled owl *flapped her* in the ivy; the firmament looking down through her 'argus eyes,'—

Ministers of heaven's mute melodies.

And lo! two strokes tolled from out the warder tower, and 'Two o'clock' re-echoed its interpreter below."

Such stories as this of "The Enigma" remind us of the pictures clever children sometimes draw 'out of their own head,' where you will see a modern villa on the right, two knights in helmets fighting in the foreground, and a tiger grinning in a jungle on the left, the several objects being brought together because the artist thinks each pretty, and perhaps still more because he remembers seeing them in other pictures.

But we like the authoress much better on her mediæval stilts than on her oracular ones,—when she talks of the *Ich* and of "subjective" and "objective," and lays down the exact line of Christian verity, between "right-hand excesses and left-hand declensions." Persons who deviate from this line are introduced with a patronizing air of charity. Of a certain Miss Inshquine she informs us, with all the lucidity of italics and small caps, that "*function*, not *form*, AS *the inevitable outer expression of the spirit in this tabernacled age*, weakly engrossed her." And *à propos* of Miss Mayjar, an evangelical lady who is a little too apt to talk of her visits to sick women and the state of their souls, we are told that the model clergyman is "not one to disallow, through the *super* crust, the undercurrent towards good in the *subject*, or the positive benefits, nevertheless, to the *object*." We imagine the double-refined accent and protrusion of chin which are feebly represented by the italics in this lady's sentences! We abstain from quoting any of her oracular doctrinal passages, because they refer to matters too serious for our pages just now.

The epithet "silly" may seem impertinent, applied to a novel which indicates so much reading and intellectual activity as "The Enigma"; but we use this epithet advisedly. If, as the world has long agreed, a very great amount of instruction will not make a wise man, still less will a very mediocre amount of instruction make a wise woman. And the most mischievous form of feminine silliness is the literary form, because it tends to confirm the popular prejudice against the more solid education of women. When men see girls wasting their time in consultations about bonnets and ball dresses, and in giggling or sentimental love-confidences, or middle-aged women mismanaging their children, and solacing themselves with acrid gossip, they can hardly help saying, "For Heaven's sake, let girls be better educated; let them have some better objects of thought—some more solid occupations." But after a few hours' conversation with an oracular literary woman, or a few hours' reading of her books, they are likely enough to say, "After all, when a woman gets some knowledge, see what use she makes of it! Her knowledge remains acquisition, instead of passing into culture; instead of being subdued into modesty and simplicity by a larger acquaintance with thought and fact, she has a feverish consciousness of her attainments; she keeps a sort of mental pocket-mirror, and is continually looking in it at her own 'intellectuality'; she spoils the taste of one's muffin by questions of metaphysics; 'puts down' men at a dinner table with her superior information; and seizes the opportunity of a *soirée* to catechise us on the vital question of the relation between mind and matter. And then, look at her writings! She mistakes vagueness for depth, bombast for eloquence, and affectation for originality; she struts on one page, rolls her eyes on another, grimaces in a third, and is hysterical in a fourth. She may have read many writings of great men, and a few writings of great women; but she is as unable to discern the difference between her own style and theirs as a Yorkshireman is to discern the difference between his own English and a Londoner's: rhodomontade is the native accent of her intellect. No—the average nature of women is too shallow and feeble a soil to bear much tillage; it is only fit for the very lightest crops."

It is true that the men who come to such a decision on such very superficial and imperfect observation may not be among the wisest in the world; but we have not now to contest their opinion—we are only pointing out how it is unconsciously encouraged by many women who have volunteered themselves as representatives of the feminine intellect. We do not believe that a man was ever strengthened in such an opinion by associating with a woman of true culture, whose mind had absorbed her knowledge instead of being absorbed by it. A really cultured woman, like a really cultured man, is all the simpler and the less obtrusive for her knowledge; it has made her see herself and her opinions in something like just proportions; she does not make it a pedestal from which she flatters herself that she commands a complete view of men and things, but makes it a point of observation from which to form a right estimate of herself. She neither spouts poetry nor quotes Cicero on slight provocation; not because she thinks that a sacrifice must be made to the prejudices of men, but because that mode of exhibiting her memory and Latinity does not present itself to her as edifying or graceful. She does not write books to confound philosophers, perhaps because she is able to write books that delight them. In conversation she is the least formidable of women, because she understands you, without wanting to make you aware that you *can't* understand her. She does not give you information, which is the raw material of culture,—she gives you sympathy, which is its subtlest essence.

A more numerous class of silly novels than the oracular, (which are generally inspired by some form of High Church, or transcendental Christianity,) is what we may call the *white neck-cloth* species, which represent the tone of thought and feeling in the Evangelical party. This species is a kind of genteel tract on a large scale, intended as a sort of medicinal sweetmeat for Low Church young ladies; an Evangelical substitute for the fashionable novel, as the May Meetings are a substitute for the Opera. Even Quaker children, one would think, can hardly have been denied the indulgence of a doll; but it must be a doll dressed in a drab gown and a coal-scuttle bonnet—not a worldly doll, in gauze and spangles. And there are no young ladies, we imagine,—unless they belong to the Church of the United Brethren, in which people are married without any love-making—who can dispense with love stories. Thus, for Evangelical young ladies there are Evangelical love stories, in which the vicissitudes of the tender passion are sanctified by saving views of Regeneration and the Atonement. These novels differ from the oracular ones, as a Low Churchwoman often differs from a High Churchwoman: they are a little less supercilious, and a great deal more ignorant, a little less correct in their syntax, and a great deal more vulgar.

The Orlando of Evangelical literature is the young curate, looked at from the point of view of the middle class, where cambric bands are understood to have as thrilling an effect on the hearts of young ladies as epaulettes have in the classes above and below it. In the ordinary type of these novels, the hero is almost sure to be a young curate, frowned upon, perhaps, by worldly mammas, but carrying captive the hearts of their daughters, who can "never forget *that* sermon"; tender glances are seized from the pulpit stairs instead of the opera-box; *tête-à-têtes* are seasoned with quotations from Scripture, instead of quotations from the poets; and questions as to the state of the heroine's affections are mingled with anxieties as to the state of her soul. The young curate always has a background of well-dressed and wealthy, if not fashionable society;—for Evangelical silliness is as snobbish as any other kind of silliness; and the Evangelical lady novelist, while she explains to you the type of the scapegoat on one page, is ambitious on another to represent the manners and conversation of aristocratic people. Her pictures of fashionable society are often curious studies considered as efforts of the Evangelical imagination; but in one particular the novels of the White Neck-cloth School are meritoriously realistic,—their favourite hero, the Evangelical young curate is always rather an insipid personage.

The most recent novel of this species that we happen to have before us, is "The Old Grey Church." It is utterly tame and feeble; there is no one set of objects on which the writer seems to have a stronger grasp than on any other; and we should be entirely at a loss to conjecture among what phases of life her experience has been gained, but for certain vulgarisms of style which sufficiently indicate that she has had the advantage, though she has been unable to use it, of mingling chiefly with men and women whose manners and characters have not had all their bosses and angles rubbed down by refined conventionalism. It is less excusable in an Evangelical novelist, than in any other, gratuitously to seek her subjects among titles and carriages. The real drama of Evangelicalism—and it has abundance of fine drama for any one who has genius enough to discern and reproduce it—lies among the middle and lower classes; and are not Evangelical opinions understood to give an especial interest in the weak things of the earth, rather than in the mighty? Why then, cannot our Evangelical lady novelists show us the operation of their religious views among people (there really are many such in the world) who keep no carriage, "not so much as a brassbound gig," who even manage to eat their dinner without a silver fork, and in whose mouths the authoress's questionable English would be strictly consistent? Why can we not have pictures of religious life among the industrial classes in England, as interesting as Mrs. Stowe's pictures of religious life among the negroes? Instead of this, pious ladies nauseate us with novels which remind us of what we sometimes see in a worldly woman recently "converted";—she is as fond of a fine dinner table as before, but she invites clergymen instead of beaux; she thinks as much of her dress as before, but she adopts a more sober choice of colours and patterns; her conversation is as trivial as before, but the triviality is flavoured with gospel instead of gossip. In "The Old Grey Church," we have the same sort of Evangelical travesty of the fashionable novel, and of course the vicious, intriguing baronet is not wanting. It is worth while to give a sample of the style of conversation attributed to this high-born rake—a style that in its profuse italics and palpable innuendoes, is worthy of Miss Squeers. In an evening visit to the ruins of the Colosseum, Eustace, the young clergyman, has been withdrawing the heroine, Miss Lushington, from the rest of the party, for the sake of a *tête-à-tête*. The baronet is jealous, and vents his pique in this way:

> There they are, and Miss Lushington, no doubt, quite safe; for she is under the holy guidance of Pope Eustace the First, who has, of course, been delivering to her an edifying homily on the wickedness of the heathens of yore, who, as tradition tells us, in this very place let loose the wild *beastises* on poor St. Paul!—Oh, no! by-the-bye, I believe I am wrong, and betraying my want of clergy, and that it was not at all St. Paul, nor was it here. But no matter, it would equally serve as a text to preach from, and from which to diverge to the degenerate *heathen* Christians of the present day, and all their naughty practices, and so end with an exhortation to "come out from among them, and be separate";—and I am sure, Miss Lushington, you have most scrupulously conformed to that injunction this evening, for we have seen nothing of you since our arrival. But every one seems agreed it has been a *charming party of pleasure*, and I am sure we all feel *much indebted* to Mr. Grey for having *suggested* it; and as he seems so capital a cicerone, I hope he will think of something else equally agreeable to *all*.

This drivelling kind of dialogue, and equally drivelling narrative, which, like a bad drawing, represents nothing, and barely indicates what is meant to be represented, runs through the book; and we have no doubt is considered by the amiable authoress to constitute an improving novel, which Christian mothers will do well to put into the hands of their daughters. But everything is relative; we have met with American vegetarians whose normal diet was dry meal, and who, when their appetite wanted stimulating, tickled it with *wet* meal; and so, we can imagine that there are Evangelical circles in which "The Old Grey Church" is devoured as a powerful and interesting fiction.

But, perhaps, the least readable of silly women's novels, are the *modern-antique* species, which unfold to us the domestic life of Jannes and Jambres, the private love affairs of Sennacherib, or the mental struggles and ultimate conversion of Demetrius the silversmith. From most silly novels we can at least extract a laugh; but those of the modern antique school have a ponderous, a leaden kind of fatuity, under which we groan. What can be more demonstrative of the inability of literary women to measure their own powers, than their frequent assumption of a task which can only be justified by the rarest concurrence of acquirement with genius? The finest effort to reanimate the past is of course only approximative—is always more or less an infusion of the modern spirit into the ancient form,

Was ihr den Geist der Zeiten heisst,
Das ist im Grund der Herren eigner Geist,
In dem die Zeiten sich bespiegeln.

What you call the spirit of the ages
Is at bottom but the gentlemen's spirit
In which the ages are reflected.

Admitting that genius which has familiarized itself with all the relics of an ancient period can sometimes, by the force of its sympathetic divination, restore the missing notes in the "music of humanity," and reconstruct the fragments into a whole which will really bring the remote past nearer to us, and interpret it to our duller apprehension,—this form of imaginative power must always be among the very rarest, because it demands as much accurate and minute knowledge as creative vigour. Yet we find ladies constantly choosing to make their mental mediocrity more conspicuous, by clothing it in a masquerade of ancient names; by putting their feeble sentimentality into the mouths of Roman vestals or Egyptian princesses, and attributing their rhetorical arguments to Jewish high-priests and Greek philosophers. A recent example of this heavy imbecility is, "Adonijah, a Tale of the Jewish Dispersion," which forms part of a series, "uniting," we are told, "taste, humour, and sound principles." "Adonijah," we presume, exemplifies the tale of "sound principles"; the taste and humour are to be found in other members of the series. We are told on the cover, that the incidents of this tale are "fraught with unusual interest," and the preface winds up thus: "To those who feel interested in the dispersed of Israel and Judea, these pages may afford, perhaps, information on an important subject, as well as amusement." Since the "important subject" on which this book is to afford information is not specified, it may possibly lie in some esoteric meaning to which we have no key; but if it has relation to the dispersed of Israel and Judea at any period of their history, we believe a tolerably well-informed school-girl already knows much more of it than she will find in this "Tale of the Jewish Dispersion." "Adonijah" is simply the feeblest kind of love story, supposed to be instructive, we presume, because the hero is a Jewish captive, and the heroine a Roman vestal; because they and their friends are converted to Christianity after the shortest and easiest method approved by the "Society for Promoting the Conversion of the Jews"; and because, instead of being written in plain language, it is adorned with that peculiar style of grandiloquence which is held by some lady novelists to give an antique colouring, and which we recognise at once in such phrases as these: "the splendid regnal talents undoubtedly possessed by the Emperor Nero"—"the expiring scion of a lofty stem"—"the virtuous partner of his couch"—"ah, by Vesta!"—and "I tell thee, Roman." Among the quotations which serve at once for instruction and ornament on the cover of this volume, there is one from Miss Sinclair, which informs us that "Works of imagination are *avowedly* read by men of science, wisdom, and piety"; from which we suppose the reader is to gather the cheering inference that Dr. Daubeny, Mr.

Mill, or Mr. Maurice, may openly indulge himself with the perusal of "Adonijah," without being obliged to secrete it among the sofa cushions, or read it by snatches under the dinner table.

"Be not a baker if your head be made of butter," says a homely proverb, which, being interpreted, may mean, let no woman rush into print who is not prepared for the consequences. We are aware that our remarks are in a very different tone from that of the reviewers who, with a perennial recurrence of precisely similar emotions, only paralleled, we imagine, in the experience of monthly nurses, tell one lady novelist after another that they "hail" her productions "with delight." We are aware that the ladies at whom our criticism is pointed are accustomed to be told, in the choicest phraseology of puffery, that their pictures of life are brilliant, their characters well drawn, their style fascinating, and their sentiments lofty. But if they are inclined to resent our plainness of speech, we ask them to reflect for a moment on the chary praise, and often captious blame, which their panegyrists give to writers whose works are on the way to become classics. No sooner does a woman show that she has genius or effective talent, than she receives the tribute of being moderately praised and severely criticised. By a peculiar thermometric adjustment, when a woman's talent is at zero, journalistic approbation is at the boiling pitch; when she attains mediocrity, it is already at no more than summer heat; and if ever she reaches excellence, critical enthusiasm drops to the freezing point. Harriet Martineau, Currer Bell, and Mrs. Gaskell have been treated as cavalierly as if they had been men. And every critic who forms a high estimate of the share women may ultimately take in literature, will, on principle, abstain from any exceptional indulgence towards the productions of literary women. For it must be plain to every one who looks impartially and extensively into feminine literature, that its greatest deficiencies are due hardly more to the want of intellectual power than to the want of those moral qualities that contribute to literary excellence—patient diligence, a sense of the responsibility involved in publication, and an appreciation of the sacredness of the writer's art. In the majority of women's books you see that kind of facility which springs from the absence of any high standard; that fertility in imbecile combination or feeble imitation which a little self-criticism would check and reduce to barrenness; just as with a total want of musical ear people will sing out of tune, while a degree more melodic sensibility would suffice to render them silent. The foolish vanity of wishing to appear in print, instead of being counter balanced by any consciousness of the intellectual or moral derogation implied in futile authorship, seems to be encouraged by the extremely false impression that to write *at all* is a proof of superiority in a woman. On this ground, we believe that the average intellect of women is unfairly represented by the mass of feminine literature, and that while the few women who write well are very far above the ordinary intellectual level of their sex, the many women who write ill are very far below it. So that, after all, the severer critics are fulfilling a chivalrous duty in depriving the mere fact of feminine authorship of any false prestige which may give it a delusive attraction, and in recommending women of mediocre faculties—as at least a negative service they can render their sex—to abstain from writing.

The standing apology for women who become writers without any special qualification is, that society shuts them out from other spheres of occupation. Society is a very culpable entity, and has to answer for the manufacture of many unwholesome commodities, from bad pickles to bad poetry. But society, like "matter," and Her Majesty's Government, and other lofty abstractions, has its share of excessive blame as well as excessive praise. Where there is one woman who writes from necessity, we believe there are three women who write from vanity; and, besides, there is something so antiseptic in the mere healthy fact of working for one's bread, that the most trashy and rotten kind of feminine literature is not likely to have been produced under such circumstances. "In all labour there is profit"; but ladies' silly novels, we imagine, are less the result of labour than of busy idleness.

Happily, we are not dependent on argument to prove that Fiction is a department of literature in which women can, after their kind, fully equal men. A cluster of great names, both living and dead, rush to our memories in evidence that women can produce novels not only fine, but among the very finest;—novels, too, that have a precious speciality, lying quite apart from masculine aptitudes and experience. No educational restrictions can shut women out from the materials of fiction, and there is no species of art which is so free from rigid requirements. Like crystalline masses, it may take any form, and yet be beautiful; we have only to pour in the right elements—genuine observation, humour, and passion. But it is precisely this absence of rigid requirement which constitutes the fatal seduction of novel-writing to incompetent women. Ladies are not wont to be very grossly deceived as to their power of playing on the piano; here certain positive difficulties of execution have to be conquered, and incompetence inevitably breaks down. Every art which has its absolute *technique* is, to a certain extent, guarded from the intrusions of mere left-handed imbecility. But in novel-writing there are no barriers for incapacity to stumble against, no external criteria to prevent a writer from mistaking foolish facility for mastery. And so we have again and again the old story of La Fontaine's ass, who puts his nose to the flute, and, finding that he elicits some sound, exclaims, "Moi, aussi, je joue de la flute";—a fable which we commend, at parting, to the consideration of any feminine reader who is in danger of adding to the number of "silly novels by lady novelists."

Matthew Arnold 1822–1888

A major Victorian poet ("Dover Beach," "The Scholar Gipsy," "Thyrsis") and the leading literary critic of his day, Arnold was the son of a famous father, Thomas Arnold, headmaster of Rugby, a militant Christian leader, and a classical scholar. Matthew Arnold possessed the imagination and sensibility of a poet, attributes his father did not have, and it was out of this lifelong tension between Arnold-as-poet and -as-rational-man that both his poetry and his views on criticism grew. Arnold saw criticism as vital and as creative as poetry. He subordinated the historical method and emphasized the use of standards (like "touchstones," examples of what he considered great literature, especially in form and subject matter) to ascertain the quality of literary works.

"The Function of Criticism at the Present Time" (1865) is one of his better-known critical essays. In it he states that criticism is equal in value to the literary works with which it deals in its demand for creative effort and literary genius. He defines "real criticism" as an attempt "to know the best that is known and thought in the world." Its goal is truth, and to be successful, criticism must be allowed to exercise "a free play of the mind on all subjects which it touches." Criticism must not be bound by the practical spirit or by any kind of bias. Arnold refers to this aloofness as "disinterestedness" and argues that criticism can be successful only when allowed to operate within the world of ideas and aesthetics.

The Function of Criticism at the Present Time

Many objections have been made to a proposition which, in some remarks of mine on translating Homer, I ventured to put forth; a proposition about criticism, and its importance at the present day. I said: "Of the literature of France and Germany, as of the intellect of Europe in general, the main effort, for now many years, has been a critical effort; the endeavour, in all branches of knowledge, theology, philosophy, history, art, science, to see the object as in itself it really is." I added, that owing to the operation in English literature of certain causes, "almost the last thing for which one would come to English literature is just that very thing which now Europe most desires,—criticism"; and that the power and value of English literature was thereby impaired. More than one rejoinder declared that the importance I here assigned to criticism was excessive, and asserted the inherent superiority of the creative effort of the human spirit over its critical effort. And the other day, having been led by a Mr. Shairp's excellent notice of Wordsworth to turn again to his biography, I found, in the words of this great man, whom I, for one, must always listen to with the profoundest respect, a sentence passed on the critic's business, which seems to justify every possible disparagement of it. Wordsworth says in one of his letters:—

"The writers in these publications" (the Reviews), "while they prosecute their inglorious employment, can not be supposed to be in a state of mind very favourable for being affected by the finer influences of a thing so pure as genuine poetry."

And a trustworthy reporter of his conversation quotes a more elaborate judgment to the same effect:—

"Wordsworth holds the critical power very low, infinitely lower than the inventive; and he said to-day that if the quantity of time consumed in writing critiques on the works of others were given to original composition, of whatever kind it might be, it would be much better employed; it would make a man find out sooner his own level, and it would do infinitely less mischief. A false or malicious criticism may do much injury to the minds of others, a stupid invention, either in prose or verse, is quite harmless."

It is almost too much to expect of poor human nature, that a man capable of producing some effect in one line of literature, should, for the greater good of society, voluntarily doom himself to impotence and obscurity in another. Still less is this to be expected from men addicted to the composition of the "false or malicious criticism" of which Wordsworth speaks. However, everybody would admit that a false or malicious criticism had better never have been written. Everybody, too, would be willing to admit, as a general proposition, that the critical faculty is lower than the inventive. But is it true that criticism is really, in itself, a baneful and injurious employment; is it true that all time given to writing critiques on the works of others would be much better employed if it were given to original composition, of whatever kind this may be? Is it true that Johnson had better have gone on producing more *Irenes* instead of writing his *Lives of the Poets;* nay, is it certain that Wordsworth himself was better employed in making his Ecclesiastical Sonnets than when he made his celebrated Preface, so full of criticism, and criticism of the works of others? Wordsworth was himself a great critic, and it is to be sincerely regretted that he has not left us more criticism; Goethe was one of the greatest of critics, and we may sincerely congratulate ourselves that he has left us so much criticism. Without wasting time over the exaggeration which Wordsworth's judgment on criticism clearly contains, or over an attempt to trace the causes,—not difficult, I think, to be traced,—which may have led Wordsworth to this exaggeration, a critic may with advantage seize an occasion for trying his own conscience, and for asking himself of what real service at any given moment the practice of criticism either is or may be made to his own mind and spirit, and to the minds and spirits of others.

The critical power is of lower rank than the creative. True; but in assenting to this proposition, one or two things are to be kept in mind. It is undeniable that the exercise of a creative power, that a free creative activity, is the highest function of man; it is proved to be so by man's finding in it his true happiness. But it is undeniable, also, that men may have the sense of exercising this free creative activity in other ways than in producing great works of literature or art; if it were not so, all but a very few men would be shut out from the true happiness of all men. They may have it in well-doing, they may have it in learning, they may have it even in criticising. This is one thing to be kept in mind. Another is, that the exercise of the creative power in the production of great works of literature or art, however high this exercise of it may rank, is not at all epochs and under all conditions possible; and that therefore labour may be vainly spent in attempting it, which might with more fruit be used in preparing for it, in rendering it possible. This creative power works with elements, with materials; what if it has not those materials, those elements, ready for its use? In that case it must surely wait till they are ready. Now, in literature,—I will limit myself to literature, for it is about literature that the question arises,—the elements with which the creative power works are ideas; the best ideas on every matter which literature touches, current at the time. At any rate we may lay it down as certain that in modern literature no manifestation of the creative power not working with these can be very important or fruitful. And I say *current* at the time, not merely accessible at the time; for creative literary genius does not principally show itself in discovering new ideas, that is rather the business of the philosopher. The grand work of literary genius is a work of synthesis and exposition, not of analysis and discovery; its gift lies in the faculty of being happily inspired by a certain intellectual and spiritual atmosphere, by a certain order of ideas, when it finds itself in them; of dealing divinely with these ideas, presenting them in the most effective and attractive combinations,—making beautiful works with them, in short. But it must have the atmosphere, it must find itself amidst the order of ideas, in order to work freely; and these it is not so easy to command. This is why great creative epochs in literature are so rare, this is why there is so much that is unsatisfactory in the productions of many men of real genius; because, for the creation of a master-work of literature two powers must concur, the power of the man and the power of the moment, and the man is not enough without the moment; the creative power has, for its happy exercise, appointed elements, and those elements are not in its own control.

Nay, they are more within the control of the critical power. It is the business of the critical power, as I said in the words already quoted, "in all branches of knowledge, theology, philosophy, history, art, science, to see the object as in itself it really is." Thus it tends, at last, to make an intellectual situation of which the creative power can profitably avail itself. It tends to establish an order of ideas, if not absolutely true, yet true by comparison with that which it displaces; to make the best ideas prevail. Presently these new ideas reach society, the touch of truth is the touch of life, and there is a stir and growth everywhere; out of this stir and growth come the creative epochs of literature.

Or, to narrow our range, and quit these considerations of the general march of genius and of society,—considerations which are apt to become too abstract and impalpable,—every one can see that a poet, for instance, ought to know life and the world before dealing with them in poetry; and life and the world being in modern times very complex things, the creation of a modern poet, to be worth much, implies a great critical effort behind it; else it must be a comparatively poor, barren, and short-lived affair. This is why Byron's poetry had so little endurance in it, and Goethe's so much; both Byron and Goethe had a great productive power, but Goethe's was nourished by a great critical effort providing the true materials for it, and Byron's was not; Goethe knew life and the world, the poet's necessary subjects, much more comprehensively and thoroughly than Byron. He knew a great deal more of them, and he knew them much more as they really are.

It has long seemed to me that the burst of creative activity in our literature, through the first quarter of this century, had about it in fact something premature; and that from this cause its productions are doomed, most of them, in spite of the sanguine hopes which accompanied and do still accompany them, to prove hardly more lasting than the productions of far less splendid epochs. And this prematureness comes from its having proceeded without having its proper data, without sufficient materials to work with. In other words, the English poetry of the first quarter of this century, with plenty of energy, plenty of creative force, did not know enough. This makes Byron so empty of matter, Shelley so incoherent, Wordsworth even, profound as he is, yet so wanting in completeness and variety. Wordsworth cared little for books, and disparaged Goethe. I admire Wordsworth, as he is, so much that I cannot wish him different; and it is vain, no doubt, to imagine such a man different from what he is, to suppose that he *could* have been different. But surely the one thing wanting to make Wordsworth an even greater poet than he is,—his thought richer, and his influence of wider application,—was that he should have read more books, among them, no doubt, those of that Goethe whom he disparaged without reading him.

But to speak of books and reading may easily lead to a misunderstanding here. It was not really books and reading that lacked to our poetry at this epoch; Shelley had plenty of reading, Coleridge had immense reading. Pindar and Sophocles—as we all say so glibly, and often with so little discernment of the real import of what we are saying—had not many books; Shakspeare was no deep reader. True; but in the Greece of Pindar and Sophocles, in the England of Shakspeare, the poet lived in a current of ideas in the highest degree animating and nourishing to the creative power; society was, in the fullest measure, permeated by fresh thought, intelligent and alive. And this state of things is the true basis for the creative power's exercise, in this it finds its data, its materials, truly ready for its hand; all the books and reading in the world are only valuable as they are helps to this. Even when this does not actually exist, books and reading may enable a man to construct a kind of semblance of it in his own mind, a world of knowledge and intelligence in which he may live and work. This is by no means an equivalent to the artist for the nationally diffused life and thought of the epochs of Sophocles or Shakspeare; but, besides that it may be a means of preparation for such epochs, it does really constitute, if many share in it, a quickening and sustaining atmosphere of great value. Such an atmosphere the many-sided learning and the long and widely-combined critical effort of Germany formed for Goethe, when he lived and worked. There was no national glow of life and thought there as in the Athens of Pericles or the England of Elizabeth. That was the poet's weakness. But there was a sort of equivalent for it in the complete culture and unfettered thinking of a large body of Germans. That was his strength. In the England of the first quarter of this century there was neither a national glow of life and thought, such as we had in the age of Elizabeth, nor yet a culture and a force of learning and criticism such as were to be found in Germany. Therefore the creative power of poetry wanted, for success in the highest sense, materials and a basis; a thorough interpretation of the world was necessarily denied to it.

At first sight it seems strange that out of the immense stir of the French Revolution and its age should not have come a crop of works of genius equal to that which came out of the stir of the great productive time of Greece, or out of that of the Renascence, with its powerful episode the Reformation. But the truth is that the stir of the French Revolution took a character which essentially distinguished it from such movements as these. These were, in the main, disinterestedly intellectual and spiritual movements; movements in which the human spirit looked for its satisfaction in itself and in the increased play of its own activity. The French Revolution took a political, practical character. The movement which went on in France under the old *régime*, from 1700 to 1789, was far more really akin than that of the Revolution itself to the movement of the Renascence; the France of Voltaire and Rousseau told far more powerfully upon the mind of Europe than the France of the Revolution. Goethe reproached this last expressly with having "thrown quiet culture back." Nay, and the true key to how much in our Byron, even in our Wordsworth, is this!—that they had their source in a great movement of feeling, not in a great movement of mind. The French Revolution, however,—that object of so much blind love and so much blind hatred,—found undoubtedly its motive-power in the intelligence of men, and not in their practical sense; that is what distinguishes it from the English Revolution of Charles the First's time. This is what makes it a more spiritual event than our Revolution, an event of much more powerful and world-wide interest, though practically less successful; it appeals to an order of ideas which are universal, certain, permanent. 1789 asked of a thing, Is it rational?

1642 asked of a thing, Is it legal? or, when it went furthest, Is it according to conscience? This is the English fashion, a fashion to be treated, within its own sphere, with the highest respect; for its success, within its own sphere, has been prodigious. But what is law in one place is not law in another; what is law here to-day is not law even here to-morrow; and as for conscience, what is binding on one man's conscience is not binding on another's. The old woman who threw her stool at the head of the surpliced minister in St. Giles's Church at Edinburgh obeyed an impulse to which millions of the human race may be permitted to remain strangers. But the prescriptions of reason are absolute, unchanging, of universal validity; *to count by tens is the easiest way of counting*—that is a proposition of which every one, from here to the Antipodes, feels the force; at least I should say so if we did not live in a country where it is not impossible that any morning we may find a letter in the *Times* declaring that a decimal coinage is an absurdity. That a whole nation should have been penetrated with an enthusiasm for pure reason, and with an ardent zeal for making its prescriptions triumph, is a very remarkable thing, when we consider how little of mind, or anything so worthy and quickening as mind, comes into the motives which alone, in general, impel great masses of men. In spite of the extravagant direction given to this enthusiasm, in spite of the crimes and follies in which it lost itself, the French Revolution derives from the force, truth, and universality of the ideas which it took for its law, and from the passion with which it could inspire a multitude for these ideas, a unique and still living power; it is—it will probably long remain—the greatest, the most animating event in history. And as no sincere passion for the things of the mind, even though it turn out in many respects an unfortunate passion, is ever quite thrown away and quite barren of good, France has reaped from hers one fruit—the natural and legitimate fruit, though not precisely the grand fruit she expected: she is the country in Europe where *the people* is most alive.

But the mania for giving an immediate political and practical application to all these fine ideas of the reason was fatal. Here an Englishman is in his element: on this theme we can all go on for hours. And all we are in the habit of saying on it has undoubtedly a great deal of truth. Ideas cannot be too much prized in and for themselves, cannot be too much lived with; but to transport them abruptly into the world of politics and practice, violently to revolutionise this world to their bidding,—that is quite another thing. There is the world of ideas and there is the world of practice; the French are often for suppressing the one and the English the other; but neither is to be suppressed. A member of the House of Commons said to me the other day: "That a thing is an anomaly, I consider to be no objection to it whatever." I venture to think he was wrong; that a thing is an anomaly *is* an objection to it, but absolutely and in the sphere of ideas: it is not necessarily, under such and such circumstances, or at such and such a moment, an objection to it in the sphere of politics and practice. Joubert has said beautifully: "C'est la force et le droit qui règlent toutes choses dans le monde; la force en attendant le droit." (Force and right are the governors of this world; force till right is ready.) *Force till right is ready;* and till right is ready, force, the existing order of things, is justified, is the legitimate ruler. But right is something moral, and implies inward recognition, free assent of the will; we are not ready for right—*right,* so far as we are concerned, *is not ready,*—until we have attained this sense of seeing it and willing it. The way in which for us it may change and transform force, the existing order of things, and become, in its turn, the legitimate ruler of the world, should depend on the way in which, when our time comes, we see it and will it. Therefore for other people enamoured of their own newly discerned right, to attempt to impose it upon us as ours, and violently to substitute their right for our force, is an act of tyranny, and to be resisted. It sets at nought the second great half of our maxim, *force till right is ready*. This was the grand error of the French Revolution, and its movements of ideas, by quitting the intellectual sphere and rushing furiously into the political sphere, ran, indeed, a prodigious and memorable course, but produced no such intellectual fruit as the movement of ideas of the Renascence, and created, in opposition to itself, what I may call an *epoch of concentration*. The great force of that epoch of concentration was England; and the great voice of that epoch of concentration was Burke. It is the fashion to treat Burke's writings on the French Revolution as superannuated and conquered by the event; as the eloquent but unphilosophical tirades of bigotry and prejudice. I will not deny that they are often disfigured by the violence and passion of the moment, and that in some directions Burke's view was bounded, and his observation therefore at fault. But on the whole, and for those who can make the needful corrections, what distinguishes these writings is their profound, permanent, fruitful, philosophical truth. They contain the true philosophy of an epoch of concentration, dissipate the heavy atmosphere which its own nature is apt to engender round it, and make its resistance rational instead of mechanical.

But Burke is so great because, almost alone in England, he brings thought to bear upon politics, he saturates politics with thought. It is his accident that his ideas were at the service of an epoch of concentration, not of an epoch of expansion; it is his characteristic that he so lived by ideas, and had such a source of them welling up within him, that he could float even an epoch of concentration and English Tory politics with them. It does not hurt him that Dr. Price and the Liberals were enraged with him; it does not even hurt him that George the Third and the Tories were enchanted with him. His greatness is that he lived in a world which neither English Liberalism nor English Toryism is apt to enter;—the world of ideas, not the world of catchwords and party habits. So far is it from being really true of him that he "to party gave up what was meant for mankind," that at the very end of his fierce struggle with the French Revolution, after all his invectives against its false pretensions, hollowness, and madness, with his sincere conviction of its mischievousness, he can close a memorandum on the best means of combating it, some of the last pages he ever wrote,—the *Thoughts on French Affairs*, in December 1791,—with these striking words:—

"The evil is stated, in my opinion, as it exists. The remedy must be where power, wisdom, and information, I hope, are more united with good intentions than they can be with me. I have done with this subject, I believe, for ever. It has given me many anxious moments for the last two years. *If a great change is to be made in human affairs, the minds of men will be fitted to it; the general opinions and feelings will draw that way. Every fear, every hope will forward it; and then they who persist in opposing this mighty current in human affairs, will appear rather to resist the decrees of Providence itself, than the mere designs of men. They will not be resolute and firm, but perverse and obstinate.*"

That return of Burke upon himself has always seemed to me one of the finest things in English literature, or indeed in any literature. That is what I call living by ideas: when one side of a question has long had your earnest support, when all your feelings are engaged, when you hear all round you no language but one, when your party talks this language like a steam-engine and can imagine no other,—still to be able to think, still to be irresistibly carried, if so it be, by the current of thought to the opposite side of the question and, like Balaam, to be unable to speak anything *but what the Lord has put in your mouth*. I know nothing more striking, and I must add that I know nothing more un-English.

For the Englishman in general is like my friend the Member of Parliament, and believes, point-blank, that for a thing to be an anomaly is absolutely no objection to it whatever. He is like the Lord Auckland of Burke's day, who, in a memorandum on the French Revolution, talks of "certain miscreants, assuming the name of philosophers, who have presumed themselves capable of establishing a new system of society." The Englishman has been called a political animal, and he values what is political and practical so much that ideas easily become objects of dislike in his eyes, and thinkers "miscreants," because ideas and thinkers have rashly meddled with politics and practice. This would be all very well if the dislike and neglect confined themselves to ideas transported out of their own sphere, and meddling rashly with practice; but they are inevitably extended to ideas as such, and to the whole life of intelligence; practice is everything, a free play of the mind is nothing. The notion of the free play of the mind upon all subjects being a pleasure in itself, being an object of desire, being an essential provider of elements without which a nation's spirit, whatever compensations it may have for them, must, in the long run, die of inanition, hardly enters into an Englishman's thoughts. It is noticeable that the word *curiosity*, which in other languages is used in a good sense, to mean, as a high and fine quality of man's nature, just this disinterested love of a free play of the mind on all subjects, for its own sake,—it is noticeable, I say, that this word has in our language no sense of the kind, no sense but a rather bad and disparaging one. But criticism, real criticism, is essentially the exercise of this very quality. It obeys an instinct prompting it to try to know the best that is known and thought in the world, irrespectively of practice, politics, and everything of the kind; and to value knowledge and thought as they approach this best, without the intrusion of any other considerations whatever. This is an instinct for which there is, I think, little original sympathy in the practical English nature, and what there was of it has undergone a long benumbing period of blight and suppression in the epoch of concentration which followed the French Revolution.

But epochs of concentration cannot well endure for ever; epochs of expansion, in the due course of things, follow them. Such an epoch of expansion seems to be opening in this country. In the first place all danger of a hostile forcible pressure of foreign ideas upon our practice has long disappeared; like the traveller in the fable, therefore, we begin to wear our cloak a little more loosely. Then, with a long peace, the ideas of Europe steal gradually and amicably in, and mingle, though in infinitesimally small quantities at a time, with our own notions. Then, too, in spite of all that is said about the absorbing and brutalising influence of our passionate material progress, it seems to me indisputable that this progress is likely, though not certain, to lead in the end to an apparition of intellectual life; and that man, after he has made himself perfectly comfortable and has now to determine what to do with himself next, may begin to remember that he has a mind, and that the mind may be made the source of great pleasure. I grant it is mainly the privilege of faith, at present, to discern this end to our railways, our business, and our fortune-making; but we shall see if, here as elsewhere, faith is not in the end the true prophet. Our ease, our travelling, and our unbounded liberty to hold just as hard and securely as we please to the practice to which our notions have given birth, all tend to beget an inclination to deal a little more freely with these notions themselves, to canvass them a little, to penetrate a little into their real nature. Flutterings of curiosity, in the foreign sense of the word, appear amongst us, and it is in these that criticism must look to find its account. Criticism first; a time of true creative activity, perhaps,—which, as I have said, must inevitably be preceded amongst us by a time of criticism,—hereafter, when criticism has done its work.

It is of the last importance that English criticism should clearly discern what rule for its course, in order to avail itself of the field now opening to it, and to produce fruit for the future, it ought to take. The rule may be summed up in one word,—*disinterestedness*. And how is criticism to show disinterestedness? By keeping aloof from what is called "the practical view of things"; by resolutely following the law of its own nature, which is to be a free play of the mind on all subjects which it touches. By steadily refusing to lend itself to any of those ulterior, political, practical considerations about ideas, which plenty of people will be sure to attach to them, which perhaps ought often to be attached to them, which in this country at any rate are certain to be attached to them quite sufficiently, but which criticism has really nothing to do with. Its business is, as I have said, simply to know the best that is known and thought in the world, and by in its turn making this known, to create a current of true and fresh ideas. Its business is to do this with inflexible honesty, with due ability; but its business is to do no more, and to leave alone all questions of practical consequences and applications, questions which will never fail to have due prominence given to them. Else criticism, besides being really false to its own nature, merely continues in the old rut which it has hitherto followed in this country, and will certainly miss the chance now given to it. For what is at present the bane of criticism in this country? It is that practical considerations cling to it and stifle it. It subserves interests not its own. Our organs of criticism are organs of men and parties having practical ends to serve, and with them those practical ends are the first thing and the play of mind the second; so much play of mind as is compatible with the prosecution of those practical ends is all that is wanted. An organ like the *Revue des Deux Mondes*, having for its main function to understand and utter the best that is known and thought in the world, existing, it may be said, as just an organ for a free play of the mind, we have not. But we have the *Edinburgh Review*, existing as an organ of the old Whigs, and for as much play of the mind as may suit its being that; we have the *Quarterly Review*, existing as an organ of the Tories and for as much play of mind as may suit its being that; we have the *British Quarterly Review*, existing as an organ of the political Dissenters, and for as much play of mind as may suit its being that; we have the *Times*, existing as an organ of the common, satisfied, well-to-do Englishman, and for as much play of mind as may suit its being that. And so on through all the various fractions, political and religious, of our society; every fraction has, as such, its organ of criticism, but the notion of combining all fractions in the common pleasure of a free disinterested play of mind meets with no favour. Directly this play of mind wants to have more scope, and to forget the pressure of practical considerations a little, it is checked, it is made to feel the chain. We saw this the other day in the extinction, so much to be regretted, of the *Home and Foreign Review*. Perhaps in no organ of criticism in this country was there so much knowledge, so much play of mind; but these could not save it. The *Dublin Review* subordinates play of mind to the practical business of English and Irish Catholicism, and lives. It must needs be that men should act in sects and parties, that each of these sects and parties should have its organ, and should make this organ subserve the interests of its action; but it would be well, too, that there should be a criticism not the minister of these interests, not their enemy, but absolutely and entirely independent of them. No other criticism will ever attain any real authority or make any real way towards its end,—the creating a current of true and fresh ideas.

It is because criticism has so little kept in the pure intellectual sphere, has so little detached itself from practice, has been so directly polemical and controversial, that it has so ill accomplished, in this country, its best spiritual work; which is to keep man from a self-satisfaction which is retarding and vulgarising, to lead him towards perfection, by making his mind dwell upon what is excellent in itself, and the absolute beauty and fitness of things. A polemical practical criticism makes men blind even to the ideal imperfection of their practice, makes them willingly assert its ideal perfection, in order the better to secure it against attack; and clearly this is narrowing and baneful for them. If they were reassured on the practical side, speculative considerations of ideal perfection they might be brought to entertain, and their spiritual horizon would thus gradually widen. Sir Charles Adderley says to the Warwickshire farmers:—

"Talk of the improvement of breed! Why, the race we ourselves represent, the men and women, the old Anglo-Saxon race, are the best breed in the whole world. . . . The absence of a too enervating climate, too unclouded skies, and a too luxurious nature, has produced so vigorous a race of people, and has rendered us so superior to all the world."

Mr. Roebuck says to the Sheffield cutlers:—

"I look around me and ask what is the state of England? Is not property safe? Is not every man able to say what he likes? Can you not walk from one end of England to the other in perfect security? I ask you whether, the world over or in past history, there is anything like it? Nothing. I pray that our unrivalled happiness may last."

Now obviously there is a peril for poor human nature in words and thoughts of such exuberant self-satisfaction, until we find ourselves safe in the streets of the Celestial City.

> *Das wenige verschwindet leicht dem Blicke*
> *Der vorwärts sieht, wie viel noch übrig bleibt—*

says Goethe; "the little that is done seems nothing when we look forward and see how much we have yet to do." Clearly this is a better line of reflection for weak humanity, so long as it remains on this earthly field of labour and trial.

But neither Sir Charles Adderley nor Mr. Roebuck is by nature inaccessible to considerations of this sort. They only lose sight of them owing to the controversial life we all lead, and the practical form which all speculation takes with us. They have in view opponents whose aim is not ideal, but practical; and in their zeal to uphold their own practice against these innovators, they go so far as even to attribute to this practice an ideal perfection. Somebody has been wanting to introduce a six-pound franchise, or to abolish church-rates, or to collect agricultural statistics by force, or to diminish local self-government. How natural, in reply to such proposals, very likely improper or ill-timed, to go a little beyond the mark, and to say stoutly, "Such a race of people as we stand, so superior to all the world! The old Anglo-Saxon race, the best breed in the whole world! I pray that our unrivalled happiness may last! I ask you whether, the world over or in past history, there is anything like it?" And so long as criticism answers this dithyramb by insisting that the old Anglo-Saxon race would be still more superior to all others if it had no church-rates, or that our unrivalled happiness would last yet longer with a six-pound franchise, so long will the strain, "The best breed in the whole world!" swell louder and louder everything ideal and refining will be lost out of sight, and both the assailed and their critics will remain in a sphere, to say the truth, perfectly unvital, a sphere in which spiritual progression is impossible. But let criticism leave church-rates and the franchise alone, and in the most candid spirit, without a single lurking thought of practical innovation, confront with our dithyramb this paragraph on which I stumbled in a newspaper immediately after reading Mr. Roebuck:—

"A shocking child murder has just been committed at Nottingham. A girl named Wragg left the workhouse there on Saturday morning with her young illegitimate child. The child was soon afterwards found dead on Mapperly Hills, having been strangled. Wragg is in custody."

Nothing but that; but, in juxtaposition with the absolute eulogies of Sir Charles Adderley and Mr. Roebuck, how eloquent, how suggestive are those few lines! "Our old Anglo-Saxon breed, the best in the whole world!"—how much that is harsh and ill-favoured there is in this best! *Wragg!* If we are to talk of ideal perfection, of "the best in the whole world," has any one reflected what a touch of grossness in our race, what an original shortcoming in the more delicate spiritual perceptions, is shown by the natural growth amongst us of such hideous names,—Higginbottom, Stiggins, Bugg! In Ionia and Attica they were luckier in this respect than "the best race in the world"; by the Ilissus there was no Wragg, poor thing! And "our unrivalled happiness";—what an element of grimness, bareness, and hideousness mixes with it and blurs it? the workhouse, the dismal Mapperly Hills,—how dismal those who have seen them will remember;—the gloom, the smoke, the cold, the strangled illegitimate child! "I ask you whether, the world over or in past history, there is anything like it?" Perhaps not, one is inclined to answer; but at any rate, in that case, the world is very much to be pitied. And the final touch,—short, bleak and inhuman: *Wragg is in custody*. The sex lost in the confusion of our unrivalled happiness; or (shall I say?) the superfluous Christian name lopped off by the straightforward vigour of our old Anglo-Saxon breed! There is profit for the spirit in such contrasts as this; criticism serves the cause of perfection by establishing them. By eluding sterile conflict, by refusing to remain in the sphere where alone narrow and relative conceptions have any worth and validity, criticism may diminish its momentary importance, but only in this way has it a chance of gaining admittance for those wider and more perfect conceptions to which all its duty is really owed. Mr. Roebuck will have a poor opinion of an adversary who replies to his defiant songs of triumph only by murmuring under his breath, *Wragg is in custody;* but in no other way will these songs of triumph be induced gradually to moderate themselves, to get rid of what in them is excessive and offensive, and to fall into a softer and truer key.

It will be said that it is a very subtle and indirect action which I am thus prescribing for criticism, and that, by embracing in this manner the Indian virtue of detachment and abandoning the sphere of practical life, it condemns itself to a slow and obscure work. Slow and obscure it may be, but it is the only proper work of criticism. The mass of mankind will never have any ardent zeal for seeing things as they are; very inadequate ideas will always satisfy them. On these inadequate ideas reposes, and must repose, the general practice of the world. That is as much as saying that whoever sets himself to see things as they are will find himself one of a very small circle; but it is only by this small circle resolutely doing its own work that adequate ideas will ever get current at all. The rush and roar of practical life will always have a dizzying and attracting effect upon the most collected spectator, and tend to draw him into its vortex; most of all will this be the case where that life is so powerful as it is in England. But it is only by remaining collected, and refusing to lend himself to the point of view of the practical man, that the critic can do the practical man any service; and it is only by the greatest sincerity in pursuing his own course, and by at last convincing even the practical man of his sincerity, that he can escape misunderstandings which perpetually threaten him.

For the practical man is not apt for fine distinctions, and yet in these distinctions truth and the highest culture greatly find their account. But it is not easy to lead a practical man,—unless you reassure him as to your practical intentions, you have no chance of leading him,—to see that a thing which he has always been used to look at from one side only, which he greatly values, and which, looked at from that side, quite deserves, perhaps, all the prizing and admiring which he bestows upon it,—that this thing, looked at from another side, may appear much less beneficent and beautiful, and yet retain all its claims to our practical allegiance. Where shall we find language innocent enough, how shall we make the spotless purity of our intentions evident enough, to enable us to say to the political Englishman that the British Constitution itself, which, seen from the practical side, looks such a magnificent organ of progress and virtue, seen from the speculative side,—with its compromises, its love of facts, its horror of theory, its studied avoidance of clear thoughts,—that, seen from this side, our august Constitution sometimes looks,—forgive me, shade of Lord Somers!—a colossal machine for the manufacture of Philistines? How is Cobbett to say this and not be misunderstood, blackened as he is with the smoke of a lifelong conflict in the field of political practice? how is Mr. Carlyle to say it and not be misunderstood, after his furious raid into this field with his *Latter-day Pamphlets*? how is Mr. Ruskin, after his pugnacious political economy? I say, the critic must keep out of the region of immediate practice in the political, social, humanitarian sphere, if he wants to make a beginning for that more free speculative treatment of things, which may perhaps one day make its benefits felt even in this sphere, but in a natural and thence irresistible manner.

Do what he will, however, the critic will still remain exposed to frequent misunderstandings, and nowhere so much as in this country. For here people are particularly indisposed even to comprehend that without this free disinterested treatment of things, truth and the highest culture are out of the question. So immersed are they in practical life, so accustomed to take all their notions from this life and its processes, that they are apt to think that truth and culture themselves can be reached by the processes of this life, and that it is an impertinent singularity to think of reaching them in any other. "We are all *terræ filii*," cries their eloquent advocate; "all Philistines together. Away with the notion of proceeding by any other course than the course dear to the Philistines; let us have a social movement, let us organise and combine a party to pursue truth and new thought, let us call it *the liberal party*, and let us all stick to each other, and back each other up. Let us have no nonsense about independent criticism, and intellectual delicacy, and the few and the many. Don't let us trouble ourselves about foreign thought; we shall invent the whole thing for ourselves as we go along. If one of us speaks well, applaud him; if one of us speaks ill, applaud him too; we are all in the same movement, we are all liberals, we are all in pursuit of truth." In this way the pursuit of truth becomes really a social, practical, pleasurable affair, almost requiring a chairman, a secretary, and advertisements; with the excitement of an occcasional scandal, with a little resistance to give the happy sense of difficulty overcome; but, in general, plenty of bustle and very little thought. To act is so easy, as Goethe says; to think is so hard! It is true that the critic has many temptations to go with the stream, to make one of the party movement, one of these *terræ filii;* it seems ungracious to refuse to be a *terræ filius*, when so many excellent people are; but the critic's duty is to refuse, or, if resistance is vain, at least to cry with Obermann: *Périssons en résistant*.

How serious a matter it is to try and resist, I had ample opportunity of experiencing when I ventured some time ago to criticise the celebrated first volume of Bishop Colenso. The echoes of the storm which was then raised I still, from time to time, hear grumbling round me. That storm arose out of a misunderstanding almost inevitable. It is a result of no little culture to attain to a clear perception that science and religion are two wholly different things. The multitude will for ever confuse them; but happily that is of no great real importance, for while the multitude imagines itself to live by its false science, it does really live by its true religion. Dr. Colenso, however, in his first volume did all he could to strengthen the confusion, and to make it dangerous. He did this with the best intentions, I freely admit, and with the most candid ignorance that this was the natural effect of what he was doing; but, says Joubert, "Ignorance, which in matters of morals extenuates the crime, is itself, in intellectual matters, a crime of the first order." I criticised Bishop Colenso's speculative confusion. Immediately there was a cry raised: "What is this? here is a liberal attacking a liberal. Do not you belong to the movement? are not you a friend of truth? Is not Bishop Colenso in pursuit of truth? then speak with proper respect of his book. Dr. Stanley is another friend of truth, and you speak with proper respect of his book; why make these invidious differences? both books are excellent, admirable, liberal; Bishop Colenso's perhaps the most so, because it is the boldest, and will have the best practical consequences for the liberal cause. Do you want to encourage to the attack of a brother liberal his, and your, and our implacable enemies, the *Church and State Review* or the *Record*,—the High Church rhinoceros and the Evangelical hyæna? Be silent, therefore; or rather speak, speak as loud as ever you can! and go into ecstasies over the eighty and odd pigeons."

But criticism cannot follow this coarse and indiscriminate method. It is unfortunately possible for a man in pursuit of truth to write a book which reposes upon a false conception. Even the practical consequences of a book are to genuine criticism no recommendation of it, if the book is, in the highest sense, blundering. I see that a lady who herself, too, is in pursuit of truth, and who writes with great ability, but a little too much, perhaps, under the influence of the practical spirit of the English liberal movement, classes Bishop Colenso's book and M. Renan's together, in her survey of the religious state of Europe, as facts of the same order, works, both of them, of "great importance"; "great ability, power, and skill"; Bishop Colenso's, perhaps, the most powerful; at least, Miss Cobbe gives special expression to her gratitude that to Bishop Colenso "has been given the strength to grasp, and the courage to teach, truths of such deep import." In the same way, more than one popular writer has compared him to Luther. Now it is just this kind of false estimate which the critical spirit is, it seems to me, bound to resist. It is really the strongest possible proof of the low ebb at which, in England, the critical spirit is, that while the critical hit in the religious literature of Germany is Dr. Strauss's book, in that of France M. Renan's book, the book of Bishop Colenso is the critical hit in the religious literature of England. Bishop Colenso's book reposes on a total misconception of the essential elements of the religious problem, as that problem is now presented for solution. To criticism, therefore, which seeks to have the best that is known as thought on this problem, it is, however well meant, of no importance whatever. M. Renan's book attempts a new synthesis of the elements furnished to us by the Four Gospels. It attempts, in my opinion, a synthesis, perhaps premature, perhaps impossible, certainly not successful. Up to the present time, at any rate, we must acquiesce in Fleury's sentence on such recastings of the Gospel-story: *Quiconque s'imagine la pourvoir mieux écrire, ne l'entend pas* [Whoever persuades himself that he could write it better, does not understand it]. M. Renan had himself passed by anticipation a like sentence on his own work, when he said: "If a new presentation of the character of Jesus were offered to me, I would not have it; its very clearness would be, in my opinion, the best proof of its insufficiency." His friends may with perfect justice rejoin that at the sight of the Holy Land, and of the actual scene of the Gospel-story, all the current of M. Renan's thoughts may have naturally changed, and a new casting of that story irresistibly suggested itself to him; and that this is just a case for applying Cicero's maxim: Change of mind is not inconsistency—*nemo doctus unquam mutationem consilii inconstantiam dixit esse* [No one learned has ever called a change of judgment inconsistency]. Nevertheless, for criticism, M. Renan's first thought must still be the truer one, as long as his new casting so fails more fully to commend itself, more fully (to use Coleridge's happy phrase about the Bible) to *find* us. Still M. Renan's attempt is, for criticism, of the most real interest and importance, since, with all its difficulty, a fresh synthesis of the New Testament *data,*—not a making war on them, in Voltaire's fashion, not a leaving them out of mind, in the world's fashion, but the putting a new construction upon them, the taking them from under the old, traditional, conventional point of view and placing them under a new one,—is the very essence of the religious problem, as now presented; and only by efforts in this direction can it receive a solution.

Again, in the same spirit in which she judges Bishop Colenso, Miss Cobbe, like so many earnest liberals of our practical race, both here and in America, herself sets vigorously about a positive reconstruction of religion, about making a religion of the future out of hand, or at least setting about making it. We must not rest, she and they are always thinking and saying, in negative criticism, we must be creative and constructive; hence we have such works as her recent *Religious Duty*, and works still more considerable, perhaps, by others, which will be in every one's mind. These works often have much ability; they often spring out of sincere convictions, and a sincere wish to do good; and they sometimes, perhaps, do good. Their fault is (if I may be permitted to say so) one which they have in common with the British College of Health, in the New Road. Every one knows the British College of Health; it is that building with the lion and the statue of the Goddess Hygeia before it; at least I am sure about the lion, though I am not absolutely certain about the Goddess Hygeia. This building does credit, perhaps, to the resources of Dr. Morrison and his disciples; but it falls a good deal short of one's idea of what a British College of Health ought to be. In England, where we hate public interference and love individual enterprise, we have a whole crop of places like the British College of Health; the grand name without the grand thing. Unluckily, creditable to individual enterprise as they are, they tend to impair our taste by making us forget what more grandiose, noble, or beautiful character properly belongs to a public institution. The same may be said of the religions of the future of Miss Cobbe and others. Creditable, like the British College of Health, to the resources of their authors, they yet tend to make us forget what more grandiose, noble, or beautiful character properly belongs to religious constructions. The historic religions, with all their faults, have had this; it certainly belongs to the religious sentiment, when it truly flowers, to have this; and we impoverish our spirit if we allow a religion of the future without it. What then is the duty of criticism here? To take the practical point of view, to applaud the liberal movement and all its works,—its New Road religions of the future into the bargain,—for their general utility's sake? By no means; but to be perpetually dissatisfied with these works, while they perpetually fall short of a high and perfect ideal.

For criticism, these are elementary laws; but they never can be popular, and in this country they have been very little followed, and one meets with immense obstacles in following them. That is a reason for asserting them again and again. Criticism must maintain its independence of the practical spirit and its aims. Even with well-meant efforts of the practical spirit it must express dissatisfaction, if in the sphere of the ideal they seem impoverishing and limiting. It must not hurry on to the goal because of its practical importance. It must be patient, and know how to wait; and flexible, and know how to attach itself to things and how to withdraw from them. It must be apt to study and praise elements that for the fulness of spiritual perfection are wanted, even though they belong to a power which in the practical sphere may be maleficent. It must be apt to discern the spiritual shortcomings or illusions of powers that in the practical sphere may be beneficent. And this without any notion of favouring or injuring, in the practical sphere, one power or the other; without any notion of playing off, in this sphere, one power against the other. When one looks, for instance, at the English Divorce Court,—an institution which perhaps has its practical conveniences, but which in the ideal sphere is so hideous; an institution which neither makes divorce impossible nor makes it decent, which allows a man to get rid of his wife, or a wife of her husband, but makes them drag one another first, for the public edification, through a mire of unutterable infamy,—when one looks at this charming institution, I say, with its crowded trials, its newspaper reports, and its money compensations, this institution in which the gross unregenerate British Philistine has indeed stamped an image of himself,—one may be permitted to find the marriage theory of Catholicism refreshing and elevating. Or when Protestantism, in virtue of its supposed rational and intellectual origin, gives the law to criticism too magisterially, criticism may and must remind it that its pretensions, in this respect, are illusive and do it harm; that the Reformation was a moral rather than an intellectual event; that Luther's theory of grace no more exactly reflects the mind of the spirit than Bossuet's philosophy of history reflects it; and that there is no more antecedent probability of the Bishop of Durham's stock of ideas being agreeable to perfect reason than of Pope Pius the Ninth's. But criticism will not on that account forget the achievements of Protestantism in the practical and moral sphere; nor that, even in the intellectual sphere, Protestantism, though in a blind and stumbling manner, carried forward the Renascence, while Catholicism threw itself violently across its path.

I lately heard a man of thought and energy contrasting the want of ardour and movement which he now found amongst young men in this country with what he remembered in his own youth, twenty years ago. "What reformers we were then!" he exclaimed; "what a zeal we had! how we canvassed every institution in Church and State, and were prepared to remodel them all on first principles!" He was inclined to regret, as a spiritual flagging, the lull which he saw. I am disposed rather to regard it as a pause in which the turn to a new mode of spiritual progress is being accomplished. Everything was long seen, by the young and ardent amongst us, in inseparable connection with politics and practical life. We have pretty well exhausted the benefits of seeing things in this connection, we have got all that can be got by so seeing them. Let us try a more disinterested mode of seeing them; let us betake ourselves more to the serener life of the mind and spirit. This life, too, may have its excesses and dangers; but they are not for us at present. Let us think of quietly enlarging our stock of true and fresh ideas, and not, as soon as we get an idea or half an idea, be running out with it into the street, and trying to make it rule there. Our ideas will, in the end, shape the world all the better for maturing a little. Perhaps in fifty years' time it will in the English House of Commons be an objection to an institution that it is an anomaly, and my friend the Member of Parliament will shudder in his grave. But let us in the meanwhile rather endeavour that in twenty years' time it may, in English literature, be an objection to a proposition that it is absurd. That will be a change so vast, that the imagination almost fails to grasp it. *Ab integro sœclorum nascitur ordo* [The succession of centuries rises anew].

If I have insisted so much on the course which criticism must take where politics and religion are concerned, it is because, where these burning matters are in question, it is most likely to go astray. I have wished, above all, to insist on the attitude which criticism should adopt towards things in general; on its right tone and temper of mind. But then comes another question as to the subject-matter which literary criticism should most seek. Here, in general, its course is determined for it by the idea which is the law of its being; the idea of a disinterested endeavour to learn and propagate the best that is known and thought in the world, and thus to establish a current of fresh and true ideas. By the very nature of things, as England is not all the world, much of the best that is known and thought in the world cannot be of English growth, must be foreign; by the nature of things, again, it is just this that we are least likely to know, while English thought is streaming in upon us from all sides, and takes excellent care that we shall not be ignorant of its existence. The English critic of literature, therefore, must dwell much on foreign thought, and with particular heed on any part of it, which, while significant and fruitful in itself, is for any reason specially likely to escape him. Again, judging is often spoken of as the critic's one business, and so in some sense it is; but the judgment which almost insensibly forms itself in a fair and clear mind, along with fresh knowledge, is the valuable one; and thus knowledge, and ever fresh knowledge, must be the critic's great concern for himself. And it is by communicating fresh knowledge, and letting his own judgment pass along with it,—but insensibly, and in the second place, not the first, as a sort of companion and clue, not as an abstract lawgiver,—that the critic will generally do most good to his readers. Sometimes, no doubt, for the sake of establishing an author's place in literature, and his relation to a central standard (and if this is not done, how are we to get at our *best in the world?*) criticism may have to deal with a subject-matter so familiar that fresh knowledge is out of the question, and then it must be all judgment; an enunciation and detailed application of principles. Here the great safeguard is never to let oneself become abstract, always to retain an intimate and lively consciousness of the truth of what one is saying, and, the moment this fails us, to be sure that something is wrong. Still, under all circumstances, this mere judgment and application of principles is, in itself, not the most satisfactory work to the critic; like mathematics, it is tautological, and cannot well give us, like fresh learning, the sense of creative activity.

But stop, some one will say; all this talk is of no practical use to us whatever; this criticism of yours is not what we have in our minds when we speak of criticism; when we speak of critics and criticism, we mean critics and criticism of the current English literature of the day; when you offer to tell criticism its function, it is to this criticism that we expect you to address yourself. I am sorry for it, for I am afraid I must disappoint these expectations. I am bound by my own definition of criticism: *a disinterested endeavour to learn and propagate the best that is known and thought in the world.* How much of current English literature comes into this "best that is known and thought in the world?" Not very much, I fear; certainly less, at this moment, than of the current literature of France or Germany. Well, then, am I to alter my definition of criticism, in order to meet the requirements of a number of practising English critics, who, after all, are free in their choice of a business? That would be making criticism lend itself just to one of those alien practical considerations, which, I have said, are so fatal to it. One may say, indeed, to those who have to deal with the mass—so much better disregarded—of current English literature, that they may at all events endeavour, in dealing with this, to try it, so far as they can, by the standard of the best that is known and thought in the world; one may say, that to get anywhere near this standard, every critic should try and possess one great literature, at least, besides his own; and the more unlike his own, the better. But, after all, the criticism I am really concerned with,—the criticism which alone can much help us for the future, the criticism which, throughout Europe, is at the present day meant, when so much stress is laid on the importance of criticism and the critical spirit,—is a criticism which regards Europe as being, for intellectual and spiritual purposes, one great confederation, bound to a joint action and working to a common result; and whose members have, for their proper outfit, a knowledge of Greek, Roman, and Eastern antiquity, and of one another. Special, local, and temporary advantages being put out of account, that modern nation will in the intellectual and spiritual sphere make most progress, which most thoroughly carries out this programme. And what is that but saying that we too, all of us, as individuals, the more thoroughly we carry it out, shall make the more progress?

There is so much inviting us!—what are we to take? what will nourish us in growth towards perfection? That is the question which, with the immense field of life and of literature lying before him, the critic has to answer; for himself first, and afterwards for others. In this idea of the critic's business the essays brought together in the following pages have had their origin; in this idea, widely different as are their subjects, they have, perhaps, their unity.

I conclude with what I said at the beginning: to have the sense of creative activity is the great happiness and the great proof of being alive, and it is not denied to criticism to have it; but then criticism must be sincere, simple, flexible, ardent, ever widening its knowledge. Then it may have, in no contemptible measure, a joyful sense of creative activity; a sense which a man of insight and conscience will prefer to what he might derive from a poor, starved, fragmentary, inadequate creation. And at some epochs no other creation is possible.

Still, in full measure, the sense of creative activity belongs only to genuine creation; in literature we must never forget that. But what true man of letters ever can forget it? It is no such common matter for a gifted nature to come into possession of a current of true and living ideas, and to produce amidst the inspiration of them, that we are likely to underrate it. The epochs of Æschylus and Shakspeare make us feel their preeminence. In an epoch like those is, no doubt, the true life of literature; there is the promised land, towards which criticism can only beckon. That promised land it will not be ours to enter, and we shall die in the wilderness: but to have desired to enter it, to have saluted it from afar, is already, perhaps, the best distinction among contemporaries; it will certainly be the best title to esteem with posterity.

Ralph Waldo Emerson 1803–1882

Ralph Waldo Emerson stands at the center of much theorizing about America and American thought. According to Harold Bloom, "from [Emerson's] moment to ours, American authors either are in his tradition, or else in a countertradition originating in opposition to him." Those in Emerson's tradition are Thoreau, Whitman, Frost, and Stevens; furthermore, his pragmatism emerges in the work of William James, Charles Sanders Peirce, and John Dewey. Emerson's vision of the self can be seen in his essays, "The American Scholar" (1837), "Self-Reliance" (1841), and "Experience" (1844). His first major work was *Nature* (1836), followed by *Essays: First Series* (1841), *Essays: Second Series*

(1844), and *The Conduct of Life* (1860). He also published two collections of poetry: *Poems* (1846) and *Mayday and Other Poems* (1867). Poems such as "Concord Hymn" (1837), "The Humble-Bee" (1839), and "Merlin" (1847) are representative of his considerable stature as a poet.

Emerson graduated from Harvard in 1821, was ordained as a Unitarian minister, and served at Second Church, Boston, from 1829 to 1832. He resigned after a conflict with the church because he refused to serve the Lord's Supper. He lectured extensively from 1835 to 1843, providing material for many of his published essays. He founded a journal, *The Dial*, in 1840 to serve the emerging Transcendentalist movement.

Given as the Phi Beta Kappa address at Harvard in 1837, "The American Scholar" defined the essence of the self struggling to embody all creation. Emerson emphasized unity of experience in contrast to Old World schemes of classification. His prophetic call for "the sluggard intellectual of this continent [to] look from under its iron lids" made a deep impression on the audience. Oliver Wendell Holmes, for example, claimed "The American Scholar" to be America's "intellectual Declaration of Independence." The challenge Emerson posed was incredible: the American Scholar should unify the experience of all Americans within himself. In this democratic variant of Platonism and romanticism, Emerson mapped out the mythic territory of America, where the individual self represents America's landscape, people, and culture.

The American Scholar

An Oration Delivered Before the Phi Beta Kappa Society, at Cambridge, August 31, 1837

Mr. President and Gentlemen,

I greet you on the re-commencement of our literary year. Our anniversary is one of hope, and, perhaps, not enough of labor. We do not meet for games of strength or skill, for the recitation of histories, tragedies, and odes, like the ancient Greeks; for parliaments of love and poesy, like the Troubadours; nor for the advancement of science, like our contemporaries in the British and European capitals. Thus far, our holiday has been simply a friendly sign of the survival of the love of letters amongst a people too busy to give to letters any more. As such, it is precious as the sign of an indestructible instinct. Perhaps the time is already come, when it ought to be, and will be something else; when the sluggard intellect of this continent will look from under its iron lids, and fill the postponed expectation of the world with something better than the exertions of mechanical skill. Our day of dependence, our long apprenticeship to the learning of other lands, draws to a close. The millions, that around us are rushing into life, cannot always be fed on the sere remains of foreign harvests.

Events, actions arise, that must be sung, that will sing themselves. Who can doubt, that poetry will revive and lead in a new age, as the star in the constellation Harp, which now flames in our zenith, astronomers announce, shall one day be the pole-star for a thousand years?

In this hope, I accept the topic which not only usage, but the nature of our association, seem to prescribe to this day,—the AMERICAN SCHOLAR. Year by year, we come up hither to read one more chapter of his biography. Let us inquire what light new days and events have thrown on his character, and his hopes.

It is one of those fables, which, out of an unknown antiquity, convey an unlooked-for wisdom, that the gods, in the beginning, divided Man into men, that he might be more helpful to himself; just as the hand was divided into fingers, the better to answer its end.

The old fable covers a doctrine ever new and sublime; that there is One Man,—present to all particular men only partially, or through one faculty; and that you must take the whole society to find the whole man. Man is not a farmer, or professor, or an engineer, but he is all. Man is priest, and scholar, and statesman, and producer, and soldier. In the *divided* or social state, these functions are parcelled out to individuals, each of whom aims to do his stint of the joint work, whilst each other performs his. The fable implies, that the individual, to possess himself, must sometimes return from his own labor to embrace all the other laborers. But unfortunately, this original unit, this fountain of power, has been so distributed to multitudes, has been so minutely subdivided and peddled out, that it is spilled into drops, and cannot be gathered. The state of society is one in which the members have suffered amputation from the trunk, and strut about so many walking monsters,—a good finger, a neck, a stomach, an elbow, but never a man.

Man is thus metamorphosed into a thing, into many things. The planter, who is Man sent out into the field to gather food, is seldom cheered by any idea of the true dignity of his ministry. He sees his bushel and his cart, and nothing beyond, and sinks into the farmer, instead of Man on the farm. The tradesman scarcely ever gives an ideal worth to his work, but is ridden by the routine of his craft, and the soul is subject to dollars. The priest becomes a form; the attorney, a statute-book; the mechanic, a machine; the sailor, a rope of a ship.

In this distribution of functions, the scholar is the delegated intellect. In the right state, he is *Man Thinking*. In the degenerate state, when the victim of society, he tends to become a mere thinker, or, still worse, the parrot of other men's thinking.

In this view of him, as Man Thinking, the theory of his office is contained. Him nature solicits with all her placid, all her monitory pictures; him the past instructs; him the future invites. Is not, indeed, every man a student, and do not all things exist for the student's behoof? And, finally, is not the true scholar the only true master? But the old oracle said, "All things have two handles: beware of the wrong one." In life, too often, the scholar errs with mankind and forfeits his privilege. Let us see him in his school, and consider him in reference to the main influences he receives.

I

The first in time and first in importance of the influences upon the mind is that of nature. Every day, the sun; and, after sunset, night and her stars. Ever the winds blow; ever the grass grows. Every day, men and women, conversing, beholding and beholden. The scholar is he of all men whom this spectacle most engages. He must settle its value in his mind. What is nature to him? There is never a beginning, there is never an end, to the inexplicable continuity of this web of God, but always circular power returning into itself. Therein it resembles his own spirit, whose beginning, whose ending, he never can find,—so entire, so boundless. Far, too, as her splendors shine, system on system shooting like rays, upward, downward, without centre, without circumference,—in the mass and in the particle, nature hastens to render account of herself to the mind. Classification begins. To the young mind, every thing in individuals, stands by itself. By and by, it finds how to join two things, and see in them one nature; then three, then three thousand; and so, tyrannized over by its own unifying instinct, it goes on tying things together, diminishing anomalies, discovering roots running under ground, whereby contrary and remote things cohere, and flower out from one stem. It presently learns, that, since the dawn of history, there has been a constant accumulation and classifying of facts. But what is classification but the perceiving that these objects are not chaotic, and are not foreign, but have a law which is also a law of the human mind? The astronomer discovers that geometry, a pure abstraction of the human mind, is the measure of planetary motion. The chemist finds proportions and intelligible method throughout matter; and science is nothing but the finding of analogy, identity, in the most remote parts. The ambitious soul sits down before each refractory fact; one after another, reduces all strange constitutions, all new powers, to their class and their law, and goes on for ever to animate the last fibre of organization, the outskirts of nature, by insight.

Thus to him, to this school-boy under the bending dome of day, is suggested, that he and it proceed from one root; one is leaf and one is flower; relation, sympathy, stirring in every vein. And what is that Root? Is not that the soul of his soul?—A thought too bold,—a dream too wild. Yet when this spiritual light shall have revealed the law of more earthly natures,—when he has learned to worship the soul, and to see that the natural philosophy that now is, is only the first gropings of its gigantic hand, he shall look forward to an ever expanding knowledge as to a becoming creator. He shall see, that nature is the opposite of the soul, answering to it part for part. One is seal, and one is print. Its beauty is the beauty of his own mind. Its laws are the laws of his own mind. Nature then becomes to him the measure of his attainments. So much of nature as he is ignorant of, so much of his own mind does he not yet possess. And, in fine, the ancient precept, "Know thyself," and the modern precept, "Study nature," become at last the one maxim.

II

The next great influence into the spirit of the scholar, is, the mind of the Past,—in whatever form, whether of literature, of art, of institutions, that mind is inscribed. Books are the best type of the influence of the past, and perhaps we shall get at the truth,—learn the amount of this influence more conveniently,—by considering their value alone.

The theory of books is noble. The scholar of the first age received into him the world around; brooded thereon; gave it the new arrangement of his own mind, and uttered it again. It came into him, life; it went out from him, truth. It came to him, short-lived actions; it went out from him, immortal thoughts. It came to him, business; it went from him, poetry. It was dead fact; now, it is quick thought. It can stand, and it can go. It now endures, it now flies, it now inspires. Precisely in proportion to the depth of mind from which it issued, so high does it soar, so long does it sing.

Or, I might say, it depends on how far the process had gone, of transmuting life into truth. In proportion to the completeness of the distillation, so will the purity and imperishableness of the product be. But none is quite perfect. As no air-pump can by any means make a perfect vacuum, so neither can any artist entirely exclude the conventional, the local, the perishable from his book, or write a book of pure thought, that shall be as efficient, in all respects, to a remote posterity, as to contemporaries, or rather to the second age. Each age, it is found, must write its own books; or rather, each generation for the next succeeding. The books of an older period will not fit this.

Yet hence arises a grave mischief. The sacredness which attaches to the act of creation,—the act of thought,—is transferred to the record. The poet chanting, was felt to be a divine man: henceforth the chant is divine also. The writer was a just and wise spirit: henceforward it is settled, the book is perfect; as love of the hero corrupts into worship of his statue. Instantly, the book becomes noxious: the guide is a tyrant. The sluggish and perverted mind of the multitude, slow to open to the incursions of Reason, having once so opened, having once received this book, stands upon it, and makes an outcry, if it is disparaged. Colleges are built on it. Books are written on it by thinkers, not by Man Thinking; by men of talent, that is, who start wrong, who set out from accepted dogmas, not from their own sight of principles. Meek young men grow up in libraries, believing it their duty to accept the views, which Cicero, which Locke, which Bacon, have given, forgetful that Cicero, Locke and Bacon were only young men in libraries, when they wrote these books.

Hence, instead of Man Thinking, we have the bookworm. Hence, the book-learned class, who value books, as such; not as related to nature and the human constitution, but as making a sort of Third Estate with the world and the soul. Hence, the restorers of readings, the emendators, the bibliomaniacs of all degrees.

Books are the best of things, well used; abused, among the worst. What is the right use? What is the one end, which all means go to effect? They are for nothing but to inspire. I had better never see a book, than to be warped by its attraction clean out of my own orbit, and made a satellite instead of a system. The one thing in the world, of value, is the active soul. This every man is entitled to; this every man contains within him, although, in almost all men, obstructed, and as yet unborn. The soul active sees absolute truth; and utters truth, or creates. In this action, it is genius; not the privilege of here and there a favorite, but the sound estate of every man. In its essence, it is progressive. The book, the college, the school of art, the institution of any kind, stop with some past utterance of genius. This is good, say they,—let us hold by this. They pin me down. They look backward and not forward. But genius looks forward: the eyes of man are set in his forehead: not in his hindhead: man hopes: genius creates. Whatever talents may be, if the man create not, the pure efflux of the Deity is not his;—cinders and smoke there may be, but not yet flame. There are creative manners, there are creative actions, and creative words; manners, actions, words, that is, indicative of no custom or authority, but springing spontaneous from the mind's own sense of good and fair.

On the other part, instead of being its own seer, let it receive from another mind its truth, though it were in torrents of light, without periods of solitude, inquest, and self-recovery, and a fatal disservice is done. Genius is always sufficiently the enemy of genius by over influence. The literature of every nation bear me witness. The English dramatic poets have Shakspearized now for two hundred years.

Undoubtedly there is a right way of reading, so it be sternly subordinated. Man Thinking must not be subdued by his instruments. Books are for the scholar's idle times. When he can read God directly, the hour is too precious to be wasted in other men's transcripts of their readings. But when the intervals of darkness come, as come they must, when the sun is hid, and the stars withdraw their shining,—we repair to the lamps which were kindled by their ray, to guide our steps to the East again, where the dawn is. We hear, that we may speak. The Arabian proverb says, "A fig tree, looking on a fig tree, becometh fruitful."

It is remarkable, the character of the pleasure we derive from the best books. They impress us with the conviction, that one nature wrote and the same reads. We read the verses of one of the great English poets, of Chaucer, of Marvell, of Dryden, with the most modern joy,—with a pleasure, I mean, which is in great part caused by the abstraction of all *time* from their verses. There is some awe mixed with the joy of our surprise, when this poet, who lived in some past world, two or three hundred years ago, says that which lies close to my own soul, that which I also had wellnigh thought and said. But for the evidence thence afforded to the philosophical doctrine of the identity of all minds, we should suppose some preëstablished harmony, some foresight of souls that were to be, and some preparation of stores for their future wants, like the fact observed in insects, who lay up food before death for the young grub they shall never see.

I would not be hurried by any love of system, by any exaggeration of instincts, to underrate the Book. We all know, that, as the human body can be nourished on any food, though it were boiled grass and the broth of shoes, so the human mind can be fed by any knowledge. And great and heroic men have existed, who had almost no other information than by the printed page. I only would say, that it needs a strong head to bear that diet. One must be an inventor to read well. As the proverb says, "He that would bring home the wealth of the Indies, must carry out the wealth of the Indies." There is then creative reading as well as creative writing. When the mind is braced by labor and invention, the page of whatever book we read becomes luminous with manifold allusion. Every sentence is doubly significant, and the sense of our author is as broad as the world. We then see, what is always true, that, as the seer's hour of vision is short and rare among heavy days and months, so is its record, perchance, the least part of his volume. The discerning will read, in his Plato or Shakspeare, only that least part,—only the authentic utterances of the oracle;—all the rest he rejects, were it never so many times Plato's and Shakspeare's.

Of course, there is a portion of reading quite indispensable to a wise man. History and exact science he must learn by laborious reading. Colleges, in like manner, have their indispensable office,—to teach elements. But they can only highly serve us, when they aim not to drill, but to create; when they gather from far every ray of various genius to their hospitable halls, and, by the concentrated fires, set the hearts of their youth on flame, Thought and knowledge are natures in which apparatus and pretension avail nothing. Gowns, and pecuniary foundations, though of towns of gold, can never countervail the least sentence or syllable of wit. Forget this, and our American colleges will recede in their public importance, whilst they grow rich every year.

III

There goes in the world a notion, that the scholar should be a recluse, a valetudinarian,—as unfit for any handiwork or public labor, as a penknife for an axe. The so-called "practical men" sneer at speculative men, as if, because they speculate or *see*, they could do nothing. I have heard it said that the clergy,—who are always, more universally than any other class, the scholars of their day,—are addressed as women; that the rough, spontaneous conversation of men they do not hear, but only a mincing and diluted speech. They are often virtually disfranchised; and, indeed, there are advocates for their celibacy. As far as this is true of the studious classes, it is not just and wise. Action is with the scholar subordinate, but it is essential. Without it, he is not yet man. Without it, thought can never ripen into truth. Whilst the world hangs before the eye as a cloud of beauty, we cannot even see its beauty. Inaction is cowardice, but there can be no scholar without the heroic mind. The preamble of thought, the transition through which it passes from the unconscious to the conscious, is action. Only so much do I know, as I have lived. Instantly we know whose words are loaded with life, and whose not.

The world,—this shadow of the soul, or *other me*, lies wide around. Its attractions are the keys which unlock my thoughts and make me acquainted with myself. I run eagerly into this resounding tumult. I grasp the hands of those next me, and take my place in the ring to suffer and to work, taught by an instinct, that so shall the dumb abyss be vocal with speech. I pierce its order; I dissipate its fear; I dispose of it within the circuit of my expanding life. So much only of life as I know by experience, so much of the wilderness have I vanquished and planted, or so far have I extended my being, my dominion. I do not see how any man can afford, for the sake of his nerves and his nap, to spare any action in which he can partake. It is pearls and rubies to his discourse. Drudgery, calamity, exasperation, want, are instructors in eloquence and wisdom. The true scholar grudges every opportunity of action past by, as a loss of power.

It is the raw material out of which the intellect moulds her splendid products. A strange process too, this, by which experience is converted into thought, as a mulberry leaf is converted into satin. The manufacture goes forward at all hours.

The actions and events of our childhood and youth, are now matters of calmest observation. They lie like fair pictures in the air. Not so with our recent actions,—with the business which we now have in hand. On this we are quite unable to speculate. Our affections as yet circulate through it. We no more feel or know it, than we feel the feet, or the hand, or the brain of our body. The new deed is yet a part of life,—remains for a time immersed in our unconscious life. In some contemplative hour, it detaches itself from the life like a ripe fruit, to become a thought of the mind. Instantly, it is raised, transfigured; the corruptible has put on incorruption. Henceforth it is an object of beauty, however base its origin and neighborhood. Observe, too, the impossibility of antedating this act. In its grub state, it cannot fly, it cannot shine, it is a dull grub. But suddenly, without observation, the selfsame thing unfurls beautiful wings, and is an angel of wisdom. So is there no fact, no event in our private history, which shall not, sooner or later, lose its adhesive, inert form, and astonish us by soaring from our body into the empyrean. Cradle and infancy, school and playground, the fear of boys, and dogs, and ferules, the love of little maids and berries, and many another fact that once filled the whole sky, are gone already; friend and relative, profession and party, town and country, nation and world, must also soar and sing.

Of course, he who has put forth his total strength in fit actions, has the richest return of wisdom. I will not shut myself out of this globe of action, and transplant an oak into a flower-pot, there to hunger and pine; nor trust the revenue of some single faculty, and exhaust one vein of thought, much like those Savoyards, who, getting their livelihood by carving shepherds, shepherdesses, and smoking Dutchmen, for all Europe, went out one day to the mountain to find stock, and discovered that they had whittled up the last of their pine-trees. Authors we have, in numbers, who have written out their vein, and who, moved by a commendable prudence, sail for Greece or Palestine, follow the trapper into the prairie, or ramble round Algiers, to replenish their merchantable stock.

If it were only for a vocabulary, the scholar would be covetous of action. Life is our dictionary. Years are well spent in country labors; in town,—in the insight into trades and manufactures; in frank intercourse with many men and women; in science; in art; to the one end of mastering in all their facts a language by which to illustrate and embody our perceptions. I learn immediately from any speaker how much he has already lived, through the poverty or the splendor of his speech. Life lies behind us as the quarry from whence we get tiles and copestones for the masonry of to-day. This is the way to learn grammar. Colleges and books only copy the language which the field and the workyard made.

But the final value of action, like that of books, and better than books, is, that it is a resource. That great principle of Undulation in nature, that shows itself in the inspiring and expiring of the breath; in desire and satiety; in the ebb and flow of the sea; in day and night; in heat and cold; and as yet more deeply ingrained in every atom and every fluid, is known to us under the name of Polarity,—these "fits of easy transmission and reflection," as Newton called them, are the law of nature because they are the law of spirit.

The mind now thinks; now acts; and each fit reproduces the other. When the artist has exhausted his materials, when the fancy no longer paints, when thoughts are no longer apprehended, and books are a weariness,—he has always the resource *to live.* Character is higher than intellect. Thinking is the function. Living is the functionary. The stream retreats to its source. A great soul will be strong to live, as well as strong to think. Does he lack organ or medium to impart his truths? He can still fall back on this elemental force of living them. This is a total act. Thinking is a partial act. Let the grandeur of justice shine in his affairs. Let the beauty of affection cheer his lowly roof. Those "far from fame," who dwell and act with him, will feel the force of his constitution in the doings and passages of the day better than it can be measured by any public and designed display. Time shall teach him, that the scholar loses no hour which the man lives. Herein he unfolds the sacred germ of his instinct, screened from influence. What is lost in seemliness is gained in strength. Not out of those, on whom systems of education have exhausted their culture, comes the helpful giant to destroy the old or to build the new, but out of unhandselled savage nature, out of terrible Druids and berserkirs, come at last Alfred and Shakspeare.

I hear therefore with joy whatever is beginning to be said of the dignity and necessity of labor to every citizen. There is virtue yet in the hoe and the spade, for learned as well as for unlearned hands. And labor is everywhere welcome; always we are invited to work; only be this limitation observed, that a man shall not for the sake of wider activity sacrifice any opinion to the popular judgments and modes of action.

I have now spoken of the education of the scholar by nature, by books, and by action. It remains to say somewhat of his duties.

They are such as become Man Thinking. They may all be comprised in self-trust. The office of the scholar is to cheer, to raise, and to guide men by showing them facts amidst appearances. He plies the slow, unhonored, and unpaid task of observation. Flamsteed and Herschel, in their glazed observatories, may catalogue the stars with the praise of all men, and, the results being splendid and useful, honor is sure. But he, in his private observatory, cataloguing obscure and nebulous stars of the human mind, which as yet no man has thought of as such,—watching days and months, sometimes, for a few facts; correcting still his old records;—must relinquish display and immediate fame. In the long period of his preparation, he must betray often an ignorance and shiftlessness in popular arts, incurring the disdain of the able who shoulder him aside. Long he must stammer in his speech; often forego the living for the dead. Worse yet, he must accept,—how often! poverty and solitude. For the ease and pleasure of treading the old road, accepting the fashions, the education, the religion of society, he takes the cross of making his own, and of course, the self-accusation, the faint heart, the frequent uncertainty and loss of time, which are the nettles and tangling vines in the way of the self-relying and self-directed; and the state of virtual hostility in which he seems to stand to society, and especially to educated society. For all this loss and scorn, what offset? He is to find consolation in exercising the highest functions of human nature. He is one, who raises himself from private considerations, and breathes and lives on public and illustrious thoughts. He is the world's eye. He is the world's heart. He is to resist the vulgar prosperity that retrogrades ever to barbarism, by preserving and communicating heroic sentiments, noble biographies, melodious verse, and the conclusions of history. Whatsoever oracles the human heart, in all emergencies, in all solemn hours, has uttered as its commentary on the world of actions,—these he shall receive and impart. And whatsoever new verdict Reason from her inviolable seat pronounces on the passing men and events of to-day—this he shall hear and promulgate.

These being his functions, it becomes him to feel all confidence in himself, and to defer never to the popular cry. He and he only knows the world. The world of any moment is the merest appearance. Some great decorum, some fetish of a government, some ephemeral trade, or war, or man, is cried up by half mankind and cried down by the other half, as if all depended on this particular up or down. The odds are that the whole question is not worth the poorest thought which the scholar has lost in listening to the controversy. Let him not quit his belief that a popgun is a popgun, though the ancient and honorable of the earth affirm it to be the crack of doom. In silence, in steadiness, in severe abstraction, let him hold by himself; add observation to observation, patient of neglect, patient of reproach; and bide his own time,—happy enough, if he can satisfy himself alone, that this day he has seen something truly. Success treads on every right step. For the instinct is sure, that prompts him to tell his brother what he thinks. He then learns, that in going down into the secrets of his own mind, he has descended into the secrets of all minds. He learns that he who has mastered any law in his private thoughts, is master to that extent of all men whose language he speaks, and of all into whose language his own can be translated. The poet, in utter solitude remembering his spontaneous thoughts and recording them, is found to have recorded that, which men in crowded cities find true for them also. The orator distrusts at first the fitness of his frank confessions,—his want of knowledge of the persons he addresses,—until he finds that he is the complement of his hearers;—that they drink his words because he fulfils for them their own nature; the deeper he dives into his privatest, secretest presentiment, to his wonder he finds, this is the most acceptable, most public, and universally true. The people delight in it; the better part of every man feels, This is my music; this is myself.

In self-trust, all the virtues are comprehended. Free should the scholar be,—free and brave. Free even to the definition of freedom, "without any hindrance that does not arise out of his own constitution." Brave; for fear is a thing, which a scholar by his very function puts behind him. Fear always springs from ignorance. It is a shame to him if his tranquillity, amid dangerous times, arise from the presumption, that, like children and women, his is a protected class; or if he seek a temporary peace by the diversion of his thoughts from politics or vexed questions, hiding his head like an ostrich in the flowering bushes, peeping into microscopes, and turning rhymes, as a boy whistles to keep his courage up. So is the danger a danger still; so is the fear worse. Manlike let him turn and face it. Let him look into its eye and search its nature, inspect its origin,—see the whelping of this lion, which lies no great way back; he will then find in himself a perfect comprehension of its nature and extent; he will have made his hands meet on the other side, and can henceforth defy it, and pass on superior. The world is his, who can see through its pretension. What deafness, what stone-blind custom, what overgrown error you behold, is there only by sufferance,—by your sufferance. See it to be a lie, and you have already dealt it its mortal blow.

Yes, we are the cowed,—we the trustless. It is a mischievous notion that we are come late into nature; that the world was finished a long time ago. As the world was plastic and fluid in the hands of God, so it is ever to so much of his attributes as we bring to it. To ignorance and sin, it is flint. They adapt themselves to it as they may; but in proportion as a man has any thing in him divine, the firmament flows before him and takes his signet and form. Not he is great who can alter matter, but he who can alter my state of mind. They are the kings of the world who give the color of their present thought to all nature and all art, and persuade men by the cheerful serenity of their carrying the matter, that this thing which they do, is the apple which the ages have desired to pluck, now at last ripe, and inviting nations to the harvest. The great man makes the great thing. Wherever Macdonald sits, there is the head of the table. Linnæus makes botany the most alluring of studies, and wins it from the farmer and the herd-woman; Davy, chemistry; and Cuvier, fossils. The day is always his, who works in it with serenity and great aims. The unstable estimates of men crowd to him whose mind is filled with a truth, as the heaped waves of the Atlantic follow the moon.

For this self-trust, the reason is deeper than

can be fathomed,—darker than can be enlightened. I might not carry with me the feeling of my audience in stating my own belief. But I have already shown the ground of my hope, in adverting to the doctrine that man is one. I believe man has been wronged; he has wronged himself. He has almost lost the light, that can lead him back to his prerogatives. Men are become of no account. Men in history, men in the world of to-day are bugs, are spawn, and are called "the mass" and "the herd." In a century, in a millennium, one or two men; that is to say,—one or two approximations to the right state of every man. All the rest behold in the hero or the poet their own green and crude being,—ripened, yes, and are content to be less, so *that* may attain to its full stature. What a testimony,—full of grandeur, full of pity, is borne to the demands of his own nature, by the poor clansman, the poor partisan, who rejoices in the glory of his chief. The poor and the low find some amends to their immense moral capacity, for their acquiescence in a political and social inferiority. They are content to be brushed like flies from the path of a great person, so that justice shall be done by him to that common nature which it is the dearest desire of all to see enlarged and glorified. They sun themselves in the great man's light, and feel it to be their own element. They cast the dignity of man from their downtrod selves upon the shoulders of a hero, and will perish to add one drop of blood to make that great heart beat, those giant sinews combat and conquer. He lives for us, and we live in him.

Men such as they are, very naturally seek money or power; and power because it is as good as money,—the "spoils," so called, "of office." And why not? for they aspire to the highest, and this, in their sleep-walking, they dream is highest. Wake them, and they shall quit the false good, and leap to the true, and leave governments to clerks and desks. This revolution is to be wrought by the gradual domestication of the idea of Culture. The main enterprise of the world for splendor, for extent, is the upbuilding of a man. Here are the materials strown along the ground. The private life of one man shall be a more illustrious monarchy,—more formidable to its enemy, more sweet and serene in its influence to its friend, than any kingdom in history. For a man, rightly viewed, comprehendeth the particular natures, of all men. Each philosopher, each bard, each actor, has only done for me, as by a delegate, what one day I can do for myself. The books which once we valued more than the apple of the eye, we have quite exhausted. What is that but saying, that we have come up with the point of view which the universal mind took through the eyes of one scribe; we have been that man, and have passed on. First, one; then, another; we drain all cisterns, and waxing greater by all these supplies, we crave a better and more abundant food. The man has never lived that can feed us ever. The human mind cannot be enshrined in a person, who shall set a barrier on any one side to this unbounded, unboundable empire. It is one central fire, which, flaming now out of the lips of Etna, lightens the capes of Sicily; and, now out of the throat of Vesuvius, illuminates the towers and vineyards of Naples. It is one light which beams out of a thousand stars. It is one soul which animates all men.

But I have dwelt perhaps tediously upon this abstraction of the Scholar. I ought not to delay longer to add what I have to say, of nearer reference to the time and to this country.

Historically, there is thought to be a difference in the ideas which predominate over successive epochs, and there are data for marking the genius of the Classic, of the Romantic, and now of the Reflective or Philosophical age. With the views I have intimated of the oneness or the identity of the mind through all individuals, I do not much dwell on these differences. In fact, I believe each individual passes through all three. The boy is a Greek; the youth, romantic; the adult, reflective. I deny not, however, that a revolution in the leading idea may be distinctly enough traced.

Our age is bewailed as the age of Introversion. Must that needs be evil? We, it seems, are critical; we are embarrassed with second thoughts; we cannot enjoy anything for hankering to know whereof the pleasure consists; we are lined with eyes; we see with our feet; the time is infected with Hamlet's unhappiness,—

> Sicklied o'er with the pale cast of thought.

Is it so bad then? Sight is the last thing to be pitied. Would we be blind? Do we fear lest we should outsee nature and God, and drink truth dry? I look upon the discontent of the literary class, as a mere announcement of the fact, that they find themselves not in the state of mind of their fathers, and regret the coming state as untried; as a boy dreads the water before he has learned that he can swim. If there is any period one would desire to be born in,—is it not the age of Revolution; when the old and the new stand side by side, and admit of being compared; when the energies of all men are searched by fear and by hope; when the historic glories of the old can be compensated by the rich possibilities of the new era? This time, like all times, is a very good one, if we but know what to do with it.

I read with joy some of the auspicious signs of the coming days, as they glimmer already through poetry and art, through philosophy and science, through church and state.

One of these signs is the fact, that the same movement which effected the elevation of what was called the lowest class in the state, assumed in literature a very marked and as benign an aspect. Instead of the sublime and beautiful; the near, the low, the common, was explored and poetized. That, which had been negligently trodden under foot by those who were harnessing and provisioning themselves for long journeys into far countries, is suddenly found to be richer than all foreign parts. The literature of the poor, the feelings of the child, the philosophy of the street, the meaning of household life, are the topics of the time. It is a great stride. It is a sign—is it not? of new vigor, when the extremities are made active, when currents of warm life run into the hands and the feet. I ask not for the great, the remote, the romantic; what is doing in Italy or Arabia; what is Greek art, or Provençal minstrelsy; I embrace the common, I explore and sit at the feet of the familiar, the low. Give me insight into today, and you may have the antique and future worlds. What would we really know the meaning of? The meal in the firkin; the milk in the pan; the ballad in the street; the news of the boat; the glance of the eye; the form and the gait of the body;—show me the ultimate reason of these matters; show me the sublime presence of the highest spiritual cause lurking, as always it does lurk, in these suburbs and extremities of nature; let me see every trifle bristling with the polarity that ranges it instantly on an eternal law; and the shop, the plough, and the ledger, referred to the like cause by which light undulates and poets sing;—and the world lies no longer a dull miscellany and lumber-room, but has form and order; there is no trifle; there is no puzzle; but one design unites and animates the farthest pinnacle and the lowest trench.

This idea has inspired the genius of Goldsmith, Burns, Cowper, and, in a newer time, of Goethe, Wordsworth, and Carlyle. This idea they have differently followed and with various success. In contrast with their writing, the style of Pope, of Johnson, of Gibbon, looks cold and pedantic. This writing is blood-warm. Man is surprised to find that things near are not less beautiful and wondrous than things remote. The near explains the far. The drop is a small ocean. A man is related to all nature. This perception of the worth of the vulgar is fruitful in discoveries. Goethe, in this very thing the most modern of the moderns, has shown us, as none ever did, the genius of the ancients.

There is one man of genius, who has done much for this philosophy of life, whose literary value has never yet been rightly estimated;—I mean Emanuel Swedenborg. The most imaginative of men, yet writing with the precision of a mathematician, he endeavored to engraft a purely philosophical Ethics on the popular Christianity of his time. Such an attempt, of course, must have difficulty, which no genius could surmount. But he saw and showed the connection between nature and the affections of the soul. He pierced the emblematic or spiritual character of the visible, audible, tangible world. Especially did his shade-loving muse hover over and interpret the lower parts of nature; he showed the mysterious bond that allies moral evil to the foul material forms, and has given in epical parables a theory of insanity, of beasts, of unclean and fearful things.

Another sign of our times, also marked by an analogous political movement, is, the new importance given to the single person. Everything that tends to insulate the individual,—to surround him with barriers of natural respect, so that each man shall feel the world is his, and man shall treat with man as a sovereign state with a sovereign state,—tends to true union as well as greatness. "I learned," said the melancholy Pestalozzi, "that no man in God's wide earth is either willing or able to help any other man." Help must come from the bosom alone. The scholar is that man who must take up into himself all the ability of the time, all the contributions of the past, all the hopes of the future. He must be an university of knowledges. If there be one lesson more than another, which should pierce his ear, it is, The world is nothing, the man is all; in yourself is the law of all nature, and you know not yet how a globule of sap ascends; in yourself slumbers the whole of Reason; it is for you to know all, it is for you to dare all. Mr. President and Gentlemen, this confidence in the unsearched might of man belongs, by all motives, by all prophecy, by all preparation, to the American Scholar. We have listened too long to the courtly muses of Europe. The spirit of the American freeman is already suspected to be timid, imitative, tame. Public and private avarice make the air we breathe thick and fat. The scholar is decent, indolent, complaisant. See already the tragic consequence. The mind of this country, taught to aim at low objects, eats upon itself. There is no work for any but the decorous and the complaisant. Young men of the fairest promise, who begin life upon our shores, inflated by the mountain winds, shined upon by all the stars of God, find the earth below not in unison with these,—but are hindered from action by the disgust which the principles on which business is managed inspire, and turn drudges, or die of disgust,—some of them suicides. What is the remedy? They did not yet see, and thousands of young men as hopeful now crowding to the barriers for the career, do not yet see, that, if the single man plant himself indomitably on his instincts, and there abide, the huge world will come round to him. Patience,—patience;—with the shades of all the good and great for company; and for solace, the perspective of your own infinite life; and for work, the study and the communication of principles, the making those instincts prevalent, the conversion of the world. Is it not the chief disgrace in the world, not to be an unit;—not to be reckoned one character;—not to yield that peculiar fruit which each man was created to bear, but to be reckoned in the gross, in the hundred, or the thousand, of the party, the section, to which we belong; and our opinion predicted geographically, as the north, or the south? Not so, brothers, and friends,—please God, ours shall not be so. We will walk on our own feet; we will work with our own hands; we will speak our own minds. The study of letters shall be no longer a name for pity, for doubt, and for sensual indulgence. The dread of man and the love of man shall be a wall of defence and a wreath of joy around all. A nation of men will for the first time exist, because each believes himself inspired by the Divine Soul which also inspires all men.

William Morris 1834–1896

Best known for his craftsmanship and artistry in interior decoration, William Morris was also a poet, a manufacturer, and a political lecturer. Morris's commitment to a socialist vision led him to promote the socialist movement and to join the ranks of its leaders in Victorian England. Born into a well-to-do family on March 24, 1834, in Walthamstow, Essex, Morris spent his boyhood in the countryside surrounding the Epping forest, an experience that proved seminal to his art and to his political beliefs. Although Morris's position as an affluent member of the middle class and his demanding sense of artistic craftsmanship might seem opposed to his role as a self-proclaimed political revolutionary, his belief in the inseparable fusion of the two perspectives invests his political vision with strength and dynamism. Morris served the Socialist League by editing its weekly journal, *Commonweal*, which flourished and became the leading socialist publication of the day. Additionally, surviving evidence reveals that Morris delivered 578 political lectures in the thirteen years before his death in 1896.

"Art under Plutocracy" was first delivered as a lecture in the hall of University College, Oxford in 1883. Here, Morris describes a project for proletarianizing art, a conception of art as a committed and responsible endeavor within a vital community, a way we might live if wasteful and bourgeois competition were eliminated. In the system Morris envisions, committed artistic labor would replace mere decoration and finery. Virtually the entire range of cultural life could be transformed if art were resituated as meaningful labor within a rationally conceived socialistic community.

Art under Plutocracy

You may well think I am not here to criticize any special school of art or artist, or to plead for any special style, or to give you any instructions, however general, as to the practice of the arts. Rather I want to take counsel with you as to what hindrances may lie in the way towards making art what it should be, a help and solace to the daily life of all men. Some of you here may think that the hindrances in the way are none, or few, and easy to be swept aside. You will say that there is on many sides much knowledge of the history of art, and plenty of taste for it, at least among the cultivated classes; that many men of talent, and some few of genius, practise it with no mean success; that within the last fifty years there has been something almost like a fresh renaissance of art, even in directions where such a change was least to be hoped for. All this is true as far as it goes; and I can well understand this state of things being a cause of gratulation amongst those who do not know what the scope of art really is, and how closely it is bound up with the general condition of society, and especially with the lives of those who live by manual labour and whom we call the working classes. For my part, I cannot help noting that under the apparent satisfaction with the progress of art of late years there lies in the minds of most thinking people a feeling of mere despair as to the prospects of art in the future; a despair which seems to me fully justified if we look at the present condition of art without considering the causes which have led to it, or the hopes which may exist for a change in those causes. For, without beating about the bush, let us consider what the real state of art is. And first I must ask you to extend the word art beyond those matters which are consciously works of art, to take in not only painting and sculpture, and architecture, but the shapes and colours of all household goods, nay, even the arrangement of the fields for tillage and pasture, the management of towns and of our highways of all kinds; in a word, to extend it to the aspect of all the externals of our life. For I must ask you to believe that every one of the things that goes to make up the surroundings among which we live must be either beautiful or ugly, either elevating or degrading to us, either a torment and burden to the maker of it to make, or a pleasure and a solace to him. How does it fare therefore with our external surroundings in these days? What kind of an account shall we be able to give to those who come after us of our dealings with the earth, which our forefathers handed down to us still beautiful, in spite of all the thousands of years of strife and carelessness and selfishness?

Surely this is no light question to ask ourselves; nor am I afraid that you will think it a mere rhetorical flourish if I say that it is a question that may well seem a solemn one when it is asked here in Oxford, amidst sights and memories which we older men at least regard with nothing short of love. He must be indeed a man of narrow incomplete mind, who, amidst the buildings raised by the hopes of our forefathers, amidst the country which they made so lovely, would venture to say that the beauty of the earth was a matter of little moment. And yet, I say, how have we of these latter days treated the beauty of the earth, or that which we call art?

Perhaps I had best begin by stating what will scarcely be new to you, that art must be broadly divided into two kinds, of which we may call the first Intellectual, and the second Decorative Art, using the words as mere forms of convenience. The first kind addresses itself wholly to our mental needs; the things made by it serve no other purpose but to feed the mind, and, as far as material needs go, might be done without altogether. The second, though so much of it as is art does also appeal to the mind, is always but a part of things which are intended primarily for the service of the body. I must further say that there have been nations and periods which lacked the purely Intellectual art but positively none which lacked the Decorative (or at least some pretence of it); and furthermore, that in all times when the arts were in a healthy condition there was an intimate connexion between the two kinds of art; a connexion so close, that in the times when art flourished most, the higher and lower kinds were divided by no hard and fast lines. The highest intellectual art was meant to please the eye, as the phrase goes, as well as to excite the emotions and train the intellect. It appealed to all men, and to all the faculties of a man. On the other hand, the humblest of the ornamental art shared in the meaning and emotion of the intellectual; one melted into the other by scarce perceptible gradations; in short, the best artist was a workman still, the humblest workman was an artist. This is not the case now, nor has been for two or three centuries in civilized countries. Intellectual art is separated from Decorative by the sharpest lines of demarcation, not only as to the kind of work produced under those names, but even in the social position of the producers; those who follow the Intellectual arts being all professional men or gentlemen by virtue of their calling, while those who follow the Decorative are workmen earning weekly wages, non-gentlemen in short.

Now, as I have already said, many men of talent and some few of genius are engaged at present in producing works of Intellectual art, paintings and sculpture chiefly. It is nowise my business here or elsewhere to criticize their works; but my subject compels me to say that those who follow the Intellectual arts must be divided into two sections, the first composed of men who would in any age of the world have held a high place in their craft; the second of men who hold their position of gentleman-artist either by the accident of their birth, or by their possessing industry, business habits, or such-like qualities, out of all proportion to their artistic gifts. The work which these latter produce seems to me of little value to the world, though there is a thriving market for it, and their position is neither dignified nor wholesome; yet they are mostly not to be blamed for it personally, since often they have gifts for art, though not great ones, and would probably not have succeeded in any other career. They are, in fact, good decorative workmen spoiled by a system which compels them to ambitious individualist effort, by cutting off from them any opportunity for co-operation with others of greater or less capacity for the production of popular art.

As to the first section of artists, who worthily fill their places and make the world wealthier by their work, it must be said of them that they are very few. These men have won their mastery over their craft by dint of incredible toil, pains, and anxiety, by qualities of mind and strength of will which are bound to produce something of value. Nevertheless they are injured also by the system which insists on individualism and forbids co-operation. For first, they are cut off from tradition, that wonderful, almost miraculous accumulation of the skill of ages, which men find themselves partakers in without effort on their part. The knowledge of the past and the sympathy with it which the artists of to-day have, they have acquired, on the contrary, by their own most strenuous individual effort; and as that tradition no longer exists to help them in their practice of the art, and they are heavily weighted in the race by having to learn everything from the beginning, each man for himself, so also, and that is worse, the lack of it deprives them of a sympathetic and appreciative audience.

Apart from the artists themselves and a few persons who would be also artists but for want of opportunity and for insufficient gifts of hand and eye, there is in the public of to-day no real knowledge of art, and little love for it. Nothing, save at the best certain vague prepossessions, which are but the phantom of that tradition which once bound artist and public together. Therefore the artists are obliged to express themselves, as it were, in a language not understanded of the people. Nor is this their fault. If they were to try, as some think they should, to meet the public half-way and work in such a manner as to satisfy at any cost those vague prepossessions of men ignorant of art, they would be casting aside their special gifts, they would be traitors to the cause of art, which it is their duty and glory to serve. They have no choice save to do their own personal individual work unhelped by the present, stimulated by the past, but shamed by it, and even in a way hampered by it; they must stand apart as possessors of some sacred mystery which, whatever happens, they must at least do their best to guard. It is not to be doubted that both their own lives and their works are injured by this isolation. But the loss of the people; how are we to measure that? That they should have great men living and working amongst them, and be ignorant of the very existence of their work, and incapable of knowing what it means if they could see it!

In the times when art was abundant and healthy, all men were more or less artists; that is to say, the instinct for beauty which is inborn in every complete man had such force that the whole body of craftsmen habitually and without conscious effort made beautiful things, and the audience for the authors of intellectual art was nothing short of the whole people. And so they had each an assured hope of gaining that genuine praise and sympathy which all men who exercise their imagination in expression most certainly and naturally crave, and the lack of which does certainly injure them in some way; makes them shy, over-sensitive, and narrow, or else cynical and mocking, and in that case well-nigh uesless. But in these days, I have said and repeat, the whole people is careless and ignorant of art; the inborn instinct for beauty is checked and thwarted at every turn; and the result on the less intellectual or decorative art is that as a spontaneous and popular expression of the instinct for beauty it does not exist at all.

It is a matter of course that everything made by man's hand is now obviously ugly, unless it is made beautiful by conscious effort; nor does it mend the matter that men have not lost the habit deduced from the times of art, of professing to ornament household goods and the like; for this sham ornament, which has no least intention of giving anyone pleasure, is so base and foolish that the words upholstery and upholsterer have come to have a kind of secondary meaning indicative of the profound contempt which all sensible men have for such twaddle.

This, so far, is what decorative art has come to, and I must break off a while here and ask you to consider what it once was, lest you think over hastily that its degradation is a matter of little moment. Think, I beg you, to go on further back in history, of the stately and careful beauty of S. Sophia at Constantinople, of the golden twilight of S. Mark's at Venice; of the sculptured cliffs of the great French cathedrals, of the quaint and familiar beauty of our own minsters; nay, go through Oxford streets and ponder on what is left us there unscathed by the fury of the thriving shop and the progressive college; or wander some day through some of the out-of-the-way villages and little towns that lie scattered about the country-side within twenty miles of Oxford; and you will surely see that the loss of decorative art is a grievous loss to the world.

Thus then in considering the state of art among us I have been driven to the conclusion that in its co-operative form it is extinct, and only exists in the conscious efforts of men of genius and talent, who themselves are injured, and thwarted, and deprived of due sympathy by the lack of co-operative art.

But furthermore, the repression of the instinct for beauty which has destroyed the Decorative and injured the Intellectual arts has not stopped there in the injury it has done us. I can myself sympathize with a feeling which I suppose is still not rare, a craving to escape sometimes to mere Nature, not only from ugliness and squalor, not only from a condition of superabundance of art, but even from a condition of art severe and well ordered, even, say, from such surroundings as the lovely simplicity of Periclean Athens. I can deeply sympathize with a weary man finding his account in interest in mere life and communion with external nature, the face of the country, the wind and weather, and the course of the day, and the lives of animals, wild and domestic; and man's daily dealings with all this for his daily bread, and rest, and innocent beast-like pleasure. But the interest in the mere animal life of man has become impossible to be indulged in in its fulness by most civilized people. Yet civilization, it seems to me, owes us some compensation for the loss of this romance, which now only hangs like a dream about the country life of busy lands. To keep the air pure and the rivers clean, to take some pains to keep the meadows and tillage as pleasant as reasonable use will allow them to be; to allow peaceable citizens freedom to wander where they will, so they do no hurt to garden or cornfield; nay, even to leave here and there some piece of waste or mountain sacredly free from fence or tillage as a memory of man's ruder struggles with nature in his earlier days: is it too much to ask civilization to be so far thoughtful of man's pleasure and rest, and to help so far as this her children to whom she has most often set such heavy tasks of grinding labour? Surely not an unreasonable asking. But not a whit of it shall we get under the present system of society. That loss of the instinct for beauty which has involved us in the loss of popular art is also busy in depriving us of the only compensation possible for that loss, by surely and not slowly destroying the beauty of the very face of the earth. Not only are London and our other great commercial cities mere masses of sordidness, filth, and squalor, embroidered with patches of pompous and vulgar hideousness, no less revolting to the eye and the mind when one knows what it means: not only have whole counties of England, and the heavens that hang over them, disappeared beneath a crust of unutterable grime, but the disease, which, to a visitor coming from the times of art, reason, and order, would seem to be a love of dirt and ugliness for its own sake, spreads all over the country, and every little market-town seizes the opportunity to imitate, as far as it can, the majesty of the hell of London and Manchester. Need I speak to you of the wretched suburbs that sprawl all round our fairest and most ancient cities?

Must I speak to you of the degradation that has so speedily befallen this city, still the most beautiful of them all; a city which, with its surroundings, would, if we had had a grain of common sense, have been treated like a most precious jewel, whose beauty was to be preserved at any cost? I say at any cost, for it was a possession which did not belong to us, but which we were trustees of for all posterity. I am old enough to know how we have treated that jewel; as if it were any common stone kicking about on the highway, good enough to throw at a dog. When I remember the contrast between the Oxford of to-day and the Oxford which I first saw thirty years ago, I wonder I can face the misery (there is no other word for it) of visiting it, even to have the honour of addressing you to-night. But furthermore, not only are the cities a disgrace to us, and the smaller towns a laughing-stock; not only are the dwellings of man grown inexpressibly base and ugly, but the very cowsheds and cart-stables, nay, the merest piece of necessary farm-engineering, are tarred with the same brush. Even if a tree is cut down or blown down, a worse one, if any, is planted in its stead, and, in short, our civilization is passing like a blight, daily growing heavier and more poisonous, over the whole face of the country, so that every change is sure to be a change for the worse in its outward aspect. So then it comes to this, that not only are the minds of great artists narrowed and their sympathies frozen by their isolation, not only has co-operative art come to a standstill, but the very food on which both the greater and the lesser art subsists is being destroyed; the well of art is poisoned at its spring.

Now I do not wonder that those who think that these evils are from henceforth for ever necessary to the progress of civilization should try to make the best of things, should shut their eyes to all they can, and praise the galvanized life of the art of the present day; but, for my part, I believe that they are not necessary to civilization, but only accompaniments to one phase of it, which will change and pass into something else, like all prior phases have done. I believe also that the essential characteristic of the present state of society is that which has so ruined art, or the pleasure of life; and that this having died out, the inborn love of man for beauty and the desire for expressing it will no longer be repressed, and art will be free. At the same time I not only admit, but declare, and think it most important to declare, that so long as the system of competition in the production and exchange of the means of life goes on, the degradation of the arts will go on; and if that system is to last for ever, then art is doomed, and will surely die; that is to say, civilization will die. I know it is at present the received opinion that the competitive or "Devil take the hindmost" system is the last system of economy which the world will see; that it is perfection, and therefore finality has been reached in it; and it is doubtless a bold thing to fly in the face of this opinion, which I am told is held even by the most learned men. But though I am not learned, I have been taught that the patriarchal system died out into that of the citizen and chattel slave, which in its turn gave place to that of the feudal lord and the serf, which, passing through a modified form, in which the burgher, the gild-craftsman and his journeyman played their parts, was supplanted by the system of so-called free contract now existing. That all things since the beginning of the world have been tending to the development of this system I willingly admit, since it exists; that all the events of history have taken place for the purpose of making it eternal, the very evolution of those events forbids me to believe.

For I am "one of the people called Socialists"; therefore I am certain that evolution in the economical conditions of life will go on, whatever shadowy barriers may be drawn across its path by men whose apparent self-interest binds them, consciously or unconsciously, to the present, and who are therefore hopeless for the future. I hold that the condition of competition between man and man is bestial only, and that of association human; I think that the change from the undeveloped competition of the Middle Ages, trammelled as it was by the personal relations of feudality, and the attempts at associations of the gild-craftsmen into the full-blown *laissez-faire* competition of the nineteenth century, is bringing to birth out of its own anarchy, and by the very means by which it seeks to perpetuate that anarchy, a spirit of association founded on that antagonism which has produced all former changes in the condition of men, and which will one day abolish all classes and take definite and practical form, and substitute association for competition in all that relates to the production and exchange of the means of life. I further believe that as that change will be beneficient in many ways, so especially will it give an opportunity for the new birth of art, which is now being crushed to death by the money-bags of competitive commerce.

My reason for this hope for art is founded on what I feel quite sure is a truth, and an important one, namely that all art, even the highest, is influenced by the conditions of labour of the mass of mankind, and that any pretensions which may be made for even the highest intellectual art to be independent of these general conditions are futile and vain; that is to say, that any art which professes to be founded on the special education or refinement of a limited body or class must of necessity be unreal and short-lived. Art is man's expression of his joy in labour. If those are not Professor Ruskin's words they embody at least his teaching on this subject. Nor has any truth more important ever been stated; for if pleasure in labour be generally possible, what a strange folly it must be for men to consent to labour without pleasure; and what a hideous injustice it must be for society to compel most men to labour without pleasure! For since all men not dishonest must labour, it becomes a question either of forcing them to lead unhappy lives or allowing them to live unhappily. Now the chief accusation I have to bring against the modern state of society is that it is founded on the art-lacking or unhappy labour of the greater part of men; and all that external degradation of the face of the country of which I have spoken is hateful to me not only because it is a cause of unhappiness to some few of us who still love art, but also and chiefly because it is a token of the unhappy life forced on the great mass of the population by the system of competitive commerce.

The pleasure which ought to go with the making of every piece of handicraft has for its basis the keen interest which every healthy man takes in healthy life, and is compounded, it seems to me, chiefly of three elements: variety, hope of creation, and the self-respect which comes of a sense of usefulness to which must be added that mysterious bodily pleasure which goes with the deft exercise of the bodily powers. I do not think I need spend many words in trying to prove that these things, if they really and fully accompanied labour, would do much to make it pleasant. As to the pleasures of variety, any of you who have ever made anything, I don't care what, will well remember the pleasure that went with the turning out of the first specimen. What would have become of that pleasure if you had been compelled to go on making it exactly the same for ever? As to the hope of creation, the hope of producing some worthy or even excellent work which without you, the craftsman, would not have existed at all, a thing which needs you and can have no substitute for you in the making of it—can we any of us fail to understand the pleasure of this? No less easy, surely, is it to see how much the self-respect born of the consciousness of usefulness must sweeten labour. To feel that you have to do a thing not to satisfy the whim of a fool or a set of fools, but because it is really good in itself, that is useful, would surely be a good help to getting through the day's work. As to the unreasoning, sensuous pleasure in handiwork, I believe in good sooth that it has more power of getting rough and strenuous work out of men, even as things go, than most people imagine. At any rate it lies at the bottom of the production of all art, which cannot exist without it even in its feeblest and rudest form.

Now this compound pleasure in handiwork I claim as the birthright of all workmen. I say that if they lack any part of it they will be so far degraded, but that if they lack it altogether they are, so far as their work goes, I will not say slaves, the word would not be strong enough, but machines more or less conscious of their own unhappiness.

I have appealed already to history in aid of my hopes for a change in the system of the conditions of labour. I wish to bring forward now the witness of history that this claim of labour for pleasure rests on a foundation stronger than a mere fantastic dream; what is left of the art of all kinds produced in all periods and countries where hope of progress was alive before the development of the commercial system shows plainly enough to those who have eyes and understanding that pleasure did always in some degree accompany its production. This fact, however difficult it may be to demonstrate in a pedantic way, is abundantly admitted by those who have studied the arts widely; the very phrases so common in criticism that such and such a piece of would-be art is done mechanically, or done without feeling, express accurately enough the general sense of artists of a standard deduced from times of healthy art; for this mechanical and feelingless handiwork did not exist till days comparatively near our own, and it is the condition of labour under plutocratic rule which has allowed it any place at all.

The craftsman of the Middle Ages no doubt often suffered grievous material oppression, yet in spite of the rigid line of separation drawn by the hierarchical system under which he lived between him and his feudal superior, the difference between them was arbitrary rather than real; there was no such gulf in language, manners, and ideas as divides a cultivated middle-class person of today, a "gentleman," from even a respectable lower-class man; the mental qualities necessary to an artist, intelligence, fancy, imagination, had not then to go through the mill of the competitive market, nor had the rich (or successful competitors) made good their claim to be the sole possessors of mental refinement.

As to the conditions of handiwork in those days, the crafts were drawn together into gilds which indeed divided the occupations of men rigidly enough, and guarded the door to those occupations jealously; but as outside among the gilds there was little competition in the markets, wares being made in the first instance for domestic consumption, and only the overplus of what was wanted at home close to the place of production ever coming into the market or requiring anyone to come and go between the producer and consumer, so inside the gilds there was but little division of labour; a man or youth once accepted as an apprentice to a craft learned it from end to end, and became as a matter of course the master of it; and in the earlier days of the gilds, when the masters were scarcely small capitalists, there was no grade in the craft save this temporary one. Later on, when the masters became capitalists in a sort, and the apprentices were, like the masters, privileged, the class of journeymen-craftsmen came into existence; but it does not seem that the difference between them and the aristocracy of the gild was anything more than an arbitrary one. In short, during all this period the unit of labour was an intelligent man. Under this system of handiwork no great pressure of speed was put on a man's work, but he was allowed to carry it through leisurely and thoughtfully; it used the whole of a man for the production of a piece of goods, and not small portions of many men; it developed the workman's whole intelligence according to his capacity, instead of concentrating his energy on one-sided dealing with a trifling piece of work; in short, it did not submit the hand and soul of the workman to the necessities of the competitive market, but allowed them freedom for due human development. It was this system, which had not learned the lesson that man was made for commerce, but supposed in its simplicity that commerce was made for man, which produced the art of the Middle Ages, wherein the harmonious co-operation of free intelligence was carried to the furthest point which has yet been attained, and which alone of all art can claim to be called Free. The effect of this freedom, and the widespread or rather universal sense of beauty to which it gave birth, became obvious enough in the outburst of the expression of splendid and copious genius which marks the Italian Renaissance. Nor can it be doubted that this glorious art was the fruit of the five centuries of free popular art which preceded it, and not of the rise of commercialism which was contemporaneous with it; for the glory of the Renaissance faded out with strange rapidity as commercial competition developed, so that about the end of the seventeenth century, both in the intellectual and the decorative arts, the commonplace or body still existed, but the romance or soul of them was gone. Step by step they had faded and sickened before the advance of commercialism, now speedily gathering force throughout civilization. The domestic or architectural arts were becoming (or become) mere toys for the competitive market through which all material wares used by civilized men now had to pass. Commercialism had by this time well-nigh destroyed the craft-system of labour, in which, as aforesaid, the unit of labour is a fully instructed craftsman, and had supplanted it by what I will ask leave to call the workshop-system, wherein, when complete, division of labour in handiwork is carried to the highest point possible, and the unit of manufacture is no longer a man, but a group of men, each member of which is dependent on his fellows, and is utterly useless by himself. This system of the workshop division of labour was perfected during the eighteenth century by the efforts of the manufacturing classes, stimulated by the demands of the ever-widening markets; it is still the system in some of the smaller and more domestic kinds of manufacture, holding much the same place amongst us as the remains of the craft-system did in the days when that of the workshop was still young. Under this system, as I have said, all the romance of the arts died out, but the commonplace of them flourished still; for the idea that the essential aim of manufacture is the making of goods still struggled with a newer idea which has since obtained complete victory, namely, that it is carried on for the sake of making a profit for the manufacturer on the one hand, and on the other for the employment of the working classes.

This idea of commerce being an end in

itself and not a means merely, being but half developed in the eighteenth century, the special period of the workshop-system, some interest could still be taken in those days in the making of wares. The capitalist-manufacturer of the period had some pride in turning out goods which would do him credit, as the phrase went; he was not willing wholly to sacrifice his pleasure in this kind to the imperious demands of commerce; even his workman, though no longer an artist, that is a free workman, was bound to have skill in his craft, limited though it was to the small fragment of it which he had to toil at day by day for his whole life.

But commerce went on growing, stimulated still more by the opening up of new markets, and pushed on the invention of men, till their ingenuity produced the machines which we have now got to look upon as necessities of manufacture, and which have brought about a system the very opposite to the ancient craft-system; that system was fixed and conservative of methods; there was no real difference in the method of making a piece of goods between the time of Pliny and the time of Sir Thomas More; the method of manufacture, on the contrary, in the present time, alters not merely from decade to decade, but from year to year; this fact has naturally helped the victory of this machine-system, the system of the Factory, where the machine-like workmen of the workshop period are supplanted by actual machines, of which the operatives (as they are now called) are but a portion, and a portion gradually diminishing both in importance and numbers. This system is still short of its full development, therefore to a certain extent the workshop-system is being carried on side by side with it, but it is being speedily and steadily crushed out by it; and when the process is complete, the skilled workman will no longer exist, and his place will be filled by machines directed by a few highly trained and very intelligent experts, and tended by a multitude of people, men, women, and children, of whom neither skill nor intelligence is required.

This system, I repeat, is as near as may be the opposite of that which produced the popular art which led up to that splendid outburst of art in the days of the Italian Renaissance which even cultivated men will sometimes deign to notice nowadays; it has therefore produced the opposite of what the old craft-system produced, the death of art and not its birth; in other words the degradation of the external surroundings of life, or simply and plainly unhappiness. Through all society spreads that curse of unhappiness: from the poor wretches, the news of whom we middle-class people are just now receiving with such naif wonder and horror: from those poor people whom nature forces to strive against hope, and to expend all the divine energy of man in competing for something less than a dog's lodging and a dog's food, from them up to the cultivated and refined person, well lodged, well fed, well clothed, expensively educated, but lacking all interest in life except, it may be, the cultivation of unhappiness as a fine art.

Something must be wrong then in art, or the happiness of life is sickening in the house of civilization. What has caused the sickness? Machine-labour will you say? Well, I have seen quoted a passage from one of the ancient Sicilian poets rejoicing in the fashioning of a water-mill, and exulting in labour being set free from the toil of the hand-quern in consequence; and that surely would be a type of a man's natural hope when foreseeing the invention of labour-saving machinery as 'tis called; natural surely, since though I have said that the labour of which art can form a part should be accompanied by pleasure, no one could deny that there is some necessary labour even which is not pleasant in itself, and plenty of unnecessary labour which is merely painful. If machinery had been used for minimizing such labour, the utmost ingenuity would scarcely have been wasted on it; but is that the case in any way? Look round the world, and you must agree with John Stuart Mill in his doubt whether all the machinery of modern times has lightened the daily work of one labourer. And why have our natural hopes been so disappointed? Surely because in these latter days, in which as a matter of fact machinery has been invented, it was by no means invented with the aim of saving the pain of labour. The phrase labour-saving machinery is elliptical, and means machinery which saves the cost of labour, not the labour itself, which will be expended when saved on tending other machines. For a doctrine which, as I have said, began to be accepted under the workshop-system, is now universally received, even though we are yet short of the complete development of the system of the Factory. Briefly, the doctrine is this, that the essential aim of manufacture is making a profit; that it is frivolous to consider whether the wares when made will be of more or less use to the world so long as any one can be found to buy them at a price which, when the workman engaged in making them has received of necessaries and comforts as little as he can be got to take, will leave something over as a reward to the capitalist who has employed him. This doctrine of the sole aim of manufacture (or indeed of life) being the profit of the capitalist and the occupation of the workman, is held, I say, by almost everyone; its corollary is, that labour is necessarily unlimited, and that to attempt to limit it is not so much foolish as wicked, whatever misery may be caused to the community by the manufacture and sale of the wares made.

It is this superstition of commerce being an end in itself, of man made for commerce, not commerce for man, of which art has sickened; not of the accidental appliances which that superstition when put in practice has brought to its aid; machines and railways and the like, which do now verily control us all, might have been controlled by us, if we had not been resolute to seek profit and occupation at the cost of establishing for a time that corrupt and degrading anarchy which has usurped the name of Society. It is my business here to-night and everywhere to foster your discontent with that anarchy and its visible results; for indeed I think it would be an insult to you to suppose that you are contented with the state of things as they are; contented to see all beauty vanish from our beautiful city, for instance; contented with the squalor of the black country, with the hideousness of London, the wen of all wens, as Cobbett called it; contented with the ugliness and baseness which everywhere surround the life of civilized man; contented, lastly, to be living above that unutterable and sickening misery of which a few details are once again reaching us as if from some distant unhappy country, of which we could scarcely expect to hear, but which I tell you is the necessary foundation on which our society, our anarchy, rests.

Neither can I doubt that every one here has formed some idea of remedies for these defects in our civilization, as we euphemistically call them, even though the ideas be vague; also I know that you are familiar with the precepts of the system of economy, that religion, I may say, which has supplanted the precepts of the old religions on the duty and blessing of giving to the needy; you understand of course that though a friend may give to a friend and both giver and receiver be better for the gift, yet a rich man cannot give to a poor one without both being the worse for it; I suppose because they are not friends. And amidst all this I feel sure, I say, that you all of you have some ideal of a state of things better than that amidst which we live, something, I mean to say, more than the application of temporary palliatives to the enduring defects of our civilization.

Now it seems to me that the ideal of better times which the more advanced in opinion of our own class have formed as possible and hopeful is something like this. There is to be a large class of industrious people not too much refined (or they could not do the rough work wanted of them), who are to live in comfort (not, however, meaning our middle-class comfort), and receive a kind of education (if they can), and not be overworked; that is, not overworked for a working man; his light day's work would be rather heavy for the refined classes. This class is to be the basis of society, and its existence will leave the consciences of the refined class quite free and at rest. From this refined class will come the directors or captains of labour (in other words the usurers), the directors of people's consciences, religious and literary (clergy, philosophers, newspaper-writers), and lastly, if that be thought of at all, the directors of art; these two classes with or without a third, the functions of which are indefinite, will live together with the greatest goodwill, the upper helping the lower without sense of condescension on one side or humiliation on the other; the lower are to be perfectly content with their position, and there is to be no grain of antagonism between the classes: although (even Utopianism of this kind being unable to shake off the idea of the necessity of competition between individuals) the lower class, blessed and respected as it is to be, will have moreover the additional blessing of hope held out to it; the hope of each man rising into the upper class, and leaving the chrysalis of labour behind him; nor, if that matters, is the lower class to lack due political or parliamentary power; all men (or nearly all) being equal before the ballot-box, except so far as they may be bought like other things. That seems to me to be the middle-class liberal ideal of reformed society; all the world turned bourgeois, big and little, peace under the rule of competitive commerce, ease of mind, a good conscience to all and several under the rule of the devil take the hindmost.

Well, for my part I have nothing, positively nothing, to say against it if it can be brought about. Religion, morality, art, literature, science, might for all I know flourish under it and make the world a heaven. But have we not tried it somewhat already? Are not many people jubilant whenever they stand on a public platform over the speedy advent of this good time? It seems to me that the continued and advancing prosperity of the working classes is almost always noted when a political man addresses an audience on general subjects, when he forgets party politics; nor seldom when he remembers them most. Nor do I wish to take away honour where honour is due; I believe there are many people who deeply believe in the realization of this ideal while they are not ignorant of how lamentably far things are from it at present; I know that there are men who sacrifice time, money, pleasure, their own prejudices even, to bring it about; men who hate strife and love peace, men hard working, kindly, unambitious. What have they done? How much nearer are they to the ideal of the bourgeois commonwealth than they were at the time of the Reform Bill, or the time of the repeal of the Corn Laws? Well, thus much nearer to a great change perhaps, that there is a chink in the armour of self-satisfaction; a suspicion that perhaps it is not the accidents of the system of competitive commerce which have to be abolished, but the system itself; but as to approaching the ideal of that system reformed into humanity and decency, they are about so much nearer to it as a man is nearer to the moon when he stands on a hayrick. I don't want to make too much of the matter of money-wages apart from the ghastly contrast between the rich and the poor which is the essence of our system; yet remember that poverty driven below a certain limit means degradation and slavery pure and simple. Now I have seen a statement made by one of the hopeful men of the rich middle class that the average yearly income of an English working man's household is one hundred pounds. I don't believe the figures because I am sure that they are swollen by wages paid in times of inflation, and ignore the precarious position of most working men; but quite apart from that, do not, I beg you, take refuge behind averages; for at least they are swelled by the high wages paid to special classes of workmen in special places, and in the manufacturing districts by the mothers of families working in factories, to my mind a most abominable custom, and by other matters of the like kind, which the average makers leave you to find out for yourselves. But even that is not the point of the matter. For my part the enormous average of one hundred pounds a year to so many millions of toiling people, while many thousands who do not toil think themselves poor with ten times the income, does not comfort me for the fact of a thousand strong men waiting at the dock gates down at Poplar the greater part of a working-day, on the chance of some of them being taken on at wretched wages, or for the ordinary wage of a farm labourer over a great part of England being ten shillings per week, and that considered ruinous by the farmers also: if averages will content us while such things as this go on, why stop at the working classes? Why not take in everybody, from the Duke of Westminster downwards, and then raise a hymn of rejoicing over the income of the English people?

I say let us be done with averages and look at lives and their sufferings, and try to realize them: for indeed what I want you to note is this; that though you may realize a part of the bourgeois or radical ideal, there is and for ever will be under the competitive system a skeleton in the cupboard. We may, nay, we have managed to create a great mass of middling well-to-do people, hovering on the verge of the middle classes, prosperous artisans, small tradesmen and the like; and I must say parenthetically that in spite of all their innate good qualities the class does little credit to our civilization; for though they live in a kind of swinish comfort as far as food is concerned, they are ill housed, ill educated, crushed by grovelling superstitions, lacking reasonable pleasures, utterly devoid of any sense of beauty. But let that pass. For aught I know we may very much increase the proportionate numbers of this class, without making any serious change in our system, but under all that still lies and will lie another class which we shall never get rid of as long as we are under the tyranny of the devil take the hindmost; that class is the Class of Victims. Now above all things I want us not to forget them (as indeed we are not likely to for some weeks to come), or to console ourselves by averages for the fact that the riches of the rich and the comfort of the well-to-do are founded on that terrible mass of undignified, unrewarded, useless misery, concerning which we have of late been hearing a little, a very little; after all we do know that is a fact, and we can only console ourselves by hoping that we may, if we are watchful and diligent (which we very seldom are), we may greatly diminish the amount of it. I ask you, is such a hope as that worthy of our boasted civilization with its perfected creeds, its high morality, its sounding political maxims? Will you think it monstrous that some people have conceived another hope, and see before them the ideal of a society in which there should be no classes permanently degraded for the benefit of the commonweal? For one thing I would have you remember, that this lowest class of utter poverty lies like a gulf before the whole of the working classes, who in spite of all averages live a precarious life; the failure in the game of life which entails on a rich man an unambitious retirement, and on a well-to-do man a life of dependence and laborious shifts, drags a working man down into that hell of irredeemable degradation. I hope there are but few, at least here, who can comfort their consciences by saying that the working classes bring this degradation on themselves by their own unthrift and recklessness. Some do, no doubt, stoic philosophers of the higher type not being much commoner among day-labourers than among the well-to-do and rich; but we know very well how sorely the mass of the poor strive, practising such thrift as is in itself a degradation to man, in whose very nature it is to love mirth and pleasure, and how in spite of all that they fall into the gulf. What! are we going to deny that when we see all round us in our own class cases of men failing in life by no fault of their own; nay, many of the failers worthier and more useful than those that succeed: as might indeed be looked for in the state of war which we call the system of unlimited competition, where the best campaigning-luggage a man can carry is a hard heart and no scruples? For indeed the fulfilment of that liberal ideal of the reform of our present system into a state of moderate class supremacy is impossible, because that system is after all nothing but a continuous implacable war; the war once ended, commerce, as we now understand the word, comes to an end, and the mountains of wares which are either useless in themselves or only useful to slaves and slave-owners are no longer made, and once again art will be used to determine what things are useful and what useless to be made; since nothing should be made which does not give pleasure to the maker and the user, and that pleasure of making must produce art in the hands of the workman. So will art be used to discriminate between the waste and the usefulness of labour; whereas at present the waste of labour is, as I have said above, a matter never considered at all; so long as a man toils he is supposed to be useful, no matter what he toils at.

I tell you the very essence of competitive commerce is waste; the waste that comes of the anarchy of war. Do not be deceived by the outside appearance of order in our plutocratic society. It fares with it as it does with the older forms of war, that there is an outside look of quiet wonderful order about it; how neat and comforting the steady march of the regiment; how quiet and respectable the sergeants look; how clean the polished cannon; neat as a new pin are the storehouses of murder; the books of adjutant and sergeant as innocent-looking as may be; nay, the very orders for destruction and plunder are given with a quiet precision which seems the very token of a good conscience; this is the mask that lies before the ruined cornfield and the burning cottage, the mangled bodies, the untimely death of worthy men, the desolated home. All this, the results of the order and sobriety which is the face which civilized soldiering turns towards us stay-at-homes, we have been told often and eloquently enough to consider; often enough we have been shown the wrong side of the glories of war, nor can we be shown it too often or too eloquently. Yet I say even such a mask is worn by competitive commerce, with its respectable prim order, its talk of peace and the blessings of intercommunication of countries and the like; and all the while its whole energy, its whole organized precision is employed in one thing, the wrenching the means of living from others; while outside that everything must do as it may, whoever is the worse or the better for it; as in the war of fire and steel, all other aims must be crushed out before that one object. It is worse than the older war in one respect at least, that whereas that was intermittent, this is continuous and unresting, and its leaders and captains are never tired of declaring that it must last as long as the world, and is the end-all and be-all of the creation of man and of his home. Of such the words are said:

For them alone do seethe
A thousand men in troubles wide and dark;
Half ignorant they turn an easy wheel
That sets sharp racks at work to pinch and peel.

What can overthrow this terrible organization so strong in itself, so rooted in the self-interest, stupidity, and cowardice of strenuous narrow-minded men; so strong in itself and so much fortified against attack by the surrounding anarchy which it has bred? Nothing but discontent with that anarchy, and an order which in its turn will arise from it, nay, is arising from it; an order once a part of the internal organization of that which it is doomed to destroy. For the fuller development of industrialism from the ancient crafts through the workshop-system into the system of the factory and machine, while it has taken from the workmen all pleasure in their labour, or hope of distinction and excellence in it, has welded them into a great class, and has by its very oppression and compulsion of the monotony of life driven them into feeling the solidarity of their interests and the antagonism of those interests to those of the capitalist class; they are all through civilization feeling the necessity of their rising as a class. As I have said, it is impossible for them to coalesce with the middle classes to produce the universal reign of moderate bourgeois society which some have dreamed of; because however many of them may rise out of their class, these become at once part of the middle class, owners of capital, even though it be in a small way, and exploiters of labour; and there is still left behind a lower class which in its own turn drags down to it the unsuccessful in the struggle; a process which is being accelerated in these latter days by the rapid growth of the great factories and stores, which are extinguishing the remains of the small workshops served by men who may hope to become small masters, and also the smaller of the tradesman class. Thus then, feeling that it is impossible for them to rise as a class, while competition naturally, and as a necessity for its existence, keeps them down, they have begun to look to association as their natural tendency, just as competition is looked to by the capitalists; in them the hope has arisen, if nowhere else, of finally making an end of class degradation.

It is in the belief that this hope is spreading to the middle classes that I stand before you now, pleading for its acceptance by you, in the certainty that in its fulfilment alone lies the other hope for the new birth of Art and the attainment by the middle classes of true refinement, the lack of which at present is so grievously betokened by the sordidness and baseness of all the external surroundings of our lives, even those of us who are rich. I know there are some to whom this possibility of the getting rid of class degradation may come, not as a hope, but as a fear. These may comfort themselves by thinking that this Socialist matter is a hollow scare, in England at least; that the proletariat have no hope, and therefore will lie quiet in this country, where the rapid and nearly complete development of commercialism has crushed the power of combination out of the lower classes; where the very combinations, the Trades Unions, founded for the advancement of the working class as a class, have already become conservative and obstructive bodies, wielded by the middle-class politicians for party purposes; where the proportion of the town and manufacturing districts to the country is so great that the inhabitants, no longer recruited by the peasantry but become townsmen bred of townsmen, are yearly deteriorating in physique; where lastly education is so backward.

It may be that in England the mass of the working classes has no hope; that it will not be hard to keep them down for a while, possibly a long while. The hope that this may be so I will say plainly is a dastard's hope, for it is founded on the chance of their degradation. I say such an expectation is that of slave-holders or the hangers-on of slave-holders. I believe, however, that hope is growing among the working classes even in England; at any rate you may be sure of one thing, that there is at least discontent. Can any of us doubt that, since there is unjust suffering? Or which of us would be contented with ten shillings a week to keep our households with, or to dwell in unutterable filth and have to pay the price of good lodging for it? Do you doubt that if we had any time for it amidst our struggle to live we should look into the title of those who kept us there, themselves rich and comfortable, under the pretext that it was necessary to society? I tell you there is plenty of discontent, and I call on all those who think there is something better than making money for the sake of making it to help in educating that discontent into hope, that is into the demand for the new birth of society; and I do this not because I am afraid of it, but because I myself am discontented and long for justice.

Yet, if any of you are afraid of the discontent which is abroad, in its present shape, I cannot say that you have no reason to be. I am representing reconstructive Socialism before you; but there are other people who call themselves Socialists whose aim is not reconstruction, but destruction; people who think that the present state of things is horrible and unbearable (as in very truth it is), and that there is nothing for it but to shake society by constant blows given at any sacrifice, so that it may at last totter and fall. May it not be worth while, think you, to combat such a doctrine by supplying discontent with hope of change that involves reconstruction? Meanwhile, be sure that, though the day of change may be long delayed, it will come at last. The middle classes will one day become conscious of the discontent of the proletariat; before that some will have renounced their class and cast in their lot with the working men, influenced by love of justice or insight into facts. For the rest, they will, when their conscience is awakened, have two choices before them; they must either cast aside their morality, of which though three parts are cant, the other is sincere, or they must give way. In either case I do believe that the change will come, and that nothing will seriously retard that new birth; yet I well know that the middle class may do much to give a peaceable or a violent character to the education of discontent which must precede it. Hinder it, and who knows what violence you may be driven into, even to the renunciation of the morality of which we middle-class men are so proud; advance it, strive single-heartedly that truth may prevail, and what need you fear? At any rate not your own violence, not your own tyranny?

Again I say things have gone too far, and the pretence at least of a love of justice is too common among us, for the middle classes to attempt to keep the proletariat in its condition of slavery to capital, as soon as they stir seriously in the matter, except at the cost of complete degradation to themselves, the middle class, whatever else may happen. I cannot help hoping that there are some here who are already in dread of the shadow of that degradation of consciously sustaining an injustice, and are eager to escape from that half-ignorant tyranny of which Keats tells, and which is, sooth to say, the common condition of rich people. To those I have a last word or two to say in begging them to renounce their class pretensions and cast in their lot with the working men. It may be that some of them are kept from actively furthering the cause which they believe in by that dread of organization, by that unpracticality in a word, which, as it is very common in England generally, is more common among highly cultivated people, and, if you will forgive the word, most common in our ancient universities. Since I am a member of a Socialist propaganda I earnestly beg those of you who agree with me to help us actively, with your time and your talents if you can, but if not, at least with your money, as you can. Do not hold aloof from us, since you agree with us, because we have not attained that delicacy of manners, that refinement of language, nay, even that prudent and careful wisdom of action which the long oppression of competitive commerce has crushed out of us.

Art is long and life is short; let us at least do something before we die. We seek perfection, but can find no perfect means to bring it about; let it be enough for us if we can unite with those whose aims are right, and their means honest and feasible. I tell you if we wait for perfection in association in these days of combat we shall die before we can do anything. Help us now, you whom the fortune of your birth has helped to make wise and refined; and as you help us in our work-a-day business toward the success of the cause, instil into us your superior wisdom, your superior refinement, and you in your turn may be helped by the courage and hope of those who are not so completely wise and refined. Remember we have but one weapon against that terrible organization of selfishness which we attack, and that weapon is Union. Yes, and it should be obvious union, which we can be conscious of as we mix with others who are hostile or indifferent to the cause; organized brotherhood is that which must break the spell of anarchical Plutocracy. One man with an idea in his head is in danger of being considered a madman; two men with the same idea in common may be foolish, but can hardly be mad; ten men sharing an idea begin to act, a hundred draw attention as fanatics, a thousand and society begins to tremble, a hundred thousand and there is war abroad, and the cause has victories tangible and real; and why only a hundred thousand? Why not a hundred million and peace upon the earth? You and I who agree together, it is we who have to answer that question.

Friedrich Nietzsche 1844–1900

Nietzsche is one of the greatest and most beguiling figures of modern literature and philosophy, a brilliant thinker and also a madman whose ideas circulate through and even seem to haunt much of twentieth-century culture. A scholar of classical studies, he was appointed to the chair of classical philology at the University of Basel, Switzerland, in 1869, where he remained until mental problems caused him to leave in 1879. In 1889 he went insane and never recovered. Ideas all through his work return to the nature of good and evil and the possibility of belief and will outside of Christianity and the Judeo-Christian tradition—a realm of philosophy and religion somehow "beyond" all that he knew. He eventually, in *Thus Spake Zarathustra*, postulated a cultural "superman" who, in fact, could live "beyond," or at least envision life beyond, the static categories of conventional morality and ethics. At its best, such visionary thought has been invigorating for modern philosophy and literary criticism, especially as interpreted recently by Michel Foucault and Jacques Derrida. Among Nietzsche's best-known works are *The Birth of Tragedy* (1872, trans. 1910), *Thus Spake Zarathustra* (1883–91, trans. 1909, 1930), and *Beyond Good and Evil* (1886, trans. 1907).

In "On Music and Words," from *Early Greek Philosophy and Other Essays* (1911), Nietzsche speculates on what could be called a modern poetics. In the potential of musical expression, for example, Nietzsche saw the most perfect embodiment for what Schopenhauer called the "metaphorless language of the heart." By this Nietzsche meant human activity exclusively in its performative dimension fused with meaning—the fusion, rather, of human activity and significance. In contrast to music, words constituted an "arbitrary" representation of the meaning of ideas and concepts that was far removed from the ideal of performance. Ideas as represented by words, rather, are not tied to a particular expression and can be conveyed in a variety of modes. In the gap between these poles of expression Nietzsche saw a peculiarly modern predicament in the fragmentation of the medium for representing experience. In fact, in this work and others he seems to be prophesying the very tensions of modern and postmodern culture, the culture of drek and high energy, the world of holocaust, alienation, and hyper- and surrealistic realities. Nietzsche ends this essay, however, with a highly romantic gesture as he imagines, finally, that these extremes of experience—represented by Apollo and Dionysus, rationality and irrationality, words and music—can be reconciled and fused into a single force of apprehension, perhaps one suitable for a superman.

On Music and Words

(Fragment, 1871)

What we here have asserted of the relationship between language and music must be valid too, for equal reasons, concerning the relationship of *Mime* to *Music*. The Mime too, as the intensified symbolism of man's gestures, is, measured by the eternal significance of music, only a simile, which brings into expression the innermost secret of music but very superficially, namely on the substratum of the passionately moved human body. But if we include language also in the category of bodily symbolism, and compare the *drama*, according to the canon advanced, with music, then I venture to think, a proposition of Schopenhauer will come into the clearest light, to which reference must be made again later on. "It might be admissible, although a purely musical mind does not demand it, to join and adapt words or even a clearly represented action to the pure language of tones, although the latter, being self-sufficient, needs no help; so that our perceiving and reflecting intellect, which does not like to be quite idle, may meanwhile have light and analogous occupation also. By this concession to the intellect man's attention adheres even more closely to music, by this at the same time, too, is placed underneath that which the tones indicate in their general metaphorless language of the heart, a visible picture, as it were a schema, as an example illustrating a general idea . . . indeed such things will even heighten the effect of music." (Schopenhauer, Parerga, II., "On the Metaphysics of the Beautiful and Æsthetics," § 224.) If we disregard the naturalistic external motivation according to which our perceiving and reflecting intellect does not like to be quite idle when listening to music, and attention led by the hand of an obvious action follows better—then the drama in relation to music has been characterised by Schopenhauer for the best reasons as a schema, as an example illustrating a general idea: and when he adds "indeed such things will even heighten the effect of music" then the enormous universality and originality of vocal music, of the connection of tone with metaphor and idea guarantee the correctness of this utterance. The music of every people begins in closest connection with lyricism and long before absolute music can be thought of, the music of a people in that connection passes through the most important stages of development. If we understand this primal lyricism of a people, as indeed we must, to be an imitation of the artistic typifying Nature, then as the original prototype of that union of music and lyricism must be regarded: *the duality in the essence of language*, already typified by Nature. Now, after discussing the relation of music to metaphor we will fathom more deeply this essence of language.

In the multiplicity of languages the fact at once manifests itself, that word and thing do not necessarily coincide with one another completely, but that the word is a symbol. But what does the word symbolise? Most certainly only conceptions, be these now conscious ones or as in the greater number of cases, unconscious; for how should a word-symbol correspond to that innermost nature of which we and the world are images? Only as conceptions we know that kernel, only in its metaphorical expressions are we familiar with it; beyond that point there is nowhere a direct bridge which could lead us to it. The whole life of impulses, too, the play of feelings, sensations, emotions, volitions, is known to us—as I am forced to insert here in opposition to Schopenhauer—after a most rigid self-examination, not according to its essence but merely as conception; and we may well be permitted to say, that even Schopenhauer's "Will" is nothing else but the most general phenomenal form of a Something otherwise absolutely indecipherable. If therefore we must acquiesce in the rigid necessity of getting nowhere beyond the conceptions we can nevertheless again distinguish two main species within their realm. The one species manifest themselves to us as pleasure-and-displeasure-sensations and accompany all other conceptions as a never-lacking fundamental basis. This most general manifestation, out of which and by which alone we understand all Becoming and all Willing and for which we will retain the name "Will," has now too in language its own symbolic sphere: and in truth this sphere is equally fundamental to the language, as that manifestation is fundamental to all other conceptions. All degrees of pleasure and displeasure—expressions of *one* primal cause unfathomable to us—symbolise themselves in *the tone of the speaker:* whereas all the other conceptions are indicated by the *gesture-symbolism* of the speaker. In so far as that primal cause is the same in all men, the *tonal subsoil* is also the common one, comprehensible beyond the difference of language. Out of it now develops the more arbitrary gesture-symbolism which is not wholly adequate for its basis: and with which begins the diversity of languages, whose multiplicity we are permitted to consider—to use a simile—as a strophic text to that primal melody of the pleasure-and-displeasure-language. The whole realm of the consonantal and vocal we believe we may reckon only under gesture-symbolism: consonants *and* vowels without that fundamental tone which is necessary above all else, are nothing but *positions* of the organs of speech, in short, gestures—; as soon as we imagine the *word* proceeding out of the mouth of man, then first of all the root of the word, and the basis of that gesture-symbolism, the *tonal subsoil,* the echo of the pleasure-and-displeasure-sensations originate. As our whole corporeality stands in relation to that original phenomenon, the "Will," so the word built out of its consonants and vowels stands in relation to its tonal basis.

This original phenomenon, the "Will," with its scale of pleasure-and-displeasure-sensations attains in the development of music an ever more adequate symbolic expression: and to this historical process the continuous effort of lyric poetry runs parallel, the effort to transcribe music into metaphors: exactly as this double-phenomenon, according to the just completed disquisition, lies typified in language.

He who has followed us into these difficult contemplations readily, attentively, and with some imagination—and with kind indulgence where the expression has been too scanty or too unconditional—will now have the advantage with us, of laying before himself more seriously and answering more deeply than is usually the case some stirring points of controversy of present-day æsthetics and still more of contemporary artists. Let us think now, after all our assumptions, what an undertaking it must be, to set music to a poem; *i.e.*, to illustrate a poem by music, in order to help music thereby to obtain a language of ideas. What a perverted world! A task that appears to my mind like that of a son wanting to create his father! Music can create metaphors out of itself, which will always however be but schemata, instances as it were of her intrinsic general contents. But how should the metaphor, the conception, create music out of itself! Much less could the idea, or, as one has said, the "poetical idea" do this. As certainly as a bridge leads out of the mysterious castle of the musician into the free land of the metaphors—and the lyric poet steps across it—as certainly is it impossible to go the contrary way, although some are said to exist who fancy they have done so. One might people the air with the phantasy of a Raphael, one might see St. Cecilia, as he does, listening enraptured to the harmonies of the choirs of angels—no tone issues from this world apparently lost in music: even if we imagined that that harmony in reality, as by a miracle, began to sound for us, whither would Cecilia, Paul and Magdalena disappear from us, whither even the singing choir of angels! We should at once cease to be Raphael: and as in that picture the earthly instruments lie shattered on the ground, so our painter's vision, defeated by the higher, would fade and die away.—How nevertheless could the miracle happen? How should the Apollonian world of the eye quite engrossed in contemplation be able to create out of itself the tone, which on the contrary symbolises a sphere which is excluded and conquered just by that very Apollonian absorption in Appearance? The delight at Appearance cannot raise out of itself the pleasure at Non-appearance; the delight of perceiving is delight only by the fact that nothing reminds us of a sphere in which individuation is broken and abolished. If we have characterised at all correctly the Apollonian in opposition to the Dionysean, then the thought which attributes to the metaphor, the idea, the appearance, in some way the power of producing out of itself the tone, must appear to us strangely wrong. We will not be referred, in order to be refuted, to the musician who writes music to existing lyric poems; for after all that has been said we shall be compelled to assert that the relationship between the lyric poem and its setting must in any case be a different one from that between a father and his child. Then what exactly?

Here now we may be met on the ground of a favourite æsthetic notion with the proposition, "It is not the poem which gives birth to the setting but the *sentiment* created by the poem." I do not agree with that; the more subtle or powerful stirring-up of that pleasure-and-displeasure-subsoil is in the realm of productive art *the* element which is inartistic in itself; indeed only its total exclusion makes the complete self-absorption and disinterested perception of the artist possible. Here perhaps one might retaliate that I myself just now predicated about the "Will," that in music "Will" came to an ever more adequate symbolic expression. My answer, condensed into an æsthetic axiom, is this: *the Will is the object of music but not the origin of it,* that is the Will in its very greatest universality, as the most original manifestation, under which is to be understood all Becoming. That, which we call *feeling,* is with regard to this Will already permeated and saturated with conscious and unconscious conceptions and is therefore no longer directly the object of music; it is unthinkable then that these feelings should be able to create music out of themselves. Take for instance the feelings of love, fear and hope: music can no longer do anything with them in a direct way, every one of them is already so filled with conceptions. On the contrary these feelings can serve to symbolise music, as the lyric poet does who translates for himself into the simile-world of feelings that conceptually and metaphorically unapproachable realm of the Will, the proper content and object of music. The lyric poet resembles all those hearers of music who are conscious of an *effect of music on their emotions;* the distant and removed power of music appeals, with them, to an *intermediate realm* which gives to them as it were a foretaste, a symbolic preliminary conception of music proper, it appeals to the intermediate realm of the emotions. One might be permitted to say about them, with respect to the Will, the only object of music, that they bear the same relation to this Will, as the analogous morning-dream according to Schopenhauer's theory, bears to the dream proper. To all those, however, who are unable to get at music except with their emotions, is to be said, that they will ever remain in the entrance-hall, and will never have access to the sanctuary of music: which, as I said, emotion cannot show but only symbolise.

With regard however to the origin of music,

I have already explained that that can never lie in the Will, but must rather rest in the lap of that force, which under the form of the "Will" creates out of itself a visionary world: *the origin of music lies beyond all individuation*, a proposition, which after our discussion on the Dionysean is self-evident. At this point I take the liberty of setting forth again comprehensively side by side those decisive propositions which the antithesis of the Dionysean and Apollonian dealt with has compelled us to enunciate:

The "Will," as the most original manifestation, is the object of music: in this sense music can be called imitation of Nature, but of Nature in its most general form.—

The "Will" itself and the feelings—manifestations of the Will already permeated with conceptions—are wholly incapable of creating music out of themselves, just as on the other hand it is utterly denied to music to represent feelings, or to have feelings as its object, while Will is its only object.—

He who carries away feelings as effects of music has within them as it were a symbolic intermediate realm, which can give him a foretaste of music, but excludes him at the same time from her innermost sanctuaries.—

The lyric poet interprets music to himself through the symbolic world of emotions, whereas he himself, in the calm of the Apollonian contemplation, is exempted from those emotions.—

When, therefore, the musician writes a setting to a lyric poem he is moved as musician neither through the images nor through the emotional language in the text; but a musical inspiration coming from quite a different sphere *chooses* for itself that song-text as allegorical expression. There cannot therefore be any question as to a necessary relation between poem and music; for the two worlds brought here into connection are too strange to one another to enter into more than a superficial alliance; the song-text is just a symbol and stands to music in the same relation as the Egyptian hieroglyph of bravery did to the brave warrior himself. During the highest revelations of music we even feel involuntarily the *crudeness* of every figurative effort and of every emotion dragged in for purposes of analogy; for example, the last quartets of Beethoven quite put to shame all illustration and the entire realm of empiric reality. The symbol, in face of the god really revealing himself, has no longer any meaning; moreover it appears as an offensive superficiality.

One must not think any the worse of us for considering from this point of view one item so that we may speak about it without reserve, namely the *last movement of Beethoven's Ninth Symphony*, a movement which is unprecedented and unanalysable in its charms. To the dithyrambic world-redeeming exultation of this music Schiller's poem, "To Joy," is wholly incongruous, yea, like cold moonlight, pales beside that sea of flame. Who would rob me of this sure feeling? Yea, who would be able to dispute that that feeling during the hearing of this music does not find expression in a scream only because we, wholly impotent through music for metaphor and word, already *hear nothing at all from Schiller's poem*. All that noble sublimity, yea the grandeur of Schiller's verses has, beside the truly naïve-innocent folk-melody of joy, a disturbing, troubling, even crude and offensive effect; only the ever fuller development of the choir's song and the masses of the orchestra preventing us from hearing them, keep from us that sensation of incongruity. What therefore shall we think of that awful æsthetic superstition that Beethoven himself made a solemn statement as to his belief in the limits of absolute music, in that fourth movement of the Ninth Symphony, yea that he as it were with it unlocked the portals of a new art, within which music had been enabled to represent even metaphor and idea and whereby music had been opened to the "conscious mind." And what does Beethoven himself tell us when he has choir-song introduced by a recitative? "Alas friends, let us intonate not these tones but more pleasing and joyous ones!" More pleasing and joyous ones! For that he needed the convincing tone of the human voice, for that he needed the music of innocence in the folk-song. Not the word, but the "more pleasing" sound, not the idea but the most heartfelt joyful tone was chosen by the sublime master in his longing for the most soul-thrilling ensemble of his orchestra. And how could one misunderstand him! Rather may the same be said of this movement as Richard Wagner says of the great "*Missa Solemnis,*" which he calls "a pure symphonic work of the most genuine Beethoven-spirit" (Beethoven, p. 42). "The voices are treated here quite in the sense of human instruments, in which sense Shopenhauer quite rightly wanted these human voices to be considered; the text underlying them is understood by us in these great Church compositions, not in its conceptual meaning, but it serves in the sense of the musical work of art, merely as material for vocal music and does not stand to our musically determined sensation in a disturbing position simply because it does not incite in us any rational conceptions but, as its ecclesiastical character conditions too, only touches us with the impression of well-known symbolic creeds." Besides I do not doubt that Beethoven, had he written the Tenth Symphony—of which drafts are still extant—would have composed just the *Tenth* Symphony.

Let us now approach, after these preparations, the discussion of the *opera*, so as to be able to proceed afterwards from the opera to its counterpart in the Greek tragedy. What we had to observe in the last movement of the Ninth, *i.e.*, on the highest level of modern music-development, viz., that the word-content goes down unheard in the general sea of sound, is nothing isolated and peculiar, but the general and eternally valid norm in the vocal music of all times, the norm which alone is adequate to the origin of lyric song. The man in a state of Dionysean excitement has a *listener* just as little as the orgiastic crowd, a listener to whom he might have something to communicate, a listener as the epic narrator and generally speaking the Apollonian artist, to be sure, presupposes. It is rather in the nature of the Dionysean art, that it has no consideration for the listener: the inspired servant of Dionysos is, as I said in a former place, understood only by his compeers. But if we now imagine a listener at those endemic outbursts of Dionysean excitement then we shall have to prophesy for him a fate similar to that which Pentheus the discovered eavesdropper suffered, namely, to be torn to pieces by the Mænads. The lyric musician sings "as the bird sings,"[1] alone, out of innermost compulsion; when the listener comes to him with a demand he must become dumb. Therefore it would be altogether unnatural to ask from the lyric musician that one should also understand the text-words of his song, unnatural because here a demand is made by the listener, who has no right at all during the lyric outburst to claim anything. Now with the poetry of the great ancient lyric poets in your hand, put the question honestly to yourself whether they can have even thought of making themselves clear to the mass of the people standing around and listening, clear with their world of metaphors and thoughts; answer this serious question with a look at Pindar and the Æschylian choir songs. These most daring and obscure intricacies of thought, this whirl of metaphors, ever impetuously reproducing itself, this oracular tone of the whole, which we, *without* the diversion of music and orchestration, so often cannot penetrate even with the closest attention—was this whole world of miracles transparent as glass to the Greek crowd, yea, a metaphorical-conceptual interpretation of music? And with such mysteries of thought as are to be found in Pindar do you think the wonderful poet could have wished to elucidate the music already strikingly distinct? Should we here not be forced to an insight into the very nature of the lyricist—the artistic man, who to *himself* must interpret music through the symbolism of metaphors and emotions, but who has nothing to communicate to the listener; an artist who, in complete aloofness, even forgets those who stand eagerly listening near him. And as the lyricist his hymns, so the people sing the folk-song, for themselves, out of inmost impulse, unconcerned whether the word is comprehensible to him who does not join in the song. Let us think of our own experiences in the realm of higher art-music: what did we understand of the text of a Mass of Palestrina, of a Cantata of Bach, of an Oratorio of Händel, if we ourselves perhaps did not join in singing? Only for *him who joins* in singing do lyric poetry and vocal music exist; the listener stands before it as before absolute music.

But now the *opera* begins, according to the clearest testimonies, with the *demand of the listener to understand the word.*

What? The listener *demands*? The word is to be understood?

But to bring music into the service of a series of metaphors and conceptions, to use it as a means to an end, to the strengthening and elucidation of such conceptions and metaphors—such a peculiar presumption as is found in the concept of an "opera," reminds me of that ridiculous person who endeavours to lift himself up into the air with his own arms; that which this fool and which the opera according to that idea attempt are absolute impossibilities. That idea of the opera does not demand perhaps an abuse from music but—as I said—an impossibility. Music never *can* become a means; one may push, screw, torture it; as tone, as roll of the drum, in its crudest and simplest stages, it still defeats poetry and abases the latter to its reflection. The opera as a species of art according to that concept is therefore not only an aberration of music, but an erroneous conception of æsthetics. If I herewith, after all, justify the nature of the opera for æsthetics, I am of course far from justifying at the same time bad opera music or bad opera-verses. The worst music can still mean, as compared with the best poetry, the Dionysean world-subsoil, and the worst poetry can be mirror, image and reflection of this subsoil, if together with the best music: as certainly, namely, as the single tone against the metaphor is already Dionysean, and the single metaphor together with idea and word against music is already Apollonian. Yea, even bad music together with bad poetry can still inform as to the nature of music and poesy.

When therefore Schopenhauer felt Bellini's "Norma," for example, as the fulfilment of tragedy, with regard to that opera's music and poetry, then he, in Dionysean-Apollonian emotion and self-forgetfulness, was quite entitled to do so, because he perceived music and poetry in their most general, as it were, philosophical value, *as* music and poetry: but with that judgment he showed a poorly educated taste,—for good taste always has historical perspective. To us, who intentionally in this investigation avoid any question of the historic value of an art-phenomenon and endeavour to focus only the phenomenon itself, in its unaltered eternal meaning, and consequently in its *highest* type, too,—to us the art-species of the "opera" seems to be justified as much as the folk-song, in so far as we find in both that union of the Dionysean and Apollonian and are permitted to assume for the opera—namely for the highest type of the opera—an origin analogous to that of the folk-song. Only in so far as the opera historically known to us has a completely different origin from that of the folk-song do we reject this "opera," which stands in the same relation to that generic notion just defended by us, as the marionette does to a living human being. It is certain, music never can become a means in the service of the text, but must always defeat the text, yet music must become bad when the composer interrupts every Dionysean force rising within himself by an anxious regard for the words and gestures of his marionettes. If the poet of the opera-text has offered him nothing more than the usual schematised figures with their Egyptian regularity, then the freer, more unconditional, more Dionysean is the development of the music; and the more she despises all dramatic requirements, so much the higher will be the value of the opera. In this sense it is true the opera is, at its best, good music, and nothing but music: whereas the jugglery performed at the same time is, as it were, only a fantastic disguise of the orchestra, above all, of the most important instruments the orchestra has: the singers; and from this jugglery the judicious listener turns away laughing. If the mass is diverted by *this very jugglery* and only *permits* the music with it, then the mob fares as all those do who value the frame of a good picture higher than the picture itself. Who treats such naïve aberrations with a serious or even pathetic reproach?

But what will the opera mean as "dramatic" music, in its possibly farthest distance from pure music, efficient in itself, and purely Dionysean? Let us imagine a passionate drama full of incidents which carries away the spectator, and which is already sure of success by its plot: what will "dramatic" music be able to add, if it does not take away something? Firstly, it *will* take away much: for in every moment where for once the Dionysean power of music strikes the listener, the eye is dimmed that sees the action, the eye that became absorbed in the individuals appearing before it: the listener now *forgets* the drama and becomes alive again to it only when the Dionysean spell over him has been broken. In so far, however, as music makes the listener forget the drama, it is not yet "dramatic" music: but what kind of music is that which is not *allowed* to exercise any Dionysean power over the listener? And how is it possible? It is possible as *purely conventional symbolism*, out of which convention has sucked all natural strength: as music which has diminished to symbols of remembrance: and its effect aims at reminding the spectator of something, which at the sight of the drama must not escape him lest he should misunderstand it: as a trumpet signal is an invitation for the horse to trot. Lastly, before the drama commenced and in interludes or during tedious passages, doubtful as to dramatic effect, yea, even in its highest moments, there would still be permitted another species of remembrance-music, no longer purely conventional, namely *emotional-music*, music, as a stimulant to dull or wearied nerves. I am able to distinguish in the so-called dramatic music these two elements only: a conventional rhetoric and remembrance-music, and a sensational-music with an effect essentially physical: and thus it vacillates between the noise of the drum and the signal-horn, like the mood of the warrior who goes into the battle. But now the mind, regaling itself on pure music and educated through comparison, demands a *masquerade* for those two wrong tendencies of music: "Remembrance" and "Emotion" are to be played, but in good music, which must be in itself enjoyable, yea, valuable; what despair for the dramatic musician, who must mask the big drum by good music, which, however, must nevertheless have no purely musical, but only a stimulating effect! And now comes the great Philistine public nodding its thousand heads and enjoys this "dramatic music" which is ever ashamed of itself, enjoys it to the very last morsel, without perceiving anything of its shame and embarrassment. Rather the public feels its skin agreeably tickled, for indeed homage is being rendered in all forms and ways to the public! To the pleasure-hunting, dull-eyed sensualist, who needs excitement, to the conceited "educated person" who has accustomed himself to good drama and good music as to good food, without after all making much out of it, to the forgetful and absent-minded egoist, who must be led back to the work of art by force and with signal-horns because selfish plans continually pass through his mind aiming at gain or pleasure. Woe-begone dramatic musicians! "Draw near and view your Patrons' faces! The half are coarse, the half are cold." "Why should you rack, poor foolish Bards, for ends like these the gracious Muses?"[2] And that the muses are tormented, even tortured and flayed, these veracious miserable ones do not themselves deny!

We had assumed a passionate drama, carrying away the spectator, which even without music would be sure of its effect. I fear that that in it which is "poetry" and *not* action proper will stand in relation to true poetry as dramatic music to music in general: it will be remembrance- and emotional-poetry. Poetry will serve as a means, in order to recall in a conventional fashion feelings and passions, the expression of which has been found by real poets and has become celebrated, yea, normal with them. Further, this poetry will be expected in dangerous moments to assist the proper "action,"—whether a criminalistic horror-story or an exhibition of witchery mad with shifting the scenes,—and to spread a covering veil over the crudeness of the action itself. Shamefully conscious that the poetry is only masquerade which cannot bear the light of day, such a "dramatic" rime-jingle clamours now for "dramatic" music, as on the other hand again the poetaster of such dramas is met after one-fourth of the way by the dramatic musician with his talent for the drum and the signal-horn and his shyness of genuine music, trusting in itself and self-sufficient. And now they see one another; and these Apollonian and Dionysean caricatures, this *par nobile fratrum*, embrace one another!

Notes

1. A reference to Goethe's ballad, "The Minstrel," st. 5:

> I sing as sings the bird, whose note
> The leafy bough is heard on.
> The song that falters from my throat
> For me is ample guerdon.
>
> Tr.

2. A quotation from Goethe's "Faust": Part I, lines 91, 92, and 95, 96.—Tr. (Maximillian A. Mügge)

Walter Pater 1839–1894

Despite T. S. Eliot's dismissal of Goethe-and-Gautier aestheticism, Pater, the most famous English critic of the 1890s, is now considered one of the four great English critics of the nineteenth century, along with Arnold, Ruskin, and Coleridge. The magnitude of Pater's influence on twentieth-century criticism is an intriguing debate among contemporary critics ranging from Harold Bloom to J. Hillis Miller. The reticent Oxford scholar, Pater was startled at the outrage caused by his "Conclusion" to *Studies in the History of the Renaissance* (1873). In that work, Pater asserts that our search for truth through philosophy and religion is futile; instead, he insists, we should find moments of wisdom in "poetic passion, the desire of beauty, the love of art for art's sake." The standard edition of Pater's works, though not complete, is the New Library edition of *The Works of Walter Pater* (1910). It includes his fiction and critical works, with topics that range from Plato's dialogues and Greek art to Leonardo da Vinci's paintings and the writings of French and English romantics.

Pater's essay "Wordsworth" appears in one of the most important volumes of nineteenth-century English criticism, *Appreciations* (1889). Pater believed critical writing, like poetry, to be an act of creation; and of each piece of art the aesthetic critic, one of refined temperament, must ask, "What is this song or picture, this engaging personality presented in life or in a book, to *me*? How is my nature modified by its presence, under its influence?" With condensed and rhythmic prose, Pater answers those questions by creating a portrait of Wordsworth as an impassioned contemplative who relies on imagination to transfigure life so that a reader can enter the consummate Paterian moment of beauty to know stimulation and nourishment. "Wordsworth," as an example of Pater's aesthetic criticism, claims for critic and artist, because they perceive and imagine the power to create and to destroy the world. "To treat life as art" is the skill of masters such as Wordsworth. Their art allows the reader to leave "the mere machinery of life" in order to perceive the "spectacle" of the universe, and this is the "aim of culture." This power, says Pater, with Nietzschean echoes, means that great art is "a continual protest."

WORDSWORTH

Some English critics at the beginning of the present century had a great deal to say concerning a distinction, of much importance, as they thought, in the true estimate of poetry, between the *Fancy*, and another more powerful faculty—the *Imagination*. This metaphysical distinction, borrowed originally from the writings of German philosophers, and perhaps not always clearly apprehended by those who talked of it, involved a far deeper and more vital distinction, with which indeed all true criticism more or less directly has to do, the distinction, namely, between higher and lower degrees of intensity in the poet's perception of his subject, and in his concentration of himself upon his work. Of those who dwelt upon the metaphysical distinction between the Fancy and the Imagination, it was Wordsworth who made the most of it, assuming it as the basis for the final classification of his poetical writings; and it is in these writings that the deeper and more vital distinction, which, as I have said, underlies the metaphysical distinction, is most needed, and may best be illustrated.

For nowhere is there so perplexed a mixture as in Wordsworth's own poetry, of work touched with intense and individual power, with work of almost no character at all. He has much conventional sentiment, and some of that insincere poetic diction, against which his most serious critical efforts were directed: the reaction in his political ideas, consequent on the excesses of 1795, makes him, at times, a mere declaimer on moral and social topics; and he seems, sometimes, to force an unwilling pen, and write by rule. By making the most of these blemishes it is possible to obscure the true æsthetic value of his work, just as his life also, a life of much quiet delicacy and independence, might easily be placed in a false focus, and made to appear a somewhat tame theme in illustration of the more obvious parochial virtues. And those who wish to understand his influence, and experience his peculiar savour, must bear with patience the presence of an alien element in Wordsworth's work, which never coalesced with what is really delightful in it, nor underwent his special power. Who that values his writings most has not felt the intrusion there, from time to time, of something tedious and prosaic? Of all poets equally great, he would gain most by a skilfully made anthology. Such a selection would show, in truth, not so much what he was, or to himself or others seemed to be, as what, by the more energetic and fertile quality in his writings, he was ever tending to become. And the mixture in his work, as it actually stands, is so perplexed, that one fears to miss the least promising composition even, lest some precious morsel should be lying hidden within—the few perfect lines, the phrase, the single word perhaps, to which he often works up mechanically through a poem, almost the whole of which may be tame enough. He who thought that in all creative work the larger part was *given* passively, to the recipient mind, who waited so dutifully upon the gift, to whom so large a measure was sometimes given, had his times also of desertion and relapse; and he has permitted the impress of these too to remain in his work. And this duality there—the fitfulness with which the higher qualities manifest themselves in it, gives the effect in his poetry of a power not altogether his own, or under his control, which comes and goes when it will, lifting or lowering a matter, poor in itself; so that that old fancy which made the poet's art an enthusiasm, a form of divine possession, seems almost literally true of him.

This constant suggestion of an absolute duality between higher and lower moods, and the work done in them, stimulating one always to look below the surface, makes the reading of Wordsworth an excellent sort of training towards the things of art and poetry. It begets in those, who, coming across him in youth, can bear him at all, a habit of reading between the lines, a faith in the effect of concentration and collectedness of mind in the right appreciation of poetry, an expectation of things, in this order, coming to one by means of a right discipline of the temper as well as of the intellect. He meets us with the promise that he has much, and something very peculiar, to give us, if we will follow a certain difficult way, and seems to have the secret of a special and privileged state of mind. And those who have undergone his influence, and followed this difficult way, are like people who have passed through some initiation, a *disciplina arcani*, by submitting to which they become able constantly to distinguish in art, speech, feeling, manners, that which is organic, animated, expressive, from that which is only conventional, derivative, inexpressive.

But although the necessity of selecting these precious morsels for oneself is an opportunity for the exercise of Wordsworth's peculiar influence, and induces a kind of just criticism and true estimate of it, yet the purely literary product would have been more excellent, had the writer himself purged away that alien element. How perfect would have been the little treasury, shut between the covers of how thin a book! Let us suppose the desired separation made, the electric thread untwined, the golden pieces, great and small, lying apart together.[1] What are the peculiarities of this residue? What special sense does Wordsworth exercise, and what instincts does he satisfy? What are the subjects and the motives which in him excite the imaginative faculty? What are the qualities in things and persons which he values, the impression and sense of which he can convey to others, in an extraordinary way?

An intimate consciousness of the expression of natural things, which weighs, listens, penetrates, where the earlier mind passed roughly by, is a large element in the complexion of modern poetry. It has been remarked as a fact in mental history again and again. It reveals itself in many forms; but is strongest and most attractive in what is strongest and most attractive in modern literature. It is exemplified, almost equally, by writers as unlike each other as Senancour and Théophile Gautier: as a singular chapter in the history of the human mind, its growth might be traced from Rousseau to Chateaubriand, from Chateaubriand to Victor Hugo: it has doubtless some latent connexion with those pantheistic theories which locate an intelligent soul in material things, and have largely exercised men's minds in some modern systems of philosophy: it is traceable even in the graver writings of historians: it makes as much difference between ancient and modern landscape art, as there is between the rough masks of an early mosaic and a portrait by Reynolds or Gainsborough. Of this new sense, the writings of Wordsworth are the central and elementary expression: he is more simply and entirely occupied with it than any other poet, though there are fine expressions of precisely the same thing in so different a poet as Shelley. There was in his own character a certain contentment, a sort of inborn religious placidity, seldom found united with a sensibility so mobile as his, which was favourable to the quiet, habitual observation of inanimate, or imperfectly animate, existence. His life of eighty years is divided by no very profoundly felt incidents: its changes are almost wholly inward, and it falls into broad, untroubled, perhaps somewhat monotonous spaces. What it most resembles is the life of one of those early Italian or Flemish painters, who, just because their minds were full of heavenly visions, passed, some of them, the better part of sixty years in quiet, systematic industry. This placid life matured a quite unusual sensibility, really innate in him, to the sights and sounds of the natural world—the flower and its shadow on the stone, and cuckoo and its echo. The poem of *Resolution and Independence* is a storehouse of such records: for its fulness of imagery it may be compared to Keats's *Saint Agnes' Eve*. To read one of his longer pastoral poems for the first time, is like a day spent in a new country: the memory is crowded for a while with its precise and vivid incidents—

> The pliant harebell swinging in the breeze
> On some grey rock;—
>
> The single sheep and the one blasted tree
> And the bleak music from that old stone wall;—
>
> In the meadows and the lower ground
> Was all the sweetness of a common dawn;—
>
> And that green corn all day is rustling in thine ears.

Clear and delicate at once, as he is in the outlining of visible imagery, he is more clear and delicate still, and finely scrupulous, in the noting of sounds; so that he conceives of noble sound as even moulding the human countenance to nobler types, and as something actually "profaned" by colour, by visible form, or image. He has a power likewise of realising, and conveying to the consciousness of the reader, abstract and elementary impressions—silence, darkness, absolute motionlessness: or, again, the whole complex sentiment of a particular place, the abstract expression of desolation in the long white road, of peacefulness in a particular folding of the hills. In the airy building of the brain, a special day or hour even, comes to have for him a sort of personal identity, a spirit or angel given to it, by which, for its exceptional insight, or the happy light upon it, it has a presence in one's history, and acts there, as a separate power or accomplishment; and he has celebrated in many of his poems the "efficacious spirit," which, as he says, resides in these "particular spots" of time.

It is to such a world, and to a world of congruous meditation thereon, that we see him retiring in his but lately published poem of *The Recluse*—taking leave, without much count of costs, of the world of business, of action and ambition, as also of all that for the majority of mankind counts as sensuous enjoyment.[2]

And so it came about that this sense of a life in natural objects, which in most poetry is but a rhetorical artifice, is with Wordsworth the assertion of what for him is almost literal fact. To him every natural object seemed to possess more or less of a moral or spiritual life, to be capable of a companionship with man, full of expression, of inexplicable affinities and delicacies of intercourse. An emanation, a particular spirit, belonged, not to the moving leaves or water only, but to the distant peak of the hills arising suddenly, by some change of perspective, above the nearer horizon, to the passing space of light across the plain, to the lichened Druidic stone even, for a certain weird fellowship in it with the moods of men. It was like a "survival," in the peculiar intellectual temperament of a man of letters at the end of the eighteenth century, of that primitive condition, which some philosophers have traced in the general history of human culture, wherein all outward objects alike, including even the works of men's hands, were believed to be endowed with animation, and the world was "full of souls"—that mood in which the old Greek gods were first begotten, and which had many strange aftergrowths.

In the early ages, this belief, delightful as its effects on poetry often are, was but the result of a crude intelligence. But, in Wordsworth, such power of seeing life, such perception of a soul, in inanimate things, came of an exceptional susceptibility to the impressions of eye and ear, and was, in its essence, a kind of sensuousness. At least, it is only in a temperament exceptionally susceptible on the sensuous side, that this sense of the expressiveness of outward things comes to be so large a part of life. That he awakened "a sort of thought in sense," is Shelley's just estimate of this element in Wordsworth's poetry.

And it was through nature, thus ennobled by a semblance of passion and thought, that he approached the spectacle of human life. Human life, indeed, is for him, at first, only an additional, accidental grace on an expressive landscape. When he thought of man, it was of man as in the presence and under the influence of these effective natural objects, and linked to them by many associations. The close connexion of man with natural objects, the habitual association of his thoughts and feelings with a particular spot of earth, has sometimes seemed to degrade those who are subject to its influence, as if it did but reinforce that physical connexion of our nature with the actual lime and clay of the soil, which is always drawing us nearer to our end. But for Wordsworth, these influences tended to the dignity of human nature, because they tended to tranquillise it. By raising nature to the level of human thought he gives it power and expression: he subdues man to the level of nature, and gives him thereby a certain breadth and coolness and solemnity. The leech-gatherer on the moor, the woman "stepping westward," are for him natural objects, almost in the same sense as the aged thorn, or the lichened rock on the heath. In this sense the leader of the "Lake School," in spite of an earnest preoccupation with man, his thoughts, his destiny, is the poet of nature. And of nature, after all, in its modesty. The English lake country has, of course, its grandeurs. But the peculiar function of Wordsworth's genius, as carrying in it a power to open out the soul of apparently little or familiar things, would have found its true test had he become the poet of Surrey, say! and the prophet of its life. The glories of Italy and Switzerland, though he did write a little about them, had too potent a material life of their own to serve greatly his poetic purpose.

Religious sentiment, consecrating the affections and natural regrets of the human heart, above all, that pitiful awe and care for the perishing human clay, of which relic-worship is but the corruption, has always had much to do with localities, with the thoughts which attach themselves to actual scenes and places. Now what is true of it everywhere, is truest of it in those secluded valleys where one generation after another maintains the same abiding-place; and it was on this side, that Wordsworth apprehended religion most strongly. Consisting, as it did so much, in the recognition of local sanctities, in the habit of connecting the stones and trees of a particular spot of earth with the great events of life, till the low walls, the green mounds, the half-obliterated epitaphs seemed full of voices, and a sort of natural oracles, the very religion of these people of the dales appeared but as another link between them and the earth, and was literally a religion of nature. It tranquillised them by bringing them under the placid rule of traditional and narrowly localised observances. "Grave livers," they seemed to him, under this aspect, with stately speech, and something of that natural dignity of manners, which underlies the highest courtesy.

And, seeing man thus as a part of nature, elevated and solemnised in proportion as his daily life and occupations brought him into companionship with permanent natural objects, his very religion forming new links for him with the narrow limits of the valley, the low vaults of his church, the rough stones of his home, made intense for him now with profound sentiment, Wordsworth was able to appreciate passion in the lowly. He chooses to depict people from humble life, because, being nearer to nature than others, they are on the whole more impassioned, certainly more direct in their expression of passion, than other men: it is for this direct expression of passion, that he values their humble words. In much that he said in exaltation of rural life, he was but pleading indirectly for that sincerity, that perfect fidelity to one's own inward presentations, to the precise features of the picture within, without which any profound poetry is impossible. It was not for their tameness, but for this passionate sincerity, that he chose incidents and situations from common life, "related in a selection of language really used by men." He constantly endeavours to bring his language near to the real language of men: to the real language of men, however, not on the dead level of their ordinary intercourse, but in select moments of vivid sensation, when this language is winnowed and ennobled by excitement. There are poets who have chosen rural life as their subject, for the sake of its passionless repose, and times when Wordsworth himself extols the mere calm and dispassionate survey of things as the highest aim of poetical culture. But it was not for such passionless calm that he preferred the scenes of pastoral life; and the meditative poet, sheltering himself, as it might seem, from the agitations of the outward world, is in reality only clearing the scene for the great exhibitions of emotion, and what he values most is the almost elementary expression of elementary feelings.

And so he has much for those who value highly the concentrated presentment of passion, who appraise men and women by their susceptibility to it, and art and poetry as they afford the spectacle of it. Breaking from time to time into the pensive spectacle of their daily toil, their occupations near to nature, come those great elementary feelings, lifting and solemnising their language and giving it a natural music. The great, distinguishing passion came to Michael by the sheepfold, to Ruth by the wayside, adding these humble children of the furrow to the true aristocracy of passionate souls. In this respect, Wordsworth's work resembles most that of George Sand, in those of her novels which depict country life. With a penetrative pathos, which puts him in the same rank with the masters of the sentiment of pity in literature, with Meinhold and Victor Hugo, he collects all the traces of vivid excitement which were to be found in that pastoral world—the girl who rung her father's knell; the unborn infant feeling about its mother's heart; the instinctive touches of children; the sorrows of the wild creatures, even—their home-sickness, their strange yearnings; the tales of passionate regret that hang by a ruined farm-building, a heap of stones, a deserted sheepfold; that gay, false, adventurous, outer world, which breaks in from time to time to bewilder and deflower these quiet homes; not "passionate sorrow" only, for the overthrow of the soul's beauty, but the loss of, or carelessness for personal beauty even, in those whom men have wronged—their pathetic wanness; the sailor "who, in his heart, was half a shepherd on the stormy seas"; the wild woman teaching her child to pray for her betrayer; incidents like the making of the shepherd's staff, or that of the young boy laying the first stone of the sheepfold;—all the pathetic episodes of their humble existence, their longing, their wonder at fortune, their poor pathetic pleasures, like the pleasures of children, won so hardly in the struggle for bare existence; their yearning towards each other, in their darkened houses, or at their early toil. A sort of biblical depth and solemnity hangs over this strange, new, passionate, pastoral world, of which he first raised the image, and the reflection of which some of our best modern fiction has caught from him.

He pondered much over the philosophy of his poetry, and reading deeply in the history of his own mind, seems at times to have passed the borders of a world of strange speculations, inconsistent enough, had he cared to note such inconsistencies, with those traditional beliefs, which were otherwise the object of his devout acceptance. Thinking of the high value he set upon customariness, upon all that is habitual, local, rooted in the ground, in matters of religious sentiment, you might sometimes regard him as one tethered down to a world, refined and peaceful indeed, but with no broad outlook, a world protected, but somewhat narrowed, by the influence of received ideas. But he is at times also something very different from this, and something much bolder. A chance expression is overheard and placed in a new connexion, the sudden memory of a thing long past occurs to him, a distant object is relieved for a while by a random gleam of light—accidents turning up for a moment what lies below the surface of our immediate experience—and he passes from the humble graves and lowly arches of "the little rock-like pile" of a Westmoreland church, on bold trains of speculative thought, and comes, from point to point, into strange contact with thoughts which have visited, from time to time, far more venturesome, perhaps errant, spirits.

He had pondered deeply, for instance, on those strange reminiscences and forebodings, which seem to make our lives stretch before and behind us, beyond where we can see or touch anything, or trace the lines of connexion. Following the soul, backwards and forwards, on these endless ways, his sense of man's dim, potential powers became a pledge to him, indeed, of a future life, but carried him back also to that mysterious notion of an earlier state of existence—the fancy of the Platonists—the old heresy of Origen. It was in this mood that he conceived those oft-reiterated regrets for a half-ideal childhood, when the relics of Paradise still clung about the soul—a childhood, as it seemed, full of the fruits of old age, lost for all, in a degree, in the passing away of the youth of the world, lost for each one, over again, in the passing away of actual youth. It is this ideal childhood which he celebrates in his famous *Ode on the Recollections of Childhood*, and some other poems which may be grouped around it, such as the lines on *Tintern Abbey*, and something like what he describes was actually truer of himself than he seems to have understood; for his own most delightful poems were really the instinctive productions of earlier life, and most surely for him, "the first diviner influence of this world" passed away, more and more completely, in his contact with experience.

Sometimes, as he dwelt upon those moments of profound, imaginative power, in which the outward object appears to take colour and expression, a new nature almost, from the prompting of the observant mind, the actual world would, as it were, dissolve and detach itself, flake by flake, and he himself seemed to be the creator, and when he would the destroyer, of the world in which he lived—that old isolating thought of many a brain-sick mystic of ancient and modern times.

At other times, again, in those periods of intense susceptibility, in which he appeared to himself as but the passive recipient of external influences, he was attracted by the thought of a spirit of life in outward things, a single, all-pervading mind in them, of which man, and even the poet's imaginative energy, are but moments—that old dream of the *anima mundi*, the mother of all things and their grave, in which some had desired to lose themselves, and others had become indifferent to the distinctions of good and evil. It would come, sometimes, like the sign of the *macrocosm* to Faust in his cell: the network of man and nature was seen to be pervaded by a common, universal life: a new, bold thought lifted him above the furrow, above the green turf of the Westmoreland churchyard, to a world altogether different in its vagueness and vastness, and the narrow glen was full of the brooding power of one universal spirit.

And so he has something, also, for those who feel the fascination of bold speculative ideas, who are really capable of rising upon them to conditions of poetical thought. He uses them, indeed, always with a very fine apprehension of the limits within which alone philosophical imaginings have any place in true poetry; and using them only for poetical purposes, is not too careful even to make them consistent with each other. To him, theories which for other men bring a world of technical diction, brought perfect form and expression, as in those two lofty books of *The Prelude*, which describe the decay and the restoration of Imagination and Taste. Skirting the borders of this world of bewildering heights and depths, he got but the first exciting influence of it, that joyful enthusiasm which great imaginative theories prompt, when the mind first comes to have an understanding of them; and it is not under the influence of these thoughts that his poetry becomes tedious or loses its blitheness. He keeps them, too, always within certain ethical bounds, so that no word of his could offend the simplest of those simple souls which are always the largest portion of mankind. But it is, nevertheless, the contact of these thoughts, the speculative boldness in them, which constitutes, at least for some minds, the secret attraction of much of his best poetry—the sudden passage from lowly thoughts and places to the majestic forms of philosophical imagination, the play of these forms over a world so different, enlarging so strangely the bounds of its humble churchyards, and breaking such a wild light on the graves of christened children.

And these moods always brought with them faultless expression. In regard to expression, as with feeling and thought, the duality of the higher and lower moods was absolute. It belonged to the higher, the imaginative mood, and was the pledge of its reality, to bring the appropriate language with it. In him, when the really poetical motive worked at all, it united, with absolute justice, the word and the idea; each, in the imaginative flame, becoming inseparably one with the other, by that fusion of matter and form, which is the characteristic of the highest poetical expression. His words are themselves thought and feeling; not eloquent, or musical words merely, but that sort of creative language which carries the reality of what it depicts, directly, to the consciousness.

The music of mere metre performs but a limited, yet a very peculiar and subtly ascertained function, in Wordsworth's poetry. With him, metre is but an additional grace, accessory to that deeper music of words and sounds, that moving power, which they exercise in the nobler prose no less than in formal poetry. It is a sedative to that excitement, an excitement sometimes almost painful, under which the language, alike of poetry and prose, attains a rhythmical power, independent of metrical combination, and dependent rather on some subtle adjustment of the elementary sounds of words themselves to the image or feeling they convey. Yet some of his pieces, pieces prompted by a sort of half-playful mysticism, like the *Daffodils* and *The Two April Mornings,* are distinguished by a certain quaint gaiety of metre, and rival by their perfect execution, in this respect, similar pieces among our own Elizabethan, or contemporary French poetry. And those who take up these poems after an interval of months, or years perhaps, may be surprised at finding how well old favourites wear, how their strange, inventive turns of diction or thought still send through them the old feeling of surprise. Those who lived about Wordsworth were all great lovers of the older English literature, and oftentimes there came out in him a noticeable likeness to our earlier poets. He quotes unconsciously, but with new power of meaning, a clause from one of Shakespeare's sonnets; and, as with some other men's most famous work, the *Ode on the Recollections of Childhood* had its anticipator.[3] He drew something too from the unconscious mysticism of the old English language itself, drawing out the inward significance of its racy idiom, and the not wholly unconscious poetry of the language used by the simplest people under strong excitement—language, therefore, at its origin.

The office of the poet is not that of the moralist, and the first aim of Wordsworth's poetry is to give the reader a peculiar kind of pleasure. But through his poetry, and through this pleasure in it, he does actually convey to the reader an extraordinary wisdom in the things of practice. One lesson, if men must have lessons, he conveys more clearly than all, the supreme importance of contemplation in the conduct of life.

Contemplation—impassioned contemplation—that, is with Wordsworth the end-in-itself, the perfect end. We see the majority of mankind going most often to definite ends, lower or higher ends, as their own instincts may determine; but the end may never be attained, and the means not be quite the right means, great ends and little ones alike being, for the most part, distant, and the ways to them, in this dim world, somewhat vague. Meantime, to higher or lower ends, they move too often with something of a sad countenance, with hurried and ignoble gait, becoming, unconsciously, something like thorns, in their anxiety to bear grapes; it being possible for people, in the pursuit of even great ends, to become themselves thin and impoverished in spirit and temper, thus diminishing the sum of perfection in the world, at its very sources. We understand this when it is a question of mean, or of intensely selfish ends—of Grandet, or Javert. We think it bad morality to say that the end justifies the means, and we know how false to all higher conceptions of the religious life is the type of one who is ready to do evil that good may come. We contrast with such dark, mistaken eagerness, a type like that of Saint Catherine of Siena, who made the means to her ends so attractive, that she has won for herself an undying place in the *House Beautiful,* not by her rectitude of soul only, but by its "fairness"—by those quite different qualities which commend themselves to the poet and the artist.

Yet, for most of us, the conception of means and ends covers the whole of life, and is the exclusive type or figure under which we represent our lives to ourselves. Such a figure, reducing all things to machinery, though it has on its side the authority of that old Greek moralist who has fixed for succeeding generations the outline of the theory of right living, is too like a mere picture or description of men's lives as we actually find them, to be the basis of the higher ethics. It covers the meanness of men's daily lives, and much of the dexterity and the vigour with which they pursue what may seem to them the good of themselves or of others; but not the intangible perfection of those whose ideal is rather in *being* than in *doing*—not those *manners* which are, in the deepest as in the simplest sense, *morals*, and without which one cannot so much as offer a cup of water to a poor man without offence—not the part of "antique Rachel," sitting in the company of Beatrice; and even the moralist might well endeavour rather to withdraw men from the too exclusive consideration of means and ends, in life.

Against this predominance of machinery in our existence, Wordsworth's poetry, like all great art and poetry, is a continual protest. Justify rather the end by the means, it seems to say: whatever may become of the fruit, make sure of the flowers and the leaves. It was justly said, therefore, by one who had meditated very profoundly on the true relation of means to ends in life, and on the distinction between what is desirable in itself and what is desirable only as machinery, that when the battle which he and his friends were waging had been won, the world would need more than ever those qualities which Wordsworth was keeping alive and nourishing.[4]

That the end of life is not action but contemplation—*being* as distinct from *doing*—a certain disposition of the mind: is, in some shape or other, the principle of all the higher morality. In poetry, in art, if you enter into their true spirit at all, you touch this principle, in a measure: these, by their very sterility, are a type of beholding for the mere joy of beholding. To treat life in the spirit of art, is to make life a thing in which means and ends are identified: to encourage such treatment, the true moral significance of art and poetry. Wordsworth, and other poets who have been like him in ancient or more recent times, are the masters, the experts, in this art of impassioned contemplation. Their work is, not to teach lessons, or enforce rules, or even to stimulate us to noble ends; but to withdraw the thoughts for a little while from the mere machinery of life, to fix them, with appropriate emotions, on the spectacle of those great facts in man's existence which no machinery affects, "on the great and universal passions of men, the most general and interesting of their occupations, and the entire world of nature,"—on "the operations of the elements and the appearances of the visible universe, on storm and sunshine, on the revolutions of the seasons, on cold and heat, on loss of friends and kindred, on injuries and resentments, on gratitude and hope, on fear and sorrow." To witness this spectacle with appropriate emotions is the aim of all culture; and of these emotions poetry like Wordsworth's is a great nourisher and stimulant. He sees nature full of sentiment and excitement; he sees men and women as parts of nature, passionate, excited, in strange grouping and connexion with the grandeur and beauty of the natural world:—images, in his own words, "of man suffering, amid awful forms and powers."

Such is the figure of the more powerful and original poet, hidden away, in part, under those weaker elements in Wordsworth's poetry, which for some minds determine their entire character; a poet somewhat bolder and more passionate than might at first sight be supposed, but not too bold for true poetical taste; an unimpassioned writer, you might sometimes fancy, yet thinking the chief aim, in life and art alike, to be a certain deep emotion; seeking most often the great elementary passions in lowly places; having at least this condition of all impassioned work, that he aims always at an absolute sincerity of feeling and diction, so that he is the true forerunner of the deepest and most passionate poetry of our own day; yet going back also, with something of a protest against the conventional fervour of much of the poetry popular in his own time, to those older English poets, whose unconscious likeness often comes out in him.

NOTES

1. Since this essay was written, such selections have been made, with excellent taste, by Matthew Arnold and Professor Knight.

2. In Wordsworth's prefatory advertisement to the first edition of *The Prelude*, published in 1850, it is stated that that work was intended to be introductory to *The Recluse;* and that *The Recluse*, if completed, would have consisted of three parts. The second part is "The Excursion." The third part was only planned; but the first book of the first part was left in manuscript by Wordsworth—though in manuscript, it is said, in no great condition of forwardness for the printers. This book, now for the first time printed *in extenso* (a very noble passage from it found place in that prose advertisement to *The Excursion*), is included in the latest edition of Wordsworth by Mr. John Morley. It was well worth adding to the poet's great bequest to English literature. A true student of his work, who has formulated for himself what he supposes to be the leading characteristics of Wordsworth's genius, will feel, we think, lively interest in testing them by the various fine passages in what is here presented for the first time. Let the following serve for a sample:—

> Thickets full of songsters, and the voice
> Of lordly birds, an unexpected sound
> Heard now and then from morn to latest eve,
> Admonishing the man who walks below
> Of solitude and silence in the sky:—
> These have we, and a thousand nooks of earth
> Have also these, but nowhere else is found,
> Nowhere (or is it fancy?) can be found
> The one sensation that is here; 'tis here,
> Here as it found its way into my heart
> In childhood, here as it abides by day,
> By night, here only; or in chosen minds
> That take it with them hence, where'er they go.
> —'Tis, but I cannot name it, 'tis the sense
> Of majesty, and beauty, and repose,
> A blended holiness of earth and sky,
> Something that makes this individual spot,
> This small abiding-place of many men,
> A termination, and a last retreat,
> A centre, come from wheresoe'er you will,
> A whole without dependence or defect,
> Made for itself, and happy in itself,
> Perfect contentment, Unity entire.

3. Henry Vaughn, in *The Retreat*.

4. See an interesting paper, by Mr. John Morley, on "The Death of Mr. Mill," *Fortnightly Review*, June 1873.

CHAPTER SIX

Twentieth-Century Literary Criticism

MODERNISM

Even with the twentieth century still in progress, it is evident that this century's literary criticism will be seen historically as a part of, or as in some measure responding to, modernism. This is not to say that modern criticism fits together compactly as a single movement, or that all modern criticism is reducible to the same program, but that the cultural phenomenon of modernism is broad and cohesive enough to encompass enormous developments. As a literary movement, modernism in the Anglo-American world dates from the early twentieth century and the influence of the French symbolist poetry of Baudelaire, Mallarmé, Valéry, and others. It is both a body of literature and criticism as well as a critical perspective—or, rather, several related perspectives—that produced some of the greatest writers and critics of our age. Sometimes the movement is said to have begun at the turn of the century with Conrad and Yeats, but others claim that it is most clearly delineated as a post–World War I phenomenon, best represented by the publication of James Joyce's *Ulysses* and T. S. Eliot's *The Waste Land* in 1922. By some accounts, the movement ended in the mid-1930s; others say it went on until World War II; and some note, as Fredric Jameson points out, and as we are suggesting, that contemporary postmodernism is simply another version of modernism.

In any case, the height of modernist fervor was surely Virginia Woolf's statement in 1924 that "in or about December, 1910, human character changed." She explained that "all human relations have shifted—those between masters and servants, husbands and wives, parents and children. And when human relations change there is at the same time a change in religion, conduct, politics, and literature." A decade earlier D. H. Lawrence had described a similarly radical reconception of human character in a letter to his editor describing the heroine of *The Rainbow:* "I don't so much care about what the woman *feels*—in the ordinary usage of the word. That presumes an *ego* to feel with. I only care about what the woman *is* . . . as a phenomenon (or as representing some greater, inhuman will), instead of what she feels according to the human conception." Like Woolf—and like Eliot in the essay included here—Lawrence is presenting an antiromantic, antiexpressionist conception of human character in literature—a conception of the subject that, as Eliot says, is "impersonal" and a conception of literature as something other than "expressive." It is one that focuses on the *forms* of literature and experience rather than on the narrowest sense of their "personal," "human" significance.

Notwithstanding the rhetoric of loss, apocalypse, and new beginnings (the rhetoric typical of modernism and the commentary about it)—and notwithstanding questionable politics such as fascism and anti-Semitism—the modernists were involved in a serious reevaluation of the limits of literary form and the possibilities for a new aesthetic in the arts generally—if not exactly new ways of being human, then at least a new paradigm of presentation for the products of twentieth-century culture. Henceforth, as Irving Babbitt said most forcefully, any romantic or sentimental tendencies in literature must be viewed as mere "emotional naturalism," a dissolving of real-world distinctions and a glossing over of important cultural demarcations. In place of nineteenth-century romantic "sloppiness," Babbitt said, is the emergent "modern spirit," "the positive and critical spirit, the spirit that refuses to take things on authority." Babbitt even called for a further movement away from supposedly "soft" and "uncritical" romanticism to "tough," "critical" modernism, a shift, as T. E. Hulme argued, into a contemporary version of the neoclassic sensibility and its modes of precise expression and carefully modulated sentiments. In short, Babbitt and Hulme called for a complete abandonment of romanticism and for the development of an emergent modern, antiromantic, formal sensibility.

This sensibility, as the essays by Eliot and Woolf show, most immediately calls for a movement away from the irrationality of what the British romantic poets had called *imagination*. T. S. Eliot is explicitly antiromantic in "Tradition and the Individual Talent" in his description of the "impersonality" of art. Rather, the modernists chose *fancy*, Coleridge's term for the human capacity to reason and to make demonstrable (in this sense, "critical") connections within and among experiences, an endless endeavor but a finite practice in that precise forms (distinct images and the like) are used to accomplish it. The modernists made this choice for epistemological reasons, particularly the belief that superior art comes out of the knowledge born of reasoned discriminations and a rational perspective, what Hulme called the poetic effect of the "hard" and "dry." They were not trying for "dry" in the sense of banality in poetry, but for the "hard, dry" presentation of precise images and a modulated use of language. Such imagery, like Eliot's "pair of ragged claws / Scuttling across the floors of silent seas," aims at a hard, or direct and detailed, presentation of sensory information; it is dry in being free of dependence on predetermined emotions that could be brought to or imposed on the text.

Further, the hard, dry language of modernism, as an ideal, does not need to impose emotions on the text because the text provides its own in the *form* of its progression—that is, in its discourse. Eliot calls these "structural emotions" and says that they are generated out of the text itself. By this he means that in reading poetry particular feelings are elicited from the reader by the formal arrangement of the poem's images. These images, in turn, are arranged in the text as an *objective correlative*, or a particular image sequence in the poem that corresponds to a human emotion. It follows that the act of reading draws forth all the feelings that combine to make up a particular emotion, which can be said to be "in" the text insofar as the text, by means of its form, specifically elicits that emotion. In short, this entire operation, from the deployment of images as an objective correlative through the received effect of a "structural emotion," takes place as a "textual" operation, a poetic experience that is not brought to the text as a personal experience but is generated precisely out of the text's particular patterning or structure. The modernist preference for fancy, in this way, means valuing the aesthetic structure of a text as conveyed in imagery—actually produced in the text—over the more personal responses that less rigorous reading (or a less "rigorous" poem) might produce.

Modernist poetics, then, as a formal explanation of poetry's function, is a scheme for art that fits into the twentieth century's broader picture of cultural discontinuity and irrationality. That is, the rational process whereby images in poetry call forth structural emotions in the reader happens against the modern background of lost connections between the cultural past and present, a world that is made over with each new work of art. For modernism, there are no ordained or natural lines of order in the world, no cultural backdrop that gives automatic meaning to a text; there is no providential plan according to which history and its outcomes are meaningfully situated. On the contrary, the disinheritance of modern culture is precisely the loss of belief in such traditional schemes as the Great Chain of Being. Pound and Eliot, in particular, do speak of grand cultural orders ("the mind of Europe," "tradition," "the past," and so on), but these are always distinctly human artifacts that must be reimagined for each poet and each culture. Eliot describes a kind of creative surrender whereby the poet interacts with conventional possibilities of form so that new possibilities may emerge as poetry—so that, in short, "new" culture will exist.

The modernists believed, in short, that through new poetic forms they were creating new worlds, whereas for prior ages there was only one world, given to humanity by one God. With the "new" poetics the modernists argued for the necessity of a modern cultural and artistic sensibility adequate to the felt quality of living in the aftermath of post-Enlightenment culture. This modernist perception of a contemporary crisis in values and artistic form is surely a concern for the history of ideas, and the modernist program for a new understanding of poetic and literary form has a direct bearing on Anglo-American and Continental criticism.

FORMALISM

One of the most visible and enduring aspects of modernism is the perspective in literary criticism called *formalism*. This broad movement took the modernist aesthetic and epistemology to heart and attempted to analyze literature not by its identifiable, or "natural" (or "representational"), content but consistently by its form—how it is constructed and how it functions so as to have meaning in the first place. This emphasis on form in literary criticism has two general applications: (1) an understanding of a text's interior patterning, or how it works; and (2) the recognition that form marks a work as belonging to a particular genre—novel, lyric, drama, and so on. Thus, formalism in the broadest sense views literatureeas a complex system of forms that may be analyzed in relation to one another at different levels of generality—from the specifics of a poetic image or line through that poem's genre. Formalism, in short, attempts to view literature not as constituted by its instrinsic ("natural") meaning, as an imitation of reality, but by relational patterns that are meaningful in a particular work and genre.

In addition to Russian formalism—a fertile movement in Moscow from 1915 to 1930 (for a discussion of this movement see "Modernism and Formalism" in Robert Con Davis and Ronald Schleifer's *Contemporary Literary Criticism*)—the most influential version of formalism in America and England is New Criticism. A single orthodoxy for this movement does not exist, but we can isolate several of the key tenets articulated by major Anglo-American critics from the late 1920s through the 1950s, the period of the New Criticism's active development. In particular, the New Criticism tried to displace "content" in literary analysis and, therein, to treat a work's form in a manner analogous to empirical research. It tried to organize the larger, generic forms of literature in accordance with the inner ordering of works as revealed in specific analyses, or "close readings."

The New Critics conceived literature to be a self-sustaining "artifact," a "spatial form" in Joseph Frank's term, and saw form as a self-contained "autonomous" entity, what Cleanth Brooks meant in his metaphor of the "well-wrought urn." Perhaps most important was the New Critical reliance on imagery as a concept with which to define form. Drawing heavily on the work of the modernist critics, New Critics like Brooks made the literary image the primary material or constituent of form itself. A New Critical "close reading" of a poem, for instance, involved a reader's preliminary identification of key images in a recurring pattern of opposition, or, as Brooks says, "tension." Only once this pattern of imagery is established do the New Critics attend to any interpretive considerations of form, what the poem means. The New Critics, thereafter, posited paradox and irony as controlling figures of tension. In making these terms a prescription for all poetry, the New Critics were substituting paradox and irony, as forms, for what used to be called "content." As Brooks says, paradox and irony are this important because they actually reflect the structure of the imagination itself. His reasoning, based on Kantian aesthetics, is simply that since it is produced by the imagination, poetry must reflect the imagination's own structure. That structure, or "form," is opposition as seen rhetorically in the figures of paradox and irony. These figures, then, although they are intended to be poetry's form, virtually become its content in that they are the ultimate referents for all the indications (largely imagistic) of meaning. From this standpoint, it makes sense to say that all poems are about, or "contain," these patterns.

The New Critics believed, further, that a work can be read objectively and accurately in light of its actual structure or form. A work can thus have a single, or "correct," interpretation. In "The Intentional Fallacy," for example, W. K. Wimsatt and Monroe C. Beardsley stipulate the manner of reading a work the "right" way. They explain the interference and inaccuracy possible when authorial intentions ("what the author meant") become a consideration in close reading—reading the "wrong" way. In "The Affective Fallacy," further, they show how at the other extreme a reader's undisciplined "affective," or emotional, responses to a text may distort the correct apprehension and interpretation of images, again highlighting the primacy of images themselves. In this way the New Critics—while as antiromantic as the modernists—retrieved from romanticism the concept of aesthetic wholeness and unity as well as a unified or single interpretation of a work. They argued that a work, in sum, will always be unified by a set of preconceived tensions, as expressed in paradox and irony, and that a work read properly is totally coherent.

CRITICISM AT MIDCENTURY

By midcentury there were two dominant formalist movements in American and European criticism: the New Criticism we have been discussing and the French version of it in *explication de texte*. Each prescribed a method of close reading and attempted to account for a variety of textual information, including imagery and image patterns, rhythm, sound, tone, and overall structure. Each method presented itself as potentially exhaustive, able to discover and catalogue *all* pertinent textual details in a manner approximating empirical observation in thoroughness and supposed objectivity. In the Anglo-American academy, however, the active development of the New Criticism came to an end in the late 1950s with the rise of archetypal criticism associated with the psychologist Carl Jung, which rapidly supplanted the New Criticism in practical influence and prestige.

Archetypal criticism exploited certain aspects of the New Criticism (mainly the deployment of paradox and irony) and then moved directly into areas that the New Criticism refused or failed to develop, particularly the relationship between literature and objects of study that exist "outside" the narrow formalist conception of literature. This included areas such as "mind," or personal psychology, history, culture, and even relations simultaneously "within" but transcending particular texts—what Northrop Frye specifically calls the "conceptual framework" of literature conceived as a "properly organized" intellectual discipline, the system of literature, that is, taken as more than "a huge aggregate or miscellaneous pile of creative efforts" (see Frye's "The Function of Criticism at the Present Time" in this section). On this issue, New Critics such as Cleanth Brooks, Wimsatt and Beardsley, John Crowe Ransom, Mark Schorer, and Joseph Frank were judged by Frye and others to be taking literary criticism dangerously outside of history—in a sense, outside of time—and were advocating a practice unable to account for changes in culture that affect literary form.

Archetypal criticism is defined by its focus on *archetypes*, cultural images apprehendable only as fragments, or incomplete representations, somewhat like the light flickering on the walls of Plato's cave. Archetypal images—that is, fragments and never the totality of an archetype—are scattered impressions cast upon the screen of conscious thought. These images constitute informative patterns that, while never quite unambiguous or completely unified, are nonetheless crucial indications of cultural organization. The definitive use of this concept in literary criticism is Frye's *Anatomy of Criticism* (1957), for which Frye's "The Function of Criticism at the Present Time" is the introduction. In this book Frye proclaimed, in effect, that archetypal criticism's success would be precisely where the prior movement had failed. He then went on to erect the monomyth's structure over the whole of culture in a "protostructuralist" reading of Western literature's archetypal development—from prehistoric and sacred myth to present-day irony. In a remarkable elaboration of literary archetypes, Frye presented a comprehensive catalogue of literary forms (genre, sound, rhythm, tone, and so on) as part of his complex presentation of the archetypal paradigm. Implicit in his discussion is a sense of the development of Western literature, its historical dimension, as Frye simultaneously suggested both an archetypal "conceptual framework" for criticism and an examination of the history of literature.

Throughout the 1960s, Frye's version of archetypalism influenced much theory and practical criticism, especially in medieval and Renaissance studies. Gradually, however, Frye's approach came under attack by historical critics, structuralists, and feminists for being neither truly historical (able to account for "real" historical change) nor consistent in the application of its principles. Most devastating, though, was the feminist critique of Frye, which attacked the Jungian paradigm and the notion of the monomyth. As feminists pointed out, the archetypal hero is at base a male figure attempting to bring reconciliation with an "original" female (the Great Mother) and with a potential "anima" figure who is both the hero's ideal mate and his reward for success on the quest. This exclusively male paradigm assumes a male subject, and nowhere in Jung's thought, or Frye's, is there a serious attempt to reconceive a woman's experience outside of the role of providing support for men.

It is common to note that critical movements develop through a kind of life cycle, eventually fade, and then may go on to stimulate new movements after them. Psychoanalysis, for example, was the intellectual parent of archetypalism; but, as it happens, psychoanalytic criticism both precedes archetypalism, with the first generation of Freudians beginning in the twenties and thirties, and succeeds it in the more recent movement, the semiotic "return to Freud," as we mention in the poststructuralist discussion here. That is, with psychoanalysis, a first generation of Freudian criticism—interested, for example, in identifying Freudian themes and oedipal complexes in literature (see Freud's "The Theme of the Three Caskets" for an intelligent version of this traditional criticism)—continued until the 1960s and included some of the better critical minds of the twentieth century: Ernest Jones, Marie Bonaparte, Edmund Wilson, Lionel Trilling, Frederick Crews, and others. This early Freudianism as an approach to literature began to weaken at midcentury, as did Jungian criticism and the New Criticism, largely because of an inability to go beyond thematic ("therapeutic") comment to deal with literary structure. There was the growing sense, in short, that the pointing out of an oedipal complex in a text was a truism and not an insight.

STRUCTURALISM

As the influence of several midcentury critical approaches waned, a new area of activity appeared in the 1960s that has come to be known as *structuralism*. Instead of examining the effects or results of language—the *communicative* function of language—structural (and semiotic) analyses attempted to examine the *conditions* that allow language and meaning to arise in the first place, seeking to know—as Roland Barthes says in "The Structuralist Activity"—"how meaning is possible." Structuralism has grown out of the great advances in twentieth-century linguistics initiated by Ferdinand de Saussure as *semiology*, what Saussure called "a science that studies the life of signs within society." Instead of asking where particular linguistic formations come from—their history—semiotics asks how the elements of language are configured in order to produce the results or effects they have. Saussure adds the crucial qualification that a semiotic sign, like a traffic light, is an arbitrary indicator of a message; all of the elements of language, in other words, could be different from what they are. "Green," for example, *could* represent "stop" as well as "go."

Structuralism—based on Claude Lévi-Strauss's use of semiotics in anthropology in the early 1950s—has had a huge impact on twentieth-century criticism and in the 1960s and early 1970s has proved to be a watershed in modern criticism. At first, the rise of structuralism was greeted with considerable hostility by critics in the United States and Europe. It was generally acknowledged that this movement was attempting an ambitious, "scientific" examination of literature in all its dimensions. To some, however, the supposed detachment of such an investigation appeared to be offensively antihumanistic and unrelated to the values of a Western liberal education. Not only was structuralism considered antihumanistic; to the Anglo-American world it was further suspect as a French import, merely an exotic dalliance for a few intellectuals who were arrogantly and blindly worshipping a foreignism. In 1975, however, the Modern Language Association awarded Jonathan Culler's *Structuralist Poetics* the annual James Russell Lowell prize for a literary study, and the Anglo-American academy (if not critics and readers generally) began to acknowledge that, for good or ill, structuralism was in place as a functioning critical system.

In retrospect, the rise of structuralism and semiotics in the 1960s vividly dramatizes—among other things—the extent to which modern theory became an interdisciplinary phenomenon. Structuralism and semiotics virtually constituted a field in themselves, designatable simply as "theory," because, by taking meaning and the varying conditions of meaning as their objects of study, they cut through, without being confined to, traditional humanities and social sciences such as literary studies, philosophy, history, linguistics, psychology, and anthropology, all of which directly influenced literary theory since the late 1960s.

In literary criticism, structuralism is closely related to literary formalism, as represented by both American New Criticism and Russian formalism. The principal aim of these movements was to displace content in literary analysis and to focus instead on literary form in a detailed manner analogous to the methods of empirical research. Both movements also sought to organize the generic structures of literature into a system consistent with the inner ordering of works that close reading revealed. In each case, literature is viewed as a complex system of forms analyzable with considerable objectivity at different levels of generality—from the specific components of a poetic image or line through the poem's genre to that genre's place in the system of literature. The New Criticism and Russian formalism, in short, promoted the view of literature as a system and a general scientific approach to literary studies. This systematizing and scientizing impulse, especially as formulated in the linguistically oriented theories of Russian formalism, is a major link between early modern formalism and the structuralism of the 1960s.

Structuralism's self-imposed limitations, however, especially its lack of concern with diachronic (temporal) change and its focus on general systems rather than on individual cases, became increasingly evident in the late 1960s. The French philosopher Jacques Derrida offered a particularly decisive critique, a central example of which is "Structure, Sign, and Play in the Discourse of the Human Sciences," which focuses on the structural anthropology of Claude Lévi-Strauss. Derrida connects structuralism with a traditional Western blindness to the "structurality" of structure, or an unwillingness to examine the theoretical and ideological implications of structure as a concept. Derrida points out that the attempt to investigate structure implies the ability to stand outside and apart from it—as if one could move outside of cultural understanding in order to take a detached view of culture. In specific terms, Derrida's critique of Lévi-Strauss (not only in "Structure, Sign, and Play" but in "Father of Logos," *On Grammatology*, and many other works) is a critique of the privileging of the opposition between nature and culture—what in a different context Lévi-Strauss calls the tangible and the intelligible. Derrida argues that since one never transcends culture, since one can never examine it from the outside, there is no standing free of structure, no so-called natural state free of the structural interplay that, in the structuralist analysis, constitutes meaning. There is no objective examination of structure. Therefore, as Derrida shows, the attempt to read and interpret cultural structures cannot be adequately translated into exacting scientific models. If structure, therefore, cannot be isolated and examined, then structuralism is seriously undermined as a method. Derrida, in fact, argued that in place of structuralism we should recognize the interplay of differences among texts, the activity that he and others call *structuration*—a blend of signification and the activity of signifying.

POSTSTRUCTURALISM

Poststructuralism is largely an outgrowth of the philosophical practice called *deconstruction* that Derrida initiated in his critique of structuralism, the general approach to structure that we have been speaking of. As J. Hillis Miller says in "The Search for Grounds in Literary Study," "the fundamental sense of [a deconstructive] 'critique' [is] discriminating, testing out." That is, a deconstructive critique examines and tests the assumptions supporting intellectual insight in order to interrogate the self-evident truths they are based on. It tests the legitimacy of the contextual "bounds" understanding both presents and requires. Rather than seeking a way of understanding—that is, a way of incorporating new phenomena into coherent (i.e., "bounded") existing or modified models—a deconstructive critique seeks to uncover the unexamined axioms that give rise to those models and their boundaries.

As it bears on literary criticism, deconstruction is precisely a *strategy* of reading. Derrida describes such deconstructive reading as starting from a philosophical hierarchy in which two opposed terms are presented as the "superior" general case and the "inferior" special case. These oppositions form some of Western culture's most important categories of thought, such as truth/error, health/disease, male/female, nature/culture, philosophy/literature, speech/writing, and seriousness/play. Jonathan Culler gives the sample opposition of language conceived as "constative" (i.e., as essentially a system of true or false meanings) versus language conceived as "performative" (i.e., the actual *activity* of using language). Another example, as the feminist essays in this collection suggest (see Woolf's "Shadow Across the Page," Ellman's "Phallic Criticism," and Gilbert's "Life's Empty Pack"), is the generally accepted use of "man" to mean "human" and "woman" to mean only the special case of a female human being. Deconstruction then strategically reverses such crucial hierarchies so as to elevate the inferior over the superior—making, as Culler says, "the constative a special case of the performative." Another example of a deconstructive "reversal," as Derrida himself says, would be Lévi-Strauss's reversal of nature and culture, making the once-superior category of nature a special case (an inferior category) of culture.

The purpose of these reversals, however, is not merely to invert value systems; doing such, Derrida says elsewhere, would only "confirm" the old system of opposition that is the object of analysis. Rather, deconstruction attempts to "explode" (in Derrida's metaphor) the original relationship of superior and inferior that gives rise to the semantic horizon—the possibility of any particular meaning—of a discourse. Deconstruction then attempts, in Derrida's words, to confront one interpretation "of interpretation, of structure, of sign, of freeplay"—one that seeks "a truth or an origin which is free from freeplay and from the order of the sign"—with another interpretation of interpretation "which is no longer turned toward the origin, [but] affirms freeplay and tries to pass beyond man and humanism."

The poststructuralist era that has followed from Derrida's work takes in a large area of literary criticism. Current psychoanalytic criticism, influenced by Jacques Lacan, decenters the traditional Freudian version of the "subject"—the isolated and sovereign "ego"—and is distinctly deconstructive in its practice. Feminism, too, especially in the work of Hélène Cixous, Barbara Johnson, Gayatri Chakravorty Spivak, and Julia Kristeva, uses deconstructive strategies for displacing maleness and "male" readings of literary texts. Marxist critics, especially Louis Althusser, Fredric Jameson, John Ellis, Rosalind Coward, and Michael Ryan have found deep affinities between the Marxist and deconstructive critiques of cultural production. All of these critics have adopted a deconstructive approach to literary texts and have attempted from different angles to understand the forces that shape and "rupture" those texts.

In one sense, poststructuralism can be said to cover all post-Derridean developments in criticism, including the contemporary rhetorical approach of Stanley Fish and other reader-response critics. It is, in any event, difficult to find the limits of deconstruction's influence. More conservatively, the poststructuralist approach to the literary texts arises from definitions of literature and criticism that have followed from Derrida's ideas about what constitutes a text and from his strategies for deciphering the text.

CULTURAL CRITIQUE

In the aftermath of poststructuralism and a dramatic foregrounding of the problems of signification, textuality, and interpretation, an approach to cultural studies that encompasses literary criticism has begun to emerge. This movement—associated with Derrida, Michel Foucault, Jacques Lacan, Mikhail Bakhtin, Julia Kristeva, Gayatri Chakravorty Spivak, Jean-François Lyotard, Fredric Jameson, and many others—suggests that the study of criticism can profitably be situated as a part, and a leading part, of the study of culture. A complete justification for this expansion would necessarily require an involved definition of culture itself, which Raymond Williams says in *Keywords* is "one of the two or three most complicated words in the English Language." In another book, *Culture*, Williams says that " 'cultural practice' and 'cultural production' are not simply derived from an otherwise constituted social order but are themselves major elements in its constitution." In this conception, culture is not some "informing spirit" within society; rather, Williams says, it is "the *signifying system* through which necessarily . . . a social system is communicated, reproduced, experienced and explored."

Williams's definitions, of course, are not the only valid description of culture, but it is clear from his ideas that literary studies conceived as a systematized critical activity—a criticism that studies "signifying systems" in a more or less systematic, exact, and generalizing way—is in a position to direct its methods and observations to the widest area of the production of meanings—to cultural activities as specific signifying practices and as a general area of inquiry.

In fact, a strong argument can be made that the texts which we customarily call "literature" constitute a privileged site where the most important social, psychological, and cultural forces combine and contend. In this way, the attention to discourse, to language in all its manifestations, in its production and in its reception, is a natural focus of literary studies and a natural outgrowth of criticism. Accordingly, as the essays by Kenneth Burke, Mikhail Bakhtin, Mary Ellman, Hélène Cixous, Barbara Christian, Robert Stepto, Stanley Fish, and Michel Foucault show, cultural studies is a dialogic relationship among political, pedagogical, historical, gender, and literary concerns. One of the most productive areas of cultural studies has been the recent examination of the institution of literary study in the academy. In books like Robert Scholes's *Textual Power*, Richard Ohmann's *English in America*, Gerald Graff's *Professing Literature*, Jonathan Culler's *Framing the Sign: Criticism and Its Institutions*, Frank Lentricchia's *Criticism and Social Change*, the very nature of the study of literature is being examined in relation to other cultural practices. In this section we have included examples of this wider conception of critical-practice-as-cultural-critique as an important informing force within contemporary criticism.

In ways that could scarcely be anticipated earlier in the century, late twentieth-century cultural studies reveal a radically modern perspective on continuity, change, and cultural diversity. Whereas modernism announced a break with the past and celebrated the emergence of cultural diversity—"multiplicity" as well as the foregrounding of arbitrariness and change and time itself in the modern world—cultural criticism is focused on the different discourses of culture and on the manner in which cultural practices come into existence. Further, cultural criticism, as it is developing in the 1970s and 1980s, is far more interested in conflict and ideology than were many previous approaches to culture. In this way—connected with gender, ideological, political, and other interdisciplinary studies—contemporary cultural studies is realizing some of the aims of modernist and avant-garde cultural projects at the beginning of the twentieth century.

FURTHER READING

Arac, Jonathan, et al. *The Yale Critics: Deconstruction in America.* Minneapolis: University of Minnesota Press, 1983.

Barthes, Roland. *S/Z.* Trans. R. Miller. New York: Hill and Wang, 1974.

Bleich, David. *Readings and Feelings: An Introduction to Subjective Criticism.* New York: Harper & Row, 1977.

Bloom, Harold. *The Anxiety of Influence: A Theory of Poetry.* New York: Oxford University Press, 1973.

———, et al. *Deconstruction and Criticism.* New York: Continuum, 1979.

Culler, Jonathan. *Framing the Sign: Criticism and Its Institutions.* Norman: University of Oklahoma Press, 1988.

———. *On Deconstruction: Theory and Criticism after Structuralism.* Ithaca, N.Y.: Cornell University Press, 1982.

———. *Structuralist Poetics.* Ithaca, N.Y.: Cornell University Press, 1975.

Davis, Robert Con, ed. *Lacan and Narration: The Psychoanalytic Difference in Narrative Theory.* Baltimore: Johns Hopkins University Press, 1984.

Davis, Robert Con, and Ronald Schleifer, eds. *Contemporary Literary Criticism: Literary and Cultural Theory.* White Plains, N.Y.: Longman, 1988.

———. *Rhetoric and Form: Deconstruction at Yale.* Norman: University of Oklahoma Press, 1985.

de Beauvoir, Simone. *The Second Sex.* Trans. H. M. Parshley. New York: Knopf, 1953.

de Man, Paul. *Allegories of Reading: Figural Language in Rousseau, Nietzsche, Rilke, and Proust.* New Haven, Conn.: Yale University Press, 1979.

Derrida, Jacques. *Dissemination.* Trans. Barbara Johnson. Chicago: University of Chicago Press, 1981.

———. *On Grammatology.* Trans. Gayatri G. Spivak. Baltimore: Johns Hopkins University Press, 1976.

Ellman, Mary. *Thinking about Women.* New York: Harcourt, Brace, 1968.

Erlich, Victor. *Russian Formalism: History and Doctrine.* 3rd ed. New Haven, Conn.: Yale University Press, 1981.

Fish, Stanley. *Is There a Text in This Class?* Cambridge, Mass.: Harvard University Press, 1980.

Frye, Northrop. *Anatomy of Criticism: Four Essays.* Princeton, N.J.: Princeton University Press, 1957.

Gilbert, Sandra M., and Susan Gubar. *The Madwoman in the Attic.* New Haven, Conn.: Yale University Press, 1979.

———. *No Man's Land: The Place of the Woman Writer in the Twentieth Century.* Vol. I. New Haven, Conn.: Yale University Press, 1988.

Graff, Gerald. *Literature Against Itself: Literary Ideas in Modern Society.* Chicago: University of Chicago Press, 1979.

———. *Professing Literature.* Chicago: University of Chicago Press, 1987.

Holland, Norman N. *The Dynamics of Literary Response.* New York: Oxford University Press, 1968.

Jacobus, Mary, ed. *Women Writing and Writing about Women.* London: Croom Helm, 1979.

Jameson, Fredric. *The Political Unconscious: Narrative as a Social Symbolic Act.* Ithaca, N.Y.: Cornell University Press, 1981.

———. *The Prison-House of Language: A Critical Account of Structuralism and Russian Formalism.* Princeton, N.J.: Princeton University Press, 1972.

Jardine, Alice. *Gynesis: Configurations of Woman and Modernity.* Ithaca, N.Y.: Cornell University Press, 1985.

Lacan, Jacques. *Ecrits: A Selection.* Trans. A. Sheridan. New York: Norton, 1977.

Lentricchia, Frank. *After the New Criticism.* Chicago: University of Chicago Press, 1980.

———. *Criticism and Social Change.* Chicago: University of Chicago Press, 1983.

Lévi-Strauss, Claude. *Structural Anthropology.* Vol. I. Trans. Clair Jacobson and Brooke Schoepf. New York: Basic Books, 1963.

———. *Structural Anthropology.* Vol. II. Trans. Monique Layton. New York: Basic Books, 1976.

———. *The Raw and the Cooked.* Trans. John and Doreen Weightman. New York: Harper & Row, 1975.

Macksey, Richard, and Eugenio Donato, eds. *The Structuralist Controversy.* Baltimore: Johns Hopkins University Press, 1970.

Mailloux, Steven. *Interpretive Conventions: The Reader in the Study of American Fiction.* Ithaca, N.Y.: Cornell University Press, 1982.

Merod, Jim. *The Political Responsibility of the Critic.* Ithaca, N.Y.: Cornell University Press, 1987.

Millett, Kate. *Sexual Politics.* Garden City, N.Y.: Doubleday, 1970.

Moi, Toril. *Sexual/Textual Politics: Feminist Literary Theory.* London: Methuen, 1985.

Ohmann, Richard. *English in America.* New York: Oxford University Press, 1976.

Propp, Vladimir. *The Morphology of the Folktale.* Trans. Laurence Scott. Austin: University of Texas Press, 1968.

Ryan, Michael. *Marxism and Deconstruction: A Critical Articulation.* Baltimore: Johns Hopkins University Press, 1982.

Said, Edward W. *Orientalism.* New York: Pantheon Books, 1978.

———. *The World, the Text, and the Critic.* Cambridge, Mass.: Harvard University Press, 1983.

Saussure, Ferdinand de. *Course in General Linguistics.* Trans. Wade Baskin. 1916; Reprint, New York: McGraw-Hill, 1966.

Scholes, Robert. *Textual Power.* New Haven, Conn.: Yale University Press, 1985.

Todorov, Tzvetan. *The Fantastic: A Structural Approach to a Literary Genre.* Trans. R. Howard. Ithaca, N.Y.: Cornell University Press, 1975.

Williams, Raymond. *Keywords.* New York: Oxford University Press, 1985.

———. *Culture.* London: Fontana, 1981.

Woolf, Virginia. *A Room of One's Own.* New York: Harcourt Brace Jovanovich, 1981.

Sigmund Freud 1856–1939

Sigmund Freud's work is unrivaled in its impact on the intellectual development of the twentieth century. Its influence reaches beyond psychology and far into literature, philosophy, political science, pedagogy, sociology, women's studies—in fact, to all of the self-conscious disciplines of the human sciences.

His most famous works include *Studies in Hysteria* (1895); *The Interpretation of Dreams* (1900); *The Psychopathology of Everyday Life* (1904); *Introductory Lectures on Psychoanalysis* (1909); *Totem and Taboo* (1913); *The Ego and the Id* (1923); *Civilization and Its Discontents* (1930); *New Introductory Lectures on Psychoanalysis* (1933); and *Moses and Monotheism* (1939). Freud's writings are collected in the Standard Edition of *The Complete Psychological Works of Sigmund Freud,* edited by James Strachey in collaboration with Anna Freud and assisted by Alix Strachey and Alan Tyson, 24 volumes (1953–74).

Freud's theories are no longer deemed, if in fact they ever were, as scientific fact. Rather, the psychoanalytic model has become—with revision—a powerful interpretive tool, for some a "system," used to make sense of the hidden, chaotic aspects of modern existence. Implicit in Freud's thought is the belief that there is an ordering principle, or principles, a superstructure, that unravels hidden meaning in unrelated symptoms and pulls them together into a sense-making, unifying explanation. Thus when the psychoanalytic method is applied to literary criticism, the reader is left with the sometimes comforting, sometimes infuriating, conclusion that "everything" signifies something. That is, while some significances are unconscious, nothing is accidental.

In "The Theme of the Three Caskets," Freud becomes a kind of literary critic and examines the motivating structures of two of Shakespeare's plays, *The Merchant of Venice* and *King Lear.* In this essay, two things are apparent. The first is that history, myth, folklore, and literature all may be read as manifestations of human unconscious motivations. The second is that woman exists only in relation to man and gives voice to man's fears and desires.

Although the plays superficially may seem unrelated, Freud contends that both *The Merchant of Venice* and *King Lear* transform timeless myths into the substance of human dreams. In *The Merchant of Venice,* Portia has been bidden to marry the one of her suitors who chooses correctly among three caskets made of gold, silver, and lead. The story has its roots in folklore and myth, and thus Freud postulates that mythic tales articulate the dreams of man; therefore, the starring role falls not to Portia but rather to her suitor. The caskets are not mere gold, silver, and lead; they are dream symbols of women. As Freud says, "the theme is a human one, a man's choice between three women."

In *King Lear,* a father makes a choice among his daughters, three women who symbolize those things which man most desires and most fears. Here

Freud invokes the concept of reaction formation: a thing consumed (or almost consumed) by its opposite. The third casket and the third daughter have been transformed into the prizes. Yet, says Freud, lead seems dull as compared to gold and silver just as Cordelia lavishes no praise on her father and then dies. According to Freud, her death—all death—is the underlying wager of such interpretive choices. To return to its mythic origins, Shakespeare's story harkens back to the bifurcation of woman as the goddess of love and the goddess of death. Cordelia and that leaden casket appear to be what man desires most: the unconditional love of a woman (his mother), but they are both imbued with the destruction that mother earth brings. Cordelia's death thus is not her own; it is the dream image of Lear's own death; "the silent Goddess of Death, will take him into her arms."

The Theme of the Three Caskets

I

Two scenes from Shakespeare, one from a comedy and the other from a tragedy, have lately given me occasion for posing and solving a small problem.

The first of these scenes is the suitors' choice between the three caskets in *The Merchant of Venice*. The fair and wise Portia is bound at her father's bidding to take as her husband only that one of her suitors who chooses the right casket from among the three before him. The three caskets are of gold, silver and lead: the right casket is the one that contains her portrait. Two suitors have already departed unsuccessful: they have chosen gold and silver. Bassanio, the third, decides in favour of lead; thereby he wins the bride, whose affection was already his before the trial of fortune. Each of the suitors gives reasons for his choice in a speech in which he praises the metal he prefers and depreciates the other two. The most difficult task thus falls to the share of the fortunate third suitor; what he finds to say in glorification of lead as against gold and silver is little and has a forced ring. If in psycho-analytic practice we were confronted with such a speech, we should suspect that there were concealed motives behind the unsatisfying reasons produced.

Shakespeare did not himself invent this oracle of the choice of a casket; he took it from a tale in the *Gesta Romanorum*,[1] in which a girl has to make the same choice to win the Emperor's son.[2] Here too the third metal, lead, is the bringer of fortune. It is not hard to guess that we have here an ancient theme, which requires to be interpreted, accounted for and traced back to its origin. A first conjecture as to the meaning of this choice between gold, silver and lead is quickly confirmed by a statement of Stucken's,[3] who has made a study of the same material over a wide field. He writes: "The identity of Portia's three suitors is clear from their choice: the Prince of Morocco chooses the gold casket—he is the sun; the Prince of Arragon chooses the silver casket—he is the moon; Bassanio chooses the leaden casket—he is the star youth." In support of this explanation he cites an episode from the Estonian folk-epic "Kalewipoeg," in which the three suitors appear undisguisedly as the sun, moon and star youths (the last being "the Pole-star's eldest boy") and once again the bride falls to the lot of the third.

Thus our little problem has led us to an astral myth! The only pity is that with this explanation we are not at the end of the matter. The question is not exhausted, for we do not share the belief of some investigators that myths were read in the heavens and brought down to earth; we are more inclined to judge with Otto Rank[4] that they were projected on to the heavens after having arisen elsewhere under purely human conditions. It is in this human content that our interest lies.

Let us look once more at our material. In the Estonian epic, just as in the tale from the *Gesta Romanorum*, the subject is a girl choosing between the three suitors; in the scene from *The Merchant of Venice* the subject is apparently the same, but at the same time something appears in it that is in the nature of an inversion of the theme: a *man* chooses between three—caskets. If what we were concerned with were a dream, it would occur to us at once that caskets are also women, symbols of what is essential in woman, and therefore of a woman herself—like coffers, boxes, cases, baskets, and so on.[5] If we boldly assume that there are symbolic substitutions of the same kind in myths as well, then the casket scene in *The Merchant of Venice* really becomes the inversion we suspected. With a wave of the wand, as though we were in a fairy tale, we have stripped the astral garment from our theme; and now we see that the theme is a human one, *a man's choice between three women.*

This same content, however, is to be found in another scene of Shakespeare's, in one of his most powerfully moving dramas; not the choice of a bride this time, yet linked by many hidden similarities to the choice of the casket in *The Merchant of Venice*. The old King Lear resolves to divide his kingdom while he is still alive among his three daughters, in proportion to the amount of love that each of them expresses for him. The two elder ones, Goneril and Regan, exhaust themselves in asseverations and laudations of their love for him; the third, Cordelia, refuses to do so. He should have recognized the unassuming, speechless love of his third daughter and rewarded it, but he does not recognize it. He disowns Cordelia, and divides the kingdom between the other two, to his own and the general ruin. Is not this once more the scene of a choice between three women, of whom the youngest is the best, the most excellent one?

There will at once occur to us other scenes from myths, fairy tales and literature, with the same situation as their content. The shepherd Paris has to choose between three goddesses, of whom he declares the third to be the most beautiful. Cinderella, again, is a youngest daughter, who is preferred by the prince to her two elder sisters. Psyche, in Apuleius's story, is the youngest and fairest of three sisters. Psyche is, on the one hand, revered as Aphrodite in human form; on the other, she is treated by that goddess as Cinderella was treated by her stepmother and is set the task of sorting a heap of mixed seeds, which she accomplishes with the help of small creatures (doves in the case of Cinderella, ants in the case of Psyche).[6] Anyone who cared to make a wider survey of the material would undoubtedly discover other versions of the same theme preserving the same essential features.

Let us be content with Cordelia, Aphrodite, Cinderella and Psyche. In all the stories the three women, of whom the third is the most excellent one, must surely be regarded as in some way alike if they are represented as sisters. (We must not be led astray by the fact that Lear's choice is between three *daughters*; this may mean nothing more than that he has to be represented as an old man. An old man cannot very well choose between three women in any other way. Thus they become his daughters.)

But who are these three sisters and why must the choice fall on the third? If we could answer this question, we should be in possession of the interpretation we are seeking. We have once already made use of an application of psycho-analytic technique, when we explained the three caskets symbolically as three women. If we have the courage to proceed in the same way, we shall be setting foot on a path which will lead us first to something unexpected and incomprehensible, but which will perhaps, by a devious route, bring us to a goal.

It must strike us that this excellent third woman has in several instances certain peculiar qualities besides her beauty. They are qualities that seem to be tending towards some kind of unity; we must certainly not expect to find them equally well marked in every example. Cordelia makes herself unrecognizable, inconspicuous like lead, she remains dumb, she "loves and is silent."[7] Cinderella hides so that she cannot be found. We may perhaps be allowed to equate concealment and dumbness. These would of course be only two instances out of the five we have picked out. But there is an intimation of the same thing to be found, curiously enough, in two other cases. We have decided to compare Cordelia, with her obstinate refusal, to lead. In Bassanio's short speech while he is choosing the casket, he says of lead (without in any way leading up to the remark):

> Thy paleness[8] moves me more than eloquence.

That is to say: "Thy plainness moves me more than the blatant nature of the other two." Gold and silver are "loud"; lead is dumb—in fact like Cordelia, who "loves and is silent."[9]

In the ancient Greek accounts of the Judgement of Paris, nothing is said of any such reticence on the part of Aphrodite. Each of the three goddesses speaks to the youth and tries to win him by promises. But, oddly enough, in a quite modern handling of the same scene this characteristic of the third one which has struck us makes its appearance again. In the libretto of Offenbach's *La Belle Hélène*, Paris, after telling of the solicitations of the other two goddesses, describes Aphrodite's behaviour in this competition for the beauty-prize:

> *La troisième, ah! la troisième . . .*
> *La troisième ne dit rien.*
> *Elle eut le prix tout de même . . .*[10]

If we decide to regard the peculiarities of our "third one" as concentrated in her "dumbness," then psycho-analysis will tell us that in dreams dumbness is a common representation of death.[11]

More than ten years ago a highly intelligent man told me a dream which he wanted to use as evidence of the telepathic nature of dreams. In it he saw an absent friend from whom he had received no news for a very long time, and reproached him energetically for his silence. The friend made no reply. It afterwards turned out that he had met his death by suicide at about the time of the dream. Let us leave the problem of telepathy on one side:[12] there seems, however, not to be any doubt that here the dumbness in the dream represented death. Hiding and being unfindable—a thing which confronts the prince in the fairy tale of Cinderella three times, is another unmistakable symbol of death in dreams; so, too, is a marked pallor, of which the "paleness" of the lead in one reading of Shakespeare's text is a reminder.[13] It would be very much easier for us to transpose these interpretations from the language of dreams to be mode of expression used in the myth that is now under consideration if we could make it seem probable that dumbness must be interpreted as a sign of being dead in productions other than dreams.

At this point I will single out the ninth story in Grimm's *Fairy Tales,* which bears the title "The Twelve Brothers."[14] A king and a queen have twelve children, all boys. The king declares that if the thirteenth child is a girl, the boys will have to die. In expectation of her birth he has twelve coffins made. With their mother's help the twelve sons take refuge in a hidden wood, and swear death to any girl they may meet. A girl is born, grows up, and learns one day from her mother that she has had twelve brothers. She decides to seek them out, and in the wood she finds the youngest; he recognizes her, but is anxious to hide her on account of the brothers' oath. The sister says: "I will gladly die, if by so doing I can save my twelve brothers." The brothers welcome her affectionately, however, and she stays with them and looks after their house for them. In a little garden beside the house grow twelve lilies. The girl picks them and gives one to each brother. At that moment the brothers are changed into ravens, and disappear, together with the house and garden. (Ravens are spirit-birds; the killing of the twelve brothers by their sister is represented by the picking of the flowers, just as it is at the beginning of the story by the coffins and the disappearance of the brothers.) The girl, who is once more ready to save her brothers from death, is now told that as a condition she must be dumb for seven years, and not speak a single word. She submits to the test, which brings her herself into mortal danger. She herself, that is, dies for her brothers, as she promised to do before she met them. By remaining dumb she succeeds at last in setting the ravens free.

In the story of "The Six Swans"[15] the brothers who are changed into birds are set free in exactly the same way—they are restored to life by their sister's dumbness. The girl has made a firm resolve to free her brothers, "even if it should cost her her life"; and once again (being the wife of the king) she risks her own life because she refuses to give up her dumbness in order to defend herself against evil accusations.

It would certainly be possible to collect further evidence from fairy tales that dumbness is to be understood as representing death. These indications would lead us to conclude that the third one of the sisters between whom the choice is made is a dead woman. But she may be something else as well—namely, Death itself, the Goddess of Death. Thanks to a displacement that is far from infrequent, the qualities that a deity imparts to men are ascribed to the deity himself. Such a displacement will surprise us least of all in relation to the Goddess of Death, since in modern versions and representations, which these stories would thus be forestalling, Death itself is nothing other than a dead man.

But if the third of the sisters is the Goddess of Death, the sisters are known to us. They are the Fates, the Moerae, the Parcae or the Norns, the third of whom is called Atropos, the inexorable.

II

We will for the time being put aside the task of inserting the interpretation that we have found into our myth, and listen to what the mythologists have to teach us about the role and origin of the Fates.[16]

The earliest Greek mythology (in Homer) only knew a single *Μοῖρα*, personifying inevitable fate. The further development of this one Moera into a company of three (or less often two) sister-goddesses probably came about on the basis of other divine figures to which the Moerae were closely related—the Graces and the Horae [the Seasons].

The Horae were originally goddesses of the waters of the sky, dispensing rain and dew, and of the clouds from which rain falls; and, since the clouds were conceived of as something that has been spun, it came about that these goddesses were looked upon as spinners, an attribute that then became attached to the Moerae. In the sun-favoured Mediterranean lands it is the rain on which the fertility of the soil depends, and thus the Horae became vegetation goddesses. The beauty of flowers and the abundance of fruit was their doing, and they were accredited with a wealth of agreeable and charming traits. They became the divine representatives of the Seasons, and it is possibly owing to this connection that there were three of them, if the sacred nature of the number three is not a sufficient explanation. For the peoples of antiquity at first distinguished only three seasons: winter, spring and summer. Autumn was only added in late Graeco-Roman times, after which the Horae were often represented in art as four in number.

The Horae retained their relation to time. Later they presided over the times of day, as they did at first over the times of the year; and at last their name came to be merely a designation of the hours (*heure, ora*). The Norns of German mythology are akin to the Horae and the Moerae and exhibit this time-signification in their names.[17] It was inevitable, however, that a deeper view should come to be taken of the essential nature of these deities, and that their essence should be transposed on to the regularity with which the seasons change. The Horae thus became the guardians of natural law and of the divine Order which causes the same thing to recur in Nature in an unalterable sequence.

This discovery of Nature reacted on the conception of human life. The nature-myth changed into a human myth: the weather-goddesses became goddesses of Fate. But this aspect of the Horae found expression only in the Moerae, who watch over the necessary ordering of human life as inexorably as do the Horae over the regular order of nature. The ineluctable severity of Law and its relation to death and dissolution, which had been avoided in the charming figures of the Horae, were now stamped upon the Moerae, as though men had only perceived the full seriousness of natural law when they had to submit their own selves to it.

The names of the three spinners, too, have been significantly explained by mythologists. Lachesis, the name of the second, seems to denote "the accidental that is included in the regularity of destiny"[18]—or, as we should say, "experience"; just as Atropos stands for "the ineluctable"—Death. Clotho would then be left to mean the innate disposition with its fateful implications.

But now it is time to return to the theme which we are trying to interpret—the theme of the choice between three sisters. We shall be deeply disappointed to discover how unintelligible the situations under review become and what contradictions of their apparent content result, if we apply to them the interpretation that we have found. On our supposition the third of the sisters is the Goddess of Death, Death itself. But in the Judgement of Paris she is the Goddess of Love, in the tale of Apuleius she is someone comparable to the goddess for her beauty, in *The Merchant of Venice* she is the fairest and wisest of women, in *King Lear* she is the one loyal daughter. We may ask whether there can be a more complete contradiction. Perhaps, improbable though it may seem, there is a still more complete one lying close at hand. Indeed, there certainly is; since, whenever our theme occurs, the choice between the women is free, and yet it falls on death. For, after all, no one chooses death, and it is only by a fatality that one falls a victim to it.

However, contradictions of a certain kind—replacements by the precise opposite—offer no serious difficulty to the work of analytic interpretation. We shall not appeal here to the fact that contraries are so often represented by one and the same element in the modes of expression used by the unconscious, as for instance in dreams.[19] But we shall remember that there are motive forces in mental life which bring about replacement by the opposite in the form of what is known as reaction-formation; and it is precisely in the revelation of such hidden forces as these that we look for the reward of this enquiry. The Moerae were created as a result of a discovery that warned man that he too is a part of nature and therefore subject to the immutable law of death. Something in man was bound to struggle against this subjection, for it is only with extreme unwillingness that he gives up his claim to an exceptional position. Man, as we know, makes use of his imaginative activity in order to satisfy the wishes that reality does not satisfy. So his imagination rebelled against the recognition of the truth embodied in the myth of the Moerae, and constructed instead the myth derived from it, in which the Goddess of Death was replaced by the Goddess of Love and by what was equivalent to her in human shape. The third of the sisters was no longer Death; she was the fairest, best, most desirable and most lovable of women. Nor was this substitution in any way technically difficult: it was prepared for by an ancient ambivalence, it was carried out along a primaeval line of connection which could not long have been forgotten. The Goddess of Love herself, who now took the place of the Goddess of Death, had once been identical with her. Even the Greek Aphrodite had not wholly relinquished her connection with the underworld, although she had long surrendered her chthonic role to other divine figures, to Persephone, or to the tri-form Artemis-Hecate. The great Mother-goddesses of the oriental peoples, however, all seem to have been both creators and destroyers—both goddesses of life and fertility and goddesses of death. Thus the replacement by a wishful opposite in our theme harks back to a primaeval identity.

The same consideration answers the question how the feature of a choice came into the myth of the three sisters. Here again there has been a wishful reversal. Choice stands in the place of necessity, of destiny. In this way man overcomes death, which he has recognized intellectually. No greater triumph of wish-fulfilment is conceivable. A choice is made where in reality there is obedience to a compulsion; and what is chosen is not a figure of terror, but the fairest and most desirable of women.

On closer inspection we observe, to be sure, that the original myth is not so thoroughly distorted that traces of it do not show through and betray its presence. The free choice between the three sisters is, properly speaking, no free choice, for it must necessarily fall on the third if every kind of evil is not to come about, as it does in *King Lear*. The fairest and best of women, who has taken the place of the Death-goddess, has kept certain characteristics that border on the uncanny, so that from them we have been able to guess at what lies beneath.[20]

So far we have been following out the myth and its transformation, and it is to be hoped that we have correctly indicated the hidden causes of the transformation. We may now turn our interest to the way in which the dramatist has made use of the theme. We get an impression that a reduction of the theme to the original myth is being carried out in his work, so that we once more have a sense of the moving significance which had been weakened by the distortion. It is by means of this reduction of the distortion, this partial return to the original, that the dramatist achieves his more profound effect upon us.

To avoid misunderstandings, I should like to say that it is not my purpose to deny that King Lear's dramatic story is intended to inculcate two wise lessons: that one should not give up one's possessions and rights during one's lifetime, and that one must guard against accepting flattery at its face value. These and similar warnings are undoubtedly brought out by the play; but it seems to me quite impossible to explain the overpowering effect of *King Lear* from the impression that such a train of thought would produce, or to suppose that the dramatist's personal motives did not go beyond the intention of teaching these lessons. It is suggested, too, that his purpose was to present the tragedy of ingratitude, the sting of which he may well have felt in his own heart, and that the effect of the play rests on the purely formal element of its artistic presentation; but this cannot, so it seems to me, take the place of the understanding brought to us by the explanation we have reached of the theme of the choice between the three sisters.

Lear is an old man. It is for this reason, as we have already said, that the three sisters appear as his daughters. The relationship of a father to his children, which might be a fruitful source of many dramatic situations, is not turned to further account in the play. But Lear is not only an old man: he is a dying man. In this way the extraordinary premiss of the division of his inheritance loses all its strangeness. But the doomed man is not willing to renounce the love of women; he insists on hearing how much he is loved. Let us now recall the moving final scene, one of the culminating points of tragedy in modern drama. Lear carries Cordelia's dead body on to the stage. Cordelia is Death. If we reverse the situation it becomes intelligible and familiar to us. She is the Death-goddess who, like the Valkyrie in German mythology, carries away the dead hero from the battlefield. Eternal wisdom, clothed in the primaeval myth, bids the old man renounce love, choose death and make friends with the necessity of dying.

The dramatist brings us nearer to the ancient theme by representing the man who makes the choice between the three sisters as aged and dying. The regressive revision which he has thus applied to the myth, distorted as it was by wishful transformation, allows us enough glimpses of its original meaning to enable us perhaps to reach as well a superficial allegorical interpretation of the three female figures in the theme. We might argue that what is represented here are the three inevitable relations that a man has with a woman—the woman who bears him, the woman who is his mate and the woman who destroys him; or that they are the three forms taken by the figure of the mother in the course of a man's life—the mother herself, the beloved one who is chosen after her pattern, and lastly the Mother Earth who receives him once more. But it is in vain that an old man yearns for the love of woman as he had it first from his mother; the third of the Fates alone, the silent Goddess of Death, will take him into her arms.

Notes

1. [A mediaeval collection of stories of unknown authorship.]—Trans.
2. Brandes (1896).

3. Stucken (1907, 655).

4. Rank (1909, 8 ff.).

5. [See *The Interpretation of Dreams* (1900*a*), *Standard Ed.*, **5**, 354.]—Trans.

6. I have to thank Dr. Otto Rank for calling my attention to these similarities. [Cf. a reference to this in Chapter XII of *Group Psychology* (1921*c*), *Standard Ed.*, **18**, 136.]—Trans.

7. [From an aside of Cordelia's, Act I, Scene 1.]—Trans.

8. "Plainness" according to another reading.

9. In Schlegel's translation this allusion is quite lost: indeed, it is given the opposite meaning: "*Dein schlichtes Wesen spricht beredt mich an.*" ["Thy plainness speaks to me with eloquence."]—Trans.

10. [Literally: "The third one, ah! the third one . . . . the third one said nothing. She won the prize all the same."—The quotation is from Act I, Scene 7, of Meilhac and Halévy's libretto. In the German version used by Freud "the third one" "*blieb stumm*"—"remained dumb."]—Trans.

11. In Stekel's *Sprache des Traumes*, too, dumbness is mentioned among the "death" symbols (1911*a*, 351). [Cf. *The Interpretation of Dreams* (1900*a*), *Standard Ed.*, **5**, 357.]—Trans.

12. [Cf. Freud's later paper on "Dreams and Telepathy" (1922*a*).]—Trans.

13. Stekel (1911*a*), loc. cit.

14. ["Die zwölf Brüder." Grimm, 1918, **1**, 42.]—Trans.

15. ["Die sechs Schwäne." Grimm, 1918, **1**, 217 (No. 49).]—Trans.

16. What follows is taken from Roscher's lexicon [1884–1937], under the relevant headings.

17. [Their names may be rendered: "What was," "What is," "What shall be."]—Trans.

18. Roscher [ibid.], quoting Preller, ed. Robert (1894).

19. [Cf. *The Interpretation of Dreams* (1900*a*), *Standard Ed.*, **4**, 318.]—Trans.

20. The Psyche of Apuleius's story has kept many traits that remind us of her relation with death. Her wedding is celebrated like a funeral, she has to descend into the underworld, and afterwards she sinks into a death-like sleep (Otto Rank).—On the significance of Psyche as goddess of the spring and as "Bride of Death," cf. Zinzow (1881).—In another of Grimm's Tales ("The Goose-girl at the Fountain" ["Die Gänsehirtin am Brunnen," 1918, **2**, 300], No. 179) there is, as in "Cinderella," an alternation between the beautiful and the ugly aspect of the third sister, in which one may no doubt see an indication of her double nature—before and after the substitution. This third daughter is repudiated by her father, after a test which is almost the same as the one in *King Lear*. Like her sisters, she has to declare how fond she is of their father, but can find no expression for her love but a comparison with salt. (Kindly communicated by Dr. Hanns Sachs.)

T. S. Eliot 1888–1965

T. S. (Thomas Sterns) Eliot is best known as a poet, but he is arguably the central modern critic writing in English because of his vast influence in several areas: he almost single-handedly brought about the reappraisal of sixteenth- and seventeenth-century drama and metaphysical poetry; he demonstrated the necessity of reading American and English literature in relation to European and non-European (especially Oriental) traditions; he helped to formulate a modern way of reading and writing that eschewed romantic values and furthered an aesthetic of "hard, dry" images and sentiments. Eliot thus directed modern readers in what and how to read and how to understand literary texts. These achievements, along with the critical revolution signaled by his own poetry, mark Eliot as a modern critic of the first rank. His major works of criticism include *The Sacred Wood* (1920) and *Notes Toward the Definition of Culture* (1949).

"Tradition and the Individual Talent" (1919) shows some of the furthest reaches of Eliot's theories and literary philosophy. He asserts the value of poetic creation as the process by which a whole culture locates itself in the present in relation to an acquired sense of the past. The past is an active force in the present, constituting "the presentness of the past," and is a channel of access to a cultural "mind" larger than any single poet's and ultimately decisive in determining the direction and import of all "significant" art in any age. These ideas had a direct influence on modernist criticism and literature, but—to a greater extent than is sometimes recognized—they also underlie some contemporary cultural theories, such as reader-response criticism and various approaches to audience-reception theory. Noteworthy for its coherence and cogency, this essay is perhaps Eliot's most important critical statement.

Tradition and the Individual Talent

I

In English writing we seldom speak of tradition, though we occasionally apply its name in deploring its absence. We cannot refer to "the tradition" or to "a tradition"; at most, we employ that adjective in saying that the poetry of So-and-so is "traditional" or even "too traditional." Seldom, perhaps, does the word appear except in a phrase of censure. If otherwise, it is vaguely approbative, with the implication, as to the work approved, of some pleasing archaeological reconstruction. You can hardly make the word agreeable to English ears without this comfortable reference to the reassuring science of archaeology.

Certainly the word is not likely to appear in our appreciations of living or dead writers. Every nation, every race, has not only its own creative, but its own critical turn of mind; and is even more oblivious of the shortcomings and limitations of its critical habits than of those of its creative genius. We know, or think we know, from the enormous mass of critical writing that has appeared in the French language the critical method or habit of the French; we only conclude (we are such unconscious people) that the French are "more critical" than we, and sometimes even plume ourselves a little with the fact, as if the French were the less spontaneous. Perhaps they are; but we might remind ourselves that criticism is as inevitable as breathing, and that we should be none the worse for articulating what passes in our minds when we read a book and feel an emotion about it, for criticizing our own minds in their work of criticism. One of the facts that might come to light in this process is our tendency to insist, when we praise a poet, upon those aspects of his work in which he least resembles anyone else. In these aspects or parts of his work we pretend to find what is individual, what is the peculiar essence of the man. We dwell with satisfaction upon the poet's difference from his predecessors, especially his immediate predecessors; we endeavour to find something that can be isolated in order to be enjoyed. Whereas if we approach a poet without this prejudice we shall often find that not only the best, but the most individual parts of his work may be those in which the dead poets, his ancestors, assert their immortality most vigorously. And I do not mean the impressionable period of adolescence, but the period of full maturity.

Yet if the only form of tradition, of handing down, consisted in following the ways of the immediate generation before us in a blind or timid adherence to its successes, "tradition" should positively be discouraged. We have seen many such simple currents soon lost in the sand; and novelty is better than repetition. Tradition is a matter of much wider significance. It cannot be inherited, and if you want it you must obtain it by great labour. It involves, in the first place, the historical sense, which we may call nearly indispensable to anyone who would continue to be a poet beyond his twenty-fifth year; and the historical sense involves a perception, not only of the pastness of the past, but of its presence; the historical sense compels a man to write not merely with his own generation in his bones, but with a feeling that the whole of the literature of Europe from Homer and within it the whole of the literature of his own country has a simultaneous existence and composes a simultaneous order. This historical sense, which is a sense of the timeless as well as of the temporal and of the timeless and of the temporal together, is what makes a writer traditional. And it is at the same time what makes a writer most acutely conscious of his place in time, of his own contemporaneity.

No poet, no artist of any art, has his complete meaning alone. His significance, his appreciation is the appreciation of his relation to the dead poets and artists. You cannot value him alone; you must set him, for contrast and comparison, among the dead. I mean this as a principle of aesthetic, not merely historical, criticism. The necessity that he shall conform, that he shall cohere, is not onesided; what happens when a new work of art is created is something that happens simultaneously to all the works of art which preceded it. The existing monuments form an ideal order among themselves, which is modified by the introduction of the new (the really new) work of art among them. The existing order is complete before the new work arrives; for order to persist after the supervention of novelty, the whole existing order must be, if ever so slightly, altered; and so the relations, proportions, values of each work of art towards the whole are readjusted; and this is conformity between the old and the new. Whoever has approved this idea of order, of the form of European, of English literature will not find it preposterous that the past should be altered by the present as much as the present is directed by the past. And the poet who is aware of this will be aware of great difficulties and responsibilities.

In a peculiar sense he will be aware also that he must inevitably be judged by the standards of the past. I say judged, not amputated, by them; not judged to be as good as, or worse or better than, the dead; and certainly not judged by the canons of dead critics. It is a judgment, a comparison, in which two things are measured by each other. To conform merely would be for the new work not really to conform at all; it would not be new, and would therefore not be a work of art. And we do not quite say that the new is more valuable because it fits in; but its fitting in is a test of its value—a test, it is true, which can only be slowly and cautiously applied, for we are none of us infallible judges of conformity. We say: it appears to conform, and is perhaps individual, or it appears individual, and may conform; but we are hardly likely to find that it is one and not the other.

To proceed to a more intelligible exposition of the relation of the poet to the past: he can neither take the past as a lump, an indiscriminate bolus, nor can he form himself wholly on one or two private admirations, nor can he form himself wholly upon one preferred period. The first course is inadmissible, the second is an important experience of youth, and the third is a pleasant and highly desirable supplement. The poet must be very conscious of the main current, which does not at all flow invariably through the most distinguished reputations. He must be quite aware of the obvious fact that art never improves, but that the material of art is never quite the same. He must be aware that the mind of Europe—the mind of his own country—a mind which he learns in time to be much more important than his own private mind—is a mind which changes, and that this change is a development which abandons nothing *en route*, which does not superannuate either Shakespeare, or Homer, or the rock drawing of the Magdalenian draughtsmen. That this development, refinement perhaps, complication certainly, is not, from the point of view of the artist, any improvement. Perhaps not even an improvement from the point of view of the psychologist or not to the extent which we imagine; perhaps only in the end based upon a complication in economics and machinery. But the difference between the present and the past is that the conscious present is an awareness of the past in a way and to an extent which the past's awareness of itself cannot show.

Someone said: "The dead writers are remote from us because we *know* so much more than they did." Precisely, and they are that which we know.

I am alive to a usual objection to what is clearly part of my programme for the *métier* of poetry. The objection is that the doctrine requires a ridiculous amount of erudition (pedantry), a claim which can be rejected by appeal to the lives of poets in any pantheon. It will even be affirmed that much learning deadens or perverts poetic sensibility. While, however, we persist in believing that a poet ought to know as much as will not encroach upon his necessary receptivity and necessary laziness, it is not desirable to confine knowledge to whatever can be put into a useful shape for examinations, drawing-rooms, or the still more pretentious modes of publicity. Some can absorb knowledge, the more tardy must sweat for it. Shakespeare acquired more essential history from Plutarch than most men could from the whole British Museum. What is to be insisted upon is that the poet must develop or procure the consciousness of the past and that he should continue to develop this consciousness throughout his career.

What happens is a continual surrender of himself as he is at the moment to something which is more valuable. The progress of an artist is a continual self-sacrifice, a continual extinction of personality.

There remains to define this process of depersonalization and its relation to the sense of tradition. It is in this depersonalization that art may be said to approach the condition of science. I therefore invite you to consider, as a suggestive analogy, the action which takes place when a bit of finely filiated platinum is introduced into a chamber containing oxygen and sulphur dioxide.

II

Honest criticism and sensitive appreciation are directed not upon the poet but upon the poetry. If we attend to the confused cries of the newspaper critics and the susurrus of popular repetition that follows, we shall hear the names of poets in great numbers; if we seek not Blue-book knowledge but the enjoyment of poetry, and ask for a poem, we shall seldom find it. I have tried to point out the importance of the relation of the poem to other poems by other authors, and suggested the conception of poetry as a living whole of all the poetry that has ever been written. The other aspect of this Impersonal theory of poetry is the relation of the poem to its author. And I hinted, by an analogy, that the mind of the mature poet differs from that of the immature one not precisely in any valuation of "personality," not being necessarily more interesting, or having "more to say," but rather by being a more finely perfected medium in which special, or varied, feelings are at liberty to enter into new combinations.

The analogy was that of the catalyst. When the two gases previously mentioned are mixed in the presence of a filament of platinum, they form sulphurous acid. This combination takes place only if the platinum is present; nevertheless the newly formed acid contains no trace of platinum, and the platinum itself is apparently unaffected: has remained inert, neutral, and unchanged. The mind of the poet is the shred of platinum. It may partly or exclusively operate upon the experience of the man himself; but, the more perfect the artist, the more completely separate in him will be the man who suffers and the mind which creates; the more perfectly will the mind digest and transmute the passions which are its material.

The experience, you will notice, the elements which enter the presence of the transforming catalyst, are of two kinds: emotions and feelings. The effect of a work of art upon the person who enjoys it is an experience different in kind from any experience not of art. It may be formed out of one emotion, or may be a combination of several; and various feelings, inhering for the writer in particular words or phrases or images, may be added to compose the final result. Or great poetry may be made without the direct use of any emotion whatever: composed out of feelings solely. Canto XV of the *Inferno* (Brunetto Latini) is a working up of the emotion evident in the situation; but the effect, though single as that of any work of art, is obtained by considerable complexity of detail. The last quatrain[1] gives an image, a feeling attaching to an image, which "came" which did not develop simply out of what precedes, but which was probably in suspension in the poet's mind until the proper combination arrived for it to add itself to. The poet's mind is in fact a receptacle for seizing and storing up numberless feelings, phrases, images, which remain there until all the particles which can unite to form a new compound are present together.

If you compare several representative passages of the greatest poetry you see how great is the variety of types of combination, and also how completely any semi-ethical criterion of "sublimity" misses the mark. For it is not the "greatness," the intensity, of the emotions, the components, but the intensity of the artistic process, the pressure, so to speak, under which the fusion takes place, that counts. The episode of Paolo and Francesca employs a definite emotion, but the intensity of the poetry is something quite different from whatever intensity in the supposed experience it may give the impression of. It is no more intense, furthermore, than Canto XXVI, the voyage of Ulysses, which has not the direct dependence upon an emotion. Great variety is possible in the process of transmutation of emotion: the murder of Agamemnon, or the agony of Othello, gives an artistic effect apparently closer to a possible original than the scenes from Dante. In the *Agamemnon*, the artistic emotion approximates to the emotion of an actual spectator; in *Othello* to the emotion of the protagonist himself. But the difference between art and the event is always absolute; the combination which is the murder of Agamemnon is probably as complex as that which is the voyage of Ulysses. In either case there has been a fusion of elements. The ode of Keats contains a number of feelings which have nothing particular to do with the nightingale, but which the nightingale, partly perhaps because of its attractive name, and partly because of its reputation, served to bring together.

The point of view which I am struggling to attack is perhaps related to the metaphysical theory of the substantial unity of the soul: for my meaning is, that the poet has, not a "personality" to express, but a particular medium, which is only a medium and not a personality, in which impressions and experiences combine in peculiar and unexpected ways. Impressions and experiences which are important for the man may take no place in the poetry, and those which become important in the poetry may play quite a negligible part in the man, the personality.

I will quote a passage which is unfamiliar enough to be regarded with fresh attention in the light—or darkness—of these observations:

> And now methinks I could e'en chide myself
> For doating on her beauty, though her death
> Shall be revenged after no common action.
> Does the silkworm expend her yellow labours
> For thee? For thee does she undo herself?
> Are lordships sold to maintain ladyships
> For the poor benefit of a bewildering minute?
> Why does yon fellow falsify highways,
> And put his life between the judge's lips,
> To refine such a thing—keeps horse and men
> To beat their valours for her? . . .[2]

In this passage (as is evident if it is taken in its context) there is a combination of positive and negative emotions: an intensely strong attraction towards beauty and an equally intense fascination by the ugliness which is contrasted with it and which destroys it. This balance of contrasted emotion is in the dramatic situation to which the speech is pertinent, but that situation alone is inadequate to it. This is, so to speak, the structural emotion, provided by the drama.

But the whole effect, the dominant tone, is due to the fact that a number of floating feelings, having an affinity to this emotion by no means superficially evident, have combined with it to give us a new art emotion.

It is not in his personal emotions, the emotions provoked by particular events in his life, that the poet is in any way remarkable or interesting. His particular emotions may be simple, or crude, or flat. The emotion in his poetry will be a very complex thing, but not with the complexity of the emotions of people who have very complex or unusual emotions in life. One error, in fact, of eccentricity in poetry is to seek for new human emotions to express; and in this search for novelty in the wrong place it discovers the perverse. The business of the poet is not to find new emotions, but to use the ordinary ones and, in working them up into poetry, to express feelings which are not in actual emotions at all. And emotions which he has never experienced will serve his turn as well as those familiar to him. Consequently, we must believe that "emotion recollected in tranquility[3] is an inexact formula. For it is neither emotion, nor recollection, nor, without distortion of meaning, tranquility. It is a concentration, and a new thing resulting from the concentration, of a very great number of experiences which to the practical and active person would not seem to be experiences at all; it is a concentration which does not happen consciously or of deliberation. These experiences are not "recollected," and they finally unite in an atmosphere which is "tranquil" only in that it is a passive attending upon the event. Of course this is not quite the whole story. There is a great deal, in the writing of poetry, which must be conscious and deliberate. In fact, the bad poet is usually unconscious where he ought to be conscious, and conscious where he ought to be unconscious. Both errors tend to make him "personal." Poetry is not a turning loose of emotion, but an escape from emotion; it is not the expression of personality, but an escape from personality. But, of course, only those who have personality and emotions know what it means to want to escape from these things.

III

> *ὁ δὲ νους ἰυως θειότερόν τι καί ἀπαθές ἐστιν.*[4]

This essay proposes to halt at the frontier of metaphysics or mysticism, and confine itself to such practical conclusions as can be applied by the responsible person interested in poetry. To divert interest from the poet to the poetry is a laudable aim: for it would conduce to a juster estimation of actual poetry, good and bad. There are many people who appreciate the expression of sincere emotion in verse, and there is a smaller number of people who can appreciate technical excellence. But very few know when there is an expression of *significant* emotion, emotion which has its life in the poem and not in the history of the poet. The emotion of art is impersonal. And the poet cannot reach this impersonality without surrendering himself wholly to the work to be done. And he is not likely to know what is to be done unless he believes in what is not merely the present, but the present moment of the past, unless he is conscious, not of what is dead, but of what is already living.

Notes

1. In the translation of Dorothy L. Sayers:

   > Then he turned around,
   > And seemed like one of those who over the
   > flat

And open course in the fields beside Verona
Run for the green cloth; and he seemed, at
that,
Not like a loser, but the winning runner.

2. Cyril Tourneur, *The Revenger's Tragedy* (1607), III, iv.

3. "Poetry is the spontaneous overflow of powerful feelings: it takes its origins from emotion recollected in tranquility." Wordsworth, Preface to *Lyrical Ballads* (1800).

4. "While the intellect is doubtless a thing more divine and is impassive." Aristotle, *De Anima*.

Mikhail Bakhtin (V. N. Volosinov) 1895–1975

Mikhail Bakhtin's greatest period of productivity—the 1920s and 1930s—were troubled first by the effects of the Russian Revolution and civil war and then by the repressive Stalin regime. During the 1920s, three books and several articles were published under the names of his friends; these include *The Formal Method in Literary Scholarship, Freudianism: A Critical Sketch, Marxism and the Philosophy of Language,* "Beyond the Social," "Contemporary Vitalism," and "Discourse in Life and Discourse in Art." In 1946 and 1949, the State Accrediting Bureau rejected his 1940 dissertation, "Rabelais and Folk Culture of the Middle Ages and Renaissance," and it remained unpublished until 1965. Since that time it has gone through several editions in Japanese, German, and English.

Bakhtin's early work was devoted to developing a philosophy of language grounded in the interplay of communication. He first defined the utterance as a dialogic process, involving both the speaker or writer and the implied or actual listener or reader, in his "Problems of Dostoevsky's Art" (1929). In the dialogic process, the importance of context becomes crucial to understanding the meaning of an utterance. Language, like all art, he defined as an "exchange" or clash of values between a work and its audience. This definition of language, a "sociological poetics," views language as both determining and determined by the historical components of particular utterances. Consequently, it rejects both the formalism that treats a text as a static, purely linguistic object and the Marxism that would define a text as determined entirely by its creator and reader.

Bakhtin's first attempt to define a theory of utterance appeared in his "Discourse in Life and Discourse in Art" (1926). He asserts here that context, including nonverbal elements, is an integral, not an external, component of utterance. Artistic form, he concludes, is largely influenced by extra-artistic reality. In the course of his discussion, Bakhtin attacks the traditional sociological method of studying art. While Bakhtin uses Marxist terminology in order to enter into a dialogue with the Marxist sociologies of literature, he proposes a more radical kind of analysis. He defines language as an "event" in which both linquistic and social elements predetermine one another in a struggle toward textual meaning.

Discourse in Life and Discourse in Art

(Concerning Sociological Poetics)

I

In the study of literature, the sociological method has been applied almost exclusively for treating historical questions while remaining virtually untouched with regard to the problems of so-called *theoretical poetics*—that whole area of issues involving artistic form and its various factors, style, and so forth.

A fallacious view, but one adhered to even by certain Marxists, has it that the sociological method becomes legitimate only at that point where poetic form acquires added complexity through the ideological factor (the content) and begins to develop historically in conditions of external social reality. Form in and of itself, according to this view, possesses its own special, not sociological but specifically artistic, nature and system of governance.

Such a view fundamentally contradicts the very basis of the Marxist method—its monism and its historicity. The consequence of this and similar views is that form and content, theory and history, are rent asunder.

But we cannot dismiss these fallacious views without further, more detailed inquiry; they are too characteristic for the whole of the modern study of the arts.

The most patent and consistent development of the point of view in question appeared recently in a work by Professor P. N. Sakulin.[1] Sakulin distinguishes two dimensions in literature and its history: the immanent and the causal. The immanent "artistic core" of literature possesses special structure and governance peculiar to itself alone; so endowed, it is capable of autonomous evolutionary development "by nature." But in the process of this development, literature becomes subject to the "causal" influence of the extra-artistic social milieu. With the "immanent core" of literature, its structure and autonomous evolution, the sociologist can have nothing to do—those topics fall within the exclusive competence of theoretical and historical poetics and their special methods.[2] The sociological method can successfully study only the causal interaction between literature and its surrounding extra-artistic social milieu. Moreover, immanent (nonsociological) analysis of the essence of literature, including its intrinsic, autonomous governance, must precede sociological analysis.[3]

Of course, no Marxist sociologist could agree with such an assertion. Nevertheless, it has to be admitted that sociology, up to the present moment, has dealt almost exclusively with concrete issues in history of literature and has not made a single serious attempt to utilize its methods in the study of the so-called "immanent" structure of a work of art. That structure has, in plain fact, been relegated to the province of aesthetic or psychological or other methods that have nothing in common with sociology.

To verify this fact we need only examine any modern work on poetics or even on the theory of art study in general. We will not find a trace of any application of sociological categories. Art is treated as if it were nonsociological "by nature" just exactly as is the physical or chemical structure of a body. Most West European and Russian scholars of the arts make precisely this claim regarding literature and art as a whole, and on this basis persistently defend the study of art as a special discipline against sociological approaches of any kind.

They motivate this claim of theirs in approximately the following way. Every item that becomes the object of supply and demand, that is, that becomes a commodity, is subject, as concerns its value and its circulation within human society, to the governing socioeconomic laws. Let us suppose that we know those laws very well; still, despite that fact, we shall understand exactly nothing about the physical and chemical structure of the item in question. On the contrary, the study of commodities is itself in need of preliminary physical and chemical analysis of the given commodity. And the only persons competent to perform such analysis are physicists and chemists with the help of the specific methods of their fields. In the opinion of these art scholars, art stands in an analogous position. Art, too, once it becomes a social factor and becomes subject to the influence of other, likewise social, factors, takes its place, of course, within the overall system of sociological governance—but from that governance we shall never be able to derive art's *aesthetic essence*, just as we cannot derive the chemical formula for this or that commodity from the governing economic laws of commodity circulation. What art study and theoretical poetics are supposed to do is to seek such a formula for a work of art—one that is *specific* to art and independent of sociology.

This conception of the essence of art is, as we have said, fundamentally in contradiction with the bases of Marxism. To be sure, you will never find a chemical formula by the sociological method, but a scientific "formula" for any domain of *ideology* can be found, and can only be found, by the methods of sociology. All the other—"immanent"—methods are heavily involved in subjectivism and have been unable, to the present day, to break free of the fruitless controversy of opinions and points of view and, therefore, are least of all capable of finding anything even remotely resembling the rigorous and exact formulas of chemistry. Neither, of course, can the Marxist method claim to provide such a "formula"; the rigor and exactness of the natural sciences are impossible within the domain of ideological study due to the very nature of what it studies. But the closest approximation to genuine scientificness in the study of ideological creativity has become possible for the first time thanks to the sociological method in its Marxist conception. Physical and chemical bodies or substances exist outside human society as well as within it, but all products of ideological creativity arise in and for human society. Social definitions are not applicable from outside, as is the case with bodies and substances in nature—*ideological formations are intrinsically, immanently sociological.* No one is likely to dispute that point with respect to political and juridical forms—what possible nonsociological, immanent property could be found in them? The most subtle formal nuances of a law or of a political system are all equally amenable to the sociological method and only to it. But exactly the same thing is true for other ideological forms. They are all *sociological through and through*, even though their structure, mutable and complex as it is, lends itself to exact analysis only with enormous difficulty.

Art, too, is just as immanently social; the extra-artistic social milieu, affecting art from outside, finds direct, intrinsic response within it. This is not a case of one foreign element affecting another but of one social formation affecting another social formation. The *aesthetic*, just as the juridical or the cognitive, is *only a variety of the social*. Theory of art, consequently, can only be a *sociology of art*.[4] No "immanent" tasks are left in its province.

II

If sociological analysis is to be properly and productively applied to the theory of art (poetics in particular), then two fallacious views that severely narrow the scope of art by operating exclusively with certain isolated factors must be rejected.

The first view can be defined as the *fetishization of the artistic work artifact*. This fetishism is the prevailing attitude in the study of art at the present time. The field of investigation is restricted to the work of art itself, which is analyzed in such a way as if everything in art were exhausted by it alone. The creator of the work and the work's contemplators remain outside the field of investigation.

The second point of view, conversely, restricts itself to the study of the psyche of the creator or of the contemplator (more often than not, it simply equates the two). For it, all art is exhausted by the experiences of the person doing the contemplating or doing the creating.

Thus, for the one point of view the object of study is only the structure of the work artifact, while for the other it is only the individual psyche of the creator or contemplator.

The first point of view advances the material to the forefront of aesthetic investigation. Form, understood very narrowly as the form of the material—that which organizes it into a single unified and complete artifact—becomes the main and very nearly exclusive object of study.

A variety of the first point of view is the so-called formal method. For the formal method, a poetic work is verbal material organized by form in some particular way. Moreover, it takes *the verbal* not as a sociological phenomenon but from an abstract linguistic point of view. That it should adopt just such a point of view is quite understandable: Verbal discourse, taken in the broader sense as a phenomenon of cultural communication, ceases to be something self-contained and can no longer be understood independently of the social situation that engenders it.

The first point of view cannot be consistently followed out to the end. The problem is that if one remains within the confines of the artifact aspect of art, there is no way of indicating even such things as the boundaries of the material or which of its features have artistic significance. The material in and of itself directly merges with the extra-artistic milieu surrounding it and has an infinite number of aspects and definitions—in terms of mathematics, physics, chemistry, and so forth as well as of linguistics. However far we go in analyzing all the properties of the material and all the possible combinations of those properties, we shall never be able to find their aesthetic significance unless we slip in the contraband of another point of view that does not belong within the framework of analysis of the material. Similarly, however far we go in analyzing the chemical structure of a body or substance, we shall never understand its value and significance as a commodity unless we draw economics into the picture.

The attempt of the second view to find the aesthetic in the individual psyche of the creator or contemplator is equally vain. To continue our economic analogy, we might say that such a thing is similar to the attempt to analyze the individual psyche of a proletarian in order thereby to disclose the objective production relations that determine his position in society.

In the final analysis, both points of view are guilty of the same fault: *They attempt to discover the whole in the part,* that is, they take the structure of a part, abstractly divorced from the whole, and claim it as the structure of the whole. Meanwhile, "the artistic" in its total integrity is not located in the artifact and not located in the separately considered psyches of creator and contemplator; it encompasses all three of these factors. It is a *special form of interrelationship between creator and contemplator fixed in a work of art.*

This *artistic communication* stems from the basis common to it and other social forms, but, at the same time, it retains, as do all other forms, its own uniqueness; it is a special type of communication, possessing a form of its own peculiar to itself. *To understand this special form of social communication realized and fixed in the material of a work of art—that precisely is the task of sociological poetics.*

A work of art, viewed outside this communication and independently of it, is simply a physical artifact or an exercise in linguistics. It becomes art only in the process of the interaction between creator and contemplator, as the essential factor in this interaction. Everything in the material of a work of art that cannot be drawn into the communication between creator and contemplator, that cannot become the "medium," the means of their communication, cannot be the recipient of artistic value, either.

Those methods that ignore the social essence of art and attempt to find its nature and distinguishing features only in the organization of the work artifact are in actuality obliged to project the social interrelationship of creator and contemplator into various aspects of the material and into various devices for structuring the material. In exactly the same way, psychological aesthetics projects the same social relations into the individual psyche of the perceiver. This projection distorts the integrity of these interrelationships and gives a false picture of both the material and the psyche.

Aesthetic communication, fixed in a work of art, is, as we have already said, entirely unique and irreducible to other types of ideological communication such as the political, the juridical, the moral, and so on. If political communication establishes corresponding institutions and, at the same time, juridical forms, aesthetic communication organizes only a work of art. If the latter rejects this task and begins to aim at creating even the most transitory of political organizations or any other ideological form, then by that very fact it ceases to be aesthetic communication and relinquishes its unique character. *What characterizes aesthetic communication is the fact that it is wholly absorbed in the creation of a work of art and in its continuous re-creations in the co-creation of contemplators, and it does not require any other kind of objectification.* But, needless to say, this unique form of communciation does not exist *in isolation;* it participates in the unitary flow of social life, it reflects the common economic basis, and it engages in interaction and exchange with other forms of communication.

The purpose of the present study is to try to reach an understanding of the poetic utterance as a form of this special, verbally implemented aesthetic communication. But in order to do so, we must first analyze in detail certain aspects of verbal utterances outside the realm of art—utterances in the *speech of everyday life and behavior*, for in such speech are already embedded the bases, the potentialities of artistic form. Moreover, the social essence of verbal discourse stands out here in sharper relief and the connection between an utterance and the surrounding social milieu lends itself more easily to analysis.

III

In life, verbal discourse is clearly not self-sufficient. It arises out of an extraverbal pragmatic situation and maintains the closest possible connection with that situation. Moreover, such discourse is directly informed by life itself and cannot be divorced from life without losing its import.

The kind of characterizations and evaluations of pragmatic, behavioral utterances we are likely to make are such things as: "that's a lie," "that's the truth," "that's a daring thing to say," "you can't say that," and so on and so forth.

All these and similar evaluations, whatever the criteria that govern them (ethical, cognitive, political, or other), take in a good deal more than what is enclosed within the strictly verbal (linguistic) factors of the utterance. *Together with the verbal factors, they also take in the extraverbal situation of the utterance.* These judgments and evaluations refer to a certain whole wherein the verbal discourse directly engages an event in life and merges with that event, forming an indissoluble unity. The verbal discourse itself, taken in isolation as a purely linguistic phenomenon, cannot, of course, be true or false, daring or diffident.

How does verbal discourse in life relate to the extraverbal situation that has engendered it? Let us analyze this matter, using an intentionally simplified example for the purpose.

Two people are sitting in a room. They are both silent. Then one of them says, "Well!" The other does not respond.

For us, as outsiders, this entire "conversation" is utterly incomprehensible. Taken in isolation, the utterance "Well!" is empty and unintelligible. Nevertheless, this peculiar colloquy of two persons, consisting of only one—although, to be sure, one expressively intoned—word, does make perfect sense, is fully meaningful and complete.

In order to disclose the sense and meaning of this colloquy, we must analyze it. But what is it exactly that we can subject to analysis? Whatever pains we take with the purely verbal part of the utterance, however subtly we define the phonetic, morphological, and semantic factors of the word *well*, we shall still not come a single step closer to an understanding of the whole sense of the colloquy.

Let us suppose that the intonation with which this word was pronounced is known to us: indignation and reproach moderated by a certain amount of humor. This intonation somewhat fills in the semantic void of the adverb *well* but still does not reveal the meaning of the whole.

What is it we lack, then? We lack the "extraverbal context" that made the word *well* a meaningful locution for the listener. This *extraverbal context* of the utterance is comprised of three factors: (1) the *common spatial purview* of the interlocutors (the unity of the visible—in this case, the room, the window, and so on), (2) the interlocutors' *common knowledge and understanding of the situation*, and (3) their *common evaluation* of that situation.

At the time the colloquy took place, both interlocutors *looked up* at the window and *saw* that it had begun to snow; *both knew* that it was already May and that is was high time for spring to come; finally, *both* were *sick and tired* of the protracted winter—*they both were looking forward* to spring and *both were bitterly disappointed* by the late snowfall. On this "jointly seen" (snowflakes outside the window), "jointly known" (the time of year—May), and "unanimously evaluated" (winter wearied of, spring looked forward to)—on all this the utterance *directly depends*, all this is seized in its actual, living import—is its very sustenance. And yet all this remains without verbal specification or articulation. The snowflakes remain outside the window; the date, on the page of a calendar; the evaluation, in the psyche of the speaker; and nevertheless, all this is *assumed* in the word *well*.

Now that we have been let in on the "assumed," that is, now that we know the *shared spatial and ideational purview*, the whole sense of the utterance "Well!" is perfectly clear to us and we also understand its intonation.

How does the extraverbal purview relate to the verbal discourse, how does the said relate to the unsaid?

First of all, it is perfectly obvious that, in the given case, the discourse does not at all reflect the extraverbal situation in the way a mirror reflects an object. Rather, the discourse here *resolves the situation*, bringing it to an *evaluative conclusion*, as it were. Far more often, behavioral utterances actively continue and develop a situation, adumbrate a plan for future action, and organize that action. But for us it is another aspect of the behavioral utterance that is of special importance: Whatever kind it be, the behavioral utterance always joins the participants in the situation together as *co-participants* who know, understand, and evaluate the situation in like manner. *The utterance*, consequently, *depends on their real, material appurtenance to one and the same segment of being and gives this material commonness ideological expression and further ideological development.*

Thus, the extraverbal situation is far from being merely the external cause of an utterance—it does not operate on the utterance from outside, as if it were a mechanical force. Rather, *the situation enters into the utterance as an essential constitutive part of the structure of its import*. Consequently, a behavioral utterance as a meaningful whole is comprised of two parts: (1) the part realized or actualized in words and (2) the assumed part. On this basis, the behavioral utterance can be likened to the enthymeme.[5]

However, it is an enthymeme of a special order. The very term enthymeme (literally translated from the Greek, something located in the heart or mind) sounds a bit too psychological. One might be led to think of the situation as something in the mind of the speaker on the order of a subjective-psychical act (a thought, idea, feeling). But that is not the case. The individual and subjective are backgrounded here by *the social and objective*. What *I* know, see, want, love, and so on cannot be assumed. Only what all of us speakers know, see, love, recognize—only those points on which we are all united can become the assumed part of an utterance. Furthermore, this fundamentally social phenomenon is completely objective; it consists, above all, of *the material unity of world that enters the speakers' purview* (in our example, the room, the snow outside the window, and so on) and of *the unity of the real conditions of life* that generate a *community of value judgments*—the speakers' belonging to the same family, profession, class, or other social group, and their belonging to the same time period (the speakers are, after all, contemporaries). Assumed value judgments are, therefore, not individual emotions but regular and essential social acts. *Individual* emotions can come into play only as *overtones* accompanying the *basic tone of social evaluation*. "I" can realize itself verbally only on the basis of "we."

Thus, every utterance in the business of life is an objective social enthymeme. It is something like a "password" known only to those who belong to the same social purview. The distinguishing characteristic of behavioral utterances consists precisely in the fact that they make myriad connections with the extraverbal context of life and, once severed from that context, lose almost all their import—a person ignorant of the immediate pragmatic context will not understand these utterances.

This immediate context may be of varying scope. In our example, the context is extremely narrow: it is *circumscribed by the room and the moment of occurrence,* and the utterance makes an intelligible statement only for the two persons involved. However, the unified purview on which an utterance depends can expand in both space and time: *The "assumed" may be that of the family, clan, nation, class and may encompass days or years or whole epochs*. The wider the overall purview and its corresponding social group, the more *constant* the assumed factors in an utterance become.

When the assumed real purview of an utterance is narrow, when, as in our example, it coincides with the actual purview of two people sitting in the same room and seeing the same thing, then even the most momentary change within that purview can become the assumed. Where the purview is wider, the utterance can operate only on the basis of constant, stable factors in life and substantive, fundamental social evaluations.

Especially great importance, in this case, belongs to assumed evaluations. The fact is that all the basic social evaluations that stem directly from the distinctive characteristics of the given social group's economic being are usually not articulated: They have entered the flesh and blood of all representatives of the group; they organize behavior and actions; they have merged, as it were, with the objects and phenomena to which they correspond, and for that reason they are in no need of special verbal formulation. We seem to perceive the value of a thing together with its being as one of its qualities; we seem, for instance, to sense, along with its warmth and light, the sun's value for us, as well. All the phenomena that surround us are similarly merged with value judgments. If a value judgment is in actual fact conditioned by the being of a given community, it becomes a matter of dogmatic belief, something taken for granted and not subject to discussion. On the contrary, whenever some basic value judgment is verbalized and justified, we may be certain that it has already become dubious, has separated from its referent, has ceased to organize life, and, consequently, has lost its connection with the existential conditions of the given group.

A healthy social value judgment remains within life and from that position organizes the very form of an utterance and its intonation, but it does not at all aim to find suitable expression in the content side of discourse. Once a value judgment shifts from formal factors to content, we may be sure that a reevaluation is in the offing. Thus, a viable value judgment exists wholly without incorporation into the content of discourse and is not derivable therefrom; instead, it determines the *very selection of the verbal material and the form of the verbal whole.* It finds its purest expression in *intonation.* Intonation establishes a firm link between verbal discourse and the extraverbal context—genuine, living intonation moves verbal discourse beyond the border of the verbal, so to speak.

Let us stop to consider in somewhat greater detail the connection between intonation and the pragmatic context of life in the example utterance we have been using. This will allow us to make a number of important observations about the social nature of intonation.

IV

First of all, we must emphasize that the word *well*—a word virtually empty semantically—cannot to any extent predetermine intonation through its own content. Any intonation—joyful, sorrowful, contemptuous, and so on—can freely and easily operate in this word; it all depends on the context in which the word appears. In our example, the context determining the intonation used (indignant-reproachful but moderated by humor) is provided entirely by the extraverbal situation that we have already analyzed, since, in this instance, there is no immediate verbal context. We might say in advance that even were such an immediate verbal context present and even, moreover, if that context were entirely sufficient from all other points of view, the intonation would still take us beyond its confines. Intonation can be thoroughly understood only when one is in touch with the assumed value judgments of the given social group, whatever the scope of that group might be. *Intonation always lies on the border of the verbal and the nonverbal, the said and the unsaid.* In intonation, discourse comes directly into contact with life. And it is in intonation above all that the speaker comes into contact with the listener or listeners—intonation is social par excellence. It is especially sensitive to all the vibrations in the social atmosphere surrounding the speaker.

The intonation in our example stemmed from the interlocutors' shared yearning for spring and shared disgruntlement over the protracted winter. This commonness of evaluations assumed between them supplied the basis for the intonation, the basis for the distinctness and certitude of its major tonality. Given an atmosphere of sympathy, the intonation could freely undergo deployment and differentiation within the range of the major tone. But if there were no such firmly dependable "choral support," the intonation would have gone in a different direction and taken on different tones—perhaps those of provocation or annoyance with the listener, or perhaps the intonation would simply have contracted and been reduced to the minimum. When a person anticipates the disagreement of his interlocutor or, at any rate, is uncertain or doubtful of his agreement, he intones his words differently. We shall see later that not only intonation but the whole formal structure of speech depends to a signficant degree on what the relation of the utterance is to the assumed community of values belonging to the social milieu wherein the discourse figures. A creatively productive, assured, and rich intonation is possible only on the basis of presupposed "choral support." Where such support is lacking, the voice falters and its intonational richness is reduced, as happens, for instance, when a person laughing suddenly realizes that he is laughing alone—his laughter either ceases or degenerates, becomes forced, loses its assurance and clarity and its ability to generate joking and amusing talk. *The commonness of assumed basic value judgments constitutes the canvas upon which living human speech embroiders the designs of intonation.*

Intonation's set toward possible sympathy, toward "choral support," does not exhaust its social nature. It is only one side of intonation—the side turned toward the listener. But intonation contains yet another extremely important factor for the sociology of discourse.

If we scrutinize the intonation of our example, we will notice that it has one "mysterious" feature requiring special explanation. In point of fact, the intonation of the word *well* voiced not only passive dissatisfaction with an occurring event (the snowfall) but also active indignation and reproach. To whom is this reproach addressed? Clearly not to the listener but to somebody else. This tack of the intonational movement patently makes an opening in the situation for a *third participant*. Who is this third participant? Who is the recipient of the reproach? The snow? Nature? Fate, perhaps?

Of course, in our simplified example of a behavioral utterance the third participant—the "hero" of this verbal production—has not yet assumed full and definitive shape; the intonation has demarcated a definite place for the hero but his semantic equivalent has not been supplied and he remains nameless. Intonation has established an active attitude toward the referent, toward the object of the utterance, an attitude of a kind verging on *apostrophe* to that object as the incarnate, living culprit, while the listener—the second participant—is, as it were, called in *as witness and ally*.

Almost any example of live intonation in emotionally charged behavioral speech proceeds as if it addressed, behind inanimate objects and phenomena, animate participants and agents in life; in other words, it has an inherent *tendency toward personification*. If the intonation is not held in check, as in our example, by a certain amount of irony, then it becomes the source of the mythological image, the incantation, the prayer, as was the case in the earliest stages of culture. In our case, however, we have to do with an extremely important phenomenon of language creativity—*the intonational metaphor:* The intonation of the utterance "Well!" makes the word sound as if it were reproaching the living culprit of the late snowfall—winter. We have in our example an instance of *pure* intonational metaphor wholly confined within the intonation; but latent within it, in cradle, so to speak, there exists the possibility of the usual *semantic metaphor*. Were this possibility to be realized, the word *well* would expand into some such metaphorical expression as: "What a *stubborn winter! It just won't give up,* though goodness knows it's time!" But this possibility, inherent in the intonation, remained unrealized and the utterance made do with the almost semantically inert adverb *well*.

It should be noted that the intonation in behavioral speech, on the whole, is a great deal more metaphorical than the words used: The aboriginal myth-making spirit seems to have remained alive in it. Intonation makes it sound as if the world surrounding the speaker were still full of animate forces—it threatens and rails against or adores and cherishes inanimate objects and phenomena, whereas the usual metaphors of colloquial speech for the most part have been effaced and the words become semantically spare and prosaic.

Close kinship unites the intonational metaphor with the *gesticulatory metaphor* (indeed, words were themselves originally lingual gestures constituting one component of a complex, omnicorporeal gesture)—the term "gesture" being understood here in a broad sense including miming as facial gesticulation. Gesture, just as intonation, requires the choral support of surrounding persons; only in an atmosphere of sympathy is free and assured gesture possible. Furthermore, and again just as intonation, gesture makes an opening in the situation and introduces a third participant—the hero. Gesture always has latent within itself the germ of attack or defence, of threat or caress, with the contemplator and listener relegated to the role of ally or witness. Often, the "hero" is merely some inanimate thing, some occurrence or circumstance in life. How often we shake our fist at "someone" in a fit of temper or simply scowl at empty space, and there is literally nothing we cannot smile at—the sun, trees, thoughts.

A point that must constantly be kept in mind (something that psychological aesthetics often forgets to do) is this: *Intonation and gesture are active and objective by tendency.* They not only express the passive mental state of the speaker but also always have embedded in them a living, forceful relation with the external world and with the social milieu—enemies, friends, allies. When a person intones and gesticulates, he assumes an active social position with respect to certain specific values, and this position is conditioned by the very bases of his social being. It is precisely this objective and sociological, and not subjective and psychological, aspect of intonation and gesture that should interest theorists of the various relevant arts, inasmuch as it is here that reside forces in the arts that are responsible for aesthetic creativity and that devise and organize artistic form.

As we see then, every instance of intonation is oriented *in two directions:* with respect to the listener as ally or witness and with respect to the object of the utterance as the third, living participant whom the intonation scolds or caresses, denigrates or magnifies. *This double social orientation is what determines all aspects of intonation and makes it intelligible.* And this very same thing is true for all the other factors of verbal utterances: They are all organized and in every way given shape in the same process of the speaker's *double orientation;* this social origin is only most easily detectable in intonation since it is the verbal factor of greatest sensitivity, elasticity, and freedom.

Thus, as we now have a right to claim, *any locution actually said aloud or written down for intelligible communication* (i.e., anything but words merely reposing in a dictionary) *is the expression and product of the social interaction of three participants: the speaker* (author), *the listener* (reader), and the *topic* (the who or what) *of speech* (the hero). Verbal discourse is a social event; it is not self-contained in the sense of some abstract linguistic quantity, nor can it be derived psychologically from the speaker's subjective consciousness taken in isolation. Therefore, both the formal linguistic approach and the psychological approach equally miss the mark: The concrete, sociological essence of verbal discourse, that which alone can make it true or false, banal or distinguished, necessary or unnecessary, remains beyond the ken and reach of both these points of view. Needless to say, it is also this very same "social soul" of verbal discourse that makes it beautiful or ugly, that is, that makes it artistically meaningful, as well. To be sure, once subordinated to the basic and more concrete sociological approach, both abstract points of view—the formal linguistic and the psychological—retain their value. Their collaboration is even absolutely indispensable; but separately, each by itself in isolation, they are inert.

The concrete utterance (and not the linguistic abstraction) is born, lives, and dies in the process of social interaction between the participants of the utterance. Its form and meaning are determined basically by the form and character of this interaction. When we cut the utterance off from the real grounds, that nurture it, we lose the key to its form as well as to its import—all we have left is an abstract linguistic shell or an equally abstract semantic scheme (the banal "idea of the work" with which earlier theorists and historians of literature dealt)—two abstractions that are not mutually joinable because there are no concrete grounds for their organic synthesis.

It remains for us now only to sum up our short analysis of utterance in life and of those *artistic potentials, those rudiments of future form and content,* that we have detected in it.

The meaning and import of an utterance in life (of whatever particular kind that utterance may be) do not coincide with the purely verbal composition of the utterance. Articulated words are impregnated with assumed and unarticulated qualities. What are called the "understanding" and "evaluation" of an utterance (agreement or disagreement) always encompass the extraverbal pragmatic situation together with the verbal discourse proper. Life, therefore, does not affect an utterance from without; it penetrates and exerts an influence on an utterance from within, as that unity and commonness of being surrounding the speakers and that unity and commonness of essential social value judgments issuing from that being without all of which no intelligible utterance is possible. Intonation lies on the border between life and the verbal aspect of the utterance; it, as it were, pumps energy from a life situation into the verbal discourse, it endows everything linguistically stable with living historical momentum and uniqueness. Finally, the utterance reflects the social interaction of the speaker, listener, and hero as the product and fixation in verbal material of the act of living communication among them.

Verbal discourse is like a "*scenario*" of a certain event. A viable understanding of the whole import of discourse must *reproduce* this event of the mutual relationship between speakers, must, as it were, "reenact" it, with the person wishing to understand taking upon himself the role of the listener. But in order to carry out that role, he must distinctly understand the positions of the other two participants, as well.

For the linguistic point of view, neither this event nor its living participants exist, of course; the linguistic point of view deals with abstract, bare words and their equally abstract components (phonetic, morphological, and so on). Therefore, the *total import of discourse* and *its ideological value*—the cognitive, political, aesthetic, or other—are inaccessible to it. Just as there cannot be a linguistic logic or a linguistic politics, so there cannot be a linguistic poetics.

V

In what way does an artistic verbal utterance—a complete work of poetic art—differ from an utterance in the business of life?

It is immediately obvious that discourse in art neither is nor can be so closely dependent on all the factors of the extraverbal context, on all that is seen and known, as in life. A poetic work cannot rely on objects and events in the immediate milieu as things "understood," without making even the slightest allusion to them in the verbal part of the utterance. In this regard, a great deal more is demanded of discourse in literature: Much that could remain outside the utterance in life must find verbal representation. Nothing must be left unsaid in a poetic work from the pragmatic-referential point of view.

Does it follow from this that in literature the speaker, listener, and hero come in contact for the first time, knowing nothing about one another, having no purview in common, and are, therefore, bereft of anything on which they can jointly rely or hold assumptions about? Certain writers on these topics are inclined to think so.

But in actuality a poetic work, too, is closely enmeshed in the unarticulated context of life. If it were true that author, listener, and hero, as abstract persons, come into contact for the first time devoid of any unifying purview and that the words used are taken as from a dictionary, then it is hardly likely that even a nonpoetic work would result, and certainly not a poetic one. Science does to some degree approach this extreme—a scientific definition has a minimum of the "assumed"; but it would be possible to prove that even science cannot do entirely without the assumed.

In literature, assumed value judgments play a role of particular importance. We might say that *a poetic work is a powerful condenser of unarticulated social evaluations*—each word is saturated with them. *It is these social evaluations that organize form as their direct expression.*

Value judgments, first of all, determine the author's *selection of words* and the reception of that selection (the coselection) by the listener. The poet, after all, selects words not from the dictionary but from the context of life where words have been steeped in and become permeated with value judgments. Thus, he selects the value judgments associated with the words and does so, moreover, from the standpoint of the incarnated bearers of those value judgments. It can be said that the poet constantly works in conjunction with his listener's sympathy or antipathy, agreement or disagreement. Furthermore, evaluation is operative also with regard to the object of the utterance—the hero. The simple selection of an epithet or a metaphor is already an active evaluative act with orientation in both directions—toward the listener and toward the hero. *Listener and hero are constant participants in the creative event*, which does not for a single instant cease to be an event of living communication involving all three.

The problem of sociological poetics would be resolved if each factor of form could be explained as the active expression of evaluation in these two directions—toward the listener and toward the object of utterance, the hero.[6] But at the present time the data are too insufficient for such a task to be carried out. All that can be done is to map out at least the preliminary steps leading toward that goal.

The formalistic aesthetics of the present day defines artistic forms as *the form of the material*. If this point of view be carried out consistently, content must necessarily be ignored, since no room is left for it in the poetic work; at best, it may be regarded as a factor of the material and in that way, indirectly, be organized by artistic form in its direct bearing on the material.[7]

So understood, form loses its active evaluative character and becomes merely a stimulus of passive feelings of pleasure in the perceiver.

It goes without saying that form is realized with the help of the material—it is fixed in material; but by virtue of *its significance* it exceeds the material. *The meaning, the import of form has to do not with the material but with the content.* So, for instance, the form of a statue may be said to be not the form of the marble but the form of the human body, with the added qualification that the form "heroicizes" the human depicted or "dotes upon" him or, perhaps, denigrates him (the caricature style in the plastic arts); that is, the form expresses some specific evaluation of the object depicted.

The evaluative significance of form is especially obvious in verse. Rhythm and other formal elements of verse overtly express a certain active attitude toward the object depicted: The form celebrates or laments or ridicules that object.

Psychological aesthetics calls this the "emotional factor" of form. But it is not the psychological side of the matter that is important for us, not the identity of the psychical forces that take part in the creation of form and the cocreative perception of form. What is important is the significance of these experiences, their active role, their bearing on content. Through the agency of artistic form the creator takes up *an active position with respect to content.* The form in and of itself need not necessarily be pleasurable (the hedonistic explanation of form is absurd); what it must be is a *convincing evaluation* of the content. So, for instance, while the form of "the enemy" might even be repulsive, the positive state, the pleasure that the contemplator derives in the end, is a consequence of the fact that the form is *appropriate to the enemy* and that it is *technically perfect* in its realization through the agency of the material. It is in these two aspects that form should be studied: with respect to content, as its ideological evaluation, and with respect to the material, as the technical realization of that evaluation.

The ideological evaluation expressed through form is not at all supposed to transpose into content as a maxim or a proposition of a moral, political, or other kind. The evaluation should remain in the rhythm, *in the very evaluative impetus* of the epithet or metaphor, *in the manner of the unfolding* of the depicted event; it is supposed to be realized by the formal means of the material only. But, at the same time, while not transposing into content, the form must not lose its connection with content, its correlation with it, otherwise it becomes a technical experiment devoid of any real artistic import.

The general definition of style that classical and neoclassical poetics had advanced, together with the basic division of style into "high" and "low," aptly brings out precisely this active evaluative nature of artistic form. The structure of form is indeed *hierarchical*, and in this respect it comes close to political and juridical gradations. Form similarly creates, in an artistically configured content, a complex system of hierarchical interrelations: Each of its elements—an epithet or a metaphor, for instance—either raises the designatum to a higher degree or lowers it or equalizes it. The selection of a hero or an event determines from the very outset the general level of the form and the admissibility of this or that particular set of configurating devices. And this basic requirement of *stylistic suitability* has in view *the evaluative-hierarchical suitability of form and content:* They must be *equally adequate* for one another. The selection of content and the selection of form constitute one and the same act establishing the creator's basic position; and in that act one and the same social evaluation finds expression.

VI

Sociological analysis can take its starting point only, of course, from the purely verbal, linguistic makeup of a work, but it must not and cannot confine itself within those limits, as linguistic poetics does. Artistic contemplation via the reading of a poetic work does, to be sure, start from the grapheme (the visual image of written or printed words), but at the very instant of perception this visual image gives way to and is very nearly obliterated by other verbal factors—articulation, sound image, intonation, meaning—and these factors eventually take us beyond the border of the verbal altogether. And so it can be said that *the purely linguistic factor of a work is to the artistic whole as the grapheme is to the verbal whole.* In poetry, as in life, verbal discourse is a *"scenario" of an event.* Competent artistic perception reenacts it, sensitively surmising from the words and the forms of their organization the specific, living interrelations of the author with the world he depicts and entering into those interrelations as a third participant (the listener's role). Where linguistic analysis sees only words and the interrelations of their abstract factors (phonetic, morphological, syntactic, and so on), there, for living artistic perception and for concrete sociological analysis, relations among *people* stand revealed, relations merely reflected and fixed in verbal material. Verbal discourse is the skeleton that takes on living flesh only in the process of creative perception—consequently, only in the process of living social communication.

In what follows here we shall attempt to provide a brief and preliminary sketch of the essential factors in the interrelationships of the participants in an artistic event—those factors that determine the broad and basic lines of poetic style as a social phenomenon. Any further detailing of these factors would, of course, go beyond the scope of the present essay.

The author, hero, and listener that we have been talking about all this time are to be understood not as entities outside the artistic event but only as entities of the very perception of an artistic work, entities that are essential constitutive factors of the work. They are the living forces that determine form and style and are distinctly detectable by any competent contemplator. This means that all those definitions that a historian of literature and society mighty apply to the author and his heroes—the author's biography, the precise qualifications of heroes in chronological and sociological terms and so on—are excluded here: They do not enter directly into the structure of the work but remain outside it. The listener, too, is taken here as the listener whom the author himself takes into account, the one toward whom the work is oriented and who, consequently, intrinsically determines the work's structure. Therefore, we do not at all mean the actual people who in fact made up the reading public of the author in question.

The first form-determining factor of content is the *evaluative rank* of the depicted event and its agent—the hero (whether named or not), taken in strict correlation with the rank of the creator and contemplator. Here we have to do, just as in legal or political life, with a *two-sided relationship:* master-slave, ruler-subject, comrade-comrade, and the like.

The basic stylistic tone of an utterance is therefore determined above all by who is talked about and what his relation is to the speaker—whether he is higher or lower than or equal to him on the scale of the social hierarchy. King, father, brother, slave, comrade, and so on, as heroes of an utterance, also determine its formal structure. And this *specific hierarchical weight* of the hero is determined, in its turn, by that unarticulated context of basic evaluations in which a poetic work, too, participates. Just as the "intonational metaphor" in our example utterance from life established an organic relationship with the object of the utterance, so also all elements of the style of a poetic work are permeated with the author's evaluative attitude toward content and express his basic social position. Let us stress once again that we have in mind here not those ideological evaluations that are incorporated into the content of a work in the form of judgments or conclusions but that deeper, more ingrained kind of *evaluation via form* that finds expression in the very manner in which the artistic material is viewed and deployed.

Certain languages, Japanese in particular, possess a rich and varied store of special lexical and grammatical forms to be used in strict accordance with the rank of the hero of the utterance (language etiquette).[8]

We might say that what is still a *matter of grammar* for the Japanese has already become for us a *matter of style*. The most important stylistic components of the heroic epic, the tragedy, the ode, and so forth are determined precisely by the hierarchical status of the object of the utterance with respect to the speaker.

It should not be supposed that this hierarchical interdefinition of creator and hero has been eliminated from modern literature. It has been made more complex and does not reflect the contemporary sociopolitical hierarchy with the same degree of distinctness as, say, classicism did in its time—but *the very principle of change of style in accordance with change in the social value of the hero of the utterance* certainly remains in force as before. After all, it is not his personal enemy that the poet hates, not his personal friend that his form treats with love and tenderness, not the events from his private life that he rejoices or sorrows over. Even if a poet has in fact borrowed his passion in good measure from the circumstances of his own private life, still, he must *socialize* that passion and, consequently, elaborate the event with which it corresponds to the level of *social significance*.

The second style-determining factor in the interrelationship between hero and creator is *the degree of their proximity to one another*. All languages possess direct grammatical means of expression for this aspect: first, second, and third persons and variable sentence structure in accordance with the person of the subject ("I" or "you" or "he"). The form of a proposition about a third person, the form of an address to a second person, the form of an utterance about oneself (and their modifications) are already different in terms of grammar. Thus, here *the very structure of the language reflects the event of the speakers' interrelationship*.

Certain languages have purely grammatical forms capable of conveying with even greater flexibility the nuances of the speakers' social interrelationship and the various degrees of their proximity. From this angle, the so-called "inclusive" and "exclusive" forms of the plural in certain languages present a case of special interest. For example, if a speaker using the form *we* has the listener in mind and includes him in the subject of the proposition, then he uses one form, whereas if he means himself and some other person (*we* in the sense of *I* and *he*), he uses a different form. Such is the use of the dual in certain Australian languages, for instance. There, too, are found two special forms of the triad: one meaning *I and you and he*; the other, *I and he and he* (with *you*—the listener—excluded).[9]

In European languages these and similar interrelationships between speakers have no special grammatical expression. The character of these languages is more abstract and not so capable of reflecting the situation of utterance via grammatical structure. However, interrelationships between speakers do find expression in these languages—and expression of far greater subtlety and diversity—*in the style and intonation of utterances*. Here the social situation of creativity finds thoroughgoing reflection in a work by means of purely artistic devices.

The form of a poetic work is determined, therefore, in many of its factors by *how the author perceives his hero*—the hero who serves as the organizing center of the utterance. The form of *objective narration*, the form of *address or apostrophe* (prayer, hymn, certain lyric forms), the form of *self-expression* (confession, autobiography, lyric avowal—an important form of the love lyric) are determined precisely by the *degree of proximity between author and hero.*

Both the factors we have indicated—the hierarchical value of the hero and the degree of his proximity to the author—are as yet insufficient, taken independently and in isolation, for the determination of artistic form. The fact is that a third participant is constantly in play as well—the listener, whose presence affects the interrelationship of the other two (creator and hero).

The interrelationship of author and hero never, after all, actually is an intimate relationship of two; all the while form makes provision for the third participant—the listener—who exerts crucial influence on all the other factors of the work.

In what way can the listener determine the style of a poetic utterance? Here, too, we must distinguish two basic factors: first, the listener's proximity to the author and, second, his relation to the hero. Nothing is more perilous for aesthetics than to ignore the autonomous role of the listener. A very commonly held opinion has it that the listener is to be regarded as equal to the author, excepting the latter's technical performance, and that the position of a competent listener is supposed to be a simple reproduction of the author's position. In actual fact this is not so. Indeed, the opposite may sooner be said to be true: The listener never equals the author. The listener has *his own independent place* in the event of artistic creation; he must occupy a special, and, what is more, a *two-sided* position in it—with respect to the author and with respect to the hero—and it is this position that has determinative effect on the style of an utterance.

How does the author sense his listener? In our example of an utterance in the business of life, we have seen to what degree the presumed agreement or disagreement of the listener shaped an utterance. Exactly the same is true regarding all factors of form. To put it figuratively, the listener normally stands *side by side* with the author as his ally, but this classical positioning of the listener is by no means always the case.

Sometimes the listener begins to lean toward the hero of the utterance. The most unmistakable and typical expression of this is the polemical style that aligns the hero and the listener together. Satire, too, can involve the listener as someone calculated to be close to the hero ridiculed and not to the ridiculing author. This constitutes a sort of *inclusive form of ridicule* distinctly different from the exclusive form where the listener is in solidarity with the jeering author. In romanticism, an interesting phenomenon can be observed where the author *concludes an alliance,* as it were, *with his hero against the listener* (Friedrich Schlegel's *Lucinda* and, in Russian literature, *Hero of Our Time* to some extent).

Of very special character and interest for analysis is the author's sense of his listener in the forms of the confession and the autobiography. All shades of feeling from humble reverence before the listener, as before a veritable judge, to contemptuous distrust and hostility can have determinative effect on the style of a confession or an autobiography. Extremely interesting material for the illustration of this contention can be found in the works of Dostoevskij. The confessional style of Ippolit's "article" (*The Idiot*) is determined by an almost extreme degree of contemptuous distrust and hostility directed toward all who are to hear this dying confession. Similar tones, but somewhat softened, determine the style of *Notes from Underground.* The style of "Stavrogin's Confession" (*The Possessed*) displays far greater trust in the listener and acknowledgments of his rights, although here too, from time to time, a feeling almost of hatred for the listener erupts, which is what is responsible for the jaggedness of its style. Playing the fool, as a special form of utterance, one, to be sure, lying on the periphery of the artistic, is determined above all by an extremely complex and tangled conflict of the speaker with the listener.

A form especially sensitive to the position of the listener is the lyric. The underlying condition for lyric intonation is *the absolute certainty of the listener's sympathy*. Should any doubt on this score creep into the lyric situation, the style of the lyric changes drastically. This conflict with the listener finds its most egregious expression in so-called lyric irony (Heine, and in modern poetry, Laforgue, Annenskij, and others). The form of irony in general is conditioned by a social conflict: It is the encounter in one voice of two incarnate value judgments and their interference with one another.

In modern aesthetics a special, so-called juridical theory of tragedy was proposed, a theory amounting essentially to the attempt to conceive of *the structure of a tragedy as the structure of a trial in court.*[10]

The interrelationshp of hero and chorus, on the one side, and the overall position of the listener, on the other, do indeed, to a degree, lend themselves to juridical interpretation. But of course this can only be meant as *an analogy*. The important common feature of tragedy—indeed of any work of art—and judicial process comes down merely to the existence of "sides," that is, the occupying by the several participants of *different positions*. The terms, so widespread in literary terminology, that define the poet as "judge," "exposer," "witness," "defender," and even "executioner" (the phraseology for "scourging satire"—Juvenal, Barbier, Nekrasov, and others), and associated definitions for heroes and listeners, reveal by way of analogy, the same social base of poetry. At all events, author, hero, and listener nowhere merge together into one indifferent mass—they occupy *autonomous positions*, they are indeed "sides," the sides not of a judicial process but of an artistic event with specific social structure the "protocol" of which is the work of art.

It would not be amiss at this point to stress once again that we have in mind, and have had in mind all this time, the listener as an immanent participant in the artistic event who has determinative effect on the form of the work from within. This listener, on a par with the author and the hero, is an essential, intrinsic factor of the work and does not at all coincide with the so-called reading public, located outside the work, whose artistic tastes and demands can be consciously taken into account. Such a conscious account is incapable of direct and profound effect on artistic form in the process of its living creation. What is more, if this conscious account of the reading public does come to occupy a position of any importance in a poet's creativity, that creativity inevitably loses its artistic purity and degrades to a lower social level.

This external account bespeaks the poet's loss of *his immanent listener*, his divorce from the *social whole* that *intrinsically*, aside from all abstract considerations, has the capability of determining *his value judgments* and the artistic form of his poetic utterances, which form is the expression of those crucial social value judgments. The more a poet is cut off from the social unity of his group, the more likely he is to take into account the *external* demands of a *particular reading public*. Only a social group alien to the poet can determine his creative work from outside. One's *own* group needs no such external definition: It exists in the poet's voice, in the basic tone and intonations of that voice—whether the poet himself intends this or not.

The poet acquires his words and learns to intone them *over the course of his entire life* in the process of his every-sided contact with his environment. The poet begins to use those words and intonations already in the *inner speech* with the help of which he thinks and becomes conscious of himself, even when he does not produce utterances. It is naive to suppose that one can assimilate as one's own *an external speech that runs counter to one's inner speech,* that is, runs counter to one's whole inner verbal manner of being aware of oneself and the world. Even if it is possible to create such a thing for some pragmatic occasion, still, as something cut off from all sources of sustenance, it will be devoid of any artistic productiveness. A poet's style is engendered from *the style of his inner speech,* which does not lend itself to control, and his inner speech is itself the product of his entire social life. "Style is the man," they say; but we might say: Style is at least two persons or, more accurately, one person plus his social group in the form of its authoritative representative, the listener—the constant participant in a person's inner and outward speech.

The fact of the matter is that no conscious act of any degree of distinctness can do without inner speech, without words and intonations—without evaluations—and, consequently, every conscious act is already a social act, an act of communication. Even the most intimate self-awareness is an attempt to translate oneself into the common code, to take stock of another's point of view, and, consequently, entails orientation toward a possible listener. This listener may be only the bearer of the value judgments of the social group to which the "conscious" person belongs. In this regard, consciousness, provided that we do not lose sight of its content, is *not just a psychological phenomenon* but also, and above all, an *ideological phenomenon, a product of social intercourse.* This constant *coparticipant* in all our conscious acts determines not only the content of consciousness but also—and this is the main point for us—the very *selection* of the content, the selection of what precisely we become conscious of, and thus determines also those *evaluations* which permeate consciousness and which psychology usually calls the "emotional tone" of consciousness. It is precisely from this constant participant in all our conscious acts that the listener who determines artistic form is engendered.

There is nothing more perilous than to conceive of this subtle social structure of verbal creativity as analogous with the conscious and cynical speculations of the bourgeois publisher who "calculates the prospects of the book market," and to apply to the characterization of the immanent structure of a work categories of the "supply-demand" type. Alas, all too many "sociologists" are likely to identify the creative writer's service to society with the vocation of the enterprising publisher.

Under the conditions of the bourgeois economy, the book market does, of course, "regulate" writers, but this is not in any way to be identified with the regulative role of the listener as a constant structural element in artistic creativity. For a historian of the literature of the capitalist era, the market is a very important factor, but for theoretical poetics, which studies the basic ideological structure of art, that external factor is irrelevant. However, even in the historical study of literature the history of the book market must not be confused with the history of literature.

VII

All the form-determining factors of an artistic utterance that we have analyzed—(1) the hierarchical value of the hero or event serving as the content of the utterance, (2) the degree of the latter's proximity to the author, and (3) the listener and his interrelationship with the author, on the one side, and the hero, on the other—all those factors are *the contact points between the social forces of extra-artistic reality and verbal art*. Thanks precisely to that kind of *intrinsically social structure* which artistic creation possesses, it is *open on all sides to the influence of other domains of life*. Other ideological spheres, prominently including the sociopolitical order and the economy, have determinative effect on verbal art not merely from outside but with direct bearing upon its intrinsic structural elements. And, conversely, the artistic interaction of author, listener, and hero may exert its influence on other domains of social intercourse.

Full and thoroughgoing elucidation of questions as to who the typical heroes of literature at some particular period are, what the typical formal orientation of the author toward them is, what the interrelationships of the author and hero with the listener are in the whole of an artistic creation—elucidation of such questions presupposes thoroughgoing analysis of the economic and ideological conditions of the time.

But these concrete historical issues exceed the scope of theoretical poetics which, however, still does include one other important task. Up to now we have been concerned only with those factors which determine form in its relation to content, that is, form as the embodied social evaluation of precisely that content, and we have ascertained that every factor of form is a product of social interaction. But we also pointed out that form must be understood from another angle, as well—as form realized with the help of *specific material*. This opens up a whole long series of questions connected with *the technical aspect of form*.

Of course, *these technical questions can be separated out from questions of the sociology of form only in abstract terms; in actuality* it is impossible to divorce the *artistic* import of some device, say, a metaphor that relates to content and expresses the formal evaluation of it (i.e., the metaphor degrades the object or raises it to a higher rank), from *the purely linguistic* specification of that device.

The extraverbal import of a metaphor—a regrouping of values—and its *linguistic covering*—a semantic shift—are merely different points of view on one and the same real phenomenon. But the second point of view is subordinate to the first: a poet uses a metaphor in order to regroup values and not for the sake of a linguistic exercise.

All questions of form can be taken in relation with material—in the given case, in relation with language in its linguistic conception. Technical analysis will then amount to the question as to *which linguistic means are used for the realization of the socioartistic purpose of the form*. But if that purpose is not known, if its import is not elucidated in advance, technical analysis will be absurd.

Technical questions of form, of course, go beyond the scope of the task we have set ourself here. Moreover, their treatment would require an incomparably more diversified and elaborated analysis of the socioartistic aspect of verbal art. Here we have been able to provide only a brief sketch of the basic directions such an analysis must take.

If we have succeeded in demonstrating even the mere possibility of a sociological approach to the immanent structure of poetic form, we may consider our task to have been fulfilled.

Notes

1. P. N. Sakulin, *Sociologičeskij metod v literaturovedenii* [*The Sociological Method in the Study of Literature*] (1925).

2. "Elements of poetic form (sound, word, image, rhythm, composition, genre), poetic thematics, artistic style in totality—all these things are studied, as preliminary matters, with the help of methods that have been worked out by theoretical poetics, grounded in psychology, aesthetics, and linguistics, and that are now practiced in particular by the so-called formal method." *Ibid.*, p. 27.

3. "Viewing literature as a social phenomenon, we inevitably arrive at the question of its causal conditioning. For us this is a matter of sociological causality. Only at the present time has the historian of literature received the right to assume the position of a sociologist and to pose 'why' questions so as to include literary facts within the general process of the social life of some particular period and so as to, thereupon, define the place of literature in the whole movement of history. It is at this point that the sociological method, as applied to the history of literature, becomes a historical-sociological method.

In the first, immanent stage, a work was conceived of as an artistic value and not in its social and historical meaning." *Ibid.*, pp. 27, 28.

4. We make a distinction between theory and history of art only as a matter of a technical division of labor. There cannot be any methodological breach between them. Historical categories are of course applicable in absolutely all the fields of the humanities, whether they be historical or theoretical ones.

5. The enthymeme is a form of syllogism, one of whose premises is not expressed but assumed. For example, "Socrates is a man, therefore he is mortal." The assumed premise: "All men are mortal."

6. We ignore technical questions of form here but will have something to say on this topic later.

7. The point of view of V. M. Žirmunskij.

8. See W. Humboldt, *Kawi-Werk* No. 2:335, and Hoffman, *Japan. Sprachlehre*, p. 75.

9. See Matthews, *Aboriginal Languages of Victoria*. Also Humboldt. *Kawi-Werk*.

10. For the most interesting development of this point of view, see Hermann Cohen, *Ästhetick des reinen Gefühls*, vol. 2.

Virginia Woolf 1882–1941

Virginia Woolf, born in London, was the daughter of Leslie Stephen, a distinguished Victorian critic, philosopher, and editor. She grew up surrounded by books and eminent writers, educating herself in her father's extensive library. After her father's death in 1904, the Stephen family settled in Bloomsbury, the district of London that later was to become associated with Woolf and the "Bloomsbury Group," the informal literary group of which she was a founding member. In 1912 she married Leonard Woolf, a journalist and political thinker; together they founded the Hogarth Press, which specialized in publishing the works of new writers. In March 1941, in a state of depression brought on by the fear that she might lose her mind and be a burden on her husband, Virginia Woolf committed suicide by drowning herself.

Woolf is considered one of the great innovators of the modern novel. After writing two novels in traditional form, she developed her own style of the "stream of consciousness" technique. Her most successful novels were written in the "new" style: *Jacob's Room* (1922), *Mrs. Dalloway* (1925), *To the Lighthouse* (1927), *The Waves* (1931), and *Between the Acts* (published posthumously in 1941). In her novels, Woolf subtly explores problems of identity and personal relationships.

In addition to writing novels, Woolf wrote a great many reviews and essays. Several of her essays addressed the position of women, especially professional women, and the restrictions imposed upon them by patriarchal society. Her most famous discussion on this subject is her book *A Room of One's Own* (1929). In this book, Woolf describes the conditions most conducive to a woman's success as a writer. She persuasively argues that these conditions, which include money, education, and "a room of one's own," have not been available for women. If available, these conditions would give women the freedom and independence to become successful writers.

Woolf was also interested in determining the conditions of the mind that are necessary for successful writing. In "The Shadow Across the Page," chapter six of *A Room of One's Own*, Woolf directly addresses this question. She postulates that the mind, like the body, has two sexes (male and female), which strive for union and balance. In a conversationally lucid style, Woolf argues that in the "normal and comfortable state" of the mind, the state most conducive to creativity, the male and female aspects of the mind "live in harmony." Her creative conclusion is that the great artist has an androgynous mind.

from A Room of One's Own

Chapter Six

Next day the light of the October morning was falling in dusty shafts through the uncurtained windows, and the hum of traffic rose from the street. London then was winding itself up again; the factory was astir; the machines were beginning. It was tempting, after all this reading, to look out of the window and see what London was doing on the morning of the twenty-sixth of October 1928. And what was London doing? Nobody, it seemed, was reading *Antony and Cleopatra*. London was wholly indifferent, it appeared, to Shakespeare's plays. Nobody cared a straw—and I do not blame them—for the future of fiction, the death of poetry or the development by the average woman of a prose style completely expressive of her mind. If opinions upon any of these matters had been chalked on the pavement, nobody would have stooped to read them. The nonchalance of the hurrying feet would have rubbed them out in half an hour. Here came an errand-boy; here a woman with a dog on a lead. The fascination of the London street is that no two people are ever alike; each seems bound on some private affair of his own. There were the businesslike, with their little bags; there were the drifters rattling sticks upon area railings; there were affable characters to whom the streets serve for clubroom, hailing men in carts and giving information without being asked for it. Also there were funerals to which men, thus suddenly reminded of the passing of their own bodies, lifted their hats. And then a very distinguished gentleman came slowly down a doorstep and paused to avoid collision with a bustling lady who had, by some means or other, acquired a spendid fur coat and a bunch of Parma violets. They all seemed separate, self-absorbed, on business of their own.

At this moment, as so often happens in London, there was a complete lull and suspension of traffic. Nothing came down the street; nobody passed. A single leaf detached itself from the plane tree at the end of the street, and in that pause and suspension fell. Somehow it was like a signal falling, a signal pointing to a force in things which one had overlooked. It seemed to point to a river, which flowed past, invisibly, round the corner, down the street, and took people and eddied them along, as the stream at Oxbridge had taken the undergraduate in his boat and the dead leaves. Now it was bringing from one side of the street to the other diagonally a girl in patent leather boots, and then a young man in a maroon overcoat; it was also bringing a taxi-cab; and it brought all three together at a point directly beneath my window; where the taxi stopped; and the girl and the young man stopped; and they got into the taxi; and then the cab glided off as if it were swept on by the current elsewhere.

The sight was ordinary enough; what was strange was the rhythmical order with which my imagination had invested it; and the fact that the ordinary sight of two people getting into a cab had the power to communicate something of their own seeming satisfaction. The sight of two people coming down the street and meeting at the corner seems to ease the mind of some strain, I thought, watching the taxi turn and make off. Perhaps to think, as I had been thinking these two days, of one sex as distinct from the other is an effort. It interferes with the unity of the mind. Now that effort had ceased and that unity had been restored by seeing two people come together and get into a taxi-cab. The mind is certainly a very mysterious organ, I reflected, drawing my head in from the window, about which nothing whatever is known, though we depend upon it so completely. Why do I feel that there are severances and oppositions in the mind, as there are strains from obvious causes on the body? What does one mean by "the unity of the mind," I pondered, for clearly the mind has so great a power of concentrating at any point at any moment that it seems to have no single state of being. It can separate itself from the people in the street, for example, and think of itself as apart from them, at an upper window looking down on them. Or it can think with other people spontaneously, as, for instance, in a crowd waiting to hear some piece of news read out. It can think back through its fathers or through its mothers, as I have said that a woman writing thinks back through her mothers. Again if one is a woman one is often surprised by a sudden splitting off of consciousness, say in walking down Whitehall, when from being the natural inheritor of that civilisation, she becomes, on the contrary, outside of it, alien and critical. Clearly the mind is always altering its focus, and bringing the world into different perspectives. But some of these states of mind seem, even if adopted spontaneously, to be less comfortable than others. In order to keep oneself continuing in them one is unconsciously holding something back, and gradually the repression becomes an effort. But there may be some state of mind in which one could continue without effort because nothing is required to be held back. And this perhaps, I thought, coming in from the window, is one of them. For certainly when I saw the couple get into the taxi-cab the mind felt as if, after being divided, it had come together again in a natural fusion. The obvious reason would be that it is natural for the sexes to co-operate. One has a profound, if irrational, instinct in favour of the theory that the union of man and woman makes for the greatest satisfaction, the most complete happiness. But the sight of the two people getting into the taxi and the satisfaction it gave me made me also ask whether there are two sexes in the mind corresponding to the two sexes in the body, and whether they also require to be united in order to get complete satisfaction and happiness. And I went on amateurishly to sketch a plan of the soul so that in each of us two powers preside, one male, one female; and in the man's brain, the man predominates over the woman, and in the woman's brain, the woman predominates over the man. The normal and comfortable state of being is that when the two live in harmony together, spiritually cooperating. If one is a man, still the woman part of the brain must have effect; and a woman also must have intercourse with the man in her. Coleridge perhaps meant this when he said that a great mind is androgynous. It is when this fusion takes place that the mind is fully fertilised and uses all its faculties. Perhaps a mind that is purely masculine cannot create, any more than a mind that is purely feminine, I thought. But it would be well to test what one meant by man-womanly, and conversely by woman-manly, by pausing and looking at a book or two.

Coleridge certainly did not mean, when he said that a great mind is androgynous, that it is a mind that has any special sympathy with women; a mind that takes up their cause or devotes itself to their interpretation. Perhaps the androgynous mind is less apt to make these distinctions than the single-sexed mind. He meant, perhaps, that the androgynous mind is resonant and porous; that it transmits emotion without impediment; that it is naturally creative, incandescent and undivided. In fact one goes back to Shakespeare's mind as the type of the androgynous, of the man-womanly mind, though it would be impossible to say what Shakespeare thought of women. And if it be true that it is one of the tokens of the fully developed mind that it does not think specially or separately of sex, how much harder it is to attain that conditon now than ever before. Here I come to the books by living writers, and there paused and wondered if this fact were not at the root of something that had long puzzled me. No age can ever have been as stridently sex-conscious as our own; those innumerable books by men about women in the British Museum are a proof of it. The Suffrage campaign was no doubt to blame. It must have roused in men an extraordinary desire for self-assertion; it must have made them lay an emphasis upon their own sex and its characteristics which they would not have troubled to think about had they not been challenged. And when one is challenged, even by a few women in black bonnets, one retaliates, if one has never been challenged before, rather excessively. That perhaps accounts for some of the characteristics that I remember to have found here, I thought, taking down a new novel by Mr. A, who is in the prime of life and very well thought of, apparently, by the reviewers. I opened it. Indeed, it was delightful to read a man's writing again. It was so direct, so straightforward after the writing of women. It indicated such freedom of mind, such liberty of person, such confidence in himself. One had a sense of physical well-being in the presence of this well-nourished, well-educated, free mind, which had never been thwarted or opposed, but had had full liberty from birth to stretch itself in whatever way it liked. All this was admirable. But after reading a chapter or two a shadow seemed to lie across the page. It was a straight dark bar, a shadow shaped something like the letter "I." One began dodging this way and that to catch a glimpse of the landscape behind it. Whether that was indeed a tree or a woman walking I was not quite sure. Back one was always hailed to the letter "I." One began to be tired of "I." Not but what this "I" was a most respectable "I"; honest and logical; as hard as a nut, and polished for centuries by good teaching and good feeding. I respect and admire that "I" from the bottom of my heart. But—here I turned a page or two, looking for something or other—the worst of it is that in the shadow of the letter "I" all is shapeless as mist. Is that a tree? No, it is a woman. But . . . she has not a bone in her body, I thought, watching Phoebe, for that was her name, coming across the beach. Then Alan got up and the shadow of Alan at once obliterated Phoebe. For Alan had views and Phoebe was quenched in the flood of his views. And then Alan, I thought, has passions; and here I turned page after page very fast, feeling that the crisis was approaching, and so it was. It took place on the beach under the sun. It was done very openly. It was done very vigorously. Nothing could have been more indecent. But . . . I had said "but" too often. One cannot go on saying "but." One must finish the sentence somehow, I rebuked myself. Shall I finish it, "But—I am bored!" But why was I bored? Partly because of the dominance of the letter "I" and the aridity, which, like the giant beech tree, it casts within its shade. Nothing will grow there. And partly for some more obscure reason. There seemed to be some obstacle, some impediment of Mr. A's mind which blocked the fountain of creative energy and shored it within narrow limits. And remembering the lunch party at Oxbridge, and the cigarette ash and the Manx cat and Tennyson and Christina Rossetti all in a bunch, it seemed possible that the impediment lay there. As he no longer hums under his breath, "There has fallen a splendid tear from the passion flower at the gate," when Phoebe crosses the beach, and she no longer replies, "My heart is like a singing bird whose nest is in a water'd shoot," when Alan approaches what can he do? Being honest as the day and logical as the sun, there is only one thing he can do. And that he does, to do him justice, over and over (I said, turning the pages) and over again. And that, I added, aware of the awful nature of the confession, seems somehow dull. Shakespeare's indecency uproots a thousand other things in one's mind, and is far from being dull. But Shakespeare does it for pleasure; Mr. A, as the nurses say, does it on purpose. He does it in protest. He is protesting against the equality of the other sex by asserting his own superiority. He is therefore impeded and inhibited and self-conscious as Shakespeare might have been if he too had known Miss Clough and Miss Davies. Doubtless Elizabethan literature would have been very different from what it is if the woman's movement had begun in the sixteenth century and not in the nineteenth.

What, then, it amounts to, if this theory of the two sides of the mind holds good, is that virility has now become self-conscious—men, that is to say, are now writing only with the male side of their brains. It is a mistake for a woman to read them, for she will inevitably look for something that she will not find. It is the power of suggestion that one most misses, I thought, taking Mr. B the critic in my hand and reading, very carefully and very dutifully, his remarks upon the art of poetry. Very able they were, acute and full of learning; but the trouble was, that his feelings no longer communicated; his mind seemed separated into different chambers; not a sound carried from one to the other. Thus, when one takes a sentence of Mr. B into the mind it falls plump to the ground—dead; but when one takes a sentence of Coleridge into the mind, it explodes and gives birth to all kinds of other ideas, and that is the only sort of writing of which one can say that it has the secret of perpetual life.

But whatever the reason may be, it is a fact that one must deplore. For it means—here I had come to rows of books by Mr. Galsworthy and Mr. Kipling—that some of the finest works of our greatest living writers fall upon deaf ears. Do what she will a woman cannot find in them that fountain of perpetual life which the critics assure her is there. It is not only that they celebrate male virtues, enforce male values and describe the world of men; it is that the emotion with which these books are permeated is to a woman incomprehensible. It is coming, it is gathering, it is about to burst on one's head, one begins saying long before the end. That picture will fall on old Jolyon's head; he will die of the shock; the old clerk will speak over him two or three obituary words; and all the swans on the Thames will simultaneously burst out singing. But one will rush away before that happens and hide in the gooseberry bushes, for the emotion which is so deep, so subtle, so symbolical to a man moves a woman to wonder. So with Mr. Kipling's officers who turn their backs; and his Sowers who sow the Seed; and his Men who are alone with their Work; and the Flag—one blushes at all these capital letters as if one had been caught eavesdropping at some purely masculine orgy. The fact is that neither Mr. Galsworthy nor Mr. Kipling has a spark of the woman in him. Thus all their qualities seem to a woman, if one may generalise, crude and immature. They lack suggestive power. And when a book lacks suggestive power, however hard it hits the surface of the mind it cannot penetrate within.

And in that restless mood in which one takes books out and puts them back again without looking at them I began to envisage an age to come of pure, of self-assertive virility, such as the letters of professors (take Sir Walter Raleigh's letters, for instance) seem to forebode, and the rulers of Italy have already brought into being. For one can hardly fail to be impressed in Rome by the sense of unmitigated masculinity; and whatever the value of unmitigated masculinity upon the state, one may question the effect of it upon the art of poetry. At any rate, according to the newspapers, there is a certain anxiety about fiction in Italy. There has been a meeting of academicians whose object it is "to develop the Italian novel." "Men famous by birth, or in finance, industry or the Fascist corporations" came together the other day and discussed the matter, and a telegram was sent to the Duce expressing the hope "that the Fascist era would soon give birth to a poet worthy of it." We may all join in that pious hope, but it is doubtful whether poetry can come out of an incubator. Poetry ought to have a mother as well as a father. The Fascist poem, one may fear, will be a horrid little abortion such as one sees in a glass jar in the museum of some county town. Such monsters never live long, it is said; one has never seen a prodigy of that sort cropping grass in a field. Two heads on one body do not make for length of life.

However, the blame for all this, if one is anxious to lay blame, rests no more upon one sex than upon the other. All seducers and reformers are responsible, Lady Bessborough when she lied to Lord Granville; Miss Davies when she told the truth to Mr. Greg. All who have brought about a state of sex-consciousness are to blame, and it is they who drive me, when I want to stretch my faculties on a book, to seek it in that happy age, before Miss Davies and Miss Clough were born, when the writer used both sides of his mind equally. One must turn back to Shakespeare then, for Shakespeare was androgynous; and so was Keats and Sterne and Cowper and Lamb and Coleridge. Shelley perhaps was sexless. Milton and Ben Jonson had a dash too much of the male in them. So had Wordsworth and Tolstoi. In our time Proust was wholly androgynous, if not perhaps a little too much of a woman. But that failing is too rare for one to complain of it, since without some mixture of the kind the intellect seems to predominate and the other faculties of the mind harden and become barren. However, I consoled myself with the reflection that this is perhaps a passing phase; much of what I have said in obedience to my promise to give you the course of my thought will seem out of date; much of what flames in my eyes will seem dubious to you who have not yet come of age.

Even so, the very first sentence that I would write here, I said, crossing over to the writing-table and taking up the page headed Women and Fiction, is that it is fatal for any one who writes to think of their sex. It is fatal to be a man or woman pure and simple; one must be woman-manly or man-womanly. It is fatal for a woman to lay the least stress on any grievance; to plead even with justice any cause; in any way to speak consciously as a woman. And fatal is no figure of speech; for anything written with that conscious bias is doomed to death. It ceases to be fertilised. Brilliant and effective, powerful and masterly, as it may appear for a day or two, it must wither at nightfall; it cannot grow in the minds of others. Some collaboration has to take place in the mind between the woman and the man before the act of creation can be accomplished. Some marriage of opposites has to be consummated. The whole of the mind must lie wide open if we are to get the sense that the writer is communicating his experience with perfect fullness. There must be freedom and there must be peace. Not a wheel must grate, not a light glimmer. The curtains must be close drawn. The writer, I thought, once his experience is over, must lie back and let his mind celebrate its nuptials in darkness. He must not look or question what is being done. Rather, he must pluck the petals from a rose or watch the swans float calmly down the river. And I saw again the current which took the boat and the undergraduate and the dead leaves; and the taxi took the man and the woman, I thought, seeing them come together across the street, and the current swept them away, I thought, hearing far off the roar of London's traffic, into that tremendous stream.

Here, then, Mary Beton ceases to speak. She has told you how she reached the conclusion—the prosaic conclusion—that it is necessary to have five hundred a year and a room with a lock on the door if you are to write fiction or poetry. She has tried to lay bare the thoughts and impressions that led her to think this. She has asked you to follow her flying into the arms of a Beadle, lunching here, dining there, drawing pictures in the British Museum, taking books from the shelf, looking out of the window. While she has been doing all these things, you no doubt have been observing her failings and foibles and deciding what effect they have had on her opinions. You have been contradicting her and making whatever additions and deductions seem good to you. That is all as it should be, for in a question like this truth is only to be had by laying together many varieties of error. And I will end now in my own person by anticipating two criticisms, so obvious that you can hardly fail to make them.

No opinion has been expressed, you may say, upon the comparative merits of the sexes even as writers. That was done purposely, because, even if the time had come for such a valuation—and it is far more important at the moment to know how much money women had and how many rooms than to theorise about their capacities—even if the time had come I do not believe that gifts, whether of mind or character, can be weighed like sugar and butter, not even in Cambridge, where they are so adept at putting people into classes and fixing caps on their heads and letters after their names. I do not believe that even the Table of Precedency which you will find in Whitaker's *Almanac* represents a final order of values, or that there is any sound reason to suppose that a Commander of the Bath will ultimately walk in to dinner behind a Master in Lunacy. All this pitting of sex against sex, of quality against quality; all this claiming of superiority and imputing of inferiority, belong to the private-school stage of human existence where there are "sides," and it is necessary for one side to beat another side, and of the utmost importance to walk up to a platform and receive from the hands of the Headmaster himself a highly ornamental pot. As people mature they cease to believe in sides or in Headmasters or in highly ornamental pots. At any rate, where books are concerned, it is notoriously difficult to fix labels of merit in such a way that they do not come off. Are not reviews of current literature a perpetual illustration of the difficulty of judgment? "This great book," "this worthless book," the same book is called by both names. Praise and blame alike mean nothing. No, delightful as the pastime of measuring may be, it is the most futile of all occupations, and to submit to the decrees of the measurers the most servile of attitudes. So long as you write what you wish to write, that is all that matters; and whether it matters for ages or only for hours, nobody can say. But to sacrifice a hair of the head of your vision, a shade of its colour, in deference to some Headmaster with a silver pot in his hand or to some professor with a measuring-rod up his sleeve, is the most abject treachery, and the sacrifice of wealth and chastity which used to be said to be the greatest of human disasters, a mere flea-bite in comparison.

Next I think that you may object that in all this I have made too much of the importance of material things. Even allowing a generous margin for symbolism, that five hundred a year stands for the power to contemplate, that a lock on the door means the power to think for oneself, still you may say that the mind should rise above such things; and that great poets have often been poor men. Let me then quote to you the words of your own Professor of Literature, who knows better than I do what goes to the making of a poet. Sir Arthur Quiller-Couch writes:[1]

"What are the great poetical names of the last hundred years or so? Coleridge, Wordsworth, Byron, Shelley, Landor, Keats, Tennyson, Browning, Arnold, Morris, Rossetti, Swinburne—we may stop there. Of these, all but Keats, Browning, Rossetti were University men; and of these three, Keats, who died young, cut off in his prime, was the only one not fairly well to do. It may seem a brutal thing to say, and it is a sad thing to say: but, as a matter of hard fact, the theory that poetical genius bloweth where it listeth, and equally in poor and rich, holds little truth. As a matter of hard fact, nine out of those twelve were University men: which means that somehow or other they procured the means to get the best education England can give. As a matter of hard fact, of the remaining three you know that Browning was well to do, and I challenge you that, if he had not been well to do, he would no more have attained to write *Saul* or *The Ring and the Book* than Ruskin would have attained to writing *Modern Painters* if his father had not dealt prosperously in business. Rossetti had a small private income; and, moreover, he painted. There remains but Keats; whom Atropos slew young, as she slew John Clare in a mad-house, and James Thomson by the laudanum he took to drug disappointment. These are dreadful facts, but let us face them. It is—however dishonouring to us as a nation—certain that, by some fault in our commonwealth, the poor poet has not in these days, nor has had for two hundred years, a dog's chance. Believe me—and I have spent a great part of ten years in watching some three hundred and twenty elementary schools—we may prate of democracy, but actually, a poor child in England has little more hope than had the son of an Athenian slave to be emancipated into that intellectual freedom of which great writings are born."

Nobody could put the point more plainly. "The poor poet has not in these days, nor has had for two hundred years, a dog's chance . . . a poor child in England has little more hope than had the son of an Athenian slave to be emancipated into that intellectual freedom of which great writings are born." That is it. Intellectual freedom depends upon material things. Poetry depends upon intellectual freedom. And women have always been poor, not for two hundred years merely, but from the beginning of time. Women have had less intellectual freedom than the sons of Athenian slaves.Women, then, have not had a dog's chance of writing poetry. That is why I have laid so much stress on money and a room of one's own. However, thanks to the toils of those obscure women in the past, of whom I wish we knew more, thanks, curiously enough, to two wars, the Crimean which let Florence Nightingale out of her drawing-room, and the European War which opened the doors to the average woman some sixty years later, these evils are in the way to be bettered. Otherwise you would not be here tonight, and your chance of earning five hundred pounds a year, precarious as I am afraid that it still is, would be minute in the extreme.

Still, you may object, why do you attach so much importance to this writing of books by women when, according to you, it requires so much effort, leads perhaps to the murder of one's aunts, will make one almost certainly late for luncheon, and may bring one into very grave disputes with certain very good fellows? My motives, let me admit, are partly selfish. Like most uneducated Englishwomen, I like reading—I like reading books in the bulk. Lately my diet has become a trifle monotonous; history is too much about wars; biography too much about great men; poetry has shown, I think, a tendency to sterility, and fiction—but I have sufficiently exposed my disabilities as a critic of modern fiction and will say no more about it. Therefore I would ask you to write all kinds of books, hesitating at no subject however trivial or however vast. By hook or by crook, I hope that you will possess yourselves of money enough to travel and to idle, to contemplate the future or the past of the world, to dream over books and loiter at street corners and let the line of thought dip deep into the stream. For I am by no means confining you to fiction. If you would please me—and there are thousands like me—you would write books of travel and adventure, and research and scholarship, and history and biography, and criticism and philosophy and science. By so doing you will certainly profit the art of fiction. For books have a way of influencing each other. Fiction will be much the better for standing cheek by jowl with poetry and philosophy. Moreover, if you consider any great figure of the past, like Sappho, like the Lady Murasaki, like Emily Brontë, you will find that she is an inheritor as well as an originator, and has come into existence because women have come to have the habit of writing naturally; so that even as a prelude to poetry such activity on your part would be invaluable.

But when I look back through these notes and criticise my own train of thought as I made them, I find that my motives were not altogether selfish. There runs through these comments and discursions the conviction—or is it the instinct?—that good books are desirable and that good writers, even if they show every variety of human depravity, are still good human beings. Thus when I ask you to write more books I am urging you to do what will be for your good and for the good of the world at large. How to justify this instinct or belief I do not know, for philosophic words, if one has not been educated at a university, are apt to play one false. What is meant by "reality"? It would seem to be something very erratic, very undependable—now to be found in a dusty road, now in a scrap of newspaper in the street, now in a daffodil in the sun. It lights up a group in a room and stamps some causal saying. It overwhelms one walking home beneath the stars and makes the silent world more real than the world of speech—and then there it is again in an omnibus in the uproar of Piccadilly. Sometimes, too, it seems to dwell in shapes too far away for us to discern what their nature is. But whatever it touches, it fixes and makes permanent. That is what remains over when the skin of the day has been cast into the hedge; that is what is left of past time and of our loves and hates. Now the writer, as I think, has the chance to live more than other people in the presence of this reality. It is his business to find it and collect it and communicate it to the rest of us. So at least I infer from reading *Lear* or *Emma* or *La Recherche du Temps Perdu*. For the reading of these books seems to perform a curious couching operation on the senses; one sees more intensely afterwards; the world seems bared of its covering and given an intenser life. Those are the enviable people who live at enmity with unreality; and those are the pitiable who are knocked on the head by the thing done without knowing and caring. So that when I ask you to earn money and have a room of your own, I am asking you to live in the presence of reality, an invigorating life, it would appear, whether one can impart it or not.

Here I would stop, but the pressure of convention decrees that every speech must end with a peroration. And a peroration addressed to women should have something, you will agree, particularly exalting and ennobling about it. I should implore you to remember your responsibilities, to be higher, more spiritual; I should remind you how much depends upon you, and what an influence you can exert upon the future. But those exhortations can safely, I think, be left to the other sex, who will put them, and indeed have put them, with far greater eloquence than I can compass. When I rummage in my own mind I find no noble sentiments about being companions and equals and influencing the world to higher ends. I find myself saying briefly and prosaically that it is much more important to be oneself than anything else. Do not dream of influencing other people, I would say, if I knew how to make it sound exalted. Think of things in themselves.

And again I am reminded by dipping into newspapers and novels and biographies that when a woman speaks to women she should have something very unpleasant up her sleeve. Women are hard on women. Women dislike women. Women—but are you not sick to death of the word? I can assure you that I am. Let us agree, then, that a paper read by a woman to women should end with something particularly disagreable.

But how does it go? What can I think of? The truth is, I often like women. I like their unconventionality. I like their subtlety. I like their anonymity. I like—but I must not run on in this way. That cupboard there,—you say it holds clean table-napkins only; but what if Sir Archibald Bodkin were concealed among them? Let me then adopt a sterner tone. Have I, in the preceding words, conveyed to you sufficiently the warnings and reprobation of mankind? I have told you the very low opinion in which you were held by Mr. Oscar Browning. I have indicated what Napoleon once thought of you and what Mussolini thinks now. Then, in case any of you aspire to fiction, I have copied out for your benefit the advice of the critic about courageously acknowledging the limitations of your sex. I have referred to Professor X and given prominence to his statement that women are intellectually, morally and physically inferior to men. I have handed on all that has come my way without going in search of it, and here is a final warning—from Mr. John Langdon Davies.[2] Mr. John Langdon Davies warns women "that when children cease to be altogether desirable, women cease to be altogether necessary." I hope you will make a note of it.

How can I further encourage you to go about the business of life? Young women, I would say, and please attend, for the peroration is beginning, you are, in my opinion, disgracefully ignorant. You have never made a discovery of any sort of importance. You have never shaken an empire or led an army into battle. The plays of Shakespeare are not by you, and you have never introduced a barbarous race to the blessings of civilisation. What is your excuse? It is all very well for you to say, pointing to the streets and squares and forests of the globe swarming with black and white and coffee-coloured inhabitants, all busily engaged in traffic and enterprise and love-making, we have had other work on our hands. Without our doing, those seas would be unsailed and those fertile lands a desert. We have borne and bred and washed and taught, perhaps to the age of six or seven years, the one thousand six hundred and twenty-three million human beings who are, according to statistics, at present in existence, and that, allowing that some had help, takes time.

There is truth in what you say—I will not deny it. But at the same time may I remind you that there have been at least two colleges for women in existence in England since the year 1866; that after the year 1880 a married woman was allowed by law to possess her own property; and that in 1919—which is a whole nine years ago—she was given a vote? May I also remind you that the most of the professions have been open to you for close on ten years now? When you reflect upon these immense privileges and the length of time during which they have been enjoyed, and the fact that there must be at this moment some two thousand women capable of earning over five hundred a year in one way or another, you will agree that the excuse of lack of opportunity, training, encouragement, leisure and money no longer holds good. Moreover, the economists are telling us that Mrs. Seton has had too many children. You must, of course, go on bearing children, but, so they say, in twos and threes, not in tens and twelves.

Thus, with some time on your hands and with some book learning in your brains—you have had enough of the other kind, and are sent to college partly, I suspect, to be uneducated—surely you should embark upon another stage of your very long, very laborious and highly obscure career. A thousand pens are ready to suggest what you should do and what effect you will have. My own suggestion is a little fantastic, I admit; I prefer, therefore, to put it in the form of fiction.

I told you in the course of this paper that Shakespeare had a sister; but do not look for her in Sir Sidney Lee's life of the poet. She died young—alas, she never wrote a word. She lies buried where the omnibuses now stop, opposite the Elephant and Castle. Now my belief is that this poet who never wrote a word and was buried at the crossroads still lives. She lives in you and in me, and in many other women who are not here tonight, for they are washing up the dishes and putting the children to bed. But she lives; for great poets do not die; they are continuing presences; they need only the opportunity to walk among us in the flesh. This opportunity, as I think, it is now coming within your power to give her. For my belief is that if we live another century or so—I am talking of the common life which is the real life and not of the little separate lives which we live as individuals—and have five hundred a year each of us and rooms of our own; if we have the habit of freedom and the courage to write exactly what we think; if we escape a little from the common sitting-room and see human beings not always in their relations to each other but in relation to reality; and the sky, too, and the trees or whatever it may be in themselves; if we look past Milton's bogey, for no human being should shut out the view; if we face the fact, for it is a fact, that there is no arm to cling to, but that we go alone and that our relation is to the world of reality and not only to the world of men and women, then the opportunity will come and the dead poet who was Shakespeare's sister will put on the body which she has so often laid down. Drawing her life from the lives of the unknown who were her forerunners, as her brother did before her, she will be born. As for her coming without that preparation, without that effort on our part, without that determination that when she is born again she shall find it possible to live and write her poetry, that we cannot expect, for that would be impossible. But I maintain that she would come if we worked for her, and that so to work, even in poverty and obscurity, is worth while.

Notes

1. *The Art of Writing*, by Sir Arthur Quiller-Couch.

2. *A Short History of Women*, by John Langdon Davies.

Kenneth Burke 1897–

In an era of critical thought that understands itself increasingly in terms of movements and schools, Kenneth Burke has produced over sixty years of criticism and theory that distances itself from any single approach to literature. This antinomian attitude is captured in one of Burke's mottoes: "When in Rome, do as the Greeks"; and it is this role of gadfly within the critical establishment that makes Burke a central figure in the development of American criticism. But to say that Burke continually opposed himself to prevailing critical schools is not to say that he disdained critical method; quite the contrary. In fact, one might characterize the trajectory of his thought as a search for a method adequate not only to an understanding of literature but adequate to an understanding of all aspects of human behavior. This broader concern with human behavior began to develop after the publication of his first book, *Counter-Statement* (1931), when he turned his attention to the question of human motivation, focusing on the nature of perspective, or what he often calls "attitude." The major publications from this early concern are *Permanence and Change* (1935) and *Attitudes Toward History* (1937). It was during this transitional period that "Literature as Equipment for Living" was written. During the following years, Burke wrote his best-known works: *A Grammar of Motives* (1945), *A Rhetoric of Motives* (1950), and the essays collected in *Language as Symbolic Action* (1966). Interest in these works, as in Burke's thought in general, has increased over the past ten years, as American critics, influenced by Continental theories of language, have rediscovered Burke's concern with the relationship of language, knowledge, and social structures.

"Literature as Equipment for Living" was published initially in 1937, in the first volume of the American leftist journal *Direction*, which Burke later joined as an associate editor. In this essay, Burke positions his critical method, more or less explicitly, in relation to three currents in American criticism, all of which, according to Burke, neutralize the vitality of literature. The first is the idea that literature is detached from everyday life and, consequently, more "pure" than the practicalities of living; but in opposition to this idea, Burke asserts that we use literature to deal with recurrent situations in our lives. The second current, which Burke discusses toward the end of the essay, is the drive toward specialization that is encouraged by academic criticism; the tendency of academic criticism, because it excludes other areas of learning, is to reify older literary classifications and thereby to stifle the development of literary criticism. In opposition to these first two currents, Burke calls for a "sociological criticism"; but, as he suggests in his opening paragraph, his idea of sociological criticism has an emphasis different from traditional sociological criticism. Burke appears to be referring to Marxist critics like Van Wyck Brooks, Granville Hicks, and V. F. Calverton, whose work he had reviewed unfavorably as positing a simplistic economic determinism between literary work and social context. In opposition to this determinism, Burke suggests a broader range of motivations that could affect the production of a literary work and redefines sociological criticism as the codifying of "the various strategies which artists have developed with relation to the naming of situations."

LITERATURE AS EQUIPMENT FOR LIVING

Here I shall put down, as briefly as possible, a statement in behalf of what might be catalogued, with a fair degree of accuracy, as a *sociological* criticism of literature. Sociological criticism in itself is certainly not new. I shall here try to suggest what partially new elements or emphasis I think should be added to this old approach. And to make the "way in" as easy as possible, I shall begin with a discussion of proverbs.

1

Examine random specimens in *The Oxford Dictionary of English Proverbs*. You will note, I think, that there is no "pure" literature here. Everything is "medicine." Proverbs are designed for consolation or vengeance, for admonition or exhortation, for foretelling.

Or they name typical, recurrent situations. That is, people find a certain social relationship recurring so frequently that they must "have a word for it." The Eskimos have special names for many different kinds of snow (fifteen, if I remember rightly) because variations in the quality of snow greatly affect their living. Hence, they must "size up" snow much more accurately than we do. And the same is true of social phenomena. Social structures give rise to "type" situations, subtle subdivisions of the relationships involved in competitive and coöperative acts. Many proverbs seek to chart, in more or less homey and picturesque ways, these "type" situations. I submit that such naming is done, not for the sheer glory of the thing, but because of its bearing upon human welfare. A different name for snow implies a different kind of hunt. Some names for snow imply that one should not hunt at all. And similarly, the names for typical, recurrent social situations are not developed out of "disinterested curiosity," but because the names imply a command (what to expect, what to look out for).

To illustrate with a few representative examples:

Proverbs designed for consolation: "The sun does not shine on both sides of the hedge at once." "Think of ease, but work on." "Little troubles the eye, but far less the soul." "The worst luck now, the better another time." "The wind in one's face makes one wise." "He that hath lands hath quarrels." "He knows how to carry the dead cock home." "He is not poor that hath little, but he that desireth much."

For vengeance: "At length the fox is brought to the furrier." "Shod in the cradle, barefoot in the stubble." "Sue a beggar and get a louse." "The higher the ape goes, the more he shows his tail." "The moon does not heed the barking of dogs." "He measures another's corn by his own bushel." "He shuns the man who knows him well." "Fools tie knots and wise men loose them."

Proverbs that have to do with foretelling: (The most obvious are those to do with the weather.) "Sow peas and beans in the wane of the moon, Who soweth them sooner, he soweth too soon." "When the wind's in the north, the skilful fisher goes not forth." "When the sloe tree is as white as a sheet, sow your barley whether it be dry or wet." "When the sun sets bright and clear, An easterly wind you need not fear. When the sun sets in a bank, A westerly wind we shall not want."

In short: "Keep your weather eye open": be realistic about sizing up today's weather, because your accuracy has bearing upon tomorrow's weather. And forecast not only the meteorological weather, but also the social weather: "When the moon's in the full, then wit's in the wane." "Straws show which way the wind blows." "When the fish is caught, the net is laid aside." "Remove an old tree, and it will wither to death." "The wolf may lose his teeth, but never his nature." "He that bites on every weed must needs light on poison." "Whether the pitcher strikes the stone, or the stone the pitcher, it is bad for the pitcher." "Eagles catch no flies." "The more laws, the more offenders."

In this foretelling category we might also include the recipes for wise living, sometimes moral, sometimes technical: "First thrive, and then wive." "Think with the wise but talk with the vulgar." "When the fox preacheth, then beware your geese." "Venture a small fish to catch a great one." "Respect a man, he will do the more."

In the class of "typical, recurrent situations" we might put such proverbs and proverbial expressions as: "Sweet appears sour when we pay." "The treason is loved but the traitor is hated." "The wine in the bottle does not quench thirst." "The sun is never the worse for shining on a dunghill." "The lion kicked by an ass." "The lion's share." "To catch one napping." "To smell a rat." "To cool one's heels."

By all means, I do not wish to suggest that this is the only way in which the proverbs could be classified. For instance, I have listed in the "foretelling" group the proverb, "When the fox preacheth, then beware your geese." But it could obviously be "taken over" for vindictive purposes. Or consider a proverb like, "Virtue flies from the heart of a mercenary man." A poor man might obviously use it either to console himself for being poor (the implication being, "Because I am poor in money I am rich in virtue") or to strike at another (the implication being, "When he got money, what else could you expect of him but deterioration?"). In fact, we could even say that such symbolic vengeance would itself be an aspect of solace. And a proverb like "The sun is never the worse for shining on a dunghill" (which I have listed under "typical recurrent situations") might as well be put in the vindictive category.

The point of issue is not to find categories that "place" the proverbs once and for all. What I want is categories that suggest their active nature. Here there is no "realism for its own sake." There is realism for promise, admonition, solace, vengeance, foretelling, instruction, charting, all for the direct bearing that such acts have upon matters of welfare.

2

Step two: Why not extend such analysis of proverbs to encompass the whole field of literature? Could the most complex and sophisticated works of art legitimately be considered somewhat as "proverbs writ large"?

Such leads, if held admissible, should help us to discover important facts about literary organization (thus satisfying the requirements of technical criticism). And the kind of observation from this perspective should apply beyond literature to life in general (thus helping to take literature out of its separate bin and give it a place in a general "sociological" picture).

The point of view might be phrased in this way: Proverbs are *strategies* for dealing with *situations*. In so far as situations are typical and recurrent in a given social structure, people develop names for them and strategies for handling them. Another name for strategies might be *attitudes*.

People have often commented on the fact that there are contrary *proverbs*. But I believe that the above approach to proverbs suggests a necessary modification of that comment. The apparent contradictions depend upon differences in *attitude*, involving a correspondingly different choice of *strategy*. Consider, for instance, the *apparently* opposite pair: "Repentance comes too late" and "Never too late to mend." The first is admonitory. It says in effect: "You'd better look out, or you'll get yourself too far into this business." The second is consolatory, saying in effect: "Buck up, old man, you can still pull out of this."

Some critics have quarreled with me about my selection of the word "strategy" as the name for this process. I have asked them to suggest an alternative term, so far without profit. The only one I can think of is "method." But if "strategy" errs in suggesting to some people an overly *conscious* procedure, "method" errs in suggesting an overly "*methodical*" one. Anyhow, let's look at the documents:

Concise Oxford Dictionary: "Strategy: Movement of an army or armies in a campaign, art of so moving or disposing troops or ships as to impose upon the enemy the place and time and conditions for fighting preferred by oneself" (from a Greek word that refers to the leading of an army).

New English Dictionary: "Strategy: The art of projecting and directing the larger military movements and operations of a campaign."

André Cheron, *Traité Complet d'Echecs:* "On entend par stratégie les manoeuvres qui ont pour but la sortie et le bon arrangement des pièces."

Looking at these definitions, I gain courage. For surely, the most highly alembicated and sophisticated work of art, arising in complex civilizations, could be considered as designed to organize and command the army of one's thoughts and images, and to so organize them that one "imposes upon the enemy the time and place and conditions for fighting preferred by oneself." One seeks to "direct the larger movements and operations" in one's campaign of living. One "maneuvers," and the maneuvering is an "art."

Are not the final results one's "strategy"? One tries, as far as possible, to develop a strategy whereby one "can't lose." One tries to change the rules of the game until they fit his own necessities. Does the artist encounter disaster? He will "make capital" of it. If one is a victim of competition, for instance, if one is elbowed out, if one is willy-nilly more jockeyed against than jockeying, one can by the solace and vengeance of art convert this very "liability" into an "asset." One tries to fight on his own terms, developing a strategy for imposing the proper "time, place, and conditions."

But one must also, to develop a full strategy, be *realistic*. One must *size things up* properly. One cannot accurately know how things *will be*, what is promising and what is menacing, unless he accurately knows how things *are*. So the wise strategist will not be content with strategies of merely a self-gratifying sort. He will "keep his weather eye open." He will not too eagerly "read into" a scene an attitude that is irrelevant to it. He won't sit on the side of an active volcano and "see" it as a dormant plain.

Often, alas, he will. The great allurement in our present popular "inspirational literature," for instance, may be largely of this sort. It is a strategy for easy consolation. It "fills a need," since there is always a need for easy consolation—and in an era of confusion like our own the need is especially keen. So people are only too willing to "meet a man halfway" who will *play down* the realistic naming of our situation and *play up* such strategies as make solace cheap. However, I should propose a reservation here. We usually take it for granted that people who consume our current output of books on "How to Buy Friends and Bamboozle Oneself and Other People" are reading as *students* who will attempt applying the recipes given. Nothing of the sort. *The reading of a book on the attaining of success is in itself the symbolic attaining of that success.* It is *while they read* that these readers are "succeeding." I'll wager that, in by far the great majority of cases, such readers make no serious attempt to apply the book's recipes. The lure of the book resides in the fact that the reader, while reading it, is then living in the aura of success. What he wants is *easy* success; and he gets it in symbolic form by the mere reading itself. To attempt applying such stuff in real life would be very difficult, full of many disillusioning difficulties.

Sometimes a different strategy may arise. The author may remain realistic, avoiding too easy a form of solace—yet he may get as far off the track in his own way. Forgetting that realism is an aspect for foretelling, he may take it as an end in itself. He is tempted to do this by two factors: (1) an *ill-digested* philosophy of science, leading him mistakenly to assume that "relentless" naturalistic "truthfulness" is a proper end in itself, and (2) a merely *competitive* desire to outstrip other writers by being "more realistic" than they. Works thus made "efficient" by tests of competition internal to the book trade are a kind of academicism not so named (the writer usually thinks of it as the *opposite* of academicism). Realism thus stepped up competitively might be distinguished from the proper sort by the name of "naturalism." As a way of "sizing things up," the naturalistic tradition tends to become as inaccurate as the "inspirational" strategy, though at the opposite extreme.

Anyhow, the main point is this: A work like *Madame Bovary* (or its homely American translation, *Babbitt*) is the strategic naming of a situation. It singles out a pattern of experience that is sufficiently representative of our social structure, that recurs sufficiently often *mutandis mutatis*, for people to "need a word for it" and to adopt an attitude towards it. Each work of art is the addition of a word to an informal dictionary (or, in the case of purely derivative artists, the addition of a subsidiary meaning to a word already given by some originating artist). As for *Madame Bovary*, the French critic Jules de Gaultier proposed to add it to our *formal* dictionary by coining the word "Bovarysme" and writing a whole book to say what he meant by it.

Mencken's book on *The American Language*, I hate to say, is splendid. I console myself with the reminder that Mencken didn't write it. Many millions of people wrote it, and Mencken was merely the amanuensis who took it down from their dictation. He found a true "vehicle" (that is, a book that could be greater than the author who wrote it). He gets the royalties, but the job was done by a collectivity. As you read that book, you see a people who were up against a new set of typical recurrent situations, situations typical of their business, their politics, their criminal organizations, their sports. Either there were no words for these in standard English, or people didn't know them, or they didn't "sound right." So a new vocabulary arose, to "give us a word for it." I see no reason for believing that Americans are unusually fertile in word-coinage. American slang was not developed out of some exceptional gift. It was developed out of the fact that new typical situations had arisen and people needed names for them. They had to "size things up." They had to console and strike, to promise and admonish. They had to describe for purposes of forecasting. And "slang" was the result. It is, by this analysis, simply *proverbs not so named*, a kind of "folk criticism."

3

With what, then, would "sociological criticism" along these lines be concerned? It would seek to codify the various strategies which artists have developed with relation to the naming of situations. In a sense, much of it would even be "timeless," for many of the "typical, recurrent situations" are not peculiar to our own civilization at all. The situations and strategies framed in Aesop's Fables, for instance, apply to human relations now just as fully as they applied in ancient Greece. They are, like philosophy, sufficiently "generalized" to extend far beyond the particular combination of events named by them in any one instance. They name an "essence." Or, as Korzybski might say, they are on a "high level of abstraction." One doesn't usually think of them as "abstract," since they are usually so concrete in their stylistic expression. But they invariably aim to discern the "general behind the particular" (which would suggest that they are good Goethe).

The attempt to treat literature from the standpoint of situations and strategies suggests a variant of Spengler's notion of the "contemporaneous." By "contemporaneity" he meant corresponding stages of different cultures. For instance, if modern New York is much like decadent Rome, then we are "contemporaneous" with decadent Rome, or with some corresponding decadent city among the Mayas, etc. It is in this sense that situations are "timeless," "nonhistorical," "contemporaneous." A given human relationship may be at one time named in terms of foxes and lions, if there are foxes and lions about; or it may now be named in terms of salesmanship, advertising, the tactics of politicians, etc. But beneath the change in particulars, we may often discern the naming of the one situation.

So sociological criticism, as here understood, would seek to assemble and codify this lore. It might occasionally lead us to outrage good taste, as we sometimes found exemplified in some great sermon or tragedy or abstruse work of philosophy the same strategy as we found exemplified in a dirty joke. At this point, we'd put the sermon and the dirty joke together, thus "grouping by situation" and showing the range of possible particularizations. In his exceptionally discerning essay, "A Critic's Job of Work," R. P. Blackmur says, "I think on the whole his (Burke's) method could be applied with equal fruitfulness to Shakespeare, Dashiell Hammett, or Marie Corelli." When I got through wincing, I had to admit that Blackmur was right. This article is an attempt to say for the method what can be said. As a matter of fact, I'll go a step further and maintain: You can't properly put Marie Corelli and Shakespeare apart until you have first put them together. First genus, then differentia. The strategy in common is the genus. The *range* or *scale* or *spectrum* of particularizations is the differentia.

Anyhow, that's what I'm driving at. And that's why reviewers sometime find in my work "intuitive" leaps that are dubious as "science." They are not "leaps" at all. They are classifications, groupings, made on the basis of some strategic element common to the items grouped. They are neither more nor less "intuitive" than *any* grouping or classification of social events. Apples can be grouped with bananas as fruits, and they can be grouped with tennis balls as round. I am simply proposing, in the social sphere, a method of classification with reference to *strategies*.

The method has these things to be said in its favor: It gives definite insight into the organization of literary works; and it automatically breaks down the barriers erected about literature as a specialized pursuit. People can classify novels by reference to three kinds, eight kinds, seventeen kinds. It doesn't matter. Students patiently copy down the professor's classification and pass examinations on it, because the range of possible academic classifications is endless. Sociological classification, as herein suggested, would derive its relevance from the fact that it should apply both to works of art and to social situations outside of art.

It would, I admit, violate current pieties, break down current categories, and thereby "outrage good taste." But "good taste" has become *inert*. The classifications I am proposing would be *active*. I think that what we need is active categories.

These categories will lie on the bias across the categories of modern specialization. The new alignment will outrage in particular those persons who take the division of faculties in our universities to be an exact replica of the way in which God himself divided up the universe. We have had the Philosophy of the Being; and we have had the Philosophy of the Becoming. In contemporary specialization, we have been getting the Philosophy of the Bin. Each of these mental localities has had its own peculiar way of life, its own values, even its own special idiom for seeing, thinking, and "proving." Among other things, a sociological approach should attempt to provide a reintegrative point of view, a broader empire of investigation encompassing the lot.

What would such sociological categories be like? They would consider works of art, I think, as strategies for selecting enemies and allies, for socializing losses, for warding off evil eye, for purification, propitiation, and desanctification, consolation and vengeance, admonition and exhortation, implicit commands or instructions of one sort or another. Art forms like "tragedy" or "comedy" or "satire" would be treated as *equipments for living*, that size up situations in various ways and in keeping with correspondingly various attitudes. The typical ingredients of such forms would be sought. Their relation to typical situations would be stressed. Their comparative values would be considered, with the intention of formulating a "strategy of strategies," the "over-all" strategy obtained by inspection of the lot.

Erich Auerbach 1892–1957

Professor of romance philology at Yale in 1950 and named Sterling professor at Yale in 1956, Auerbach began his academic career in 1913, when he received a doctor of law degree from Heidelberg University. Upon completion of military service in the German army in World War I, he returned to academic study, earning a Ph.D. in romance philology from the University of Greifswald in 1921. He worked as librarian for the Prussian State Library in Berlin from 1923 to 1929, when he was appointed to the chair of romance philology at the University of Marburg, a post he held for six years until the Nazis revoked his position. In 1936, he left for Turkey, where he taught at the Turkish State University. Following his move to the United States in 1947, he taught at Pennsylvania State University and then at Princeton. His works include *Dante, Poet of the Secular World* (1929); "Figura," a study of the development of Dante's allegories (1939); *Mimesis: The Representation of Reality In Western Literature* (1946); *Literary Language and Its Public in Late Antiquity and in the Middle Ages* (1958).

The following essay, "Odysseus' Scar," is the first chapter of *Mimesis*, the beginning of Auerbach's aesthetic discussion of realism. In this chapter, Auerbach contrasts the traditional Greek narrative style of Homer with that of the Judeo-Christian narrative style as demonstrated in the biblical story of the sacrifice of Isaac. Although it is never defined explicitly, realism emerges as an interpretive style or thesis working its way toward the realization of some future ideal.

For Auerbach, a brief passage of literature, such as a historical event, works like a trope or a character, carrying universal meaning from the past into the future, prefiguring what is to follow. These figural models are always changing with historical contexts; only the phenomenon is "real." Thus, the story of Isaac is more "real" than that of Odysseus, for the narrative of the sacrifice of Isaac is a link in the chain of Judeo-Christian history, prefiguring the crucifixion of Christ. Not only is the biblical story more "real" at the structural level but also at the level of the particular. Homer presents a narrative of the upper class, unlike the story of Isaac, which reflects the more domestic and supranatural concerns of a nomadic people. A paradox arises in that the particularization of event and time becomes an abstraction in Homer, while the figural models of the Old Testament speak of the general as the "truth" of history. Homer tells a story (as opposed to a history that interprets the meaning of human experience); whereas the narrative of Isaac, though less particularized, is more real in that it performs both diachronically and synchronically. The tension between the universal context of the story of Isaac and the deuniversalization of particulars is constant. Realism is a "guise," a historical way of seeing. Narrative is the performance of a culture of a moment in history, history being a rhetorical construct.

Odysseus' Scar

Readers of the *Odyssey* will remember the well-prepared and touching scene in book 19, when Odysseus has at last come home, the scene in which the old housekeeper Euryclea, who had been his nurse, recognizes him by a scar on his thigh. The stranger has won Penelope's good will; at his request she tells the housekeeper to wash his feet, which, in all old stories, is the first duty of hospitality toward a tired traveler. Euryclea busies herself fetching water and mixing cold with hot, meanwhile speaking sadly of her absent master, who is probably of the same age as the guest, and who perhaps, like the guest, is even now wandering somewhere, a stranger; and she remarks how astonishingly like him the guest looks. Meanwhile Odysseus, remembering his scar, moves back out of the light; he knows that, despite his efforts to hide his identity, Euryclea will now recognize him, but he wants at least to keep Penelope in ignorance. No sooner has the old woman touched the scar than, in her joyous surprise, she lets Odysseus' foot drop into the basin; the water spills over, she is about to cry out her joy; Odysseus restrains her with whispered threats and endearments; she recovers herself and conceals her emotion. Penelope, whose attention Athena's foresight had diverted from the incident, has observed nothing.

All this is scrupulously externalized and narrated in leisurely fashion. The two women express their feelings in copious direct discourse. Feelings though they are, with only a slight admixture of the most general considerations upon human destiny, the syntactical connection between part and part is perfectly clear, no contour is blurred. There is also room and time for orderly, perfectly well-articulated, uniformly illuminated descriptions of implements, ministrations, and gestures; even in the dramatic moment of recognition, Homer does not omit to tell the reader that it is with his right hand that Odysseus takes the old woman by the throat to keep her from speaking, at the same time that he draws her closer to him with his left. Clearly outlined, brightly and uniformly illuminated, men and things stand out in a realm where everything is visible; and not less clear—wholly expressed, orderly even in their ardor—are the feelings and thoughts of the persons involved.

In my account of the incident I have so far passed over a whole series of verses which interrupt it in the middle. There are more than seventy of these verses—while to the incident itself some forty are devoted before the interruption and some forty after it. The interruption, which comes just at the point when the housekeeper recognizes the scar—that is, at the moment of crisis—describes the origin of the scar, a hunting accident which occurred in Odysseus' boyhood, at a boar hunt, during the time of his visit to his grandfather Autolycus. This first affords an opportunity to inform the reader about Autolycus, his house, the precise degree of the kinship, his character, and, no less exhaustively than touchingly, his behavior after the birth of his grandson; then follows the visit of Odysseus, now grown to be a youth; the exchange of greetings, the banquet with which he is welcomed, sleep and waking, the early start for the hunt, the tracking of the beast, the struggle, Odysseus' being wounded by the boar's tusk, his recovery, his return to Ithaca, his parents' anxious questions—all is narrated, again with such a complete externalization of all the elements of the story and of their interconnections as to leave nothing in obscurity. Not until then does the narrator return to Penelope's chamber, not until then, the digression having run its course, does Euryclea, who had recognized the scar before the digression began, let Odysseus' foot fall back into the basin.

The first thought of a modern reader—that this is a device to increase suspense—is, if not wholly wrong, at least not the essential explanation of this Homeric procedure. For the element of suspense is very slight in the Homeric poems; nothing in their entire style is calculated to keep the reader or hearer breathless. The digressions are not meant to keep the reader in suspense, but rather to relax the tension. And this frequently occurs, as in the passage before us. The broadly narrated, charming, and subtly fashioned story of the hunt, with all its elegance and self-sufficiency, its wealth of idyllic pictures, seeks to win the reader over wholly to itself as long as he is hearing it, to make him forget what had just taken place during the foot-washing. But an episode that will increase suspense by retarding the action must be so constructed that it will not fill the present entirely, will not put the crisis, whose resolution is being awaited, entirely out of the reader's mind, and thereby destroy the mood of suspense; the crisis and the suspense must continue, must remain vibrant in the background. But Homer—and to this we shall have to return later—knows no background. What he narrates is for the time being the only present, and fills both the stage and the reader's mind completely. So it is with the passage before us. When the young Euryclea (vv. 401ff.) sets the infant Odysseus on his grandfather Autolycus' lap after the banquet, the aged Euryclea, who a few lines earlier had touched the wanderer's foot, has entirely vanished from the stage and from the reader's mind.

Goethe and Schiller, who, though not referring to this particular episode, exchanged letters in April 1797 on the subject of "the retarding element" in the Homeric poems in general, put it in direct opposition to the element of suspense—the latter word is not used, but is clearly implied when the "retarding" procedure is opposed, as something proper to epic, to tragic procedure (letters of April 19, 21, and 22). The "retarding element," the "going back and forth" by means of episodes, seems to me, too, in the Homeric poems, to be opposed to any tensional and suspensive striving toward a goal, and doubtless Schiller is right in regard to Homer when he says that what he gives us is "simply the quiet existence and operation of things in accordance with their natures"; Homer's goal is "already present in every point of his progress." But both Schiller and Goethe raise Homer's procedure to the level of a law for epic poetry in general, and Schiller's words quoted above are meant to be universally binding upon the epic poet, in contradistinction from the tragic. Yet in both modern and ancient times, there are important epic works which are composed throughout with no "retarding element" in this sense but, on the contrary, with suspense throughout, and which perpetually "rob us of our emotional freedom"—which power Schiller will grant only to the tragic poet. And besides it seems to me undemonstrable and improbable that this procedure of Homeric poetry was directed by aesthetic considerations or even by an aesthetic feeling of the sort postulated by Goethe and Schiller. The effect, to be sure, is precisely that which they describe, and is, furthermore, the actual source of the conception of epic which they themselves hold, and with them all writers decisively influenced by classical antiquity. But the true cause of the impression of "retardation" appears to me to lie elsewhere—namely, in the need of the Homeric style to leave nothing which it mentions half in darkness and unexternalized.

The excursus upon the origin of Odysseus' scar is not basically different from the many passages in which a newly introduced character, or even a newly appearing object or implement, though it be in the thick of a battle, is described as to its nature and origin; or in which, upon the appearance of a god, we are told where he last was, what he was doing there, and by what road he reached the scene; indeed, even the Homeric epithets seem to me in the final analysis to be traceable to the same need for an externalization of phenomena in terms perceptible to the senses. Here is the scar, which comes up in the course of the narrative; and Homer's feeling simply will not permit him to see it appear out of the darkness of an unilluminated past; it must be set in full light, and with it a portion of the hero's boyhood—just as, in the *Iliad*, when the first ship is already burning and the Myrmidons finally arm that they may hasten to help, there is still time not only for the wonderful simile of the wolf, not only for the order of the Myrmidon host, but also for a detailed account of the ancestry of several subordinate leaders (16, vv. 155ff.). To be sure, the aesthetic effect thus produced was soon noticed and thereafter consciously sought; but the more original cause must have lain in the basic impulse of the Homeric style: to represent phenomena in a fully externalized form, visible and palpable in all their parts, and completely fixed in their spatial and temporal relations. Nor do psychological processes receive any other treatment: here too nothing must remain hidden and unexpressed. With the utmost fullness, with an orderliness which even passion does not disturb, Homer's personages vent their inmost hearts in speech; what they do not say to others, they speak in their own minds, so that the reader is informed of it. Much that is terrible takes place in the Homeric poems, but it seldom takes place wordlessly: Polyphemus talks to Odysseus; Odysseus talks to the suitors when he begins to kill them; Hector and Achilles talk at length, before battle and after; and no speech is so filled with anger or scorn that the particles which express logical and grammatical connections are lacking or out of place. This last observation is true, of course, not only of speeches but of the presentation in general. The separate elements of a phenomenon are most clearly placed in relation to one another; a large number of conjunctions, adverbs, particles, and other syntactical tools, all clearly circumscribed and delicately differentiated in meaning, delimit persons, things, and portions of incidents in respect to one another, and at the same time bring them together in a continuous and ever flexible connection; like the separate phenomena themselves, their relationships—their temporal, local, causal, final, consecutive, comparative, concessive, antithetical, and conditional limitations—are brought to light in perfect fullness; so that a continuous rhythmic procession of phenomena passes by, and never is there a form left fragmentary or half-illuminated, never a lacuna, never a gap, never a glimpse of unplumbed depths.

And this procession of phenomena takes place in the foreground—that is, in a local and temporal present which is absolute. One might think that the many interpolations, the frequent moving back and forth, would create a sort of perspective in time and place; but the Homeric style never gives any such impression. The way in which any impression of perspective is avoided can be clearly observed in the procedure for introducing episodes, a syntactical construction with which every reader of Homer is familiar; it is used in the passage we are considering, but can also be found in cases when the episodes are much shorter. To the word scar (v. 393) there is first attached a relative clause ("which once long ago a boar . . ."), which enlarges into a voluminous syntactical parenthesis; into this an independent sentence unexpectedly intrudes (v. 396: "A god himself gave him . . ."), which quietly disentangles itself from syntactical subordination, until, with verse 399, an equally free syntactical treatment of the new content begins a new present which continues unchallenged until, with verse 467 ("The old woman now touched it . . ."), the scene which had been broken off is resumed. To be sure, in the case of such long episodes as the one we are considering, a purely syntactical connection with the principal theme would hardly have been possible; but a connection with it through perspective would have been all the easier had the content been arranged with that end in view; if, that is, the entire story of the scar had been presented as a recollection which awakens in Odysseus' mind at this particular moment. It would have been perfectly easy to do; the story of the scar had only to be inserted two verses earlier, at the first mention of the word scar, where the motifs "Odysseus" and "recollection" were already at hand. But any such subjectivistic-perspectivistic procedure, creating a foreground and background, resulting in the present lying open to the depths of the past, is entirely foreign to the Homeric style; the Homeric style knows only a foreground, only a uniformly illuminated, uniformly objective present. And so the excursus does not begin until two lines later, when Euryclea has discovered the scar—the possibility for a perspectivistic connection no longer exists, and the story of the wound becomes an independent and exclusive present.

The genius of the Homeric style becomes even more apparent when it is compared with an equally ancient and equally epic style from a different world of forms. I shall attempt this comparison with the account of the sacrifice of Isaac, a homogeneous narrative produced by the so-called Elohist. The King James version translates the opening as follows (Genesis 22:1): "And it came to pass after these things, that God did tempt Abraham, and said to him, Abraham! and he said, Behold, here I am." Even this opening startles us when we come to it from Homer. Where are the two speakers? We are not told. The reader, however, knows that they are not normally to be found together in one place on earth, that one of them, God, in order to speak to Abraham, must come from somewhere, must enter the earthly realm from some unknown heights or depths. Whence does he come, whence does he call to Abraham? We are not told. He does not come, like Zeus or Poseidon, from the Aethiopians, where he has been enjoying a sacrificial feast. Nor are we told anything of his reasons for tempting Abraham so terribly. He has not, like Zeus, discussed them in set speeches with other gods gathered in council; nor have the deliberations in his own heart been presented to us; unexpected and mysterious, he enters the scene from some unknown height or depth and calls: Abraham! It will at once be said that this is to be explained by the particular concept of God which the Jews held and which was wholly different from that of the Greeks. True enough—but this constitutes no objection. For how is the Jewish concept of God to be explained? Even their earlier God of the desert was not fixed in form and content, and was alone; his lack of form, his lack of local habitation, his singleness, was in the end not only maintained but developed even further in competition with the comparatively far more manifest gods of the surrounding Near Eastern world. The concept of God held by the Jews is less a cause than a symptom of their manner of comprehending and representing things.

This becomes still clearer if we now turn to the other person in the dialogue, to Abraham. Where is he? We do not know. He says, indeed: Here I am—but the Hebrew word means only something like "behold me," and in any case is not meant to indicate the actual place where Abraham is, but a moral position in respect to God, who has called to him—Here am I awaiting thy command. Where he is actually, whether in Beersheba or elsewhere, whether indoors or in the open air, is not stated; it does not interest the narrator, the reader is not informed; and what Abraham was doing when God called to him is left in the same obscurity. To realize the difference, consider Hermes' visit to Calypso, for example, where command, journey, arrival and reception of the visitor, situation and occupation of the person visited, are set forth in many verses; and even on occasions when gods appear suddenly and briefly, whether to help one of their favorites or to deceive or destroy some mortal whom they hate, their bodily forms, and usually the manner of their coming and going, are given in detail. Here, however, God appears without bodily form (yet he "appears"), coming from some unspecified place—we only hear his voice, and that utters nothing but a name, a name without an adjective, without a descriptive epithet for the person spoken to, such as is the rule in every Homeric address; and of Abraham too nothing is made perceptible except the words in which he answers God: *Hinne-ni,* Behold me here—with which, to be sure, a most touching gesture expressive of obedience and readiness is suggested, but it is left to the reader to visualize it. Moreover the two speakers are not on the same level: if we conceive of Abraham in the foreground, where it might be possible to picture him as prostrate or kneeling or bowing with outspread arms or gazing upward, God is not there too: Abraham's words and gestures are directed toward the depths of the picture or upward, but in any case the undetermined, dark place from which the voice comes to him is not in the foreground.

After this opening, God gives his command, and the story itself begins: everyone knows it; it unrolls with no episodes in a few independent sentences whose syntactical connection is of the most rudimentary sort. In this atmosphere it is unthinkable that an implement, a landscape through which the travelers passed, the serving-men, or the ass, should be described, that their origin or descent or material or appearance or usefulness should be set forth in terms of praise; they do not even admit an adjective: they are serving-men, ass, wood, and knife, and nothing else, without an epithet; they are there to serve the end which God has commanded; what in other respects they were, are, or will be, remains in darkness. A journey is made, because God has designated the place where the sacrifice is to be performed; but we are told nothing about the journey except that it took three days, and even that we are told in a mysterious way: Abraham and his followers rose "early in the morning" and "went unto" the place of which God had told him; on the third day he lifted up his eyes and saw the place from afar. That gesture is the only gesture, is indeed the only occurrence during the whole journey, of which we are told; and though its motivation lies in the fact that the place is elevated, its uniqueness still heightens the impression that the journey took place through a vacuum; it is as if, while he traveled on, Abraham had looked neither to the right nor to the left, had suppressed any sign of life in his followers and himself save only their footfalls.

Thus the journey is like a silent progress

through the indeterminate and the contingent, a holding of the breath, a process which has no present, which is inserted, like a blank duration, between what has passed and what lies ahead, and which yet is measured: three days! Three such days positively demand the symbolic interpretation which they later received. They began "early in the morning." But at what time on the third day did Abraham lift up his eyes and see his goal? The text says nothing on the subject. Obviously not "late in the evening," for it seems that there was still time enough to climb the mountain and make the sacrifice. So "early in the morning" is given, not as an indication of time, but for the sake of its ethical significance; it is intended to express the resolution, the promptness, the punctual obedience of the sorely tried Abraham. Bitter to him is the early morning in which he saddles his ass, calls his serving-men and his son Isaac, and sets out; but he obeys, he walks on until the third day, then lifts up his eyes and sees the place. Whence he comes, we do not know, but the goal is clearly stated: Jeruel in the land of Moriah. What place this is meant to indicate is not clear—"Moriah" especially may be a later correction of some other word. But in any case the goal was given, and in any case it is a matter of some sacred spot which was to receive a particular consecration by being connected with Abraham's sacrifice. Just as little as "early in the morning" serves as a temporal indication does "Jeruel in the land of Moriah" serve as a geographical indication; and in both cases alike, the complementary indication is not given, for we know as little of the hour at which Abraham lifted up his eyes as we do of the place from which he set forth—Jeruel is significant not so much as the goal of an earthly journey, in its geographical relation to other places, as through its special election, through its relation to God, who designated it as the scene of the act, and therefore it must be named.

In the narrative itself, a third chief character appears: Isaac. While God and Abraham, the serving-men, the ass, and the implements are simply named, without mention of any qualities or any other sort of definition, Isaac once receives an appositive; God says, "Take Isaac, thine only son, whom thou lovest." But this is not a characterization of Isaac as a person, apart from his relation to his father and apart from the story; he may be handsome or ugly, intelligent or stupid, tall or short, pleasant or unpleasant—we are not told. Only what we need to know about him as a personage in the action, here and now, is illuminated, so that it may become apparent how terrible Abraham's temptation is, and that God is fully aware of it. By this example of the contrary, we see the significance of the descriptive adjectives and digressions of the Homeric poems; with their indications of the earlier and as it were absolute existence of the persons described, they prevent the reader from concentrating exclusively on a present crisis; even when the most terrible things are occurring, they prevent the establishment of an overwhelming suspense. But here, in the story of Abraham's sacrifice, the overwhelming suspense is present; what Schiller makes the goal of the tragic poet—to rob us of our emotional freedom, to turn our intellectual and spiritual powers (Schiller says "our activity") in one direction, to concentrate them there—is effected in this Biblical narrative, which certainly deserves the epithet epic.

We find the same contrast if we compare the two uses of direct discourse. The personages speak in the Bible story too; but their speech does not serve, as does speech in Homer, to manifest, to externalize thoughts—on the contrary, it serves to indicate thoughts which remain unexpressed. God gives his command in direct discourse, but he leaves his motives and his purpose unexpressed; Abraham, receiving the command, says nothing and does what he has been told to do. The conversation between Abraham and Isaac on the way to the place of sacrifice is only an interruption of the heavy silence and makes it all the more burdensome. The two of them, Isaac carrying the wood and Abraham with fire and a knife, "went together." Hesitantly, Isaac ventures to ask about the ram, and Abraham gives the well-known answer. Then the text repeats: "So they went both of them together." Everything remains unexpressed.

It would be difficult, then, to imagine styles more contrasted than those of these two equally ancient and equally epic texts. On the one hand, externalized, uniformly illuminated phenomena, at a definite time and in a definite place, connected together without lacunae in a perpetual foreground; thoughts and feeling completely expressed; events taking place in leisurely fashion and with very little of suspense. On the other hand, the externalization of only so much of the phenomena as is necessary for the purpose of the narrative, all else left in obscurity; the decisive points of the narrative alone are emphasized, what lies between is nonexistent; time and place are undefined and call for interpretation; thoughts and feeling remain unexpressed, are only suggested by the silence and the fragmentary speeches; the whole, permeated with the most unrelieved suspense and directed toward a single goal (and to that extent far more of a unity), remains mysterious and "fraught with background."

I will discuss this term in some detail, lest it be misunderstood. I said above that the Homeric style was "of the foreground" because, despite much going back and forth, it yet causes what is momentarily being narrated to give the impression that it is the only present, pure and without perspective. A consideration of the Elohistic text teaches us that our term is capable of a broader and deeper application. It shows that even the separate personages can be represented as possessing "background"; God is always so represented in the Bible, for he is not comprehensible in his presence, as is Zeus; it is always only "something" of him that appears, he always extends into depths. But even the human beings in the Biblical stories have greater depths of time, fate, and consciousness than do the human beings in Homer; although they are nearly always caught up in an event engaging all their faculties, they are not so entirely immersed in its present that they do not remain continually conscious of what has happened to them earlier and elsewhere; their thoughts and feelings have more layers, are more entangled. Abraham's actions are explained not only by what is happening to him at the moment, nor yet only by his character (as Achilles' actions by his courage and his pride, and Odysseus' by his versatility and foresightedness), but by his previous history; he remembers, he is constantly conscious of, what God has promished him and what God has already accomplished for him—his soul is torn between desperate rebellion and hopeful expectation; his silent obedience is multilayered, has background. Such a problematic psychological situation as this is impossible for any of the Homeric heroes, whose destiny is clearly defined and who wake every morning as if it were the first day of their lives: their emotions, though strong, are simple and find expression instantly.

How fraught with background, in comparison, are characters like Saul and David! How entangled and stratified are such human relations as those between David and Absalom, between David and Joab! Any such "background" quality of the psychological situation as that which the story of Absalom's death and its sequel (II Samuel 18 and 19, by the so-called Jahvist) rather suggests than expresses, is unthinkable in Homer. Here we are confronted not merely with the psychological processes of characters whose depth of background is veritably abysmal, but with a purely geographical background too. For David is absent from the battlefield; but the influence of his will and his feelings continues to operate, they affect even Joab in his rebellion and disregard for the consequences of his actions; in the magnificent scene with the two messengers, both the physical and psychological background is fully manifest, though the latter is never expressed. With this, compare, for example, how Achilles, who sends Patroclus first to scout and then into battle, loses almost all "presentness" so long as he is not physically present. But the most important thing is the "multilayeredness" of the individual character; this is hardly to be met with in Homer, or at most in the form of a conscious hesitation between two possible courses of action; otherwise, in Homer, the complexity of the psychological life is shown only in the succession and alternation of emotions; whereas the Jewish writers are able to express the simultaneous existence of various layers of consciousness and the conflict between them.

The Homeric poems, then, though their intellectual, linguistic, and above all syntactical culture appears to be so much more highly developed, are yet comparatively simple in their picture of human beings; and no less so in their relation to the real life which they describe in general. Delight in physical existence is everything to them, and their highest aim is to make that delight perceptible to us. Between battles and passions, adventures and perils, they show us hunts, banquets, palaces and shepherds' cots, athletic contests and washing days—in order that we may see the heroes in their ordinary life, and seeing them so, may take pleasure in their manner of enjoying their savory present, a present which sends strong roots down into social usages, landscape, and daily life. And thus they bewitch us and ingratiate themselves to us until we live with them in the reality of their lives; so long as we are reading or hearing the poems, it does not matter whether we know that all this is only legend, "make-believe." The oft-repeated reproach that Homer is a liar takes nothing from his effectiveness, he does not need to base his story on historical reality, his reality is powerful enough in itself; it ensnares us, weaving its web around us, and that suffices him. And this "real" world into which we are lured, exists for itself, contains nothing but itself; the Homeric poems conceal nothing, they contain no teaching and no secret second meaning. Homer can be analyzed, as we have essayed to do here, but he cannot be interpreted. Later allegorizing trends have tried their arts of interpretation upon him, but to no avail. He resists any such treatment; the interpretations are forced and foreign, they do not crystallize into a unified doctrine. The general considerations which occasionally occur (in our episode, for example, v. 360: that in misfortune men age quickly) reveal a calm acceptance of the basic facts of human existence, but with no compulsion to brood over them, still less any passionate impulse either to rebel against them or to embrace them in an ecstasy of submission.

It is all very different in the Biblical stories. Their aim is not to bewitch the senses, and if nevertheless they produce lively sensory effects, it is only because the moral, religious, and psychological phenomena which are their sole concern are made concrete in the sensible matter of life. But their religious intent involves an absolute claim to historical truth. The story of Abraham and Isaac is not better established than the story of Odysseus, Penelope, and Euryclea; both are legendary. But the Biblical narrator, the Elohist, had to believe in the objective truth of the story of Abraham's sacrifice—the existence of the sacred ordinances of life rested upon the truth of this and similar stories. He had to believe in it passionately; or else (as many rationalistic interpreters believed and perhaps still believe) he has to be a conscious liar—no harmless liar like Homer, who lied to give pleasure, but a political liar with a definite end in view, lying in the interest of a claim to absolute authority.

To me, the rationalistic interpretation seems psychologically absurd; but even if we take it into consideration, the relation of the Elohist to the truth of his story still remains a far more passionate and definite one than is Homer's relation. The Biblical narrator was obliged to write exactly what his belief in the truth of the tradition (or, from the rationalistic standpoint, his interest in the truth of it) demanded of him—in either case, his freedom in creative or representative imagination was severely limited; his activity was perforce reduced to composing an effective version of the pious tradition. What he produced, then, was not primarily oriented toward "realism" (if he succeeded in being realistic, it was merely a means, not an end); it was oriented toward truth. Woe to the man who did not believe it! One can perfectly well entertain historical doubts on the subject of the Trojan War or of Odysseus' wanderings, and still, when reading Homer, feel precisely the effects he sought to produce; but without believing in Abraham's sacrifice, it is impossible to put the narrative of it to the use for which it was written. Indeed, we must go even further. The Bible's claim to truth is not only far more urgent than Homer's, it is tyrannical—it excludes all other claims. The world of the Scripture stories is not satisfied with claiming to be a historically true reality—it insists that it is the only real world, is destined for autocracy. All other scenes, issues, and ordinances have no right to appear independently of it, and it is promised that all of them, the history of all mankind, will be given their due place within its frame, will be subordinated to it. The Scripture stories do not, like Homer's, court our favor, they do not flatter us that they may please us and enchant us—they seek to subject us, and if we refuse to be subjected we are rebels.

Let no one object that this goes too far, that not the stories, but the religious doctrine, raises the claim to absolute authority; because the stories are not, like Homer's, simply narrated "reality." Doctrine and promise are incarnate in them and inseparable from them; for that very reason they are fraught with "background" and mysterious, containing a second, concealed meaning. In the story of Isaac, it is not only God's intervention at the beginning and the end, but even the factual and psychological elements which come between, that are mysterious, merely touched upon, fraught with background; and therefore they require subtle investigation and interpretation, they demand them. Since so much in the story is dark and incomplete, and since the reader knows that God is a hidden God, his effort to interpret it constantly finds something new to feed upon. Doctrine and the search for enlightenment are inextricably connected with the physical side of the narrative—the latter being more than simple "reality"; indeed they are in constant danger of losing their own reality, as very soon happened when interpretation reached such proportions that the real vanished.

If the text of the Biblical narrative, then, is so greatly in need of interpretation on the basis of its own content, its claim to absolute authority forces it still further in the same direction. Far from seeking, like Homer, merely to make us forget our own reality for a few hours, it seeks to overcome our reality: we are to fit our own life into its world, feel ourselves to be elements in its structure of universal history. This becomes increasingly difficult the further our historical environment is removed from that of the Biblical books; and if these nevertheless maintain their claim to absolute authority, it is inevitable that they themselves be adapted through interpretative transformation. This was for a long time comparatively easy; as late as the European Middle Ages it was possible to represent Biblical events as ordinary phenomena of contemporary life, the methods of interpretation themselves forming the basis for such a treatment. But when, through too great a change in environment and through the awakening of a critical consciousness, this becomes impossible, the Biblical claim to absolute authority is jeopardized; the method of interpretation is scorned and rejected, the Biblical stories become ancient legends, and the doctrine they had contained, now dissevered from them, becomes a disembodied image.

As a result of this claim to absolute authority, the method of interpretation spread to traditions other than the Jewish. The Homeric poems present a definite complex of events whose boundaries in space and time are clearly delimited; before it, beside it, and after it, other complexes of events, which do not depend upon it, can be conceived without conflict and without difficulty. The Old Testament, on the other hand, presents universal history: it begins with the beginning of time, with the creation of the world, and will end with the Last Days, the fulfilling of the Covenant, with which the world will come to an end. Everything else that happens in the world can only be conceived as an element in this sequence; into it everything that is known about the world, or at least everything that touches upon the history of the Jews, must be fitted as an ingredient of the divine plan; and as this too became possible only by interpreting the new material as it poured in, the need for interpretation reaches out beyond the original Jewish-Israelitish realm of reality—for example to Assyrian, Babylonian, Persian, and Roman history; interpretation in a determined direction becomes a general method of comprehending reality; the new and strange world which now comes into view and which, in the form in which it presents itself, proves to be wholly unutilizable within the Jewish religious frame, must be so interpreted that it can find a place there. But this process nearly always also reacts upon the frame, which requires enlarging and modifying. The most striking piece of interpretation of this sort occurred in the first century of the Christian era, in consequence of Paul's mission to the Gentiles: Paul and the Church Fathers reinterpreted the entire Jewish tradition as a succession of figures prognosticating the appearance of Christ, and assigned the Roman Empire its proper place in the divine plan of salvation. Thus while, on the one hand, the reality of the Old Testament presents itself as complete truth with a claim to sole authority, on the other hand that very claim forces it to a constant interpretative change in its own content; for millennia it undergoes an incessant and active development with the life of man in Europe.

The claim of the Old Testament stories to represent universal history, their insistent relation—a relation constantly redefined by conflicts—to a single and hidden God, who yet shows himself and who guides universal history by promise and exaction, gives these stories an entirely different perspective from any the Homeric poems can possess. As a composition, the Old Testament is incomparably less unified than the Homeric poems, it is more obviously pieced together—but the various components all belong to one concept of universal history and its interpretation. If certain elements survived which did not immediately fit in, interpretation took care of them; and so the reader is at every moment aware of the universal religio-historical perspective which gives the individual stories their general meaning and purpose. The greater the separateness and horizontal disconnection of the stories and groups of stories in relation to one another, compared with the *Iliad* and the *Odyssey*, the stronger is their general vertical connection, which holds them all together and which is entirely lacking in Homer. Each of the great figures of the Old Testament, from Adam to the prophets, embodies a moment of this vertical connection. God chose and formed these men to the end of embodying his essence and will—yet choice and formation do not coincide, for the latter proceeds gradually, historically, during the earthly life of him upon whom the choice has fallen. How the process is accomplished, what terrible trials such a formation inflicts, can be seen from our story of Abraham's sacrifice. Herein lies the reason why the great figures of the Old Testament are so much more fully developed, so much more fraught with their own biographical past, so much more distinct as individuals, than are the Homeric heroes. Achilles and Odysseus are splendidly described in many well-ordered words, epithets cling to them, their emotions are constantly displayed in their words and deeds—but they have no development, and their life-histories are clearly set forth once and for all. So little are the Homeric heroes presented as developing or having developed, that most of them—Nestor, Agamemnon, Achilles—appear to be of an age fixed from the very first. Even Odysseus, in whose case the long lapse of time and the many events which occurred offer so much opportunity for biographical development, shows almost nothing of it. Odysseus on his return is exactly the same as he was when he left Ithaca two decades earlier. But what a road, what a fate, lie between the Jacob who cheated his father out of his blessing and the old man whose favorite son had been torn to pieces by a wild beast!—between David the harp player, persecuted by his lord's jealousy, and the old king, surrounded by violent intrigues, whom Abishag the Shunnamite warmed in his bed, and he knew her not! The old man, of whom we know how he has become what he is, is more of an individual than the young man; for it is only during the course of an eventful life that men are differentiated into full individuality; and it is this history of a personality which the Old Testament presents to us as the formation undergone by those whom God has chosen to be examples. Fraught with their development, sometimes even aged to the verge of dissolution, they show a distinct stamp of individuality entirely foreign to the Homeric heroes. Time can touch the latter only outwardly, and even that change is brought to our observation as little as possible; whereas the stern hand of God is ever upon the Old Testament figures; he has not only made them once and for all and chosen them, but he continues to work upon them, bends them and kneads them, and, without destroying them in essence, produces from them forms which their youth gave no grounds for anticipating. The objection that the biographical element of the Old Testament often springs from the combination of several legendary personages does not apply; for this combination is a part of the development of the text. And how much wider is the pendulum swing of their lives than that of the Homeric heroes! For they are bearers of the divine will, and yet they are fallible, subject to misfortune and humiliation—and in the midst of misfortune and in their humiliation their acts and words reveal the transcendent majesty of God. There is hardly one of them who does not, like Adam, undergo the deepest humiliation—and hardly one who is not deemed worthy of God's personal intervention and personal inspiration. Humiliation and elevation go far deeper and far higher than in Homer, and they belong basically together. The poor beggar Odysseus is only masquerading, but Adam is really cast down, Jacob really a refugee, Joseph really in the pit and then a slave to be bought and sold. But their greatness, rising out of humiliation, is almost superhuman and an image of God's greatness. The reader clearly feels how the extent of the pendulum's swing is connected with the intensity of the personal history—precisely the most extreme circumstances, in which we are immeasurably forsaken and in despair, or immeasurably joyous and exalted, give us, if we survive them, a personal stamp which is recognized as the product of a rich existence, a rich development. And very often, indeed generally, this element of development gives the Old Testament stories a historical character, even when the subject is purely legendary and traditional.

Homer remains within the legendary with all his material, whereas the material of the Old Testament comes closer and closer to history as the narrative proceeds; in the stories of David the historical report predominates. Here too, much that is legendary still remains, as for example the story of David and Goliath; but much—and the most essential—consists in things which the narrators knew from their own experience or from firsthand testimony. Now the difference between legend and history is in most cases easily perceived by a reasonably experienced reader. It is a difficult matter, requiring careful historical and philological training, to distinguish the true from the synthetic or the biased in a historical presentation; but it is easy to separate the historical from the legendary in general. Their structure is different. Even where the legendary does not immediately betray itself by elements of the miraculous, by the repetition of well-known standard motives, typical patterns and themes, through neglect of clear details of time and place, and the like, it is generally quickly recognizable by its composition. It runs far too smoothly. All cross-currents, all friction, all that is casual, secondary to the main events and themes, everything unresolved, truncated, and uncertain, which confuses the clear progress of the action and the simple orientation of the actors, has disappeared. The historical event which we witness, or learn from the testimony of those who witnessed it, runs much more variously, contradictorily, and confusedly; not until it has produced results in a definite domain are we able, with their help, to classify it to a certain extent; and how often the order to which we think we have attained becomes doubtful again, how often we ask ourselves if the data before us have not led us to a far too simple classification of the original events! Legend arranges its material in a simple and straightforward way; it detaches it from its contemporary historical context, so that the latter will not confuse it; it knows only clearly outlined men who act from few and simple motives and the continuity of whose feelings and actions remains uninterrupted. In the legends of martyrs, for example, a stiff-necked and fanatical persecutor stands over against an equally stiff-necked and fanatical victim; and a situation so complicated—that is to say, so real and historical—as that in which the "persecutor" Pliny finds himself in his celebrated letter to Trajan on the subject of the Christians, is unfit for legend. And that is still a comparatively simple case. Let the reader think of the history which we are ourselves witnessing; anyone who, for example, evaluates the behavior of individual men and groups of men at the time of the rise of National Socialism in Germany, or the behavior of individual peoples and states before and during the last war, will feel how difficult it is to represent historical themes in general, and how unfit they are for legend; the historical comprises a great number of contradictory motives in each individual, a hesitation and ambiguous groping on the part of groups; only seldom (as in the last war) does a more or less plain situation, comparatively simple to describe, arise, and even such a situation is subject to division below the surface, is indeed almost constantly in danger of losing its simplicity; and the motives of all the interested parties are so complex that the slogans of propaganda can be composed only through the crudest simplification—with the result that friend and foe alike can often employ the same ones. To write history is so difficult that most historians are forced to make concessions to the technique of legend.

It is clear that a large part of the life of David as given in the Bible contains history and not legend. In Absalom's rebellion, for example, or in the scenes from David's last days, the contradictions and crossing of motives both in individuals and in the general action have become so concrete that it is impossible to doubt the historicity of the information conveyed. Now the men who composed the historical parts are often the same who edited the older legends too; their peculiar religious concept of man in history, which we have attempted to describe above, in no way led them to a legendary simplification of events; and so it is only natural that, in the legendary passages of the Old Testament, historical structure is frequently discernible—of course, not in the sense that the traditions are examined as to their credibility according to the methods of scientific criticism; but simply to the extent that the tendency to a smoothing down and harmonizing of events, to a simplification of motives, to a static definition of characters which avoids conflict, vacillation, and development, such as are natural to legendary structure, does not predominate in the Old Testament world of legend. Abraham, Jacob, or even Moses produces a more concrete, direct, and historical impression than the figures of the Homeric world—not because they are better described in terms of sense (the contrary is the case) but because the confused, contradictory multiplicity of events, the psychological and factual cross-purposes, which true history reveals, have not disappeared in the representation but still remain clearly perceptible. In the stories of David, the legendary, which only later scientific criticism makes recognizable as such, imperceptibly passes into the historical; and even in the legendary, the problem of the classification and interpretation of human history is already passionately apprehended—a problem which later shatters the framework of historical composition and completely overruns it with prophecy; thus the Old Testament, in so far as it is concerned with human events, ranges through all three domains: legend, historical reporting, and interpretative historical theology.

Connected with the matters just discussed is the fact that the Greek text seems more limited and more static in respect to the circle of personages involved in the action and to their political activity. In the recognition scene with which we began, there appears, aside from Odysseus and Penelope, the housekeeper Euryclea, a slave whom Odysseus' father Laertes had bought long before. She, like the swineherd Eumaeus, has spent her life in the service of Laertes' family; like Eumaeus, she is closely connected with their fate, she loves them and shares their interests and feelings. But she has no life of her own, no feelings of her own; she has only the life and feelings of her master. Eumaeus too, though he still remembers that he was born a freeman and indeed of a noble house (he was stolen as a boy), has, not only in fact but also in his own feeling, no longer a life of his own; he is entirely involved in the life of his masters. Yet these two characters are the only ones whom Homer brings to life who do not belong to the ruling class. Thus we become conscious of the fact that in the Homeric poems life is enacted only among the ruling class—others appear only in the role of servants to that class. The ruling class is still so strongly patriarchal, and still itself so involved in the daily activities of domestic life, that one is sometimes likely to forget their rank. But they are unmistakably a sort of feudal aristocracy, whose men divide their lives between war, hunting, marketplace councils, and feasting, while the women supervise the maids in the house. As a social picture, this world is completely stable; wars take place only between different groups of the ruling class; nothing ever pushes up from below. In the early stories of the Old Testament the patriarchal condition is dominant too, but since the people involved are individual nomadic or half-nomadic tribal leaders, the social picture gives a much less stable impression; class distinctions are not felt. As soon as the people completely emerges—that is, after the exodus from Egypt—its activity is always discernible, it is often in ferment, it frequently intervenes in events not only as a whole but also in separate groups and through the medium of separate individuals who come forward; the origins of prophecy seem to lie in the irrepressible politico-religious spontaneity of the people. We receive the impression that the movements emerging from the depths of the people of Israel-Judah must have been of a wholly different nature from those even of the later ancient democracies—of a different nature and far more elemental.

With the more profound historicity and the more profound social activity of the Old Testament text, there is connected yet another important distinction from Homer: namely, that a different conception of the elevated style and of the sublime is to be found here. Homer, of course, is not afraid to let the realism of daily life enter into the sublime and tragic; our episode of the scar is an example, we see how the quietly depicted, domestic scene of the foot-washing is incorporated into the pathetic and sublime action of Odysseus' homecoming. From the rule of the separation of styles which was later almost universally accepted and which specified that the realistic depiction of daily life was incompatible with the sublime and had a place only in comedy or, carefully stylized, in idyl—from any such rule Homer is still far removed. And yet he is closer to it than is the Old Testament. For the great and sublime events in the Homeric poems take place far more exclusively and unmistakably among the members of a ruling class; and these are far more untouched in their heroic elevation than are the Old Testament figures, who can fall much lower in dignity (consider, for example, Adam, Noah, David, Job); and finally, domestic realism, the representation of daily life, remains in Homer in the peaceful realm of the idyllic, whereas, from the very first, in the Old Testament stories, the sublime, tragic, and problematic take shape precisely in the domestic and commonplace: scenes such as those between Cain and Abel, between Noah and his sons, between Abraham, Sarah, and Hagar, between Rebekah, Jacob, and Esau, and so on, are inconceivable in the Homeric style. The entirely different ways of developing conflicts are enough to account for this. In the Old Testament stories the peace of daily life in the house, in the fields, and among the flocks, is undermined by jealousy over election and the promise of a blessing, and complications arise which would be utterly incomprehensible to the Homeric heroes. The latter must have palpable and clearly expressible reasons for their conflicts and enmities, and these work themselves out in free battles; whereas, with the former, the perpetually smouldering jealousy and the connection between the domestic and the spiritual, between the paternal blessing and the divine blessing, lead to daily life being permeated with the stuff of conflict, often with poison. The sublime influence of God here reaches so deeply into the everyday that the two realms of the sublime and the everyday are not only actually unseparated but basically inseparable.

We have compared these two texts, and, with them, the two kinds of style they embody, in order to reach a starting point for an investigation into the literary representation of reality in European culture. The two styles, in their opposition, represent basic types: on the one hand fully externalized description, uniform illumination, uninterrupted connection, free expression, all events in the foreground, displaying unmistakable meanings, few elements of historical development and of psychological perspective; on the other hand, certain parts brought into high relief, others left obscure, abruptness, suggestive influence of the unexpressed, "background" quality, multiplicity of meanings and the need for interpretation, universal-historical claims, development of the concept of the historically becoming, and preoccupation with the problematic.

Homer's realism is, of course, not to be equated with classical-antique realism in general; for the separation of styles, which did not develop until later, permitted no such leisurely and externalized description of everyday happenings; in tragedy especially there was no room for it; furthermore, Greek culture very soon encountered the phenomena of historical becoming and of the "multilayeredness" of the human problem, and dealt with them in its fashion; in Roman realism, finally, new and native concepts are added. We shall go into these later changes in the antique representation of reality when the occasion arises; on the whole, despite them, the basic tendencies of the Homeric style, which we have attempted to work out, remained effective and determinant down into late antiquity.

Since we are using the two styles, the Homeric and the Old Testament, as starting points, we have taken them as finished products, as they appear in the texts; we have disregarded everything that pertains to their origins, and thus have left untouched the question whether their peculiarities were theirs from the beginning or are to be referred wholly or in part to foreign influences. Within the limits of our purpose, a consideration of this question is not necessary; for it is in their full development, which they reached in early times, that the two styles exercised their determining influence upon the representation of reality in European literature.

Cleanth Brooks 1906–

During the 1930s in the United States a group of critics led by John Crowe Ransom and including Cleanth Brooks, Robert Penn Warren, Donald Davidson, Allen Tate, and Yvor Winters, became a powerful force in the formal criticism of literature. Their position is known as New Criticism, after Ransom's book of the same name, and they have played a major role in literary criticism during this century in the United States. Perhaps the quintessential New Critic, Brooks wrote two books with Robert Penn Warren, *Understanding Poetry* (1938) and *Understanding Fiction* (1943), both of which have become standards in modern poetics and pedagogy. His best-known work is *The Well Wrought Urn* (1947) from which this essay, "What Does Poetry Communicate?", was taken.

This essay, like the others in *The Well Wrought Urn*, grew out of a summer class Brooks taught in 1942 at the University of Michigan. In it his focus is the question posed by the essay's title: what does poetry communicate? To answer the question, Brooks closely examines Robert Herrick's poem, "Corrina's Going a-Maying," and shows that understanding what a poem means is the result of several factors working together: the poetic form, the literary tradition of which it is a willing part, the methods characteristic of poetry, and the willingness of the reader to accept the responsibility for reading the poem "as poetry." Brooks emphasizes the need for careful, close examination of the poem and states that both the writing of the poem and the understanding of it are "a process of exploration."

What Does Poetry Communicate?

The question of what poetry communicates, if anything, has been largely forced upon us by the advent of "modern" poetry. Some of that poetry is admittedly highly difficult—a very great deal of it is bound to *appear* difficult to the reader of conventional reading habits, even in spite of the fact—actually, in many cases, *because* of the fact—that he is a professor of literature.

For this reason, the difficult moderns are often represented as untraditional and generally irresponsible. (The War, incidentally, has encouraged the tendency: critics who ought to know better lend themselves to the popular plea that we should go back to the good old days when a poet meant what he said and there was no nonsense about it.)

The question, however, allows only one honest answer: modern poetry (if it is really poetry, and, at its best, it is really poetry) communicates whatever any other poetry communicates. The fact is that the question is badly asked. What does traditional poetry communicate? What does a poem like Herrick's "Corinna's going a-Maying" communicate? The example is a fair one: the poem has been long praised, and it is not noted for its difficulty.

The textbook answer is easy: the poem is a statement of the *carpe diem* theme. So it is, of course. But what does the poem do with the theme—specifically: Does the poet accept the theme? How seriously does he accept it? Within what context? etc., etc. These are questions of the first importance, a point that becomes obvious when we come to deal with such a matter as the following: after describing the joys of the May-day celebration, the poet prefaces his final invitation to Corinna to accept these joys by referring to them as "the harmlesse follie of the time." Unless we are absentmindedly dictating a stock answer to an indifferent freshman, we shall certainly feel constrained to go further in describing what the poem "says."

Well, let us try again. Herrick's poem says that the celebration of nature is a beautiful but harmless folly, and his invitation to Corinna, thus, is merely playful, not serious. The Anglican parson is merely pretending for the moment that he is Catullus and that his Corinna is a pagan nymph. The poem is a pretense, a masquerade.

But there are the closing lines of the poem:

> Our life is short; and our dayes run
> As fast away as do's the Sunne:
> And as a vapour, or a drop of raine
> Once lost, can ne'er be found againe:
> So when or you or I are made
> A fable, song, or fleeting shade;
> All love, all liking, all delight
> Lies drown'd with us in endlesse night.
> Then while time serves, and we are but decaying;
> Come, my *Corinna*, come, let's goe a-Maying.

Obviously, there is a sense in which the invitation is thoroughly serious.

Confronted with this apparent contradiction, we can conclude, if we like, that Herrick is confused; or, softening the censure, we can explain that he was concerned only with providing some sort of framework for a description of the Devonshire spring. But if Herrick is confused about what he is saying in the poem, he behaves very strangely for a man in that plight. Far from being unconscious of the contradictory elements in the poem, he quite obviously has them in mind. Indeed, he actually takes pains to stress the clash between the Christian and pagan world views; or rather, while celebrating the pagan view, he refuses to suppress references to the Christian. For instance, for all the dew-besprinkled description of the morning, he makes the ominous, unpagan word "sin" run throughout the poem. While the flowers are rejoicing and the birds are singing their hymns of praise, it is a "sin" and a "profanation" for Corinna to remain within doors. In the second stanza, the clash between paganism and Christianity becomes quite explicit: Corinna is to be "briefe in praying:/ Few Beads are best" on this morning which is dedicated to the worship of the nature god. And in the third stanza, paganism becomes frankly triumphant. Corinna is to

> . . . sin no more, as we have done, by staying. . . .

Moreover, a great deal that is usually glossed over as decorations or atmosphere in this poem is actually used by the poet to point up this same conflict. Herrick persists (with a shrewdness worthy of Sir James Frazer) in seeing the May-day rites as religious rites, though, of course, those of a pagan religion. The flowers, like worshippers, bow to the east; the birds sing "Mattens" and "Hymnes"; and the village itself, bedecked with greenery, becomes a cluster of pagan temples:

> Devotion gives each House a Bough,
> Or Branch: Each Porch, each doore, ere this,
> An Arke a Tabernacle is. . . .

The religious terms—"devotion," "ark," "tabernacle"—appear insistently. Corinna is actually being reproached for being late to church—the church of nature. The village itself has become a grove, subject to the laws of nature. One remembers that the original sense of "pagan" was "country-dweller" because the worship of the old gods and goddesses persisted longest there. On this May morning, the country has come into the village to claim it, at least on this one day, for its own. Symbolically, the town has disappeared and its mores are superseded.

I cannot see how we can avoid admitting that all this is communicated by the poem. Here it is in the poem. And its repercussions on the theme (if we still want to view the poem as a communication of a theme) are important. Among other things, they qualify the theme thus: the poem is obviously not a brief for the acceptance of the pagan ethic so much as it is a statement that the claims of the pagan ethic—however much they may be overlaid—exist, and on occasion emerge, as on this day.

The description of Corinna herself supplies another important qualification of the theme. The poet suggests that she properly falls under the dominion of nature as do the flowers and birds and trees. Notice the opening of the second stanza:

> Rise; and put on your Foliage. . . .

And this suggestion that she is a part of nature, like a plant, is reinforced throughout the poem. The trees drenched in dew will shake down dew-drops on her hair, accepting her as a companion and equal. Her human companions, the boys and girls of the village, likewise are plants—

> There's not a budding Boy, or Girle, this day,
> But is got up, and gone to bring in May.

Indeed, as we go through the first three stanzas of the poem, the old friendships gradually dissolve: the street itself turns into a park, and the boys and girls returning with their arms loaded with branches of white-thorn, merge into the plants themselves. Corinna, like them, is subject to nature, and to the claims of nature; and the season of springtime cannot, and ought not, to be denied. Not to respond is to "sin" against nature itself.

All this is "communicated" by the poem, and must be taken into account when we attempt to state what the poem "says." No theory of communication can deny that this is part of what the poem communicates, however awkwardly a theory of communication may be put to it to handle the problem.

We have still not attempted to resolve the conflict between the Christian and pagan attitudes in the poem, though the qualifications of each of them, as Herrick qualifies each in the poem, may make it easier to discover possible resolutions which would have appealed to Herrick the Anglican parson who lived so much of his life in Devonshire and apparently took so much interest, not only in the pagan literature of Rome and Greece, but in the native English survivals of the old fertility cults.

Something of the nature of the poet's reconcilement of the conflicting claims of paganism and Christianity—and this, again, is part of what the poem communicates—is foreshadowed in the fourth stanza. The paganism with which the poem is concerned is clearly not an abstract and doctrinaire paganism. It comes to terms with the authoritative Christian mores, casually and without undue thought about the conflict—at least the paganism in action does: the village boys and the girls with their grass-stained gowns, coming to the priest to receive the blessing of the church.

> And some have wept, and woo'd, and plighted Troth,
> And chose their Priest, ere we can cast off sloth. . . .

After the poet's teasing play between attitudes in the first three stanzas, we are apparently approaching some kind of viable relation between them in this most realistic stanza of the poem with its

> Many a jest told of the Keyes betraying
> This night, and Locks pickt. . . .

The explicit resolution, of course, is achieved, with a change of tone, in the last stanza, with its

> Come, let us goe, while we are in our prime;
> And take the harmlesse follie of the time.
> We shall grow old apace, and die. . .

I shall not try to indicate in detail what the resolution is. Here one must refer the reader to the poem itself. Yet one can venture to suggest the tone. The tone would be something like this: All right, let's be serious. Dismiss my pagan argument as folly. Still, in a sense, we are a part of nature, and are subject to its claims, and participate in its beauty. Whatever may be true in reality of the life of the soul, the body does decay, and unless we make haste to catch some part of that joy and beauty, that beauty—whatever else may be true—is lost.

If my clumsy paraphrase possesses any part of the truth, then this is still another thing which the poem communicates, though I shall hardly be able to "prove" it. As a matter of fact, I do not care to insist upon this or any other paraphrase. Indeed it is just because I am suspicious of such necessarily abstract paraphrases that I think our initial question, "What does the poem communicate?" is badly asked. It is not that the poem communicates nothing. Precisely the contrary. The poem communicates so much and communicates it so richly and with such delicate qualifications that the thing communicated is mauled and distorted if we attempt to convey it by any vehicle less subtle than that of the poem itself.

This general point is reinforced if we consider the function of particular words and phrases within the poem. For instance, consider

> Our life is short; and our dayes run
> As fast away as do's the Sunne:
> And as a vapour, or a drop of raine
> Once lost, can ne'er be found againe. . . .

Why does the rain-drop metaphor work so powerfully? It is hardly because the metaphor is startlingly novel. Surely one important reason for its power is the fact that the poet has filled the first two stanzas of his poem with references to the dew. And the drops of dew have come to stand as a symbol of the spring and early dawn and of the youth of the lovers themselves. The dewdrops are the free gift of nature, spangling every herb and tree; they sparkle in the early light like something precious, like gems; they are the appropriate decoration for the girl; but they will not last—Corinna must hasten to enjoy them if she is to enjoy them at all. Thus, in the context of the poem they become a symbol heavily charged with meanings which no dictionary can be expected to give. When the symbol is revived at the end of the poem, even though in somewhat different guise, the effect is powerful; for the poet has made the little globule of moisture come to stand for the brief beauty of youth. And this too is part of what the poem says, though it is said indirectly, and the dull or lazy reader will not realize that it has been said at all.

The principle of rich indirection applies even to the individual word. Consider

> Then while time serves, and we are but decaying;
> Come, my *Corinna*, come, let's goe a-Maying.

"While time serves" means loosely "while there is yet time," but in the full context of the poem it also means "while time serves us," while time is still servant, not master—

before we are mastered by time. Again, mere recourse to the dictionary will not give us this powerful second meaning. The poet is exploiting the potentialities of language—indeed, as all poets must do, he is remaking language.

To sum up: our examination of the poem has not resulted in our locating an idea or set of ideas which the poet has communicated with certain appropriate decorations. Rather, our examination has carried us further and further into the poem itself in a process of exploration. As we have made this exploration, it has become more and more clear that the poem is not only the linguistic vehicle which conveys the thing communicated most "poetically," but that it is also the sole linguistic vehicle which conveys the things communicated accurately. In fact, if we are to speak exactly, the poem itself is the *only* medium that communicates the particular "what" that is communicated. The conventional theories of communication offer no easy solution to our problem of meanings: we emerge with nothing more enlightening than this graceless bit of tautology: the poem says what the poem says.

There is a further point that comes out of our examination: our examination tends to suggest that not only our reading of the poem is a process of exploration, but that Herrick's process of making the poem was probably a process of exploration too. To say that Herrick "communicates" certain matters to the reader tends to falsify the real situation. The old description of the poet was better and less dangerous: the poet is a maker, not a communicator. He explores, consolidates, and "forms" the total experience that is the poem. I do not mean that he fashions a replica of his particular experience of a certain May morning like a detective making a moulage of a footprint in wet clay. But rather, out of the experiences of many May mornings, and out of his experience of Catullus, and possibly out of a hundred other experiences, he fashions, probably through a process akin to exploration, the total experience which is the poem.

This experience is *communicable*, partially so, at least. If we are willing to use imaginative understanding, we can come to know the poem as an object—we can share in the experience. But the poet is most truthfully described as a *poietes* or maker, not as an expositor or communicator. I do not mean to split hairs. It is doubtless possible to elaborate a theory of communication which will adequately cover these points. I believe that I. A. Richards, if I understand him correctly, has attempted to qualify his theory in precisely this way. At any rate, the net effect of his criticism has been to emphasize the need of a more careful reading of poetry and to regard the poem as an organic thing.

But most proponents of poetry as communication have been less discerning, and have used this view of poetry to damn the modern poets. I refer to such typical critics as Max Eastman and F. L. Lucas. But perhaps the most hard-bitten and vindictive of all the adherents of the theory is a man to whom the phrase "theory of communication" may seem novel and unfamiliar: I mean the average English professor. In one form or another, whether in a conception which makes poetry a romantic raid on the absolute, or in a conception of more didactic persuasion which makes poetry an instrument of edification, some form of the theory of communication is to be found deeply embedded in the average teacher's doctrine of poetry. In many contexts it does little or no harm; but it can emerge to becloud the issues thoroughly when one confronts poetry which is unfamiliar or difficult.

Much modern poetry is difficult. Some of

it may be difficult because the poet is snobbish and definitely wants to restrict his audience, though this is a strange vanity and much rarer than Mr. Eastman would have us think. Some modern poetry is difficult because it is bad—the total experience remains chaotic and incoherent because the poet could not master his material and give it a form. Some modern poetry is difficult because of the special problems of our civilization. But a great deal of modern poetry is difficult for the reader simply because so few people, relatively speaking, are accustomed to reading *poetry as poetry*. The theory of communication throws the burden of proof upon the poet, overwhelmingly and at once. The reader says to the poet: Here I am; it's your job to "get it across" to me—when he ought to be assuming the burden of proof himself.

Now the modern poet has, for better or worse, thrown the weight of the responsibility upon the reader. The reader must be on the alert for shifts of tone, for ironic statement, for suggestion rather than direct statement. He must be prepared to accept a method of indirection. He is further expected to be reasonably well acquainted with the general tradition—literary, political, philosophical, for he is reading a poet who comes at the end of a long tradition and who can hardly be expected to write honestly and with full integrity and yet ignore this fact. But the difficulties are not insuperable, and most of them can be justified in principle as the natural results of the poet's employment of his characteristic methods. For example, surely there can be no objection to the poet's placing emphasis on methods characteristic of poetry—the use of symbol rather than abstraction, of suggestion rather than explicit pronouncement, of metaphor rather than direct statement.

In stressing such methods, it is true, the modern poet has not produced a poetry which easily yields manageable abstractions in the way that some of the older poetry seems to do. But this is scarcely a conclusion that is flattering to the antagonists of modern poetry. What does an "older poem" like "Corinna's going a-Maying?" say? What does this poem communicate? If we are content with the answer that the poem says that we should enjoy youth before youth fades, and if we are willing to write off everything else in the poem as "decoration," then we can properly censure Eliot or Auden or Tate for not making poems so easily tagged. But in that case we are not interested in poetry; we are interested in tags. Actually, in a few years, when time has wrought its softening changes, and familiarity has subdued the modern poet's frightful mien, and when the tags have been obligingly supplied, we may even come to terms with our difficult moderns.

Postscript

In a recent essay, Arthur Mizener connects the reference to "the god unshorn" in the first lines of Herrick's poem with a comparable passage in Spenser.

At last the golden Orientall gate
 Of greatest heaven gan to open faire,
 And *Phoebus* fresh, a bridegrome to his mate,
 Came dauncing forth, shaking his deawie haire:
 And hurled his glistring beames through gloomy aire.
 Which when the wakeful Elf perceiu'd streight way
 He started up, and did him selfe arraye:
 In sun-bright armes, and battailovs array:
For with that Pagan proud he combat will that day.

"There is," Mizener comments, "a nice fusion, if, to our tastes, not a complete ordering of Pagan and Christian elements here. Phoebus, fresh as the Psalmist's bridegroom, comes dancing (with, I suppose, both a pagan grace and the rejoicing of a strong man to run a race) from the gate of a heaven which is actually felt simultaneously in terms of the clear and lovely classical fantasy on nature and in terms of a Christian vision of the metaphysical source of the meaning of life." And a little later in the essay Mizener goes on to say: "Certainly the Red Cross Knight's 'sun-bright armes' ('the armour of a Christian man') are intended to be compared to the 'glistring beames' with which Apollo attacks the darkness, as the virtuous and enlightened Elf is about to attack the darkly evil Pagan. And it is tempting to suppose that since the strength of Holiness is that of the sun, of 'the god unshorn,' the references to Apollo's hair and to the bridegroom's energy are also significant."

Later still in his essay, Mizener quotes the following passage from Paradise Lost:

> . . . . nor appear'd
> Less than Arch Angel ruin'd, and th' excess
> Of Glory obscur'd: As when the Sun new ris'n
> Looks through the Horizontal misty Air
> Shorn of his Beams, or from behind the Moon
> In dim Eclipse disastrous twilight sheds
> On half the Nations, and with fear of change
> Perplexes Monarchs.

"By the first of these sun comparisons," Mizener points out, "the archangel ruined is the sun deprived of its power to dispel with its beams the foul mists of winter and make the earth fruitful once more; the fallen angel is Apollo, shorn. . . . Nor is it easy to believe the epithet insignificant here; with all his learning Milton must certainly have known how common a symbol of virility the hair was among the Greeks. Herrick, a much less learned man, knew this, as his use of it in 'Corinna's going a-Maying' clearly shows:

> Get up, get up, for shame, the Blooming
> Morn
> Upon her wings presents the god unshorne."

It is unfair, of course, to quote from Mizener's essay without reference to his general thesis, and to quote only those bits of it which bear directly upon the dawn passage in Herrick's poem. (The essay, by the way, should be read in entirety and for its own sake: "Some Notes on the Nature of English Poetry," *The Sewanee Review*, Winter, 1943.) Even so, the passage quoted may be of value in demonstrating to the skeptical reader, suspicious that too much is being "read into" Herrick's innocent poem, how other poets of the same general period used the sun figure.

In Herrick's poem, "the god unshorne" is obviously the prepotent bridegroom of nature, the fertility god himself, toward whom the plants bow in adoration and whose day is now to be celebrated.

Corinna's Going a-Maying

Get up, get up for shame, the Blooming Morne
Upon her wings presents the god unshorne.
 See how *Aurora* throwes her faire
 Fresh-quilted colours through the aire:
 Get up, sweet-Slug-a-bed, and see
 The Dew bespangling Herbe and Tree.
Each Flower has wept, and bow'd toward
 the East,

Above an houre since; yet you not drest,
Nay! not so much as out of bed?
When all the Birds have Mattens seyd,
And sung their thankful Hymnes: 'tis sin,
Nay, profanation to keep in,
When as a thousand Virgins on this day,
Spring, sooner than the Lark, to fetch in May.

Rise; and put on your Foliage, and be seene
To come forth, like the Spring-time, fresh and greene;
And sweet as *Flora*. Take no care
For Jewels for your Gowne, or Haire:
Feare not; the leaves will strew
Gemms in abundance upon you:
Besides, the childhood of the Day has kept,
Against you come, some *Orient Pearls* unwept:
Come, and receive them while the light
Hangs on the Dew-locks of the night:
And *Titan* on the Eastern hill
Retires himselfe, or else stands still
Till you come forth. Wash, dresse, be briefe in praying:
Few beads are best, when once we goe a-Maying.

Come, my *Corinna*, come: and comming, marke
How each field turns a street; each street a Parke
Made green, and trimm'd with trees: see how
Devotion gives each House a Bough,
Or Branch: Each Porch, each doore, ere this,
An Arke a Tabernacle is
Made up of white-thorn neatly enterwove;
As if here were those cooler shades of love.
Can such delights be in the street,
And open fields, and we not see't?
Come, we'll abroad; and let's obay
The Proclamation made for May:
And sin no more, as we have done, by staying;
But my *Corinna*, come, let's goe a-Maying.

There's not a budding Boy, or Girle, this day,
But is got up, and gone to bring in May.
A deale of Youth, ere this, is come
Back, and with *White-thorn* laden home,
Some have dispatcht their Cakes and Creame,
Before that we have left to dreame:
And some have wept, and woo'd, and plighted Troth,
And chose their Priest, ere we can cast off sloth:
Many a green-gown has been given;
Many a kisse, both odde and even:
Many a glance too has been sent
From out the eye, Loves Firmament:
Many a jest told of the Keyes betraying
This night, and Locks pickt, yet w'are not a-Maying.

Come, let us goe, while we are in our prime;
And take the harmlesse follie of the time.
We shall grow old apace, and die
Before we know our liberty.
Our life is short; and our dayes run
As fast away as do's the Sunne:
And as a vapour, or a drop of raine
Once lost, can ne'er be found againe:
So when or you or I are made
A fable, song, or fleeting shade;
All love, all liking, all delight
Lies drown'd with us in endlesse night.
Then while time serves, and we are but decaying;
Come, my *Corinna*, come, let's goe a-Maying.

Northrop Frye 1912–

Northrop Frye's most acclaimed work is *Anatomy of Criticism* (1957), in which he introduced his systematic approach to literature. Among his other works are *The Well-Tempered Critic* (1963), *The Critical Path* (1971), and *The Stubborn Structure* (1970). He also authored two books on Shakespeare: *The Fools of Time* (1967) and *A Natural Perspective* (1965). His two in-depth studies of romanticism are *Fearful Symmetry: A Study of William Blake* (1947) and *A Study of English Romanticism* (1968).

In his work Frye offers a concise, fully developed, systematic approach to the study of literature. Unlike the preceding theories of formalism (which concentrate on individual works), historicism (emphasizing the author as creator), and later reader response (affirming the individual interpretive process), his method identifies the whole of literature as a culturally structured entity consisting of the entire canon of poems, dramas, and prose. Frye uses a mythological model to illustrate the morphology of literature: it consists of birth (melodrama), zenith (comedy), death (tragedy), and darkness (ironic literature).

In "The Function of Criticism at the Present Time" Frye considers it the responsibility of the critic to systematize the previously unorganized study of literature. As the shaper of intellectual tradition, the critic must organize the material within a critical framework that follows the natural contours of the literature. Before criticism can exist as an organized system, it must thoroughly—even scientifically—classify its sense of literature as entity, context, and genre while carefully reconsidering the all-too-frequent use of unsupported value judgments by many writers. To truly understand literature, says Frye, one must see it as a system of word-symbols, not unlike mathematics, which must be considered as part of its greater structure, separate from the world that gave rise to the ideas it depicts.

The Function of Criticism at the Present Time

The subject-matter of literary criticism is an art, and criticism is presumably an art too. This sounds as though criticism were a parasitic form of literary expression, an art based on pre-existing art, a second-hand imitation of creative power. The conception of the critic as a creator *manque* is very popular, especially among artists. Yet the critic has specific jobs to do which the experience of literature has proved to be less ignoble. One obvious function of criticism is to mediate between the artist and his public. Art that tried to do without criticism is apt to get involved in either of two fallacies. One is the attempt to reach the public directly through "popular" art, the assumption being that criticism is artificial and public taste natural. Below this is a further assumption about natural taste which goes back to Rousseau. The opposite fallacy is the conception of art as a mystery, an initiation into an esoteric community. Here criticism is restricted to masonic signs of occult understanding, to significant exclamations and gestures and oblique cryptic comments. This fallacy is like the other one in assuming a rough correlation between the merit of art and the degree of public response to it, though the correlation it assumes is inverse. But art of this kind is cut off from society as a whole, not so much because it retreats from life—the usual charge against it—as because it rejects criticism.

On the other hand, a public that attempts to do without criticism, and asserts that it knows what it likes, brutalizes the arts. Rejection of criticism from the point of view of the public, or its guardians, is involved in all forms of censorship. Art is a continuously emancipating factor in society, and the critic, whose job it is to get as many people in contact with the best that has been and is being thought and said, is, at least ideally, the pioneer of education and the shaper of cultural tradition. There is no immediate correlation either way between the merits of art and its general reception. Shakespeare was more popular than Webster, but not because he was a greater dramatist; W. H. Auden is less popular than Edgar Guest, but not because he is a better poet. But after the critic has been at work for a while, some positive correlation may begin to take shape. Most of Shakespeare's current popularity is due to critical publicity.

Why does criticism have to exist? The best and shortest answer is that it can talk, and all the arts are dumb. In painting, sculpture, or music it is easy enough to see that the art shows forth, and cannot *say* anything. And, although it sounds like a frantic paradox to say that the poet is inarticulate or speechless, literary works also are, for the critic, mute complexes of facts, like the data of science. Poetry is a *disinterested* use of words: it does not address a reader directly. When it does so, we feel that the poet has a certain distrust in the capacity of readers and critics to interpret his meaning without assistance, and has therefore stopped creating a poem and begun to talk. It is not merely tradition that impels a poet to invoke a Muse and protest that his utterance is involuntary. Nor is it mere paradox that causes Mr. MacLeish, in his famous "Ars Poetica," to apply the words, "mute," "dumb," and "wordless" to a poem. The poet, as Mill saw in a wonderful flash of critical insight, is not heard, but overheard. The first assumption of criticism, and the assumption on which the autonomy of criticism rests, is not that the poet does not know what he is talking about, but that he cannot talk about what he knows, any more than the painter or composer can.

The poet may of course have some critical ability of his own, and so interpret his own work; but the Dante who writes a commentary on the first canto of the *Paradiso* is merely one more of Dante's critics. What he says has a peculiar interest, but not a peculiar authority. Poets are too often the most unreliable judges of the value or even the meaning of what they have written. When Ibsen maintains that *Emperor and Galilean* is his greatest play and that certain episodes in *Peer Gynt* are not allegorical, one can only say that Ibsen is an indifferent critic of Ibsen. Wordsworth's Preface to the *Lyrical Ballads* is a remarkable document, but as a piece of Wordsworthian criticism nobody would give it more than about a B plus. Critics of Shakespeare are often supposed to be ridiculed by the assertion that if Shakespeare were to come back from the dead he would not be able to understand their criticism and would accuse them of reading far more meaning into his work than he intended. This, though pure hypothesis, is likely enough: we have very little evidence of Shakespeare's interest in criticism, either of himself or of anyone else. But all that this means is that Shakespeare, though a great dramatist, was not also the greatest Shakespearean critic. Why should he be?

The notion that the poet is necessarily his own best interpreter is indissolubly linked with the conception of the critic as a parasite or jackal of literature. Once we admit that he has a specific field of activity, and that he has autonomy within that field, we are forced to concede that criticism deals with literature in terms of a specific conceptual framework. This framework is not that of literature itself, for this is the parasite theory again, but neither is it something outside literature, for in that case the autonomy of criticism would again disappear, and the whole subject would be assimilated to something else.

Here, however, we have arrived at another conception of criticism which is different from the one we started with. This autonomous organizing of literature may be criticism, but it is not the activity of mediating between the artist and his public which we at first ascribed to criticism. There is one kind of critic, evidently, who faces the public and another who is still as completely involved in literary values as the poet himself. We may call this latter type the critic proper, and the former the critical reader. It may sound like quibbling to imply such a distinction, but actually the whole question of whether the critic has a real function, independent both of the artist at his most explicit and of the public at its most discriminating, is involved in it.

Our present-day critical traditions are rooted in the age of Hazlitt and Arnold and Sainte-Beuve, who were, in terms of our distinction, critical readers. They represented, not another conceptual framework within literature, but the reading public at its most expert and judicious. They conceived it to be the task of a critic to exemplify how a man of taste uses and evaluates literature, and thus how literature is to be absorbed into society. The nineteenth century has bequeathed to us the conception of the *causerie*, the man of taste's reflections on works of literature, as the normal form of critical expression. I give one example of the difference between a critic and a critical reader which amounts to a head-on collision. In one of his curious, brilliant, scatter-brained footnotes to *Munera Pulveris*, John Ruskin says:

> Of Shakespeare's names I will afterwards speak at more length; they are curiously—often barbarously—mixed out of various traditions and languages. Three of the clearest in meaning have been already noticed. Desdemona—"δυσδαιμονία," *miserable fortune*—is also plain enough. Othello is, I believe, "the careful"; all the calamity of the tragedy arising from the single flaw and error in his magnificently collected strength. Ophelia, "serviceableness," the true, lost wife of Hamlet, is marked as having a Greek name by that of her brother, Laertes; and its signification is once exquisitely alluded to in that brother's last word of her, where her gentle preciousness is opposed to the uselessness of the churlish clergy: "A *ministering* angel shall my sister be, when thou liest howling."

On this passage Matthew Arnold comments as follows:

> Now, really, what a piece of extravagance all that is! I will not say that the meaning of Shakespeare's names (I put aside the question as to the correctness of Mr. Ruskin's etymologies) has no effect at all, may be entirely lost

> sight of; but to give it that degree of prominence is to throw the reins to one's whim, to forget all moderation and proportion, to lose the balance of one's mind altogether. It is to show in one's criticism, to the highest excess, the note of provinciality.

Ruskin is a critic, perhaps the only important one that the Victorian age produced, and, whether he is right or wrong, what he is attempting is genuine criticism. He is trying to interpret Shakespeare in terms of a conceptual framework which belongs to the critic alone, and yet relates itself to the plays alone. Arnold is perfectly right in feeling that this is not the sort of material that the public critic can directly use. But he does not suspect the existence of criticism as we have defined it above. Here it is Arnold who is the provincial. Ruskin has learned his trade from the great iconological tradition which comes down through classical and biblical scholarship into Dante and Spenser, both of whom he knew how to read, and which is incorporated in the medieval cathedrals he had pored over in such detail. Arnold is assuming, as a universal law of nature, certain "plain sense" critical assumptions which were hardly heard of before Dryden's time and which can assuredly not survive the age of Freud and Jung and Frazer and Cassirer. What emerges from this is that the critic and critical reader are each better off when they know of one another's existence, and perhaps best off when their work forms different aspects of the same thing.

However, the *causerie* does not, or at least need not, involve any fallacy in the theory of criticism itself. The same cannot be said of the reaction against the *causerie* which has produced the leading twentieth-century substitute for criticism. This is the integrated system of religious, philosophical, and political ideas which takes in, as a matter of course, a critical attitude to literature. Thus Mr. Eliot defines his outlook as classical in literature, royalist in politics, anglo-catholic in religion; and it is clear that the third of these has been the spark-plug, the motivating power that drives the other two. Mr. Allen Tate describes his own critical attitude as "reactionary" in a sense intended to include political and philosophical overtones, and the same is true of Hulme's *Speculations*, which are primarily political speculations. Mr. Yvor Winters collects his criticism under the title "In Defence of Reason." What earthly business, one may inquire, has a literary critic to defend reason? He might as well be defending virtue. And so we could go through the list of Marxist, Thomist, Kierkegaardian, Freudian, Jungian, Spenglerian, or existential critics, all determined to substitute a critical attitude for criticism within literature, but to attach criticism to one of a miscellany of frameworks outside it.

The anxious and postulates of criticism have to grow out of the art that the critic is dealing with. The first thing that the literary critic has to do is to read literature, to make an inductive survey of his own field and let his critical principles shape themselves solely out of his knowledge of that field. Critical principles cannot be taken over ready-made from theology, philosophy, politics, science, or any combination of these. Further, an inductive survey of his own field is equally essential for the critic of painting or of music, and so each art has its own criticism. Aesthetics, or the consideration of art as a whole, is not a form of criticism but a branch of philosophy. I state all this as dogma, but I think the experience of literature bears me out. To subordinate criticism to a critical attitude is to stereotype certain values in literature which can be related to the extra-literary source of the value-judgment. Mr. Eliot does not mean to say that Dante is a greater poet than Shakespeare or perhaps even Milton;

yet he imposes on literature an extra-literary schematism, a sort of religio-political colour-filter, which makes Dante leap into prominence, shows Milton up as dark and faulty, and largely obliterates the outlines of Shakespeare. All that the genuine critic can do with this colour-filter is to murmur politely that it shows things in a new light and is indeed a most stimulating contribution to criticism.

If it is insisted that we cannot criticize literature until we have acquired a coherent philosophy of criticism with its centre of gravity in something else, the existence of criticism as a separate subject is still being denied. But there is one possibility further. If criticism exists, it must be, we have said, an examination of literature in terms of a conceptual framework derivable from an inductive survey of the literary field. The word "inductive" suggests some sort of scientific procedure. What if criticism is a science as well as an art? The writing of history is an art, but no one doubts that scientific principles are involved in the historian's treatment of evidence, and that the presence of this scientific element is what distinguishes history from legend. Is it also a scientific element in criticism which distinguishes it from *causerie* on the one hand, and the superimposed critical attitude on the other? For just as the presence of science changes the character of a subject from the casual to the causal, from the random and intuitive to the systematic, so it also safeguards the integrity of a subject from external invasions. So we may find in science a means of strengthening the fences of criticism against enclosure movements coming not only from religion and philosophy, but from the other sciences as well.

If criticism is a science, it is clearly a social science, which means that it should waste no time in trying to assimilate its methods to those of the natural sciences. Like psychology, it is directly concerned with the human mind, and will only confuse itself with statistical methodologies. I understand that there is a Ph.D. thesis somewhere that displays a list of Hardy's novels in the order of the percentages of gloom that they contain, but one does not feel that that sort of procedure should be encouraged. Yet as the field is narrowed to the social sciences the distinctions must be kept equally sharp. Thus there can be no such thing as a sociological "approach" to literature. There is no reason why a sociologist should not work exclusively on literary material, but if he does he should pay no attention to literary values. In his field Horatio Alger and the writer of the Elsie books are more important than Hawthorne or Melville, and a single issue of the *Ladies' Home Journal* is worth all of Henry James. The literary critic using sociological data is similarly under no obligation to respect sociological values.

It seems absurd to say that there *may* be a scientific element in criticism when there are dozens of learned journals based on the assumption that there is, and thousands of scholars engaged in a scientific procedure related to literary criticism. Either literary criticism is a science, or all these highly trained and intelligent people are wasting their time on a pseudo-science, one to be ranked with phrenology and election forecasting. Yet one is forced to wonder whether scholars as a whole are consciously aware that the assumptions on which their work is based are scientific ones. In the growing complication of secondary sources which constitutes literary scholarship, one misses, for the most part, that sense of systematic progressive consolidation which belongs to a science. Research begins in what is known as "background," and one would expect it, as it goes on, to organize the foreground as well. The digging up of relevant information about a poet should lead to a steady consolidating progress in the criticism of his poetry. One feels a certain failure of nerve in coming out of the background into the foreground, and research seems to prefer to become centrifugal, moving away from the works of art into more and more research projects. I have noticed this particularly in two fields in which I am interested, Blake and Spenser. For every critic of Spenser who is interested in knowing what, say, the fourth book of *The Faerie Queene* actually means as a whole, there are dozens who are interested primarily in how Spenser used Chaucer, Malory, and Ariosto in putting it together. So far as I know there is no book devoted to an analysis of *The Faerie Queene* itself, though there are any number on its sources, and, of course, background. As for Blake, I have read a whole shelf of books on his poetry by critics who did not know what any of his major poems meant. The better ones were distinguishable only by the fact that they did not boast of their ignorance.

The reason for this is that research is ancillary to criticism, but the critic to whom the researcher should entrust his materials hardly exists. What passes for criticism is mainly the work of critical readers or spokesmen of various critical attitudes, and these make, in general, a random and haphazard use of scholarship. Such criticism is therefore often regarded by the researcher as a subjective and regressive dilettantism, interesting in its place, but not real work. On the other hand, the critical reader is apt to treat the researcher as Hamlet did the grave-digger, ignoring everything he throws out except an odd skull that he can pick up and moralize about. Yet unless research consolidates into a criticism which preserves the scientific and systematic element in research, the literary scholar will be debarred by his choice of profession from ever making an immediately significant contribution to culture. The absence of direction in research is, naturally, clearest on the very lowest levels of all, where it is only a spasmodic laying of unfertilized eggs in order to avoid an administrative axe. Here the research is characterized by a kind of desperate tentativeness, an implied hope that some synthesizing critical Messiah of the future will find it useful. A philologist can show the relationship of even the most minute study of dialect to his subject as a whole, because philology is a properly organized science. But the researcher who collects all a poet's references to the sea or God or beautiful women does not know who will find this useful or in what ways it could be used, because he has no theory of imagery.

I am not, obviously, saying that literary scholarship at present is doing the wrong thing or should be doing something else: I am saying that it should be possible to get a clearer and more systematic comprehension of what it is doing. Most literary scholarship could be described as prior criticism (the so-called "lower" criticism of biblical scholarship), the editing of texts and the collecting of relevant facts. Of the posterior (or "higher") criticism that is obviously the final cause of this work we have as yet no theory, no tradition, and above all no systematic organization. We have, of course, a good deal of the thing itself. There is even some good posterior criticism of Spenser, though most of it was written in the eighteenth century. And in every age the greater scholar will do the right thing by the instinct of genius. But genius is rare, and scholarship is not.

2

Sciences normally begin in a state of naïve induction: they come immediately in contact with phenomena and take the things to be explained as their immediate data. Thus physics began by taking the immediate sensations of experience, classified as hot, cold, moist, and dry, as fundamental principles. Eventually physics turned inside out, and discovered that its real function was to explain what heat and moisture were. History began as chronicle; but the difference between the old chronicler and the modern historian is that to the chronicler the events he recorded were also the structure of history, whereas the historian sees these events as historical phenomena, to be explained in terms of a conceptual framework different in shape from them. Similarly each modern science has had to take what Bacon calls (though in another context) an inductive leap, occupying a new vantage ground from which it could see its former principles as new things to be explained. As long as astronomers regarded the movements of heavenly bodies as the *structure* of astronomy, they were compelled to regard their own point of view as fixed. Once they thought of movement as itself an explainable phenomenon, a mathematical theory of movement became the conceptual framework, and so the way was cleared for the heliocentric solar system and the law of gravitation. As long as biology thought of animal and vegetable forms of life as constituting its subject, the different branches of biology were largely efforts of cataloguing. As soon as it was the existence of forms of life themselves that had to be explained, the theory of evolution and the conceptions of protoplasm and the cell poured into biology and completely revitalized it.

It occurs to me that literary criticism is now in such a state of naïve induction as we find in a primitive science. Its materials, the masterpieces of literature, are not yet regarded as phenomena to be explained in terms of a conceptual framework which criticism alone possesses. They are still regarded as somehow constituting the framework or form of criticism as well. I suggest that it is time for criticism to leap to a new ground from which it can discover what the organizing or containing forms of its conceptual framework are. And no one can examine the present containing forms of criticism without being depressed by an overwhelming sense of unreality. Let me give one example.

In confronting any work of literature, one obvious containing form is the genre to which it belongs. And criticism, incredible as it may seem, has as yet no coherent conception of genres. The very word sticks out in an English sentence as the unpronounceable and alien thing it is. In poetry, the common-sense Greek division by methods of performance, which distinguishes poetry as lyric, epic, or dramatic according to whether it is sung, spoken, or shown forth, survives vestigially. On the whole it does not fit the facts of Western poetry, though in Joyce's *Portrait* there is an interesting and suggestive attempt made to re-define the terms. So, apart from a drama which belongs equally to prose, a handful of epics recognizable as such only because they are classical imitations, and a number of long poems also called epics because they are long, we are reduced to the ignoble and slovenly practice of calling almost the whole of poetry "lyric" because the Greeks had no other word for it. The Greeks did not need to develop a classification of prose forms: we do, but have never done so. The circulating-library distinction between fiction and non-fiction, between books which are about things admitted not to be true and books which are about everything else, is apparently satisfactory to us. Asked what the forms of prose fiction are, the literary critic can only say, "well, er—the novel." Asked what form of prose fiction *Gulliver's Travels*, which is clearly not a novel, belongs to, there is not one critic in a hundred who could give a definite answer, and not one in a thousand who would regard the answer (which happens to be "Menippean satire") as essential to the critical treatment of the book. Asked what he is working on, the critic will invariably say that he is working on Donne, or Shelley's thought, or the period from 1640 to 1660, or give some other answer which implies that history, or philosophy, or literature itself, constitutes the structural basis of criticism. It would never occur to any critic to say, for instance, "I am working on the theory of genres." If he actually were interested in this, he would say that he was working on a "general" topic; and the work he would do would probably show the marks of naïve induction: that is, it would be an effort to classify and pigeonhole instead of clarifying the tradition of the genre.

If we do not know how to handle even the genre, the most obvious of all critical conceptions, it is hardly likely that subtler instruments will be better understood. In any work of literature the characteristics of the language it is written in form an essential critical conception. To the philologist, literature is a function of language, its works linguistic documents, and to the philologist the phrase "English literature" makes sense. It ought not to make any sense at all to a literary critic. For while the philologist sees English literature as illustrating the organic growth of the English language, the literary critic can only see it as the miscellaneous pile of literary works that happened to get written in English. (I say in English, not in England, for the part of "English literature" that was written in Latin or Norman French has a way of dropping unobtrusively into other departments.) Language is an important secondary aspect of literature, but when magnified into a primary basis of classification it becomes absurdly arbitrary.

Critics, of course, maintain that they know this, and that they keep the linguistic categories only for convenience. But theoretical fictions have a way of becoming practical assumptions, and in no time the meaningless convenience of "English literature" expands into the meaningless inconvenience of the "history of English literature." Now, again, the historian must necessarily regard literature as an historical product and its works as historical documents. It is also quite true that the time a work was written in forms an essential critical conception. But again, to the literary critic, as such, the phrase "history of English literature" ought to mean nothing at all. If he doubts this, let him try writing one, and he will find himself confronted by an insoluble problem of form, or rather by an indissoluble amorphousness. The "history" part of his project is an abstract history, a bald chronicle of names and dates and works and influences, deprived of all the real historical interest that a real historian would give it, however much enlivened with discussions of "background." This chronicle is periodically interrupted by conventional judgments of value lugged in from another world, which confuse the history and yet are nothing by themselves. The *form* of literary history has not been discovered, and probably does not exist, and every successful one has been either a textbook or a *tour de force*. Linear time is not an exact enough category to catch literature, and all writers whatever are subtly belittled by a purely historical treatment.

Biography, a branch of history, presents a similar fallacy to the critic, for the biographer turns to a different job and a different kind of book when he turns to criticism. Again, the man who wrote the poem is one of the legitimate containing forms of criticism. But here we have to distinguish the poet *qua* poet, whose work is a single imaginative body, from the poet as man, who is something else altogether. The latter involves us in what is known as the personal heresy, or rather the heroic fallacy. For a biographer, poetry is an emanation of a personality; for the literary critic it is not, and the problem is to detach it from the personality and consider it on impersonal merits. The no man's land between biography and criticism, the process by which a poet's impressions of his environment are transmuted into poetry, has to be viewed by biographer and critic from opposite points of view. The process is too complex ever to be completely unified, Lowes's *Road to Xanadu* being the kind of exception that goes a long way to prove the rule. In Johnson's *Lives of the Poets* a biographical narrative is followed by a critical analysis, and the break between them is so sharp that it is represented in the text by a space.

In all these cases, the same principle recurs. The critic is surrounded by biography, history, philosophy, and language. No one doubts that he has to familiarize himself with these subjects. But is his job only to be the jackal of the historian, the philologist, and the biographer, or can he use these subjects in his own way? If he is not to sell out to all his neighbours in turn, what is distinctive about his approach to the poet's life, the time when he lived, and the language he wrote? To ask this is to raise one of the problems involved in the whole question of what the containing forms of literature are as they take their place in the conceptual framework of criticism. This confronts me with the challenge to make my criticism of criticism constructive. All I have space to do is to outline what I think the first major steps should be.

We have to see what literature is, and try to distinguish the category of literature among all the books there are in the world. I do not know that criticism has made any serious effort to determine what literature is. Next, as discussed above, we should examine the containing forms of criticism, including the poet's life, his historical context, his language, and his thought, to see whether the critic can impose a unified critical form on these things, without giving place to or turning into a biographer, an historian, a philologist, or a philosopher. Next, we should establish the broad distinctions, such as that between prose and poetry, which are preparatory to working out a comprehensive theory of genres. I do not know that critics have clearly explained what the difference between prose and poetry, for instance, really is. Then we should try to see whether the critic, like his neighbours the historian and the philosopher, lives in his own universe. To the historian there is nothing that cannot be considered historically; to the philosopher nothing that cannot be considered philosophically. Does the critic aspire to contain all things in criticism, and so swallow history and philosophy in his own synthesis, or must he be forever the historian's and philosopher's pupil? If I have shown up Arnold in a poor light, I should say that he is the only one I know who suggests that criticism can be, like history and philosophy, a total attitude to experience. And finally, since criticism may obviously deal with anything in a poem from its superficial texture to its ultimate significance, the question arises whether there are different levels of meaning in literature, and, if so, whether they can be defined and classified.

It follows that arriving at value-judgments is not, as it is so often said to be, part of the immediate tactic of criticism. Criticism is not well enough organized as yet to know what the factors of value in a critical judgment are. For instance, as was indicated above in connection with Blake and Spenser, the question of the quality of a poet's thinking as revealed in the integration of his argument is an essential factor in a value-judgment, but many poets are exhaustively discussed in terms of value without this factor being considered. Contemporary judgments of value come mainly from either the critical reader or from the spokesman of a critical attitude. That is, they must be on the whole either unorganized and tentative, or over-organized and irrelevant. For no one can jump directly from research to a value-judgment. I give one melancholy instance. I recently read a study of the sources of mythological allusions in some of the romantic poets, which showed that for the second part of *Faust* Goethe had used a miscellany of cribs, some of dubious authenticity. "I have now, I hope," said the author triumphantly at the end of his investigation, "given sufficient proof that the second part of *Faust* is not a great work of art." I do not deny the ultimate importance of the value-judgment. I would even consider the suggestion that the value-judgment is precisely what distinguishes the social from the natural science. But the more important it is, the more careful we should be about getting it solidly established.

What literature is may perhaps best be understood by an analogy. We shall have to labour the analogy, but that is due mainly to the novelty of the idea here presented. Mathematics appears to begin in the counting and measuring of objects, as a numerical commentary on the world. But the mathematician does not think of his subject as the counting and measuring of physical objects at all. For him it is an autonomous language, and there is a point at which it becomes in a measure independent of that common field of experience which we think of as the physical world, or as existence, or as reality, according to our mood. Many of its terms, such as irrational numbers, have no direct connection with the common field of experience, but depend for their meaning solely on the interrelations of the subject itself. Irrational numbers in mathematics may be compared to prepositions in verbal languages, which, unlike nouns and verbs, have no external symbolic reference. When we distinguish pure from applied mathematics, we are thinking of the former as a disinterested conception of numerical relationships, concerned more and more with its inner integrity, and less and less with its reference to external criteria.

Where, in that case, is pure mathematics going? We may gain a hint from the final chapter of Sir James Jeans' *Mysterious Universe*, which I choose because it shows some of the characteristics of the imaginative leap to a new conceptual framework already mentioned. There, the author speaks of the failure of physical cosmology in the nineteenth century to conceive of the universe as ultimately mechanical, and suggests that a mathematical approach to it may have better luck. The universe cannot be a machine, but it may be an interlocking set of mathematical formulas. What this means is surely that pure mathematics exists in a mathematical universe which is no longer a commentary on an "outside" world, but contains that world within itself. Mathematics is at first a form of understanding an objective world regarded as its content, but in the end it conceives of the content as being itself mathematical in form, so that when the conception of the mathematical universe is reached, form and content become the same thing.

Jeans was a mathematician, and thought of his mathematical universe as *the* universe. Doubtless it is, but it does not follow that the only way of conceiving it is mathematical. For we think also of literature at first as a commentary on an external "life" or "reality." But just as in mathematics we have to go from three apples to three, and from a square field to a square, so in reading Jane Austen we have to go from the faithful reflection of English society to the novel, and pass from literature as symbol to literature as an autonomous language. And just as mathematics exists in a mathematical universe which is at the circumference of the common field of experience, so literature exists in a verbal universe, which is not a commentary on life or reality, but contains life and reality in a system of verbal relationships. This conception of a verbal universe, in which life and reality are inside literature, and not outside it and being described or represented or approached or symbolized by it, seems to me the first postulate of a properly organized criticism.

It is vulgar for the critic to think of literature as a tiny palace of art looking out upon an inconceivably gigantic "life." "Life" should be for the critic only the seed-plot of literature, a vast mass of potential literary forms, only a few of which will grow up into the greater world of the verbal universe. Similar universes exist for all the arts. "We make to ourselves pictures of facts," says Wittgenstein, but by pictures he means representative illustrations, which are not pictures. Pictures as pictures are themselves facts, and exist only in a pictorial universe. It is easy enough to say that while the stars in their courses may form the subject of a poem, they will still remain the stars in their courses, forever outside poetry. But this is pure regression to the common field of experience, and nothing more; for the more strenuously we try to conceive the stars in their courses in non-literary ways, the more assuredly we shall fall into the idioms and conventions of some other mental universe. The conception of a constant external reality acts as a kind of censor principle in the arts. Painting has been much bedevilled by it, and much of the freakishness of modern painting is clearly due to the energy of its revolt against the representational fallacy. Music on the other hand has remained fairly free of it: at least no one, so far as I know, insists that it is flying in the face of common sense for music to do anything but reproduce the sounds heard in external nature. In literature the chief function of representationalism is to neutralize its opposing fallacy of an "inner" or subjective reality.

These different universes are presumably different ways of conceiving the same universe. What we call the common field of experience is a provisional means of unifying them on the level of sense-perception, and it is natural to infer a higher unity, a sort of beatification of common sense. But it is not easy to find any human language capable of reaching such exalted heights. If it is true, as is being increasingly asserted, that metaphysics is a system of verbal constructions with no direct reference to external criteria by means of which its truth or falsehood may be tested, it follows that metaphysics forms part of the verbal universe. Theology postulates an ultimate reality in God, but it does not assume that man is capable of describing it in his own terms, nor does it claim to be itself such a description. In any case, if we assert this final unity too quickly we may injure the integrity of the different means of approaching it. It does not help a poet much to tell him that the function of literature is to empty itself into an ocean of superverbal significance, when the nature of that significance is unknown.

Pure mathematics, we have said, does not relate itself directly to the common field of experience, but indirectly, not to avoid it, but with the ultimate design of swallowing it. It thus presents the appearance of a series of hypothetical possibilities. It by-passes the confirmation from without which is the goal of applied mathematics, and seeks it only from within: its conclusions are related primarily to its own premises. Literature also proceeds by hypothetical possibilities. The poet, said Sidney, never affirmeth. He never says "this is so"; he says "let there be such a situation," and poetic truth, the validity of his conclusion, is to be tested primarily by its coherence with his original postulate. Of course, there is applied literature, just as there is applied mathematics, which we test historically, by its lifelikeness, or philosophically, by the cogency of its propositions. Literature, like mathematics, is constantly useful, a word which means having a continuing relationship to the common field of experience. But pure literature, like pure mathematics, is disinterested, or useless: it contains its own meaning. Any attempt to determine the category of literature must start with a distinction between the verbal form which is primarily itself and the verbal form which is primarily related to something else. The former is a complex verbal fact, the latter a complex of verbal symbols.

We have to use the mathematical analogy once more before we leave it. Literature is, of course, dependent on the haphazard and unpredictable appearance of creative genius. So actually is mathematics, but we hardly notice this because in mathematics a steady consolidating process goes on, and the work of its geniuses is absorbed in the evolving and expanding pattern of the mathematical universe. Literature being as yet unorganized by criticism, it still appears as a huge aggregate or miscellaneous pile of creative efforts. The only organizing principle so far discovered in it is chronology, and when we see the miscellaneous pile strung out along a chronological line, some coherence is given to it by the linear factors in tradition. We can trace an epic tradition by virtue of the fact that Virgil succeeded Homer, Dante Virgil, and Milton Dante. But, as already suggested, this is very far from being the best we can do. Criticism has still to develop a theory of literature which will see this aggregate within a verbal universe, as forms integrated within a total form. An epic, besides occurring at a certain point in time, is also something of a definitive statement of the poet's imaginative experience, whereas a lyric is usually a more fragmentary one. This suggests the image of a kind of radiating circle of literary experience in which the lyric is nearer to a periphery and the epic nearer to a centre. It is only an image, but the notion that literature, like any other form of knowledge, possesses a centre and a circumference seems reasonable enough.

If so, then literature is a single body, a vast organically growing form, and, though of course works of art do not improve, yet it may be possible for criticism to see literature as showing a progressive evolution in time, of a kind rather like what Newman postulates for Catholic dogma. One could collect remarks by the dozen from various critics, many of them quite misleading, to show that they are dimly aware, on some level of consciousness, of the possibility of a critical progress toward a total comprehension of literature which no critical history gives any hint of. When Mr. Eliot says that the whole tradition of Western poetry from Homer down ought to exist simultaneously in the poet's mind, the adverb suggests a transcending by criticism of the tyranny of historical categories. I even think that the consolidation of literature by criticism into the verbal universe was one of the things that Matthew Arnold meant by culture. To begin this process seems to me the function of criticism at the present time.

Tzvetan Todorov 1939–

Born in Sofia, Bulgaria, Tzvetan Todorov attended the University of Sofia (M.A., 1961) and the University of Paris (Doctorat de Troisième Cycle, 1966; Doctorat des Lettres, 1970). He has been on the staff of the Centre National de la Recherche Scientifique in Paris since 1968. Todorov has been a pioneer in structuralism and much of his work has been translated into English and other languages. His books include *Literature and Signification* (1967), *The Fantastic: A Structural Approach to a Literary Genre* (1970), *The Poetics of Prose* (1971), *Introduction to Poetics* (1973), *Theories of the Symbol* (1973), and *The Conquest of America: The Question of the Other* (1982).

Todorov's structuralist approach to literature is evident in "The Uncanny and the Marvelous," the second chapter of *The Fantastic,* where his thesis is that the fantastic is a frontier between two adjacent genres: the uncanny (the supernatural explained) and the marvelous (the supernatural accepted). In keeping with his belief that literature is a vehicle in which language creates an internal system through a large, complex system of signs that produces structure, Todorov examines the differences and similarities between the fantastic, the uncanny, and the marvelous. In this essay he positions the genres in relation to one another in much the same way Saussure positions the elements of language in relation to other elements of language. He states that these three genres emphasize ambiguity and the supernatural but explains that the end of a work determines in which of the three categories that work falls. By defining each of the three categories and juxtaposing the uncanny and the marvelous with the fantastic, Todorov opens the door to further discussion of all three and also lays the foundation for his definition and discussion of the fantastic as a clearly defined genre based on structural criticism.

The Uncanny and the Marvelous

The fantastic, we have seen, lasts only as long as a certain hesitation: a hesitation common to reader and character, who must decide whether or not what they perceive derives from "reality" as it exists in the common opinion. At the story's end, the reader makes a decision even if the character does not; he opts for one solution or the other, and thereby emerges from the fantastic. If he decides that the laws of reality remain intact and permit an explanation of the phenomena described, we say that the work belongs to another genre: the uncanny. If, on the contrary, he decides that new laws of nature must be entertained to account for the phenomena, we enter the genre of the marvelous.

The fantastic therefore leads a life full of dangers, and may evaporate at any moment. It seems to be located on the frontier of two genres, the marvelous and the uncanny, rather than to be an autonomous genre. One of the great periods of supernatural literature, that of the Gothic novel, seems to confirm this observation. Indeed, we generally distinguish, within the literary Gothic, two tendencies: that of the supernatural explained (the "uncanny"), as it appears in the novels of Clara Reeves and Ann Radcliffe; and that of the supernatural accepted (the "marvelous"), which is characteristic of the works of Horace Walpole, M. G. Lewis, and Mathurin. Here we find not the fantastic in the strict sense, only genres adjacent to it. More precisely, the effect of the fantastic is certainly produced, but during only a portion of our reading: in Ann Radcliffe, up to the moment when we are sure that everything which has happened is susceptible of a rational explanation; in M. G. Lewis, up to the moment when we are sure that the supernatural events will receive *no* explanation. Once we have finished reading, we understand—in both cases—that what we call the fantastic has not existed.

We may ask how valid a definition of genre may be if it permits a work to "change genre" by a simple sentence like: "At this moment, he awakened and saw the walls of his room. . . ." But there is no reason not to think of the fantastic as an evanescent genre. Such a category, moreover, has nothing exceptional about it. The classic definition of the *present*, for example, describes it as a pure limit between the past and the future. The comparison is not gratuitous: the marvelous corresponds to an unknown phenomenon, never seen as yet, still to come—hence to a future; in the uncanny, on the other hand, we refer the inexplicable to known facts, to a previous experience, and thereby to the past. As for the fantastic itself, the hesitation which characterizes it cannot be situated, by and large, except in the present.

Here we also are faced with the problem of the work's unity. We take this unity as self-evident, and we assert that a sacrilege has been committed when cuts are made. But matters are probably more complicated; let us not forget that in school, where our first, and decisive, experience of literature occurred, we read only "selected passages" or "extracts" from most works. A certain fetishism of the book survives in our own day and age: the literary work is transformed both into a precious and motionless object and into a symbol of plentitude, and the act of cutting it becomes an equivalent of castration. How much freer was the attitude of a Khlebnikov, who composed his poems out of fragments of preceding poems and who urged his editors and even his printers to revise his text! Only an identification of the book with its author explains our horror of cuts.

If we do decide to proceed by examining certain parts of the work in isolation, we discover that by temporarily omitting the end of the narrative we are able to include a much larger number of texts within the genre of the fantastic. The modern (French or English) editions of *The Saragossa Manuscript* precisely confirm this: without its end, which resolves the hesitation, the book clearly belongs to the fantastic. Charles Nodier, one of the pioneers of the fantastic in France, thoroughly understood this, and deals with it in one of his tales, "Inès de las Sierras." This text consists of two apparently equal parts, and the end of the first part leaves us in utter perplexity: we are at a loss to explain the strange phenomena which occur; on the other hand, we are not as ready to admit the supernatural as we are to embrace the natural. The narrator hesitates between two procedures: to break off his narrative (and remain in the fantastic) or to continue (and abandon it). His own preference, he declares to his hearers, is to stop, with the following justification: "Any other outcome would be destructive to my story, for it would change its nature."

Yet it would be wrong to claim that the fantastic can exist only in a part of the work, for there are certain texts which sustain their ambiguity to the very end, i.e., even beyond the narrative itself. The book closed, the ambiguity persists. A remarkable example is supplied by Henry James' tale "The Turn of the Screw," which does not permit us to determine finally whether ghosts haunt the old estate, or whether we are confronted by the hallucinations of a hysterical governess victimized by the disturbing atmosphere which surrounds her. In French literature, Mérimée's tale "La Vénus d'Ille" affords a perfect example of this ambiguity. A statue seems to come alive and to kill the bridegroom; but we remain at the point of "seems," and never reach certainty.

Whatever the case, we cannot exclude from a scrutiny of the fantastic either the marvelous or the uncanny, genres which it overlaps. But we must not, on the other hand, forget Louis Vax's remark that "an ideal art of the fantastic must keep to indecision."

Let us take a closer look, then, at these two neighbors. We find that in each case, a transitory sub-genre appears: between the fantastic and the uncanny on the one hand, between the fantastic and the marvelous on the other. These sub-genres include works that sustain the hesitation characteristic of the true fantastic for a long period, but that ultimately end in the marvelous or in the uncanny. We may represent these subdivisions with the help of the following diagram:

uncanny	*fantastic-uncanny*	*fantastic-marvelous*	*marvelous*

The fantastic in its pure state is represented here by the median line separating the fantastic-uncanny from the fantastic-marvelous. This line corresponds perfectly to the nature of the fantastic, a frontier between two adjacent realms.

Let us begin with the fantastic-uncanny. In this sub-genre events that seem supernatural throughout a story receive a rational explanation at its end. If these events have long led the character and the reader alike to believe in an intervention of the supernatural, it is because they have an unaccustomed character. Criticism has described, and often condemned, this type under the label of "the supernatural explained."

Let us take as an example of the fantastic-uncanny the same *Saragossa Manuscript*. All of the "miracles" are explained rationally at the end of the narrative. Alfonso meets in a cave the hermit who had sheltered him at the beginning, and who is the grand sheik of the Gomélez himself. This man reveals the machinery of all the foregoing events:

> Don Emmanuel de Sa, the Governor of Cadiz, is one of the initiates. He had sent you Lopez and Moschite, who abandoned you at the spring of Alcornoques. . . . By means of a sleeping potion you were made to waken the next day under the gallows of the Zoto brothers. Whence you came to my hermitage, where you encountered the dreadful Pascheco, who is in fact a Basque dancer. . . . The following day, you were subjected to a far crueler ordeal: the false inquisition which threatened you with horrible tortures but did not succeed in shaking your courage.

Doubt had been sustained up to this point, as we know, between two poles: the existence of the supernatural and a series of rational explanations. Let us now enumerate the types of explanation that erode the case for the supernatural: first, accident or coincidence—for in the supernatural world, instead of chance there prevails what we might call "pandeterminism" (an explanation in terms of chance is what works against the supernatural in "Inès de las Sierras"); next, dreams (a solution proposed in *Le Diable Amoureux*); then the influence of drugs (Alfonso's dreams during the first night); tricks and prearranged apparitions (an essential solution in *The Saragossa Manuscript*); illusion of the senses (we shall find examples of this in Théophile Gautier's "La Morte Amoureuse" and John Dickson Carr's *The Burning Court*); and lastly madness, as in Hoffmann's "Princess Brambilla." There are obviously two groups of "excuses" here which correspond to the oppositions real/imaginary and real/illusory. In the first group, there has been no supernatural occurrence, for nothing at all has actually occurred: what we imagined we saw was only the fruit of a deranged imagination (dream, madness, the influence of drugs). In the second group, the events indeed occurred, but they may be explained rationally (as coincidences, tricks, illusions).

We recall that in the definitions of the fantastic cited above, the rational solution was decided as "completely stripped of internal probability" (Solovyov) or as a loophole "small enough to be unusable" (M.R. James). Indeed, the realistic solutions given in *The Saragossa Manuscript* or "Inès de las Sierras" are altogether improbable; supernatural solutions would have been, on the contrary, quite probable. The coincidences are too artificial in Nodier's tale. As for *The Saragossa Manuscript*, its author does not even try to concoct a credible ending: the story of the treasure, of the hollow mountain, of the empire of the Gomélez is more incredible than that of the women transformed into corpses! The probable is therefore not necessarily opposed to the fantastic: the former is a category that deals with internal coherence, with submission to the genre; the *fantastic* refers to an ambiguous perception shared by the reader and one of the characters. Within the genre of the fantastic, it is *probable* that "fantastic" reactions will occur.

In addition to such cases as these, where we find ourselves in the uncanny rather in spite of ourselves—in order to explain the fantastic—there also exists the uncanny in the pure state. In works that belong to this genre, events are related which may be readily accounted for by the laws of reason, but which are, in one way or another, incredible, extraordinary, shocking, singular, disturbing or unexpected, and which thereby provoke in the character and in the reader a reaction similar to that which works of the fantastic have made familiar. The definition is, as we see, broad and vague, but so is the genre which it describes: the uncanny is not a clearly delimited genre, unlike the fantastic. More precisely, it is limited on just one side, that of the fantastic; on the other, it dissolves into the general field of literature (Dostoievsky's novels, for example, may be included in the category of the uncanny). According to Freud, the sense of the uncanny is linked to the appearance of an image which originates in the childhood of the individual or the race (a hypothesis still to be verified; there is not an entire coincidence between Freud's use of the term and our own). The literature of horror in its pure state belongs to the uncanny—many examples from the stories of Ambrose Bierce could serve as examples here.

The uncanny realizes, as we see, only one

of the conditions of the fantastic: the description of certain reactions, especially of fear. It is uniquely linked to the sentiments of the characters and not to a material event defying reason. (The marvelous, by way of contrast, may be characterized by the mere presence of supernatural events, without implicating the reaction they provoke in the characters.)

Poe's tale "The Fall of the House of Usher" is an instance of the uncanny bordering on the fantastic. The narrator of this tale arrives at the house one evening summoned by his friend Roderick Usher, who asks him to stay for a time. Usher is a hypersensitive, nervous creature who adores his sister, now seriously ill. When she dies some days later, the two friends, instead of burying her, leave her body in one of the vaults under the house. Several days pass. On a stormy night the two men are sitting in a room together, the narrator reading aloud an ancient tale of chivalry. The sounds that are described in the chronicle seem to correspond to the noises they hear in the house itself. At the end, Roderick Usher stands up and says, in a scarcely audible voice: "We have put her living in the tomb!" And, indeed, the door opens, the sister is seen standing on the threshold. Brother and sister rush into each other's arms, and fall dead. The narrator flees the house just in time to see it crumble into the environing tarn.

Here the uncanny has two sources. The first is constituted by two coincidences (there are as many of these as in a work of the *supernatural explained*). Although the resurrection of Usher's sister and the fall of the house after the death of its inhabitants may appear supernatural, Poe has not failed to supply quite rational explanations for both events. Of the house, he writes: "Perhaps the eye of a scrutinizing observer might have discovered a barely perceptible fissure, which, extending from the roof of the building in front, made its way down the wall in a zigzag direction, until it became lost in the sullen waters of the tarn." And of Lady Madeline: "Frequent although transient affections of a partially cataleptical character were the unusual diagnosis." Thus the supernatural explanation is merely suggested, and one need not accept it.

The other series of elements that provoke the sense of the uncanny is not linked to the fantastic but to what we might call "an experience of limits," which characterizes the whole of Poe's *oeuvre*. Indeed, Baudelaire wrote of Poe: "No man has more magically described the *exceptions* of human life and of nature." Likewise Dostoievsky: "He almost always chooses the most exceptional reality, puts his character in the most exceptional situation, on the external or psychological level. . . ." (Poe, moreover, wrote a tale on this theme, a "meta-uncanny" tale entitled "The Angel of the Odd.") In "The Fall of the House of Usher," it is the extremely morbid condition of the brother and sister which disturbs the reader. In other tales, scenes of cruelty, delight in evil, and murder will provoke the same effect. The sentiment of the uncanny originates, then, in certain themes linked to more or less ancient taboos. If we grant that primal experience is constituted by transgression, we can accept Freud's theory as to the origin of the uncanny.

Thus the fantastic is ultimately excluded from "The Fall of the House of Usher." As a rule, we do not find the fantastic in Poe's works, in the strict sense, with the exception perhaps of "The Black Cat." His tales almost all derive their effect from the uncanny, and several from the marvelous. Yet Poe remains very close to the authors of the fantastic both in his themes and in the techniques that he applies.

We also know that Poe originated the detective story or murder mystery, and this relationship is not a matter of chance. It has often been remarked, moreover, that for the reading public, detective stories have in our time replaced ghost stories. Let us consider the nature of this relationship. The murder mystery, in which we try to discover the identity of the criminal, is constructed in the following manner: on the one hand there are several easy solutions, initially tempting but turning out, one after another, to be false; on the other, there is an entirely improbable solution disclosed only at the end and turning out to be the only right one. Here we see what brings the detective story close to the fantastic tale. Recalling Solovyov's and James's definitions, we note that the fantastic narrative, too, involves two solutions, one probable and supernatural, the other improbable and rational. It suffices, therefore, that in the detective story this second solution be so inaccessible as to "defy reason" for us to accept the existence of the supernatural rather than to rest with the absence of any explanation at all. A classical example of this situation is Agatha Christie's *Ten Little Indians*. Ten characters are isolated on an island; they are told (by a recording) that they will all die, punished for a crime which the law cannot punish. The nature of each death, moreover, is described in the counting-rhyme "Ten Little Indians." The doomed characters—and the reader along with them—vainly try to discover who is carrying out the successive executions. They are alone on the island and dying one after another, each in a fashion announced by the rhyme; down to the last one, who—and it is this that arouses an aura of the supernatural—does not commit suicide but is killed in his turn. No rational explanation seems possible; we must admit the existence of invisible beings or spirits. Obviously this hypothesis is not really necessary: the rational explanation will be given. The murder mystery approaches the fantastic, but it is also the contrary of the fantastic: in fantastic texts, we tend to prefer the supernatural explanation; the detective story, once it is over, leaves no doubt as to the absence of supernatural events. This relationship, moreover, is valid only for a certain type of detective story (the "sealed room") and a certain type of uncanny narrative (the "supernatural explained"). Further, the emphasis differs in the two genres: in the detective story, the emphasis is placed on the solution to the mystery; in the texts linked to the uncanny (as in the fantastic narrative), the emphasis is on the reactions which this mystery provokes. This structural proximity nonetheless produces a resemblance which we must take into account.

An author who deserves a more extended scrutiny when we deal with the relation between detective stories and fantastic tales is John Dickson Carr. Among his books there is one in particular which raises the problem in an exemplary fashion, *The Burning Court*. As in *Ten Little Indians*, we are confronted with an apparently insoluble problem: four men open a crypt in which a corpse had been placed a few days before; the crypt is empty, but it is not possible that anyone could have opened it in the meantime. Throughout the story, moreover, ghosts and supernatural phenomena are evoked. There is a witness to the crime that had taken place, and this witness asserts he has seen the murderess leave the victim's room, passing through the wall at a place where a door existed two hundred years earlier. Furthermore, one of the persons implicated in the case, a young woman, believes herself to be a witch, or more precisely, a poisoner (the murder was the result of poison) who belongs to a particular type of human beings, *the non-dead*: "Briefly, the non-dead are those persons—commonly women—who have been condemned to death for the crime of poisoning, and whose bodies have been burnt at the stake, whether alive or dead," we learn later on. While leafing through a manuscript he has received from the publishing house that he works for, Stevens, the young woman's husband, happens on a photograph whose caption reads: *Marie d'Aubray: Guillotined for Murder, 1861*. The text continues: "He was looking at a photograph of his own wife." How could this young woman, some seventy years later, be the same person as a famous nineteenth-century poisoner, guillotined into the bargain? Quite simply, according to Stevens' wife, who is ready to assume responsibility for the present murder. A series of further coincidences seems to confirm the presence of the supernatural. Finally, a detective arrives, and everything begins to be explained. The woman who had been seen passing through the wall was an optical illusion caused by a mirror. The corpse had not vanished after all, but was cunningly concealed. Young Marie Stevens had nothing in common with a long-dead poisoner, though an effort had been made to make her believe that she had. The entire supernatural atmosphere had been created by the murderer in order to confuse the case, to avert suspicion. The actual guilty parties are discovered, even if they are not successfully punished.

Then follows an epilogue, as a result of which *The Burning Court* emerges from the class of detective stories that simply evoke the supernatural, to join the ranks of the fantastic. We see Marie once again, in her house, thinking over the case; and the fantastic reemerges. Marie asserts once again (to the reader) that she is indeed the poisoner, that the detective was in fact her friend (which is not untrue), and that he has provided the entire rational explanation in order to save her ("It was clever of him to pluck a physical explanation, a thing of sizes and dimensions and stone walls").

The world of the non-dead reclaims its rights, and the fantastic with it: we are thrown back on our hesitation as to which solution to choose. But it must be noted, finally, that we are less concerned here with a resemblance between two genres than with their synthesis.

If we move to the *other* side of that median line which we have called the fantastic, we find ourselves in the fantastic-marvelous, the class of narratives that are presented as fantastic and that end with an acceptance of the supernatural. These are the narratives closest to the pure fantastic, for the latter, by the very fact that it remains unexplained, unrationalized, suggests the existence of the supernatural. The frontier between the two will therefore be uncertain; nonetheless, the presence or absence of certain details will always allow us to decide.

Gautier's "La Morte Amoureuse" can serve as an example. This is the story of a monk (Romuald) who on the day of his ordination falls in love with the courtesan Clarimonde. After several fleeing encounters, Romuald attends Clarimonde's deathbed—whereupon she begins to appear in his dreams, dreams that have a strange property: instead of conforming to impressions of each passing day, they constitute a continuous narrative. In his dreams, Romuald no longer leads the austere life of a monk, but lives in Venice in continuous revelry. And at the same time he realizes that Clarimonde has been keeping herself alive by means of blood she sucks from him during the night. . . .

Up to this point, all the events are susceptible of rational explanations. The explanations are largely furnished by the dreams themselves ("May God grant that it is a dream!" Romuald exclaims, in this resembling Alvaro in *Le Diable Amoureux*). Illusions of the senses furnish another plausible explanation. Thus: "One evening, strolling along the box-lined paths of my little garden, *I seemed to see* through the hedgerow a woman's shape . . ."; "For a moment *I thought* I saw her foot move . . ."; *"I do not know if this was an illusion or a reflection of the lamp, but it seemed* that the blood began to circulate once more beneath that lustreless pallor," etc. (italics mine). Finally, a series of events can be considered as simply uncanny and due to chance. But Romuald himself is ready to regard the matter as a diabolic intervention:

> The strangeness of the episode. Clarimonde's supernatural [!] beauty, the phosphorescent lustre of her eyes, the burning touch of her hand, the confusion into which she had thrown me, the sudden change that had occurred in me—all of this clearly proved the presence of the Devil; and that silken hand was perhaps nothing but the glove in which he had clad his talons.

It might be the Devil, indeed, but it might also be chance and no more than that. We remain, then, up to this point in the fantastic in its pure state. At this moment there occurs an event which causes the narrative to swerve. Another monk, Sérapion, learns (we do not know how) of Romuald's adventure. He leads the latter to the graveyard in which Clarimonde lies buried, unearths the coffin, opens it, and Clarimonde appears, looking just as she did on the day of her death, a drop of blood on her lips. . . . Seized by pious rage, Abbé Sérapion flings holy water on the corpse. "The wretched Clarimonde had no sooner been touched by the holy dew than her lovely body turned to dust; nothing was left but a shapeless mass of ashes and half-consumed bones." This entire scene, and in particular the metamorphosis of the corpse, cannot be explained by the laws of nature as they are generally acknowledged. We are here in the realm of the fantastic-marvelous.

A similar example is to be found in Villiers de l'Isle-Adam's "Véra." Here again, throughout the tale, we may hesitate between believing in life-after-death or thinking that the count who so believes is mad. But at the end, the count discovers the key to Véra's tomb in his own room, though he himself had flung it into the grave; it must therefore be Véra, his dead wife, who has brought it to him.

There exists, finally, a form of the marvelous in the pure state which—just as in the case of the uncanny in the pure state—has no distinct frontiers (we have seen in the preceding chapter that extremely diverse works contain elements of the marvelous). In the case of the marvelous, supernatural elements provoke no particular reaction in either the characters or in the implicit reader. It is not an attitude toward the events described which characterizes the marvelous, but the nature of these events.

We note, in passing, how arbitrary the old distinction was between form and content: the event, which traditionally belonged to "content," here becomes a "formal" element. The converse is also true: the stylistic (hence "formal") procedure of modalization can have, as we have seen in connection with *Aurélia*, a precise content.

We generally link the genre of the marvelous to that of the fairy tale. But as a matter of fact, the fairy tale is only one of the varieties of the marvelous, and the supernatural events in fairy tales provoke no surprise: neither a hundred years' sleep, nor a talking wolf, nor the magical gifts of the fairies (to cite only a few elements in Perrault's tales). What distinguishes the fairy tale is a certain kind of writing, not the status of the supernatural. Hoffmann's tales illustrate this difference perfectly: "The Nutcracker and the Mouse-King," "The Strange Child," and "The King's Bride" belong, by stylistic properties, to the fairy tale. "The Choice of a Bride," while preserving the same status with regard to the supernatural, is not a fairy tale at all. One would also have to characterize the *Arabian Nights* as marvelous tales rather than fairy tales (a subject which deserves a special study all its own).

In order to delimit the marvelous in the pure state, it is convenient to isolate it from several types of narrative in which the supernatural is somewhat justified.

1. We may speak first of all of *hyperbolic marvelous*. In it, phenomena are supernatural only by virtue of their dimensions, which are superior to those that are familiar to us. Thus in the *Arabian Nights* Sinbad the Sailor declares he has seen "fish one hundred and even two hundred ells long" or "serpents so great and so long that there was not one which could not have swallowed an elephant." But perhaps this is no more than a simple manner of speaking (we shall study this question when we deal with the poetic or allegorical interpretation of the text); one might even say, adapting a proverb, that "fear has big eyes." In any case, this form of the supernatural does not do excessive violence to reason.

2. Quite close to this first type of the marvelous is the *exotic marvelous*. In this type, supernatural events are reported without being presented as such. The implicit reader is supposed to be ignorant of the regions where the events take place, and consequently he has no reason for calling them into question. Sinbad's second voyage furnishes some excellent examples, such as the *roc*, a bird so tremendous that it concealed the sun and "one of whose legs . . . was as great as a great tree-trunk." Of course, this bird does not exist for contemporary zoology, but Sinbad's hearers were far from any such certainty and, five centuries later, Galland himself writes: "Marco Polo, in his travels, and Father Martini, in his *History of China*, speak of this bird," etc. A little later, Sinbad similarly describes the rhinoceros, which however is well known to us:

> There is, on the same island, a rhinoceros, a creature smaller than the elephant and larger than the buffalo: it bears a single horn upon its snout, about one ell long; this horn is solid and severed through the center, from one end to the other. Upon it may be seen white lines which represent the face of a man. The rhinoceros attacks the elephant, pierces it with its horn through the belly, carries it off and bears it upon its head; but when the elephant's blood flows over its eyes and blinds it, the rhinoceros falls to the ground, and—what will amaze you [indeed], the roc comes and bears off both creatures in its talons, in order to feed its young upon their bodies.

This virtuoso passages shows, by its mixture of natural and supernatural elements, the special character of the *exotic marvelous*. The mixture exists of course, only for the modern reader; the narrator implicit in the tale situates everything on the same level (that of the "natural").

3. A third type of the marvelous might be called the *instrumental marvelous*. Here we find the gadgets, technological developments unrealized in the period described but, after all, quite possible. In the "Tale of Prince Ahmed" in the *Arabian Nights*, for instance, the marvelous instruments are, at the beginning: a flying carpet, an apple that cures diseases, and a "pipe" for seeing great distances; today, the helicopter, antibiotics, and binoculars, endowed with the same qualities, do not belong in any way to the marvelous. The same is true of the flying horse in the "Tale of the Magic Horse." Similarly in the case of the revolving stone in the "Tale of Ali

Baba," we need only think of recent espionage films in which a safe opens only when its owner's voice utters certain words. We must distinguish these objects, products of human skill, from certain instruments that are often similar in appearance but whose origin is magical, and that serve to communicate with other worlds. Thus Aladdin's lamp and ring, or the horse in "The Third Calender's Tale," which belong to a different kind of marvelous.

4. The "instrumental marvelous" brings us very close to what in nineteenth-century France was called the *scientific marvelous*, which today we call *science fiction*. Here the supernatural is explained in a rational manner, but according to laws which contemporary science does not acknowledge. In the high period of fantastic narratives, stories involving magnetism are characteristic of the scientific marvelous: magnetism "scientifically" explains supernatural events, yet magnetism itself belongs to the supernatural. Examples are Hoffmann's "Spectre Bridegroom" or "The Magnetizer," and Poe's "The Facts in the Case of M. Valdemar" or Maupassant's "Un Fou?" Contemporary science fiction, when it does not slip into allegory, obeys the same mechanism: these narratives, starting from irrational premises, link the "facts" they contain in a perfectly logical manner. (Their plot structure also differs from that of the fantastic tale; we shall discuss science fiction plots in Chapter 10.)

All these varieties of the marvelous—"excused," justified, and imperfect—stand in opposition to the marvelous in its pure—unexplained—state. We shall not consider it here: first, because the elements of the marvelous, as themes, will be examined below in Chapters 7 and 8; and also because the aspiration to the marvelous, as an anthropological phenomenon, exceeds the context of a study limited to literary aspects. In any case, the marvelous has been, from this perspective, the object of several penetrating books; and in conclusion, I shall borrow from one of these, Pierre Mabille's *Miroir du Merveilleux*, a sentence which neatly defines the meaning of the marvelous:

> Beyond entertainment, beyond curiosity, beyond all the emotions such narratives and legends afford, beyond the need to divert, to forget, or to achieve delightful or terrifying sensations, the real goal of the marvelous journey is the total exploration of universal reality.

Mary Ellmann 19—

In *The Female Imagination*, author Patricia Meyer Spacks describes Mary Ellmann's rhetorical politics of "evasiveness" as "the triumph and limitation of *Thinking About Women*." Spacks identifies Ellmann's advocacy of evasiveness as "a primary resource of women in their social victimization." That same evasiveness of Ellmann's literary style obviously shapes her lifestyle as well. No biographical information is available on her beyond the fact that she was educated at the University of Massachusetts and at Yale and currently teaches at Oxford University. Her critical work includes articles on such authors as

John Barth, Nabokov, Joyce Carol Oates, Sylvia Plath, Rebecca West, and J.R.R. Tolkien, among others. "Phallic Criticism" is from her *Thinking About Women* (1968), a collection of essays that adds a remarkably trenchant perspective and spirited voice to the body of feminist criticism.

Phallic Criticism

This Neary that does not love Miss Counihan, nor need his Needle, any more, may he soon get over Murphy and find himself free, following his drift, to itch for an ape, or a woman writer.

—Samuel Beckett, *Murphy*

Through practice, begun when they begin to read, women learn to read about women calmly. Perhaps there have been some, but I have not heard of women who killed themselves simply and entirely because they were women.[1] They are evidently sustained by the conviction that I can never be They, by the fact that the self always, at least to itself, eludes identification with others. And, in turn, this radical separateness is fortified in some of us by phlegm, in others by vanity or most of all by ignorance (the uneducated are humiliated by class rather than by sex)—by all the usual defenses against self-loathing. Moreover, both men and women are now particularly accustomed, not so much to the resolution of issues, as to the proliferation of irreconcilable opinions upon them. In this intellectual suspension, it is possible for women, most of the time, to be more interested in what *is* said about them than in what presumably and finally *should* be said about them. In fact, none of them knows what should be said.

Their detachment is perhaps especially useful in reading literary criticism. Here, the opinions of men about men and of women about women are at least possibly esthetic, but elsewhere they are, almost inescapably, sexual as well. Like eruptions of physical desire, this intellectual distraction is no less frequent for being gratuitous as well. With a kind of inverted fidelity, the discussion of women's books by men will arrive punctually at the point of preoccupation, which is the fact of femininity. Books by women are treated as though they themselves were women, and criticism embarks, at its happiest, upon an intellectual measuring of busts and hips. Of course, this preoccupation has its engaging and compensatory sides.[2] Like such minor physical disorders as shingles and mumps, it often seems (whether or not it *feels* to the critic) comical as well as distressing. Then too, whatever intellectual risks this criticism runs, one of them is not abstraction. Any sexual reference, even in the most dryasdust context, shares the power which any reference to food has, of provoking fresh and immediate interest. As lunch can be mentioned every day without boring those who are hungry, the critic can always return to heterosexual (and, increasingly, to homosexual) relations and opinions with certainty of being read.

Admittedly, everyone is amused by the skillful wrapping of a book, like a negligee, about an author. Stanley Kauffmann opened a review of Françoise Sagan's *La Chamade* with this simile:

> Poor old Françoise Sagan. Just one more old-fashioned old-timer, bypassed in the rush for the latest literary vogue and for youth. Superficially, her career in America resembles the lifespan of those medieval beauties who flowered at 14, were deflowered at 15, were old at 30 and crones at 40.[3]

A superior instance of the mode—the play, for example, between *flowered* and *deflowered* is neat. And quite probably, of course, women might enjoy discussing men's books in similar terms. Some such emulative project would be diverting for a book season or two, if it were possible to persuade conventional journals to print its equivalent remarks. From a review of a new novel by the popular French novelist, François Sagan:

> Poor old François Sagan. . . . Superficially, his career in America resembles the life-span of those medieval troubadours who masturbated at 14, copulated at 15, were impotent at 30 and prostate cases at 40.

Somehow or other, No. It is not that male sexual histories, in themselves, are not potentially funny—even though they seem to be thought perceptibly less so than female sexual histories. It is rather that the literal fact of masculinity, unlike femininity, does not impose an erogenic form upon all aspects of the person's career.

I do not mean to suggest, however, that this imposition necessarily results in injustice. (Stanley Kauffmann went on to be more than just, *merciful* to Françoise Sagan.) In fact, it sometimes issues in fulsome praise. Excess occurs when the critic, like Dr. Johnson congratulating the dog who walked like a man, is impressed that the woman has—not so much written well, as written at all. But unfortunately, benign as this upright-pooch predisposition can be in the estimate of indifferent work, it can also infect the praise of work which deserves (what has to be called) asexual approval. In this case, enthusiasm issues in an explanation of the ways in which the work is free of what the critic ordinarily dislikes in the work of a woman. He had despaired of ever seeing a birdhouse built by a woman; now *here* is a birdhouse built by a woman. Pleasure may mount even to an admission of male envy of the work examined: an exceptionally sturdy birdhouse at that! In *Commentary*, Warren Coffey has expressed his belief that "a man would give his right arm to have written Flannery O'Connor's 'Good Country People'."[4] And here, not only the sentiment but the confidence with which the cliché is wielded, is distinctly phallic. It is as though, merely by thinking about Flannery O'Connor or Mrs. Gaskell or Harriet Beecher Stowe, the critic experienced acute sensations of his own liberty. The more he considers a feeble, cautious and timid existence, the more devil-may-care he seems to himself. This exhilaration then issues, rather tamely, in a daring to be commonplace.

And curiously, it often issues in expressions of contempt for delicate men as well. In this piece, for example, Flannery O'Connor is praised not only as a woman writer who writes as well as a man might wish to write, but also as a woman writer who succeeds in being less feminine than some men. She is less "girlish" than Truman Capote or Tennessee Williams.[5] In effect, once the critic's attention is trained, like Sweeney's, upon the Female Temperament, he invariably sideswipes at effeminacy in the male as well. The basic distinction becomes nonliterary: it is less between the book under review and other books, than between the critic and other persons who seem to him, regrettably, less masculine than he is. The assumption of the piece is that no higher praise of a woman's work exists than that such a critic should like it or think that other men will like it. The same ploy can also be executed in reverse. Norman Mailer, for example, is pleased to think that Joseph Heller's *Catch-22* is a man's book to read, a book which merely "puzzles" women. Women cannot comprehend male books, men cannot tolerate female books. The working rule is simple, basic: there must always be two literatures like two public toilets, one for Men and one for Women.

Sometimes it seems that no achievement can override this division. When Marianne Moore received the Poetry Society of America's Gold Medal for Poetry, she received as well Robert Lowell's encomium, "She is the best woman poet in English." The late Langston Hughes added, "I consider her the most famous Negro woman poet in America," and others would have enjoyed "the best blue-eyed woman poet." [6] Lowell has also praised Sylvia Plath's last book of poems, *Ariel*. His foreword begins:

> In these poems, written in the last months of her life and often rushed out at the rate of two or three a day, Sylvia Plath becomes herself, becomes something imaginary, newly, wildly and subtly created—hardly a person at all, or a woman, certainly not another "poetess," but one of those super-real, hypnotic, great classical heroines. The character is feminine, rather than female, though almost everything we customarily think of as feminine is turned on its head. The voice is now coolly amused, witty, now sour, now fanciful, girlish, charming, now sinking to the strident rasp of the vampire—a Dido, Phaedra, or Medea, who can laugh at herself as "cow-heavy and floral in my Victorian nightgown."

A little cloudburst, a short heavy rain of sexual references. The word *poetess*, whose gender killed it long ago, is exhumed—to be denied. Equivalently, a critic of W. H. Auden would be at pains, first of all, to deny that Auden is a poetaster. But *poetess* is only part of the general pelting away at the single fact that Sylvia Plath belonged to a sex (that inescapable membership) and that her sex was not male—*woman, heroines, feminine, female, girlish, fanciful, charming, Dido, Phaedra, Medea. Vampire*, too. And it would of course be this line, "Cow-heavy and floral in my Victorian nightgown," which seizes attention first and evokes the surprised pleasure of realizing that Sylvia Plath "can laugh at herself." Self-mockery, particularly sexual self-mockery, is not expected in a woman, and it is irresistible in the criticism of women to describe what was expected: the actual seems to exist only in relation to the preconceived.

Lowell's distinction between *feminine* and *female* is difficult, though less difficult, than a distinction between *masculine* and *male* would be—say, in an introduction to Blake's *Songs of Innocence*. What helps us with the first is our all knowing, for some time now, that femaleness is a congenital fault, rather like eczema or Original Sin. An indicative denunciation, made in 1889: "They are no ladies. The only word good enough for them is the word of opprobrium—females." But fortunately, some women can be saved. By good manners, they are translated from females into ladies; and by talent, into feminine creatures (or even into "classical heroines"). And we are entirely accustomed to this generic mobility on their part: the individual is assumed into the sex and loses all but typical meaning within it. The emphasis is finally macabre, as though women wrote with breasts instead of pens—in which event it would be remarkable, as Lowell feels that it is, if one of them achieved ironic detachment.

When the subject of the work by a woman

is also women (as it often has to be, since everyone has to eat what's in the cupboard), its critical treatment is still more aberrant. Like less specialized men, critics seem to fluctuate between attraction and surfeit. An obsessive concern with femininity shifts, at any moment, into a sense of being confined or suffocated by it. In the second condition, a distaste for books *before they are read* is not uncommon, as in Norman Mailer's unsolicited confession of not having been able to read Virginia Woolf, or in Anthony Burgess's inhibitory "impression of high-waisted dresses and genteel parsonage flirtation" [7] in Jane Austen's novels. More luckily, the work may be patronized by mild minds already persuaded that the human temperament combines traits of both sexes and that even masculine natures may respond, through their subterranean femininity, to the thoroughly feminine book.

A similar indulgence is fostered by any association, however tenuous, which the critic forms between the woman writer and some previous student of his own.[8] Now that almost everyone who writes teaches too, the incidence of this association is fairly high. Robert Lowell remembers that Sylvia Plath once audited a class of his at Boston University:

> She was never a student of mine, but for a couple of months seven years ago, she used to drop in on my poetry seminar at Boston University. I see her dim against the bright sky of a high window, viewless unless one cared to look down on the city outskirts' defeated yellow brick and square concrete pillbox filling stations. She was willowy, long-waisted, sharp-elbowed, nervous, giggly, gracious—a brilliant tense presence embarrassed by restraint. Her humility and willingness to accept what was admired seemed at times to give her an air of maddening docility that hid her unfashionable patience and boldness.[9]

It is not easy, of course, to write about a person whom one knew only slightly in the past. The strain is felt here, for example, in the gratuitous street scene from the classroom window. And in general, there is a sense of physical recollection emended by a much later intellectual and poetic impression. The "brilliant tense presence" of the final poetry is affixed, generously enough, to the original figure of a young girl. The "maddening docility" too must have been a sexual enlargement, now reduced to an "air" of docility, since again the poems demonstrate the artistic (rather than "feminine") union of "patience and boldness." (Elsewhere they are, according to Lowell, "modest" poems too, they are uniquely "modest" *and* "bold.") But then the poet Anne Sexton's recollections, which originate in the same poetry seminar, make no reference to elbows or giggles or docility. Miss Sexton seems to have seen even at that time a woman entirely congruous with her later work. After class, the two used to drink together—at the Ritz bar, some distance away from those "concrete pillbox filling stations"—and conduct workmanlike discussions of suicidal techniques:

> *But suicides have a special language.*
> *Like carpenters they want to know* which
>   tools.
> *They never ask* why build.
>
> ("Wanting to Die")[10]

Lowell seems honestly caught between two ways of comprehending what exists outside the self. And certainly there is nothing of the stag posture about his remarks, no pretense of writing only for other men about women. All critics are of course secretly aware that no literary audience, except perhaps in Yemen, is any longer restricted to men. The man's-man tone is a deliberate archaism, coy and even flirtatious, like wearing spats. No one doubts that some silent misogyny may be dark and deep, but written misogyny is now generally a kind of chaffing, and not frightfully clever, gambit. For the critic in this style, the writer whose work is most easily related to established stereotypes of femininity is, oddly, the most welcome. What-to-say then flows effortlessly from the stereotypes themselves. The word *feminine* alone, like a grimace, expresses a displeasure which is not less certain for its being undefined. In a review of Fawn Brodie's biography of Sir Richard Burton, *The Devil Drives*, Josh Greenfeld remarked on the "feminine biographer's attachment to subject," and suggested that this quality (*or else* a "scholarly objectivity") prevented Mrs. Brodie's conceding Burton's homosexuality.[11] So her book is either too subjective or too objective: we will never know which.

But the same word can be turned upon men too. John Weightman has remarked that Genet's criminals cannot play male and female effectively because "a convicted criminal, however potent, has been classified as an object, and therefore feminized, by society."[12] An admirably simple social equation: a man in prison amounts to a woman. Similarly, *feminine* functions as an eight-letter word in the notorious Woodrow Wilson biography by Freud and William Bullitt. At one heated point, Clemenceau calls Wilson feminine, Wilson calls Clemenceau feminine, then both Freud and Bullitt call Wilson feminine again. The word means that all four men thoroughly dislike each other. It is also sufficient for Norman Mailer to say that Herbert Gold reminds him "of nothing so much as a woman writer,"[13] and for Richard Gilman to consign Philip Roth to the "ladies' magazine" level.[14] In fact, chapters of *When She Was Good* were first published, and seemed to settle in snugly, at the *haut bourgeois* level of *Harper's* and the *Atlantic*. But, except perhaps in the *Daily Worker*, the consciousness of class is less insistent than that of sex: the phrase "ladies' magazine" is one of those which refuses not to be written once a month.[15]

But at heart most of these "the-ladies-bless-them" comments are as cheerful and offhand as they are predictable. When contempt, like anything else, has an assigned route to follow, and when it is accustomed to its course, it can proceed happily. This is evident, for example, in Norman Mailer's lively, even jocular, essay on the deplorable faults of Mary McCarthy's *The Group*. What accounts for these high spirits, except the fact that Mailer rejoices in what he spanks so loudly? The pleasure lies in Mary McCarthy's having capitulated, as it seems to Mailer, having at last written what he can securely and triumphantly call a female novel.[16] Not that Mailer's treatment of *The Group*, even in these familiar terms, is not still remarkable—even frightening, and that is a rare treat in criticism. One does not expect a disdain for feminine concerns, which is entirely commonplace, to mount to cloacal loathing. Mary McCarthy has soiled an abstraction, a genre, the novel-yet-to-be: "Yes, Mary deposited a load on the premise, and it has to be washed all over again, this little long-lived existential premise."[17]

But few rise to that kind of washing-up with Mailer's alacrity. In most critics, revulsion is an under-developed area. What rouses a much more interesting hostility in many is the work which does not conform to sexual preconception. That is, if feminine concerns can be found, they are conventionally rebuked; but their absence is shocking. While all women's writing should presumably strive for a suprafeminine condition, it is profoundly distrusted for achieving it. So for all Anthony Burgess's resistance to Jane Austen, he is still less pleased by George Eliot

("The male impersonation is wholly successful") or by Ivy Compton-Burnett ("A big sexless nemesic force"). Similarly, he cannot leave alone what strikes him as the contradiction between Brigid Brophy's appearance and her writing.[18] His review of her book of essays, *Don't Never Forget*, opens in this sprightly manner:

> An American professor friend of mine, formerly an admirer of Miss Brophy's work, could no longer think of her as an author once he'd seen her in the flesh. "That girl was made for love," he would growl. Various writers who have smarted from her critical attentions might find it hard to agree.[19]

It is as though Elizabeth Hardwick, asked to review William Manchester's *Death of a President*, was obliged to refuse, growling, "That man was made for love." The same notion of an irreconcilable difference between the nature of woman and the mind of man prompts the hermaphroditic fallacy according to which one half the person, separating from the other half, produces a book by binary fission. So Mary McCarthy has been complimented, though not by Norman Mailer, on her "masculine mind" while, through the ages, poor Virgil has never been complimented on his "effeminacy." (Western criticism begins with this same tedious distinction—between manly Homer and womanish Virgil.) At the same time, while sentiment is a disadvantage, the alternative of feminine coolness is found still more disagreeable. Mary McCarthy used to be too *formidable*, Jean Stafford has sometimes been *clinical*, and others (going down, down) are *perverse*, *petulant*, *catty*, *waspish*.

The point is that comment upon Violette Leduc, who is not directly assertive, will be slurring; but the slur hardens into resentment of those writers who seem to endorse the same standards of restraint and reason which the critic presumably endorses. If for nothing else, for her tolerance of Sade, Simone de Beauvoir must be referred to (scathingly!) as "the lady," and then even her qualifications of tolerance must be described as a reluctance "to give herself unreservedly" to Sade.[20] Similarly, it is possible that much of the voluble male distaste for Jane Austen is based, not upon her military limitations (her infamous failure to discuss the Napoleonic Wars), but upon her antipathetic detachment. So a determined counteremphasis was first placed by her relatives, and has been continued since by most of her critics, upon her allegiance to domestic ideals—when, in fact, she is read only for her mockery of them.

What seems to be wanted, insisted upon, is the critic's conception of women expressed in his conception of feminine terms—that is, confirmation of the one sex's opinions by the imagination of the other, a difficult request which can seldom be gratified. It is perhaps this request which explains Louis Auchincloss's erratic view of Mary McCarthy in his *Pioneers and Caretakers*. Suddenly she is sister to Ellen Glasgow and Sarah Orne Jewett, as one of our feminine "caretakers of the culture," a guise in which few other readers can easily recognize her. But if one's thesis is sexual, the attachment of women to the past and the incapacity of women for "the clean sweep," then Mary McCarthy only seems to hate a few present things and actually loves many past things. One might as well argue that it was Swift's finding babies so sweet that made him think of eating them for dinner.

The vague and ominous critical implications of femininity, with which we generally make do now, were more precisely defined by Walter Pater:

> Manliness in art, what can it be, as distinct from that which in opposition to it must be called the feminine quality there,—what but a full consciousness of what one does, of art itself in the work of art, tenacity of intuition and of consequent purpose, the spirit of construction as opposed to what is literally incoherent or ready to fall to pieces, and, in opposition to what is hysteric or works at random, the maintenance of a standard. Of such art ήθος rather than πάθος will be the predominant mood. To use Plato's own expression, there will be here no παραλειπόμενα, no "negligences," no feminine forgetfulness of one's self, nothing in the work of art unconformed to the leading intention of the artist, who will but increase his power by reserve. An artist of this kind will be apt, of course, to express more than he seems actually to say. He economizes. He will not spoil good things by exaggeration. The rough, promiscuous wealth of nature he reduces to grace and order: reduces, it may be, lax verse to staid and temperate prose. With him, the rhythm, the music, the notes, will be felt to follow, or rather literally accompany as ministers, the sense,—ἀκολουθειν τόν λόγον.[21]

The intellectual consequences of unmanliness are prodigal. The feminine is the not fully conscious, not fully assembled, the intemperate, incoherent, hysterical, extravagant and capricious. In the rush of his contrasts, Pater comes to the verge of dismissing poetry: "verse" is a slut, and "staid, temperate prose" is a don. A limited view of the two forms, but understandable in the light of Pater's own twin employments as lecturer on the Renaissance and prose stylist. "The rough, promiscuous wealth of nature" anticipates (unlikely as any association between the two may seem) such a later fancy as Leslie Fiedler's image of the sculpture as male, and the tree out of which the sculpture is carved, as female. Here too, male art imposes form upon female nature. The homosexual contrast is between two possible partners: *nature*, the coarse, indiscriminate and blowsy woman, and *art*, the ordered, graceful and exquisite boy.

Pater foreshadows our present situation, however, in that his concern for "manliness" in art expends itself as much upon the contraindications to masculinity as upon its intrinsic properties. We are now wholly familiar with this emphasis upon the difficulties, rather than the capacities, of the male artist. The same emphasis has, in fact, mounted now to a sense of armies fighting openly against his accomplishment. Danger is unanimously confirmed, only its nature or origin is less agreed upon. Philip Roth has suggested the increasing difficulty of fiction's competing with actuality. What political novelist, he asks, could *imagine* Eisenhower, who yet seems an effect casually thrown off by society? Reality, then, is inimical to the writer, having itself grown incomparably fantastic. On the other hand, Saul Bellow argues that the writer is impeded by literary intellectuals whose respect for past achievements depresses present efforts. And Norman Mailer finds that it is ubiquitous corruption which prevents art. In architecture, for example:

> There is so much corruption in the building codes, overinflation in the value of land, featherbedding built into union rules, so much graft, so much waste, so much public relations, and so much emptiness that no one tries to do more with the roof than leave it flat.[22]

Mailer is forever Gothic and aspirant, possessed by a vision of renewal and of total accomplishment. But meanwhile hostile forces remain in the ascendancy, suppressing and flattening talent. The threat of these forces steadily diverts the writer—not from writing, but from writing what he would write if he did not feel threatened. In self-defense, he does quasi-military exercises for writing in the future, a kind of shadow-typing until the date is set for a real match. For the time being, communiqués are issued, protesting the present and improper circumstances of art and thereby adding to them—rather as people bang on their ceilings to make the upstairs people stop banging on their floors.

I do not mean to underestimate this conviction on the part of many writers that they live among strangers and aliens. On the contrary, I am alienated in turn by the habitual identification of this complex and all-encompassing enmity with the relatively narrow circumstance of sexuality. It is through this identification that phallic criticism regularly and rapidly shifts from writing by women, which can be dismissed as innocuous, to their vicious influence upon writing by men. It is clear that sexual conflict has become the specific focus, literal as well as metaphoric, of a general and amorphous sense of intellectual conflict. A simple instance is this last novel of Philip Roth's, *When She Was Good,* in which a pimple of a young woman is created only to be squeezed, interminably, to death—a small self-gratification which none of us would deny each other, but still prefer not to witness. And yet this tiny tumor, this Emma Bovary in galoshes, is supposed to define the Morality of the Middle West. Nothing much must stand for everything.

But the metaphoric focus is ordinarily more interesting. The capacity to write, even as it is held more and more precariously, is made synonymous with sexual capacity, whereupon the woman becomes the enemy of both. She appears as the risk that the writer has to take, or the appetite, at once sluggish and gargantuan, which must be roused and then satisfied in order to prove that the writer is capable of giving satisfaction of any kind. So she is all that offers stubborn and brute resistance to achievement even as she is its only route. Her range is limitless, all internal obstacle as well as external impediment, all that within the writer himself may prevent his accomplishing his aim—weakness, dullness, caution, fear, dishonesty, triviality.

At the crudest level of this metaphoric struggle, the writer finds his professional and sexual activities incompatible, on the grounds of the distribution of resources. This anxiety seems distinctly modern. The association of the two faculties, intellectual and sexual, is ancient, but the expressed inability to reconcile them is recent. Blake, for example, celebrated "the lineaments of gratified desire," and seemed to sense no contradiction between them and artistic gratification. In fact, he considered sexual intercourse, rather like having breakfast or a walk in the garden, an essential prelude to composition. Hemingway, instead, found a young writer to warn against making love during periods of composition: the best ideas would be lost in bed. An intense frugality has set in, a determination not to squander vital spirits. Goods produced or released by the self, like semen and words, become oddly equivalent and interdependent. The Samson law: the consumption or removal of one product, particularly by a woman, must inevitably diminish another. Naturally then, the minds which so balance the books of themselves frequently remark upon the materiality of women. The impression is deflected from their own sense of possessing a warehouse of scarce, conglomerate materials, all subtracting strength from each other, and all consequently in need of vigilant supervision. A loss of all one's buttons will inevitably mean a strain on one's supply of safety pins. A fear of insufficiency develops, a terror of running out. All sexual difficulties have therefore shifted in fiction from women to men, from feminine barrenness to masculine impotence or sterility or utter indifference. The women are uniformly and insatiably greedy (again, of course, in fiction) for conception. The men cannot afford to give them, indiscriminately, all the children they demand. The expenditure could only mean their going, as writers, into debtors' prison.

And yet there is an opposite dilemma: the testing of talent is confounded with the testing of sexual resources. Both must engage themselves, even though each engagement risks depletion or failure. In this metaphoric distortion, the actual energy and excess of nature is forgotten or does not convince. The rich, against all reason, describe their poverty, and every spermatozoon stands for an item of talent, infinitesimal and yet precious. It is all like (a literary) India, where men are commonly convinced of the debilitating consequences of intercourse even as the population increases by a million a month. In such a context, Milton's old cause for concern,

> And that one talent which is death to hide
> Lodged with me useless,

seems cavalier—at least the talent is eager and impatient. Instead now, the cause of death seems to be the extravagant and unguarded employment of talent. It should be housed and protected and kept ready for a crucial moment in the indefinite future. And this future engagement is envisaged as a quarrel which the fighter-lover-writer will probably lose, or (at best) a prize of which he will probably be cheated. The possibility of failure, either of one's own nerve or of the other's loyalty, is always present. The best preparation is to stockpile animosity. In this connection, Norman Mailer has described one of the prize fighter Harry Greb's "training methods":

> That is, before he had a fight he would go to a brothel, and he would have two prostitutes, not one, taking the two of them into the same bed. And this apparently left him feeling like a wild animal. Don't ask me why. Perhaps he picked the two meanest whores in the joint and so absorbed into his system all the small, nasty, concentrated evils which had accumulated from carloads of men. Greb was known as the dirtiest fighter of his time.[23]

The thin chance held by the fighting talent is intertwined with sexual chance, and the possibilities of subversion or treachery are contained, like mutated ova, in the female. The commonplace sexual fiction must now regularly describe a man—preferably gifted, but a fool will do in a pinch—who cannot get his work done because he is involved with a deficient woman. His abilities are either wasted on her stupidity or poisoned by her malice. No one, again, distrusted women more than Milton, and yet it was possible for him to retain a conception of at least a sombre accord, founded upon an unremitting discipline.

> Therefore God's universal law
> Gave to the man despotic power
> Over his female in due awe,
> Nor from that right to part an hour
> Smile she or lour:
> So shall he least confusion draw
> On his whole life, not swayed
> By female usurpation, nor dismayed.
> (*Samson Agonistes*,
> II.1053–60)

Occasionally, Mailer attempts the terms of this past coexistence: "she had fled the domination which was liberty for her" ("The Time of Her Time"), but this is only in bed and besides the mood has collapsed. Allowed domination, or at least imaginative domination, Milton also furnished confident images of fructification. The abyss upon which the Holy Ghost broods (rather like a *hen*) is vast and yet yielding to impregnation. The abyss for Mailer is an enticing image of terror, an irresistible descent into horror. At best, it is like a point on Bunyan's map, a Pit of Responsibility. The writer descends to face truths which will diminish previous self-estimations.

Women are waiting in this pit, like large, pallid insects under stones, and whatever grace—or rather *significance,* there must always be some moral significance—the sexual encounter retains is at once masculine and dour: it is a test of courage, a persistence in the face of disgust. Conception is difficult: either the spermatozoa are wasted (thrown away! squandered! from fortune to farm) on contraceptives or they must be assisted by fury: "Satan, if it takes your pitchfork up my gut, let me blast a child into this bitch."[24] And yet these encounters are more intellectual than physical statements, since the effect upon women is premonitory of the effect upon words, of failure (always the more likely) or success in writing: "Every child is a poem someone conceived in short space."[25] (Conceived? Then a *poetess* is meant?) So the hero of Mailer's story, "The Time of Her Time," Sergius O'Shaughnessy, attaches symbolic meaning to his (hardly unparalleled) effort to bring his partner to orgasm. Achieving that, ". . . it was more likely that I would win the next time I gambled my stake on something more appropriate for my ambition."

The concept of femininity is static and resistant, that of masculinity at once dynamic and striving:

> Masculinity is not something given to you, something you're born with, but something you gain. And you gain it by winning small battles with honor. Because there is very little honor left in American life, there is a certain built-in tendency to destroy masculinity.[26]

That is, it is difficult not only to pass a test but to find a test to pass. Everything conspires to make occasions of courage, in the formal and stylized sense of such occasions in the past, hard to come by. Hemingway was reduced to fighting fish, and the only land test in constant supply is fighting females. So armed intercourse must subsume all other single tournaments. In *An American Dream,* the mythomaniac Rojack combats social evil with his honorable penis, cousin to Sergius O'Shaughnessy's chivalric "avenger." And like O'Shaughnessy, Rojack scores by sodomy, his only way with a German housemaid of rebuking the immense social horror of Nazism.

But the avenger-writer, even as he engages with the enemy, risks deception. If the whore-novel (with her "feminine taste for the mortal wound") is not quite deadly, she is always at least devious:

> Every novelist who has slept with the Bitch (only poets and writers of short stories have a *Muse*) comes away bragging afterward like a G.I. tumbling out of a whorehouse spree—"Man, I made her moan," goes the cry of the young writer. But the Bitch laughs afterward in her empty bed. "He was so sweet in the beginning," she declares, "but by the end he just went, 'Peep, peep, peep.' "[27]

The sympathetic role is shuffled: the writer is the Orpheus now, too vulnerable or too impressionable not to be victimized by the cruelties of inspiration. Or deluded into vanity by false success. And worse, in having to deal with dishonesty, writers may grow dishonest too. The Bitch is full of "swilling crafts" by which they can be contaminated. The vision, then, must be of an achievement beyond craft, something wildly and spontaneously pure, beyond practice or calculation or skill. If a writer is always in training, it is nevertheless in order to accomplish something in the end which is quite alien to training. It is as though one prepared regularly, through sexual promiscuity, for the future assumption of an absolute virginity.

At the lowest level of writing as sexual act, in pornography, the exercise is frankly masturbatory. But actually, in any persistent association of the two experiences, even a metaphoric association, the impression of onanism (which is perhaps appropriate to writing) is inescapable. Mailer has almost forgiven J. D. Salinger's *Raise High the Roof Beam, Carpenters*, in these terms:

> Now, all of us have written as badly. There are nights when one comes home after a cancerously dull party, full of liquor but not drunk, leaden with boredom, somewhere out of Fitzgerald's long dark night. Writing at such a time is like making love at such a time. It is hopeless, it desecrates one's future, but one does it anyway because at least it is an act.[28]

Here, the "act" of making love is as solitary as the act of defecating or of writing, or, for that matter, of dying. ("Herr Hemingway, can you sum up your feelings about death?" and Herr Hemingway: "Yes—just another whore.") All that seems active outside the impacted consciousness, and therefore all that can pierce it, is time: hence, that familiar anxiety for abstractions like the genre or the "future." The only sensation attributed to concrete forms outside the self is implacability, an obscure inimical urge to resist domination. But some signature must be left upon these surroundings, some exertion made, even hopelessly. Encircled by blank forms, one fills them out, one writes over them. In that sense, composition and copulation are now considered identical twins.

Notes

1. Men, however, have been known to kill themselves for this reason. Otto Weininger, the German author of *Sex and Character*, killed himself because of the femininity which he ascribed to Jews, of whom he was one.

2. It has an unnerving side as well, though this appears less often in criticism, I think, than in fiction or poetry. For example, James Dickey's poem "Falling" expresses an extraordinary concern with the underwear of a woman who has fallen out of an airplane. While this woman, a stewardess, was in the airplane, her girdle obscured, to the observation of even the most alert passenger, her mesial groove. The effect was, as the poem recalls, "monobuttocked." As the woman falls, however, she undresses and "passes her palms" over her legs, her breasts, and "deeply between her thighs." Beneath her, "widowed farmers" are soon to wake with futile (and irrelevant?) erections. She lands on her back in a field, naked, and dies. The sensation of the poem is necrophilic: it mourns a vagina rather than a person crashing to the ground.

3. Stanley Kauffmann, "Toujours Tristesse," *New Republic*, October 29, 1966, p. 2.

4. Warren Coffey, *Commentary*, November 1965, p. 98.

5. Though Tennessee Williams is cited here to enhance Flannery O'Connor's virtues, he is just as easily cited to prove other women's defects. For example, Dr. Karl Stern has resorted to Williams and Edward Albee as witnesses to the modern prevalence of the Castrating Woman. (*Barat Review*, January 1967, p. 46) Naturally, in this context, both playwrights assume a status of unqualified virility.

6. Miss Moore's femininity leaves her vulnerable even to the imagination of John Berryman:

> Fancy a lark with Sappho,
> a tumble in the bushes with Miss Moore,
> a spoon with Emily, while Charlotte glare.
> Miss Bishop's too noble-O.

("Four Dream Songs," *Atlantic,* February 1968, p. 68.)

7. *New York Times Book Review,* December 4, 1966, p. 1.

8. For the especial amicability of this sexual relationship, see "The Student," p. 119.

9. Foreward to Sylvia Plath's *Ariel,* p. xi.

10. Anne Sexton, "The barfly ought to sing," *Tri-Quarterly,* Fall 1966, p. 90.

11. *Book Week,* May 28, 1967, p. 2. Mrs. Brodie had still more trouble in the *Times Literary Supplement* (January 11, 1968, p. 32), where her nationality as well as her sex was at fault: "So immense is this gulf, so inalienably remote are the societies that produced biographer and subject, *so difficult is it, even now, for a woman to get beneath a man's skin,* that only some imaginative genius could really have succeeded in the task Mrs. Brodie so boldly undertook." [My italics.]

12. *New York Review of Books,* August 24, 1967, p. 8.

13. *Advertisements for Myself,* p. 435.

14. Richard Gilman, "Let's Lynch Lucy," *New Republic,* June 24, 1967, p. 19.

15. The phrase is at least sociologically interesting: it suggests the impossibility of remarking that some bad novel is fit for the "men's magazines." For fiction, there is none. At the same level of intelligence and cultivation, women evidently prefer stories (*McCall's, Redbook, The Ladies' Home Journal,* etc.) and men prefer facts (or quasi-facts) and photographs (*Time, Life, Look, Dude, Gent,* etc.). *Playboy* is exceptional in presupposing an eclectic male audience (does it exist?) for both photographs *and* fiction.

16. A female novel, Mailer indicates, is one which deals with the superficial details of women's lives instead of their lower depths. Such a book is at once tedious and cowardly. On the other hand, Joseph Heller's *Catch-22* is a book for men (rather than a male novel) which deals with the superficial details of men's lives. It speaks, according to Mailer, to the man who "prefers to become interested in quick proportions and contradictions; in the practical surface of things." Both novels, then, are tedious but the first is a disgrace while the second has "a vast appeal." Obviously, it all depends on which practical surface of things the commentator himself is glued to.

17. *Cannibals and Christians,* p. 138.

18. Burgess has also furnished this country, in a "Letter from London" (*Hudson Review,* Spring 1967), the following couplet:

> People who read Brigid Brophy
> Should contend for the Krafft-Ebing Trophy.

In fact, he seems unfailingly exhilarated by Miss Brophy's faults, thrilled by them as Norman Mailer is by Mary McCarthy's. Burgess's most recent agitation was a review of *Fifty Works of English Literature We Could Do Without* (by Miss Brophy, Michael Levey and Charles Osborne): "The authors are now rubbing themselves in an ecstasy of the kind granted only to Exclusive Brethren." (*Encounter,* August 1967, p. 71.)

19. *Manchester Guardian Weekly,* November 24, 1966, p. 11. There is, incidentally, an American Professor who exists only in the minds of English journalists. The *Times Literary Supplement* would be halved without him.

20. Leslie Schaeffer, *New Republic,* August 19, 1967, p. 28.

21. Walter Pater, "Plato's Esthetics," *Plato and Platonism* (New York, 1899), pp. 253–54. The only term associated with women which Pater seems to have enjoyed was preg*nancy,* and that only in references to men instead: Goethe, then in all the pregnancy of his wonderful youth. . . ." (*The Renaissance*, Cleveland and New York, The World Publishing Co., 1961, p. 193.)

22. *Cannibals and Christians*, p. 234.

23. *Cannibals and Christians*, p. 217.

24. *An American Dream*, p. 240.

25. *Cannibals and Christians*, p. 202.

26. *Cannibals and Christians*, p. 201.

27. *Cannibals and Christians*, p. 107. From this it follows, as the belch the gas, that "a good novelist can do without everything but the remnant of his balls." (*Advertisements for Myself*, p. 435.)

28. *Cannibals and Christians*, pp. 123–24.

Barbara T. Christian 1943–

Barbara T. Christian received her B.A. from Marquette University and her M.A. and Ph.D. from Columbia University. She has been extensively involved in developing and implementing programs directed at America's underprivileged and undervalued, including the SEEK program at City College in New York for disadvantaged black and Puerto Rican students and numerous projects for black and women's communities in and around Berkeley. She was the first black woman to receive tenure at the University of California at Berkeley, where she presently teaches. She has written and edited numerous books, including *Black Women Novelists: The Development of a Tradition* (1983); *Teaching Guide to Accompany Black Foremothers: Three Lives* (1980); *Black Feminist Criticism: Perspectives on Black Women Writers* (1985); *and From the Inside Out: Afro-American Women's Literacy and the State* (1987).

In "Images of Black Women in Afro-American Literature," Barbara Christian begins the work of articulating the tradition of Afro-American women writers. She does so by discussing—chronologically—the writings of several black women authors: Zora Neal Hurston, Gwendolyn Brooks, Paule Marshall, Nikki Giovanni, and Toni Morrison. As Christian herself recognizes, her essay is not exhaustive—the tradition she alludes to requires more extensive and rigorous analysis. Yet her essay celebrates "the diversity of the black woman's experience in America, what she has made of it and how she is transforming it." No longer is the black American female stranded in the literary stereotypes of an enslaved century—mere mammies and tragic mulattoes who are more caricature than character.

Images of Black Women in Afro-American Literature: From Stereotype to Character

This essay was originally written for inclusion in an anthology on Afro-American literature to be published by the University of Ibaden Press. Its editor, Adam David Miller, believed that Africans wanted to know more about the literature of their brothers and sisters here in North America. We agreed, without realizing the importance of our decision, that the inclusion of an essay on Afro-American women writers was critical to the anthology. Such inclusion was by no means usual in 1975.

For me, this essay was an extremely important one, since it was my first attempt to organize the research I had been doing on Afro-American women writers. It is actually the first sketch of my book. *Black Women Novelists, The Development of a Tradition (1892–1976),* which I finished in 1979.

It is interesting for me to note what I selected for use in that book, since the scope of this essay was far too ambitious. In it, I look at Afro-American poets as well as fiction writers, at male writers' treatment of women, as well as female writers. More important is what was missing in the essay. Although it does indicate that the concept of images was one of my major concerns, it does not demonstrate the depth of historical investigation and analysis necessary for the establishment of my thesis—that a tradition of Afro-American women writers existed. Instead, the essay is organized around a few women writers, chosen rather quixotically, according to historical epoch. There is, for example, little discussion of Jessie Fauset or Alice Walker. Still, the sections of Paule Marshall and Toni Morrison are clearly the kernel of the work I would do on these writers in *Black Women Novelists.*

Since this present collection of essays does not include any excerpt from that book, "Images . . ." is necessary background for the essays that follow. It shows how far literary criticism on black women writers has come in a decade. By now, most of the writers I mention have received some degree of attention from an emerging group of black feminist critics. As importantly, this essay's omissions illustrate how significant the few historical books on Afro-American women published since 1975 have been to the development of this new body of criticism.

1

Until the 1940s, black women in both Anglo- and Afro-American literature have been usually assigned stereotyped roles—their images being a context for some other major dilemma or problem the society cannot resolve. Throughout the novels of the slavery and reconstruction periods, Anglo-American literature, particularly southern white literature, fashioned an image of the black woman intended to further create submission, conflict between the black man and woman, and importantly, a dumping ground for those female functions a basically Puritan society could not confront.

The mammy figure, Aunt Jemima, the most prominent black female figure in southern white literature,[1] is in direct contrast to the ideal white woman, though both images are dependent on each other for their effectiveness. Mammy is black in color, fat, nurturing, religious, kind, above all strong, and as Faulkner would call Dilsey, enduring. She relates to the world as an all embracing figure, and she herself needs or demands little, her identity derived mainly from a nurturing service. She must be plump and have big breasts and arms—she is the mammy in the unconscious of the South, desired and needed since ideal white women would have to debase themselves in order to be a mother. In contrast, the white woman was supposed to be frail, alabaster white, incapable of doing hard work, shimmering with the beauty of fragile crystal. These images are dependent on one another, since the white woman could not be ornamental, descriptive, fussy, if she nursed and brought up children. In the mythology of the South, men did not fight duels or protect the honor of a woman who was busy cooking, scrubbing floors, or minding children, since the exclusive performance of this kind of work precluded the intrigue necessary to be a person as ornament. In other words leisure time on one's pretty hands made one weak enough to need protection.

The image of the ideal white woman tries to deny the gross physical aspects of being female, gross from the southern point of view. In contrast, all the functions of mammy are magnificently physical. They involve the body as sensuous, as funky, the part of woman that white southern America was profoundly afraid of. Mammy, then, harmless in her position as a slave, unable because of her all-giving nature to do harm is needed as an image, a surrogate to contain all those fears of the physical female.

One could analyze the other prominent black female images in white southern literature, the concubine, in much the same way. Even the conjure woman is a reservoir for fears—fears, in this case, of the unknown spiritual world, so that particularly in New Orleans, the center of Catholicism in the South, Marie Laveau, the great voodoo mambo, could emerge as one of its most powerful citizens for half a century.

During the same period, Afro-American literature moved in a different direction. While southern white literature had focused on the mammy as the dominant black female image, with some glimpses at the concubine and the conjure woman, black literature centered mainly on the image of the tragic mulatta. Such novels as *Clotell* (1850) by William Wells Brown and Frances Harper's *Iola LeRoy* (1892), the first published novel by a black woman, set the stage for this heroine as a lasting image in black literature for decades to come.[2]

The tragic mulatta theme reveals the conflict of values that blacks faced as a *conquered* people. In her very being, the mulatta called up the illicit crossing between cultures. She is American in that she emerges out of the sexual relationship between a black slave mother and a white slave master, a sexual relationship denying the most basic philosophical concept of slavery—that blacks were not human beings. Do humans mate with nonhumans, and if they do, what is the product, human or nonhuman? As the white slave master entered the bodies of countless black women, he knew of her being, her humanness. His mind could attempt to deny it for economic and social reasons, but he knew in his loins her humanness.

Therefore, the plight of the mulatta arose

as reading material for the ears of white folks. And we cannot forget that the first black novels were written for a white audience, since black people, according to the laws of many states, were not permitted to read or write. White audiences lapped up the stories of mulattos and their tragedies in the ironic way that the guilty and powerful always delight in looking obliquely at their guilt. The existence of the mulatta, who combined the physical characteristics of both races, denied their claim that blacks were not human, while allowing them the argument that they were lifting up the race by lightening it. Most, though, knew that in lightening the black race they were also darkening the white race, hence the laws against miscegenation in so many southern states.

In this devious circle of logic, the mulatta becomes the vehicle for cultural transference as well, since in literature, she is usually the house slave, much to the chagrin of the white mistresses who had to face their husbands' promiscuity in their most intimate slaves. By living in the Big House, the slave saw the master's way of life, its comforts and pleasures but also its disharmony and deceptiveness and could relate either to the power inherent in the master's position by identifying with him or by rejecting him in fury. In either case, however, the die is cast, for the mulatta may be light but never white and hence could not have the power or the pleasures of the Big House no matter how much she identified with her master. If independence were a virtue, as it was among white slave masters, the mulatta who identified with that spirit was in deep trouble. If refinement were a goal of life, the leisure necessary for such a quality was simply not obtainable to the slave.

Hence, the tragedy of the mulatta. The alienation that was an essential part of her being was complicated by the knowledge she represented to the black slave. To the black field slave mother, whose mulatta baby is taken away from her at an early age to be raised in the Big House, the child itself must have called up mixed emotions within her. For the black slave man who knows his lack of power to prevent the union between slave woman and master, this child must have represented his powerlessness. The birth of such a child heightened the emotional pain of being a slave. And on the practical level, the black field slave must have wondered about the loyalty of the mulatta. Is she loyal to her father or to her mother?

"Softly speak," the spirituals say, "softly speak of freedom." But what does freedom mean? The lot of the tragic mulatta challenges the easy definition of that dream. *Clotell* and subsequent novels of that gender present the mulatta as a person worthy to be free—because she is beautiful, courageous and refined: beautiful because she represents those qualities of white standards of beauty, denied automatically to the darky; refined because she has learned the manners and customs of the Big House; courageous because she knows and relates to the code of conduct defined by the South. And in order to refute the slaveowners' argument that black people are inferior, writers liked William Wells Brown present heroines who say, "See, I can be like you and even be better than you by your very own standards."

It is important that the mulatto woman rather than the man is the one more often chosen in literature to project this argument since until recently in America, the women of any group represented the body of ideals that the group measured itself by. Woman, because she bears and raises children, has, for better or worse, embodied those intangibles of a culture deemed worthy to be passed on more than any code of law or written philosophy. And of course woman in white culture is not as powerful as man, so to pose the existence of a mulatto slave man who embodies the qualities of the master is so great a threat, so dangerous an idea, even in fiction, that it is seldom tried.

The image of the mulatta is a stereotype that reaches a peak in the essence of mulattas presented by Jean Toomer (himself a black man who could pass as white) in *Cane* (1923), a work principally about physical, cultural, and emotional miscegenation, and in the novels of Nella Larson, such as *Passing* (1929).

Before we move from the images of black women projected in slavery and reconstruction literature, we must look at the images fashioned by another tradition, the oral tradition, the witnessing of black people as seen through narratives and songs. The slave narrative as a genre has tended to be represented by those extraordinary slaves, usually men such as Frederick Douglass, who escaped from bondage. Yet there are many narratives of slaves, and of women slaves, who considered themselves the common folk and remained in slavery most of their lives.[3]

As would be expected, within the genre, the image of mammy persists. She is there as cook, housekeeper, nursemaid, seamstress, always nurturing and caring for her folk. But unlike the white southern image of mammy, she is cunning, prone to poisoning her master, and not at all content with her lot. It is interesting and ironic that Sojourner Truth, the flamboyant orator who advocated the abolition of slavery and fought for women's rights, would fit the stereotype, at least the physical stereotype, of the mammy southern gentlemen wanted to perceive as harmless. Sojourner Truth is not the only mammy who fought to protect her own children or who rose up against slavery. Mammies kicked, fought, connived, plotted, most often covertly, to throw off the chains of bondage. Mammy saw herself as a mother, but to her that role embodied a certain dignity and responsibility, rather than a physical debasement, doubtless a carry-over from the African view that every mother is a symbol of the marvelous creativity of the earth.[4] Mammy is an important figure in the mythology of Africa. The way in which this theme of African culture is distorted by the white southern perspective testifies to its inability to relate femaleness and femininity, as countless southern belles in antebellum American movies illustrate.

The tragic mulatta also appears in slave narratives. And indeed, she is tragic, as are almost all of the accounts. The contrast of comic darky and tragic mulatto developed in the literature of that period certainly does not stand the test of reality. There is little romanticism in the accounts mulattas give of their lives. There are tales of mulattas who as mistresses were abused and sold, their children scattered to the ends of the land, tales of mad mulattas who hated their fathers if they were acknowledged by them at all. There were sullen, cynical mulattas reared to be sold as high class courtesans. The narratives abound with tales of woman—be she field nigger or house nigger, mulatta or darky—as breeder, nurser, nurse maid, concubine, whipping block, put on the rack of everlasting work and debasing servitude.[5] And in the tales of these women, be they yaller or chocolate, the trivial underscores the abuses they faced: having to sleep outside the mistress's door so that little sexual relationship with one's husband was possible, having to take care of mistresses' children so that one's babies were born dead, time after time. The list of trivia goes on—trivia to the minds of the slavemaster—near death, in a particularly female way, for these slaves. The narratives are particularly poignant in the equalization of abuse they suggest, for the advantages that the mulatta might have because of her link to the master were easily offset by the disadvantages of alienation and frustration.

The narratives tend to focus on the relationship between slave and master, but the work-songs give us another view of how the slave woman viewed herself and was viewed by others. Since music is usually so intensely personal and need not be sanctioned by a publisher in order to be heard and spread, the songs about and by women tend to peer into the relationship between the black man and woman in their identity as man and woman. Courting, lovemaking, success and disappointment in love, all these aspects appear in the songs. Some men revel in their women. "Pretty Girl" is representative of this group:

Rubber is a pretty thing.
You rub it to make it shine.
If you want to see a pretty girl,
Take a peep at mine, take a peep at mine.

Talking about a pretty girl
You jus' ought-a-see mine.
She is not so pretty
But she is jus' so fine.
She gives me sugar,
She gives me lard,
She works all the while
In the white folks' yard.[6]

And at the same time, there is often the recurring theme that:

De woman am de cause of it all,
De woman am de cause of it all,
She's de cause of po' Adam's fall
De woman's de cause of it all.[7]

The songs also mirror the tingling clash between the dark woman and the yaller woman, often in a humorous tone:

De mulatto gal got yaller skin, yaller skin,
De mulatto gal got yaller skin, yaller skin,
De mulatto gal got yaller skin, yaller skin,
De mulatto gal got yaller skin,
Den she got a devilish grin, daddy.

De chocolate gal got greasy hair, greasy hair,
De chocolate gal got greasy hair, greasy hair,
De chocolate gal got greasy hair, greasy hair,
De chocolate gal got greasy hair,
She is de gal can cuss and rare, daddy.[8]

Yet within the confines of their own space, threatened as it was by a more powerful society with different standards, there does not emerge a hard and fast line about the value of a woman simply because she has got some white blood. Unlike the literary products of the day, the heroines of these songs might or might not be cinnamon, coffee, chocolate, or yaller:

If 'twant for de ter'pin pie
And sto-bought ham,
Dese country women
Couldn't git nowhere.

Some say, give me a high yaller,
I say, give me a teasin brown,
For it takes a teasin brown
To satisfy my soul.

For some folkies say
A yaller is low down,
But teasin brown
Is what I's crazy about.[9]

Almost always the substances of work-songs about or by women are sifted through the cry of hard times and how that affects relationships: The men who caught trains and left for whatever reasons, the lack of money, the pervasive sense of danger, the need for a woman to be independent of men, an independence imposed rather than desired, all shape the songs and give even the gayest song an undertone of plaintiveness. Slave narrative and worksong alike project black women as caught in the vise of hard times, their spirits occasionally rising to the heights of heroism but more often tempered by the nibbling need to always be practical.

2

There is no single-face in nature, because every eye that looks upon it, sees it from its own angle. So every man's spice-box seasons his own food.[10]

Zora Neale Hurston, *Dust Tracks on the Road*

Zora Neale Hurston arrived in New York City with her own unique spice box, at a time when the Harlem Renaissance was just beginning to swing. In the decade preceding her arrival, blacks had migrated in large numbers from the rural South to cities like New York. Out of that great migration emerged Harlem, the mecca of the black world in the twenties, where jazz and urban blues, a new race pride, and a wealth of black literature blossomed. Black women, of course, had made that migration to the city looking for a new life and found that the substance remained the same, though the apparel looked different. Instead of being housekeepers, cooks, and cotton pickers, they became domestics, garment factory workers, prostitutes—the hard bottom of the labor market.[11]

The literature had yet to catch up with the new reality. The women in *Cane* (1923) that you remember are the southern women who do not speak but are spoken of, tragic mulattas whose existences were metaphors for the blend of sweetness and madness Toomer tasted in the South. Jessie Fauset's women in her novels such as *The Chinaberry Tree* (1931) were genteel ladies whose conflicts about color and class tended to be closer to fairytale than anyone's imagined or factual reality. Nella Larsen's characters in *Quicksand* (1928) and *Passing* (1929) are again mulattas plagued by the tragedy of shade. A literature of the tragic mulatta emerged—stereotyped par excellence.

In the journey from the image of the tragic mulatta to a more varied, more complex view of the black woman as she appears in American literature, Zora Neale Hurston's work is transitional. Her autobiography, *Dust Tracks on the Road* (1942), told in the roving conversational tone Zora developed, breaks down stereotype and paints a canvas of multicolors that reflects Zora's mental and emotional life. Born in Eatonville, Florida, a black town founded and governed by black men, Zora tells us about the store porch where people gathered and performed lying sessions, where they whispered about those who dabbled in hoodoo, about who was courting who, in a speech that was to hold wonder for her most of her life. Her wanderings in Eatonville, Washington, D.C., Barnard in New York, the South, and the West Indies chart the intellectual and artistic development of this black woman with a richness of detail not seen before in the literature.

In her novels, Hurston incorporates the complexity of character into a marvel of a tale, for she is foremost a storyteller, attempting and sometimes succeeding to capture the gestures and tones of the folk on Joe Clarke's store porch. Her heroines are not the women of New York City—they move in that mythology of the South, the roots still for the race, the place where the black culture of the previous century had reached a particular peak, though that culture was now undergoing changes in the North.

Zora's urbaneness, her sophistication did not lead her down the path to genteel literature. Her roots were so strong that the "cityfying" gave her skill, articulation, and discipline as she pursued her double role as anthropologist and writer. In her autobiography as woman, she is independent, flamboyant, humorous, and always dedicated to the work she *must* do. And as a woman, her work collided with the view of woman held high in the general society. Men could not, would not accept, she tells us, that they *and* her work were the important things to her. It had to be one or the other. For Zora Neale Hurston, nothing was ever this or that; there were too many spice boxes around to make it that clear cut. So she is a controversial figure on every issue except one, the wonderful richness and beauty of black folk culture.

Her works exude this feel for variedness—her characters move in their own space, pinching bits of their spices, applying sage or basil to different types of menus as only they can. *Their Eyes Were Watching God* (1937), her most acclaimed novel, has the Hurston blend of complexity of character within the frame of a good story.

Janie, the heroine of this tale, in some ways fits the outlines of the conventional tragic mulatta. Her grandmother Nanny tells the budding Janie how she was raped by her master and ran off with her child when threatened by her mistress. When Nanny's child, (Janie's mother) is seventeen, she is also raped and goes slightly out of her mind leaving Nanny to bring up Janie. So Janie's birth and the birth of her mother are results of rape, the genesis of the mulatto in southern literature. The outline has been drawn, but within it a portraiture begins that is Janie's and hers alone. Searching for a center, a means to clarity and harmony, Janie wanders through two unhappy marriages, one with an old man who is jealous of her youth and beauty, the other with Jody Stark, the black entrepreneur who creates a town partly to establish Janie as its queen, seated on the porch, aloof and apart from everyone. The mulatta usually sits there, regal in her imitation of the white folks' ways, content that she has gotten to the peak of colored society. But Janie cannot stand this isolation. She wants to know herself, and she wants to know her husband, a desire he perceives as a threat. When he dies, she falls in love with Tea Cake, a man younger than she, who is interested not in her money or in her long black hair but in her essence. Their love story forms the hard kernel of this book, romantic in its abandon, but tingling with a poignancy borne of a dream dreamt so long that it had to come true. That Janie must kill Tea Cake because he is mad with rabies leads us back to the stereotype of the tragic mulatta, except that to Janie, her life has not been tragic but rich:

> She pulled her horizon like a great fish net. Pulled it from around the waist of the world and draped it over her shoulder. So much of life in its meshes. She called in her soul to come and see.[12]

Such a tale could be schematic or trite in its romanticism, but it is Zora Neale Hurston's precise grasp of black peoples' ways, their speech, and wisdom that gives the novel earth's rich feel:

> Man know all dem sitters-and-talkers goin tuh worry they guts into fiddle strings til dey find out whut we been talkin' about. Dat's all right Pheoby, tell 'em. Dey goin tuh make 'miration 'cause mah love didn't wok lak they *love*, if dey ever had any. Then you must tell 'em dat love ain't somethin' lak uh grindstone dat's de same thing everywhere and do de same thing tuh everything it touch. Love is lak de sea. It's uh movin' thing, but still and all, it takes its shape from de shore it meets, and it different with every shore.[13]

Zora Neale Hurston also grasped in her works a theme of black folklore, the delving into the nature of man, the nature of woman, and how these two natures blend or conflict. She delighted in the folk's continuous interest, whether devastatingly cynical, tender, or humorous, in the push and pull of human sexual relationships. Woman, viewing and viewed, is part of the theme of *Their Eyes Were Watching God*, as if the writer were illuminating one part of a canvas in order to give meaning to the entire painting. The novel begins:

> Ships at a distance have every man's wish on board. For some they come in with the tide. For others they sail forever on the horizon, never out of sight, never landing until the Watcher turns his eyes away in resignation, his dreams mocked to death by Time. That is the life of men.
>
> Now women forget all those things they don't want to remember, and remember everything they don't want to forget. The dream is the truth. They act and do things accordingly.[14]

Throughout the novel, as Janie tells her story to Phoeby, her friend, observances about black women, almost adage-like, probe not only Janie's nature but the condition of all black women. So Nanny tells Janie when she becomes a woman that

> Honey, de white man is de ruler of everything as fur as Ah been able tuh find out. Maybe it's some place off in de ocean where de black man is in power, but we don't know nothin' but what we see. So de white man throw down de load and tell de nigger man to pick it up. He pick it up because he have to but he don't tote it. He hand it to his womenfolks. De nigger woman is de mule uh de world so fur as Ah can see. Ah been praying fuh it toh be different wid you. Lawd, Lawd, Lawd![15]

And Zora puts in print conversations held usually within the confines of one's own circle:

> She (Janie) took a room at the boarding house for the night and heard the men talking around the front.
>
> "Aw you know dem white mens wuzn't goin' tuh do nothin' tuh no woman dat look lak her."
>
> "She didn't kill no white man, did she? Well, as long as she don't shoot no white man she kin kill jus' as many niggers as she please."
>
> "Yeah de nigger women kin kill up all de mens day wants tuh, but you bet' not kill one uh dem. De white folks will sho hang you if yuh do."
>
> "Well you know whut de say 'uh white man and uh nigger woman is the freest thing on the earth.' Dey do as de please."[16]

Part of the workings of the novel tests such adages, since we know Janie's story as the characters within the book do not. We, the readers, can judge the truth of these sayings. But we know, even as we read the words, that they were not created by Zora Hurston. We have heard them or perhaps even spoken them ourselves and are now being confronted with them in stark relief, set aside from the particularity of our own lives.

Zora Neale Hurston, in her life and in her work, moved the image of the black woman beyond stereotype, as she sought the ever-evolving ways of the folk. She grafted onto the nineteenth century mode, a new way of looking at the mulatta and the southern black woman, preparing the way for different spice boxes in the twentieth century.

In 1946, five years after Zora Neale Hurston published her autobiography, a newcomer, Ann Petry, published *The Street*. Along with Hurston's work, this novel functions as a transition from the tragic mulatta pattern and/or the rural southern woman as heroine to a more contemporary view of the black novel. As Hurston's novels had emphasized complexity of character, so *The Street* drew the outlines of the urban black woman's existence. Petry's novel belonged to the new black literary approach of the day, pioneered and symbolized by Richard Wright. In many ways *The Street* is akin to *Native Son* (1941) and its relentless presentation of the dreary despair of the inner cities and the illumination of the casual relationship between social and personal crime. As Bigger Thomas typified an alienated black male created partially by the concrete plantations of the North, so Lutie Johnson in *The Street* is the lost black female, alone and struggling. Both characters become literary types used so often by writers in later years that they have become stereotypes.

Lutie Johnson of *The Street* combines some of the characteristics of the various black female stereotypes of the previous century. She is a domestic working in the rich white folks' home, northern style. She is a mother struggling to protect her child, not only from overt physical danger, but also from the more hidden patterns of castration and debasement sketched by the concrete plantations of the North. She is a "brown, good-looking girl," plagued by the sexual advances of men, both black and white, who would use her as a sexual object in much the same way the black female slave was used. She is struggling to survive, working overtime, no longer bearing the legal status of the slave, but a slave nonetheless in the framework of society.

The novel also portrays the fragmentation of the black community which was more prevalent in the concrete plantations of the North than in the rural southern town. Here, husbands leave their wives not because they are sold or had to leave town, but because they are unable to be a man in their own eyes (i.e., find a job, protect their women and children). The apparel may be different, but the substance remains the same. Here, the spiritualists are not conjure women revered by both the master and the slave, but commercial salesmen selling powders and herbs to the highest bidder. In the North, one's child would not be sold into slavery, but might be taken away to jail or reform school. The lack of money becomes the jailer; hidden and overt racisim becomes the lock. And the alienation of people, one from the other, separated by concrete and the ache to survive, strangles friendship and family ties. Everyone suspects each other as slaves were expected to. The apparel changes but the substance remains the same, except for one important factor. One was told one was free, and therefore part of the mind believed this, incorporating the attitudes of a free person into one's value systems. Frustration and confusion about who one really was further intensified an already harrowing situation.

It is on situation, setting, and environment that this novel focuses. Lutie Johnson might be one of many hundreds of thousands of black women who lived in Harlem in 1946, women whose hope for a better life was the only thing that kept them going. Lutie is seldom further delineated as a particular person, with a particular make-up. Her plight is actually the major character of the novel, a plight that can only lead to crime and tragedy. To some, this novel is unbelievable precisely because it is so grim and Lutie so alone. Yet it is as horribly true as the treatment of black slaves in southern plantations.

The Street marks a change in setting and tone in the literature of the black woman. It brings the literature into the twentieth century, for the concrete plantation became the dwelling place of more and more blacks in this century. After the publication of this novel, the black city woman could not be forgotten. The particular brand of slavery under which she exists meant that new changes in the literature would have to occur.

3

The poet has always been a synthesizer and a thermometer, whether she is aware of it or not. Somehow, poets allow the facility of sensing the present, a facility we all originally have, to have its own way, in spite of the world's attempt to divide time into past, present, and future. Most of us, for lack of time and stubbornness, live within the forms of the past as we dream about the possibilities of the future. Poets sense the present, and keep reminding us that the present is both past and future as it is now.

Gwendolyn Brooks' work springs from her abiding with the present. She synthesizes the work of the poets of her tradition, both Afro- and Anglo-American, and tests the temperature of the waters of our time. Her poetry (1946–present) and her only novel *Maud Martha* (1953) are Chicago, Cottage Grove, the Mecca or to put it more generically, are urban. And yet her work does not sacrifice the harshness of setting to the inner realities of her characters, who may be hampered by the envrionment but are not completely made of or by it. One feels both the lyricism, a soul-singing that is found in Zora Neal Hurston's work, and the harsh cutting edges of Petry's *The Street*. The major characters in her work, whether verse or fiction, are in process, flowing in and out of themselves and the world around them. We feel this process because Gwendolyn Brooks is so much in the present, sensing, perceiving, and translating those perceptions into precise words. The words become the perceptions:

> Abortions will not let you forget.
> You remember the children you got that you did not get
> The damp small pulps with a little or no hair,
> The singers and workers that never handled the air.
> You will never neglect or beat
> Them, or silence or buy with a sweet
> You will never wind up the sucking-thumb
> Or scuttle off ghosts that come
> You will never leave them, controlling your luscious sigh,
> Return for a snack of them, with gobbling mother-eye.[17]

Her language may not have the "hip" sound of the stereotyped ghetto mother, and some may say that we don't talk this way. Perhaps that is why some people find Gwendolyn Brooks's poetry distant at first. It is not dramatic, in the sense of being flamboyant; rather it strives always for the way we would put it, if we had the time, had all words at our disposal, could caress each perception as it happened.

Details are crucial to Gwendolyn Brooks's work, not the tedious details of legal documents but those who often determine why we feel this emotion now and cannot exactly understand why. Her characters (for there are characters in her poetry) are intense perceivers. Often these perceivers are women trying to know themselves, exhausted by the seeming trivia of the commonplace yet finding truths through continuously experiencing everyday life. There are few grand topics in her works, as we have come to recognize them. Her themes are commonplace and therefore great, as birth and death are, as growing old or losing a man is. And always the tone is understated, dramatic because it *is* muted.

The women that we remember from her poetry are not so much complex as they are distinct. Maude, Sadie, Cousin Vit, Pearlie May Lee, Maude Martha, Mary, the Shakedancer's daughter, even as general a name as "the mother" are distinct, one from another, in the way that they comment on our perceptions that we may have forgotten we had or may have had not the time or patience to really crystallize into permanence. These characters are thinking and feeling people, as black women always have been, despite the clay stereotypes in which we are perpetually cast.

As part of the dominant colors of the fabric of Gwendolyn Brooks's works, the impact of racism, subtle or hidden is also woven. Her earlier works do not address this theme as directly as do the later pieces. Yet in the earlier works it is there as part of the larger theme of her works—the perceptions of her characters. Because her characters are black, their perceptions are about birth and death, common to all human beings. Because they are black, their perceptions are about racism and its ramifications to nonwhites. Because they are black, their experience of and expression of their reality is culturally distinct; therefore their perception is as strong a statement about their condition as any manifesto. Here is a section from *Maud Martha*. Maud Martha has come to work as a maid at the home of the Burns-Coopers:

> The two of them, richly dressed, and each with that health in the face that bespeaks, or seems to bespeak, much milk drinking from earliest childhood, looked at Maud Martha. There was no remonstrance; no firing. They just looked. But for the first time she understood what Paul endured daily. For so—she could gather from a Paul-word here, a Paul-curse there—his Boss! When, squared upright, terribly upright, superior to the President, commander of the world, he wished to underline Paul's lacks, to indicate soft shock, controlled incredulity. As his boss looked at Paul, so these people looked at her. As though she were a child, a ridiculous one, and one that ought to be given a little shaking, except that shaking was not quite the thing, would not quite do. One held up one's finger (if one did anything), cocked one's head, was arch. As in the old song one hinted, "Tut, tut! now now! come come!" Metal rose, all built, in one's eye.
>
> I'll never come back, Maud Martha assured herself when she hung up her apron at eight in the evening. She knew Mrs. Burns-Cooper would be puzzled. The wages were very good. Indeed, what could be said in explanation? Perhaps the hours were long. I couldn't explain my explanation, she thought.
>
> One walked out from that almost perfect wall, spitting at the firing squad. What difference did it make whether the firing squad understood or did not understand the manner of one's retaliation or why one had to retaliate?
>
> Why, one was a human being. One wore clean nightgowns. One loved one's baby. One drank cocoa by the fire—or the gas range—come the evening, in the wintertime.[18]

The human correlative of such an abstract sociological concept as racism gives this passage and much of Gwendolyn Brooks's work its impact. Her perceivers think tangibles. In all their muted glory, they defy abstraction.

Gwendolyn Brooks published her first book of poetry, *A Street in Bronzeville*, in 1945. Since then, many black women writers have emerged, each with her particular focus, style, and world view. I cannot comment on every significant black woman writer of that time. Instead I will try to give a sense of that richness and diversity in the spectrum by concentrating on the works of three black women writers: Paule Marshall, Nikki Giovanni, and Toni Morrison.

The works of these writers cannot be discussed without some understanding of dominant literary themes in contemporary Afro-American literature. The period 1945–1975 is such a rich one that it would take many books to fully cover it. I will only sketch certain characteristics that are particularly relevant to the images of black women projected in Afro-American literature.

It is safe to say that in the genre of the novel from 1945–1960, four novelists dominate: Richard Wright, James Baldwin, Chester Himes, and Ralph Ellison. In Wright's major works, such as *Native Son* or *The Outsider*, black women are seldom seen except in the role of a slightly outlined mama or as a victim, like Bessie in *Native Son*, whose fate is given little thought by the society around her. In *Black Boy*, we do get glimpses of Wright's grandmother and mother, both long-suffering, fanatically religious women whom the author remembers primarily as being in pain. Ellison's major work, *Invisible Man,* again projects the black woman in the solo role of mammy. Mary, the woman who rescues our nameless narrator from illness, disappears from the book after she nurses him back to health.

Baldwin's novels present women in more diverse roles. Ida in *Another Country* is a perceptive person, though she shares with many of Baldwin's other women that grating quality that some call the "sapphire," named after Sapphire in the "Amos and Andy" series. Baldwin's 1973 book, *If Beale Street Could Talk,* has a black woman as its central character. However, this novel appears at the end of this thirty-year period and has yet to have its impact. Chester Himes's women veer toward another stereotype, the sex kitten, women created and used for sex, as in *Pinktoes.* Himes pushed his characterizations of women to the heights of caricature, perhaps a caricature intended as a comment on the stereotype itself.

In effect, the black women that appear in the novels of these four literary giants come painfully close to the stereotypes about the black woman projected by white southern literature in the latter part of the nineteenth century. Perhaps images do inform reality.

The poetry of the sixties reflects the growing need to include women as central figures in literature, since much of it is socio-political in nature. Poetry advocating nationhood, by writers such as Imamu Baraka and Don Lee, assume that there have been wedges placed between black men and women and that work must be done to remove these wedges. Because of this, black women are often idealized in this poetry, saluted as queens, as Mothers of the Universe, or exhorted to change their ways (i.e., stop being Sapphires or loose women) in order to deserve these titles. A different stereotype begins to emerge: the idealized black woman poised on a pedestal somewhat in reaction to the previously projected stereotypes. Black women become symbolic holders of the moral condition of blacks in much of the nationalist poetry. In some ways, though, this kind of stereotype assumes the existence of Sapphire, Aunt Jemima, the black mammy, the sex kitten, and the evil woman—images germinated in the white southern mythology and enhanced and enriched by film, television, and social programs even up to the present.

This is not to say that one of the thrusts of contemporary male Afro-American literature was to denigrate the black woman. Rather, the black woman herself had to illuminate her own situation, reflect on her own identity and growth, her relationship to men, children, society, history, and philosophy as she had experienced it. And during these explosive years some black women writers began to project the intensity, complexity, and diversity of the experience of black women from their own point of view.

Certain trends do characterize the writings of black women writers during this period. The image of the tragic mulatta no longer dominates the literature and is replaced by a diversity of physical and psychological types. The role of mammy is carefully and continually moved from the level of stereotype to that of a living human being with her own desires and needs. The relationship between black men and women is also scrutinized, often in less generic and more particular terms, with special emphasis placed on the societal forces that strain marriage. And most importantly, black women themselves are projected as thinkers, feelers, human beings, not only used by others, but as conscious beings. There are many black women, these voices say. They have culture, race, sex, sometimes situations in common, but they are not just push button automatons who scream when given this cue, cuddle up when given that smile. They are not just stereotypes, for stereotype is the very opposite of humanness; stereotype, whether positive or negative, is a byproduct of racism, is one of the vehicles through which racism tries to reduce the human being to a nonhuman level.

4

Paule Marshall is supremely devoted to the creation of character. In her work and in her lectures on the craft of novel writing she emphasizes the necessity she feels to create distinct human beings who are affected by culture and society, but who also affect these two important elements. She consistently delves into the psychology of her characters, why they act as they do, as well as into the psychology of the place and time within which they exist. The essential aspects of her work—descriptions of characters and settings, storyline and themes—are all integrally related to her characters. The black women in her books are particularly complex, or at least rounded out. Daringly, she presents women who seem at first to be familiar types—the domineering mother, the prostitute, the martyred mother—only to investigate their personalities so thoroughly that the stereotype is forever broken in the mind of the reader.

Such are the people in Paule Marshall's first novel: *Browngirl, Brownstones* (1959). The central figure in this work about West Indian immigrants in New York is Selina, who as a first generation American woman must reconcile her West Indian heritage with the new world culture within which she is living. But Selina is not only type, she is an honest, sensitive young girl who struggles to understand her strong, practical, and difficult mother as she loves her marvelous dreamer father. Both mother, Silla, and father, Deighton, at first seem to be types: the mother, materialistic, bitter, set on owning a house at all costs; the father, dreaming about imagined triumphs, an artist lacking a form. But almost immediately, stereotype is dispelled by the space Paule Marshall somehow creates for them.

Because the domineering mother has been so much a part of black mythology, at least in terms of white society, Paule Marshall's development of the character of Silla is particularly instructive. We first see her as Selina looks at a family photograph taken many years before:

> The young woman in the 1920s dress with a headband around her forehead could not be the mother. The mother had a shy beauty, there was a girlish expectancy in her smile.[19]

A few pages later we see Silla Boyce as she is now:

> Silla Boyce brought the theme of winter into the park with her dark dress amid the summer green and the bright-figured housedresses of the women lounging on the benches there. Not only that, every line of her strong-made body seemed to reprimand the women for the idleness and the park for its senseless summer display. Her lips, set in a permanent protest against life, implied that there was no time for gaiety. And the park, the women, the sun even gave way for her dark force; the flushed summer colors ran together and faded as she passed.[20]

Paule Marshall's descriptions of her characters are particularly important as a technique, for they not only give us visual pictures but suggest questions, probe inner tensions. The question, subtly posed to the reader by the juxtaposition of these two descriptions, is one of the themes of the novel. How does Silla Boyce, the woman with the shy beauty and girlish expectations, become this dark foreboding force? And what are the ramifications of this change, if indeed the change is complete?

The struggle between Silla and Deighton, as seen by Selina, is an intense and harrowing one. Their differences: the mother's desire for security, symbolized by the possession of a brownstone, the father's need for creativity, beauty, meaning in his life, set them in life-long conflict. And their backgrounds illuminate the reasons for the intensity with which they view each other. Deighton had come from the town scene in Barbados, where his wit and the adulation of his mother had given him a sense of worth. Silla, in contrast, came from the harsh countryside, from cutting cane, and knowing how it was to starve. Their respective descriptions of their past life in Barbados is one contributing factor to their final confrontation, a confrontation that ends in tragedy. Deighton describes his youth in Barbados in this way:

> ". . . I's a person live in town and always had plenty to do. I not like yuh mother and the mounts of these Bajan that come from down some gully or up some hill behind God's back and ain' use to nothing. 'pon a Sat'day I would walk 'bout town like I was a full-full man. All up Broad Street and Swan Street like I did own the damn place."[21]

Silla's experience is quite different:

> "Iris, you know what it is to work hard and still never having to work for next skin to nothing. The white people treating we like slaves still and we taking it. The rum shop and the church join together to keep we pacify and in ignorance. That's Barbados. It's a terrible thing to know you gon be poor all yuh life, no matter how hard you work. You does stop trying after a time. People does see you so and call you lazy. But it ain laziness. It just that you does give up. You does kind of die inside."[22]

In the end, we know that Silla is the defeated one, left without the love and appreciation she desires, not giving herself the opportunity to fully develop that "odd softness" that stood out so in the old photograph and sometimes peeps out from behind her perpetual rage. She is defeated, except that at least Selina, her daughter, begins to understand her mother's need for independence:

> Quickly Selina found her coat and, putting it on, stared at her mother's bowed face, seeing there the finely creased flesh around her eyes, the hair graying at her temples and, on her brow the final frightening loneliness that was to be her penance. "Mother," she said gently, "I have to disappoint you. Maybe it's as you once said: that in making your own way you always hurt someone. I don't know. . . . Everybody used to call me Deighton's Selina but they were wrong. Because you see I'm truly your child. Remember how you used to talk about how you left home and came here alone as a girl of eighteen and was your own woman? I used to love hearing that. And that's what I want. I want it!"[23]
>
> Silla's pained eyes searched her adamant face, and after a long time a wistfulness softened her mouth. It was as if she somehow glimpsed in Selina the girl she had once been. For that moment, as the softness pervaded her and her hands lay open like a girl's on her lap, she became the girl who had stood, alone and innocent, at the ship's rail, watching the city rise glittering with promise from the sea.[24]

Both Silla and Deighton are trapped by the conditions of their world. The world will not give Deighton, a black man, the sense of dignity and worth he desires, unless he perverts his nature and becomes a money-grubbing businessman; it will not allow him imagination. Since Deighton cannot seek the security she needs, the dreams he had set in motion when he courted her, Silla must pursue them herself, ruthlesssly, with no holds barred. She ends up partially hating herself and Deighton for her having to do it at all. Yet these people are caught not only by the circumstances of their worlds. It is their personal responses to their conditions that make their story what it is.

Browngirl, Brownstones is also about the culture from which its characters spring and how this culture mediates between them and their world. In her next book, *The Chosen Place, the Timeless People* (1969), Paule Marshall investigates the cultural levers even more, while maintaining the rich comprehensiveness of her characters. Stereotyped forms are cracked, new forms are sculpted to become characters who instruct us about their particular lives and therefore about the general themes of the culture. In Paule Marshall's books, characters and culture transform each other. And the women, who tend to be her central characters, give voice to that continual transformation.

5

it's funny that smells and sounds return
so all alone uncalled unheeded
on a sweaty night as i sit around
with coffee and cigarettes waiting

sometimes it seems
my life is a scrapbook[25]

Nikki Giovanni is as close to a superstar poet as any black woman poet has been in this century. At 30 she had published three books of poetry; *Black Feeling, Black Talk, Black Judgement, Re:Creation,* and *My House,* a book of poetry for children, *Spin a Soft Black Song,* edited an anthology of black women poets, *Night Comes Softly,* and written an autobiography, *Gemini.* She has read her poetry on a solo, mass distributed album, *Truth Is On Its Way.* She has appeared on countless television talk shows, particularly *Soul,* interviewed such literary figures as James Baldwin and Yevtushenko, and has written articles for popular magazines, black and white alike. She is a popular poet in the sense that Aretha Franklin (a favorite singer of hers) is a popular singer; Nikki's books sell well.

What accounts for this poet's popularity in a country where poets are usually read primarily in the colleges? Or to be more precise, what are the societal forces that have created a phenomenon such as the contemporary popular black poet? Poets like Nikki Giovanni and Don Lee, her male counterpart, sprang out of the cultural-political atmosphere of the sixties when a more intense race pride manifested itself in black America. That pride had always been there, but at certain times in history such as the 1920s and the 1960s it erupted with more force and flair. The rhetoric of the sixties, a political nationalistic rhetoric, is preceded by a language of protest, revolt, self and cultural investigation that fostered a linguistic correlative to the changing mood in the inner cities of America. Poets broadcasted that change as they helped to make it. In the late fifties, poets like Bob Kaufman, Ted Joans, and the ever-enduring Langston Hughes were not only writing their poems to be printed, but spoke them at church gatherings, in coffee houses, at political rallies, wherever they might be heard. The oral tradition was revitalized.

The oral rendering of poems, though not immediately heard by as many people as read the printed word, set up a new chain of vibrations and created another kind of audience different from the audience who read poetry. And in the case of television, perhaps even more people heard the word than read it. Not only was the craft of poetry writing important to the oral performance, but also the way the poem was spoken, the flair and personality of the poet, so that the message be gotten across in as engaging a manner as possible. The new poetry sound, released by this revival of the oral, lent itself well to emotionally involving the audience in the message the poet was sending. In the sixties that message was generally of a political-cultural nature. Social questions, political comment, and cultural insight meshed with sound to elicit audience response—if not action.

Nikki Giovanni began her career as an oral poet. Charming, petite, articulate, her image as well as her poetry communicated the message. Her first book, *Black Feeling, Black Talk, Black Judgement* (1968), first published by a black press, Broadsides, was celebrated for its hard-hitting nationalistic language:

> Nigger
> Can you kill
> Can you kill
> Can a nigger kill
> Can a nigger kill a honkie
> Can a nigger kill the Man
> Can you kill nigger
> Huh? Nigger can you
> Kill[26]

It is the rhythm the poem is written in as well as the controversial thoughts that elicit the audience's response, for it is the rapping style of the sixties associated with the language of the ghetto stylized by the politicos of the period. Social protest in poetry has become associated with this rapping style, a style that is named after Rap Brown, one of the political spokesmen of that period.

A distinctive quality of Nikki's poetry is her sense of humor, her sense of irony about the political rhetoric of the day:

> one day
> you gonna walk in this house
> and i'm gonna have on a long African gown
> you'll sit down and say "The Black . . ."
> and i'm gonna take one arm out
> then you—not noticing me at all—will say
> "What about this brother . . ."
> and i'm gonna be slipping it over my head
> and you'll rap on about "the revolution . . ."
> while i rest your hand against my stomach
> you'll go on—as you always do—saying "i
> just can't dig . . ."
> while i'm moving your hand up and down
> and i'll be taking your dashiki off
> then you'll say—"What we really need . . ."
> and i'll be licking your arm
> and "The way i see it we ought to . . ."
> and unbuckling your pants
> "And what about the situation . . ."
> and taking your shorts off
> and then you'll notice
> your state of undress
> and knowing you you'll just say
> "Nikki,
> isn't this counterrevolutionary . . .?"[27]

You can hear the audience roar with laughter at the end of the poem.

As a woman poet, Nikki Giovanni expresses her particular view of what it is to be black and to be a woman. All of her work peaks at this point of juncture, as she traces her own girlhood in poems like "Nikki Rosa," her coming to age, her growing understanding of her parents, her own motherhood, her loves and disappointments in love. Particularly in these poems, the rapping style is underlined by the rhythms of the popular music, rhythm 'n' blues:

> i wanta say just gotta say something
> bout those beautiful outasight
> black men
> with they afros
> walking down the street
> is the same ol danger
> but a brand new pleasure[28]

And when she addresses herself to the problems of the black woman she puts all her poetic force, rap, and rhythm into illuminating the situation:

> it's a sex object if you're pretty
> and no love
> or love and no sex if you're fat
> get back fat black woman be a mother
> grandmother strong thing but not woman
> gameswoman romantic woman love needer
> man seeker dick eater sweat getter
> fuck needing love seeking woman[29]

"Woman Poem" is often anthologized and is as popular a poem today from printed as well as oral response as any poem written about black women during the last ten years. Again, it is the style, a putting together of the facts we all know in a voice that sounds familiar even as it changes from type to type.

Because the oral poet must register his/her message immediately, Nikki Giovanni's poetry is dynamic, dramatic, headed almost always for a punch line. And the advantages of this style carry with it some disadvantages—particularly the paring away of any factor that will not elicit an immediate response. Sometimes depth, precision, hard strategy is sacrificed to drama, whim, technique. But then the poet has got her audience's ear. Now they might want to go deeper with her or others, since they have at least begun to listen.

Giovanni's poetry is also urban, in the sense that the fast talk, the setting, the conflicts and confrontations feel like Harlem, the South Side of Chicago, Detroit, the glamorous though harsh, swinging inner cities of the North. And her words emphasize their glamour, their vibrancy instead of their horror or death-anguish. In some ways she idealizes their inhabitants, making them feel magnificent in their fine clothes and hip talk and therefore capable of stronger action.

Giovanni's poetry is often discussed in terms of its social themes, but especially with the publication of *My House* (1972) her poetry becomes more personal, even more impressionistic. Her view of her mother in the poem "Mothers" is one of the most touching poems in the book:

i remember the first time
i consciously saw her
we were living in a three room
apartment on burns avenue

mommy always sat in the dark
i don't know how i knew that but she did

that night i stumbled into the kitchen
maybe because i've always been
a night person or perhaps because i had
wet the bed
she was sitting on a chair
the room was bathed in moonlight diffused
through thousands of panes landlords who
rented
to people with children were prone to put
in windows
she may have been smoking but maybe not
her hair was three-quarters her height
which made me a strong believer in the
Samson myth and very black[30]

Many of her personal poems are pieces written to her women friends. They are sympathetic listeners as she talks to them about her feelings and thoughts. While her woman poems celebrate friendship, her love poems to men waver between grief and ecstasy and always ask that awful question:

and i'm asking you baby please
please somehow show me what i need
to know so i can love you right
now[31]

As a popular poet, Nikki Giovanni has been consistently asked about the women's liberation movement, its relationship to black women, and about women and their sense of the world. In *Gemini*, her autobiography, there are two sections that come as close to synthesizing her many comments as any two I could find. I think it is important that these two comments appear in an essay called *Gemini*, a prolonged autobiographical statement on why she decided to become a writer.

And sometimes you say, that's all right; if he takes advantage of me, so what? At nineteen that's cool. Or maybe at twenty-three. But around twenty-five or thirty you say, maybe men and women aren't meant to live with each other. Maybe they have a different sort of thing going where they come together during mating season and produce beautiful useless animals who then go on to love, you hope, each of you . . . but living together there are too many games to be gotten through. And the intimacies still seem to be left to his best friend and yours. I mean, the incidence is too high to be ignored. The guy and girl are inseparable until they get married; then he's out with his friends and she's out with hers or home alone, and there's no reason to think he's lying when he says he loves her. . . . She's just not the other half of him. He is awed and frightened by her screams and she is awed and cautious about his tears. Which is not to say there is not one man or one woman who can't make a marriage—i.e., home—run correctly and many even happily but it happens so infrequently. Or as a relative of mine in one of her profound moments said, "Marriage is give and take—you give and he takes." And I laughed because it was the kind of hip thing I was laughing about then. And even if that's true, so what? Somebody has to give and somebody has to take. But people set roles out, though the better you play them the more useless you are to that person. People move in conflicts. To me sex is an essence. . . . . It's a basic of human relationships. And sex is conflict; it could be considered a mini-war between two people. Really. I think so. So i began to consider being a writer.[32]

We Black women are the single group in the West intact. And anybody can see we're pretty shaky. We are, however, (all praises), the only group that derives its identity from itself. I think its been rather unconscious but we measure ourselves by ourselves, and I think that's a practice we can ill afford to lose. For whatever combination of events that made us turn inward, we did. And we are watching the world trying to tear us apart. I don't think it will happen. I think the Lena Youngers will always survive and control in the happy sort of way they do. I don't really think it's bad to be used by someone you love. As Verta Mae pointed out, "What does it mean to walk five paces behind him?" If he needs it to know he's leading, then do it—or stop saying he isn't leading. Because it's clear that no one can outrun us. We Black Women have obviously underestimated our strength. I used to think why don't they just run ahead of us? But obviously we are moving pretty fast. The main thing we have to deal with is, What makes a woman? Once we decide that everything else will fall into plan. As perhaps everything has. Black men have to decide what makes a man.[33]

6

While Nikki Giovanni's poetry is urban social realism, Toni Morrison's work is earthy fantastic realism. Deeply rooted in history and mythology, her work resonates with mixtures of pleasures and pain, wonder and horror. There is something primal about her characters. They come at you with the force and beauty of gushing water, seemingly fantastic but as basic as the earth they stand on. While Paule Marshall carefully sculpts her characters, Toni Morrison lets her erupt out of the wind, sometimes gently, often with force and horror. Her work is sensuality combined with an intrigue that only a piercing intellect could create.

She has written two novels: *The Bluest Eye* (1970) and *Sula* (1974). Her novels illustrate the growth of a theme as it goes through many transformations, in much the way a good jazz musician finds the hidden melodies within a phrase. Both novels chronicle the search for beauty amidst the restrictions of life, both from without and within. In both novels, the black woman, as girl then grown woman, is the turning character looking at the world outside as she peers inside herself. In both novels friendship between two women or girls serves as the periscope through which the overwhelming contradictions of life are measured. Her heroines are double-faced—looking outward and searching inward, trying to find some continuity between the seasons, the earth, other people, the cycles of life and themselves. Her novels are rich not only with characterizations, but also with signs, symbols, omens sent by nature. Wind and fire, robins in the spring, marigolds that won't grow are as much characterizations in her novels as the human beings who people them.

The Bluest Eye startles the reader with its straight-arrow aim as well as its experimentation, for Toni Morrison finds the language to describe the psychic trauma experienced by so many black girls growing up in a culture where blue eyes and blonde hair are the culmination of beauty. Because she takes risks with the language, she communicates a link between one's sense of one's physical self and the developing spiritual psyche. The beauty searched for in the book is not just the possession of blue eyes, but the harmony that they symbolize:

> It had occurred to Pecola sometime ago that if her eyes, those eyes that held the pictures, and knew the sights—if those eyes of hers were different, that is to say, beautiful, she herself would be different. Her teeth were good, and at least her nose was not big and flat like some of those who were thought so cute. If she looked different, beautiful, maybe Cholly would be different and Mrs. Breedlove, too. Maybe they'd say, "Why look at pretty-eyed Pecola. We musn't do bad things in front of those pretty eyes."
>
> Pretty eyes. Pretty blue eyes. Big blue pretty eyes. Run, Jip, run. Jip runs. Alice runs. . . . They run with their blue eyes. Four blue eyes. Four pretty blue eyes. Blue-jay eyes, blue-like-Mrs. Forrest's-blue-blouse eyes. Morning-glory-blue eyes. Alice-and-Jerry-blue storybook eyes.
>
> Each night, without fail she prayed for blue eyes.[34]

Pecola's search for blue eyes ends in visible madness because she does not transfer the physical thing itself into a symbolic aim. Others also seek their version of the bluest eye, only within the accepted mores of the society:

> They go to land-grant colleges, normal schools and learn how to do the white man's work with refinement: home economics to prepare his food; teacher education to instruct black children in education; music to soothe the weary master and entertain his blunted soul. Here they learn the rest of the lesson; the careful development of thrift, patience, high morals and good manners. In short, how to get rid of the funkiness. The dreadful funkiness of passion, the funkiness of nature, the funkiness of the wide range of human emotions.
>
> Wherever it erupts, this Funk, they wipe it away; where it crusts they dissolve it, wherever it drips, flowers or clings they find it and fight it until it dies. They fight the battles all the way to the grave. The laugh that is a little too loud; the enunciation a little too round; the gesture a little too generous. They hold their behind in for fear of a sway too free; when they wear lipstick, they never cover the entire mouth for fear of lips too thick, and they worry, worry, worry, about the edges of their hair.[35]

Pecola and Sula, Toni Morrison's heroine in her next book, share many qualities in common. They are women who become scapegoats in their communities because they look at the truth of things and will not or cannot disguise it, becoming the dumping ground for those feelings of helplessness and horror people have about their own lives. Pecola's madness makes everyone feel sane. Sula's evilness highlights everyone's goodness.

In *Sula*, Toni Morrison takes us further down those dangerous paths her characters tread to find personal wholeness. In this book her setting becomes even more important than in *The Bluest Eye*, for the town emphasizes the restrictions of living that are the very nature of life itself. The Bottom had started as a nigger joke, a joke played on a nigger by a white man:

> A good white farmer promised freedom and a piece of bottom land to his slave if he would perform some very difficult chores. When the slave completed the work, he asked the farmer to keep his end of the bargain. Freedom was easy—the farmer had no objection to that but he didn't want to give up any land. So he told the slave that he was very sorry that he had to give him valley land. He had hoped to give him a piece of the Bottom. The slave blinked and said he thought the valley land was bottom land. The master said, "Oh no! See those hills? That's bottom land rich and fertile." "But it's high up in the hills," said the slave. "High up from us," said the master, "but when God looks down it's the bottom. That's why we call it so. It's the bottom of heaven—best land there is." So the slave pressed his master to try to get him some. He preferred it to the valley. And it was done. The nigger got the hilly land, where planting was backbreaking, where soil slid down and washed away the seeds, and where the wind lingered all through the winter.[36]

It is in this place that Sula is born and grows up. It is to this place that she returns after long years of searching for that wholeness she must have. And it is to her only friend Nel, with whom she shared adolescence, the accidental drowning of a young boy, and the intimacies of being female that she returns. But the two women are no longer one. Sula wants everything or nothing and therefore flies in the face of compromising traditions that keep this community intact. It is her honesty, her absolute resolve to face the meanness of life that binds her to Shadrack, the shell-shock soldier who started National Suicide Day. Nel, on the other hand, marries, has children, tries to suit her desires to the restrictions of life. In one of the cruical passages of the book, Sula sees Nel as "one of those spiders whose only thought was the next rung of the web, who dangled in dark dry places suspended by their own spittle, more terrified of the free fall than the snake's breath below."[37] Nel has become like those who are "Bent into grimy sickles of concern":

> The narrower their lives, the wider their hips. Those with husbands had folded themselves into starched coffins, their sides bursting with other people's skinned dreams and bony regrets. Those without men were like sour-tipped needles featuring one constant empty eye.[38]

In contrast, Sula Peace recalls the spiraling roads she has run:

> Nel was one of the reasons she had drifted back to Medallion, that and the boredom she found in Nashville, Detroit, New Orleans, New York, Philadelphia, Macon and San Diego. All these cities held the same people, working the same mouths, sweating the same sweat. The men who took her to one or another of those places had merged into one large personality: the same language of love, the same entertainments of love, the same cooling of love. Whenever she introduced her private thoughts into their rubbings or goings, they hooded their eyes. They taught her nothing but love tricks, shared nothing but worry, gave nothing but money. She had been looking for a friend, and it took her a while to discover that a lover was not a comrade and could never be—for a woman.[39]

Toni Morrison then brings this passage to a climax:

> Had she [Sula] paints, clay, or knew the discipline of the dance, or string; had she anything to engage her tremendous curiosity and her gift for metaphor, she might have exchanged the restlessness and preoccupation with whim for an activity that provided her with all she yearned for. And like any artist with no art form, she became dangerous.[40]

Either way you lose. Nel loses her husband to Sula, begins to see that her children will grow old and leave her with nothing to fill in the spaces. Sula dies from boredom and spiritual malnutrition as much as from anything else. Their broken friendship is a measure of their broken lives, lives that are cramped from the very start. As counterpoints, all the other women in this book must either fit themselves into the place life has set for them or defy it with tragic circumstances proportionate to their degree of nonaccommodation.

Sula's grandmother, Eva, is as fine an example of the mama who is both sacrificer and sacrifice, as woman who learns to accommodate to life's meanness but only with a vengenance. She is forceful, conniving, intriguing. It is rumored that when she could no longer support her children she had a train run over her leg so that she could collect money for the rest of her life. When her only son Plum returns from the war and continues to cling to her—as she puts it, tries to climb back into her womb—she lovingly burns him to death. In simple justice, she sees her daughter Harriet (Sula's mother) burned to death beneath her window before she can prevent it. Eva is Sula's opponent from that day, for she sees her granddaughter watching her own mother burn with interest rather than horror. Eva knows Sula is much like her, and so enters into combat with her. Sula puts her grandmother in an old folk's home, but Eva outlives her and has the last word when many years later Nel visits her. Then she accuses Nel, and therefore Sula, of having drowned that little boy. If the warm, all-nourishing mama stereotype were alive and well, the creation of Eva has done away with it. Eva as mother both gives and takes life away. She is as complex a character because of and in spite of her motherhood as any I have read about. She is as mean as life, as energetic as the cold wind up in the Bottom, as unpredictable as warm weather in January.

Toni Morrison's characters illustrate how far we have moved from the stereotypes of the nineteenth century. How could one classify Eva, Sula, even Nel? Into what category could one put Nikki Giovanni as she projects herself in her poetry? What stereotypes would suit Paule Marshall's Selina or Silla? If there is one prevalent trend in this literature it is the movement away from stereotype, whatever the price. Stereotype can be comforting as well as denigrating, and to go beyond set images can be painful. There are so many fine black Afro-American women writers, including June Jordan, Mari Evans, Toni Cade, Alice Walker, Sonia Sanchez, Jane Cortez, not to mention the playwrights whom I have neglected in this analysis. Whether they be primarily political, cultural, historical, philosophical, or eclectic in their point of reference, whether they write about the city, country, or suburbs, whether they weave fantasies or tend toward social realism, whether they are experimental or traditional in style, they leave us with the diversity of the black woman's experience in America, what she has made of it and how she is transforming it.

NOTES

1. Sterling Brown, *The Negro in American Fiction* (1937; reprint, New York: Atheneum, 1969), pp. 1–89.

2. Ibid.

3. Gerda Lerner, ed., *Black Women in White America* (New York: Vintage Press, 1972), pp. 7–72.

4. John Mbiti, *African Religions & Philosophy* (New York: Doubleday Anchor, 1970).

5. Lerner, *Black Women*, pp. 7–72.

6. Howard Odum and Guy Johnson, *Negro Workaday Songs* (Chapel Hill: University of North Carolina Press, 1926), p. 145.

7. Ibid., pp. 142–143.
8. Ibid., pp. 153–154.
9. Ibid., p. 146.
10. Zora Neale Hurston, *Dust Tracks on the Road* (Philadelphia: J. B. Lippincott Co., 1942), p. 61.
11. Florette Henri, *Black Migration, Movement North 1900–1920* (New York: Doubleday Anchor, 1975).
12. Zora Neale Hurston, *Their Eyes Were Watching God* (New York: J. B. Lippincott, 1937; reprint, New York: Fawcett Publishers, 1965). p. 159.
13. Ibid.
14. Ibid.
15. Ibid., p. 16.
16. Ibid.
17. Gwendolyn Brooks, *Selected Poems* (New York: Harper & Row, 1963), p. 4.
18. Gwendolyn Books, "Maud Martha," *The World of Gwendolyn Books* (New York: Harper & Row, 1971), pp. 228–289.
19. Paule Marshall, *Browngirl, Brownstones* (New York: Avon, 1959), p. 11.
20. Ibid.
21. Ibid.
22. Ibid., p. 60.
23. Ibid., pp. 143–144.
24. Ibid., p. 252.
25. Nikki Giovanni, "Scrapbooks," *My House* (New York: Morrow, 1972). p. 33.
26. Nikki Giovanni, "The True Importance of Present Dialogues, Black vs. Negro," *Black Feeling/Black Talk/Black Judgment* (New York: Morrow, 1970), p. 19.
27. Giovanni, *Black Feeling*, p. 38.
28. Ibid., p. 77.
29. Ibid., p. 78.
30. Giovanni, *My House*, pp. 6–7.
31. Ibid., p. 16.
32. Nikki Giovanni, *Gemini* (New York: Morrow, 1971), p. 37.
33. Ibid., p. 145.
34. Toni Morrison, *The Bluest Eye* (New York: Holt, Rinehart & Winston, 1970), p. 40.
35. Ibid., p. 68.
36. Toni Morrison, *Sula* (New York: Knopf, 1974), p. 5.
37. Ibid., p. 121.
38. Ibid., p. 122.
39. Ibid., p. 121.
40. Ibid.

Roland Barthes 1915–1980

Barthes is regarded by some as the preeminent structuralist in literary studies, the structuralist who developed the method for deciphering cultural signs and discourses and applied it more rigorously, more extensively, than anyone else. There are even some who also argue that it was Barthes who prepared the way for Derrida, deconstruction, and much that has happened in poststructuralism. Barthes was a critic and theorist but also a consummate essayist and writer addressing his special subject, writing. A writer with theoretical interests, therefore, can easily find Barthes's work appealing because it is always possible to detect in that work a writer's concerns. It is easy then when reading Barthes to understand his claim that the "text's unity lies not in its origin but in its destination" and that "the text is a collaborative effort with the author that the reader inherits." Among his many prominent works are *Writing Degree Zero* (1953; trans. 1967), *Elements of Semiology* (1964; trans. 1964), *Mythologies* (1957; trans. 1972), *Image-Music-Text* (1966; trans. 1977), and *A Lover's Discourse* (1977; trans. 1978).

"From Work to Text" (1971), taken from *Image-Music-Text* (1977), makes a distinction between "work" and "text" that informs much of Barthes's work. The work is a fixed product, a document of stable and exact meaning, that a reader may read and, therein, consume. A work, in other words, and as Barthes says, is what one can "put on the shelf." The "text," on the other hand, is that which is situated in language and remains in a state of production. It has no fixed "signifieds," or stable meanings, and "exists," as Barthes says, only "in the movement of a discourse." The text, in other words, is the work seen in the very activity of reading and interpretation. Barthes uses very similar formulations of the static and dynamic text in *The Pleasure of the Text*, when he expands his idea of work/text to include the "classic," the text that we know well and return to for enjoyment again and again, and the avant-garde text that we encounter without comparisons and must read without familiar recognition.

FROM WORK TO TEXT

Over the past several years, a change has been taking place in our ideas about language and, as a consequence, about the (literary) work which owes at least its phenomenal existence to language. This change is obviously linked to current developments in, among other fields, linguistics, anthropology, Marxism, and psychoanalysis (the word "link" is used here in a deliberately neutral fashion: it implies no decision about a determination, be it multiple and dialectical). The change affecting the notion of the work does not necessarily come from the internal renewal of each of these disciplines, but proceeds, rather, from their encounter at the level of an object that traditionally depends on none of them. *Interdisciplinary* activity, valued today as an important aspect of research, cannot be accomplished by simple confrontations between various specialized branches of knowledge. Interdisciplinary work is not a peaceful operation: it begins *effectively* when the solidarity of the old disciplines breaks down—a process made more violent, perhaps, by the jolts of fashion—to the benefit of a new object and a new language, neither of which is in the domain of those branches of knowledge that one calmly sought to confront.

It is precisely this uneasiness with classification that allows for the diagnosis of a certain mutation. The mutation that seems to be taking hold of the idea of the work must not, however, be overestimated: it is part of an epistemological shift [*glissement*] rather than of a real break [*coupure*], a break of the kind which, as has often been remarked, supposedly occurred during the last century, with the appearance of Marxism and Freudianism. No new break seems to have occurred since, and it can be said that, in a way, we have been involved in repetition for the past hundred years. Today history, our history, allows only displacement, variation, going-beyond, and rejection. Just as Einsteinian science requires the inclusion of the *relativity of reference points* in the object studied, so the combined activity of Marxism, Freudianism, and structuralism requires, in the case of literature, the relativization of the *scriptor*'s, the reader's, and the observer's (the critic's) relationships. In opposition to the notion of the *work*—a traditional notion that has long been and still is thought of in what might be called Newtonian fashion—there now arises a need for a new object, one obtained by the displacement or overturning of previous categories. This object is the *Text*. I realize that this word is fashionable and therefore suspect in certain quarters, but that is precisely why I would like to review the principal propositions at the intersection of which the Text is situated today. These propositions are to be understood as enunciations rather than arguments, as mere indications, as it were, approaches that "agree" to remain metaphoric. Here, then, are those propositions: they deal with method, genre, the sign, the plural, filiation, reading (in an active sense), and pleasure.

(1) The Text must not be thought of as a defined object. It would be useless to attempt a material separation of works and texts. One must take particular care not to say that works are classical while texts are avant-garde. Distinguishing them in not a matter of establishing a crude list in the name of modernity and declaring certain literary productions to be "in" and others "out" on the basis of their chronological situation. A very ancient work can contain "some text," while many products of contemporary literature are not texts at all. The difference is as follows: the work is concrete, occupying a portion of book-space (in a library, for example); the Text, on the other hand, is a methodological field.

This opposition recalls the distinction proposed by Lacan between "reality" and the "real": the one is displayed, the other demonstrated. In the same way, the work can be seen in bookstores, in card catalogues, and on course lists, while the text reveals itself, articulates itself according to or against certain rules. While the work is held in the hand, the text is held in language: it exists only as discourse. The Text is not the decomposition of the work; rather it is the work that is the Text's imaginary tail. In other words, *the Text is experienced only in an activity, a production*. It follows that the Text cannot stop, at the end of a library shelf, for example; the constitutive movement of the Text is a *traversal* [*traversée*]: it can cut across a work, several works.

(2) Similarly, the Text does not come to a stop with (good) literature; it cannot be apprehended as part of a hierarchy or even a simple division of genres. What constitutes the Text is, on the contrary (or precisely), its subversive force with regard to old classifications. How can one classify Georges Bataille? Is this writer a novelist, a poet, an essayist, an economist, a philosopher, a mystic? The answer is so uncertain that manuals of literature generally chose to forget about Bataille; yet Bataille wrote texts—even, perhaps, always one and the same text.

If the Text raises problems of classification, that is because it always implies an experience of limits. Thibaudet used to speak (but in a very restricted sense) about limit-works (such as Chateaubriand's *Life of Rancé*, a work that today indeed seems to be a "text"): the Text is that which goes to the limit of the rules of enunciation (rationality, readability, and so on). The Text tries to situate itself exactly *behind* the limit of *doxa* (is not public opinion—constitutive of our democratic societies and powerfully aided by mass communication—defined by its limits, its energy of exclusion, its *censorship*?). One could literally say that the Text is always *paradoxical*.

(3) Whereas the Text is approached and experienced in relation to the sign, the work closes itself on a signified. Two modes of signification can be attributed to this signified: on the one hand, one can assume that it is obvious, in which case the work becomes the object of a "science of the letter" (philology); on the other hand, one can assume that the signified is secret and ultimate, in which case one must search for it, and the work then depends upon a hermeneutic, an interpretation (Marxist, psychoanalytic, thematic, for example). In brief, the work itself functions as a general sign and thus represents an institutional category of the civilization of the Sign. The Text, on the contrary, practices the infinite deferral of the signified [*le recul infini du signifié*]: the Text is *dilatory;* its field is that of the signifier. The signifier must not be conceived as "the first stage of meaning," its material vestibule, but rather, on the contrary, as its *aftermath* [*après-coup*]. In the same way, the signifier's *infinitude* does not refer back to some idea of the ineffable (of an unnamable signified) but to the idea of *play*. The engendering of the perpetual signifier within the field of the text should not be identified with a organic process of maturation or a hermeneutic process of deepening, but rather with a serial movement of dislocations, overlappings, and variations. The logic that governs the Text is not comprehensive (seeking to define "what the work means") but metonymic; and the activity of associations, contiguities, and cross-references coincides with a liberation of symbolic energy. The work (in the best of cases) is moderately symbolic (its symbolism runs out, comes to a halt), but the Text is *radically* symbolic. *A work whose integrally symbolic nature one conceives, perceives, and receives is a text.*

In this way the Text is restored to language: like language, it is structured but decentered, without closure (here one might note, in reply to the scornful insinuation of "faddishness" which is often directed against structuralism, that the epistemological privilege presently granted to language proceeds precisely from our discovery in language of a paradoxical idea of structure, a system without end or center).

(4) The Text is plural. This does not mean just that it has several meanings, but rather that it achieves plurality of meaning, an *irreducible* plurality. The Text is not coexistence of meanings but passage, traversal; thus it answers not to an interpretation, liberal though it may be, but to an explosion, a dissemination. The Text's plurality does not depend on the ambiguity of its contents, but rather on what could be called the *stereographic plurality* of the signifiers that weave it (etymologically the text is a cloth; *textus*, from which text derives, means "woven").

The reader of the Text could be compared to an idle subject (a subject having relaxed his "imaginary"[1]): this fairly empty subject strolls along the side of a valley at the bottom of which runs a *wadi* (I use *wadi* here to stress a certain feeling of unfamiliarity). What he sees is multiple and irreducible; it emerges from substances and levels that are heterogeneous and disconnected: lights, colors, vegetation, heat, air, bursts of noise, high-pitched bird calls, children's cries from the other side of the valley, paths, gestures, clothing of close and distant inhabitants. All these *occurrences* are partially identifiable: they proceed from known codes, but their combination is unique, founding the stroll in difference that can be repeated only as difference. This is what happens in the case of the Text: it can be itself only in its difference (which does not mean its "individuality"); its reading is semelfactive (which renders all inductive-deductive sciences of texts illusory—there is no "grammar" of the text) and yet completely woven with quotations, references, and echoes. These are cultural languages (and what language is not?), past or present, that traverse the text from one end to the other in a vast stereophony.

Every text, being itself the intertext of another text, belongs to the intertextual, which must not be confused with a text's origins; the search for the "sources of" and "influence upon" a work is to satisfy the myth of filiation. The quotations from which a text is constructed are anonymous, irrecoverable, and yet *already read:* they are quotations without quotation marks. The work does not upset monistic philosophies, for which plurality is evil. Thus, when it is compared with the work, the text might well take as its motto the words of the man possessed by devils: "My name is legion, for we are many" (Mark 5:9).

The plural or demonic texture that divides text from work can carry with it profound modifications in the activity of reading and precisely in the areas where monologism seems to be the law. Some of the "texts" of the Scriptures that have traditionally been recuperated by theological (historical or anagogical) monism may perhaps lend themselves to a diffraction of meaning, while the Marxist interpretation of the work, until now resolutely monistic, may be able to materialize itself even further by pluralizing itself (if, of course, Marxist "institutions" allow this).

(5) The work is caught up in a process of filiation. Three things are postulated here: a *determination* of the work by the outside world (by race, then by history), a *consecution* of works among themselves, and an *allocation* of the work to its author. The author is regarded as the father and the owner of his work; literary research therefore learns to *respect* the manuscript and the author's declared intentions, while society posits the legal nature of the author's relationship with his work (these are the "author's rights," which are actually quite recent; they were not legalized in France until the Revolution).

The Text, on the other hand, is read without the father's signature. The metaphor that describes the Text is also distinct from that describing the work. The latter refers to the image of an *organism* that grows by vital expansion, by "development" (a significantly ambiguous word, both biological and rhetorical). The Text's metaphor is that of the *network:*[2] if the Text expands, it is under the effect of a *combinatorial,* a *systematics*[3] (an image which comes close to modern biology's views on the living being).

Therefore, no vital "respect" is owed to the Text: it can be broken (this is exactly what the Middle Ages did with two authoritative texts, the Scriptures and Aristotle). The Text can be read without its father's guarantee: the restitution of the intertext paradoxically abolishes the concept of filiation. It is not that the author cannot "come back" into the Text, into his text; however, he can only do so as a "guest," so to speak. If the author is a novelist, he inscribes himself in his text as one of his characters, as another figure sewn into the rug; his signature is no longer privileged and paternal, the locus of genuine truth, but rather, ludic. He becomes a "paper author": his life is no longer the origin of his fables, but a fable that runs concurrently with his work. There is a reversal, and it is the work which affects the life, not the life which affects the work: the work of Proust and Genet allows us to read their lives as a text. The word "bio-graphy" reassumes its strong meaning, in accordance with its etymology. At the same time, the enunciation's sincerity, which has been a veritable "cross" of literary morality, becomes a false problem: that *I* that writes the text is never, itself, anything more than a paper *I*.

(6) The work is ordinarily an object of consumption. I intend no demagoguery in referring here to so-called consumer culture, but one must realize that today it is the work's "quality" (this implies, ultimately, an appreciation in terms of "taste") and not the actual process of reading that can establish differences between books. There is no structural difference between "cultured" reading and casual subway reading. The Text (if only because of its frequent "unreadability") decants the work from its consumption and gathers it up as play, task, production, and activity. This means that the Text requires an attempt to abolish (or at least to lessen) the distance between writing and reading, not by intensifying the reader's projection into the work, but by linking the two together in a single signifying process [*pratique signifiante*].

The distance separating writing from reading is historical: during the era of greatest social divison (before the institution of democratic cultures), both reading and writing were class privileges. Rhetoric, the great literary code of those times, taught *writing* (even though speeches and not texts were generally produced). It is significant that the advent of democracy reversed the order: (secondary) school now prides itself on teaching how to *read* (well), and not how to *write*.

In fact, *reading* in the sense of *consuming* is not *playing* with the text. Here "playing" must be understood in all its polysemy. The text itself *plays* (like a door on its hinges, like a device in which there is some "play"); and the reader himself plays twice over: playing the Text as one plays a game, he searches for a practice that will re-produce the Text; but, to keep that practice from being reduced to a passive, inner mimesis (the Text being precisely what resists such a reduction), he also *plays* the Text in the musical sense of the term. The history of music (as practice, not as "art") happens to run quite parallel to the history of the Text. There was a time when "practicing" music lovers were numerous (at least within the confines of a certain class), when "playing" and "listening" constituted an almost undifferentiated activity. Then two roles appeared in succession: first, that of the *interpreter*, to whom the bourgeois public delegated its playing; second, that of the music lover who listened to music without knowing how to play it. Today, post-serial music has disrupted the role of the "interpreter" by requiring him to be, in a certain sense, the coauthor of a score which he completes rather than "interprets."

The Text is largely a score of this new type: it asks the reader for an active collaboration. This is a great innovation, because it compels us to ask "who *executes* the work?" (a question raised by Mallarmé, who wanted the audience to *produce* the book). Today only the critic *executes* the work (in both senses). The reduction of reading to consumption is obviously responsible for the "boredom" that many people feel when confronting the modern ("unreadable") text, or the avant-garde movie or painting: to suffer from boredom means that one cannot produce the text, play it, open it out, *make it go*.

(7) This suggests one final approach to the Text, that of pleasure. I do not know if a hedonistic aesthetic ever existed, but there certainly exists a pleasure associated with the work (at least with certain works). I can

enjoy reading and rereading Proust, Flaubert, Balzac, and even—why not?—Alexandre Dumas; but this pleasure, as keen as it may be and even if disengaged from all prejudice, remains partly (unless there has been an exceptional critical effort) a pleasure of consumption. If I can read those authors, I also know that I cannot *rewrite* them (that today, one can no longer write "like that"); that rather depressing knowledge is enough to separate one from the production of those works at the very moment when their remoteness founds one's modernity (for what is "being modern" but the full realization that one cannot begin to write the same works once again?). The Text, on the other hand, is linked to enjoyment [*jouissance*], to pleasure without separation. Order of the signifier, the Text participates in a social utopia of its own: prior to history, the Text achieves, if not the transparency of social relations, at least the transparency of language relations. It is the space in which no one langauge has a hold over any other, in which all languages circulate freely.

These few propositions, inevitably, do not constitute the articulation of a theory of the Text. This is not just a consequence of the presenter's insufficiencies (besides, I have in many respects only recapitulated what is being developed around me); rather, it proceeds from the fact that a theory of the Text cannot be fully satisfied by a metalinguistic exposition. The destruction of metalanguage, or at least (since it may become necessary to return to it provisionally) the questioning of it, is part of the theory itself. Discourse on the Text should itself be only "text," search, and textual toil, since the Text is that *social* space that leaves no language safe or untouched, that allows no enunciative subject to hold the position of judge, teacher, analyst, confessor, or decoder. The theory of the Text can coincide only with the activity of writing.

Notes

1. "Qui aurait détendu en lui tout imaginaire." *Imaginary* is not simply the opposite of real. Used in the Lacanian sense, it is the register, the dimension of all images, conscious or unconscious, perceived or imagined.—Trans.

2. Barthes uses here the word *réseau*. I have chosen to translate it by "network" (rather than "web," for instance) at the risk of overemphasizing the mechanical implications of the metaphor.—Trans.

3. *Systematics* is the science (or method) of classification of living forms.—Trans.

Michel Foucault 1926–1984

Along with Jacques Derrida, Michel Foucault has become one of the most prominent European influences directing the pursuit of theory in recent American literary studies. Foucault's thought, however, has not been as readily integrated into literary criticism as have the ideas of Derrida and the poststructuralist work of Roland Barthes, Jacques Lacan, and Julia Kristeva (even though he has written on Gustave Flaubert, Maurice Blanchot, and Raymond Roussel). This difficulty of integration results from the specific concerns of his work.

Unlike most poststructuralists, Foucault is less concerned with language at the level of the sign and much more concerned with the relationship of language and social institutions, a relationship that he calls "discourse." To examine language at the level of discourse is to identify the institutional rules that make possible particular significations and, consequently, make possible particular forms of knowledge.

This concern with underlying rules that govern the production of knowledge is found in Foucault's early major work, in which he identifies the conditions that made possible the emergence and development of modern areas of knowledge and their corresponding institutions: the diagnosis of madness and the emergence of asylums (*Madness and Civilization*, 1961; trans. 1965), scientific medicine and the emergence of clinics (*The Birth of the Clinic*, 1963; trans. 1973), and the emergence of the human sciences in eighteenth-century Europe (*The Order of Things*, 1966; trans, 1970). Though Foucault, in his later work, remained interested in the social conditions of knowledge, his focus shifted following the failed leftist uprising in Paris during May 1968. The failure of this uprising led Foucault to an analysis of the exercise of power through social practices, including uses of language, or "discursive practices." This shift of interest coincided with a prestigious appointment to the Collège de France in 1970. His inaugural lecture in this position, *The Discourse on Language* (1971; trans. 1972), set the agenda for future work by outlining the ways in which "in every society the production of discourse is at once controlled, selected, organized, and redistributed according to a certain number of procedures. . . ." In *Discipline and Punish* (1975; trans. 1977), Foucault combined his interest in the emergence of social institutions (in this case, the rise of prisons in the early nineteenth century) and the exercise of power through discipline, especially discipline of the body. This interest in the application of discipline though discursive and other practices continues in the last of Foucault's major works, the three volumes of *The History of Sexuality* (1976, 1984; trans. 1978, 1986). Foucault's thought, then, does not lend itself to commentaries on individual literary works as much as it directs us to view literature as a socially determined discursive practice. Foucault's work has also influenced several American critics to examine literary criticism (and its history) as a discursive practice. Foucault died in 1984.

"What Is an Author?" was first published in 1969; while it probes the institutional forces that affect writing and knowledge (a project that Foucault theorized in *The Archeology of Knowledge*, 1969; trans. 1972), it was the first work to reflect his new concern with the exercise of power. Foucault frames the essay by observing a contradiction in modern culture: in many ways our culture regards the author as unimportant (for example, formalist literary criticism and the structuralist approach to the human sciences), yet in our criticism we do not hesitate to use the names of authors. On the basis of this contradiction, Foucault sets the direction of his inquiry: "I am not certain that consequences derived from the disappearance or death of the author have been fully explored or that the importance of this event has been appreciated." Foucault, then, in posing the question, What is an author? is asking, In what ways do we use the notion of author? Foucault observes that we use the name of an author to do more than to refer to a person; instead, the notion of author, unlike the notion of writer, is used to *authorize* certain writings, to privilege those writings. Thus by focusing on the notion of author, Foucault raises the more general questions of what conditions and interests allow one writer to be regarded as an author and another writer not. Foucault also uses this insight into the social/political nature of the notion of author to problematize the subjectivity of the writer—that is, to assert that a text is never the product of a unified consciousness (the author) but consists in several socially determined roles, or "author-functions."

What Is an Author?

The coming into being of the notion of "author" constitutes the privileged moment of *individualization* in the history of ideas, knowledge, literature, philosophy, and the sciences. Even today, when we reconstruct the history of a concept, literary genre, or school of philosophy, such categories seem relatively weak, secondary, and superimposed scansions in comparison with the solid and fundamental unit of the author and the work.

I shall not offer here a sociohistorical analysis of the author's persona. Certainly it would be worth examining how the author became individualized in a culture like ours, what status he has been given, at what moment studies of authenticity and attribution began, in what kind of system of valorization the author was involved, at what point we began to recount the lives of authors rather than of heroes, and how this fundamental category of "the-man-and-his-work criticism" began. For the moment, however, I want to deal solely with the relationship between text and author and with the manner in which the text points to this "figure" that, at least in appearance, is outside it and antecedes it.

Beckett nicely fomulates the theme with which I would like to begin: " 'What does it matter who is speaking,' someone said, 'what does it matter who is speaking.' " In this indifference appears one of the fundamental ethical principles of contemporary writing [*écriture*]. I say "ethical" because this indifference is not really a trait characterizing the manner in which one speaks and writes, but rather a kind of immanent rule, taken up over and over again, never fully applied, not designating writing as something completed, but dominating it as a practice. Since it is too familiar to require a lengthy analysis, this immanent rule can be adequately illustrated here by tracing two of its major themes.

First of all, we can say that today's writing has freed itself from the dimension of expression. Referring only to itself, but without being restricted to the confines of its interiority, writing is identified with its own unfolded exteriority. This means that it is an interplay of signs arranged less according to its signified content than according to the very nature of the signifier. Writing unfolds like a game [*jeu*] that invariably goes beyond its own rules and transgresses its limits. In writing, the point is not to manifest or exalt the act of writing, nor is it to pin a subject within language; it is rather a question of creating a space into which the writing subject constantly disappears.

The second theme, writing's relationship with death, is even more familiar. This link subverts an old tradition exemplified by the Greek epic, which was intended to perpetuate the immortality of the hero: if he was willing to die young, it was so that his life consecrated and magnified by death, might pass into immortality; the narrative then redeemed this accepted death. In another way, the motivation, as well as the theme and the pretext of Arabian narratives—such as *The Thousand and One Nights*—was also the eluding of death: one spoke, telling stories into the early morning, in order to forestall death, to postpone the day of reckoning that would silence the narrator. Scheherazade's narrative is an effort, renewed each night, to keep death outside the circle of life.

Our culture has metamorphosed this idea of narrative, or writing, as something designed to ward off death. Writing has become linked to sacrifice, even to the sacrifice of life: it is now a voluntary effacement which does not need to be represented in books, since it is brought about in the writer's very existence. The work, which once had the duty of providing immortality, now possesses the right to kill, to be its author's murderer, as in the cases of Flaubert, Proust, and Kafka. That is not all, however: this relationship between writing and death is also manifested in the effacement of the writing subject's individual characteristics. Using all the contrivances that he sets up between himself and what he writes, the writing subject cancels out the signs of his particular individuality. As a result, the mark of the writer is reduced to nothing more than the singularity of his absence; he must assume the role of the dead man in the game of writing.

None of this is recent; criticism and philosophy took note of the disappearance—or death—of the author some time ago. But the consequences of their discovery of it have not been sufficiently examined, nor has its import been accurately measured. A certain number of notions that are intended to replace the privileged position of the author actually seem to preserve that privilege and suppress the real meaning of his disappearance. I shall examine two of these notions, both of great importance today.

The first is the idea of the work. It is a very familiar thesis that the task of criticism is not to bring out the work's relationships with the author, nor to reconstruct through the text a thought or experience, but rather, to analyze the work through its structure, its architecture, its intrinsic form, and the play of its internal relationships. At this point, however, a problem arises: "What is a work? What is this curious unity which we designate as a work? Of what elements is it composed? Is it not what an author has written?" Difficulties appear immediately. If an individual were not an author, could we say that what he wrote, said, left behind in his papers, or what has been collected of his remarks, could be called a "work"? When Sade was not considered an author, what was the status of his papers? Were they simply rolls of paper onto which he ceaselessly uncoiled his fantasies during his imprisonment?

Even when an individual has been accepted as an author, we must still ask whether everything that he wrote, said, or left behind is part of his work. The problem is both theoretical and technical. When undertaking the publication of Nietzsche's works, for example, where should one stop? Surely everything must be published, but what is "everything"? Everything that Nietzsche himself published, certainly. And what about the rough drafts for his works? Obviously. The plans for his aphorisms? Yes. The deleted passages and the notes at the bottom of the page? Yes. What if, within a workbook filled with aphorisms, one finds a reference, the notation of a meeting or of an address, or a laundry list: is it a work, or not? Why not? And so on, ad infinitum. How can one define a work amid the millions of traces left by someone after his death? A theory of the work does not exist, and the empirical task of those who naively undertake the editing of works often suffers in the absence of such a theory.

We could go even further: does *The Thousand and One Nights* constitute a work? What about Clement of Alexandria's *Miscellanies* or Diogenes Laertius' *Lives*? A multitude of questions arises with regard to this notion of the work. Consequently, it is not enough to declare that we should do without the writer (the author) and study the work in itself. The word "work" and the unity that it designates are probably as problematic as the status of the author's individuality.

Another notion which has hindered us from taking full measure of the author's disappearance, blurring and concealing the moment of this effacement and subtly preserving the author's existence, is the notion of writing [*écriture*]. When rigorously applied, this notion should allow us not only to circumvent references to the author, but also to situate his recent absence. The notion of writing, as currently employed, is concerned with neither the act of writing nor the indication—be it symptom or sign—of a meaning which someone might have wanted to express. We try, with great effort, to imagine the general condition of each text, the condition of both the space in which it is dispersed and the time in which it unfolds.

In current usage, however, the notion of writing seems to transpose the empirical characteristics of the author into a transcendental anonymity. We are content to efface the more visible marks of the author's empiricity by playing off, one against the other, two ways of characterizing writing, namely, the critical and the religious approaches. Giving writing a primal status seems to be a way of retranslating, in transcendental terms, both the theological affirmation of its sacred character and the critical affirmation of its creative character. To admit that writing is, because of the very history that it made possible, subject to the test of oblivion and repression, seems to represent, in transcendental terms, the religious principle of the hidden meaning (which requires interpretation) and the critical principle of implicit significations, silent determinations, and obscured contents (which gives rise to commentary). To imagine writing as absence seems to be a simple repetition, in transcendental terms, of both the religious principle of inalterable and yet never fulfilled tradition, and the aesthetic principle of the work's survival, its perpetuation beyond the author's death, and its enigmatic excess in relation to him.

This usage of the notion of writing runs the risk of maintaining the author's privileges under the protection of writing's a priori status: it keeps alive, in the grey light of neutralization, the interplay of those representations that formed a particular image of the author. The author's disappearance, which, since Mallarmé, has been a constantly recurring event, is subject to a series of transcendental barriers. There seems to be an important dividing line between those who believe that they can still locate today's discontinuities [*ruptures*] in the historico-transcendental tradition of the nineteenth century, and those who try to free themselves once and for all from that tradition.[1]

It is not enough, however, to repeat the empty affirmation that the author has disappeared. For the same reason, it is not enough to keep repeating (after Nietzsche) that God and man have died a common death. Instead, we must locate the space left empty by the author's disappearance, follow the distribution of gaps and breaches, and watch for the openings that this disappearance uncovers.

First, we need to clarify briefly the problems arising from the use of the author's name. What is an author's name? How does it function? Far from offering a solution, I shall only indicate some of the difficulties that it presents.

The author's name is a proper name, and therefore it raises the problems common to all proper names. (Here I refer to Searle's analyses, among others.[2]) Obviously, one cannot turn a proper name into a pure and simple reference. It has other than indicative functions: more than an indication, a gesture, a finger pointed at someone, it is the equivalent of a description. When one says "Aristotle," one employs a word that is the equivalent of one, or a series of, definite descriptions, such as "the author of the *Analytics*," "the founder of ontology," and so forth. One cannot stop there, however, because a proper name does not have just one signification. When we discover that Rimbaud did not write *La Chasse spirituelle*, we cannot pretend that the meaning of this proper name, or that of the author, has been altered. The proper name and the author's name are situated between the two poles of description and designation: they must have a certain link with what they name, but one that is neither entirely in the mode of designation nor in that of description; it must be a *specific* link. However—and it is here that the particular difficulties of the author's name arise—the links between the proper name and the individual named and between the author's name and what it names are not isomorphic and do not function in the same way. There are several differences.

If, for example, Pierre Dupont does not have blue eyes, or was not born in Paris, or is not a doctor, the name Pierre Dupont will still always refer to the same person; such things do not modify the link of designation. The problems raised by the author's name are much more complex, however. If I discover that Shakespeare was not born in the house that we visit today, this is a modification which, obviously, will not alter the functioning of the author's name. But if we proved that Shakespeare did not write those sonnets which pass for his, that would constitute a significant change and affect the manner in which the author's name functions. If we proved that Shakespeare wrote Bacon's *Organon* by showing that the same author wrote both the works of Bacon and those of Shakespeare, that would be a third type of change which would entirely modify the functioning of the author's name. The author's name is not, therefore, just a proper name like the rest.

Many other facts point out the paradoxical singularity of the author's name. To say that Pierre Dupont does not exist is not at all the same as saying that Homer or Hermes Trismegistus did not exist. In the first case, it means that no one has the name Pierre Dupont; in the second, it means that several people were mixed together under one name, or that the true author had none of the traits traditionally ascribed to the personae of Homer or Hermes. To say that X's real name is actually Jacques Durand instead of Pierre Dupont is not the same as saying that Stendhal's name was Henri Beyle. One could also question the meaning and functioning of propositions like

"Bourbaki is so-and-so, so-and-so, etc." and "Victor Eremita, Climacus, Anticlimacus, Frater Taciturnus, Constantine Constantius, all of these are Kierkegaard."

These differences may result from the fact that an author's name is not simply an element in a discourse (capable of being either subject or object, of being replaced by a pronoun, and the like); it performs a certain role with regard to narrative discourse, assuring a classificatory function. Such a name permits one to group togther a certain number of texts, define them, differentiate them from and contrast them to others. In addition, it establishes a relationship among the texts. Hermes Trismegistus did not exist, nor did Hippocrates—in the sense that Balzac existed—but the fact that several texts have been placed under the same name indicates that there has been established among them a relationship of homogeneity, filiation, authentification of some texts by the use of others, reciprocal explication, or concomitant utilization. The author's name serves to characterize a certain mode of being of discourse: the fact that the discourse has an author's name, that one can say "this was written by so-and-so" and "so-and-so is its author," shows that this discourse is not ordinary everyday speech that merely comes and goes, not something that is immediately consumable. On the contrary, it is a speech that must be received in a certain mode and that, in a given culture, must receive a certain status.

It would seem that the author's name, unlike other proper names, does not pass from the interior of a discourse to the real and exterior individual who produced it; instead, the name seems always to be present, marking off the edges of the text, revealing, or at least characterizing, its mode of being. The author's name manifests the appearance of a certain discursive set and indicates the status of this discourse within a society and a culture. It has no legal status, nor is it located in the fiction of the work; rather, it is located in the break that founds a certain discursive construct and its very particular mode of being. As a result, we could say that in a civilization like our own there are a certain number of discourses that are endowed with the "author-function," while others are deprived of it. A private letter may well have a signer—it does not have an author; a contract may well have a guarantor—it does not have an author. An anonymous text posted on a wall probably has a writer—but not an author. The author-function is therefore characteristic of the mode of existence, circulation, and functioning of certain discourses within a society.

Let us analyze this "author-function" as we have just described it. In our culture, how does one characterize a discourse containing the author-function? In what way is this discourse different from other discourses? If we limit our remarks to the author of a book or a text, we can isolate four different characteristics.

First of all, discourses are objects of appropriation. The form of ownership from which they spring is of a rather particular type, one that has been codified for many years. We should note that, historically, this type of ownership has always been subsequent to what one might call penal appropriation. Texts, books, and discourses really began to have authors (other than mythical, "sacralized" and "sacralizing" figures) to the extent that authors became subject to punishment, that is, to the extent that discourses could be transgressive. In our culture (and doubtless in many others), discourse was not originally a product, a thing, a kind of goods; it was essentially an act—an act placed in the bipolar field of the sacred and the profane, the licit and the illicit, the religious and the blasphemous. Historically, it was a gesture fraught with risks before becoming goods caught up in a circuit of ownership.

Once a system of ownership for texts came into being, once strict rules concerning author's rights, author-publisher relations, rights of reproduction, and related matters were enacted—at the end of the eighteenth and the beginning of the nineteenth century—the possiblity of transgression attached to the act of writing took on, more and more, the form of an imperative peculiar to literature. It is as if the author, beginning with the moment at which he was placed in the system of property that characterizes our society, compensated for the status that he thus acquired by rediscovering the old bipolar field of discourse, systematically practicing transgression and thereby restoring danger to a writing which was now guaranteed the benefits of ownership.

The author-function does not affect all discourses in a universal and constant way, however. This is its second characteristic. In our civilization, it has not always been the same types of texts which have required attribution to an author. There was a time when the texts that we today call "literary" (narratives, stories, epics, tragedies, comedies) were accepted, put into circulation, and valorized without any question about the identity of their author; their anonymity caused no difficulties since their ancientness, whether real or imagined, was regarded as a sufficient guarantee of their status. On the other hand, those texts that we now would call scientific—those dealing with cosmology and the heavens, medicine and illnesses, natural sciences and geography—were accepted in the Middle Ages, and accepted as "true," only when marked with the name of their author. "Hippocrates said," "Pliny recounts," were not really formulas of an argument based on authority; they were the markers inserted in discourses that were supposed to be received as statements of demonstrated truth.

A reversal occurred in the seventeenth or eighteenth century. Scientific discourses began to be received for themselves, in the anonymity of an established or always redemonstrable truth; their membership in a systematic ensemble, and not the reference to the individual who produced them, stood as their guarantee. The author-function faded away, and the inventor's name served only to christen a theorem, proposition, particular effect, property, body, group of elements, or pathological syndrome. By the same token, literary discourses came to be accepted only when endowed with the author-function. We now ask of each poetic or fictional text: from where does it come, who wrote it, when, under what circumstances, or beginning with what design? The meaning ascribed to it and the status or value accorded it depend upon the manner in which we answer these questions. And if a text should be discovered in a state of anonymity—whether as a consequence of an accident or the author's explicit wish—the game becomes one of rediscovering the author. Since literary anonymity is not tolerable, we can accept it only in the guise of an enigma. As a result, the author-function today plays an important role in our view of literary works. (These are obviously generalizations that would have to be refined insofar as recent critical practice is concerned.)

The third characteristic of this author-function is that it does not develop spontaneously as the attribution of a discourse to an individual. It is, rather, the result of a complex operation which constructs a certain rational being that we call "author." Critics doubtless try to give this intelligible being a realistic status, by discerning, in the individual, a "deep" motive, a "creative" power, or a "design," the milieu in which writing originates. Nevertheless, these aspects of an individual which we designate as making him an author are only a projection, in more or less psychologizing terms, of the operations that we force texts to undergo, the connections that we make, the traits that we establish as pertinent, the continuities that we recognize, or the exclusions that we practice. All these operations vary according to periods and types of discourse. We do not construct a "philosophical author" as we do a "poet," just as, in the eighteenth century, one did not construct a novelist as we do today. Still, we can find through the ages certain constants in the rules of author-construction.

It seems, for example, that the manner in which literary criticism once defined the author—or rather constructed the figure of the author beginning with existing texts and discourses—is directly derived from the manner in which Christian tradition authenticated (or rejected) the texts at its disposal. In order to "rediscover" an author in a work, modern criticism uses methods similar to those that Christian exegesis employed when trying to prove the value of a text by its author's saintliness. In *De viris illustribus*, Saint Jerome explains that homonymy is not sufficient to identify legitimately authors of more than one work: different individuals could have had the same name, or one man could have, illegitimately, borrowed another's patronymic. The name as an individual trademark is not enough when one works within a textual tradition.

How then can one attribute several discourses to one and the same author? How can one use the author-function to determine if one is dealing with one or several individuals? Saint Jerome proposes four criteria: (1) if among several books attributed to an author one is inferior to the others, it must be withdrawn from the list of the author's works (the author is therefore defined as a constant level of value); (2) the same should be done if certain texts contradict the doctrine expounded in the author's other works (the author is thus defined as a field of conceptual or theoretical coherence); (3) one must also exclude works that are written in a different style, containing words and expressions not ordinarily found in the writer's production (the author is here conceived as a stylistic unity); (4) finally, passages quoting statements that were made, or mentioning events that occurred after the author's death must be regarded as interpolated texts (the author is here seen as a historical figure at the crossroads of a certain number of events).

Modern literary criticism, even when—as is now customary—it is not concerned with questions of authentication, still defines the author the same way: the author provides the basis for explaining not only the presence of certain events in a work, but also their transformations, distortions, and diverse modifications (through his biography, the determination of his individual perspective, the analysis of his social position, and the revelation of his basic design). The author is also the principle of a certain unity of writing—all differences having to be resolved, at least in part, by the principles of evolution, maturation, or influence. The author also serves to neutralize the contradictions that may emerge in a series of texts: there must be—at a certain level of his thought or desire, of his consciousness or unconscious—a point where contradictions are resolved, where incompatible elements are at last tied together or organized around a fundamental or originating contradiction. Finally, the author is a particular source of expression that, in more or less completed forms, is manifested equally well, and with similar validity, in works, sketches, letters, fragments, and so on. Clearly, Saint Jerome's four criteria of authenticity (criteria which seem totally insufficient for today's exegetes) do define the four modalities according to which modern criticism brings the author-function into play.

But the author-function is not a pure and simple reconstruction made secondhand from a text given as passive material. The text always contains a certain number of signs referring to the author. These signs, well known to grammarians, are personal pronouns, adverbs of time and place, and verb conjugation. Such elements do not play the same role in discourses provided with the author-function as in those lacking it. In the latter, such "shifters" refer to the real speaker and to the spatio-temporal coordinates of his discourse (although certain modifications can occur, as in the operation of relating discourses in the first person). In the former, however, their role is more complex and variable. Everyone knows that, in a novel narrated in the first person, neither the first person pronoun, nor the present indicative refer exactly either to the writer or to the moment in which he writes, but rather to an alter ego whose distance from the author varies, often changing in the course of the work. It would be just as wrong to equate the author with the real writer as to equate him with the fictitious speaker; the author-function is carried out and operates in the scission itself, in this division and this distance.

One might object that this is a characteristic peculiar to novelistic or poetic discourse, a "game" in which only "quasi-discourses" participate. In fact, however, all discourses endowed with the author-function do possess this plurality of self. The self that speaks in the preface to a treatise on mathematics—and that indicates the circumstances of the treatise's composition—is identical neither in its position nor in its functioning to the self that speaks in the course of a demonstration, and that appears in the form of "I conclude" or "I suppose." In the first case, the "I" refers to an individual without an equivalent who, in a determined place and time, completed a certain task; in the second, the "I" indicates an instance and a level of demonstration which any individual could perform provided that he accept the same system of symbols, play of axioms, and set of previous demonstrations. We could also, in the same treatise, locate a third self, one that speaks to tell the work's meaning, the obstacles encountered, the results obtained, and the remaining problems; this self is situated in the field of already existing or yet-to-appear mathematical discourses. The author-function is not assumed by the first of these selves at the expense of the other two, which would then be nothing more than a fictitious splitting in two of the first one. On the contrary, in these discourses the author-function operates so as to effect the dispersion of these three simultaneous selves.

No doubt analysis could discover still more characteristic traits of the author-function. I will limit myself to these four, however, because they seem both the most visible and the most important. They can be summarized as follows: (1) the author-function is linked to the juridical and institutional system that encompasses, determines, and articulates the universe of discourses; (2) it does not affect all discourses in the same way at all times and in all types of civilization; (3) it is not defined by the spontaneous attribution of a discourse to its producer, but rather by a series of specific and complex operations; (4) it does not refer purely and simply to a real individual, since it can give rise simultaneously to several selves, to several subjects—positions that can be occupied by different classes of individuals.

Up to this point I have unjustifiably limited my subject. Certainly the author-function in painting, music, and other arts should have been discussed, but even supposing that we remain within the world of discourse, as I want to do, I seem to have given the term "author" much too narrow a meaning. I have discussed the author only in the limited sense of a person to whom the production of a text, a book, or a work can be legitimately attributed. It is easy to see that in the sphere of discourse one can be the author of much more than a book—one can be the author of a theory, tradition, or discipline in which other books and authors will in their turn find a place. These authors are in a position which we shall call "transdiscursive." This is a recurring phenomenon—certainly as old as our civilization. Homer, Aristotle, and the Church Fathers, as well as the first mathematicians and the originators of the Hippocratic tradition, all played this role.

Furthermore, in the course of the nineteenth century, there appeared in Europe another, more uncommon, kind of author, whom one should confuse with neither the "great" literary authors, nor the authors of religious texts, nor the founders of science. In a somewhat arbitrary way we shall call those who belong in this last group "founders of discursivity." They are unique in that they are not just the authors of their own works. They have produced something else: the possibilities and the rules for the formation of other texts. In this sense, they are very different, for example, from a novelist, who is, in fact, nothing more than the author of his own text. Freud is not just the author of *The Interpretation of Dreams* or *Jokes and Their Relation to the Unconscious;* Marx is not just the author of the *Communist Manifesto* or *Capital:* they both have established an endless possiblity of discourse.

Obviously, it is easy to object. One might say that it is not true that the author of a novel is only the author of his own text; in a sense, he also, provided that he acquires some "importance," governs and commands more than that. To take a very simple example, one could say that Ann Radcliffe not only wrote *The Castles of Athlin and Dunbayne* and several other novels, but also made possible the appearance of the Gothic horror novel at the beginning of the nineteenth century; in that respect, her author-function exceeds her own work. But I think there is an answer to this objection. These founders of discursivity (I use Marx and Freud as examples, because I believe them to be both the first and the most important cases) make possible something altogether different from what a novelist makes possible. Ann Radcliffe's texts opened the way for a certain number of resemblances and analogies which have their model or principle in her work. The latter contains characteristic signs, figures, relationships, and structures which could be reused by others. In other words, to say that Ann Radcliffe founded the Gothic horror novel means that in the nineteenth-century Gothic novel one will find, as in Ann Radcliffe's works, the theme of the heroine caught in the trap of her own innocence, the hidden castle, the character of the black, cursed hero devoted to making the world expiate the evil done to him, and all the rest of it.

On the other hand, when I speak of Marx or Freud as founders of discursivity, I mean that they made possible not only a certain number of analogies, but also (and equally important) a certain number of differences. They have created a possibility for something other than their discourse, yet something belonging to what they founded. To say that Freud founded psychoanalysis does not (simply) mean that we find the concept of the libido or the technique of dream analysis in the works of Karl Abraham or Melanie Klein; it means that Freud made possible a certain number of divergences—with respect to his own texts, concepts, and hypotheses—that all arise from the psychoanalytical discourse itself.

This would seem to present a new difficulty, however: is the above not true, after all, of any founder of a science, or of any author who has introduced some important transformation into a science? After all, Galileo made possible not only those discourses that repeated the laws that he had formulated, but also statements very different from what he himself had said. If Cuvier is the founder of biology or Saussure the founder of linguistics, it is not because they were imitated, nor because people have since taken up again the concept of organism or sign; it is because Cuvier made possible, to a certain extent, a theory of evolution diametrically opposed to his own fixism; it is because Saussure made possible a generative grammar radically different from his structural analyses. Superficially, then, the initiation of discursive practices appears similiar to the founding of any scientific endeavor.

Still, there is a difference, and a notable one. In the case of a science, the act that founds it is on an equal footing with its future transformations; this act becomes in some respects part of the set of modifications that it makes possible. Of course, this belonging can take several forms. In the future development of a science, the founding act may appear as little more than a particular instance of a more general phenomenon which unveils itself in the process. It can also turn out to be marred by intuition and empirical bias; one must then reformulate it, making it the object of a certain number of supplementary theoretical operations which establish it more rigorously, etc. Finally, it can seem to be a hasty generalization which must be limited, and whose restricted domain of validity must be retraced. In other words, the founding act of a science can always be reintroduced within the machinery of those transformations that derive from it.

In contrast, the initiation of a discursive practice is heterogeneous to its subsequent transformations. To expand a type of discursivity, such as psychoanalysis as founded by Freud, is not to give it a formal generality that it would not have permitted at the outset, but rather to open it up to a certain number of possible applications. To limit psychoanalysis as a type of discursivity is, in reality, to try to isolate in the founding act an eventually restricted number of propositions or statements to which, alone, one grants a founding value, and in relation to which certain concepts or theories accepted by Freud might be considered as derived, secondary, and accessory. In addition, one does not declare certain propositions in the work of these founders to be false: instead, when trying to seize the act of founding, one sets aside those statements that are not pertinent, either because they are deemed inessential, or because they are considered "prehistoric" and derived from another type of discursivity. In other words, unlike the founding of a science, the initiation of a discursive practice does not participate in its later transformations.

As a result, one defines a proposition's theoretical validity in relation to the work of the founders—while, in the case of Galileo and Newton, it is in relation to what physics or cosmology *is* (in its intrinsic structure and "normativity") that one affirms the validity of any proposition that those men may have put forth. To phrase it very schematically:

the work of initiators of discursivity is not situated in the space that science defines; rather, it is the science or the discursivity which refers back to their work as primary coordinates.

In this way we can understand the inevitable necessity, within these fields of discursivity, for a "return to the origin." This return, which is part of the discursive field itself, never stops modifying it. The return is not a historical supplement which would be added to the discursivity, or merely an ornament; on the contrary, it constitutes an effective and necessary task of transforming the discursive practice itself. Re-examination of Galileo's text may well change our knowledge of the history of mechanics, but it will never be able to change mechanics itself. On the other hand, re-examining Freud's texts modifies psychoanalysis itself just as a re-examination of Marx's would modify Marxism.[3]

What I have just outlined regarding the initiation of discursive practices is, of course, very schematic; this is true, in particular, of the oppostion that I have tried to draw between discursive initiation and scientific founding. It is not always easy to distinguish between the two; moreover, nothing proves that they are two mutually exclusive procedures. I have attempted the distinction for only one reason: to show that the author-function, which is complex enough when one tries to situate it at the level of a book or a series of texts that carry a given signature, involves still more determining factors when one tries to analyze it in larger units, such as groups of works or entire disciplines.

To conclude, I would like to review the reasons why I attach a certain importance to what I have said.

First, there are theoretical reasons. On the one hand, an analysis in the direction that I have outlined might provide for an approach to a typology of discourse. It seems to me, at least at first glance, that such a typology cannot be constructed solely from the grammatical features, formal structures, and objects of discourse: more likely there exist properties or relationships peculiar to discourse (not reducible to the rules of grammar and logic), and one must use these to distinguish the major categories of discourse. The relationship (or nonrelationship) with an author, and the different forms this relationship takes, constitute—in a quite visible manner—one of these discursive properties.

On the other hand, I believe that one could find here an introduction to the historical analysis of discourse. Perhaps it is time to study discourses not only in terms of their expressive value or formal transformations, but according to their modes of existence. The modes of circulation, valorization, attribution, and appropriation of discourses vary with each culture and are modified within each. The manner in which they are articulated according to social relationships can be more readily understood, I believe, in the activity of the author-function and in its modifications, than in the themes or concepts that discourses set in motion.

It would seem that one could also, beginning with analyses of this type, re-examine the privileges of the subject. I realize that in undertaking the internal and architectonic analysis of a work (be it a literary text, philosophical system, or scientific work), in setting aside biographical and psychological references, one has already called back into question the absolute character and founding role of the subject. Still, perhaps one must return to this question, not in order to re-establish the theme of an originating subject, but to grasp the subject's points of insertion, modes of functioning, and system of dependencies. Doing so means overturning the traditional problem, no longer raising the questions "How can a free subject penetrate the substance of things and give it meaning? How can it activate the rules of a language from within and thus give rise to the designs which are properly its own?" Instead, these questions will be raised: "How, under what conditions and in what forms can something like a subject appear in the order of discourse? What place can it occupy in each type of discourse, what functions can it assume, and by obeying what rules?" In short, it is a matter of depriving the subject (or its substitute) of its role as originator, and of analyzing the subject as a variable and complex function of discourse.

Second, there are reasons dealing with the "ideological" status of the author. The question then becomes: How can one reduce the great peril, the great danger with which fiction threatens our world? The answer is: One can reduce it with the author. The author allows a limitation of the cancerous and dangerous proliferation of significations within a world where one is thrifty not only with one's resources and riches, but also with one's discourses and their significations. The author is the principle of thrift in the proliferation of meaning. As a result, we must entirely reverse the traditional idea of the author. We are accustomed, as we have seen earlier, to saying that the author is the genial creator of a work in which he deposits, with infinite wealth and generosity, an inexhaustible world of significations. We are used to thinking that the author is so different from all other men, and so transcendent with regard to all languages that, as soon as he speaks, meaning begins to proliferate, to proliferate indefinitely.

The truth is quite the contrary: the author is not an indefinite source of significations which fill a work; the author does not precede the works, he is a certain functional principle by which, in our culture, one limits, excludes, and chooses; in short, by which one impedes the free circulation, the free manipulation, the free composition, decomposition, and recomposition of fiction. In fact, if we are accustomed to presenting the author as a genius, as a perpetual surging of invention, it is because, in reality, we make him function in exactly the opposite fashion. One can say that the author is an ideological product, since we represent him as the opposite of his historically real function. (When a historically given function is represented in a figure that inverts it, one has an ideological production.) The author is therefore the ideological figure by which one marks the manner in which we fear the proliferation of meaning.

In saying this, I seem to call for a form of culture in which fiction would not be limited by the figure of the author. It would be pure romanticism, however, to imagine a culture in which the fictive would operate in an absolutely free state, in which fiction would be put at the disposal of everyone and would develop without passing through something like a necessary or constraining figure. Although, since the eighteenth century, the author has played the role of the regulator of the fictive, a role quite characteristic of our era of industrial and bourgeois society, of individualism and private property, still, given the historical modifications that are taking place, it does not seem necessary that the author-function remain constant in form, complexity, and even in existence. I think that, as our society changes, at the very moment when it is in the process of changing, the author-function will disappear, and in such a manner that fiction and its polysemic texts will once again function according to another mode, but still with a system of constraint—one which will no longer be the author, but which will have to be determined or, perhaps, experienced.

All discourses, whatever their status, form, value, and whatever the treatment to which they will be subjected, would then develop in the anonymity of a murmur. We would no longer hear the questions that have been rehashed for so long: "Who really spoke? Is it really he and not someone else? With what authenticity or originality? And what part of his deepest self did he express in his discourse?" Instead there would be other questions, like these: "What are the modes of existence of this discourse? Where has it been used, how can it circulate, and who can appropriate it for himself? What are the places in it where there is room for possible subjects? Who can assume these various subject-functions?" And behind all these questions, we would hear hardly anything but the stirring of an indifference: "What difference does it make who is speaking?"

Notes

1. For a discussion of the notions of discontinuity and historical tradition see Foucault's *Les Mots et les choses* (Paris: Gallimard, 1966), translated as *The Order of Things* (New York: Pantheon, 1971).—TRANS.

2. John Searle, *Speech Acts: An Essay in the Philosophy of Language* (Cambridge: Cambridge University Press, 1969), pp. 162–174.—TRANS.

3. To define these returns more clearly, one must also emphasize that they tend to reinforce the enigmatic link between an author and his works. A text has an inaugurative value precisely because it is the work of a particular author, and our returns are conditioned by this knowledge. As in the case of Galileo, there is no possibility that the rediscovery of an unknown text by Newton or Cantor will modify classical cosmology or set theory as we know them (at best, such an exhumation might modify our historical knowledge of their genesis). On the other hand, the discovery of a text like Freud's "Project for a Scientific Psychology"—insofar as it is a text by Freud—always threatens to modify not the historical knowledge of psychoanalysis, but its theoretical field, even if only by shifting the accentuation or the center of gravity. Through such returns, which are part of their makeup, these discursive practices maintain a relationship with regard to their "fundamental" and indirect author unlike that which an ordinary text entertains with its immediate author.—TRANS.

Hélène Cixous 1937–

Hélène Cixous, although considered a "French" writer, academic, and feminist theorist, was born in Oran, Algeria. In 1968, she received a *doctorat* in literature and then published her 900-page thesis, *The Exile of James Joyce*. In that same year, Cixous became a founder of France's revolutionary University of Paris VIII at Vincennes (now at Saint-Denis), where she began her tenure as professor of English literature. After the turbulent student-worker uprisings of May 1968, Cixous emerged as a leading radical academic and avant-garde feminist writer. Her fictional autobiography, *Dedans* (*Inside*) was awarded the Prix Médicis in 1969.

With *Portrait du soleil* (*Portrait of the Sun*) (1973), Cixous started to write specifically about the question of sexual difference; and a year later, she established the Centre de Recherches en Études Feminine (Center of Research in Feminine Studies) at Paris VIII. To show her political commitment to the women's movement, in 1976 Cixous began publishing all her work at Des Femmes, a publishing house founded by women. However, in 1982 she discontinued her association with Des Femmes in order to find greater poetic freedom.

The result of this poetic freedom is a series of bold, enthusiastic feminist writings. These writings address the problem of writing as a woman and question the traditional concept that defines women as passive. Cixous is interested in reading and writing texts in order to displace the existing repressive concepts of femininity in the major discourses that govern Western patriarchal society. She meditates on the possibility of social change through writing.

In "The Laugh of the Medusa" (1976), Cixous offers her theory of *écriture feminine* ("feminine writing"), a guide to reading and writing like a woman. With effusive energy, she calls on women to break their silence and to write. She challenges women to become more than they have been: "Write! Writing is for you, you are for you; your body is yours, take it." Advancing the theory that writing takes place in a "masculine" or a "feminine" economy, Cixous makes her case for the reality and force of the feminine economy. Whereas Cixous sees the masculine economy as linear, rule-conscious, and tyrannical, the feminine economy is the "overflow" of "luminous torrents" with an "openness" that is not repressed by masculine rules of order. This openness of feminine writing is clearly evident in the innovative style of "The Laugh of the Medusa."

The Laugh of the Medusa

I shall speak about women's writing: about *what it will do*. Woman must write her self: must write about women and bring women to writing, from which they have been driven away as violently as from their bodies—for the same reasons, by the same law, with the same fatal goal. Woman must put herself into the text—as into the world and into history—by her own movement.

The future must no longer be determined by the past. I do not deny that the effects of the past are still with us. But I refuse to strengthen them by repeating them, to confer upon them an irremovability the equivalent of destiny, to confuse the biological and the cultural. Anticipation is imperative.

Since these reflections are taking shape in an area just on the point of being discovered, they necessarily bear the mark of our time—a time during which the new breaks away from the old, and, more precisely, the (feminine) new from the old (*la nouvelle de l'ancien*). Thus, as there are no grounds for establishing a discourse, but rather an arid millennial ground to break, what I say has at least two sides and two aims: to break up, to destroy; and to foresee the unforeseeable, to project.

I write this as a woman, toward women. When I say "woman," I'm speaking of woman in her inevitable struggle against conventional man; and of a universal woman subject who must bring women to their senses and to their meaning in history. But first it must be said that in spite of the enormity of the repression that has kept them in the "dark"—that attribute—there is, at this time, no general woman, no one typical woman. What they have *in common* I will say. But what strikes me is the infinite richness of their individual constitutions: you can't talk about *a* female sexuality, uniform, homogeneous, classifiable into codes—any more than you can talk about one unconscious resembling another. Women's imagery is inexhaustible, like music, painting, writing: their stream of phantasms is incredible.

I have been amazed more than once by a description a woman gave me of a world all her own which she had been secretly haunting since early childhood. A world of searching, the elaboration of a knowledge, on the basis of a systematic experimentation with the bodily functions, a passionate and precise interrogation of her erotogeneity. This practice, extraordinarily rich and inventive, in particular as concerns masturbation, is prolonged or accompanied by a production of forms, a veritable aesthetic activity, each stage of rapture inscribing a resonant vision, a composition, something beautiful. Beauty will no longer be forbidden.

I wished that that woman would write and proclaim this unique empire so that other women, other unacknowledged sovereigns, might exclaim: I, too, overflow; my desires have invented new desires, my body knows unheard-of songs. Time and again I, too, have felt so full of luminous torrents that I could burst—burst with forms much more beautiful than those which are put up in frames and sold for a stinking fortune. And I, too, said nothing, showed nothing; I didn't open my mouth, I didn't repaint my half of the world. I was ashamed. I was afraid, and I swallowed my shame and my fear. I said to myself: You are mad! What's the meaning of these waves, these floods, these outbursts? Where is the ebullient, infinite woman who, immersed as she was in her naiveté, kept in the dark about herself, led into self-disdain by the great arm of parental-conjugal phallocentrism, hasn't been ashamed of her strength? Who, surprised and horrified by the fantastic tumult of her drives (for she was made to believe that a well-adjusted normal woman has a . . . divine composure), hasn't accused herself of being a monster? Who, feeling a funny desire stirring inside her (to sing, to write, to dare to speak, in short, to bring out something new), hasn't thought she was sick? Well, her shameful sickness is that she resists death, that she makes trouble.

And why don't you write? Write! Writing is for you, you are for you; your body is yours, take it. I know why you haven't written. (And why I didn't write before the age of twenty-seven.) Because writing is at once too high, too great for you, it's reserved for the great—that is, for "great men"; and it's "silly." Besides, you've written a little, but in secret. And it wasn't good, because it was in secret, and because you punished yourself for writing, because you didn't go all the way; or because you wrote, irresistibly, as when we would masturbate in secret, not to go further, but to attenuate the tension a bit, just enough to take the edge off. And then as soon as we come, we go and make ourselves feel guilty—so as to be forgiven; or to forget, to bury it until the next time.

Write, let no one hold you back, let nothing stop you: not man; not the imbecilic capitalist machinery, in which publishing houses are the crafty, obsequious relayers of imperatives handed down by an economy that works against us and off our backs; and not *yourself*. Smug-faced readers, managing editors, and big bosses don't like the true texts of women—female-sexed texts. That kind scares them.

I write woman: woman must write woman. And man, man. So only an oblique consideration will be found here of man; it's up to him to say where his masculinity and feminity are at: this will concern us once men have opened their eyes and seen themselves clearly.[1]

Now women return from afar, from always: from "without," from the heath where witches are kept alive; from below, from beyond "culture"; from their childhood which men have been trying desperately to make them forget, condemning it to "eternal rest." The little girls and their "ill-mannered" bodies immured, well-preserved, intact unto themselves, in the mirror. Frigidified. But are they ever seething underneath! What an effort it takes—there's no end to it—for the sex cops to bar their threatening return. Such a display of forces on both sides that the struggle has for centuries been immobilized in the trembling equilibrium of a deadlock.

Here they are, returning, arriving over and again, because the unconscious is impregnable. They have wandered around in circles, confined to the narrow room in which they've been given a deadly brainwashing. You can incarcerate them, slow them down, get away with the old Apartheid routine, but for a time only. As soon as they begin to speak, at the same time as they're taught their name, they can be taught that their territory is black: because you are Africa, you are black. Your continent is dark. Dark is dangerous. You can't see anything in the dark, you're afraid. Don't move, you might fall. Most of all, don't go into the forest. And so we have internalized this horror of the dark.

Men have committed the greatest crime against women. Insidiously, violently, they have led them to hate women, to be their own enemies, to mobilize their immense strength against themselves, to be the executants of their virile needs. They have made for women an antinarcissism! A narcissism which loves itself only to be loved for what women haven't got! They have constructed the infamous logic of antilove.

We the precocious, we the repressed of culture, our lovely mouths gagged with pollen, our wind knocked out of us, we the labyrinths, the ladders, the trampled spaces, the bevies—we are black and we are beautiful.

We're stormy, and that which is ours breaks loose from us without our fearing any debilitation. Our glances, our smiles, are spent; laughs exude from all our mouths; our blood flows and we extend ourselves without ever reaching an end; we never hold back our thoughts, our signs, our writing; and we're not afraid of lacking.

What happiness for us who are omitted, brushed aside at the scene of inheritances; we inspire ourselves and we expire without running out of breath, we are everywhere!

From now on, who, if we say so, can say no to us? We've come back from always.

It is time to liberate the New Woman from the Old by coming to know her—by loving her for getting by, for getting beyond the Old without delay, by going out ahead of what the New Woman will be, as an arrow quits the bow with a movement that gathers and separates the vibrations musically, in order to be more than her self.

I say that we must, for, with a few rare exceptions, there has not yet been any writing that inscribes femininity; exceptions so rare, in fact, that, after plowing through literature across languages, cultures, and ages,[2] one can only be startled at this vain scouting mission. It is well known that the number of women writers (while having increased very slightly from the nineteenth century on) has always been ridiculously small. This is a useless and deceptive fact unless from their species of female writers we do not first deduct the immense majority whose workmanship is in no way different from male writing, and which either obscures women or reproduces the classic representations of women (as sensitive—intuitive—dreamy, etc.)[3]

Let me insert here a parenthetical remark. I mean it when I speak of male writing. I maintain unequivocally that there is such a thing as *marked* writing; that, until now, far more extensively and repressively than is ever suspected or admitted, writing has been run by a libidinal and cultural—hence political, typically masculine—economy; that this is a locus where the repression of women has been perpetuated, over and over, more or less consciously, and in a manner that's frightening since it's often hidden or adorned with the mystifying charms of fiction; that this locus has grossly exaggerated all the signs of sexual opposition (and not sexual difference), where woman has never *her* turn to speak—this being all the more serious and unpardonable in that writing is precisely *the very possibility of change*, the space that can serve as a springboard for subversive thought, the precursory movement of a transformaton of social and cultural structures.

Nearly the entire history of writing is confounded with the history of reason, of which it is at once the effect, the support, and one of the privileged alibis. It has been one with the phallocentric tradition. It is indeed that same self-admiring, self-stimulating, self-congratulatory phallocentrism.

With some exceptions, for there have been failures—and if it weren't for them, I wouldn't be writing (I-woman, escapee)—in that enormous machine that has been operating and turning out its "truth" for centuries. There have been poets who would go to any lengths to slip something by at odds with tradition—men capable of loving love and hence capable of loving others and of wanting them, of imagining the woman who would hold out against oppression and constitute herself as a superb, equal, hence "impossible" subject, untenable in a real social framework. Such a woman the poet could desire only by breaking the codes that negate her. Her appearance would necessarily bring on, if not revolution—for the bastion was supposed to be immutable—at least harrowing explosions. At times it is in the fissure caused by an earthquake, through that radical mutation of things brought on by a material upheaval when every structure is for a moment thrown off balance and an ephemeral wildness sweeps order away, that the poet slips something by, for a brief span, of woman. Thus did Kleist expend himself in his yearning for the existence of sister-lovers, maternal daughters, mother-sisters, who never hung their heads in shame. Once the palace of magistrates is restored, it's time to pay: immediate bloody death to the uncontrollable elements.

But only the poets—not the novelists, allies of representationalism. Because poetry involves gaining strength through the unconscious and because the unconscious, that other limitless country, is the place where the repressed manage to survive: women, or as Hoffmann would say, fairies.

She must write her self, because this is the invention of a *new insurgent* writing which, when the moment of her liberation has come, will allow her to carry out the indispensable ruptures and transformations in her history, first at two levels that cannot be separated.

a) Individually. By writing her self, woman will return to the body which has been more than confiscated from her, which has been turned into the uncanny stranger on display—the ailing or dead figure, which so often turns out to be the nasty companion, the cause and location of inhibitions. Censor the body and you censor breath and speech at the same time.

Write your self. Your body must be heard. Only then will the immense resources of the unconscious spring forth. Our naphtha will spread, throughout the world, without dollars—black or gold—nonassessed values that will change the rules of the old game.

To write. An act which will not only "realize" the decensored relation of woman to her sexuality, to her womanly being, giving her access to her native strength; it will give her back her goods, her pleasures, her organs, her immense bodily territories which have been kept under seal; it will tear her away from the superegoized structure in which she has always occupied the place reserved for the guilty (guilty of everything, guilty at every turn: for having desires, for not having any; for being frigid, for being "too hot"; for not being both at once; for being too motherly and not enough; for having children and for not having any; for nursing and for not nursing. . .)—tear her away by means of this research, this job of analysis and illumination, this emancipation of the marvelous text of her self that she must urgently learn to speak. A woman without a body, dumb, blind, can't possibly be a good fighter. She is reduced to being the servant of the militant male, his shadow. We must kill the false woman who is preventing the live one from breathing. Inscribe the breath of the whole woman.

b) An act that will also be marked by woman's *seizing* the occasion to *speak*, hence her shattering entry into history, which has always been based *on her suppression*. To write and thus to forge for herself the antilogos weapon. To become *at will* the taker and initiator, for her own right, in every symbolic system, in every political process.

It is time for women to start scoring their feats in written and oral language.

Every woman has known the torment of getting up to speak. Her heart racing, at times entirely lost for words, ground and language slipping away—that's how daring a feat, how great a transgression it is for a woman to speak—even just open her mouth—in public. A double distress, for even if she transgresses, her words fall almost always upon the deaf male ear, which hears in language only that which speaks in the masculine.

It is by writing, from and toward women, and by taking up the challenge of speech which has been governed by the phallus, that women will confirm women in a place other than that which is reserved in and by the symbolic, that is, in a place other than silence. Women should break out of the snare of silence. They shouldn't be conned into accepting a domain which is the margin or the harem.

Listen to a woman speak at a public gathering (if she hasn't painfully lost her wind). She doesn't "speak," she throws her trembling body forward; she lets go of herself, she flies; all of her passes into her voice, and it's with her body that she vitally supports the "logic" of her speech. Her flesh speaks true. She lays herself bare. In fact, she physically materializes what she's thinking; she signifies it with her body. In a certain way she *inscribes* what she's saying, because she doesn't deny her drives the intractable and impassioned part they have in speaking. Her speech, even when "theoretical" or political, is never simple or linear or "objectified," generalized: she draws her story into history.

There is not that scission, that division made by the common man between the logic of oral speech and the logic of the text, bound as he is by his antiquated relation—servile, calculating—to mastery. From which proceeds the niggardly lip service which engages only the tiniest part of the body, plus the mask.

In women's speech, as in their writing, that

element which never stops resonating, which, once we've been permeated by it, profoundly and imperceptibly touched by it, retains the power of moving us—that element is the song: first music from the first voice of love which is alive in every woman. Why this privileged relationship with the voice? Because no woman stockpiles as many defenses for countering the drives as does a man. You don't build walls around yourself, you don't forego pleasure as "wisely" as he. Even if phallic mystification has generally contaminated good relationships, a woman is never far from "mother" (I mean outside her role functions: the "mother" as nonname and as source of goods). There is always within her at least a little of that good mother's milk. She writes in white ink.

Woman for women.—There always remains in woman that force which produces/is produced by the other—in particular, the other woman. *In* her, matrix, cradler; herself giver as her mother and child; she is her own sister-daughter. You might object, "What about she who is the hysterical offspring of a bad mother?" Everything will be changed once woman gives woman to the other woman. There is hidden and always ready in woman the source; the locus for the other. The mother, too, is a metaphor. It is necessary and sufficient that the best of herself be given to woman by another woman for her to be able to love herself and return in love the body that was "born" to her. Touch me, caress me, you the living no-name, give me my self as myself. The relation to the "mother," in terms of intense pleasure and violence, is curtailed no more than the relation to childhood (the child that she was, that she is, that she makes, remakes, undoes, there at the point where, the same, she others herself). Text: my body—shot through with streams of song; I don't mean the overbearing, clutchy "mother" but, rather, what touches you, the equivoice that affects you, fills your breast with an urge to come to language and launches your force; the rhythm that laughs you; the intimate recipient who makes all metaphors possible and desirable; body (body? bodies?), no more describable than god, the soul, or the Other; that part of you that leaves a space between yourself and urges you to inscribe in language your woman's style. In women there is always more or less of the mother who makes everything all right, who nourishes, and who stands up against separation; a force that will not be cut off but will knock the wind out of the codes. We will rethink womankind beginning with every form and every period of her body. The Americans remind us, "We are all Lesbians"; that is, don't denigrate woman, don't make of her what men have made of you.

Because the "economy" of her drives is prodigious, she cannot fail, in seizing the occasion to speak, to transform directly and indirectly *all* systems of exchange based on masculine thrift. Her libido will produce far more radical effects of political and social change than some might like to think.

Because she arrives, vibrant, over and again, we are at the beginning of a new history, or rather of a process of becoming in which several histories intersect with one another. As subject for history, woman always occurs simultaneously in several places. Woman un-thinks[4] the unifying, regulating history that homogenizes and channels forces, herding contradictions into a single battlefield. In woman, personal history blends together with the history of all women, as well as national and world history. As a militant, she is an integral part of all liberations. She must be farsighted, not limited to a blow-by-blow interaction. She foresees that her liberation will do more than modify power relations or toss the ball over to the other camp; she will bring about a mutation in human relations, in thought, in all praxis: hers is not simply a class struggle, which she carries forward into a much vaster movement. Not that in order to be a woman-in-struggle(s) you have to leave the class struggle or repudiate it; but you have to split it open, spread it out, push it forward, fill it with the fundamental struggle so as to prevent the class struggle, or any other struggle for the liberation of a class or people, from operating as a form of repression, pretext for postponing the inevitable, the staggering alteration in power relations and in the production of individualities. This alteration is already upon us—in the United States, for example, where millions of night crawlers are in the process of undermining the family and disintegrating the whole of American sociality.

The new history is coming; it's not a dream, though it does extend beyond men's imagination, and for good reason. It's going to deprive them of their conceptual orthopedics, beginning with the destruction of their enticement machine.

It is impossible to *define* a feminine practice of writing, and this is an impossibility that will remain, for this practice can never be theorized, enclosed, coded—which doesn't mean that it doesn't exist. But it will always surpass the discourse that regulates the phallocentric system, it does and will take place in areas other than those subordinated to philosophico-theoretical domination. It will be conceived of only by subjects who are breakers of automatisms, by peripheral figures that no authority can ever subjugate.

Hence the necessity to affirm the flourishes of this writing, to give form to its movement, its near and distant byways. Bear in mind to begin with (1) that sexual opposition, which has always worked for man's profit to the point of reducing writing, too, to his laws, is only a historico-cultural limit. There is, there will be more and more rapidly pervasive now, a fiction that produces irreducible effects of femininity. (2) That it is through ignorance that most readers, critics, and writers of both sexes hesitate to admit or deny outright the possibility or the pertinence of a distinction between feminine and masculine writing. It will usually be said, thus disposing of sexual difference: either that all writing, to the extent that it materializes, is feminine; or, inversely—but it comes to the same thing—that the act of writing is equivalent to masculine masturbation (and so the woman who writes cuts herself out a paper penis), or that writing is bisexual, hence neuter, which again does away with old differentiation. To admit that writing is precisely working (in) the in-between, inspecting the process of the same and of the other without which nothing can live, undoing the work of death—to admit this is first to want the two, as well as both, the ensemble of the one and the other, not fixed in sequences of struggle and expulsion or some other form of death but infinitely dynamized by an incessant process of exchange from one subject to another. A process of different subjects knowing one another and beginning one another anew only from the living boundaries of the other: a multiple and inexhaustible course with millions of encounters and transformations of the same into the other and into the in-between, from which woman takes her forms (and man, in his turn, but that's his other history).

In saying "bisexual, hence neuter," I am referring to the classic conception of bisexuality, which, squashed under the emblem of castration fear and along with the fantasy of a "total" being (though composed of two halves), would do away with the difference experienced as an operation incurring loss, as the mark of dreaded sectility.

To this self-effacing, merger-type bisexuality, which would conjure away castration (the writer who puts up his sign: "bisexual written here, come and see," when the odds are good that it's neither one nor the other), I oppose the *other bisexuality* on which every subject not enclosed in the false theater of phallocentric representationalism has founded his/her erotic universe. Bisexuality: that is, each one's location in self (*répérage en soi*) of the presence—variously manifest and insistent according to each person, male or female—of both sexes, nonexclusion either of the difference or of one sex, and, from this "self-permission," multiplication of the effects of the inscription of desire, over all parts of my body and the other body.

Now it happens that at present, for historico-cultural reasons, it is women who are opening up to and benefiting from this vatic bisexuality which doesn't annul differences but stirs them up, pursues them, increases their number. In a certain way, "woman is bisexual"; man—it's a secret to no one—being poised to keep glorious phallic monosexuality in view. By virtue of affirming the primacy of the phallus and of bringing it into play, phallocratic ideology has claimed more than one victim. As a woman, I've been clouded over by the great shadow of the scepter and been told: idolize it, that which you cannot brandish. But at the same time, man has been handed that grotesque and scarcely enviable destiny (just imagine) of being reduced to a single idol with clay balls. And consumed, as Freud and his followers note, by a fear of being a woman! For, if psychoanalysis was constituted from woman, to repress femininity (and not so successful a repression at that—men have made it clear), its account of masculine sexuality is now hardly refutable; as with all the "human" sciences, it reproduces the masculine view, of which it is one of the effects.

Here we encounter the inevitable man-with-rock, standing erect in his old Freudian realm, in the way that, to take the figure back to the point where linguistics is conceptualizing it "anew," Lacan preserves it in the sanctuary of the phallos (ϕ) "sheltered" from *castration's lack*! Their "symbolic" exists, it holds power—we, the sowers of disorder, know it only too well. But we are in no way obliged to deposit our lives in their banks of lack, to consider the constitution of the subject in terms of a drama manglingly restaged, to reinstate again and again the religion of the father. Because we don't want that. We don't fawn around the supreme hole. We have no womanly reason to pledge allegiance to the negative. The feminine (as the poets suspected) affirms: ". . . And yes," says Molly, carrying *Ulysses* off beyond any book and toward the new writing; "I said yes, I will Yes."

The Dark Continent is neither dark nor unexplorable.—It is still unexplored only because we've been made to believe that it was too dark to be explorable. And because they want to make us believe that what interests us is the white continent, with its monuments to Lack. And we believed. They riveted us between two horrifying myths: between the Medusa and the abyss. That would be enough to set half the world laughing, except that it's still going on. For the phallologocentric sublation[5] is with us, and it's militant, regenerating the old patterns, anchored in the dogma of castration. They haven't changed a thing: they've theorized their desire for reality! Let the priests tremble, we're going to show them our sexts!

Too bad for them if they fall apart upon discovering that women aren't men, or that the mother doesn't have one. But isn't this fear convenient for them? Wouldn't the worst be, isn't the worst, in truth, that women aren't castrated, that they have only to stop listening to the Sirens (for the Sirens were men) for history to change its meaning? You only have to look at the Medusa straight on to see her. And she's not deadly. She's beautiful and she's laughing.

Men say that there are two unrepresentable things: death and the feminine sex. That's because they need femininity to be associated with death; it's the jitters that gives them a hard-on! for themselves! They need to be afraid of us. Look at the trembling Perseuses moving backward toward us, clad in apotropes. What lovely backs! Not another minute to lose. Let's get out of here.

Let's hurry: the continent is not impenetrably dark. I've been there often. I was overjoyed one day to run into Jean Genêt. It was in *Pompes funèbres*.[6] He had come there led by his Jean. There are some men (all too few) who aren't afraid of femininity.

Almost everything is yet to be written by women about femininity: about their sexuality, that is, its infinite and mobile complexity, about their eroticization, sudden turn-ons of a certain miniscule-immense area of their bodies; not about destiny, but about the adventure of such and such a drive, about trips, crossings, trudges, abrupt and gradual awakenings, discoveries of a zone at one time timorous and soon to be forthright. A woman's body, with its thousand and one thresholds of ardor—once, by smashing yokes and censors, she lets it articulate the profusion of meanings that run through it in every direction—will make the old single-grooved mother tongue reverberate with more than one language.

We've been turned away from our bodies, shamefully taught to ignore them, to strike them with that stupid sexual modesty; we've been made victims of the old fool's game: each one will love the other sex. I'll give you your body and you'll give me mine. But who are the men who give women the body that women blindly yield to them? Why so few texts? Because so few women have as yet won back their body. Women must write through their bodies, they must invent the impregnable language that will wreck partitions, classes, and rhetorics, regulations and codes, they must submerge, cut through, get beyond the ultimate reserve-discourse, including the one that laughs at the very idea of pronouncing the word "silence," the one that, aiming for the impossible, stops short before the word "impossible" and writes it as "the end."

Such is the strength of women that, sweeping away syntax, breaking that famous thread (just a tiny little thread, they say) which acts for men as a surrogate umbilical cord, assuring them—otherwise they couldn't come—that the old lady is always right behind them, watching them make phallus, women will go right up to the impossible.

When the "repressed" of their culture and their society returns, it's an explosive, *utterly* destructive, staggering return, with a force never yet unleashed and equal to the most forbidding of suppressions. For when the Phallic period comes to an end, women will have been either annihilated or borne up to the highest and most violent incandescence. Muffled throughout their history, they have lived in dreams, in bodies (though muted), in silences, in aphonic revolts.

And with such force in their fragility; a fragility, a vulnerability, equal to their incomparable intensity. Fortunately, they haven't sublimated; they've saved their skin, their energy. They haven't worked at liquidating the impasse of lives without futures. They have furiously inhabited these sumptuous bodies; admirable hysterics who made Freud succumb to many voluptuous moments impossible to confess, bombarding his Mosaic statue with their carnal and passionate body words, haunting him with their inaudible and thundering denunciations, dazzling, more than naked underneath the seven veils of modesty. Those who, with a single word of the body, have inscribed the vertiginous immensity of a history which is sprung like an arrow from the whole history of men and from biblico-capitalist society, are the women, the supplicants of yesterday, who come as forebears of the new women, after whom no intersubjective relation will ever be the same. You, Dora, you the indomitable, the poetic body, you are the true "mistress" of the Signifier. Before long your efficacity will be seen at work when your speech is no longer suppressed, its point turned in against your breast, but written out over against the other.

In body.—More so than men who are coaxed toward social success, toward sublimation, women are body. More body, hence more writing. For a long time it has been in body that women have responded to persecution, to the familial-conjugal enterprise of domestication, to the repeated attempts at castrating them. Those who have turned their tongues 10,000 times seven times before not speaking are either dead from it or more familiar with their tongues and their mouths than anyone else. Now, I-woman am going to blow up the Law: an explosion henceforth possible and ineluctable; let it be done, right now, *in* language.

Let us not be trapped by an analysis still encumbered with the old automatisms. It's not to be feared that language conceals an invincible adversary, because it's the language of men and their grammar. We mustn't leave them a single place that's any more theirs alone than we are.

If woman has always functioned "within" the discourse of man, a signifier that has always referred back to the opposite signifier which annihilates its specific energy and diminishes or stifles its very different sounds, it is time for her to dislocate this "within," to explode it, turn it around, and seize it; to make it hers, containing it, taking it in her own mouth, biting that tongue with her very own teeth to invent for herself a language to get inside of. And you'll see with what ease she will spring forth from that "within"—the "within" where once she so drowsily crouched—to overflow at the lips she will cover the foam.

Nor is the point to appropriate their instruments, their concepts, their places, or to begrudge them their position of mastery. Just because there's a risk of identification doesn't mean that we'll succumb. Let's leave it to the worriers, to masculine anxiety and its obsession with how to dominate the way things work—knowing "how it works" in order to "make it work." For us the point is not to take possession in order to internalize or manipulate, but rather to dash through and to "fly."[7]

Flying is woman's gesture—flying in language and making it fly. We have all learned the art of flying and its numerous techniques; for centruies we've been able to possess anything only by flying; we've lived in flight, stealing away, finding, when desired, narrow passageways, hidden crossovers. It's no accident that *voler* has a double meaning, that it plays on each of them and thus throws off the agents of sense. It's no accident: women take after birds and robbers just as robbers take after women and birds. They (*illes*)[8] go by, fly the coop, take pleasure in jumbling the order of space, in disorienting it, in changing around the furniture, dislocating things and values, breaking them all up, emptying structures, and turning propriety upside down.

What woman hasn't flown/stolen? Who

hasn't felt, dreamt, performed the gesture that jams sociality? Who hasn't crumbled, held up to ridicule, the bar of separation? Who hasn't inscribed with her body the differential, punctured the system of couples and opposition? Who, by some act of transgression, hasn't overthrown successiveness, connection, the wall of circumfusion?

A feminine text cannot fail to be more than subversive. It is volcanic; as it is written it brings about an upheaval of the old property crust, carrier of masculine investments; there's no other way. There's no room for her if she's not a he. If she's a her-she, it's in order to smash everything, to shatter the framework of institutions, to blow up the law, to break up the "truth" with laughter.

For once she blazes *her* trail in the symbolic, she cannot fail to make of it the chaosmos of the "personal"—in her pronouns, her nouns, and her clique of referents. And for good reason. There will have been the long history of gynocide. This is known by the colonized peoples of yesterday, the workers, the nations, the species off whose backs the history of men has made its gold; those who have known the ignominy of persecution derive from it an obstinate future desire for grandeur; those who are locked up know better than their jailers the taste of free air. Thanks to their history, women today know (how to do and want) what men will be able to conceive of only much later. I say woman overturns the "personal," for if, by means of law, lies, blackmail, and marriage, her right to herself has been extorted at the same time as her name, she has been able, through the very movement of mortal alienation, to see more closely the inanity of "propriety," the reductive stinginess of the masculine-conjugal subjective economy, which she doubly resists. On the one hand she has constituted herself necessarily as that "person" capable of losing a part of herself without losing her integrity. But secretly, silently, deep down inside, she grows and multiplies, for, on the other hand, she knows far more about living and about the relation between the economy of the drives and the management of the ego than any man. Unlike man, who holds so dearly to his title and his titles, his pouches of value, his cap, crown, and everything connected with his head, woman couldn't care less about the fear of decapitation (or castration), adventuring, without the masculine temerity, into anonymity, which she can merge with without annihilating herself, because she's a giver.

I shall have a great deal to say about the whole deceptive problematic of the gift. Woman is obviously not that woman Nietzsche dreamed of who gives only in order to.[9] Who could ever think of the gift as a gift-that-takes? Who else but man, precisely the one who would like to take everything?

If there is a "propriety of woman," it is paradoxically her capacity to depropriate unselfishly: body without end, without appendage, without principal "parts." If she is a whole, it's a whole composed of parts that are wholes, not simple partial objects but a moving, limitlessly changing ensemble, a cosmos tirelessly traversed by Eros, an immense astral space not organized around any one sun that's any more of a star than the others.

This doesn't mean that she's an undifferentiated magma, but that she doesn't lord it over her body or her desire. Though masculine sexuality gravitates around the penis, engendering that centralized body (in political anatomy) under the dictatorship of its parts, woman does not bring about the same regionalization which serves the couple head/genitals and which is inscribed only within boundaries. Her libido is cosmic, just as her unconscious is worldwide. Her writing can only keep going, without ever inscribing or discerning contours, daring to make these vertiginous crossings of the other(s) ephemeral and passionate sojourns in him, her, them, whom she inhabits long enough to look at from the point closest to their unconscious from the moment they awaken, to love them at the point closest to their drives; and then further, impregnated through and through with these brief, identificatory embraces, she goes and passes into infinity. She alone dares and wishes to know from within, where she, the outcast, has never ceased to hear the resonance of fore-language. She lets the other language speak—the language of 1,000 tongues which knows neither enclosure nor death. To life she refuses nothing. Her language does not contain, it carries; it does not hold back, it makes possible. When id is ambiguously uttered—the wonder of being several—she doesn't defend herself against these unknown women whom she's surprised at becoming, but derives pleasure from this gift of alterability. I am spacious, singing flesh, on which is grafted no one knows which I, more or less human, but alive because of transformation.

Write! and your self-seeking text will know itself better than flesh and blood, rising, insurrectionary dough kneading itself, with sonorous, perfumed ingredients, a lively combination of flying colors, leaves, and rivers plunging into the sea we feed. "Ah, there's her sea," he will say as he holds out to me a basin full of water from the little phallic mother from whom he's inseparable. But look, our seas are what we make of them, full of fish or not, opaque or transparent, red or black, high or smooth, narrow or bankless; and we are ourselves sea, sand, coral, seaweed, earth, sky—what matter would rebuff us? We know how to speak them all.

Heterogeneous, yes. For her joyous benefit she is erogenous; she is the erotogeneity of the heterogeneous; airborne swimmer, in flight, she does not cling to herself; she is dispersible, prodigious, stunning, desirous and capable of others, of the other woman that she will be, of the other woman she isn't, of him, of you.

Woman be unafraid of any other place, of any same, or any other. My eyes, my tongue, my ears, my nose, my skin, my mouth, my body-for-(the)-other—not that I long for it in order to fill up a hole, to provide against some defect of mine, or because, as fate would have it, I'm spurred on by feminine "jealousy"; not because I've been dragged into the whole chain of substitutions that brings that which is substituted back to its ultimate object. That sort of thing you would expect to come straight out of "Tom Thumb," out of the *Penisneid* whispered to us by old grandmother ogresses, servants to their father-sons. If they believe, in order to muster up some self-importance, if they really need to believe that we're dying of desire, that we are this hole fringed with desire for their penis—that's their immemorial business. Undeniably (we verify it at our own expense—but also to our amusement), it's their busienss to let us know they're getting a hard-on, so that we'll assure them (we the maternal mistresses of their little pocket signifier) that they still can, that it's still there—that men structure themselves only by being fitted with a leather. In the child it's not the penis that the woman desires, it's not that famous bit of skin around which every man gravitates. Pregnancy cannot be traced back, except within the historical limits of the ancients, to some form of fate, to those mechanical substitutions brought about by the unconscious of some eternal "jealous woman"; not to penis envies; and not to narcissism or to some sort of homosexuality linked to the ever-present mother! Begetting a child doesn't mean that the woman or the man must fall ineluctably into patterns or must recharge the circuit of reproduction. If there's a risk there's not an inevitable trap: may women be spared the pressure, under the guise of consciousness-raising, of a supplement of interdictions. Either you want a kid or you don't—*that's your business.* Let nobody threaten you; in satisfying your desire, let not the fear of becoming the accomplice to a sociality succeed the old-time fear of being "taken." And man, are you still going to bank on everyone's blindness and passivity, afraid lest the child make a father and, consequently, that in having a kid the woman land herself more than one bad deal by engendering all at once child—mother—father—family? No; it's up to you to break the old circuits. It will be up to man and woman to render obsolete the former relationship and all its consequences, to consider the launching of a brand-new subject, alive, with defamilialization. Let us demater-paternalize rather than deny woman, in an effort to avoid the co-optation of procreation, a thrilling era of the body. Let us defetishize. Let's get away from the dialectic which has it that the only good father is a dead one, or that the child is the death of his parents. The child is the other, but the other without violence, bypassing loss, struggle. We're fed up with reuniting of bonds forever to be severed, with the litany of castration that's handed down and genealogized. We won't advance backward anymore; we're not going to repress something so simple as the desire for life. Oral drive, anal drive, vocal drive—all these drives are our strengths, and among them is the gestation drive—just like the desire to write: a desire to live self from within, a desire for the swollen belly, for language, for blood. We are not going to refuse, if it should happen to strike our fancy, the unsurpassed pleasures of pregnancy which have actually been always exaggerated or conjured away—or cursed—in the classic texts. For if there's one thing that's been repressed here's just the place to find it: in the taboo of the pregnant woman. This says a lot about the power she seems invested with at the time, because it has always been suspected, that, when pregnant, the woman not only doubles her market value, but—what's more important—takes on intrinsic value as a woman in her own eyes and, undeniably, acquires body and sex.

There are thousands of ways of living one's pregnancy; to have or not to have with that still invisible other a relationship of another intensity. And if you don't have that particular yearning, it doesn't mean that you're in any way lacking. Each body distributes in its own special way, without model or norm, the nonfinite and changing totality of its desires. Decide for yourself on your position in the arena of contradictions, where pleasure and reality embrace. Bring the other to life. Women know how to live detachment; giving birth is neither losing nor increasing. It's adding to life an other. Am I dreaming? Am I mis-recognizing? You, the defenders of "theory," the sacrosanct yes-men of Concept, enthroners of the phallus (but not of the penis):

Once more you'll say that all this smacks of "idealism," or what's worse, you'll splutter that I'm a "mystic."

And what about the libido? Haven't I read the "Signification of the Phallus"? And what about separation, what about that bit of self for which, to be born, you undergo an ablation—an ablation, so they say, to be forever commemorated by your desire?

Besides, isn't it evident that the penis gets around in my texts, that I give it a place and appeal? Of course I do. I want all. I want all of me with all of him. Why should I deprive myself of a part of us? I want all of us. Woman of course has a desire for a "loving desire" and not a jealous one. But not because she is gelded; not because she's deprived and needs to be filled out, like some wounded person who wants to console herself or seek vengeance: I don't want a penis to decorate my body with. But I do desire the other for the other, whole and entire, male or female; because living means wanting everything that is, everything that lives, and wanting it alive. Castration? Let others toy with it. What's a desire originating from a lack? A pretty meager desire.

The woman who still allows herself to be threatened by the big dick, who's still impressed by the commotion of the phallic stance, who still leads a loyal master to the beat of the drum: that's the woman of yesterday. They still exist, easy and numerous victims of the oldest of farces: either they're cast in the original silent version in which, as titanesses lying under the mountains they make with their quivering, they never see erected that theoretic monument to the golden phallus looming, in the old manner, over their bodies. Or, coming today out of their *infans* period and into the second, "enlightened" version of their virtuous debasement, they see themselves suddenly assaulted by the builders of the analytic empire and, as soon as they've begun to formulate the new desire, naked, nameless, so happy at making an appearance, they're taken in their bath by the new old men, and then, whoops! Luring them with flashy signifiers, the demon of interpretation—oblique, decked out in modernity—sells them the same old handcuffs, baubles, and chains. Which castration do you prefer? Whose degrading do you like better, the father's or the mother's? Oh, what pwetty eyes, you pwetty little girl. Here, buy my glasses and you'll see the Truth-Me-Myself tell you everything you should know. Put them on your nose and take a fetishist's look (you are me, the other analyst—that's what I'm telling you) at your body and the body of the other. You see? No? Wait, you'll have everything explained to you, and you'll know at last which sort of neurosis you're related to. Hold still, we're going to do your portrait, so that you can begin looking like it right away.

Yes, the naives to the first and second degree are still legion. If the New Women, arriving now, dare to create outside the theoretical, they're called in by the cops of the signifier, fingerprinted, remonstrated, and brought into the line of order that they are supposed to know, assigned by force of trickery to a precise place in the chain that's always formed for the benefit of a privileged signifier. We are pieced back to the string which leads back, if not to the Name-of-the-Father, then, for a new twist, to the place of the phallic-mother.

Beware, my friend, of the signifier that would take you back to the authority of the signified! Beware of diagnoses that would reduce your generative powers. "Common" nouns are also proper nouns that disparage your singularity by classifying it into species. Break out of the circles; don't remain within the psychoanalytic closure. Take a look around, then cut through!

And if we are legion, it's because the war of liberation has only made as yet a tiny breakthrough. But women are thronging to it. I've seen them, those who will be neither dupe nor domestic, those who will not fear the risk of being a woman; will not fear any risk, any desire, any space still unexplored in themselves, among themselves and others or anywhere else. They do not fetishize, they do not deny, they do not hate. They observe, they approach, they try to see the other woman, the child, the lover—not to strengthen their own narcissism or verify the solidity or weakness of the master, but to make love better, to invent

Other love.—In the beginning are our differences. The new love dares for the other, wants the other, makes dizzying, precipitous flights between knowledge and invention. The woman arriving over and over again does not stand still; she's everywhere, she exchanges, she is the desire-that-gives. (Not enclosed in the paradox of the gift that takes nor under the illusion of unitary fusion. We're past that.) She comes in, comes-in-between herself me and you, between the other me where one is always infinitely more than one and more than me, wihout the fear of ever reaching a limit; she thrills in our becoming. And we'll keep on becoming! She cuts though defensive loves, motherages, and devourations: beyond selfish narcissism, in the moving, open, transitional space, she runs her risks. Beyond the struggle-to-the-death that's been removed to the bed, beyond the love-battle that claims to represent exchange, she scorns at an Eros dynamic that would be fed by hatred. Hatred: a heritage, again, a remainder, a duping subservience to the phallus. To love, to watch-think-seek the other in the other, to despecularize, to unhoard. Does this seem difficult? It's not impossible, and this is what nourishes life—a love that has no commerce with the apprehensive desire that provides against the lack and stultifies the strange; a love that rejoices in the exchange that multiplies. Wherever history still unfolds as the history of death, she does not tread. Opposition, hierarchizing exchange, the struggle for mastery which can end only in at least one death (one master—one slave, or two nonmasters ≠ two dead)—all that comes from a period in time governed by phallocentric values. The fact that this period extends into the present doesn't prevent woman from starting the history of life somewhere else. Elsewhere, she gives. She doesn't "know" what she's giving, she doesn't measure it; she gives, though, neither a counterfeit impression nor something she hasn't got. She gives more, with no assurance that she'll get back even some unexpected profit from what she puts out. She gives that there may be life, thought, transformation. This is an "economy" that can no longer be put in economic terms. Wherever she loves, all the old concepts of management are left behind. At the end of a more or less conscious computation, she finds not her sum but her differences. I am for you what you want me to be at the moment you look at me in a way you've never seen me before: at every instant. When I write, it's everything that we don't know we can be that is written out of me, without exclusions, without stipulation, and everything we will be calls us to the unflagging, intoxicating, unappeasable search for love. In one another we will never be lacking.

Notes

1. Men still have everything to say about their sexuality, and everything to write. For what they have said so far, for the most part, stems from the opposition activity/passivity, from the power relation between the fantasized obligatory virility meant to invade, to colonize, and the consequential phantasm of woman as a "dark continent" to penetrate and to "pacify." (We know what "pacify" means in terms of scotomizing the other and misrecognizing the self.) Conquering her, they've made haste to depart from her borders, to get out of sight, out of body. The way man has of getting out of himself and into her whom he takes not for the other but for his own, deprives him, he knows, of his own bodily territory. One can understand how man, confusing himself with his penis and rushing in for the attack, might feel resentment and fear of being "taken" by the woman, of being lost in her, absorbed, or alone.

2. I am speaking here only of the place "reserved" for women by the Western world.

3 Which works, then, might be called feminine? I'll just point out some examples: one would have to give them full readings to bring out what is pervasively feminine in their significance. Which I shall do elsewhere. In France (have you noted our infinite poverty in this field?—the Anglo-Saxon countries have shown resources of distinctly greater consequence), leafing through what's come out of the twentieth century—and it's not much—the only inscriptions of femininity that I have seen were by Colette, Marguerite Duras, . . . and Jean Genêt.

4. "*Dé-pense*," a neologism formed on the verb *penser*, hence "unthinks," but also "spends" (from *dépenser*) (translator's note).

5. Standard English term for the Hegelian *Aufhebung*, the French *la relève*.

6. Jean Genêt, *Pompes funèbres* (Paris, 1948), p. 185.

7. Also, "to steal." Both meanings of the verb *voler* are played on, as the text itself explains in the following paragraph (translator's note).

8. *Illes* is a fusion of the masculine pronoun *ils*, which refers back to birds and robbers, with the feminine pronoun *elles*, which refers to women (translator's note).

9. Reread Derrida's text. "Le Style de la femme," in *Nietzsche aujourd'hui* (Paris: Union Générale d'Editions, Coll. 10/18), where the philosopher can be seen operating an *Aufhebung* of all philosophy in its systematic reducing of woman to the place of seduction: she appears as the one who is taken for; the bait in person, all veils unfurled, the one who doesn't give but who gives only in order to (take).

Jacques Derrida 1930–

A leading figure in the history of philosophy, Jacques Derrida teaches an annual spring course in comparative literature at the University of California at Irvine, as well as courses in philosophy at the École Normale Supérieure in Paris during the rest of the academic year. English translations of his 1968 book publications in France appeared in the 1970s as *Speech and Phenomena* (1973), *Of Grammatology* (1974), and *Writing and Difference* (1978). In 1972, three new books of Derrida's appeared in France. These have been translated in English as *Positions* (1981), *Dissemination* (1981), and *Margins of Philosophy* (1982). The complete text of "Plato's Pharmacy" appears in *Dissemination*.

In 1966, this Algiers-born French philosopher arrived in Baltimore to address a conference at Johns Hopkins University called "The Languages of Criticism and the Sciences of Man." He worked with others—among them, Roland Barthes, Lucien Goldmann, Jean Hyppolite, Jacques Lacan, Georges Poulet, and Tzvetan Todorov—to introduce structuralism to the American academy. However, his paper, "Structure, Sign, and Play in the Discourse of the Human Sciences," a critical discussion of the work of Claude Lévi-Strauss, contributed to that introduction only to signal that the structuralist enterprise was dead.

Derrida contended that the "structurality of structure," as presented according to structuralist commitments to a coherence determined by a "center" or "fixed origin" of interpretive structures, had to be seen in light of the notion of "freeplay" and "interplay of absence and presence" prior to absence and presence. Derrida challenged, in other words, some fundamental notions of coherence and structure crucial to Western thought.

At Johns Hopkins Derrida created a controversial focus typical of his philosophic work in criticism. This work, despite its decisive and stunning—and often brilliant—reworking of the fabric of Western metaphysics, can be difficult even for those trained in the Continental philosophic tradition. The following selection, "The Father of Logos," from "Plato's Pharmacy" is a case in point. "Plato's Pharmacy" challenges the customary relation of writing as supplementary to speech, with speech "the better half" as it were, in opposition to writing. What, for example, is the status of speech for Plato in the very dialogues in which he attacks writing for being inferior to speech because it stands alone, "fatherless" without the presence of the speaker?

According to Plato, writing is "repeating without knowing"—in Derrida's phrase—a kind of degenerate mnemonics used for rote recollection that cannot recapture the Soul's forgotten memory of the time of union with the True or the Good. Writing, in other words, can only serve as a secondary imitation of speech as a primary imitation. Derrida's point, however, is that writing is not such a mnemonic and that it is no more imitative than speech. Speech and writing, therefore, are mutual efforts to render that which is "other" to language. Such renderings are "tracings," elaborations of an original that is present only in the trace signified in language.

Derrida's rendering in "Plato's Pharmacy" of Plato's *Phaedrus*, the dialogue introducing the myth of Theuth, is a deconstruction, or displacement, of that dialogue's traditional structure and meaning. This deconstruction is accomplished by taking an off-center approach to the myths Plato appropriated and presented. With the myth of Theuth, for example, that decentering takes place via Derrida's addressing the issue of authority, an issue that appears to be secondary—in other words, marginal—in the original text. It is significant in "The Father of Logos" that Derrida stops his recounting of Theuth's presentation just before the king rejects the worth of writing on the grounds that a system for recapturing the contents of memory will be bad, because it will encourage the activity of empty rote recollection. Derrida's particular account focuses on Theuth's gift as a potential challenge to the authority of the king and develops a notion of logocentrism as a prohibition against patricide, writing's denial of its origin in speech.

THE FATHER OF LOGOS

The story begins like this:

SOCRATES: Very well. I heard, then, that at Naucratis in Egypt there lived one of the old gods of that country, the one whose sacred bird is called the ibis; and the name of the divinity was Theuth. It was he who first invented numbers and calculation, geometry and astronomy, not to speak of draughts and dice, and above all writing (*grammata*). Now the King of all Egypt at that time was Thamus who lived in the great city of the upper region which the Greeks call the Egyptian Thebes; the god himself they call Ammon. Theuth came to him and exhibited his arts and declared that they ought to be imparted to the other Egyptians. And Thamus questioned him about the usefulness of each one; and as Theuth enumerated, the King blamed or praised what he thought were the good or bad points in the explanation. Now Thamus is said to have had a good deal to remark on both sides of the question about every single art (it would take too long to repeat it here); but when it came to writing, Theuth said, "This discipline (*to mathēma*), my King, will make the Egyptians wiser and will improve their memories (*sophōterous kai mnēmonikōterous*): my invention is a recipe (*pharmakon*) for both memory and wisdom." But the King said . . . etc. (274*c*–*e*).

Let us cut the King off here. He is faced with the *pharmakon*. His reply will be incisive.

Let us freeze the scene and the characters and take a look at them. Writing (or, if you will, the *pharmakon*) is thus presented to the King. Presented: like a kind of present offered up in homage by a vassal to his lord (Theuth is a demigod speaking to the king of the gods), but above all as a finished work submitted to his appreciation. And this work is itself an art, a capacity for work, a power of operation. This artefactum is an art. But the value of this gift is still uncertain. The value of writing—or of the *pharmakon*—has of course been spelled out to the King, but it is the King who will give it its value, who will set the price of what, in the act of receiving, he constitutes or institutes. The king or god (Thamus represents[1] Ammon, the king of the gods, the king of kings, the god of gods. Theuth says to him: *O basileu*) is thus the other name for the origin of value. The value of writing will not be itself, writing will have no value, unless and to the extent that god-the-king approves of it. But god-the-king nonetheless experiences the *pharmakon* as a product, an *ergon*, which is not his own, which comes to him from outside but also from below, and which awaits his condescending judgment in order to be consecrated in its being and value. God the king does not know how to write, but that ignorance or incapacity only testifies to his sovereign independence. He has no need to write. He speaks, he says, he dictates, and his word suffices. Whether a scribe from his secretarial staff then adds the supplement of a transcription or not, that consignment is always in essence secondary.

From this position, without rejecting the homage, the god-king will depreciate it, pointing out not only its uselessness but its menace and its mischief. Another way of not receiving the offering of writing. In so doing, god-the-king-that-speaks is acting like a father. The *pharmakon* is here presented to the father and is by him rejected, belittled, abandoned, disparaged. The father is always suspicious and watchful toward writing.

Even if we did not want to give in here to the easy passage uniting the figures of the king, the god, and the father, it would suffice to pay systematic attention—which to our knowledge has never been done—to the permanence of a Platonic schema that assigns the origin and power of speech, precisely of *logos*, to the paternal position. Not that this happens especially and exclusively in Plato. Everyone knows this or can easily imagine it. But the fact that "Platonism," which sets up the whole of Western metaphysics in its conceptuality, should not escape the generality of this structural constraint, and even illustrates it with incomparable subtlety and force, stands out as all the more significant.

Not that logos *is* the father, either. But the origin of logos is *its father*. One could say anachronously that the "speaking subject" is the *father* of his speech. And one would quickly realize that this is no metaphor, at least not in the sense of any common, conventional effect of rhetoric. *Logos* is a son, then, a son that would be destroyed in his very *presence* without the present *attendance* of his father. His father who answers. His father who speaks for him and answers for him. Without his father, he would be nothing but, in fact, writing. At least that is what is said by the one who says: it is the father's thesis. The specificity of writing would thus be intimately bound to the absence of the father. Such an absence can of course exist along very diverse modalities, distinctly or confusedly, successively or simultaneously: to have lost one's father, through natural or violent death, through random violence or patricide; and then to solicit the aid and attendance, possible or impossible, of the paternal presence, to solicit it directly or to claim to be getting along without it, etc. The reader will have noted Socrates' insistence on the misery, whether pitiful or arrogant, of a *logos* committed to writing: ". . . It always needs its father to attend it, being quite unable to defend itself or attend to its own needs" (275*e*).

This misery is ambiguous: it is the distress of the orphan, of course, who needs not only an attending presence but also a presence that will attend to its needs; but in pitying the orphan, one also makes an accusation against him, along with writing, for claiming to do away with the father, for achieving emancipation with complacent self-sufficiency. From the position of the holder of the scepter, the desire of writing is indicated, designated, and denounced as a desire for orphanhood and patricidal subversion. Isn't this *pharmakon* then a criminal thing, a poisoned present?

The status of this orphan, whose welfare cannot be assured by any attendance or assistance, coincides with that of a *graphein* which, being nobody's son at the instant it reaches inscription, scarcely remains a son at all and no longer *recognizes* its origins, whether legally or morally. In contrast to writing, living *logos* is alive in that it has a living father (whereas the orphan is already half dead), a father that is *present, standing* near it, behind it, within it, sustaining it with his rectitude, attending it in person in his own name. Living *logos*, for its part, recognizes its debt, lives off that recognition, and forbids itself, thinks it can forbid itself patricide. But prohibition and patricide, like the relations between speech and writing, are structures surprising enough to require us later on to articulate Plato's text between a particle prohibited and a patricide proclaimed. The deferred murder of the father and rector.

The *Phaedrus* would already be sufficient

to prove that the responsibility for *logos*, for its meaning and effects, goes to those who attend it, to those who are present with the presence of a father. These "metaphors" must be tirelessly questioned. Witness Socrates, addressing Eros: "If in our former speech Phaedrus or I said anything harsh against you, blame Lysias the father of the subject (*ton tou logou patera*)" (275*b*). *Logos*—"discourse"—has the meaning here of argument, line of reasoning, guiding thread animating the spoken discussion (the *Logos*). To translate it by "subject" [*sujet*], as Robin does, is not merely anachronistic. The whole intention and the organic unity of signification is destroyed. For only the "living" discourse, only a spoken word (and not a speech's theme, object, or subject) can have a father; and, according to a necessity that will not cease to become clearer to us from now on, the *logoi* are the children. Alive enough to protest on occasion and to let themselves be questioned; capable, too, in contrast to written things, of responding when their father is there. They are their father's responsible presence.

Some of them, for example, descend from Phaedrus, who is sometimes called upon to sustain them. Let us refer again to Robin, who translates *logos* this time not by "subject" but by "argument," and disrupts in a space of ten lines the play on the *tekhnē tō logōn*. (What is in question is the *tekhnē* the sophists and rhetors had or pretended to have at their disposal, which was at once an art and an instrument, a recipe, an occult but transmissible "treatise," etc. Socrates considers the then classical problem in terms of the opposition between persuasion [*peithō*] and truth [*alētheia*] [260 *a*].)

Socrates: I agree—if, that is, the arguments (*logoi*) that come forward to speak for oratory should give testimony that is an art (*tekhnē*). Now I seem, as it were, to hear some arguments advancing to give their evidence that it tells lies, that it is not an art at all, but an artless routine. "Without a grip on truth," says the Spartan, "there can be no genuine art of speaking (*tou de legein*) either now or in the future."

Phaedrus: Socrates, we need these arguments (*Toutō dei tōn logōn, ō Sōkrates*). Bring the witnesses here and let's find out what they have to say and how they'll say it (*ti kai pōs legousin*).

Socrates: Come here, then, noble brood (*gennaia*), and convince Phaedrus, father of such fine children (*kallipaida te Phaidron*), that if he doesn't give enough attention to philosophy, he will never become a competent speaker on any subject. Now let Phaedrus answer (260*e*–261*a*).

It is again Phaedrus, but this time in the *Symposium*, who must speak first because he is both "head of the table" and "father of our subject" (*patēr tou logou*) (177*d*).

What we are provisionally and for the sake of convenience continuing to call a metaphor thus in any event belongs to a whole system. If *logos* has a father, if it is a *logos* only when attended by its father, this is because it is always a being (*on*) and even a certain species of being (the *Sophist*, 260*a*), more precisely a *living* being. *Logos* is a *zōon*. An animal that is born, grows, belongs to the *phusis*. Linguistics, logic, dialectics, and zoology are all in the same camp.

In describing *logos* as a *zōon*, Plato is following certain rhetors and sophists before him who, as a contrast to the cadaverous rigidity of writing, had held up the living spoken word, which infallibly conforms to the necessities of the situation at hand, to the expectations and demands of the interlocutors present, and which sniffs out the spots where it ought to produce itself, feigning to bend and adapt at the moment it is actually achieving maximum persuasiveness and control.[2]

Logos, a living, animate creature, is thus also an organism that has been engendered. An *organism*: a differentiated body *proper*, with a center and extremities, joints, a head, and feet. In order to be "proper," a written discourse *ought* to submit to the laws of life just as a living discourse does. Logographical necessity (*anangkē logographikē*) ought to be analogous to biological, or rather zoological, necessity. Otherwise, obviously, it would have neither head nor tail. Both *structure* and *constitution* are in question in the risk run by *logos* of losing through writing both its tail and its head:

Socrates: And what about the rest? Don't you think the different parts of the speech (*ta tou logou*) are tossed in hit or miss? Or is there really a cogent reason for starting his second point in the second place? And is that the case with the rest of the speech? As for myself, in my ignorance, I thought that the writer boldly set down whatever happened to come into his head. Can you explain his arrangement of the topics in the order he has adopted as the result of some principle of composition, some logographic necessity?

Phaedrus: It's very kind of you to think me capable of such an accurate insight into his methods.

Socrates: But to this you will surely agree: every discourse (*logon*), like a living creature (*ōsper zōon*), should be so put together (*sunestanai*) that it has its own body and lacks neither head nor foot, middle nor extremities, all composed in such a way that they suit both each other and the whole (264*b*–*c*).

The organism thus engendered must be well born, of noble blood: "*gennaia!*," we recall, is what Socrates called the *logoi*, those "noble creatures." This implies that the organism, having been engendered, must have a beginning and an end. Here, Socrates' standards become precise and insistent: a speech must have a beginning and an end, it must begin with the beginning and end with the end: "It certainly seems as though Lysias, at least, was far from satisfying our demands: it's from the end, not the beginning, that he tries to swim (on his back!) upstream through the current of his discourse. He starts out with what the lover ought to say at the very end to his beloved!" (264*a*). The implications and consequences of such a norm are immense, but they are obvious enough for us not to have to belabor them. It follows that the spoken discourse behaves like someone attended in origin and present in person. *Logos: "Sermo tanquam persona ipse loquens,"* as one Platonic Lexicon puts it.[3] Like any person, the *logos-zōon* has a father.

But what is a father?

Should we consider this known, and with this term—the known—classify the other term within what one would hasten to classify as a metaphor? One would then say that the origin or cause of *logos* is being compared to what we know to be the cause of a living son, his father. One would understand or imagine the birth and development of *logos* from the standpoint of a domain foreign to it, the transmission of life or the generative relation. But the father is not the generator or procreator in any "real" sense prior to or outside all relation to language. In what way, indeed, is the father/son relation distinguishable from a mere cause/effect or generator/engendered relation, if not by the instance of logos? Only a power of speech can have a father. The father is always father to a speaking/living being. In other words, it is precisely *logos* that enables us to perceive and investigate something like paternity. If there were a simple metaphor in the expression "father of logos," the first word, which seemed the more *familiar,* would nevertheless receive more meaning *from* the second than it would transmit *to* it. The first familiarity is always involved in a relation of cohabitation with *logos.* Living-beings, father and son, are announced to us and related to each other within the household of *logos.* From which one does not escape, in spite of appearances, when one is transported, by "metaphor," to a foreign territory where one meets fathers, sons, living creatures, all sorts of beings that come in handy for explaining to anyone that doesn't know, by comparison, what *logos,* that strange thing, is all about. Even though this hearth is the heart of all metaphoricity, one would have to make the statement that some living creature incapable of language, if anyone still wished to believe in such a thing, has a father. One must thus proceed to undertake a general reversal of all metaphorical directions, no longer asking whether *logos* can have a father but understanding that what the father claims to be the father of cannot go without the essential possibility of *logos.*

A *logos indebted* to a father, what does that mean? At least how can it be read within the stratum of the Platonic text that interests us here?

The figure of the father, of course, is also that of the good (*agathon*). Logos *represents* what it is indebted to: the father who is also chief, capital, and good(s). Or rather *the* chief, *the* capital, *the* good(s). *Patēr* in Greek means all that at once. Neither translators nor commentators of Plato seem to have accounted for the play of these schemas. It is extremely difficult, we must recognize, to respect this play in a translation, and the fact can at least be explained in that no one has ever raised the question. Thus, at the point in the *Republic* where Socrates backs away from speaking of the good in itself (VI, 506e), he immediately suggests replacing it with its *ekgonos,* its son, its offspring:

> . . . let us dismiss for the time being the nature of the good in itself, for to attain to my present surmise of that seems a pitch above the impulse that wings my flight today. But what seems to be the offspring (*ekgonos*) of the good and most nearly made in its likeness I am willing to speak if you too wish it, and otherwise to let the matter drop.
>
> Well, speak on, he said, for you will duly pay me the tale of the parent another time.
>
> I could wish, I said, that I were able to make and you to receive the payment, and not merely as now the interest (*tokous*). But at any rate receive this interest and the offspring of the good (*tokon te kai ekgonon autou tou agathou*).

Tokos, which is here associated with *ekgonos,* signifies production and the product, birth and the child, etc. This word functions with this meaning in the domains of agriculture, of kinship relations, and of fiduciary operations. None of these domains, as we shall see, lies outside the investment and possibility of a *logos.*

As product, the *tokos* is the child, the human or animal brood, as well as the fruits of the seed sown in the field, and the interest on a capital investment: it is a *return* or *revenue.* The distribution of all these meanings can be followed in Plato's text. The meaning of *patēr* is sometimes even inflected in the exclusive sense of financial capital. In the *Republic* itself, and not far from the passage we have just quoted. One of the drawbacks of democracy lies in the role that capital is often allowed to play in it: "But these moneymakers with down-bent heads, pretending not even to see the poor, but inserting the sting of their money into any of the remainder who do not resist, and harvesting from them in interest as it were a manifold progeny of the parent sum (*tou patros ekgonous tokous pollaplasious*), foster the drone and pauper element in the state" (555*e*).

Now, about this father, this capital, this good, this origin of value and of appearing beings, it is not possible to speak simply or directly. First of all because it is no more possible to look them in the face than to stare at the sun. On the subject of this bedazzlement before the face of the sun, a rereading of the famous passage of the *Republic* (VII, 515*c* ff) is strongly recommended here.

Thus will Socrates evoke only the visible sun, the son that resembles the father, the *analogon* of the intelligible sun: "It was the sun, then, that I meant when I spoke of that offspring of the Good (*ton tou agathou ekgonon*), which the Good has created in its own image (*hon tagathon egennēsen analogon heautōi*), and which stands in the visible world in the same relation to vision and visible things at that which the good itself bears in the intelligible world to intelligence and to intelligible objects" (508*c*).

How does *logos* intercede in this *analogy* between the father and the son, the *nooumena* and the *horōmena?*

The Good, in the visible-invisible figure of the father, the sun, or capital, is the origin of all *onta*, responsible for their appearing and their coming into *logos*, which both assembles and distinguishes them: "We predicate 'to be' of many beautiful things and many good things, saying of them severally that they *are*, and so define them in our speech (*einai phamen te kai diorizomen tōi logōi*)" (507 *b*).

The good (father, sun, capital) is thus the hidden illuminating, blinding source of *logos*. And since one cannot speak of that which enables one to speak (being forbidden to speak of it or to speak to it face to face), one will speak only of that which speaks and of things that, with a single exception, one is constantly speaking of. And since an account or reason cannot be given of what *logos* (account or reason: *ratio*) is accountable or owing *to*, since the capital cannot be counted nor the chief looked in the eye, it will be necessary, by means of a discriminative, diacritical operation, to count up the plurality of interests, returns, products, and offspring: "Well, speak on (*lege*), he said, for you will duly pay me the tale of the parent another time—I could wish, I said, that I were able to make and you to receive the payment, and not merely as now the interest. But at any rate receive this interest and the offspring of the good. Have a care, however, lest I deceive you unintentionally with a false reckoning (*ton logon*) of the interest (*tou tokou*)" (507*a*).

From the foregoing passage we should also retain the fact that, along with the account (*logos*) of the supplements (to the father-good-capital-origin, etc.), along with what comes above and beyond the One in the very movement through which it absents itself and becomes invisible, thus requiring that its place be supplied along with difference and diacriticity, Socrates introduces or discovers the ever open possibility of the *kibdēlon*, that which is falsified, adulterated, mendacious, deceptive, equivocal. Have a care, he says, lest I deceive you with a false reckoning of the interest (*kibdēlon apodidous ton logon tou tokou*). *Kibdēleuma* is fraudulent merchandise. The corresponding verb (*kibdēleuō*) signifies "to tamper with money or merchandise, and, by extension, to be of bad faith."

This recourse to *logos*, from fear of being blinded by any direct intuition of the face of the father, of good, of capital, of the origin of being in itself, of the form of forms, etc., this recourse to logos as that which *protects us from the sun*, protects us under it and from it, is proposed by Socrates elsewhere, in the *analogous* order of the sensible or the visible. We shall quote at length from that text. In addition to its intrinsic interest, the text, in its official Robin translation, manifests a series of slidings, as it were, that are highly significant.[4] The passage in question is the critique, in the *Phaedo*, of "physicalists":

Socrates proceeded: —I thought that as I had failed in the contemplation of true existence (*ta onta*), I ought to be careful that I did not lose the eye of my soul; as people may injure their bodily eye by observing and gazing on the sun during an eclipse, unless they take the precaution of only looking at the image (*eikona*) reflected in the water, or in some analogous medium. So in my own case, I was afraid that my soul might be blinded altogether if I looked at things with my eyes or tried to apprehend them with the help of the senses. And I thought that I had better have recourse to the world of *idea* (*en logois*) and seek there the truth of things. . . . So, basing myself in each case on the idea (*logon*) that I judged to be the strongest . . ." (99*d*–100*a*).

Logos is thus a *resource*. One must *turn* to it, and not merely when the solar source is *present* and risks burning the eyes if stared at; one has also to turn away toward *logos* when the sun seems to withdraw during its eclipse. Dead, extinguished, or hidden, that star is more dangerous than ever.

We will let these yarns of suns and sons spin on for a while. Up to now we have only followed this line so as to move from *logos* to the father, so as to tie speech to the *kurios*, the master, the lord, another name given in the *Republic* to the good-sun-capital-father (508*a*). Later, within the same tissue, within the same texts, we will draw on other filial filaments, pull the same strings once more, and witness the weaving or unraveling of other designs.

Notes

1. For Plato, Thamus is doubtless another name for Ammon, whose figure (that of the sun king and of the father of the gods) we shall sketch out later for its own sake. On this question and the debate to which it has given rise, see Frutiger, *Mythes*, p. 233, n. 2, and notably Eisler, "Platon und das ägyptische Alphabet," *Archiv für Geschichte der Philosophie*, 1922; Pauly-Wissowa, *Real-encyclopädie der classischen Altertumswissenschaft* (art. Ammon); Roscher, *Lexikon der griechischen und römischen Mythologie* (art. Thamus).

2. The association *logos-zōon* appears in the discourse of Isocrates *Against the Sophists* and in that of Alcidamas *On the Sophists*. Cf. also W. Süss, who compares these two discourses line by line with the *Phaedrus*, in *Ethos: Studien zur älteren griechischen Rhetorik* (Leipzig, 1910), pp. 34 ff; and A. Diès, "Philosophie et rhétorique," in *Autour de Platon* (Paris: Gabriel Beauchesne, 1927), I, 103.

3. Fr. Ast, *Lexique platonicien*. Cf. also B. Parain, *Essai sur le logos platonicien* (Paris: Gallimard, 1942), p. 211; and P. Louis, *Les Métaphores de Platon* (Paris: Les Belles Lettres, 1945), pp. 43–44.

4. I am indebted to the friendship and alertness of Francine Markovits for having brought this to my attention. This text should of course be placed alongside those of books VI and VII of the *Republic*.

Stanley E. Fish 1938–

Stanley Fish has taught at the University of California at Berkeley and at Johns Hopkins University (he is currently at Duke). His training was in seventeenth-century British literature, but as a critic he has been identified with the development of reader-response criticism since the publication of *Surprised by Sin: The Reader in "Paradise Lost"* (1967). His approach to reading is fiercely pragmatic, and he tends to shun any philosophical or abstract formulation of his methods. The temperament and tone of his work place it close to that of ordinary-language philosophers (especially John L. Austin). His method consists largely of anticipating the direction of narrative development and then discussing in detail how closely actual development coincides with or frustrates what was expected. He tends to think of interpretive strategies as guided by a reader's "interpretive community." His work, in addition to many essays, includes *John Skelton's Poetry* (1965); *Self-Consuming Artifacts: The Experience of Seventeenth-Century Literature* (1972); and *Is There a Text in This Class?* (1980).

Fish's "Interpreting the *Variorum*" (1980) is a critical document remarkable for its insight into reading and for its candor. Fish looks at the problems of interpretation raised by publication of the first two volumes of the Milton *Variorum Commentary*, noting that again and again the *Variorum* gives evidence for multiple readings of key passages in Milton's work. Fish then does two things. First, he demonstrates how a reader transforms an interpretive dispute by making it "signify, first by regarding it as evidence of an experience and then by specifying for that experience a meaning." This reader-oriented approach, however, is marked by its "inability to say how it is that one ever begins" to read and interpret. Fish's answer is that readers are guided by "interpretive communities" of readers. Second, Fish asks, How can any one of us know whether or not he is a member of the same interpretive community as any other of us? His answer is that we can never be sure, but that our commonsense experience tends to confirm the existence of such reading communities.

INTERPRETING THE *Variorum*

I

The first two volumes of the Milton *Variorum Commentary* have now appeared, and I find them endlessly fascinating. My interest, however, is not in the questions they manage to resolve (although these are many) but in the theoretical assumptions which are responsible for their occasional failures. These failures constitute a pattern, one in which a host of commentators—separated by as much as two hundred and seventy years but contemporaries in their shared concerns—are lined up on either side of an interpretive crux. Some of these are famous, even infamous: what is the two-handed engine in *Lycidas*? what is the meaning of Haemony in *Comus*? Others, like the identity of whoever or whatever comes to the window in *L'Allegro*, line 46, are only slightly less notorious. Still others are of interest largely to those who make editions: matters of pronoun referents, lexical ambiguities, punctuation. In each instance, however, the pattern is consistent: every position taken is supported by wholly convincing evidence—in the case of *L'Allegro* and the coming to the window there is a persuasive champion for every proper noun within a radius of ten lines—and the editorial procedure always ends either in the graceful throwing up of hands, or in the recording of a disagreement between the two editors themselves. In short, these are problems that apparently cannot be solved, at least not by the methods traditionally brought to bear on them. What I would like to argue is that they are not *meant* to be solved, but to be experienced (they signify), and that consequently any procedure that attempts to determine which of a number of readings is correct will necessarily fail. What this means is that the commentators and editors have been asking the wrong questions and that a new set of questions based on new assumptions must be formulated. I would like at least to make a beginning in that direction by examining some of the points in dispute in Milton's sonnets. I choose the sonnets because they are brief and because one can move easily from them to the theoretical issues with which this paper is finally concerned.

Milton's twentieth sonnet—"Lawrence of virtuous father virtuous son"—has been the subject of relatively little commentary. In it the poet invites a friend to join him in some distinctly Horation pleasures—a neat repast intermixed with conversation, wine, and song; a respite from labor all the more enjoyable because outside the earth is frozen and the day sullen. The only controversy the sonnet has inspired concerns its final two lines:

Lawrence of virtuous father virtuous son,
  Now that the fields are dank, and ways are mire,
  Where shall we sometimes meet, and by the fire
  Help waste a sullen day; what may be won
From the hard season gaining; time will run
  On smoother, till Favonius reinspire
  The frozen earth; and clothe in fresh attire
  The lily and rose, that neither sowed nor spun.
What neat repast shall feast us, light and choice,
  Of Attic taste, with wine, whence we may rise
  To hear the lute well touched, or artful voice
Warble immortal notes and Tuscan air?
  He who of those delights can judge, and spare
  To interpose them oft, is not unwise.[1]

The focus of the controversy is the word "spare," for which two readings have been proposed: leave time for and refrain from. Obviously the point is crucial if one is to resolve the sense of the lines. In one reading "those delights" are being recommended—he who can leave time for them is not unwise; in the other, they are the subject of a warning—he who knows when to refrain from them is not unwise. The proponents of the two interpretations cite as evidence both English and Latin syntax, various sources and analogues, Milton's "known attitudes" as they are found in his other writings, and the unambiguously expressed sentiments of the following sonnet on the same question. Surveying these arguments, A. S. P. Woodhouse roundly declares: "It is plain that all the honours rest with" the meaning "refrain from" or "forbear to." This declaration is followed immediately by a bracketed paragraph initialled D. B. for Douglas Bush, who, writing presumably after Woodhouse has died, begins "In spite of the array of scholarly names the case for 'forbear to' may be thought much weaker, and the case for 'spare time for' much stronger, than Woodhouse found them."[2] Bush then proceeds to review much of the evidence marshaled by Woodhouse and to draw from it exactly the opposite conclusion. If it does nothing else, this curious performance anticipates a point I shall make in a few moments: evidence brought to bear in the course of formalist analyses—that is, analyses generated by the assumption that meaning is embedded in the artifact—will always point in as many directions as there are interpreters; that is, not only will it prove something, it will prove anything.

It would appear then that we are back at square one, with a controversy that cannot be settled because the evidence is inconclusive. But what if that controversy is *itself* regarded as evidence, not of an ambiguity that must be removed, but of an ambiguity that readers have always experienced? What, in other words, if for the question "what does 'spare' mean?" we substitute the question "what does the fact that the meaning of 'spare' has always been an issue mean"? The advantage of this question is that it can be answered. Indeed it has already been answered by the readers who are cited in the *Variorum Commentary*. What these readers debate is the judgment the poem makes on the delights of recreation; what their debate indicates is that the judgment is blurred by a verb that can be made to participate in contradictory readings. (Thus the important thing about the evidence surveyed in the *Variorum* is not how it is marshaled, but that it could be marshaled at all, because it then becomes evidence of the equal availability of both interpretations.) In other words, the lines first generate a pressure for judgment—"he who of those delights can judge"—and then decline to deliver it; the pressure, however, still exists, and it is transferred from the words on the page to the reader (the reader is "he who"), who comes away from the poem not with a statement, but with a responsibility, the responsibility of deciding when and how often—if at all—to indulge in "those delights" (they remain delights in either case). This transferring of responsibility from the text to its readers is what the lines ask us to do—it is the essence of their experience—and in my terms it is therefore what the lines *mean*. It is a meaning the *Variorum* critics attest to even as they resist it, for what they are laboring so mightily to do by fixing the sense of the lines is to give the responsibility back. The text, however, will not accept it and remains determinedly evasive, even in its last two words, "not unwise." In their position these words confirm the impossibility of extracting from the poem a moral formula, for the assertion (certainly too strong a word) they complete is of the form, "He who does such and such, of him it cannot be said that he is unwise"; but of course neither can it be said that he is wise. Thus what Bush correctly terms the "defensive" "not unwise" operates to prevent us from attaching the label "wise" to any action including *either* of the actions—leaving time for or refraining from—represented by the ambiguity of "spare." Not only is the pressure of judgment taken off the poem, it is taken off the activity the poem at first pretended to judge. The issue is finally not the moral status of "those delights"—they become in seventeenth-century terms "things indifferent"—but on the good or bad uses to which they can be put by readers who are left, as Milton always leaves them, to choose and manage by themselves.

Let us step back for a moment and see how far we've come. We began with an apparently insoluble problem and proceeded, not to solve it, but to make it signify; first by regarding it as evidence of an experience and then by specifying for that experience a meaning. Moreover, the configurations of that experience, when they are made available by a reader-oriented analysis, serve as a check against the endlessly inconclusive adducing of evidence which characterizes formalist analysis. That is to say, any determination of what "spare" means (in a positivist or literal sense) is liable to be upset by the bringing forward of another analogue, or by a more complete computation of statistical frequencies, or by the discovery of new biographical information, or by anything else; but if we first determine that everything in the line before "spare" creates the expectation of an imminent judgment, then the ambiguity of "spare" can be assigned a significance in the context of that expectation. (It disappoints it and transfers the pressure of judgment to us.) That context is experiential, and it is within its contours and constraints that significances are established (both in the act of reading and in the analysis of that act). In formalist analyses the only constraints are the notoriously open-ended possibilities and combinations of possibilities that emerge when one begins to consult dictionaries and grammars and histories; to consult dictionaries, grammars, and histories is to assume that meanings can be specified independently of the activity of reading; what the example of "spare" shows is that it is in and by that activity that meanings—experiential, not positivist—are created.

In other words, it is the structure of the reader's experience rather than any structures available on the page that should be the object of description. In the case of Sonnet XX, that experiential structure was uncovered when an examination of formal structures led to an impasse; and the pressure to remove that impasse led to the substitution of one set of questions for another. It will more often be the case that the pressure of a spectacular failure will be absent. The sins of formalist-positivist analysis are primarily sins of omission, not an inability to explain phenomena, but an inability to see that they are there because its assumptions make it inevitable that they will be overlooked or suppressed. Consider, for example, the concluding lines of another of Milton's sonnets, "Avenge O Lord thy slaughtered saints."

> Avenge O Lord thy slaughtered saints, whose bones
> Lie scattered on the Alpine mountains cold,
> Even them who kept thy truth so pure of old
> When all our fathers worshipped stocks and stones,
> Forget not: in thy book record their groans
> Who were thy sheep and in their ancient fold
> Slain by the bloody Piedmontese that rolled
> Mother with infant down the rocks. Their moans
> The vales redoubled to the hills, and they
> To heaven. Their martyred blood and ashes sow
> O'er all the Italian fields where still doth sway
> The triple Tyrant: that from these may grow
> A hundredfold, who having learnt thy way
> Early may fly the Babylonian woe.

In this sonnet, the poet simultaneously petitions God and wonders aloud about the justice of allowing the faithful—"Even them who kept thy truth"—to be so brutally slaughtered. The note struck is alternately one of plea and complaint, and there is more than a hint that God is being called to account for what has happened to the Waldensians. It is generally agreed, however, that the note of complaint is less and less sounded and that the poem ends with an affirmation of faith in the ultimate operation of God's justice. In this reading, the final lines are taken to be saying something like this: From the blood of these martyred, O God, raise up a new and more numerous people, who, by virtue of an early education in thy law, will escape destruction by fleeing the Babylonian woe. Babylonian woe has been variously glossed[3]: but whatever it is taken to mean it is always read as part of a statement that specifies a set of conditions for the escaping of destruction or punishment; it is a warning to the reader as well as a petition to God. As a warning, however, it is oddly situated since the conditions it seems to specify were in fact met by the Waldensians, who of all men most followed God's laws. In other words, the details of their story would seem to undercut the affirmative moral the speaker proposes to draw from it. It is further undercut by a reading that is fleetingly available, although no one has acknowledged it because it is a function, not of the words on the page, but of the experience of the reader. In that experience, line 13 will for a moment be accepted as a complete sense unit and the emphasis of the line will fall on "thy way" (a phrase that has received absolutely no attention in the commentaries). At this point "thy way" can refer only to the way in which God has dealt with the Waldensians. That is, "thy way" seems to pick up the note of outrage with which the poem began, and if we continue to so interpret it, the conclusion of the poem will be a grim one indeed: since by this example it appears that God rains down punishment indiscriminately, it would be best perhaps to withdraw from the arena of his service, and thereby hope at least to be safely out of the line of fire. This is not the conclusion we carry away, because as line 14 unfolds, another reading of "thy way" becomes available, a reading in which "early" qualifies "learnt" and refers to something the faithful should do (learn thy way at an early age) rather than to something God has failed to do (save the Waldensians). These two readings are answerable to the pulls exerted by the beginning and ending of the poem: the outrage expressed in the opening lines generates a pressure for an explanation, and the grimmer reading is answerable to that pressure (even if it is also disturbing): the ending of the poem, the forward and upward movement of lines 10–14, creates the expectation of an affirmation, and the second reading fulfills that expectation. The criticism shows that in the end we settle on the more optimistic reading—it feels better—but even so the other has been a part of our experience, and because it has been a part of our experience, it *means*. What it means is that while we may be able to extract from the poem a statement affirming God's justice, we are not allowed to forget the evidence (of things seen) that makes the extraction so difficult (both for the speaker and for us). It is a difficulty we experience in the act of reading, even though a criticism which takes no account of that act has, as we have seen, suppressed it.

II

In each of the sonnets we have considered, the significant word or phrase occurs at a line break where a reader is invited to place it first in one and then in another structure of syntax and sense. This moment of hesitation, of semantic or syntactic slide, is crucial to the experience the verse provides, but, in a formalist analysis, that moment will disappear, either because it has been flattened out and made into an (insoluble) interpretive crux, or because it has been eliminated in the course of a procedure that is incapable of finding value in temporal phenomena. In the case of "When I consider how my light is spent" these two failures are combined.

> When I consider how my light is spent,
> Ere half my days, in this dark world and wide,
> And that one talent which is death to hide,
> Lodged with me useless, though my soul more bent
> To serve therewith my maker, and present
> My true account, lest he returning chide,
> Doth God exact day-labour, light denied,
> I fondly ask; but Patience to prevent
> That murmur, soon replies, God doth not need
> Either man's work or his own gifts, who best
> Bear his mild yoke, they serve him best, his state
> Is kingly. Thousands at his bidding speed
> And post o'er land and ocean without rest:
> They also serve who only stand and wait.

The interpretive crux once again concerns the final line: "They also serve who only stand and wait." For some this is an unqualified acceptance of God's will, while for others the note of affirmation is muted or even forced. The usual kinds of evidence are marshaled by the opposing parties, and the usual inconclusiveness is the result. There are some areas of agreement. "All the interpretations," Woodhouse remarks, "recognize that the sonnet commences from a mood of depression, frustration [and] impatience."[4] The object of impatience is a God who would first demand service and then take away the means of serving, and the oft noted allusion to the parable of the talents lends scriptural support to the accusation the poet is implicitly making: you have cast the wrong servant into unprofitable darkness. It has also been observed that the syntax and rhythm of these early lines, and especially of lines 6–8, are rough and uncertain; the speaker is struggling with his agitated thoughts and he changes directions abruptly, with no regard for the line as a unit of sense. The poem, says one critic, "seems almost out of control."[5]

The question I would ask is "whose control?"; for what these formal descriptions point to (but do not acknowledge) is the extraordinary number of adjustments required of readers who would negotiate these lines. The first adjustment is the result of the expectations created by the second half of line 6—"lest he returning chide." Since there is no full stop after "chide," it is natural to assume that this will be an introduction to reported speech, and to assume further that what will be reported is the poet's anticipation of the voice of God as it calls him, to an unfair accounting. This assumption does not survive line 7—"Doth God exact day-labour, light denied"—which rather than chiding the poet for his inactivity seems to rebuke him for having expected that chiding. The accents are precisely those heard so often in the Old Testament when God answers a reluctant Gideon, or a disputatious Moses, or a self-justifying Job: do you presume to judge my ways or to appoint my motives? Do you think I would exact day labor, light denied? In other words, the poem seems to turn at this point from a questioning of God to a questioning of that questioning; or, rather, the reader turns from the one to the other in the act of revising his projection of what line 7 will say and do. As it turns out, however, that revision must itself be revised because it had been made within the assumption that what we are hearing is the voice of God. This assumption falls before the very next phrase "I fondly ask," which requires not one, but two adjustments. Since the speaker of line 7 is firmly identified as the poet, the line must be reinterpreted as a continuation of his complaint—Is that the way you operate,

God, denying light, but exacting labor?—but even as that interpretation emerges, the poet withdraws from it by inserting the adverb "fondly," and once again the line slips out of the reader's control.

In a matter of seconds, then, line 7 has led four experiential lives, one as we anticipate it, another as that anticipation is revised, a third when we retroactively identify its speaker, and a fourth when that speaker disclaims it. What changes in each of these lives is the status of the poet's murmurings—they are alternately expressed, rejected, reinstated, and qualified—and as the sequence ends, the reader is without a firm perspective on the question of record: does God deal justly with his servants?

A firm perspective appears to be provided by Patience, whose entrance into the poem, the critics tell us, gives it both argumentative and metrical stability. But in fact the presence of Patience in the poem finally assures its continuing instability by making it impossible to specify the degree to which the speaker approves, or even participates in, the affirmation of the final line: "They also serve who only stand and wait." We know that Patience to prevent the poet's murmur soon replies (not soon enough however to prevent the murmur from registering), but we do not know when that reply ends. Does Patience fall silent in line 12, after "kingly"? or at the conclusion of line 13? or not at all? Does the poet appropriate these lines or share them or simply listen to them, as we do? These questions are unanswerable, and it is because they remain unanswerable that the poem ends uncertainly. The uncertainty is not in the statement it makes—in isolation line 14 is unequivocal—but in our inability to assign that statement to either the poet or to Patience. Were the final line marked unambiguously for the poet, then we would receive it as a resolution of his earlier doubts; and were it marked for Patience, it would be a sign that those doubts were still very much in force. It is marked for neither, and therefore we are without the satisfaction that a firmly conclusive ending (in *any* direction) would have provided. In short, we leave the poem unsure, and our unsureness is the realization (in our experience) of the unsureness with which the affirmation of the final line is, or is not, made. (This unsureness also operates to actualize the two possible readings of "wait": wait in the sense of expecting, that is waiting for an opportunity to serve actively; or wait in the sense of waiting *in* service, a waiting that is itself fully satisfying because the impulse to self-glorifying action has been stilled.)

The question debated in the *Variorum Commentary* is, how far from the mood of frustration and impatience does the poem finally move? The answer given by an experiential analysis is that you can't tell, and the fact that you can't tell is responsible for the uneasiness the poem has always inspired. It is that uneasiness which the critics inadvertently acknowledge when they argue about the force of the last line, but they are unable to make analytical use of what they acknowledge because they have no way to dealing with or even recognizing experiential (that is, temporal) structures. In fact, more than one editor has eliminated those structures by punctuating them out of existence: first by putting a full stop at the end of line 6 and thereby making it unlikely that the reader will assign line 7 to God (there will no longer be an expectation of reported speech), and then by supplying quotation marks for the sestet in order to remove any doubts one might have as to who is speaking. There is of course no warrant for these emendations, and in 1791 Thomas Warton had the grace and honesty to admit as much. "I have," he said, "introduced the turned commas both in the question and answer, not from any authority, but because they seem absolutely necessary to the sense."[6]

III

Editorial practices like these are only the most obvious manifestations of the assumptions to which I stand opposed: the assumption that there *is* a sense, that it is embedded or encoded in the text, and that it can be taken in at a single glance. These assumptions are, in order, positivist, holistic, and spatial, and to have them is to be committed both to a goal and to a procedure. The goal is to settle on a meaning, and the procedure involves first stepping back from the text, and then putting together or otherwise calculating the discrete units of significance it contains. My quarrel with this procedure (and with the assumptions that generate it) is that in the course of following it through the reader's activities are at once ignored and devalued. They are ignored because the text is taken to be self-sufficient—everything is *in* it—and they are devalued because when they are thought of at all, they are thought of as the disposable machinery of extraction. In the procedures I would urge, the reader's activities are at the center of attention, where they are regarded, not as leading to meaning, but as *having* meaning. The meaning they have is a consequence of their not being empty; for they include the making and revising of assumptions, the rendering and regretting of judgments, the coming to and abandoning of conclusions, the giving and withdrawing of approval, the specifying of causes, the asking of questions, the supplying of answers, the solving of puzzles. In a word, these activities are interpretive—rather than being preliminary to questions of value they are at every moment settling and resettling questions of value—and because they are interpretive, a description of them will also be, and without any additional step, an interpretation, not after the fact, but of the fact (of experiencing). It will be a description of a moving field of concerns, at once wholly present (not waiting for meaning, but constituting meaning) and continually in the act of reconstituting itself.

As a project such a description presents enormous difficulties, and there is hardly time to consider them here;[7] but it should be obvious from my brief examples how different it is from the positivist-formalist project. Everything depends on the temporal dimension, and as a consequence the notion of a mistake, at least as something to be avoided, disappears. In a sequence where a reader first structures the field he inhabits and then is asked to restructure it (by changing an assignment of speaker or realigning attitudes and positions) there is no question of priority among his structurings; no one of them, even if it is the last, has privilege; each is equally legitimate, each equally the proper object of analysis, because each is equally an event in his experience.

The firm assertiveness of this paragraph only calls attention to the questions it avoids. Who is this reader? How can I presume to describe his experiences, and what do I say to readers who report that they do not have the experiences I describe? Let me answer these questions or rather make a beginning at answering them in the context of another example, this time from Milton's *Comus*. In line 46 of *Comus* we are introduced to the villain by way of genealogy:

> Bacchus that first from out the purple grape,
> Crushed the sweet poison of misused wine.

In almost any edition of this poem, a footnote will tell you that Bacchus is the god of wine. Of course most readers already know that, and because they know it, they will be anticipating the appearance of "wine" long before they come upon it in the final position. Moreover, they will also be anticipating a negative judgment on it, in part because of the association of Bacchus with revelry and excess, and especially because the phrase "sweet poison" suggests that the judgment has already been made. At an early point then, we will have both filled in the form of the assertion and made a decision about its moral content. That decision is upset by the word "misused"; for what "misused" asks us to do is transfer the pressure of judgment from wine (where we have already placed it) to the abusers of wine, and therefore when "wine" finally appears, we must declare it innocent of the charges we have ourselves made.

This, then, is the structure of the reader's experience—the transferring of a moral label from a thing to those who appropriate it. It is an experience that depends on a reader for whom the name Bacchus has precise and immediate associations; another reader, a reader for whom those associations are less precise will not have that experience because he will not have rushed to a conclusion in relation to which the word "misused" will stand as a challenge. Obviously I am discriminating between these two readers and between the two equally real experiences they will have. It is not a discrimination based simply on information, because what is important is not the information itself, but the action of the mind which its possession makes possible for one reader and impossible for the other. One might discriminate further between them by noting that the point at issue—whether value is a function of objects and actions or of intentions—is at the heart of the seventeenth-century debate over "things indifferent." A reader who is aware of that debate will not only *have* the experience I describe; he will recognize at the end of it that he has been asked to take a position on one side of a continuing controversy; and that recognition (also a part of his experience) will be part of the disposition with which he moves into the lines that follow.

It would be possible to continue with this profile of the optimal reader, but I would not get very far before someone would point out that what I am really describing is the intended reader, the reader whose education, opinions, concerns, linguistic competences, etc. make him capable of having the experience the author wished to provide. I would not resist this characterization because it seems obvious that the efforts of readers are always efforts to discern and therefore to realize (in the sense of becoming) an author's intention. I would only object if that realization were conceived narrowly, as the single act of comprehending an author's purpose, rather than (as I would conceive it) as the succession of acts readers perform in the continuing assumption that they are dealing with intentional beings. In this view discerning an intention is no more or less than understanding, and understanding includes (is constituted by) all the activities which make up what I call the structure of the reader's experience. To describe that experience is therefore to describe the reader's efforts at understanding, and to describe the reader's efforts at understanding is to describe his realization (in two senses) of an author's intention. Or to put it another way, what my analyses amount to are descriptions of a succession of decisions made by readers about an author's intention; decisions that are not limited to the specifying of purpose but include the specifying of every aspect of successively intended worlds; decisions that are precisely the shape, because they are the content, of the reader's activities.

Having said this, however, it would appear that I am open to two objections. The first is that the procedure is a circular one. I describe the experience of a reader who in his strategies is answerable to an author's intention, and I specify the author's intention by pointing to the strategies employed by that same reader. But this objection would have force only if it were possible to specify one independently of the other. What is being specified from either perspective are the conditions of utterance, of what could have been understood to have been meant by what was said. That is, intention and understanding are two ends of a conventional act, each of which necessarily stipulates (includes, defines, specifies) the other. To construct the profile of the informed or at-home reader is at the same time to characterize the author's intention and vice versa, because to do either is to specify the *contemporary* conditions of utterance, to identify, by becoming a member of, a community made up of those who share interpretive strategies.

The second objection is another version of the first: if the content of the reader's experience is the succession of acts he performs in search of an author's intentions, and if he performs those acts at the bidding of the text, does not the text then produce or contain everything—intention *and* experience—and have I not compromised my antiformalist position? This objection will have force only if the formal patterns of the text are assumed to exist independently of the reader's experience, for only then can priority be claimed for them. Indeed, the claims of independence and priority are one and the same; when they are separated it is so that they can give circular and illegitimate support to each other. The question "do formal features exist independently?" is usually answered by pointing to their priority: they are "in" the text before the reader comes to it. The question "are formal features prior?" is usually answered by pointing to their independent status: they are "in" the text before the reader comes to it. What looks like a step in an argument is actually the spectacle of an assertion supporting itself. It follows then that an attack on the independence of formal features will also be an attack on their priority (and vice versa), and I would like to mount such an attack in the context of two short passages from *Lycidas*.

The first passage (actually the second in the poem's sequence) begins at line 42:

> The willows and the hazel copses green
> Shall now no more be seen,
> Fanning their joyous leaves to thy soft lays.
> [Ll. 42–44]

It is my thesis that the reader is always making sense (I intend "making" to have its literal force), and in the case of these lines the sense he makes will involve the assumption (and therefore the creation) of a completed assertion after the word "seen," to wit, the death of Lycidas has so affected the willows and the hazel copses green that, in sympathy, they will wither and die (will no more be seen by *anyone*). In other words at the end of line 43 the reader will have hazarded an interpretation, or performed an act of perceptual closure, or made a decision as to what is being asserted. I do not mean that he has done four things, but that he has done one thing the description of which might take any one of four forms—making sense, interpreting, performing perceptual closure, deciding about what is intended. (The importance of this point will become clear later.) Whatever he has done (that is, however we characterize it) he will undo it in the act of reading the next line; for here he discovers that his closure, or making of sense, was premature and that he must make a new one in which the relationship between man and nature is exactly the reverse of what was first assumed. The willows and the hazel copses green will in fact be seen, but they will not be seen by Lycidas. It is he who will be no more, while they go on as before, fanning their joyous leaves to someone else's soft lays (the whole of line 44 is now perceived as modifying and removing the absoluteness of "seen"). Nature is not sympathetic, but indifferent, and the notion of her sympathy is one of those "false surmises" that the poem is continually encouraging and then disallowing.

The previous sentence shows how easy it is to surrender to the bias of our critical language and begin to talk as if poems, not readers or interpreters, did things. Words like "encourage" and "disallow" (and others I have used in this paper) imply agents, and it is only "natural" to assign agency first to an author's intentions and then to the forms that assumedly embody them. What really happens, I think, is something quite different: rather than intention and its formal realization producing interpretation (the "normal" picture), interpretation creates intention and its formal realization by creating the conditions in which it becomes possible to pick them out. In other words, in the analysis of these lines from *Lycidas* I did what critics always do: I "saw" what my interpretive principles permitted or directed me to see, and then I turned around and attributed what I had "seen" to a text and an intention. What my principles direct me to "see" are readers performing acts; the points at which I find (or to be more precise, declare) those acts to have been performed become (by a sleight of hand) demarcations *in* the text; those demarcations are then available for the designation "formal features," and as formal features they can be (illegitimately) assigned the responsibility for producing the interpretation which in fact produced them. In this case, the demarcation my interpretation calls into being is placed at the end of line 42; but of course the end of that (or any other) line is worth noticing or pointing out only because my model *demands* (the word is not too strong) perceptual closures and therefore locations at which they occur; in that model this point will be one of those locations, although (1) it needn't have been (not every line ending occasions a closure) and (2) in another model, one that does not give value to the activities of readers, the possibility of its being one would not have arisen.

What I am suggesting is that formal units are always a function of the interpretive model one brings to bear; they are not "in" the text, and I would make the same argument for intentions. That is, intention is no more embodied "in" the text than are formal units; rather an intention, like a formal unit, is made when perceptual or interpretive closure is hazarded; it is verified by an interpretive act, and I would add, it is not verifiable in any other way. This last assertion is too large to be fully considered here, but I can sketch out the argumentative sequence I would follow were I to consider it: intention is known when and only when it is recognized; it is recognized as soon as you decide about it; you decide about it as soon as you make a sense; and you make a sense (or so my model claims) as soon as you can.

Let me tie up the threads of my argument with a final example from *Lycidas:*

> He must not float upon his wat'ry bier
> Unwept . . .
>
> [Ll. 13–14]

Here the reader's experience has much the same career as it does in lines 42–44: at the end of line 13 perceptual closure is hazarded, and a sense is made in which the line is taken to be a resolution bordering on a promise: that is, there is now an expectation that something will be done about this unfortunate situation, and the reader anticipates a call to action, perhaps even a program for the undertaking of a rescue mission. With "Unwept," however, that expectation and anticipation are disappointed, and the realization of that disappointment will be inseparable from the making of a new (and less comforting) sense: nothing will be done; Lycidas will continue to float upon his wat'ry bier, and the only action taken will be the lamenting of the fact that no action will be efficacious, including the actions of speaking and listening to this lament (which in line 15 will receive the meretricious and self-mocking designation "melodious tear"). Three "structures" come into view at precisely the same moment, the moment when the reader having resolved a sense unresolves it and makes a new one; that moment will also be the moment of picking out a formal pattern or unit, end of line/beginning of line, and it will also be the moment at which the reader having decided about the speaker's intention, about what is meant by what has been said, will make the decision again and in so doing will make another intention.

This, then, is my thesis: that the form of the reader's experience, formal units, and the structure of intention are one, that they come into view simultaneously, and that therefore the questions of priority and independence do not arise. What does arise is another question: what produces *them*? That is, if intention, form, and the shape of the reader's experience are simply different ways of referring to (different perspectives on) the same interpretive act, what is that act an interpretation *of*? I cannot answer that question, but neither, I would claim, can anyone else, although formalists try to answer it by pointing to patterns and claiming that they are available independently of (prior to) interpretation. These patterns vary according to the procedures that yield them: they may be statistical (number of two-syllable words per hundred words), grammatical (ratio of passive to active constructions, or of right-branching to left-branching sentences, or of anything else); but whatever they are I would argue that they do not lie innocently in the world but are themselves constituted by an interpretive act, even if, as is often the case, that act is unacknowledged. Of course, this is as true of my analyses as it is of anyone else's. In the examples offered here I appropriate the notion "line ending" and treat it as a fact of nature; and one might conclude that as a fact it is responsible for the reading experience I describe. The truth I think is exactly the reverse: line endings exist by virtue of perceptual strategies rather than the other way around. Historically, the strategy that we know as "reading (or hearing) poetry" has included paying attention to the line as a unit, but is precisely that attention which has made the line as a unit (either of print or of aural duration) available. A reader so practiced in paying that attention that he regards the line as a brute fact rather than as a convention will have a great deal of difficulty with concrete poetry; if he overcomes that difficulty, it will not be because he has learned to ignore the line as a unit but because he will have acquired a new set of interpretive strategies (the strategies constitutive of "concrete poetry reading") in the context of which the line as a unit no longer exists. In short, what is noticed is what has been made noticeable, not by a clear and undistorting glass, but by an interpretive strategy.

This may be hard to see when the strategy has become so habitual that the forms it yields seem part of the world. We find it easy to assume that alliteration as an effect depends on a "fact" that exists independently of an interpretive "use" one might make of it, the fact that words in proximity begin with the same letter. But it takes only a moment's reflection to realize that the sameness, far from being natural, is enforced by an orthographic convention; that is to say it is the product of an interpretation. Were we to substitute phonetic conventions for orthographic ones (a "reform" traditionally urged by purists), the supposedly "objective" basis for alliteration would disappear because a phonetic transcription would require that we distinguish between the initial sounds of those very words that enter into alliterative relationships; rather than conforming to those relationships the rules of spelling make them. One might reply that, since alliteration is an aural rather than a visual phenomenon when poetry is heard, we have unmediated access to the physical sounds themselves and hear "real" similarities. But phonological "facts" are no more uninterpreted (or less conventional) than the "facts" of orthography; the distinctive features that make articulation and reception possible are the product of a system of differences that must be *imposed* before it can be recognized; the patterns the ear hears (like the patterns the eye sees) are the patterns its perceptual habits make available.

One can extend this analysis forever, even to the "facts" of grammar. The history of linguistics is the history of competing paradigms each of which offers a different account of the constituents of language. Verbs, nouns, cleft sentences, transformations, deep and surface structures, semes, rhemes, tagmemes—now you see them, now you don't, depending on the descriptive apparatus you employ. The critic who confidently rests his analyses on the bedrock of syntactic descriptions is resting on an interpretation; the facts he points to *are* there, but only as a consequence of the interpretive (man-made) model that has called them into being.

The moral is clear: the choice is never between objectivity and interpretation but between an interpretation that is unacknowledged as such and an interpretation that is at least aware of itself. It is this awareness that I am claiming for myself, although in doing so I must give up the claims implicitly made in the first part of this paper. There I argue that a bad (because spatial) model had suppressed what was really happening, but by my own declared principles the notion "really happening" is just one more interpretation.

IV

It seems then that the price one pays for denying the priority of either forms or intentions is an inability to say how it is that one ever begins. Yet we do begin, and we continue, and because we do there arises an immediate counter-objection to the preceding pages. If interpretive acts are the source of forms rather than the other way around, why isn't it the case that readers are always performing the same acts or a random succession of forms? How, in short, does one explain these two random succession of forms. How, in short, does one explain these two "facts" of reading?: (1) the same reader will perform differently when reading two "different" (the word is in quotation marks because its status is precisely what is at issue) texts; and (2) different readers will perform similarly when reading the "same" (in quotes for the same reason) text. That is to say, both the stability of interpretation among readers and the variety of interpretation in the career of a single reader would seem to argue for the existence of something independent of and prior to interpretive acts, something which produces them. I will answer this challenge by asserting that both the stability and the variety are functions of interpretive strategies rather than of texts.

Let us suppose that I am reading *Lycidas.* What is it that I am doing? First of all, what I am not doing is "simply reading," an activity in which I do not believe because it implies the possibility of pure (that is, disinterested) perception. Rather, I am proceeding on the basis of (at least) two interpretive decisions: (1) that *Lycidas* is a pastoral and (2) that it was written by Milton. (I should add that the notions "pastoral" and "Milton" are also interpretations; that is they do not stand for a set if indisputable objective facts: if they did, a great many books would not now be getting written.) Once these decisions have been made (and if I had not made these I would have made others, and they would be consequential in the same way), I am immediately predisposed to perform certain acts, to "find," by looking for, themes (the relationship between natural processes and the careers of men, the efficacy of poetry or of any other action), to confer significances (on flowers, streams, shepherds, pagan deities), to mark out "formal" units (the lament, the consolation, the turn, the affirmation of faith, etc.). My disposition to perform these acts (and others; the list is not meant to be exhaustive) constitutes a set of interpretive strategies, which, when they are put into execution, become the large act of reading. That is to say, interpretive strategies are not put into execution after reading (the pure act of perception in which I do not believe); they are the shape of reading, and because they are the shape of reading, they give texts their shape, making them rather than, as it is usually assumed, arising from them. Several important things follow from this account:

1. I did not have to execute this particular set of interpretive strategies because I did not have to make those particular interpretive (pre-reading) decisions. I could have decided, for example, that *Lycidas* was a text in which a set of fantasies and defenses find expression. These decisions would have entailed the assumption of another set of interpretive strategies (perhaps like that put forward by Norman Holland in *The Dynamics of Literary Response*) and the execution of that set would have made another text.

2. I could execute this same set of strategies when presented with texts that did not bear the title (again a notion which is itself an interpretation) *Lycidas, A Pastoral Monody. . . .* I could decide (it is a decision some have made) that *Adam Bede* is a pastoral written by an author who consciously modeled herself on Milton (still remembering that "pastoral" and "Milton" are interpretations, not facts in the public domain); or I could decide, as Empson did, that a great many things not usually considered pastoral were in fact to be so read; and either decision would give rise to a set of interpretive strategies, which, when put into action, would *write* the text I write when reading *Lycidas.* (Are you with me?)

3. A reader other than myself who, when presented with *Lycidas,* proceeds to put into execution a set of interpretive strategies similar to mine (how he could do so is a question I will take up later), will perform the same (or at least a similar) succession of interpretive acts. He and I then might be tempted to say that we agree about the poem (thereby assuming that the poem exists independently of the acts either of us performs); but what we really would agree about is the way to write it.

4. A reader other than myself who, when presented with *Lycidas* (please keep in mind that the status of *Lycidas* is what is at issue), puts into execution a different set of interpretive strategies will perform a different succession of interpretive acts. (I am assuming, it is the article of my faith, that a reader will always execute some set of interpretive strategies and therefore perform some succes-

sion of interpretive acts.) One of us might then be tempted to complain to the other that we could not possibly be reading the same poem (literary criticism is full of such complaints) and he would be right; for each of us would be reading the poem he had made.

The large conclusion that follows from these four smaller ones is that the notions of the "same" or "different" texts are fictions. If I read *Lycidas* and *The Waste Land* differently (in fact I do not), it will not be because the formal structures of the two poems (to term them such is also an interpretive decision) call forth different interpretive strategies but because my predisposition to execute different interpretive strategies will *produce* different formal structures. That is, the two poems are different because I have decided that they will be. The proof of this is the possibility of doing the reverse (that is why point 2 is so important). That is to say, the answer to the question "why do different texts give rise to different sequences of interpretive acts?" is that *they don't have to,* an answer which implies strongly that "they" don't exist. Indeed it has always been possible to put into action interpretive strategies designed to make all texts one, or to put it more accurately, to be forever making the same text. Augustine urges just such a strategy, for example, in *On Christian Doctrine* where he delivers the "rule of faith" which is of course a rule of interpretation. It is dazzlingly simple: everything in the Scriptures, and indeed in the world when it is properly read, points to (bears the meaning of) God's love for us and our answering responsibility to love our fellow creatures for His sake. If only you should come upon something which does not at first seem to bear this meaning, that "does not literally pertain to virtuous behavior or to the truth of faith," you are then to take it "to be figurative" and proceed to scrutinize it "until an interpretation contributing to the reign of charity is produced." This then is both a stipulation of what meaning there is and a set of directions for finding it, which is of course a set of directions—of interpretive strategies—for making it, that is, for the endless reproduction of the same text. Whatever one may think of this interpretive program, its success and ease of execution are attested to by centuries of Christian exegesis. It is my contention that any interpretive program, any set of interpretive strategies, can have a similar success, although few have been as spectacularly successful as this one. (For some time now, for at least a hundred years, the most successful interpretive program has gone under the name "ordinary language.") In our own discipline programs with the same characteristic of always reproducing one text include psychoanalytic criticism, Robertsonianism (always threatening to extend its sway into later and later periods), numerology (a sameness based on the assumption of innumerable fixed differences).

The other challenging question—"why will different readers execute the same interpretive strategy when faced with the 'same' text?"—can be handled in the same way. The answer is again that *they don't have to,* and my evidence is the entire history of literary criticism. And again this answer implies that the notion "same text" is the product of the possession by two or more readers of similar interpretive strategies.

But why should this ever happen? Why should two or more readers ever agree, and why should regular, that is, habitual, differences in the career of a single reader ever occur? What is the explanation on the one hand of the stability of interpretation (at least among certain groups of certain times) and on the other of the orderly variety of interpretation if it is not the stability and variety of texts? The answer to all of these questions is to be found in a notion that has been implicit in my argument, the notion of *interpretive communities*. Interpretive communities are made up of those who share interpretive strategies not for reading (in the conventional sense) but for writing texts, for constituting their properties and assigning their intentions. In other words these strategies exist prior to the act of reading and therefore determine the shape of what is read rather than, as is usually assumed, the other way around. If it is an article of faith in a particular community that there are a variety of texts, its members will boast a repertoire of strategies for making them. And if a community believes in the existence of only one text, then the single strategy its members employ will be forever writing it. The first community will accuse the members of the second of being reductive, and they in turn will call their accusers superficial. The assumption in each community will be that the other is not correctly perceiving the "true text," but the truth will be that each perceives the text (or texts) its interpretive strategies demand and call into being. This, then, is the explanation both for the stability of interpretation among different readers (they belong to the same community) and for the regularity with which a single reader will employ different interpretive strategies and thus make different texts (he belongs to different communities). It also explains why there are disagreements and why they can be debated in a principled way: not because of a stability in texts, but because of a stability in the makeup of interpretive communities and therefore in the opposing positions they make possible. Of course this stability is always temporary (unlike the longed for and timeless stability of the text). Interpretive communities grow larger and decline, and individuals move from one to another; thus while the alignments are not permanent, they are always there, providing just enough stability for the interpretive battles to go on, and just enough shift and slippage to assure that they will never be settled. The notion of interpretive communities thus stands between an impossible ideal and the fear which leads so many to maintain it. The ideal is of perfect agreement and it would require texts to have a status independent of interpretation. The fear is of interpretive anarchy, but it would only be realized if interpretation (text making) were completely random. It is the fragile but real consolidation of interpretive communities that allows us to talk to one another, but with no hope or fear of ever being able to stop.

In other words interpretive communities are no more stable than texts because interpretive strategies are not natural or universal, but *learned*. This does not mean that there is a point at which an individual has not yet learned any. The ability to interpret is not acquired; it is constitutive of being human. What is acquired are the ways of interpreting and those same ways can also be forgotten or supplanted, or complicated or dropped from favor ("no one reads that way anymore"). When any of these things happens, there is a corresponding change in texts, not because they are being read differently, but because they are being written differently.

The only stability, then, inheres in the fact (at least in my model) that interpretive strategies are always being deployed, and this means that communication is a much more chancy affair than we are accustomed to think it. For if there are no fixed texts, but only interpretive strategies making them; and if interpretive strategies are not natural, but learned (and are therefore unavailable to a finite description), what is it that utterers (speakers, authors, critics, me, you) do? In the old model utterers are in the business of handing over ready made or prefabricated meanings. These meanings are said to be encoded, and the code is assumed to be in the world independently of the individuals who are obliged to attach themselves to it (if they do not they run the danger of being declared deviant). In my model, however, meanings are not extracted but made and made not by encoded forms but by interpretive strategies that call forms into being. It follows then that what utterers do is give hearers and readers the opportunity to make meanings (and texts) by inviting them to put into execution a set of strategies. It is presumed that the invitation will be recognized, and that presumption rests on a projection on the part of a speaker or author of the moves *he* would make if confronted by the sounds or marks he is uttering or setting down.

It would seem at first that this account of things simply reintroduces the old objection: for isn't this an admission that there is after all a formal encoding, not perhaps of meanings, but of the directions for making them, for executing interpretive strategies? The answer is that they will only *be* directions to those who already have the interpretive strategies in the first place. Rather than producing interpretive acts, they are the product of one. An author hazards his projection, not because of something "in" the marks, but because of something he assumes to be in his reader. The very existence of the "marks" is a function of an interpretive community, for they will be recognized (that is, made) only by its members. Those outside that community will be deploying a different set of interpretive strategies (interpretation cannot be withheld) and will therefore be making different marks.

So once again I have made the text disappear, but unfortunately the problems do not disappear with it. If everyone is continually executing interpretive strategies and in that act constituting texts, intentions, speakers, and authors, how can any one of us know whether or not he is a member of the same interpretive community as any other of us? The answer is that he can't, since any evidence brought forward to support the claim would itself be an interpretation (especially if the "other" were an author long dead). The only "proof" of membership is fellowship, the nod of recognition from someone in the same community, someone who says to you what neither of us could ever prove to a third party: "we know," I say it to you now, knowing full well that you will agree with me (that is, understand) only if you already agree with me.

Notes

1. All references are to *The Poems of John Milton*, ed. John Carey and Alastair Fowler (London, 1968).

2. *A Variorum Commentary on the Poems of John Milton*, vol. 2, pt. 2, ed. A.S.P. Woodhouse and Douglas Bush (New York, 1972), p. 475.

3. It is first of all a reference to the city of iniquity from which the Hebrews are urged to flee in Isaiah and Jeremiah. In Protestant polemics Babylon is identified with the Roman Church, whose destruction is prophesied in the book of Revelation. And in some Puritan tracts, Babylon is the name for Augustine's earthly city, from which the faithful are to flee inwardly in order to escape the fate awaiting the unregenerate. See *Variorum Commentary*, pp. 440–41.

4. *Variorum Commentary*, p. 469.

5. Ibid., p. 457.

6. *Poems Upon Several Occasions, English, Italian, and Latin, With Translations, By John Milton*, ed. Thomas Warton (London, 1791), p. 352.

7. See my *Surprised by Sin: The Reader*

in Paradise Lost (London and New York, 1967); *Self-Consuming Artifacts: The Experience of Seventeenth-Century Literature* (Berkeley, 1972); "What Is Stylistics and Why Are They Saying Such Terrible Things About It?" in *Approaches to Poetics*, ed. Seymour Chatman (New York, 1973), pp. 109–52; "How Ordinary Is Ordinary Language?" in *New Literary History*, 5 (Autumn 1973): 41–54; "Facts and Fictions: A Reply to Ralph Rader," *Critical Inquiry*, 1 (June 1975): 883–91.

Raymond Williams 1921–1988

The work of British critic Raymond Williams represents an important contribution to that area of critical discussion where literary and historical, cultural and political concerns are seen to be interrelated and necessarily dependent upon one another. Williams, born in 1921, was the son of a railway signalman in the Welsh border village of Pandy. The influence of his working-class background on his critical thinking and writing has been significant and is reflected in two works, *Border Country* (1960) and *Second Generation* (1964). He received his education through government scholarships, first at Abergavenny Grammar School and then at Trinity College, Cambridge—personal circumstances representative of a generation of postwar British intellectuals who were educated at state expense but who never felt themselves to be a part of the social and academic status quo. After military service he became an adult education tutor at Oxford University. In 1961 he was elected fellow of Jesus College, Cambridge, where he was a reader in English until 1974, when he became professor of drama, a position he held until his death in 1988.

The critical heir of both F.R. Leavis and Karl Marx, Williams's approach to literary study assumes a vital relationship between literature and life and foregrounds literature's ability to analyze and critique the dominant social, political, and discursive systems in which it operates. In 1958 he published *Culture and Society* , in which he traced the "idea of culture" as it developed in Britain from 1780 to 1950. In his work since then he has continued to practice a kind of cultural analysis that focuses on both literary and historical materials and considers their complex interactions and development. In *Drama from Ibsen to Brecht* (1968), Williams examines the conventions of modern drama in a broad survey of European and British works and finds that they embody specific "structures of feeling" that have their origin in the historical moment and a sense of lived life and, specifically, in the limitations and alienating features of bourgeois society.

In *The Country and the City* (1973) he explores the dichotomy between rural life and urban experience in both English history and literature. "Country" and "city" are viewed not only as particular forms of social organization centered around historically specifiable modes of production but also as conceptual and ideological constructs that have, through their altering relationships, borne various meanings and values throughout British history and within the literary tradition. *Marxism and Literature* (1977), his most rigorously theoretical work, attempts a theory of cultural materialism through an integration of Marxist theories on language and literature. Within his critical practice, Marxism operates as a theoretical position from which to focus his concerns in a number of areas that "converge but in general do not meet"—literature, history, political economy, sociology. His analysis is always incisive and complex and combines intellectual acumen with ideological passion. His insistence on the interconnectedness of life and art places him squarely within the tradition of liberal humanism.

In *Keywords* (1983), he explores, via historical semantics, the networks of meaning and semantic resonance emitted by a set of terms crucial to social and cultural discussion. His aim is not to specify meaning in a definitive sense, but rather to expose the mutability of key terms and to explore the dynamic of semantic transformation and exchange within critical discourse, a process characterized as much by rupture and displacement as by continuity and progression. His method is to begin by placing the word within the context of its historical use and development, then to situate the term both within and between the systems of critical and theoretical discourse that have appropriated it (often in surprisingly contradictory ways), and finally to situate it within the larger but less stable system of actual, practical language use. His glosses focus on both the "internal developments and structures" of the word as well as its various specifying contexts—literary, historical, and political.

All the terms in *Keywords* represent particular problems and complexities that bear heavily on the clarity and precision of the critical discourses to which they are so integral. Williams readily acknowledges the provisional and fragmentary nature of this project and invites further discussion and amendment. Yet in the range of terms selected for inclusion and in his approach to semantic analysis, we can get a clear idea of both the theoretical issues and concerns that inform his work generally, and more particularly, a sense of the strategy that underlies his critical methodology.

from KEYWORDS

CRITICISM

Criticism has become a very difficult word, because although its predominant general sense is of fault-finding, it has an underlying sense of judgment and a very confusing specialized sense, in relation to art and literature, which depends on assumptions that may now be breaking down. The word came into English in eC17, from **critic** and **critical** mC16, fw *criticus*, L, *kritikos*, Gk, rw *kritos*, Gk—a judge. Its predominant early sense was of fault-finding: "stand at the marke of criticisme . . . to bee shot at," Dekker (1607). It was also used for commentary on literature and especially from lC17 for a sense of the act of judging literature and the writing which embodied this. What is most interesting is that the general sense of fault-finding, or at least of negative judgment, has persisted as primary. This has even led to the distinction of *appreciation* as a softer word for the judgment of literature. But what is significant in the development of **criticism,** and of **critic** and **critical,** is the assumption of judgment as the predominant and even natural response. (**Critical** has another specialized but important and persistent use, not to describe judgment, but from a specialized use in medicine to refer to a turning point; hence decisive. *Crisis* itself has of course been extended to any difficulty as well as to any turning point.)

While **criticism** in its most general sense developed towards *censure* (itself acquiring from C17 an adverse rather than a neutral implication), **criticism** in its specialized sense developed towards TASTE (q.v.), *cultivation,* and later CULTURE (q.v.) and *discrimination* (itself a split word, with this positive sense for good or informed judgment, but also a strong negative sense of unreasonable exclusion or unfair treatment of some outside group). The formation which underlies this development is very difficult to understand because it has taken so strong a hold on our minds. In its earliest period the association is with learned or "informed" ability. It still often tries to retain this sense. But its crucial development, from lC17, depended on the isolation of the reception of impressions: the reader, one might now say, as the CONSUMER (q.v.) of a range of works. Its generalization, within a particular class and profession, depended on the assumptions best represented by *taste* and *cultivation:* a form of social development of personal impressions and responses, to the point where they could be represented as the STANDARDS (q.v.) of *judgment.* The notion that response was judgment depended, of course, on the social confidence of a class and later a profession. The confidence was variously specified, originally as *learning* or scholarship, later as *cultivation* and *taste,* later still as SENSIBILITY (q.v.). At various stages, forms of this confidence have broken down, and especially in C20 attempts have been made to replace it by *objective* (cf. SUBJECTIVE) methodologies, providing another kind of basis for judgment. What has not been questioned is the assumption of "judgment." In its pretensions to authority it has of course been repeatedly challenged, and **critic** in the most common form of this specialized sense—as a reviewer of plays, films, books and so on—has acquired an understandable derogatory sense. But this cannot be resolved by distinctions of status between **critic** and *reviewer.* What is at issue is not only the association between **criticism** and faultfinding but the more basic association between **criticism** and judgment as apparently general and natural processes. As a term for the social or professional generalization of the processes of reception of any but especially the more formal kinds of COMMUNICATION (q.v.), **criticism** is ideological not only in the sense that it assumes the position of the *consumer* but also in the sense that it masks this position by a succession of abstractions of its real terms of response (as *judgment, taste, cultivation, discrimination, sensibility; disinterested, qualified, rigorous* and so on). This then actively prevents that understanding of response which does not assume the habit (or right or duty) of judgment. The continuing sense of **criticism** as fault-finding is the most useful linguistic influence against the confidence of this habit, but there are also signs, in the occasional rejection of **criticism** as a definition of conscious response, of a more significant rejection of the habit itself. The point would then be, not to find some other term to replace it, while continuing the same kind of activity, but to get rid of the habit, which depends, fundamentally, on the abstraction of response from its real situation and circumstances: the elevation to judgment, and to an apparently general process, when what always needs to be understood is the specificity of the response, which is not a judgment but a practice, in active and complex relations with the situation and conditions of the practice, and, necessarily, with all other practices.

Formalist

Formalist is quite an old English word, but in C20 it has been widely used in a relatively new context, following uses of the corresponding word in Russian. Two senses of **formalist** appeared in English from eC17: (i) an adherent of the "mere forms" or "outward shows" of religion: "formalists and time-servers" (1609); (ii) one who explains a matter from its superficial rather than its substantial qualities: "it is a ridiculous thing . . . to see what shiftes theis Formalists have . . . to make superficies to seeme body, that hath depth and bulk" (Bacon, 1607–12). These uses, and some of the intricate confusions of more recent usage, can be understood only by reference to the complicated development of **form** itself. From fw *forme,* oF, *forma,* L—shape, *form* repeated in English the complications of its Latin development, of which two are principally relevant: (i), a visible or outward shape, with a strong sense of the physical body: "an angel bi wai he mette, In mannes fourm" (c. 1325); "forme is most frayle, a fading flattering showe" (1568); (ii), an essential shaping principle, making indeterminate material into a determinate or specific being or thing: "the body was only mater, of which (the soul) were the fourme" (1413); "according to the diversity of inward forms, things of the world are distinguished into their kinds" (Hooker, 1594). It is clear that in these extreme senses **form** spanned the whole range from the external and superficial to the inherent and determining. **Formality** spanned the same range, from "the attyre . . . being a matter of meere formalitie" (Hooker, 1597), to "those Formalities, wherein their Essence doth consist" (1672). In common use, **form** retained its full range but **formality, formalist** and (from mC19) **formalism** were predominantly used in negative or dismissive ways: "the Ceremonies are Idols to Formalists" (1637); "oh ye cold-hearted, frozen, formalists" (Young, 1742); "useless formalism" (Kingsley, 1850); "cant and formalism" (1878). Two examples have some relevance to the later specific development: "Formalists who demand Explications of the least ambiguous Word" (1707); "the formalist of dramatic criticism" (1814).

Given the complications of **form,** and the received implications of **formalist,** it is not surprising that the **formal method** and **formalist school** which can be distinguished, under those names, in Russian literary studies from about 1916, should have been so variously understood. Moreover, as **formalism** itself developed, it showed many different tendencies and emphases. Its predominant emphasis was on the specific, intrinsic characteristics of a literary work, which required analysis "in its own terms" before any other kind of discussion, and especially social or ideological analysis, was relevant or even possible. The intricacies of the subsequent argument are extraordinary. There was a simple opposition (bringing into play a received distinction between *form* (i) and *content*) between a **formalism** limited to "merely" AESTHETIC (q.v.) interests and a *Marxism* concerned with social content and ideological tendency. In the actual disposition and development of historical forces, it was this strongly negative sense of **formalism** which first became widely known in English, where it was used as if equivalent to ideas of "art for art's sake." At the same time, in some developments of **formalism,** notably in the idea of a quite separate category of "poetic language," and in some tendency to deny the relevance of "social content" or "social meaning" at *any* stage, this was, quite often, the position really held. The debate (it is better to call it that than an argument) between these two schools (in the specialized senses of **formalist** and *Marxist*) dominated usage until c. 1950. The earlier English senses of "outward show" and "superficial appearance" undoubtedly compromised **formalist** in this stage. What was more interesting, but still extremely difficult, was the notion of **form** (ii) as a shaping principle, either in its widest sense (where it overlapped with genre) or in its most specific sense, where it was a discoverable organizing principle within a work (cf. "no work of true genius dares want its appropriate form," Coleridge). With this sense of **form,** (ii) as distinct from (i), the *Marxist* emphasis could be reasonably described as a **formalism of content,** using the unfavourable sense (i) of "outward show," and different questions that could be asked about the real **formation** (form (ii)) of a work, which requires specific analysis of its elements in a particular organization. Moreover, as to some extent happened (though with much transfer and confusion of names) this kind of emphasis, allowing for or actually involving extension from the specific form to wider forms, and to forms of consciousness and relationship (*society*), was one of the tendencies within **formalism.** The point was confused by distinctions (involving deep disagreements which were not always fully articulated) between *intersubjective* and SOCIAL (q.v.) processes, and between *synchronic* and *diachronic* analyses: terms derived from a tendency in linguistics, and used either to express an absolute distinction between a self-sufficient system in language and a system as part of an historical process, or to express alternative emphases, now on the system, now on the process of development of which it is a moment, with real and dynamic relations between them. On the whole **formalism** (cf. *structuralism*) has followed the former (*intersubjective,* and the duality of *synchronic* and *diachronic*) rather than the latter emphasis, but while it is opposed only by a *Marxism* which treats **form** as the "mere expression" or "outward show" of *content,* its qualities of specification in analysis remain powerful. It has still to be seen whether the negative associations of the word will prevent general recognition of the important though partial redirection of emphasis which **formalism** and the **formalists** contributed.

IDEOLOGY

Ideology first appeared in English in 1796, as a direct translation of the new French word *idéologie* which had been proposed in that year by the rationalist philosopher Destutt de Tracy. Taylor (1796): "Tracy read a paper and proposed to call the philosophy of mind, ideology." Taylor (1797): ". . . ideology, or the science of ideas, in order to distinguish it from the ancient metaphysics." In this scientific sense, **ideology** was used in epistemology and linguistic theory until lC19.

A different sense, initiating the main modern meaning, was introduced by Napoleon Bonaparte. In an attack on the proponents of democracy—"who misled the people by elevating them to a sovereignty which they were incapable of exercising"—he attacked the principles of the Enlightenment as "ideology."

> It is to the doctrine of the ideologues—to this diffuse metaphysics, which in a contrived manner seeks to find the primary causes and on this foundation would erect the legislation of peoples, instead of adapting the laws to a knowledge of the human heart and of the lessons of history—to which one must attribute all the misfortunes which have befallen our beautiful France.

This use reverberated throughout C19. It is still very common in conservative criticism of any social policy which is in part or in whole derived from social theory *in a conscious way*. It is especially used of democratic or socialist policies, and indeed, following Napoleon's use, **ideologist** was often in C19 generally equivalent to *revolutionary*. But **ideology** and **ideologist** and **ideological** also acquired, by a process of broadening from Napoleon's attack, a sense of abstract, impractical or fanatical theory. It is interesting in view of the later history of the word to read Scott (*Napoleon*, vi, 251): "ideology, by which nickname the French ruler used to distinguish every species of theory, which, resting in no respect upon the basis of self-interest, could, he thought, prevail with none save hot-brained boys and crazed enthusiasts" (1827). Carlyle, aware of this use, tried to counter it: "does the British reader . . . call this unpleasant doctrine of ours ideology?" (*Chartism*, vi, 148; 1839).

There is then some direct continuity between the pejorative sense of **ideology**, as it had been used in eC19 by conservative thinkers, and the pejorative sense popularized by Marx and Engels in *The German Ideology* (1845–7) and subsequently. Scott had distinguished ideology as theory "resting in no respect upon the basis of self-interest," though Napoleon's alternative had actually been the (suitably vague) "knowledge of the human heart and of the lessons of history." Marx and Engels, in their critique of the thought of their radical German contemporaries, concentrated on its abstraction from the real processes of history. Ideas, as they said specifically of the ruling ideas of an epoch, "are nothing more than the ideal expression of the dominant material relationships, the dominant material relationships grasped as ideas." Failure to realize this produced **ideology:** an upside-down version of reality.

> If in all ideology men and their circumstances appear upside down as in a *camera obscura*, this phenomenon arises just as much from their historical life process as the inversion of objects on the retina does from their physical life process. (*German Ideology*, 47)

Or as Engels put it later:

> Every ideology . . . once it has arisen develops in connection with the given concept-material, and develops this material further; otherwise it would cease to be ideology, that is, occupation with thoughts as with independent entities, developing independently and subject only to their own laws. That the material life-conditions of the persons inside whose heads this thought process goes on in the last resort determines the course of this process remains of necessity unknown to these persons, for otherwise there would be an end to all ideology. (*Feuerbach*, 65–6)

Or again:

> Ideology is a process accomplished by the so-called thinker consciously indeed but with a false consciousness. The real motives impelling him remain unknown to him, otherwise it would not be an ideological process at all. Hence he imagines false or apparent motives. Because it is a process of thought he derives both its form and its content from

> pure thought, either his own or his predecessors'. (*Letter to Mehring*, 1893)

Ideology is then abstract and false thought, in a sense directly related to the original conservative use but with the alternative—knowledge of real material conditions and relationships—differently stated. Marx and Engels then used this idea critically. The "thinkers" of a ruling class were "its active conceptive ideologists, who make the perfecting of the illusion of the class about itself their chief source of livelihood" (*German Ideology*, 65). Or again: "the official representatives of French democracy were steeped in republican ideology to such an extent that it was only some weeks later that they began to have an inkling of the significance of the June fighting" (*Class Struggles in France*, 1850). This sense of **ideology** as illusion, false consciousness, unreality, upside-down reality, is predominant in their work. Engels believed that the "higher ideologies"—philosophy and religion—were more removed from material interests than the direct ideologies of politics and law, but the connection, though complicated, was still decisive (*Feuerbach*, 277). They were "realms of ideology which soar still higher in the air . . . various false conceptions of nature, of man's own being, of spirits, magic forces, etc. . . ." (*Letter to Schmidt*, 1890). This sense has persisted.

Yet there is another, apparently more neutral sense of **ideology** in some parts of Marx's writing, notably in the well-known passage in the *Contribution to the Critique of Political Philosophy* (1859):

> The distinction should always be made between the material transformation of the economic conditions of production . . . and the legal, political, religious, aesthetic or philosophic—in short, ideological—forms in which men become conscious of this conflict and fight it out.[1]

This is clearly related to part of the earlier sense: the ideological forms are expressions of (changes in) economic conditions of production. But they are seen here as the forms in which men become *conscious* of the conflict arising from conditions and changes of condition in economic production. This sense is very difficult to reconcile with the sense of **ideology** as mere illusion.

In fact, historically, this sense of **ideology** as the set of ideas which arise from a given set of material interests has been at least as widely used as the sense of **ideology** as illusion. Moreover, each sense has been used, at times very confusingly, within the Marxist tradition. There is clearly no sense of illusion or false consciousness in a passage such as this from Lenin:

> Socialism, insofar as it is the ideology of struggle of the proletarian class, undergoes the general conditions of birth, development and consolidation of an ideology, that is to say it is founded on all the material of human knowledge, it presupposes a high level of science, demands scientific work, etc. . . . In the class struggle of the proletariat which develops spontaneously, as an elemental force, on the basis of capitalist relations, socialism is *introduced* by the ideologists. (*Letter to the Federation of the North*)

Thus there is now "proletarian ideology" or "bourgeois ideology," and so on, and **ideology** in each case is the system of ideas appropriate to that class. One ideology can be claimed as correct and progressive as against another ideology. It is of course possible to add that the other ideology, representing the class enemy, is, while a true expression of their interests, false to any general human interest, and something of the earlier sense of illusion or false consciousness can then be loosely associated with what is primarily a description of the class character of certain ideas. But the neutral sense of **ideology,** which usually needs to be qualified by an adjective describing the class or social group which it represents or serves, has in fact become common in many kinds of argument. At the same time, within Marxism but also elsewhere, there has been a standard distinction between **ideology** and SCIENCE (q.v.), in order to retain the sense of illusory or merely abstract thought. This develops the distinction suggested by Engels, in which ideology would end when men realized their real life-conditions and therefore their real motives, after which their consciousness would become genuinely *scientific* because they would then be in contact with reality. This attempted distinction between Marxism as *science* and other social thought as **ideology** has of course been controversial, not least among Marxists. In a very much broader area of the "social sciences," comparable distinctions between **ideology** (speculative systems) and *science* (demonstrated facts) are commonplace.

Meanwhile, in popular argument, **ideology** is still mainly used in the sense given by Napoleon. Sensible people rely on *experience*, or have a *philosophy;* silly people rely on **ideology.** In this sense **ideology,** now as in Napoleon, is mainly a term of abuse.

LITERATURE

Literature is a difficult word, in part because its conventional contemporary meaning appears, at first sight, so simple. There is no apparent difficulty in phrases like **English literature** or **contemporary literature,** until we find occasion to ask whether all books and writing are **literature** (and if they are not, which kinds are excluded and by what criteria) or until, to take a significant example, we come across a distinction between **literature** and *drama* on the grounds, apparently, that drama is a form primarily written for spoken performance (though often also to be read). It is not easy to understand what is at stake in these often confused distinctions until we look at the history of the word.

Literature came into English, from C14, in the sense of polite learning through reading. Its fw, *littérature,* F, *litteratura,* L, had the same general sense. The rw is *littera,* L—letter (of the alphabet). Thus a man of **literature,** or of *letters,* meant what we would now describe as a man of wide reading. Thus: "hes nocht sufficient literatur to undirstand the scripture" (1581); "learned in all literature and erudition, divine and humane" (Bacon, 1605). It can be seen from the Bacon example that the noun of condition—being well-read—is at times close to the objective noun—the books in which a man is well-read. But the main sense can be seen from the normal adjective, which was **literate,** from C15, rather than **literary,** which appeared first in C17 as a simple alternative to **literate** and only acquired its more general meaning in C18. As late as Johnson's *Life of Milton,* this original usage was still normal: "he had probably more than common literature, as his son addresses him in one of his most elaborate Latin poems" (1780).

Literature, that is to say, corresponded mainly to the modern meanings of **literacy,** which, probably because the older meaning had then gone, was a new word from lC19. It meant both an ability to read and a condition of being well-read. This can be confirmed from the negatives. **Illiterate** usually meant poorly-read or ill-educated: "Judgis illitturate" (1586); "my illeterate and rude stile" (1597); and as late as Chesterfield (1748); "the word *illiterate,* in its common acceptance, means a man who is ignorant of those two languages" (Greek and Latin). Even more clearly there was the now obsolete **illiterature,** from lC16: "the cause . . . ignorance

. . . and . . . illiterature" (1592). By contrast, from eC17, the **literati** were the highly-educated.

But the general sense of "polite learning," firmly attached to the idea of printed books, was laying the basis for the later specialization. Colet, in C16, distinguished between **literature** and what he called **blotterature;** here the sense of inability to write clear letters is extended to a kind of book which was below the standards of polite learning. But the first certain signs of a general change in meaning are from C18. **Literary** was extended beyond its equivalence to **literate:** probably first in the general sense of well-read but from mC18 to refer to the practice and profession of writing: "literary merit" (Goldsmith, 1759); "literary reputation" (Johnson, 1773). This appears to be closely connected with the heightened self-consciousness of the profession of authorship, in the period of transition from patronage to the bookselling market. Where Johnson had used **literature** in the sense of being highly literate in his *Life of Milton,* in his *Life of Cowley* he wrote, in the newly objective sense: "an author whose pregnancy of imagination and elegance of language have deservedly set him high in the ranks of literature." Yet **literature** and **literary,** in these new senses, still referred to the whole body of books and writing; or if distinction was made it was in terms of falling below the level of polite learning rather than of particular kinds of writing. A philosopher such as Hume quite naturally described his "Love of literary Fame" as his "ruling passion." All works within the orbit of polite learning came to be described as **literature** and all such interests and practices as **literary.**

What has then to be traced is the attempted and often successful specialization of **literature** to certain kinds of writing. This is difficult just because it is incomplete; a **literary editor** or a **literary supplement** still deals generally with all kinds of books. But there has been a specialization to a sense which is sometimes emphasized (because of the remaining uncertainty) in phrases like **creative literature** and **imaginative literature** (cf. CREATIVE and IMAGINATIVE as descriptions of kinds of writing; cf. also FICTION). In relation to the past, **literature** is still a relatively general word: Carlyle and Ruskin, for example, who did not write novels or poems or plays, belong to **English literature.** But there has been a steady distinction and separation of other kinds of writing—philosophy, essays, history, and so on—which may or may not possess **literary merit** or be of **literary interest** (meaning that "in addition to" their intrinsic interest as philosophy or history or whatever they are "well written") but which are not now normally described as **literature,** which may be understood as well-written books but which is even more clearly understood as well-written books of an *imaginative* or *creative* kind. The teaching of English, especially in universities, is understood as the teaching of **literature,** meaning mainly poems and plays and novels; other kinds of "serious" writing are described as *general* or *discursive.* Or there is **literary criticism**—judgment of how a (*creative* or *imaginative*) work is written—as distinct, often, from discussion of "ideas" or "history" or "general subject-matter." At the same time many, even most poems and plays and novels are not seen as **literature;** they fall below its level, in a sense related to the old distinction of *polite learning;* they are not "substantial" or "important" enough to be called **works of literature.** A new category of **popular literature** or the **sub-literary** has then to be instituted, to describe works which may be *fiction* but which are not *imaginative* or *creative,* which are therefore devoid of AESTHETIC (q.v.) interest, and which are not ART (q.v.).

Clearly the major shift represented by the modern complex of **literature,** *art, aesthetic,* *creative* and *imaginative* is a matter of social and cultural history. **Literature** itself must be seen as a late medieval and Renaissance isolation of the skills of reading and of the qualities of the book; this was much emphasized by the development of printing. But the sense of *learning* was still inherent, and there were also the active arts of *grammar* and *rhetoric*. Steadily, with the predominance of print, *writing* and *books* became virtually synonymous; hence the subsequent confusion about *drama*, which was writing for speech (but then Shakespeare is obviously **literature**, though with the *text* proving this). Then **literature** was specialized towards *imaginative writing*, within the basic assumptions of Romanticism. It is interesting to see what word did service for this before the specialization. It was, primarily, *poetry*, defined in 1586 as "the arte of making: which word as it hath alwaies beene especially used of the best of our English Poets, to expresse the very faculty of speaking or wryting Poetically" (note the inclusion of *speaking*). Sidney wrote in 1581: "verse being but an ornament and no cause to Poetry: sith there have been many most excellent Poets, that never versified." The specialization of *poetry* to metrical composition is evident from mC17, though this was still contested by Wordsworth: "I here use the word 'Poetry' (though against my own judgment) as opposed to the word 'Prose,' and synonymous with metrical composition" (1798). It is probable that this specialization of *poetry* to verse, together with the increasing importance of prose forms such as the NOVEL (q.v.), made **literature** the most available general word. But this was in its turn affected by an emphatic definition of an appropriate subject-matter. *Poetry* had been the high skills of writing and speaking in the special context of high imagination; the word could be moved in either direction. **Literature**, in its C19 sense, repeated this, though excluding speaking. But it is then problematic, not only because of the further specialization to *imaginative* and *creative* subject-matter (as distinct from *imaginative* and *creative* writing) but also because of the new importance of many forms of writing for speech (*broadcasting* as well as *drama*) which the specialization to books seemed by definition to exclude.

Significantly in recent years **literature** and **literary**, though they still have effective currency in post-C18 senses, have been increasingly challenged, on what is conventionally their own ground, by concepts of *writing* and *communication* which seek to recover the most active and general senses which the extreme specialization had seemed to exclude. Moreover, in relation to this reaction, **literary** has acquired two unfavourable senses, as belonging to the printed book or to past literature rather than to active contemporary writing and speech; or as (unreliable) evidence from books rather than "factual inquiry." This latter sense touches the whole difficult complex of the relations between *literature* (poetry, *fiction*, *imaginative* writing) and real or *actual* experience. Meanwhile **literacy** and **illiteracy** have become key social concepts, in a much wider perspective than in the pre-C19 sense. **Illiteracy** was extended, from C18, to indicate general inability to read and write, and **literacy**, from lC19, was a new word invented to express the achievement and possesson of what were increasingly seen as general and necessary skills.

THEORY

Theory has an interesting development and range of meanings, and a significant distinction from (later an opposition to) *practice*. The earliest English form was *theorique* (C14), followed by *theory* (C16), from fw *theoria*, lL, *theoria*, Gk—contemplation, spectacle, mental conception (from *theoros*, Gk—spectator, rw *thea*, Gk—sight: cf. *theatre*). In C17 it had a wide range: (i) spectacle: "a Theory or Sight" (1605); (ii) a contemplated sight: "the true Theory of death when I contemplate a skull" (Browne, 1643); "all their theory and contemplation (which they count Science) represents nothing but waking men's dreams, and sick men's phantasies" (Harvey, 1653); (iii) scheme (of ideas): "to execute their owne Theorie in this Church" (Hooker, 1597); (iv) explanatory scheme: "leave such theories to those that study Meteors" (1638). A distinction between **theory** and *practice* was widely made in C17, as in Bacon (1626); "Philosophy . . . divided into two parts, namely, speculative and practical" (1657); "only pleasing in the Theory, but not in the Practice" (1664); "Theorie without Practice will serve but for little" (1692).

It is interesting that **theory** and *speculation*, **theoretic(al)** and *speculative*, were ready alternatives, with the same root senses. In our own time, one use of **theory** is sharply distinguished from *speculation*, and, even more strongly, one use of **theoretical** from the relevant sense of *speculative* (the commercial sense of *speculative* is from C18). This depends on an important development of the sense of **theory**, basically from sense (iv), which is in effect "a scheme of ideas which explains practice." There is still a qualification in "scheme"; cf. "were a theory open to no objection it would cease to be theory and would become a law" (1850). But **theory** in this important sense is always in active relation to *practice*: an interaction between things done, things observed and (systematic) explanation of these. This allows a necessary distinction between **theory** and *practice*, but does not require their opposition. At the same time it is clear that forms of senses (ii) and (iii) survive actively, and the **theory**/*practice* relation, which is neutral or positive in sense (iv), is radically affected by them, at times confusingly. In sense (ii) the clearer word is now *speculation*: a projected idea, with no necessary reference to practice. In sense (iii) the relevant words are *doctrine* or IDEOLOGY (q.v.), a largely programmatic idea of how things should be. Of course these senses interact; (ii) may lead to (iii) and especially (iv); in certain areas of the human sciences, as distinct from the physical sciences, (iii) and (iv) are often inseparable, because *practice* itself is complex. There is *practice* in the sense of a particular thing done (and observed) which can be immediately related to **theory** (iv). There is also *practice* in the sense of a repeated or customary action (cf. *practise* as a verb), in which the **theory**/*practice* relation is often a contrast between one way of doing a thing and another, the **theoretical** being that which is proposed and the *practical* that which is now usually done. It is especially important to distinguish this relation not only from the relation in sense (iv), which it often confuses, but from the weaker forms of the relation in sense (ii), where "waking men's dreams, and sick men's phantasies" can be powerfully contrasted with *practice* in the sense of doing anything (though to ignore the stronger forms of sense (ii), overlapping with sense (iii), would be damaging; cf. IDEALISM). It also needs to be noted that the very strength of **theory** (iv), its (systematic) explanation of *practice*, with which it is in regular and active relation, can be made prejudicial. *Practice* which has become CONVENTIONAL (q.v.) or habitual can be traced to (or made conscious as) a base in **theory** ((iii) or (iv)), and **theory** is then used derogatively just because it explains and (implicitly or explicitly) challenges some customary action.

The word *praxis* is now increasingly used, in specialized contexts, to express a sense related to **theory** (iv) but in a new relation to *practice*. **Theory** (iv) is simple in relation to the physical sciences: an active interrelation between explanation and things happening or made to happen in controlled conditions. *Praxis* (fw *praxis*, mL, *praxis*, Gk—practice, action) has been used in English since lC16 to express the practice or exercise of an art or an idea, a set of examples for practice, and accepted practice. In none of these is it quite separate from *practice*, though the notion of a "scheme for practice" obviously distinguishes it from **theory**/*practice* oppositions: the *praxis* is systematic exercise in an understood and organized skill. But this was not predominant in the English development. As late as 1800 Coleridge used the wider sense: "in theory false, and pernicious in praxis." The specialized modern sense comes from a development in German, c. 1840, in origin late Hegelian but now especially Marxist, where *praxis* is *practice* informed by **theory** and also, though less emphatically, **theory** informed by *practice*, as distinct both from *practice* uninformed by or unconcerned with **theory** and from **theory** which remains **theory** and is not put to the test of *practice*. In effect it is a word intended to unite **theory** (iii) and (iv) with the strongest sense of *practical* (but not conventional or customary) activity: *practice* as action. *Praxis* is then also used, derivatively, to describe a whole mode of activity in which, by analysis but only by analysis, **theoretical** and *practical* elements can be distinguished, but which is always a whole activity, to be judged as such. The opposition between *theory* and *practice* is then, it is said, broken down, by the interactive redefinition of each term.

Note

1. Marx's German reads: . . . *kurz, ideologischen Formen, worin sich die Menschen diesen Konflikts bewusst werden* . . .

Sandra Gilbert 1936–

Sandra M. Gilbert holds an M.A. from New York University and a Ph.D. from Columbia University. A writer of fiction and poetry as well as of literary criticism, she has taught English at a number of institutions, including Indiana University and the University of California at Davis. Currently on the faculty at Princeton University, she is one of the dominant voices in American feminist criticism. She is the coauthor with Susan Gubar of the ground-breaking *The Madwoman in the Attic* (1979) and of the newly published *No Man's Land: The Place of the Woman Writer in the Twentieth Century* (1988). Also with Susan Gubar, Sandra Gilbert edited *Shakespeare's Sisters: Feminist Essays on Women Poets*, as well as the pioneering *Norton Anthology of Literature by Women* (1985).

In "Life's Empty Pack: Notes Toward a Literary Daughteronomy," Gilbert draws on Freudian and Lacanian psychoanalytic theory, Lévi-Strauss's work in anthropology, and recent feminist theory to argue that "a prescription for father-daughter incest lies at the heart of female psychosexual development in patriarchal society." Gilbert locates this determining paradigm in George Eliot's culturally central *Silas Marner,* as well as in *Summer,* a revisionary tale by Edith Wharton, and "Allerleirauh," a Grimm brothers fairy tale. Gilbert's concern is not simply to identify the myth she defines as so chillingly pervasive: she argues that no woman writer can ever fully extricate herself from this myth, for the message inscribed by her literary foremothers is that the daughter must give herself to the father. Gilbert's feminist analysis thus indicates that patriarchal values control even the most rebellious (and creative) of women. The "mother tongue" teaches submission to the Father's Law.

Life's Empty Pack: Notes Toward a Literary Daughteronomy

No mother gave me birth. Therefore the father's claim
And male supremacy in all things . . .
. . . wins my whole heart's loyalty.
—Athene, in Aeschylus, *The Eumenides*

If underneath the water
You comb your golden hair
With a golden comb, my daughter,
Oh would that I were there!
—Christina Rosetti, "Father and Lover"

Sad and weary I go back to you, my cold father, my cold mad father,
my cold mad feary father . . . I rush, my only, into your arms.
—Anna Livia Plurabelle, in James Joyce, *Finnegans Wake*

O father, all by yourself
You are pithy and historical as the Roman Forum.
—Sylvia Plath, "The Colossus"

For the first time all of us, men and women alike, can look back on nearly two centuries of powerful literary ancestresses. Aside from the specifically literary-historical implications of such a phenomenon—an issue that Susan Gubar and I have addressed elsewhere[1]—what effects has this unprecedented situation had? In particular, what paradigms of female sexuality have strong female precursors passed on to other women writers? These are questions I want to begin to address here—specifically, by exploring an aspect of female psychosexual development. A dark, indeed problematic, pattern emerges when we juxtapose the accounts of female maturation and obligation that are offered by theorists like Sigmund Freud and Claude Lévi-Strauss with the meaning that George Eliot's frequently studied *Silas Marner* may have had for the women who are in a sense that powerful literary mother's aesthetic daughters.

I choose Eliot as my paradigm of the female precursor because, as Virginia Woolf put it, she was "the first woman of the age," a thinker who became, in one historian's words, a "Man of Ideas," her official importance sanctioned by the biography Woolf's own father dutifully produced for the English Men of Letters Series.[2] At the same time, however, I see Eliot as paradigmatic because her very power—the success that made her into what we call a "precursor"—evidently disquieted so many of her female contemporaries and descendants. As Elaine Showalter reminds us, "most nineteenth-century women novelists seem to have found [Eliot] a troubling and demoralizing competitor, one who had created an image of the woman artist they could never equal." "George Eliot *looks* awful. Her picture frightens me!" exclaims a character in Elizabeth Robins' novel *George Mandeville's Husband*.[3] Even Eliot's most fervent female admirers, moreover, express ambivalence toward her in the rhetoric through which they try to come to terms with her. Two of these notable Eliotian heiresses are Emily Dickinson and Edith Wharton. Both offer commentaries curiously haunted by ambiguities, and though these commentaries are ostensibly about the writer's life story, they provide a dramatic set of metaphors that can help us interpret the messages these literary daughters extracted from such an apparently "legendary" story as *Silas Marner*.[4]

In 1883, after having waited with great anxiety to receive a copy of the Eliot biography written by John Walter Cross, the novelist's husband in the last year of her life, Dickinson wrote a thank-you note to the Boston publisher Thomas Niles, in which she succinctly mythologizes the career of her English precursor. "The Life of Marian Evans had much I never knew," she begins. "A Doom of Fruit without the Bloom, like the Niger Fig," and a poem follows this strange introduction.

> Her Losses make our Gains ashamed—
> She bore Life's empty Pack
> As gallantly as if the East
> Were swinging at her Back.
> Life's empty Pack is heaviest,
> As every Porter knows—
> In vain to punish Honey—
> It only sweeter grows.[5]

"A Doom of Fruit without the Bloom." "Life's empty Pack." "In vain to punish Honey." These are striking but mysterious phrases. Where do they come from, and what do they mean?

Several remarks by Wharton, though almost equally paradoxical, begin to provide some clarification. Reviewing Leslie Stephen's English Men of Letters Series volume on Eliot, Wharton writes that "unconsciously, perhaps, [the Victorian novelist] began to use her books as a vehicle of rehabilitation, a means, not of defending her own course, but of proclaiming, with increasing urgency and emphasis, her allegiance to the law she appeared to have violated." Earlier in her essay, Wharton offers a metaphorical, almost Dickinsonian statement of what she means by "the law": "The stern daughter of the voice of God," she writes, "stands ever at the side of Romola and Dorothea, of Lydgate and Maggie, and lifts even Mr. Farebrother and poor Gwendolyn to heights of momentary heroism."[6]

Putting statements like these together with Woolf's sense of Eliot's success and centrality, we can begin to see why the author of *Silas Marner* was both a paradigmatic and a problematic female precursor. Metaphorically speaking, such a conflation of reactions suggests that Eliot represents the conundrum of the empty pack which until recently has confronted every woman writer. Specifically, this conundrum is the riddle of daughterhood, a figurative empty pack with which—as it has seemed to many women artists—not just every powerful literary mother but every literal mother presents her daughter. For such artists, the terror of the female precursor is not that she is an emblem of power but, rather, that when she achieves her greatest strength, her power becomes self-subverting: in the moment of psychic transformation that is the moment of creativity, the literary mother, even more than the literal one, becomes the "stern daughter of the voice of God" who paradoxically proclaims her "allegiance to the law" she herself appears to have violated.

As such a preceptor, the literary mother necessarily speaks both of and for the father, reminding her female child that she is not and cannot be his inheritor: like her mother and like Eliot's Dorothea, the daughter must inexorably become a "foundress of nothing."[7] For human culture, says the literary mother, is bound by rules which make it possible for a woman to speak but which oblige her to speak of her own powerlessness, since such rules might seem to constitute what Jacques Lacan calls the "Law of the Father," the law that means culture is by definition both patriarchal and phallocentric and must therefore transmit the empty pack of disinheritance to every daughter.[8] Not surprisingly, then, even while the literary daughter, like the literal one, desires the matrilineal legitimation incarnated in her precursor/mother, she fears her literary mother: the more fully the mother represents culture, the more inexorably she tells the daughter that she cannot have a mother because she has been signed with and assigned to the Law of the Father.[9] Like Eliot, who aspired to be a "really cultured woman," this "culture-mother" uses her knowledge, as Eliot advised in her scornful essay "Silly Novels by Lady Novelists," "to form a right estimate of herself"—that is, to put herself (and, by implication, her daughters) in the "right" place.[10]

This speculation rests of course on syntheses of Freud and Lévi-Strauss that psychoanalytic thinkers like Lacan and Juliet Mitchell have lately produced. Concentrating on the Oedipus complex, such writers have argued that every child enters the language-defined system of kinship exchange that we call "culture" by learning that he or she cannot remain permanently in the state of nature signified by the embrace of the mother; instead, the child must be assigned a social place denoted by the name (and the Law) of the Father, the potent symbol of human order who disrupts the blissful mother-child dyad. What this means for the boy—a temporary frustration of desire coupled with the promise of an ultimate accession to power—has been elaborately and famously explored by both Freud and Lacan (and also, in a different way, by Lévi-Strauss). What it means for the girl is much less clearly understood; hence, in meditating on the empty pack of daughterhood, I am necessarily improvising both literary and psychoanalytic theory. But my task will, I hope, be made possible by Eliot's status as paradigmatic female precursor, or symbolic culture-mother, and made plausible by the juxtaposition of one of Eliot's texts, *Silas Marner*, with what we might call a revisionary daughter-text, Wharton's *Summer*.

* * *

A definition of Eliot as renunciatory culture-mother may seem an odd preface to a discussion of *Silas Marner* since, of all her novels, this richly constructed work is the one in which the empty pack of daughterhood appears fullest, the honey of femininity most unpunished. I want to argue, however, that this "legendary tale," whose status as a schoolroom classic makes it almost as much a textbook as a novel, examines the relationship between woman's fate and the structure of society in order to explicate the meaning of the empty pack of daughterhood. More specifically, this story of an adoptive father, an orphan daughter, and a dead mother broods on events that are actually or symbolically situated on the margins or boundaries of society, where culture must enter into a dialectical struggle with nature, in order to show how the young female human animal is converted into the human daughter, wife, and mother. Finally, then, this fictionalized "daughteronomy" becomes a female myth of origin narrated by a severe literary mother who uses the vehicle of a half-allegorical family romance to urge acquiescence in the law of the Father.

If *Silas Marner* is not obviously a story about the empty pack of daughterhood, it is plainly, of course, a "legendary tale" about a wanderer with a heavy yet empty pack. In fact, it is through the image of the packman that the story, in Eliot's own words, "came *across* my other plans by a sudden inspiration"—and, clearly, her vision of this burdened outsider is a re-vision of the Romantic wanderer who haunts the borders of society, seeking a local habitation and a name.[11] I would argue further, though, that Eliot's depiction of Silas Marner's alienation begins to explain Ruby Redinger's sense that the author of this "fluid and metamorphic" story "is" both Eppie, the redemptive daughter, and Silas, the redeemed father. For in examining the outcast weaver's marginality, this novelist of the "hidden life" examines also her own female disinheritance and marginality.[12]

Almost everything that we learn about Silas and the tribe of pack-bearing wanderers he represents tends to reinforce our sense that he belongs in what anthropologists call a "liminal zone."[13] Pallid, undersized, alien-looking, he is one of the figures ordinary country folk see at the edges of time and place—"on the upland, dark against the early winter sunset," "far away among the lanes, or deep in the bosom of the hills." As a weaver, moreover, he is associated with those transformations that take place on the borders of culture—activities that seem to partake "of the nature of conjuring."[14] Again, he is liminal because, both shortsighted and cataleptic, he cannot participate meaningfully in the social world. That he dwells on the edge of Raveloe, near the disused Stone-pits, and never strolls "into the village to drink a pint at [the local pub called] the Rainbow" further emphasizes his alienation, as does the story of his Job-like punishment when the casting of lots in Lantern Yard "convicted" him of a theft he had not committed (*SM*, 1. 1). Finally, his obsessive hoarding, in which gold is drained of all economic signification, reduces the currency of society to absurdity, further emphasizing his alienation.

Considering all these deprivations and denials of social meaning, it is no wonder that this wanderer's pack seems to be heavy with emptiness. Psychologically, moreover, it is no wonder that Eliot in some sense "is" the Silas whom we first encounter at the Stone-pits, if only because through him she examines the liminality that Marian Evans experienced in fact and Maggie Tulliver in fiction. Her own metaphors frequently remind us, furthermore, that just as he weaves textiles, she "weaves" texts—and at the time his story "thrust itself" into the loom of her art, her texts were turning to gold as surely (and as problematically) as his textiles did.[15] In addition, as the man without a place, Silas carries with him the dispossession that she herself had experienced as part of the empty pack of daughterhood. Perhaps, indeed, it is because he shares to some extent in what Sherry Ortner has seen as woman's liminal estate that Silas is often associated not only with the particulars of Marian Evans' femaleness but also with a number of socially defined female characteristics, including a domestic expertise which causes him, in the words of one Raveloer, to be "partly as handy as a woman" (*SM*, 1. 14).[16]

Paradoxically, however, it is his handily maternal rearing of Eppie that redeems Silas as a *man* even while his transformation from outcast to parent reflects a similar but more troubled metamorphosis that Marian Evans was herself undergoing at the time she wrote the novel. Significantly, at the moment the plot of *Silas Marner* began to "unfold" in her mind, George Eliot was becoming a "mother" to George Henry Lewes' children. But where her ambiguous status as "mother" of "a great boy of eighteen . . . as well as two other boys, almost as tall" isolated her further from the society that had cast her out, Silas' status as father of a golden-haired daughter definitively integrates him into a community that had previously thought him diabolic.[17] His transformations of role and rank, therefore, suggest at least one kind of redemption a fallen literary woman might want to imagine for herself: becoming a father.

Silas' redemptive fatherhood, which originates at Christmastime, is prepared for by Eliot's long meditation on the weaver's relationship to his gold, perhaps the most compelling passage of psychological analysis in the novel and the one that most brilliantly propounds the terms of the submerged metaphor that is to govern the book's dramatic action. For the miser, as I noted earlier, what would ordinarily be a kind of language that links members of society is empty of signification and therefore not only meaningless but dead-ended. Halted, static, even regressive, the currency does not flow: nothing goes out into the world, and therefore nothing returns.[18] Silas' history is thus a history without a story because it is without characters—without, that is, both persons and signifiers. Yet its terror consists not merely in the absence of meaning but in the presence of empty matter: the shining purposeless heaps of coins which "had become too large for the iron pot to hold them" (SM, 1. 2). It is this mass of lifeless matter that must be imprinted with vital signification if the outcast weaver is to be resurrected and redeemed. And ultimately, indeed, Silas' transformation from fall to fatherhood is symbolized, in a kind of upside-down myth of Midas, by the metamorphosis of his meaningless gold into a living and meaningful child, a child whose Christmas coming marks her as symbolically divine but whose function as divine daughter rather than sacred son is to signify, rather than to replace, the power of her newly created father.

To make way for Eppie, who is his gold made meaningful, Silas must first, of course, be separated from his meaningless gold. What is surely most important about this loss, however, is that the absence of the gold forces the miser to confront the absence that his gold represented. In addition, if we think of this blank, this empty pack, in relation to the Christmas myth for which Eliot is preparing us, we can see that Silas' dark night of the soul is the long dark night of the winter solstice, when dead matter must be kindled and dead flesh made Word if culture is to survive. That "the invisible wand of catalepsy" momentarily freezes the weaver in his open doorway on the crucial New Year's Eve that is to lead to his resurrection merely emphasizes this point. His posture is that of the helpless virgin who awaits annunciation "like a graven image . . . powerless to resist either the good or evil that might enter there" (SM, 1. 12).

Because it depends on drastic role reversals, however, Eliot's deliberate parody of the Christmas story suggests that she is half-consciously using the basic outlines of a central culture myth to meditate not on the traditionally sanctified relationship of Holy Mother and Divine Son but on another, equally crucial, bond—that of Holy Father and Divine Daughter. In doing so, she clarifies for herself and for her readers the key differences between sonship and daughterhood. For when the divine child is a son he is, as the Christian story tells us, an active spiritual agent for his mother. To put the matter in a Freudian or Lacanian way, he is the "phallus" for her, an image of sociocultural as well as sexual power.[19] But when the divine child is a daughter, or so the story of Silas Marner tells us, she is a treasure, a gift the father is given so that he can give it to others, thereby weaving himself into the texture of society. To put the matter in a Lévi-Straussian way, she is the currency whose exchange constitutes society, a point Eliot stunningly anticipated in her submerged metaphor of the girl who is not only as good as but better than gold because her very existence is a pot of gold not at the end but at the beginning of the Rainbow covenant between man and man.

This last allusion is, of course, a reference to the central notion of *The Elementary Structures of Kinship*, in which Lévi-Strauss argues that both the social order, which distinguishes culture from nature, and the incest taboo, which universally manifests the social order, are based upon the exchange of women.[20] In this anthropological view, a daughter is a treasure whose potential passage from man to man insures psychological and social well-being: if the very structure of a patrilineage guarantees that ultimately, inexorably, a man's son will *take* his place and his name, it also promises that a daughter will never be such a usurper since she is an instrument—rather than an agent—of culture. In fact, because she is the father's wealth, his treasure, she is what he *has*, for better or worse.

That Silas christens his Christmas child "Hephzibah" dramatizes this point even while it begins to weave him deeply into the common life of "Bible names" and knit him back into his own past (*SM*, 1. 14). "Hephzibah," or "Eppie," was the name of both Silas' mother and his sister: in gaining a new Hephzibah, he has regained the treasure of all his female kin. Even more significantly, the name itself, drawn from Isaiah, refers to the title Zion will be given after the coming of the Messiah. Literally translated as "my delight is in her," "Hephzibah" magically signifies both a promised land and a redeemed land (see Isa. 62:4 and 5). Diffusely female, this delightful land incarnates the treasure that is possessed and exchanged by male citizens, and therefore it represents the culture that is created by the covenant between man and man as well as between God and man. A philological fact upon which Eliot herself once meditated enriches further such an association. According to an etymology given by the *Oxford English Dictionary* and based upon Grimm's law, the Anglo-Saxon word "daughter" can be traced back to the Indo-European root *dhugh*, meaning "to milk." Hence, this daughter named Hephzibah is not only milkmaid but milk giver, she who nurtures as well as she who is nurtured—for, as defined by the Law and reinforced by the lexicon of the Father, a daughter *is* the promised land of milk and honey, the gift of wealth that God the Father gives to every human father.[21]

Most of these points are made quite explicit in the concern with weddings that permeates *Silas Marner*, a concern which surfaces in the famous conversation that happens to be taking place at the Rainbow Tavern just when Silas is discovering the loss of his gold. Old Mr. Macey, the parish clerk, is recounting the story of the Lammeter marriage, a ceremony in which the minister got his phrases oddly turned around. The tale asks the question, "Is't the meanin' or the words as makes folks fast i' wedlock?" and answers that "it's neither the meaning nor the words—its the regester does it—that's the glue" (*SM*, 1. 16). But of course, as we learn by the end of *Silas Marner*, it is the very idea of the wedding itself, the having and giving of the daughter, that is the glue.[22] For as Silas and Eppie, Aaron and Dollie parade through Raveloe on their way back to Silas' enlarged cottage after

Eppie's marriage to Aaron, the harmony of the bridal party contrasts strikingly with our memory of Silas' former isolation. In marrying Aaron, Silas' daughter has married Silas—married him both to the world and to herself.[23] What had been the "shrunken rivulet" of his love has flowed into a larger current and a dearer currency, a treasure he has given so that it can return to him. And it has returned: "O father," says Eppie, just as if she had married *him*, "What a pretty home ours is" (*SM*, "Conclusion"). Unlike that other Romantic wanderer, the Ancient Mariner, Silas Marner is a member of the wedding. But then, the Ancient Mariner never got the Christian Christmas gift of a daughter.

How does the gift feel about herself, however? What does it mean to Eppie to mean all this for Silas? Certainly Eliot had long been concerned with the social significance and cultural possibilities of daughterhood. Both *The Mill on the Floss*—the novel that precedes *Silas Marner*—and *Romola*—the one that follows it—are elaborate examinations of the structural inadequacies of a daughter's estate. As for Marian Evans, moreover, her real life had persistently confronted her with the problematic nature of daughterhood and its corollary condition, sisterhood. As biographers have shown, her feelings for her own father were ambivalent not only during his lifetime but throughout hers; yet his superegoistic legacy pervaded other relationships she formed. When she was in her early twenties, for instance, she became a dutiful disciple to the Casaubon-like Dr. Brabant, who "punningly baptized her *Deutera* because she was to be a second daughter to him."[24] And even when she was a middle-aged woman, she remembered her older brother Isaac as a kind of miniature father, "a Like unlike, a Self that self restrains," observing wistfully that "were another childhood-world my share,/ I would be born a little sister there."[25] Since "Eppie" was the name of Silas' little sister, it seems likely that, in being "born" again to the mild weaver, Marian Evans did in fiction if not in fact re-create herself as both daughter and little sister.

Certainly Eppie's protestations of daughterly devotion suggest that she is in some sense a born-again daughter. "I should have no delight i' life any more if I was forced to go away from my father," she tells Nancy and Godfrey Cass (*SM*, 2. 19). Like the Marian Evans who became "Deutera," Eppie is not so much a second daughter as twice a daughter—a doubly daughterly daughter. As such a "Deutera," she is the golden girl whose being reiterates those cultural commandments Moses set forth for the second time in Deuteronomy. Thus, although scrupulous Nancy Lammeter Cass has often been seen as articulating Eliot's moral position on the key events of this novel, it is really the more impulsive Eppie who is the conscience of the book.

This becomes clearest when Nancy argues that "there's a duty you owe to your lawful father." Eppie's instant reply, with its counterclaim that "I can't feel as I've got any father but one," expresses a more accurate understanding of the idea of fatherhood (*SM*, 2. 19). For in repudiating *God-free* Cass, who is only by chance (*casus*) her natural father, and affirming Silas Marner, who is by choice her cultural father, Eppie rejects the lawless father in favor of the lawful one, indicating her clear awareness that fatherhood itself is both *a* social construct (or, in Stephen Dedalus' words, "a legal fiction") and *the* social construct that constructs society.[26] Having achieved and acted on this analysis, she is rewarded with a domestic happiness which seems to prove Dickinson's contention that it is "vain to punish Honey / It only sweeter grows." At the same time, in speaking such a law, this creature of milk and honey initiates the reeducation and redemption of Godfrey Cass: the cultural code of Deuteronomy speaks through her, suggesting that, even if she is a Christmas child, she is as much a daughter of the Old Testament as of the New, of the first telling of the law as of its second telling.[27]

Happy and dutiful as she is, however, Eppie is not perfectly contented, for she has a small fund of anxiety that is pledged to her other parent—her lost mother. This intermittent sadness, which manifests itself as a preoccupation with her mother's wedding ring, directs our attention to a strange disruption at the center of *Silas Marner*: the history of Eppie's dead mother. On the surface, of course, the ring that Silas has saved for his adopted daughter is an aptly ironic symbol of that repressed plot, since there never was any bond beyond an artificial one between Molly Farren and Godfrey Cass, the lawless father "of whom [the ring] was the symbol." But Eppie's frequent ruminations on the questions of "how her mother looked, whom she was like, and how [Silas] had found her against the furze bush" suggest that there is something more problematic than a traditional bad marriage at issue here (*SM*, 2. 16). As so often in this "legendary tale," what seems like a moral point also offers an eerily accurate account of what Freud sees as the inexorable psychosexual growth and entry of the daughter into a culture shaped by the codes of the father. "Our insight into [the pre-Oedipus] phase in the little girl's development comes to us as a surprise, comparable . . . with . . . the discovery of the Minoan-Mycenaean civilization behind that of Greece," remarks Freud, explaining that "everything connected with this first mother-attachment has . . . seemed to me . . . lost in a past so dim and shadowy . . . that it seemed as if it had undergone some specially inexorable repression."[28]

Indeed, Molly Farren *has* undergone a "specially inexorable repression" in this novel. Three or four pages of a single chapter are devoted to her, though her damned and doomed wanderings in the snow strikingly recapitulate the lengthier wanderings of fallen women like Hetty Sorel and Maggie Tulliver. I suggest that Eliot attempts this drastic condensation precisely because *Silas Marner*, in allowing her to speak symbolically about the meaning of daughterhood, also allowed her to speak in even more resonant symbols about the significance of motherhood. What she said was what she saw: that it is better to be a daughter than a mother and better still to be a father than a daughter. For when the Deuteronomy of culture formulates the incest laws that lie at the center of human society, that severe code tells the son: "You may not have your mother; you may not kill your father." But when it is translated into a "Daughteronomy" preached for the growing girl, it says: "You must bury your mother; you must give yourself to your father."[29] Since the daughter has inherited an empty pack and cannot *be* a father, she has no choice but to be *for* the father—to be his treasure, his land, his voice.

Yet, as Eliot shows, the growing girl is haunted by her own difficult passage from mother to father, haunted by the primal scene in the snow when she was forced to turn away from the body of the mother, the emblem of nature which can give only so much and no more, and seek the hearth of the father, the emblem of culture that must compensate for nature's inadequacies.[30] This moment is frozen into the center of *Silas Marner* like the dead figure of Molly Farren Cass, whose final posture of self-abandonment brings about Eppie's "effort to regain the pillowing arm and bosom; but mammy's ear was deaf, and the pillow seemed to be slipping away backward" (*SM*, 1. 12). Indeed, for women the myth that governs personality may be based on such a moment, a confrontation of the dead mother that is as enduring and horrifying to daughters as Freud (in *Totem and Taboo*) claimed the nightmare of the dead father was to sons. Finally, the garden that Eppie and Silas plant at the end of the novel memorializes this moment. " 'Father,' " says the girl "in a tone of gentle gravity. . . , 'we shall take the furze bush into the garden' "—for it was against the bush that Molly died (*SM*, 2. 16). Now, fenced in by the garden of the law, the once "straggling" bush will become a symbol of nature made meaningful, controlled and confined by culture (*SM*, 1. 12).

In the end, then, it is Silas Marner, the meek weaver of Raveloe, who inherits the milk and honey of the earth, for he has affirmed the Law of the Father that weaves kin and kindness together. Not coincidentally, when Silas' adopted daughter's engagement to Aaron knits him definitively into the world, Dunstan Cass' skeleton is uncovered and the gold is restored: since Silas has been willing to give his treasure to another, his treasure is given back to him. The intricate web of nemesis and apotheosis that Eliot has woven around Silas reminds us, moreover, that the very name "Raveloe" preserves two conflicting meanings along with an allegorical pun on the word "law." According to *Webster's*, to "ravel" means both to "entangle" or "make intricate" and to "unravel" or "disentangle." And indeed, in this "legendary" domain the nots and knots of the law are unraveled—untangled and clarified—in an exemplary manner, even while the *Ravel* or entanglement of the *Law* weaves people together with Rainbow threads of custom and ceremony.

Finally, too, all is for the best in this domain because this tale of ravelings and unravelings has been told both by and about a daughter of wisdom. Indeed, though Silas as Job is, of course, no Jove and the daughter of his single parenthood is no Minerva, the structure of the relationship between innocently wise Eppie and her lawful father repeats the structure of the relationship between the goddess of wisdom and her lawgiving father, just as the frozen burial of Molly Farren Cass affirms the fateful judgment of *The Oresteia* that the mother "is not the true parent of the child / Which is called hers."[31] In Hélène Cixous' wry words, there is "no need for mother—provided that there is something of the maternal: and it is the father then who acts as—is—the mother."[32] With no Eumenides in sight, the redeemed land of Raveloe belongs to fathers and daughters. It is no wonder that Wharton begins her revisionary *Summer* with Charity Royall, an angry transformation of Eppie, trapped in a library ruled by a plaster bust of Minerva.

* * *

Writing to Wharton in 1912 about *The Reef*, perhaps the most Jamesian of her novels, Henry James thought of Eliot and suggested that his friend's revisionary clarification of Eliot's message was so radical that the American writer had made herself, metaphorically speaking, into her English culture-mother's primordial precursor. "There used to be little notes in you that were like fine benevolent finger-marks of the good George Eliot—the echo of much reading of that excellent woman," he told Wharton. "But now you are like a lost and recovered 'ancient' whom *she* might have got a reading of (especially were he a Greek) and of whom in *her* texture some weaker reflection were to show."[33] In fact, James' remarks were more prophetic than analytic, for if the not altogether successful *Reef* was quasi-Jamesian rather than proto-Eliotian, the brilliantly coherent *Summer* does surface the *Ur*-myth, and specifically the dark "Daughteronomy," on which *Silas Marner* is based.

It may seem odd to argue that *Summer*, a sexy story of an illicit love affair, has anything in common with Eliot's pedagogically respectable *Silas Marner*. Yet, like *Silas Marner*, *Summer* is a family romance which also incorporates a female *Bildungsroman*, the account of a daughter's growth to maturity. As in *Silas Marner*, too, both the covert symbolic romance and the overt educational *roman* are resolved through the relationship between an adopted daughter and a man who seems to act as both her father and her mother. Again, like *Silas Marner*, *Summer* broods on the winter of civilization's discontent and the summer of reproduction; in doing so, moreover, Wharton's romance, like Eliot's fable, explores events that are situated on the margins of society, where culture must enter into a dialectical struggle with nature in order to transform "raw" female reality into "cooked" feminine sex roles.[34] In addition, as a corollary of this exploration, *Summer*, like *Silas Marner*, traces the redemption that the father achieves through his possession of the daughter. Finally, therefore, the two novels illuminate each other with striking reciprocity: in the conciliatory coziness with which it evades desire, *Silas Marner* is the story Wharton might have liked to tell, while in the relentless rigor with which it renounces desire, *Summer* is the tale Eliot may have feared to confront.

As James' remark about her "ancient" quality implied, Wharton had begun to become a fierce mythologist by the time she wrote this short novel; in particular, she had started to read Joseph Conrad, whose grasp of archaic symbolism she much admired and imported into *Summer*, strengthening her implicit reading of *Silas Marner* with a quest plot that mimics the psychic journey at the heart of his *Heart of Darkness*. Thus, as my epigraph from Sylvia Plath's poem "The Colossus" is meant to suggest, "a blue sky out of the Oresteia" does arch over *Summer*, infusing and illuminating every detail of a mythic narrative that revolves around three figures: a father who "all by [himself is] pithy and historical as the Roman Forum," a daughter who marries the "winter of [his] year" as helplessly as Aeschylus' Electra or Plath's "Electra on Azalea Path" marry the shadow of Agamemnon, and a dead mother who must be as definitively consigned to barren ground as Clytemnestra or the Eumenides.[35] Appropriately enough, therefore, *Summer* begins as its heroine, teenage Charity Royall, walks down the main street of the New England village of North Dormer to her part-time job in a library presided over by a plaster cast of "sheep-nosed" Minerva,[36] the divine daddy's girl who resolved *The Oresteia* by ruling in favor of "the father's claim / And male supremacy in all things." A representative of nature bewildered by culture, Charity is a sort of foundling who, we learn, was "brought down" from a nearby mountain (always mysteriously called "the Mountain,"with an ominous capital *M*) when she was very little, an origin which places her among the "humblest of the humble even in North Dormer, where to come from the Mountain was the worst disgrace." At the same time, however, both her job as librarian and the odd fact that she keeps the lace she is making "wound about the buckram back of a disintegrated copy of 'The Lamplighter' " significantly qualify her humbleness (S, pp.

22, 14). For, like Eliot's Eppie and like Gerty, the heroine of Maria Cummins' 1854 best-seller, Wharton's Charity is the ward of a solitary older man who dotes on and delights in her youth, her dependence.[37]

Where both Eliot's Silas Marner and Cummins' Trueman Flint are sympathetic men almost from the first, however, Charity's guardian is an equivocal figure, and his difference begins to reveal the secret dynamics such apparently divergent works as Cummins' and Eliot's novels share with Wharton's. For Lawyer Royall, says the narrator of *Summer*, "ruled in North Dormer; and Charity ruled in Lawyer Royall's house. . . . But she knew her power, knew what it was made of, and hated it." *Lawyer* Royall: so far as we know, this "magnificent monument of a man" has no other name (S, pp. 23, 27). Indeed, as Charity's father/guardian/suitor and (eventually) husband, he is, ultimately, no more than the role his professional title and allegorical surname together denote: a regal lawgiver, a mythologized superego whose occupation links him with the library and with culture, that is, with the complex realm of patriarchal history that both puzzles and imprisons the wild child he is trying to make into a desirable daughter/bride.

Even while he is a "towering" public man, however, Lawyer Royall is a notably pathetic private man. From the first, Wharton deconstructs the colossus of the father to make explicit the ways in which the paradigmatic patriarch is as dependent on his Charity as Silas Marner was on his Eppie or, indeed, as Agamemnon was on Iphigenia or Electra, Oedipus on Antigone and Ismene, or the biblical Jephthah on his (nameless) daughter. To begin with, we learn that Charity had long ago perceived Lawyer Royall as "too lonesome" for her to go away to school (S, p. 26); later, more dramatically, we discover that his "lonesomeness" manifested itself in an abortive attempt to rape her. Finally, we are told that it was this episode which drove the girl to try to establish her independence by taking her deathly job in the library. But, of course, this attempt at escape, as in some Sophoclean case history, simply impels her even more inexorably toward her fate.

For it is in "Minerva's" library that Charity meets her lover-to-be, a handsome architect named Lucius Harney—a far more glamourously equivocal representative of culture than the aging Lawyer Royall. Town-bred, easy with books, this dashing young man is culture's heir; at the same time, he is a golden boy whose "lusciousness," as Andrea Hammer has observed, links him to nature, even seems to make him nature's emissary—and that is why *he* is an equivocal figure. Young, sensual, magnetic, he is frequently associated with the grass, the sky, the "flaming breath" of summer; indeed, he and Charity conduct their affair while is is "camping" halfway up the Mountain in a little abandoned house surrounded by a fallen fence, "crowding grasses," and rosebushes that have "run wild" (S, p. 166).[38] That he is often connected in Charity's mind with her mysterious Mountain relative Liff Hyatt, whose initials echo his, seems at first to suggest, moreover, that, like Liff, Lucius is a brother figure—and his earliest advances *are* described as "more fraternal than lover-like" (S, p. 95).[39] Yet, just as Eppie Marner's marriage to the brother figure Aaron also marries her definitively to her father, Silas, so Charity's apparently illegitimate romance with Lucius Harney moves her inexorably into the arms of Lawyer Royall, and this not just because it is Lawyer Royall who marries her to "rescue" her from unwed motherhood but because it eventually becomes plain that even Lucius Harney's desire for her is entangled in feelings of rival-rous identification with the patriarchally "majectic" lawyer (see *S*, p. 191).

For Charity, in every sense of that word, must be given to the father. And, as *Summer's* denouement finally makes clear, even while Harney has seemed to act against the patriarchal Royall, he has also acted *for* the lawyer, appearing as if by magic in the library to deflower Charity and impregnate her so that she is at last ready for the marriage to her guardian that she had earlier persistently refused. Indeed, it is arguable that throughout the affair in which he seems to have functioned as nature's emissary by drawing the girl into the wilderness of her own sexuality, Harney has really performed as culture's messenger and, specifically, as a vivid and vital "Phallus" whose glamour seduces the daughter into the social architecture from which she would otherwise have tried to flee. For in patriarchal marriage, says Wharton's plot, the brother/equal inevitably turns into the father/rule. Not surprisingly, therefore, when Charity and Lawyer Royall start on their journey toward the allegorically named town of *Nettle*ton, where the girl's sexual initiation began and where she is finally going to be married to her legal guardian, Charity briefly imagines that she is "sitting beside her lover with the leafy arch of summer bending over them." But "this illusion [is] is faint and transitory" because it implies a deceptive liberty of desire (*S*, p. 273). As Wharton reluctantly observed, the daughter's summer of erotic content blooms only to prepare her for what Dickinson called "a Doom of Fruit without the Bloom"—an autumn and winter of civilized discontent in which, like her precursor, the first Mrs. Royall, she will be "sad and timid and weak" (*S*, p. 24). As in Wharton's pornographic "Beatrice Palmato" fragment—a more melodramatic tale of father-daughter incest which makes overt some of the psychodynamics that even in *Summer* are only covert—the symbolic father will "reap [the] fruit" borne from the son/lover's deflowering of the daughter.[40]

Charity does, however, make one last frantic effort to flee the wintry prison house of culture that is closing around her, and that is in her wild pilgrimage up the Mountain in search of her mother. As the girl's affair with Lucius Harney has progressed, she has become increasingly concerned about her origins and begun to try, the way Eppie did in *Silas Marner*, to explain to herself what it means both to have and to be a mother. Finally, when she realizes she is pregnant, she also understands that there is "something in her blood that [makes] the Mountain the only answer to her questioning," and in an astonishing episode, which includes some of the most fiercely imagined scenes in American fiction, she journeys toward the originary heart of darkness where she will find and lose her mother (*S*, p. 236).

Appropriately enough, Charity's mother's name is *Mary* Hyatt. Equally appropriately, Charity arrives in the outlaw community on the Mountain only to discover that the woman has just died. It is as if the very idea of the daughter's quest must necessarily kill her female progenitor, not only to emphasize the unavailability of female power but also to underscore the Oresteian dictum that "The mother is not the true parent of the child / Which is called hers. She is [merely] a nurse who tends the growth / Of young seed planted by its true parent, the male."[41] Worse still, this anti-Virgin Mary is not only dead, she is horrifyingly dead, dead "like a dead dog in a ditch," "lips parted in a frozen gasp above . . . broken teeth," one leg drawn up under a torn skirt and the other "swollen glistening leg" flung out, "bare to the knee," in a death paroxysm that parodies the paroxysm of birth and suggests the nausea of nakedness in which the flesh of the mother expels and repels the flesh of the child (S, pp. 250, 248). As Mr. Miles, the clergyman who ascends the Mountain only for funerals, prepares to bury the woman's uncoffined body in frozen ground, nameless and undistinguishable squatters, Charity's undefinable relatives, squabble over the pitiful furnishings in the shanty where Mary Hyatt died on a mattress on the floor. Nothing, they say, was hers: "She never had no bed"; "And the stove warn't hers." Nor does the reading of the Bible, the Book of patriarchal Law, offer any hope of redemption for the dead woman. When Mr. Miles intones "yet in my flesh shall I see God," Charity thinks of "the gaping mouth and stony eyes [and] glistening leg," and when he proposes that Jesus Christ shall change this "vile body that it may be like unto His glorious body," a last spadeful of earth falls heavily "on the vile body of Mary Hyatt" (S, pp. 251, 255).

Where women poets from Elizabeth Barrett Browning and Emily Dickinson transformed mothers into "multitudinous mountains sitting in / [A] magic circle, with [a] mutual touch /Electric," and "Sweet Mountains" into "Strong Madonnas," Wharton, like her culture-mother George Eliot, saw the mother as blind, deaf, and stony and the maternal Mountain as a place of mourning.[42] As if Eliot anticipated the French feminist psychoanalyst Christiane Olivier's contention that the mirror which man holds toward woman "contains only the image of a dead woman" and, more specifically, a dead Jocasta, the morbid moment of Molly Farren Cass' death in the snow and her daughter Eppie's discovery that "mammy's ear was deaf" is—as we saw—frozen into the center of *Silas Marner*.[43] Similarly, frozen into the center of *Summer* is the moment of Mary Hyatt's burial in the snow and her daughter Charity's mortifying discovery that there is no salvation from or for her mother's "vile body."

Neither is there salvation or even significant charity for Charity from other women in the novel. To be sure, one of the girl's unnamed relatives—Liff Hyatt's mother—lets her spend the night on a mattress on the floor "as her dead mother's body had lain," but as that simile suggests, such an act of kindness only promises to induct Charity into the "passive promiscuity" lived by the matriarchal horde on the Mountain, a life entirely outside the comforts and controls of culture, a life in which the mother—possessionless and unpossessed—is "glad to have the child go" (S, pp. 258, 260). As for the other women, the semisenile figure of Verena Marsh, the Royalls' housekeeper, "with her old deaf-looking eyes" foreshadows the blind deaf stony figure of Charity's mother; the "fallen" Julia Hawes and her impoverished sister Ally, together with the "indestructible" Annabel Balch, reemphasize women's dependence on male legal and financial protection; and the pseudomotherly abortionist, Dr. Merkel, suggests that a daughter who wants to live apart from the father must kill her baby or else, like Mary Hyatt, be "cut down" and killed by the "savage misery" of a life apart from culture (S, pp. 155, 254, 259).

Taken together, therefore, the decisions and destinies of all these women italicize Charity's own perception that "in the established order of things as she [knows] them, [there is] no place for her individual adventure." In fact, the pregnancy that signals her transformation from girl to woman, from daughter to mother, has so severely depersonalized her that she feels herself "a mere speck in the lonely circle of the sky." Like dead Mary Hyatt, she has nothing and is nothing but a vessel for her child; thus the impersonal biological imperative of the coming life is, as Wharton brilliantly puts it, "like a load that [holds] her down, and yet like a hand that pull[s] her to her feet" (S, pp. 235, 264, 265). The annunciation of summer, Charity discovers, inexorably entails the renunciation that is winter, a divestment of desire that definitively prepares her for her final turn toward the rescuing father. Fated to move from father to library to lover to father, she goes to Nettleton and marries her guardian. And by now even the Romantic nature she had experienced with her lover has been transmuted into culture—that is, into a set of cultural artifacts: an engraving of a couple in a boat that decorates her bridal chamber, and a pin set with a lake blue gem which implies that in the bloomless winter of her maturity the lake itself must turn to stone.

But if a stone is all Charity has, Charity is what Lawyer Royall has, an emblem of redemption that he needs as much as Silas Marner needs "his" Eppie. For if, as Freud argues, the girl arrives at "the ultimate normal feminine attitude in which she takes her father as love-object" only after "a lengthy process of [symbolically castrating] development" ("FS," p. 199) which, in Helene Deutsch's words, "drive[s]" her "into her constitutionally predetermined passive role," then the daughter's desire for the father must be understood to be, like Charity's need for Lawyer Royall, constructed by a patriarchal order that forces her to renounce what might be more "natural" desires—for lover/brother, for mother, for self.[44] But as the ambiguous allegory of Charity's name suggests, the father's desire for the daughter is inevitable, a desire not only to give but to receive charity. Standing outside the girl's room after proposing to her (and being rejected) for the second time, Lawyer Royall seems to understand this: "his hand on the door knob[,] 'Charity!' he plead[s]" (S, p. 119). For not only is the "daughter" a milk-giving creature, a suitably diminished and dependent mother, she is also, as a living manifestation of the father's wealth, the charity to which he is culturally entitled.

Finally, therefore, from Charity's point of view, *Summer* is very much a novel about both renunciation and resignation. When her last hope for escape is buried with her mother, she must resign herself, or, rather, reassign herself, to her symbolic father.[45] After her marriage she will be Charity Royall Royall, a name whose redundancy emphasizes the proprietorial power by which her guardian/husband commands her loyalty. But from Lawyer Royall's point of view or, for that matter, from Lucius Harney's, *Summer* is a novel about assignment—that is, about the roles of cultural authority to which men are assigned and about the women who are assigned—marked out, given over—to them to signify that authority. No wonder, then, that Lawyer Royall's first gesture after his marriage to Charity is to give his new bride the munificent sum of forty dollars to buy clothes so that, like an illustration from Thorstein Veblen's *Theory of the Leisure Class*, she will prove his wealth by "beating" all the other girls "hollow" (S, p. 285). "Of course, *he's* the book," said Wharton enigmatically about Lawyer Royall.[46] Consciously, she no doubt meant that he is the novel's most complex personality—indeed, its only Jamesian adult—and therefore the only character whose redemption is worth tracing in detail. But, less consciously, she might have meant that, as law-giving patriarch, he is the "book" in which Charity's fate must be inscribed; for it is, after all, the text of his desire that determines the destiny of hers.

* * *

Apart from fictions like *Silas Marner* and *Summer*, what evidence have we that father-daughter incest is a culturally constructed paradigm of female desire? Equally to the point, what proof is there that the father may need, even desire, the daughter at least as much as she needs him? Though psychoanalytic and sociological replies to both these questions have been disputed, many answers have been offered, particularly in recent years. From Phyllis Chesler to Judith Lewis Herman, for instance, feminist theorists have argued that in a patriarchal culture women are encouraged by society, in Chesler's words, "to commit incest as a way of life." "As opposed to marrying our fathers, we marry men like our fathers," Chesler declares, "men who are older than us, [and] have more money [and] more power [and are taller]." Similarly, in her study of literal father-daughter incest, Herman claims that "overt incest represents only the furthest point on a continuum—an exaggeration of patriarchal family norms, but not a departure from them."[47] Less extravagantly but along the same lines, Nancy Chodorow has observed, following Talcott Parsons, that "father-daughter incest does not threaten a daughter [with a return to infantile dependency] in the same way" in which "mother-son incest . . . threatens a son," so that "mother-son and mother-*daughter* [not father-daughter] incest are the major threats to the formation of new families (as well as to the male-dominant family)."[48]

Nor are any of these views incompatible with Freud's own belief that what he called the "female Oedipus complex"—the process through which the little girl relinquishes her earliest mother-attachment and transfers her affection to her father—is both the end result of an extraordinarily difficult procedure and, as he puts it, a "positive" development. Only by a "very circuitous path," he admits in his late essay "Female Sexuality" (1931), does the girl "arrive at the ultimate normal feminine attitude in which she takes her father as love-object." And because *her* Oedipus complex (unlike the boy's) represents the "final result of a lengthy process, . . . it escapes the strong hostile influences which, in men, tend to its destruction"—that is, because the female Oedipus complex is not destroyed but created by the "castration complex" (which signifies the recognition of sexual difference), many women in Freud's view, never surmount the female Oedipus complex at all and perhaps never should ("FS," p. 199).

As the researches of Judith Herman and Lisa Hirschman have shown, however, and as Deutsch argued, the desire of the father for the daughter is frequently complicitous, even essential in constructing the desire for him that she manifests in the "positive" female Oedipus complex. Proposing a theory of what has come to be called "reciprocal role learning," Deutsch suggested in *The Psychology of Women* that the father functions "as a seducer, with whose help the girl's aggressive instinctual components are transformed into masochistic ones."[49] Recent investigators have suggested that girls do "learn to behave in a feminine fashion through complementing the masculine behavior of their fathers." Tellingly, though, "there is no evidence that reciprocal role learning is of any significance in the development of masculinity."[50] In other words, boys are not encouraged to learn to be boys by responding with precocious virility to seductive behavior by their mothers. This last point, however, leads to my second question—What proof is there that the father needs the daughter at least as much as she needs him?—and to a related query—Why *should* the father desire the daughter? If men have not developed masculinity through reciprocal role learning with mothers, why should they interact "reciprocally" with their daughters? I have extrapolated from my readings of *Silas Marner* and *Summer* the idea that the father needs the daughter because she is a suitably diminished "milk giver," a miniaturized version of the mother whom patriarchal culture absolutely forbids him to desire. Beyond the often ambiguous configurations that shape literary texts like Eliot's and Wharton's, there is considerable evidence that this is so.

The empirical investigations of Herman and Hirschman, for instance, have yielded crucial information: in studying surveys of "white, predominantly middle-class, urban, educated women," these clinical psychologists discovered that "between four and twelve percent of all women reported a sexual experience with a relative, and one woman in one hundred reported a sexual experience with her father or stepfather." Examining individual incest cases, moreover, they learned that, often because of a wife's illness, absence, or alleged frigidity, a father had transferred his affections to his daughter in an attempt "to continue to receive female nurturance." More generally, they observed that "in the father's fantasy life, the daughter becomes the source of all the father's infantile longings for nurturance and care. He thinks of her first as the idealized childhood bride or sweetheart, and finally as the all-good, all-giving mother." Reasoning both from anthropological studies and from the Bible, they conclude that "in patriarchal societies [where] the rights of ownership and exchange of women within the family are vested primarily in the father[, t]hese rights find their most complete expression in the father's relationship with his daughter" because—of all female relatives—"the daughter belongs to the father alone." They then cite a key passage from Leviticus in which, while forbidding sexual union with every other female blood relative or in-law, "the patriarchal God sees fit to pass over father-daughter incest in silence."[51]

Freud's theories of psychoanalysis began, of course, with the hypothesis that just such incest was the root cause of the hysteria manifested by the female patients he and Josef Breuer treated in the 1890s. But traditional interpretations of the history of psychoanalysis propose that, as Diane Sadoff puts it, "Freud realized that his female patients' stories of remembered paternal seduction did not necessarily report reality and may have reported fantasy [so that] the scene of paternal seduction retroactively seeks to represent and solve a major enigma confronting the daughter: the origin or upsurge of her sexuality."[52] In fact, explains O. Mannoni, "the theory of trauma, of the seduction by the father . . . served as [Freud's] defense against knowledge of the Oedipus complex."[53] Even the feminist theorist Juliet Mitchell acquiesces in this view, observing that "the fact that, as Freud himself was well aware, *actual* paternal seduction or rape occurs not infrequently, has nothing to do with the essential concepts of psychoanalysis" (which are, after all, founded on the hypothesis of filial rather than paternal desire) (*PF*, p. 9). Yet, interestingly enough, we have from the Father of Psychoanalysis himself strikingly direct evidence of the reality of paternal desire.

In May 1897, shortly before abandoning his theory that hysteria was caused by paternal seduction or rape, Freud had a dream about "feeling over-affectionately towards" his oldest daughter, Mathilde. "The dream," he wrote to his friend Wilhelm Fliess, "of course fulfills my wish to pin down a father as the originator of neurosis and put an end to my persistent doubts."[54] Yet, on the one hand, the experience clearly troubled him, while, on the other hand, it does seem to have functioned as a screen for what troubled him even more: the sequence of dreams and memories Freud recorded in the letters of spring–summer 1897 shows that many of the psychic events he examined as part of the self-analysis he was conducting at this time had to do with desires for or anxieties about mature women—his mother or figures for her. The sequence culminated in his crucial speculation that "(between the ages of two and two-and-a-half) libido towards *matrem* was aroused" at a time when he "had the opportunity of seeing her *nudam*."[55] Embedded in this dramatic series of reveries is his equally dramatic decision that though "in every case [of female hysteria] blame was laid on perverse acts by the father . . . it was hardly credible that perverted acts against children were so general," a decision that, despite its negative implications for a career he had been building on theories about paternal seduction, left him feeling inexplicably exhilarated.[56]

Careful analysis of these materials suggests that Freud's brilliant self-interrogations both reveal and conceal a slippage in his thinking. His no doubt accurate discovery of feelings for his mother is quite unaccountably associated with the notion, which he later repudiated, that his female patients would naturally have had equivalent desires for their *fathers*. That even as he surfaced his own Oedipal wishes, he may have disguised them (for instance, reporting awful dreams about an ugly elderly nurse who washed him in "reddish water") implies his own *resistance* to these wishes, however, a resistance also expressed in his dream of Mathilde. As Mitchell observes, even "Freud . . . found it more acceptable to be the father than the incest-desiring or rival-castrating son—as do most men" (*PF*, p. 75). Thus the theory of paternal seduction appropriately led to Freud's understanding of the son's desire for the mother, of which the father's desire for the daughter is a belated but more socially acceptable transformation. Nevertheless, the father's desire for the daughter was not so acceptable to Freud that he could persist in his "wish to pin down a father as the originator of neurosis."[57] Rather, having admitted his own filial desire, he seems to have wished to "pin down" daughters as equivalent sources of desire. Yet as his later formulations of female psychosexual development were to suggest, erotic feelings of daughters for fathers symmetrical with those of sons for mothers were not necessarily implicit in the accounts of paternal seduction that he called his patients' "fantasies." In fact, as recent reports about the unpublished portions of his letters to Fliess, along with analyses of the alterations and evasions in *Studies on Hysteria* have suggested, Freud himself was, in Mitchell's phrase, "well aware" that many of these patients were not fantasizing, that they actually had been seduced or in some sense seductively manipulated by their fathers or by father figures. Their "hysteria" may therefore have constituted not a rejection of their own desire but a refusal of the paternal demands that not only their own families but also their culture defined as psychologically "right."[58] Even so early in his career, in other words, Freud's fruitful transformation of speculations about father-daughter seduction into a theory about son-mother incest, with its corollary evasion of a theory of father-daughter desire, expresses his proleptic awareness that he would eventually have to construct a far more complicated model of female psychosexual development in order to trace the girl's circuitous path" to what he was to define as mature (heterosexual) femininity.

That path, with its obstacles, its terrors, and its refusals, is the road studied in *Silas*

Marner and *Summer*—in *Silas Marner*'s exploration of the powers the daughter gives the father and in *Summer*'s examination of the powers the father takes away from the daughter. But of course countless other literary texts—written by both men and women—focus on the submerged paradigm of father-daughter incest that shapes the plots and possibilities inscribed in these novels. From *The Oresteia*'s repudiation and repression of the matriarchal Furies and its concomitant aggrandizement of Athene, the dutiful father's daughter, to *Oedipus at Colonus*' praise of Antigone and Ismene, the two loyal daughters who have been their father's sole guardians in the blinded exile to which his incestuous marriage with his mother condemned him, Greek literature consistently valorizes such a paradigm. That Oedipus' daughters, in particular, functioned as their father's "eyes" reminds us, moreover, that "the word for daughter in Greek is *Kore*, the literal meaning of which is pupil of the eye."[59] Similarly, the violent obliteration of the mother in these works and many others recalls one version of the story of Athene's origin: after raping Metis the Titaness, the father-god *swallowed her*, having heard that, though she was now pregnant with a daughter, she would bear a son who would depose him if she had another child; then, "in due time . . . seized by a raging headache," he himself gave birth to Athene, who "sprang fully armed" from his skull.[60] In just the way that Antigone and Ismene properly replace Jocasta as Oedipus' helpmeets—indeed, as the "eyes" who, according to Freud, would signify his continuing sexual potency—so Athene supplants Metis as Zeus' true child/bride.

To be sure, these archaic texts enact the prescriptions and proscriptions of patriarchal culture with exceptional clarity; yet such imperatives also underlie a surprising number of other, later works, ranging from Shakespeare's *King Lear* to Percy Bysshe Shelley's *Cenci*, from Mary Shelley's *Mathilda* to Christina Stead's *Man Who Loved Children*, from some of Sylvia Plath's and Anne Sexton's most striking poems to Toni Morrison's *Bluest Eye*. Whereas the stories of such heroines as Antigone and her later, more angelically Victorian avatar Eppie Marner—the creation of a novelist long haunted by Antigone—had recounted the daughter's acquiescence in her filial destiny, however, these works, like Wharton's *Summer*, record her ambivalence toward a fate in which, as Beatrice Cenci cries, "all things" terrifyingly transform themselves into "my father's spirit, / His eye, his voice, his touch surrounding me."[61] Specifically, in each of these works a father more or less explicitly desires a daughter. His incestuous demands may be literal or they may be figurative, but in either case the heroine experiences them as both inexorable and stifling. Thus, in each work the girl struggles with more or less passion to escape, arguing that "I love your Majesty according to my bond, no more, no less." And in almost all these works, she discovers, finally, just what the nature of that bond is: no more, no less, than—on the one hand—death or on the other hand—a surrender to the boundless authority of paternal desire that governs the lives of mothers and daughters in what Adrienne Rich has called "the kingdom of the sons" and the fathers.[62] Indeed, in the few works (for instance, Plath's "Daddy" and Stead's *Man Who Loved Children*) where the daughter neither dies nor acquiesces, she becomes a murderess and an outlaw.

* * *

Reducing the plot, as fairy tales so often do, to its most essential psychic outline, a narrative recorded by the brothers Grimm provides a resonant summary of the father-daughter "story" I have been exploring here. The fairy tale "Allerleirauh" (which means "many different kinds of fur") introduces us to a king whose dying wife has made him promise not to remarry unless he can find a new bride who is as beautiful as she is and who has "just such golden hair as I have."[63] Grief-stricken, the king keeps his word until one day he looks at his growing daughter, sees that she is "just as beautiful as her dead mother, and ha[s] the same golden hair," "suddenly [feels] a violent love for her," and resolves to marry *her*. Shocked, the daughter tries to escape by setting him impossible tasks—she asks for three magical dresses and a "mantle of a thousand different kinds of fur"—but when he fulfills her requests, she has no choice but to run away. Taking her three dresses and three tiny domestic treasures, she wraps herself in her fur mantle and escapes to a great forest. There she is asleep in a hollow tree when "the King to whom this forest belong[s]" passes through with some huntsmen who capture her, thinking she is "a wondrous beast." When she tells them she is simply a poor orphan child, they bring her to this king's palace, where they set her to work, like Cinderella, in the kitchen ("A," pp. 327, 328).[64]

Of course, however, the king at this palace soon manages to discover her identity. He gives a series of three feasts, at each of which she appears in one of her magic dresses; he admires the soup she cooks while she is disguised in her furry Cinderella garb; and he finally manages to tear off her protective mantle, revealing her magic dress and her golden hair so that, in the words of the story, "she [can] no longer hide herself," and the pair are wed soon after this epiphany ("A," p. 331). Like such texts as *Summer*, *Mathilda*, and *The Cenci*, then, this tale records the case history of a daughter who tries to escape paternal desire, and like the heroines of many such works (for instance, Charity Royall journeying to the Mountain), the "fair princess" who becomes "Allerleirauh" flees from culture (her father's palace) to nature (the great wood), trying to transform herself into a creature of nature (a "hairy animal") rather than acquiesce in the extreme demands culture is making upon her ("A," pp. 329, 330).[65] Like a number of other protagonists of these stories and case histories, however, Allerleirauh cannot altogether abandon the imperatives her cultures has impressed upon her: she brings with her the three magical dresses and the three domestic tokens which will eventually reveal her identity and knit her back into society. Like countless other heroines in such tales, moreover, she is motherless, a fact which, the story emphasizes, has brought about the seductive paternal persecution she is trying to evade. Finally, like that of so many of these heroines—perhaps most notably *Silas Marner*'s Eppie—her function as a "treasure" to both kinds is manifested by the golden hair that she is at last unable to conceal.

That there are in fact two kinds in "Allerleirauh" may at first seem to controvert my argument that this tale offers us a paradigm of the prescription for father-daughter incest that lies at the heart of female psychosexual development in patriarchal society. Not just the princess but also the first king's courtiers, after all, express dismay at his desire to marry his daughter. In addition, the second king is distinguished from the first by a restrictive clause: he is not "the king, who owns this forest"—that is, the king from whose palace Allerleirauh has just fled—but, rather, "the king who owns this forest." Yet structurally and psychologically, if not grammatically, the two kinds are one: paternal figures from both of whom the "fair princess" tries to escape, though not, perhaps, with equal vigor. In fact, for all practical purposes, the distinction between the two is best expressed by a single comma, the linguistic mark that marks the difference between illegitimate and legitimate incest, a difference Allerleirauh herself involuntarily acknowledges by the ambivalance with which at one moment she decks herself in glorious apparel and then, soon after, retreats into her old life as a wild child.

To be sure, given such ambivalence, some readers might see this tale simply as an account of the advances and retreats through which an adolescent girl comes to terms with her own mature desires. At the same time, however, what gives the tale a good deal of its force is the fatality it shares with subtler works like *Silas Marner* and *Summer*—specifically, a fatality provided by the *mother*'s complicity in her daughter's destiny. For it is, after all, Allerleirauh's mother who has set the girl's story going with her admonition to the father that he must marry only a bride as beautiful as she. Lost to the daughter, like Molly Farren Cass and Mary Hyatt, she nevertheless rules her daughter's life with the injunctions of the culture-mother: "You must bury your mother, you must give yourself to your father." In such novels as *Silas Marner* and *Summer*, the authors themselves replace her, splitting the maternal function between the ignominy of the dead mother and the qualified triumph of the male-identified maternal authority. But in all these stories, as even in more apparently rebellious works, the text itself discovers no viable alternative to filial resignation. Certainly, paradigmatic culture-mothers like Eliot and Wharton do not suggest (at least not in works like *Silas Marner* and *Summer*) that the daughter has any choice but that of acquiescence.[66] Though the "empty Pack" of daughteronomy may be heavy, as Dickinson saw perhaps more clearly than they, it is vain to "punish" the cultural "Honey" it manufactures; for the daughter who understands her duty and her destiny, such honey "only sweeter" grows. Under "a blue sky out of the Oresteia," Eppie Marner, Charity Royall, and the fair princess Allerleirauh, along with many others, and each in her own way, obey the implicit command of patriarchal society and marry the winter of the Father's year.

Notes

This essay was researched and written with the assistance of grants from the Rockefeller and Guggenheim foundations, to both of which I am very grateful. In addition, I have profited greatly from criticisms and suggestions offered by many friends and colleagues, including (as always) Susan Gubar and Elliot Gilbert, as well as Andrea Hammer, Susan Lurie, Elyse Blankley, Peter Hays, Suzanne Graver, and Michael Wolfe. Finally, I have learned much from audiences at a number of institutions where this paper was "tried out" in various forms, among them helpful and incisive respondents at the Rutgers University George Eliot Centenary Conference, and at Harvard University, the University of Colorado, the University of Washington, Yale University, the University of Southern California, and Princeton University.

1. See Sandra M. Gilbert and Susan Gubar, "Tradition and the Female Talent," *Proceedings of the Northeastern University Center for Literary Studies* 2 (1984), and " 'Forward Into the Past': The Complex Female Affiliation Complex," in *Historical Studies in Literary Criticism*, ed. Jerome J. McGann (Madison, Wis., 1985).

2. Virginia Woolf to Lady Robert Cecil [26 Jan.? 1919] (no. 1010), *The Letters of Virginia Woolf*, ed, Nigel Nicolson and Joanne Trautmann, 6 vols. (New York, 1975–80), 2:322; the historian Shelton Rothblatt called George

Eliot a "Man of Ideas" (paper delivered at the George Eliot Centenary Conference, Rutgers University, Sept. 1980); and see Leslie Stephen, *George Eliot*, English Men of Letters Series (London and New York, 1902).

3. Elaine Showalter, *A Literature of Their Own: British Women Novelists from Brontë to Lessing* (Princeton, N.J., 1977), p. 108; Elizabeth Robins, *George Mandeville's Husband*, quoted in *A Literature of Their Own*, p. 109.

4. Eliot had said that *Silas Marner* "came to me first of all, quite suddenly, as a sort of legendary tale" (Eliot to John Blackwood, 24 Feb. 1861, quoted in Gordon S. Haight, *George Eliot: A Biography* [New York, 1968], p. 341).

5. Emily Dickinson to Thomas Niles, Apr. 1883 (no. 814), *The Letters of Emily Dickinson*, ed. Thomas H. Johnson, 3 vols. (Cambrige, Mass., 1965), 3:769–70; and see Dickinson, *The Complete Poems of Emily Dickinson*, ed. Johnson (Boston, 1960), no. 1562, p. 650.

6. Edith Wharton, review of *George Eliot* by Stephen, *Bookman* 15 (May 1902): 251, 250.

7. Eliot, "Prelude," *Middlemarch*, ed. W. J. Harvey (Harmondsworth, 1965), p. 26.

8. Jacques Lacan, "On a Question Preliminary to Any Possible Treatment of Psychosis," *Ecrits: A Selection*, trans. Alan Sheridan (New York, 1977), p. 199. Anika Lemaire succinctly summarizes this Lacanian position:

> Society and its structures are always present in the form of the family institution and the father, the representative of the law of society into which he will introduce his child by forbidding dual union with the mother (the register of the imaginary, of nature). By identifying with the father, the child receives a name and a place in the family constellation; restored to himself, he discovers that he is to be made in and by a world of Culture, language and civilization. [*Jacques Lacan*, trans. David Macey (London, 1977), p. 92]

Elsewhere, Lacan observes: "That the woman should be inscribed in an order of exchange of which she is the object, is what makes for the fundamentally conflictual, and, I would say, insoluble character of her position: the symbolic order literally submits her, it transcends her" (Lacan, "Seminar 2" [1954–55], quoted in Jacqueline Rose, intro. to *Feminine Sexuality: Jacques Lacan and the "école freudienne,"* ed. Juliet Mitchell and Rose, trans. Rose [New York, 1983], p. 45).

9. For female "anxiety of authorship" and women's corollary need for matrilineal legitimation, see Gilbert and Gubar, *The Madwoman in the Attic: The Woman Writer and the Nineteenth-Century Literary Imagination* (New Haven, Conn., 1979), chap. 2.

10. Eliot, "Silly Novels by Lady Novelists," *The Writings of George Eliot*, 25 vols. (Boston and New York, 1907–8), 22:209. In a study of Eliot's stance toward paternal authority, Dianne F. Sadoff makes a point similar to this one, noting that Eliot seeks "to usurp [paternal authority] as the discourse of a male narrator, the authority of a male author" (*Monsters of Affection: Dickens, Eliot, and Brontë on Fatherhood* [Baltimore, 1982], p. 3).

11. Eliot to Blackwood, 12 Jan. 1861, quoted in Ruby V. Redinger, *George Eliot: The Emergent Self* (New York, 1975), p. 436. As Susan Gubar has suggested to me, the resonant image of the "packman" may be associated with the figure of Bob Jakin in *The Mill on the Floss* (which Eliot had just completed), the itinerant pack-bearing peddler who brings Maggie Tulliver a number of books, the most crucial of which is Thomas à Kempis' treatise on Christian renunciation (so that its subject metaphorically associates it with Silas Marner's pack full of emptiness).

12. Redinger, *George Eliot*, p. 439; Eliot, "Finale," *Middlemarch*, p. 896.

13. For "liminal zone," see Victor Turner, "Passages, Margins, and Poverty: Religious Symbols of Communitas," *Dramas, Fields, and Metaphors: Symbolic Action in Human Society* (Ithaca, N.Y., 1974), pp. 231–71, and "Betwixt and Between: The Liminal Period in *Rites de Passage*," *The Forest of Symbols: Aspects of Ndembu Ritual* (Ithaca, N.Y., 1967), pp. 93–111.

14. Eliot, *Silas Marner: The Weaver of Raveloe*, ed. Q. D. Leavis (Harmondsworth, 1967), pt. 1, chap. 1, pp. 51, 52; all further references to this work, abbreviated *SM*, will be included in the text, with only part and chapter numbers (or chapter title) for the convenience of those using other editions.

15. Eliot herself consciously exploits the text-textile analogy in *Silas Marner*, referring to the "tale" of cloth Silas weaves and letting Silas accuse William Dane of having "woven a plot" against him (*SM*, 1. 2, 1). For discussions of her more general use of webs, weaving, and spinning as metaphors, see Gilbert and Gubar, *The Madwoman in the Attic*, pp. 522–28; Reva Stump, *Movement and Vision in George Eliot's Novels* (Seattle, 1959), pp. 172–214; and J. Hillis Miller, "Optic and Semiotic in *Middlemarch*," in *The Worlds of Victorian Fiction*, ed. Jerome H. Buckley (Cambridge, Mass., 1975), pp. 125–45. On Eliot's own tendency to avarice—an inclination that, at least in the view of Blackwood, her publisher, became problematic just at the time she was composing *Silas Marner*—see Lawrence Jay Dessner, "The Autobiographical Matrix of *Silas Marner*," *Studies in the Novel* 11 (Fall 1979): 258–59.

16. See Sherry B. Ortner, "Is Female to Male as Nature Is to Culture?" in *Women, Culture, and Society*, ed. Michelle Zimbalist Rosaldo and Louise Lamphere (Stanford, Calif., 1974), pp. 67–87. In connection with Silas' "female" qualities, it is interesting that the villagers respond to his herbal knowlege by trying to make him take the place of "the Wise Woman," a role he at first vigorously resists (see *SM*, 1. 2).

17. Eliot, quoted in Haight, *George Eliot*, p. 336. U. C. Knoepflmacher has pointed out that Silas, like Shakespeare's Pericles, will become "another passive Job . . . redeemed through the miraculous gift of a daughter" (*George Eliot's Early Novels: The Limits of Realism* [Berkeley and Los Angeles, 1968], p. 229).

18. In a psychoanalytic study of Eliot's work, Laura Comer Emery points out "the connection of [Silas'] guineas" to a solipsistic "anality" (*George Eliot's Creative Conflict: The Other Side of Silence* [Berkeley and Los Angeles, 1976], pp. 62, 63).

19. See Sigmund Freud's observaton that, as the girl enters the Oedipal stage, her "libido slips into a new position by means—there is no other way of putting it—of the equation 'penis = child.' She gives up her wish for a penis and puts in place of it a wish for a child" ("Some Psychological Consequences of the Anatomical Distinction between the Sexes" [1925], trans. James Strachey, *Sexuality and the Psychology of Love*, ed. Philip Rieff [New York, 1963], p. 191). On the special qualities of a boy-child, see Nancy Chodorow, *The Reproduction of Mothering: Psychoanalysis and the Sociology of Gender* (Berkeley and Los Angeles, 1978), pp. 107 and 131–32.

20. See Claude Lévi-Strauss: "Even with regard to our own society, where marriage appears to be a contract between persons, . . . the relationship of reciprocity which is the basis of marriage is not established between men and women, but between men by means of women, who are merely the occasion of this relationship" (*The Elementary Structures of Kinship,* trans. James Harle Bell, John Richard von Sturmer, and Rodney Needham, ed. Needham [Boston, 1969], pp. 115–16).

21. See Eliot, *A Writer's Notebook, 1854–1879, and Uncollected Writings,* ed. Joseph Wiesenfarth (Charlottesville, Va., 1981), p. 98, where Eliot looks at Grimm's law, which traces the evolution of *dhugh* into "daughter." The theme of the daughter as treasure is, in addition, one that Eliot might have picked up from Honoré de Balzac's *Eugénie Grandet* (1833), a novel which treats the relationship of a miserly father and a "treasured" only daughter far more cynically than *Silas Marner* does; also, in an unpublished discussion of *Romola,* Robin Sheets has proposed to analyze this theme.

22. It is arguable that the very name "George Eliot" represents Marian Evans' own concern with this question. Unable legally to marry the man to whom she felt herself to be married, she still wanted, like a dutiful wife, to "take" his name. Since George Henry Lewes' surname was not available to her—his first "wife" had preempted it—she had to content herself with his Christian name. In this way, though she was ostensibly a lawbreaker, she was able symbolically to signal that even "so substantive and rare a creature" as Marian Evans had been properly (if only partially) "absorbed into the life of another," as, according to the laws of her society, every woman ought to be (Eliot, "Finale," *Middlemarch,* p. 894).

23. Emery observes that at the end of *Silas Marner* "it is almost as though Eppie and her father were being married" (*George Eliot's Creative Conflict,* p. 70). Similarly, Sadoff suggests that Eliot "portrays . . . daughterly desire as fabled fantasy in *Silas Marner* and *Felix Holt,*" adding in a general analysis of the (father-daughter) "scene of seduction" that "the story the daughter relates about this scene, this moment in her history, symbolizes the emergence of her sexuality expressed as desire for her father and represents her attempt to solve this enigma of childhood history" (*Monsters of Affection,* pp. 78, 104). Although Sadoff cites an early, unpublished version of my "Life's Empty Pack" essay as making some of the same points she makes, we differ radically in our interpretation of the meaning that the female Oedipus complex has for Eliot and other culture-mothers. Sadoff takes as a given the "emergence" of female sexuality and its inevitable expression as "daughterly desire"; I am interested in the coercive cultural construction of "daughterly desire," a point Mitchell emphasizes when she remarks that "the father, so crucial for the development of femininity, and the men that follow him, so essential for the preservation of 'normal' womanhood, are only secondary figures, for pride of place as love-object is taken by the mother—for both sexes [so that] in a sense, the father is only second-best anyway" (*Psychoanalysis and Feminism* [New York, 1975], p. 111; all further references to this work, abbreviated *PF,* will be included in the text).

24. Haight, *George Eliot,* p. 49.

25. Eliot, "Brother and Sister," *The Poems of George Eliot* (New York, n.d.), pp. 356, 357.

26. James Joyce, *Ulysses* (New York, 1934), p. 205; on the significance of the name "Cass," see Knoepflmacher, *George Eliot's Early Novels,* p. 239.

27. Because of her metonymic as well as coincidental connection with the gold stolen by Godfrey Cass' brother Dunstan, Eppie represents the law in yet another way, reinforcing our sense that its curses as well as its blessings cannot be averted. The place in society that Silas' false brother, William *Dane*, stole from him is ironically restored to him through an act of theft perpetrated by Godfrey's false brother, *Duns*tan Cass. Though he has tried to flee culture on the horse Wildfire, moreover, Dunstan falls inexorably into the Stone-pits of damnation—the abyss the law has prepared for him. Similarly, his Godfree brother, who tries to flee his cultural responsibility as father, loses not one but all children and inherits an empty house, a mere shell or box (a "case," so to speak) devoid of meaning because devoid both of sons who can carry on its name and daughters who can link it into society. Even his refusal to be his prodigal brother's keeper eventually brings about Godfrey's nemesis, for it is the discovery of Dunstan's skeleton in the Stone-pits that causes this rejecting father to make his rejected proposal to Eppie. In all these cases, essentially, the machinations of murderous brothers dramatize failures of just those Mosaic Laws of the Father which should make transactions between man and man both orderly and faithful.

28. Freud, "Female Sexuality" [1931], trans. John Riviere, *Sexuality and the Psychology of Love*, p. 195; all further references to this work, abbreviated "FS," will be included in the text.

29. According to Freud, the Oedipus complex means for the girl an attachment to the father which parallels the boy's attachment to his mother; but for the girl, her attachment to the father is a "positive" phenomenon that succeeds an earlier "negative" phase in which she experiences the same "first mother-attachment" that the boy feels. When the girl learns that her mother has not "given" her a penis, however—i.e., in Lacan's sense, that the mother has not given her the power represented by the "Phallus"—she turns in disgust and despair to the father, the one who has the phallus and may therefore be able to give her some of its power (see Freud, "FS," pp. 195, 199, and passim, and "Some Psychological Consequences of the Anatomical Distinction between the Sexes"). Interestingly in this regard, Sadoff observes that a "pattern of the displaced mother occurs throughout Eliot's novels and serves the story of father-daughter seduction" (*Monsters of Affection*, p. 69).

30. Observing that "a boy's repression of his Oedipal maternal attachment (and his preoedipal dependence) seems to be *more* complete than a girl's"—in part, no doubt, because the boy can look forward to a future in which he will "have" at least a figure of the mother, Chodorow quotes Alice Balint's assertion that "the amicable loosening of the bond between daughter and mother is one of the most difficult tasks of education" (*The Reproduction of Mothering*, p. 130).

31. Aeschylus, *The Eumenides, The Oresteian Trilogy*, trans. Philip Vellacott (Harmondsworth, 1959), p. 169; this is Apollo's argument.

32. Hélène Cixous, "Sorties," trans. Ann Liddle, in *New French Feminisms: An Anthology*, ed. Elaine Marks and Isabelle de Courtivron (Amherst, Mass., 1980), p. 92.

33. Henry James to Wharton, Dec. 1912, quoted in Millicent Bell, *Edith Wharton and Henry James: The Story of Their Friendship* (New York, 1965), p. 274.

34. On the analogy between nature ("raw") and culture ("cooked"), see Lévi-Strauss, *Introduction to a Science of Mythology*, vol. 1, *The Raw and the Cooked* (New York, 1969).

35. Sylvia Plath, "The Colossus," *The Collected Poems*, ed. Ted Hughes (New York, 1981), pp. 129; "The Beekeeper's Daughter," *Collected Poems*, p. 118; and see "Electra on Azalea Path," pp. 116–17.

36. Wharton, *Summer* [with an intro. by Cynthia Griffin Wolff] (New York, 1980), p. 44; all further references to this work, abbreviated *S*, will be included in the text.

37. See Maria Cummins, *The Lamplighter* (Boston, 1854); a major best-seller in its day, it tells the story of orphaned Gerty's daughterly devotion to the adoptive father, Trueman Flint, who rescued her from poverty and starvation. For a discussion of the book's appeal in its day, see Nina Baym, *Woman's Fiction: A Guide to Novels by and About Women in America, 1820–1870* (Ithaca, N.Y., 1978), pp. 164–69.

38. Andrea Hammer's remark was made in an unpublished paper on *Summer*. Wolff notes that Charity Royall's feelings for Lucius Harney are "explicitly sexual" and her view of him "inescapably phallic" (intro. to *Summer*, p. xi).

39. It is possible that in recounting Charity's desire for Lucius Harney, Wharton is recording nostalgic details of her affair with Morton Fullerton (see R. W. B. Lewis, *Edith Wharton: A Biography* [New York, 1975], pp. 203–328). In addition, by implying that Charity at first experiences her passion for Lucius Harney as a desire for a brotherly equal, she may be meditating on Fullerton's long erotic relationship with his cousin Katharine, who had been brought up to believe she was his half-sister (see pp. 200–203). Further resonance might have been added to the relationship by the brother-sister romance of Siegmund and Sieglinde in Richard Wagner's *Die Walküre*, a work Wharton surely knew.

40. Wharton, "Beatrice Palmato," in Lewis, *Edith Wharton*, p. 548; and see pp. 544–48. For a related analysis of father-daughter incest in *Summer* and "Beatrice Palmato," see Elizabeth Ammons' suggestion that *Summer* is "Wharton's bluntest criticism of the patriarchal sexual economy" and her ensuing discussion of the two texts (*Edith Wharton's Argument with America* (Athens, Ga., 1980], p. 133; and see pp. 133–43). I agree with many points in Ammons' reading of *Summer* but do not believe that Wharton was consciously "criticizing" the "patriarchal sexual economy"; rather, like Eliot, she was transcribing a myth that nonjudgmentally (if painfully) "explains" woman's position in patriarchal culture.

41. Aeschylus, *The Eumenides*, p. 169; and see Lewis, *Edith Wharton*, p. 397.

42. Elizabeth Barrett Browning, *Aurora Leigh*, *"Aurora Leigh" and Other Poems* (London, 1978), bk. 1, II. 622–34, p. 57; Dickinson, Complete Poems, no. 722, p. 354. For a more general discussion of maternal images in the works of Barrett Browning, see Gilbert, "From Patria to Matria: Elizabeth Barrett Browning's *Risorgimento*," *PMLA* 99 (Mar. 1984): 194–211; for a discussion of Dickinson's use of such imagery, see Gilbert and Gubar, *The Madwoman in the Attic*, pp. 642–50.

43. Christiane Olivier, *Les Enfants de Jocaste: L'Empreinte de la mère* (Paris, 1980), p. 149; my translation ("Or dans [le miroir tendu par l'homme] la femme ne voit pas son image mais celle que l'homme a d'elle. Jocaste a imprime au coeur de l'homme sa trace indelebile car ce miroir ne contient que l'image d'une femme 'morte' ").

44. Helene Deutsch, *The Psychology of Women: A Psychoanalytic Interpretation*, 2 vols. (New York, 1944–45), 1:252.

45. In his essay "Fathers and Daughters," the psychoanalyst Joseph H. Smith makes a similar case for the inevitability of what I am calling "resignation" in women; see "Fathers and Daughters," *Man and World: An International Philosophical Review* 13 (1980): esp. 391 and 395. For a different formulation of the same point, see Freud, "Analysis Terminable and Interminable" [1937], trans. Riviere, *Therapy and Technique*, ed. Rieff (New York, 1963), esp. pp. 268–71. Freud's n. 14, a quotation from Sandor Ferenczi, is particularly telling in this regard: "In every male patient the sign that his castration-anxiety has been mastered . . . is a sense of equality of rights with the analyst; and every female patient . . . must have . . . become able to *submit without bitterness* to thinking in terms of her feminine role" (p. 270 n. 14; italics mine).

46. Wharton, quoted in Wolff, intro. to *Summer*, p. xv.

47. Phyllis Chesler, "Rape and Psychotherapy," in *Rape: The First Sourcebook for Women*, ed. Noreen Connell and Cassandra Wilson (New York, 1974), p. 76; Judith Lewis Herman, with Lisa Hirschman, *Father-Daughter Incest* (Cambridge, Mass., 1981), p. 110.

48. Chodorow, *The Reproduction of Mothering*, p. 132. Chodorow also notes that "sociologist Robert Winch reports that marked attachment to the opposite gender parent retards courtship progress for male college students and accelerates it for females" (p. 133); thus, the father-daughter bond is actually "healthful" for women while the mother-son bond is "unhealthy" for men.

49. Deutsch, *The Psychology of Women*, 1:252.

50. Michael E. Lamb, Margaret Tresch Owen, and Lindsay Chase-Lansdale, "The Father-Daughter Relationship: Past, Present, and Future," in *Becoming Female: Perspectives on Development*, ed. Claire B. Kopp, in collaboration with Martha Kirkpatrick (New York, 1979), p. 94.

51. Herman, with Hirschman, *Father-Daughter Incest*, pp. 12, 87, 60, 61.

52. Sadoff, *Monsters of Affection*, p. 68.

53. O. Mannoni, *Freud*, trans. Renaud Bruce (New York, 1971), p. 45.

54. Freud to Wilhelm Fliess, 31 May 1897 (no. 64), *The Origins of Psycho-Analysis: Letters to Wilhelm Fliess, Drafts and Notes: 1887–1902*, ed. Marie Bonaparte, Anna Freud, and Ernst Kris, trans. Eric Mosbacher and Strachey (New York, 1977), p. 206.

55. Freud to Fliess, 3 Oct. 1897 (no. 70), *Origins*, p. 219; and see the dreams and memories reported on pp. 215–25.

56. Freud to Fliess, 21 Sept. 1897 (no. 69), *Origins*, pp. 215–16.

57. An article in *Newsweek* in 1981 reported interviews with a number of scholars who speculated, on the basis of recently discovered documents relating to the Freud family and unpublished portions of the letters to Fliess, that Freud's anxiety about his own father "prevented him from recognizing the primal guilt of Laius"—that is, of all fathers (David Gelman, "Finding the Hidden Freud," *Newsweek*, 30 Nov. 1981, p. 67; and see pp. 64–70).

58. As Kris points out in a footnote to the Fliess letters, Freud later observed that "seduction still retains a certain aetiological importance, and I still consider that some of the psychological views expressed [in the first theory] meet the case" (*Origins*, p. 217 n.1). Herman declares that "Freud falsified his incest cases," that he named uncles instead of fathers as seducers in several instances, because he wanted to exercise "discretion" (*Father-Daughter Incest*, p. 9). The *Newsweek* article asserts that "in unpublished passages of the Fliess letters [Freud] continued to describe cases of sexual brutality by fathers" ("Finding the Hidden Freud," p. 67). In a pioneering essay on this subject, Robert Seidenberg and Evangelos Papathomopoulos discuss the pressures put on late-Victorian daughters by ill or tyrannical fathers and the implications of those pressures for *Studies on Hysteria* (see "Daughters Who Tend Their Fathers: A Literary Survey," *Psychoanalytic Study of Society* 2 [1962]: esp. 135–39).

59. Seidenberg and Papathomopoulos, "Daughters Who Tend Their Fathers," p. 150. They observe, in addition, that "the word, *Kore*, is also used to designate the female figures who act as supports, the Caryatids of the Holy Temples" (p. 150).

60. Robert Graves, quoted in ibid., p. 151.

61. Percy Bysshe Shelley, *The Cenci, Poetical Works,* ed. Thomas Hutchinson (New York, 1967), act. 5, sc. 4, II. 60–61, p. 332. For discussions of Eliot's views of Antigone, see Gilbert and Gubar, *The Madwoman in the Attic,* p. 494, and Redinger, *George Eliot,* pp. 314–15 and 325; both these analyses emphasize the rebellious heroine of *Antigone,* but, significantly, Eliot had the eponymous heroine of *Romola* sit for a portrait of Antigone at Colonus—the dutiful daughter.

62. Adrienne Rich, "Sibling Mysteries," *The Dream of a Common Language: Poems, 1974–1977* (New York, 1978), p. 49.

63. "Allerleirauh," *The Complete Grimm's Fairy Tales,* trans. Margaret Hunt and James Stern, rev. ed. (New York, 1972), pp. 326–27; all further references to this work, abbreviated "A," will be included in the text.

64. In a brief discussion of this tale, Herman argues that "Allerleirauh" is a version of "Cinderella"; see *Father-Daughter Incest,* p. 2. Even more interestingly, the folklorist Alan Dundes argues a connection between the plot of this story ("tale type 923, Love Like Salt"), "Cinderella," and *King Lear,* although he claims—as perhaps Sadoff would—that this basic plot functions as "*a projection of incestuous desires on the part of the daughter*" ("To Love My Father All': A Psychoanalytic Study of the Folktale Source of *King Lear,*" *Southern Folklore Quarterly* 40 [Sept.–Dec. 1976]: 355, 360; italics his).

65. Psychologically speaking, in fact, Allerleirauh's flight could even be compared to the seizures of hysteria suffered by so many of Freud's and Josef Breuer's patients, daddy's girls who sought to escape the imprisonment of the father by rejecting not only the modes and manners but also the language of "his" culture and speaking instead through a more "natural" body language.

66. To be sure, in, e.g., *Romola* and *Middlemarch* and in, e.g., *The Age of Innocence,* Eliot and Wharton, respectively, embed fantasies of female, and sometimes even matriarchal, autonomy, fantasies which clearly function as covertly compensatory gestures toward liberation from the father-daughter scripts elaborated in works like *Silas Marner* and *Summer.*

J. Hillis Miller 1928–

J. Hillis Miller, a distinguished critic and scholar, received a Ph.D. from Harvard University in 1951. He taught for more than two decades at Johns Hopkins University and fourteen years at Yale University. He is now Distinguished Professor of English and Comparative Literature at the University of California,

Irvine. At Yale with Geoffrey Hartman and Paul de Man, Miller had been vital in introducing Continental literary studies and philosophy to the Anglo-American academic community, practicing versions of deconstructive and post-structuralist criticism. Miller's work has always been at the forefront of critical discourse in the United States; in fact, his career—including a formalist dissertation, books that approach texts from a phenomenological perspective, and his present work in deconstructive criticism—epitomizes postwar American literary studies. His major works include *Charles Dickens: The World of His Novels* (1958), *The Disappearance of God* (1963), *The Poets of Reality: Six Twentieth-Century Writers* (1965), *The Form of Victorian Fiction* (1968), *Thomas Hardy: Distance and Desire* (1970), *Fiction and Repetition* (1982), *The Linguistic Moment* (1985), and *The Ethics of Reading* (1987).

The most striking aspect of Miller's work is his lucid faithfulness to literary or critical texts as he profoundly questions those texts. Throughout his career, Miller has sought in many ways for such a "metaphysical" reading of literature, but never without maintaining a close sense of the literary texts themselves. As he wrote in *Fiction and Repetition*, "A theory is all too easy to refute or deny, but a reading can be controverted only by going through the difficult task of rereading the work in question and proposing an alternative reading."

In "The Search for Grounds in Literary Study" (1985) Miller specifically returns to Matthew Arnold in the kind of rereading he is calling for. In this essay he is attempting to do several things simultaneously. First of all, he is trying to account for the *experience* of reading, to make sense of—or at least to describe—the strange, uncanny experience reading sometimes gives rise to. Second, he is trying to articulate the unconscious assumptions that govern critical writing: he argues that there are four "grounds" upon which to base reading—linguistic, social, psychological, and ontological or metaphysical—and that various critics and schools of critics assume one or the other of these. Moreover, these grounds have two striking qualities: first, they are "imperialist," by which Miller means that they tend to reduce all understanding to their own base; and second, they each occasion remarkable resistance, almost hysterical denial (in the Freudian sense of the word) in readers to other bases. A third aim of this essay is to question the larger ground of literary study, to ask why it is that literature, since Arnold's time, has been burdened with the weight of carrying and maintaining cultural values. For Miller, this is not a necessary aspect of literature, and one can, indeed, question why so many people have seen this as a function of literature. Finally, Miller is also providing a method of criticism, what he calls the "scrupulously slow reading" that Nietzsche speaks of in his call, "back to the texts!"

THE SEARCH FOR GROUNDS IN LITERARY STUDY

You ask me in what I think or have thought you going wrong: in this: that you would never take your assiette as something determined final and unchangeable for you and proceed to work away on the basis of that: but were always poking and patching and cobbling at the assiette itself—

(Matthew Arnold, *Letters to Clough*)[1]

. . . perhaps one is a philologist still, that is to say, a teacher of slow reading [*ein Lehrer des langsamen Lesens*].

(Friedrich Nietzsche, "Preface" to *Daybreak*)[2]

An important passage in George Eliot's *Daniel Deronda* (1876) speaks of the liability of the heroine, Gwendolen Harleth, to sudden, inexplicable fits of hysterical terror or of "spiritual dread." She has these fits when faced with open spaces: "Solitude in any wide scene impressed her with an undefined feeling of immeasurable existence aloof from her, in the midst of which she was helplessly incapable of asserting herself."[3]

A strange little paragraph by Maurice Blanchot entitled "Une scène primitive," "A Primitive Scene," and published just a century later, in 1976, describes a "similar" "experience," ascribed this time to a child of seven or eight standing at the window and looking at a wintry urban or suburban scene outside:

> Ce qu'il voit, le jardin, les arbres d'hiver, le mur d'une maison; tandis qu'il voit, sans doute à la manière d'un enfant, son espace de jeu, il se lasse et lentement regarde en haut vers le ciel ordinaire, avec les nuages, la lumière grise, le jour terne et sans lointain. Ce qui se passe ensuite: le ciel, le *même* ciel, soudain ouvert, noir absolument et vide absolument, révélant (comme par la vitre brisée) une telle absence que tout s'y est depuis toujours et à jamais perdu, au point que s'y affirme et s'y dissipe le savoir vertigineux que rien est ce qu'il y a, et d'abord rien au-delà.
>
> [What he saw, the garden, the winter trees, the wall of a house; while he looked, no doubt in the way a child does, at his play area, he got bored and slowly looked higher toward the ordinary sky, with the clouds, the grey light, the day flat and without distance. What happened then: the sky, the *same* sky, suddenly opened, black absolutely and empty absolutely, revealing (as if the window had been broken) such an absence that everything is since forever and for forever lost, to the point at which there was affirmed and dispersed there the vertiginous knowledge that nothing is what there is there, and especially nothing beyond.][4]

"Rien est ce qu'il y a, et d'abord rien audelà": nothing is what there is there, and first of all nothing beyond. As in the case of Wallace Stevens' "The Snow Man," where the listener and watcher in the snow, "nothing himself, beholds / Nothing that is not there and the nothing that is,"[5] the devastating experience of a transfiguration of the scene which leaves it nevertheless exactly the same, the *same* sky, is the confrontation of a nothing which somehow is, has being, and which absorbs into itself any beyond or transcendence. In this primitive scene, original and originating, for Blanchot's child, or possibly even for Blanchot as a child, the sky definitely does not open to reveal heavenly light or choirs of angels singing "Glory, glory, glory." If the effect on Gwendolen Harleth in Eliot's novel of confronting open space in solitude is sometimes hysterical outbursts, the effect on Blanchot's child of an opening of the sky which does not open is seemingly endless tears of a "ravaging joy [joie ravagéant]."

I take these details from *Daniel Deronda* and from Blanchot's little scene, quite arbitrarily, or almost quite arbitrarily, as parables for the terror or dread readers may experience when they confront a text which seems irreducibly strange, inexplicable, perhaps even mad, for example Blanchot's *Death Sentence* [*L'arrêt de mort*]. As long as we have not identified the law by which the text can be made reasonable, explicable, it is as if we have come face to face with an immeasurable existence aloof from us, perhaps malign, perhaps benign, in any case something we have not yet mastered and assimilated into what we already know. It is as if the sky had opened, while still remaining the same sky, for are not those words there on the page familiar and ordinary words, words in our own language or mother tongue, words whose meaning we know? And yet they have suddenly opened and become terrifying, inexplicable. On the one hand, our task as readers is to transfer to reading Henry James's injunction to the observer of life, the novice writer: "Try to be one of those on whom nothing is lost." A good reader, that is, especially notices oddnesses, gaps, anacoluthons, non sequiturs, apparently irrelevant details, in short, all the marks of the inexplicable, all the marks of the unaccountable, perhaps of the mad, in a text. On the other hand, the reader's task is to reduce the inexplicable to the explicable, to find its reason, its law, its ground, to make the mad sane. The task of the reader, it will be seen, is not too different from the task of the psychoanalyst.

Current criticism tends to propose one or another of the three following grounds on the basis of which the anomalies of literature may be made lawful, the unaccountable accountable: society, the more or less hidden social or ideological pressures which impose themselves on literature and reveal themselves in oddnesses; individual psychology, the more or less hidden psychic pressures which impose themselves on a work of literature and make it odd, unaccountable; language, the more or less hidden rhetorical pressures, or pressures from some torsion within language itself as such, which impose themselves on the writer and make it impossible for his work to maintain itself as an absolutely lucid and reasonable account.

The stories or *récits* of Maurice Blanchot, as well as his criticism, propose a fourth possibility. Though this possiblity is, in the case of Blanchot at least, exceedingly difficult to name in so many words, and though the whole task of the reader of Blanchot could be defined as an (perhaps impossible) attempt to make this definition clear to oneself or to others, it can be said that this fourth possibility for the disturber of narrative sanity and coherence, a disruptive energy neither society nor individual psychology nor language itself, is properly religious, metaphysical, or ontological, though hardly in a traditional or conventional way. To borrow a mode of locution familiar to readers of Blanchot it is an ontology without ontology. Nor is it to be defined simply as a species of negative theology. Blanchot gives to this "something" that enters into the words or between the words the names, among others, of it [*il*]; the thing [*la chose*]; dying [*mourir*]; the neutral [*le neutre*]; the non-presence of the eternal return [*le retour éternel*]; writing [*écrire*]; the thought [*la pensée*]; the truth [*la verité*]; the other of the other [*l'autre de l'autre*]; meaning something encountered in our relations to other people, especially relations involving love, betrayal, and that ultimate betrayal by the other of our love for him or her, the death of the other. To list these names in this way cannot possibly convey very much, except possibly, in their multiplicity and incoherence, a glimpse of the inadequacy of any one of them and of the fact that all of them must in one way or another be figurative rather than literal. What sort of "thing" is it which cannot be pinned down and labelled with one single name, so that all names for it are improper, whether proper or generic? All Blanchot's writing is a patient, continual, long-maintained attempt to answer this question, the question posed by the experience recorded in "A Primitive Scene."

Two further features may be identified of my four proposed modes of rationalizing or accounting for or finding grounds for the irrational or unaccountable in any literary account.

The first feature seems obvious enough, though it is evaded often enough to need emphasizing. This is the exclusivity or imperialism of any one of the four. Each has a mode of explanation or of grounding the anomalous in literature demands to exercise sovereign control over the others, to make the others find their ground in *it*. You cannot have all four at once or even any two of them without ultimately grounding, or rather without having already implicitly grounded, all but one in the single regal ur-explanation. Psychological explanations tend to see linguistic, religious, or social explanations as ultimately finding *their* cause in individual human psychology. Social explanations see human psychology, language, and religion as epiphenomena of underlying and determining social forces, the "real" conditions of class, production, consumption, exchange. Linguistic explanations tend to imply or even openly to assert that society, psychology, and religion are "all language," generated by language in the first place and ultimately to be explained by features of language. Metaphysical explanations see society, psychology, and language as secondary, peripheral. Each of these modes of grounding explanation asserts that it is the true "principle of reason," the true *Satz vom Grund*, the others bogus, an abyss not a ground. Each asserts a jealous will to power over the others.

The second feature of these four modes of explaining oddnesses in literature is the strong resistance each of them seems to generate in those to whom they are proposed. Their resistance, for example, to Sigmund Freud's assertion of a universal unconscious sexual etiology for neurosis is notorious, and that resistance has by no means subsided. In Marxist theory, for example that of Louis Althusser in *For Marx*, "ideology" is the name given to the imaginary structures, whereby men and women resist facing directly the real economic and social conditions of their exsitence. "Ideology, then," says Althusser, "is the expression of the relation between men and their 'world,' that is, the (overdetermined) unity of the real relation and the imaginary relation between them and their real conditions of existence."[6] There is a tremendous resistance to totalizing explanations which say, "It's all language," the resistance encountered, for example, by structuralism, semiotics, and by misunderstandings of so-called "deconstruction" today. Many people, finally, seem able to live on from day to day and year to year, even as readers of literature, without seeing religious or metaphysical questions as having any sort of force or substance. It is not the case that man is everywhere and universally a religious or metaphysical animal. George Eliot, speaking still of Gwendolen, describes eloquently the latter's resistance to two of my sovereign principles of grounding:

> She had no permanent consciousness of other fetters, or of more spiritual restraints, having always disliked whatever was presented to her under the name of religion, in the same way that people dislike arithmetic and accounts: it had raised no other emotion in her, no alarm, no longing; so that the question whether she believed it had not occurred to

> her, any more than it had occurred to her to inquire into the conditions of colonial property and banking, on which, as she had had many opportunities of knowing, the family fortune was dependent. (pp. 89–90)

Why this resistance to looking into things, including works of literature, all the way down to the bottom is so strong and so universal I shall not attempt here to explain. Perhaps it is inexplicable. Perhaps it is a general consensus that, as Conrad's Winnie Verloc in *The Secret Agent* puts it, "life doesn't stand much looking into."[7] It might be better not to know.

Is it legitimate to seek in literature a serious concern for such serious topics, to see works of literature as in one way or another interrogations of the ground, taking ground in the sense of a sustaining metaphysical foundation outside language, outside nature, and outside the human mind? The role granted to poetry or to "literature" within our culture and in particular within our colleges and universities today is curiously contradictory. The contradiction is an historical inheritance going back at least to Kant and to eighteenth-century aesthetic theory or "critical philosophy." The tradition comes down from the enlightenment through romantic literary theory and later by way of such figures as Matthew Arnold (crucial to the development of the "humanities" in American higher education) to the New Criticism and the academic humanism of our own day. On the one hand the enjoyment of poetry is supposed to be the "disinterested" aesthetic contemplation of beautiful or sublime organic forms made of words. It is supposed to be "value free," without contamination by use of the poem for any cognitive, practical, ethical, or political purposes. Such appropriations, it is said, are a misuse of poetry. According to this aestheticizing assumption one ought to be able to read Dante and Milton, for example, or Aeschylus and Shelley, without raising either the question of the truth or falsity of their philosophical and religious beliefs, or the question of the practical consequences of acting on those beliefs. Cleanth Brooks, for example, in a recent essay vigorously reaffirming the tenets of the New Criticism, presents *Paradise Lost* as a case in point: "Milton tells us in the opening lines of *Paradise Lost* that his purpose is to 'justify the ways of God to men,' and there is no reason to doubt that this was what he hoped to do. But what we actually have in the poem is a wonderful interconnected story of events in heaven and hell and upon earth, with grand and awesome scenes brilliantly painted and with heroic actions dramatically rendered. In short, generations of readers have found that the grandeur of the poem far exceeds any direct statement of theological views. The point is underscored by the fact that some readers who reject Milton's theology altogether nevertheless regard *Paradise Lost* as a great poem."[8]

On the other hand, literature has been weighted down in our culture with the burden of carrying from generation to generation the whole freight of the values of that culture, what Matthew Arnold called "the best that is known and thought in the world."[9] Cleanth Brooks elsewhere in his essay also reiterates this traditional assumption about literature. Walter Jackson Bate, in a recent polemical essay, sees specialization, including the New Criticism's specialization of close reading, as greatly weakening the humanities generally and departments of English in particular. Bate regrets the good old days (from 1930 to 1950) when departments of English taught everything under the sun but reading as such, in a modern reincarnation of the Renaissance ideal of *litterae humaniores*. The literature components of the humanities in our colleges and universities, and departments of English in particular, have with a good conscience undertaken, after hurrying through a soupçon of rhetoric and poetics, to teach theology, metaphysics, psychology, ethics, politics, social and intellectual history, even the history of science and natural history, in short, "Allerleiwissenschaft," like Carlyle's Professor Diogenes Teufelsdröck.[10]

The implicit reasoning behind this apparently blatant contradiction may not be all that difficult to grasp, though the reasoning will only reinstate the contradiction. It is just because, and only because, works of literature are stable, self-contained, value-free objects of disinterested aesthetic contemplation that they can be trustworthy vehicles of the immense weight of values they carry from generation to generation uncontaminated by the distortions of gross reality. Just because the values are enshrined in works of literature, uninvested, not collecting interest, not put out to vulgar practical use, they remain pure, not used up, still free to be reappropriated for whatever use we may want to make of them. Has not Kant in the third critique, the *Critique of Judgment,* once and for all set works of art as reliable and indispensible middle member (*Mittelglied*), between cognition (pure reason, theory, the subject of the first critique) and ethics (practical reason, praxis, ethics, the subject of the second critique)? And has not Kant defined beauty, as embodied for example in a poem, as "the symbol of morality [*Symbol der Sittlichkeit*]"?[11] Both Bate and René Wellek, the latter in another outspoken polemical essay with the nice title of "Destroying Literary Studies," invoke Kant, or rather their understanding of Kant, as having settled these matters once and for all, as if there were no more need to worry about them, and as if our understanding of Kant, or rather theirs, could safely be taken for granted: ". . . Why not," asks Bate, "turn to David Hume, the greatest skeptic in the history of thought . . . and then turn to Kant, by whom so much of this is answered?" (p. 52); "One can doubt the very existence of aesthetic experience," says Wellek, "and refuse to recognize the distinctions, clearly formulated in Immanuel Kant's *Critique of Judgment,* between the good, the true, the useful, and the beautiful."[12] So much is at stake here that it is probably a good idea to go back and read Kant for ourselves, no easy task to be sure, in order to be certain that he says what Bate and Wellek say he says.

When Matthew Arnold, the founding father, so to speak, of the American concept of the humanities, praises the virtues of disinterested contemplation, he is being faithful to the Kantian inheritance, no doubt by way of its somewhat vulgarizing distortions in Schiller. It was, and is, by no means necessary to have read Kant to be a Kantian of sorts. Arnold's full formulaic definition of criticism, in "The Function of Criticism at the Present Time" (1864), is "a disinterested endeavour to learn and propagate the best that is known and thought in the world."[13] He speaks elsewhere in the same essay of the "disinterested love of a free play of the mind on all subjects, for its own sake."[14] When Arnold, in a well-known statement in "The Study of Poetry" (1880) which has echoed down the decades as the implicit credo of many American departments of English, says: "The future of poetry is immense, because in poetry, where it is worthy of its high destinies, our race, as time goes on, will find an ever surer and surer stay," he goes on to make it clear that poetry is a "stay" just because it is detached from the question of its truth or falsity as fact. Poetry can therefore replace religion when the fact fails religion. Poetry is cut off from such questions, sequestered in a realm of disinterested fiction. Just for this reason poetry is a "stay," a firm resting place when all else gives way, like a building without a solid foundation. "There is not a creed which is not shaken," says Arnold in his melancholy litany, "not an accredited dogma which is not shown to be questionable, not a received tradition which does not threaten to dissolve. Our religion has materialized itself in the fact, in the supposed fact; it has attached its emotion to the fact, and now the fact is failing it. But for poetry the idea is everything; the rest is a world of illusion, of divine illusion. Poetry attaches its emotions to the idea; the idea is the fact."[15] The image here is that of a self-sustaining linguistic fiction or illusion which holds itself up by a kind of intrinsic magic of levitation over the abyss, like an aerial floating bridge over chaos, as long as one does not poke and patch at the assiette. This bridge or platform may therefore hold up also the ideas the poem contains and the readers who sustain themselves by these ideas.

Arnold had this double or even triple notion of the staying power of poetry already in mind when, in 1848 or 1849, many years before writing "The Study of Poetry," he wrote to Arthur Hugh Clough: "Those who cannot read G[ree]k sh[ou]ld read nothing but Milton and parts of Wordsworth: the state should see to it. . . ."[16] Most Freshman and Sophomore courses in American colleges and universities in "Major English Authors" are still conceived in the spirit of Arnold's categorical dictum. The uplifting moral value of reading Milton and parts of Wordsworth, so important that it should be enforced by the highest civil authority, is initially stylistic. Arnold opposes the solemn, elevated, composing "grand" style of Homer, or, failing that, of Milton and parts of Wordsworth, to the "confused multitudinousness" (*ibid.*) of Browning, Keats, and Tennyson, the romantics and Victorians generally, excepting that part of Wordsworth. The occasion of Arnold's letter to Clough is the devastating effect on him of reading Keats's letters: "What a brute you were to tell me to read Keats's Letters. However it is over now: and reflexion resumes her power over agitation" (p. 96). From Keats Arnold turns to the Greeks, to Milton, and to those parts of Wordsworth to subdue his inner agitation as well as to protect himself from the agitation without.

Only secondary to the sustaining effect of the grand style as such are the "ideas" expressed in that style. A writer, says Arnold, "must begin with an Idea of the world in order not to be prevailed over by the world's multitudinousness" (*ibid.*, p. 97). The Idea, so to speak, is the style or, the style is the Idea, since the grand style is nothing but the notion of composure, elevation, coherence, objectivity, that is, just the characteristics of the grand style. This combination of grand elevated style and presupposed, preconceived, or pre-posited grand comprehensive Idea of the world (never mind whether it is empirically verifiable) not only composes and elevates the mind but also fences it off from the confused multitudinousness outside and the danger therefore of confused multitudinousness within. The latter, Arnold, in the "Preface" of 1853, calls "the dialogue of the mind with itself."[17] He associates it especially with the modern spirit, and fears it more than anything else. It is the dissolution of the mind's objectivity, calm, and unity with itself. This composing, lifting up, and fencing out through literature takes place, to borrow from one of the authors Arnold tells us excusively to read, as God organizes chaos in the work of creation, or as Milton, at the beginning of *Paradise Lost*, prays that his interior chaos, likened to the unformed Abyss, may be illuminated, elevated, impregnated, and grounded by the Holy Spirit or heavenly muse: "Thou from the first / Was present, and with mighty wings outspread / Dove-like satst brooding on the vast Abyss / And madst it pregnant: What in me is dark / Illumine, what is low raise and support" (*Paradise Lost*, I, 19–23).

It is only a step from Kant's image in paragraph 59 of the *Critique of Judgment* of art of poetry as *hypotyposis* [*Hypotypose*], indirect symbols of intuitions for which there is not direct expression,[18] to Hegel's assertion that sublime poetry, like parable, fable, and apologue, is characterized by the non-adequation and dissimilarity between symbol and symbolized, what he calls the *Sichnichtentsprechen beider*, the noncorrespondence of the two.[19] It is only another step beyond that to I. A. Richards' assertion, in *Principles of Literary Criticism*, with some help from Jeremy Bentham's theory of fictions, that the function of poetry is to produce an equilibrium among painfully conflicting impulses and thereby to provide fictive solutions to real psychological problems. Another step in this sequence (which is not even a progression, radicalizing or deepening, but a movement in place), takes us to Wallace Stevens' resonant formulation in the *Adagia* of what all these writers in somewhat different ways are saying: "The final belief is to believe in a fiction, which you know to be a fiction, there being nothing else. The exquisite truth is to know that it is a fiction and that you believe in it willingly."[20]

Proof that Matthew Arnold still plays an indispensible role within this sequence as the presumed base for a conservative humanism is a forceful recent article by Eugene Goodheart, "Arnold at the Present Time," with accompanying essays and responses by George Levine, Morris Dickstein, and Stuart M. Tave.[21] As is not surprising, the oppositions among these essays come down to a question of how one reads Arnold. If Goodheart grossly misrepresents "deconstruction" and the sort of "criticism as critique" I advocate (which is not surprising), he is also a bad reader or a non-reader of Arnold. Goodheart takes for granted the traditional misreading of Arnold which has been necessary to make him, as Goodheart puts it, "the inspiration of humanistic study in England and America" (p. 451). Levine, Dickstein, and Tave are, it happens, far better and more searching readers of Arnold. Adjudication of differences here is of course possible only by a response to that call, "Back to the texts!," which must be performed again and again in literary study. Nothing previous critics have said can be taken for granted, however authoritative it may seem. Each reader must do again for himself the laborious task of a scrupulous slow reading, trying to find out what the texts actually say rather than imposing on them what she or he wants them to say or wishes they said. Advances in literary study are not made by the free invention of new conceptual or historical schemes (which always turn out to be old ones anew in any case), but by that grappling with the texts which always has to be done over once more by each new reader. In the case of Arnold the poetry and prose must be read together, not assumed to be discontinuous units or an early negative stage and a late affirmative stage negating the earlier negation. Far from offering a firm "assiette" to the sort of humanism Goodheart advocates, such a careful reading of Arnold will reveal him to be a nihilist writer through and through, nihilist in the precise sense in which Nietzsche or Heidegger defines the term: as a specifically historical designation of the moment within the development of Western metaphysics when the highest values devalue themselves and come to nothing as their transcendent base dissolves:[22] "There is not a creed which is not shaken, not an accredited dogma which is not shown to be questionable, not a received tradition which does not threaten to dissolve. "I am nothing and very probably never shall be anything," said Arnold in one of the letters to Clough.[23]

A house built on sand, in this case a humanistic tradition built on the shaky foundation of a misreading of Matthew Arnold, cannot stand firmly. To put this another way, the affirmations of Goodheart, Bate, Wellek, and others like them participate inevitably in the historical movement of nihilism ("the history of the next two centuries," Nietzsche called it)[24] which they contest. Most of all they do this in the act itself of contestation. "The question arises," says Heidegger in the section on nihilism in his *Nietzsche*, "whether the innermost essence of nihilism and the power of its dominion do not consist precisely in considering the nothing merely as a nullity [*nur für etwas Nichtiges*], considering nihilism as an apotheosis of the merely vacuous [*der blossen Leere*], as a negation [*eine Verneinung*] that can be set to rights at once by an energetic affirmation."[25]

In a brilliant essay on "The Principle of Reason: The University in the Eyes of its Pupils,"[26] Jacques Derrida identifies the way the modern university and the study of literature within it are based on the domination of the Leibnizian principle of reason, what in German is called "der Satz vom Grund," the notion that everything can and should be accounted for, *Omnis veritatis reddi ratio potest*, that nothing is without reason, *nihil est sine ratione*. Following Nietzsche and Heidegger, Derrida also argues that so-called nihilism is an historical moment which is "completely symmetrical to, thus dependent on, the principle of reason" (p. 15). Nihilism arises naturally and inevitably during a period, the era of technology, when the principle of universal accountability holds sway in the organization of society and of the universities accountable to that society. "For the principle of reason," says Derrida, "may have obscurantist and nihilist effects. They can be seen more or less everywhere, in Europe and America among those who believe they are defending philosophy, literature and the humanities against these new modes of questioning that are also a new relation to language and tradition, a new affirmation, and new ways of taking responsibility. We can easily see on which side obscurantism and nihilism are lurking when on occasion great professors or representatives of prestigious institutions lose all sense of proportion and control; on such occasions they forget their principles that they claim to defend in their work and suddenly begin to heap insults, to say whatever comes into their heads on the subject of texts that they obviously have never opened or that they have encountered through a mediocre journalism that in other circumstances they would pretend to scorn" (p. 15). Obviously much is at stake here, and we must go carefully, looking before and after, testing the ground carefully, taking nothing for granted.

If such a tremendous burden is being placed on literature throughout all the period from Kant to academic humanists of our own day like Bate and Goodheart, it is of crucial importance to be sure that literature is able to bear the weight, or that it is a suitable instrument to perform its function. The question is too grave for its answer to be left untested. To raise the question of the weight-bearing capacities of the medium of poetry is of course not the only thing criticism can do or ought to do, but I claim it is one all-important task of literary study. The question in question here is not of the thematic content of or the assertions made by works of literature but of the weight-bearing characteristics of the medium of literature, that is, of language. It is a question of what the language of poetry is and does. Is it indeed solid enough and trustworthy enough to serve, according to the metaphor Kant proposes at the end of the introduction to the *Critique of Judgment*, as the fundamentally necessary bridge passing back and forth between pure cognition and moral action, between *theoria* and *praxis?* "The realm of the natural concept under the one legislation," says Kant, "and that of the concept of freedom under the other are entirely removed [*gänzlich abgesondert*] from all mutual influence [*wechselseitigen Einfluss*] which they might have on one another (each according to its fundamental laws) by the great gulf [*die grosse Kluft*] that separates the supersensible from phenomena [*das Übersinnliche von den Erscheinungen*]. The concept of freedom determines nothing in respect of the theoretical cognition of nature, and the internal concept determines nothing in respect of the practical laws of freedom. So far, then, it is not possible to throw a bridge from the one realm to the other [*eine Brücke von einem Gebiete zu dem andern hinüber zu schlagen*]"[27]

Art or the aesthetic experience is the only candidate for a possible bridge. The whole of the *Critique of Judgment* is written to test out the solidity, so to speak, of the planks by which this indispensable bridge from the realm of knowledge to the realm of moral action might be built, across the great gulf that separates them. If the "beauty" of the work of art is the sensible symbol of morality, it is, on the other hand, the sensible embodiment of the pure idea, what Hegel was to call, in a famous formulation, and in echo of Kant's word *Erscheinungen*, "the sensible shining forth of the idea [*das sinnliche 'scheinen' der Idee*]."[28] As Hegel elsewhere puts it, "art occupies the intermediate ground between the purely sensory and pure thought [*steht in der 'Mitte' zwischen der umittelbaren Sinnlichkeit und dem ideellen Gedanken*]" (*Ibid.*, I, 60, my trans.). Whether Kant or Hegel establish satisfactorily the solidity of this ground, its adequacy as a bridge, is another question, one that a full reading of Kant's third *Kritik* and of Hegel's *Ästhetik* would be necessary to answer. That the answer is affirmative does not go without saying, nor of course that it is negative either. Others are at work on this task of re-reading Kant and Hegel.

The sort of interrogation for which I am calling is neither a work of "pure theory" nor a work of pure praxis, a series of explications. It is something between those two or preparatory to them, a clearing of the ground and an attempt to sink foundations. It is "criticism" in the fundamental sense of "critique," discriminating testing out, in this case a testing of the medium of which the bridge between theory and practice is made. If criticism as critique is between theory and practice, it is also neither to be identified with hermeneutics, or the search for intentional meaning, on the one side, nor with poetics, or the theory of how texts have meaning, on the other side, though it is closely related to the latter. Critique, however, is a testing of the grounding of language in this or that particular text, not in the abstract or in abstraction from any particular case.

If this sort of investigation of the weight-bearing features of language is often an object of suspicion these days from the point of view of a certain traditional humanism, the humanism of *litterae humaniores*, it is also under attack from the other direction, from the point of view of those who see the central work of literary study as the reinsertion of the work of literature within its social context. The reproaches from the opposite political directions are strangely similar or symmetrical. They often come to the same thing or are couched in the same words. It is as if there were an unconscious alliance of the left and the right to suppress something which is the bad conscience of both a conservative humanism and a "radical" politicizing or sociologizing of the study of literature. A specific problematic is associated with the latter move, which attempts to put literature under the law of economy, under the laws of economic change and social power. I shall examine this problematic in detail elsewhere,[29] but it may be said here that the most resolute attempts to bracket linguistic considerations in the study of literature, to take the language of literature for granted and shift from the study of the relations of word with word to the study of the relations of words with things or with subjectivities, will only lead back in the end to the study of language. Any conceivable encounter with things or with subjectivities in literature or in discourse about literature must already have represented things and subjects in words, numbers, or other signs. Any conceivable representation of the relations of words to things, powers, persons, modes of production and exchange, juridical or political systems (or whatever name the presumably non-linguistic may be given) will turn out to be one or another figure of speech. As such, it will require a rhetorical interpretaion, such as that given by Marx in *Capital* and in the *Grundrisse*. Among such figures are that of mimesis, mirroring reflection or representation. This turns out to be a species of metaphor. Another such figure is that of part to whole, work to surrounding and determining milieu, text to context, container to thing contained. This relation is one variety or another of synecdoche or of metonymy. Another figure of the relation of text to social context is that of anamorphosis or of ideology, which is a species of affirmation by denial, abnegation, what Freud called *Verneinung*. Sociologists of literature still all too often do no more than set some social fact side by side with some citation from a literary work and assert that the latter reflects the former, or is accounted for by it, or is determined by it, or is an intrinsic part of it, or is grounded in it. It is just in this place, in the interpretation of this asserted liaison, that the work of rhetorical analysis is indispensable. The necessary dialogue between those practicing poetics or rhetoric and sociologists of literature have this at least in common: both tend to suppress, displace, or replace what I call the linguistic moment in literature.[30] Here, too, however, denegation is affirmation. The covering over always leaves traces behind, tracks which may be followed back to those questions about language I am raising.

Kant, once more, in the "Preface" to the *Critique of Judgment* has admirably formulated the necessity of this work of critique: "For if such a system is one day to be completed [*einmal zu Stande kommen soll*] under the general name of metaphysic. . . , the soil for the ediface [*den Boden zu diesem Gebaude*] must be explored by critique [*die Kritik*] as deep down as the foundation [*die erste Grundlage*] of the faculty of principles independent of experience, in order that it may sink in no part [*damit es nicht an irgend einem Teile sinke*], for this would inevitably bring about the downfall [*Einsturz*] of the whole" (Eng. 4; Ger. 74–75). Elsewhere, in the *Critique of Pure Reason*, the same metaphor has already been posited as the foundation of the edifice of pure thought: "But though the following out of these considerations is what gives to philosophy its peculiar dignity, we must meantime occupy ourselves with a less resplendent [*nicht so glänzenden*], but still meritorious task, namely, to level the ground, and to render it sufficiently secure for moral edifices of these majestic dimensions [*den Boden zu jenen majestätischen sittlichen Gebäuden eben und baufest zu machen*]. For this ground has been honeycombed by subterranean workings [*allerlei Maulwurfsgänge:* all sorts of mole tunnels: Smith's translation effaces the figure] which reason, in its confident but fruitless search for hidden treasures has carried out in all directions, and which threaten the security of the superstructures [*und die jenes Bauwerk unsicher machen*]."[31]

Which is critique? It is groundbreaking to be distinguished from mole-tunneling and a repair of it, as the second quotation claims, or is critique, as the first quotation affirms, the work of tunnelling itself, the underground search for bedrock which in that process hollows out the soil? Does this contradiction in Kant's formulations not have something to do with the fact that Kant uses a metaphor from art, or to put this another way, throws out a little artwork of his own in the form of an architectural metaphor, in order to define the work of criticism which is supposed to be a testing out of the very instrument of bridging of which the definition makes use? This is an example of a *mise en abyme* in the technical sense of placing within the larger sign system a miniature image of that larger one, a smaller one potentially within that, and so on, in a filling in and covering over of the abyss, gulf, or *Kluft* which is at the same time an opening of the abyss. Such a simultaneous opening and covering over is the regular law of the *mise en abyme*.

Have I not, finally, by an intrinsic and unavoidable necessity, done the same thing as Kant, with my images of bridges, tunnels, bedrock, pathways, and so on, and with my strategy of borrowing citations from Arnold, Kant, and the rest to describe obliquely my own enterprise? This somersaulting, self-constructing, self-undermining form of language, the throwing out of a bridge where no firm bedrock exists, in place of the bedrock, as, to quote Milton again, beneath the lowest deep a lower deep still opens.

I end by drawing several conclusions from what I have said, and by briefly relating what I have said to the question of genre. The first conclusion is a reiteration of my assertion that the stakes are so large in the present quarrels among students of literature that we must go slowly and circumspectly, testing the ground carefully and taking nothing for granted, returning once more to those founding texts of our modern tradition of literary study and reading them anew with patience and care. To put this another way, the teaching of philology, of that "slow reading" or *langsamen Lesen* for which Nietzsche calls, is still a fundamental responsibility of the humanities, at no time more needed than today. Second conclusion: Disagreements among students of literature can often be traced to often more covert disagreement about the presupposed ground of literature—whether that ground is assumed to be society, the self, language, or the "thing." One of these four presuppositions may be taken so for granted by a given critic that he is not even aware that it determines all his procedures and strategies of interpretation. Much will be gained by bringing the fundamental causes of these disagreements into the open. Third conclusion: Though the intellectual activity of ground-testing and of testing out the very idea of the ground or of the principle of reason, through slow reading, has a long and venerable tradition under the names of philology and of critical philosophy, nevertheless such testing has a peculiar role in the university. It is likely to seem subversive, threatening, outside the pale of what is a legitimate activity within the university, if research within the university, including research and teaching in the humanities, is all under the sovereign and unquestioned rule of the principle of reason. Nevertheless, moving forward to the necessary new affirmation and the new taking of responsibility for the humanities and within the humanities depends now, as it always has, on allowing that interrogation to take place.

This new taking of responsibility for language and literature, for the language of literature, which I am calling critique, has, finally, important implications for genre theory or for generic criticism. What I have said would imply not that generic classifications or distinctions and the use of these as a guide to interpretation and evaluation are illegitimate, without grounds, but that they are in a certain sense superficial. They do not go all the way to the ground, and the choice of a ground (or being chosen by one) may be more decisive for literary interpretation than generic distinctions and even determine those generic distinctions and their import. It is only on the grounds of a commitment to language, society, the self, or the "it," one or another of these, that generic distinctions make sense and have force. The choice of a ground determines both the definition of each genre and the implicit or explicit hierarchy among them. It is possible, it makes sense, to say "This is a lyric poem," or "This is a novel," and to proceed on the basis of that to follow certain interpretative procedures and ultimately to say, "This is a good lyric poem," or "This is a bad novel." Nevertheless, it is possible and makes sense to do these things only on the grounds of a prior commitment, perhaps one entirely implicit or even unthought, to founding assumptions about the ultimate ground on which all these genres are erected as so many different dwelling places or cultural forms for the human spirit to live in and use.

Beyond that, it might be added that what I am calling critique, in its double emphasis on rhetoric as the study of tropes, on the one hand, in a work of whatever genre, and, on the other hand, on the way any work of literature, of whatever genre, tells a story with beginning, middle, end, and underlying *logos* or *Grund* and at the same time interrupts or deconstructs that story—this double emphasis tends to break down generic distinctions and to recognize, for example, the fundamental role of tropes in novels, the way any lyric poem tells a story and can be interpreted as a narrative, or the way a work of philosophy may be read in terms of its tropological patterns or in terms of the story it tells. Much important criticism today goes against the grain of traditional generic distinctions, while at the same time perpetuating them in new ways in relation to one or another of my four grounds, just as many important works of recent primary literature do not fit easily into any one generic pigeonhole.

Notes

1. *The Letters of Matthew Arnold to Arthur Hugh Clough*, ed. H. F. Lowry (London and New York: Oxford University Press, 1932), p. 130.

2. Friedrich Nietzsche, *Daybreak: Thoughts on the Prejudices of Morality*, trans. R. J. Hollingdale (Cambridge: Cambridge University Press, 1982), p. 5, trans. slightly altered; German: Friedrich Nietzsche, *Morgenröte*, "Vorrede," *Werke in Drei Bänden*, ed. Karl Schlecta, I (Munich: Carl Hanser Verlag, 1966), 1016. Further citations will be from these editions.

3. George Eliot, *Daniel Deronda*, I, *Works*, Cabinet Edition (Edinburgh and London: William Blackwood and Sons, n. d.), Ch. 6, p. 90. Further references will be to this volume of this edition.

4. In *Première Livraison* (1976), my trans.

5. Wallace Stevens, *The Collected Poems* (New York: Alfred A. Knopf, 1954), p. 10.

6. Louis Althusser, *For Marx*, trans. Ben Brewster (New York: Vintage Books, 1970), pp. 233–34.

7. Joseph Conrad. *The Secret Agent* (Garden City, N.Y.: Doubleday, Page, 1925), p. xiii.

8. Cleanth Brooks, "The Primacy of the Author," *The Missouri Review*, 6 (1982), 162.

9. Matthew Arnold, "The Function of Criticism at the Present Time," *Lectures and Essays in Criticism, The Complete Prose Works*, ed. R. H. Super, III (Ann Arbor: The University of Michigan Press, 1962), 270.

10. See Walter Jackson Bate, "The Crisis in English Studies," *Harvard Magazine*, 85, No. 1, (1982), 46–53, esp. pp. 46–47. For a vigorous reply to Bate's essay see Paul de Man, "The Return to Philology," *The Times Literary Supplement*, No. 4, 158 (Friday, December 10, 1982), 1355–56.

11. Immanuel Kant, paragraph 59, "Of Beauty as the Symbol of Morality," *Critique of Judgment*, trans. J. H. Bernard (New York: Hafner Publishing Company, 1951), p. 196; German: *Kritik der Urteilskraft, Werkausgabe*, ed. Wilhelm Weischedel, X (Frankfurt am Main: Suhrkamp Verlag, 1979), 294.

12. René Wellek, "Destroying Literary Studies," *The New Criterion* (December 1983), p. 2.

13. Matthew Arnold, "The Function of Criticism at the Present Time," p. 282.

14. *Ibid.*, p. 268.

15. Matthew Arnold, "The Study of Poetry," *English Literature and Irish Politics, The Complete Prose Works*, ed. R. H. Super, IX (Ann Arbor: The University of Michigan Press, 1973), 161.

16. *Letters to Clough*, p. 97.

17. Matthew Arnold, *Poems*, ed. Kenneth Alott (London: Longmans, Green and Co. Ltd., 1965), p. 591.

18. See Kant, *Critique of Judgment*, eds. cit.: Eng. pp. 197–98; Ger., pp. 295–297.

19. G. W. F. von Hegel, *Aesthetics: Lectures on Fine Art*, trans. T. M. Knox, I (New York: Oxford University Press, 1975), 378; *Vorlesungen über die Ästhetik*, I (Frankfurt am Main: Suhrkamp, 1970), 486.

20. Wallace Stevens, *Opus Posthumous* (New York: Alfred A. Knopf, 1957), p. 163.

21. "The Function of Matthew Arnold at the Present Time," *Critical Inquiry*, 9 (1983), 451–516. Goodheart's essay, "Arnold at the Present Time," is on pp. 451–68.

22. See Friedrich Nietzsche, "European Nihilism," *The Will to Power*, trans. Walter Kaufmann and R. J. Hollingdale (New York: Vintage Books, 1968), pp. 5–82. These notes are dispersed in chronological order with the other notes traditionally making up *Der Wille zur Macht* in Nietzsche, "Aus dem Nachlass der Achtzigerjahre," *Werke in Drei Bänden*, III, 415–925. See also Martin Heidegger, "Nihilism," *Nietzsche*, trans. Frank A. Capuzzi, IV (San Francisco: Harper & Row, Publishers, 1982); German: *Nietzsche*, II (Pfullingen: Verlag Günther Neske, 1961), 31–256; 335–98.

23. *Letters to Clough*, p. 135.

24. *The Will to Power*, p. 3.

25. Heidegger, "Nihilism," *Nietzsche*, IV, 21; German: *Nietzsche*, II, 53.

26. Trans. Catherine Porter and Edward P. Morris, *Diacritics*, 13 (1983), 3–20.

27. Kant, *Critique of Judgment*, Eng., p. 32; Ger., p. 106.

28. Hegel, *Ästhetik*, I, 151, my trans.

29. In "Economy," in *Penelope's Web: On the External Relations of Narrative*, forthcoming.

30. A book on nineteenth- and twentieth-century poetry with that title is forthcoming from Princeton University Press.

31. Immanuel Kant, *Critique of Pure Reason*, trans. Norman Kemp Smith (New York:

St. Martin's Press, 1965), pp. 313–14; German: *Kritik der reinen Vernunft*, A (1781), p. 319; B (1787), pp. 375–76, *Werkausgabe*, ed. cit., III, 325–26. For a discussion of the image of the mole in Kant, Hegel, and Nietzsche see David Farrell Krell, "*Der Maulwurf: Die philosophische Wühlarbeit bei Kant, Hegel und Nietzsche*/The Mole: Philosophic Burrowings in Kant, Hegel, and Nietzsche," *Boundary* 2, 9 and 10 (Spring/Fall, 1981), 155–79.

Robert Burns Stepto 1945–

Robert Stepto, a leading Afro-American literary critic, received his B.A. from Trinity College in Hartford, Connecticut, in 1966 and his Ph.D. from Stanford University in 1974. Professor Stepto teaches in the English department at Yale University. His writings include *Chant of Saints* (1977); *Afro-American Literature* (1978); *From Behind the Veil* (1979); *Toward a New Century* (1981); *The Collected Papers of Sterling Brown*, Vol. I (1981); and *Selected Poems of Jay Wright* (1987).

In "Distrust of the Reader in Afro-American Narratives," Stepto describes how the black writer, who for so long had fiercely coveted the power and privilege of reading, comes to distrust writing and the reader. In this reader-response analysis, Stepto explores the critical ramifications of the black author writing for a generic American audience: not just the white reader, but all readers affected by the fictions and distortions of a society dominated by one race.

The "discourse of distrust" he posits—where black authors write about their distrust—is most clearly isolated in the differences between storytelling and storywriting. The frame tale allows the illusion of the telling of a tale, which just happens to appear in print. Although he illustrates several variations on a theme, "the basic written tale is fundamentally a framed tale in which either the framed or framing narrative depicts a black storyteller's white listener socially and morally maturing into competency." This kind of storytelling engages the reader—making the reader hear and actively participate in the making of meaning—which opens up possibilities for both writer and reader. Thus, Afro-American literature engages the reader from the framework of an oral and written tradition.

Distrust of the Reader in Afro-American Narratives

You know everything . . . A black mama birthed you, let you suck her titty, cleaned your dirty drawers, and you will look at us through paper and movie plots . . . "Now this is the way it happened," . . . I want you to write it on whatever part of your brain that ain't already covered with page print.

James Alan McPherson,
"The Story of a Scar"

One does not have to read very far into the corpus of Afro-American letters to find countless examples of the exaltation of literacy and the written word. In Frederick Douglass' *Narrative* of 1845, he proclaims that learning his "A, B, C"—and overhearing that, as a slave, he wasn't supposed to was his "pathway from slavery to freedom." In Frances E. W. Harper's "Sketches of Southern Life" (1872), the persona of the "Aunt Chloe" poem, "Learning to Read," declares:

So I got a pair of glasses,
And straight to work I went,
And never stopped till I could read
The hymns and Testament.

Then I got a little cabin,
A place to call my own—
And I felt as independent
As a queen upon her throne.

Du Bois's *The Souls of Black Folk* (1903) offers many eloquent testimonials to literacy, including the famous passage that begins, "I sit with Shakespeare and he winces not." Richard Wright's *Black Boy* (1945) is essentially the chronicle of how, as a youth, the author/persona "burned to learn to read," partly so that he might leave the South for a full, literate life upon "undreamed-of shores of knowing." Such examples appear in every period; somewhere in the canon of nearly every Afro-American writer, literacy is extolled and the written word minted as the coin of freedom's realm.

I have argued that the Afro-American quest for freedom has been more precisely a quest for freedom *and* literacy—and that this dual quest has provided not just a subject but a narrative structure for much of the culture's written literature. There is a decided value to this argument: it enables discussion of the literature and culture alike in literary terms.[1] But my focus here is quite different, not opposed but broader and dialectical. What I will argue here is that Afro-American literature has developed as much because of the culture's distrust of literacy as because of its abiding faith in it.

Let me begin with two of literacy's most fervent advocates, Frederick Douglass and Richard Wright. In the years just after the publication of his great *Narrative*, Douglass encountered hostility from friend and foe alike, apparently because of his increasing skills as a speaker and writer. In his autobiography *My Bondage and My Freedom*, he tells us that friends urged that he confine his acts of literacy to the narrow straits of what they insisted was his story, while foes declared in so many words that his literacy in and of itself made them suspect that neither his story nor Douglass himself existed. It was in response to his foes, but possibly to his friends as well, that Douglass soon composed the *Narrative*. But recall: these annoying encounters with censorship of one form or another proved to be grist not for the *Narrative*, but for the autobiography still to come. While it was Douglass' audience's distrust of him that led to the *Narrative*, it was his increasing distrust of *them* that prompted *My Bondage* as well as his newspapers, his novella, "The Heroic Slave," and his removal, in fine American form, to the "West."[2] In short, the illiteracy of the allegedly literate spurred Douglass the speaker to become also Douglass the writer and editor.

Richard Wright's career at times shows remarkable parallels to Douglass'. In what both men choose to recall of their early years in their autobiographies, the effort to gain literacy is a subject matched only by that of how each had to cloak or disavow his skills once even a measure of literacy was attained. The incidents they recall in this regard are often strikingly similar: at some point each had to find whites who were sufficiently unsuspecting to impart lessons or advice; each had to endure the distrust from and occasional betrayals by fellow blacks; each had to hide the few books they had. For each, youth was a time in which one had to learn how to perform, as it were, before unreliable audiences, white and black, especially if one aspired to a condition of literacy which, if realized and inadvertently displayed, would render those audiences all the more distrustful and hostile.

What Douglass and Wright learned as black youths in the South was just as useful to them once each gained a degree of freedom in the North. For all the obvious differences, personal and cultural, there are significant parallels between Wright's experiences among the American Communists and Douglass' among New England's abolitionists. The censoring of Wright by the Communists, for example, is unquestionably of a piece with the censorship to which Garrisonians subjected Douglass. In both cases, sympathizers, men and women who strove to see through race to the individual and to champion that individual's right to free access to literacy, became confused about the distinction between employing and exploiting an individual as a race representative. And in both cases, they were also confused about whether access to literacy for that individual was to be for their purposes or those which the individual might construe. When one thinks of how Douglass' newspapers were soon blacklisted by the Garrisonians and of how Wright was barred from Communist May Day parades, it is not difficult to see why Douglass removed to the West or why Wright expatriated to France. Friends found on "undreamed-of shores" had turned out to be the most distrustful sort of unfriendly natives.

Just as Douglass wrote his *Narrative* in response to his audience's distrust of him, so Wright composed *Uncle Tom's Children* (1938) and *Twelve Million Black Voices* (1941) partly to appease the distrust he encountered from blacks and whites alike once he came North. Similarly, Douglass' many writerly activities of the 1850s express *his* distrust of those who distrusted him, while Wright increasingly vented his own distrust of the American left, first in "Blueprint for Negro Literature" (1937), then in *Native Son* (1940), and finally in the whole of *American Hunger*, of which only the first section, *Black Boy*, was published in 1945. More specifically, *My Bondage and My Freedom* revises the *Narrative* in accord with Douglass' distrust of his audiences, much as the whole of *American Hunger* (that is, the original manuscript) revises *Black Boy*.[3]

For the most part, distrust of the American reader prompted Douglass and Wright to write, and affected the choices they made regarding what they would write about. Distrust motivated them to improve their writing skills and to venture into new areas of inquiry and writerly performance, including those which were designated by custom, ideology, and an implicit racism as the provinces of others. (In *American Hunger*, for example, Wright asks, "Didn't Lenin read bourgeois books?" and a "comrade" replies, "But you're not Lenin.") Once we consider distrust of the American reader and of American acts of reading to be a primary and pervasive motivation for Afro-American writing, we are equipped to read the autobiographies of Douglass, Wright, and many other writers in fresh and useful ways. This distrust is not merely a subject or theme of certain autobiographies. Nor is it something that exists in some festering form within the writer, or within his or her act of writing as distinct from the resulting texts. While distrust prompts some Afro-American writers to write about almost anything and everything, it has led others to write about distrust itself—to create and refine what I call a discourse of distrust. In short, a study of distrust in Afro-American writing can (and should) lead to new perceptions of the various strains and historical contours within Afro-American literature as a whole.

In the following section I offer a few of my thoughts in this regard, principally by choosing to see the distinction between distrusting writers who write and those who write about their distrust as being more precisely that between storywriters and (writing) storytellers. Part of what allows this last distinction in the requisite presence, and frequently active role, of the distrusting American reader—thinly guised as an unreliable story listener—in storytelling texts. With this in view, I then raise questions about the adequacies of the "social models" for reader-response literary analysis, especially since they do not seem to be, in Du Bois's terms, "frank and fair" about the American "race rituals" which invariably affect American acts of reading. In the concluding section, I describe the narrative strategies of several storytelling texts, mostly contemporary ones, to provide thereby a morphology of the Afro-American storytelling narrative.

The Afro-American discourse of distrust assumes many narrative forms and infiltrates many literary genres. My focus here is not on the autobiographical or confessional modes of this literature (for example, the Douglass and Wright autobiographies), or on literary essays such as Ralph Ellison's "The World and the Jug"—which is justly famous in part because it so eloquently expresses Ellison's distrust of Irving Howe as a reader of modern black fiction. Nor will I turn to poems such as Gwendolyn Brooks's "Negro Hero" or Michael Harper's "Nightmare Begins Responsibility," even though both poems are major texts largely because they portray how a "distrusting [black] self" may cope with that self as well as with those "audiences" which "read" him or her, often cavalierly or distrustingly. My concern is instead with fiction, and with coming to some understanding of why some Afro-American storywriters and novelists distrust the term "fiction," and choose to see themselves as storytellers instead of storywriters, even though they can hardly surmount the fact that they *are* writing, and that simulations of storytelling performances in written art are, no matter how artful, simulations and little more. In the texts of these writers, distrust is not so much a subject as a basis for specific narrative plottings and rhetorical strategies. Moreover, the texts are fully "about" the communicative prospects of Afro-Americans writing for American readers, black and white, given the race rituals which color reading and/or listening. If we can understand these prospects, we can have a surer sense of how American culture is developing and in what direction.

The effort to draw a distinction between storytelling and storywriting in a written Afro-American literature is by no means unique on my part. Authors and critics alike have engaged in this task for years. Novelist Gayl Jones, for example, remarks in a 1975 interview,

> . . . for me fiction and storytelling are different. I say I'm a fiction writer if I'm asked, but I really think of myself as a storyteller. When I say "fiction," it evokes a lot of different kinds of abstractions, but when I say "storyteller," it always has its human connections . . . There is always that kind of relationship between a storyteller and a hearer—the seeing of each other. The hearer has to see/hear the storyteller, but the storyteller has to see/hear the hearer, which the written tradition doesn't usually acknowledge.[4]

What Jones attempts to describe here is a mode, if not exactly a genre, in written narrative which accommodates the perfomative aesthetic or oral storytelling by fashioning characters (voices) who pose as tellers and hearers and occasion thereby certain types of narrative structuring. In acknowledging and discussing this mode, several Afro-Americanist scholars have produced a useful intrinsic criticism of storytelling within texts. I think here of John F. Callahan's essays on the "spoken in the written word," Robert O'Meally's discussions of the written "preacherly" voice, and of the recent studies which strive to make distinctions between black speech and literary dialect.[5]

However, I believe that Jones is making another point as well, one which both complicates our notion of written storytelling and challenges us to discuss the texts in ways which are not exclusively intrinsic. Jones suggests that storytelling narratives not only present voices as tellers and hearers but also coerce authors and readers (or, if you will, texts and readers) into teller-hearer relationships. In other words, storytelling narratives create "interpretive communities"[6] in which authors, texts, and readers collectively assert that telling and hearing may be occasioned by written tales, and that the distinctions between telling and writing on the one hand, and hearing and reading on the other, are far more profound than they are usually determined to be in those interpretive groupings constituted by other types of fictive narrative.

The role of the reader is the key issue here, and not just because examinations of the reader require new, less intrinsic approaches to storytelling texts. I would submit that the reader in the storytelling paradigm is what makes that model different. Many models accommodate rather easily the idea of an author or text "telling" a story but only the storytelling paradigm posits that the reader, in "constituting" himself through engaging the text, becomes a hearer, with all that that implies in terms of how one may sustain through reading the *responsibilities* of listenership as they are defined in purely performative contexts. In reading experiences occasioned by storytelling texts, the reader may be an "implied," "informed," or "competent" figure, as Wolfgang Iser, Stanley Fish, and Jonathan Culler have declared the engaged readers of most written traditions to be.[7] But within the storytelling interpretive community, implication (especially insofar as it embraces complicity), knowledge, and competency area all measured according to a different scale. That scale measures hearing, not reading, the distinction being most apparent when the acts of authoring that hearing and reading spawn are compared.

To speak of the authoring a reader performs is to refer as well to the risks assumed when a reader is invited to partake in either type of communicative event. The written traditions that encourage fiction-making incite competitive authoring; readers of these writerly texts author competing texts both when they attempt to articulate what the prompting text means (or what its author intends) and when they go the other, "deconstructionist route" and playfully mime the prompting text's apparent deviousness or meaninglessness. In either case, the risk undertaken is that the prompting text will be rightfully or wrongfully superseded by one of its competing offspring—as countenanced, of course, by the jury of "informed" authors engendered by text. Glory and probable canonization come either through angst or anxiety. In the first scenario, the reader is in varying degrees defeated as an author but left with the consolation of knowing that the competing text he can imagine (but not yet or perhaps ever fully render) has at least a pedagogic or scholarly value. In the second scenario, the reader is characteristically triumphant as an author, which is to say that the prompting text has entered the firmament precisely because its authorship has been not so much passed along as conquered. In either case, the prompting text "lives" because its authorship has been contested.

Competition of a kind occurs in storytelling, but most of the communicative impulses within that tradition discourage competition of the order found in most written traditions, and risk is defined in new terms. While fictionmaking and its kindred activities incite competitive authoring, storytelling invites comparable authoring; the "hearer" within the storytelling model is encouraged to compose what are essentially authenticating texts for the prompting story narrative.[8] What this means in part is that competition within the model is largely a matter of hearers vying with hearers as authenticators, and not one of readers attempting to create through their "reading" a stronger text than that which initiated their interpretive community. The risks that written storytelling undertakes are thus at least twofold: one is that the reader will become a hearer but not manage an authenticating response; the other is that the reader will *remain a reader* and not only belittle or reject storytelling's particular "keen disturbance,"[9] but also issue confrontational responses which sustain altogether different definitions of literature, of literacy, and of appropriate reader response. The threat to most texts in the written tradition is that readers will hasten its death.

While the risks to written storytelling are just this high, the rewards are equally great, especially in terms of the opportunities provided for authors and texts alike to be an advancing force within various literary traditions *and* a subversive factor within them as well. Subversion is probably most apparent in storytelling's persistent efforts to sustain the tenets of a performative aesthetic in an artistic medium ostensibly hostile to that aesthetic. Consider, for example, how subversive it is for storytelling to pursue various explicitly didactic strategies ("Now this is the way it happened, . . . I want you to *write* it on whatever part of your brain that ain't already covered with page print.") in an era in which most critics proclaim that "true art ignores the audience"[10] and most writers write accordingly. Subversion is also apparent in the previously discussed notion that the competent reader must become a competent *hearer* who eventually tells authenticating stories, especially since it is obviously "bad form" for any author or text to insist upon that degree of "submission" as an element of reading well. However, the most subversive, and hence most interesting, claim that storytelling makes is that, contrary to what most modern critics and even some writers tell us, it is the reader—not the author or text and certainly not the storyteller in the text—who is unreliable.

Most theories of creative reading and/or authoring offer episodes in which a devious or elusive text is grappled, if not altogether subdued, by a comparably ingenious reader. All such assaults are rationalized as a necessary, creative activity: it is the reader's lot to control or "reauthor" a text, which, by its taunting deviousness or playfulness—its *unreliability*—has actually invited the reader's aggression. Storytelling seeks to turn this model inside out. In Afro-American storytelling texts especially, rhetoric and narrative strategy combine time and again to declare that the principal unreliable factor in the storytelling paradigm is the reader (white American readers, obviously, but blacks as well), and that acts of creative communication are fully initiated not when the text is assaulted but when the reader gets "told"—or "told off"—in such a way that he or she finally begins to *hear*. It is usually in this way that most written tales express their distrust not just of readers but of official literate culture in general.[11] It is also in this way that they sustain the instructional nature of performed storytelling in a cultural context which devalues didactic art.

Wayne Booth has written, "Much of our scholarly and critical work of the highest seriousness has . . . employed . . . [a] dialectical opposition between artful showing and inartistic, merely rhetorical, telling."[12] It should not be surprising, then, to find that in American literary studies, the biographies of Mark Twain are generally superior to the critical studies of his works, that the many fine examinations of Faulkner and Ellison usually minimize their subversive activities as storytellers, and that within the realm of Afro-American letters alone, the studies of storywriters (for example, Wright and Baldwin) are both more voluminous and more thoughtful than those of storytellers (Gaines, McPherson, and Jones).[13] And so we must ask how literary history may be reconstituted to accommodate the storytelling strain in its own right.

The challenge occurs on two fronts: the intrinsic analysis of what is most minimally conceived to be the text, and the extrinsic analysis of what might be termed the text seen "large," that is, the text performing itself as well as its subversive activities. In the first case, the scholar of written literatures must consider the extent to which current *oral* literature theories illuminate the inner workings of a written text. These theories are primarily structuralist and thereby immune (for the most part) to the seductions of ferreting out intrinsic meaning or intention. It also occurs because most of the theories proceed from assumptions regarding the contextual origins of oral stories (and storytelling) which yield a critical language that usefully examines written tales as well.[14] What oral literature scholars mean in their use of familiar terms such as "theme" and "repetition" is often different from what scholars of written literatures mean, and those differences encourage fresh approaches to written literatures. To argue, for example, as Albert Lord did some twenty years ago, that a theme is not so much a "central or dominating idea" but a repeated incident or description—a "narrative building block"—is to confront most literary scholars with a new idea of thematic criticism.[15] Similarly, Harold Scheub's notion that narrative repetition finds its form in "expansible and patterned and parallel image-sets" usefully takes one beyond conventional considerations of the reiterated work or phrase or of the reworded idea.[16] Generally, what the oral literature scholars provide are methods and terms for critical discourse on the large units of narrative structure—the "macro-units," if you will—which most readily identify tales as the distilled products of various artistic impulses both collected and controlled. Since even the written Afro-American tale is similarly multigeneric in intention and often in result, it is also open to "macronic" analysis.

Regarding the extrinsic analysis of written storytelling, I should acknowledge at once that what I have just described as an intrinsic method could equally be seen as extrinsic. Oral literature scholars always assume that narratives are performed art forms and accordingly view the written texts of narratives as necessary but altogether limited approximations of complex events. When David Buchan directs our attention to the stanzaic units in Scottish ballads rather than to the stanzas themselves, he does so because the clustering of stanzas into larger structural units has a far greater bearing on the production and reception of ballads than that of the stanza itself.[17] Buchan is aware of the solitary stanza's autonomy and authority on the printed page; yet he submits not to that authority but to that of stanzas-in-performance and fashions his narrative analysis accordingly. In sum, his intrinsic analysis is distinctly extrinsic.

Nonetheless, I find it useful to distinguish between discussions of narrative structure and those of reader or listener response, and to refer to these respectively as intrinsic and extrinsic critical discourse. Written tales present at least two challenges to most reader-response theories. One is offered by the framed tale readily found in both nineteenth- and twentieth-century Afro-American writing. Framed tales by their nature invent storylisteners within their narratives and storyreaders, through their acts of reading, may be transformed into storylisteners. In tale after tale, considerable artistic energy is brought to the task of persuading the reader to constitute himself as a listener, the key issue affecting that activity being whether the reader is to pursue such self-transformations in accord with or at variance with the model of the listener found within the narrative itself. In other words, the competent reader of framed tales always must decide just how much he will or can submit to the model of listening which almost always is the dominating meta-plot of the tale. He must decide as well to what extent a refusal to submit endangers his or her competency.

What this suggests is that framed tales seem to require two kinds of "reader-response" analysis, one of teller-listener relations within the narrative, another of those relations incorporating the "outside" reader. Moreover, a full extrinsic study of a framed tale does not declare as supreme the latter analysis, as most reader-response theories aggressively do, but attempts to fashion an accommodation of both analyses. The challenge is to manage such accommodations.

Beyond this lies the specific challenge presented by the Afro-American framed tale in particular. In its depictions within narratives of demonstrably white or black listeners, and in its presumption that most of its readers are white (and specifically, white Americans), the Afro-American framed tale confronts interracial and intraracial rituals of behavior while fashioning various models of readership. While these features invariably distinguish the Afro-American framed tale from other framed tales, they do not remove these tales from the mainstream of the Afro-American written story. Tales that aren't framed are much like those that are, especially since the narrating voices within them are normally those of whites or blacks who have undergone listenership and who are now attempting storytelling at a level comparable to that which first engaged their attention. Once we acknowledge as well that non-framed Afro-American tales also assume a white readership, we may say that, in their narrative intentions and recognition of communicative prospects, both types of written tales are far more candid than the reader-response literary critics have been about how acts of listening and reading may be complicated by race.

The second kind of challenge that written storytelling presents to reader-response theories is therefore obvious: to what extent are the psychological, intersubjective, and even the social models of reader-response analysis articulate about the communicative situations black authors in the Americas have confronted for two hundred years? While something useful may be gleaned from all three models, the social models of Stanley Fish (in his most recent phase) and Steven Mailloux are the most useful, even though they are relatively underdeveloped for these purposes.[18]

Fish advances a sophisticated concept of the "authority" invested in interpretive communities by acts of reading, which is useful, for example, in suggesting how written tales manage authority in simulated performative communities. On the other hand, he seems rather naive about interpretive arbitration within those bodies comprising readership on a large scale. Mailloux criticizes Fish's notion of interpretive communities for referring only to "one aspect (though a most important one) of historical communities—shared constitutive conventions for making sense of reality" (p. 137). He argues that "More often, however, historical communities are made up of several conflicting interpretive communities," (p. 137), from which I infer that Mailloux envisions America as being made up of many historical *and* interpretive communities often contending with each other over the prime issues of which conventions are shared and which render the world real.

However, one must ask—as Afro-Americanists always must of Americanists—which working definition of community underlies Mailloux's assertion? I say "working" because quite often the bone of contention between Afro-Americanists and Americanists is less a matter of pure definition than one of how terms are put to use. For example, it is difficult to find fault with Mailloux's claim that "common ties remain the most relevant general criteria for defining community," or with what he understands "common ties" to be: "shared traditions, imposed or agreed upon behavior patterns, and common ways of making sense—that is, as traditional, regulative, and constitutive conventions" (p. 137). However, where these thoughts lead Mailloux is, I think, a curious matter, especially in light of his posture as a revisionist literary historian.

After usefully citing Jessie Bernard's definition of communities as " 'clubs' whose conventions constitute a kind of boundary-maintenance device," Mailloux then argues that

> the historical communities that fill the category of "literature" can be whole societies, but more often they are social groups based on economic organization (for example, the network of authors, publishers, periodical editors, and book reviewers), social rank (for instance, intelligentsia and governing classes), or institutional and professional position (such as English professor). (pp. 137–138)

What is exposed here is the bare outline of an all too familiar story: intentionally or not, another Americanist is shying away from confronting the role that race has played in America in creating communities (black *and* white) veritably bristling with traditional, regulative, and constitutive conventions. Should Mailloux argue that racial societal groups in America are not as pertinent or substantial as those based upon economic organization, social rank, or professional position, he would be sadly mistaken. Should he contend instead that America's racial societal groups have not "filled" the category of American literature, he would be more mistaken still. In either case, Mailloux offers no guidance on this considerable issue. Just as his new readings of Hawthorne, Melville, and Crane are illuminating but in no way reflective of the *many* historical and interpretive communities in nineteenth-century America, his social model for what might be called the American act of reading is insufficiently social.

It is quite possible that the most useful, amending model—useful especially in terms of comprehending the abiding link in America between race and readership—is to be found in rough form within the aggregate literature of the Afro-American written tale. We must therefore attempt to extract and formalize the social mode of reading collectively authored by Afro-American writers as various as Frederick Douglass, Charles Chesnutt, Jean Toomer, Zora Neale Hurston, Ralph Ellison, Ernest Gaines, Toni Morrison, Gayl Jones, James Alan McPherson, Alice Walker, and David Bradley. In doing so, we should be less concerned with offering a chronology or even a history of Afro-American literature based upon those authors than with suggesting how the "basic" written tale has been modified over time, usually in an effort to accommodate the changing subtleties of America's race rituals, so that appropriately revised models of competent readership can be advanced.

The basic written tale is fundamentally a framed tale in which either the framed or framing narrative depicts a black storyteller's white listener socially and morally maturing into competency. In thus presenting a very particular reader in the text, the basic written tale squarely addresses the issue of its probable audience while raising an issue for some or most of its readers regarding the extent to which they can or will identify with the text's "reader" while pursuing (if not always completing) their own act of reading. Where matters develop beyond this is the subject of the next section.

Let me begin by noting that while there are many white storytellers throughout the Afro-American written canon, they are always novices—freshly elevated to the rank of teller by virtue of their newly acquired competency as listeners—and never master storytellers. Many black storytellers, especially in modern and contemporary narratives, also are novices, but a few (Charles Chesnutt's Uncle Julius, Ernest Gaines's Miss Jane Pittman, David Bradley's Old Jack Hawley) are master storytellers, custodians of the prompting tales. They seem to pass from knowing to possessing the tales (as a curator "possesses" a fine painting) as they share them. We may thus recognize several tale types which are created by the presence or absence in narratives of master tellers, novice tellers, and unreliable listeners in varying combinations, and by the positioning of these figures as primary or ancillary tellers or listeners in narratives as wholes. The accompanying chart will be of assistance here.

Type A stories are the basic tales in the written storytelling tradition. By "basic" I do not mean that they are primitive or unsophisticated, or that they are numerically dominant within the canon. Rather, these are the stories in which (a) the primary narrators are black master storytellers, (b) tales of a didactic nature are told to conspicuously incompetent listeners, largely out of distrust of them, (c) the listeners are fully present as characters or voices and not as "implied" personages, (d) the tales within the stories are autobiographical only insofar as they partake of episodes from the master teller's personal history, and (e) the framed-tale structure of the narrative as a whole is fully intact and seemingly inviolate.

Type A and A′ stories differ in terms of

the race of the listener—and hence in terms of the stated or implied performative context in which the master teller's tale is told. The story types also differ as to the frequency with which they are composed as discrete written stories. While a number of type A stories appear in the canon as full-fledged narratives—such as James Alan McPherson's "Problems of Art"—they emerge more often as the tales within the type B story cited in the chart. In contrast, type A′ stories frequently are discrete stories. McPherson's "Solo Song: For Doc" and "The Story of a Scar" enhance this category, as does Zora Neale Hurston's *Their Eyes Were Watching God*.

Storytellers and Tales in Afro-American Framed Tales

TYPE A: BASIC STORY	TYPE A′: BASIC STORY WITH BLACK LISTENER
Master teller—white listener Tale, usually with veiled instructions for listener	Master teller—black listener Tale, usually with veiled instructions for listener
TYPE B: BASIC NOVICE STORY	TYPE B′: BASIC NOVICE STORY WITH BLACK NOVICES
White novice teller—readers Tale = basic story A	Black novice teller—readers Tale = basic story A′
TYPE C: NOVICE STORY II	TYPE C′: NOVICE STORY II WITH BLACK NOVICE
White novice teller—readers Tale = framing narrative of basic story A	Black novice teller—readers Tale = framing narrative of basic story A′
TYPE D: NOVICE STORY III	TYPE D′: NOVICE STORY III WITH BLACK NOVICE
White novice teller—readers Tale = type C tale varied without master teller	Black novice teller—readers Tale = type C tale varied without master teller

Type B tales are told by novice storytellers who have just recently achieved competency as listeners. This fact is important for it explains why the tale offered is basically an account of the storytelling event which occasioned the novice teller's competency, and why the master teller *and* his or her tale fully dominate that account. In other words, the novice teller is seemingly still too close to the moment when competency was achieved, and too overwhelmed by the teller, tale, and other features of that moment, to author a story which is anything other than a strict account of that moment.

The characteristics of Type B (and B′) stories are therefore as follows: (a) although the story's primary narrator is a novice teller (white or black), the black master teller is fully present as the teller of the story's tale; (b) although the novice teller may tell the tale of his or her previous incompetency to listeners situated within the tale's frame, direct address to the "listener" outside the story (the "outside" reader) is both possible and likely; (c) although the predominating autobiographical statement is still that offered by the master teller in the tale, the novice teller's self-history also has a place, sometimes a significant one, in the story as a whole; (d) although the story is normally a framed tale, with this type we begin to see improvisations upon that structure, especially in those instances where the story is repeated and otherwise developed for the needs and purposes of novellas and novels.

Two points must be stressed here, both involving story features which the basic novice's story initiates. One is that the novice teller's story is essentially autobiographical, the other is that his or her act of composing the narrative whole is a form of what I have described before as comparable storytelling. What makes the basic novice's story "basic" is that both of these features are pursued at an elementary level. Invariably, a single episode passes for autobiography, and repetition of the master teller's tale—albeit with some record of how the teller, when a listener, thwarted and/or abetted a given performance of the tale—passes for comparable telling. Once we see that these resolutions to the two most basic impulses within the novice's story are the obvious resolutions, we can also see why at least two more types of novice stories have developed. There is room in the form for a larger measure of the novice teller's autobiography and room as well for acts of comparable telling which exclude the master teller and do not repeat any of his or her specific tales. This is not to say that type B stories are unremarkable; Douglass' sole fiction, "The Heroic Slave," and Charles Chesnutt's Uncle Julius stores are type B stories, and the type B′ category includes such estimable texts as Ernest Gaines's *The Autobiography of Miss Jane Pittman*, Hurston's *Mules and Men*, McPherson's "The Story of a Dead Man," and Gayl Jones's *Corregidora*. However, these stories offer but one solution to how one may create a written art out of the storytelling event most accurately simulated in story types A and A′.

I have devised story type C chiefly to acknowledge that for some novice tellers the event (or events) of storytelling which initiated their transformation from listeners to tellers may be appropriately recognized and recounted without full reference to the tale the master teller told at that time. The tale is thus incidental to the event in some accounts; in others, no one tale stands out as central to the former listener's epiphanic experience. In the type C story, the master teller is nonetheless on the scene, though full versions of his or her story are not. This means that his or her presence in the type C story is often more figurative than literal.

These economies in the rendering of master teller and master tale alike are usually to some major purpose. In Chesnutt's "The Dumb Witness," reducing the role Julius (the master teller) and his tale play leaves a space which John (the novice teller) fills with fragments of the tale he himself has collected. On the other hand, in the "Kabnis" section of Jean Toomer's *Cane*, the great effect of Father John (the master teller) saying so little so cryptically is that the novice/persona can be that much more autobiographical in his account of the advent of his competency. In either case, the larger role the novice plays in telling every aspect of the story leads to certain manipulations or dismantlings of the basic framed-tale structure. "The Dumb Witness" is a framed tale, but the fact that John's voice dominates both the frame and the tale means that, in this particular Julius story, we cannot distinguish between the frame and the tale in terms of what Alan Dundes and other folklorists would call linguistic textures. Toomer's "Kabnis" modifies the storytelling story in precisely the opposite way. While the encounter with Father John is framed, and while differing vernaculars or textures are employed to distinguish his voice from that of the novice (and from those of the other figures assembled), there quite simply is no tale of any expected sort residing within either the frame or the language presumably created for tale telling.

These developments suggest that a new concept of comparable authoring emerges in the type C story. The manipulation of the framed-tale structure, diminution of the master tale, and virtual transformation of the master teller from voice to trope all seem to constitute acts of authorial competition; but I would contend that each of these activities is pursued in an effort to create a story that authenticates the essentials or essences of storytelling instead of the details of any one story or story event. The framed-tale structure is manipulated so that the novice teller may confirm in a fresh way that *telling grows out of listening*. Both acts are nearly simultaneously initiated by the acquisition of competency. Such confirmations may be possible in story types A and B, but because they are far better managed in structures which do not segregate acts of telling for those of listening to the degree commonly found in rigidly executed framed tales. Moreover, the cost of reducing or deleting the master tale is willingly paid if the result is a self-portrait of the novice teller that persuades us that something more has been accomplished on the order of cultural integration (or reintegration) than that of tale memorization.

This feature yields our best clue as to why the master teller appears more as trope than voice. Something has to embody the historical and/or interpretive community of which the novice teller is now presumably a part, and of which he or she now tells stories. That "something" is commonly the master teller who, in one sense, began the whole business. If the pursuit of these activities in a type C story fashions a narrative which authenticates the communal context from which master teller and tale alike emerge, and which authenticates as well the essential oneness of context, teller, and tale, then it is a good and comparable story within the tradition. If any of this is mismanaged, the aesthetics of storytelling counsel us to receive the novice teller not as a promising competitive author, but as one who is still at base an unreliable listener. This is one of the several points at which the aesthetics of storytelling also urge us to subvert our usual critical habits, for the disapproval with which we are to greet the erring novice is also to be freely bestowed upon his or her author.

Much of the description just offered for the type C story holds for the type D story as well. However, the type D story attempts comparable storytelling without the outward presence of a master teller in a narrative. What this generally means is that the historical and/or interpretive community embodied by the master teller is configured in different but comparable terms. "Comparable" is a key word here. This is not just because we are discussing modes of comparable storytelling; it is essential to see that in these stories of configurations such as family, kin, menfolk, womenfolk, the neighborhood, the black belt, the South, the ghetto, our people, and home (among others) occupy much the same space in the story that a master teller solely occupies in a type C tale. Indeed, one might say that they are identical to the master teller as signs for the same referent. However, this does not mean that master tellers are altogether absent from these stories. In many instances, it is impossible to evoke fully a given family, neighborhood, or "club" without acknowledging the storytellers who are unquestionably presences in the group. In other words, these storytellers no longer stand for the group as a whole, nor do they function as intermediaries between the group and the novice. When and if they appear in type D stories as tropes, what they configure is not so much a community as one or more of that body's shared conventions. Moreover, insofar as mediation between a community and "outsiders" occurs, it is pursued in varying degrees of explicitness by the novice teller. Central to all such mediations, especially in the type D story, is the manner in which the novice first forges, then wields, and then at strategic moments forsakes *his* distrust of outsiders. In this respect above all others, his act of mediation is yet another aspect of an attempt to manage comparable authorship.

Much of this comes clear when one thinks of the luminous figures of the South—and especially of the palpable presence of Georgia—in Toomer's *Cane*. Zora Neale Hurston's all-black town of Eatonville also is a communal context for storytelling, as are the black enclaves in Toni Morrison's novels and the Louisiana plantations in the fiction of Ernest Gaines. Each of these communities offers an unusually rich display of nearly archetypal characters, including a fair number of estimable raconteurs. And yet each of these communities looms larger than any one master teller or tale, and indeed subsumes teller and tale alike while becoming in every sense the major presence in a type D story.

I am well aware, of course, that certain texts do not neatly fall into one of my four categories, or mischievously blur them. As is often the case, there is something to be learned from such exceptions to the rule. Most of the "problem" texts are very new—some written yesterday, as it were. Many of them are long narratives—novellas or novels. Many can be usefully described as long narratives which in some measure are long precisely because they *combine* the story types just described. The texts include such acclaimed titles as Toni Morrison's *Song of Solomon* (1977), James Alan McPherson's "Elbow Room" (1977), David Bradley's *The Chaneysville Incident* (1981), and Alice Walker's *The Color Purple* (1982). The combinations achieved are various and at times stunningly comprehensive. The Bradley novel, for example, traces the career of a young historian who, after forsaking his stacks of note cards (his totems of official literacy), is transformed into an increasingly reliable listener and then into a better and better storyteller. In this fashion, the novel combines key aspects of the B′, C′, and D′ story types as it unfolds, only to become, rather remarkably, a type A basic written tale at its closure.

Stories of this sort figure in this discussion partly because they challenge my categories, but mostly because they confirm, in their storytelling *about* storytelling, that storytelling has developed its own store of artistic conventions. They are "artistic" conventions, not strictly "literary" ones, chiefly because they have their origins in both oral and written artmaking—for example, in both the oral and written versions of Frederick Douglass' story of the slave revolt hero, Madison Washington. When our contemporary writers employ these conventions, they acknowledge that a particular tradition in Afro-American writing exists, and, knowingly or not, they place themselves within it. In this way, the tradition endures, and necessarily complicates, in rich and complex ways, our thinking about the points of congruence between Afro-American and other Western literatures.

Notes

1. I pursue this argument further in "Teaching Afro-American Literature: Survey or Tradition; or, The Reconstruction of Instruction" in Dexter Fisher and Robert B. Stepto, eds., *Afro-American Literature: The Reconstruction of Instruction* (New York: MLA, 1979), pp. 8–24, and in my *From Behind the Veil: A study of Afro-American Narrative* (Urbana: University of Illinois Press, 1979).

2. For Douglass, the "West" was, in this instance, Rochester, New York.

3. Regarding the latter revision, it must be noted that while Wright composed both portions of his autobiography in the 1940s, many readers were not aware of both until the second, "American Hunger," saw print in 1977. While we can speculate about the whys and wherefores of this curious publishing history, one result of it seems clear: Wright's most explicit statement of distrust of the audiences which initially supported him was virtually suppressed for thirty years; intentionally or not, the act of reading Wright was manipulated.

4. Michael S. Harper, "Gayl Jones: An Interview," in Michael S. Harper and Robert B. Stepto, eds., *Chant of Saints: A Gathering of Afro-American Literature, Art, and Scholarship* (Urbana: University of Illinois Press, 1979), pp. 355, 374–375.

5. John F. Callahan, "Image-Making: Tradition and the Two Versions of the Autobiography of Miss Jane Pittman," *Chicago Review*, 29 (Autumn 1977), 45–62, and two as yet unpublished essays, "Storytelling Narrative and Rhetorical Tradition in Afro-American Letters" and "The Spoken in the Written Word: Narrative Form and Afro-American Personality in the Tales of Joel Chandler Harris and Charles Chesnutt"; Myron Simon, "Dunbar and Dialect Poetry," in Jay Martin, ed., *A Singer in the Dawn: Reinterpretations of Paul Laurence Dunbar* (New York: Dodd, Mead, 1975), pp. 114–134; Houston A. Baker, Jr., *The Journey Back: Issues in Black Literature and Criticism* (Chicago: University of Chicago Press, 1980), pp. 1–52, passim. This list is hardly inclusive and is only meant to be suggestive.

6. The phrase is Stanley Fish's: see his *Is There a Text in This Class?* (Cambridge, Mass.: Harvard University Press, 1980), passim, but esp. pp. 171–173.

7. Wolfgang Iser, *The Implied Reader* (Baltimore: Johns Hopkins University Press, 1974); Stanley E. Fish, *Self-Consuming Artifacts* (Berkeley: University of California Press, 1972); Jonathan Culler, *Structuralist Poetics* (Ithaca, N.Y.: Cornell University Press, 1975). Appropriate selections from these studies conveniently appear in Jane P. Tompkins, ed., *Reader-Response Criticism* (Baltimore: Johns Hopkins University Press, 1980).

8. See my discussion of authenticating narratives in *From Behind the Veil*. pp. 5, 26–31.

9. Iser's phrase; see Wolfgang Iser, "Indeterminancy and the Reader's Response," in J. H. Miller, ed., *Aspects of Narrative* (New York: Columbia University Press, 1971), p. 2.

10. Wayne C. Booth discusses this "truism" in *The Rhetoric of Fiction* (Chicago: University of Chicago Press, 1961), esp. in chap 4, pp. 89–116.

11. The "Americanness" of this Afro-American activity should be apparent. Mark Twain—to cite the most obvious example—also fashioned written tales expressing distrust of the reader. Indeed, it is fair to argue that some twentieth-century Afro-American writers (Sterling Brown and Ralph Ellison in particular) are in their storytelling as much American as Afro-American precisely because of their reading of Twain. But let us not lose sight of when this activity is distinctly "Afro-American" as well: while both traditions may pit teller against hearer in terms of country versus city, South versus North, West versus East, commonsense versus booksense, and New World versus the Old, it is mainly, and perhaps exclusively, in Afro-American letters that this match may be fully played out across the ubiquitous net of America's color line.

12. Booth, *The Rhetoric of Fiction*, p. 27.

13. The obvious exception is the rush of good work on Zora Neale Hurston.

14. Part of my point here is that new concepts for the scholar of written literatures, such as Harold Scheub's theory of the expansible image, advance one's discussion of the written tale. See Scheub, "The Technique of the Expansible Image in Xhosa Ntsomi-

Performances," *Research in African Literatures,* 1, 2 (1970), 119–146.

15. Albert Lord, "Umbundu: A Comparative Analysis," in Merlin Ennis, ed., *Umbundu: Folktales from Angola* (Boston: Beacon Press, 1962), p. xvi.

16. Scheub discusses narrative repetition at length in "Oral Narrative Process and the Use of Models, in Alan Dundes, ed., *Varia Folklorica* (Mouton, 1978), pp. 71–89. Also useful is his "Performance of Oral Narrative," in William R. Bascom, ed., *Frontiers of Folklore* (1977), pp. 54–78.

17. David Buchan, *The Ballad and the Folk* (London: Routledge and Kegan Paul, 1972), pp. 87–104.

18. I refer to Fish's "most recent phase" because I distinguish as others do between his concept of the early 1970s of the informed reader and his more recent idea of the interpretive community. See again the essays collected in *Is There a Text in This Class?* Regarding Mailloux, see his *Interpretive Conventions: The Reader in the Study of American Fiction* (Ithaca, N.Y.: Cornell University Press, 1982), pp. 126–139; further references are by page number in the text.

Barbara T. Christian 1943–

Barbara T. Christian received her B.A. from Marquette University in Milwaukee and her M.A. and Ph.D. from Columbia University. She has been extensively involved in developing and implementing programs directed at America's underprivileged and undervalued: these include the SEEK program at City College in New York for disadvantaged black and Puerto Rican students and numerous projects for black and women's communities in and around Berkeley. She was the first black woman to receive tenure at the University of California at Berkeley, where she presently teaches. She has written or edited numerous books, including *Black Women Novelists* (1983), *Teaching Guide to Accompany Black Foremothers: Three Lives* (1980), *Black Feminist Criticism* (1985), and *From the Inside Out: Afro-American Women's Literacy and the State* (1987).

In "The Race for Theory" (1988), Christian questions the need for theoretical approaches to the literary issues of Afro-American theory. She argues for the primacy of literary experience, for a kind of trueness to that experience, without the need for great amplification by theoretical discourse. She believes, further, that the academic preoccupation with theory may be detrimental to Third-World scholars, who have the great responsibility of creating institutional room for a literature that has been ignored or even suppressed by the dominant culture. In this discussion she enters a contemporary debate with Henry Louis Gates, Jr., Joyce A. Joyce, and Houston Baker concerning the place of theory in the cultural life and struggles of black America. She also joins Horace, Schlegel, Dante, Wordsworth, and many others in the debate over the value of nature versus nurture, in this case preferring the nature of literature to theoretical nurture.

The Race for Theory

I have seized this occasion to break the silence among those of us, critics, as we are now called, who have been intimidated, devalued by what I call the race for theory. I have become convinced that there has been a takeover in the literary world by Western philosopers from the old literary élite, the neutral humanists. Philosophers have been able to effect such a takeover because so much of the literature of the West has become pallid, laden with despair, self-indulgent, and disconnected. The New Philosophers, eager to understand a world that is today fast escaping their political control, have redefined literature so that the distinctions implied by that term, that is, the distinctions between everything written and those things written to evoke feeling as well as to express thought, have been blurred. They have changed literary critical language to suit their own purposes as philosophers, and they have reinvented the meaning of theory.

My first response to this realization was to ignore it. Perhaps, in spite of the egocentrism of this trend, some good might come of it. I had, I felt, more pressing and interesting things to do, such as reading and studying the history and literature of black women, a history that had been totally ignored, a contemporary literature bursting with originality, passion, insight, and beauty. But unfortunately it is difficult to ignore this new takeover, since theory has become a commodity which helps determine whether we are hired or promoted in academic institutions—worse, whether we are heard at all. Due to this new orientation, works (a word which evokes labor) have become texts. Critics are no longer concerned with literature, but with other critics' texts, for the critic yearning for attention has displaced the writer and has conceived of himself as the center. Interestingly in the first part of this century, at least in England and America, the critic was usually also a writer of poetry, plays, or novels. But today, as a new generation of professionals develops, he or she is increasingly an academic. Activities such as teaching or writing one's response to specific works of literature have, among this group, become subordinated to one primary thrust, that moment when one creates a theory, thus fixing a constellation of ideas for a time at least, a fixing which no doubt will be replaced in another month or so by somebody else's competing theory as the race accelerates. Perhaps because those who have effected the takeover have the power (although they deny it) first of all to be published, and thereby to determine the ideas which are deemed valuable, some of our most daring and potentially radical critics (and by *our* I mean black, women, third world) have been influenced, even coopted, into speaking a language and defining their discussion in terms alien to and opposed to our needs and orientation. At least so far, the creative writers I study have resisted this language.

For people of color have always theorized—but in forms quite different from the Western form of abstract logic. And I am inclined to say that our theorizing (and I intentionally use the verb rather than the noun) is often in narrative forms, in the stories we create, in riddles and proverbs, in the play with language, since dynamic rather than fixed ideas seem more to our liking. How else have we managed to survive with such spiritedness the assault on our bodies, social institutions, countries, our very humanity? And women, at least the women I grew up around, continuously speculated about the nature of life through pithy language that unmasked the power relations of their world. It is this language, and the grace and pleasure with which they played with it, that I find celebrated, refined, critiqued in the works of writers like Morrison and Walker. My folk, in other words, have always been a race for theory—though more in the form of the hieroglyph, a written figure which is both sensual and abstract, both beautiful and communicative. In my own work I try to illuminate and explain these hieroglyphs, which is, I think, an activity quite different from the creating of the hieroglyphs themselves. As the Buddhists would say, the finger pointing at the moon is not the moon.

In this discussion, however, I am more concerned with the issue raised by my first use of the term, *the race for theory*, in relation to its academic hegemony, and possibly of its inappropriateness to the energetic emerging literatures in the world today. The pervasiveness of this academic hegemony is an issue continually spoken about—but usually in hidden groups, lest we, who are disturbed by it, appear ignorant to the reigning academic élite. Among the folk who speak in muted tones are people of color, feminists, radical critics, creative writers, who have struggled for much longer than a decade to make their voices, their various voices, heard, and for whom literature is not an occasion for discourse among critics but is necessary nourishment for their people and one way by which they come to understand their lives better. Clichéd though this may be, it bears, I think, repeating here.

The race for theory, with its linguistic jargon, its emphasis on quoting its prophets, its tendency towards "Biblical" exegesis, its refusal even to mention specific works of creative writers, far less contemporary ones, its preoccupations with mechanical analyses of language, graphs, algebraic equations, its gross generalizations about culture, has silenced many of us to the extent that some of us feel we can no longer discuss our own literature, while others have developed intense writing blocks and are puzzled by the incomprehensibility of the language set adrift in literary circles. There have been, in the last year, any number of occasions on which I had to convince literary critics who have pioneered entire new areas of critical inquiry that they did have something to say. Some of us are continually harassed to invent wholesale theories regardless of the complexity of the literature we study. I, for one, am tired of being asked to produce a black feminist literary theory as if I were a mechanical man. For I believe such theory is prescriptive—it ought to have some relationship to practice. Since I can count on one hand the number of people attempting to be black feminist literary critics in the world today, I consider it presumptuous of me to invent a theory of how we *ought* to read. Instead, I think we need to read the works of our writers in our various ways and remain open to the intricacies of the intersection of language, class, race, and gender in the literature. And it would help if we share our process, that is, our practice, as much as possible since, finally, our work *is* a collective endeavor.

The insidious quality of this race for theory is symbolized for me by the very name of this special issue—Minority Discourse—a label which is borrowed from the reigning theory of the day and is untrue to the literatures being produced by our writers, for many of our literatures (certainly Afro-American literature) are central, not minor, and by the titles of many of the articles, which illuminate language as an assault on the other, rather than as possible communication, and play with, or even affirmation of another. I have used the passive voice in my last sentence construction, contrary to the rules of Black English, which like all languages has a particular value system, since I have not placed responsibility on any particular person or group. But that is precisely because this new ideology has become so prevalent among us that it behaves like so many of the other ideologies with which we have had to contend. It appears to have neither head nor center. At the least, though, we can say that the terms "minority" and "discourse" are located firmly in a Western dualistic or "binary" frame which sees the rest of the world as minor, and tries to convince the rest of the world that it *is* major, usually through force and then through language, even as it claims many of the ideas that we, its "historical" other, have known and spoken about for so long. For many of us have never conceived of ourselves only as somebody's *other*.

Let me not give the impression that by objecting to the race for theory I ally myself with or agree with the neutral humanists who see literature as pure expression and will not admit to the obvious control of its production, value, and distribution by those who have power, who deny, in other words, that literature is, of necessity, political. I am studying an entire body of literature that has been denigrated for centuries by such terms as *political*. For an entire century Afro-American writers, from Charles Chesnutt in the nineteenth century through Richard Wright in the 1930s, Imamu Baraka in the 1960s, Alice Walker in the 1970s, have protested the literary hierarchy of dominance which declares when literature is literature, when literature is great, depending on what it thinks is to its advantage. The Black Arts Movement of the 1960s, out of which Black Studies, the Feminist Literary Movement of the 1970s, and Women's Studies grew, articulated precisely those issues, which came *not* from the declarations of the New Western philosophers but from these groups' reflections on their own lives. That Western scholars have long believed their ideas to be universal has been strongly opposed by many such groups. Some of my colleagues do not see black critical writers of previous decades as eloquent enough. Clearly they have not read Wright's "Blueprint for Negro Writing," Ellison's *Shadow and Act*, Chesnutt's resignation from being a writer, or Alice Walker's "Search for Zola Neale Hurston." There are two reasons for this general ignorance of what our writer-critics have said. One is that black writing has been generally ignored in this country. Since we, as Toni Morrison has put it, are seen as a discredited people, it is no surprise, then, that our creations are also discredited, but this is also due to the fact that until recently dominant critics in the Western World have also been creative writers who have had access to the upper middle class institutions of education and until recently our writers have decidedly been excluded from these institutions and in fact have often been opposed to them. Because of the academic world's general ignorance about the literature of black people and of women, whose work too has been discredited, it is not surprising that so many of our critics think that the position arguing that literature is political begins with these New Philosophers. Unfortunately, many of our young critics do not investigate the reasons *why* that statement—literature is political—is now acceptable when before it was not; nor do we look to our own antecedents for the sophisticated arguments upon which we can build in order to change the tendency of any established Western idea to become hegemonic.

For I feel that the new emphasis on literary critical theory is as hegemonic as the world which it attacks. I see the language it creates as one which mystifies rather than clarifies our condition, making it possible for a few people who know that particular language to control the critical scene—that language surfaced, interestingly enough, just when the literature of peoples of color, of black women, of Latin Americans, of Africans began to move to "the center." Such words as *center* and *periphery* are themselves instructive. *Discourse, canon, texts,* words as latinate as the tradition from which they come, are quite familiar to me. Because I went to a Catholic Mission school in the West Indies I must confess that I cannot hear the word "canon" without smelling incense, that the word "text" immediately brings back agonizing memories of Biblical exegesis, that "discourse" reeks for me of metaphysics forced down my throat in those courses that traced *world* philosophy from Aristotle through Thomas Aquinas to Heidegger. "Periphery" too is a word I heard throughout my childhood, for if anything was seen as being at the periphery, it was those small Caribbean islands which had neither land mass nor military power. Still I noted how intensely important this periphery was, for U.S. troups were continually invading one island or another if any change in political control even seemed to be occurring. As I lived among folk for whom language was an absolutely necessary way of validating our existence, I was told that the minds of the world lived only in the small continent of Europe. The metaphysical language of the New Philosophy, then, I must admit, is repulsive to me and is one reason why I raced from philosophy to literature, since the latter seemed to me to have the possibilities of rendering the world as large and as complicated as I experienced it, as sensual as I knew it was. In literature I sensed the possibility of the integration of feeling/knowledge, rather than the split between the abstract and the emotional in which Western philosophy inevitably indulged.

Now I am being told that philosophers are the ones who write literature, that authors are dead, irrelevant, mere vessels through which their narratives ooze, that they do not work nor have they the faintest idea what they are doing; rather they produce texts as disembodied as the angels. I am frankly astonished that scholars who call themselves Marxists or post-Marxists could seriously use such metaphysical language even as they attempt to deconstruct the philosophical tradition from which their language comes. And as a student of literature, I am appalled by the sheer ugliness of the language, its lack of clarity, its unnecessarily complicated sentence constructions, its lack of pleasurableness, its alienating quality. It is the kind of writing for which composition teachers would give a freshman a resounding F.

Because I am a curious person, however, I postponed readings of black women writers I was working on and read some of the prophets of this new literary orientation. These writers did announce their dissatisfaction with some of the cornerstone ideas of their own tradition, a dissatisfaction with which I was born. But in their attempt to change the orientation of Western scholarship, they, as usual, concentrated on themselves and were not in the slightest interested in the worlds they had ignored or controlled. Again I was supposed to know *them*, while they were not at all interested in knowing *me*. Instead they sought to "deconstruct" the tradition to which they belonged even as they used the same forms, style, language of that tradition, forms which necessarily embody its values. And increasingly as I read them and saw their substitution of their philosophical writings for literary ones, I began to have the uneasy feeling that their folk were not producing any literature worth mentioning. For they always harkened back to the masterpieces of the past, again reifying the very texts they said they were deconstructing. Increasingly, as *their* way, *their* terms, *their* approaches remained central and became the means by which one defined literary critics, many of my own peers who had previously been concentrating on dealing with the other side of the equation, the reclamation and discussion of past and *present* third world literatures, were diverted into continually discussing the new literary theory.

From my point of view as a critic of contemporary Afro-American women's writing, this orientation is extremely problematic. In attemping to find the deep structures in the literary tradition, a major preoccupation of the new New Criticism, many of us have become obsessed with the nature of reading itself to the extent that we have stopped writing about literature being written today. Since I am slightly paranoid, it has begun to occur to me that the literature being produced *is* precisely one of the reasons why this new philosophical-literary-critical theory of relativity is so prominent. In other words, the literature of blacks, women of South America and Africa, etc., as overtly "political" literature was being preempted by a new Western concept which proclaimed that reality does not exist, that everything is relative, and that every text is silent about something—which indeed it must necessarily be.

There is, of course, much to be learned from exploring how we know what we know, how we read what we read, an exploration which, of necessity, can have no end. But there also has to be a "what," and that "what," when it is even mentioned by the new philosophers, are texts of the past, primarily Western male texts, whose norms are again being transferred onto third world, female texts as theories of reading proliferate. Inevitably a hierarchy has now developed between what is called theoretical criticism and practical criticism, as mind is deemed superior to matter. I have no quarrel with those who wish to philosophize about how we know what we know. But I do resent the fact that this particular orientation is so privileged and has diverted so many of us from doing the first readings of the literature being written today as well as of past works about which nothing has been written. I note, for example, that there is little work done on Gloria Naylor, that most of Alice Walker's works have not been commented on—despite the rage around *The Color Purple*—that there has yet to be an in-depth study of Frances Harper, the nineteenth-century abolitionist poet and novelist. If our emphasis on theoretical criticism continues, critics of the future may have to reclaim the writers we are now ignoring, that is, if they are even aware these artists exist.

I am particularly perturbed by the movements to exalt theory, as well, because of my own adult history. I was an active member of the Black Arts Movement of the sixties and know how dangerous theory can become. Many today may not be aware of this, but the Black Arts Movement tried to create Black Literary Theory and in doing so became prescriptive. My fear is that when Theory is not rooted in practice, it becomes prescriptive, exclusive, élitist.

An example of this prescriptiveness is the approach the Black Arts Movement took towards language. For it, blackness resided in the use of black talk which they defined as hip urban language. So that when Nikki Giovanni reviewed Paule Marshall's *Chosen Place, Timeless People*, she criticized the novel on the grounds that it was not black, for the language was too elegant, too white. Blacks, she said, did not speak that way. Having come from the West Indies where we do, some of the time, speak that way, I was amazed by the narrowness of her vision. The emphasis on *one way* to be black resulted in the works of Southern writers being seen as non-black since the black talk of Georgia does not sound like the black talk of Philadelphia. Because the ideologues, like Baraka, come from the urban centers they tended to privilege their way of speaking, thinking, writing, and to condemn other kinds of writing as not being black enough. Whole areas of the canon were assessed according to the dictum of the Black Arts Nationalist point of view, as in Addison Gayle's *The Way of the New World,* while other works were ignored because they did not fit the scheme of cultural nationalism. Older writers like Ellison and Baldwin were condemned because they saw that the intersection of Western and African influences resulted in a new Afro-American culture, a position with which many of the Black Nationalist idealogues disagreed. Writers were told that writing love poems was not being black. Further examples abound.

It is true that the Black Arts Movement resulted in a necessary and important critique both of previous Afro-American literature and of the white-established literary world. But in attempting to take over power, it, as Ishmael Reed satirizes so well in *Mumbo Jumbo,* became much like its opponent, monolithic and downright repressive.

It is this tendency towards the monolithic, monotheistic, etc., which worries me about the race for theory. Constructs like the *center* and the *periphery* reveal that tendency to want to make the world less complex by organizing it according to one principle, to fix it through an idea which is really an ideal. Many of us are particularly sensitive to monolithism since one major element of ideologies of dominance, such as sexism and racism, is to dehumanize people by stereotyping them, by denying them their variousness and complexity. Inevitably, monolithism becomes a metasystem, in which there is a controlling ideal, especially in relation to pleasure. Language as one form of pleasure is immediately restricted, and becomes heavy, abstract, prescriptive, monotonous.

Variety, multiplicity, eroticism are difficult to control. And it may very well be that these are the reasons why writers are often seen as *persona non grata* by political states, whatever form they take, since writers/artists have a tendency to refuse to give up their way of seeing the world and of playing with possibilities; in fact, their very expression relies on that insistence. Perhaps that is why creative literature, even when written by politically reactionary people, can be so freeing, for in having to embody ideas and recreate the world, writers cannot merely produce "one way."

The characteristics of the Black Arts Movement are, I am afraid, being repeated again today, certainly in the other area to which I am especially tuned. In the race for theory, feminists, eager to enter the halls of power, have attempted their own prescriptions. So often I have read books on feminist literary theory that restrict the definition of what *feminist* means and overgeneralize about so much of the world that most women as well as men are excluded. Nor seldom do feminist theorists take into account the complexity of life—that women are of many races and ethnic backgrounds with different histories and cultures and that as a rule women belong to different classes that have different concerns. Seldom do they note these distinctions, because if they did they could not articulate a theory. Often as a way of clearing themselves they do acknowledge that women of color, for example, do exist, then go on to do what they were going to do anyway, which is to invent a theory that has little relevance for us.

That tendency towards monolithism is precisely how I see the French feminist theorists. They concentrate on the female body as the means to creating a female language, since language, they say, is male and necessarily conceives of woman as other. Clearly many of them have been irritated by the theories of Lacan for whom language is phallic. But suppose there are peoples in the world whose language was invented primarily in relation to women, who after all are the ones who relate to children and teach language. Some Native American languages, for example, use female pronouns when speaking about non-gender specific activity. Who knows who, according to gender, created languages. Further, by positing the body as the source of everything French feminists return to the old myth that biology determines everything and ignore the fact that gender is a social rather than a biological construct.

I could go on critiquing the positions of French feminists who are themselves more various in their points of view than the label which is used to describe them, but that is not my point. What I am concerned about is the authority this school now has in feminist scholarship—the way it has become *authoritative discourse*, monologic, which occurs precisely because it does have access to the means of promulgating its ideas. The Black Arts Movement was able to do this for a time because of the political movements of the 1960s—so too with the French feminists who could not be inventing "theory" if a space had not been created by the Women's Movement. In both cases, both groups posited a theory that excluded many of the people who made that space possible. Hence one of the reasons for the surge of Afro-American women's writing during the 1970s and its emphasis on sexism in the black community is precisely that when the ideologues of the 1960s said *black*, they meant *black male*.

I and many of my sisters do not see the world as being so simple. And perhaps that is why we have not rushed to create abstract theories. For we know there are countless women of color, both in America and in the rest of the world to whom our singular ideas would be applied. There is, therefore, a caution we feel about pronouncing black feminist theory that might be seen as a decisive statement about Third World women. This is not to say we are not theorizing. Certainly our literature is an indication of the ways in which our theorizing, of necessity, is based on our multiplicity of experiences.

There is at least one other lesson I learned from the Black Arts Movement. One reason for its monolithic approach had to do with its desire to destroy the power which controlled black people, but it was a power which many of its ideologues wished to achieve. The nature of our context today is such that an approach which desires power singlemindedly must of necessity become like that which it wishes to destroy. Rather than wanting to change the whole model, many of us want to be at the center. It is this point of view that writers like June Jordan and Audre Lorde continually critique even as they call for empowerment, as they emphasize the fear of difference among us and our need for leaders rather than a reliance on ourselves.

For one must distinguish the desire for power from the need to become empowered—that is, seeing oneself as capable of and having the right to determine one's life. Such empowerment is partially derived from a knowledge of history. The Black Arts Movement did result in the creation of Afro-American Studies as a concept, thus giving it a place in the university where one might engage in the reclamation of Afro-American history and culture and pass it on to others. I am particularly concerned that institutions such as Black Studies and Women's Studies, fought for with such vigor and at some sacrifice, are not often seen as important by many of our black or women scholars precisely because the old hierarchy of traditional departments is seen as superior to these "marginal" groups. Yet, it is in this context that many others of us are discovering the extent of our complexity, the interrelationships of different areas of knowledge in relation to a distinctly Afro-American or female experience. Rather than having to view our world as subordinate to others, or rather than having to work as if we were hybrids, we can pursue ourselves as subjects.

My major objection to the race for theory, as some readers have probably guessed by now, really hinges on the question, "for whom are we doing what we are doing when we do literary criticism?" It is, I think, the central question today especially for the few of us who have infiltrated the academy enough to be wooed by it. The answer to that question determines what orientation we take in our work, the language we use, the purposes for which it is intended.

I can only speak for myself. But what I write and how I write is done in order to save my own life. And I mean that literally. For me literature is a way of knowing that I am not hallucinating, that whatever I feel/know *is*. It is an affirmation that sensuality is intelligence, that sensual language is language that makes sense. My response, then, is directed to those who write what I read and to those who read what I read—put concretely—to Toni Morrison and to people who read Toni Morrison (among whom I would count few academics). That number is increasing, as is the readership of Walker and Marshall. But in no way is the literature Morrison, Marshall, or Walker create supported by the academic world. Nor given the political context of our society, do I expect that to change soon. For there is no reason, given who controls these institutions, for them to be anything other than threatened by these writers.

My readings do presuppose a need, a desire among folk who like me also want to save their own lives. My concern, then, is a passionate one, for the literature of people who are not in power has always been in danger of extinction or of cooptation, not because we do not theorize, but because what we can even imagine, far less who we can reach, is constantly limited by societal structures. For me, literary criticism is promotion as well as understanding, a response to the writer to whom there is often no response, to folk who need the writing as much as they need anything. I know, from literary history, that writing disappears unless there is a response to it. Because I write about writers who are now writing, I hope to help ensure that their tradition has continuity and survives.

So my "method," to use a new "lit. crit." word, is not fixed but relates to what I read and to the historical context of the writers I read *and* to the many critical activities in which I am engaged, which may or may not involve writing. It is a learning from the language of creative writers, which is one of surprise, so that I might discover what language I might use. For my language is very much based on what I read and how it affects me, that is, on the surprise that comes from reading something that compels you to read differently, as I believe literature does. I, therefore, have no set method, another prerequisite of the new theory, since for me every work suggests a new approach. As risky as that might seem, it is, I believe, what intelligence means—a tuned sensitivity to that which is alive and therefore cannot be known until it is known. Audre Lorde puts it in a far more succinct and sensual way in her essay "Poetry is not a Luxury":

> As they become known to and accepted by us, our feelings and the honest exploration of them become sanctuaries and spawning grounds for the most radical and daring of ideas. They become a safe-house for that dif-

ference so necessary to change and the conceptualization of any meaningful action. Right now, I could name at least ten ideas I would have found intolerable or incomprehensible and frightening, except as they came after dreams and poems. This is not idle fantasy, but a disciplined attention to the true meaning of "it feels right to me." We can train ourselves to respect our feelings and to transpose them into a language so they can be shared. And where that language does not yet exist, it is our poetry which helps to fashion it. Poetry is not only dream and vision; it is the skeleton architecture of our lives. It lays the foundations for a future of change, a bridge across our fears of what has never been before.[1]

Note

1. Audre Lord, *Sister Outsider* (Trumansburg, N.Y.: The Crossing Press, 1984), 37.

PART 2

CRITICAL GUIDES TO FOUR GENERAL TOPICS

Women, Gender, and Criticism

Kristina Straub

"Seeing is believing." This old adage suggests the close connection between vision and what we believe to be the truth. Since criticism has been, among other things, an ongoing attempt to tell the truth about literature, writers, society, and people in general, it is perhaps not surprising that observation is a metaphor dear to literary critics from the eighteenth century to the present. In the early years of the eighteenth century, Joseph Addison and Richard Steele embodied this metaphor of watching in their Spectator, the persona they created to comment on English customs, social mores, and literature. The very first issue of their periodical, *The Spectator,* introduces us to their fictional observer, a man who is distinguished by his capacity to see the faults and beauties of human life and letters. Indeed, he tells us that he sees all the more clearly for not being an active participant, a part of the human show that he observes: "as Standers-by discover Blots, which are apt to escape those who are in the Game."[1] The Spectator of Addison and Steele is a fictional example of one extremely important kind of critic: the ostensibly objective observer whose authority rests upon his ability to keep his eyes focused on the object of his observations while his heart remains sympathetic, perhaps, but separate from, not implicated in what he watches. Unlike the poet who is licensed, as Sir Philip Sidney says, to write lies in the interest of a "higher truth," the critic has traditionally been bound to "objective" assessments of the objects he criticizes.

While modern critical thinking has called into question the possibility of objectivity in any strictly empirical, positivist sense, the stance of the detached observer is still very much a part of writing and reading criticism. And, indeed, this authoritative position is hard to avoid if one takes on the task of explaining, analyzing, and assessing literary texts to any audience, even an audience of one's peers. This critical model, so much a part of scholarship and teaching, implies a particular kind of power. The observer's authority depends upon his implicit or explicit superiority over the observed, or at least his detachment and separation from what he is watching. This kind of power excludes or suppresses the observer's complicity in what he observes, the sense that in critiquing what he sees he may also be criticizing his own practices or ideas. The critic's effort to understand the object of his criticism and to articulate his understanding is, therefore, never quite clear of, never quite free from the issue of his power over the object of his criticism. The position of observer implicitly makes the critic more authoritative, at least in the context of his critique, than the human object that he critiques.

I've used the masculine pronoun in the above paragraph quite deliberately, for this model of criticism is traditionally and historically masculine. A glance at the table of contexts of this text suggests that the model might be male because, in fact, many of the critics whom we consider most important today were (and are) male. What, then, is the place of women in the paradigm of critic as observer? "Don't make a spectacle out of yourself" is, as feminist critic Mary Russo points out,[2] a warning that many of us heard from our elders while we were growing up. For women, "making a spectacle" of themselves means not just being silly, but also opening themselves to attacks that focus on their sexuality and render them the objects of others' desires. The sixteen-year-old who dresses in a fashion that her mother fears will be too provocative might make a spectacle of herself in a way that, say, the male class clown does not. Exhibitionism, a delight in self-display, may be involved in the spectacle into which either gender "makes" itself, but women lose control through self-display as men do not. The point is that femininity is implicitly aligned with what is *seen*, not with the one who observes. Translated into literary and textual terms, this paradigm of women as seen and men as seers has meant that women simply have been written about more than they have written. And when women did write, they often did so with the clear sense that they were more acceptable to their largely male audiences when they were seen rather than heard. Hence, when Christine de Pisan criticizes the misogynistic objectification of women in Jean de Meun's *Romance of the Rose*, she writes, somewhat defensively, with the awareness that women are more commonly "seen" as the subjects of men's writing than as themselves in the role of critical judges. Indeed, in responding to John of Montrevil's praise of Meun's work, she claims not her own authority, but the authority given her by her male interlocutor's approval of her "reasoning," despite her "feminine debility." Gender, then, may be the subtext underlying the power relationship between the critic/observer and the object of his critical gaze, and it also informs the ways in which women seek to engage in criticism.

Many social institutions and traditions, from Freudian psychology to heterosexual romance, reinforce the traditions and institutions of criticism that give men the power of the critic/observer while positioning women as the objects of men's critical gaze. Femininity, as it has been traditionally conceived in British and American culture, complicates women's entry into the critical paradigm of observation. The criticism of detached observation is, therefore, not, by social definition, a "natural" activity for women.

Another look at the table of contents will tell you, however, that women, especially lately, *have* taken on the role of the observer/critic. Women have a long history of ambivalence about this role, and this ambivalence has produced an important tradition in women's criticism. Women since the eighteenth century—and probably before (where my expertise does not go)—have struggled both to gain and to subvert the masculinized power implicit in critical observation. They have, indeed, accepted, rejected, adapted, and/or subverted the model of the "objective" observer inherited from their male predecessors; modern feminist criticism is only the most recent and perhaps the most intentionally political manifestation of women's historical ambivalence toward the power of the critical gaze, the latest episode in a long historical process of feminine ambivalence toward the role of the critic/observer. Pisan, for instance, chooses a literal subversion of Meun's own words, turning them around to indict their own misogyny: "Just as his priest's Genius says: 'Flee! flee woman, the evil serpent lurking under the grass!' I can say: 'Flee! flee the covert malice beneath the shadow of goodness and virtue!' " Although women writers have long seen criticism's potential for empowering women's point of view and for challenging dominant social and literary conventions, their willingness to use the observer's critical stance has often been qualified by strong reservations about participating in an activity that has so constantly been one of the means of their own oppression. As a result, women who practice the critic/observer role have often done so with considerable self-consciousness about the effects of this power on others and about their own social and moral responsibility to use that power carefully.

George Eliot wields the power of critical observation with devastating authority, for instance, in "Silly Novels by Lady Novelists." Eliot's critique of several contemporary women novelists seems, at first blush, an unforgivable power play by a strong woman writer against her weaker sisters. But Eliot's criticisms, however devastating to the hapless writers who come under her critical gaze, are concerned with the gender politics of critical, literary judgment. "Silly novels by lady novelists" are all too prone, Eliot says, to confirm men in their tendencies to dismiss women's minds as shallow and their education as wasted. While Eliot condemns "the men who come to such a decision on such very superficial and imperfect observation," she also holds women's incautious assumption of authorial observation responsible for encouraging these men's bad judgment; the knowledge of the "really cultured woman" "has made her see herself and her opinions in something like just proportions; she does not make it a pedestal from which she flatters herself that she commands a complete view of men and things, but makes it a point of observation from which to form a right estimate of herself." The authority of observation must be used self-consciously, self-critically, and with an awareness of the gender politics implicit in the act of women, as an oppressed class, writing, and being read, in turn, by their male oppressors. Eliot exposes the cultural power differential between men and women that comes into play when a woman writes unself-consciously and is encouraged to do so by male critics: "The foolish vanity of wishing to appear in print, instead of being counter balanced by any consciousness of the intellectual or moral derogation implied by futile authorship, seems to be encouraged by the extremely false impression that to write *at all* is a proof of superiority in a woman." In other words, the woman writer who unwarily assumes the authoritative role of writerly observer is all too likely to be made a spectacle of by her male audience. Eliot assumes the authority of the critical observer over other women's texts in order to expose the foolish unself-consciousness with which these women help reinscribe their own cultural definition as second-rate thinkers, writers, and human beings.

Similarly, Virginia Woolf assumes the critic's role with an awareness of the gender politics implicit in critical observation as well as an awareness of the gender politics of writing. Her critique of "Mr. A's" novel confronts directly the authoritarian ego informing the masculine literary vision: "a shadow seemed to lie across the page. It was a straight dark bar, a shadow shaped something like the letter 'I.' . . . The worst of it is that in the shadow of the letter 'I' all is shapeless as mist. Is that a tree? No, it is a woman. But . . . she has not a bone in her body." Ironically, the clarity of male vision in Mr. A's novel is to blame for the reduction of women to boneless ciphers, as Woolf goes on to explain: "Then Alan got up and the shadow of Alan at once obliterated Phoebe. For Alan had views and Phoebe was quenched in the flood of his views. . . . The crisis was approaching, and so it was. It took place on the beach under the sun. It was done very openly. It was done very vigorously. Nothing could have been more indecent." The brightly lit clarity of Mr. A's novel is, in fact, an assertion of male ego that paradoxically blots out women, among other things, by the very power of its illumination.

Woolf's observations on the hypothetical Mr. A's hypothetical novel may also shed light on her own practice as a critic. As several of my students point out, with some frustration, in a recent seminar on Woolf's *A Room of One's Own* and *The Three Guineas*, Woolf asks probing and disturbing questions about relations between the genders and the sexual politics of literary and cultural institutions, but she withholds from the reader a clear sense of having the answers to these questions. For starters, she begins *A Room of One's Own* by rejecting "the first duty of a lecturer—to hand you after an hour's discourse a nugget of pure truth to wrap up between the pages of your notebooks and keep on the mantelpiece forever."[3] And Woolf ends her critical lectures on women and fiction with the observation that "truth is only to be had by laying together many varieties of error"—a formulation that frustrated our seminar's desire for a truth that we could walk out of the classroom with and put to good use in our lives. Woolf's failure to satisfy us seems less perverse, however, when considered in contrast to the smothering "I" that she identifies with masculine writing. Woolf seeks to avoid the authoritarian role of a writer whose very clarity is domination by leaving her questions open-ended and still in process in her readers' minds. The history of women writing criticism, is, in one sense, a continual and ongoing struggle to use the critic's power without replicating the structures of literary dominance that discourage women from writing in the first place.

The Little Man Who Wasn't There

Eliza Haywood published her counterpart to Addison's and Steele's famous *Spectator, The Female Spectator*, in 1745. Haywood, whose literary output runs to over eighty titles in several different literary genres, was one of the dozens of middle-class women in the first half of the eighteenth century who made subsistence livings with their pens. As Dale Spender, Mary Poovey, and other critics and historians of eighteenth-century women's writing have shown, the number of women writing in order to make or supplement an income would have been greater had the social strictures against women taking on the public role of a published author been less pervasive and less effective.[4] Women's place, according to eighteenth-century thinking about femininity, was in the home, and women who ventured to do work which took them down from their domestic pedestals as wives, mothers, and daughters and placed them in the public eye often met with harsh criticism, even social ostracism. Not all women had the sort of "home" that was supposed to protect and support them, however, and Haywood was one of many women whose inclinations to publish might have been encouraged by financial need. Her literary efforts brought her a living of sorts, but they also exposed her to attacks such as Alexander Pope's in *The Dunciad*, in which Haywood is depicted as the cowlike, sluttish prize won in a pissing contest by publishers that Pope despised. Haywood knew through first hand experience what it was like to be made a spectacle of, and *The Female Spectator* shows her self-consciousness about making a spectacle out of others.

Addison begins the first issue of *The Spectator* by allowing his readers a peep at the fictional Spectator, who introduces himself in concession to this readers' curiosity: "I HAVE observed, that a Reader seldom peruses a Book with Pleasure 'till he knows whether the Writer of it be a black or a fair Man, of a mild or choleric Disposition, Married or a Batchelor, with other Particulars of the like nature, that conduce very much to the right Understanding of an Author" (I: 1). Haywood begins her *Spectator* "in imitation of my learned Brother, of ever precious memory," by giving a similarly incomplete portrait of her persona. Like her brother Spectator, the Female Spectator does not allow readers too much knowledge of her, a knowledge that might curtail her abilities as an anonymous observer. Unlike her brother, Haywood's persona is aware of being herself subjected to an examination: she sketches her portrait "that the reader, on *casting his eye* over the four or five first pages, may judge how far the book may, or may not be qualified to entertain" (my emphasis).[5] The Female Spectator's awareness of her role as critic/observer is never completely separate from her awareness of herself as the object of observation, the spectacle itself.

It is not surprising, therefore, that Haywood tempers the role of critic/observer with a consciousness of what it is like to be the object of criticism. In the opening issue of *The Female Spectator*, the Haywood persona explains that her qualifications as spectator are based on her complicity in, as well as on her distance from, the "scenes of vanity and folly" that will be the object of her criticisms. Addison's Spectator stresses his lack of involvement in the human scenes that are his subject: "Thus I live in the World, rather as a Spectator of Mankind, than as one of the Species; by which means I have made myself a Speculative Statesman, Soldier, Merchant, and Artisan, without ever meddling with any Practical Part in Life. I am very well versed in the Theory of an Husband, or a Father, and can discern the Errors in the Oeconomy, Business, and Diversion of others, better than those who are engaged in them" (I: 4–5). The Female Spectator, by contrast, owes her authority to involvement as well as to detachment. Her experience with people has been "general and by consequence [it] furnished me, not only with the knowledge of many occurrences, . . . but also enabled me, when the too great vivacity of my nature became tempered with reflection, to see into the secret springs which gave rise to the actions I had either heard or been witness of" (I: 2). The Female Spectator's authority to criticize depends on *both* her practical involvement in human experience and her ability to stop back and reflect on that experience. She rejects the male Spectator's too neat distinction between the observer and the observed, the critic and the social "text"—in short, between knowledge and experience.

The Female Spectator's vision is not, then, the infallible, detached gaze, but a vision informed by "reflection" upon *and* involvement in the experiences she critiques. She sees double, in the sense that her vision involves two traditionally opposed positions in criticism, the perspective of the viewer and that of the viewed, and this doubleness leads, I would argue, to a kind of critical authority that is highly self-conscious about the uses of power in language and the oppression that criticism can impose upon the critiqued. The Female Spectator tells the story of "A Certain noble person, who in his time was looked upon as the arbiter of wit" and a young author who subjects his work to the latter's critical assessment. The critic impatiently and thoughtlessly quips that the piece is so bad that the young writer should go hang himself and burn his play—the first part of which advice the devastated author then follows. Haywood's Spectator critiques as sadistic the critic's thoughtless detachment from any possible effects that his words might have: "It is certainly a fiend-like disposition to be pleased with giving pain" (I: 270). She goes on to admonish her readers to "consider who are the objects on whom we have the power of discharging our ill-humor.—Are they not such as fate has in some measure subjected to us?" (I: 273). But she also uses the power of criticism herself against the sadistic critique of the young author's piece by noting that it is illogical and ridiculous to tell a man, first, to hang himself and *then* to burn his play.

Haywood sees quite clearly that critical observation might be turned to fighting social injustices instead of functioning merely as the tool of an oppressive authoritarianism. The Female Spectator critiques, especially, the oppression of women in patriarchal culture. Following again in the footsteps of her "learned Brother," she writes, in the guise of "Cleora," a correspondent, of the abuses in women's education that keep her sex locked in ignorance. But perhaps because she is herself female, Cleora shifts from the voice of an objective observer, speaking of "the Ladies" in the third person, to the point of view of a feminine "we" who suffers from, and is therefore angry at, the inferior education imposed upon women by men: "it is therefore only the men, and the men of understanding, too, who, in effect, merit the blame of this, and are answerable for all the misconduct we are guilty of. —Why do they call us silly women, and not endeavour to make us otherwise? —God and Nature has endowed them with means, and custom has established them in the power of rendering our Minds such as they ought to be;—how highly ungenerous is it then to give us a wrong turn, and then despise us for it!" (II: 191). Haywood seizes the potential of criticism for initiating and encouraging social reform, while rejecting its tendency to subject a helpless "them" to the power of a critical "we" or "I." Her double position as woman and critic seems to have instilled in her work an acute awareness of the politics of power, especially the politics of power between the genders.

Haywood's use of the observer/critic role in *the Female Spectator* suggests a model for telling the truth that takes into account and, indeed, privileges social relation. While observation is important to the process of knowing the truth, and while abstract moral systems—ethics and religion—certainly play a role in measuring and assessing observations, the final standard by which Haywood regulates critical inquiry is social accountability. The modern feminist theorist Carol Gilligan has argued that women are more likely to base their moral decisions on the effects that the resulting action may have on other members of their social group. Men are more likely, Gilligan says, to make decisions according to an abstract set of standards and/or the effects that the decision may have on themselves.[6] Haywood's manner of criticism seems an instance of this privileging of the welfare of the group over both self and ideals. In fact, as we are told, the Female Spectator does not operate by herself; rather *The Female Spectator* is the product of a fictional committee of women—the Female Spectator, a young married woman named Mira, a widow, and Euphrosina, a young spinster—all of whom meet to discuss possible topics for publication. Unlike the male Spectator's committee, this group calls into question the solitary detachment of the Female Spectator, even calls into question the solitariness of the act of writing itself. This fiction of a community of women disperses and decentralizes the authority of the critic/observer: at one point, for instance, Mira physically removes the pen from the Female Spectator's hand when she thinks her fellow writer has gone too far in arguing a point. The Female Spectator's critical survey of truth must answer to the dictates of a community. Moreover, the well-being of that community often takes precedence over the subject of inquiry itself. The Female Spectator and her friends enter into an astrological dispute on the existence of other worlds, at one point, but the group drops the topic by unspoken consensus when it appears that arguing further might bring more distress to the group than light to the subject (III:262).

Haywood's Female Spectator uses the authority of the critic/observer's detached stance—the stance of her masculine spectatorial predecessor—to arrive at moral "readings" of human behavior. Unlike the male Spectator, however, she concurrently reshapes that authority to admit complicity with the object of criticism, to self-consciously expose and thereby regulate unconscious critical sadism, and, finally, to operate out of a relational moral system, rather than a set of abstract, ideal truths. The problem that Haywood cannot completely solve, however, is that her refashioned model of the critic/observer partakes of femininity's marginalization, its devaluation by a male-dominated intellectual community. The Female Spectator simply has less authority over her audience, particularly the male part, because she is feminine: "I had not a sufficient idea of my own capacity to imagine, that any thing offered by a Female Censor would have so much weight with the men as is requisite to make that change in their conduct and oeconomy, which I cannot help acknowledging a great many of them stand in too much need of" (III:158). If the model for critical authority is masculine, can a female critic restyle it along lines more culturally feminine without diluting the power of that authority? On the other hand, if the female critic simply puts on the masculine model of the critic/observer without revision or retailoring, does she fully put on the authority of that role? Or does she rather become a sort of intellectual transvestite, a woman dressed up in the trappings of male power?[7]

Haywood's follow-up to *The Female Spectator, The Invisible Spy* (1755) seeks to avoid both transvestism and the Female Spectator's explicitly feminine model for criticism by presenting her readers with an ambiguously gendered "spy" whose observational authority depends on a literal invisibility that magically obfuscates the issue of the observer's role in social relations: she/he is simply not there. Like the Wizard of Oz in the classic Hollywood film, the Invisible Spy conceals gender, class, all the socially defined aspects of individual identity, through magical illusion, the "Belt of Invisibility" that enables her/him to observe others without the self-identification that would inevitably tie the critic/observer into a system of gender-linked differences in public authority. And like the Wizard, who is finally unmasked as all too human, the Invisible Spy is ultimately exposed as a pleasant but dangerous illusion. Magic hides the oppressive social relations implicit in critical observation, but it does not do away with them.

Like both the Spectator and the Female Spectator, the Spy begins by acknowledging readers' desire to know who the man (or woman) behind the curtain of spectatorial authority might be. While ostensibly intending to satisfy this desire, the Spy actually substitutes a narrative of how she/he obtained the gift of invisibility for information about who or even what she/he is:

> I expect to hear an hundred different names inscribed to the Invisible,—some of which I should, perhaps be proud of, others as much ashamed to own. — Some will doubtless take me for a philosopher,—others for a fool;—with some I shall pass for a man of pleasure, with others for a stoic;—some will look upon me as a courtier,—others as a patriot;—but whether I am any one of these, or whether I am even a man or a woman, they will find it, after all their conjectures, as difficult to discover as the longitude."[8]

By blotting out personal identity, the Spy imitates the shadowy identity of the male Spectator. But her/his anonymity obfuscates gender identity as well, translating Addison's fiction of a neutral observer into terms of sexual as well as social identity. The narrative that follows tells the tale of how the Spy was given both a magic belt that allows the wearer to watch others while remaining unseen and a set of magic tablets that take on the impression of words spoken in their proximity. The latter allow the Spy to relay the audio portion of her/his observations without the distorting medium of memory. This narrative—complete with a key to the mysterious room at "the top of the house," winding staircases, magic powder, a sympathetic bell, shrinking cap, and other fairy-tale-like paraphernalia—answers the question of how they Spy came to be the critic/observer in fantastic terms that free the Spy from having to answer to gender-linked assumptions about authority. The magical belt and tablets guarantee the Spy's authority; in this fantasy realm, neither the observational talents of the male Spectator nor the communal system of moral checks and balances of the Female Spectator are necessary.

The Spy is no amoral Ariel, however, and she/he is as conscientious about the critic/observer's moral and social responsibilities as the Spectators, male and female. The Spy's purposes in writing, however fantastically achieved through magic belt and tablets, are social and didactic. Social responsibility becomes a problem to the Spy within the fiction of the narrative, however, in ways it did not for the Spectators, because of the very fantasy of invisibility. The very magic belt that releases the Spy from the gendered power relationships of criticism renders her/him ineffectual at stopping injustice. On at least two occasions, the Spy observes an injustice that could have been prevented if action were taken against it. But the Spy cannot stop injustice because of the very means that allow her/him to observe it: the anonymity afforded by being invisible. The Spy is caught in a double bind. To act against what is wrong, she/he must relinquish the power of detection, the authority of the critic/observer. A comparison with the comic-book character of Superman clarifies the Spy's handicap. Clark Kent, the reporter, observes the trouble that Superman, after a quick trip to a phonebooth, can then fix; the Spy's invisibility allows her/him to observe injustice but gives her/him no alter-ego in which to fight that injustice with direct intervention. Haywood reveals a contradiction between the otherworldly magic of her critic/observer and her/his social and moral goal of preventing injustice and protecting the oppressed. The Spy cannot protect women from the social injustices that oppress them, a failure that may gesture towards the limitations of the Spy's ability to act, like the Female Spectator, as a champion of women's rights.

The Invisible Spy's very fiction of magical powers, a fiction that seems to obfuscate the problems of gender and power, also serves to expose them. Invisibility itself gives *only* the power of observation, not the power of criticism. The magical tablets enable the Spy to record and relay her/his observations to readers, to become the critic/observer, and when this power is taken from the Spy, as it is at the end of the second and last volume, criticism ends. While the Spy retains the magic belt, she/he cannot continue as critic by invisibility alone. The use of these tablets depends, according to the magic formula, on its being periodically erased "by the breath of a virgin, of so pure an innocence as not to have even thought on the difference of sexes." This virgin, who "must exceed twelve years of age," presents a problem to the Spy who initially finds that several young ladies "tho' I dare answer for their virtue," are not sufficiently ignorant of sexual difference to suit the conditions of the magic directions (I: 8–10). The Spy solves this problem by buying and imprisoning a three-year-old girl, the daughter of a "very poor widow," for the purpose of raising her in complete ignorance of sexual difference:

> The little creature was kept in an upper-room, which had no window in it but a sky-light in the roof of the house, so could be witness of nothing that pass'd below;—her diet was thin and very sparing;—she was not permitted to sleep above half the time generally allow'd for repose, and saw no living thing but the old woman who lay with her, gave her food, and did all that was necessary about her. (I: 10–11).

When the girl turns thirteen, the Spy is able to use her for her/his purposes until she accidently sees a picture of a "lovely Youth," is attracted to him, and comes to know the "difference of the sexes." The Spy's ability to parlay observation into criticism depends on the food, sleep, and stimulus deprivation of a girl who is, past the time of her menses, kept ignorant of all sexuality. In short, the Spy's critical abilities depend on the denial of physical, emotional, mental, and sexual human status to a woman purchased by her/his superior economic power.

Haywood underscores this sordid system of class and gender oppression that supports her critic/observer's authority by having the Spy relate, almost immediately after introducing readers to the workings of her/his magic powers, the story of Alinda, a young woman who is victimized and hounded into a loveless early death by a father who insists on her total ignorance of men and sexuality and by an exploitative tutor who takes cruel advantage of this ignorance for his own sexual and economic enrichment. Alinda is sexually molested by the tutor at the age of thirteen, the same age at which the Spy begins to exploit her/his little virgin. Alinda explains that her enforced ignorance left her vulnerable to victimization: "It will perhaps seem a little strange, that a girl turned of thirteen, as I then was, should think or act in the manner I did; but the way in which I had been brought up, left me in the same ignorance and innocence as others of six or seven years old" (I: 22). She blames "the caprice and credulity of her father, and the base designs of the person appointed to be her governor and instructor" for her misery and impending death (I: 30). The Spy does not compare the treatment of Alinda by her male protectors with her/his oppressive guardianship of the little virgin, but the connection is hard to miss. Haywood reveals what the Spy conceals: that the authority of the critic/observer actually rests on power, dominance over other human beings rather than simple detachment: the empowered "spectator," in other words, oppresses and exploits the woman who enables her/him to write the "truth." Haywood uses this authority as a tool for exposing social injustice, but she also reveals the injustice and oppression of other human beings that can be implicit in the very act of "detached" criticism. The critic/observer is not simply "the little man who wasn't there," an invisible entity watching the "truth" from a neutral site, but rather a role that one cannot play without victimizing others.

Finally, the Spy's inability to continue to write after her/his little virgin sees the image of an attractive young man and feels the first stirrings of desire suggests that once a woman "looks," takes on the role of spectator, the authority of the detached spectator is rendered useless by the intervention of feminine desire. The issue of what women want and need, excluded from an "objective" (masculine) view of the world, shakes and then ends, once and for all, the cool control of a supposedly detached criticism that ignores the power differential between men and women. The little virgin and the Invisible Spy together articulate a dilemma facing women who seek to use criticism, as it has developed in Anglo-American traditions, as a means to bring the wants and needs of feminine experience into literary culture: how do women assume the stance of critic/observer without replicating the social structures of their own oppression in patriarchal culture? While detached observation may serve as a mask for masculine desire, a socially acceptable means of power over those outside of the definition of dominant masculinity, can feminine desire effectively masquerade as critical observation? For that matter, should it? Does a mere reversal of the gendered paradigm of boys-watching-girls effect the kinds of structural, basic changes in sexual politics that many feminists see as far more important and desirable than the rather dubious goal of simply dividing up the means of power between certain men and certain women? Feminist critics have often cannily avoided being "just like men," in the knowledge that accepting male standards of critical performance is not the way to empower either themselves or other women. To write criticism like a man may bring the feminist critic a measure of acceptance in a male-dominated line of work, but (as George Eliot warns the lady novelists) it also makes her into that most dangerously trivialized being—a token, the exception to the rule that women can't write criticism. The important question for feminists, then, is not how women can make themselves into critics but, rather, how criticism can be refashioned to call into question its own gender-linked premises of power and authority.

Watching the Detectives

Feminist critics do not, then, simply aspire to the masculine model of the critic/observer, to be empowered by their spectatorship whatever little virgins suffer. The question is, then, What should feminist critics be? The ambivalence that Haywood seems to have felt towards a critical model that she wants both to use for women's empowerment and that she distrusts as conducive to women's oppression does not stop with the eighteenth century, and many modern feminist critics evince a similar attraction to and distrust of the critic/observer role. At the same time, they are posed with the problem of what other role to play if not this traditionally empowering one. Sensitive to the oppressiveness of this model as it has been shaped by masculine critics, feminists seek to use its capacity for the social critique of which, as Haywood says, patriarchal culture is in all too much need. Often, like Haywood in *The Invisible Spy*, they expose the mechanisms of power and social control that underlie the supposed objectivity of criticism even as they speak with the authority traditionally granted the critic/observer. Since Kate Millett's 1970 *Sexual Politics* (a Ph.D. thesis institutionally if not philosophically within the academic tradition), feminist criticism has sought to dismantle patriarchal literary institutions from within, through the very authority of the critic supported by those institutions.

Throughout this process of disruption from within, feminist critics have sought grounds for critical authority other than the "objectivity" of the observer. The idea of women's experience has played an important part in women's criticism, and modern feminist criticism often foregrounds the issue of women's experience in the struggle to reshape criticism to fit women's needs. The modern emphasis on women's experience is not without historical precedent. Christine de Pisan, for example, claims her own particular feminine experience as a part of the "pure truth" that is missing from male assessments of femininity and feminine experience: "in that I am indeed a woman, I can better bear witness on this aspect than he who has no experience of it." George Eliot calls on women novelists to look to their own experience for the material of good fiction. Feminist critical texts such as Arlyn Diamond's and Lee R. Edward's *The Authority of Experience*, an anthology published in 1977, dismantle masculine "objectivity," and look to the woman critic's own experience and the experience of other women instead of accepting the supposedly gender-neutral but actually biased view of the dominant masculine critical tradition. The issue of "experience" is central to Jonathan Culler's reading of feminist criticism in one of the few recent, male-written texts that deal with feminist theory.[9] But the authority of women's experience as the basis for criteria for literature raises the problem of deciding what women's experience *is;* in other words, the critic consciously or unconsciously decides *whose* experience, of which women, in what circumstances, should serve as a basis for interpretation and judgement. And the feminist critic is back to the problem of assuming the authority of the observer over the women whose experiences she may not share: women of class, color, or sexual object choice other than her own.

The recent history of feminist criticism has taught us that feminists can too readily duplicate the Spy's unconscious oppression of women less empowered than those critics who are paid, however poorly, to teach and write by academic institutions. Feminist critics have, despite their subversion of the ostensibly neutral spectator model of criticism, found themselves acting as spectators—at the expense of other women less privileged than they. Black women, women of color, poor women, women of the Third World, and lesbians are often placed in the position of Haywood's little virgin by academic feminist criticism. By and large, the feminist critics whose essays are anthologized, whose books are published, whose work is recognized in the academies of America, England, and Europe are white, heterosexual, and very much privileged in relation to women who do not fit into these narrow categories. In this exclusivity, academic feminist criticism would differ from its masculine counterpart only in its awareness of gender—except for the recurring emergence, in feminist criticism, of awareness of, and attention to, power relations that can oppress and exploit any marginalized people in relation to the culturally dominant group or groups. The erasure by omission of those oppressed on grounds of race, class, and/or sexual object choice can and does make feminist criticism complicit in the very social assumptions and institutions that oppress women as well; but, like Haywood, modern feminists struggle with the aspects of their own criticism that are oppressive to other women, and the recent history of feminist criticism is marked by many instances of both collective and individual consciousness of this complicity and the need to remedy it with a heightened awareness of the differences that divide women as well as men. Like the Female Spectator, many feminist critics seek to privilege social relations between women in their critical discourse.

Collectivity plays a corrective role in many traditions and kinds of criticism: the critic/observer only *appears* to be a lone spectator in the landscape of her or his text. Despite the solitary stance of critics since the Spectator of Addison and Steele, criticism often proceeds collectively, collaboratively, with critic reminding critic of what she or he is missing or omitting.

Collective assessment of feminist criticism frequently points out feminism's responsibility to *all* the collective, to the feminist critic's responsibility to speak with an awareness of women different from her specific class, race, and sexual identification. The little virgin—what Jane Gallop has called "the other woman"[10]—must not be hidden from view, but given a voice in the writings of her more empowered sisters. Better yet, she should be listened to when she writes criticism herself. The recent history of feminist criticism is characterized by a collective struggle for the awareness and articulation of differences among women. In 1980, the journal *Feminist Studies* published Annette Kolodny's survey of feminist criticism to date, an apparently comprehensive overview essay in which she called for the acceptance of a plentiful range of feminist viewpoints, while omitting to speak of criticism written by and for lesbians, black women, and women of color. In 1982, *Feminist Studies* published heated, often angry correctives by Judith Kegan Gardiner, Elly Bulkin, and Rena Grasso Patterson reminding the readers of *Feminist Studies* that Kolodny's call for a "playful pluralism" of critical interpretation rather nonplayfully excluded criticism by black women, women of color and lesbians. In another instance of the collective corrective to individual critical blindspots, Audre Lorde replied to Mary Daly's *Gyn/Ecology* in an open letter that reminded Daly and her readers that "What you excluded from *Gyn/Ecology* dismissed my heritage and the heritage of all other non-European women, and denied the real connections that exist between us."[11] In a 1980 article in the prestigious American journal *Critical Inquiry*, Gayatri Chakravorty Spivak also raised the problem of the liberal, well-intentioned feminist critic's complicity (again, through the sin of omission) in the torture, rape, and murder of Third-World women in an introduction to her translation of Mahasveta Devi's short story "Draupadi." Similarly, her 1981 *Yale French Studies* essay in a volume devoted to feminist criticism aligned with French and American "high theories" of deconstruction and psychoanalysis exhorted the critical elite not to forget the oppressed women of the Third World. If individual feminist critics forget to point out the oppressive potential of their own observations, the collective body of feminist critics exacerbates the problem of the critic/observer's authority over women she either patronizes and belittles or fails to see at all.

Individual feminists working within this collective awareness of sexual, class, and racial difference often find themselves, despite and—more significantly—*because of* their best intentions, struggling with the question of what it means for a woman and a feminist to be writing criticism within a tradition and an academy that are largely premised on exclusionary, elitest values oppressive to the overwhelming majority of women. Spivak's *Critical Inquiry* article is a rebuke to feminists who forget the "other woman," but it is also a part of Spivak's own struggle against her complicity in elitism: this feminist critic with a political commitment is also a translator of one of the most powerful of male high theorists, Jacques Derrida. The struggle of feminists to articulate their political commitments within the university is often internal as well as external. The traditions of academic criticism have become a part of the feminist critic at the same time that she is marginalized within the academy.

Feminist critics' connections with the academic institutions that facilitate their very ability to write place them awkwardly in relation to the critical tradition that they seek to subvert. In "Gender Theory and the Yale School," Barbara Johnson tries to place herself, as a "Yale daughter," in relation to high-powered masculine theory and, in particular, Paul de Man, the now-dead "father" of the deconstructive theory she practices. Asked to speak in the just-deceased de Man's place at a conference on "Genre Theory and the Yale School," Johnson notes her position at the conference as the only woman and the fact that she has been asked to speak, not about her own work, but about de Man's. Johnson is not altogether the obedient daughter, however, and the end of her published talk takes a hard, critical look at her work and its place in relation to the Yale School of theory. She notes, in a "meditation on a possible female version of the Yale School," her own erasure of difference in a book *about* difference, *The Critical Difference*:

> What happens when one raises Mary Jacobus's question: "Is there a woman in this text?" The answer is rather surprising. For no book produced by the Yale School seems to have excluded women as effectively as *The Critical Difference*. No woman authors are studied. Almost no women critics are cited. And, what is even more surprising, there are almost no female characters in any of the stories analyzed. . . . In a book that announces itself as a study of difference, the place of the woman is constantly being erased.[12]

Johnson goes on to muse that "There may, however, be something accurate about this repeated dramatization of woman as simulacrum, erasure, or silence. For it would not be easy to assert that the existence and knowledge of the female subject could simply be produced, without difficulty or epistemological damage, within the existing patterns of culture and language." How, in other words, is she to articulate an elusive, feminine experience when the critical modes, even the very language she has learned preclude this experience? "It would be no easy task," Johnson concludes, "to undertake the effort of reinflection or translation required to retrieve the lost knowledge of the gypsy, or to learn to listen with retrained ears to Edith Bunker's patient elaboration of an answer to the question, 'What *is* the difference'?"[13]

No easy task, indeed. How is Barbara Johnson, trained in the male-dominated Yale School, to listen to textual voices devalued as marginal or trivial by those who have trained her? Johnson, along with Alice Jardine, Jane Gallop, Nancy Miller, and Naomi Schor, among others, may be extreme examples of critics with strong commitments both to feminism and the current avant-garde of male-dominated critical theory, but many feminists in the academy experience a similar self-division, a split between the critical values and training of the academy and the feminist values that are just becoming part of that academy. In fact, feminism shares a critique of the "objective" critic/observer with many recent deconstructive and Marxist critical theorists, and many feminist critics have found their politicized work facilitated rather than blocked by such theory, however male-dominated.[14] But as several feminists have recently pointed out, while deconstruction might constructively transform feminism into a more radically revolutionary attack on male-dominated institutions, feminism must also transform deconstruction into a more politicized critical discourse.[15] The feminist critic must not *become* the deconstructionist, in other words, but rather retain a sense of her own inner difference, an internal division that reflects the external differences too often suppressed in academic criticism.

In "Watching the Detectives," an article from which I take the title for this section of my essay, Nathalie F. Anderson has likened the feminist critic/observer to the institutionally disaffected but morally committed private detective of modern fiction. Anderson says that, like the fictional private detective, caught between her commitment to law and order and her hatred of the means of oppression by which law and order are maintained, the feminist critic is in an ambivalent position. She seeks to subvert the academic and critical tradition of "objective" observer, a tradition that has historically kept patriarchal order at the cost of oppressing women, while she herself is enabled by that tradition. The sympathies of the private detective may be divided between the criminal she investigates and the police who seek, unequivocally, to enforce the law against criminal behavior. The feminist critic is also divided in her allegiance to the institutions and traditions that support and empower her and her sympathy with those—including often herself—who live outside and even seek to disrupt those institutions and traditions. Anderson points out the difficulty of this position, asking "Can one be a private eye in the [police] academy?"[16] Can one watch, can one look, can one play the critic/observer, I would add, while retaining one's own feminist difference from the institutions that enable that observation?

Barbara Johnson, in "Thresholds of Difference: Structures of Address in Zora Neale Hurston," seems to be seeking a form of the private eye's ambiguous relation to both the subject of her detection—Zora Neale Hurston—and the academic critical traditions that empower her interpretation of that subject. To do so, she turns her relation to Hurston into one of student to teacher: "It was as though I were asking Zora Neale Hurston for answers to questions I did not even know I was unable to formulate. I had a lot to learn, then, from Hurston's way of dealing with multiple agendas and heterogeneous implied readers."[17] Johnson turnes the critic/observer's authoritative stance into one of subservience and questioning; like the private detectives of popular fiction by writers such as Dorothy Sayers, Sara Paretsky, and Barbara Wilson, she investigates not by a show of authority—like a policeman/woman—but by a querying relationship between the student who needs to know and doesn't, and the teacher who knows and can teach. As Anderson's insights suggest, however, this apparently pedagogical situation involves a certain duplicity on the critic/detective's part since she is, after all, asking the questions and formulating the answers—as she has been trained to do by academic institutions that are in large part resistant to giving a place to writers such as Hurston. Anderson asks, "can one be duplicitous and not con oneself?"[18] The feminist critic finds herself as both the critic/observer, supported by male-dominated and oppressive traditions and institutions, and a "private eye" subverting the very authority of critic/observer she deploys.

Seeing Double

The ambiguity of Johnson's position suggests that the detectives must watch themselves, must be alert to their own thoughts and feelings as constituents in a racist, sexist, homophobic culture. As Johnson says, just being a woman—even just being a feminist—is not sufficient for the thoroughgoing examination and understanding of sexual, racial, and class difference that would help dismantle the social institutions and assumptions oppressive to women, among others. The "authority" of feminists' experience, left uncritiqued, may well be the unwitting means to reinforcing rigid categories of race, gender, sexuality, and class, all of which are integral parts of a capitalist patriarchy oppressive to all but a select few of its constituents. Whatever the dangers of self-deceit and self-division encountered by Anderson's feminist critics/detectives, their ambiguous positions allow for a criticism informed by perspectives other than those of the male-dominated academy and culture in which they write and pose healthy alternatives to the oppressive authority of the "objective" critical observer. Living and writing as both spectators and spectacles, feminists are inclined to cultivate a double vision that derives from being both a part of, and marginal to, the traditions of critical observation in which the academy trains them. Looking at patriarchy from the position of the marginalized, as well as writing from that position, allows the critic to see what is harder to see from a position of centrality and empowerment within patriarchy.

Some feminists are more marginalized in the academy than others, as I have already suggested, and the feminist critic's failure to remember this fact may silence other women and other feminists, keeping them locked up, like the Spy's little virgin, in their own marginality. Feminist critics have also, however, recognized the connection between their own marginalization and that of others, and this recognition has led to the dissemination of ways of seeing that are traditionally connected most explicitly with certain marginalized groups. Judith McDaniel, for instance, writes in *Sinister Wisdom* that "lesbian feminist criticism is a political or thematic perspective, a kind of imagination that can see beyond the barriers of heterosexuality, role stereotypes, patterns of language and culture that may be repressive to female sexuality and expression."[19] Bonnie Zimmerman argues that the lesbian perspective articulated by McDaniel and others might open up vantage points for feminist critics at large:

> Because feminism concerns itself with the removal of limitations and impediments in the way of female imagination, and lesbian criticism helps to expand our notions of what is *possible* for women, then all women would grow by adopting for themselves a lesbian vision. Disenfranchised groups have had to adopt a double vision for survival; one of the political transformations of recent decades has been the realization that enfranchised groups—men, whites, heterosexuals, the middle class—would do well to adopt that double vision for the survival of us all.[20]

Zimmerman's "What Has Never Been: An Overview of Lesbian Feminist Literary Criticism" was first published in *Feminist Studies* and later reprinted in Elaine Showalter's *The New Feminist Criticism*, a widely read and taught anthology; while white middle-class heterosexual critics undoubtedly still dominate American feminist criticism, voices from the sexual, social, and economic margins of feminist criticism disrupt and counteract the tendency of feminist critical authority to harden, to become set as one politically correct vision.

Some form of double vision is implicit in the feminist awareness of women's—and the critic's own—marginalization in the public realm in which criticism is spoken and written in patriarchal society. Feminism has enabled women to see their separateness from as well as their complicity in patriarchal institutions. From a feminist perspective, women are dualities, partaking of both their marginalized position and the dominant culture of which they are a marginalized part. Women critics, as we can see from Haywood to the present, write out of two points of view emanating from the two "identities" implicit in the two terms of the title "woman critic." On the one hand, dominant Anglo-American tradition has defined "woman" as belonging to the domestic, the private, and as not having a place to speak outside that realm. On the other hand, a woman who reads, thinks, and writes criticism has access to the male-dominated public domain of literature and politics. Hence, the woman critic is automatically constructed as double, as engaging in two mutually exclusive kinds of activity: witness Haywood's double vision from the point of view of both oppressor and oppressed. While this doubleness may lead to confusion, contradiction, perhaps an inability to sustain dual roles, it might also, as Joan Kelly suggests, develop into a more enabling perspective for twentieth-century feminists dedicated to critiquing and changing the social systems that oppress women. Kelly argues that the twentieth-century feminist theorist, by her concern for and stake in *both* the private and public "sexual and social domains," is able to attain a "unified, 'doubled' view of the social order."[21] By seeing double and reading double, the feminist critic sees connections between the exclusion of women from the public realm and their incarceration in the private realm and is able to work against women's oppression in both spheres.

But Kelly's description of this vision as "unified" suggests the totalizing capacity of a double vision unproblematically conceived of as "adding up to" an authoritative view by women in society. While this totalizing, unified "double vision" might give feminism an authority in a critical tradition inclined towards seeking totalizing visions, it also suppresses the differences internal to feminism: what about, for instance, the women who are not empowered to move so easily between the sexual domains of private and public? As we have seen, attempts to reach a feminist consensus on critical vision have often unwittingly excluded others for whom the critic was supposedly trying to speak. In a reading of Showalter's anthology, Jane Gallop has pointed out that this exclusion is, in part, "the effect of a certain structure, the recurrent tendency in the establishment of a subfield to generate exclusionary definitions."[22] Gallop argues that exclusionary definitions arise, ironically, out of the need to define feminist criticism as distinct from an exclusionary critical tradition—a vicious critical cycle. A definition that fails to make clear the differences between feminism and other forms of criticism may blunt the edge of its political difference. A definition too exclusive may erase the differences within feminism and unwittingly prevent feminist political stategies from breaking down social hierarchies that silence some and allow others voice.

The lesbian double vision noted by Zimmerman offers an alternative model for writing the definitions of feminism as well as for seeing critically. Gallop offers Zimmerman's method of considering the problem of defining lesbianism as a model for defining feminism: "[Zimmerman's] 'double vision' allows her to see the advantages and disadvantages of both sides of the argument. Rather than following the polemical necessity of choosing sides, a necessity that draws a halt to exploratory thinking, her 'double vision' makes it possible to think through the connections between the two positions."[23] Unlike the "unified" double view celebrated by Kelly, this lesbian double vision does not seek to unify or reconcile contradictory views: it does not, therefore, erase difference. Double vision, translated into writing double, can articulate possibilities for definition without oppressive totalizations.

Writing double also, of course, implies reading double. Zimmerman can incorporate varying definitions of lesbianism in her writing because she is able to read in a way that is open to oppositional possibilities. Gallop can read in Showalter's use of an epigraph on the impossibility of definition (drawn from the French feminist Hélène Cixous) the inclusion of a voice oppositional to Showalter's own attempts to define feminist criticism. Doubleness—double vision, double reading, double writing—is, then, as it was for Haywood, a way of articulating the marginal as well as the central. The feminist critic can speak from both her marginal position as a woman and her authority as a critic, and it allows her, like Haywood duplicitously critiquing the very means to authority she uses, to include feminine perspectives other than her relatively privileged one. Double vision would seem, then, to acquire a privileged position in feminist discourse; I would argue, however, that while double vision has been and is a useful strategy, it may vary in its usefulness to feminism in relation to the specific historical contexts in which it is used. Gallop, in discussing the problem of how to define feminist criticism, notes that timing is a crucial factor in the making or postponing of definitions. While the openness to possibility implicit in feminist double vision, double reading, and double writing is conducive to a process that does not allow definition to rigidify into the means to somebody's oppression, definition—choosing one side of the feminist double vision—can be a necessary defense against a hostile political and intellectual environment. The problem, as Gallop says, is how to know when to use which strategy.

The pervasiveness of double vision as a metaphor for feminist critical vision suggests, however, that the long struggle to be both feminist and critical in a tradition that tends to make these terms contradict each other has reached a point at which feminist consciousness and the authority of the critic/observer are beginning to affect the very terms of each other's existence. Feminism has begun to depend less and less, in its political struggles against patriarchy, on the authority of some wished-for, but nonexistent essential female experience or some utopian vision of the feminine. And the postmodern masculine criticism of the last thirty years is becoming increasingly self-conscious of criticism's potential for oppressing those not empowered by it. But the mutual effect of the terms on each other does not mean that the problems of contradiction, grappled with by Haywood and others, are solved. The feminist critic who seeks to see, read, and write double still faces the problem of not being "clear" or authoritative enough to be taken seriously—not just by traditional critic/observers, but by other feminists as well. Naomi Schor, for example, is aware of the dangers of being misread by both feminists and nonfeminist critics when she sums up the advantages and dangers of her double reading strategy of "tricksterism":

> To read beyond difference is inescapably to run the risk of reinforcing the canon and its founding sexual hierarchies and exclusions, while to read for difference is to risk relapsing into essentialism and its inevitable consequence, marginalization. Reading double presents, of course, its own dangers, those inherent in tricksterism: ambiguity and equivocation. But, as I hope to show, it offers a possible way out of the current impasse, by suggesting a way of reconceptualizing the problematics of sexual difference.[24]

Schor's opposition between reading beyond and for difference identifies those aspects of a totalizing feminist criticism and a totalizing masculine criticism that she wishes to avoid. By choosing not to choose between the two, she allows herself to read as a feminist *and* an observer/critic. But, as she says, this choice is still a dangerous one, fraught with "ambiguity and equivocation." It could conduce to her being misread either as stuck in her own feminine difference—not objective enough—or as a traitor to a feminist politics of difference.

The feminist trickster may, then, still unintentionally make a spectacle out of herself just as Haywood inadvertently did when she caught the satiric attention of Alexander Pope. Double vision may help the feminist critic understand and articulate her own difference from and complicity in the critical tradition, but it does not necessarily force her audience to see the reasons for her doubleness. Many feminists may not find her feminist enough, and her nonfeminist colleagues may see her in the light of a long, misogynistic tradition: as duplicitous, two-faced, about as trustworthy as Spencer's treacherous half-monster, half-woman Duessa. But as Mary Russo has wisely pointed out, making a spectacle of oneself, while risky, may lead to possibilities for empowerment that are automatically foreclosed by allowing someone else to do it for you.[25] The feminist observer/critic has become a spectator as well as a spectacle, and, in doing so, she may embody our best hope for restructuring the unself-consciously oppressive critical model of "objective" observation.

Notes

I want to thank my friends, students, and colleagues, Dale Bauer, Art Casciato, Danae Clark, Leslie Harris, and Melissa Hill for their feedback and support. Laurie Finke and Bob Markley also gave me many useful suggestions in preparing the final draft.

1. Donald Bond, ed., *The Spectator* (Oxford, Eng.: Clarendon Press, 1965), I: 5. Subsequent references to Addison's and Steele's *Spectator* are to this edition and will be noted parenthetically in the text.
2. Mary Russo, "Female Grotesques: Carnival and Theory," *Feminist Studies/Critical Studies*, ed. Teresa de Lauretis (Bloomington: Indiana University Press, 1986), p. 213.
3. Virginia Woolf, *A Room of One's Own* (San Diego: Harcourt Brace Jovanovich, 1957), pp. 1–2.
4. See Dale Spender's first two chapters in *Mothers of the English Novel* (London: Pandora Press, 1986), and Mary Poovey's Introduction to *The Proper Lady and the Woman Writer: Ideology as Style in the Works of Mary Wollstonecraft, Mary Shelley, and Jane Austen* (Chicago: University of Chicago Press, 1984) for good overviews of the economic and social conditions of women writing in the eighteenth century.
5. *The Female Spectator* (London: Millar, 1775), I: 1. Subsequent references to *The Female Spectator* are to this edition and will be noted parenthetically in the text.
6. See *In a Different Voice: Psychological Theory and Women's Development* (Cambridge, Mass.: Harvard University Press, 1982) for a full account of Gilligan's work with psychological theory and women's socialization.
7. Elaine Showalter admonishes feminists that "Feminist criticism cannot go around forever in men's ill-fitting hand-me-downs, the Annie Hall of English studies; but must, as John Stuart Mill wrote about women's literature in 1869, 'emancipate itself from the influence of accepted models, and guide itself by its own impulses.' . . ." See "Towards a Feminist Poetics," reprinted in *The New Feminist Criticism: Essays on Women, Literature, and Theory*, ed. Elaine Showalter (New York: Pantheon Books, 1985), pp. 125–143.

8. *The Invisible Spy, by Explorabilis* (London: Harrison, 1788), I: 1–2. Subsequent references to the *Spy* are to this edition and will be noted parenthetically in the text.
9. See "Reading as a Woman" in *On Deconstruction: Theory and Criticism after Structuralism* (Ithaca, N.Y.: Cornell University Press, 1982), pp. 43–63.
10. See "Annie LeClerc Writing a Letter, with Vermeer," in *The Poetics of Gender*, ed. Nancy K. Miller (New York: Columbia University Press, 1986), p. 154, for an explanation of how the feminist critic's attempts to be seen as creditable by masculine-dominated "high theory" can lead to her complicity in the erasure of other women.
11. "An Open Letter to Mary Daly," *This Bridge Called My Back: Writings by Radical Women of Color* (Watertown, Mass.: Persephone Press, 1981), pp. 98–101.
12. *A World of Difference* (Baltimore: Johns Hopkins University Press, 1987), p. 39.
13. Ibid., pp. 40–41.
14. See Laurie Finke, "The Rhetorics of Marginality: Why I Do Feminist Theory," *Tulsa Studies in Women's Literature*, 5(1986): 251–272, for a clear statement of this position.
15. This position has been taken, with variations, by Elizabeth Meese in *Crossing the Double Cross: The Practice of Feminist Criticism* (Chapel Hill: University of North Carolina Press, 1986); by Catherine Belsey in "Constructing the Subject: Deconstructing the Text," *Feminist Criticism and Social Change: Sex, Class and Race in Literature and Culture*, eds. Judith Newton and Deborah Rosenfelt (New York: Methuen, 1985), pp. 45–64; and by Mary Poovey, in "Deconstruction and Feminism," a paper delivered at Miami University, April 8, 1987.
16. "Watching the Detectives," a paper presented for discussion in "Feminism and Other Discourses," a session of the Society for Critical Exchange, MMLA, November 1987. Forthcoming in *Critical Exchange*.
17. Johnson, *World of Difference*, p. 172.
18. Anderson, "Watching the Detectives," p. 8.
19. Quoted by Bonnie Zimmerman, "What Has Never Been: An Overview of Lesbian Feminist Criticism," *The New Feminist Criticism*, p. 218.
20. Ibid., p. 219.
21. "The Doubled Vision of Feminist Theory," *Sex and Class in Women's History*, eds. Judith L. Newton, Mary P. Ryan, Judith Walkowitz (London: Routledge & Kegan Paul, 1983), p. 259.
22. "The Problem of Definition," a paper delivered at Swarthmore College, February 1987, p. 19. A printed version of this essay is forthcoming in *Genre*, 20, 2 (1987): 111–132.
23. Gallop, "Problem of Definition," p. 10.
24. "Reading Double: Sand's Difference," *The Poetics of Gender*, p. 250.
25. Russo, pp. 225–227.

History, Literature, and Criticism

Robert Markley

"How do you define history?" is not a question over which most of us lose much sleep. At first glance, the answer seems obvious: history is what we learn in school, what we read in textbooks, what we are taught to memorize. History of this sort takes the form of lists of names, dates, facts, and artifacts: it is the stuff of encyclopedia articles, monuments, tombstones, old books, old newsreels, and documentaries. But the more we think about what history actually is, the more difficult it becomes to pin down a single definition. Ezra Pound defined history as "time remembered," a workable definition, were it not for the fact that it is never simply our memory that is involved. The memories that constitute history are available only through materials—books, photographs, films, deeds, wills, diaries, and so on—that have already structured both the reality that they sought in their own times to represent and our perceptions of that reality. In this regard, the more we deal with history as a series of specific texts and artifacts, the more likely we are to perceive it not as an abstract entity or a truthful account of what "really" happened but as a series of arguments and debates, of differing viewpoints about the significance of various events, individuals, policies, and crises. History, in this respect, can never simply be taken for granted or presumed to be a set of objective observations about "time remembered." It is always a part of what it attempts to describe.

Most of us would agree that much of what we regard as history really happened: Rome really fell, the American colonies really rebelled against the British in 1776, the Nazis really shoved men, women, and children into ovens and gas chambers. But we would also be tempted to acknowledge that we can experience these events only in the retelling, only as a set of narratives about or depictions (including photographic representations) of what happened. We cannot witness the actual events, we can only read and interpret the accounts that are themselves interpretations of what "really" happened. If we need a thumbnail description of history, we could do worse than to borrow Hayden White's observation that history is the collection of narratives we tell ourselves in order to create a past from which we would like to be descended.[1] To accept White's description is *not,* I think, to buy into the dubious notion that all events are *simply* textual events, ungrounded and susceptible to an infinite number of interpretations, or to reduce Auschwitz or Biafra to mere signs that have no fixed, "real" meaning. Instead, White points us towards a view of history as a set of textual and discursive practices by which we try to explain what happened, to investigate how it happened, and to suggest how past events have helped to shape the way we are now.

All social, political, and cultural struggles, in an important sense, are vitally concerned with who gets to write these accounts of what happened, with whose literary and cultural practices survive and are taken to be, to greater or lesser extents, "true." History—including literary history—is generally written by the winners of these struggles, and their victories influence subsequent interpretations in ways that even the participants themselves may not fully recognize. In the late 1640s during the English Civil War, the radicals in Cromwell's victorious New Model Army attempted to gain a measure of political power; one offshoot of their efforts was the Leveller Agreement of the People, a protodemocratic document that asserted the rights of the common people of England to own their own property, practice their own forms of religion, and elect their own leaders. Had the radicals been successful, this document would today be invoked, revered, and memorized; instead it survives only as an obscure footnote in British history. The radicals lost, the British Commonwealth did not become a democracy, and the Agreement of the People had little discernible influence in shaping the ways in which the history of seventeenth-century Britain was written.[2] History belongs to the winners.

Seeing history as the complex set of discursive practices that represent material reality complicates the problem of how we define its relationship to literature. Traditionally, literary critics have viewed history as a backdrop against which novels, plays, and poems take place. History is itself not a text to be interpreted but the scenery for "timeless" human dramas that transcend their immediate circumstances. To this way of thinking, Shakespeare's history plays, for example, are interesting not primarily because they offer a particular view of political infighting during the fourteenth and fifteenth centuries but because they represent "timeless" spectacles of human love, hate, loyalty, betrayal, courage, fear, and patriotism. But recent critics—particularly the practitioners of what is called the new historicism—have questioned both specific interpretations of individual works (like Shakespeare's history plays) and larger assumptions about the relationship between literature and history. For Stephen Greenblatt, Jonathan Dollimore, and Leonard Tennenhouse, among others, no firm distinctions exist between Renaissance literature and Renaissance history.[3] In fact, Greenblatt argues, literary works help to constitute what we mean by "history" and help to define our relationship to it. Literature does not passively reflect actual events or uncover timeless, universal truths in particular actions (the argument that Sir Philip Sidney makes in his *Apology for Poetry*). Instead, literary works shape our view of historical reality and influence—often in quite subtle ways—what reality itself may be. In this sense, literary narratives, like historical narratives, are often the sites of struggles to interpret and control what we might call the politics of representation. What is at stake in differing readings of, say, Shakespeare's *Othello* may be something more than scholarly questions about the nature of tragedy; different interpretations of the play may reveal different attitudes about race, sexual relationships, and the politics of a mercantile society—like the Venice that Shakespeare depicts in the play.

If we conceive of history, then, as *both* a set of narrative constructs *and* as specific economic, political, and cultural practices, we can begin to understand why it is that within particular periods, genres, and literary works the definition of history becomes so maddeningly complex. By its very nature history is impure, what Bakhtin would call the site of a dialogical struggle to define—and therefore control—its potential range of meanings.[4] Within the essays collected in this anthology, we can identify and describe numerous struggles among competing notions of history. These struggles are often implicit rather than explicit. Precisely because few literary critics agonize over what they see as the meaning of history—that is, *their* meaning of history—we often have to explore for ourselves the half-articulated assumptions and values that shape their responses to particular works, to particular periods, and to particular notions of literature itself. With the understanding that any scheme of classification is going to be open to question, we might tentatively define five versions of history that roughly coincide with historical periods: the classical (ancient Greece and Rome), Christian (medieval Europe), humanist (Renaissance Europe), neoclassical (seventeenth- and eighteenth-century Europe), Marxist (nineteenth- and twentieth-century Europe and America), and postmodern. What complicates this scheme is that older notions of history persist and frequently absorb or modify newer descriptions that are intended, in part, to replace them. From the Renaissance on, theories of history grow more flexible and more muddled as historians seek to discern patterns or "meanings" in historical events by constructing narrative accounts to explain why things happen in particular ways. It is also important to realize that within, say, classical or neoclassical versions of history all sorts of contradictions abound. Again, if we keep in mind the accounts of Bakhtin and Hayden White, we will be less inclined to view history as a self-consistent description of what really happened than as a series of utterances that compete for our attention by attacking other voices, other versions of "time remembered." At the risk of generalizing, we might say that history is forever wracked by contradictory assumptions that, on the one hand, what it describes is meaningless, the mere flux of events (as the ancient philosopher Heraclitus would have it), and, on the other, that it is the sole repository of meaning for whatever political faction happens at the time to dictate the terms under which history is written. From the Golden Age of Athens, to the global empire of nineteenth-century Britain, to the Manifest Destiny of the United States in the nineteenth and twentieth centuries, to the Nazis' thousand-year Reich, to the Revolutionary Republic of contemporary Iran, there are always those who believe that history is on their side, that a particular form of political, economic, cultural, or religious authority represents a final turn of history, an ultimate meaning. What is interesting from our point of view are the ways in which these views of history have shaped the cultural, literary, and critical practices that we have inherited.

Classical views of history were generally fatalistic. Humankind was at the mercy of the whims of the gods. Regardless of our efforts, we could not understand the inscrutable and inexorable workings of fate. Paradoxically, however, even as these fatalistic views of history blocked the development of sophisticated theories to account for specific historical changes, they encouraged historians like Thucydides (the great historian of the Peloponnesian War between Athens and Sparta in the fifth century B.C.) to develop complex historiographical methods for uncovering the "truth." Fatalistic accounts of historical process underlie, for example, Aristotle's description of tragedy in the *Poetics*. The tragic hero is depicted as both the victim of fate, and through the notion of *harmatia* (literally "missing the target"), or what is conventionally referred to as the "tragic flaw," as also guilty of some error of judgment. Because he is both a symbol of a political community and a fallible human being, the Aristotelian tragic hero, like Oedipus in Sophocles' play *Oedipus Rex*, is obsessed with trying to make sense of his place in the narrative of historical events. This attempt, however, must be seen as tragic because history—or fate—has no ultimate meaning or transcendent pattern that either the hero or the audience can discover. For this reason, philosophy—the study of timeless forms and universal truths—frequently in Greek thought takes precedence over specific materialistic accounts that attempt to make history meaningful. History is the flux of events, philosophy the speculative inquiry into metaphysical order.

In contrast to the Greeks, the ancient Hebrews developed notions of history that were teleological. History is perceived as a process with an identifiable end: the return to the promised land, the creation of an ideal state, the rebuilding of Jerusalem. In the Old Testament, God becomes the controlling agent, the determining force behind history. Unlike the Greeks, who see history as chaotic and meaningless, the ancient Hebrews perceive it as the working out of prophecy, the fulfillment of God's promise to restore the ancient kingdoms of Judea and Israel to power and prosperity. In the third and fourth centuries A.D. Christian theologians adapted this teleological view of history in two important ways: history is defined as both a progress toward the millenium, toward the Second Coming and Christ's thousand-year rule on earth, and as a fallen state that is always about to end, to be redeemed by the serene timelessness of earthly perfection that will follow the Second Coming. In this respect, what we think of as historical time is seen, from a Christian vantage point, as a sinful, corrupt state. Time itself—like death—is an unfortunate consequence of Adam's and Eve's having sinned in and been banished from Eden. In Christian theology, then, the external, political, and socioeconomic history of particular events pales in significance to the individual history of the Christian soul's timeless struggle with temptation and sin. Historical process is, at least in theory, subordinated to questions of individual salvation. Throughout the Middle Ages, then, and specifically in the works of Augustine and Aquinas, problems of representation are cast in terms of finding appropriate means to present in a fallen, corrupted language the mysteries of divine perfection.

Matters become more complicated in the Renaissance with the advent of humanism—the "rediscovery" and celebration of the classical world view within a Christian context—and in the eighteenth century with neoclassicism, which may be defined as a series of strategies intended to reestablish the model of classical aesthetic and cultural values as a guide to contemporary poetic and critical practices. Neither Renaissance humanism nor seventeenth- and eighteenth-century neoclassicism dispense with Christian or more broadly teleological notions of history; instead, a variety of writers between the sixteenth and late eighteenth centuries try to reconcile the increasingly complicated traditions of historical thinking that they have inherited. Abstract or providential notions of progress are frequently pressed into service to justify the particular moral, cultural, and political authority of the countries or political parties that critics wish to defend or celebrate. At the risk of generalizing, we might say that literary criticism in the sixteenth, seventeenth, and eighteenth centuries is concerned with adapting classical and Christian models so that they can be used to justify specific cultural and political practices, to create narratives (in other words) that have as their heroes specific political factions or sociopolitical philosophies. A good example of how complex notions of history inform literary criticism during the period is Dryden's *Essay of Dramatic Poesy*.

At first glance, the aesthetic issues in this well-known critical essay seem clear-cut: Dryden, in the person of Neander, argues for the superiority of British drama to the rule-bound drama of France and offers (in passages that seem strange to most modern readers) defenses of Shakespeare, Ben Jonson, and the playwrighting team of Francis Beaumont and John Fletcher for their respective accomplishments. But Dryden's critical argument is more complex than simply tub-thumping for the virtues of a handful of English dramatists. It rests on a number of assumptions about history, politics, and the function of the theater that need to be examined before we can get a good sense of what the *Essay of Dramatic Poesy* is trying to accomplish as both a critical and cultural document.

Dryden was a civil servant in the government of Oliver Cromwell in 1657 and 1658. Like many of his countrymen, he changed his political colors in 1660 and celebrated the restoration of Charles II to the throne in June of that year in an effusive heroic poem, "Astraea Redux." The poem concludes with lines that attempt to establish Charles as the savior of an England politically and religiously divided against itself, as a reincarnation of the greatest of the ancient Roman emperors, Augustus Caesar, and as the embodiment of a new, seemingly endless, period of power and prosperity for England:

> O happy Prince, whom Heav'n hath taught the way
> By paying Vowes, to have more Vowes to pay!
> O Happy Age! O times like those alone
> By Fate reserv'd for Great *Augustus* Throne!
> When the joint growth of Armes and Arts foreshew
> The World a Monarch, and that Monarch *You* (318–23).[5]

In these lines, Dryden alludes to both Christian—implicitly millenial—notions of the end of history and classical ideas of fate, of the heroic leader who brings together "Armes and Arts" to solidify and extend national power. History, in effect, becomes the theater for staging the works of God's providence—in this case the Augustan age heralded by Charles' return. In this sense, the restoration of the monarch is taken as evidence of a coherent pattern, a divinely ordained narrative that plots worldly events.

The sceptics among us might note, however, that Dryden in 1659 had written a poem entitled "Heroique Stanzas to the Glorious Memory of Cromwell," the man who in 1649 helped to have Charles I executed. Charles I, of course, was the father of Charles II. Dryden's career after 1660—particularly his politically risky conversion to Catholicism in the 1680s—suggests that something more than crass political opportunism may be involved in his praise of first Cromwell, then Charles II. In both the "Heroique Stanzas" and "Astraea Redux," Dryden defines his and his country's immediate political situation within a larger framework of assumptions about history and divine providence. Cromwell's triumphs and Charles II's restoration are not random or unrelated events; they are evidence, for Dryden, of God's guiding hand at work in the affairs of men and nations. They are parts of a narrative structure—of history—that must be seen as a whole in order for us to make sense of any of its parts, specifically the otherwise bewildering political events that occurred between 1658 and 1660. For Dryden, "Astraea Redux" is not simply an attempt to curry favor with a new political regime, but an effort to mythologize the return of the heir to the English throne as a crucial event in a narrative structure that offers us a vision of progress from rebellion and political chaos to order, power, and national prosperity.

This analysis of Dryden's view of history, however, creates problems when we return to his *Essay* (written in 1664 but not published until four years later). How can Dryden uphold a theory of history as the progress of England from chaos to order and, at the same time, celebrate the achievements of Shakespeare, Jonson, and Beaumont and Fletcher, dramatists who wrote during a comparatively primitive and "unrefined" era? If poetry is a barometer of cultural achievement, how does Dryden reconcile the high regard he holds for the works of these playwrights to the thinly disguised contempt he and his contemporaries have for the cruder aspects of early seventeenth-century culture? If Dryden celebrates the restoration of Charles II as the dawning of a new golden age for English arms and arts, how does he deal with the fact that Shakespeare and his contemporaries were the immediate forebears of the generation who lost the Civil War and failed to prevent the execution of Charles I?

The most convincing answer to these questions may be that Dryden's remarks on the literary qualities of Shakespeare, Jonson, and Beaumont and Fletcher both depend upon and help to shape his views of seventeenth-century history. For Dryden, the idea of cultural and political progress—that is, of history as an unfolding of God's design—becomes a means to celebrate the literary achievements of Restoration England and to construct a narrative of his own, a coherent literary history of English drama that supports and is supported by his larger views of historical progress. In his mind, Shakespeare offers a comprehensive view of human nature; Jonson, in his plays, demonstrates the proper way to adapt the "models" of ancient authors; and Beaumont and Fletcher develop a form of dramatic verse that most closely imitates the "language of gentleman," the refined speech of the upper classes. Taken together, the achievements of these figures (Dryden has Neander declare) surpass those of French dramatists, who are more rigidly bound to neoclassical ideals of decorum, moral instruction, and the unities of time, place, and action. In this respect, by celebrating the "perfections" of Shakespeare, Jonson, and Beaumont and Fletcher, Dryden is able to advance claims for British cultural superiority against those of French critics who maintain that literary and artistic excellence depend on a rigorous policing of literature, criticism, and the people who write them. At the same time, however, Dryden's elevating Beaumont and Fletcher to the status of Shakespeare and Jonson indicates the importance that he places on what we might call the ideological nature of literature. Significantly, Dryden's argument for Beaumont's and Fletcher's greatness (a familiar one throughout the seventeenth century) rests on the fact that their verse most closely mirrors the sociopolitical values embodied in upper-class conversation. In other words, Dryden sees Beaumont and Fletcher as his precursors, as the dramatists who brought polite conversation to the English stage. Their literary standards, he believes, are his; and, consequently, so too is their vision of a hierarchical society based on class privilege and on the glories of monarchial rule.

By trying to understand something of what "history" may have meant to Dryden, we can begin to see why his *Essay of Dramatic Poesy* occupies an important position in our critical and cultural heritage. The *Essay* does not passively reflect "objective" qualities of early seventeenth-century plays; almost no critic now writing would maintain that Dryden somehow got it "right," that his specific judgments of the enduring qualities of Shakespeare and Jonson, and the not-so-enduring qualities of Beaumont and Fletcher, are somehow "objectively" better than everything else that has been written before or after 1668. Nor does the *Essay* claim our attention simply because it presents a model of neoclassical attitudes towards drama that we can dust off, remark on how quaint those seventeenth-century critics were, and put back on the shelf. What it does offer is a penetrating view of how Dryden's historical situation—his sense of his own political function in justifying England's claims to cultural prominence—informs his judgments of individual works and, by implication, his notions of how we should go about reading literature. In one sense, the success of Dryden's critical argument is that he convinces us that his particular historical reaction to literature is valuable beyond its immediate sociopolitical situation. Good criticism is an opinion that still seems fresh, still seems worth justifying. It is what has been culturally integrated into our very conception of what it means to read, form an opinion of, and write about literature. If Dryden's assessments of Shakespeare and Jonson seem somehow familiar to us, if his implicit elevating of English drama over French has us nodding our heads in silent agreement, it is because the *Essay* represents part of what we already "know" about literature, part of what we have been taught as "general principles" or as proper critical standards, though often without its author's name being mentioned.

Reading Dryden's *Essay* within the context of late seventeenth-century culture and politics, we get some sense of why the history of criticism becomes so complex when we begin to examine how literary works have been evaluated and canonized over the course of the last 2,500 years. As critics from generation to generation reread the classics of literature, they bring to bear on their reading new, evolving sets of cultural, political, economic, religious, and moral values. Their writings, however, are also necessarily influenced by what previous critics have said about particular works and about the function of literature in general. Without too much difficulty, we can pick out in Dryden's *Essay* a number of allusions to both ancient and "modern" critics—Aristotle, Horace, Jonson, Bossu, and others—who have influenced his thinking on the drama. But Dryden is not simply a passive recipient of traditions or ideas that are already in place; he is both an active synthesizer and an original thinker who is reformulating cultural and critical values in his discussions of the nature of drama.

Dryden, of course, like all other critics, becomes part of the tradition that his successors can draw on and adapt to their own ends. Samuel Johnson, for example, is often considered, like Dryden, to be a "neoclassical" critic, and in many conventional histories of English criticism he is treated as a later exemplar of principles that remained more or less the same between the 1660s and the 1760s. But Johnson, although in some respects as politically conservative as Dryden, demonstrates a very different attitude toward the Restoration and its literary productions from his predecessor's lavish praise of its arms and arts. The era that Dryden celebrated as the dawning of a new Augustan age, Johnson savagely attacked as a period of moral depravity, unbridled sexual corruption, political opportunism, and abject flattery of the rich and powerful. In his biography of Dryden in his *Lives of the English Poets* (first published in ten volumes between 1779 and 1781), Johnson criticizes his predecessor for "accommodating himself to the corruption of the times" (1: 404) and, in his often lavish dedications of his works to his aristocratic patrons, demonstrating a "meanness and servility in hyperbolical adulation" (1: 399).[6] The basis of Johnson's attack is his conviction that Dryden demeaned his art by mixing "politics with poetry" and allowing himself to become "profitably employed in [political] controversy and flattery" (1: 384). Significantly, Johnson's criticism is historical and political rather than personal; it is an attack on the age rather than on the man. "Dryden," he says, "has never been charged with any personal agency unworthy of a good character: he abetted vice and vanity only with his pen" (1: 398). This distinction between the writer and the man is crucial to our understanding of the basis of Johnson's response to Dryden and of the principles that underlie his criticism as a whole.

Johnson's depiction of Dryden as writer corrupted by the "vice and vanity" of his time should serve as a warning to those traditionalists who see the history of literary criticism either as a succession of brilliant, individual insights into universally acknowledged masterpieces or as brilliant illustrations of the dominant ideas of distinct historical epochs. What separates Johnson's criticism of Shakespeare from Dryden's is not simply individual temperament or the advent of a new set of literary standards that can be impartially applied to the plays; it is a complex of cultural and historical differences that suggest, to Johnson, new ways of describing the nature and function of Shakespearean drama. Shakespeare's plays have not somehow changed between 1668 and 1765 (although Johnson's edition provides a better text than had been available a century earlier), but the historical context in which they are read and performed has.

Johnson brings to bear on Shakespeare's works a different set of cultural, political, and aesthetic attitudes from Dryden's. Although there are obvious similarities in the critical vocabularies that the two critics employ—"wit," "judgment," and "fancy" occur repeatedly in both their works—these terms often take on different shades of meaning, different emphases. Dryden, for example, defines wit as "a propriety of words and thoughts," and, as he makes clear in his praise of Beaumont and Fletcher, sees it as a social attribute, as a function of one's place among the upper reaches of a hierarchically ordered society. For Johnson, however, wit is not primarily a verbal construct. He attacks Pope's definition of wit in the *Essay on Criticism* ("True Wit is Nature to advantage dress'd;/ What oft was thought, but ne'er so well express'd") as "undoubtedly erroneous," and offers in its place the notion of "*discordia concors*[,] a combination of dissimilar images, or discovery of occult resemblances in things apparently unlike" (1: 19, 20). Johnson emphasizes that wit is a mental operation, a process of discovery that exists less as a general definition than as particular examples of what "is at once natural and new," what is, if not at first "obvious, [then] acknowledged to be just" (1: 20). If Johnson has borrowed elements from Dryden's social and Pope's verbal definitions of wit (or relied on similar assumptions about the relationships of polite language and social class), he has also redescribed wit in a manner that allows him to comment critically, and he would no doubt say disinterestedly, on its prior manifestations in Pope, Cowley, Donne, and the metaphysical poets. The point, however, is not that Johnson necessarily offers a better definition of wit than either Dryden or Pope but that he brings different conceptions of poetry and propriety to bear on an important critical term. His definition ultimately tells us more about the processes of his thought than about wit as an abstract, ahistorical entity.

To describe in detail how Johnson's conceptions of poetry and propriety differ from Dryden's or Pope's would require several volumes. One example from the "Preface to Shakespeare," though, should indicate some of the ways in which his criticism diverges from Dryden's. Johnson, for example, has no truck with "the supposed necessity" of drama's maintaining the unities of time and place. He dismisses this fundamental tenet of neoclassical criticism by observing that the unities celebrated by Corneille and tolerated by Dryden "have given more trouble to the poet, than pleasure to the auditor." Rather than ensuring a proximity to nature, the neoclassical unities produce a rule-bound drama that should "be contemplated [only] as an elaborate curiosity, as the product of superfluous and ostentatious art." In the place of rules as a criterion of dramatic judgment, Johnson offers a version of Horace's maxim: "the greatest graces of a play, are to copy nature and instruct life." These standards explain both Shakespeare's strengths and weaknesses as a writer in the Horatian tradition: although his "drama is the mirror of life," he "seems to write without any moral purpose." Consequently, Johnson sees in Shakespeare's history plays a conception of history that—paradoxically—he finds both credible and morally lacking: "History [in his plays] was a series of actions, with no other than chronological succession, independent [of] each other, and without any tendency to introduce or regulate the conclusion." Unlike Dryden, Johnson does not assume that Shakespeare was trying to write in a "proper" Restoration manner, to imitate the "conversation of gentlemen" on the one hand and the providential designs of history on the other. But what Johnson perceives as Shakespeare's lack of "moral purpose" clearly troubles him. He attributes it less to the dramatist's personal failings than to the fact that the "English nation, in the time of Shakespeare, was yet struggling to emerge from barbarity." Elizabethan England was effectively "a country unenlightened by learning," and its people were "vulgar." As in his attack on Dryden, Johnson defines the writer in terms of his time. "Every writer's performances, to be rightly estimated," he tells us, "must be compared with the state of the age in which he lived, and with his own particular opportunities." This, in effect, is the basis of Johnson's criticism of Shakespeare. He does not dispense with the Horatian notion that literature should instruct and delight, nor does he violate eighteenth-century notions that virtue, justice, and loyalty transcend particular times and places. But Johnson adapts these views to his own sense of historical difference, to his notion that we are all, to some extent, historically bounded in our writing and thinking. In this sense, the value of his "Preface to Shakespeare" lies in the fact that it articulates a fundamental tension inherent in many, if not most, forms of literary criticism: the desire, on the one hand, to impose some sense of order or value on works of literature, to discover (or invent) standards of judgment that will yield definitive interpretations of both particular works and their authors; and the desire, on the other, to allow authors to speak for themselves, to recover as precisely as possible the historical circumstances in which they wrote, to read their works without the mediation of intervening years or centuries.

I have devoted a fair amount of time to discussing Dryden, Pope, and Johnson because their criticism represents a particularly important formative period in the development of literary criticism as both a rhetoric and an institution. In brief, our current assumptions about what it is to write and read criticism are, in a number of ways, indebted to the attempts of these authors to formulate historically specific standards of judgment and to use them to develop a canon of English literature, a set of works worthy to stand beside the masterpieces of ancient Greece and Rome precisely because they appeal to transhistorical values of cultural, social, and literary values. It is important, however, to recognize that the history of criticism embodied in this anthology and in others like it does not conform to a simple linear or progressive pattern. In other words, to trace a line from Dryden in the seventeenth century to Pope and Johnson in the eighteenth to, say, Matthew Arnold in the nineteenth and T. S. Eliot in the twentieth is to accept tacitly the sorts of assumptions about history that are embedded in the works of these critics. And, as Kristina Straub points out in her essay in this volume, to take this sort of construction of history as objectively true or somehow natural is to exclude those critics—women, people of color, and social and political radicals—whose opinions do not fit neatly into the narrative pattern demanded by a linear or progressive view of the history of criticism. What one finds, for example, in the works of nineteenth- and early twentieth-century critics like Arnold and Eliot is not a continuation or a further elaboration of set principles legislated by their predecessors but a process of redefining and recontextualizing notions of literary and cultural value. If Eliot, like Pope, continues to be concerned with assessing the literary quality of specific works and with keeping alive a sense of tradition as a vital and creative poetic force, he is also concerned, in ways very different from his predecessors, with reshaping his readers' perception of tradition in a manner that is neither historically nor politically innocent.

Eliot, a political and religious conservative, is drawn in "Tradition and the Individual Talent" to images of poetry and the poet that either erase distinctions between past and present or remove poetry from what most of us would recognize as history. "The emotion of art," he asserts, "is impersonal"; "poetry is not a turning loose of emotion, but an escape from emotion[,] . . . an escape from personality." The poet is a "catalyst," and his "progress . . . is a continual self-sacrifice, a continual extinction of personality." Poetry, therefore, attains a timeless impersonality, and the poet writes with a "historical sense [that] compels [him]" to experience "a feeling that the whole of the literature of Europe from Homer and within it the whole of the literature of his own country has a simultaneous existence and composes a simultaneous order." The process of writing poetry, for Eliot, approaches an ahistorical condition of transcendence; it marks the poet's entry into a privileged realm of Aristotelian "intelligence" (as he argues in his essay "The Perfect Critic") that guarantees he has depersonalized himself enough to become part of tradition, "the present moment of the past." At the end of "Tradition and the Individual Talent," Eliot "proposes to halt at the frontier of metaphysics or mysticism," but, given his emphasis on a quasi-mystical "tradition," this proposal comes rather late in the day. In effect, he has defined history as "tradition," not as a material structuring of sociopolitical realities by and through literature. Eliot's history, like the Ghost in *Hamlet*, demands of the Hamlet-like poet an obedience that precludes questioning its "impersonal" dictates. In this respect, even as tradition is presented as a "living" force, it also seems oddly ethereal, detached, disembodied. Despite Eliot's protestations to the contrary, "Tradition and the Individual Talent" crosses the threshold of metaphysics in its insistence on rendering history imagistically as an "order" that transcends time. This essay, then, anticipates the kind of history that we see dramatized in Eliot's later play *Murder in the Cathedral* (1935). Like the ideal poet in "Tradition and the Individual Talent," Thomas à Becket (Eliot's twelfth-century hero) must learn to depersonalize himself and accept his martyrdom as a fulfillment of divinely inspired history. In this play, as in Eliot's criticism, history becomes a backdrop against which timeless dramas of worldly temptation and self-sacrifice are staged.

But even as Eliot was writing in the aftermath of World War I, crucial debates (particularly in Russia and Eastern Europe) were challenging conventional notions of the timelessness of literary discourse and critical judgment. The most significant of these challenges came from Marxist critics, particularly Mikhail Bakhtin and members of his circle, and the Russian formalists, Viktor Shklovsky, Boris Eichenbaum, Jurij Tynyanov, and Roman Jakobson, who became prominent in the decade after the October Revolution of 1917.[7] Writing before the advent of Stalinist repression, the Marxist critics of the 1920s were concerned with demonstrating that literature was historical, sociological, and political. The purpose of criticism, they maintained, was to indicate how the sociohistorical dimension of literature supported, challenged, or sought to overturn dominant ideological and economic systems. Obviously, their work owed a great deal to Marx's economic thought, but what is significant about the varieties of Marxism that have developed since the 1920s is the ways in which they have reshaped and reformulated traditional Marxist notions of literature and culture.

Marx held that history was a dialectical and progressive process. It could be represented as an evolutionary (or revolutionary) line that depicted the development of humankind from primitive to gradually more sophisticated forms of economic and political organization. All forms of culture, including literature and criticism, formed part of what Marx termed the "superstructure" that rested upon a materialist "base." This superstructure may best be understood as a set of practices which, though often complex in themselves, were determined by the economic conditions that produced them. For Marx, Engels, and their early followers, then, the study of literature involved investigating the ways in which class conflict and economic oppression were either reflected or suppressed in specific works and in the cultural practices—like criticism—that sought to celebrate and evaluate them. Underlying this analysis was the assumption that criticism, as a form of social activity, was itself inherently political; no writer, artist, or critic could opt out of politics or out of history, as Eliot tried to do, because writers themselves were products of the socioeconomic systems in which they wrote.

However deterministic orthodox Marxism may seem in retrospect, its cultural critique in the first third of the twentieth century had the important effect of shifting questions of aesthetic value from a self-sustaining and historically transcendent tradition of literature to the processes of history itself. As Bakhtin's work demonstrates, this redefinition of the relationship between history and literature opens up the possibility of investigating a number of constructions that had been taken, by more traditionally minded critics like Arnold and Eliot, as self-evident truths; as the entries from Raymond Williams's *Keywords* reprinted in this volume indicate, these include notions of literature, theory, and ideology, and, as Foucault's essay suggests, ultimately the notion of authorship, even of subjectivity itself. In this respect, the Marxist critiques of Bakhtin and, later, Williams open up areas of cross-disciplinary investigation that had, for the most part in nineteenth-century criticism, been neglected or dismissed as irrelevant. At the risk of oversimplifying, we might note that Marxist criticism after Bakhtin locates questions of meaning and value in the contingencies of what he calls a "dialogics of culture" rather than within the literary realm of tradition and individual talent.[8]

Yet the increasing importance of Marxist literary criticism in the latter half of the twentieth century paradoxically calls into question the basic Marxist assumption that history moves in a straight line, that progress from capitalist inequality to socialist equality is a process that is impersonally propelled by the workings of dialectical materialism, of history itself. One upshot of Bakhtin's argument for a dialogics of culture rather than simply a dialectics of literature or history is that culture becomes the site of sociopolitical conflict, of ongoing battles among different constructions of what value and meaning are or should be. For Bakhtin, this ongoing struggle is class-based; it is not a free-for-all among literary critics, or cultural historians, or economic theorists trying to interpret a given number of canonical texts. Instead, these competing constructions of culture represent complex forms of conflict that may be mediated by specific works of literature or art but can never be solely identified with them. Significantly, Bakhtin's account of culture takes the form of literary-historical analyses of works by, among others, Rabelais, Dostoevsky, and, interestingly enough, eighteenth-century English novelists (notably Henry Fielding and Laurence Sterne). In effect, Bakhtin's view of the relationships among literature, culture, class politics, economics, and criticism arrives at formulations reminiscent of the points argued by Pope and Johnson. Like these eighteenth-century critics, Bakhtin rejects narrow notions of formalism for a sociopolitical description of what literature is and how it functions. To be sure, there are vast differences between, say, Johnson's conservative defense of Christian culture and Bakhtin's radical rewriting of the relationships between literature and history. But their descriptions of literature should alert us to the ways in which both writers attempt to use history as a means to make what we might call narrative sense of a seemingly chaotic or absurd reality of the type that Johnson satirizes in his poetic adaptations of Juvenal, "London," and "The Vanity of Human Wishes." In this regard, Bakhtin, a Christian communist, and Johnson offer two historically different conceptions of literature as a historical process.

In recent years, Marxist reformulations of traditional conceptions of history have themselves been challenged by postmodern attempts to deny any "grounding," any repository of meaning to writing. Postmodernism, on the one hand, shares with Marxist analyses a concern with revealing the internal inconsistencies and gaps within what had previously been considered the artistic whole of the literary text. But unlike Marxist strategies of demystification, postmodern readings seek to deconstruct history itself as a means of making sense of cultural and political events. In extreme, neoformalist versions of postmodern or deconstructive analysis, history threatens to become a series of texts that resist determinant meanings of the sort on which both traditional Anglo-American and Marxist criticism depend. In practice, however, postmodern readings of specific literary and philosophical works seldom become as nihilistic as they are occasionally accused of being. Because deconstruction, for example, in its various forms, relies on the revolutionary potential of any language or work to be read against itself, against the assumptions that have brought it into being, it can no more escape its historical situation than any other form of criticism. At its most routine, the deconstructive analysis of literary texts becomes a kind of low-grade philosophy that parodies the important assertions made by Derrida, Barthes, and Miller in their essays reprinted in this volume. In different ways, all three critics suggest that postmodernism is a cross-disciplinary as well as textual undertaking that seeks to decenter notions of the holistic text, authoritative meaning, and the autonomous subject in order to explore the ways in which philosophical certainties contain within themselves the means by which they may be questioned, subverted, and rewritten.

Postmodernism and Marxism, then, are not necessarily antithetical undertakings, although the relationship between them is often complex. Both share strategies of questioning the sorts of premises that underlie classical and much Anglo-American criticism of the nineteenth and twentieth centuries; both take advantage of the energy released by the process of turning a language against itself; and both challenge traditional notions of imitation, of the essential congruence between "reality" and the "literary text." But once we have noted these similarities, we find ourselves in the middle of an ongoing political argument between those critics, like Michael Ryan, for whom Marxism and deconstruction share important fundamental goals and those, like Terry Eagleton, who see postmodernism as fundamentally ahistorical, as a continuation of the formalist assumptions of New Criticism.[9] Because neither Marxism nor postmodernism exists as a single discourse—a single party line that all its practitioners echo—their areas of agreement and contention cannot be reduced to simple sets of conflicting oppositions. Bakhtin is relevant in this context. His notion of the dialogics of culture offers us a way of seeing current critical debates as part of the inherent conflicts that are characteristic of modern culture. When we read a textbook like this one, we are confronted with competing notions of literature and criticism that cannot be neatly resolved by invoking a single authoritative voice. Criticism, in an important sense, is part of the complex processes of writing our own history. If the debate between various postmodernisms and various Marxisms resists our efforts to reduce it to a conflict of opposing extremes, it is in part because we cannot separate ourselves from this dialogic history—or, more accurately, histories—that we are telling ourselves. Even as we attempt to formulate a definitive history of our times, history—including the contemporary history of criticism—has a way of slipping out from under fast and easy generalizations.

Paradoxically, however, it is the very difficulty of writing a history of literature or criticism that sends us back to canonical texts in order to rewrite them, to reinterpret them in light of our own historical situation, our own sense of priorities, our own political agendas. If, in their different ways, Johnson and Bakhtin are convincing about the historical function of criticism, they should help convince us that our own writing cannot escape the sociopolitical conditions of its creation, any more than a work of art can completely transcend the conditions under which it was produced. If there is an identifiable movement in contemporary criticism, it may be evident in the ways in which many critics—Williams, Gilbert, Cixous, Christian, and Stepto—acknowledge their polemical intentions, the political effects that they want their critical writing to produce. In particular, recent developments in feminist and black criticism have challenged the sorts of literary history—and sociopolitical history—that the works of Arnold, Eliot, Frye, and others have helped to produce. For critics otherwise as different as Woolf and Christian, the rewriting of the history of literature and literary criticism is a fundamentally political act.

As Gilbert argues in "Life's Empty Pack: Towards a Literary Daughteronomy," the creation of a feminist literary history necessitates a rewriting of history itself to allow people who traditionally have been denied a voice—

women, people of color, servants, and members of the lower classes—to articulate their resistance to strategies of social exclusion and repression. Traditionally, members of these groups have not been allowed to speak within the canon of literature. In Daniel Defoe's *Robinson Crusoe*, for example, we never hear Friday, the narrator's nonwhite servant/slave, talk directly to us; his voice is always represented to us by his white, middle-class English master. No women poets are represented in Johnson's *Lives of the Poets*, though some women, like Aphra Behn, were certainly better known as writers in the eighteenth century than some of the male poets who are included. Many of us who went through college and graduate school before the late 1970s never read a poem, novel, play, or essay by a black writer. These exclusions in some instances may represent deliberate strategies to keep literature exclusively white, middle-class, and male, but they also can represent unconscious or semiconscious conceptions of literature and history at work that silently resist intrusions by "female wits" like Behn and black revolutionaries like the contemporary playwright and poet, Imamu Amiri Baraka. In one sense, what is at stake in both the overt and covert battles being waged about what belongs in the canon are notions of history. The traditional literary establishment, in invoking notions of what "everyone" knows are great or "timeless" works, is also silently evoking a vision of history of the kind Pope projects in his *Essay*. History, in this sense, is a single narrative, a line connecting the great critics of the past—Aristotle, Horace, and Longinus—to the present. Its concerns are timeless; they transcend, as Sidney claims, the vicissitudes of history. In contrast, the history envisioned by Gilbert and Christian is effectively multiple or dialogic, not a single narrative but a group of narratives. In the essays of these critics, history is decentered; it is no longer the master discourse that silences "marginal" figures—women, blacks, Indians, and the poor—but a series of discourses that give voice to both traditional figures like Aristotle and Johnson and to those people who have previously been ignored by the narratives of history.

The selections in the final section of this anthology from twentieth-century critics should indicate the general directions in which criticism has moved during the past two decades. It is a relatively simple task to see that since the mid-1960s new forms of criticism have developed to challenge traditional notions of what literature is and what role it should play in society. The history that these essays represent is not the history that Pope, Burke, Arnold, or even Brooks had in mind when they wrote. In effect, history has been pluralized as well as decentered. Its narratives have grown more complex, its claims on our literary and political allegiances more demanding. Just as the literary canon is now under pressure to include the voices of those who had been previously silenced, so too is the canon of criticism. This dialogic competition of competing critical voices affords both opportunities and dilemmas. In fact, one could argue that the notion of a canon itself has been destabilized by theorists such as Derrida, Foucault, and Cixous. The master narrative of critical history is, as this anthology demonstrates by including figures like Christine de Pisan, Aphra Behn, and Eliza Haywood, itself being rewritten to take into account new political understandings of how the histories of literature and criticism have been constituted. One consequence of this rewriting is that our own position as twentieth-century consumers of literary criticism has become more ambiguous, more difficult. Do we search for nuggets of Johnsonian authority in the criticism of eighteenth-century women writers to demonstrate their "value"? or do we redefine what we value in literary criticism? Do we extend the canon of literature to include female as well as male writers, black as well as white authors? Or do we restructure literature itself to exclude what previously had been considered canonical works? If we write some writers into the canon, should we then write others out? To correct past "mistakes," should we overtly politicize the canons of literature and criticism, judging writers on the basis of, say, their socioeconomic views rather than on their "timeless" appeal to "universal" truths? Do we even need to answer these kinds of questions? What happens when and if we begin to grapple with them?

The sixty or so selections in this anthology offer different answers to these questions, some more convincing than others. However we choose to answer them will tell us something about our own historical position, our own desires to construct the kind of narratives from which we would like to see ourselves descended. In effect, even to begin to ask these kinds of questions is to demonstrate that criticism is never an escape from history but a charge, full-bore, into it.

Notes

1. Hayden White, *The Content of the Form: Narrative Discourse and Historical Representation* (Baltimore: Johns Hopkins University Press, 1987). See also White's earlier studies, *Metahistory: The Historical Imagination in Nineteenth-Century Europe* (Baltimore: Johns Hopkins University Press, 1973) and *Tropics of Discourse: Essays in Cultural Criticism* (Baltimore: Johns Hopkins University Press, 1978).
2. On the radicals during the English Civil War, see Christopher Hill, *The World Turned Upside Down: Radical Ideas During the English Revolution* (1971; rpt. Harmondsworth, Eng.: Penguin, 1975).
3. Stephen Greenblatt, *Renaissance Self-Fashioning: From More to Shakespeare* (Chicago: University of Chicago Press, 1980) and *Shakespearean Negotiations: The Circulation of Social Energy in Renaissance England* (Berkeley and Los Angeles: University of California Press, 1988); Jonathan Dollimore, *Radical Tragedy: Religion, Ideology and Power in the Drama of Shakespeare and His Contemporaries* (Chicago: University of Chicago Press, 1984).
4. In addition to Bakhtin's essay in this collection, see *The Dialogical Imagination: Four Essays by M. M. Bakhtin*, ed. Michael Holquist, trans. Caryl Emerson and Michael Holquist (Austin: University of Texas Press, 1981).
5. "Astraea Redux," in *Works of John Dryden*, vol. 1, ed. Edward Niles Hooker

and H. T. Swedenberg, Jr. (Berkeley and Los Angeles: University of California Press, 1956).

6. Samuel Johnson, *Lives of the English Poets*, 3 vols., ed. George Birkbeck Hill (1905; rpt. New York: Octagon Books, 1967). All quotations are from this edition.
7. On Bakhtin and his circle, see Katerina Clark and Michael Holquist, *Mikhail Bakhtin* (Cambridge, Mass.: Harvard University Press, 1984); on the Russian formalists, see Tony Bennett, *Formalism and Marxism* (New York: Methuen, 1979) and Peter Steiner, *Russian Formalism: A Metapoetics* (Ithaca, N.Y.: Cornell University Press, 1984).
8. The phrase "dialogics of culture" is from a passage of Bakhtin's in Tzvetan Todorov, *Mikhail Bakhtin: The Dialogical Principle*, trans. Wlad Godzich (Minneapolis: University of Minnesota Press, 1984), p. 124.
9. Michael Ryan, *Marxism and Deconstruction: A Critical Articulation* (Baltimore: Johns Hopkins University Press, 1982); Terry Eagleton, *Literary Theory: An Introduction* (Minneapolis: University of Minnesota Press, 1983), especially pp. 142–50.

Semiotics and Criticism

Ronald Schleifer

The World of Signs

In the third voyage of *Gulliver's Travels* Gulliver visits the School of Languages at the Grand Academy of Lagado, where he encounters a strange scheme for the abolition of all words in order to preserve the health of our lungs. Instead of using words, people would simply carry around with them "such *Things* as were necessary to express the particular Business they are to discourse on." This scheme, Gulliver noted, "hath only this Inconvenience attending it; that if a Man's Business be very great, and of various Kinds, he must be obliged in Proportion to carry a great Bundle of *Things* upon his Back, unless he can afford one or two strong Servants to attend him." Such a scheme, as Swift well knew, is impracticable and wrongheaded: not only would such discoursers sink "under the Weight of their Packs, like Pedlars among us," more strikingly, as Swift demonstrates in the next voyage of *Gulliver's Travels,* such a conception of the nature of language as "only Names for *Things*" would not allow for one of the most powerful aspects of language, the ability of language to say *"the Thing which was not"*: to make promises, to imagine and define worlds different from our own (like those of *Gulliver's Travels*), to describe the future, to lie, to articulate values, to assert negations—all things that cannot fit in the packs people would have to carry with them to replace language.

In this negative example, Swift is describing the great convenience of language, the power it affords us to represent or "signify" absent entities. The science of such signification—which studies language more carefully, I think, than the scholars of Lagado—is semiotics. The term *semiotics* comes from the Greek word *semeion,* which means "sign," and semiotics is the study—or the science—of the functioning of signs. Signs function all around us every time we use one entity to *signify* or *represent* another. For instance, the sounds that comprise the word *tree* in English signify the physical object of a tree; and the graphic marks "tree" signify the sounds *tree,* and so on. Signification takes place all the time, even when we are not intentionally attending to some discursive business or another: this is part of Swift's mockery of the single-minded nearsightedness of the scholars of Lagado. But signification does more than allow us to signify absent entities in thought or speech or other modes of communication; it saves us from more than the heavy bundle of things Swift's scholars carry. More complexly than simple representation, signification helps determine experience and perception: the fact that English has a sign *tree*—especially in relation to the sign *shrub,* for instance—contributes to the determination of experience and perception so that the world takes on an orderly shape and gains both value and a future.

This is perhaps clearer in my second example, in which the seemingly precise sound of the word "tree" is designated by a graphic sign (or a combination of graphic signs, *t-r-e-e*). Even though most of the pronunciations of the sound of the word "tree," spoken by old men and young women, by children, by people with accents from different parts of the country, in screams and whispers, are measurably different in terms of the physical properties of sound, we experience or perceive these manifestations of the word as the same. In fact, some variations of the sound *tree* are far more different from one another than the difference between *tree* and *three,* just as scrub oaks and palm trees are far more different from one another than scrub oaks and woody shrubs, yet the designation—the sign *tree*—helps us delimit the object the sign represents. This conception of signification does not assume that signs represent *preexisting* entities (which we could carry around in a sack). Rather, it sees the process of signification as one in which signs designate mental images or thoughts or ideas, but in such a way that such ideas or thoughts do not preexist the process of signification but rather gain their definition by means of signification. In this conception, a sign does not "re-present" some entity or thought, but rather the process of signification gives definition to an idea—it *realizes* it—when that idea, like a promised future, was only a vague, indefinite possibility before.

In this conception, the ways in which signs *refer* to objects (including mental objects) in the world are less important than the generative capacities of signification, the ways in which signs create the possibility of definition and intelligibility. In fact, Claude Lévi-Strauss describes the function of signs as the expression of "intelligible" meaning by means of "tangible" physical entities. When we think about it, the fact that intelligibility—the apparently private experience of understanding—can be expressed and communicated by means of things that can be tangibly perceived is remarkable. Yet, as I shall argue, semiotics teaches us that this seemingly private process is socially determined in such a way that we must rethink not only the ordinary conceptions of what meaning and understanding are, but even rethink the apparently simple opposition between meaning and fact. If signification helps determine the entities it seemingly represents, then private understanding may not preexist its public communication: signification becomes less an activity we engage in, like taking things out of a sack, than a world we inhabit.

In any case, the complex relationship between perception and meaning—between the tangible and the intelligible—is woven closely into everything we do. A striking part of being human is the ability to discern meaning—to apprehend signs—wherever we look: not only in stories we hear or experiences we remember, but in things as subtle as tones of voice, facial expressions, the accidental ways in which light strikes a tree, the color of cloth, and the sequences of sounds. Literature, of course, teaches us to apprehend such signs better than we might; it does so, I believe, by making the accidental an unacceptable mode of explaining (i.e., "understanding") the perceptions it presents to us. If this is so, then semiotics, the science of signs, can teach us how literature achieves its ends. Later in this essay I will examine how semiotics can help us to read and understand literary texts more fully (and how literature can help us understand semiotics), but here I want to emphasize that semiotics does not aim to discover particular meanings in its objects of study. Rather, semiotics seeks to understand the conditions of meaning, to isolate and describe those conditions under which signification can take place. The great questions of semiotics are How is meaning possible? What is its nature? How does it work? How is it possible to "represent" something that is absent? What, finally, is the nature of intelligibility and what is its relationship to representation and signification?

Humanities and the Human Sciences

A striking fact about the history of science is the ways in which the great revolutionary figures—Newton, Darwin, Einstein, and perhaps Freud—gained their insights by asking questions where most people had seen simple, self-evident truths. For instance, Darwin asked, "Why are there so many species?" Marx asked, "Do belief systems do more than articulate general truths, and if so, what particular social ends do they serve?" Einstein asked, "What is the significance of the nature of light for understanding the relationship between time and space?" In each case—and, of course, they could be significantly multiplied—science is asserting that there is a question to be asked concerning the human situation and experience that is so close to everyday life that no one ever stopped to notice that it *was* a question. In each case, as Northrop Frye says in "The Function of Criticism at the Present Time," science transforms itself from the condition of "naive induction," which attempts to classify the immediate sensations of experience, to more sophisticated questioning that attempts to explain the very phenomenon it examines "in terms of a conceptual framework different in shape" from that phenomenon itself.

The same is true of semiotics. Just as scientific physics was impossible for the ancients because they did not imagine that the different elements so close to human life—earth, fire, air, and water—could be understood beyond the simple recounting of their existence, so the semiotic science of the signifying process could not be formulated as a science until basic questions about the nature of meaning that focused on self-evident truths could be asked. One such question (which I have already touched upon) examines the concept of the sameness of different entities or events: what makes two sounds or two concepts or two experiences the same? Such a question—which became more and more pressing to philosophers in the course of the nineteenth century, to the precursors of semiotics such as Marx, Durkheim, Nietzsche, Freud—is basic to larger questions of *how* it is that signification is possible? What takes place when one entity stands for or signifies another? And finally, how is it possible for such signification to be *interpersonal* communication? Roman Jakobson, the great linguist and semiotician, defines meaning itself as the translation of one set of signs into another set of signs, a definition of meaning that, raising these questions, is closely tied to the conception of the "same."

The science of semiotics attempts to create a conceptual framework in which such questions about language, signification, and communication can be rigorously addressed and answered. As Lévi-Strauss has argued, at the heart of signification is the process of translation:

> I have tried to transcend the contrast between the tangible and the intelligible by operating from the outset at the sign level. The function of signs, is, precisely, to express the one by means of the other. Even when very restricted in number, they lend themselves to rigorously organized combinations which can translate even the finest shades of the whole range of sense experience. We can thus hope to reach a plane where logical properties, as attributes of things, will be manifested as directly as flavors or perfumes; perfumes are unmistakably identifiable, yet we know that they result from combinations of elements which, if subjected to a different selection and organization, would have created awareness of a different perfume.[1]

In this passage Lévi-Strauss is articulating the great ambition of semiotics: to be a science of signs that can account for the myraid meanings of signification—the "phenomenal" or "felt" sense of meaning that experience continuously presents to us—with the same rigor as the laws of chemistry. Just as the smell of perfume is a phenomenal effect of chemical combinations whose invariant elements and active properties can be formulated, recorded, and predicted to behave in certain ways in certain situations, so, Lévi-Strauss hopes, "meaning" is also a phenomenal effect that can be accounted for and predicted by the scientific isolation and discovery of invariant elements and processes of signification.

In other words, Lévi-Strauss assumes that the intelligible effects of meaning are in no way mysterious or spiritual or intangible or unique. Rather, he assumes they are recurrent phenomena which, like the other phenomena science studies, can be understood in terms of what Frye calls the "conceptual framework different in shape from them" of science. Science begins by assuming that phenomena are more than a collection of unique events; it assumes that they are related to one another and can be explained within a framework that articulates the relationships—the repetition of the same invariant elements—across seemingly unique events. In the same way, Lévi-Strauss assumes that different meanings are related to one another as palpable effects on human perception that can be accounted for in the same way the effect of smell is accountable in relation to the general laws of chemical combinations. How else, Lévi-Strauss implies, could meanings present so many seeming invariables (such as the word *tree*)? How else could meaning be shared? How else could the ability to speak and understand an almost infinite number of sentences be acquired in the first three years of life?

For this reason A. J. Greimas, an important follower of Lévi-Strauss, notes that the science of semiotics assumes that the phenomenon of meaning can be understood in the same way other phenomena are understood. In *Structural Semantics* (1966) he says

> It may be—it is a philosophic and not linguistic question—that the phenomenon of language as such is mysterious, but there are no mysteries in language.
>
> The "piece of wax" of Descartes is no less mysterious than the symbol of the moon. It is simply that chemistry has succeeded in giving an account of its elementary composition. It is toward an analysis of the same type that structural semantics must proceed. It is true the *effects of meaning* do hold good in both cases, but the new analytic plane of reality—whether it is in chemistry or semiology—is not less legitimate.[2]

The piece of wax Greimas is talking about is the fact that Descartes notes in his *Meditations* that wax manifests itself variously—changing its qualities when he brings it close to a fire—so that, while all the qualities "which fall under taste, smell, sight, touch, and hearing, are found to be changed, . . . yet the same wax remains."[3] Since Descartes' time chemistry has developed as a science insofar as it can reduce a large number of phenomena such as the perceptions of the different qualities of wax Descartes describes to variations governed by invariant chemical laws and substances. Greimas hopes that semiotics can achieve the same simplicity, coherence, and scope for the science of meaning and signification: that it can account for the effects of meaning such as the symbolic meanings associated with the moon in the same way chemistry accounts for the phenomenal effects that chemical compounds produce.

Behind this assumption—as it is behind those of Lévi-Strauss and Frye—is a reconception of those areas of knowledge that have traditionally examined the nature of meaning in human affairs, the humanities. The humanities—

whether the study of literary texts, musical compositions, philosophical treatises, or works of art—have always assumed that each object of study was a unique and unrepeatable event. After all, Shakespeare wrote *Hamlet* only once; Descartes meditated on the nature of the human mind once at a particular moment in the history of ideas; and Mozart's "Hunt" quartet is an unrepeatable event in the history of music. But since the humanities have always understood the objects of their attention to be unique events, they have always limited themselves as a body of knowledge to description and paraphrase. Thus literary criticism has interpreted literary works by paraphrasing their meanings in other words or describing them in terms of their unique elements.

As the linguist Louis Hjelmslev has noted, according to this traditional view "humanistic, as opposed to natural phenomena are nonrecurrent and for that very reason cannot, like natural phenomena, be subjected to exact and generalizing treatment. . . . In the field of the humanities," he continues, "consequently, there would have to be a different method [from that of science]—namely, mere description, which would be nearer to poetry than to exact science—or, at any event, a method that restricts itself to a discursive form of presentation in which the phenomena pass by, one by one, without being interpreted through a system."[4] This method, Hjelmslev suggests, is history in its most chronological manifestation. Since the objects of humanistic study are unique, they can be catalogued only in chronological order. For this reason the humanities have traditionally been historical studies: the history of philosophy, the history of art, history itself, the history of science, literary history, and so forth. Frye says a similar thing in "The Function of Criticism": "literature as yet being unorganized by criticism, it still appears as a huge aggregate or miscellaneous pile of creative efforts. The only organizing principle so far discovered in it is chronology. . . ."

Implicit in Frye's and Hjelmslev's statements is the basic of assumption of semiotics: that the humanities can reorient themselves and adopt a scientific model in their study. Instead of pursuing the "naive induction" of cataloguing unique events, they can, as Hjelmslev says, attempt "to rise above the level of mere primitive description to that of a systematic, exact, and generalizing science, in the theory of which all events (possible combinations of elements) are foreseen and the conditions for their realization established."[5] Such a discipline could examine signification from a host of different points of view. It could examine the elements that combine to create the meaning effects Greimas describes; it could study the recurrent elements of myth and narrative Lévi-Strauss examines; it could explore the ways in which signification takes place in language as Saussure and Hjelmslev do. In more particularly literary examples, it could study the systematic nature of literature itself, such as the general theory of genre that Frye suggests and that Tzvetan Todorov pursues in relation to the fantastic; it could examine the systematic relationship among the objects of humanistic study conceived as textuality (and, elsewhere, intertextuality) that Roland Barthes describes in "From Work to Text"; it could examine the relationship among the assumptions that govern particular modes of interpretation as J. Hillis Miller does in "The Search for Grounds in Literary Study"; it could study racism and misogyny within more general patterns of cultural signification as Barbara Christian and Hélène Cixous do; it could study the role of writing and authors in culture as Jacques Derrida and Michel Foucault do; and it could offer, as this anthology does, topical and systematic alternatives to the chronological presentation of critical texts.

In these ways the traditional humanities can reconceptualize themselves as the "human sciences." In such a conception, as Frye notes, criticism would take its place among the social sciences rather than the natural sciences. In fact, the same opposition between the humanities and the human sciences can be seen in the social sciences themselves. For instance, Ferdinand de Saussure notes in the *The Course in General Linguistics* the difference between two methods of studying economics—economic history and the "synchronic" study of the economic system at any particular moment. Most of the social sciences are divided in this way: psychology, for instance, encompasses both the analysis of unique case histories in clinical psychology and attempts to articulate the general functioning of mental activity in experimental psychology. Anthropology encompasses both the study of unique cultures and, as in Lévi-Strauss's work, the general functioning of aspects of culture. Even history, the model of humanistic study of unique and unrepeatable events, is sometimes taken to be a social science in whose conceptual framework, as Frye says, "there is nothing that cannot be considered historically."

In this way, literary study also can be seen to offer two methods of study: literary history and more or less systematizing criticism. What allows the systematization of criticism, however, is the common and most recurrent element of traditional humanistic study, the fact that, as Hjelmslev notes, all the humanities deal in the study of language and discourse, the study of signification. In other words, if the humanities all participate in areas of the social sciences, they do so because the *foundation* of society is the signifying systems that allow for intelligible social intercourse. In this way, the overarching social science is semiotics: it studies the functioning of signs as an always *social* functioning basic to psychology, sociology, history, economics, and the other social sciences. In this way, literary criticism would take its place among the social and, more broadly speaking, the "human" sciences. Its study of the signifying forms of literature would be a special case of the study of signification altogether, the study of semiotics. Such a human science would attempt to describe what distinguishes literature from other signifying practices and what literature shares with them. It would attempt, as many have already attempted, to situate literary practice within other cultural practices (including linguistics, teaching, politics, psychology, history, philosophy, ideology, sociology, and so forth). It would study literary works not as special cases, but as representative cases, as possessing and presenting the forms of signification that can help us to understanding the nature and generation of meaning in general.

Structural Linguistics

Lévi-Strauss, Greimas, and Hjelmslev base their understanding of signification on the studies of the great linguists of the twentieth century, and especially the work of Continental (as opposed to Anglo-American) linguists. At the head of this tradition is the great Swiss linguist, Ferdinand de Saussure whom I've already mentioned in passing. In fact, Saussure called for a science of semiology in the several courses in general linguistics he offered at the University of Geneva from 1907 to 1911. Almost simultaneously in the first decade of the twentieth century the American philosopher and logician Charles Sanders Peirce used the term "semiotic" to describe the general science of the functioning of signs in various sciences—what Jonathan Culler describes as the "science of sciences."[6] (In the 1970s the International Association for Semiotic Studies opted for Peirce's term, "semiotics.") Peirce saw semiotics in relation to logic and developed elaborate taxonomies of types of signs. Saussure, on the other hand, has exerted much greater influence by calling for semiotics to model itself as a discipline in relation to linguistics (even if, as some recent writers have noted, this modelling has produced a narrow definition of the sign based upon the special properties of linguistic signs.)[7]

In any case, the coincidental articulation of a neologism to describe a science which did not exist but which, as Saussure said, had "a right to exist"[8] is one of the remarkable events in the history of ideas, comparable to the coincidental development of calculus by Isaac Newton and G. W. Leibniz at the turn of the eighteenth century. Moreover, like the introduction of calculus, which allowed Newton to calculate and predict in a short time the planetary motions that Johann Kepler recorded over the course of more than twenty years, and like the linguistic science Saussure developed and the discovery of "the truth about the general reference of symbols to their objects" that Peirce was pursuing, semiotics is an attempt to reduce the myriad facts about signification—that is, about meaning in human affairs—to a manageable number of propositions about the functioning of the signifying process in human life within a rigorous conceptual framework.[9]

Saussure defined semiology as the science "*that studies the life of signs within society*" which "would be part of social psychology and consequently of general psychology." "Semiology," he goes on, "would show what constitutes signs, what laws govern them. . . . Linguistics is only a part of the general science of semiology; the laws discovered by semiology will be applicable to linguistics, and the latter will circumscribe a well-defined area within the mass of anthropological facts."[10] Whether linguistics is part of semiotics, as Saussure contends here, or whether semiotics is modelled upon linguistics is a debate that has received a good deal of attention in the last three decades. At the other extreme is Roland Barthes' contention that *all* semiotic systems—including the "natural semiotics" of animal sign and signal languages, the connotations (as opposed to the denotations) of human linguistic systems, and nonverbal semiotic systems such as music and painting—can be understood as species of what Umberto Eco has called *translinguistics*, the examination of "all sign systems with reference to linguistic laws."[11] It is Barthes' position that linguistic science, rather than psychology, has developed the conceptual framework in which to understand signification in general.

Whether scholars assume that semiotics simply *extends* linguistics beyond the sentence or that it *subsumes* linguistics in its understanding of the functioning of signs in general, it is clear that linguistics has offered the most rigorous examination of the process of signification of all the branches of semiotic science. I believe this is because the object of linguistics has been more rigorously defined than other semiotic systems.[12] Saussure describes semiology as belonging to general psychology. However, the rigor of structural linguistics and semiotics has established itself, as we shall see, in their avoidance of psychological and cognitive explanations—causal explanations—in defining the linguistic (and semiotic) sign. That definition begins with Saussure's reorientation of linguistics in the *Course of General Linguistics* from the historical study of language—and especially etymology—to the "systemic" study of language that he inaugurated in his work. Saussure's reexamination of language is based upon three assumptions. The first of these, which I have already touched upon, is the assumption that the scientific study of language needs to develop and study the *system* rather than the history of linguistic phenomena. Saussure distinguishes between the particular occurrences of language—its particular speech-events, which he designates as *parole*—and the proper object of linguistics, the system that governs those events—its code, which he designates as *langue*. Moreover, he argues for the "synchronic" study of the relationship among the elements of language at a particular instant rather than the "diachronic" study of the development of language through history.

This assumption gave rise to what Jakobson came to call *structuralism* in 1929:

> Were we to comprise the leading idea of present-day science in its most various manifestations, we could hardly find a more appropriate designation that *structuralism*. Any set of phenomena examined by contemporary science is treated not as a mechanical agglomeration but as a structural whole, and the basic task is to reveal the inner . . . laws of this system. What appears to be the focus of scientific preoccupations is no longer the outer stimulus, but the internal premises of the development: now the mechanical conception of processes yields to the question of their function.[13]

In this dense passage Jakobson is articulating the scientific aim of linguistics I have described more generally as the aim of semiotics. But more than this, he is also describing the second foundational assumption in Saussurean—we can now call it "structural"—linguistics. The second assumption is that the basic elements of language—and of signification more generally—can be studied only in relation to their *function* rather than their *cause*. Instead of studying particular and unique events and entities, those events and entities have to be situated within a systemic framework in which they are related to other so-called events and entities. This is a radical reorientation in conceiving of the world, one whose importance the philosopher Ernst Cassirer has compared "to the new science of Galileo which in the seventeenth century changed our whole concept of the physical world."[14]

I have already touched upon this matter when I attempted to define "sign" at the beginning of this essay. Saussure describes the nature of the linguistic sign as the union of "a concept and a sound image," which he called "signified" (*signifié*) and "signifier" (*signifiant*).[15] But the nature of their combination is what makes this conception functional: for Saussure, neither the signified nor the signifier is the cause of the other. Rather, they exist within the linguistic sign in what Greimas calls a relationship of "reciprocal presupposition": the signifier presupposes the signified that, after all, it signifies; but at the same time the signified presupposes the signifier: otherwise it couldn't be "signified [by something]." In this way, Saussure defines the basic element of language, the sign, *relationally;* and in doing so he can explain the problem of the *identity* of units of language and signification I mentioned at the beginning of this essay: the reason we can recognize different pronunciations of the word *tree* as the same word is that the word is not defined by inherent qualities—it is not a "mechanical agglomeration" of such qualities—but rather it is defined as an element in a system—a "structural whole"—of language.

Such a relational definition of an entity—it is sometimes also called a diacritical definition—governs the conception of all the elements of signification. This is clearest in the most impressive achievement of Saussurean linguistics, the development of the concepts of *phonemes* and *distinctive features* of language. Phonemes are the smallest articulated and signifying units of a language. They are opposed to *phones,* which are the actual sounds that a language utilizes. Phonemes are not the sounds that occur in language, but the sounds that are phenomenally apprehended as conveying meaning: for instance, in English the [t] can be pronounced with an aspiration (a slight "h" sound seemingly added to it) as in an emphatic pronunciation of the word *take* [t']; or it can be pronounced unaspirated as in *steak;* but in both cases an English speaker will recognize it as variations (or "allophones") of a /t/ phoneme so that someone speaking with an accent that aspirates all /t/s could still be understood. What are phonemic variations in one language constitute distinct phonemes in another: thus English, unlike Chinese, distinguishes between /l/ and /r/, and native Chinese speakers have great trouble with the distinction between these English phonemes precisely because in their native language they are simply variations of the "same" sound. In every natural language, the vast number of possible words is a combination of a small number of phonemes. English, for instance, possesses less than forty phonemes that combine to form over a million different words and the infinite number of different pronunciations these words are susceptible to.

The phonemes of language, however, are themselves systematically organized. In the twenties and thirties, following the lead of Saussure, Jakobson and the great Russian phonologist N. S. Trubetzkoy isolated the *distinctive features* of phonemes. These features are based upon the physiological structure of the speech organs—tongue, teeth, vocal chords, and so on—and they combine to form phonemes in "bundles." No distinctive feature can exist outside of combination with others within a phonemic articulation (one cannot engage the vocal chords without doing other things to produce a sound); but, more important, they organize and *define* themselves through a logic of binary opposition in terms of their presence and absence. For instance, in English the difference between /t/ and /d/ is the presence or absence of "voice" (the engagement of the vocal chords), and on the level of voicing these phonemes reciprocally define one another; the difference between /p/ and /t/ is that the former possesses the feature of "labiality" (i.e., it is produced by the lips), while the latter is "dental," and again they are defined in relation to one another. In this way, phonology is a specific example of a general rule of language Saussure describes:

> . . . in language there are only differences. Even more important: a difference generally implies positive terms between which the difference is set up; but in language there are only differences *without positive terms.* Whether we take the signified or the signifier, language has neither ideas nor sound that existed before the linguistic system, but only conceptual and phonic differences that have issued from the system. The idea or phonic substance that a sign contains is of less importance than the other signs that surround it.[16]

In this framework, "positive" identities—what constitutes sameness and, finally, meaning itself—are determined not by inherent qualities but by systemic—"structural"—relationships.

This conception of the elements of signification being diacritically determined through a system suggests a third assumption governing Saussurean linguistics and semiotics: what Saussure calls "the arbitrary nature of the sign." By this he means that the relationship between the signifier and signified in language is never necessary (or "motivated"): one could just as easily find the sound signifier *arbre* as the signifier *tree* to unite with the concept of "tree." But more than this, it means that the *signified* is arbitrary as well: one could as easily define the concept "tree" by its woody quality (which would exclude palm trees) as by its size (which excludes the "low woody plants" we call shrubs). This relationship is not necessary because it is not based upon inherent qualities of signifier or signified: the nature of the sign—and of signifiers and signifieds—is governed by systematic diacritical relationships. Moreover, this should make clear that the numbering of assumptions I have been making is not an order of priority. Each assumption—the systemic nature of signification (best apprehended by studying language synchronically); the relational, or diacritical, nature of the elements of signification; the arbitrary nature of signs—is in a relationship of reciprocal presupposition with the others.

In this we can see that the science of signification, like that of chemistry, is governed by a conceptual framework that understands the phenomena it studies in overarching relationships of *contrast* and *combination*. The elements of language are defined on any particular level of understanding in terms of the ways in which they contrast with other elements on that level (just as the periodic table offers the chemical elements in a systematic framework of contrasts); while they combine with elements from their own level to create the elements of the next linguistic level (just as chemical elements combine in a systematic fashion determined by their contrasting qualities). Thus distinctive features combine to form phonemes, and phonemes combine to form morphemes (the smallest units of meaning such as prefixes, suffixes, and so on), and morphemes combine to form words, and words combine to form sentences. In each instance, the whole of an element is greater than the sum of its parts (just as water, H_2O, is more than the mechanical agglomeration of hydrogen and oxygen).

The great difference, however, between a semiotic (or "human") science such as linguistics and a natural science such as chemistry is Saussure's third assumption, the arbitrary nature of the sign. In chemistry the elements of the framework of understanding—particles, chemical elements, molecules—are not arbitrary, but rather inherent and necessary within the object of study. In studying meaning, on the other hand, the elements *are* arbitrary: signification can use any phenomenon to signify. This is clearest, I think, in those instances when language uses the *absence* of some feature as part of its signifying system, when, as Saussure says, "a material sign is not necessary for the expression of an idea; language is satisfied with the opposition between something and nothing."[17] In chemistry material is always necessary, and the absence of oxygen, say, is simply its absence. But in language—in signification—the absence of voicing is more than the simple absence of the sound produced by air rushing across vocal chords. It also produces a signification that, in English, can be perceived in the difference between *site* and *side*, *dew* and *two*. Absence here is not simple; as Jacques Derrida says in another context, it—and signification in general—is "irreducibly nonsimple."[18] Such nonsimplicity is what Friedrich Nietzsche means in "On Music and Words" when he describes "the duality in the essence of language."

Such an understanding of the arbitrary nature of the sign leads to the great difference between the natural sciences and the human sciences. As linguist Emile Benveniste has argued,

> . . . one should draw a fundamental distinction between two orders of phenomena: on the one side the physiological and biological data, which present a "simple" nature (no matter what their complexity may be) because they hold entirely within the field in which they appear. . . ; on the other side, the phenomena belonging to the interhuman milieu, which have the characteristic that they can never be taken as simple data or defined in the order of their own nature but must always be understood as double from the fact that they

> are connected to something else, whatever their "referent" may be. A fact of culture is such only insofar as it refers to something else.[19]

The overriding "fact" of culture is signification, the fact that a phenomenon—whatever we can "perceive"—always means something, always signifies. Semiotics studies such signifying cultural phenomena—the phenomenon of signification itself—in as exact and generalizing a way as the natural sciences study physical and biological phenomena, even if, as the poststructuralist critique of semiotics suggests, the irreducible "nonsimplicity" of signifying interhuman phenomena undermines, in significant ways, this scientific project.

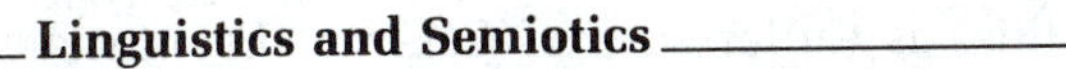

Linguistics and Semiotics

The remarkable and revolutionary assumptions about meaning and the explanations for signification developed by structural linguistics led Cassirer to claim that semiotics changed our whole concept of the world. "For this to happen," Culler says of this claim, linguistics "would have to become a model for thinking about social and cultural activities in general . . . [so that we would] come to think about our social and cultural world as a series of sign systems comparable with languages."[20] In other words, because of the linguistic concepts of the arbitrary nature of sign and the relational nature of the elements of signification, semiotics can study signifying phenomena beyond the limits of the sentence—the usual limit of linguistic analysis—within a conceptual framework similar to, if not identical with, that of structural linguistics. Thus in *Elements of Semiology* Barthes argues that the connotations of language arise systematically when language takes up the accidental variants of its elements and uses them, arbitrarily, within a relational system of signification: "the rolled r is a mere combinative variant at the denotative level," he writes, "but in the speech of the theatre, for instance, it signals a country accent and therefore is part of a code, without which the message of 'ruralness' could not be either emitted or perceived."[21] In the same way, discourse can take up a whole sign—*wine* in French culture, for example—and have it, as the union of its signifier and signified ("an alcoholic drink made from grapes") function, connotatively, to signify, as Barthes argues, the French nation itself.[22]

Besides such more-or-less linguistic phenomena, semiotics studies various social forms that function in the manner of a language: Barthes' work on the mythologies of culture is an example in which he describes the significance of such nonverbal phenomena as wrestling or wine or Greta Garbo's face as signifiers in culture. In a similar way, Lévi-Strauss analyzed kinship structures in so-called primitive cultures in a manner analogous to that in which Saussure and Jakobson analyze the elementary structures of language. In this analysis, Lévi-Strauss asserts that women are exchanged between men of different tribes according to systems of binary oppositions. In later studies Lévi-Strauss pursues this structuralist analysis in cultural myths, but he is less interested in myths as linguistic phenomena than as semiotic, cultural phenomena that serve social ends. Thus, he argues that myths are structured like languages on a level higher than linguistic analysis—on the level of the narrative discourse as a whole. Mythic structure defines "a 'universe of the tale,' analyzable in pairs of opposition interlocked within each character, who—far from constituting a single entity—form a bundle of distinctive features like the phoneme in Roman Jakobson's theory."[23] In one example, he notes that "in a tale a 'king' is not only king and a 'shepherdess' not only a shepherdess; these words and what they signify become recognizable means of constructing a system formed by the oppositions *male/female* (with regard to *nature*) and *high/low* (with regard to *culture*), as well as permutations among the six terms."[24]

In this, as Culler says of Cassirer, Lévi-Strauss is creating a model for thinking about social and cultural activities by raising the largest questions about the relationship of nature and culture in a conceptual framework that is coherent and systematic. In this way semiotics has examined phenomena as different as the general semiotics of the natural world and the special semiotics of the legal system. In *A Theory of Semiotics* Eco describes the range of semiotics from the study of the "the communicative behavior of non-human . . . communities" in *Zoosemiotics* through olfactory signs, tactile communication, codes of taste, visual communication to specific cultural codes like those of medicine, music, writing, text theory, aesthetic texts, and mass communication. Some of the most important work in semiotics is being done in film studies. But more than this, semiotics can also examine social and political phenomena: as I have suggested, it can help us understand racism and sexism as functioning signifying systems. All these areas of study clearly indicate the arbitrary nature of signs: signification (or, the broader sense of signification, "semiosis"), as I have said, can and will use anything at hand—sound, color, gender, skin color—for the sake of its meanings, its process of signification. But these studies also share two other assumptions of linguistics: (1) a belief in the need to describe the system rather than the particular manifestations of social and cultural activities—what I have called the "conditions" that give rise to and determine the meanings of these activities; and (2) an understanding that the elements of semiosis are relationally defined.

In the wider scope of semiotics the relational nature of signs might be better understood as the *positionality* of signification. Nietzsche attempts to create such positions in the relationship of words and music, and Michel Foucault does this when he describes the author's place in the interpretive process. In "What Is an Author?" he writes: "we must locate the space left empty by the author's disappearance, follow the distribution of gaps and breaches, and watch for the openings that this disappearance uncovers." Further, in "The Search for Grounds in Literary Study," Hillis Miller describes the competing grounding assumptions of literary criticism in terms of four relationally defined positions: psychological, social, linguistic, and (negatively) ontological. These positions all exist in relation to one another; and Miller's essay—like that of Todorov in his definition of the fantastic as a literary genre and like that of Derrida in his description of the assignment of "the origin and power of speech, precisely of *logos*, to the paternal position"—is an attempt to describe the assumptions of literary criticism in terms of functional position rather than cause and effect. In fact, he is attempting to *account for* disparate understandings of literature just as semiotics attempts to account for the myriad and disparate meanings that inhabit human life.

Semiotics and Literary Study

In this we can see that literary criticism has a central, and perhaps a leading role in semiotics. Moreover, it should be equally clear that the semiotic study of literary texts as signifying systems has an important role in literary studies. Literature is important to semiotics because the nature of literary texts underlines the central importance of semiosis in human life. In fact, many literary texts make the processes of signification their very theme. I am thinking not only of more or less experimental texts, like *Tristram Shandy* or *Ulysses* or *Pale Fire,* but even more traditional texts such as *Moby-Dick* or *Mansfield Park* or *The Prelude.* Literature makes the process of finding meaning in the world—of signifying—something to be examined, and when the life of Fanny Price is described in *Mansfield Park,* it is described as the narrative of her learning how things signify in a social class different from her own.

Moreover, literature forces us to attend to signification. When Augustine distinguishes between "things" and "signs" in *On Christian Doctrine,* he defines a thing as "that which is not used to signify something else," and his theological semiotics requires such a distinction as part of its faith that doctrine—that is, Christian significations—is more than one sign system among others. But nothing (no *thing*) in a literary text is not used to signify something else—any literary text is simply one sign system (or subsystem) among others—so that, as I mentioned already, literature cannot be satisfactorily explained by accident or by saying that this is simply the way things are. Literature (and literary criticism) needs to account for everything it contains in terms of its *function,* what sense it makes. In this, literature lends itself, perhaps more strikingly than other signifying phenomena, to demonstrating semiosis.

But more than this, the study of literature—with its self-conscious use of figurative language, its constant foregrounding not only of the contents of meaning but the process of its presentation—can help to situate semiotics and the human sciences, to "locate" semiotics in the same way Foucault attempts to locate the space of an author. For instance, in a novel like *Moby-Dick,* or even *Gulliver's Travels,* the ways in which the narrator understands the world are as important to the text as the worlds these books present. And this doubling—always present in literature precisely because literature, as Culler says, "is cut off from the immediate pragmatic purposes which simplify other sign situations" so that in it "the potential complexities of signifying processes work freely"—not only makes clear Benveniste's distinction between natural and human science, it also marks the limits of semiotics.[25] That is, as Derrida and Foucault and others demonstrate in their poststructuralist critique, the scientific aim of semiotics is undermined by the doubleness of signification. If all things signify—if, as Derrida says, *logos* has a "father" to which it is "connected" within the human milieu—neither that father nor that signification, as Derrida says, is "in any 'real' sense prior to or outside all relation to language. . . . In other words, it is precisely *logos* that enables us to perceive and investigate something like paternity." In the same way, signification allows us to investigate semiotics: the arbitrary nature of the sign means that signs can signify their own meaninglessness, that if signification is everywhere, it is also "nowhere." In other words, if semiotics teaches us that literature can be studied scientifically, then literature teaches us that science (and especially semiotic science) can be understood as unique rhetorical events that can also be situated—like the concept of the "death" of the "author"—within historical frameworks.

Still, if literature has a central role in semiotics, then semiotics can help us reconceive and understand more fully the nature and functioning of literary texts. Frye is perhaps most clear about this in his essay calling for the "scientific" study of literature, and his book, *Anatomy of Criticism*, is a sustained argument for the systematization of literary studies in ways that would produce knowledge comparable to the discoveries of knowledge that physics and chemistry—and linguistics, for that matter—have achieved. That is, semiotics can raise important new questions about the nature of literature and the "meaning-effects" semiotics achieves—from the minute particulars of metaphors and rhetoric through the largest questions, such as those that Miller and others have raised, about social function: how semiotics helps to create desire and social roles (e.g. sexual and racial roles) and carries the "burden" of cultural values in general that Miller describes. The study of signs in culture has been one of the ways people have attempted to understand what Locke calls "human understanding" and Augustine describes as more than human understanding from the beginnings of our culture in the West. And such understanding, as this anthology demonstrates, has consistently focused on language and literature. Semiotics is attempting to systematize that understanding so that we can know how literature functions to affect us individually and socially.

Notes

1. Claude Lévi-Strauss, *The Raw and the Cooked*, trans. John and Doreen Weightman (New York: Harper Torchbooks, 1975), p. 14.
2. A. J. Greimas, *Structural Semantics*, trans. Daniele MacDowell, Ronald Schleifer, and Alan Velie (Lincoln: University of Nebraska Press, 1983), p. 65.

3. René Descartes, *Philosophical Works*, trans. Elizabeth Haldane and G. R. T. Ross (Cambridge, Eng.: Cambridge University Press, 1911), p. 154.
4. Louis Hjelmslev, *Prolegomena to a Theory of Language*, trans. Francis J. Whitfield (Madison: University of Wisconsin Press, 1961), pp. 8–9.
5. Ibid.
6. Jonathan Culler, *The Pursuit of Signs* (Ithaca, N.Y.: Cornell University Press, 1981), p. 23; Marshall Blonsky, "Introduction" to *On Signs*, ed. Marshall Blonsky (Baltimore: Johns Hopkins University Press, 1985), p. xvii.
7. Culler, *Pursuit of Signs*, p. 23.
8. Ferdinand de Saussure, *Course in General Linguistics*, trans. Wade Baskin (New York: McGraw-Hill, 1959), p. 16.
9. Charles S. Peirce, *Selected Writings* (New York: Dover Books, 1958), p. 403.
10. Saussure, *General Linguistics*, p. 16.
11. Umberto Eco., *A Theory of Semiotics* (Bloomington: University of Indiana Press, 1976), p. 30.
12. Ronald Schleifer, *A. J. Greimas and the Nature of Meaning: Linguistics, Semiotics, and Discourse Theory* (Lincoln: University of Nebraska Press, 1987), pp. 169–172.
13. Roman Jakobson, *Selected Writings: Volume II, Word and Language* ('S-Gravenhage: Mouton, 1971), p. 711.
14. Culler, *Pursuit of Signs*, p. 24.
15. Saussure, *General Linguistics*, pp. 66–67.
16. Ibid.
17. Ibid.
18. Jacques Derrida, *Margins of Philosophy*, trans. Alan Bass (Chicago: University of Chicago Press, 1982), p. 13.
19. Emile Benveniste, *Problems in General Linguistics*, trans. Mary E. Meek (Coral Gables, Fla.: University of Miami Press, 1977), pp. 38–39.
20. Culler, *Pursuit of Signs*, p. 25.
21. Roland Barthes, *Elements of Semiology*, trans. Annette Lavers and Colin Smith. (Boston: Beacon Press, 1968), p. 20.
22. Roland Barthes, *Mythologies*, trans. Annette Lavers (London: Granada, 1973), pp. 58–61.
23. Claude Lévi-Strauss, "Structure and Form: Reflections on a Work by Vladimir Propp," trans. Monique Layton, rev. Anatoly Liberman. In *Theory and History of Folklore*, ed. Vladimir Propp (Minneapolis: University of Minnesota Press, 1984), p. 182.
24. Ibid., p. 187.
25. Culler, *Pursuit of Signs*, p. 35.

Psychology, the Subject, and Criticism

Herman Rapaport

It is a striking truth that literary analysis, like Freud's dream analysis, does no more and no less than disclose a life in images or words that has its own momentum.

—Geoffrey Hartman, "The Interpreter's Freud"

I

Long before we have begun taking courses in college we have been taught what to expect in literary works. For example, we assume that poems, plays, and stories will probably have characters, settings, plots, and figurative language. In E. M. Forster's *Aspects of the Novel,* the assumption is made that "since the novelist is himself a human being, there is an affinity between him and his subject-matter which is absent in many other forms of art."[1] Forster believes that because a novelist will necessarily compose sentences that contain a subject (an agency that bears on a predicate), it will be more than merely probable that the novelist will identify himself or herself with such an agency and develop what is called a character. Neither the painter nor the musical composer are as destined by their media to make characters as is the literary writer.

Of course the moment Forster raises character in this way, he immediately recognizes the need to distinguish people in daily life from represented people in literature, and, as one might expect, this leads to questions of psychology.

> In daily life we never understand each other, neither complete clairvoyance nor complete confessional exists. We know each other approximately, by external signs, and these serve well enough as a basis for society and even form intimacy. But people in a novel can be understood completely by the reader, if the novelist wishes; their inner as well as their outer life can be exposed. And this is why they often seem more definite than characters in history, or even our own friends; we have been told all about them that can be told;

even if they are imperfect or unreal they do not contain any secrets, whereas our friends do and must, mutual secrecy being one of the conditions of life upon this globe.[2]

Forster's point is that we can know James Joyce's Molly Bloom or Charlotte Brontë's Jane Eyre better than we can know real people with whom we are on intimate terms, since we can see into fictional characters and not into the people around us. Literature, then, even if it only represents people as fictionalized characters has the effect of appearing more real than daily or real experience, because it directly reflects the psychology of character and allows us to understand or know another's mind from within.

Yet few great literary characters are devoid of any secrets. No matter how much we know about the thoughts of Maggie Verver in Henry James's *The Golden Bowl*, or the minute details of a day in the life of James Joyce's Leopold Bloom, we can never completely understand their motivations and actions. Even Stendhal's transparent Julien Sorel in *Le rouge et le noir* is not easy to comprehend. If he is motivated out of some fundamental inferiority complex that is rooted in his relationship to his father, this still does not adequately explain why he is as emotionally destructive as he is. This is not to say that the novelist does not give us enough information with which to speculate on such matters, but that character is rarely fully disclosed and that what makes a novel entertaining for critics is its availability for protracted and open ended speculations about the motivation and psychology of character.

Indeed, when a feminist critic like Diane Sadoff decides that "what critics call 'masochism' in Brontë's novels, then, we may interpret as stories about the female fantasy in a patriarchal and phallocentric culture [such as] 'I am being beaten by my father,' " she is attempting to develop a psychological hypothesis about character motivation that speculates with a large range of textual features specific to Brontë's work.[3] That this hypothesis also draws from feminist theories of Freudian psychoanalysis is implicitly justified on the grounds that Brontë is an established writer who has succeeded in realistically portraying the human condition in her characters along the lines noted by Forster. That is, since Brontë exposes the psychology of her female characters at great length, a critic like Sadoff may feel quite free to apply psychological models that have a certain applicability to represented figures who take on the appearance of being more real than real people themselves.

Indeed, much psychological criticism relies on there being literary characters who make perfect "subjects" for those trying to develop psychological theories by means of speculating with literary texts. But for readers of authors such as Henry James or Robert Musil, there is often the assumption that a story in and of itself represents an aspect of the psyche. In Dorrit Cohn's *Transparent Minds* we read of Robert Musil's "The Performing of a Love,"

This story portrays the mind of a woman involved in a paradoxical experience: during a brief voyage she 'perfects' her love for her husband by way of a sordid affair with a stranger. Musil's own summation: 'an unfaithfulness can

> be a union in a deeper inner zone' points to the stratum of the psyche that is the exclusive site of the story.[4]

Here the critic not only probes the psychology of individual characters, but more generally feels justified in reading the whole narrative as that which "points to the stratum of the psyche."

This is an approach also developed at great length by readers like Norman Holland who in a study such as *The I* attempts to synthesize as many of the major narratives by a writer as one can in order to find a narrative condensation or identity theme that serves as the key to the writer's identity. Of course, reading this literary identity theme back into the writer's biography is essential for Holland.

> I can use the term "identity theme" for the continuing core of personality that I see a person bringing to every new experience, their theme or style or, to borrow a French term, *cachet spécifique*. I would arrive at someone's identity theme as I would a personal style, by abstracting it from its many, many various expressions. Then I can use the term "identity" for the history of that theme and the history of its variations over a lifetime.[5]

Undoubtedly, it is difficult to read a writer like Marguerite Duras or watch the films of Erich Rohmer without noticing some very strong identity themes. As Holland correctly assumes, it is not unusual for artists to write or produce works that directly reflect their own psychologies, and we can see in Holland's researches an attempt to use the work of art as a clue to understanding the psychology of the artist and also of the relationship between art and life. And again, as in Forster, we notice the assumption that literature, particularly, serves as an ideal text for disclosing character, since it is here that we can see what is hidden from view in real life.

The attempt to read a text as psyche also motivates many of the recent developments in French Freudian thought. However, in France notions like subject, character, or self have been under attack as false categories that are based on what Michael Riffaterre has called the "mimetic fallacy," the assumption that art directly mirrors life and that the categories of ordinary or common-sense experience may be used more or less uncritically to determine the definition of the elements of literature. It is in this context that a text such as Forster's *Aspects of the Novel* could come under severe and withering critique. Still, even when a figure as radical as Jacques Lacan analyzes Hamlet, one realizes rather quickly that Shakespeare's play does exemplify the linguistic dimensions of psychological disorder. When Lacan asks "What is the connection between mourning and the constitution of the object in desire?"[6] he develops such topics at length in terms of Hamlet's actions and speeches. Again, despite Lacan's well-known and highly sophisticated deconstructions of the Cartesian subject, there is a fundamental optimism about the capacity of a literary work to expose some general pathological features of behavior that are reflected in and as language. Hence, even if Hamlet is to be considered but an effect or purely linguistic point of reference or locus within the textures of language, it is still possible, by means of studying how language behaves, to discover those general laws of linguistic pathology by means of which the clinician can better study the analysand's madness.

Even such a canny reader as Alice Jardine, who is very careful not to perform character analyses and works instead on the linguistic features of a text, will ultimately succumb in *Gynesis* to the same tug of realism that one can detect in Lacan. Certainly Jardine's choice of reading Philippe Sollers' *Drame* is strategically set up to avoid discussing realist characters. Still, in her effort to discuss gender, Alice Jardine must necessarily analyse Sollers' pronouns and their placement in *Drame*. This, in part, is what Jardine discovers.

> Sollers' radical explorations of alterity, like those of the writers we looked at earlier, involve a putting into discourse of the feminine—feminine pronouns in this case—as that which makes possible the displacement of the monological and mono-vocal structures of representation. The erotic merging with the Other (sex) is that which allows the male subject of enunciation enough distance from his 'self' to explore language as the performance as act, as text, as writing itself.[7]

Jardine is very expert in demonstrating that one cannot simply read a literary work as if it were the direct expression of a set of positions that are each very unique and self-consistent. In other words, Jardine makes the point, often overlooked in literature classes, that a literary work cannot be broken down into a kind of debate on which one can easily take sides. One cannot simply oppose Stendhal's Madame de Rânal to Mathilde de la Mole, because their discourses cannot be reduced to self-identical subjects that exist independent of the text and of the various linguistic formations out of which Stendhal was himself writing. Especially in Sollers' *Drame*, a new French novel of the 1960s, it would be naive to reduce the text to a set of "mono-vocal structures of representation." Yet, if *Drame's* pronouns are strategically placed in order to confuse the familiar realist discourses of gender, these pronouns still reveal a psychology in a way not so inconsistent with the assumptions of critics like Forster. That is, the pronouns in Sollers' *Drame* expose psychological relations that we can know as if from the inside of a certain consciousness. Hence Jardine can read the psychology of the text's pronoun behavior in order to argue that a male subject of enunciation is displaying a desire for an erotic merging with women whose consequence is an exploration of the performance of language. Reductively put, Jardine is exploring language as a substitute for sexual performance, and the feminine pronouns are analyzed as evidence for developing this approach.

There is, of course, the temptation for an unsympathetic reader to say that Jardine merely switches her focus from the traditional analysis of character to that of language in order to arrive at what is, finally, a very similar point. Yet one has to caution that for writers like Jardine and Lacan these psychological conclusions are not meant to be considered as the fundamental ground upon which we come to understand a text. If Lacan does, in fact, learn something about pathology through the disfunctioning of Hamlet's speech, that is not to say one should consider *Hamlet* definitively read. Rather, one has merely penetrated aspects of the drama wherein a certain subjectivity or psyche reveals itself not according to a global theory of analysis that would systematically explain all the features of the play, but according to more localized theories of analysis which respect the heterogeneity of a text's discourses. The difference of the French approach with respect to the kind of formalist analysis advanced by Forster and drawn upon by many psychoanalytic critics who have implicitly accepted his views is that it does not reduce the literary work to subjects or characters who exist as ideal but never fully articulate forms in the imagination of the reader against which a homogeneous and self-identical set of constructions is asked to correspond. If Jardine discloses a male psychology operative in *Drame*, it is a psychology to which the text as a whole is not relevant. Nor is it necessarily a determining psychology, though it may have its effects. However, at the same time—and this is where matters become quite problematic—Jardine is still largely concerned as a feminist critic with finding the "male subject" and its deteminations in a text whose value for such a critic resides in the fact that in fiction the psychology of man is better disclosed and therefore more realistically or adequately represented than in daily life wherein men's psychologies are less accessible.

The purpose of these comments is not only to discuss in general some of the psychological approaches to literary analysis, but to raise a specific point for consideration: can psychoanalytic criticism ever completely shake off Forster's most basic perceptions above on how and why authors write what they do? I am raising this issue not because I want to take sides (I rather admire Lacan's and Jardine's approaches), but because it raises the question of whether or not psychological readings of literature have radically changed over the last thirty years—have we genuinely abandoned or deconstructed the subject? In other words, to what extent does this "subject" that we seek to dismantle in analysis return in various forms?

Having said that, I would like to turn to yet a couple of other questions. Is it possible to unearth a coherent theory of the subject or ego in the psychology of Freud? And, more important, does not, in fact, the subject that we find in the literary work substitute for a subject that is really not quite there in psychoanalytic theory? This is the rhetorical question that makes up the thesis of my essay. Before developing it, I must alert us to some of the consequences that are being suggested: that if psychological readings of texts necessarily drag along with them the protocols of realist literary assumptions (such as those outlined by Forster), the psychoanalysis of Freud and many of his followers have curiously resisted this "subject" of literary analysis: the positing of the ego. What I want to demonstrate for you now, however, is a very curious phenomenon: that even Freud and his followers practice this contradiction in their own writings. For it is often when they themselves turn to literature that the "subject" in psychoanalysis returns.

II

In the *Introductory Lectures on Psychoanalysis* Sigmund Freud argued that the "artist is once more in rudiments an introvert, not far removed from neurosis" whose wishes entertain phantasies that could well lead to pathological results. However, the artist, unlike the neurotic, "finds a path back to reality."[8] It is quite noteworthy that already in 1916 Freud views the artist as one who occupies the place of the ego, which defends against both the pressures of the id and the outside world. Unlike the neurotic who has paid too high a price for ego defenses, the artist "knows, moreover, how to link so large a yield of pleasure to this representation of his unconscious phantasy that, for the time being at least, repressions are outweighed and lifted by it."[9] That is, the artist exposes aspects of the unconscious that most people simply deny or repress; moreover, the artist is capable of translating such unconscious phenomena into socially acceptable forms that take on a certain objectivity or reality. Early followers of Freud, like Ernest Jones and Marie Bonaparte, accepted this characterization of the literary writer. As we will see, the approach to a literary psychoanalysis wherein the ego or notion of self takes center stage is not unproblematic, given Freud's own theories of the ego, or the way in which both Freud's writings and those of his followers have come to understand how the social subject is constituted in analysis.

Our point of departure will be the literary analyses of Ernest Jones and Marie Bonaparte, largely because these analyses presuppose a notion of the subject that many influential psychoanalytical readers of literature still assume and that, of course, has come under considerable attack in recent years. Particularly interesting is that Freud grounded his own literary interpretations much more in terms of a "subject" than he did in most of his theoretical texts, and this suggests that within the Freudian canon literature could be said to mark a resistance to what is often called the "decentering of the subject." This resistance is amply reflected in *The Interpretation of Dreams*, wherein Freud wrote of Shakespeare's Hamlet, "if anyone is inclined to call [Hamlet] a hysteric, I can only accept the fact as one that is implied by my interpretation."[10] Here, as in many other passages, Freud is considering the subject as self or selfhood, and this consideration has been influential for the early followers of Freud's literary remarks.

Ernest Jones's "The Oedipus Complex as an Explanation of Hamlet's Mystery" (1910), for example, expands upon Freud's remarks on Hamlet in *The Interpretation of Dreams* and considers the protagonist of Shakespeare's *Hamlet* as if he were a patient undergoing the "talking cure." Of particular interest to Jones is how Hamlet's language and actions closely approximate real clinical cases. One of the underlying presuppositions in Jones's study, borrowed from Freud himself, is that Shakespeare not only exposes and meticulously scripts numerous psychological phenomena related to the id that had gone largely unnoticed by his contemporaries, but that Shakespeare does so in a way that ingeniously accords with findings that can be scientifically proven to characterize general psychological behavior. Shakespeare, therefore, mediates the subjectivity of individual psychological phenomena with an objectivized or real characterization of human psychology that is as true today as in Shakespeare's time. Hence literature functions to confirm psychoanalytical theory even as it provides additional forms of clinical evidence.

Hamlet's delay in murdering Claudius is motivated out of identification with the usurper. Hamlet apparently had never accepted his real father's claim on his mother and has always secretly wished that his real father be murdered so that Hamlet himself could take his mother, Gertrude. Freud acknowledged this as an Oedipal wish that all male children shared, though in normal development conflict with the father is supposed to be resolved. In Hamlet's case, however, the conflict has only been repressed or pushed out of consciousness. When Claudius kills Hamlet's father and marries his mother, Claudius does what Hamlet has wished to do all along and therefore becomes a figure with whom Hamlet closely identifies. For Hamlet to kill Claudius becomes, then, merely a means of contemplating his own suicide. This line of reasoning, however, only pertains to thoughts that remain latent and do not occur to Hamlet's consciousness, for at that level Hamlet feels he must avenge himself on Claudius as murderer of his father and, too, on Claudius as father substitute, the one who has the mother. Claudius is, therefore, an extremely ambivalent figure. He is both a substitute for the son and for the father, and because of this Hamlet cannot resolve his allegiances and therefore cannot take action. Indeed Jones notices that Hamlet's discourse betrays this neurotic Oedipal confict, neurotic (Freud calls it hysterical) because it is a conflict that depends upon the inaccessibility of the love object, Gertrude, as a precondition for a denial of all sexual partners. Hence the curious relationship to Ophelia: while she lives Hamlet spurns her, but when he finds her dead he proclaims his love. The language of Shakespeare's play is particularly important for Jones because it is here that evidence of such neurosis becomes not only noticeable but analyzable as symptomatic for Hamlet's conflicts in identification. One example that Jones cites is the slip of the tongue wherein Hamlet addresses Claudius as "dear mother."[11] This, it seems to Jones, represents but another part of Hamlet's conflicts: he also wants to kill the mother in order to resolve his relation with the paternal figures.

Jones's expansion of Freud's intuitions is an important example of early psychoanalytical criticism, placing Shakespeare in the role of an artistic ego who mediates the processes of the id with an objective understanding of human development and behavior. Because of *Hamlet*, Jones implies, the artist has made people more aware of their inner conflicts and how they interrelate with the real world. This reading, however, presupposes that the author, the protagonist, and the reader are independent social subjects and that the main purpose of Shakespeare's work is to show the dynamics of maladjustments in ego identification. Moreover, from a methodological point of view, Jones's study suggests that characters in literature have the same subjecthood as patients in analysis and that we can interrogate such subjecthood through the language which the characters enunciate. This realist approach assumes not only that there is fundamentally no difference between art and life, but that methodologically one can explain artistic works with the same models one uses to explain developmental neurotic conflicts.

In 1933 Princess Marie Bonaparte published a very detailed and lengthy study entitled *The Life and Work of Edgar Allan Poe: A Psycho-Analytic Interpretation*. Today we might be inclined to call this study a psychobiography, since its aim is to form a psychological portrait of Poe by means of integrating his biography and his works according to insights provided by Freudian analysis. Bonaparte's work differs markedly from that of Jones, because it is less interested in proving or applying the logic of a Freudian model to an analogous literary situation for the sake of establishing the universality of developmental patterns. Rather, Bonaparte wants to understand how an artist's works represent phantasy structures that reflect traumatic psychological experiences in early childhood of which the artist may no longer be entirely conscious. In his remarks on Hamlet, Freud pointed the way by arguing that "It can, of course, only be the poet's own mind which confronts us in *Hamlet*," meaning that the drama is symptomatic of Shakespeare's own hysterical psychology.[12] This manner of symptomatic interpretation is precisely what Bonaparte will carry forward in her study of Poe.

However, whereas Freud and Jones used a unified or singular logical model through which to read *Hamlet*, Bonaparte relies on the gradual accumulation of biographical and literary detail, suspecting that through repetition of themes, symbols, and conceptual patterns some very fundamental structures will emerge, providing the key to Poe's psychological identity. In other words, whereas Freud's approach was deductive, Bonaparte's approach is inductive. Indeed, her study does not suggest that the identity of Poe's subjecthood ought to be considered part of a universal developmental model, such as the Oedipus complex, but that both Poe's literary works and his biography reflect very unique and even pathological characteristics that must be considered as part of a very subjective experience about one's being-in-the-world that we cannot inherently share as part of a universal existential mode of experiencing the world. What makes Bonaparte's study very remarkable is that it risks an intimacy between analyst and analysand that many literary critics would find objectionable. That is, Bonaparte allows herself to advance numerous impressionistic interpretations whose purpose is to recreate the conditions of the repressed or unconscious phantasies that appear to be directly related to verifiable traumatic experiences that Poe must have encountered when very young.

The Life and Work of Edgar Allan Poe is divided roughly into three parts. Part one is a chronological biography, part two consists of detailed psychological readings of Poe's entire oeuvre, and part three attempts some general applications of what has been learned in the previous sections. Bonaparte's thesis is that Poe remained fixated on the image of his dying mother, Elizabeth Arnold, who died when Poe was only two and a half years old. Both his biography and his literary works attempt to restore the fragile figure of the mother to the son, whose desire for her is incestuous. When Poe marries the tubercular Virginia Eliza Clemm, he marries a mother substitute who was

> a pale, fragile thing, in whom the marks of her disease were soon apparent. Thus, she approximated still more cloely to the type, which we saw, constituted Poe's sexual ideal. Poe, therefore, in remaining chaste, would do so partly from fidelity to the loved, dead woman and again to defend himself from temptations, sado-necrophilist in kind, which living and disease-tainted women would evoke, by transference from his original love-object.[13]

Bonaparte suspects that Poe's attraction to Virginia is unconsciously morbid and perverse: it is an attempt to occupy the position of his father, who deserted wife and children and probably died himself of consumption, and to consummate a love relation with the dying mother. But this is confused with the wish of Poe as a little child to hold on to the mother's corpse as well as the anger that the child feels at the mother's being taken away from him. The result is sado-necrophilia. Poe's love for Virginia Clemm has pathological roots because it gives expression to sado-necrophilia—Bonaparte's study could be read as a genetic study of misogyny—even as it must respect the fragile condition of the beloved, which requires Poe's chastity. The beloved, Bonaparte suggests, is a figure of repression wherein the repressed returns.

In a very remarkable passage anticipating French structuralist psychoanalysis of the 1960s, Marie Bonaparte treats the name Annabel Lee as what the French psychoanalyst Nicolas Abraham would much later call a *mot tabou*, an acrostic wherein the names Elizabeth (Poe's mother), Rosalie (Poe's sister), and Annie (Annie Richmond) are condensed or "encrypted." We recall that in the poem, "Annabel Lee," Poe narrates the heroine's entombment; however, Bonaparte is noticing already in the early 1930s that the name functions as a crypt for names in the unconscious that have undergone acrostic condensation and emerge as sound shapes, "Li," "belle," "beth," "lie," "[Ro] . . . salie." The names of the beloveds are mutilated and encrypted (put in the sepulcher, scrambled) even as an imaginery figure of feminine loveliness is established whom the narrator will lose. Bonaparte realizes, of course, that this loss is one the subject sadistically wishes, that, were it not for Poe's literary talent and his writing down of such a phantasy, he might well have acted such wishes out in the real. Annabel Lee is the name that signs in place of women who might have been murdered by a criminal psychopath. What interests

Bonaparte, then, is how the act of writing literature takes the place of acting out crimes against women.

Perhaps most important in Bonaparte's study are the individual analyses of Poe's tales. These might appear at first sight to exemplify the most naive or crude sort of psychological interpretation: the impressionistic assignment of psychosexual symbolism. In fact, it has been because of analyses such as these that many students of literature have discounted the psychological interpretation of art as reductive and even degrading. We should realize, however, that such views miss some essential points. In the analysis of "The Fall of the House of Usher," for example, Bonaparte discusses the vault wherein Madeline is entombed as follows. "This vault, in the Mother-Mansion, brings to mind the maternal *cloaca* from which Madeline, like Usher, issued. In analytic terms, this would be described as a phantasy of the return to the mother's womb, which seems to confirm that, in phantasy, Poe had established a blood-relationship between himself and Virginia." The whiteness of the vault is also mother symbolism, and its blackness is related to anality. This "suggests those intestinal regions from which children, in their infantile sexual theories, imagine themselves to emerge."[14] While these psycho-sexual readings may seem gratuitous, they do, in fact, support Bonaparte's thesis that Poe is unconsciously reflecting sado-necrophiliac phantasies, with the emphasis, here, on sadism. Assuming she does not have to explain the underlying theory, Bonaparte is pointing out to the educated reader that Poe's story contains residues from an infantile stage wherein the difference between the mother's vagina and her anus is not perceivable and wherein it is assumed by the infant that children are born in the same way feces are aggressively expelled. In other words, we notice some examples of how infantile memories, long forgotten by consciousness and preserved in the unconscious, emerge through phantasy as Poe composes his story, though, of course, Poe himself is probably unaware of their taking place. Bonaparte's aim, I think, is not to say that the vault is only the ambivalent womb/anus of the mother, but that behind whatever else we may think the story is saying, this phantasy structure is making itself apparent to the psychoanalyst. The significance, of course, is that such a phantasy structure affects the figure of Madeline as an object of sadistic desire, that the psychological construction of a brutal misogyny is being witnessed.

It has not been generally recognized that the recent French reinterpretation of Freud by Jacques Lacan has been very indebted to the research of Marie Bonaparte, even if Lacan had greatly distanced himself from her mainly because of political strife within the psychoanalytic community wherein Bonaparte had considerable power. Still, Lacan's "Seminar on the Purloined Letter" could be seen in relation to Bonaparte's work somewhat in the same perspective that Jones's essay relates to Freud's remarks in *The Interpretation of Dreams*. Like Freud's remarks on Hamlet, Bonaparte's consideration of Poe's story is limited to just a few paragraphs. However, Bonaparte does establish two major points that Lacan will in the 1950s take over: the role of repetition compulsion in the story, and the construction of a female phallus. These concerns relate to her psychobiographical reading of Poe in that they establish, once more, a repeated phantasy that reflects an infantile confusion over the mother's anatomy that is fundamental to a sadistic pre-Oedipal stage. At issue in "The Purloined Letter" is that the phantasy concerns a masculine conceptual reorganization of female sexuality which Bonaparte believes was not only critical for Poe's psychology but for the general development of his literary works.

According to Bonaparte, "The Purloined Letter" is mainly a story about the circulation of the phallus-that-mother-never-had. We recall that the story concerns a queen who has left a letter exposed that she doesn't want the king to know about. A malevolent minister steals the letter in plain sight of the queen, who is powerless to call attention to the theft for fear of the king, and Dupin, a detective, is hired by the queen to recover the stolen material. After the police have thoroughly searched the minister's home without luck, Dupin enters and discovers the letter in plain sight. The letter is the "very symbol of the maternal penis," Bonaparte says, and it hangs "from a little brass knob just beneath the middle of the mantelpiece." That knob symbolizes the clitoris. Bonaparte stresses that Dupin substitutes one letter or penis for another, because the phantasy that the clitoris is like a female phallus must be maintained by men through repetition, both in terms of stealing the female phallus and replacing it. Only in terms of taking it away and putting it back does an imaginary structure acquire an ontological illusion of being subject to either presence or absence. Bonaparte's remarks develop Freud's remarks in "The Infantile Genital Organization" (1923) that children react to their first impression of the woman's absence of the penis by "[disavowing] the fact and [believing] all the same that they *do* see a penis, all the same." Again, "Women, whom he [the child] respects, like his mother, retain a penis for a long time."[15] According to Freud, this female phallus is merely a phantasy which especially males construct as a means for representing a sexuality that is inconceivable to them without their being signs of phallic organization. What Bonaparte's reading adds to these remarks is the manner in which the female phallus is supplied by processes of exchange. It is this idea of the imaginary phallus that Bonaparte considers of major importance to the Poe story, and Lacan, of course, borrows from Bonaparte's interpretation.

Although Bonaparte's study reflects Freud's impulse to view literature as the "poet's own psychology," a notion explicitly maintained in Bonaparte's theoretical remarks, Bonaparte's analyses implicitly demonstrate what Freud in *The Ego and the Id* (1923) attributed to George Groddeck: "what we call our ego behaves essentially passively in life[. . .] we are 'lived' by unknown and uncontrollable forces."[16] Bonaparte's study examines how the "subject" is not an artistic ego with a path back to reality, but one that passively records fantasized narratives coming in large part from the id. These narratives maintain perverse psychological orientations to the world wherein the boundaries of the ego give way to the reaches of the id.

III

Having discussed early psychoanalytical literary interpretations that consider the "subject," it is also important to review some of Freud's remarks on the ego, beginning with *The Interpretation of Dreams*. Such remarks reveal the ambivalence with which Freud approached this issue, not to say his resistances to the ego. I am leaving aside Freud's earlier formulations in the studies on hysteria and the *Scientific Project* because they will implicitly recur in the material we will be covering. Freud's remarks on the ego were constantly revised, though without necessarily resulting in an entirely systematic model of the subject wherein the ego was definitively conceptualized. A most useful place to begin is with the remark by Jean Laplanche and J. B. Pontalis that in *The Interpretation of Dreams*, "the new theory distinguishes the systems of the unconscious, preconscious and conscious, and these provide the framework for an 'apparatus" in which the ego is allotted no place."[17] To put this remark in deconstructionist terms, in the *Interpretation of Dreams* there are places where the "subject" is decentered, where it does not "take place" as ego. Instead, the mind is perceived as paralleling registers of mental processes that can be studied through the representation of thoughts and feelings. The analysis of dreams is intended to explore not only how the unconscious, preconscious, and conscious translate psychical representations from one register to another, but how these representations themselves obey semantic and syntactic laws. In "The Function and Field of Speech and Language," Jacques Lacan takes this approach as fundamental to his conception of the subject.

> The important part begins with the translation of the text, the important part that Freud tells us is given in the elaboration of the dream—that is to say, in its rhetoric. Ellipsis and pleonasm, hyperbaton or syllepsis, regression, repetition, apposition—these are the syntactical displacements; metaphor, catachresis, autonomasis, allegory, metonymy, and synecdoche—these are the semantic condensations in which Freud teaches us to read the intentions—ostentatious or demonstrative, dissimulating or persuasive, retaliatory or seductive—out of which the subject modulates his oneiric discourse.[18]

Lacan clarifies that such dream rhetoric is the result of language becoming more functional at the level of mental processes rather than at the level of interpersonal communication. "As language becomes more functional, it becomes improper for speech, and as it becomes too particular for us, it loses its function as language."[19] Freud argued that in dreams there are both "dream contents" and "dream thoughts." "The dream-thoughts and the dream-content are presented to us like two versions of the same subject-matter in two different languages. Or, more properly, the dream-content seems like a transcript of the dream-thoughts into another mode of expression, whose characters and syntactic laws it is our business to discover by comparing the original and the translation."[20] In such passages there can be little doubt that Freud was thinking of dreams as texts or as linguistic structures. This applies even to visual representations. "The dream-content, on the other hand, is expressed as it were in a pictographic script, the characters of which have to be transposed individually into the language of the dream-thoughts."[21] Freud insists that these hieroglyphics are not to be viewed as pictures, but rather as symbols belonging to a rebus. In analysis, then, one ought to take the trouble to replace each image by a syllable or word that it may represent by virtue of some allusion or relation. "The words which are put together in this way are no longer nonsensical but may form a poetical phrase of the greatest beauty and significance."[22]

Among the most well-known remarks of *The Interpretation of Dreams*, these thoughts are fundamental to the influential Lacanian reading of Freud that considers the dream to be like a sentence[23] and the "Ich" or "I" as "the complete, total locus of the network of signifiers, that is to say, the subject, *where it was*, where it has always been, the dream."[24] When Lacan says that the unconscious is structured like a language, he merely intensifies what was already in Freud's thoughts on the dream work and reminds us that the analysis of dreams is essentially a linguistic activity. However, whereas linguists are used to working with "speech" or language defined in terms of a determinate speaker who is at least hypothetically real, psychoanalysis must appreciate language as more functional within psychical apparatuses wherein no unified locus of address can be established. Rather, language is functioning in accordance with psychic forces which "strips the elements which have a high psychical value of their intensity, and on the other hand, *by means of overdetermination*, creates from elements of low psychical value new values which afterwards find their way into the dream-content."[25]

But what is the speaking agency in all of these linguistic transformations? Who is ensuring that the dream is "differently centered from the dream-thoughts"?[26] And who sees to it that the dream thoughts are always camouflaged or "displaced" in terms that prohibit us from easily deciphering their real content? We could also ask who sees to it that dream thoughts are not only displaced but compressed in representations that one cannot unscramble without extensive analysis? Or, who sees to it that the dream manages to omit precisely that which is not only central but most important? Freud's answer is that no subject in particular is orchestrating these processes; rather, the dream is a consequence of how instinctual impulses come into conflict with organized thought structures. "We may therefore suppose that dreams are given their shape in individual human beings by the operation of two psychical forces (or we may describe them as currents or systems); and that one of these forces constructs the wish which is expressed by the dream, while the other exercises a censorship upon this dream-wish and, by the use of that censorship, forcibly brings about a distortion in the expression of the wish."[27]

When Lacan reread Freud, he made a very influential modification. Instead of reading the word "wish," Lucan substituted the term "desire." Freud argued that all dreams reflect a wish for something that necessarily came into conflict with various psychical processes. Lacan, however, argued that all dreams are expressions of desire that concern an "Other." Lacan has said on a number of occasions that "the unconscious is the discourse of the Other," by which he meant, in part, that there is something functioning in the mind that has the effect of ensuring that the rhetoric of dreams is not arbitrary. Lacan's point is not that there is an ego of the unconscious, but that even when language loses its function as interpersonal communicative speech when determined at the level of psychical apparatuses, it does not ignore the functions of addresser and addressee but articulates them within a structure of desire. The Other, therefore, is not some kind of agency that controls the language of the unconscious; rather it is the function of speech in whose name that discourse makes an appeal.

In Freud's essay on Shakespeare's *King Lear*, "Theme of the Three Caskets" (1913), the situation of a man's having to choose between three women is studied from the perspective not of the ego but the dream. First, Freud establishes numerous instances in literature and folklore wherein the action of choice is situated, as if they were distant or half-forgotten memories that Shakespeare, like any one of us, would have absorbed over time. Freud knows that Shakespeare has thought about this scene before: it occurs in displaced form in *The Merchant of Venice*. A man has to choose between three caskets. Freud, assuming that literary works can be analyzed in ways similar to dreams, points out that the syntax of the scene governs its meaning. In other words, it matters less what the man is choosing between than that there are three of them to choose from. However, it is interesting to Freud that the caskets may well be metaphors for the female fates, of whom the third is called Atropos, the inexorable. In fact, Freud draws from many literary examples in order to convince us that when it is the third figure who is chosen in the familiar folk ritual of choosing between three, this third will have associations with death. The argument is not that Shakespeare's psychology is reflected in an artistic decision, conscious or unconscious, to associate Cordelia with coffins. Rather, the tragic affect at the end of *Lear* is so strong or, as Freud says, "overpowering" that we can sense the "poet's creative instincts" going far beyond the illustration of the play's essential maxims that say we must guard against flattery and that we shouldn't give up our privileges and possessions in our lifetime. Whatever Shakespeare might have been thinking, consciously or unconsciously, the play's emotional affect strikes Freud as much too negative, given what the play is ostensibly about. Hence Freud intervenes with an interpretation that explains the reason for this affect: in Shakespeare's unconscious drawing from folk tradition, he has constituted Cordelia as the goddess of death. It is not she whom Lear is carrying in his arms, but he whom Cordelia has come to take away, she who has come from the shades of death to lay claim on Lear. However, the scene we see is displaced. It is the reverse of the scene wherein the goddess of death arrives, for here the dead Cordelia is being carried by Lear. Are his remonstrations actually an expression of a desire to see the goddess of death dead? In this possibility lies the power of the play's ending.

This kind of literary interpretation is aggressive in its refusal to get caught up in all the dynamics and details of an organic or formalist reading of a literary work. In other words, Freud does not have anything to say about the majority of actions and characterizations presented in *King Lear*. Neither the structure of the play, the represented motivations of all the figures, nor the historical conditions that the play was meant to reflect seem to have any influence on this reading. Yet, when compared to much more complex and comprehensive scholarly studies, Freud's analysis stands out as much more incisive. Given one's experience of seeing the work, Freud is extremely convincing because his analysis drastically changes the way in which we *feel* about the end rather than the way in which we merely think about or interpret it. Indeed, if one reads "Theme of the Three Caskets" shortly before watching or perhaps even reading the drama, there is a good likelihood that one will feel a resolution of a once-painful or traumatic scene. In short, Freud's essay has the potential of allaying the anxiety that the play produces. Of course, there are those who think that drama is most effective when anxiety producing, that nothing is worse than neutralizing the affect of a work of art. However, Freud's point is that *Lear*'s affect is not artistic. Rather, it is really an affect or effect of pathology. And this again raises the interesting specter of the "subject," in that Freud has interpreted *Lear* not as an artistic work but as the discourse of a patient in analysis whom it is the psychotherapist's charge to heal.

If we turn to Geoffrey Hartman's "The Interpreter's Freud" (1984), we will notice a very similar approach to the reading of William Wordsworth. Much as been written on "A Slumber Did My Spirit Seal," but, again, as in the case of the *Lear* scholarship, little of that critical literature has much effect on how one reads the work. Hartman's insights are another matter. Reading the first line of the poem, Hartman notices that what follows should be a dream vision. "The formula is, I fell asleep, and behold!" But there is no vision. The difference between vision and sleep is elided, Hartman says, and that the poet has no human fears or feels emotionally anesthetized "may be what he names a slumber."[28] The problem here is the inverse of that which Freud considers in Shakespeare: in Wordsworth's poem there is too little feeling or affect rather than too much. And here, again, the question of the "subject" is necessarily raised in terms of the issue, "who feels?"

Hartman knows, of course, that the voluminous critical discourse on this poem is prompted by the peculiar "idolatrous charm" that is so out of keeping with the subject matter. "Is there nothing which betrays how deeply disturbing the fantasy may have been?"[29] Hartman recalls that the poem may enact a death wish, that the poet as subject may be addressing his sister, for whom he has an incestuous desire and which he inhibits by means of a fantasy suggesting her death. But in recalling F. W. Bateson's thesis, Hartman asks why such a wish "does not disturb the poet's language more"? If we are considering psychical conflicts of a subject, shouldn't the poem's language reflect the same kinds of distortions and tensions that one might find in dreams, especially since sleep is so central an issue in "A Slumber Did My Spirit Seal"? With this in mind, Hartman writes, "I want to suggest that Wordsworth's curious yet powerful complacency is related to euphemism. . . ."[30] In short, these ordinary or plain words in Wordsworth's poem do not say what they say. Here it is not just a question of saying one thing and meaning another, but of saying something entirely other, of saying something else in place of what is said. "Diurnal" covers for "die . . . urn," and "course" covers for "corpse." The phrase, "Rolled round in earth's diurnal course," suggests gravitation in which we can read the word "grave." "Trees" becomes "tears" and so on. This reading depends much more on the psychical processes wherein language functions not to communicate an interpersonal message but to translate dream thoughts that require censoring.

Given Hartman's analysis, "A Slumber Did My Spirit Seal" is less the representation of a narrator's thoughts (that is to say, of a "subject's" discourse) than it is the process of dreaming itself, wherein dream thoughts are disguised as a dream content by way of euphemism. From a Lacanian perspective, Hartman might have argued that the poem is "the discourse of the other," something he confirms by noting a transference in the poem whereby the girl appears to be speaking for the narrator, discoursing in his place. The euphemisms, then, allow for both speakers to be heard. They facilitate the "appeal" of the poem in all senses. And these euphemisms, therefore, complicate our ability to attribute words to particular, self-identical agencies or subjects. Hartman's implicit claim is that this poem requires Freudian analysis because its thoughts are not transparently embedded in the words. Therefore, one has to force matters considerably, even to the point of breaking with conventional poetic analyses generally considered to be more satisfactory, such as the interpretation of intentional tropes or rhyme schemes rather than finding in a word like "trees" the word "tears." As in Marie Bonaparte's literary readings, Hartman's interpretation approaches what will seem to some a network of gratuitous associations. However, one must be aware that when psychoanalytical readings of literature stress how language works according to the dynamics of the royal road to the dream, this attention to language is most subtle and insightful when it breaks with the usual conventions of formalist literary analysis. It is as if by abandoning the subjecthood of formalist literary analysis characteristic of someone like Forster, that another, much more adequate, notion of subjecthood can be recovered within psychoanalysis, one that is not monovocal. For this reason the most striking and brilliant of psychoanalytical interpretations comes into conflict with the principles of exhaustive close reading, whose protocols are based on the study of formal literary conventions wherein the function of language, to recall Lacan, is radically different from what it is at the level of an analysis of the dream, or, "discourse of the other." Still, the "other" speaks, or, at least, critics like Hartman attempt to speak about it. Yet despite Hartman's evocative analysis, one senses that basic to this type of analysis is Hartman's perception that "It is a striking truth that literary analysis, like Freud's dream analysis, does no more and no less than disclose a life in images or words that has its own momentum."[31]

IV

Clearly Freud's metapsychology of the unconscious, preconscious, and conscious in *The Interpretation of Dreams* has encouraged readings of literary texts that emphasize the id or unconscious and preconscious processes rather than what Freud already in the studies on hysteria called the "ego," a mental formation wherein conscious thoughts defend the subject against unwanted or unpleasurable ideas. Still, we should realize that even in *The Interpretation of Dreams* Freud writes, that "All of them [the dreams] are completely egoistic: the beloved ego appears in all of them, even though it may be disguised. The wishes that are fulfilled in them are invariably the ego's wishes, and if a dream seems to have been provoked by an altruistic interest, we are only being deceived by appearances."[32] From 1900 to 1923 Freud made a number of attempts to reconcile himself with some sort of theory about the ego, though the evidence shows that at a fundamental intellectual level Freud distrusted this notion.

This is most evident in the *Introductory Lectures on Psychoanalysis* (1916), wherein even a cursory look at the chapter titles reflect a bias for studying psychology from the standpoint of the unconscious, beginning with parapraxis, dreams, the archaic, and moving on to wishfulfillment, symptoms, fixation, repression, sexual development, repression, neurosis, anxiety, narcissism, transference, and, finally, therapy. It is noteworthy that even after having written the famous essay "On Narcissism: An Introduction" (1914), wherein Freud began exploring various "ego instincts" and the "ego ideal," that the *Introductory Lectures* reneges a theory of the ego itself. Yet, the *Introductory Lectures* reflects some important shifts in Freud's thinking on the ego that was occurring in essays written during the First World War. In "The Unconscious" (1915), "Mourning and Melancholia" (1917), and "On Narcissism: An Introduction," Freud approached the ego as a structure resulting from various processes of identification. It is crucial to note that in these papers the ego is not considered an inherent structure with which we are born: it develops as a consequence of processes wherein identifications come about. The ego therefore represents an often unstable objectivization of these identifications to which we accord the role of an agency who is responsible for thoughts and actions. Crucial to the development of the ego are what Freud in the essay on mourning and melancholia saw as object relations, wherein the ego may become overly attached to objects that are lost so that "the shadow of the object has fallen on the ego" and the destruction that has befallen the object is transformed into a lack in the ego. In the essay on narcissism, Freud suggests that the ego develops as the infant comes to terms with relinquishing love objects, such as the mother's breast, and introjects them into the ego. The ego is established by the setting up of objects inside itself. In so doing, the ego makes itself an object to be loved by another.

In *Group Psychology and the Analysis of the Ego* (1921), Freud summarized his approach to the ego as a relatively unstable set of identifications. The rejection of the ego as something determinate or central to consciousness was reinforced by Freud's situating the ego within an analysis of group behavior. Drawing from the work of Le Bon, which took a very pessimistic view of group behavior, Freud related the ego to group identifications that were essentially libidinal, even if their sexual aims were directed away from sexual objects, and unconscious, since as Le Bon maintained, people in large groups behave under a sort of mass hypnosis. Nevertheless, Freud broaches many of the earlier points about the ego's individual development in the chapter entitled "Identification." The infant boy, Freud says, has emotional ties to both the mother and the father that come into conflict during the Oedipal period. He wants the mother, but the father stands in the way. By passing through this conflict, the identity of the child is strengthened because its desire has been strongly positioned and identifications chosen between. Yet, Freud says, identification is also brought about through the assimilation of objects by physical or imaginary interiorization.

Melanie Klein, whose early papers date from this period, worked on the Freudian theory of identification for some forty years, developing what has become known as the English "object relations" school. Klein argued very convincingly that infants internalize, or "introject," objects experienced as both positive and negative. Klein's work with child patients supported Freud's guess that identifications are highly unstable in younger infants because both the mother's and father's bodies are perceived as being at once good and bad objects. Klein noticed, furthermore, that if the infant internalizes objects with the result of establishing an ego, there is also an additional mental faculty that is being constructed by means of these introjections, and this is the superego, wherein the young child experiences extreme guilt and inhibition. Klein argued that the superego was much stronger and more developed in infants than the ego, and much of her analysis of children consisted in relieving tensions initiated by the superego so that the ego could gain strength. Klein maintained that girls had much stronger capacities for introjection and what she called projection (empathy, identification with others, the wish to be someone else) than did boys, and that not only did adult women therefore have stronger ties to objects than men, but their egos had developed differently. Although Klein's rhetoric would alarm feminists—women are portrayed as naturally inclining towards "deceit" and "intrigue"—her point is that women are probably more aware of internalized objects than men because the child is itself an internalized object for a woman. In fact, it is the capacity to carry this internalized object that, in part, distinguishes the psychology of the genders from one another.

Klein's interest in object relations were broadened and developed further by D. W. Winnicott, another analyst of the so-called English School. Particularly interesting about Winnicott's work in studies like *Playing and Reality* is that a theory of the ego is established most clearly when one studies transitional objects that in later life, according to Winnicott, can be identified with art. The transitional object is a structure with which the psychical apparatuses play. In early development the child's blanket or teddy bear is such an object occupying a borderline between internalized objects that the child can magically manipulate and fully externalized objects that are in the control of others. It is important that the object avails itself to imagining even as it exists in the real as a real object. The transitional object, of course, need not be a thing. For example it can be the voice of the mother. Thus lullabies can be transitional phenomena. Some characteristics of object-relating to transitional phenomena are emotional attachment, the infant's right over the object, survival of aggressive handling, and eventual letting go. Although the transitional object is symbolically a replacement for the mother's breast, its significance is that it is *not* the mother but something else, an object in and of itself. The main theoretical consequence is that Winnicott does not see the object as a "displacement" or part of any dream logic, as Klein would have. What the transitional object represents, from Winnicott's viewpoint, is precisely a possession, at once real and imagined, that facilitates the integration of psychical processes with the real world by providing a means of gently bringing internal and external phenomena into proximity. Transitional phenomena provide, then, an intermediate area for experience wherein inner and outer senses of reality can be "shared."

> This intermediate area of experience, unchallenged in respect of its belonging to inner or external (shared) reality, constitutes the greater part of the infant's experience, and throughout life is retained in the intense experiencing that belongs to the arts and to religion and to imaginative living, and to creative scientific work.[33]

The significance of transitional phenomena, then, is not just relevant to infants but concerns many of those objects in adult life that are extremely important to individuals, although their practical use may seem nil. Poems, novels, plays, films, paintings, and music, for example, could be considered to be transitional objects wherein highly sensitive internal thoughts and feelings are brought before oneself and perhaps others by means of an attachment, however temporary, to the object. Whereas Winnicott's theory of transitional objects may not provide us a method with which to interpret a literary work's verbal unconscious as well as Freud's theory of the dream, it does allow us to better understand the act of reading as an emotional and intellectual play that is creative and also therapeutic. Also important is that particularly in terms of art, the transitional object becomes the locus of identification wherein the "subject" begins to emerge as a stable structure. One of Winnicott's points has been that the transitional object, even if it prompts a close attachment, is still part of reality and as such resistant to our omnipotent wishes. That we can never establish an interpretation of a work that will stand for all time as the definitive reading wherein the work's complete truth is revealed, establishes our relation to a work of art as one that must respect the fact that it resists our projections and introjections, that it is always "something else" than we imagine it to be. Because of this, the work brings out our finitude as subjects and helps us understand ego boundaries. Cultural objects, then, provide a structure wherein experience phenomenologically brings inner mental phenomena into an intimate relation with external wordly phenomena and in such a way that we grasp the whole as part of a continuity than can be shared with others. This approach, then, rests on the assumption that the subject in psychology and cultural criticism is one that is constituted in relation to a complex notion of the object as a transitional phenomenon wherein the ego and reality are brought into an adjustment that can be objectified and shared.

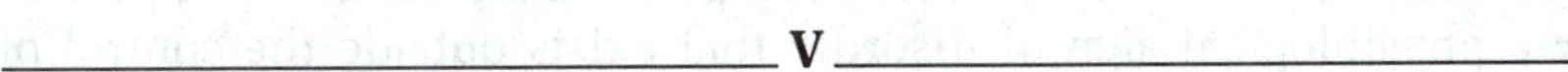

V

In the *Ego and the Id* Freud already distanced himself somewhat from the sort of decentralized identification theories advanced in *Group Psychology* from which the English School took its cue. Yet if Freud cleared even more space for a notion of the ego, he nevertheless wrote that "it is easy to see that the ego is that part of the id which has been modified by the direct influence of the external world. . . ."[34] Even in this theoretical account, the ego is by no means the foundation of thoughts and feelings but merely an outer layer of the id that undergoes modification through tensions with the outside world. Moreover, the previous views on identification remain salient in that Freud argues that "The ego is formed to a great extent out of identifications which take the place of abandoned cathexes [investments] by the id,"[35] suggesting once more that the ego begins as a residual entity and that whatever dynamic interplay the infant has with its mother, it is, from the ego's perspective, but a residue of something that took place at the level of the unconscious or id, but which the ego has not only taken over but censored for the sake of not feeling unpleasure. This censoring notion, which has its roots in Freud's much earlier studies on hysteria of the nineteenth century, contributes to the theory that the ego has defense mechanisms against both the id and the real, that the ego can be defined as that which allows for a majority of conscious thoughts to be integrated and protected from these two sources of threat that are, ultimately, aimed against the ego's capacity to preserve self-identity.

But in *Inhibitions, Symptoms, and Anxiety* (1926) Freud again resists such a conclusion.

> We should be quite wrong if we pictured the ego and the id as two opposing camps and if we supposed that, when the ego tries to suppress a part of the id by means of repression, the remainder of the id comes to the rescue of the endangered part and measures its strength with the ego. This may often be what happens, but it is certainly not the initial situation in repression. As a rule the instinctual impulse which is to be repressed remains isolated. Although the act of repression demonstrates the strength of the ego, in one particular it reveals the ego's powerlessness and how impervious to influence are the separate instinctual impulses of the id. For the mental process which has been turned into a symptom owing to repression now maintains its existence outside the organization of the ego and independently of it. Indeed, it is not that process alone but all its derivatives which enjoy, as it were, this same privilege of extra-territoriality.[36]

Departing from the interrogation of narcissistic identification through objects, Freud stresses how the ego is not a structure in and of itself that can always be clearly distinguished from the id. Yet, when the ego acts on its own behalf by censoring objectionable thoughts emanating from the id, the ego proves powerless. For the ego's censorship of a thought or impulse only drives it underground as a symptom. Therefore, in place of the censored impulse there is now a physiological sign of disorder that exists outside the control of the ego, a sign that represents an instinctual desire for something that has been successfully repressed. Yet, since the ego is an organization that binds, Freud argues it is very capable of adapting to not only the real world but to symptom formations. In fact, the ego binds the symptoms to itself in such a way that such symptoms become important to the ego's structure. "In this way the symptom gradually comes to be the representative of important interests."[37] Of major interest is that even if Freud views the ego as an organizational entity that through adaptation binds or synthesizes psychological phenomena, that ego is still constituted very much as id, since it is the symptom that becomes crucial to the ego's organization and in such a way that the symptom successfully remains out of the ego's grasp even as it is given sanction by the ego's binding structure.

Finally, in his late career Freud, in "Splitting of the Ego in the Process of Defence" (1940), put his resistance aside in denying the central role of the ego in analysis and wrote that "the synthetic function of the ego" is of "extraordinary importance."[38] In "Analysis Terminable and Interminable" (1937) he wrote that the "analytic situation consists in our allying ourselves with the ego of the person under treatment, in order to subdue portions of his id which are uncontrolled—that is to say to include them in the synthesis of his ego."[39] At this time Freud also talked of "ego modification" and of the "normal ego," arguing, as he did much earlier, that the ego acts as intermediary between id and outside world. "In the one case we want to make something from the id conscious, in the other we want to correct something in the ego."[40] Again, these comments reflect a strong departure from Freud's earlier reluctance to accord the ego the status of a central agency wherein mental processes are "synthesized" or "unified." However, in late pieces like those cited above and the well-known "Analysis Terminable and Interminable," the ego is given much more independence and prestige than in many of Freud's earlier major studies, and it is made explicit by Freud that during this period he is following the path of Anna Freud's commitment to an "ego psychology."

VI

It has become commonplace for literary critics influenced by recent developments in French psychoanalysis to assume that American ego psychology developed theories wherein the subject or self has been rigidly posited as a central, controlling agency of the psychological process. In fact, nothing could be more unrepresentative. Although ego psychology addresses the later Freud, it has been very sensitive to the fact that one cannot study patients in isolation but must, rather, consider them in terms of their family histories; furthermore, it has also been concerned with exploring the subject in terms of social structures as a whole. It is important to recognize that many American analysts revised Freud's often-unsynthesized accounts of the ego into theories that were often much more rigorously unified and even more philosophically sophisticated than Freud's, though by no means did they attempt to reify the ego. Quite the opposite. A particularly good example of how even American ego psychology resists the construction of a naive notion of the Cartesian subject in analysis is well documented in Hans Loewald's "Ego and Reality" (1949), whose starting point is the question of whether the ego is in fundamental antagonism with the reality principle, as claimed by Freud in *The Ego and the Id*. Loewald asks this question because he feels that Freud introduces a bifurcation of subject and object that is philosophically much to simplistic. Accepting Freud's argument that the ego is not an a priori faculty of mental processes but an organized structure that is constituted through psychical development, Loewald agrees with Freud that the ego begins to form at that moment the infant becomes aware of its mother's body as something that is either present and gratifying or absent and unsatisfying. Loewald also agrees that somewhat later the ego will begin to take shape as various outside structures replace the maternal body.

> The emancipation from the mother, which entails the tension system between child and mother and the constitution of libidinal forces directed towards her, as well as of libidinal forces on the part of the mother toward the child—this emancipation and tension culminate in the phallic phase of the psychosexual development, lead to the Oedipus situation, and to the emergence of the superego.[41]

Loewald notices that at some point the figure of the mother becomes less important for ego development, while the figure of the father becomes extraordinarily crucial. The phallic phase (the infant's perception of his or her own genitals as either present [phallic] or lacking), the Oedipus complex (recognition of the father's desire for the mother as more primary than the infant's desire for her), the castration complex (the infant's fear of the father's power to separate the child from its sexual object), and the development of the superego are all crucial to the formation of the ego and rest upon the role of the father. As Loewald remarks, "Reality, then, is represented by the father who as an alien, hostile, jealous force interferes with the intimate ties between mother and child, forces the child into submission, so that he seeks the father's protection."[42]

Although Loewald's remarks seem to follow Freud's assumption that the ego is mainly to be considered the product of the mind's defending itself against the real (i.e., a father who is alien, hostile, and so forth), Loewald will point out that instead of viewing ego and reality as separate and opposed, we should view the ego from the beginning as integral to the real and as developing the capacities to maintain the sense of its original unity with the world (primary narcissism) even as it experiences complex levels of differentiation and objectification with respect to reality. "What the ego defends itself, or the psychic apparatus, against is not reality but the loss of reality, that is, the loss of an integration with the world such as it exists in the libidinal relationship with the mother, and with which the father seems to interfere in the Oedipus situation (castration threat)."[43] Loewald, taking a clue from Karen Horney's important paper "The Dread of Women" (1932), points out that the castration threat of the father is not to be reduced to a reality the ego must defend itself against but should be viewed as that which is accepted in place of a much worse threat, that of the mother's vulva, whose psychological effects are fear of drowning, being sucked in, overpowered, and so on. Loewald's argument is that both paternal castration and maternal annihilation threaten the development of the ego but that because paternal castration is much less threatening than the dread of the mother's vulva, identification with the father occurs and, instead of submitting to a catastrophe, the ego undergoes further structural development. In short, the subject has the capacity to come into its own.

Loewald's argument, however, is not that the subject, in coming into its own, ever stands alone over and against the real. For the concept of reality is established in terms of libidinal attachments which ensure that the ego in its relationship to reality "evolve together in successive stages of ego-reality integration."[44] Far from establishing an autonomous self separate from reality that integrates experience to suit itself, Loewald demonstrates that it would be difficult to talk about the ego independently of its being structured by reality. Moreover, he shows that this structuring occurs through profoundly ambivalent relationships to parent figures that stimulate levels of both differentiation or objectification and identification or subjectification. For example, "Primary identification with father and 'dread of womb' in mutual reinforcement drive toward further structuralization of this tension system [ego and reality], which is held together as a system, as it were, by the continuing libidinal urge towards the mother."[45] Evidently, the ego's development does not occur in a simple progression of stages, merely, but within complex overlapping relationships wherein father and mother mirror one another, even as they present themselves very differently to the ego.

The conclusions of Loewald's analysis need to be cited in full.

> In the formation of the ego, the libido does not turn to objects that, so to speak, lie ready for it, waiting to be turned to. In the developmental process, reality, at first without boundaries against an ego, later in magical communication with it, becomes objective at last. As the ego goes through its transformations from primitive beginnings, so libido and reality go through stages of transformation, until the ego, to the extent to which it is "fully developed," has an objective reality, detached from itself, before it, not in it, yet holding this reality to itself in the ego's synthetic activity. Then the ego's libido has become object relationship. Only then does the ego live in what we call an objective reality.[46]

Loewald's interpretation of the ego, then, does not presuppose it to be a separate regulative entity in the mind—what centuries ago was called the seat of reason—but a mental articulation capable of acknowledging an objective realm detached from itself even while such a realm is significant as a constitutive structure whereupon the ego partly depends for its organization.

Although adherents of the structuralist or poststructuralist Freud routinely dismiss American psychoanalytical theories of the ego as philosophically and psychologically reductive (Lacan's writings treat these with utter contempt), it has to be recognized that, in fact, a position such as that of Loewald's is quite close to what we might call a phenomenological account of consciousness wherein the subject is perceived not as an a priori self in the way Descartes formulated it in his *Discourse on Method*, but as an apparatus of psychical phenomena whose structure depends upon its capacity to be as a being-in-the-world as opposed to being merely something in itself. Thus, once more, we see in a school that one might expect to promulgate a realist notion of the subject (as central relay point wherein all psychical phenomena are unified), a very sophisticated theory that is by no means egocentric. In fact, it has to be kept in mind that many ego psychologists have been interested in divesting Freudian terminology of all anthropomorphic jargon in order to head off precisely the charge that Lacanian analysts have made: that American psychology perverts Freud by supplying his theories with an ego or subject they inherently deny.

A French psychoanalyst influenced by Lacan who is surprisingly not so far removed from Loewald is Julia Kristeva. Known in France as part of a new vanguard of theorists working in the fields of linguistics, literature, social theory, and gender, Kristeva started practicing psychoanalysis in the late 1970s. Without doubt her book, *Powers of Horror*, is one of the most significant theoretical breakthroughs in psychoanalysis to have appeared in recent decades. Trained in the study of Husserl, Kristeva too believes that the ego is a structure of consciousness that cannot be disentangled from its identifications. Like Loewald, she believes very strongly in the account that the development of the ego is threatened by both paternal castration and maternal annihilation and that the maternal threat is even more dangerous to the ego than the paternal threat. Kristeva too recognizes that the ego cannot develop independently of its being structured by reality. And, as in Loewald, Kristeva's writings reflect the perception that the ego's development does not occur in terms of simple progression through stages, but that it involves the complex overlapping of relationships wherein parental figures are mirrored in one another, even as they present themselves as highly individualized.

However, whereas Loewald is concerned with the constitution of the ego in what he calls objective reality, Kristeva is concerned with the neurotic defenses against the breakup of the ego that are motivated by the surfacing of pre-Oedipal phantasies wherein maternal identifications are especially threatening. One of Kristeva's hypotheses is that when the symbolic agency of the father becomes very weak, the subject will experience something analogous to that father's death, after which the mother comes to be as a threatening agency. At once fascinating and terrifying, the mother is an extremely ambivalent figure that the subject claims for himself or herself in terms of abject loathing. Not unlike Lacan, Kristeva focuses not so much on the individual per se but upon language. Indeed, her theory is that the powers of horror are situated in language, which has been the means whereby the subject comes to terms with the maternal as something approaching pure loathing. Whereas the hysteric outwardly or somatically displays and exhibits symptoms, the one overcome by abjection internalizes his or her relation to the mother in language. Yet, the moment this is enacted the subject's psychology implodes and the subject itself suddenly vanishes. Yet something remains in his or her place: a language of abjection, a delegation of "spurious egos" that take on undesirable objects. Eminently clear is that the subject undecidably identifies with and flees from terrifying objects of incredible loathing. So remarkable is this defensive demolition of the subject that the undecidability of identification is converted to absolute separation. Kristeva calls this condition "an abyss without any possible means of conveyance between its two edges. No subject, no object: petrification on one side, falsehood on the other."[47] The only thing that bridges the abyss is defilement: the symbolicity of fear.

Yet, given this deconstructed picture of a psychology of abjection, *Powers of Horror* turns to a reading of Ferdinand Céline that typifies our perception that often a practical literary analysis will recover the subject which a theoretical analysis has subverted. Indeed, Céline's fiction is read like a case history of abjection whereby we work back from the verbal symbol to psychological experience. "And yet it is the human corpse that occasions the greatest concentration of abjection and fascination. All of Céline's narratives converge on a scene of massacres or death. . . ."[48] Kristeva's argument will be that Céline's anti-semitism relates to a psychology of abjection insofar as the figure of the Jew functions in several capacities: symbol of defilement, feminine figure, image of the corpse, exotic attraction, and so on. And the bottom line for Kristeva seems to be that Nazi anti-semitism is nothing other than Hitler's having unconsciously decided that since there is no God, God's law has to be sublimated in the abyss his absence opens up by way of abject objects: his chosen. Céline's writings make up the particular case study that proves the general theory. Again, literature appears more real than life to the extent that we can increase our understandings of actual people and events through literary analysis. In fact, Kristeva's reading affirms that

> Céline's narrative is a narrative of suffering and horror, not only because the "themes" are there, as such, but because his whole narrative stance seems controlled by the necessity of going through abjection, whose intimate side is suffering and horror its public feature.[49]

Wholly unlike the more delirious theoretical style of the earlier sections of this book where psychoanalytic thought alone is presented, the literary reading does appear to once more bear out Forster's perception that "since the novelist is himself a human being, there is an affinity between him and his subject-matter." What was disarticulated in the theory of abjection now reappears in a most familiar guise: the subject of literature as the subject of psychoanalysis.

The question on which I would like to end is whether or not, from the standpoint of a sophisticated psychoanalytical theory that resists the notion of a self-identical subject, the introduction of a literary psychoanalysis is not a threat in and of itself? For does it not compromise the sophisticated analyses that theory develops? Or is literary psychoanalysis itself a necessary corrective wherein the notion of the subject can be reinstated within that theory from which it has been expelled? However we answer or even formulate such questions, it appears that psychoanalytical literary criticism does not distance itself as much from Forster's very rudimentary observations as we have been led to believe by those who claim to have deconstructed the psychologism of the subject by means of linguistic and literary analysis. In fact, it would appear that the subject we find in the practice of literary analysis does take the place of what is being resisted in the theory of psychoanalysis. That this is a general and not a particular phenomenon should alert us to the possibility that literary criticism (and cultural criticism more generally) may be fundamentally incompatible with various aspects of those psychoanalytic theories whose aims are to resist the distortions of the subject, what in even such a brilliantly skeptical essay as Cynthia Chase's " 'Transference' as Trope and Persuasion" is called with respect to a poem by Baudelaire, "the totalizing movement that unites thoughts and sensations, the senses and the mind."[50]

Notes

1. E. M. Forster, *Aspects of the Novel* (New York: Harcourt Brace Jovanovich, 1927), p. 44.
2. Ibid., p. 47.
3. Diane Sadoff, *Monsters of Affection* (Baltimore: Johns Hopkins University Press, 1982), p. 134.
4. Dorrit Cohen, *Transparent Minds* (Princeton, N.J.: Princeton University Press, 1979), p. 41.
5. Norman Holland, *The I* (New Haven, Conn.: Yale University Press, 1985). p. 35.
6. Jacques Lacan, "Desire and the Interpretation of Desire in *Hamlet*," in *Literature and Psychoanalysis*, ed. S. Felman, *Yale French Studies*, No. 55/56, p. 36.
7. Alice Jardine, *Gynesis* (Ithaca, N.Y.: Cornell University Press, 1985), p. 243.
8. Sigmund Freud, *The Standard Edition of the Complete Psychological Works of Sigmund Freud*, trans. James Strachey, et al. (London: Hogarth, 1957), XVI: 376.
9. Ibid., XVI: 376.
10. Ibid., IV: 265.
11. Ernest Jones, *Hamlet and Oedipus* (New York: Norton, 1976), p. 99.
12. Sigmund Freud, *Standard Edition*, IV: 265.
13. Marie Bonaparte, *The Life and Works of Edgar Allen Poe* (London: Imago, 1949), pp. 86–87.
14. Ibid., p. 245.
15. Sigmund Freud, *Standard Edition*, XIX: 143–145.
16. Sigmund Freud, *Standard Edition*, XIX: 23.
17. Jean Laplanche and J. B. Pontalis, *The Language of Psychoanalysis* (New York: Norton, 1973), p. 135.
18. Jacques Lacan, *Ecrits*, trans. A. Sheridan (New York: Norton, 1977), p. 58.
19. Ibid., p. 85.
20. Sigmund Freud, *Standard Edition*, IV: 277.
21. Ibid.
22. Ibid., p. 278.
23. Lacan, *Ecrits*, p. 57.
24. Jacques Lacan, *Four Fundamental Concepts of Psychoanalysis* (New York: Norton, 1978). p. 44.
25. Sigmund Freud, *Standard Edition*, IV: 307.
26. Ibid., p. 305.
27. Ibid., pp. 143–144.
28. Geoffrey Hartman, "The Interpreter's Freud," in *Easy Pieces* (New York: Columbia University Press, 1985), p. 145.
29. Ibid., p. 146.
30. Ibid., pp. 147–148.
31. Ibid., p. 138.

32. Sigmund Freud, *Standard Edition*, IV: 267.
33. D. W. Winnicott, *Playing and Reality* (London: Tavistock, 1976), p. 14.
34. Sigmund Freud, *Standard Edition*, XIX: 25.
35. Ibid., p. 48.
36. Ibid., XX: pp. 97–98.
37. Ibid., p. 99.
38. Ibid., XXIII: 276.
39. Ibid., p. 235.
40. Ibid., p. 238.
41. Hans W. Loewald, *Papers on Psychoanalysis* (New Haven, Conn.: Yale University Press, 1980), p. 6.
42. Ibid., p. 7.
43. Ibid., p. 12.
44. Ibid., p. 18.
45. Ibid., p. 16.
46. Ibid., pp. 19–20.
47. Julia Kristeva, *Powers of Horror* (New York: Columbia University Press, 1982), p. 47.
48. Ibid., p. 149.
49. Ibid., p. 140.
50. " 'Transference' as Trope and Persuasion," in *Discourse in Psychoanalysis and Literature*, ed. S. Rimmon-Kenan (New York: Methuen, 1987), p. 228.

Index

Boldface figures refer to essay selections.